USING FINANCIAL ACCOUNTING INFORMATION
The Alternative to Debits and Credits

5e

Gary A. **Porter**

+

Curtis L. **Norton**
Northern Illinois University

THOMSON ™

SOUTH-WESTERN

Australia · Brazil · Canada · Mexico · Singapore · Spain · United Kingdom · United States

THOMSON

SOUTH-WESTERN

Using Financial Accounting Information: The Alternative to Debits and Credits, Fifth Edition

Gary A. Porter, Curtis L. Norton

VP/Editorial Director:
Jack W. Calhoun

Publisher:
Rob Dewey

Acquisitions Editor:
Matthew Filimonov

Senior Developmental Editor:
Craig Avery

Marketing Manager:
Steve Joos

Associate Content Project Manager:
Joanna Grote

Manager, Editorial Media:
John Barans

Technology Project Manager:
Robin K. Browning

Manufacturing Coordinator:
Doug Wilke

Production House:
LEAP Publishing Services, Inc.

Compositor:
International Typesetting and Composition

Printer:
Transcontinental Printing
Beauceville, QC

Art Director:
Linda Helcher

Internal Designers:
Chris A. Miller Design
Stratton Design

Cover Designers:
Beckmeyer Design

Photography Manager:
Deanna Ettinger

Photo Researcher:
Charlotte Goldman

Library of Congress Control Number:
2007920206

For more information about our products, contact us at:

Thomson Learning
Academic Resource Center

1-800-423-0563

Thomson Higher Education
5191 Natorp Boulevard
Mason, OH 45040
USA

To those who really "count":
Melissa
Kathy, Amy, Andrew

User Perspective. Decision-Making Focus. Discover the Best of Both with

Porter/Norton's

Using Financial Accounting Information: The Alternative to Debits and Credits, 5e

A student finishing a financial accounting course needs to understand how to read and comprehend a simple annual report. Even more, that student needs to be able to discern what information is needed to make sound business decisions. This is why, from the very first edition, we pursued a **User Perspective** with a clear focus on **Decision Making.** The text clearly presents transactions in a spreadsheet format that indicates the effect on the accounting equation—giving you the ability to keep your students focused on business decisions.

Discover the strength of a conceptual, user approach with an emphasis on the importance of business decision making—all in a single solution.

WE INVITE you to discover the best of both with *Using Financial Accounting Information: The Alternative to Debits and Credits, 5e.* P N

REVISION GOALS

Based on extensive feedback from both students and educators, we revised the book with the following convictions in mind:

A Book Should Motivate and Focus Students. The fifth edition adopts a more streamlined approach that emphasizes key points. By streamlining complex accounting topics and emphasizing readability and usefulness, the result is an uncluttered, straightforward financial accounting textbook that will help students succeed.

Students Succeed When They Know Why Accounting is Important. Using real-world, relevant flagship companies like Nike, Finish Line, Foot Locker, and Coca-Cola helps show why accounting is important to a business. Experience has shown that knowing the why helps students succeed.

Getting an 'A' in Accounting is Still About Homework. Experience shows that student success is still largely a measure of doing homework. That is why this book contains a range of problems and exercises—including A & B problems, review problems, warm-up exercises, and more—that are designed to motivate and build skills in a systematic, step-by-step manner. Enhancing this emphasis on student success are homework aids—warm-up exercises and solutions, review problems and solutions, key terms quizzes and solutions, among others—that help prepare students to turn in homework of the highest quality.

The following goals are consistent with and complement the approach we adopted in the first edition and have maintained through each revision:

1. **To enhance decision making.** For the fifth edition we have included three decision-making models that will help students throughout their accounting and business careers: the **Ratio Decision Model,** introduced in Chapter 2 and appearing in most subsequent chapters; a **Financial Decision Framework** for making business decisions, in Chapter 1; and an **Ethical Decision-Making Model,** also in Chapter 1. Decision Cases in the end-of-chapter material focus on Reading and Interpreting Financial Statements, Making Financial Decisions, and Ethical Decision Making. In these and many other ways, we continue to be dedicated to guiding students' acquisition of decision skills.

2. **To create a book that accommodates students' changing learning styles.** Students will benefit directly from our new design featuring visual enhancement of key topics, use of bulleted lists, a new Study Highlights format, a new Study Links feature at the start of each chapter—all designed to make studying more effective, efficient, and tailored to students' time constraints.

3. **To demonstrate accounting by using actual public companies.** Each chapter features an actual public company as the central example for topics along with key industry competitive companies in all chapters.

KEY FEATURES IN THIS EDITION

The fifth edition carries on a tradition of focusing on the use of financial information so students understand how and why financial statements drive business decision making. Three decision models now complement the approach of the fifth edition:

- **Shows how transactions affect the financial statements.** The fifth edition, like previous editions, replaces nearly all journal entries with a **transaction-effects equation** that reflects how each transaction affects the income statement and balance sheet. This more conceptual approach focuses students on the use of financial accounting, not the preparation of journal entries and debits and credits.

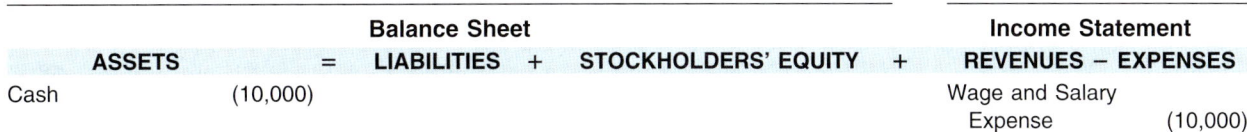

	Balance Sheet					Income Statement	
ASSETS		**=**	**LIABILITIES**	**+**	**STOCKHOLDERS' EQUITY**	**+**	**REVENUES − EXPENSES**
Cash	(10,000)					Wage and Salary Expense	(10,000)

- *NEW* **Financial Decision Framework.** Chapter 1 introduces a framework for financial decision making as a process that illustrates how to use financial information to make business and investment decisions:

  1. **Formulate the Question**
  2. **Gather Information**
  3. **Read the Financials**
  4. **Analyze the Financials**
  5. **Make the Decision**
  6. **Assess the Decision**

  Using this model, students learn not only what accounting is and who uses financial information, but also how that information is the basis for decision making.

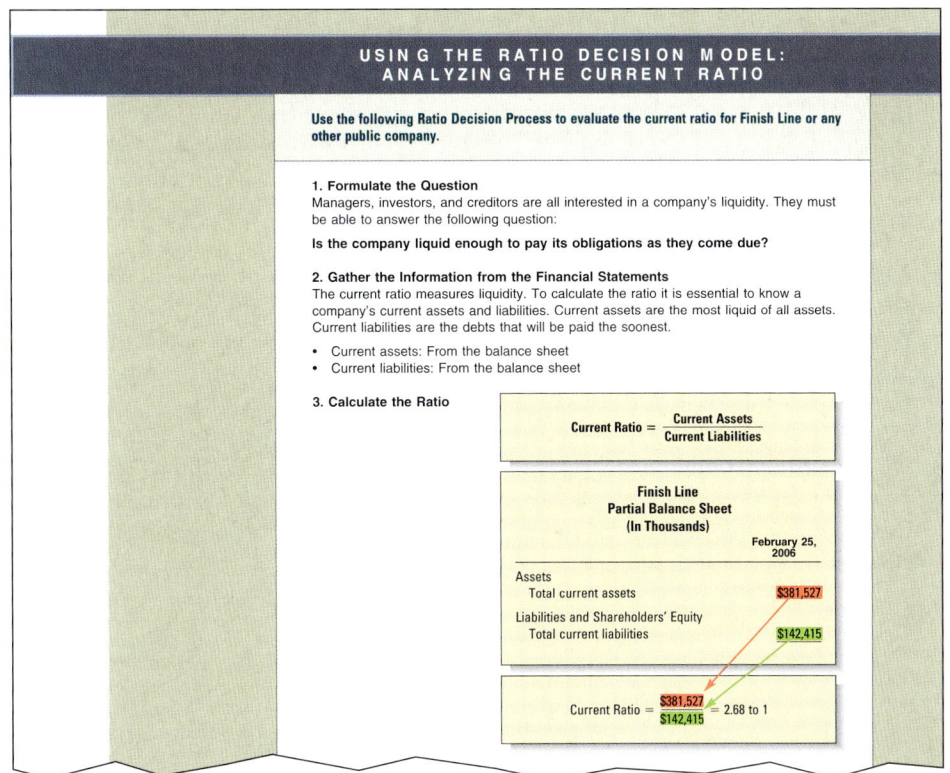

The Ratio Decision Model on current ratio excerpted here is introduced in Chapter 2. The Model appears in most chapters to help focus on ratios as a tool for decision making and to show where in the financial statements the ratio items are found.

- *NEW* **Ratio Decision Model.** Each time a ratio is introduced, the Ratio Decision Model walks students step-by-step through developing and using a financial ratio, from financial statement excerpts that highlight ratio terms. The model depicts the financial statement line items that actually make up the ratio, to help students understand where the numbers come from. Most importantly, the model highlights the interrelationship of the statements and the numbers, and emphasizes the importance of comparing the results with both prior performance and industry competitors.

- **Ethical Decision Model.** In the wake of accounting and business scandals of the last few years, the fifth edition provides a step-by-step ethical analysis and decision tool that students can rely on to help them base their business decisions on ethical and social principles throughout their careers.

- *REVISED* **Concentration on fewer real-world financial statements.** Examples are generated from the chapter-opening company to reinforce concepts with clear, easy-to-follow examples. A focus on fewer companies and examples minimizes distracting and complicated alternative financial formats and numbers. Students can concentrate on learning one business or one industry, and one set of financial statements that apply to the company example within the chapter.

- *UPDATED* **Coverage of the PCAOB, Sarbanes-Oxley, and auditing standards for internal control.** In response to the accounting and reporting scandals that have occurred in the last few years, the fifth edition introduces the role of Sarbanes-Oxley and the PCAOB in Chapter 1. Chapter 6 devotes an entire section to Sarbanes-Oxley in the context of internal control. Students are exposed to Section 404 of SOX and the new management report on internal control required by this monumental legislation.

- *NEW* **Chapter order and organization.** The order of chapters 5, 6, and 7 has been changed. For the fifth edition, inventories and cost of goods sold has been moved up to Chapter 5, with cash and internal control now discussed in Chapter 6 and investments and receivables covered in Chapter 7. This change was made to better reflect the order of a business cycle, in which a business first holds inventories, then converts those inventories to cash, receivables, and investments; Another important change in this edition was the movement of much of the material on accounting for stock and bonds to an appendix to Chapter 7—one more indication of our attempt to streamline the coverage whenever possible.

- *NEW* **Study Highlights.** Key concepts highlighted by **Learning Outcomes** make it easier than ever for students to review the key ideas in the chapter.

- *NEW* **Study Links.** This feature, found in earlier editions of the text, returns for the fifth edition to help students keep the big picture of the course in mind as they study. Study Links let them look back at the main concepts of the prior chapter, preview the concepts of the chapter under study, and look ahead to the chapter they will study next.

- *NEW* **Learning Outcomes Approach.** A change from Learning Objectives to **Learning Outcomes** reflects a fundamental shift in our philosophy about how instructors should be able to access and use quizzing and testing for pre-testing, post-testing, and assessment.

SUPPLEMENTS

HELPING STUDENTS SUCCEED

Excel® Templates. Many problems in each chapter may be solved on a Microsoft Excel spreadsheet to increase student awareness of basic software applications. Those selected assignments that may be solved using the Excel spreadsheets are identified by icons in the text. Downloadable from the Student Resources page of the product Web site.

Web Resources. Many helpful web resources including quizzes, topical discussions and more are available for students to access. These items help reinforce and shed light on text topics. We invite you to discover more by logging into the text Web site.

HELPING INSTRUCTORS SHINE

An unsurpassed package of supplementary resources helps you **plan, manage,** and **teach** your course. Additionally, special resources are available to help **assess** the progress of your students.

Instructor's Resource CD-ROM (ISBN 0324648901). This all-in-one resource contains all of the key instructor ancillaries (solutions manual, instructor's manual, test item files, ExamView® test bank, and PowerPoint® presentation slides), giving instructors the ultimate tool for customizing lectures and presentations.

Instructor's PowerPoint® Slides Located on the Instructor's Resource CD-ROM and on the text's Web site, these colorful slides, by Catherine Lumbattis (Southern Illinois University), reinforce chapter content and provide a rich tool for in-class lectures and out-of-class reviewing.

Assessment Tools The testing materials accompanying the fifth edition were revised to accommodate your need to accurately assess student performance and measure progress towards achieving departmental and college objectives.

ACKNOWLEDGMENTS

REVIEWERS

Throughout the course of our writing, we are indebted to those individuals who provided valuable guidance to our ongoing efforts. These include:

Sheryl J. Alley, Ball State University

Cynthia E. Bolt, The Citadel

Angele Brill, Castleton State College

Marcia Croteau, University of Maryland, Baltimore County

Louann Cummings, The University of Findlay

Araya Debessay, University of Delaware

J. Allen Jinnette, Trevecca Nazarene University

Cathy Xanthaky Larson, Middlesex Community College

Joseph M. Larkin, Saint Joseph's University

Xiaohui (Gloria) Liu, University of Texas at Dallas

Donald W. McFall, Jr., Kent State University

Yaw M. Mensah, Rutgers University

Susan Minke, University of Indiana Purdue at Ft. Wayne

Susan Mundy, City University, Washington

Volkan Muslu, The University of Texas at Dallas

Marshall K. Pitman, University of Texas at San Antonio

Robert W. Rouse, College of Charleston

Gary Schader, Kean University

Lynette E. Teal, Western Wisconsin Technical College

Craig Vilhauer, Merced College

REVIEWERS OF PRIOR EDITIONS

Throughout the first four editions, many other individuals have contributed helpful suggestions that have resulted in many positive changes. Although they are not cited here, we remain grateful for their assistance.

THE PUBLISHING TEAM

We wish to thank these individuals for their insights, skill, and attention to detail in important aspects of the project: We are grateful to Leslie Kauffman at LEAP Publishing for her work on the spreadsheet templates and to Malvine Litten and LEAP Publishing for their great help in production of the text and the solutions manual. We are especially grateful to Elise Hasbrook of The Finish Line, Inc., and Eugene Kim of Foot Locker, Inc., for their careful review and their permission in allowing extensive use of the company's financial information in the development of the text. We thank the team at Thomson Learning for their efforts in all phases of planning, development, marketing, production, and technology: Matt Filimonov, acquisitions editor; Craig Avery, senior developmental editor; Steve Joos, marketing manager; Bob Dreas and Joanna Grote, content project managers; Robin Browning, technology project manager; and Deanna Ettinger, photography manager.

Gary A. Porter
Curtis L. Norton
December 2006

MEET THE AUTHORS

Gary A. Porter earned Ph.D. and M.B.A. degrees from the University of Colorado and his B.S.B.A. from Drake University. Recently retired as Professor of Accounting, Dr. Porter served as Department Chair and taught at numerous universities. He has published in the *Journal of Accounting Education, Journal of Accounting, Auditing & Finance,* and *Journal of Accountancy,* among others, and has conducted numerous workshops on the subjects of introductory accounting education and corporate financial reporting.

Dr. Porter's professional activities include experience as a staff accountant with Deloitte & Touche in Denver, a participant in KPMG Peat Marwick Foundation's Faculty Development program, and a leader in numerous bank training programs. He has won an Excellence in Teaching Award from the University of Colorado and Outstanding Professor Awards from both San Diego State University and the University of Montana.

He served on the Illinois CPA Society's Innovations in Accounting Education Grants Committee, the steering committee of the Midwest region of the American Accounting Association, and the board of directors of the Chicago chapter of Financial Executives International.

Curtis L. Norton has been a professor at Northern Illinois University in DeKalb, Illinois, since 1976. He earned his Ph.D. from Arizona State University, his M.B.A. from the University of South Dakota, and his B.S. from Jamestown College, North Dakota. His extensive list of publications include articles in *Accounting Horizons, The Journal of Accounting Education, Journal of Accountancy, Journal of Corporate Accounting, Journal of the American Taxation Association, Real Estate Review, The Accounting Review, CPA Journal,* and many others. In 1988–1989, Dr. Norton received the University Excellence in Teaching Award, the highest university-wide teaching recognition at NIU. He is also a consultant and has conducted training programs for governmental authorities, bank, utilities, and other entities.

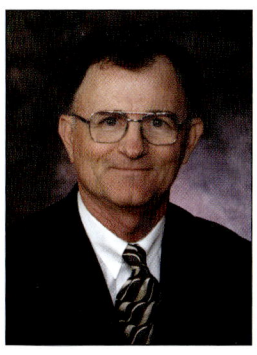

Dr. Norton is a member of the American Accounting Association and a member and officer of Financial Executives International.

BRIEF CONTENTS

INTRODUCTION	Getting Started in Business	2
CHAPTER 1	Accounting as a Form of Communication	12
CHAPTER 2	Financial Statements and the Annual Report	58
CHAPTER 3	Processing Accounting Information	104
CHAPTER 4	Income Measurement and Accrual Accounting	152
CHAPTER 5	Inventories and Cost of Goods Sold	202
CHAPTER 6	Cash and Internal Control	270
CHAPTER 7	Investments and Receivables	304
CHAPTER 8	Operating Assets: Property, Plant, and Equipment, Natural Resources, and Intangibles	348
CHAPTER 9	Current Liabilities, Contingencies, and the Time Value of Money	392
CHAPTER 10	Long-Term Liabilities	454
CHAPTER 11	Stockholders' Equity	498
CHAPTER 12	The Statement of Cash Flows	550
CHAPTER 13	Financial Statement Analysis	612
APPENDIX A	Excerpts from The Finish Line, Inc., Form 10–K for 2006	A-1
APPENDIX B	Excerpts from Foot Locker, Inc., Form 10–K for 2005	B-1

GLOSSARY   G-1

COMPREHENSIVE INDEX   I-1

CONTENTS

Introduction: Getting Started in Business   2

The Finish Line, Inc.: Making Business Decisions   3

What Is Business?   4

Forms of Organization   5

    Business Entities   5

    Nonbusiness Entities   7

    Organizations and Social Responsibility   7

The Nature of Business Activity   7

    Financing Activities   7

    Investing Activities   8

    Operating Activities   8

Starting Your Study of Accounting   9

CHAPTER 1   Accounting as a Form of Communication   12

The Finish Line, Inc.: Making Business Decisions   13

What Is Accounting?   14

Users of Accounting Information and Their Needs   15

    Internal Users   15

    External Users   15

    Using Financial Accounting Information   16

Using the Ratio Decision Model: *A Financial Decision Framework*   17

Financial Statements: How Accountants Communicate   18

    The Accounting Equation   18

    The Balance Sheet   18

    The Income Statement   19

    The Statement of Retained Earnings   20

    The Statement of Cash Flows   21

    Relationships Among the Financial Statements   22

Looking at Financial Statements for a Real Company: Finish Line   23

    Finish Line's Balance Sheet   23

    Finish Line's Income Statement   23

The Conceptual Framework: Foundation for Financial Statements   26

    Conceptual Framework for Accounting   26

    Economic Entity Concept   26

    Cost Principle   26

    Going Concern   26

    Time Period Assumption   27

    Generally Accepted Accounting Principles   27

    Accounting as a Social Science   27

    Who Determines the Rules of the Game?   28

Introduction to Ethics in Accounting   28

    Accountants and Ethical Judgments   31

    The Changing Face of the Accounting Profession   31

The Accounting Profession   32

    Employment by Private Business   32

    Employment by Nonbusiness Entities   33

    Employment in Public Accounting   33

    Accountants in Education   35

    Accounting as a Career   35

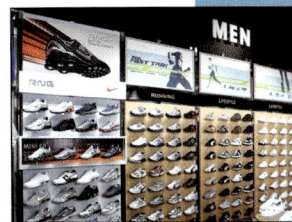

Each chapter contains some or all of the following end-of-chapter material:
• Study Highlights • Ratio Review • Accounts Highlighted • Key Terms Quiz
• Alternate Terms • Warmup Exercises & Solutions • Review Problem &
Solution • Questions • Exercises • Multi-Concept Exercises • Problems
• Multi-Concept Problems • Alternate Problems • Alternate Multi-Concept
Problems • Decision Cases • Solutions to Key Terms Quiz

CHAPTER 2   Financial Statements and the Annual Report   58

The Finish Line, Inc.: Making Business Decisions   59
What Financial Statements Tell about a Business   61
Objectives of Financial Reporting   61
   The Primary Objective of Financial Reporting   61
   Secondary Objectives of Financial Reporting   62
What Makes Accounting Information Useful? Qualitative
Characteristics   62
   Understandability   63
   Relevance   63
   Reliability   63
   Comparability and Consistency   64
   Materiality   64
   Conservatism   65
Financial Reporting: An International Perspective   65
Looking at Financial Statements   66
What Are the Parts of the Balance Sheet? Understanding the
Operating Cycle   66
The Classified Balance Sheet   67
   Current Assets   67
   Noncurrent Assets   68
   Current Liabilities   69
   Long-Term Liabilities   70
   Stockholders' Equity   70
Using a Classified Balance Sheet: Introduction
to Ratios   71
   Working Capital   71
   Current Ratio   72
   The Income Statement   73
   What Appears on the Income Statement?   73
   Format of the Income Statement   73
   Using an Income Statement   76
The Statement of Retained Earnings   76
The Statement of Cash Flows   77
Looking at Financial Statements for a Real Company: The
Finish Line, Inc.   78
   Finish Line's Condensed Balance Sheet   79
Using the Ratio Decision Model: *Analyzing the Current Ratio   80*
   Finish Line's Income Statement   81
Using the Ratio Decision Model: *Analyzing the Profit Margin   82*
   Other Elements of an Annual Report   82

CHAPTER 3   Processing Accounting Information   104

Foot Locker, Inc.: Making Business Decisions   105
Economic Events: The Basis for Recording Transactions   106
   External and Internal Events   106
   The Role of Source Documents in Recording Transactions   107
   *Analyzing the Effects of Transactions on the Accounting
   Equation   107*
   *Balance Sheet and Income Statement for Glengarry
   Health Club   111*

What Is an Account? 113
   Chart of Accounts 113
   The General Ledger 113
Processing Accounting Information 114
APPENDIX—Accounting Tools: The Double-Entry System 116

CHAPTER 4   Income Measurement and Accrual Accounting   **152**

Foot Locker, Inc.: Making Business Decisions 153
Recognition and Measurement in Financial Statements 155
   Recognition 155
   Measurement 155
   Summary of Recognition and Measurement in Financial
   Statements 157
The Accrual Basis of Accounting 157
   Comparing the Cash and Accrual Bases of Accounting 157
   What the Income Statement and the Statement
   of Cash Flows Reveal 158
   Accrual Accounting and Time Periods 159
   The Revenue Recognition Principle 160
   Expense Recognition and the Matching Principle 161
Accrual Accounting and Adjustments 163
   Types of Adjustments 163
   Accruals and Deferrals 168
   Summary of Adjustments 169
   Comprehensive Example of Adjustments 170
   Adjustments at the End of January 170
   Income Statement and Balance Sheet for Duffy Transit 172
   Ethical Considerations for a Company on the Accrual Basis 173
The Accounting Cycle 174
   The Use of a Work Sheet 175
   The Closing Process 175
   Interim Financial Statements 175
Integrative Problem 200

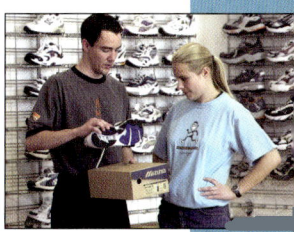

CHAPTER 5   Inventories and Cost of Goods Sold   **202**

The Finish Line, Inc.: Making Business Decisions 203
The Nature of Inventory 204
   Three Types of Inventory Cost and Three Forms of Inventory 205
The Income Statement for a Merchandiser 206
Net Sales of Merchandise 207
   Sales Returns and Allowances 207
   Credit Terms and Sales Discounts 208
The Cost of Goods Sold 208
   The Cost of Goods Sold Model 208
   Inventory Systems: Perpetual and Periodic 210
   Beginning and Ending Inventories in a Periodic System 211
   The Cost of Goods Purchased 211
   The Gross Profit Ratio 215
Using the Ratio Decision Model: *Analyzing the Gross Profit Ratio 216*
Inventory Valuation and the Measurement of Income 217
   Inventory Costs: What Should Be Included? 217
Inventory Costing Methods with a Periodic System 218
   Specific Identification Method 219
   Weighted Average Cost Method 220
   First-in, First-out Method (FIFO) 220
   Last-in, First-out Method (LIFO) 221
   Selecting an Inventory Costing Method 221
   Costing Methods and Cash Flow 222

LIFO Liquidation 223
The LIFO Conformity Rule 223
The LIFO Reserve: Estimating LIFO's Effect on Income
and on Taxes Paid 224
Costing Methods and Inventory Profits 224
Changing Inventory Methods 225
Inventory Valuation in Other Countries 225
Inventory Errors 226
Valuing Inventory at Lower of Cost or Market 229
Why Replacement Cost Is Used as a Measure of Market 229
Conservatism Is the Basis for the Lower-of-Cost-or-Market Rule 230
Application of the LCM Rule 231
Methods for Estimating Inventory Value 231
Gross Profit Method 231
Retail Inventory Method 233
Analyzing the Management of Inventory 233
Using the Ratio Decision Model: *Analyzing the Management*
of Inventory 234
How Inventories Affect the Cash Flows Statement 235
APPENDIX—Accounting Tools: Inventory Costing Methods with
the Use of a Perpetual Inventory System 236

CHAPTER 6 Cash and Internal Control 270

The Finish Line, Inc.: Making Business Decisions 271
What Constitutes Cash? 272
Cash Equivalents and the Statement of Cash Flows 272
Control over Cash 273
Cash Management 273
Reading a Bank Statement 273
The Bank Reconciliation 276
The Bank Reconciliation and the Need for Adjustments
to the Records 278
Establishing a Petty Cash Fund 278
An Introduction to Internal Control 279
The Sarbanes-Oxley Act of 2002 279
The Control Environment 282
The Accounting System 282
Internal Control Procedures 283
Limitations on Internal Control 284
Computerized Business Documents and Internal Control 285
Control over Cash Receipts 286
The Role of Computerized Business Documents in Controlling
Cash Disbursements 287

CHAPTER 7 Investments and Receivables 304

Apple Computer Company: Making Business Decisions 305
Accounting for Investments 306
Investments in Highly Liquid Financial Instruments 307
Investing Idle Cash 307
Accounting for an Investment in a Certificate of Deposit (CD) 307
Investments in Stocks and Bonds 308
Accounts Receivable 310
The Use of a Subsidiary Ledger 310
The Valuation of Accounts Receivable 311
Two Methods to Account for Bad Debts 311
Write-Offs of Uncollectible Accounts with the Allowance
Method 312
Two Approaches to the Allowance Method of Accounting
for Bad Debts 313

The Accounts Receivable Turnover Ratio   316
Using the Ratio Decision Model: Analyzing the Accounts Receivable
Rate of Collection   316
Notes Receivable   318
   Important Terms Connected with Promissory Notes   318
Accelerating the Inflow of Cash from Sales   320
   Credit Card Sales   320
   Discounting Notes Receivable   321
How Liquid Assets Affect the Statement of Cash Flows   321
APPENDIX—Accounting for Investments in Stocks
and Bonds   323

CHAPTER 8   Operating Assets: Property, Plant, and Equipment,
Natural Resources, and Intangibles   348

Nike: Making Business Decisions   349
Operating Assets: Property, Plant, and Equipment   350
   Balance Sheet Presentation   350
   Acquisition of Property, Plant, and Equipment   351
   Use and Depreciation of Property, Plant,
   and Equipment   353
   Capital versus Revenue Expenditures   358
   Environmental Aspects of Operating Assets   360
   Disposal of Property, Plant, and Equipment   360
Operating Assets: Natural Resources   361
   Balance Sheet Presentation   361
   Depletion of Natural Resources   361
Operating Assets: Intangible Assets   362
   Balance Sheet Presentation   363
   Acquisition Cost of Intangible Assets   364
   Amortization of Intangibles   365
How Long-Term Assets Affect the Statement
of Cash Flows   367
Analyzing Long-Term Assets for Average Life
and Asset Turnover   368
Using the Ratio Decision Model: Analyzing Average Life
and Asset Turnover   369
Integrative Problem   389

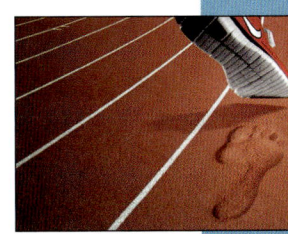

CHAPTER 9   Current Liabilities, Contingencies, and the Time
Value of Money   392

Jacuzzi: Making Business Decisions   393
Current Liabilities   395
   Accounts Payable   396
   Notes Payable   396
   Current Maturities of Long-Term Debt   398
   Taxes Payable   398
   Other Accrued Liabilities   398
   Reading the Statement of Cash Flows for Changes in Current
   Liabilities   399
Contingent Liabilities   401
   Contingent Liabilities That Are Recorded   401
   Contingent Liabilities That Are Disclosed   402
   Contingent Liabilities versus Contingent Assets   404
Time Value of Money Concepts   405
   Simple Interest   406
   Compound Interest   406
   Interest Compounding   406
   Future Value of a Single Amount   407

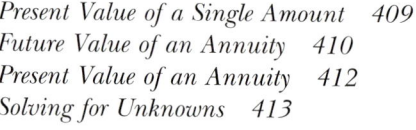

Present Value of a Single Amount   409
Future Value of an Annuity   410
Present Value of an Annuity   412
Solving for Unknowns   413

APPENDIX A—Accounting Tools: Payroll Accounting   419

APPENDIX B—Accounting Tools: Using Excel for Problems Involving Interest Calculations   423

CHAPTER 10   Long-Term Liabilities   454

Coca-Cola: Making Business Decisions   455
Balance Sheet Presentation   457
Bonds Payable   458
 Characteristics of Bonds   458
 Issuance of Bonds   460
 Factors Affecting Bond Price   460
 Premium or Discount on Bonds   462
 Bond Amortization   464
 Redemption of Bonds   467
Liability for Leases   469
 Leases   469
Analyzing Debt to Assess a Firm's Ability to Pay Its Liabilities   473
How Long-Term Liabilities Affect the Statement of Cash Flows   474
Using the Ratio Decision Model: *Analyzing the Debt-to-Equity and Times Interest Earned Ratios   474*

APPENDIX—Accounting Tools: Other Liabilities   476

CHAPTER 11   Stockholders' Equity   498

Jacuzzi: Making Business Decisions   499
An Overview of Stockholders' Equity   500
 Equity as a Source of Financing   500
 Stockholders' Equity on the Balance Sheet   501
 How Income and Dividends Affect Retained Earnings   502
 Identifying the Components of the Stockholders' Equity Section of the Balance Sheet   502
What Is Preferred Stock?   505
Issuance of Stock   506
 Stock Issued for Cash   506
 Stock Issued for Noncash Consideration   506
What Is Treasury Stock?   507
Retirement of Stock   508
Dividends: Distribution of Income to Shareholders   509
 Cash Dividends   509
 Cash Dividends for Preferred and Common Stock   509
 Stock Dividends   510
 Stock Splits   512
Statement of Stockholders' Equity   513
What Is Comprehensive Income?   514
What Analyzing Stockholders' Equity Reveals About a Firm's Value   516
 Book Value per Share   516
Using the Ratio Decision Model: *Analyzing Book Value per Share   516*
 Calculating Book Value When Preferred Stock Is Present   518
 Market Value per Share   519
How Changes in Stockholders' Equity Affect the Statement of Cash Flows   519

APPENDIX—Accounting Tools: Unincorporated Businesses **521**

Integrative Problem 547

CHAPTER 12 The Statement of Cash Flows 550

Best Buy: Making Business Decisions 551
Cash Flows and Accrual Accounting 553
Purpose of the Statement of Cash Flows 554
  An Example 554
Reporting Requirements for a Statement of Cash Flows 555
  The Definition of Cash: Cash and Cash Equivalents 556
  Classification of Cash Flows 557
  Two Methods of Reporting Cash Flow from Operating Activities 560
  Noncash Investing and Financing Activities 562
How the Statement of Cash Flows Is Put Together 564
  The Accounting Equation and the Statement of Cash Flows 564
  An Approach to Preparing the Statement of Cash Flows: Direct Method 565
  An Approach to Preparing the Statement of Cash Flows: Indirect Method 575
  Comparison of the Indirect and Direct Methods 576
The Use of Cash Flow Information 577
  Creditors and Cash Flow Adequacy 577
Using the Ratio Decision Model: *Analyzing Cash Flow Adequacy 578*
  Stockholders and Cash Flow per Share 580

APPENDIX—Accounting Tools: A Work-Sheet Approach to the Statement of Cash Flows 580

CHAPTER 13 Financial Statement Analysis 612

Wm. Wrigley Jr. Company: Making Business Decisions 613
Precautions in Statement Analysis 614
  Watch for Alternative Accounting Principles 614
  Take Care When Making Comparisons 614
  Understand the Possible Effects of Inflation 615
Analysis of Comparative and Common-Size Statements 616
  Horizontal Analysis 616
  Vertical Analysis 621
Liquidity Analysis and the Management of Working Capital 623
  Working Capital 623
  Current Ratio 624
  Acid-Test Ratio 624
  Cash Flow from Operations to Current Liabilities 625
  Accounts Receivable Analysis 626
  Inventory Analysis 627
  Cash Operating Cycle 628
Solvency Analysis 628
  Debt-to-Equity Ratio 628
  Times Interest Earned 629
  Debt Service Coverage 629
  Cash Flow from Operations to Capital Expenditures Ratio 630
Profitability Analysis 631
  Rate of Return on Assets 631
  Components of Return on Assets 632
  Return on Common Stockholders' Equity 633
  Return on Assets, Return on Equity, and Leverage 633
  Earnings per Share 634
  Price/Earnings Ratio 635

Dividend Ratios   636

Summary of Selected Financial Ratios   636

APPENDIX—Accounting Tools: Reporting and Analyzing Other Income Statement Items   638

Integrative Problem   671

EXCERPTS FROM THE FINISH LINE, INC., FORM 10-K FOR 2006   A-1

EXCERPTS FROM FOOT LOCKER, INC., FORM 10-K FOR 2005   B-1

GLOSSARY   G-1

COMPREHENSIVE INDEX   I-1

USING FINANCIAL ACCOUNTING INFORMATION

The Alternative to Debits and Credits

5e

Gary A. **Porter**

+

Curtis L. **Norton**

Northern Illinois University

Getting Started in Business

Study Links

A Look at This Introduction
Business is the foundation upon which accounting rests. This introduction explains the nature of business, the different forms of organization, and the types of activities in which businesses engage.

A Look at the Upcoming Chapter
Chapter 1 introduces you to accounting and the output of an accounting system, the financial statements. As a form of communication, we will explore how accounting provides useful information to a variety of users and the various roles that accountants play in organizations.

Learning Outcomes

After studying this module, you should be able to:

LO1 Understand what business is about.
LO2 Distinguish among the forms of organization.
LO3 Describe the various types of business activities.

The Finish Line, Inc.

MAKING BUSINESS DECISIONS

Pick your favorite company. Maybe it is The Gap, because you buy all of your clothes there. Or maybe it is The Tribune Company because it owns your favorite team, the Chicago Cubs. Or is it The Coca-Cola Company because you like its commercials? At any rate, have you ever wondered how the company got started? Consider the case of The Finish Line, Inc. The familiar, mall-based retailer of athletic shoes and fitness apparel got its start back in 1976 when two childhood friends decided to take a risk. Alan Cohen and David Klapper opened the first Finish Line (at the time a franchise of Athlete's Foot) in Indianapolis, Indiana. The company is now the second largest athletic retailer, and by November 2006 it was operating over 690 Finish Line stores in 47 states.

In its 2005 fiscal year, a mere thirty years after its start with that one franchise, Finish Line's sales topped the one billion dollar mark for the first time. Most impressive is the growth achieved since 1998, when sales were $500 million, half of those reported in 2005. Certainly our fitness-minded society has been a significant factor in Finish Line's tremendous growth. However, any successful company owes a major part of its success to its ability to make *financial decisions*. Initially, Alan Cohen and David Klapper made a crucial decision to invest their own money and open a shoe store. Would *you* have been willing to risk your savings to start a business from the ground up? This was a financial decision the two founders of Finish Line had to make.

Along the way, there were other major decisions to be made. Because their Athlete's Foot franchise rights were limited to Indiana (with the exception of the city of Louisville, Kentucky) the two men decided in 1981 to start their own company, called Finish Line, and in the process add two more partners. Like all retailers that continue to grow, Finish Line needed to add more retail outlets, which in turn took more cash. One way to get cash is to borrow it. However, bankers will lend only a certain amount of money before they want to see additional investments by the owners of the business. So, in 1992, the four partners made another crucial decision in the life of their relatively young company and "took it public." That is, they sold stock to the public and allowed others to become part owners of the business. As is the case for most companies, a public offering of stock gave Finish Line the additional money it needed to continue to grow and become an industry leader.

All of the major events in the history of Finish Line have involved a need to take risks and make decisions. For example, every time the company considers adding a new store in a mall, it must take a risk and decide whether sales in a new location will warrant the sizeable upfront investment and the continuing costs of running the store. In all decisions, the decision makers must rely on financial information. We all use financial information in making decisions. For example, when you were deciding whether or not to enroll at your present school, you needed information on the tuition and, in some cases, the room-and-board costs at the different schools you were considering. When a stockbroker decides whether or not to recommend to a client the purchase of stock in a company, the broker needs information on the company's profits and whether it pays dividends. When trying to decide whether or not to lend money to a company, a banker must consider the company's current debts.

In this book, we explore how accounting can help all of us make informed financial decisions. Before we turn to the role played by accounting in decision making, we need to explore business in more detail:

- What is business? (See pp. 4–5)
- What forms of organization carry on business activities? (See pp. 5–7)
- In what types of business activities do those organizations engage? (See pp. 7–9)

Source: The information reported here is provided in more detail on Finish Line's Web site primarily in the section titled "Our Company—History."

What Is Business?

LO1 Understand what business is about.

Business
All the activities necessary to provide the members of an economic system with goods and services.

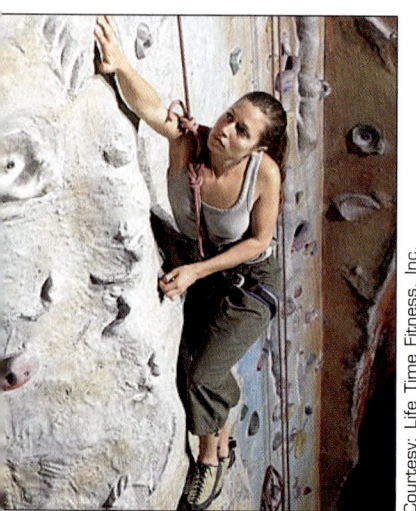

Like rock climbing, starting and growing a business takes focus, energy, endurance, a sense of responsibility, inner strength, and an ability to balance a number of demands.

Just as Finish Line got its start with its store in Indianapolis, your study of accounting has to start somewhere. All disciplines have a foundation on which they rest. For accounting, that foundation is business.

Broadly defined, **business** consists of all the activities necessary to provide the members of an economic system with goods and services. Certain business activities focus on the providing of goods or products, such as ice cream, running shoes, and computers. Some of these companies produce or manufacture the products. Others are involved in the distribution of the goods, either as wholesalers (who sell to retail outlets) or retailers (who sell to consumers). Other business activities by their nature are service oriented. Corporate giants such as **Citicorp**, **Walt Disney**, **Time Warner**, and **United Airlines** remind us of the prominence of service activities in the world today. The relatively recent phenomenon of various "service providers," such as health-care organizations and Internet companies, is a testimony to the growing importance of the service sector in the U.S. economy.

To appreciate the kinds of business enterprises in our economy, consider the various types of companies that have a stake in the delivery of a pint of ice cream to the grocery store. We will use as an example the case of Daisy's Dairy, a producer of super-premium ice cream. First, Daisy's Dairy must contract with a local milk *supplier,* Cramden Creamery. As a *manufacturer* or *producer,* Daisy's Dairy takes the milk and other various raw materials, such as sugar and chocolate, and transforms them into a finished product. At this stage, a *distributor* or *wholesaler* gets involved. For example, Daisy's Dairy sells a considerable amount of its ice cream to Duffy's Distributors. Duffy's Distributors, in turn, sells the products to many different *retailers,* such as **Albertson's** and **Safeway**. Although maybe less obvious, any number of *service* companies are also involved in the process. For example, ABC Transport hauls the milk to Daisy's Dairy for production, and others move the ice cream along to Duffy's Distributors. Still others get it to supermarkets and other retail outlets. Exhibit I-1 summarizes the process.

EXHIBIT I-1   Types of Businesses

Forms of Organization

There are many different types of organizations in our society. One convenient way to categorize the myriad types is to distinguish between those that are organized to earn money and those that exist for some other purpose. Although the lines can become blurred, *business entities* generally are organized to earn a profit, whereas *nonbusiness entities* generally exist to serve various segments of society. Both types are summarized in Exhibit I-2.

LO2 Distinguish among the forms of organization.

BUSINESS ENTITIES

Business entities are organized to earn a profit. Legally, a profit-oriented company is one of three types: a sole proprietorship, a partnership, or a corporation.

Business entity
Organization operated to earn a profit.

Sole Proprietorships This form of organization is characterized by a single owner. Many small businesses are organized as **sole proprietorships.** Very often the

Sole proprietorship
Form of organization with a single owner.

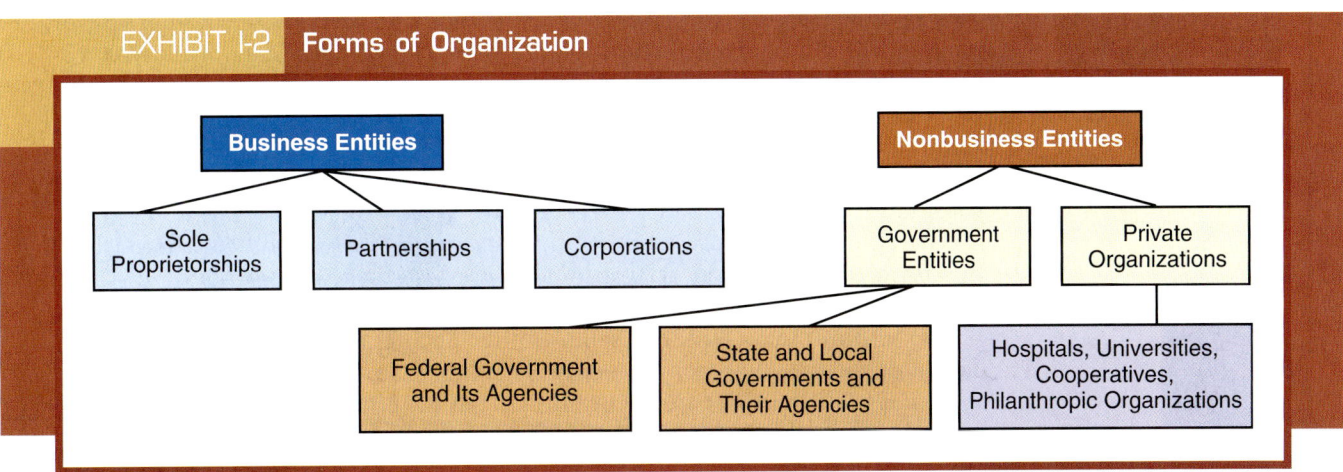

EXHIBIT I-2   Forms of Organization

Economic entity concept
The assumption that a single, identifiable unit must be accounted for in all situations.

business is owned and operated by the same person. Because of the close relationship between the owner and the business, the affairs of the two must be kept separate. This is one example in accounting of the **economic entity concept,** which requires that a single, identifiable unit of organization be accounted for in all situations. For example, assume that Bernie Berg owns a neighborhood grocery store. In paying the monthly bills, such as utilities and supplies, Bernie must separate his personal costs from the costs associated with the grocery business. In turn, financial statements prepared for the business must not intermingle Bernie's personal affairs with the company affairs.

Unlike the distinction made for accounting purposes between an individual's personal and business affairs, the IRS does not recognize the separate existence of a proprietorship from its owner. That is, a sole proprietorship is not a taxable entity; any profits earned by the business are taxed on the return of the individual.

Partnership
A business owned by two or more individuals; organization form often used by accounting firms and law firms.

Partnerships A **partnership** is a business owned by two or more individuals. Many small businesses begin as partnerships. When two or more partners start out, they need some sort of agreement as to how much each will contribute to the business and how they will divide any profits. In many small partnerships, the agreement is often just an oral understanding between the partners. In large businesses, the partnership agreement is formalized in a written document.

Although a partnership may involve just two owners, some have thousands of partners. Public accounting firms, law firms, and other types of service companies are often organized as partnerships. Like a sole proprietorship, a partnership is not a taxable entity. The individual partners pay taxes on their proportionate shares of the profits of the business.

Corporation
A form of entity organized under the laws of a particular state; ownership evidenced by shares of stock.

Share of stock
A certificate that acts as evidence of ownership in a corporation.

Corporations Although sole proprietorships and partnerships dominate in sheer number, corporations control an overwhelming majority of the private resources in this country. A **corporation** is an entity organized under the laws of a particular state. Each of the 50 states is empowered to regulate the creation and operation of businesses organized as corporations in it. The Finish Line, Inc., is incorporated under the laws of the state of Indiana.

To start a corporation, one must file articles of incorporation with the state. If the articles are approved by the state, a corporate charter is issued, and the corporation can begin to issue stock. A **share of stock** is a certificate that acts as evidence of ownership in a corporation. Although not always the case, stocks of many corporations are traded on organized stock exchanges, such as the New York and American Stock Exchanges.

What are the advantages of running a business as a corporation? One of the primary advantages of the corporate form of organization is the ability to raise large amounts of money in a relatively brief period of time. This is what prompted Finish Line to "go public" in 1992. To raise money, the company sold a specific type of security: stock. As stated earlier, a share of stock is simply a certificate that evidences ownership in a corporation. Sometimes, corporations issue another type of security called a bond. A **bond** is similar in that it is a certificate or piece of paper issued to someone. However, it is different from a share of stock in that a bond represents a promise by the company to repay a certain amount of money at a future date. In other words, if you were to buy a bond from a company, you would be lending it money. Interest on the bond is usually paid semiannually. You will learn more about stocks and bonds later.

Bond
A certificate that represents a corporation's promise to repay a certain amount of money and interest in the future.

The ease of transfer of ownership in a corporation is another advantage of this form of organization. If you hold shares of stock in a corporation whose stock is actively traded and you decide that you want out, you simply call your broker and put in an order to sell. Another distinct advantage is the limited liability of the stockholder. Generally speaking, a stockholder is liable only for the amount contributed to the business. That is, if a company goes out of business, the most the stockholder stands to lose is the amount invested. On the other hand, both proprietors and general partners usually can be held personally liable for the debts of the business.

NONBUSINESS ENTITIES

Most **nonbusiness entities** are organized for a purpose other than to earn a profit. They exist to serve the needs of various segments of society. For example, a hospital is organized to provide health care to its patients. A municipal government is operated for the benefit of its citizens. A local school district exists to meet the educational needs of the youth in the community.

All these entities are distinguished by the lack of an identifiable owner. The lack of an identifiable owner and of the profit motive changes to some extent the type of accounting used by nonbusiness entities. This type, called *fund accounting*, is discussed in advanced accounting courses. Regardless of the lack of a profit motive in nonbusiness entities, there is still a demand for the information provided by an accounting system. For example, a local government needs detailed cost breakdowns in order to levy taxes. A hospital may want to borrow money and will need financial statements to present to the prospective lender.

Nonbusiness entity
Organization operated for some purpose other than to earn a profit.

ORGANIZATIONS AND SOCIAL RESPONSIBILITY

Although nonbusiness entities are organized specifically to serve members of society, U.S. business entities also have become more sensitive to their broader social responsibilities. Because they touch the lives of so many members of society, most large corporations recognize the societal aspects of their overall mission and have established programs to meet their social responsibilities. Some companies focus their efforts on local charities, while others donate to national or international causes. All of the companies showcased in the chapter openers of this book have programs in place to meet their corporate giving objectives.

The Nature of Business Activity

Because corporations dominate business activity in the United States, in this book we will focus on this form of organization. Corporations engage in a multitude of different types of activities. It is possible to categorize all of them into one of three types, however: financing, investing, and operating.

LO3 Describe the various types of business activities.

FINANCING ACTIVITIES

All businesses must start with financing. Simply put, money is needed to start a business. The founders of Finish Line needed money in 1976 to open their first store. As described earlier, the company found itself in need of additional financing in 1992 and thus made the decision to sell stock to the public. Most companies not only sell stock to raise money but also borrow from various sources to finance their operations.

Accounting has its own unique terminology. In fact, accounting is often referred to as *the language of business*. The discussion of financing activities brings up two important accounting terms: "liabilities" and "capital stock." A **liability** is an obligation of a business; it can take many different forms. When a company borrows money at a bank, the liability is called a *note payable*. When a company sells bonds, the obligation is termed *bonds payable*. Amounts owed to the government for taxes are called *taxes payable*. Assume Finish Line buys cleaning supplies to be used in one of its stores. Assume the supplier gives Finish Line 30 days to pay the amount owed. During this 30-day period, Finish Line has an obligation called *accounts payable*.

Capital stock is the term used by accountants to indicate the dollar amount of stock sold to the public. Capital stock differs from liabilities in one very important

Liability
An obligation of a business.

Capital stock
Indicates the owners' contributions to a corporation.

Stockholder
One of the owners of a corporation. *Alternate term: Shareholder*

Creditor
Someone to whom a company or person has a debt. *Alternate term: Lender*

respect. Those who buy stock in a corporation are not lending money to the business, as are those who buy bonds in the company or make a loan in some other form to the company. Someone who buys stock in a company is called a **stockholder,** and that person is providing a permanent form of financing to the business. In other words, there is not a due date at which time the stockholder will be repaid. Normally, the only way for a stockholder to get back his or her original investment from buying stock is to sell it to someone else. Someone who buys bonds in a company or in some other way makes a loan to it is called a **creditor.** A creditor does *not* provide a permanent form of financing to the business. That is, the creditor expects repayment of the amount loaned and, in many instances, payment of interest for the use of the money.

INVESTING ACTIVITIES

There is a natural progression in a business from financing activities to investing activities. That is, once funds are generated from creditors and stockholders, money is available to invest. For example, Finish Line used some of the money it received from selling stock to the public in 1992 to open new stores.

Asset
A future economic benefit.

An **asset** is a future economic benefit to a business. For example, cash is an asset to a company. To Finish Line, its furniture and fixtures in its stores are assets. Those stores are filled with all sorts of athletic footwear and apparel. These products on hand in the stores that are awaiting sale to customers are called *inventories* and are another valuable asset of the company.

An asset represents the right to receive some sort of benefit in the future. The point is that not all assets are tangible in nature, as are inventories and buildings and equipment. For example, assume that Finish Line sells a product and allows the customer to pay at the end of 30 days. At the time of the sale, Finish Line doesn't have cash yet, but it has another valuable asset. The right to collect the amount due from the customer in 30 days is an asset called an *account receivable.* As a second example, assume that a company acquires from an inventor a patent that will allow the company the exclusive right to manufacture a certain product. The right to the future economic benefits from the patent is an asset. In summary, an asset is a valuable resource to the company that controls it.

At this point, you should notice the inherent tie between assets and liabilities. How does a company satisfy its liabilities, that is, its obligations? Although there are some exceptions, most liabilities are settled by transferring assets. The asset most often used to settle a liability is cash.

OPERATING ACTIVITIES

Once funds are obtained from financing activities and investments are made in productive assets, a business is ready to begin operations. Every business is organized with a purpose in mind. The purpose of some businesses is to sell a *product.* For example, **Nike** was organized to manufacture and sell shoes. Other companies provide *services.* Service-oriented businesses are becoming an increasingly important sector of the U.S. economy. Some of the largest corporations in this country, such as banks and airlines, sell services rather than products.

Revenue
An inflow of assets resulting from the sale of goods and services.

Accountants have a name for the sale of products and services. **Revenue** is the inflow of assets resulting from the sale of products and services. When a company makes a cash sale, the asset it receives is cash. When a sale is made on credit, the asset received is an account receivable. Revenue represents the dollar amount of sales of products and services for a specific period of time.

We have thus far identified one important operating activity: the sale of products and services. However, costs must be incurred to operate a business. Finish Line must pay its employees salaries and wages. Suppliers must be paid for purchases of inventory, and the utility company has to be paid for heat and electricity. The government must be paid the taxes owed it. All of these are examples of important operating activities of a business. Accountants use a specific name for the costs incurred in operating a business. An **expense** is the outflow of assets resulting from the sale of goods and services.

Exhibit I-3 summarizes the three types of activities conducted by a business. Our discussion and the exhibit present a simplification of business activity, but actual businesses are in a constant state of motion with many different financing, investing, and operating activities going on at any one time. Still, the model as portrayed in Exhibit I-3 should be helpful as you begin the study of accounting. To summarize, a company obtains money from various types of financing activities, uses the money raised to invest in productive assets, and then provides goods and services to its customers.

Expense
An outflow of assets resulting from the sale of goods and services.

EXHIBIT I-3   A Model of Business Activities

Financing Activities
Raising money to start the business

Finish Line started with owner investments.

Money raised through financing is needed for investing.

Some profits are used to pay creditors

while other profits are reinvested in productive assets—such as those needed to open new stores.

Operating Activities
Generating revenues (and profits) via sales

Finish Line sells products to its customers.

Assets are used to generate revenues.

Investing Activities
Buying assets

Finish Line invested in assets such as inventory to start its business.

Starting Your Study of Accounting

The purpose of this module is to introduce you to business and help you to understand why it is the foundation on which accounting is based. Now that you have a basic understanding of what business is, the types of organizations that engage in business, and the various activities they conduct, you are ready to begin the study of accounting itself.

This module introduced you to business and decision making by telling a brief story of how Finish Line got started. You will learn more about the company and its financial statements in the next two chapters. Other new companies will be featured at the start of other chapters as a way of introducing the material in that chapter.

If you do not own stock in one of these companies, how can you get access to its financial statements and other information about it? One way is by calling or writing to the company's investor relations department. A much more efficient and timely approach to gathering this information, however, is to use the Internet. Nearly all major corporations, as well as many smaller ones, now post financial statements and other information on their Web sites.

KEY TERMS QUIZ

Note to the student: We conclude each chapter with a quiz on the key terms, which are in bold where they appear in the chapter. We have included a quiz for the numerous important terms introduced in this introduction.

Read each definition below and then write the number of that definition in the blank beside the appropriate term it defines. The first one has been done for you. The solution appears at the end of this introduction. When reviewing terminology, come back to your completed key terms quiz. Study tip: Also check the glossary in the margin or at the end of the book.

_____ Business	_____ Nonbusiness entity
_____ Business entity	_____ Liability
_____ Sole proprietorship	_____ Capital stock
_____ Economic entity concept	_____ Stockholder
_____ Partnership	_____ Creditor
_____ Corporation	__1__ Asset
_____ Share of stock	_____ Revenue
_____ Bond	_____ Expense

1. A future economic benefit.
2. A business owned by two or more individuals; organization form often used by accounting firms and law firms.
3. An inflow of assets resulting from the sale of goods and services.
4. A form of entity organized under the laws of a particular state; ownership evidenced by shares of stock.
5. Organization operated for some purpose other than to earn a profit.
6. An outflow of assets resulting from the sale of goods and services.
7. An obligation of a business.
8. A certificate that acts as evidence of ownership in a corporation.
9. A certificate that represents a corporation's promise to repay a certain amount of money and interest in the future.
10. One of the owners of a corporation.
11. Someone to whom a company or person has a debt.
12. The assumption that a single, identifiable unit must be accounted for in all situations.
13. Form of organization with a single owner.
14. Indicates the owners' contributions to a corporation.
15. All the activities necessary to provide the members of an economic system with goods and services.
16. Organization operated to earn a profit.

ALTERNATE TERMS

Creditor Lender
Stockholder Shareholder

QUESTIONS

1. What is business about? What do all businesses have in common?

2. What is an asset? Give three examples.

3. What is a liability? How does the definition of *liability* relate to the definition of *asset*?

4. Business entities are organized as one of three distinct forms. What are these three forms?

5. What are the three distinct types of business activity in which companies engage? Assume you start your own company to rent bicycles in the summer and skis in the winter. Give an example of at least one of each of the three types of business activities in which you would engage.

SOLUTIONS TO KEY TERMS QUIZ

15	Business	5	Nonbusiness entity
16	Business entity	7	Liability
13	Sole proprietorship	14	Capital stock
12	Economic entity concept	10	Stockholder
2	Partnership	11	Creditor
4	Corporation	1	Asset
8	Share of stock	3	Revenue
9	Bond	6	Expense

HOMEWORK

1

Accounting as a Form of Communication

Study Links

A Look at This Chapter

We begin the study of accounting by considering what accounting is and who uses the information it provides. We will see that accounting is an important form of communication and that financial statements are the medium that accountants use to communicate with those who have some interest in the financial affairs of a company.

A Look at Upcoming Chapters

Chapter 1 introduces you to accounting and financial statements. In Chapter 2, we look in more detail at the composition of the statements and the conceptual framework that supports the work of an accountant. Chapter 3 steps back from financial statements and examines how companies process economic events as a basis for preparing the statements. Chapter 4 completes our introduction to the accounting model by considering the importance of accrual accounting in this communication process.

Learning Outcomes

After studying this chapter, you should be able to:

LO1 Identify the primary users of accounting information and their needs.

LO2 Explain the purpose of each of the financial statements and the relationships among them, and prepare a set of simple statements.

LO3 Identify and explain the primary assumptions made in preparing financial statements.

LO4 Explain the critical role that ethics play in providing useful financial information.

LO5 Describe the various roles of accountants in organizations.

The Finish Line, Inc.

MAKING BUSINESS DECISIONS

All businesses have a few key measures of success in reaching their goals. Some of these measures, such as sales, are financial in nature while others are not. Even though the number of Finish Line stores and total retail square footage are nonfinancial statistics, it is easy to understand how these numbers relate to the company's financial success. Finish Line reported in the Financial Summary included in its annual report and reproduced here a healthy 12 percent increase in net sales during fiscal 2006. The prior period was a pivotal year, with net sales topping a billion dollars for the first time, and 2006 continued the upward trend with over $1.3 billion in sales of footwear, apparel, and accessories. And to emphasize what has been driving sales growth, the company reported that its total retail square footage was up by 10 percent in 2006.

For most of its 30-year existence, the company has stayed close to its roots by focusing on its running shoe stores under the Finish Line name. It wasn't until 2005 that it broadened its scope with the acquisition of the Man Alive stores, one of the country's

leading hip-hop fashion retailers. As the summary indicates, 14 new Man Alive stores were added to the existing 37 during 2006, bringing the total to 51 by year-end. While this represents less than 10 percent of the company's total stores, it plans to open 35 new Man Alive locations in 2007. Another signal of the company's intentions to broaden its appeal to the mall shopper was the creation of a new venture in 2006 called Paiva. The first of these premium athletic stores for women was opened in Austin, Texas, in April 2006, with plans to have 15 stores open by the end of the 2007 fiscal year.

Certainly it takes more than just opening additional outlets to improve a retailer's financial performance. First, those stores need to prove their ability to attract shoppers and add to the company's sales growth. But even that isn't enough. Along with new stores come added costs, and the ability to control these costs is what ultimately determines whether a company improves its "bottom line," or net income. How the company measures the number of new stores is easy. But how did Finish Line come up with total revenue of $1.3 billion in 2006? And how did it determine that its net income for the same year was $60.5 million? As you study this chapter, look for answers to these key questions:

- What is revenue and how is it measured? (See pp. 23–25)

- What is net income and how is it measured? (See pp. 23–25)

- How do revenue and net income relate to a company's assets? (See pp. 23–25)

- Where do these various items appear on a company's financial statements? (See pp. 23–25)

As you study Chapter 1, consider how answers to these questions can help you decide whether Finish Line had a successful year and is on the right track.

2006 FINANCIAL SUMMARY

Dollars in thousands except per share data

	Fiscal 2006	Fiscal 2005	Fiscal 2004
Net sales	$1,306,045	$1,166,767	$985,891
Operating income	$94,905	$96,947	$75,716
Operating income as a % of net sales	7.3%	8.3%	7.7%
Net income	$60,533	$61,263	$47,347
Net income as a % of net sales	4.6%	5.3%	4.8%
Diluted earnings per share	$1.23	$1.24	$.98
Total assets	$627,816	$575,019	$460,742
Cash and marketable securities	$96,563	$113,166	$95,852
Total debt	$0	$0	$0
Total shareholders' equity	$428,542	$385,971	$320,653
Finish Line stores	657	598	531
Man Alive stores	51	37	–
Avg. Finish Line store size	5,641	5,710	5,802
Avg. Man Alive store size	3,110	2,831	–
Total retail square footage	3,864,739	3,519,114	3,080,995

Record $1.3 billion in sales

Sales topped $1 billion for first time

Net income of over $60 million in each of last two years

The Company's fiscal year ends on the Saturday nearest to the end of February. As used in this report, "Fiscal 2002," "Fiscal 2003," "Fiscal 2004," "Fiscal 2005" and "Fiscal 2006" refer to the company's fiscal years ended March 2, 2002; March 1, 2003; February 28, 2004; February 26, 2005; and February 25, 2006, respectively. "Fiscal 2007" and "Fiscal 2008" refer to the company's fiscal years ending March 3, 2007, and March 2, 2008, respectively.

Net Sales (in millions) — +12%

Total Retail Sq. Footage (000's) — +10%

Total Finish Line Stores — +10%

Total Man Alive Stores — +38%

Source: Finish Line's 2006 Annual Report.

What Is Accounting?

Accounting
The process of identifying, measuring, and communicating economic information to various users.

Many people have preconceived notions about what accounting is. They think of it as a highly procedural activity practiced by people who are "good in math." This notion of accounting is very narrow and focuses only on the record-keeping or bookkeeping aspects of the discipline. Accounting is in fact much broader than this in its scope. Specifically, **accounting** is "the process of identifying, measuring, and communicating economic information to permit informed judgments and decisions by users of the information.[1]

Each of the three activities in this definition—*identifying, measuring,* and *communicating*—requires the judgment of a trained professional. We will return later in this chapter to accounting as a profession and the various roles of accountants in our society. Note that the definition refers to the users of economic information and the decisions they make. Who *are* the users of accounting information? We turn now to this important question.

Users of Accounting Information and Their Needs

It is helpful to categorize users of accounting information on the basis of their relationship to the organization. Internal users, primarily the managers of a company, are involved in the daily affairs of the business. All other groups are external users.

LO1 Identify the primary users of accounting information and their needs.

INTERNAL USERS

The management of a company is in a position to obtain financial information in a way that best suits its needs. For example, if management of a Finish Line store needs to know whether or not the store's revenues are enough to cover its operating costs, this information exists in the accounting system and can be reported. If the manager wants to find out if the monthly payroll is more or less than the budgeted amount, a report can be generated to provide the answer. **Management accounting** is the branch of accounting concerned with providing internal users (management) with information to facilitate planning and control. The ability to produce management accounting reports is limited only by the extent of the data available and the cost involved in generating the relevant information.

Management accounting
The branch of accounting concerned with providing management with information to facilitate planning and control.

EXTERNAL USERS

External users, those not involved directly in the operations of a business, need information that differs from that needed by internal users. In addition, the ability of external users to obtain the information is more limited. Without the day-to-day contact with the affairs of the business, outsiders must rely on the information presented to them by the management of the company.

Certain external users, such as the Internal Revenue Service, require that information be presented in a very specific manner, and they have the authority of the law to ensure that they get the required information. Stockholders, bondholders, and other creditors must rely on *financial statements* for their information.[2] **Financial accounting** is the branch of accounting concerned with communication with outsiders through financial statements.

Financial accounting
The branch of accounting concerned with the preparation of financial statements for outsider use.

Stockholders and Potential Stockholders Both existing and potential stockholders need financial information about a business. If you currently own stock in Finish Line, you need information that will aid in your decision either to continue to hold the stock or to sell it. If you are considering buying stock, you need financial information that will help in choosing among competing alternative investments. What has been the recent performance of the company in the stock market? What were its profits for the most recent year? How do these profits compare with those of the prior year? Did the company pay any dividends? One source for much of this information is the company's financial statements.

---

1 American Accounting Association, *A Statement of Basic Accounting Theory* (Evanston, Ill.: American Accounting Association, 1966), p. 1.

2 Technically, stockholders are insiders because they own stock in the business. In most large corporations, however, it is not practical for stockholders to be involved in the daily affairs of the business. Thus, they are better categorized here as external users because they normally rely on general-purpose financial statements, as do creditors.

Bondholders, Bankers, and Other Creditors Before buying a bond in a company (remember you are lending money to the company), you need to feel comfortable that the company will be able to pay you the amount owed at maturity and the periodic interest payments. Financial statements can help you to decide whether or not to purchase a bond. Similarly, before lending money, a bank needs information that will help it to determine the company's ability to repay both the amount of the loan and interest. Therefore, a set of financial statements is a key ingredient in a loan proposal.

Government Agencies Numerous government agencies have information needs specified by law. For example, the Internal Revenue Service (IRS) is empowered to collect a tax on income from both individuals and corporations. Every year a company prepares a tax return to report to the IRS the amount of income it earned. Another government agency, the Securities and Exchange Commission (SEC), was created in the aftermath of the Great Depression. This regulatory agency sets the rules under which financial statements must be prepared for corporations that sell their stock to the public on organized stock exchanges. Similar to the IRS, the SEC prescribes the manner in which financial information is presented to it. Companies operating in specialized industries submit financial reports to other regulatory agencies, such as the Interstate Commerce Commission and the Federal Trade Commission.

Other External Users Many other individuals and groups rely on financial information given to them by businesses. A supplier of raw material needs to know the creditworthiness of a company before selling it a product on credit. To promote its industry, a trade association must gather financial information on the various companies in the industry. Other important users are stockbrokers and financial analysts. They use financial reports in advising their clients on investment decisions. In reaching their decisions, all of these users rely to a large extent on accounting information provided by management. Exhibit 1-1 summarizes the various users of financial information and the types of decisions they must make.

USING FINANCIAL ACCOUNTING INFORMATION

As stated earlier, financial accounting is concerned with communication with external users. One of the primary external users of accounting information is a stockholder. The box on page 17 contains a Financial Decision Framework that can be

EXHIBIT 1-1	Users of Accounting Information		
Categories of Users	**Examples of Users**	**Common Decision**	**Relevant Question**
Internal	Management	Should Finish Line open a new store?	What will be the cost to open the new store?
External	Stockholder	Should I buy shares of Finish Line stock?	How much did the company earn last year?
	Banker	Should I lend money to Finish Line?	What existing debts or liabilities does the company have?
	Employee	Should I ask for a raise?	How much are the company's revenues, and how much is it paying out in salaries and wages? Is the compensation it is paying reasonable compared to its revenues?
	Supplier	Should I allow Finish Line to buy supplies from me and pay me later?	What is the current amount of the company's accounts payable?

used to help make investment decisions using financial accounting information. Here you'll consider whether or not to buy a company's stock.

For example, for the last few months you have been eagerly awaiting an earnings announcement from Finish Line, the mall-based retailer of athletic footwear and apparel. You regularly shop at one of its stores but never gave much thought to the financial side of the company's business.

You log on to Finish Line's Web site and after clicking on the link to "Investor Relations," you begin to wonder . . . should I or shouldn't I buy stock in the company? Use the Financial Decision Framework to make your decision.

USING THE RATIO DECISION MODEL: A FINANCIAL DECISION FRAMEWORK

Use the following Decision Process to help you make an investment decision on Finish Line or any other public company.

1. Formulate the Question
For about the same as I spend in a year for running shoes and apparel at the store ($500), I could buy 20 shares of Finish Line stock at $25 per share.

- Should I invest $500 in Finish Line?

2. Gather Information from the Financial Statements and Other Sources
The information needed will come from a variety of sources:

- My personal finances at the present time
- Alternative uses for the $500
- The outlook for the industry
- Publicly available information about Finish Line, including its financial statements

3. Analyze the Financials
The information in the financial statements can be used to perform:

- Ratio analysis (looking at relationships among financial statement items)
- Horizontal analysis (looking at trends over time)
- Vertical analysis (comparing financial statement items in a single period)
- Comparisons with competitors
- Comparisons with industry averages

4. Make the Decision
Taking into account all of the various sources of information, you decide to either:

- Use the $500 for something else
- Invest the $500 in Finish Line

5. Interpret the Results
If you do decide to invest, you will want to periodically monitor your investment. Whether or not you made a good decision will be based on the answers to these two questions:

- Have I received any dividends on my shares?
- Has the price of the stock increased above the $25 per share I paid?

One of the most critical steps in this framework is gathering information from the financial statements, the means by which an accountant communicates information about a company to those interested in it. We explore these statements in the next section.

Financial Statements: How Accountants Communicate

LO2 Explain the purpose of each of the financial statements and the relationships among them, and prepare a set of simple statements.

Study Tip

The accounting equation and the financial statements are at the heart of this course. Memorize the accounting equation, and make sure you study this introduction to how the financial statements should look, how to read them, and what they say about a company.

Owners' equity
The owners' claims on the assets of an entity.

Stockholders' equity
The owners' equity in a corporation. *Alternate term: Shareholders' equity.*

Retained earnings
The part of owners' equity that represents the income earned less dividends paid over the life of an entity.

Balance sheet
The financial statement that summarizes the assets, liabilities, and owners' equity at a specific point in time. *Alternate term: Statement of financial position.*

The primary focus of this book is financial accounting. This branch of accounting is concerned with informing management and outsiders about a company through financial statements. We turn now to the composition of the four major statements: the balance sheet, the income statement, the statement of retained earnings, and the statement of cash flows.

THE ACCOUNTING EQUATION

The accounting equation is the foundation for the entire accounting system:

$$\text{Assets} = \text{Liabilities} + \text{Owners' Equity}$$

- **The left side of the accounting equation refers to the *assets* of the company.** Those items that are valuable economic resources and will provide future benefit to the company should appear on the left side of the equation.
- **The right side of the equation indicates who provided, or has a claim to, those assets.** Some of the assets were provided by creditors, and they have a claim to them. For example, if a company has a delivery truck, the dealer that provided the truck to the company has a claim to the assets until the dealer is paid. The delivery truck would appear on the left side of the equation as an asset to the company; the company's *liability* to the dealer would appear on the right side of the equation. Other assets are provided by the owners of the business. Their claims to these assets are represented by the portion of the right side of the equation called **owners' equity.**

This book focuses on corporations. The term *stockholders' equity* is used to refer to the owners' equity of a corporation. **Stockholders' equity** is the mathematical difference between a corporation's assets and its obligations or liabilities. That is, after the amounts owed to bondholders, banks, suppliers, and other creditors are subtracted from the assets, the amount remaining is the stockholders' equity, the amount of interest or claim that the owners have on the assets of the business. **Because we focus on corporations, from now on we will refer to stockholders' equity rather than owners' equity:**

$$\text{Assets} = \text{Liabilities} + \text{Stockholders' Equity}$$

Stockholders' equity arises in two distinct ways. First, it is created when a company issues stock to an investor. As we noted earlier, capital stock reflects ownership in a corporation in the form of a certificate. It represents the amounts contributed by the owners to the company. Second, as owners of shares in a corporation, stockholders have a claim on the assets of a business when it is profitable. **Retained earnings** represents the owners' claims to the company's assets that result from its earnings that have not been paid out in dividends. It is the earnings accumulated or retained by the company.

THE BALANCE SHEET

The balance sheet (sometimes called the *statement of financial position*) is the financial statement that summarizes the assets, liabilities, and owners' equity of a company. It is a "snapshot" of the business at a certain date. A balance sheet can be prepared on any day of the year, although it is most commonly prepared on the last day of a month, quarter, or year. At any point in time, the balance sheet must be "in balance." That is, assets must equal liabilities and owners' equity.

For a company like Finish Line, real financial statements can be quite complex, especially this early in your study of accounting. Therefore, before we attempt to read Finish Line's statements, we will start with a hypothetical company. Top of the World owns and operates a ski resort in the Rockies. The company's balance sheet on June 30, 2007, the end of its first year of business, is presented in Exhibit 1-2. As you study the exhibit, note the descriptions for each item to help you understand them better.

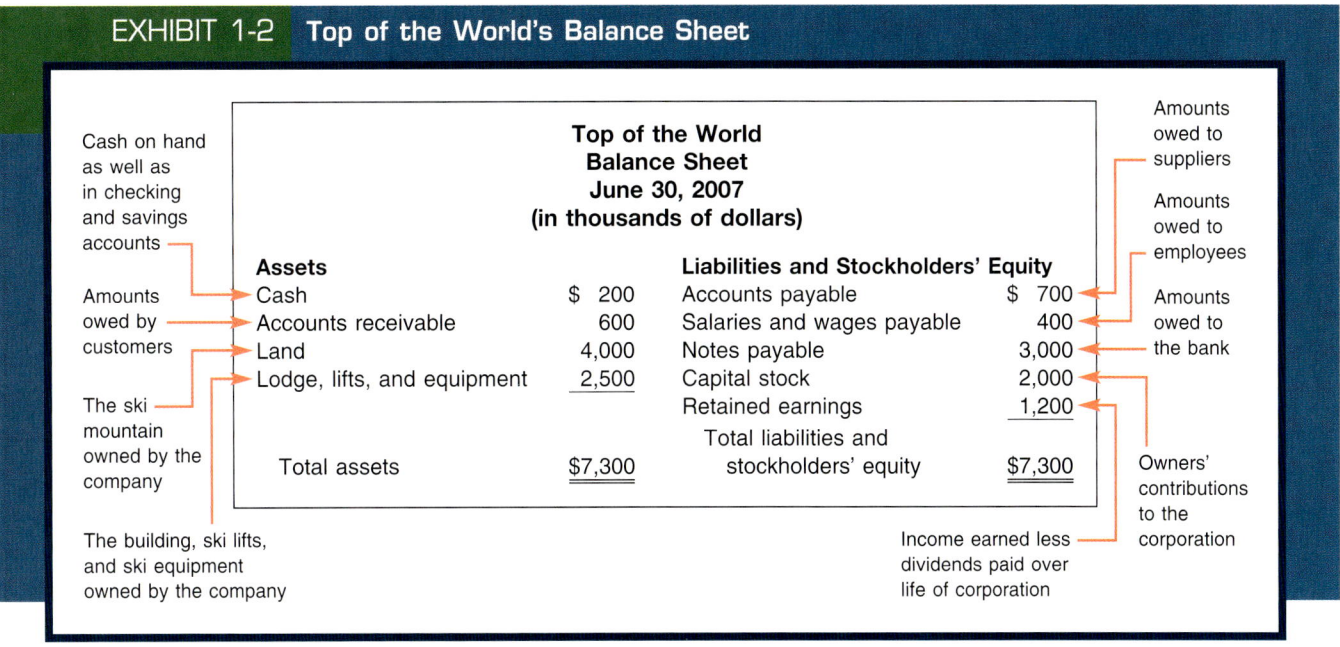

EXHIBIT 1-2   Top of the World's Balance Sheet

Cash on hand as well as in checking and savings accounts

Amounts owed by customers

The ski mountain owned by the company

The building, ski lifts, and ski equipment owned by the company

Top of the World
Balance Sheet
June 30, 2007
(in thousands of dollars)

Assets		**Liabilities and Stockholders' Equity**	
Cash	$ 200	Accounts payable	$ 700
Accounts receivable	600	Salaries and wages payable	400
Land	4,000	Notes payable	3,000
Lodge, lifts, and equipment	2,500	Capital stock	2,000
		Retained earnings	1,200
		Total liabilities and	
Total assets	$7,300	stockholders' equity	$7,300

Amounts owed to suppliers

Amounts owed to employees

Amounts owed to the bank

Owners' contributions to the corporation

Income earned less dividends paid over life of corporation

Two items should be noted in the heading of the statement. First, the company chose a date other than December 31, the calendar year-end, to finish its accounting or fiscal year. Although December 31 is the most common year-end, some companies choose a date other than this to conclude their year. Often this choice is based on when a company's peak selling season is over. For example, **The Gap** ends its accounting year on the Saturday closest to January 31, after the busy holiday season. By June 30, Top of the World's ski season has ended and the company can devote its attention to preparing its financial statements. The second item to note in the heading of the statements is the last line: "in thousands of dollars." This means, for example, that rather than cash being $200, the amount is actually 1,000 × $200, or $200,000.

Exhibit 1-3 summarizes the relationship between the accounting equation and the items that appear on a balance sheet.

THE INCOME STATEMENT

An income statement, or statement of income, as it is sometimes called, summarizes the revenues and expenses of a company for a period of time. An income statement for Top of the World for its first year in business is shown in Exhibit 1-4. **Unlike the balance sheet, an income statement is a *flow* statement.** That is, it summarizes the flow of revenues and expenses for the year. The top portion of Exhibit 1-4 makes it clear that the ski company has two distinct types of revenues: those from selling lift tickets and those from renting ski equipment. For example, if you paid the company $50 for a one-day lift ticket and another $30 to rent your equipment for the day, each of these amounts would be included in Top of the World's revenues for

Income statement
A statement that summarizes revenues and expenses. *Alternate term: Statement of income.*

EXHIBIT 1-3   The Relationship between the Accounting Equation and the Balance Sheet

Assets	**=**	**Liabilities**	**+**	**Stockholders' Equity**

Economic resources	**Creditors' claims to the assets**	**Owners' claims to the assets**
Examples:	Examples:	Examples:
• Cash	• Accounts payable	• Capital stock
• Accounts receivable	• Notes payable	• Retained earnings
• Land		

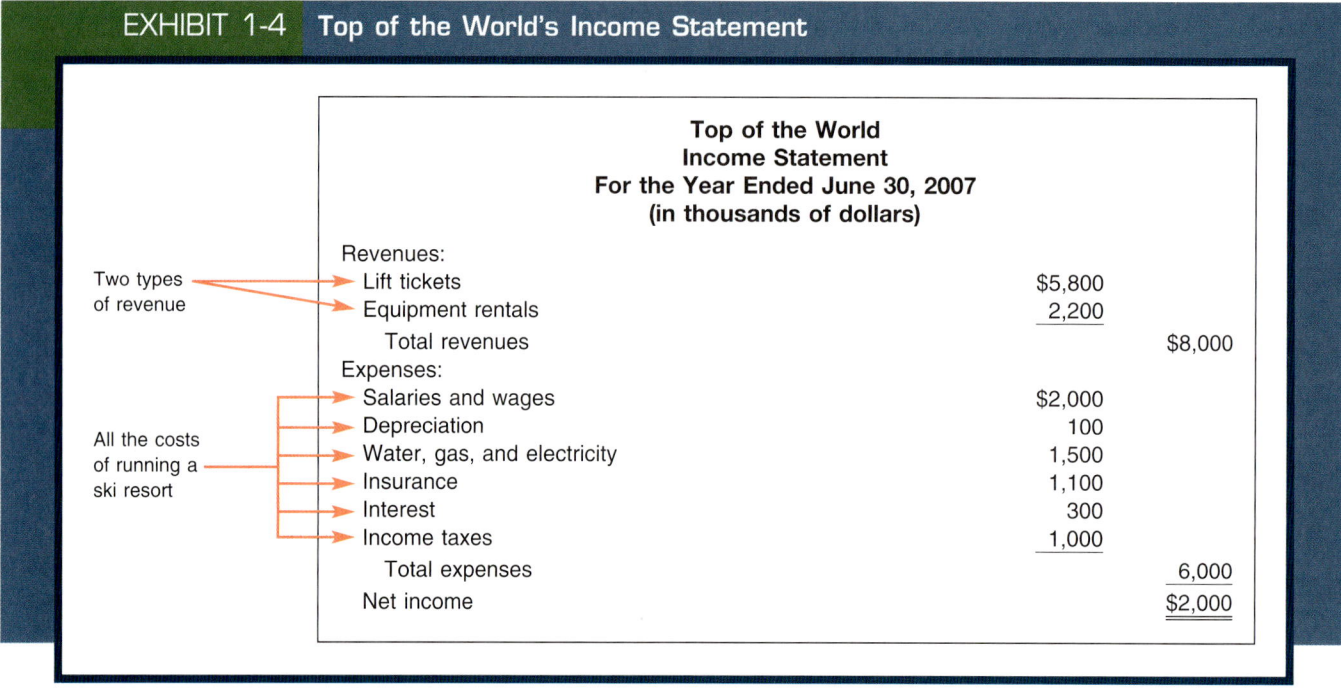

EXHIBIT 1-4 Top of the World's Income Statement

Top of the World
Income Statement
For the Year Ended June 30, 2007
(in thousands of dollars)

Two types of revenue →

Revenues:		
Lift tickets	$5,800	
Equipment rentals	2,200	
Total revenues		$8,000
Expenses:		
Salaries and wages	$2,000	
Depreciation	100	
Water, gas, and electricity	1,500	
Insurance	1,100	
Interest	300	
Income taxes	1,000	
Total expenses		6,000
Net income		$2,000

All the costs of running a ski resort →

the year. The expenses reported on the income statement represent all of the various costs necessary to run a ski resort. For example, a significant cost for such an operation is its payroll, as represented by salaries and wages on the income statement. At this point in your study, note that the amount reported for salaries and wages expense on the income statement is not the same amount that appeared as salaries and wages payable on the balance sheet. The expense of $2,000 on the income statement represents the total cost for the year, while the payable of $400 on the balance sheet is the amount owed to employees on June 30, 2007. We will have much more to say in later chapters about differences between balance sheet and income statement items. Finally, note that the excess of revenues over expenses, or **net income** as it is called, appears as the bottom line on the income statement. A company's net income is sometimes referred to as its profits or earnings.

Net income
The excess of revenues over expenses. *Alternate term: Profits or earnings.*

THE STATEMENT OF RETAINED EARNINGS

As discussed earlier, Retained Earnings represents the accumulated earnings of a corporation less the amount paid in dividends to stockholders. **Dividends** are distributions of the net income or profits of a business to its stockholders. Not all businesses pay cash dividends. Among those companies that do pay dividends, the frequency with which they pay differs. For example, most companies that pay dividends do so four times a year.

A **statement of retained earnings** explains the change in retained earnings during the period. The basic format for the statement is as follows:

Dividends
A distribution of the net income of a business to its owners.

Statement of retained earnings
The statement that summarizes the income earned and dividends paid over the life of a business.

Beginning balance	$xxx,xxx
Add: Net income for the period	xxx,xxx
Deduct: Dividends for the period	xxx,xxx
Ending balance	$xxx,xxx

A statement of retained earnings for Top of the World is shown in Exhibit 1-5. Revenues minus expenses, or net income, is an increase in retained earnings, and dividends are a decrease in the balance. Why are dividends shown on a statement of retained earnings instead of on an income statement? Dividends are not an expense and thus are not a component of net income, as are expenses. Instead, they are a *distribution* of the income of the business to its stockholders.

Recall that stockholders' equity consists of two parts: capital stock and retained earnings. In lieu of a separate statement of retained earnings, many corporations

---

EXHIBIT 1-5   Top of the World's Statement of Retained Earnings

Top of the World
Statement of Retained Earnings
For the Year Ended June 30, 2007
(in thousands of dollars)

Retained earnings, beginning of the year	$ 0
Add: Net income for the year	2,000
Deduct: Dividends for the year	(800)
Retained earnings, end of the year	$1,200

---

prepare a comprehensive statement to explain the changes both in the various capital stock accounts and in retained earnings during the period. Finish Line, for example, presents the more comprehensive statement of shareholders' equity.

THE STATEMENT OF CASH FLOWS

The statement of cash flows summarizes the cash flow effects of a company's operating, investing, and financing activities for the period. In essence, it shows the reader where a company got cash during the year and how it used that cash. (We will have more to say about this in Chapter 2.)

A statement of cash flows for Top of the World is shown in Exhibit 1-6. Note the three categories of cash flow: operating, investing, and financing. The major source of cash to the company from its operations was the cash it collected from its customers.

Statement of cash flows
The financial statement that summarizes a company's cash receipts and cash payments during the period from operating, investing, and financing activities.

EXHIBIT 1-6   Top of the World's Statement of Cash Flows

Top of the World
Statement of Cash Flows
For the Year Ended June 30, 2007
(in thousands of dollars)

Cash flows from operating activities:		
Cash collected from customers		$ 7,400
Cash payments for:		
Salaries and wages	$ 1,600	
Water, gas, and electricity	1,500	
Insurance	400	
Interest	300	
Income taxes	1,000	
Total cash payments		4,800
Net cash provided by operating activities		$ 2,600
Cash flows from investing activities:		
Purchase of land	$(4,000)	
Purchase of lodge, lifts, and equipment	(2,600)	
Net cash used by investing activities		(6,600)
Cash flows from financing activities:		
Proceeds from issuance of long-term note	$ 3,000	
Proceeds from issuance of capital stock	2,000	
Dividends declared and paid	(800)	
Net cash provided by financing activities		4,200
Net increase in cash		$ 200
Cash at beginning of year		0
Cash at end of year		$ 200

After deducting cash payments for operating activities, the ski company generated $2,600 from its operations. During the period, the company spent $6,600 on various assets. The last category shows that the issuance of a note generated $3,000 of cash and the issuance of stock another $2,000. Finally, the company paid dividends of $800. The net increase in cash from these three categories is $200, and since the company was new this year, this number is also its ending cash balance.

RELATIONSHIPS AMONG THE FINANCIAL STATEMENTS

Note the natural progression in the items from one statement to another. Normally, a company starts the period with balances in each of the items on its balance sheet. Because Top of the World is a new company, Exhibit 1-7 shows zero balances on

---

EXHIBIT 1-7 | **Relationships among Financial Statements**

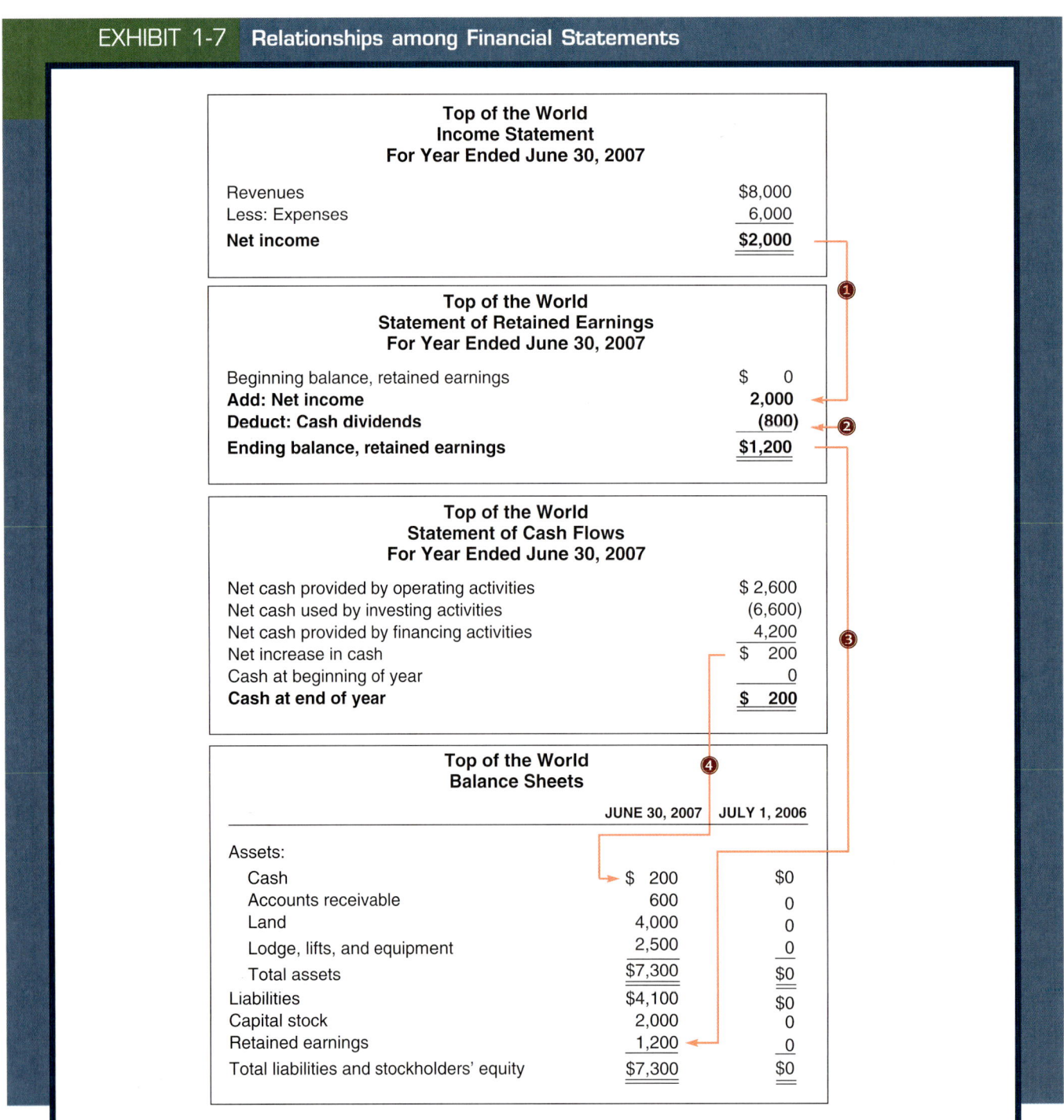

Top of the World
Income Statement
For Year Ended June 30, 2007

Revenues	$8,000
Less: Expenses	6,000
Net income	**$2,000**

Top of the World
Statement of Retained Earnings
For Year Ended June 30, 2007

Beginning balance, retained earnings	$ 0
Add: Net income	**2,000**
Deduct: Cash dividends	**(800)**
Ending balance, retained earnings	**$1,200**

Top of the World
Statement of Cash Flows
For Year Ended June 30, 2007

Net cash provided by operating activities	$ 2,600
Net cash used by investing activities	(6,600)
Net cash provided by financing activities	4,200
Net increase in cash	$ 200
Cash at beginning of year	0
Cash at end of year	**$ 200**

Top of the World
Balance Sheets

	JUNE 30, 2007	JULY 1, 2006
Assets:		
Cash	$ 200	$0
Accounts receivable	600	0
Land	4,000	0
Lodge, lifts, and equipment	2,500	0
Total assets	$7,300	$0
Liabilities	$4,100	$0
Capital stock	2,000	0
Retained earnings	1,200	0
Total liabilities and stockholders' equity	$7,300	$0

July 1, 2006, the beginning of its first year in business. Next, the company operated during the year and the result was net income of $2,000 as shown on the income statement in the top of the exhibit. The net income naturally flows ❶ onto the statement of retained earnings. Again, because the ski company is new, its beginning retained earnings balance is zero. After the distribution of $800 to the owners in cash dividends ❷, ending retained earnings amounts to $1,200. The ending retained earnings number flows ❸ onto the ending balance sheet along with the other June 30, 2007, balance sheet items. Finally, the net increase in cash at the bottom of the statement of cash flows equals ❹ the amount shown on the June 30, 2007, balance sheet.

Looking at Financial Statements for a Real Company: Finish Line

You would certainly expect the financial statements of companies in the real world to be more complex than those for a hypothetical company such as Top of the World. Still, even this early in your study of accounting, there are certain fundamental points about all financial statements, real-world or otherwise, that you can appreciate.

FINISH LINE'S BALANCE SHEET

Balance sheets for Finish Line at the end of two recent years are shown in Exhibit 1-8. For comparative purposes, the company reports its financial position not only at the end of the most recent year, February 25, 2006, but also on February 26, 2005. Note also in the statement under the headings for the two years that the amounts are in thousands of dollars. For example, this means that Finish Line had $627,816 × 1,000 or $627,816,000 of total assets at the end of 2006 (Finish Line chooses to refer to the year that ends on February 25, 2006, as its 2006 fiscal year):

TOTAL ASSETS: $627,816 × 1,000 = $627,816,000 = almost ⅔ billion dollars!

A quick comparison of Finish Line's assets with those for Top of the World reveals one significant difference. Because the ski company is a service company, it does not have an inventory account on its balance sheet. Conversely, "Merchandise inventories, net" is Finish Line's largest asset, accounting for over 40% of its total assets on February 25, 2006. Finish Line's inventory of over $268 million represents the dollar amount of the various products that it sells in its stores, such as running shoes, clothing, and other apparel. It is logical that inventories would be a major asset for a retailer. The second largest asset for Finish Line is "Leasehold improvements." It is common for retailers in malls to lease (rent) the space they occupy. Even though their space is rented, they often are responsible for making improvements to the stores, such as adding display cases, sales racks, and lighting. These are called *leasehold improvements* and amount to over $243 million at year-end.

Various types of liabilities are reported on Finish Line's balance sheets, and we will return to look more closely at many of these in later chapters. For now, it is worth noting that total liabilities amount to just under $200 million at the end of 2006. Total shareholders' equity amounts to over $428 million, of which the balance in retained earnings is about $320 million.

FINISH LINE'S INCOME STATEMENT

Comparative income statements for three recent years are shown in Exhibit 1-9.

As was the case for the balance sheet, you are not expected at this point to understand fully all the complexities involved on the income statement of a real company. However, note the two largest items on the income statement: Net sales and Cost of sales. For now, it is sufficient to understand that the former is the revenue Finish Line earned from selling its various products and the

1-1 Real World Practice

Reading Finish Line's Income Statement

Finish Line's income statement reports that its "Net Sales" increased in 2006 from the prior year. Does it seem logical that "Cost of Sales" would also increase? Explain your answer and compute the percentage increase from 2005 to 2006 for both Net Sales and Cost of Sales.

EXHIBIT 1-8 Finish Line's Balance Sheet

THE FINISH LINE, INC.
CONSOLIDATED BALANCE SHEETS
(in thousands)

	February 25, 2006	February 26, 2005
Assets $\boxed{A}$		
Current Assets:		
Cash and cash equivalents	$ 47,488	$ 55,991
Marketable securities	49,075	57,175
Accounts receivable, net	11,999	14,230
Merchandise inventories, net	268,590	241,242
Other	4,375	3,162
Total current assets	381,527	371,800
Property and Equipment		
Land	1,557	315
Building	33,757	23,309
Leasehold improvements	243,312	217,371
Furniture, fixtures, and equipment	93,221	77,945
Construction in progress	10,753	10,616
	382,600	329,556
Less accumulated depreciation	161,418	141,258
	221,182	188,298
Deferred income taxes	11,118	3,578
Goodwill and intangible assets	13,989	11,343
Total assets	$627,816	$575,019

The products sold in the stores account for nearly 43% of total assets.

Improvements to rented retail space account for nearly 39% of total assets.

Total assets of almost $628 million

=

	February 25, 2006	February 26, 2005
Liabilities and Shareholders' Equity $\boxed{L}$		
Current Liabilities:		
Accounts payable	$ 84,006	$ 92,378
Employee compensation	12,026	12,883
Accrued property and sales tax	8,254	6,914
Deferred income taxes	12,429	7,645
Other liabilities and accrued expenses	25,700	17,196
Total current liabilities	142,415	137,016

Creditors' claims are about $200 million.

	February 25, 2006	February 26, 2005
Commitments and contingencies		
Deferred credits from landlords	56,859	50,532
Other long-term liabilities	—	1,500

+

	February 25, 2006	February 26, 2005
Shareholders' Equity $\boxed{SE}$		
Preferred stock, $.01 par value; 1,000 shares authorized; none issued	—	—
Common stock, $.01 par value		
Class A:		
Shares authorized—100,000		
Shares issued—47,649		
Shares outstanding (2006—42,865; 2005—43,578)	476	476
Class B:		
Shares authorized—10,000		
Shares issued and outstanding—5,141	52	52
Additional paid-in capital	142,645	138,130
Retained earnings	319,656	263,971
Treasury stock (2006—4,784, 2005—4,071)	(34,287)	(16,658)
Total shareholders' equity	428,542	385,971
Total liabilities and shareholders' equity	$627,816	$575,019

Creditors' claims and shareholders' equity is the same as total assets.

[See accompanying notes in the book appendix.]

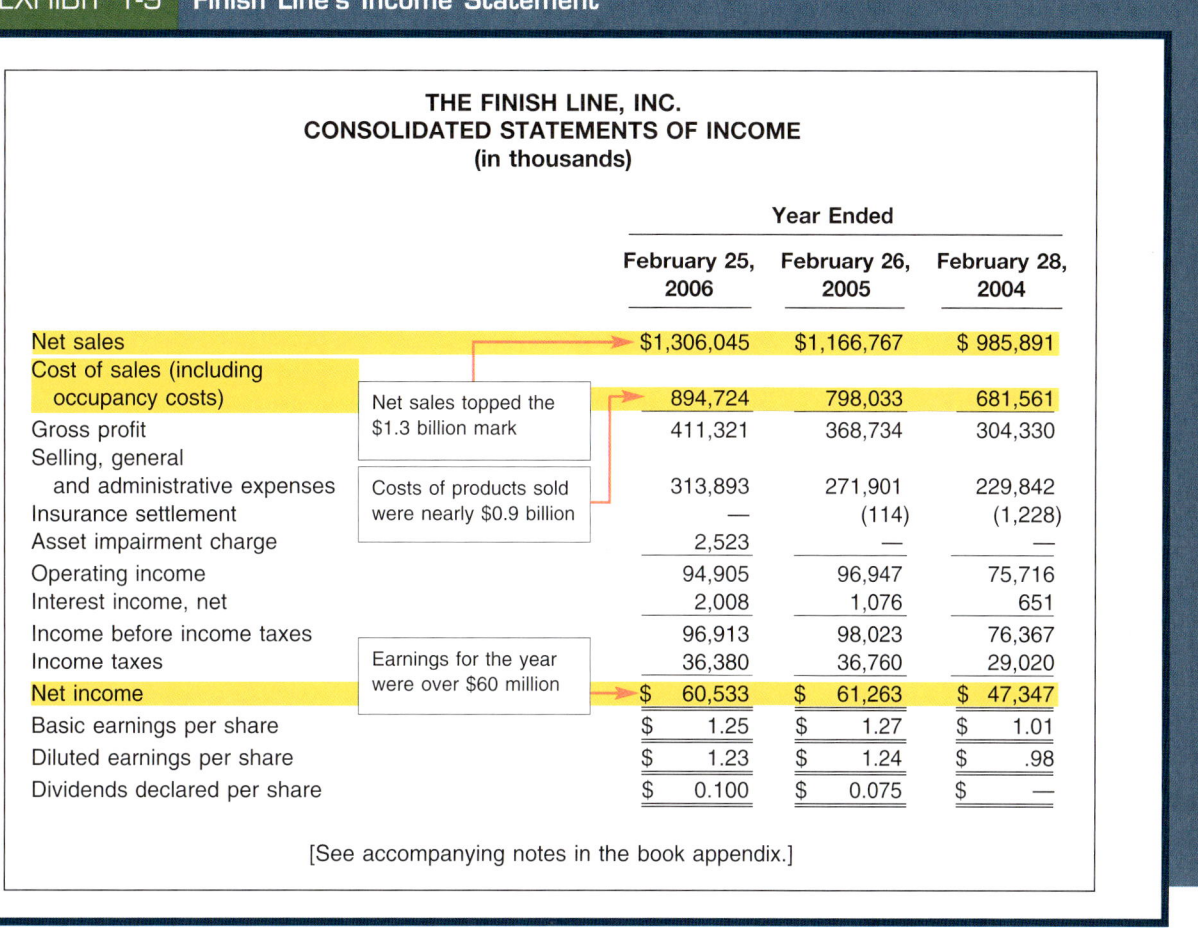

| EXHIBIT 1-9 | Finish Line's Income Statement |

THE FINISH LINE, INC.
CONSOLIDATED STATEMENTS OF INCOME
(in thousands)

| | Year Ended | | |
	February 25, 2006	February 26, 2005	February 28, 2004
Net sales	$1,306,045	$1,166,767	$ 985,891
Cost of sales (including occupancy costs)	894,724	798,033	681,561
Gross profit	411,321	368,734	304,330
Selling, general and administrative expenses	313,893	271,901	229,842
Insurance settlement	—	(114)	(1,228)
Asset impairment charge	2,523	—	—
Operating income	94,905	96,947	75,716
Interest income, net	2,008	1,076	651
Income before income taxes	96,913	98,023	76,367
Income taxes	36,380	36,760	29,020
Net income	$ 60,533	$ 61,263	$ 47,347
Basic earnings per share	$ 1.25	$ 1.27	$ 1.01
Diluted earnings per share	$ 1.23	$ 1.24	$ .98
Dividends declared per share	$ 0.100	$ 0.075	$ —

Net sales topped the $1.3 billion mark

Costs of products sold were nearly $0.9 billion

Earnings for the year were over $60 million

[See accompanying notes in the book appendix.]

latter is the cost of those products. Net sales for the most recent year topped the $1.3 billion mark, and the cost of sales was just under $0.9 billion. After selling, general and administrative expenses, income taxes, and other minor items are taken into account, net income for the year amounted to approximately $60.5 million.

2 minute review

1. State the accounting equation, and indicate what each term means.

2. What are the four financial statements presented in this chapter?

3. How do amounts in the four statements interrelate?

Answers

1. *Assets = Liabilities + Owners' Equity or Assets = Liabilities + Stockholders' Equity*
   Assets are economic resources. Liabilities are creditors' claims against assets. Owners' Equity (or Stockholders' Equity) is owners' claims against assets. See Exhibit 1-3.

2. *The four financial statements are the balance sheet, the income statement, the statement of retained earnings, and the statement of cash flows.*

3. *Net income on the income statement increases retained earnings on the statement of retained earnings. The ending balance in retained earnings is transferred to the balance sheet. The net increase in cash from the statement of cash flows is added to the beginning cash on the balance sheet to produce the ending balance. See Exhibit 1-7.*

The Conceptual Framework: Foundation for Financial Statements

Study Tip

The concepts in this section underlie everything you will learn throughout the course. You'll encounter them later in the context of specific topics.

Many people perceive the work of an accountant as being routine. In reality, accounting is anything but routine and requires a great deal of judgment on the part of the accountant. The record-keeping aspect of accounting—what we normally think of as bookkeeping—is the routine part of the accountant's work and is only a small part of it. Most of the job deals with communicating relevant information to financial statement users.

CONCEPTUAL FRAMEWORK FOR ACCOUNTING

The accounting profession has developed a *conceptual framework for accounting* that aids accountants in their role as interpreters and communicators of relevant information. The purpose of the framework is to act as a foundation for the specific principles and standards needed by the profession. An important part of the conceptual framework is a set of assumptions accountants make in preparing financial statements. We will briefly consider these assumptions, returning to a more detailed discussion of them in later chapters.

ECONOMIC ENTITY CONCEPT

The *economic entity concept* was discussed in the introduction to the book when we first discussed different types of business entities. This assumption requires that an identifiable, specific entity be the subject of a set of financial statements. For example, even though some of Finish Line's employees are stockholders and therefore own part of Finish Line, their personal affairs must be kept separate from the business affairs. When we look at a balance sheet for the company, we need assurance that it shows the financial position of that entity only and does not intermingle the personal assets and liabilities of the employees or any of the other stockholders.

COST PRINCIPLE

Cost principle
Assets are recorded at the cost to acquire them.
Alternate term: Original cost or historical cost.

The **cost principle** requires that accountants record assets at the cost paid to acquire them and continue to show this amount on all balance sheets until the company disposes of them. With a few exceptions, companies do not carry assets at their market value (how much they could sell the asset for today) but at original cost. Accountants use the term *historical cost* to refer to the original cost of an asset. Why not show an asset such as land at market value? The *subjectivity* inherent in determining market values supports the practice of carrying assets at their historical cost. The cost of an asset is verifiable by an independent observer and is much more *objective* than market value.

GOING CONCERN

Going concern
The assumption that an entity is not in the process of liquidation and that it will continue indefinitely.

Accountants assume that the entity being accounted for is a **going concern**. That is, they assume that Finish Line is not in the process of liquidation and that it will continue indefinitely into the future. Another important reason for using historical cost rather than market value to report assets is the going concern assumption. If we assume that a business is *not* a going concern, then we assume that it is in the process of liquidation. If this is the case, market value might be more relevant than cost as a basis for recognizing the assets. But if we are able to assume that a business will continue indefinitely, cost can be more easily justified as a basis for valuation. The **monetary unit** used in preparing the statements of Finish Line is the dollar. The reason for using the dollar as the monetary unit is that it is the recognized medium of exchange in the United States. It provides a convenient yardstick to measure the position and earnings of the business. As a yardstick, however, the dollar, like the currencies of all other countries, is subject to instability. We are all well aware that a dollar will not buy as much today as it did 10 years ago.

Monetary unit
The yardstick used to measure amounts in financial statements; the dollar in the United States.

Inflation is evidenced by a general rise in the level of prices in an economy. Its effect on the measuring unit used in preparing financial statements is an important concern to the accounting profession. Although accountants have experimented with financial statements adjusted for the changing value of the measuring unit, the financial statements now prepared by corporations are prepared under the assumption that the monetary unit is relatively stable. At various times in the past, this has been a reasonable assumption and at other times not so reasonable.

TIME PERIOD ASSUMPTION

Under the **time period** assumption, accountants assume that it is possible to prepare an income statement that accurately reflects net income or earnings for a specific time period. In the case of Finish Line, this time period is one year. It is somewhat artificial to measure the earnings of a business for a period of time indicated on a calendar, whether it be a month, a quarter, or a year. Of course, the most accurate point in time to measure the earnings of a business would be at the end of its life. Accountants prepare periodic statements, however, because the users of the statements demand information about the entity on a regular basis.

Time period
Artificial segment on the calendar, used as the basis for preparing financial statements.

GENERALLY ACCEPTED ACCOUNTING PRINCIPLES

Financial statements prepared by accountants must conform to **generally accepted accounting principles (GAAP)**. This term refers to the various methods, rules, practices, and other procedures that have evolved over time in response to the need for some form of regulation over the preparation of financial statements. As changes have taken place in the business environment over time, GAAP have developed in response to these changes.

Generally accepted accounting principles (GAAP)
The various methods, rules, practices, and other procedures that have evolved over time in response to the need to regulate the preparation of financial statements.

ACCOUNTING AS A SOCIAL SCIENCE

Accounting is a service activity. As we have seen, its purpose is to provide financial information to decision makers. Thus, accounting is a *social* science. Accounting principles are much different from the rules that govern the *physical* sciences. For example, it is a rule of nature that an object dropped from your hand will eventually hit the ground rather than be suspended in air. There are no rules comparable to this in accounting. The principles that govern financial reporting are not governed by nature but instead develop in response to changing business conditions. For example, consider the lease of an office building. Leasing has developed in response to the need to have access to valuable assets, such as office space, without spending the large sum necessary to buy the asset. As leasing has increased in popularity, it has been left to the accounting profession to develop guidelines, some of which are quite complex, to be followed in accounting for leases. Those guidelines are now part of GAAP.

⏱ *2 minute review*

1. Name the four concepts (other than the economic entity concept) in the conceptual framework presented in this section.

2. Give a brief example of each concept.

3. What is "GAAP"?

Answers

1. Cost principle, going concern, monetary unit, and time period assumption.

2. Under the cost principle, we record assets at their cost rather than at market value. Example: Finish Line would record new lighting for one of its stores at its purchase price. Under going concern, we assume that the company will continue existing indefinitely. Example: Finish Line will continue to operate rather than begin liquidating its assets. The monetary unit, such as the dollar, is the company's recognized medium of exchange. Example: Finish Line uses the dollar as the monetary unit. The time period assumption imposes, for reporting purposes, an arbitrary time period (such as a year) that is shorter

Securities and Exchange Commission (SEC)
The federal agency with ultimate authority to determine the rules for preparing statements for companies whose stock is sold to the public.

Financial Accounting Standards Board (FASB)
The group in the private sector with authority to set accounting standards.

American Institute of Certified Public Accountants (AICPA)
The professional organization for certified public accountants.

Certified Public Accountant (CPA)
The designation for an individual who has passed a uniform exam administered by the AICPA and met other requirements as determined by individual states.

Public Company Accounting Oversight Board (PCAOB)
A five-member body created by an act of Congress in 2002 to set auditing standards.

International Accounting Standards Board (IASB)
The organization formed to develop worldwide accounting standards.

than the company's life span. Example: *Finish Line's income statement is for the year ended February 25, 2006.*

3. *GAAP is the methods, rules, practices, and other procedures that have evolved to govern the preparation of financial statements.*

WHO DETERMINES THE RULES OF THE GAME?

Who determines the rules to be followed in preparing an income statement or a balance sheet? No one group is totally responsible for setting the standards or principles to be followed in preparing financial statements. The process is a joint effort among the following groups.

The federal government, through the **Securities and Exchange Commission (SEC)**, has the ultimate authority to determine the rules for preparing financial statements by companies whose securities are sold to the general public. However, for the most part, the SEC has allowed the accounting profession to establish its own rules.

The **Financial Accounting Standards Board (FASB)** sets these accounting standards in the United States. A small independent group with a large staff, the board has issued more than 150 financial accounting standards and seven statements of financial accounting concepts since its creation in the early 1970s. These standards deal with a variety of financial reporting issues, such as the proper accounting for lease arrangements and pension plans, and the concepts are used to guide the board in setting accounting standards.

The **American Institute of Certified Public Accountants (AICPA)** is the professional organization of **certified public accountants (CPAs)**. The CPA is the designation for an individual who has passed a uniform exam administered by the AICPA and met other requirements as determined by individual states. AICPA advises the FASB and in the past was involved in setting the auditing standards to be followed by public accounting firms. However, the **Public Company Accounting Oversight Board (PCAOB)** was created by an Act of Congress in 2002 and this five-member body now has the authority to set the standards for conducting audits.

Finally, if you are considering buying stock in **Porsche,** the German-based car manufacturer, you'll want to be sure that the rules Porsche follows in preparing its statements are similar to those the FASB requires for U.S. companies. Unfortunately, accounting standards can differ considerably from one country to another. The **International Accounting Standards Board (IASB)** was created in 2001. Prior to that time, the organization was known as the International Accounting Standards Committee (IASC), which was formed in 1973 to develop worldwide accounting standards. Organizations from many different countries, including the FASB in this country, participate in the IASB's efforts to develop international reporting standards. Although the group has made considerable progress, compliance with the standards of the IASB is strictly voluntary, and much work remains to be done in developing international accounting standards.

Introduction to Ethics in Accounting

LO4 Explain the critical role that ethics play in providing useful financial information.

In the modern business world, rapidly changing markets, technological improvements, and business innovation all affect financial decisions. Decision makers consider information received from many sources, such as other investors in the marketplace, analysts' forecasts, and companies whose corporate officers and executives may be encouraging "aggressive" accounting and reporting practices.

In recent years, the news has been filled with reports of questionable accounting practices by some companies. As a decision maker outside of a company, you should be aware of the potential for ethical conflicts that arise within organizations and ask questions, do research, and not just accept everything as fact. If you are a decision maker within a company, you should stay alert for potential pressures on you or others to make choices that are not in the best interest of the company, its owners, and its employees as a whole. Companies may use aggressive accounting practices to misrepresent their earnings; executives may misuse their companies' funds. You may encounter a corporate board of directors that undermines the goals of its own company or a public accounting firm that fails its auditing duty to watch for and to disclose wrongdoing.

As a decision maker, you may analyze business information to project capital expansion, to open markets for new products, or to anticipate tax liabilities. You may be responsible for making financial reporting decisions that will affect others inside or outside of the organization. Knowledge of the professional standards of accounting procedures will be critical for your decision-making process. It will also help you recognize when information is not consistent with the standards and needs to be questioned.

It is important to note that you may encounter circumstances when it appears as if generally accepted accounting principles (GAAP) may not have been used to resolve particular accounting issues. This may occur because there are several conflicting rules, because no specific GAAP rules seem applicable, or as a result of fraud. In such situations, an ethical dilemma is likely to exist. Resolving the dilemma may involve one or more decision makers. In most instances, an accountant plays a significant role in the process.

As accountants analyze and attempt to solve the ethical dilemmas posed by certain financial transactions and complex business reporting decisions, they can turn to their profession's conceptual framework. (You will learn more about this framework in Chapter 2.) According to the profession, "Financial reporting should provide information that is useful to present and potential investors and creditors and other users in making rational investment, credit, and similar decisions."[3]

When the accountant asks: "Is the quality of the information that is disclosed good or does it need to be improved?", the answer (which shapes all accounting decisions that follow) is: "If the information is *both* relevant and reliable, its quality is good."

Relevant information is information that is useful to the decision-making process. Relevant information may provide clear information about past financial events that is helpful for predicting the future. To be relevant, the information must also be timely; that is, it must be available at the time the decision is being made.

Accounting information should also be reliable; it should accurately represent what it claims to represent. Reliability includes *verifiability;* thus, there is documentation, from one or more independent parties, that supports the accuracy of the information. Reliability also includes *neutrality*, which means the presentation of information is free from bias toward a particular result. Neutral information can be used by anyone, and it does not try to influence the decision in one direction. Basically, accounting information that is reliable will report economic activity that accurately represents the situation, without trying to influence behavior in any particular direction.[4]

Normally, the uncertainties of business transactions and reporting decisions must be resolved in accordance with generally accepted accounting principles (GAAP) following the Financial Accounting Standards Board (FASB) statements. However, the appropriate application of accounting principles may not be easy to determine. You must be alert to pressures on the decision-making process that may be due to the self-interests of one or more of the decision makers. Bias, deception, and even fraud may distort the disclosed information. Whatever the circumstances, the dilemmas should be resolved by questioning and analyzing the situation.

All decision makers should consider the moral and social implications of their decisions. How will the decisions affect others, such as shareholders, creditors, employees, suppliers, customers, and the local community? The process of determining the most ethical choice involves identifying the most significant facts of the situation. For financial reporting, this includes identifying who may be affected and how, the relevant GAAP principles, and a realistic appraisal of the possible consequences of

---

3 *Original Pronouncements: Accounting Standards* (New York: John Wiley and Sons, Inc. 2001–2002 edition), III, Concept One, paragraph 34, p. 1014.

4 *Original Pronouncements: Accounting Standards* (New York: John Wiley and Sons, Inc. 2001–2002 edition), III, p. 1022; FASB, paragraphs 46, 47, 48, 56, 63, 77, 81; pp. 48–49, 51–53, 56–59.

EXHIBIT 1-10 Ethics and Accounting: A Decision-Making Model

Recognize an ethical dilemma.

Times when an ethical dilemma is likely to occur are when a company is considering a decision about accounting methods or disclosures and:
- There are conflicting accounting rules,
- There are no GAAP to follow, or
- Fraud or other questionable actions have occurred.

Analyze the key elements in the situation.

Examples of:
- Those who may benefit or be harmed—management; shareholders; potential investors; the auditor; creditors; employees.
- Benefits—higher pay; promotion; increased status in the community.
- Harm—loss of job; bankruptcy; customer's failure to pay debt.
- Rights/claims—payments to creditors; obligations to customers.
- Conflicting interests—a member of the board of directors who is also a company employee; a manager whose bonus is based on sales.
- Responsibilities—providing the most accurate information; reporting fraud.

List alternatives and evaluate the impact of each on those affected.

Among the alternatives, which provides:
- The most useful and timely information to decision makers?
- The most reliable information to decision makers?
- Information that most accurately represents what it claims to report?
- Information that is free from bias toward any certain result?

What is the likely impact of each alternative on those affected?

Select the best alternative.

Among the alternatives, which provides decision makers with the most relevant, most reliable, most accurate, and most neutral information?

the decision. To assist your decision making for the cases and assignments, we offer an ethical decision model, shown in Exhibit 1-10 and explained here.

IDENTIFICATION

1. Recognize the ethical dilemma. A dilemma occurs when this awareness is combined with the inability to clearly apply accounting principles to represent the situation accurately.

ANALYSIS

2. Analyze the key elements in the situation by answering these questions in sequence:
   a. Who may benefit or be harmed?
   b. How are they likely to benefit or be harmed?
   c. What rights or claims may be violated?
   d. What specific interests are in conflict?
   e. What are my responsibilities and obligations?

3. Determine what alternative methods are available to report the transaction, situation, or event. Answer the following questions:

    a. How relevant and reliable are the alternatives? Timeliness should be considered; potential bias must be identified.

    b. Does the report accurately represent the situation it claims to describe?

    c. Is the information free from bias?

RESOLUTION

4. Select the best or most ethical alternative, considering all the circumstances and the consequences.

ACCOUNTANTS AND ETHICAL JUDGMENTS

Remember the primary goal of accounting: to provide useful information to aid in the decision-making process. As we discussed, the work of the accountant in providing useful information is anything but routine and requires the accountant to make subjective judgments about what information to present and how to present it. The latitude given accountants in this respect is one of the major reasons accounting is a profession and its members are considered professionals. Along with this designation as a professional, however, comes a serious responsibility. As we noted, financial statements are prepared for external parties who must rely on these statements to provide information on which to base important decisions.

At the end of each chapter are cases titled "Ethical Decision Making." The cases require you to evaluate difficult issues and make a decision. Judgment is needed in deciding which accounting method to select or how to report a certain item in the statements. As you are faced with these decisions, keep in mind the trust placed in the accountant by various financial statement users. This is central to reaching an ethical decision.

THE CHANGING FACE OF THE ACCOUNTING PROFESSION

Probably no time in the history of the accounting profession in the United States has seen more turmoil and change than the period since the start of the new millennium. Corporate scandals have led to some of the largest bankruptcies in the history of business. The involvement of the auditors in one of these scandals resulted in the demise of one of the oldest and most respected public accounting firms in the world. Many have referred to the "financial reporting crisis" that grew out of this time period.

Although the issues involved in the financial reporting crisis are complex, the accounting questions in these cases were often very basic. For example, the most fundamental accounting issue involved in the **Enron** case revolved around the entity concept that was explained earlier in the introduction to this book. Specifically, should various entities under the control of Enron have been included in the company's financial statements? Similarly, the major question in the **WorldCom** case was whether certain costs should have been treated as expenses when incurred rather than accounted for as assets.

Earlier in the chapter we described the various services provided by accounting firms to their clients. The scandals of the last few years have resulted in a major focus on the nonaudit services provided by these firms and the issue of auditor independence. For example, is it possible for an accounting firm to remain independent in rendering an opinion on a company's financial statements while simultaneously advising the company on other matters?

In 2002 Congress passed the **Sarbanes-Oxley Act**. The act was a direct response to the corporate scandals mentioned earlier and was an attempt to bring about major reforms in corporate accountability and stewardship, given the vast numbers of stockholders, creditors, employees, and others affected in one way or another by these scandals. Among the most important provisions in the act are the following:

Sarbanes-Oxley Act
An act of Congress in 2002 intended to bring reform to corporate accountability and stewardship in the wake of a number of major corporate scandals.

1. **The establishment of a new Public Company Accounting Oversight Board.**
2. **A requirement that the external auditors report directly to the company's audit committee.**
3. **A clause to prohibit public accounting firms who audit a company from providing any other services that could impair their ability to act independently in the course of their audit.**

Events of the last few years have placed accountants and the work they do in the spotlight more than ever before. Increasingly, accountants realize the burden of responsibility they have to communicate openly and honestly with the public concerning the financial well being of businesses. Whether you will someday be an accountant or simply a user of the information an accountant provides, it is important to appreciate the critical role accounting plays in the smooth functioning of the free enterprise system.

The Accounting Profession

LO5 Describe the various roles of accountants in organizations.

Accountants play many different roles in society. Understanding the various roles will help you to appreciate more fully the importance of accounting in organizations.

EMPLOYMENT BY PRIVATE BUSINESS

Many accountants work for business entities. Regardless of the types of activities companies engage in, accountants perform a number of important functions for them. A partial organization chart for a corporation is shown in Exhibit 1-11.

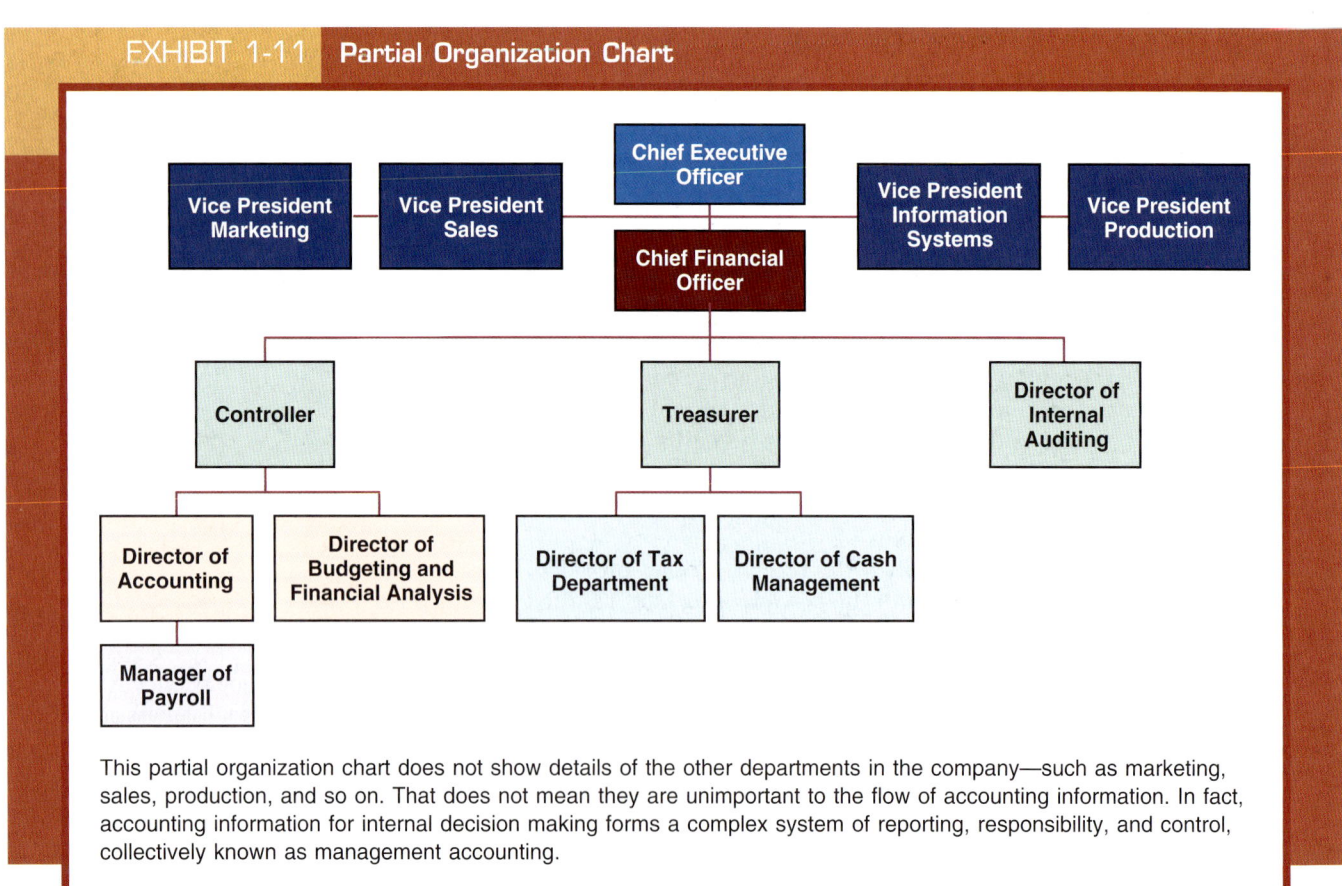

EXHIBIT 1-11   **Partial Organization Chart**

This partial organization chart does not show details of the other departments in the company—such as marketing, sales, production, and so on. That does not mean they are unimportant to the flow of accounting information. In fact, accounting information for internal decision making forms a complex system of reporting, responsibility, and control, collectively known as management accounting.

The chart indicates that three individuals report directly to the chief financial officer: the controller, the treasurer, and the director of internal auditing.

The **controller** is the chief accounting officer for a company and typically has responsibility for the overall operation of the accounting system. Accountants working for the controller record the company's activities and prepare periodic financial statements. In this organization, the payroll function is assigned to the controller's office, as well as responsibility for the preparation of budgets.

The **treasurer** of an organization is typically responsible for both the safeguarding and efficient use of the company's liquid resources, such as cash. Note that the director of the tax department in this corporation reports to the treasurer. Accountants in the tax department are responsible for both preparing the company's tax returns and planning transactions in such a way that the company pays the least amount of taxes possible within the laws of the Internal Revenue Code.

Internal auditing is the department responsible in a company for the review and appraisal of accounting and administrative controls. The department must determine whether the company's assets are properly accounted for and protected from losses. Recommendations are made periodically to management for improvements in the various controls.

EMPLOYMENT BY NONBUSINESS ENTITIES

Nonbusiness organizations, such as hospitals, universities, and various branches of the government, have as much need for accountants as do companies organized to earn a profit. Although the profit motive is not paramount to nonbusiness entities, all organizations must have financial information to operate efficiently. A county government needs detailed cost information in determining the taxes to levy on its constituents. A university must pay close attention to its various operating costs in setting the annual tuition rates. Accountants working for nonbusiness entities perform most of the same tasks as their counterparts in the business sector. In fact, many of the job titles in business entities, such as controller and treasurer, are also used by nonbusiness entities.

EMPLOYMENT IN PUBLIC ACCOUNTING

Public accounting firms provide valuable services in much the same way as do law firms or architectural firms. They provide a professional service for their clients in return for a fee. The usual services provided by public accounting firms include auditing and tax and management consulting services.

Auditing Services The auditing services rendered by public accountants are similar in certain respects to the work performed by internal auditors. However, there are key differences between the two types of auditing. Internal auditors are more concerned with the efficient operation of the various segments of the business, and therefore, the work they do is often called *operational auditing*. On the other hand, the primary objective of the external auditor, or public accountant, is to assure stockholders and other users that the statements are fairly presented. In this respect, **auditing** is the process of examining the financial statements and the underlying records of a company in order to render an opinion as to whether the statements are fairly presented.

As we discussed earlier, the financial statements are prepared by the company's accountants. The external auditor performs various tests and procedures to be able to render his or her opinion. The public accountant has a responsibility to the company's stockholders and any other users of the statements. Because most stockholders are not actively involved in the daily affairs of the business, they must rely on the auditors to ensure that management is fairly presenting the financial statements of the business.

Note that the **auditors' report** is an *opinion*, not a statement of fact. For example, one important procedure performed by the auditor to obtain assurance as to the validity of a company's inventory is to observe the year-end physical count of

---

Controller
The chief accounting officer for a company.

Treasurer
The officer responsible in an organization for the safeguarding and efficient use of a company's liquid assets.

Internal auditing
The department responsible in a company for the review and appraisal of its accounting and administrative controls.

Auditing
The process of examining the financial statements and the underlying records of a company in order to render an opinion as to whether the statements are fairly presented.

Auditors' report
The opinion rendered by a public accounting firm concerning the fairness of the presentation of the financial statements.
Alternate term: *Report of independent accountants.*

inventory by the company's employees. However, this is done on a sample basis. It would be too costly for the auditors to make an independent count of every single item of inventory.

The auditors' report on the financial statements for Finish Line is shown in Exhibit 1-12. Note first that the report is directed to the company's shareholders and board of directors. The company is audited by **Ernst & Young LLP**, a large international accounting firm. Public accounting firms range in size from those with a single owner to others, such as Ernst & Young, that have thousands of partners. The opinion given by Ernst & Young on the company's financial statements is the *standard auditors' report*. The first paragraph indicates that the firm has examined the company's balance sheet and the related statements of operations,

---

EXHIBIT 1-12   **Finish Line's Auditors' Report**

REPORT OF INDEPENDENT REGISTERED PUBLIC ACCOUNTING FIRM

The Board of Directors and Shareholders of The Finish Line, Inc.

We have audited the accompanying consolidated balance sheets of The Finish Line, Inc. as of February 25, 2006 and February 26, 2005, and the related consolidated statements of income, changes in shareholders' equity and cash flows for each of the three years in the period ended February 25, 2006. These financial statements are the responsibility of the Company's management. Our responsibility is to express an opinion on these financial statements based on our audits.

We conducted our audits in accordance with the standards of the Public Company Accounting Oversight Board (United States). Those standards require that we plan and perform the audit to obtain reasonable assurance about whether the financial statements are free of material misstatement. An audit includes examining, on a test basis, evidence supporting the amounts and disclosures in the financial statements. An audit also includes assessing the accounting principles used and significant estimates made by management, as well as evaluating the overall financial statement presentation. We believe that our audits provide a reasonable basis for our opinion.

In our opinion, the consolidated financial statements referred to above present fairly, in all material respects, the consolidated financial position of The Finish Line, Inc. at February 25, 2006 and February 26, 2005, and the consolidated results of its operations and its cash flows for each of the three years in the period ended February 25, 2006, in conformity with U.S. generally accepted accounting principles.

We also have audited, in accordance with the standards of the Public Company Accounting Oversight Board (United States), the effectiveness of The Finish Line, Inc.'s internal control over financial reporting as of February 25, 2006, based on criteria established in Internal Control—Integrated Framework issued by the Committee of Sponsoring Organizations of the Treadway Commission and our report dated May 4, 2006, expressed an unqualified opinion thereon.

Ernst & Young LLP

Indianapolis, Indiana
May 4, 2006

Standard Auditors' Report

First Paragraph	**Second Paragraph**	**Third Paragraph**
says that the auditor has examined the statements.	indicates that evidence was gathered on a test basis.	states the auditors' opinion.

shareholders' equity, and cash flows. Note that the second paragraph of the report indicates that evidence supporting the amounts and disclosures in the statements was examined on a *test* basis. The third paragraph states the firm's *opinion* that the financial statements are fairly presented in conformity with GAAP.

Tax Services In addition to auditing, public accounting firms provide a variety of tax services. Firms often prepare the tax returns for the companies they audit. They also usually work throughout the year with management to plan acquisitions and other transactions to take full advantage of the tax laws. For example, if tax rates are scheduled to decline next year, a public accounting firm would advise its client to accelerate certain expenditures this year as much as possible to receive a higher tax deduction than would be possible by waiting until next year.

Management Consulting Services By working closely with management to provide auditing and tax services, a public accounting firm becomes very familiar with various aspects of a company's business. This vantage point allows the firm to provide expert advice to the company to improve its operations. In the past, management consulting services rendered by public accounting firms to their clients took a variety of forms. For example, the firm might advise the company on the design and installation of a computer system to fill its needs. However, as we will see later in this section, serious doubts have been raised about an auditor's ability to remain independent while providing these other services. These doubts have caused the federal government to place restrictions on the nonaudit services the auditor can provide.

ACCOUNTANTS IN EDUCATION

Some accountants choose a career in education. As the demand for accountants in business entities, nonbusiness organizations, and public accounting has increased, so has the need for qualified professors to teach this discipline. Accounting programs range from two years of study at community colleges to doctoral programs at some universities. All these programs require the services of knowledgeable instructors. In addition to their teaching duties, many accounting educators are actively involved in research. The **American Accounting Association** is a professional organization of accounting educators and others interested in the future of the profession. The group advances its ideas through its many committees and the publication of a number of journals.

American Accounting Association
The professional organization for accounting educators.

ACCOUNTING AS A CAREER

As you can see, a number of different career paths in accounting are possible. The stereotypical view of the accountant as a "numbers person and not a people person" is a seriously outdated notion. Various specialties are now emerging, including tax accounting, environmental accounting, forensic accounting, software development, and accounting in the entertainment and telecommunications industries. Some of these opportunities exist in both the business and the nonbusiness sectors. For example, forensic accounting has become an exciting career field as both corporations and various agencies of the federal government, such as the FBI, concern themselves with fraud and white-collar crime.

As in any profession, salaries in accounting vary considerably, depending on numerous factors, including educational background and other credentials, number of years of experience, and size of the employer. For example, most employers pay a premium for candidates with a master's degree and professional certification, such as the CPA. Exhibit 1-13 indicates salaries for various positions within the accounting field.[5]

---

5 The information in this section regarding career opportunities and salaries was drawn primarily from the AICPA's Web site (http://www.aicpa.org), which reports data from the Robert Half 2006 Salary Guide.

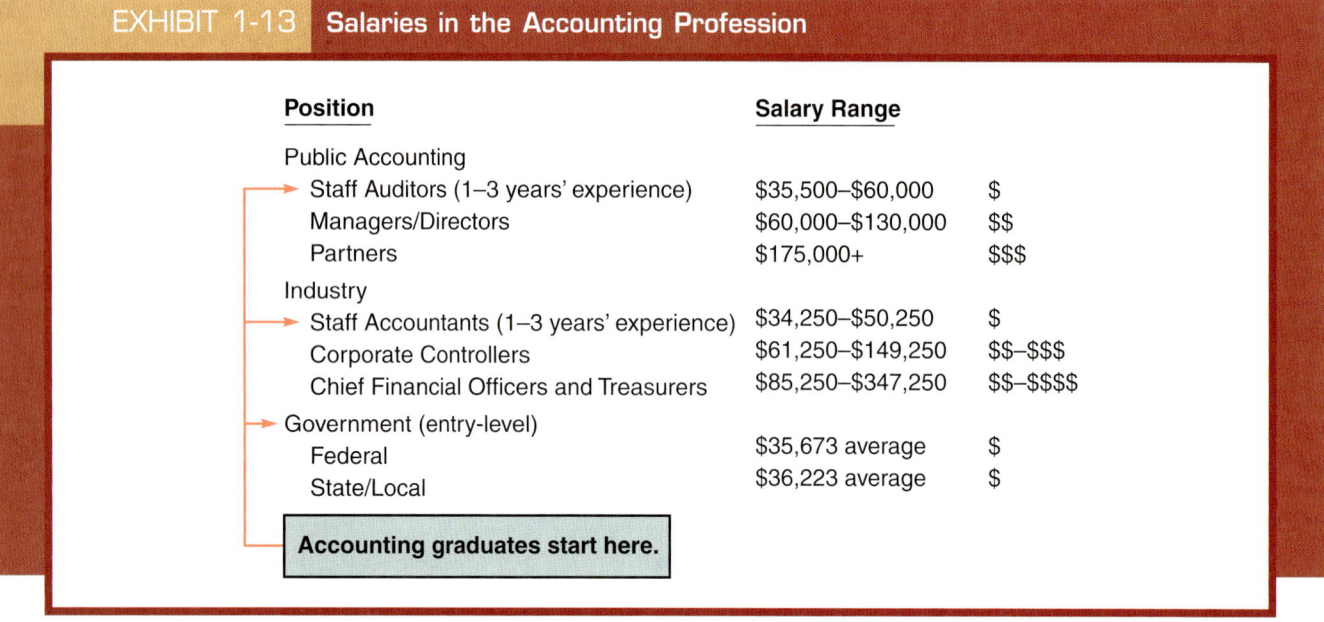

EXHIBIT 1-13 Salaries in the Accounting Profession

Position	Salary Range	
Public Accounting		
Staff Auditors (1–3 years' experience)	$35,500–$60,000	$
Managers/Directors	$60,000–$130,000	$$
Partners	$175,000+	$$$
Industry		
Staff Accountants (1–3 years' experience)	$34,250–$50,250	$
Corporate Controllers	$61,250–$149,250	$$–$$$
Chief Financial Officers and Treasurers	$85,250–$347,250	$$–$$$$
Government (entry-level)		
Federal	$35,673 average	$
State/Local	$36,223 average	$

Accounting graduates start here.

STUDY HIGHLIGHTS

LO1 **Identify the primary users of accounting information and their needs (p. 15).**

- The primary users of financial statements are those who depend upon the economic information conveyed in those statements to make decisions. Primary users may be broadly classified as internal users and those external to the company.
  - Internal users are usually managers of a company.
  - External users include stockholders, investors, creditors, and government agencies.

LO2 **Explain the purpose of each of the financial statements and the relationships among them, and prepare a set of simple statements (p. 18).**

- There are four major financial statements covered in this chapter: balance sheet, income statement, statement of retained earnings, and statement of cash flows.
  - The balance sheet is a snapshot of a company's financial position at the end of the period. It reflects the assets, liabilities, and stockholders' equity accounts.
  - The income statement summarizes the financial activity for a period of time. Items of revenues, expenses, gains, and losses are reflected in the income statement.
  - Ultimately, all net income (loss) and dividends are reflected in retained earnings on the balance sheet. The statement of retained earnings links the income statement to the balance sheet by showing how net income (loss) and dividends affect the retained earnings account.
  - The statement of cash flows summarizes the cash flow effects of a company's operating, investing, and financing activities.

LO3 **Identify and explain the primary assumptions made in preparing financial statements (p. 26).**

- The usefulness of accounting information is enhanced through the various assumptions set forth in the conceptual framework developed by the accounting profession. This conceptual framework is the foundation for the methods, rules, and practices that comprise generally accepted accounting principles (GAAP).

- Important assumptions in the conceptual framework are:
  - Economic entity concept
  - Cost principle
  - Going concern
  - Monetary unit
  - Time period

Explain the critical role that ethics play in providing useful financial information (p. 28).   **L04**

- All decision makers must consider the moral and social implications of their decisions.
- Recent news of questionable accounting practices has placed increased scrutiny on the accounting profession. Professional judgement is often needed to arrive at appropriate decisions when some question arises about the application of generally accepted accounting principles.

Describe the various roles of accountants in organizations (p. 32).   **L05**

- Accountants play an important role in the measurement, analysis, and communication of financial information and are employed by for-profit, not-for-profit, and governmental entities.
- Public accounting also employs many accountants that provide auditing, tax, and management consulting services.

KEY TERMS QUIZ

Read each of the following definitions and then write the number of that definition in the blank beside the appropriate term it defines. The quiz solutions appear at the end of the chapter.

_____ Accounting	_____ Securities and Exchange Commission (SEC)
_____ Management accounting	_____ Financial Accounting Standards Board (FASB)
_____ Financial accounting	_____ American Institute of Certified Public Accountants (AICPA)
_____ Owners' equity	_____ Certified Public Accountant (CPA)
_____ Stockholders' equity	_____ Public Company Accounting Oversight Board (PCAOB)
_____ Retained earnings	_____ International Accounting Standards Board (IASB)
_____ Balance sheet	_____ Sarbanes-Oxley Act
_____ Income statement	_____ Controller
_____ Net income	_____ Treasurer
_____ Dividends	_____ Internal auditing
_____ Statement of retained earnings	_____ Auditing
_____ Statement of cash flows	_____ Auditors' report
_____ Cost principle	_____ American Accounting Association
_____ Going concern	
_____ Monetary unit	
_____ Time period	
_____ Generally accepted accounting principles (GAAP)	

1. A statement that summarizes revenues and expenses for a period of time.
2. The statement that summarizes the income earned and dividends paid over the life of a business.
3. The owners' equity of a corporation.

4. The process of identifying, measuring, and communicating economic information to various users.
5. The branch of accounting concerned with communication with outsiders through financial statements.
6. The owners' claims to the assets of an entity.
7. The financial statement that summarizes the assets, liabilities, and owners' equity at a specific point in time.
8. The part of owners' equity that represents the income earned less dividends paid over the life of an entity.
9. The branch of accounting concerned with providing management with information to facilitate the planning and control functions.
10. A distribution of the net income of a business to its stockholders.
11. The various methods, rules, practices, and other procedures that have evolved over time in response to the need to regulate the preparation of financial statements.
12. Assets are recorded and reported at the cost paid to acquire them.
13. The federal agency with ultimate authority to determine the rules for preparing statements for companies whose stock is sold to the public.
14. The professional organization for accounting educators.
15. The officer of an organization who is responsible for the safeguarding and efficient use of the company's liquid assets.
16. The assumption that an entity is not in the process of liquidation and that it will continue indefinitely.
17. The group in the private sector with authority to set accounting standards.
18. The yardstick used to measure amounts in financial statements; the dollar in the United States.
19. The professional organization for certified public accountants.
20. The department in a company responsible for the review and appraisal of a company's accounting and administrative controls.
21. A length of time on the calendar used as the basis for preparing financial statements.
22. The chief accounting officer for a company.
23. The process of examining the financial statements and the underlying records of a company in order to render an opinion as to whether the statements are fairly presented.
24. The organization formed to develop worldwide accounting standards.
25. The opinion rendered by a public accounting firm concerning the fairness of the presentation of the financial statements.
26. An act of Congress in 2002 intended to bring reform to corporate accountability and stewardship in the wake of a number of major corporate scandals.
27. The excess of revenues over expenses.
28. The designation for an individual who has passed a uniform exam administered by the AICPA and met other requirements as determined by individual states.
29. A five-member body created by an act of Congress in 2002 to set auditing standards.
30. The financial statement that summarizes a company's cash receipts and cash payments during the period from operating, investing, and financing activities.

ALTERNATE TERMS

Auditors' report Report of independent accountants

Balance sheet Statement of financial position

Cost principle Original cost; historical cost

Income statement Statement of income or statement of operations

Net income Profits or earnings

Stockholders' equity Shareholders' equity

REVIEW

WARMUP EXERCISES & SOLUTIONS

LO2 **Warmup Exercise 1-1** Your Assets and Liabilities

Consider your own situation in terms of assets and liabilities.

Required
1. Name three of your financial assets.
2. Name three of your financial liabilities.

Key to the Solution Refer to Exhibit 1-3 for definitions of assets and liabilities.

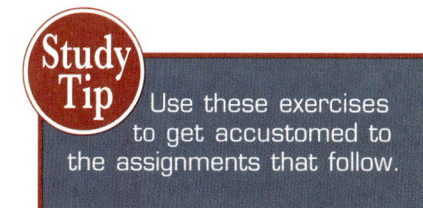

Study Tip

Use these exercises to get accustomed to the assignments that follow.

LO2 **Warmup Exercise 1-2** Finish Line's Assets and Liabilities

Think about **Finish Line**'s business in balance sheet terms.

Required
1. Name three of Finish Line's assets.
2. Name three of Finish Line's liabilities.

Key to the Solution Refer to Exhibit 1-8 if you need to see Finish Line's balance sheet.

LO2 **Warmup Exercise 1-3** Finish Line and the Accounting Equation

Place **Finish Line**'s total assets, total liabilities, and total stockholders' equity in the form of the accounting equation. (Use the February 25, 2006, amounts.)

Key to the Solution Refer to Exhibit 1-8.

SOLUTIONS TO WARMUP EXERCISES

Warmup Exercise 1-1

1. Possible personal financial assets might include checking accounts, savings accounts, certificates of deposit, money market accounts, stocks, bonds, and mutual funds.
2. Possible personal financial liabilities might include student loans, car loans, home mortgages, and amounts borrowed from relatives.

Warmup Exercise 1-2

1. Finish Line's assets include the following: Cash and cash equivalents; Marketable securities; Accounts receivable, net; Merchandise inventories, net; Other; Land; Building; Leasehold improvements; Furniture, fixtures, and equipment; Construction in progress; Deferred income taxes; and Goodwill and intangible assets.
2. Finish Line's liabilities include the following: Accounts payable; Employee compensation; Accrued property and sales tax; Deferred income taxes; Other liabilities and accrued expenses; and Deferred credits from landlords.

Warmup Exercise 1-3

$$\text{Assets} = \text{Liabilities} + \text{Stockholders' Equity}$$
$$\$627,816,000 = \$199,274,000 + \$428,542,000$$

REVIEW PROBLEM & SOLUTION

Greenway Corporation was organized on June 1, 2007. The company will provide lawn-care and tree-trimming services on a contract basis. Following is an alphabetical list of the items that should appear on its income statement for the first month and on its balance sheet at the end of the first month (you will need to determine on which statement each should appear).

REVIEW

Study Tip

At the end of each chapter is a problem to test your understanding of some of the major ideas presented in the chapter. Try to solve the problem before turning to the solution that follows it.

Accounts payable	$ 800
Accounts receivable	500
Building	2,000
Capital stock	5,000
Cash	3,300
Gas, utilities, and other expenses	300
Land	4,000
Lawn-care revenue	1,500
Notes payable	6,000
Retained earnings (beginning balance)	0
Salaries and wages expense	900
Tools	800
Tree-trimming revenue	500
Truck	2,000

Required

1. Prepare an income statement for the month of June.
2. Prepare a balance sheet at June 30, 2007. *Note:* You will need to determine the balance in Retained Earnings at the end of the month.
3. The financial statements you have just prepared are helpful, but in many ways they are a starting point. Assuming this is your business, what additional questions do they raise that you need to consider?

SOLUTION TO REVIEW PROBLEM

1.

Greenway Corporation
Income Statement
For the Month Ended June 30, 2007

Revenues:		
Lawn care	$1,500	
Tree trimming	500	$2,000
Expenses:		
Salaries and wages	$ 900	
Gas, utilities, and other expenses	300	1,200
Net income		$ 800

2.

Greenway Corporation
Balance Sheet
June 30, 2007

Assets		Liabilities and Stockholders' Equity	
Cash	$ 3,300	Accounts payable	$ 800
Accounts receivable	500	Notes payable	6,000
Truck	2,000	Capital stock	5,000
Tools	800	Retained earnings	800
Building	2,000		
Land	4,000	Total liabilities and	
Total assets	$12,600	stockholders' equity	$12,600

3. Following are examples of questions that the financial statements raise:
   - During June, 75% of the revenue was from lawn care and the other 25% from trimming trees. Will this relationship hold in future months?
   - Are the expenses representative of those that will be incurred in the future? Will any other expenses arise, such as advertising and income taxes?
   - When can we expect to collect the accounts receivable? Is there a chance that not all will be collected?
   - How soon will the accounts payable need to be paid?
   - What is the interest rate on the note payable? When is interest paid? When is the note itself due?

REVIEW

QUESTIONS

1. What is accounting? Define it in terms understandable to someone without a business background.

2. How do financial accounting and management accounting differ?

3. What are five different groups of users of accounting information? Briefly describe the types of decisions each group must make.

4. How does stockholders' equity or owners' equity fit into the accounting equation?

5. What are the two distinct elements of owners' equity in a corporation? Define each element.

6. What is the purpose of a balance sheet?

7. How should a balance sheet be dated: as of a particular day or for a particular period of time? Explain your answer.

8. What does the term *cost principle* mean?

9. What is the purpose of an income statement?

10. How should an income statement be dated: as of a particular day or for a particular period of time? Explain your answer.

11. Rogers Corporation starts the year with a Retained Earnings balance of $55,000. Net income for the year is $27,000. The ending balance in Retained Earnings is $70,000. What was the amount of dividends for the year?

12. What is the purpose of a statement of cash flows?

13. How do the duties of the controller of a corporation typically differ from those of the treasurer?

14. What are the three basic types of services performed by public accounting firms?

15. How would you evaluate the following statement: "The auditors are in the best position to evaluate a company because they have prepared the financial statements"?

16. What is the relationship between the cost principle and the going concern assumption?

17. Why does inflation present a challenge to the accountant? Relate your answer to the monetary unit assumption.

18. What is meant by the phrase *generally accepted accounting principles*?

19. What role has the Securities and Exchange Commission played in setting accounting standards? Contrast its role with that played by the Financial Accounting Standards Board.

EXERCISES

LO1

Exercise 1-1 Users of Accounting Information and Their Needs

Listed below are a number of the important users of accounting information. Below the list are descriptions of a major need of each of these various users. Fill in the blank with the one user group that is most likely to have the need described to the right of the blank.

Company management	Banker
Stockholder	Supplier
Securities and Exchange Commission	Labor union
Internal Revenue Service	

User Group

Needs Information About

_____ 1. The profitability of each division in the company

_____ 2. The prospects for future dividend payments

_____ 3. The profitability of the company since the last contract with the work force was signed

_____ 4. The financial status of a company issuing securities to the public for the first time

_____ 5. The prospects that a company will be able to meet its interest payments on time

_____ 6. The prospects that a company will be able to pay for its purchases on time

_____ 7. The profitability of the company based on the tax code

HOMEWORK

LO2

Exercise 1-2 The Accounting Equation

For each of the following independent cases, fill in the blank with the appropriate dollar amount.

	Assets	=	Liabilities	+	Stockholders' Equity
Case 1	$125,000		$ 75,000		$ ____
Case 2	400,000		_____		100,000
Case 3	_____		320,000		95,000

LO2

Exercise 1-3 The Accounting Equation

Ginger Enterprises began the year with total assets of $500,000 and total liabilities of $250,000. Using this information and the accounting equation, answer each of the following independent questions.

1. What was the amount of Ginger's stockholders' equity at the beginning of the year?
2. If Ginger's total assets increased by $100,000 and its total liabilities increased by $77,000 during the year, what was the amount of Ginger's stockholders' equity at the end of the year?
3. If Ginger's total liabilities increased by $33,000 and its stockholders' equity decreased by $58,000 during the year, what was the amount of its total assets at the end of the year?
4. If Ginger's total assets doubled to $1,000,000 and its stockholders' equity remained the same during the year, what was the amount of its total liabilities at the end of the year?

LO2

Exercise 1-4 The Accounting Equation

Using the accounting equation, answer each of the following independent questions.

1. Burlin Company starts the year with $100,000 in assets and $80,000 in liabilities. Net income for the year is $25,000, and no dividends are paid. How much is stockholders' equity at the end of the year?
2. Chapman Inc. doubles the amount of its assets from the beginning to the end of the year. Liabilities at the end of the year amount to $40,000, and stockholders' equity is $20,000. What is the amount of Chapman's assets at the beginning of the year?
3. During the year, the liabilities of Dixon Enterprises triple in amount. Assets at the beginning of the year amount to $30,000, and stockholders' equity is $10,000. What is the amount of liabilities at the end of the year?

LO2

Exercise 1-5 Changes in Stockholders' Equity

The following amounts are available from the records of Coaches and Carriages Inc. at the end of the years indicated:

December 31	Total Assets	Total Liabilities
2005	$ 25,000	$ 12,000
2006	79,000	67,000
2007	184,000	137,000

Required

1. Compute the changes in Coaches and Carriages' stockholders' equity during 2006 and 2007.
2. Compute the amount of Coaches and Carriages' net income (or loss) for 2006 assuming that no dividends were paid during the year.
3. Compute the amount of Coaches and Carriages' net income (or loss) for 2007 assuming that dividends paid during the year amounted to $10,000.

LO2

Exercise 1-6 The Accounting Equation

For each of the following independent cases, fill in the blank with the appropriate dollar amount.

	Case 1	Case 2	Case 3	Case 4
Total assets, end of period	$40,000	$ ____	$75,000	$50,000
Total liabilities, end of period	_____	15,000	25,000	10,000
Capital stock, end of period	10,000	5,000	20,000	15,000
Retained earnings, beginning of period	15,000	8,000	10,000	20,000
Net income for the period	8,000	7,000	_____	9,000
Dividends for the period	2,000	1,000	3,000	_____

LO2   **Exercise 1-7** Classification of Financial Statement Items

Classify each of the following items according to (1) whether it belongs on the income statement (IS) or balance sheet (BS) and (2) whether it is a revenue (R), expense (E), asset (A), liability (L), or stockholders' equity (SE) item.

Item	Appears on the	Classified as
Example: Cash	BS	A
1. Salaries expense	_____	_____
2. Equipment	_____	_____
3. Accounts payable	_____	_____
4. Membership fees earned	_____	_____
5. Capital stock	_____	_____
6. Accounts receivable	_____	_____
7. Buildings	_____	_____
8. Advertising expense	_____	_____
9. Retained earnings	_____	_____

LO2   **Exercise 1-8** Net Income (or Loss) and Retained Earnings

The following information is available from the records of Prestige Landscape Design Inc. at the end of the 2007 calendar year:

Accounts payable	$ 5,000	Office equipment	$ 7,500
Accounts receivable	4,000	Rent expense	6,500
Capital stock	8,000	Retained earnings,	
Cash	13,000	beginning of year	8,500
Dividends paid		Salary and wage expense	12,000
during the year	3,000	Supplies	500
Landscaping revenues	25,000		

Required

Use the information above to answer the following questions:

1. What is Prestige's net income for the year ended December 31, 2007?
2. What is Prestige's retained earnings balance at the end of the year?
3. What is the total amount of Prestige's assets at the end of the year?
4. What is the total amount of Prestige's liabilities at the end of the year?
5. How much stockholders' equity does Prestige have at the end of the year?
6. What is Prestige's accounting equation at December 31, 2007?

LO2   **Exercise 1-9** Statement of Retained Earnings

Ace Corporation has been in business for many years. Retained earnings on January 1, 2007, is $235,800. The following information is available for the first two months of 2007:

	January	February
Revenues	$83,000	$96,000
Expenses	89,000	82,000
Dividends paid	0	5,000

Required

Prepare a statement of retained earnings for the month ended February 28, 2007.

LO3   **Exercise 1-10** Accounting Principles and Assumptions

The following basic accounting principles and assumptions were discussed in the chapter:

     Economic entity

     Monetary unit

     Cost principle

     Going concern

     Time period

H O M E W O R K

Fill in each of the blanks with the accounting principle or assumption that is relevant to the situation described.

_____ 1. Genesis Corporation is now in its 30th year of business. The founder of the company is planning to retire at the end of the year and turn the business over to his daughter.

_____ 2. Nordic Company purchased a 20-acre parcel of property on which to build a new factory. The company recorded the property on the records at the amount of cash given to acquire it.

_____ 3. Jim Bailey enters into an agreement to operate a new law firm in partnership with a friend. Each partner will make an initial cash investment of $10,000. Jim opens a checking account in the name of the partnership and transfers $10,000 from his personal account into the new account.

_____ 4. Multinational Corp. has a division in Japan. Prior to preparing the financial statements for the company and all its foreign divisions, Multinational translates the financial statements of its Japanese division from yen to U.S. dollars.

_____ 5. Camden Company has always prepared financial statements annually, with a year-end of June 30. Because the company is going to sell its stock to the public for the first time, quarterly financial reports will also be required by the Securities and Exchange Commission.

LO5   **Exercise 1-11** Organizations and Accounting

Match each of the organizations listed below with the statement that most adequately describes the role of the group.

Securities and Exchange Commission

International Accounting Standards Board

Financial Accounting Standards Board

American Institute of Certified Public Accountants

American Accounting Association

_____ 1. Federal agency with ultimate authority to determine rules used for preparing financial statements for companies whose stock is sold to the public

_____ 2. Professional organization for accounting educators

_____ 3. Group in the private sector with authority to set accounting standards

_____ 4. Professional organization for certified public accountants

_____ 5. Organization formed to develop worldwide accounting standards

MULTI-CONCEPT EXERCISES

LO1,2   **Exercise 1-12** Users of Accounting Information and the Financial Statements

Listed on the following page are a number of users of accounting information and examples of questions they need answered before making decisions. Fill in each blank to indicate whether the user is most likely to find the answer by looking at the income statement (IS), the balance sheet (BS), the statement of retained earnings (RE), or the statement of cash flows (SCF).

User	Question	Financial Statement
Stockholder	How did this year's sales compare to last year's?	_____
Banker	How much debt does the company already have on its books?	_____
Banker	How much did the company borrow in the past year?	_____
Supplier	How much does the company currently owe to its suppliers?	_____
Stockholder	How much did the company pay in dividends this past year?	_____
Advertising account manager	How much did the company spend this past year to generate sales?	_____
Banker	What collateral or security can the company provide to ensure that any loan I make will be repaid?	_____

LO2,3 **Exercise 1-13** Finish Line's Land

Refer to **Finish Line**'s balance sheet reproduced in the chapter.

Required

What was the amount of Land at February 25, 2006? What does this amount represent (i.e., cost, market value)? Why does Finish Line carry its land at one or the other?

LO1,5 **Exercise 1-14** Roles of Accountants

One day on campus, you overhear two nonbusiness majors discussing the reasons each did not major in accounting. "Accountants are bean counters. They just sit in a room and play with the books all day. They do not have people skills, but I suppose it really doesn't matter because no one ever looks at the statements they prepare," said the first student. The second student replied, "Oh, they are very intelligent, though, because they must know all about the tax laws, and that's too complicated for me."

Required

Comment on the students' perceptions of the roles of accountants in society. Do you agree that no one ever looks at the statements they prepare? If not, identify who the primary users are.

PROBLEMS

LO1 **Problem 1-1** You Won the Lottery

You have won a lottery! You will receive $200,000, after taxes, each year for the next five years.

Required

Describe the process you will go through in determining how to invest your winnings. Consider at least two options and make a choice. You may consider the stock of a certain company, bonds, real estate investments, bank deposits, and so on. Be specific. What information do you need to make a final decision? How will your decision be affected by the fact that you will receive the winnings over a five-year period rather than in one lump sum? Would you prefer one payment? Explain.

LO1 **Problem 1-2** Users of Accounting Information and Their Needs

Havre Company would like to buy a building and equipment to produce a new product line. Some information about Havre is more useful to some people involved in the project than to others.

Required

Complete the chart in the margin on the next page by identifying the information listed on the left with the user's need to know the information. Identify the information as

a. *need* to know;
b. *helpful* to know; or
c. *not necessary* to know.

H O M E W O R K

Information	User of the Information		
	Management	**Stockholders**	**Banker**
1. Amount of current debt, repayment schedule, and interest rate	_____	_____	_____
2. Fair market value of the building	_____	_____	_____
3. Condition of the roof and heating and cooling, electrical, and plumbing systems	_____	_____	_____
4. Total cost of the building, improvements, and equipment to set up production	_____	_____	_____
5. Expected sales from the new product, variable production costs, related selling costs	_____	_____	_____

LO2

Problem 1-3 Balance Sheet

The following items are available from records of Freescia Corporation at the end of the 2007 calendar year:

Accounts payable	$12,550	Notes payable	$50,000
Accounts receivable	23,920	Office equipment	12,000
Advertising expense	2,100	Retained earnings, end of year	37,590
Buildings	85,000	Salary and wage expense	8,230
Capital stock	25,000	Sales revenue	14,220
Cash	4,220		

Required

Prepare a balance sheet. *Hint:* Not all the items listed should appear on a balance sheet. For each of these non-balance-sheet items, indicate where it should appear.

LO2

Problem 1-4 Corrected Balance Sheet

Dave is the president of Avon Consulting Inc. Avon began business on January 1, 2007. The company's controller is out of the country on business. Dave needs a copy of the company's balance sheet for a meeting tomorrow and asked his assistant to obtain the required information from the company's records. She presented Dave with the following balance sheet. He asks you to review it for accuracy.

Avon Consulting Inc.
Balance Sheet
For the Year Ended December 31, 2007

Assets		Liabilities and Stockholders' Equity	
Accounts payable	$13,000	Accounts receivable	$16,000
Cash	21,000	Capital stock	20,000
Cash dividends paid	16,000	Net income for 2007	72,000
Furniture and equipment	43,000	Supplies	9,000

Required

1. Prepare a corrected balance sheet.
2. Draft a memo explaining the major differences between the balance sheet Dave's assistant prepared and the one you prepared.

LO2

Problem 1-5 Income Statement, Statement of Retained Earnings, and Balance Sheet

Shown below, in alphabetical order, is a list of the various items that regularly appear on the financial statements of Maple Park Theatres Corp. The amounts shown for balance sheet items are balances as of September 30, 2007 (with the exception of Retained Earnings, which is the balance on September 1, 2007), and the amounts shown for income statement items are balances for the month ended September 30, 2007:

Accounts payable	$17,600	Furniture and fixtures	$34,000
Accounts receivable	6,410	Land	26,000
Advertising expense	14,500	Notes payable	20,000
Buildings	60,000	Projection equipment	25,000
Capital stock	50,000	Rent expense—movies	50,600
Cash	15,230	Retained earnings	73,780
Concessions revenue	60,300	Salaries and wages expense	46,490
Cost of concessions sold	23,450	Ticket sales	95,100
Dividends paid during the month	8,400	Water, gas, and electricity	6,700

Required

1. Prepare an income statement for the month ended September 30, 2007.
2. Prepare a statement of retained earnings for the month ended September 30, 2007.
3. Prepare a balance sheet at September 30, 2007.
4. You have $1,000 to invest. On the basis of the statements you prepared, would you use it to buy stock in Maple Park? What other information would you want before making a final decision?

LO2

Problem 1-6 Income Statement and Balance Sheet

Green Bay Corporation began business in July 2007 as a commercial fishing operation and passenger service between islands. Shares of stock were issued to the owners in exchange for cash. Boats were purchased by making a down payment in cash and signing a note payable for the balance. Fish are sold to local restaurants on open account, and customers are given 15 days to pay their account. Cash fares are collected for all passenger traffic. Rent for the dock facilities is paid at the beginning of each month. Salaries and wages are paid at the end of the month. The following amounts are from the records of Green Bay Corporation at the end of its first month of operations:

Accounts receivable	$18,500	Notes payable	$60,000
Boats	80,000	Passenger service revenue	12,560
Capital stock	40,000	Rent expense	4,000
Cash	7,730	Retained earnings	???
Dividends	5,400	Salary and wage expense	18,230
Fishing revenue	21,300		

Required

1. Prepare an income statement for the month ended July 31, 2007.
2. Prepare a balance sheet at July 31, 2007.
3. What information would you need about Notes Payable to assess fully Green Bay's long-term viability? Explain your answer.

LO2

Problem 1-7 Corrected Financial Statements

Hometown Cleaners Inc. operates a small dry-cleaning business. The company has always maintained a complete and accurate set of records. Unfortunately, the company's accountant left in a dispute with the president and took the 2007 financial statements with him. The following income statement and balance sheet were prepared by the company's president.

Hometown Cleaners Inc.
Income Statement
For the Year Ended December 31, 2007

Revenues:		
Accounts receivable	$15,200	
Cleaning revenue—cash sales	32,500	$47,700
Expenses:		
Dividends	$ 4,000	
Accounts payable	4,500	
Utilities	12,200	
Salaries and wages	17,100	37,800
Net income		$ 9,900

Hometown Cleaners Inc.
Balance Sheet
December 31, 2007

Assets		Liabilities and Stockholders' Equity	
Cash	$ 7,400	Cleaning revenue—	
Building and equipment	80,000	credit sales	$26,200
Less: Notes payable	(50,000)	Capital stock	20,000
Land	40,000	Net income	9,900
		Retained earnings	21,300
		Total liabilities and	
Total assets	$77,400	stockholders' equity	$77,400

The president is very disappointed with the net income for the year because it has averaged $25,000 over the last 10 years. She has asked for your help in determining if the reported net income accurately reflects the profitability of the company and if the balance sheet is prepared correctly.

Required
1. Prepare a corrected income statement for the year ended December 31, 2007.
2. Prepare a statement of retained earnings for the year ended December 31, 2007. (The actual balance of retained earnings on January 1, 2007, was $42,700. Note that the December 31, 2007, retained earnings balance shown is incorrect. The president simply "plugged" this amount in to make the balance sheet balance.)
3. Prepare a corrected balance sheet at December 31, 2007.
4. Draft a memo to the president explaining the major differences between the income statement she prepared and the one you prepared.

LO2 **Problem 1-8** Statement of Retained Earnings for The Walt Disney Company

The Walt Disney Company reported the following amounts in various statements included in its 2004 annual report (all amounts are stated in millions of dollars):

Net income for 2004	$ 2,345
Dividends declared and paid in 2004	430
Retained earnings, September 30, 2003	13,817
Retained earnings, September 30, 2004	15,732

Required
1. Prepare a statement of retained earnings for The Walt Disney Company for the year ended September 30, 2004.
2. The Walt Disney Company does not actually present a statement of retained earnings in its annual report. Instead, it presents a broader statement of shareholders' equity. Describe the information that would be included on this statement and that is not included on a statement of retained earnings.

LO5 **Problem 1-9** Role of the Accountant in Various Organizations

The following positions in various entities require a knowledge of accounting practices:

1. Chief financial officer for the subsidiary of a large company
2. Tax adviser to a consolidated group of entities
3. Independent computer consultant
4. Financial planner in a bank
5. Real estate broker in an independent office
6. Production planner in a manufacturing facility
7. Quality control adviser
8. Superintendent of a school district
9. Manager of one store in a retail clothing chain
10. Salesperson for a company that offers subcontract services, such as food service and maintenance to hospitals

Required
For each position listed identify the entity in which it occurs as business or nonbusiness and describe the kind of accounting knowledge (such as financial, managerial, taxes, not-for-profit) required by each position.

LO1 **Problem 1-10** Information Needs and Setting Accounting Standards

The Financial Accounting Standards Board requires companies to supplement their consolidated financial statements with disclosures about segments of their businesses. To comply with this standard, **Time Warner Inc.**'s 2004 annual report provides various disclosures for the five segments in which it operates: AOL, Cable, Filmed Entertainment, Networks, and Publishing.

Required
Which users of accounting information do you think the Financial Accounting Standards Board had in mind when it set this standard? What types of disclosures do you think these users would find helpful?

MULTI-CONCEPT PROBLEM

LO2,3 **Problem 1-11** Primary Assumptions Made in Preparing Financial Statements

Joe Hale opened a machine repair business in leased retail space, paying the first month's rent of $300 and a $1,000 security deposit with a check on his personal account. He took the tools, worth about $7,500, from his garage to the shop. He also bought some equipment to get started. The new equipment had a list price of $5,000, but Joe was able to purchase it on sale at Sears for only $4,200. He charged the new equipment on his personal Sears charge card. Joe's first customer paid $400 for services rendered, so Joe opened a checking account for the company. He completed a second job, but the customer has not paid Joe the $2,500 for his work. At the end of the first month, Joe prepared the following balance sheet and income statement.

Joe's Machine Repair Shop
Balance Sheet
July 31, 2007

Cash	$ 400		
Equipment	5,000	Equity	$5,400
Total	$5,400	Total	$5,400

Joe's Machine Repair Shop
Income Statement
For the Month Ended July 31, 2007

Sales		$ 2,900
Rent	$ 300	
Tools	4,200	4,500
Net loss		$(1,600)

Joe believes that he should show a greater profit next month because he won't have large expenses for items such as tools.

Required
Identify the assumptions that Joe has violated and explain how each event should have been handled. Prepare a corrected balance sheet and income statement.

ALTERNATE PROBLEMS

LO1 **Problem 1-1A** What to Do with a Million Dollars

You have inherited $1 million!

Required
Describe the process you will go through in determining how to invest your inheritance. Consider at least two options and choose one. You may consider the stock of a certain company, bonds, real estate investments, bank deposits, and so on. Be specific. What information do you need to make a final decision? Where do you find the information you need? What additional information will you need to consider if you want to make a change in your investment?

LO1 **Problem 1-2A** Users of Accounting Information and Their Needs

Billings Inc. would like to buy a franchise to provide a specialized service. Some information about Billings is more useful to some people involved in the project than to others.

Required
Complete the chart in the margin by identifying the information listed on the left with the user's need to know the information. Identify the information as

a. *need* to know;
b. *helpful* to know; or
c. *not necessary* to know.

HOMEWORK

Information	User of the Information		
	Manager	**Stockholders**	**Franchisor**
1. Expected revenue from the new service.	____	____	____
2. Cost of the franchise fee and recurring fees to be paid to the franchisor.	____	____	____
3. Cash available to Billings, the franchisee, to operate the business after the franchise is purchased.	____	____	____
4. Expected overhead costs of the service outlet.	____	____	____
5. Billings' required return on its investment.	____	____	____

LO2   **Problem 1-3A** Balance Sheet

The following items are available from the records of Victor Corporation at the end of its fiscal year, July 31, 2007:

Accounts payable	$16,900	Delivery expense	$ 4,600
Accounts receivable	5,700	Notes payable	50,000
Buildings	35,000	Office equipment	12,000
Butter and cheese inventory	12,100	Retained earnings, end of year	26,300
Capital stock	25,000	Salary and wage expense	8,230
Cash	21,800	Sales revenue	14,220
Computerized mixers	25,800	Tools	5,800

Required

Prepare a balance sheet. *Hint:* Not all the items listed should appear on a balance sheet. For each of these non-balance-sheet items, indicate where it should appear.

LO2   **Problem 1-4A** Corrected Balance Sheet

Pete is the president of Island Enterprises. Island Enterprises began business on January 1, 2007. The company's controller is out of the country on business. Pete needs a copy of the company's balance sheet for a meeting tomorrow and asked his assistant to obtain the required information from the company's records. She presented Pete with the following balance sheet. He asks you to review it for accuracy.

Island Enterprises
Balance Sheet
For the Year Ended December 31, 2007

Assets		Liabilities and Stockholders' Equity	
Accounts payable	$ 29,600	Accounts receivable	$ 23,200
Building and equipment	177,300	Supplies	12,200
Cash	14,750	Capital stock	100,000
Cash dividends paid	16,000	Net income for 2007	113,850

Required

1. Prepare a corrected balance sheet.
2. Draft a memo explaining the major differences between the balance sheet Pete's assistant prepared and the one you prepared.

LO2   **Problem 1-5A** Income Statement, Statement of Retained Earnings, and Balance Sheet

Shown below, in alphabetical order, is a list of the various items that regularly appear on the financial statements of Sterns Audio Book Rental Corp. The amounts shown for balance sheet items are balances as of December 31, 2007 (with the exception of retained earnings, which is the balance on January 1, 2007), and the amounts shown for income statement items are balances for the year ended December 31, 2007:

Accounts payable	$ 4,500	Dividends paid during the year	$ 12,000
Accounts receivable	300	Notes payable	10,000
Advertising expense	14,500	Rental revenue	125,900
Audio tape inventory	70,000	Rent paid on building	60,000
Capital stock	50,000	Retained earnings	35,390
Cash	2,490	Salaries and wages expense	17,900
Display fixtures	45,000	Water, gas, and electricity	3,600

Required

1. Prepare an income statement for the year ended December 31, 2007.
2. Prepare a statement of retained earnings for the year ended December 31, 2007.
3. Prepare a balance sheet at December 31, 2007.
4. You have $1,000 to invest. On the basis of the statements you prepared, would you use it to buy stock in this company? What other information would you want before deciding?

LO2   **Problem 1-6A** Income Statement and Balance Sheet

Fort Worth Corporation began business in January 2007 as a commercial carpet cleaning and drying service. Shares of stock were issued to the owners in exchange for cash. Equipment was purchased by making a down payment in cash and signing a note payable for the balance. Services are performed for local restaurants and office buildings on open account, and customers are given 15 days to pay their accounts. Rent for office and storage facilities is paid at the beginning of each month. Salaries and wages are paid at the end of the month. The following amounts are from the records of Fort Worth Corporation at the end of its first month of operations:

Accounts receivable	$24,750	Equipment	$62,000
Capital stock	80,000	Notes payable	30,000
Cash	51,650	Rent expense	3,600
Cleaning revenue	45,900	Retained earnings	???
Dividends	5,500	Salary and wage expense	8,400

Required

1. Prepare an income statement for the month ended January 31, 2007.
2. Prepare a balance sheet at January 31, 2007.
3. What information would you need about Notes Payable to fully assess Fort Worth's long-term viability? Explain your answer.

LO2   **Problem 1-7A** Corrected Financial Statements

Heidi's Bakery Inc. operates a small pastry business. The company has always maintained a complete and accurate set of records. Unfortunately, the company's accountant left in a dispute with the president and took the 2007 financial statements with her. The balance sheet and the income statement shown below were prepared by the company's president.

Heidi's Bakery Inc.
Income Statement
For the Year Ended December 31, 2007

Revenues:		
Accounts receivable	$15,500	
Pastry revenue—cash sales	23,700	$39,200
Expenses:		
Dividends	$ 5,600	
Accounts payable	6,800	
Utilities	9,500	
Salaries and wages	18,200	40,100
Net loss		$ (900)

Heidi's Bakery Inc.
Balance Sheet
December 31, 2007

Assets		Liabilities and Stockholders' Equity	
Cash	$ 3,700	Pastry revenue—	
Building and equipment	60,000	credit sales	$22,100
Less: Notes payable	(40,000)	Capital stock	30,000
Land	50,000	Net loss	(900)
		Retained earnings	22,500
		Total liabilities and	
Total assets	$73,700	stockholders' equity	$73,700

The president is very disappointed with the net loss for the year because net income has averaged $21,000 over the last 10 years. He has asked for your help in determining if the reported net loss accurately reflects the profitability of the company and if the balance sheet is prepared correctly.

Required

1. Prepare a corrected income statement for the year ended December 31, 2007.
2. Prepare a statement of retained earnings for the year ended December 31, 2007. (The actual amount of Retained Earnings on January 1, 2007, was $39,900. The December 31, 2007, retained earnings balance shown is incorrect. The president simply "plugged" this amount in to make the balance sheet balance.)
3. Prepare a corrected balance sheet at December 31, 2007.
4. Draft a memo to the president explaining the major differences between the income statement he prepared and the one you prepared.

LO2 **Problem 1-8A** Statement of Retained Earnings for Brunswick Corporation

Brunswick Corporation reported the following amounts in various statements included in its 2004 annual report (all amounts are stated in millions of dollars):

Net earnings for 2004	$ 269.8
Cash dividends declared and paid in 2004	58.1
Retained earnings, December 31, 2003	1,202.0
Retained earnings, December 31, 2004	1,413.7

Required

1. Prepare a statement of retained earnings for Brunswick Corporation for the year ended December 31, 2004.
2. Brunswick does not actually present a statement of retained earnings in its annual report. Instead, it presents a broader statement of shareholders' (stockholders') equity. Describe the information that would be included on this statement and that is not included on a statement of retained earnings.

LO5 **Problem 1-9A** Role of the Accountant in Various Organizations

The following positions in various entities require a knowledge of accounting practices:

_____ 1. Chief financial officer for the subsidiary of a large company

_____ 2. Tax adviser to a consolidated group of entities

_____ 3. Accounts receivable computer analyst

_____ 4. Financial planner in a bank

_____ 5. Budget analyst in a real estate office

_____ 6. Production planner in a manufacturing facility

_____ 7. Quality control adviser

_____ 8. Manager of the team conducting an audit on a state lottery

_____ 9. Assistant superintendent of a school district

_____ 10. Manager of one store in a retail clothing chain

_____ 11. Controller in a company that offers subcontract services, such as food service and maintenance to hospitals

_____ 12. Staff accountant in a large audit firm

Required

For each position listed, fill in the blank to classify the position as one of the general categories of accountants listed below.

Financial accountant	**Accountant for not-for-profit organization**
Managerial accountant	**Auditor**
Tax accountant	**Not an accounting position**

LO1 **Problem 1-10A** Information Needs and Setting Accounting Standards

The Financial Accounting Standards Board requires companies to supplement their consolidated financial statements with disclosures about segments of their businesses. To comply with this standard, **Marriott International**'s 2004 annual report provides various disclosures for the five segments in which it operates: Full-Service Lodging, Select-Service Lodging, Extended-Stay Lodging, Timeshare, and Synthetic Fuel.

Required

Which users of accounting information do you think the Financial Accounting Standards Board had in mind when it set this standard? What types of disclosures do you think these users would find helpful?

ALTERNATE MULTI-CONCEPT PROBLEM

LO2,3   **Problem 1-11A** Primary Assumptions Made in Preparing Financial Statements

Millie Abrams opened a ceramic studio in leased retail space, paying the first month's rent of $300 and a $1,000 security deposit with a check on her personal account. She took molds and paint, worth about $7,500, from her home to the studio. She also bought a new firing kiln to start the business. The new kiln had a list price of $5,000, but Millie was able to trade in her old kiln, worth $500 at the time of trade, on the new kiln, and therefore she paid only $4,500 cash. She wrote a check on her personal checking account. Millie's first customers paid a total of $1,400 to attend classes for the next two months. She opened a checking account in the company's name with the $1,400. She has conducted classes for one month and has sold for $3,000 unfinished ceramic pieces called *greenware*. Greenware sales are all cash. Millie incurred $1,000 of personal cost in making the greenware. At the end of the first month, Millie prepared the following balance sheet and income statement.

Millie's Ceramic Studio
Balance Sheet
July 31, 2007

Cash	$1,400		
Kiln	5,000	Equity	$6,400
Total	$6,400	Total	$6,400

Millie's Ceramic Studio
Income Statement
For the Month Ended July 31, 2007

Sales		$4,400
Rent	$300	
Supplies	600	900
Net income		$3,500

Millie needs to earn at least $3,000 each month for the business to be worth her time. She is pleased with the results.

Required

Identify the assumptions that Millie has violated and explain how each event should have been handled. Prepare a corrected balance sheet and income statement.

DECISION CASES

READING AND INTERPRETING FINANCIAL STATEMENTS

LO1,2   **Decision Case 1-1** An Annual Report as Ready Reference

Refer to **Finish Line**'s annual report, reprinted at the back of the book, and identify where each of the following users of accounting information would first look to answer their respective questions about Finish Line:

1. Investors: How much did the company earn for each share of stock I own? Were any dividends paid, and how much was reinvested in the company?
2. Potential investors: What amount of earnings can I expect to see from Finish Line in the near future?

3. Suppliers: Should I extend credit to Finish Line? Does it have sufficient cash or cash-like assets to repay accounts payable?
4. IRS: How much does Finish Line owe for taxes?
5. Potential employees: Does the company sponsor a retirement plan? If so, how much does it contribute to the plan?

LO2

Decision Case 1-2 Reading and Interpreting Finish Line's Financial Statements

Refer to the financial statements for **Finish Line** reproduced in the chapter and answer the following questions:

1. What was the company's net income for 2006?
2. State Finish Line's financial position on February 25, 2006, in terms of the accounting equation.
3. Explain the reasons for the change in retained earnings from a balance of $263,971,000 on February 26, 2005, to a balance of $319,656,000 on February 25, 2006.

LO2,4

Decision Case 1-3 Comparing Two Companies in the Same Industry: Finish Line and Foot Locker

Refer to the financial information for **Finish Line** and **Foot Locker** reproduced at the end of the book and answer the following questions:

1. What was the sales amount for each company for the most recent year? (Note that Finish Line uses the term "net sales" rather than sales.) Did each company's sales increase or decrease from its total amount in the prior year?
2. What was each company's net income for the most recent year? Did each company's net income increase or decrease from its net income for the prior year?
3. What was the total asset balance for each company at the end of its most recent year? Among its assets, what was the largest asset each reported on its year-end balance sheet?
4. Did either company pay its stockholders any dividents during the most recent year? Explain how you can tell whether they did or did not pay any dividends.
5. Compare the auditors' report for the two companies. Is the form of the reports the same? Do they contain the same basic information?

MAKING FINANCIAL DECISIONS

LO1

Decision Case 1-4 An Investment Opportunity

You have saved enough money to pay for your college tuition for the next three years when a high school friend comes to you with a deal. He is an artist who has spent most of the past two years drawing on the walls of old buildings. The buildings are about to be demolished and your friend thinks you should buy the walls before the buildings are demolished and open a gallery featuring his work. Of course, you are levelheaded and would normally say "No!" Recently, however, your friend has been featured on several local radio and television shows and is talking to some national networks about doing a feature on a well-known news show. To set up the gallery would take all your savings, but your friend feels that you will be able to sell his artwork for 10 times the cost of your investment. What kinds of information about the business do you need before deciding to invest all your savings? What kind of profit split would you suggest to your friend if you decide to open the gallery?

LO2

Decision Case 1-5 Preparation of Projected Statements for a New Business

Upon graduation from MegaState University, you and your roommate decide to start your respective careers in accounting and salmon fishing in Remote, Alaska. Your career as a CPA in Remote is going well, as is your roommate's job as a commercial fisherman. After one year in Remote, he approaches you with a business opportunity.

As we are well aware, the DVD rental business has yet to reach Remote, and the nearest rental facility is 250 miles away. We each put up our first year's savings of $5,000 and file for articles of incorporation with the state of Alaska to do business as Remote DVD World. In return for our investment of $5,000, we will each receive equal shares of capital stock in the corporation. Then we go to the Corner National Bank and apply for a $10,000 loan. We take the total cash of $20,000 we have now raised and buy 2,000 DVDs at $10 each from a mail-order supplier. We rent the movies for $3 per title and sell monthly memberships for $25, allowing a member to check out an unlimited number of movies during the month. Individual rentals would be a cash-and-carry business, but we would give customers until the 10th of the following month to pay for a monthly membership. My most conservative estimate is that during the first month alone, we will rent 800 movies and sell 200 memberships. As I see it, we will have only two expenses. First, we will hire four high school students to run the store for 15 hours each per week and pay them $5 per hour. Second, the landlord of a vacant store in town will rent us space in the building for $1,000 per month.

Required

1. Prepare a projected income statement for the first month of operations.
2. Prepare a balance sheet as it would appear at the end of the first month of operations.
3. Assume that the bank is willing to make the $10,000 loan. Would you be willing to join your roommate in this business? Explain your response. Also, indicate any information other than what he has provided that you would like to have before making a final decision.

ETHICAL DECISION MAKING

LO1,2,4 **Decision Case 1-6** Identification of Errors in Financial Statements and Preparation of Revised Statements

Lakeside Slammers Inc. is a minor-league baseball organization that has just completed its first season. You and three other investors organized the corporation; each put up $10,000 in cash for shares of capital stock. Because you live out of state, you have not been actively involved in the daily affairs of the club. However, you are thrilled to receive a dividend check for $10,000 at the end of the season—an amount equal to your original investment! Included with the check are the following financial statements, along with supporting explanations.

Lakeside Slammers Inc.
Income Statement
For the Year Ended December 31, 2007

Revenues:		
Single-game ticket revenue	$420,000	
Season-ticket revenue	140,000	
Concessions revenue	280,000	
Advertising revenue	100,000	$940,000
Expenses:		
Cost of concessions sold	$110,000	
Salary expense—players	225,000	
Salary and wage expense—staff	150,000	
Rent expense	210,000	695,000
Net income		$245,000

Lakeside Slammers Inc.
Statement of Retained Earnings
For the Year Ended December 31, 2007

Beginning balance, January 1, 2007	$ 0
Add: Net income for 2007	245,000
Deduct: Cash dividends paid in 2007	(40,000)
Ending balance, December 31, 2007	$205,000

Lakeside Slammers Inc.
Balance Sheet
December 31, 2007

Assets		Liabilities and Stockholders' Equity	
Cash	$ 5,000	Notes payable	$ 50,000
Accounts receivable:		Capital stock	40,000
Season tickets	140,000	Additional owners' capital	80,000
Advertisers	100,000	Parent club's equity	125,000
Auxiliary assets	80,000	Retained earnings	205,000
Equipment	50,000		
Player contracts	125,000		
Total assets	$500,000	Total liabilities and stockholders' equity	$500,000

Additional information:

a. Single-game tickets sold for $4 per game. The team averaged 1,500 fans per game. With 70 home games × $4 per game × 1,500 fans, single-game ticket revenue amounted to $420,000.

b. No season tickets were sold during the first season. During the last three months of 2007, however, an aggressive sales campaign resulted in the sale of 500 season tickets for the 2008 season. Therefore, the controller (who is also one of the owners) chose to record an Account Receivable—Season Tickets and corresponding revenue for 500 tickets × $4 per game × 70 games, or $140,000.

c. Advertising revenue of $100,000 resulted from the sale of the 40 signs on the outfield wall at $2,500 each for the season. However, none of the advertisers have paid their bills yet (thus, an account receivable of $100,000 on the balance sheet) because the contract with Lakeside required them to pay only if the team averaged 2,000 fans per game during the 2007 season. The controller believes that the advertisers will be sympathetic to the difficulties of starting a new franchise and be willing to overlook the slight deficiency in the attendance requirement.

d. Lakeside has a working agreement with one of the major-league franchises. The minor-league team is required to pay $5,000 *every* year to the major-league team for each of the 25 players on its roster. The controller believes that each of the players is certainly an asset to the organization and has therefore recorded $5,000 × 25, or $125,000, as an asset called Player Contracts. The item on the right side of the balance sheet entitled Parent Club's Equity is the amount owed to the major league team by February 1, 2008, as payment for the players for the 2007 season.

e. In addition to the cost described in (d), Lakeside directly pays each of its 25 players a $9,000 salary for the season. This amount—$225,000—has already been paid for the 2007 season and is reported on the income statement.

f. The items on the balance sheet entitled Auxiliary Assets on the left side and Additional Owners' Capital on the right side represent the value of the controller's personal residence. She has a mortgage with the bank for the full value of the house.

g. The $50,000 note payable resulted from a loan that was taken out at the beginning of the year to finance the purchase of bats, balls, uniforms, lawn mowers, and other miscellaneous supplies needed to operate the team (equipment is reported as an asset for the same amount). The loan, with interest, is due on April 15, 2008. Even though the team had a very successful first year, Lakeside is a little short of cash at the end of 2007 and has therefore asked the bank for a three-month extension of the loan. The controller reasons, "By the due date of April 15, 2008, the cash due from the new season ticket holders will be available, things will be cleared up with the advertisers, and the loan can be easily repaid."

Required

1. Identify any errors that you think the controller has made in preparing the financial statements.

2. On the basis of your answer in (1), prepare a revised income statement, statement of retained earnings, and balance sheet.

3. On the basis of your revised financial statements, identify any ethical dilemma you now face. Does the information regarding the season ticket revenue provide reliable information to an outsider? Does the $100,000 advertising revenue on the income statement represent the underlying economic reality of the transaction? Do you have a responsibility to share these revisions with the other three owners? What is your responsibility to the bank?

4. Using Exhibit 1-10 and the related text as your guide, analyze the key elements in the situation and answer the following questions. Support your answers by explaining your reasoning.
   a. Who may benefit or be harmed?
   b. How are they likely to benefit or be harmed?
   c. What rights or claims may be violated?
   d. What specific interests are in conflict?
   e. What are your responsibilities and obligations?
   f. Do you believe the information provided by the organization is relevant, is reliable, accurately represents what it claims to report, and is unbiased?

LO4,5 **Decision Case 1-7** Responsibility for Financial Statements and the Role of the Auditor

Financial statements are the means by which accountants communicate to external users. Recent financial reporting scandals have focused attention on the accounting profession and its role in the preparation of these statements and the audits performed on the statements.

1. Who is responsible for the preparation of the financial statements that are included in a company's annual report?
2. Who performs an audit of the financial statements referred to in (1) above?
3. Why is it important for those who are responsible for an audit of the financial statements to be independent of those who prepare the statements? Explain your answer.
4. What are some services that an auditor might perform that could call into question that professional's independence? Do you think these other types of services do, in fact, affect the ability of the auditor to remain independent?

SOLUTIONS TO KEY TERMS QUIZ

4	Accounting	13	Securities and Exchange Commission (SEC)
9	Management accounting	17	Financial Accounting Standards Board (FASB)
5	Financial accounting	19	American Institute of Certified Public Accountants (AICPA)
6	Owners' equity		
3	Stockholders' equity	28	Certified Public Accountant (CPA)
8	Retained earnings	29	Public Company Accounting Oversight Board (PCAOB)
7	Balance sheet		
1	Income statement	24	International Accounting Standards Board (IASB)
27	Net income		
10	Dividends	26	Sarbanes-Oxley Act
2	Statement of retained earnings	22	Controller
30	Statement of cash flows	15	Treasurer
12	Cost principle	20	Internal auditing
16	Going concern	23	Auditing
18	Monetary unit	25	Auditors' report
21	Time period	14	American Accounting Association
11	Generally accepted accounting principles (GAAP)		

HOMEWORK

2

Financial Statements and the Annual Report

Study Links

A Look at the Previous Chapter

Chapter 1 introduced how investors, creditors, and others use accounting and the outputs of the accounting system—financial statements—in making business decisions. Chapter 1 introduced the Financial Decision Model and the Ethical Decision Framework—two of the three key decision tools needed for informed and ethical decision making.

A Look at This Chapter

Chapter 2 takes a closer look at the financial statements as well as other elements that make up an annual report. It also introduces the third decision model needed for making financial decisions, the Ratio Decision Process. Here you'll learn how to use financial statement numbers to develop ratios that reflect the financial trends of a business.

A Look at the Upcoming Chapter

Chapter 3 steps back from a firm's financial statements to look at how business transactions and the resulting accounting information are handled. We begin by looking at transactions—what they are, how they are analyzed, and how accounting procedures facilitate turning them into journal entries, ledger accounts, and trial balances on which financial statements are based.

Learning Outcomes

After studying this chapter, you should be able to:

LO1 Describe the objectives of financial reporting.

LO2 Describe the qualitative characteristics of accounting information.

LO3 Explain the concept and purpose of a classified balance sheet and prepare the statement.

LO4 Use a classified balance sheet to analyze a company's financial position.

LO5 Explain the difference between a single-step and a multiple-step income statement and prepare each type of income statement.

LO6 Use a multiple-step income statement to analyze a company's operations.

LO7 Identify the components of the statement of retained earnings and prepare the statement.

LO8 Identify the components of the statement of cash flows and prepare the statement.

LO9 Read and use the financial statements and other elements in the annual report of a publicly held company.

The Finish Line, Inc.

MAKING BUSINESS DECISIONS

Like all public companies, Finish Line produces an annual report which it hopes will be of value to both existing stockholders as well as anyone else considering buying stock in the company. While no two annual reports look the same, they generally contain similar information. Finish Line's 2006 annual report is no exception. It begins with a "Message to Shareholders." In the message titled "Investing in Our Future," the CEO and the President of the company together share with stockholders their excitement for the future.

Growth is the key ingredient in the long-term success of any business and Finish Line's leaders are confident that plans are in place to ensure the success of their company. As shown in the Company Overview, reproduced here, those plans include new locations for its flagship Finish Line stores, rapid growth in the Man Alive stores that were acquired in 2005, and the opening of 15 Paiva stores. However, the fastest growing segment is what the company calls "Direct-to-Consumer." Like all retailers, Finish Line uses the Internet to sell its products and this mode of selling grew by over 40% in the 2006 fiscal year. The lack of a need to invest in fixtures, display racks, and lighting for a new store, and the lack of overhead that naturally comes with mall locations are certainly incentives to grow this segment of the business.

The letter to shareholders naturally focuses to a large extent on plans for the future. But what can an annual report tell us about how successful a company like Finish Line has been in the past year in achieving its goals? The financial statements and the notes that accompany them, along with management's discussion and analysis of company performance, are central to answering this question. In this chapter, we will explore not only the various components in an annual report but also the characteristics that make the information in a report useful. Here are some of the key questions you should look for answers to:

- What makes a set of financial statements understandable? (See p. 63)

- What distinguishes a current asset from a long-term asset? A current liability from a long-term liability? (See pp. 66–70)

- How can the numbers on a classified balance sheet be used to measure a company's liquidity? (See pp. 80–81)

- How can the numbers on an income statement be used to measure a company's profitability? (See p. 82)

- What useful nonfinancial information can be found in a company's annual report? (See pp. 82–85)

59

THE FINISH LINE, INC.

COMPANY OVERVIEW (as of February 25, 2006)

- The Finish Line, Inc. is the parent company of three retail concepts: Finish Line, Man Alive, and Paiva

- The Finish Line, Inc. has 708 retail stores nationwide

- The Finish Line, Inc. has 13,000 employees nationwide

- The Finish Line, Inc. is headquartered in Indianapolis, Indiana

- The company was created in 1976 and completed its IPO in June 1992

Finish Line.

- Finish Line is one of the nation's leading athletic specialty retailers offering the best selection of footwear, apparel and accessories for men, women and kids.

- Finish Line operates 657 stores nationwide, totaling 3.7 million square feet of retail space

- New Finish Line stores for FY 2006 averaged approximately 4,800 square feet

- In FY 2006, merchandise mix was 80 percent footwear and 20 percent softgoods

- Finish Line's primary customers are 12 to 24 year-old males and females, but the format and product appeals to a broad audience

- Web address is www.finishline.com

- Finish Line plans to open 50 new stores in FY 2007

MAN Alive.

- Man Alive is one of the nation's leading hip-hop fashion retailers with a long tradition of bringing bold, cutting edge, brand name style from across the nation into each store.

- The Finish Line, Inc. acquired Man Alive in January 2005

- Man Alive operates 51 stores in 13 states, totaling 159,000 square feet of retail space

- In FY 2006, new Man Alive stores averaged approximately 3,600 square feet

- Merchandise mix is primarily apparel, with some footwear and accessories

- Man Alive's primary customers are trend conscious 15 to 25 year-olds whose fashion is primarily influenced by the entertainment industry

- Web address is www.man-alive.com

- Man Alive plans to open 35 new stores during FY 2007

paiva.

- Paiva is a unique, inspiring, premium athletic store created exclusively for active women who demand an elevated level of service and style.

- Merchandise mix is primarily apparel, with some footwear and accessories

- The first Paiva store opened at Barton Creek Square in Austin, Texas, in April 2006

- Paiva's primary customers are active, upscale women seeking a blend of performance and style

- Paiva stores will average 4,000 square feet

- Web address is www.paiva.com

- Paiva plans to open 15 stores during FY 2007

What Financial Statements Tell about a Business

As we saw in Chapter 1, a variety of external users need information to make sound business decisions. These users include stockholders, bondholders, bankers, and other types of creditors, such as suppliers. All of these users must make an initial decision about investing in a company, regardless of whether it is in the form of a stock, a bond or a note. The balance sheet, the income statement, the statement of cash flows, along with the supporting notes and other information found in an annual report, are the key sources of information needed to make sound decisions.

- **The balance sheet tells what obligations will be due in the near future and what assets will be available to satisfy them.**
- **The income statement tells the revenues and expenses for a period of time.**
- **The statement of cash flows tells where cash came from and how it was used during the period.**
- **The notes provide essential details about the company's accounting policies and other key factors that affect its financial condition and performance.**

To use the basic information that is found, decision makers must understand the underlying accounting principles that have been applied to create the reported information in the statements. In preparing financial statements, accountants consider:

- **The objectives of financial reporting.**
- **The characteristics that make accounting information useful.**
- **The most useful way to display the information found in the balance sheet, the income statement, and the statement of cash flows.**

Objectives of Financial Reporting

The users of financial information are the main reason financial statements are prepared. After all, it is the investors, creditors, and other groups and individuals outside and inside the company who must make economic decisions based on these statements. Therefore, as we learned in Chapter 1, financial statements must be based on agreed-upon assumptions like time period, going concern, and other generally accepted accounting principles.

Moreover, when the accountants for companies like **Finish Line** and **Foot Locker** prepare their financial statements, they must keep in mind financial reporting objectives, which are focused on providing the most understandable and useful information possible. **Financial reporting has one overall objective and a set of related objectives, all of them concerned with how the information may be most useful to the readers.**

LO1 Describe the objectives of financial reporting.

THE PRIMARY OBJECTIVE OF FINANCIAL REPORTING

The primary objective of financial reporting is to provide economic information to permit users of the information to make informed decisions. Users include both the management of a company (internal users) and others not involved in the daily operations of the business (external users). The external users usually do not have access to the detailed records of the business and don't have the benefit of daily involvement in the affairs of the company. They make their decisions based on *financial statements* prepared by management. According to the Financial Accounting Standards Board (FASB), "Financial reporting should provide information that is useful to present and potential investors and creditors and other users in making rational investment, credit, and similar decisions."[1]

---

1 *Statement of Financial Accounting Concepts [SFAC] No. 1,* "Objectives of Financial Reporting by Business Enterprises" (Stamford, Conn.: Financial Accounting Standards Board, November 1978), par. 34.

EXHIBIT 2-1 **The Application of Financial Reporting Objectives**

Financial Reporting Objective	Potential Investor's Questions
1. The primary objective: Provide information for decision making.	"Based on the financial information, should I buy shares of stock in Finish Line?"
2. Secondary objective: Reflect prospective cash receipts to investors and creditors.	"How much cash, if any, will I receive in dividends each year and how much from the sale of the stock of Finish Line in the future?"
3. Secondary objective: Reflect prospective cash flows to an enterprise.	"After paying its suppliers and employees, and meeting all of its obligations, how much cash will Finish Line take in during the time I own the stock?"
4. Secondary objective: Reflect resources and claims to resources.	"How much has Finish Line invested in new stores?"

We see from this statement how closely the objective of financial reporting is tied to decision making. **The purpose of financial reporting is to help the users reach their decisions in an informed manner.**

SECONDARY OBJECTIVES OF FINANCIAL REPORTING

Three secondary objectives follow from the primary objective of financial reporting. These are:

- **Reflect Prospective Cash Receipts to Investors and Creditors**

  Investor: If I buy stock in this company, how much cash will I receive:
  - In dividends?
  - From the sale of the stock?

  Banker: If I lend money to this company, how much cash will I receive:
  - In interest on the loan?
  - When and if the loan is repaid?

- **Reflect Prospective Cash Flows to the Company**

  Investors, bankers, and other users ultimately care about their cash receipts, but this depends to some extent on the company's skills in managing its *own* cash flows.

- **Reflect the Company's Resources and Claims to its Resources**

  A company's cash flows are inherently tied to the information on the:
  - Balance sheet (assets, liabilities, and owners' equity)
  - Income statement (revenues and expenses)

Exhibit 2-1 summarizes the objectives of financial reporting as they pertain to someone considering whether to buy stock in Finish Line. The exhibit should help you to understand how something as abstract as a set of financial reporting objectives can be applied to a decision-making situation.

What Makes Accounting Information Useful? Qualitative Characteristics

LO2 Describe the qualitative characteristics of accounting information.

Since accounting information must be useful for decision making, what makes this information useful? This section focuses on the qualities that accountants strive for in their financial reporting and on some of the challenges they face in making reporting judgments. It also reveals what users of financial information expect from financial statements.

Quantitative considerations, such as tuition costs, certainly were a concern when you chose your current school. In addition, your decision required you to make subjective judgments about the *qualitative* characteristics you were looking for in a college. Similarly, there are certain qualities that make accounting information useful.

UNDERSTANDABILITY

For anything to be useful, it must be understandable.

Usefulness and understandability go hand in hand. However, **understandability** of financial information varies considerably, depending on the background of the user. For example, should financial statements be prepared so that they are understandable by anyone with a college education? Or should it be assumed that all readers of financial statements have completed at least one accounting course? Is a background in business necessary for a good understanding of financial reports, regardless of one's formal training? As you might expect, there are no simple answers to these questions. However, the FASB believes that **financial information should be comprehensible to** *those who are willing to spend the time to understand it*:

Understandability
The quality of accounting information that makes it comprehensible to those willing to spend the necessary time.

> *"Financial information is a tool and, like most tools, cannot be of much direct help to those who are unable or unwilling to use it or who misuse it. Its use can be learned, however, and financial reporting should provide information that can be used by all— nonprofessionals as well as professionals—who are willing to learn to use it properly."*[2]

RELEVANCE

Understandability alone is certainly not enough to render information useful.

To be useful, information must be relevant.

Relevance is the capacity of information to make a difference in a decision.[3] For example, assume that you are a banker evaluating the financial statements of a company that has come to you for a loan. All of the financial statements point to a strong and profitable company. However, today's newspaper revealed that the company has been named in a multimillion-dollar lawsuit. Undoubtedly, this information would be relevant to your talks with the company, and disclosure of the lawsuit in the financial statements would make them even more relevant to your lending decision.

Relevance
The capacity of information to make a difference in a decision.

RELIABILITY

What makes accounting information reliable? According to the FASB, "Accounting information is reliable to the extent that users can depend on it to represent the economic conditions or events that it purports to represent."[4]

Reliability has three basic characteristics:

Reliability
The quality that makes accounting information dependable in representing the events that it purports to represent.

1. *Verifiability* Information is verifiable when we can make sure that it is free from error—for example, by looking up the cost paid for an asset in a contract or an invoice.
2. *Representational faithfulness* Information is representationally faithful when it corresponds to an actual event—such as when the purchase of land corresponds to a transaction in the company's records.
3. *Neutrality* Information is neutral when it is not slanted to portray a company's position in a better or worse light than the actual circumstances would dictate— such as when the probable losses from a major lawsuit are disclosed accurately in the notes to the financial statements, with all its potential effects on the company, rather than minimized as a very remote possible loss.

---

2 *SFAC No. 1*, par. 36.
3 *Statement of Financial Accounting Concepts [SFAC] No. 2*, "Qualitative Characteristics of Accounting Information" (Stamford, Conn.: Financial Accounting Standards Board, May 1980), par. 47.
4 *SFAC No. 2*, par. 62.

COMPARABILITY AND CONSISTENCY

Comparability allows comparisons to be made *between or among companies*.

Comparability
For accounting information, the quality that allows a user to analyze two or more companies and look for similarities and differences.

Generally accepted accounting principles (GAAP) allow a certain amount of freedom in choosing among competing alternative treatments for certain transactions.

For example, under GAAP, companies may choose from a number of methods of accounting for the depreciation of certain long-term assets. **Depreciation** is the *process of allocating* the cost of a long-term tangible asset, such as a building or equipment, over its useful life. Each method may affect the value of the assets differently. How does this freedom of choice affect the ability of investors to make comparisons between companies?

Depreciation
The process of allocating the cost of a long-term tangible asset over its useful life.

Assume that you are considering buying stock in one of three companies. As their annual reports indicate, one of the companies uses what is called the "accelerated" depreciation method, and the other two companies use what is called the "straight-line" depreciation method. (We'll learn about these methods in Chapter 8.) Does this lack of a common depreciation method make it impossible for you to compare the performance of the three companies?

Obviously, comparisons among the companies would be easier and more meaningful if all three used the same depreciation method. However, comparisons are not impossible just because companies use different methods. Certainly, the more alike—that is, uniform—statements are in terms of the principles used to prepare them, the more comparable they will be. However, the profession allows a certain freedom of choice in selecting from among alternative generally accepted accounting principles.

To render statements of companies using different methods more meaningful, *disclosure* assumes a very important role. For example, as we will see later in this chapter, the first note in the annual report of a publicly traded company is the disclosure of its accounting policies. The reader of this note for each of the three companies is made aware that the companies do not use the same depreciation method. Disclosure of accounting policies allows the reader to make some sort of subjective adjustment to the statements of one or more of the companies and thus to compensate for the different depreciation method being used.

Consistency
For accounting information, the quality that allows a user to compare two or more accounting periods for a single company.

Consistency is closely related to the concept of comparability. Both involve the relationship between two numbers. However, whereas financial statements are comparable when they can be compared between one company and another, statements are consistent when they can be compared within a single company from one accounting period to the next.

Occasionally, companies decide to change from one accounting method to another. Will it be possible to compare a company's earnings in a period in which it switches methods with its earnings in prior years if the methods differ? Like the different methods used by different companies, changes in accounting methods from one period to the next do not make comparisons impossible, only more difficult. When a company makes an accounting change, accounting standards require various disclosures to help the reader evaluate the impact of the change.

MATERIALITY

For accounting information to be useful, it must be relevant to a decision.

Materiality
The magnitude of an accounting information omission or misstatement that will affect the judgment of someone relying on the information.

The concept of **materiality** is closely related to relevance and deals with the size of an error in accounting information. The issue is whether the error is large enough to affect the judgment of someone relying on the information. Consider the following example. A company pays cash for two separate purchases: one for a $5 pencil sharpener and the other for a $50,000 computer. Theoretically, each expenditure results in the acquisition of an asset that should be depreciated over its useful life. However, what if the company decides to account for the $5 paid for the pencil sharpener as an expense of the period rather than treat it in the theoretically correct manner by depreciating it over the life of the pencil sharpener? *Will this error in any way affect the judgment of someone relying on the financial statements?* Because such a slight error will *not* affect any decisions, minor expenditures of this nature are considered *immaterial* and are accounted for as an expense of the period.

EXHIBIT 2-2	What Characteristics Make Information Useful?

Characteristic	Why Important?
Understandability	Must understand information to use it
Relevance	Must be information that could affect a decision
Reliability	Must be able to rely on the information
Comparability	Must be able to compare with other companies
Consistency	Must be able to compare with prior years
Materiality	Must be an amount large enough to affect a decision
Conservatism	If any doubt, use the least optimistic estimate

The *threshold* for determining materiality will vary from one company to the next, depending to a large extent on the size of the company. Many companies establish policies that *any* expenditure under a certain dollar amount should be accounted for as an expense of the period. The threshold might be $50 for the corner grocery store but $1,000 for a large corporation. Finally, in some instances the amount of a transaction may be immaterial by company standards but may still be considered significant by financial statement users. For example, a transaction involving either illegal or unethical behavior by a company officer would be of concern, regardless of the dollar amounts involved.

CONSERVATISM

The concept of **conservatism** is a holdover from earlier days when the primary financial statement was the balance sheet and the primary user of this statement was the banker. It was customary to deliberately understate assets on the balance sheet because this resulted in an even larger margin of safety that the assets being provided as collateral for a loan were sufficient.

Today, the balance sheet is not the only financial statement, and deliberate understatement of assets is no longer considered desirable. The practice of conservatism is reserved for those situations in which there is *uncertainty* about how to account for a particular item or transaction: "Thus, if two estimates of amounts to be received or paid in the future are about equally likely, conservatism dictates using the less optimistic estimate; however, if two amounts are not equally likely, conservatism does not necessarily dictate using the more pessimistic amount rather than the more likely one."[5]

Various accounting rules are based on the concept of conservatism. For example, inventory held for resale is reported on the balance sheet at *the lower-of-cost-or-market value.* This rule requires a company to compare the cost of its inventory with the market price, or current cost to replace that inventory, and report the lower of the two amounts on the balance sheet at the end of the year. In Chapter 5 we will more fully explore the lower-of-cost-or-market rule as it pertains to inventory.

Exhibit 2-2 summarizes the qualities that make accounting information useful.

Conservatism
The practice of using the least optimistic estimate when two estimates of amounts are about equally likely.

Financial Reporting: An International Perspective

In Chapter 1 we introduced the International Accounting Standards Board (IASB) and its efforts to improve the development of accounting standards around the world. Interestingly, four of the most influential members of this group, representing the standard-setting bodies in the United States, the United Kingdom, Canada, and Australia, agree on the primary objective of financial reporting. All recognize that the primary objective is to provide information useful in making economic decisions.

---

5 *SFAC No. 2*, par. 95.

The standard-setting body in the United Kingdom distinguishes between qualitative characteristics that relate to *content* of the information presented and those that relate to *presentation*. Similar to the FASB, this group recognizes relevance and reliability as the primary characteristics related to content. Comparability and understandability are the primary qualities related to the presentation of the information.

The concept of conservatism is also recognized in other countries. For example, both the IASB and the standard-setting body in the United Kingdom list "prudence" among their qualitative characteristics. Prudence requires the use of caution in making the various estimates required in accounting. Like the U.S. standard-setting body, these groups recognize that prudence does not justify the deliberate understatement of assets or revenues or the deliberate overstatement of liabilities or expenses.

Looking at Financial Statements

LO3 Explain the concept and purpose of a classified balance sheet and prepare the statement.

Now that we have learned about the conceptual framework of accounting, we turn to the outputs of the system: the financial statements. First, using a hypothetical company, Dixon Sporting Goods, we will consider the significance of a *classified balance sheet*. We will then examine the *income statement*, the *statement of retained earnings*, and the *statement of cash flows* for this company. The chapter concludes with a brief look at the financial statements of a real company, Finish Line, and at the other elements in an annual report.

WHAT ARE THE PARTS OF THE BALANCE SHEET? UNDERSTANDING THE OPERATING CYCLE

In the first part of this chapter, we stressed the importance of *cash flow*. For a company that sells a product, the **operating cycle** begins when cash is invested in inventory and ends when cash is collected by the enterprise from its customers.

Consider Finish Line's typical operating cycle. Assume that on August 1 it buys a pair of running shoes from Nike for $70. At this point, Finish Line has merely substituted one asset, cash, for another, inventory. Assume that on August 20, twenty days after buying the running shoes from Nike, that it sells them to Jane Jet for $100. If Jane pays cash for the shoes, Finish Line will have completed its cash-to-cash operating cycle in a total of 20 days, as shown in Exhibit 2-3.

Operating cycle
The period of time between the purchase of inventory and the collection of any receivable from the sale of the inventory.

EXHIBIT 2-3 Operating Cycle: Cash Sale

Cash $70

August 1:
Finish Line buys shoes from Nike for $70 in cash.

Cycle starts again when Finish Line buys another pair of shoes for resale.

Cash $100

Inventory $70

Length of operating cycle: 20 days
Finish Line sells and collects 20 days after purchase.

August 20:
Finish Line sells shoes to Jane Jet for $100 in cash.

EXHIBIT 2-4 Operating Cycle: Sale on Credit

Although it is common in retail to make most sales for cash, Finish Line does make some sales on credit, as evidenced by the accounts receivable that appears on its balance sheet. Consider how Finish Line's operating cycle is extended if it sells the same pair of running shoes to Carl Quick on August 20 and allows him to pay for them in 30 days. Instead of an operating cycle of 20 days, a total of 50 days has passed between the use of cash to buy the shoes from Nike and the collection of cash from the customer, as shown in Exhibit 2-4.

The Classified Balance Sheet

CURRENT ASSETS

The basic distinction on a classified balance sheet is between current and noncurrent items. **Current assets** are "cash and other assets that are reasonably expected to be realized in cash or sold or consumed during the normal operating cycle of a business or within one year if the operating cycle is shorter than one year."[6]

The current assets section of Dixon Sporting Goods' balance sheet appears as follows:

Current asset
An asset that is expected to be realized in cash or sold or consumed during the operating cycle or within one year if the cycle is shorter than one year.

Dixon Sporting Goods Partial Balance Sheet	
Current assets	
Cash	$ 5,000
Marketable securities	11,000
Accounts receivable	23,000
Merchandise inventory	73,500
Prepaid insurance	4,800
Store supplies	700
Total current assets	$ 118,000

6 Accounting Principles Board, *Statement of the Accounting Principles Board, No. 4*, "Basic Concepts and Accounting Principles Underlying Financial Statements of Business Enterprises" (New York: American Institute of Certified Public Accountants, 1970), par. 198.

Most businesses have an operating cycle shorter than one year. For example, Finish Line's cycle in Exhibit 2-4 was assumed to be 50 days. Therefore, for most companies the cutoff for current classification is one year. We will use the one-year cutoff for current classification in the remainder of this chapter. Thus, on Dixon's balance sheet, cash, accounts receivable, and inventory are classified as current assets because they *are* cash or will be *realized* in (converted to) cash (accounts receivable) or will be *sold* (inventory) within one year.

In addition to cash, accounts receivable, and inventory, the two other most common types of current assets are marketable securities and prepaid expenses. Excess cash is often invested in the stocks and bonds of other companies, as well as in various government instruments. If the investments are made for the short term, they are classified as current and are typically called either *short-term investments* or *marketable securities.* (Alternatively, some investments are made for the purpose of exercising influence over another company and thus are made for the long term. These investments are classified as noncurrent assets.) Various prepayments, such as office supplies, rent, and insurance, are classified as *prepaid expenses* and thus are current assets. These assets qualify as current because they will usually be *consumed* within one year.

NONCURRENT ASSETS

Any asset not meeting the definition of a current asset is classified as *long-term* or *noncurrent.* Three common categories of long-term assets are: investments; property, plant, and equipment; and intangibles. For Dixon, these are:

Dixon Sporting Goods
Partial Balance Sheet

Investments			
Land held for future office site			$150,000
Property, plant, and equipment			
Land		$100,000	
Buildings	$150,000		
Less: Accumulated depreciation	60,000	90,000	
Store furniture and fixtures	$ 42,000		
Less: Accumulated depreciation	12,600	29,400	
Total property, plant, and equipment			219,400
Intangible assets			
Franchise agreement			55,000

Investments Recall from the discussion of current assets, that stocks and bonds expected to be sold within the next year are classified as current assets. Securities not expected to be sold within the next year are classified as *investments.* In many cases, the investment is in the common stock of another company. Sometimes companies invest in another company either to exercise some influence over it or actually to control its operations. Other types of assets classified as investments are land held for future use and buildings and equipment not currently used in operations. For example, Dixon classifies as an investment some land it holds for a future office site. A special fund held for the retirement of debt or for the construction of new facilities is also classified as an investment.

Property, Plant, and Equipment This category consists of the various *tangible, productive assets* used in the operation of a business. Land, buildings, equipment, machinery, furniture and fixtures, trucks, and tools are all examples of assets held for use in the *operation* of a business rather than *resale.* The distinction between inventory and equipment, for instance, depends on the company's *intent* in acquiring the asset. For example, **IBM** classifies a computer system as inventory because its intent in manufacturing the asset is to offer it for resale. However, this same computer in the hands of a law firm would be classified as equipment because its intent in buying the asset from IBM is to use it in the long-term operation of the business.

The relative size of property, plant, and equipment depends largely on a company's business. Consider **Xcel Energy**, a utility company with over $20 billion in total assets at the end of 2004. Almost 70 percent of the total assets was invested in property, plant, and equipment. On the other hand, property and equipment represented less than 3 percent of the total assets of **Microsoft**, the highly successful software company. Regardless of the relative size of property, plant, and equipment, all assets in this category are subject to depreciation, with the exception of land. A separate accumulated depreciation account is used to account for the depreciation recorded on each of these assets over its life.

Intangibles Intangible assets are similar to property, plant, and equipment in that they provide benefits to the firm over the long term. The distinction, however, is in the *form* of the asset. *Intangible assets lack physical substance.* Trademarks, copyrights, franchise rights, patents, and goodwill are examples of intangible assets. The cost principle governs the accounting for intangibles, just as it does for tangible assets. For example, the amount paid to an inventor for the patent rights to a new project is recorded as an intangible asset. Similarly the amount paid to purchase a franchise for a fast-food restaurant for the exclusive right to operate in a certain geographic area is recorded as an intangible asset. With a few exceptions, intangibles are written off to expense over their useful lives. *Depreciation* is the name given to the process of writing off tangible assets; the same process for intangible assets is called *amortization.* Depreciation and amortization are both explained more fully in Chapter 8.

2 minute review

1. Give at least three examples of current assets.

2. Give the three common categories of noncurrent assets.

Answers

1. Cash, accounts receivable, marketable securities, inventories, and prepaid expenses.

2. Investments; property, plant, and equipment; and intangibles.

CURRENT LIABILITIES

The definition of a current liability is closely tied to that of a current asset. A **current liability** is an obligation that will be satisfied within the next operating cycle or within one year, if the cycle (as is normally the case) is shorter than one year. For example, the classification of a note payable on the balance sheet depends on its maturity date. If the note will be paid within the next year, it is classified as current; otherwise, it is classified as a long-term liability. On the other hand, accounts payable, wages payable, and income taxes payable are all short-term or current liabilities, as seen on Dixon's balance sheet:

Current liability
An obligation that will be satisfied within the next operating cycle or within one year if the cycle is shorter than one year.

Dixon Sporting Goods
Partial Balance Sheet

Current liabilities		
Accounts payable	$15,700	
Salaries and wages payable	9,500	
Income taxes payable	7,200	
Interest payable	2,500	
Bank loan payable	25,000	
Total current liabilities		$ 59,900

Most liabilities are satisfied by the payment of cash. However, certain liabilities are eliminated from the balance sheet when the company performs services.

For example, the liability Subscriptions Received in Advance, which would appear on the balance sheet of a magazine publisher, is satisfied not by the payment of any cash but by the delivery of the magazine to the customers. Finally, it is possible to satisfy one liability by substituting another in its place. For example, a supplier might ask a customer to sign a written promissory note to replace an existing account payable if the customer is unable to pay at the present time.

LONG-TERM LIABILITIES

Any obligation that will not be paid or otherwise satisfied within the next year or the operating cycle, whichever is longer, is classified as a long-term liability, or long-term debt. Notes payable and bonds payable, both promises to pay money in the future, are two common forms of long-term debt. Some bonds have a life as long as 25 or 30 years. Dixon's notes payable for $120,000 is classified as a long-term liability because it is not due in the next year:

Dixon Sporting Goods
Partial Balance Sheet

Long-term debt

Notes payable, due December 31, 2018 $120,000

STOCKHOLDERS' EQUITY

Recall that stockholders' equity represents the owners' claims on the assets of the business. These claims arise from two sources: *contributed capital* and *earned capital.* The stockholders' equity section of Dixon's balance sheet reports:

Dixon Sporting Goods
Partial Balance Sheet

Contributed capital		
Capital stock, $10 par, 5,000 shares issued and outstanding	$ 50,000	
Paid-in capital in excess of par value	25,000	
Total contributed capital	$ 75,000	
Retained earnings	287,500	
Total stockholders' equity		$362,500

Contributed capital appears on the balance sheet in the form of capital stock, and earned capital takes the form of retained earnings. *Capital stock* indicates the owners' investment in the business. *Retained earnings* represents the accumulated earnings, or net income, of the business since its inception less all dividends paid during that time.

Most companies have a single class of capital stock called *common stock.* This is the most basic form of ownership in a business. All other claims against the company, such as those of *creditors* and *preferred stockholders*, take priority. *Preferred stock* is a form of capital stock that, as the name implies, carries with it certain preferences. For example, the company must pay dividends on preferred stock before it makes any distribution of dividends on common stock. In the event of liquidation, preferred stockholders have priority over common stockholders in the distribution of the entity's assets.

Capital stock may appear as two separate items on the balance sheet: *Par Value* and *Paid-in Capital in Excess of Par Value.* The total of these two items tells us the amount that has been paid by the owners for the stock. We will take a closer look at these items in Chapter 11.

Exhibit 2-5 shows a complete classified balance sheet for Dixon Sporting Goods.

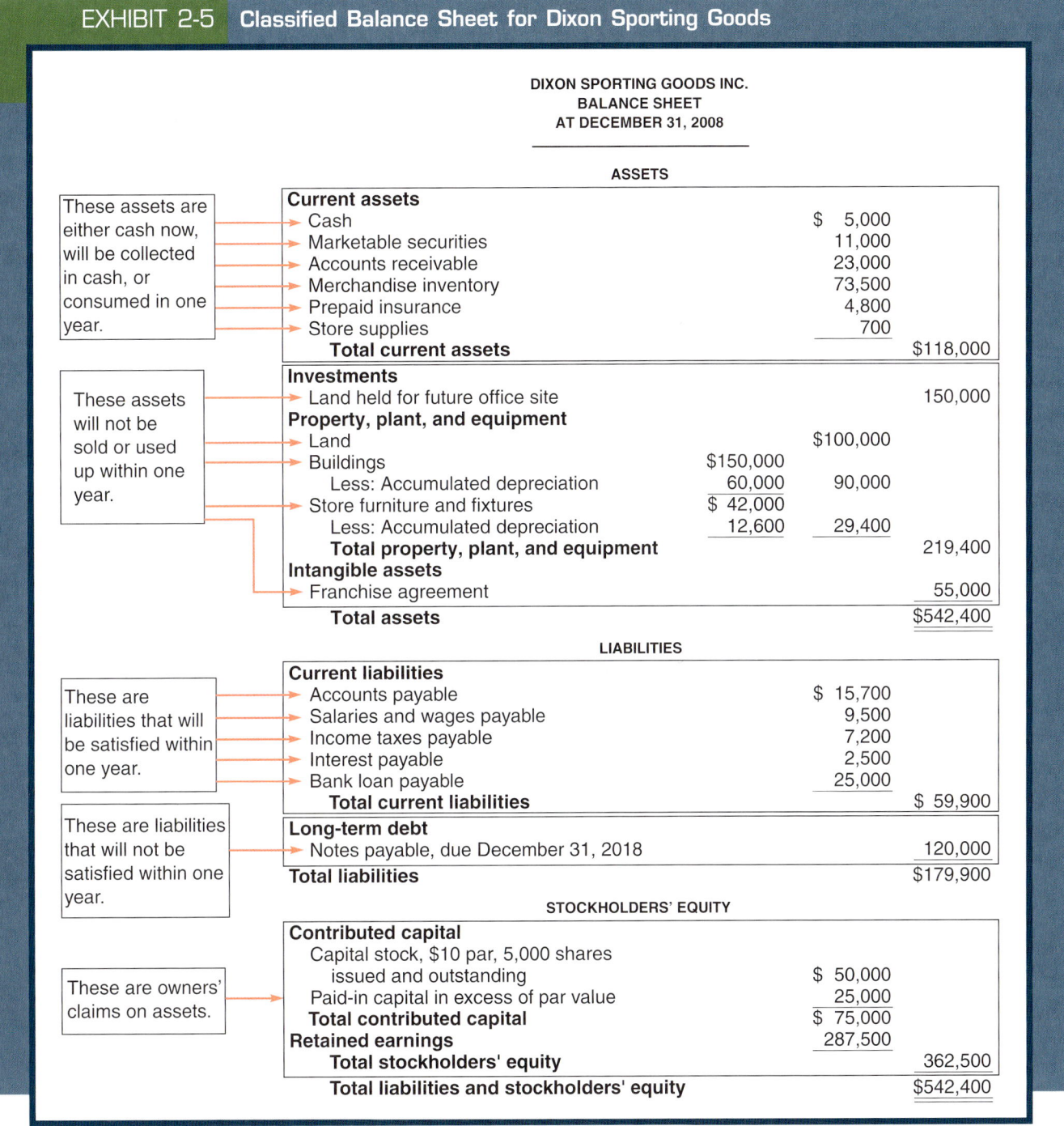

EXHIBIT 2-5 Classified Balance Sheet for Dixon Sporting Goods

DIXON SPORTING GOODS INC.
BALANCE SHEET
AT DECEMBER 31, 2008

ASSETS

These assets are either cash now, will be collected in cash, or consumed in one year.

Current assets		
Cash		$ 5,000
Marketable securities		11,000
Accounts receivable		23,000
Merchandise inventory		73,500
Prepaid insurance		4,800
Store supplies		700
Total current assets		$118,000

These assets will not be sold or used up within one year.

Investments			
Land held for future office site			150,000
Property, plant, and equipment			
Land		$100,000	
Buildings	$150,000		
Less: Accumulated depreciation	60,000	90,000	
Store furniture and fixtures	$ 42,000		
Less: Accumulated depreciation	12,600	29,400	
Total property, plant, and equipment			219,400
Intangible assets			
Franchise agreement			55,000
Total assets			$542,400

LIABILITIES

These are liabilities that will be satisfied within one year.

Current liabilities		
Accounts payable		$ 15,700
Salaries and wages payable		9,500
Income taxes payable		7,200
Interest payable		2,500
Bank loan payable		25,000
Total current liabilities		$ 59,900

These are liabilities that will not be satisfied within one year.

Long-term debt		
Notes payable, due December 31, 2018		120,000
Total liabilities		$179,900

STOCKHOLDERS' EQUITY

These are owners' claims on assets.

Contributed capital		
Capital stock, $10 par, 5,000 shares issued and outstanding		$ 50,000
Paid-in capital in excess of par value		25,000
Total contributed capital		$ 75,000
Retained earnings		287,500
Total stockholders' equity		362,500
Total liabilities and stockholders' equity		$542,400

Using a Classified Balance Sheet: Introduction to Ratios

A classified balance sheet separates both assets and liabilities into those that are current and those that are noncurrent. This distinction is very useful in any analysis of a company's financial position.

LO4 Use a classified balance sheet to analyze a company's financial position.

WORKING CAPITAL

Investors, bankers, and other interested readers use the balance sheet to evaluate the liquidity of a business. **Liquidity** is a relative term and deals with the ability of a company to pay its debts as they come due. As you might expect, bankers and other creditors are particularly interested in the liquidity of businesses to which they have lent money. A comparison of current assets and current liabilities is

Liquidity
The ability of a company to pay its debts as they come due.

Working capital
Current assets minus current liabilities.

a starting point in evaluating the ability of a company to meet its obligations. **Working capital** is the difference between current assets and current liabilities at a point in time. Referring back to Exhibit 2-5, we see that the working capital for Dixon Sporting Goods on December 31, 2008, is as follows:

Working Capital

Formula	For Dixon Sporting Goods
Current Assets − Current Liabilities	$118,000 − $59,900 = $58,100

The management of working capital is an important task for any business. A company must continually strive for a *balance* in managing its working capital. For example, too little working capital—or in the extreme, negative working capital—may signal the inability to pay creditors on a timely basis. However, an overabundance of working capital could indicate that the company is not investing enough of its available funds in productive resources, such as new machinery and equipment.

CURRENT RATIO

Current ratio
Current assets divided by current liabilities.

Because it is an absolute dollar amount, working capital is limited in its informational value. For example, $1 million may be an inadequate amount of working capital for a large corporation but far too much for a smaller company. In addition, a certain dollar amount of working capital may have been adequate for a company earlier in its life but is inadequate now. However, a related measure of liquidity, the **current ratio**, allows us to *compare* the liquidity of companies of different sizes and of a single company over time. The ratio is computed by dividing current assets by current liabilities. Dixon Sporting Goods has a current ratio of just under 2 to 1:

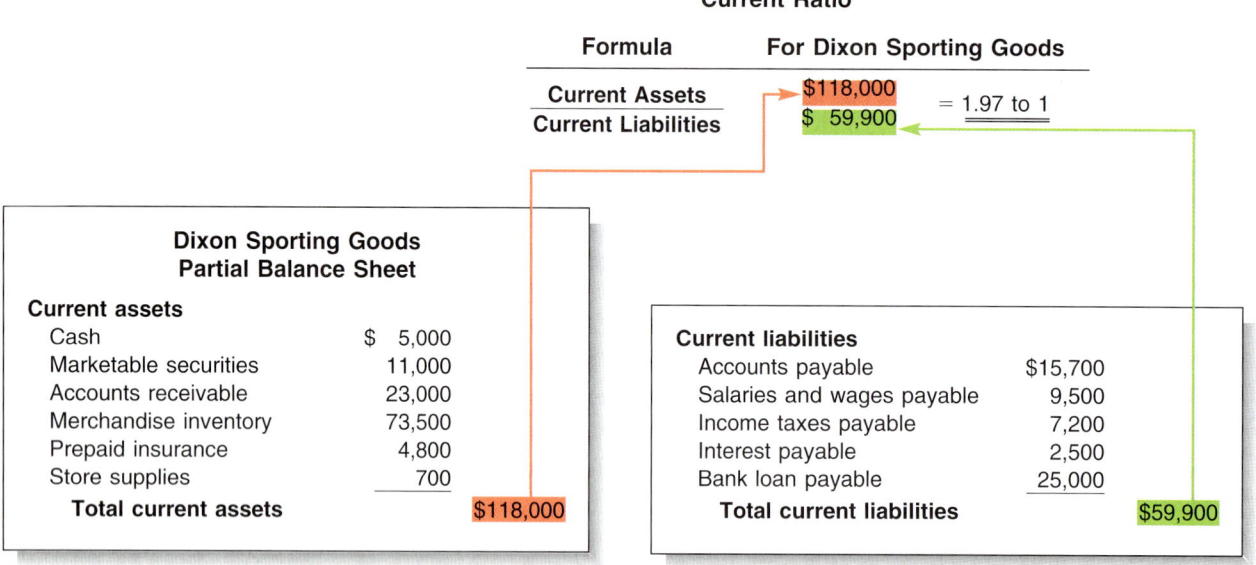

In general, the higher the current ratio, the more liquid the company is. Some analysts use a rule of thumb of 2 to 1 for the current ratio as a sign of short-term financial health. However, rules of thumb can be dangerous. Historically, companies in certain industries have operated quite efficiently with a current ratio of less than 2 to 1, whereas a ratio much higher than this is necessary to survive in other industries. Consider **Gap Inc.**, the popular clothing company. On January 29, 2005, it had a current ratio of 2.81 to 1. On the other hand, companies in the telephone communication business routinely have current ratios from well under 1 to 1. **Verizon**'s current ratio at the end of 2004 was only 0.84 to 1.

Unfortunately, neither the amount of working capital nor the current ratio tells us anything about the *composition* of current assets and current liabilities. For example, assume two companies both have total current assets equal to $100,000. Company A has cash of $10,000, accounts receivable of $50,000, and inventory of $40,000. Company B also has cash of $10,000 but accounts receivable of $20,000 and inventory of $70,000. All other things being equal, Company A is more liquid than Company B because more of its total current assets are in receivables than inventory. Receivables are only one step away from being cash, whereas inventory must be sold and then the receivable collected. Note that Dixon's inventory of $73,500 makes up a large portion of its total current assets of $118,000. An examination of the *relative* size of the various current assets for a company may reveal certain strengths and weaknesses not evident in the current ratio.

In addition to the composition of the current assets, the *frequency* with which they are "turned over" is important. For instance, how long does it take to sell an item of inventory? How long is required to collect an account receivable? Many companies could not exist with the current ratio of 0.94 reported by **Southwest Airlines** at the end of 2005. However, think about the nature of the airline business. Without large amounts in either inventories or accounts receivable, an airline can operate with a lower current ratio than a manufacturing company, for example.

The Income Statement

The income statement summarizes the results of operations of an entity for a *period of time*. At a minimum, all companies prepare income statements at least once a year. Companies that must report to the Securities and Exchange Commission prepare financial statements, including an income statement, every three months. Monthly income statements are usually prepared for internal use by management.

WHAT APPEARS ON THE INCOME STATEMENT?

From an accounting perspective, it is important to understand what transactions of an entity should appear on the income statement. In general, the income statement reports the excess of revenue over expense—that is, the *net income*, or in the event of an excess of expense over revenue, the net loss of the period. As a reference to the "bottom line" on an income statement, it is common to use the terms *profits* or *earnings* as synonyms for *net income*.

As discussed in Chapter 1, *revenue* is the inflow of assets resulting from the sale of products and services. It represents the dollar amount of sales of products and services for a period of time. An *expense* is the outflow of assets resulting from the sale of goods and services for a period of time. Wages and salaries, utilities, and taxes are all examples of expenses.

Certain special types of revenues, called *gains*, are sometimes reported on the income statement, as are certain special types of expenses, called *losses*. For example, assume that Sanders Company holds a parcel of land for a future building site. The company paid $50,000 for the land 10 years ago. The state pays Sanders $60,000 for the property to use in a new highway project. Sanders has a special type of revenue from the condemnation of its property. It will recognize a *gain* of $10,000: the excess of the cash received from the state, $60,000, over the cost of the land, $50,000.

FORMAT OF THE INCOME STATEMENT

Different formats are used by corporations to present their results. The major choice a company makes is whether to prepare the income statement in a single-step or a multiple-step form. Both forms are generally accepted although many more companies use the multiple-step form. Next, we'll explain the differences between the two forms and their variations.

LO5 Explain the difference between a single-step and a multiple-step income statement and prepare each type of income statement.

Single-step income statement
An income statement in which all expenses are added together and subtracted from all revenues.

Single-Step Format for the Income Statement In a **single-step income statement**, all expenses and losses are added together and then are deducted *in a single step* from all revenues and gains to arrive at net income. A single-step format for the income statement of Dixon Sporting Goods is presented in Exhibit 2-6. The primary advantage of the single-step form is its simplicity. No attempt is made to classify either revenues or expenses or to associate any of the expenses with any of the revenues.

Multiple-step income statement
An income statement that shows classifications of revenues and expenses as well as important subtotals.

Multiple-Step Format for the Income Statement The purpose of the **multiple-step income statement** is to subdivide the income statement into specific sections and provide the reader with important subtotals. This format is illustrated for Dixon Sporting Goods in Exhibit 2-7.

The multiple-step income statement for Dixon indicates three important subtotals. First, ❶ cost of goods sold is deducted from sales to arrive at **gross profit:**

Gross profit
Sales less cost of goods sold.

Gross Profit = Sales − Cost of Goods Sold	
Sales	$357,500
Cost of goods sold	218,300
Gross profit	$139,200

Cost of goods sold, as the name implies, is the cost of the units of inventory sold during the year. It is logical to associate cost of goods sold with the sales revenue for the year because the latter represents the *selling price* of the inventory sold during the period.

The second important subtotal on Dixon's income statement is ❷ *income from operations* of $73,600. This is found by subtracting *total operating expenses* of $65,600 from the gross profit of $139,200. Operating expenses are further subdivided between *selling expenses* and *general and administrative expenses.* For example, note that two depreciation amounts are included in operating expenses. Depreciation on store furniture and fixtures is classified as a selling expense because the store is

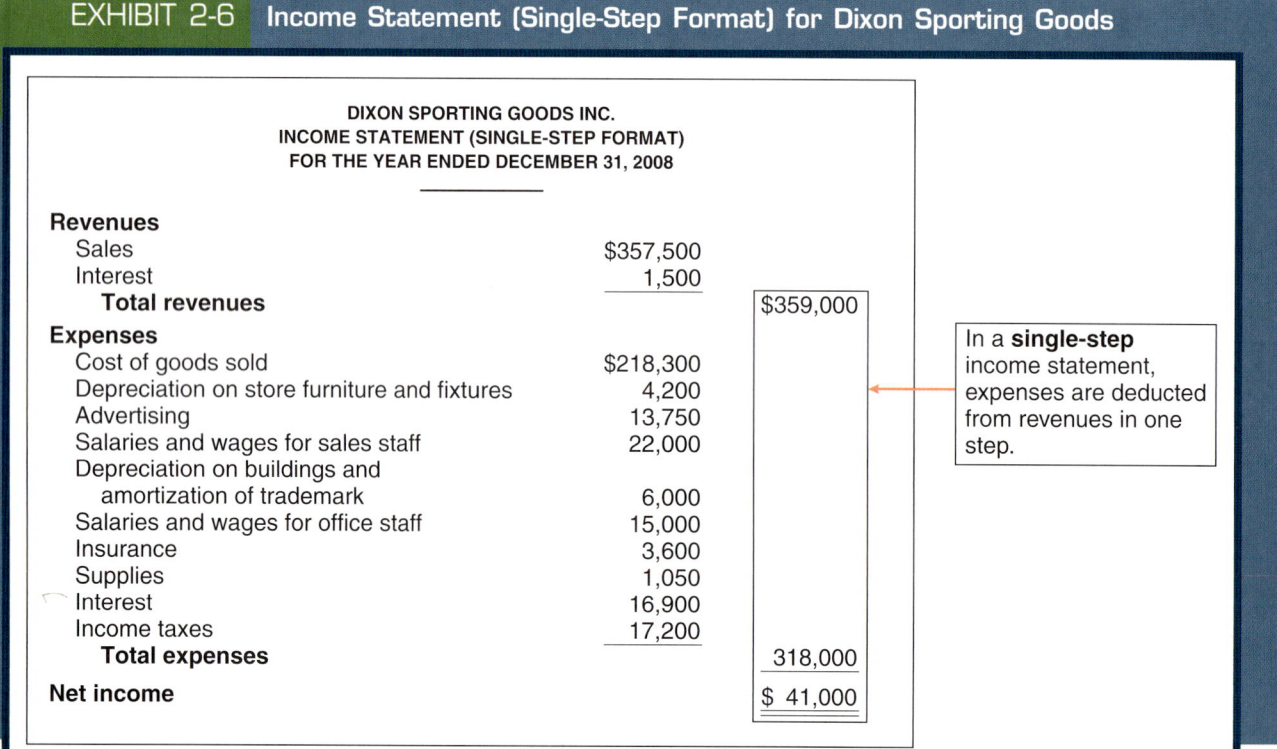

EXHIBIT 2-6 Income Statement (Single-Step Format) for Dixon Sporting Goods

DIXON SPORTING GOODS INC.
INCOME STATEMENT (SINGLE-STEP FORMAT)
FOR THE YEAR ENDED DECEMBER 31, 2008

Revenues		
Sales	$357,500	
Interest	1,500	
Total revenues		$359,000
Expenses		
Cost of goods sold	$218,300	
Depreciation on store furniture and fixtures	4,200	
Advertising	13,750	
Salaries and wages for sales staff	22,000	
Depreciation on buildings and amortization of trademark	6,000	
Salaries and wages for office staff	15,000	
Insurance	3,600	
Supplies	1,050	
Interest	16,900	
Income taxes	17,200	
Total expenses		318,000
Net income		$ 41,000

In a **single-step** income statement, expenses are deducted from revenues in one step.

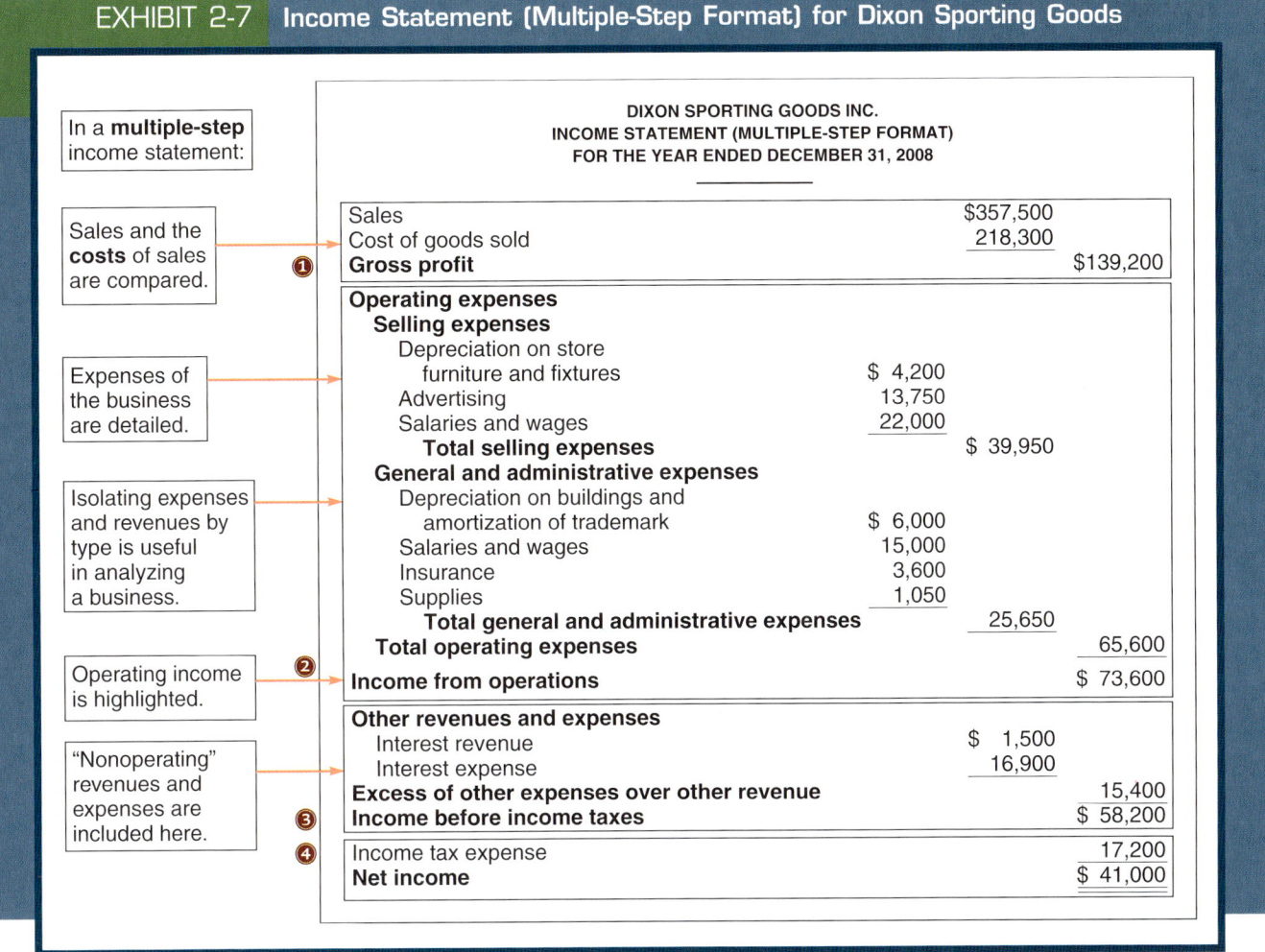

EXHIBIT 2-7 Income Statement (Multiple-Step Format) for Dixon Sporting Goods

In a **multiple-step** income statement:

Sales and the **costs** of sales are compared.

Expenses of the business are detailed.

Isolating expenses and revenues by type is useful in analyzing a business.

Operating income is highlighted.

"Nonoperating" revenues and expenses are included here.

DIXON SPORTING GOODS INC.
INCOME STATEMENT (MULTIPLE-STEP FORMAT)
FOR THE YEAR ENDED DECEMBER 31, 2008

Sales		$357,500	
Cost of goods sold		218,300	
Gross profit			$139,200
Operating expenses			
Selling expenses			
Depreciation on store furniture and fixtures	$ 4,200		
Advertising	13,750		
Salaries and wages	22,000		
Total selling expenses		$ 39,950	
General and administrative expenses			
Depreciation on buildings and amortization of trademark	$ 6,000		
Salaries and wages	15,000		
Insurance	3,600		
Supplies	1,050		
Total general and administrative expenses		25,650	
Total operating expenses			65,600
Income from operations			$ 73,600
Other revenues and expenses			
Interest revenue		$ 1,500	
Interest expense		16,900	
Excess of other expenses over other revenue			15,400
Income before income taxes			$ 58,200
Income tax expense			17,200
Net income			$ 41,000

where sales take place. On the other hand, we will assume that the buildings are offices for the administrative staff and thus depreciation on the buildings is classified as a general and administrative expense.

The third important subtotal on the income statement is ❸ *income before income taxes* of $58,200. Interest revenue and interest expense, neither of which is an operating item, are included in *other revenues and expenses*. The excess of interest expense of $16,900 over interest revenue of $1,500, which equals $15,400, is subtracted from income from operations to arrive at income before income taxes. Finally, ❹ *income tax expense* of $17,200 is deducted to arrive at *net income* of $41,000.

⏱ *2 minute review*

1. Give at least two examples of items that would appear on a multiple-step income statement but not a single-step statement.

2. Classify each of the following expenses as either selling or general and administrative: advertising, depreciation on office building, salespersons' commissions and office salaries.

A n s w e r s

1. Gross profit, income from operations, and income before income taxes.

2. Advertising: selling; depreciation on office building: general and administrative; salespersons' commissions: selling; office salaries: general and administrative.

USING AN INCOME STATEMENT

An important use of the income statement is to evaluate the *profitability* of a business. For example, a company's **profit margin** is the ratio of its net income to its sales or revenues. Some analysts refer to a company's profit margin as its *return on sales.* If the profit margin is high, this generally means that the company is generating revenue but that it is also controlling its costs. Dixon Sporting Goods would compute its profit margin by dividing its net income by its total sales as follows:

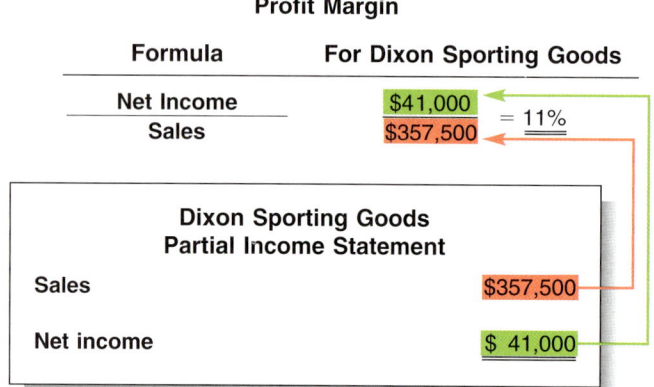

A profit margin of 11% tells us that for every dollar of sales, Dixon has $0.11 in net income.

Keep two key factors in mind when evaluating any financial statement ratio.

- **How does this year's ratio differ from ratios of prior years?** For example, a decrease in the profit margin may indicate that the company is having trouble this year controlling certain costs.

- **How does the ratio compare with industry norms?** For example, in some industries the profit margin is considerably lower than in many others, such as in mass merchandising (**Wal-Mart**'s profit margin was only 3.6% for the year ended January 31, 2005). It is always helpful to compare key ratios, such as the profit margin, with an industry average or with the same ratio for a close competitor of the company.

The Statement of Retained Earnings

The purpose of a statement of stockholders' equity is to explain the changes in the components of owners' equity during the period. Retained earnings and capital stock are the two primary components of stockholders' equity. If there are no changes during the period in a company's capital stock, it may choose to present a statement of retained earnings instead of a statement of stockholders' equity. A statement of retained earnings for Dixon Sporting Goods is shown in Exhibit 2-8.

The statement of retained earnings provides an important link between the income statement and the balance sheet. Dixon's net income of $41,000, as detailed on the income statement, is an *addition* to retained earnings. Note that the dividends declared and paid of $25,000 do not appear on the income statement because they are a payout, or *distribution,* of net income to stockholders rather than one of the expenses deducted to arrive at net income. Accordingly, they appear as a direct deduction on the statement of retained earnings. The beginning balance in retained earnings is carried forward from last year's statement of retained earnings.

EXHIBIT 2-8 | **Statement of Retained Earnings for Dixon Sporting Goods**

Dixon Sporting Goods
Statement of Retained Earnings
For the Year Ended December 31, 2008

Retained earnings, January 1, 2008	$271,500
Add: Net income for 2008	41,000
	$312,500
Less: Dividends declared and paid in 2008	(25,000)
Retained earnings, December 31, 2008	$287,500

The Statement of Cash Flows

All publicly held corporations are required to present a statement of cash flows in their annual reports. **The purpose of the statement is to summarize the cash flow effects of a company's operating, investing, and financing activities for the period.** The statement of cash flows for Dixon Sporting Goods consists of three categories:

LO8 Identify the components of the statement of cash flows and prepare the statement.

   Operating activities
   Investing activities
   Financing activities

Each of these three categories can result in a net inflow or a net outflow of cash.

- Dixon's **operating activities** generated $56,100 of cash during the period. Operating activities ❶ concern the purchase and sale of a product, in this case the acquisition of sporting goods from distributors and the subsequent sale of those goods. As we can readily see, Dixon had one major source of cash, the collection from its customers of $362,500. Similarly, Dixon's largest use of cash was the $217,200 it paid for inventory. In Chapter 12, we will discuss the statement of cash flows in detail and the preparation of this section of the statement.

Dixon Sporting Goods
Partial Statement of Cash Flows

CASH FLOWS FROM OPERATING ACTIVITIES		
Cash collected from customers	$362,500	
Cash collected in interest	1,500	
Total cash collections		$364,000
Cash payments for:		
Inventory	$217,200	
Salaries and wages	38,500	
Interest	16,900	
Store supplies	850	
Insurance	4,800	
Advertising	13,750	
Income taxes	15,900	
Total cash payments		307,900
Net cash provided by operating activities		$ 56,100

   Investing and financing activities were described in this text's Getting Started module.

- **Investing activities** involve the acquisition and sale of long-term or noncurrent assets, such as long-term investments, property, plant, and equipment, and intangible assets.

Dixon Sporting Goods Partial Statement of Cash Flows	
CASH FLOWS FROM INVESTING ACTIVITIES	
Purchase of land for future office site	$(150,000)

Dixon spent $150,000 for land for a future office site. This is an investing activity.

- **Financing activities** result from the issuance and repayment, or retirement, of long-term liabilities and capital stock and the payment of dividends.

Dixon Sporting Goods Partial Statement of Cash Flows		
CASH FLOWS FROM FINANCING ACTIVITIES		
Dividends declared and paid	$(25,000)	
Proceeds from issuance of long-term note	120,000	
Net cash provided by financing activities		$95,000

The company had two financing activities: dividends of $25,000 required the use of cash, and the issuance of a long-term note generated cash of $120,000.

The complete cash flow statement for Dixon Sporting Goods is shown in Exhibit 2-9. The balance of cash on the bottom of the statement of $5,000 must agree with the balance for this item as shown on the balance sheet in Exhibit 2-5.

Looking at Financial Statements for a Real Company: The Finish Line, Inc.

LO9 Read and use the financial statements and other elements in the annual report of a publicly held company.

The financial statements for our sporting goods company introduced the major categories on each of the statements. We now turn to these categories on the financial statements of an actual company, Finish Line. The statements for a real company are more complex and require additional analysis and a better understanding of accounting to fully appreciate them. Therefore, we will concentrate on certain elements of the statements.

As we will see later, the notes to a set of financial statements give the reader a variety of information about a company. Like the statements of many other companies, Finish Line's financials include a note that describes its business:

Nature of Operations.

Finish Line is a specialty retailer of men's, women's and children's brand-name athletic, lifestyle and outdoor footwear, activewear and accessories. Man Alive is a hip-hop fashion retailer offering men's and ladies' name brand fashions from the industry's leading designers. Paiva, Inc. is the Company's new concept for the active woman, which premiered with its first store opening on April 14, 2006. The Company manages its business on the basis of one reportable segment. Finish Line stores average approximately 5,641 square feet, Man Alive stores average approximately 3,110 square feet, and Paiva, Inc. stores will average approximately 4,000 square feet in size and all are primarily located in enclosed malls throughout most of the United States.

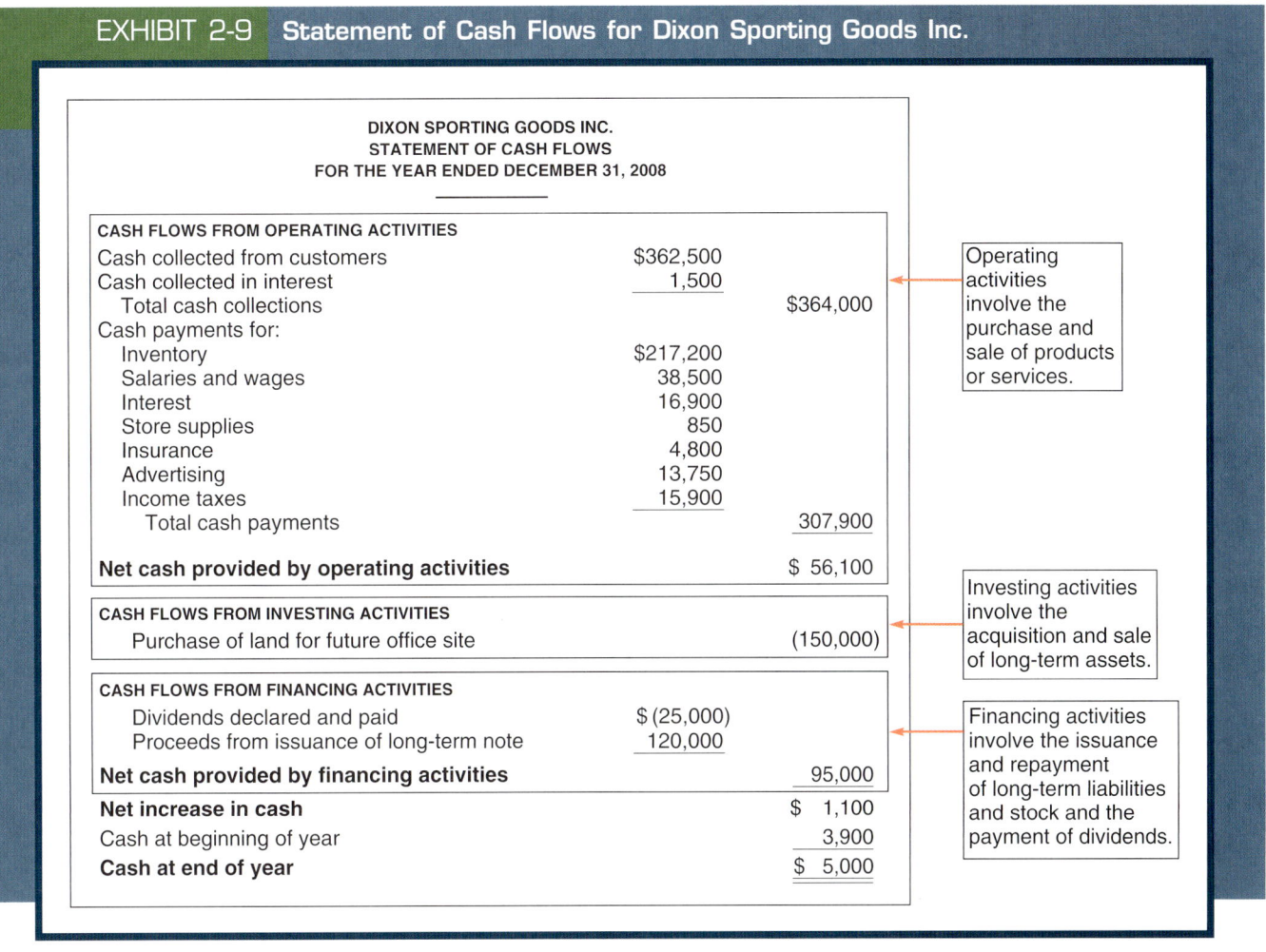

EXHIBIT 2-9   Statement of Cash Flows for Dixon Sporting Goods Inc.

DIXON SPORTING GOODS INC.
STATEMENT OF CASH FLOWS
FOR THE YEAR ENDED DECEMBER 31, 2008

CASH FLOWS FROM OPERATING ACTIVITIES

Cash collected from customers	$362,500	
Cash collected in interest	1,500	
Total cash collections		$364,000
Cash payments for:		
Inventory	$217,200	
Salaries and wages	38,500	
Interest	16,900	
Store supplies	850	
Insurance	4,800	
Advertising	13,750	
Income taxes	15,900	
Total cash payments		307,900
Net cash provided by operating activities		**$ 56,100**

Operating activities involve the purchase and sale of products or services.

CASH FLOWS FROM INVESTING ACTIVITIES

Purchase of land for future office site	(150,000)

Investing activities involve the acquisition and sale of long-term assets.

CASH FLOWS FROM FINANCING ACTIVITIES

Dividends declared and paid	$ (25,000)	
Proceeds from issuance of long-term note	120,000	
Net cash provided by financing activities		95,000
Net increase in cash		$ 1,100
Cash at beginning of year		3,900
Cash at end of year		$ 5,000

Financing activities involve the issuance and repayment of long-term liabilities and stock and the payment of dividends.

In 2006, the Company purchased approximately 80% of its merchandise from its five largest suppliers. The largest supplier, Nike, accounted for approximately 59%, 58% and 56% of merchandise purchases in 2006, 2005 and 2004, respectively.[7]

FINISH LINE'S CONDENSED BALANCE SHEET

Condensed balance sheets for Finish Line at the end of each of two years are shown in Exhibit 2-10. Finish Line releases what are called *consolidated financial statements*, which reflect the position and results of all operations that are controlled by a single entity. Like most other large corporations, Finish Line owns other companies. Often these companies are legally separate and are called *subsidiaries*. For example, one of Finish Line's subsidaries operates the Man Alive stores. How a company accounts for its investment in a subsidiary is covered in advanced accounting courses.

Finish Line presents comparative balance sheets to indicate its financial position at the end of each of the last two years. As a minimum standard, the Securities and Exchange Commission requires that the annual report include balance sheets as of the two most recent years and income statements for each of the three most recent years. Note that all amounts on the balance sheet are stated in thousands of dollars. This type of rounding is a common practice in the financial statements of large corporations and is justified under the materiality concept. Knowing the exact dollar amount of each asset would not change a decision made by an investor.

The current ratio was introduced earlier in the chapter. We will now use the information on Finish Line's balance sheet to analyze its current ratio.

2-1   Real World Practice

Reading Finish Line's Balance Sheet

What was the amount of working capital at February 25, 2006? at February 26, 2005? Did the company's total assets increase or decrease during the year?

---

7 *The Finish Line, Inc. 2006 Annual Report*, p. 32.

EXHIBIT 2-10 Condensed Comparative Balance Sheets for The Finish Line, Inc.

> Always look at the headings on comparative balance sheets to see whether the most recent year-end is placed before or after the prior year's year-end. Finish Line places the latest year on the left, which is the most common technique.

The Finish Line, Inc.
Consolidated Balance Sheets
(In thousands)

	February 25, 2006	February 26, 2005
Total current assets	$ 381,527	$ 371,800
Total noncurrent assets	246,289	203,219
Total assets	$ 627,816	$ 575,019
Total current liabilities	$ 142,415	$ 137,016
Total noncurrent liabilities	56,859	52,032
Total liabilities	$ 199,274	$ 189,048
Total shareholders' equity	$ 428,542	$ 385,971
Total liabilities and shareholders' equity	$ 627,816	$ 575,019

USING THE RATIO DECISION MODEL: ANALYZING THE CURRENT RATIO

Use the following Ratio Decision Process to evaluate the current ratio for Finish Line or any other public company.

1. Formulate the Question

Managers, investors, and creditors are all interested in a company's liquidity. They must be able to answer the following question:

Is the company liquid enough to pay its obligations as they come due?

2. Gather the Information from the Financial Statements

The current ratio measures liquidity. To calculate the ratio it is essential to know a company's current assets and liabilities. Current assets are the most liquid of all assets. Current liabilities are the debts that will be paid the soonest.

- Current assets: From the balance sheet
- Current liabilities: From the balance sheet

3. Calculate the Ratio

$$\text{Current Ratio} = \frac{\text{Current Assets}}{\text{Current Liabilities}}$$

Finish Line
Partial Balance Sheet
(In Thousands)

	February 25, 2006
Assets	
Total current assets	$381,527
Liabilities and Shareholders' Equity	
Total current liabilities	$142,415

$$\text{Current Ratio} = \frac{\$381,527}{\$142,415} = 2.68 \text{ to } 1$$

(continued)

4. Compare the Ratio with Others

Ratios can never be of any use in a vacuum. It is always necessary to compare them with both prior years and with competitors.

	Finish Line		Foot Locker	
	February 25, 2006	**February 26, 2005**	**January 28, 2006**	**January 29, 2005**
	2.68 to 1	2.71 to 1	2.81 to 1	2.68 to 1

5. Interpret the Results

In general, the higher the current ratio is, the more liquid the company is. However, earlier in the chapter we learned that rules of thumb do not always apply. It is necessary to take into account the nature of a company's business when evaluating ratios and other measures of performance. Also, ratios should be compared with prior years and with the same ratios for competitors. Both companies' current ratios indicate a relatively high degree of liquidity.

FINISH LINE'S INCOME STATEMENT

We have examined two basic formats for the income statement: the single-step format and the multiple-step format. In practice, numerous variations on these two basic formats exist, depending to a large extent on the nature of a company's business.

Multiple-step income statements for Finish Line for a three-year period are presented in Exhibit 2-11. The inclusion of three years allows the reader to note certain general trends during this period. For example, note the steady increase in net sales during this period. In fact, the increase in net sales from the first year, 2004, to the third year, 2006, can be calculated as:

$$\frac{\text{Increase in net sales from 2004 to 2006:}}{\text{Net sales in 2004}} = \frac{\$1,306,045 - \$985,891}{\$985,891} = \frac{\$320,154}{\$985,891} = \underline{\underline{32.5\%}}$$

We now turn our attention to the calculation of Finish Line's profit margin and what it can tell us about the company's profitability.

2-2 **Real World Practice**

Reading Finish Line's Income Statements

Compute the percentage increase in Finish Line's net income over the three years, i.e., by what percent did it increase from 2004 to 2006? Compare the percentage increase in net income to the percentage increase in net sales. What does a comparison of the two tell you?

EXHIBIT 2-11 **Comparative Income Statements for The Finish Line, Inc.**

The Finish Line, Inc.
Consolidated Statements of Income
(in thousands)

	Year Ended		
	February 25, 2006	**February 26, 2005**	**February 28, 2004**
Net sales	$1,306,045	$1,166,767	$ 985,891
Cost of sales (including occupancy costs)	894,724	798,033	681,561
Gross profit	411,321	368,734	304,330
Selling, general and administrative expenses	313,893	271,901	229,842
Insurance settlement	—	(114)	(1,228)
Asset impairment charge	2,523	—	—
Operating income	94,905	96,947	75,716
Interest income, net	2,008	1,076	651
Income before income taxes	96,913	98,023	76,367
Income taxes	36,380	36,760	29,020
Net income	$ 60,533	$ 61,263	$ 47,347

USING THE RATIO DECISION MODEL: ANALYZING THE PROFIT MARGIN

Use the following Ratio Decision Process to evaluate the profit margin for Finish Line or any other public company.

1. Formulate the Question

Managers, investors, and creditors are all interested in a company's profitability. They must be able to answer the following question:

How profitable has the company been in recent years?

2. Gather the Information from the Financial Statements

The profit margin is a measure of a company's profitability. To calculate the ratio it is essential to know a company's sales and expenses and the difference between the two, net income.

- Net income—from the income statement
- Net sales—from the income statement

3. Calculate the Ratio

$$\text{Profit Margin} = \frac{\text{Net Income}}{\text{Net Sales}}$$

**Finish Line
Partial Income Statement**

For the year ending February 25, 2006

| Net sales | $1,306,045 |
| Net income | 60,533 |

$$\text{Profit Margin} = \frac{\$60,533}{\$1,306,045} = 4.6\%$$

4. Compare the Ratio with Others

A comparison with prior performance helps determine whether profitability is increasing or decreasing.

	Finish Line		Foot Locker	
	Year Ended February 25, 2006	Year Ended February 26, 2005	Year Ended January 28, 2006	Year Ended January 29, 2005
	4.6%	5.3%	4.7%*	4.8%*

*Based on income from continuing operations.

5. Interpret the Results

A high profit margin indicates that the company is controlling its expenses. This is because sales minus expenses equals net income; if the ratio of net income to sales is high, the company is not only generating revenue but also minimizing its expenses. Also, ratios should be compared with prior years and with the same ratios for competitors. Both companies' profit margins indicate that the companies are able to control their expenses while increasing their sales.

OTHER ELEMENTS OF AN ANNUAL REPORT

No two annual reports look the same. The appearance of an annual report depends not only on the size of a company but also on the budget devoted to the preparation of the report. Some companies publish "bare-bones" annual reports, whereas others issue a glossy report complete with pictures of company products and employees. In recent years, many companies, as a cost-cutting measure, have scaled back the amount spent on the annual report.

Privately held companies tend to distribute only financial statements, without the additional information normally included in the annual reports of public companies. For the annual reports of public companies, however, certain basic elements are considered standard.

- A letter to the stockholders from either the president or the chairman of the board of directors appears in the first few pages of most annual reports.
- A section describing the company's products and markets is usually included.
- At the heart of any annual report is the financial report or review, which consists of the financial statements accompanied by notes to explain various items on the statements. We will now consider these other elements as presented in the 2006 annual report of The Finish Line, Inc.

Report of Independent Accountants As you see in Exhibit 2-12, Finish Line is audited by **Ernst & Young LLP,** one of the largest international accounting firms. Two key phrases should be noted in the first sentence of the third paragraph of the independent accountants' report: *in our opinion* and *present fairly*. The report indicates that responsibility for the statements rests with Finish Line and that the auditors' job is to *express an opinion* on the statements, based on certain tests. It

---

EXHIBIT 2-12 | **Report of Independent Accountants for The Finish Line, Inc.**

REPORT OF INDEPENDENT REGISTERED PUBLIC ACCOUNTING FIRM

The Board of Directors and Shareholders of The Finish Line, Inc.

We have audited the accompanying consolidated balance sheets of The Finish Line, Inc. as of February 25, 2006 and February 26, 2005, and the related consolidated statements of income, changes in shareholders' equity and cash flows for each of the three years in the period ended February 25, 2006. These financial statements are the responsibility of the Company's management. Our responsibility is to express an opinion on these financial statements based on our audits.

We conducted our audits in accordance with the standards of the Public Company Accounting Oversight Board (United States). Those standards require that we plan and perform the audit to obtain reasonable assurance about whether the financial statements are free of material misstatement. An audit includes examining, on a test basis, evidence supporting the amounts and disclosures in the financial statements. An audit also includes assessing the accounting principles used and significant estimates made by management, as well as evaluating the overall financial statement presentation. We believe that our audits provide a reasonable basis for our opinion.

In our opinion, the consolidated financial statements referred to above present fairly, in all material respects, the consolidated financial position of The Finish Line, Inc. at February 25, 2006 and February 26, 2005, and the consolidated results of its operations and its cash flows for each of the three years in the period ended February 25, 2006, in conformity with U.S. generally accepted accounting principles.

We also have audited, in accordance with the standards of the Public Company Accounting Oversight Board (United States), the effectiveness of The Finish Line, Inc.'s internal control over financial reporting as of February 25, 2006, based on criteria established in Internal Control—Integrated Framework issued by the Committee of Sponsoring Organizations of the Treadway Commission and our report dated May 4, 2006, expressed an unqualified opinion thereon.

Ernst & Young LLP

Indianapolis, Indiana
May 4, 2006

would be impossible for an auditing firm to spend the time or money to retrace and verify every single transaction entered into during the year by Finish Line. Instead, the auditing firm performs various tests of the accounting records to be able to assure itself that the statements are free of *material misstatement.* Auditors do not "certify" the total accuracy of a set of financial statements but render an opinion as to the reasonableness of those statements.

The Ethical Responsibility of Management and the Auditors The management of a company and its auditors share a common purpose: to protect the interests of stockholders. In large corporations, the stockholders are normally removed from the daily affairs of the business. The need for a professional management team to run the business is a practical necessity, as is the need for a periodic audit of the company's records. Because stockholders cannot run the business themselves, they need assurances that the business is being operated effectively and efficiently and that the financial statements presented by management are a fair representation of the company's operations and financial position. The management and the auditors have a very important ethical responsibility to their constituents, the stockholders of the company.

Management Discussion and Analysis Preceding the financial statements is a section of Finish Line's annual report titled "Management's Discussion and Analysis of Financial Condition and Results of Operations." This report gives management the opportunity to discuss the financial statements and provide the stockholders with explanations for certain amounts reported in the statements. For example, management explains the change in its net sales as follows:

Fiscal 2006 Compared to Fiscal 2005 *Net sales for fiscal 2006 were $1.3 billion, an increase of $139.3 million or 11.9% over fiscal 2005. Of this increase, $68.9 million was attributable to an increase from the 71 existing stores open only part of fiscal 2005 and the 37 Man Alive stores acquired in fiscal 2005, and $65.0 million was attributable to an 11.5% increase in the total number of stores (66 Finish Line stores opened less 7 Finish Line stores closed plus 14 Man Alive stores opened) during the period from 635 stores at the end of fiscal 2005 to 708 stores at the end of fiscal 2006. The balance of the increase in net sales was attributable to a comparable store net sales increase of 0.7% in fiscal 2006. Comparable net footwear sales increased 1.5% for fiscal 2006 while comparable net softgoods sales decreased by 2.2%. The 2.2% decrease in comparable net softgood sales was primarily due to a decline in the average retail selling price of softgoods. This is primarily related to the shift in fashion from licensed jerseys to more branded and private label sold during fiscal 2006 vs. fiscal 2005.*[8]

Notes to Consolidated Financial Statements The sentence "See accompanying notes" appears at the bottom of each of Finish Line's four financial statements. These comments, or *notes,* as they are commonly called, are necessary to satisfy the need for *full disclosure* of all the facts relevant to a company's results and financial position. Note 1 is a summary of *significant accounting policies.* The company's policies for depreciating assets and recognizing revenue are among the important items contained in this note. For example, Finish Line describes its policy for depreciating its property and equipment as follows:

> *Property and equipment are stated at cost and depreciated on a straight-line basis over the estimated useful lives of the assets: 30 years for buildings and 3 to 10 years for furniture, fixtures and equipment.*[9]

In addition to the summary of significant accounting policies, other notes discuss such topics as income taxes and stock option plans.

This completes our discussion of the makeup of the annual report. By now you should appreciate the flexibility that companies have in assembling the report, aside

---

8 *The Finish Line, Inc. 2006 Annual Report, p. 20.*
9 *The Finish Line, Inc. 2006 Annual Report, p. 33.*

from the need to follow generally accepted accounting principles in preparing the statements. The accounting standards followed in preparing the statements, as well as the appearance of the annual report itself, differ in other countries. As has been noted elsewhere, although many corporations operate internationally, accounting principles are far from being standardized.

STUDY HIGHLIGHTS

Describe the objectives of financial reporting (p. 61).   **LO1**

- The main objective of financial statements is to convey useful and timely information to parties for making economic decisions.
  - Decision makers include investors, creditors, and other individuals or groups inside and outside the firm.
- Secondary objectives include providing information to evaluate cash flows, resources of the company, and claims to those resources.

Describe the qualitative characteristics of accounting information (p. 62).   **LO2**

- Qualitative characteristics of accounting information are those attributes which make the information useful to users of the financial statements and include:
  - Understandability—that is to those who are willing to spend the time to understand the information.
  - Relevance—the capacity of information to make a difference in a decision.
  - Reliability—information that investors can depend on must be verifiable, neutral (not biased), and faithful in what it represents.
  - Comparable and consistent—GAAP provides guidelines that help to standardize accounting practices and make information from one company to another or from one period to the next period for the same company comparable.
  - Conservatism—where uncertainty about how to account for economic activity exists, accounting choices that result in the least optimistic amount should be employed.

Explain the concept and purpose of a classified balance sheet and prepare the statement (p. 66).   **LO3**

- The classified balance sheet classifies items of assets, liabilities, and stockholders' equity in a way that makes them useful to users of this financial statement.
  - Assets and liabilities are classified according to the length of time that they will serve the company or require its resources.
    - Current assets or liabilities are those whose expected lives are one year or one operating cycle, whichever is longer. Noncurrent assets or liabilities are expected to last beyond this period of time.
    - Within current or noncurrent classifications, assets and liabilities are further subclassified into categories that describe the nature of these assets and liabilities; for example, "Property, Plant, and Equipment."

Use a classified balance sheet to analyze a company's financial position (p. 71).   **LO4**

- Classifications within the balance sheet allow users to analyze various aspects of a company's financial position; for example, its liquidity.
  - Liquidity relates to the ability of a company to pay its obligations as they come due.
  - Working capital and the current ratio are two measures of liquidity.

Explain the difference between a single-step and a multiple-step income statement and prepare each type of income statement (p. 73).   **LO5**

- The multiple-step income statement classifies revenues and expenses in a manner that makes the statement more useful than the simple single-step income

(continued)

statement. Important subtotals are presented in the multiple-step income statement, including:

- Gross profit
- Income from operations
- Income before income taxes

LO6   **Use a multiple-step income statement to analyze a company's operations (p. 76).**

- The multiple-step income statement can be used to evaluate different aspects of a company's profitability.
  - Profit margin is one useful ratio to evaluate the relative profitability.

LO7   **Identify the components of the statement of retained earnings and prepare the statement (p. 76).**

- The statement of retained earnings provides a link between the income statement and balance sheet.
  - It explains the changes in retained earnings during the period, of which net income (loss) is an important component.

LO8   **Identify the components of the statement of cash flows and prepare the statement (p. 77).**

- The statement of cash flows classifies cash inflows and outflows as originating from three activities: operating, investing, and financing.
  - Operating activities are related to the primary purpose of a business.
  - Investing activities are those generally involved with the acquisition and sale of noncurrent assets.
  - Financing activities are related to the acquisition and repayment of capital that ultimately funds the operations of a business; for example, borrowing or the issuance of stock.

LO9   **Read and use the financial statements and other elements in the annual report of a publicly held company (p. 78).**

- The classified balance sheet and multiple-step income statement are more complex than simpler versions of these financial statements and yield more useful information to decision makers.
- Annual reports contain more information than just the financial statements. This information can be used alone or in conjunction with the financial statements to gain a more complete financial picture of a company.
  - Management's Discussion and Analysis provides explanatory comments about certain results reflected in the financial statements and sometimes forward-looking commentary.
  - The Report of Independent Accountants is provided by the company's auditor, whose job it is to express an opinion on whether the financial statements fairly represent the accounting treatment of a company's economic activity for the year.
  - Notes to the Consolidated Financial Statements are generally supplementary disclosures required by GAAP that help to explain detail behind the accounting treatment of certain items in the financial statements.

REVIEW

RATIO REVIEW

Working Capital = Current Assets (balance sheet) − Current Liabilities (balance sheet)

$$\text{Current Ratio} = \frac{\text{Current Assets (balance sheet)}}{\text{Current Liabilities (balance sheet)}}$$

$$\text{Profit Margin} = \frac{\text{Net Income (income statement)}}{\text{Sales or Revenues (income statement)}}$$

KEY TERMS QUIZ

Read each definition below and then write the number of that definition in the blank beside the appropriate term it defines. The quiz solutions appear at the end of the chapter.

_____ **Understandability**	_____ **Current asset**
_____ **Relevance**	_____ **Current liability**
_____ **Reliability**	_____ **Liquidity**
_____ **Comparability**	_____ **Working capital**
_____ **Depreciation**	_____ **Current ratio**
_____ **Consistency**	_____ **Single-step income statement**
_____ **Materiality**	_____ **Multiple-step income statement**
_____ **Conservatism**	_____ **Gross profit**
_____ **Operating cycle**	_____ **Profit margin**

1. An income statement in which all expenses are added together and subtracted from all revenues.

2. The magnitude of an omission or misstatement in accounting information that will affect the judgment of someone relying on the information.

3. The capacity of information to make a difference in a decision.

4. An income statement that provides the reader with classifications of revenues and expenses as well as with important subtotals.

5. The practice of using the least optimistic estimate when two estimates of amounts are about equally likely.

6. The quality of accounting information that makes it comprehensible to those willing to spend the necessary time.

7. Current assets divided by current liabilities.

8. The quality of accounting information that makes it dependable in representing the events that it purports to represent.

9. An obligation that will be satisfied within the next operating cycle or within one year if the cycle is shorter than one year.

10. Current assets minus current liabilities.

11. Net income divided by sales.

12. The quality of accounting information that allows a user to analyze two or more companies and look for similarities and differences.

13. An asset that is expected to be realized in cash or sold or consumed during the operating cycle or within one year if the cycle is shorter than one year.

14. The ability of a company to pay its debts as they come due.

15. The quality of accounting information that allows a user to compare two or more accounting periods for a single company.

16. The allocation of the cost of a tangible, long-term asset over its useful life.

17. The period of time between the purchase of inventory and the collection of any receivable from the sale of the inventory.

18. Sales less cost of goods sold.

ALTERNATE TERMS

Balance sheet Statement of financial position or condition	**Net income** Profits or earnings
Capital stock Contributed capital	**Profit margin** Return on sales
Income statement Statement of income	**Report of independent accountants** Auditors' report
Income tax expense Provision for income taxes	**Retained earnings** Earned capital
Long-term assets Noncurrent assets	**Stockholders' equity** Shareholders' equity
Long-term liability Long-term debt	

R E V I E W

WARMUP EXERCISES & SOLUTIONS

Warmup Exercise 2-1 Identifying Ratios

State the equation for each of the following:

1. Working capital
2. Current ratio
3. Profit margin

Key to the Solution Review the various ratios as discussed in the chapter.

Warmup Exercise 2-2 Calculating Ratios

Bridger reported net income of $150,000 and sales of $1,000,000 for the year. Its current assets were $300,000 and its current liabilities were $200,000 at year-end.

Required

Compute each of the following ratios for Bridger:

1. Current ratio
2. Profit margin

Key to the Solution Recall the equation for each of these ratios as presented in the chapter.

Warmup Exercise 2-3 Determining Liquidity

Big has current assets of $500,000 and current liabilities of $400,000. Small reports current assets of $80,000 and current liabilities of $20,000.

Required

Which company is more liquid? Why?

Key to the Solution Calculate the current ratio for each company and compare them.

SOLUTIONS TO WARMUP EXERCISES

Warmup Exercise 2-1
1. Working Capital = Current Assets − Current Liabilities
2. $\text{Current Ratio} = \dfrac{\text{Current Assets}}{\text{Current Liabilities}}$
3. $\text{Profit Margin} = \dfrac{\text{Net Income}}{\text{Sales or Revenues}}$

Warmup Exercise 2-2

1. $\dfrac{\$300,000}{\$200,000} = \underline{\underline{1.5 \text{ to } 1}}$

2. $\dfrac{\$150,000}{\$1,000,000} = \underline{\underline{15\%}}$

Warmup Exercise 2-3
Small Company appears on the surface to be more liquid. Its current ratio of $80,000/$20,000, or 4 to 1, is significantly higher than Big's current ratio of $500,000/$400,000, or 1.25 to 1.

REVIEW PROBLEM & SOLUTION

The following review problem will give you the opportunity to apply what you have learned by preparing both an income statement and a balance sheet.

Shown on the following page, in alphabetical order, are items taken from the records of Grizzly Inc., a chain of outdoor recreational stores in the Northwest. Use the items to prepare two statements. First, prepare an income statement for the year ended December 31, 2008.

The income statement should be in multiple-step form. Second, prepare a classified balance sheet at December 31, 2008. All amounts are in thousands of dollars.

Accounts payable	$ 6,500
Accounts receivable	8,200
Accumulated depreciation—buildings	25,000
Accumulated depreciation—furniture and fixtures	15,000
Advertising expense	3,100
Buildings	80,000
Capital stock, $1 par, 10,000 shares issued and outstanding	10,000
Cash	2,400
Commissions expense	8,600
Cost of goods sold	110,000
Depreciation on buildings	2,500
Depreciation on furniture and fixtures	1,200
Furniture and fixtures	68,000
Income taxes payable	2,200
Income tax expense	13,000
Insurance expense	2,000
Interest expense	12,000
Interest payable	1,000
Interest revenue	2,000
Land	100,000
Long-term notes payable, due December 31, 2016	120,000
Merchandise inventories	6,000
Office supplies	900
Paid-in capital in excess of par value	40,000
Prepaid rent	3,000
Rent expense for salespersons' autos	9,000
Retained earnings	48,800
Salaries and wages for office staff	11,000
Sales revenue	190,000

SOLUTION TO REVIEW PROBLEM

1. Multiple-step income statement:

Grizzly Inc.
Income Statement
For the Year Ended December 31, 2008
(In thousands of dollars)

Sales revenue		$190,000	
Cost of goods sold		110,000	
Gross profit			$ 80,000
Operating expenses:			
Selling expenses:			
Advertising expense	$ 3,100		
Depreciation on furniture and fixtures	1,200		
Rent expense for salespersons' autos	9,000		
Commissions expense	8,600		
Total selling expenses		$ 21,900	
General and administrative expenses:			
Depreciation on buildings	$ 2,500		
Insurance expense	2,000		
Salaries and wages for office staff	11,000		
Total general and administrative expenses		15,500	
Total operating expenses			37,400
Income from operations			$ 42,600
Other revenues and expenses:			
Interest revenue		$ 2,000	
Interest expense		12,000	
Excess of other expenses over other revenue			10,000
Income before income taxes			$ 32,600
Income tax expense			13,000
Net income			$ 19,600

(continued)

2. Classified balance sheet:

Grizzly Inc.
Balance Sheet
At December 31, 2008
(In thousands of dollars)

Assets

Current assets:			
Cash		$ 2,400	
Accounts receivable		8,200	
Merchandise inventories		6,000	
Office supplies		900	
Prepaid rent		3,000	
Total current assets			$ 20,500
Property, plant, and equipment:			
Land		$100,000	
Buildings	$ 80,000		
Less: Accumulated depreciation	25,000	55,000	
Furniture and fixtures	$ 68,000		
Less: Accumulated depreciation	15,000	53,000	
Total property, plant, and equipment			208,000
Total assets			$228,500

Liabilities

Current liabilities:			
Accounts payable		$ 6,500	
Income taxes payable		2,200	
Interest payable		1,000	
Total current liabilities			$ 9,700
Long-term notes payable, due December 31, 2016			120,000
Total liabilities			$129,700

Stockholders' Equity

Contributed capital:			
Capital stock, $1 par, 10,000 shares issued and outstanding		$ 10,000	
Paid-in capital in excess of par value		40,000	
Total contributed capital		$ 50,000	
Retained earnings		48,800	
Total stockholders' equity			98,800
Total liabilities and stockholders' equity			$228,500

QUESTIONS

1. How would you evaluate the following statement: "The cash flows to a company are irrelevant to an investor; all the investor cares about is the potential for receiving dividends on the investment"?

2. A key characteristic of useful financial information is understandability. How does this qualitative characteristic relate to the background of the user of the information?

3. What does *relevance* mean with regard to the use of accounting information?

4. What is the qualitative characteristic of comparability, and why is it important in preparing financial statements?

5. What is the difference between comparability and consistency as they relate to the use of accounting information?

6. How does the concept of materiality relate to the size of a company?

7. How does the concept of the operating cycle relate to the definition of a current asset?

8. How would you evaluate the following statement: "A note payable with an original maturity of five years will be classified on the balance sheet as a long-term liability until it matures"?

9. How do the two basic forms of owners' equity items for a corporation—capital stock and retained earnings—differ?

10. What are the limitations of working capital as a measure of the liquidity of a business as opposed to the current ratio?

HOMEWORK

11. What is meant by a company's capital structure?

12. What is the major weakness of the single-step form for the income statement?

13. How does a statement of retained earnings act as a link between an income statement and a balance sheet?

14. In auditing the financial statements of a company, does the auditor *certify* that the statements are totally accurate and without errors of any size or variety?

15. What is the first note in the annual report of all publicly held companies, and what is its purpose?

EXERCISES

LO2   **Exercise 2-1** Characteristics of Useful Accounting Information

Fill in the blank with the qualitative characteristic for each of the following descriptions:

_____ 1. Information that users can depend on to represent the events that it purports to represent

_____ 2. Information that has the capacity to make a difference in a decision

_____ 3. Information that is valid, that indicates an agreement between the underlying data and the events represented

_____ 4. Information that allows for comparisons to be made from one accounting period to the next

_____ 5. Information that is free from error

_____ 6. Information that is meaningful to those who are willing to learn to use it properly

_____ 7. Information that is not slanted to portray a company's position any better or worse than the circumstances warrant

_____ 8. Information that allows for comparisons to be made between or among companies

LO3   **Exercise 2-2** Classification of Assets and Liabilities

Indicate the appropriate classification of each of the following as a current asset (CA), noncurrent asset (NCA), current liability (CL), or long-term liability (LTL):

_____ 1. Inventory
_____ 2. Accounts payable
_____ 3. Cash
_____ 4. Patents
_____ 5. Notes payable, due in six months
_____ 6. Taxes payable
_____ 7. Prepaid rent (for the next nine months)
_____ 8. Bonds payable, due in 10 years
_____ 9. Machinery

LO5   **Exercise 2-3** Selling Expenses and General and Administrative Expenses

Operating expenses are subdivided between selling expenses and general and administrative expenses when a multiple-step income statement is prepared. From the following list, identify each item as a selling expense (S) or general and administrative expense (G&A):

_____ 1. Advertising expense
_____ 2. Depreciation expense—store furniture and fixtures
_____ 3. Office rent expense
_____ 4. Office salaries expense
_____ 5. Store rent expense
_____ 6. Store salaries expense
_____ 7. Insurance expense
_____ 8. Supplies expense
_____ 9. Utilities expense

HOMEWORK

LO5

Exercise 2-4 Missing Income Statement Amounts

For each of the following independent cases, fill in the blank with the appropriate dollar amount:

	Sara's Coffee Shop	Amy's Deli	Jane's Bagels
Net sales	$35,000	$_____	$78,000
Cost of goods sold	_____	45,000	_____
Gross profit	7,000	18,000	_____
Selling expenses	3,000	_____	9,000
General and administrative expenses	1,500	2,800	_____
Total operating expenses	_____	8,800	13,600
Net income	$ 2,500	$ 9,200	$25,400

LO6

Exercise 2-5 Income Statement Ratio

The 2007 income statement of Holly Enterprises shows operating revenues of $134,800, selling expenses of $38,310, general and administrative expenses of $36,990, interest expense of $580, and income tax expense of $13,920. Holly's stockholders' equity was $280,000 at the beginning of the year and $320,000 at the end of the year. The company has 20,000 shares of stock outstanding at December 31, 2007.

Required

Compute Holly's profit margin. What other information would you need to be able to comment on whether this ratio is favorable?

LO7

Exercise 2-6 Statement of Retained Earnings

Landon Corporation was organized on January 2, 2005, with the investment of $100,000 by each of its two stockholders. Net income for its first year of business was $85,200. Net income increased during 2006 to $125,320 and to $145,480 during 2007. Landon paid $20,000 in dividends to each of the two stockholders in each of the three years.

Required

Prepare a statement of retained earnings for the year ended December 31, 2007.

LO8

Exercise 2-7 Components of the Statement of Cash Flows

From the following list, identify each item as operating (O), investing (I), financing (F), or not on the statement of cash flows (N):

_____ 1. Paid for supplies

_____ 2. Collected cash from customers

_____ 3. Purchased land (held for resale)

_____ 4. Purchased land (for construction of new building)

_____ 5. Paid dividend

_____ 6. Issued stock

_____ 7. Purchased computers (for use in the business)

_____ 8. Sold old equipment

LO9

Exercise 2-8 Basic Elements of Financial Statements

Most financial reports contain the list of basic elements shown below. For each element, identify the person(s) who prepared the element and describe the information a user would expect to find in each element. Some information is verifiable; other information is subjectively chosen by management. Comment on the verifiability of information in each element.

1. Management discussion and analysis
2. Product/markets of company
3. Financial statements
4. Notes to financial statements
5. Independent accountants' report

HOMEWORK

MULTI-CONCEPT EXERCISES

LO3,5,7 **Exercise 2-9** Financial Statement Classification

Potential stockholders and lenders are interested in a company's financial statements. For the following list, identify the statement—balance sheet (BS), income statement (IS), retained earnings statement (RE)—on which each item would appear.

_____ 1. Accounts payable	_____ 11. Land held for future expansion
_____ 2. Accounts receivable	_____ 12. Loan payable
_____ 3. Advertising expense	_____ 13. Office supplies
_____ 4. Bad debt expense	_____ 14. Patent
_____ 5. Bonds payable	_____ 15. Patent amortization expense
_____ 6. Buildings	_____ 16. Prepaid insurance
_____ 7. Cash	_____ 17. Retained earnings
_____ 8. Common stock	_____ 18. Sales
_____ 9. Depreciation expense	_____ 19. Utilities expense
_____ 10. Dividends	_____ 20. Wages payable

LO5,6 **Exercise 2-10** Single- and Multiple-Step Income Statement

Some headings and/or items are used on either the single-step or the multiple-step income statement. Some are used on both. For the list below, indicate the following: single-step (S), multiple-step (M), both formats (B), or not used on either income statement (N).

_____ 1. Sales	_____ 7. Net income
_____ 2. Cost of goods sold	_____ 8. Supplies on hand
_____ 3. Selling expenses	_____ 9. Accumulated depreciation
_____ 4. Total revenues	_____ 10. Income before income taxes
_____ 5. Utilities expense	_____ 11. Gross profit
_____ 6. Administrative expense	

LO5,6 **Exercise 2-11** Multiple-Step Income Statement

Gaynor Corporation's partial income statement follows:

Sales	$1,200,000
Cost of sales	450,000
Selling expenses	60,800
General and administrative expenses	75,000

Required
Determine the profit margin. Would you consider investing in Gaynor Corporation? Explain your answer.

PROBLEMS

LO2 **Problem 2-1** Materiality

Joseph Knapp, a newly hired accountant, wanting to impress his boss, stayed late one night to analyze the office supplies expense. He determined the cost by month, for the previous 12 months, of each of the following: computer paper, copy paper, fax paper, pencils and pens, note pads, postage, stationery, and miscellaneous items.

Required
1. What did Joseph think his boss would learn from this information? What action might be taken as a result of knowing it?
2. Would this information be more relevant if Joseph worked for a hardware store or for a real estate company? Discuss.

HOMEWORK

LO2

Problem 2-2 Costs and Expenses

The following costs are incurred by a retailer:

1. Display fixtures in a retail store
2. Advertising
3. Merchandise for sale
4. Incorporation (i.e., legal costs, stock issue costs)
5. Cost of a franchise
6. Office supplies
7. Wages and salaries
8. Computer software
9. Computer hardware

Required

For each of these costs, explain whether all of the cost or only a portion of the cost would appear as an expense on the income statement for the period in which the cost was incurred. If not all of the cost would appear on the income statement for that period, explain why not.

LO3

Problem 2-3 Classified Balance Sheet

The following balance sheet items, listed in alphabetical order, are available from the records of Ruth Corporation at December 31, 2007:

Accounts payable	$ 18,255
Accounts receivable	23,450
Accumulated depreciation—automobiles	22,500
Accumulated depreciation—buildings	40,000
Automobiles	112,500
Bonds payable, due December 31, 2011	160,000
Buildings	200,000
Capital stock, $10 par value	150,000
Cash	13,230
Income taxes payable	6,200
Interest payable	1,500
Inventory	45,730
Land	250,000
Long-term investments	85,000
Notes payable, due June 30, 2008	10,000
Office supplies	2,340
Paid-in capital in excess of par value	50,000
Patents	40,000
Prepaid rent	1,500
Retained earnings	311,095
Salaries and wages payable	4,200

Required

1. Prepare in good form a classified balance sheet as of December 31, 2007.
2. Compute Ruth's current ratio.
3. On the basis of your answer to requirement 2, does Ruth appear to be liquid? What other information do you need to fully answer this question?

LO4

Problem 2-4 Financial Statement Ratios

The items below, in alphabetical order, are available from the records of Walker Corporation as of December 31, 2007 and 2006:

	December 31, 2007	December 31, 2006
Accounts payable	$ 8,400	$ 5,200
Accounts receivable	27,830	35,770
Cash	20,200	19,450
Cleaning supplies	450	700
Interest payable	–0–	1,200
Inventory	24,600	26,200
Marketable securities	6,250	5,020
Note payable, due in six months	–0–	12,000
Prepaid rent	3,600	4,800
Taxes payable	1,450	1,230
Wages payable	1,200	1,600

Required

1. Calculate the following, as of December 31, 2007, and December 31, 2006:
   a. Working capital
   b. Current ratio
2. On the basis of your answers to 1, comment on the relative liquidity of the company at the beginning and the end of the year. As part of your answer, explain the change in the company's liquidity from the beginning to the end of 2007.

LO4   **Problem 2-5** Working Capital and Current Ratio

The balance sheet of Stevenson Inc. includes the following items:

Cash	$23,000	Accounts payable	$ 54,900
Accounts receivable	13,000	Salaries payable	1,200
Inventory	45,000	Capital stock	100,000
Prepaid insurance	800	Retained earnings	5,700
Land	80,000		

Required

1. Determine the current ratio and working capital.
2. Beyond the information provided in your answers to 1, what does the composition of the current assets tell you about Stevenson's liquidity?
3. What other information do you need to fully assess Stevenson's liquidity?

LO5   **Problem 2-6** Single-Step Income Statement

The following income statement items, arranged in alphabetical order, are taken from the records of Shaw Corporation for the year ended December 31, 2007:

Advertising expense	$ 1,500
Commissions expense	2,415
Cost of goods sold	29,200
Depreciation expense—office building	2,900
Income tax expense	1,540
Insurance expense—salesperson's auto	2,250
Interest expense	1,400
Interest revenue	1,340
Rent revenue	6,700
Salaries and wages expense—office	12,560
Sales revenue	48,300
Supplies expense—office	890

Required

1. Prepare a single-step income statement for the year ended December 31, 2007.
2. What weaknesses do you see in this form for the income statement?

LO5   **Problem 2-7** Multiple-Step Income Statement and Profit Margin

Refer to the list of income statement items in Problem 2-6. Assume that Shaw Corporation classifies all operating expenses into two categories: (1) selling and (2) general and administrative.

Required

1. Prepare a multiple-step income statement for the year ended December 31, 2007.
2. What advantages do you see in this form for the income statement?
3. Compute Shaw's profit margin.
4. Comment on Shaw's profitability. What other factors need to be taken into account to assess Shaw's profitability?

LO8   **Problem 2-8** Statement of Cash Flows

Colorado Corporation was organized on January 1, 2007, with the investment of $250,000 in cash by its stockholders. The company immediately purchased an office building for $300,000, paying $210,000 in cash and signing a three-year promissory note for the balance. Colorado signed a five-year, $60,000 promissory note at a local bank during 2007 and received

(continued)

cash in the same amount. During its first year, Colorado collected $93,970 from its customers. It paid $65,600 for inventory, $20,400 in salaries and wages, and another $3,100 in taxes. Colorado paid $5,600 in cash dividends.

Required

1. Prepare a statement of cash flows for the year ended December 31, 2007.
2. What does this statement tell you that an income statement does not?

LO9 **Problem 2-9** Basic Elements of Financial Reports

Comparative income statements for Grammar Inc. are presented below.

	2007	2006
Sales	$ 1,000,000	$500,000
Cost of sales	500,000	300,000
Gross profit	$ 500,000	$200,000
Operating expenses	120,000	100,000
Operating income	$ 380,000	$100,000
Loss on sale of subsidiary	(400,000)	—
Net income (loss)	$ (20,000)	$100,000

Required

The president and management believe that the company performed better in 2007 than it did in 2006. Write the president's letter to be included in the 2007 annual report. Explain why the company is financially sound and why shareholders should not be alarmed by the $20,000 loss in a year when operating revenues increased significantly.

MULTI-CONCEPT PROBLEMS

LO2,4 **Problem 2-10** Comparing Coca-Cola and PepsiCo

The current items, listed in alphabetical order, are taken from the consolidated balance sheets of **Coca-Cola** and **PepsiCo** as of December 31, 2005 (all amounts are in millions of dollars):

Coca-Cola

Accounts payable and accrued expenses	$4,493
Accrued income taxes	797
Cash and cash equivalents	4,701
Current maturities of long-term debt	28
Inventories	1,424
Loans and notes payable	4,518
Marketable securities	66
Prepaid expenses and other assets	1,778
Trade accounts receivable, less allowance of $72	2,281

PepsiCo

Accounts and notes receivable, net	$3,261
Accounts payable and other current liabilities	5,971
Cash and cash equivalents	1,716
Income taxes payable	546
Inventories	1,693
Prepaid expenses and other current assets	618
Short-term investments	3,166
Short-term obligations	2,889

Required

1. Compute working capital and the current ratio for both companies.
2. On the basis of your answers to 1 above, which company appears to be more liquid?
3. As you know, other factors affect a company's liquidity in addition to its working capital and current ratio. Comment on the *composition* of each company's current assets and how this composition affects its liquidity.

LO2,5 **Problem 2-11** Comparability and Consistency in Income Statements

The following income statements were provided by Gleeson Company, a retailer:

2007 Income Statement		2006 Income Statement	
Sales	$1,700,000	Sales	$1,500,000
Cost of sales	520,000	Cost of sales	$ 450,000
Gross profit	$1,180,000	Sales salaries	398,000
Selling expense	$ 702,000	Advertising	175,000
Administrative expense	95,000	Office supplies	54,000
Total selling and		Depreciation—building	40,000
administrative		Delivery expense	20,000
expense	$ 797,000	Total expenses	$1,137,000
Net income	$ 383,000	Net income	$ 363,000

Required
1. Identify each income statement as either single-step or multiple-step format.
2. Convert the 2006 income statement to the same format as the 2007 income statement.

LO1,4,8 **Problem 2-12** Cash Flow

Franklin Co., a specialty retailer, has a history of paying quarterly dividends of $0.50 per share. Management is trying to determine whether the company will have adequate cash on December 31, 2008, to pay a dividend if one is declared by the board of directors. The following additional information is available:

- All sales are on account, and accounts receivable are collected one month after the sale. Sales volume has been increasing 5% each month.
- All purchases of merchandise are on account, and accounts payable are paid one month after the purchase. Cost of sales is 40% of the sales price. Inventory levels are maintained at $75,000.
- Operating expenses in addition to the mortgage are paid in cash. They amount to $3,000 per month and are paid as they are incurred.

Franklin Co.
Balance Sheet
September 30, 2008

Cash	$ 5,000	Accounts payable	$ 5,000
Accounts receivable	12,500	Mortgage note**	150,000
Inventory	75,000	Common stock—$1 par	50,000
Note receivable*	10,000	Retained earnings	66,500
Building/Land	169,000	Total liabilities and	
Total assets	$271,500	stockholders' equity	$271,500

*Note receivable represents a one-year, 5% interest-bearing note, due November 1, 2008.
**Mortgage note is a 30-year, 7% note due in monthly installments of $1,200.

Required
Determine the cash that Franklin will have available to pay a dividend on December 31, 2008. Round all amounts to the nearest dollar. What can Franklin's management do to increase the cash available? Should management recommend that the board of directors declare a dividend?

ALTERNATE PROBLEMS

LO2 **Problem 2-1A** Materiality

Jane Erving, a newly hired accountant, wanting to impress her boss, stayed late one night to analyze the long-distance calls by area code and time of day placed. She determined the monthly cost, for the previous 12 months, by hour and area code called.

(continued)

Required

1. What did Jane think her boss would learn from this information? What action might be taken as a result of knowing it?
2. Would this information be more relevant if Jane worked for a hardware store or for a real estate company? Discuss.

LO2

Problem 2-2A Costs and Expenses

The following costs are incurred by a retailer:

1. Point of sale systems in a retail store
2. An ad in the yellow pages
3. An inventory-control computer software system
4. Shipping merchandise for resale to chain outlets

Required

For each of these costs, explain whether all of the cost or only a portion of the cost would appear as an expense on the income statement for the period in which the cost is incurred. If not all of the cost would appear on the income statement for that period, explain why not.

LO3

Problem 2-3A Classified Balance Sheet

The following balance sheet items, listed in alphabetical order, are available from the records of Singer Company at December 31, 2007:

Accounts payable	$ 34,280	Land	$250,000
Accounts receivable	26,700	Marketable securities	15,000
Accumulated depreciation—buildings	40,000	Merchandise inventory	112,900
Accumulated depreciation—equipment	12,500	Notes payable, due April 15, 2008	6,500
Bonds payable, due December 31, 2013	250,000	Office supplies	400
Buildings	150,000	Paid-in capital in excess of par value	75,000
Capital stock, $1 par value	200,000	Patents	45,000
Cash	60,790	Prepaid rent	3,600
Equipment	84,500	Retained earnings	113,510
Income taxes payable	7,500	Salaries payable	7,400
Interest payable	2,200		

Required

1. Prepare a classified balance sheet as of December 31, 2007.
2. Compute Singer's current ratio.
3. On the basis of your answer to 2, does Singer appear to be liquid? What other information do you need to fully answer this question?

LO4

Problem 2-4A Financial Statement Ratios

The following items, in alphabetical order, are available from the records of Quinn Corporation as of December 31, 2007 and 2006:

	December 31, 2007	December 31, 2006
Accounts payable	$10,500	$ 6,500
Accounts receivable	16,500	26,000
Cash	12,750	11,800
Interest receivable	200	–0–
Note receivable, due 12/31/2009	12,000	12,000
Office supplies	900	1,100
Prepaid insurance	400	250
Salaries payable	1,800	800
Taxes payable	10,000	5,800

Required

1. Calculate the following, as of December 31, 2007, and December 31, 2006:
   a. Working capital
   b. Current ratio
2. On the basis of your answers to 1, comment on the relative liquidity of the company at the beginning and the end of the year. As part of your answer, explain the change in the company's liquidity from the beginning to the end of 2007.

LO4   **Problem 2-5A** Working Capital and Current Ratio

The balance sheet of Kapinski Inc. includes the following items:

Cash	$23,000	Accounts payable	$ 84,900
Accounts receivable	43,000	Salaries payable	3,200
Inventory	75,000	Capital stock	100,000
Prepaid insurance	2,800	Retained earnings	35,700
Land	80,000		

Required
1. Determine the current ratio and working capital.
2. Kapinski appears to have a positive current ratio and a large net working capital. Why would it have trouble paying bills as they come due?
3. Suggest three things that Kapinski can do to help pay its bills on time.

LO5   **Problem 2-6A** Single-Step Income Statement

The following income statement items, arranged in alphabetical order, are taken from the records of Corbin Enterprises for the year ended December 31, 2007:

Advertising expense	$ 9,000	Rent expense—office	$ 26,400
Cost of goods sold	150,000	Rent expense—salesperson's car	18,000
Depreciation expense—computer	4,500	Sales revenue	350,000
Dividend revenue	2,700	Supplies expense—office	1,300
Income tax expense	30,700	Utilities expense	6,750
Interest expense	1,900	Wages expense—office	45,600

Required
1. Prepare a single-step income statement for the year ended December 31, 2007.
2. What weaknesses do you see in this form for the income statement?

LO5   **Problem 2-7A** Multiple-Step Income Statement and Profit Margin

Refer to the list of income statement items in Problem 2-6A. Assume that Corbin Enterprises classifies all operating expenses into two categories: (1) selling and (2) general and administrative.

Required
1. Prepare a multiple-step income statement for the year ended December 31, 2007.
2. What advantages do you see in this form for the income statement?
3. Compute Corbin's profit margin.
4. Comment on Corbin's profitability. What other factors need to be taken into account to assess Corbin's profitability?

LO8   **Problem 2-8A** Statement of Cash Flows

Wisconsin Corporation was organized on January 1, 2007, with the investment of $400,000 in cash by its stockholders. The company immediately purchased a manufacturing facility for $300,000, paying $150,000 in cash and signing a five-year promissory note for the balance. Wisconsin signed another five-year note at the bank for $50,000 during 2007 and received cash for the same amount. During its first year, Wisconsin collected $310,000 from its customers. It paid $185,000 for inventory, $30,100 in salaries and wages, and another $40,000 in taxes. Wisconsin paid $4,000 in cash dividends.

Required
1. Prepare a statement of cash flows for the year ended December 31, 2007.
2. What does this statement tell you that an income statement does not?

LO9   **Problem 2-9A** Basic Elements of Financial Reports

Comparative income statements for Thesaurus Inc. are presented below.

	2007	2006
Operating revenues	$500,000	$200,000
Operating expenses	120,000	100,000
Operating income	$380,000	$100,000
Gain on the sale of subsidiary	—	400,000
Net income	$380,000	$500,000

(continued)

Required

The president and management believe that the company performed better in 2007 than it did in 2006. Write the president's letter to be included in the 2007 annual report. Explain why the company is financially sound and why shareholders should not be alarmed by the reduction in income in a year when operating revenues increased significantly.

ALTERNATE MULTI-CONCEPT PROBLEMS

LO2,4 **Problem 2-10A** Comparing Starwood Hotels & Resorts and Hilton Hotels

The following current items, listed in alphabetical order, are taken from the consolidated balance sheets of **Starwood Hotels & Resorts** and **Hilton Hotels** as of December 31, 2004 (all amounts are in millions of dollars). Any assets or liabilities that you may not be familiar with are noted parenthetically.

Starwood Hotels & Resorts

Accounts payable	$200
Accounts receivables, net of allowance for doubtful accounts	482
Accrued expenses (liability)	872
Accrued salaries, wages and benefits	299
Accrued taxes and other	138
Cash and cash equivalents	326
Inventories	371
Prepaid expenses and other	157
Restricted cash	347
Short-term borrowings and current maturities of long-term debt	619

Hilton Hotels

Accounts payable and accrued expenses	$553
Accounts receivable, net	246
Cash and cash equivalents	9
Current maturities of long-term debt	338
Current portion of notes receivable, net	32
Deferred income taxes (asset)	78
Income taxes payable	4
Inventories	193
Other current assets	64
Receivable from Caesars Entertainment, Inc.	325
Restricted cash	73

Required

1. Compute working capital and the current ratio for both companies.
2. On the basis of your answers to 1 above, which company appears to be more liquid?
3. As you know, other factors affect a company's liquidity in addition to its working capital and current ratio. Comment on the *composition* of each company's current assets and how this composition affects its liquidity.

LO2,5 **Problem 2-11A** Comparability and Consistency in Income Statements

The following income statements were provided by Chisholm Company, a wholesale food distributor:

	2007	2006
Sales	$1,700,000	$1,500,000
Cost of sales	$ 612,000	$ 450,000
Sales salaries	427,000	398,000
Delivery expense	180,000	175,000
Office supplies	55,000	54,000
Depreciation—truck	40,000	40,000
Computer line expense	23,000	20,000
Total expenses	$1,337,000	$1,137,000
Net income	$ 363,000	$ 363,000

Required
1. Identify each income statement as either single-step or multiple-step format.
2. Restate each item in the income statements as a percentage of sales. Why did net income remain unchanged when sales increased in 2007?

LO1,4,8 **Problem 2-12A** Cash Flow

Roosevelt Inc., a consulting service, has a history of paying annual dividends of $1 per share. Management is trying to determine whether the company will have adequate cash on December 31, 2008, to pay a dividend if one is declared by the board of directors. The following additional information is available:

- All sales are on account, and accounts receivable are collected one month after the sale. Sales volume has been decreasing 5% each month.
- Operating expenses are paid in cash in the month incurred. Average monthly expenses are $10,000 (excluding the biweekly payroll).
- Biweekly payroll is $4,500, and it will be paid December 15 and December 31.
- Unearned revenue is expected to be earned in December. This amount was taken into consideration in the expected sales volume.

Roosevelt Inc.
Balance Sheet
December 1, 2008

Cash	$ 15,000	Unearned revenue	$ 2,000
Accounts receivable	40,000	Note payable*	30,000
Computer equipment	120,000	Common stock—$2 par	50,000
		Retained earnings	93,000
		Total liabilities and	
Total assets	$175,000	stockholders' equity	$175,000

*The note payable plus 3% interest for six months is due January 15, 2008.

Required
Determine the cash that Roosevelt will have available to pay a dividend on December 31, 2008. Round all amounts to the nearest dollar. Should management recommend that the board of directors declare a dividend?

DECISION CASES

READING AND INTERPRETING FINANCIAL STATEMENTS

LO4 **Decision Case 2-1** Comparing Two Companies in the Same Industry: Finish Line and Foot Locker

Refer to the financial information for **Finish Line** and **Foot Locker** reproduced at the end of the book for the information needed to answer the following questions.

Required
1. Compute each company's working capital at the end of the two most recent years. Also, for each company, compute the change in working capital during the most recent year.
2. Compute each company's current ratio at the end of the two most recent years. Compute the percentage change in the ratio during the most recent year.
3. How do the two companies differ in terms of the accounts that made up their current assets at the end of the most recent year? What is the largest current asset each reports on the balance sheet at the end of the most recent year?
4. On the basis of your answers to questions (2) and (3), comment on each company's liquidity.

LO4 **Decision Case 2-2** Reading Finish Line's Balance Sheet

Refer to **Finish Line**'s balance sheet reproduced at the end of the book to answer the following questions.

(continued)

HOMEWORK

Required

1. Which is the largest of Finish Line's assets on February 25, 2006? What percentage of total assets does it represent? Given the nature of the company's business, does it seem logical that this would be the largest of its assets? Explain your answer.
2. Which is the second largest of Finish Line's assets on February 25, 2006? What percentage of total assets does it represent? Explain what this asset represents and why it is such a significant asset for a company such as Finish Line.
3. By what amount and by what percentage did each of the assets identified in (1) and (2) above increase during the most recent year? Explain what would cause a company such as Finish Line to increase its investment in each of these assets during the year.

MAKING FINANCIAL DECISIONS

LO8   **Decision Case 2-3** Analysis of Cash Flow for a Small Business

Charles, a financial consultant, has been self-employed for two years. His list of clients has grown, and he is earning a reputation as a shrewd investor. Charles rents a small office, uses the pool secretarial services, and has purchased a car that he is depreciating over three years. The following income statements cover Charles's first two years of business:

	Year 1	Year 2
Commissions revenue	$ 25,000	$65,000
Rent	$ 12,000	$12,000
Secretarial services	3,000	9,000
Car expenses, gas, insurance	6,000	6,500
Depreciation	15,000	15,000
Net income	$(11,000)	$22,500

Charles believes that he should earn more than $11,500 for working very hard for two years. He is thinking about going to work for an investment firm where he can earn $40,000 per year. What would you advise Charles to do?

LO9   **Decision Case 2-4** Factors Involved in an Investment Decision

As an investor, you are considering purchasing stock in a chain of theaters. The annual reports of several companies are available for comparison.

Required

Prepare an outline of the steps you would follow to make your comparison. Start by listing the first section that you would read in the financial reports. What would you expect to find there, and why did you choose that section to read first? Continue with the other sections of the financial report.

ETHICAL DECISION MAKING

LO2   **Decision Case 2-5** The Expenditure Approval Process

Roberto is the plant superintendent of a small manufacturing company that is owned by a large corporation. The corporation has a policy that any expenditure over $1,000 must be approved by the chief financial officer in the corporate headquarters. The approval process takes a minimum of three weeks. Roberto would like to order a new labeling machine that is expected to reduce costs and pay for itself in six months. The machine costs $2,200, but Roberto can buy the sales rep's demo for $1,800. Roberto has asked the sales rep to send two separate bills for $900 each.

What would you do if you were the sales rep? Do you agree or disagree with Roberto's actions? What do you think about the corporate policy?

LO4,6   **Decision Case 2-6** Susan Applies for a Loan

Susan Spiffy, owner of Spiffy Cleaners, a drive-through dry cleaners, would like to expand her business from its current one location to a chain of cleaners. Revenues at the one location have been increasing an average of 8% each quarter. Profits have been increasing accordingly. Susan is conservative in spending and a very hard worker. She has an appointment with a banker to apply for a loan to expand the business. To prepare for the appointment, she instructs you, as chief financial officer and payroll clerk, to copy the quarterly income statements for the past two years but not to include a balance sheet. Susan already has a substantial loan from another bank. In fact, she has very little of her own money invested in the business.

Required

Before answering the following questions, you may want to refer to Exhibit 1-10 and the related text on page 30. Support each answer with your reasoning.

1. What is the ethical dilemma in this case? Who would be affected and how would they be affected if you follow Susan's instructions? (Would they benefit? Would they be harmed?) What responsibility do you have in this situation?
2. If the banker does not receive the balance sheet, will he have all of the relevant and reliable information needed for his decision-making process? Why or why not? Will the information provided by Susan be free from bias?
3. What should you do? Might anyone be harmed by Susan's accounting decision?

SOLUTIONS TO KEY TERMS QUIZ

6	Understandability		13	Current asset
3	Relevance		9	Current liability
8	Reliability		14	Liquidity
12	Comparability		10	Working capital
16	Depreciation		7	Current ratio
15	Consistency		1	Single-step income statement
2	Materiality		4	Multiple-step income statement
5	Conservatism		18	Gross profit
17	Operating cycle		11	Profit margin

HOMEWORK

3

Processing Accounting Information

Study Links

A Look at Previous Chapters
Up to this point, we have focused on the role of accounting in decision making and the way accountants use financial statements to communicate useful information to the various users of the statements.

A Look at This Chapter
In this chapter, we consider how accounting information is processed. We begin by considering the *inputs* to an accounting system, that is, the transactions entered into by a business. We look at how transactions are analyzed, and then we turn to a number of accounting tools and procedures designed to facilitate the preparation of the *outputs* of the system, the financial statements. Ledger accounts, journal entries, and trial balances are tools that allow a company to process vast amounts of data efficiently.

A Look at the Upcoming Chapter
Chapter 4 concludes our overview of the accounting model. We will examine the accrual basis of accounting and its effect on the measurement of income. Adjustments, which are the focus of the accrual basis, will be discussed in detail in Chapter 4, along with the other steps in the accounting cycle.

Learning Outcomes

After studying this chapter, you should be able to:

LO1 Explain the difference between an external and an internal event.

LO2 Explain the role of source documents in an accounting system.

LO3 Analyze the effects of transactions on the accounting equation.

LO4 Describe the use of the account and the general ledger to accumulate amounts of financial statement items.

LO5 Explain the rules of debits and credits (Appendix).

LO6 Explain the purposes of a journal and the posting process (Appendix).

LO7 Explain the purpose of a trial balance (Appendix).

Foot Locker, Inc.

MAKING BUSINESS DECISIONS

In its 2005 annual report, Foot Locker, Inc., touts itself as the world's leading retailer of athletic footwear and apparel. The company operates approximately 4,000 stores in 20 countries in North America, Europe, and Australia. If you have spent any time in a mall recently, you likely have seen one of its stores, either in the form of one of its flagship Foot Locker locations, or one of a number of other brand names, such as Footaction, Lady Foot Locker, Kids Foot Locker, and Champs Sports. In addition, Eastbay, the unit that sells direct to customers via the Internet and catalogs, posted the highest division profit margin.

The Financial Highlights, shown here, provide evidence of Foot Locker's ability to capitalize on its size. The first line shows a steady growth in sales over the last five years, topping the $5.6 billion mark in 2005. The 5.6% increase in sales during 2005 was matched by a similar 5.1% increase in operating profit, an indication that the company was successful in controlling its costs.

Nearly all mall retailers lease rather than own the space they occupy. And as you could guess, the cost for every square foot of retail space leased in these large malls is not cheap. Thus, it is imperative that management develop strategies to maximize its sales productivity in each of its stores. One key "performance metric," as Foot Locker calls it, is the "sales per average gross square foot." Management was particularly pleased that the goal it had set earlier this decade was achieved in 2005 when it exceeded $350 of sales per average gross square foot. The Financial Highlights reports that this metric reached $361 in 2005.

We haven't yet in our study of accounting given any thought to how the numbers reported in Financial Highlights and on the various financial statements are actually determined. After all, before the information on the statements can be used for decision making, someone had to decide how to record the various transactions that underlie the amounts reported on the statements. When and how does Foot Locker record the sale of a pair of running shoes? At what point does it record the salaries and wages it must pay for all of the personnel to run its stores? As you study this chapter, look for answers to these key questions:

- What source documents are used as the necessary evidence to record transactions? (See p. 107)

- How do these transactions affect the financial statements? (See pp. 107–110)
- What are some of the tools that accountants use to effectively and efficiently process the information

that eventually appears on financial statements? (See pp. 122–125)

Financial Highlights

(Millions, except per share amounts)

	2001	2002	2003	2004	2005
Sales	$4,379	$4,509	$4,779	$5,355	$5,653
Total operating profit	$ 197	$ 269	$ 342	$ 389	$ 409
Income from continuing operations	$ 111	$ 162	$ 209	$ 255	$ 263
Diluted EPS from continuing operations	$ 0.77	$ 1.10	$ 1.40	$ 1.64	$ 1.67
Cash, cash equivalents and short-term investment position, net of debt	$ (184)	$ —	$ 113	$ 127	$ 261
Athletic stores sales per average gross square foot (dollars)	$ 306	$ 316	$ 335	$ 345	$ 361

Source: Foot Locker, Inc., 2005 Annual Report.

Economic Events: The Basis for Recording Transactions

LO1 Explain the difference between an external and an internal event.

Many different types of economic events affect an entity during the year. A sale is made to a customer. Inventory is purchased from a supplier. A loan is taken out at the bank. A fire destroys a warehouse. A new contract is signed with the union. In short, "An **event** is a happening of consequence to an entity."[1]

EXTERNAL AND INTERNAL EVENTS

Two types of events affect an entity: internal and external.

Event
A happening of consequence to an entity.

External event
An event involving interaction between an entity and its environment.

Internal event
An event occurring entirely within an entity.

Transaction
Any event that is recognized in a set of financial statements.

- An **external event** "involves interaction between the entity and its environment."[2] For example, the *payment* of wages to an employee is an external event, as is a *sale* to a customer.
- An **internal event** occurs entirely within the entity. The use of a piece of equipment is an internal event.

We will use the term **transaction** to refer to any event, external or internal, that is recognized in a set of financial statements.[3]

What is necessary to recognize an event in the records? Are all economic events recognized as transactions by the accountant? The answers to these questions involve the concept of *measurement*. An event must be measured to be recognized. Certain events are relatively easy to measure: the payroll for the week, the amount of equipment destroyed by an earthquake, or the sales for the day. Not all events

---

1 *Statement of Financial Accounting Concepts (SFAC) No. 3*, "Elements of Financial Statements of Business Enterprises" (Stamford, Conn.: Financial Accounting Standards Board, 1982), par. 65.

2 *SFAC No. 3*.

3 Technically, a *transaction* is defined by the Financial Accounting Standards Board as a special kind of external event in which the entity exchanges something of value with an outsider. Because the term *transaction* is used in practice to refer to any event that is recognized in the statements, we will use this broader definition.

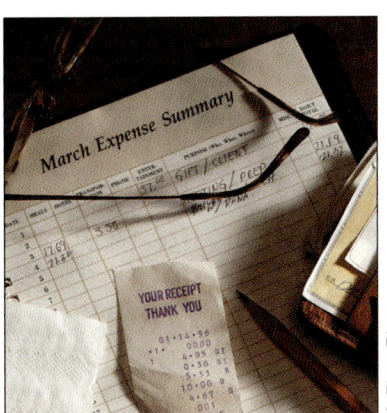

Source documents like these receipts are records that document transactions that the business engages in. Shown here are an employee's travel expense receipts, which will be turned in to the company for reimbursement. Other source documents may be contracts, lease agreements, invoices, delivery vouchers, check stubs, and deposit slips.

© PhotoDisc

that affect an entity can be measured *reliably*, however. For example, how does a manufacturer of breakfast cereal measure the effect of a drought on the price of wheat? A company hires a new chief executive. How can it reliably measure the value of the new officer to the company? There is no definitive answer to the measurement problem in accounting. It is a continuing challenge to the accounting profession and something we will return to throughout the text.

THE ROLE OF SOURCE DOCUMENTS IN RECORDING TRANSACTIONS

LO2 Explain the role of source documents in an accounting system.

The first step in the recording process is *identification.* A business needs a systematic method for recognizing events as transactions. A **source document** provides the evidence needed in an accounting system to record a transaction. Source documents take many different forms. An invoice received from a supplier is the source document for a purchase of inventory on credit. A cash register tape is the source document used by a retailer to recognize a cash sale. The payroll department sends the accountant the time cards for the week as the necessary documentation to record wages.

Source document
A piece of paper that is used as evidence to record a transaction.

Not all recognizable events are supported by a standard source document. For certain events, some form of documentation must be generated. For example, no standard source document exists to recognize the financial consequences from a fire or the settlement of a lawsuit. Documentation is just as important for these types of events as it is for standard, recurring transactions.

ANALYZING THE EFFECTS OF TRANSACTIONS ON THE ACCOUNTING EQUATION

LO3 Analyze the effects of transactions on the accounting equation.

Economic events are the basis for recording transactions in an accounting system. For every transaction, it is essential to analyze its effect on the accounting equation:

$$\text{Assets} = \text{Liabilities} + \text{Stockholders' Equity}$$

We will now consider a series of events and their recognition as transactions for a hypothetical corporation, Glengarry Health Club. The transactions are for the month of January 2007, the first month of operations for the new business.

(1) *Issuance of capital stock.* The company is started when Mary Jo Kovach and Irene McGuinness file articles of incorporation with the state to obtain a charter. Each invests $50,000 in the business. In return, each receives 5,000 shares of capital stock. Thus, at this point, each of them owns 50% of the outstanding stock of the company and has a claim to 50% of its assets. The effect of this transaction on the accounting equation is to increase both assets and stockholders' equity:

		Assets				=	Liabilities		+	Stockholders' Equity	+ Revenues − Expenses
TRANS. NO.	CASH	ACCT. REC.	EQUIP.	BLDG.	LAND		ACCT. PAY.	NOTES PAY.		CAPITAL STOCK	RET. EARN.
1	$100,000									$100,000	
Totals			$100,000							$100,000	

As you see, each side of the accounting equation increases by $100,000. Cash is increased, and because the owners contributed this amount, their claim to the assets is increased in the form of Capital Stock.

(2) *Acquisition of property in exchange for a note.* The company buys a piece of property for $200,000. The seller agrees to accept a five-year promissory note. The note is given by the health club to the seller and is a written promise to repay the principal amount of the loan at the end of five years. To the company, the promissory note is a liability. The property consists of land valued at $50,000 and a newly constructed building valued at $150,000. The effect of this transaction on the accounting equation is to increase both assets and liabilities by $200,000:

		Assets				=	Liabilities		+	Stockholders' Equity	+ Revenues − Expenses
TRANS. NO.	CASH	ACCT. REC.	EQUIP.	BLDG.	LAND		ACCT. PAY.	NOTES PAY.		CAPITAL STOCK	RET. EARN.
Bal.	$100,000									$100,000	
2				$150,000	$50,000			$200,000			
Bal.	$100,000			$150,000	$50,000			$200,000		$100,000	
Totals			$300,000							$300,000	

(3) *Acquisition of equipment on an open account.* Mary Jo and Irene contact an equipment supplier and buy $20,000 of exercise equipment: treadmills, barbells, and stationary bicycles. The supplier agrees to accept payment in full in 30 days. The health club has acquired an asset and at the same time incurred a liability:

		Assets				=	Liabilities		+	Stockholders' Equity	+ Revenues − Expenses
TRANS. NO.	CASH	ACCT. REC.	EQUIP.	BLDG.	LAND		ACCT. PAY.	NOTES PAY.		CAPITAL STOCK	RET. EARN.
Bal.	$100,000			$150,000	$50,000			$200,000		$100,000	
3			$20,000				$20,000				
Bal.	$100,000		$20,000	$150,000	$50,000		$20,000	$200,000		$100,000	
Totals			$320,000							$320,000	

(4) *Sale of monthly memberships on account.* The owners open their doors for business. During January, they sell 300 monthly club memberships for $50 each, or a total of $15,000. The members have until the 10th of the following month to pay. Glengarry does not have cash from the new members but instead has a promise from each member to pay cash in the future. The promise from a customer to pay an amount owed is an asset called an *account receivable*. The other side of this transaction is an increase in the stockholders' equity (specifically, Retained Earnings) in the business. In other words, the assets have increased by $15,000 without any increase in a liability or decrease in another asset. The increase in stockholders' equity indicates that the owners' residual interest in the assets of the business has increased by this amount. More specifically, an inflow of assets resulting from the sale of goods and services by a business is called *revenue*, and in this case, membership revenue. Note in the accounting equation at the top of the following page that $15,000 is added to the column head "Revenues − Expenses."

The last column in the equation is treated as an extension of, or addition to, stockholders' equity on the right side of the accounting equation. This is because the inflow of cash is due to the sale of memberships, and therefore, the owners'

	Assets					=	Liabilities		+ Stockholders' Equity		+ Revenues	− Expenses
TRANS. NO.	CASH	ACCT. REC.	EQUIP.	BLDG.	LAND		ACCT. PAY.	NOTES PAY.	CAPITAL STOCK	RET. EARN.		
Bal.	$100,000		$20,000	$150,000	$50,000		$20,000	$200,000	$100,000			
4		$15,000									$15,000	
Bal.	$100,000	$15,000	$20,000	$150,000	$50,000		$20,000	$200,000	$100,000		$15,000	
Totals			$335,000						$335,000			

claims to the assets of the business have increased by $15,000. More specifically, the retained earnings portion of stockholders' equity has increased by this amount. However, rather than treat the revenue as a direct increase in retained earnings, we account for it separately. Later we will see how the excess of revenue over expense makes its way into retained earnings.

(5) *Sale of court time for cash.* In addition to memberships, Glengarry sells court time. Court fees are paid at the time of use and amount to $5,000 for the first month:

	Assets					=	Liabilities		+ Stockholders' Equity		+ Revenues	− Expenses
TRANS. NO.	CASH	ACCT. REC.	EQUIP.	BLDG.	LAND		ACCT. PAY.	NOTES PAY.	CAPITAL STOCK	RET. EARN.		
Bal.	$100,000	$15,000	$20,000	$150,000	$50,000		$20,000	$200,000	$100,000		$15,000	
5	5,000										5,000	
Bal.	$105,000	$15,000	$20,000	$150,000	$50,000		$20,000	$200,000	$100,000		$20,000	
Totals			$340,000						$340,000			

The only difference between this transaction and (4) is that cash is received rather than a promise to pay at a later date. Both transactions result in an increase in an asset and an increase in the owners' claim to the assets. In both cases, there is an inflow of assets, in the form of either Accounts Receivable or Cash. Thus, in both cases, the company has earned revenue.

(6) *Payment of wages and salaries.* The wages and salaries for the first month amount to $10,000. The payment of this amount results in a decrease in Cash and a decrease in the owners' claim on the assets, that is, a decrease in Retained Earnings. More specifically, an outflow of assets resulting from the sale of goods or services is called an *expense.* In this case, the club recognizes $10,000 of *wages and salaries* expense. The effect of this transaction is to decrease both sides of the accounting equation:

	Assets					=	Liabilities		+ Stockholders' Equity		+ Revenues	− Expenses
TRANS. NO.	CASH	ACCT. REC.	EQUIP.	BLDG.	LAND		ACCT. PAY.	NOTES PAY.	CAPITAL STOCK	RET. EARN.		
Bal.	$105,000	$15,000	$20,000	$150,000	$50,000		$20,000	$200,000	$100,000		$20,000	
6	−10,000											−10,000
Bal.	$ 95,000	$15,000	$20,000	$150,000	$50,000		$20,000	$200,000	$100,000		$10,000	
Totals			$330,000						$330,000			

(7) *Payment of utilities.* The cost of utilities for the first month is $3,000. Glengarry pays this amount in cash. Both the utilities and the salaries and wages are expenses, and they have the same effect on the accounting equation. Cash is decreased, accompanied by a corresponding decrease in the right side of the equation due to the expense recognized:

	Assets					=	Liabilities		+ Stockholders' Equity		+ Revenues	− Expenses
TRANS. NO.	CASH	ACCT. REC.	EQUIP.	BLDG.	LAND		ACCT. PAY.	NOTES PAY.	CAPITAL STOCK	RET. EARN.		
Bal.	$95,000	$15,000	$20,000	$150,000	$50,000		$20,000	$200,000	$100,000		$10,000	
7	−3,000											−3,000
Bal.	$92,000	$15,000	$20,000	$150,000	$50,000		$20,000	$200,000	$100,000		$ 7,000	
Totals			$327,000						$327,000			

(8) *Collection of accounts receivable.* Even though the January monthly memberships are not due until the 10th of the following month, some of the members pay their bills by the end of January. The amount received from members in payment of their accounts is $4,000. The effect of the collection of an open account is to increase Cash and decrease Accounts Receivable:

	Assets					=	Liabilities		+ Stockholders' Equity		+ Revenues − Expenses
TRANS. NO.	CASH	ACCT. REC.	EQUIP.	BLDG.	LAND	ACCT. PAY.	NOTES PAY.	CAPITAL STOCK	RET. EARN.		
Bal.	$92,000	$15,000	$20,000	$150,000	$50,000	$20,000	$200,000	$100,000			$7,000
8	4,000	−4,000									
Bal.	$96,000	$11,000	$20,000	$150,000	$50,000	$20,000	$200,000	$100,000			$7,000
Totals		$327,000						$327,000			

This is the first transaction we have seen that affects only one side of the accounting equation. In fact, the company simply traded assets: Accounts Receivable for Cash. Thus, note that the totals for the accounting equation remain at $327,000. Also note that Retained Earnings is not affected by this transaction because revenue was recognized earlier, in **(4)**, when Accounts Receivable was increased.

(9) *Payment of dividends.* At the end of the month, Mary Jo and Irene, acting on behalf of Glengarry Health Club, decide to pay a dividend of $1,000 on the shares of stock owned by each of them, or $2,000 in total. The effect of this dividend is to decrease both Cash and Retained Earnings. That is, the company is returning cash to the owners, based on the profitable operations of the business for the first month. The transaction not only reduces Cash but also decreases the owners' claims on the assets of the company. Dividends are not an expense but rather a direct reduction of Retained Earnings. The effect on the accounting equation follows:

	Assets					=	Liabilities		+ Stockholders' Equity		+ Revenues − Expenses
TRANS. NO.	CASH	ACCT. REC.	EQUIP.	BLDG.	LAND	ACCT. PAY.	NOTES PAY.	CAPITAL STOCK	RET. EARN.		
Bal.	$96,000	$11,000	$20,000	$150,000	$50,000	$20,000	$200,000	$100,000			$7,000
9	−2,000								−2,000		
Bal.	$94,000	$11,000	$20,000	$150,000	$50,000	$20,000	$200,000	$100,000	$−2,000		$7,000
Totals		$325,000						$325,000			

The Cost Principle An important principle governs the accounting for both the exercise equipment in **(3)** and the building and land in **(2)**. **The *cost principle* requires that we record an asset at the cost to acquire it and continue to show this amount on all balance sheets until we dispose of the asset.** With a few exceptions, an asset is not carried at its market value but at its original cost. *Why not show the land on future balance sheets at its market value?* Although this might seem more appropriate in certain instances, the subjectivity inherent in determining market values is a major reason behind the practice of carrying assets at their historical cost. The cost of an asset can be verified by an independent observer and is much more *objective* than market value.

2 minute review

Assume that on February 1 Glengarry buys additional exercise equipment for $10,000 in cash.

1. Indicate which two accounts are affected and the increase or decrease in each.

2. What will be the total dollar amount of each of the two sides of the accounting equation after this transaction is recorded?

Answers

1. *Equipment will increase by $10,000, and Cash will decrease by $10,000.*

2. *$325,000 (the effect of the transaction is to increase and decrease assets by the same amount).*

BALANCE SHEET AND INCOME STATEMENT FOR GLENGARRY HEALTH CLUB

To summarize, Exhibit 3-1 indicates the effect of each transaction on the accounting equation, specifically the individual items increased or decreased by each transaction. Note the *dual* effect of each transaction. At least two items were involved in each transaction. For example, the initial investment by the owners resulted in an increase in an asset and an increase in Capital Stock. The payment of the dividends caused a decrease in an asset and a decrease in Retained Earnings.

You can now see the central idea behind the accounting equation: Even though individual transactions may change the amount and composition of the assets and liabilities, the *equation* must always balance *for* each transaction, and the *balance sheet* must balance *after* each transaction.

An income statement for Glengarry is shown in Exhibit 3-2. An income statement summarizes the revenues and expenses of a company for a period of time. In our example, the statement is for the month of January, as indicated on the third line of the heading of the statement. Glengarry earned revenues from two sources: (1) memberships and (2) court fees. Two types of expenses were incurred: (1) salaries and wages and (2) utilities. The difference between the total revenues of $20,000 and the total expenses of $13,000 is the net income for the month of $7,000.

Glengarry's statement of retained earnings is shown in Exhibit 3-3 on p. 112. Recall from Chapter 1 that a statement of retained earnings provides a bridge between a company's income statement and its balance sheet. Because the health club only began operating in January of 2004, the beginning balance in retained earnings is zero. January's net income of $7,000, as reported on the income statement in Exhibit 3-2, is added to the beginning balance, and the dividends of

Companies engage in transactions in many ways. The company from which this woman is ordering supports sales transactions over the phone using a credit card number. A sales representative may be inputting the card number and the order information into an order database. The company links its order-processing system and other business systems to this customer input.

© Peter Beck/Corbis

EXHIBIT 3-1   Glengarry Health Club Transactions for the Month of January

TRANS. NO.	Assets					=	Liabilities		+ Stockholders' Equity		+ Revenues − Expenses
	CASH	ACCOUNTS RECEIVABLE	EQUIPMENT	BUILDING	LAND		ACCOUNTS PAYABLE	NOTES PAYABLE	CAPITAL STOCK	RETAINED EARNINGS	
1	$100,000								$100,000		
2				$150,000	$50,000			$200,000			
Bal.	$100,000			$150,000	$50,000			$200,000	$100,000		
3			$20,000				$20,000				
Bal.	$100,000		$20,000	$150,000	$50,000		$20,000	$200,000	$100,000		
4		$15,000									$ 15,000
Bal.	$100,000	$15,000	$20,000	$150,000	$50,000		$20,000	$200,000	$100,000		$ 15,000
5	5,000										5,000
Bal.	$105,000	$15,000	$20,000	$150,000	$50,000		$20,000	$200,000	$100,000		$ 20,000
6	− 10,000										−10,000
Bal.	$ 95,000	$15,000	$20,000	$150,000	$50,000		$20,000	$200,000	$100,000		$ 10,000
7	− 3,000										− 3,000
Bal.	$ 92,000	$15,000	$20,000	$150,000	$50,000		$20,000	$200,000	$100,000		$ 7,000
8	4,000	− 4,000									
Bal.	$ 96,000	$11,000	$20,000	$150,000	$50,000		$20,000	$200,000	$100,000		$ 7,000
9	− 2,000									−2,000	
Bal.	$ 94,000	$11,000	$20,000	$150,000	$50,000		$20,000	$200,000	$100,000	$−2,000	$ 7,000

Total assets: $325,000   Total liabilities and stockholders' equity: $325,000

EXHIBIT 3-2 **Income Statement for Glengarry Health Club**

Glengarry Health Club
Income Statement
For the Month Ended January 31, 2007

Revenues:		
Memberships	$15,000	
Court fees	5,000	$20,000
Expenses:		
Salaries and wages	$10,000	
Utilities	3,000	13,000
Net income		$ 7,000

EXHIBIT 3-3 **Statement of Retained Earnings for Glengarry Health Club**

Glengarry Health Club
Statement of Retained Earnings
For the Month Ended January 31, 2007

Beginning balance, January 1, 2007	$ 0
Add: Net income for January	7,000
Deduct: Dividends for January	2,000
Ending balance, January 31, 2007	$5,000

$2,000 are deducted. The reason that the dividends appear directly on the statement of retained earnings in Exhibit 3-3, rather than on the income statement, is because they are a distribution of net income for the period, not a determinant of net income as are expenses.

A balance sheet for the business appears in Exhibit 3-4. Note that the ending retained earnings from the statement of retained earnings appears on the right side of the balance sheet. All of the other information needed to prepare this statement is available in Exhibit 3-1. The balances at the bottom of this exhibit are entered on the balance sheet, with assets on the left side and liabilities and stockholders' equity on the right side.

We have seen how transactions are analyzed and how they affect the accounting equation and ultimately the financial statements. While the approach we took

---

EXHIBIT 3-4 **Balance Sheet for Glengarry Health Club**

Glengarry Health Club
Balance Sheet
January 31, 2007

Assets		Liabilities and Stockholders' Equity	
Cash	$ 94,000	Accounts payable	$ 20,000
Accounts receivable	11,000	Notes payable	200,000
Equipment	20,000	Capital stock	100,000
Building	150,000	Retained earnings	5,000
Land	50,000	Total liabilities	
Total assets	$325,000	and stockholders' equity	$325,000

in analyzing the nine transactions of the Glengarry Health Club was manageable, can you imagine using this type of analysis for a company with *thousands* of transactions in any one month? We now turn to various *tools* used by the accountant to process a large volume of transactions effectively and efficiently.

What Is an Account?

An **account** is the basic unit for recording transactions. It is the record used to accumulate monetary amounts for each asset, liability, and component of owners' equity, such as Capital Stock, Retained Earnings, and Dividends. It is the basic recording unit for each element in the financial statements. Each revenue and expense has its own account. In the Glengarry Health Club example, ten accounts were used: Cash, Accounts Receivable, Equipment, Building, Land, Accounts Payable, Notes Payable, Capital Stock, Retained Earnings, and Revenues minus Expenses. In the real world, a company might have hundreds, or even thousands, of individual accounts.

No two entities have exactly the same set of accounts. To a certain extent, the accounts used by a company depend on its business. For example, a manufacturer normally has three inventory accounts: Raw Materials, Work in Process, and Finished Goods. A retailer uses just one account for inventory, a merchandise inventory account. A service business has no need for an inventory account.

CHART OF ACCOUNTS

Companies need a way to organize the large number of accounts they use to record transactions. A **chart of accounts** is a numerical list of all of the accounts an entity uses. The numbering system is a convenient way to identify accounts. For example, all asset accounts might be numbered from 100 to 199, liability accounts from 200 to 299, equity accounts from 300 to 399, revenues from 400 to 499, and expenses from 500 to 599. A chart of accounts for a hypothetical company, Widescreen Theaters Corporation, is shown in Exhibit 3-5. Note the division of account numbers within each of the financial statement categories. Within the asset category, the various cash accounts are numbered from 100 to 109, receivables from 110 to 119, etc. Not all of the numbers are currently assigned. For example, only three of the available nine numbers are currently utilized for cash accounts. This allows the company to add accounts as needed.

THE GENERAL LEDGER

Companies store their accounts in different ways, depending on their accounting system. In a manual system, a separate card or sheet is used to record the activity in each account. A **general ledger** is simply the file or book that contains the accounts.[4] For example, the general ledger for Widescreen Theaters Corporation might consist of a file of cards in a cabinet, with a card for each of the accounts listed in the chart of accounts.

In today's business world, most companies have an automated accounting system. The computer is ideally suited for the job of processing vast amounts of data rapidly. *All of the tools discussed in this chapter are as applicable to computerized systems as they are to manual systems. It is merely the appearance of the tools that differs between manual and computerized systems.* For example, the ledger in an automated system might be contained on a computer file server rather than stored in a file cabinet. Throughout the book, we will use a manual system to explain the various tools,

Account
Record used to accumulate amounts for each individual asset, liability, revenue, expense, and component of owners' equity.

Chart of accounts
A numerical list of all the accounts used by a company.

LO4 Describe the use of the account and the general ledger to accumulate amounts of financial statement items.

General ledger
A book, file, hard drive, or other device containing all the accounts. *Alternate term: Set of accounts*

---

4 In addition to a general ledger, many companies maintain subsidiary ledgers. For example, an accounts receivable subsidiary ledger contains a separate account for each customer. The use of a subsidiary ledger for Accounts Receivable is discussed further in Chapter 7.

EXHIBIT 3-5	Chart of Accounts for a Theater

100–199:	ASSETS	300–399:	STOCKHOLDERS' EQUITY
100–109:	Cash	301:	Preferred Stock
101:	Cash, Checking, Second National Bank	302:	Common Stock
102:	Cash, Savings, Third State Bank	303:	Retained Earnings
103:	Cash, Change, or Petty Cash Fund (coin and currency)	400–499:	REVENUES
		401:	Tickets
110–119:	Receivables	402:	Video Rentals
111:	Accounts Receivable	403:	Concessions
112:	Due from Employees	404:	Interest
113:	Notes Receivable	500–599:	EXPENSES
120–129:	Prepaid Assets	500–509:	Rentals
121:	Cleaning Supplies	501:	Films
122:	Prepaid Insurance	502:	Videos
130–139:	Property, Plant, and Equipment	510–519:	Concessions
131:	Land	511:	Candy
132:	Theater Buildings	512:	Soda
133:	Projection Equipment	513:	Popcorn
134:	Furniture and Fixtures	520–529:	Wages and Salaries
200–299:	LIABILITIES	521:	Hourly Employees
200–209:	Short-Term Liabilities	522:	Salaries
201:	Accounts Payable	530–539:	Utilities
202:	Wages and Salaries Payable	531:	Heat
203:	Taxes Payable	532:	Electric
203.1:	Income Taxes Payable	533:	Water
203.2:	Sales Taxes Payable	540–549:	Advertising
203.3:	Unemployment Taxes Payable	541:	Newspaper
204:	Short-Term Notes Payable	542:	Radio
204.1:	Six-Month Note Payable to First State Bank	550–559:	Taxes
210–219:	Long-Term Liabilities	551:	Income Taxes
211:	Bonds Payable, due in 2013	552:	Unemployment Taxes

such as ledger accounts. The reason is that it is easier to illustrate and visualize the tools in a manual system. However, all of the ideas apply just as well to a computerized system of accounting.

Processing Accounting Information

In this chapter, we analyzed the effects of the transactions of Glengarry Health Club on the accounting equation. Because the accounting equation is the basis for financial statements, the ability to analyze transactions in terms of their effect on the equation is an essential skill to master. In the appendix to this chapter, tools used by the accountant to effectively and efficiently process large volumes of transactions during the period are examined. One of the key tools used by the accountant is a system of debits and credits.

The emphasis throughout this book is on the *use* of financial statements to make decisions, as opposed to the tools used by accountants to process information. Therefore, in future chapters, our emphasis will not be on the accountant's various tools, such as debits and credits, but on the effects of transactions on the accounting equation and financial statements. Recall transaction 4 for the Glengarry Health Club, as it was originally summarized in Exhibit 3-1:

		Assets				=	Liabilities		+	Stockholders' Equity	+ Revenues − Expenses
NO.	CASH	ACCT. REC.	EQUIP.	BLDG.	LAND		ACCT. PAY.	NOTES PAY.		CAPITAL STOCK	RET. EARN.
4		$15,000									$15,000

Recall also that the sale of memberships increased both accounts receivable and revenue. **In future chapters, we will use a variation of the format in Exhibit 3-1 to demonstrate the effects of various transactions on the accounting equation.** For example, the sale of memberships would appear as follows in this version of the equation (and see Exhibit 3-6):

Balance Sheet				Income Statement
ASSETS	**=**	**LIABILITIES**	**+**	**STOCKHOLDERS' EQUITY** +	**REVENUES – EXPENSES**

Accounts Receivable 15,000   Membership Revenue 15,000

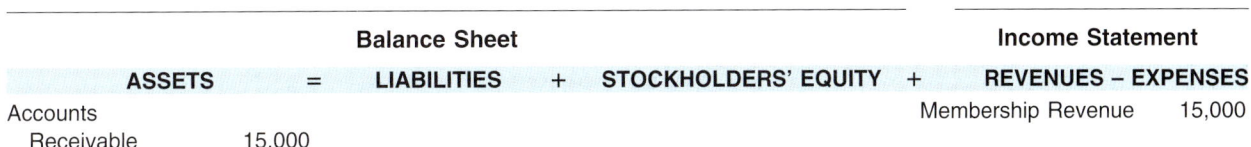

EXHIBIT 3-6 **Using the Transaction Effects Equation**

Transaction Analysis Form
- Shows how transactions are analyzed into account names and accounting equation categories for use in recording transactions (Amounts are eventually reflected in the financial statements.)
- Used in Chapter 3.

		Assets				=	**Liabilities**		+ **Stockholders' Equity**	+ **Revenues – Expenses**
NUMBER	CASH	ACCOUNTS RECEIVABLE	EQUIPMENT	BUILDING	LAND		ACCOUNTS PAYABLE	NOTES PAYABLE	CAPITAL STOCK RETAINED EARNINGS	
4		$15,000								$15,000

Transaction Effects Form
- Shows how statements—balance sheet and income statement—are affected by the transactions.
- Used in Chapters 4–13.

Amounts in these columns reflect accounts on the balance sheet.

Amounts in these columns reflect accounts on the income statement.

Balance Sheet				Income Statement
ASSETS	**=**	**LIABILITIES**	**+**	**STOCKHOLDERS' EQUITY** +	**REVENUES – EXPENSES**

Accounts Receivable 15,000   Membership Revenue 15,000

This line will display transactions discussed in each chapter—account titles, amounts, and whether increases or decreases. Decreases will be shown as negative numbers, e.g., (10,000).

Note that revenues and expenses appear on the income statement, and net income increases retained earnings, which is part of stockholders' equity.

Note two important changes in this version of the equation. First, rather than having a separate column for each individual financial statement item, the items are simply listed under the appropriate categories. For example, this transaction results in an increase in Accounts Receivable, which is shown in the assets category. Second, in this expanded version of the accounting equation, the income statement is viewed as an extension of the balance sheet. As you are aware, revenues do result in an increase in retained earnings and thus stockholders' equity, but they must first be recorded on the income statement.

To illustrate one additional transaction with this new format, recall transaction 6 for Glengarry in which $10,000 was paid in wages and salaries. The effect of this transaction on the accounting equation is:

Balance Sheet				Income Statement
ASSETS	**= LIABILITIES**	**+ STOCKHOLDERS' EQUITY**	**+**	**REVENUES – EXPENSES**
Cash (10,000)				Wage and Salary Expense (10,000)

- **Exhibit 3-6 (page 115) summarizes how the new transaction effects equation will be used in Chapters 4–13.**

Accounting Tools: The Double-Entry System

APPENDIX

The origin of the double-entry system of accounting can be traced to Venice, Italy, in 1494. In that year, Fra Luca Pacioli, a Franciscan monk, wrote a mathematical treatise. Included in his book was the concept of debits and credits that is still used almost universally today.

The T Account

The form for a general ledger account will be illustrated later in the chapter. However, the form of account often used to analyze transactions is called the *T account,* so named because it resembles the capital letter T. The name of the account appears across the horizontal line. One side is used to record increases and the other side decreases, but as you will see, the same side is not used for increases for every account. As a matter of convention, the *left* side of an *asset* account is used to record *increases* and the *right* side to record *decreases.* To illustrate a T account, we will look at the Cash account for Glengarry Health Club. The transactions recorded in the account can be traced to Exhibit 3-1.

Cash			
Increases		**Decreases**	
Investment by owners	100,000	Wages and salaries	10,000
Court fees collected	5,000	Utilities	3,000
Accounts collected	4,000	Dividends	2,000
	109,000		15,000
Bal.	94,000		

The amounts $109,000 and $15,000 are called *footings*. They represent the totals of the amounts on each side of the account. Neither these amounts nor the balance of $94,000 represents transactions. They are simply shown to indicate the totals and the balance in the account.

Debits and Credits

Rather than refer to the left or right side of an account, accountants use specific labels for each side. The *left* side of any account is the **debit** side, and the *right* side of any account is the **credit** side. We will also use the terms *debit* and *credit* as verbs. If we *debit* the Cash account, we enter an amount on the left side. Similarly, if we want to enter an amount on the right side of an account, we *credit* the account. To *charge* an account has the same meaning as to *debit* it. No such synonym exists for the act of crediting an account.

Note that *debit* and *credit* are *locational* terms. They simply refer to the left or right side of a T account. They do *not* represent increases or decreases. As we will see, when one type of account is increased (for example, the Cash account), the increase is on the left or *debit* side. When certain other types of accounts are increased, however, the entry will be on the right or *credit* side.

As you would expect from your understanding of the accounting equation, the conventions for using T accounts for assets and liabilities are opposite. Assets are future economic benefits, and liabilities are obligations to transfer economic benefits in the future. If an asset is *increased* with a *debit,* how do you think a liability would be increased? *Because assets and liabilities are opposites, if an asset is increased with a debit, a liability is increased with a credit.* Thus, the right side, or credit side, of a liability account is used to record an increase. Like liabilities, stockholders' equity (owners' equity) accounts are on the opposite side of the accounting equation from assets. *Thus, like a liability, a stockholders' equity account is increased with a credit.* We can summarize the logic of debits and credits, increases and decreases, and the accounting equation in the following way:

Assets		=	Liabilities		+	Stockholders' Equity	
Debits	Credits		Debits	Credits		Debits	Credits
Increases	Decreases		Decreases	Increases		Decreases	Increases
+	−		−	+		−	+

Note again that debits and credits are location-oriented. Debits are always on the left side of an account and credits on the right side.

Debits and Credits for Revenues, Expenses, and Dividends

Revenues In our Glengarry Health Club example, revenues increased the right side of the accounting equation. The sale of memberships was not only an increase in the asset Accounts Receivable but also an increase in the owners' claim on the assets of the business. Rather than being recorded directly in Retained Earnings,

LO5 Explain the rules of debits and credits.

Debit
An entry on the left side of an account.

Credit
An entry on the right side of an account.

Study Tip Once you know the rule to increase an asset with a debit, the rules for the other increases and decreases follow logically. For example, because a liability is the opposite of an asset, it is increased with a credit. And it follows logically that it would be decreased with a debit.

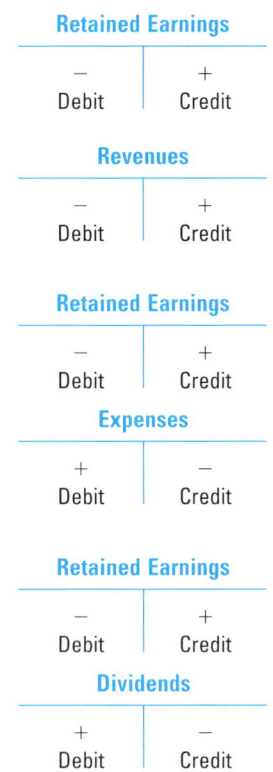

however, each revenue item is maintained in a separate account. The following logic is used to arrive at the rules for increasing and decreasing revenues:[5]

1. **Retained Earnings is increased with a credit.**
2. **Revenue is an increase in Retained Earnings.**
3. **Revenue is increased with a credit.**
4. **Because revenue is increased with a credit, it is decreased with a debit.**

Expenses The same logic is applied to the expenses recognized in transactions **(6)** and **(7)**. The rules for increasing and decreasing expense accounts are:

1. **Retained Earnings is decreased with a debit.**
2. **Expense is a decrease in Retained Earnings.**
3. **Expense is increased with a debit.**
4. **Because expense is increased with a debit, it is decreased with a credit.**

Dividends Recall that dividend transaction **(9)** reduced cash. But dividends also reduce the owners' claim on the assets of the business. Earlier we recognized this decrease in the owners' claim as a reduction of Retained Earnings. As we do for revenue and expense accounts, we will use a separate Dividends account:

1. **Retained Earnings is decreased with a debit.**
2. **Dividends are a decrease in Retained Earnings.**
3. **Dividends are increased with a debit.**
4. **Because dividends are increased with a debit, they are decreased with a credit.**

Summary of the Rules for Increasing and Decreasing Accounts

Using the accounting equation, the rules for increasing and decreasing the various types of accounts can be summarized as follows:

Normal Account Balances

Each account has a "normal" balance. For example, assets normally have debit balances. Would it be possible for an asset such as Cash to have a credit balance? Assume that a company has a checking account with a bank. A credit balance in the account would indicate that the decreases in the account, from checks written and other bank charges, were more than the deposits into the account. If this were the case, however,

---

[5] We normally think of both revenues and expenses as being only increased, not decreased. Because we will need to decrease them as part of the closing procedure, it is important to know how to reduce these accounts as well as increase them.

the company would no longer have an asset, Cash, but instead would have a liability to the bank. The normal balances for the accounts we have looked at are as follows:

Debits Aren't Bad, and Credits Aren't Good

Students often approach their first encounter with debits and credits with preconceived notions. The use of the terms *debit* and *credit* in everyday language leads to many of these notions. "Joe is a real credit to his team." "Nancy should be credited with saving Mary's career." These both appear to be very positive statements. You must resist the temptation to associate the term *credit* with something good or positive and the term *debit* with something bad or negative. **In accounting, debit means one thing: an entry made on the left side of an account. A credit means an entry made on the right side of an account.**

Debits and Credits Applied to Transactions

Recall the first transaction recorded by Glengarry Health Club earlier in the chapter: the owners invested $100,000 cash in the business. The transaction resulted in an increase in the Cash account and an increase in the Capital Stock account. Applying the rules of debits and credits, we would *debit* the Cash account for $100,000 and *credit* the Capital Stock account for the same amount:[6]

Cash	Capital Stock
100,000	100,000

You now can see why we refer to the **double-entry system** of accounting. Every transaction is recorded so that the equality of debits and credits is maintained, and in the process, the accounting equation is kept in balance. **Every transaction is entered in at least two accounts on opposite sides of T accounts. Our first transaction resulted in an increase in an asset account and an increase in a stockholders' equity account. For every transaction, the debit side must equal the credit side. The debit of $100,000 to the Cash account equals the credit of $100,000 to the Capital Stock account.** It naturally follows that if the debit side must equal the credit side for every transaction, at any point in time the total of all debits recorded must equal the total of all credits recorded. Thus, the fundamental accounting equation remains in balance.

Double-entry system
A system of accounting in which every transaction is recorded with equal debits and credits and the accounting equation is kept in balance.

Transactions for Glengarry Health Club

Three distinct steps are involved in recording a transaction in the accounts.

1. *Analyze* **the transaction.** That is, decide what accounts are increased or decreased and by how much.
2. *Recall* **the rules of debits and credits** as they apply to the transaction being analyzed.
3. *Record* **the transaction** using the rules of debits and credits.

---

6 We will use the numbers of each transaction, as they were labeled earlier in the chapter, to identify the transactions. In practice, a formal ledger account is used, and transactions are entered according to their date.

We have already explained the logic for the debit to the Cash account and the credit to the Capital Stock account for the initial investment by the health club owners. We now analyze the remaining eight transactions for the month. Refer to Exhibit 3-1 for a summary of the transactions.

(2) *Acquisition of property in exchange for a note.* **A building and land are exchanged for a promissory note.**

Analyze: **Two asset accounts are increased: Building and Land. The liability account Notes Payable is also increased.**

Recall: **An asset is increased with a debit, and a liability is increased with a credit.**

Record:

Building	Notes Payable
(2) 150,000	200,000 (2)

Land
(2) 50,000

(3) *Acquisition of equipment on an open account.* **Exercise equipment is purchased from a supplier on open account. The purchase price is $20,000.**

Analyze: **An asset account, Equipment, is increased. A liability account, Accounts Payable, is also increased. Thus, the transaction is identical to the last transaction in that an asset or assets are increased and a liability is increased.**

Recall: **An asset is increased with a debit, and a liability is increased with a credit.**

Record:

Equipment	Accounts Payable
(3) 20,000	20,000 (3)

(4) *Sale of monthly memberships on account.* **Three hundred club memberships are sold for $50 each. The members have until the 10th of the following month to pay.**

Analyze: **The asset account Accounts Receivable is increased by $15,000. This amount is an asset because the company has the right to collect it in the future. The owners' claim to the assets is increased by the same amount. Recall, however, that we do not record these claims—revenues—directly in an owners' equity account but instead use a separate revenue account. We will call the account Membership Revenue.**

Recall: **An asset is increased with a debit. Stockholders' equity is increased with a credit. Because revenue is an increase in stockholders' equity, it is increased with a credit.**

Record:

Accounts Receivable	Membership Revenue
(4) 15,000	15,000 (4)

(5) *Sale of court time for cash.* Court fees are paid at the time of use and amount to $5,000 for the first month.

Analyze: The asset account Cash is increased by $5,000. The owners' claim to the assets is increased by the same amount. The account used to record the increase in the owners' claim is Court Fee Revenue.

Recall: An asset is increased with a debit. Stockholders' equity is increased with a credit. Because revenue is an increase in stockholders' equity, it is increased with a credit.

Record:

Cash		Court Fee Revenue	
(1) 100,000			5,000 (5)
(5) 5,000			

(6) *Payment of wages and salaries.* Wages and salaries amount to $10,000, and they are paid in cash.

Analyze: The asset account, Cash, is decreased by $10,000. At the same time, the owners' claim to the assets is decreased by this amount. However, rather than record a decrease directly to Retained Earnings, we set up an expense account, Wage and Salary Expense.

Recall: An asset is decreased with a credit. Stockholders' equity is decreased with a debit. Because expense is a decrease in stockholders' equity, it is increased with a debit.

Record:

Cash		Wage and Salary Expense	
(1) 100,000	10,000 (6)	(6) 10,000	
(5) 5,000			

(7) *Payment of utilities.* The utility bill of $3,000 for the first month is paid in cash.

Analyze: The asset account Cash is decreased by $3,000. At the same time, the owners' claim to the assets is decreased by this amount. However, rather than record a decrease directly to Retained Earnings, we set up an expense account, Utilities Expense.

Recall: An asset is decreased with a credit. Stockholders' equity is decreased with a debit. Because expense is a decrease in stockholders' equity, it is increased with a debit.

Record:

Cash		Utilities Expense	
(1) 100,000	10,000 (6)	(7) 3,000	
(5) 5,000	3,000 (7)		

(8) *Collection of accounts receivable.* Cash of $4,000 is collected from members for their January dues.

Analyze: Cash is increased by the amount collected from the members. Another asset, Accounts Receivable, is decreased by the same amount. Glengarry has simply traded one asset for another.

Recall: **An asset is increased with a debit and decreased with a credit. Thus, one asset is debited, and another is credited.**

Record:

Cash		Accounts Receivable	
(1) 100,000	10,000 (6)	(4) 15,000	**4,000 (8)**
(5) 5,000	3,000 (7)		
(8) 4,000			

(9) *Payment of dividends.* **Dividends of $2,000 are distributed to the owners.**

Analyze: **The asset account Cash is decreased by $2,000. At the same time, the owners' claim to the assets is decreased by this amount. Earlier in the chapter, we decreased Retained Earnings for dividends paid to the owners. Now we will use a separate account, Dividends, to record these distributions.**

Recall: **An asset is decreased with a credit. Retained earnings is decreased with a debit. Because dividends are a decrease in retained earnings, they are increased with a debit.**

Record:

Cash		Dividends	
(1) 100,000	10,000 (6)	**(9) 2,000**	
(5) 5,000	3,000 (7)		
(8) 4,000	**2,000 (9)**		

⏱ *2 minute review*

1. Assume Glengarry pays the supplier the amount owed on open account. Record this transaction in the appropriate T accounts.

2. Assume Glengarry collects the remaining amount owed by members for dues. Record this transaction in the appropriate T accounts.

Answers

1.

Cash		Accounts Payable	
	20,000	20,000	

2.

Cash		Accounts Receivable	
11,000			11,000

The Journal: The Firm's Chronological Record of Transactions

LO6 Explain the purposes of a journal and the posting process.

Each of the nine transactions was entered directly in the ledger accounts. By looking at the Cash account, we see that it increased by $5,000 in transaction (5). But what was the other side of this transaction? That is, what account was credited? To have a record of *each entry,* transactions are recorded first in a journal. A **journal** is a chronological record of transactions entered into by a business. Because a journal lists transactions in the order in which they took place, it is called the *book of original entry.* Transactions are recorded first in a journal and then are posted to the ledger accounts. **Posting** is the process of transferring a journal entry to the ledger accounts:

Transactions are
entered in

| The Journal | and then posted to → | **Ledger Accounts**
Cash
Land
Other accounts |

Journal
A chronological record of transactions. *Alternate* **term:** *Book of original entry.*

Posting
The process of transferring amounts from a journal to the ledger accounts.

Note that posting does not result in any change in the amounts recorded. It is simply a process of resorting the transactions from a chronological order to a topical arrangement.

A journal entry is recorded for each transaction. **Journalizing** is the process of recording entries in a journal. A standard format is normally used for recording journal entries. Consider the original investment (see Transaction 1, Issuance of capital stock, on page 108) by the owners of Glengarry Health Club. The format of the journal entry is as follows:

Journalizing
The act of recording journal entries.

		Debit	Credit
Jan. xx	Cash	100,000	
	Capital Stock		100,000
	To record the issuance of 10,000 shares of stock for cash.		

Each journal entry contains a date with columns for the amounts debited and credited. Accounts credited are indented to distinguish them from accounts debited. A brief explanation normally appears on the line below the entry.

Transactions are normally recorded in a **general journal.** Specialized journals may be used to record repetitive transactions. For example, a cash receipts journal may be used to record all transactions in which cash is received. Special journals accomplish the same purpose as a general journal, but they save time in recording similar transactions. In this chapter, we will use a general journal to record all transactions.

General journal
The journal used in place of a specialized journal.

An excerpt from Glengarry Health Club's general journal appears in the top portion of Exhibit 3-7. One column needs further explanation. *Post. Ref.* is an abbreviation for *Posting Reference.* As part of the posting process explained below, the debit and credit amounts are posted to the appropriate accounts, and this column is filled in with the number assigned to the account.

Journal entries and ledger accounts are both *tools* used by the accountant. The end result, a set of financial statements, is the most important part of the process. Journalizing provides us with a chronological record of each transaction. So why not just prepare financial statements directly from the journal entries? Isn't it just extra work to *post* the entries to the ledger accounts? In our simple example of Glengarry Health Club, it would be possible to prepare the statements directly from the journal entries. In real-world situations, however, the number of transactions in any given period is so large that it would be virtually impossible, if not terribly inefficient, to bypass the accounts. Accounts provide us with a convenient summary of the activity, as well as the balance, for a specific financial statement item.

The posting process for Glengarry Health Club is illustrated in Exhibit 3-7 for the health club's fifth transaction, in which cash is collected for court fees. Rather than a T-account format for the general ledger accounts, the *running balance form* is illustrated. A separate column indicates the balance in the ledger account after each transaction. The use of the explanation column in a ledger account is optional. Because an explanation of the entry in the account can be found by referring to the journal, this column is often left blank.

EXHIBIT 3-7 **Posting from the Journal to the Ledger**

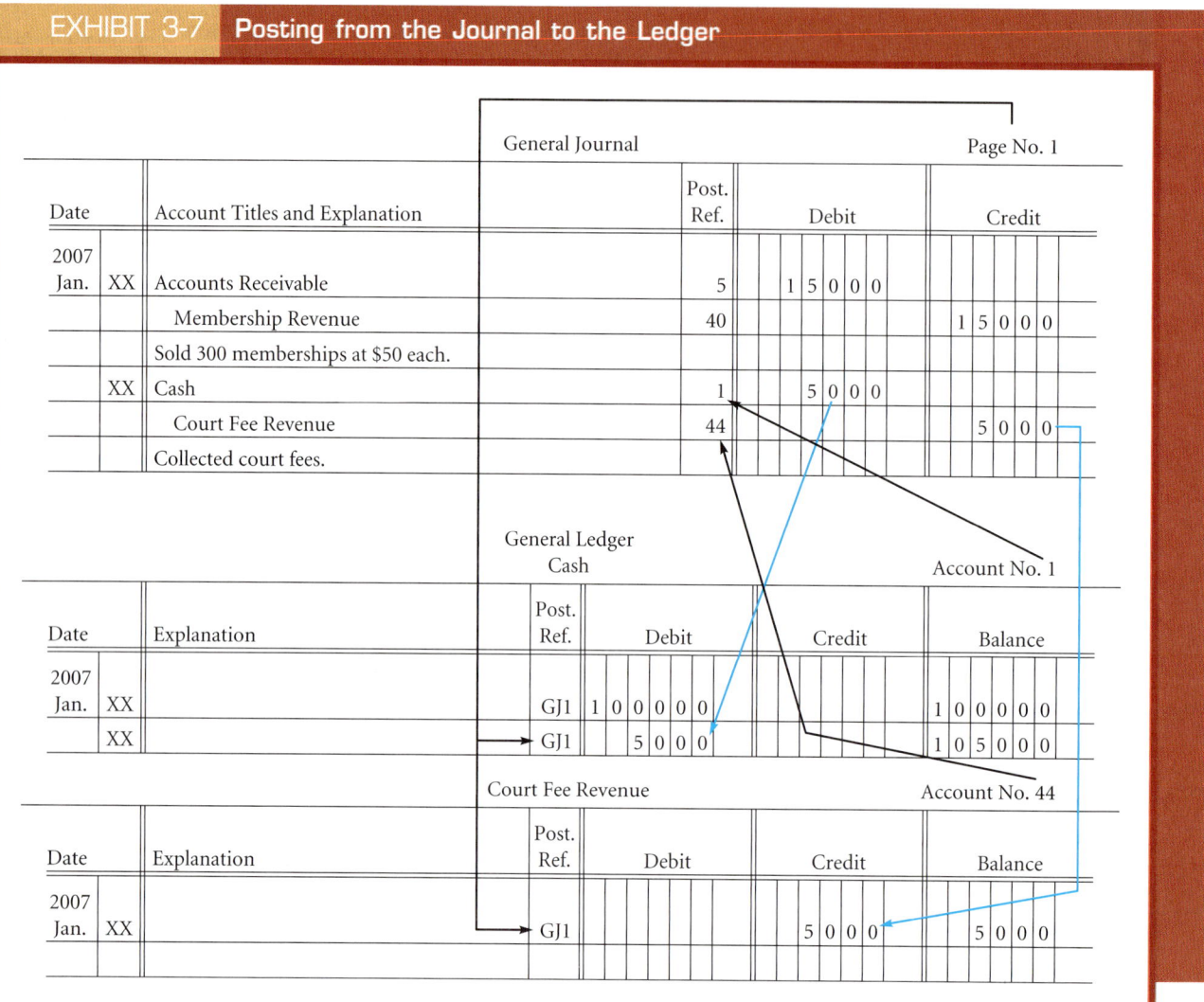

Note the cross-referencing between the journal and the ledger. As amounts are entered in the ledger accounts, the Posting Reference column is filled in with the page number of the journal. (For example, GJ1 indicates page 1 from the general journal.) At the same time, the Posting Reference column of the journal is filled in with the appropriate account number.

The frequency of posting differs among companies, partly based on the degree to which their accounting system is automated. For example, in some computerized systems, amounts are posted to the ledger accounts at the time an entry is recorded in the journal. In a manual system, posting is normally done periodically; for example, daily, weekly, or monthly. Regardless of when performed, the posting process changes nothing. It simply reorganizes the transactions by account.

The Trial Balance

LO7 Explain the purpose of a trial balance.

Accountants use one other tool to facilitate the preparation of a set of financial statements. A **trial balance** is a list of each account and its balance at a specific point in time. The trial balance is *not* a financial statement but merely a convenient device to prove the equality of the debit and credit balances in the accounts. It can be as informal as an adding-machine tape with the account titles penciled in next to the debit and credit amounts. A trial balance for Glengarry Health Club as of January 31, 2007, is shown in Exhibit 3-8. The balance in each account was

EXHIBIT 3-8 Trial Balance for Glengarry Health Club

Glengarry Health Club
Trial Balance
January 31, 2007

Account Titles	Debits	Credits
Cash	$ 94,000	
Accounts Receivable	11,000	
Equipment	20,000	
Building	150,000	
Land	50,000	
Accounts Payable		$ 20,000
Notes Payable		200,000
Capital Stock		100,000
Membership Revenue		15,000
Court Fee Revenue		5,000
Wage and Salary Expense	10,000	
Utilities Expense	3,000	
Dividends	2,000	
Totals	$340,000	$340,000

determined by adding the increases and subtracting the decreases for the account for the transactions detailed earlier.

Certain types of errors are detectable from a trial balance. For example, if the balance of an account is incorrectly computed, the total of the debits and credits in the trial balance will not equal. If a debit is posted to an account as a credit, or vice versa, the trial balance will be out of balance. The omission of part of a journal entry in the posting process will also be detected by the preparation of a trial balance.

Do not attribute more significance to a trial balance, however, than is warranted. It does provide a convenient summary of account balances for preparing financial statements. It also assures us that the balances of all the debit accounts equal the balances of all the credit accounts. But an equality of debits and credits does not necessarily mean that the *correct* accounts were debited and credited in an entry. For example, the entry to record the purchase of land by signing a promissory note *should* result in a debit to Land and a credit to Notes Payable. If the accountant incorrectly debited Cash instead of Land, the trial balance would still show an equality of debits and credits. A trial balance can be prepared at any time; it is usually prepared before the release of a set of financial statements.

Trial balance
A list of each account and its balance; used to prove equality of debits and credits.

Study Tip Remember from p. 118 that every account has a normal balance, either debit or credit. Note the normal balances for each account on this trial balance.

STUDY HIGHLIGHTS

Explain the difference between an external and an internal event (p. 106).

LO1

- Both of these different types of events affect an entity and are usually recorded in the accounting system as a transaction.
  - External events are interactions between an entity and its environment.
  - Internal events are interactions entirely within an entity.

Explain the role of source documents in an accounting system (p. 107).

LO2

- Source documents provide the evidence needed to begin the procedures for recording and processing a transaction.
- These documents need not be in hard copy form and can come from parties both internal and external to the company.

(continued)

LO3 **Analyze the effects of transactions on the accounting equation (p. 107).**

- The accounting equation illustrates the relationship between assets, liabilities, and stockholders' equity accounts. Understanding these relationships helps to see the logic behind the double-entry system in recording transactions.
  - The accounting equation: Assets = Liabilities + Stockholders' Equity
  - This equality must always be maintained. The equation can be expanded to show the linkage between the balance sheet and the income statement through the Retained Earnings account:

$$\text{Assets} = \text{Liabilities} + \text{Capital Stock} + \text{Retained Earnings}$$

LO4 **Describe the use of the account and the general ledger to accumulate amounts of financial statement items (p. 113).**

- The general ledger is a crucial part of the accounting system that lists all accounts and their balances. Financial statements may be prepared from current account balances in the general ledger.
- T accounts are a convenient way to analyze the activity in any particular account. The left side of a T account represents debits made to an account, and the right represents credits made to an account.

LO5 **Explain the rules of debits and credits (Appendix p. 117).**

- Debits and credits represent the left and right-hand side of a T account, respectively. They only take on meaning when associated with the recording of transactions involving asset, liability, and equity accounts.
  - In general, debits increase asset accounts, and credits increase liability and equity accounts.
  - The double-entry system requires that total debits equal total credits for any transaction recorded in the accounting system.

LO6 **Explain the purposes of a journal and the posting process (Appendix p. 122).**

- A journal documents the details of transactions by date. Entries are made to a journal every time a transaction occurs.
  - Similar transactions that occur regularly may be recorded in special journals.
- Ultimately, information is posted from the journal to the ledgers for each individual account.

LO7 **Explain the purpose of a trial balance (Appendix p. 124).**

- At the end of a period, a trial balance may be prepared that lists all the accounts in the general ledger along with their debit or credit balances.
- The purpose of the trial balance is to see whether total debits equals total credits. This provides some assurance that the accounting equation was adhered to in the processing of transactions but is no guarantee that transactions have been recorded properly.

KEY TERMS QUIZ

Note: A separate quiz is available for the terms in the appendix to this chapter.

Read each definition below, and then write the number of the definition in the blank beside the appropriate term it defines. The quiz solutions appear at the end of the chapter.

Quiz 1: Processing Accounting Information

_____ Event	_____ Source document
_____ External event	_____ Account
_____ Internal event	_____ Chart of accounts
_____ Transaction	_____ General ledger

REVIEW

1. A numerical list of all the accounts used by a company.
2. A happening of consequence to an entity.
3. An event occurring entirely within an entity.
4. A piece of paper, such as a sales invoice, that is used as the evidence to record a transaction.
5. An event involving interaction between an entity and its environment.
6. The record used to accumulate monetary amounts for each individual asset, liability, revenue, expense, and component of owners' equity.
7. A book, file, hard drive, or other device containing all of a company's accounts.
8. Any event, external or internal, that is recognized in a set of financial statements.

Quiz 2: Appendix

_____	Debit	_____	Posting
_____	Credit	_____	Journalizing
_____	Double-entry system	_____	General journal
_____	Journal	_____	Trial balance

1. A list of each account and its balance at a specific point in time; used to prove the equality of debits and credits.
2. An entry on the right side of an account.
3. The act of recording journal entries.
4. An entry on the left side of an account.
5. The process of transferring amounts from a journal to the appropriate ledger accounts.
6. A chronological record of transactions, also known as the *book of original entry*.
7. The journal used in place of a specialized journal.
8. A system of accounting in which every transaction is recorded with equal debits and credits and the accounting equation is kept in balance.

ALTERNATE TERMS

Credit side of an account Right side of an account

Debit an account Charge an account

Debit side of an account Left side of an account

General ledger Set of accounts

Journal Book of original entry

Journalize an entry Record an entry

Posting an account Transferring an amount from the journal to the ledger

WARMUP EXERCISES & SOLUTIONS

Warmup Exercise 3-1 Your Accounting Equation   **LO3**

Assume that you borrow $1,000 from your roommate by signing an agreement to repay the amount borrowed in six months.

Required
What is the effect of this transaction on your own accounting equation?

Key to the Solution Recall Exhibit 3-1 for the effects of transactions on the accounting equation.

Warmup Exercise 3-2 A Bank's Accounting Equation   **LO3**

The Third State Bank loans a customer $5,000 in exchange for a promissory note.

Required
What is the effect of this transaction on the bank's accounting equation?

Key to the Solution Recall Exhibit 3-1 for the effects of the transaction on the accounting equation.

REVIEW

LO3 **Warmup Exercise 3-3** Accounting Equation for Foot Locker

Assume that Foot Locker goes to its bank and borrows $50,000 by signing a promissory note. The next day the company uses the money to buy a new computer system for its offices.

Required

What is the effect of each of these two transactions on Foot Locker's accounting equation?

Key to the Solution Recall Exhibit 3-1 for the effects of transactions on the accounting equation.

SOLUTIONS TO WARMUP EXERCISES

Warmup Exercise 3-1

If you borrow $1,000 from your roommate, assets in the form of cash increase $1,000 and liabilities in the form of a note payable increase $1,000.

Warmup Exercise 3-2

If a bank loans a customer $5,000 the bank's assets in the form of a note receivable increase $5,000 and its assets in the form of cash decrease $5,000.

Warmup Exercise 3-3

If Foot Locker borrows $50,000 from its bank, assets in the form of cash increase $50,000 and liabilities in the form of a note payable increase $50,000. If the company uses the money to buy a new computer, assets in the form of equipment increase $50,000 and assets in the form of cash decrease $50,000.

REVIEW PROBLEM & SOLUTION

The following transactions are entered into by Sparkle Car Wash during its first month of operations:

a. Articles of incorporation are filed with the state, and 20,000 shares of capital stock are issued. Cash of $40,000 is received from the new owners for the shares.
b. A five-year promissory note is signed at the local bank. The cash received from the loan is $120,000.
c. An existing car wash is purchased for $150,000 in cash. The values assigned to the land, building, and equipment are $25,000, $75,000, and $50,000, respectively.
d. Cleaning supplies are purchased on account for $2,500 from a distributor. All of the supplies are used in the first month.
e. During the first month, $1,500 is paid to the distributor for the cleaning supplies. The remaining $1,000 will be paid next month.
f. Gross receipts from car washes during the first month of operations amount to $7,000.
g. Wages and salaries paid in the first month amount to $2,000.
h. The utility bill of $800 for the month is paid.
i. A total of $1,000 in dividends is paid to the owners.

Required

1. Prepare a table to summarize the preceding transactions as they affect the accounting equation. Use the format in Exhibit 3-1. Identify each transaction by letter.
2. Prepare an income statement for the month.
3. Prepare a balance sheet at the end of the month.

REVIEW

SOLUTION TO REVIEW PROBLEM

1.

Sparkle Car Wash
Transactions for the Month

	Assets				=	Liabilities		+	Stockholders' Equity		+ Revenues − Expenses
TRANS.	CASH	LAND	BUILDING	EQUIPMENT		ACCOUNTS PAYABLE	NOTES PAYABLE		CAPITAL STOCK	RETAINED EARNINGS	
a.	$ 40,000								$40,000		
b.	120,000						$120,000				
Bal.	$160,000						$120,000		$40,000		
c.	−150,000	$25,000	$75,000	$50,000							
Bal.	$ 10,000	$25,000	$75,000	$50,000			$120,000		$40,000		
d.						$2,500					$−2,500
Bal.	$ 10,000	$25,000	$75,000	$50,000		$2,500	$120,000		$40,000		$−2,500
e.	−1,500					−1,500					
Bal.	$ 8,500	$25,000	$75,000	$50,000		$1,000	$120,000		$40,000		$−2,500
f.	7,000										7,000
Bal.	$ 15,500	$25,000	$75,000	$50,000		$1,000	$120,000		$40,000		$ 4,500
g.	−2,000										−2,000
Bal.	$ 13,500	$25,000	$75,000	$50,000		$1,000	$120,000		$40,000		$ 2,500
h.	−800										− 800
Bal.	$ 12,700	$25,000	$75,000	$50,000		$1,000	$120,000		$40,000		$ 1,700
i.	−1,000									−1,000	
Bal.	$ 11,700	$25,000	$75,000	$50,000		$1,000	$120,000		$40,000	$−1,000	$ 1,700

Total assets: $161,700

Total liabilities and stockholders' equity: $161,700

2.

Sparkle Car Wash
Income Statement
For the Month Ended XX/XX/XX

Car wash revenue		$7,000
Expenses:		
Supplies	$2,500	
Wages and salaries	2,000	
Utilities	800	5,300
Net income		$1,700

3.

Sparkle Car Wash
Balance Sheet
XX/XX/XX

Assets		Liabilities and Stockholders' Equity	
Cash	$ 11,700	Accounts payable	$ 1,000
Land	25,000	Notes payable	120,000
Building	75,000	Capital stock	40,000
Equipment	50,000	Retained earnings	700
		Total liabilities and	
Total assets	$161,700	stockholders' equity	$161,700

REVIEW

QUESTIONS

1. What are the two types of events that affect an entity? Describe each.

2. What is the significance of source documents to the recording process? Give two examples of source documents.

3. What are four different forms of cash?

4. How does an account receivable differ from a note receivable?

5. What is meant by the statement "One company's account receivable is another company's account payable"?

6. Stockholders' equity represents the claim of the owners on the assets of the business. What is the distinction relative to the owners' claim between the Capital Stock account and the Retained Earnings account?

7. What do accountants mean when they refer to the "double-entry system" of accounting? (Appendix)

8. If an asset account is increased with a debit, what is the logic for increasing a liability account with a credit? (Appendix)

9. A friend comes to you with the following plight: "I'm confused. An asset is something positive, and it is increased with a debit. However, an expense is something negative, and it is also increased with a debit. I don't get it." How can you straighten your friend out? (Appendix)

10. The payment of dividends reduces cash. If the Cash account is reduced with a credit, why is the Dividends account debited when dividends are paid? (Appendix)

11. If Cash is increased with a debit, why does the bank credit your account when you make a deposit? (Appendix)

12. Your friend presents the following criticism of the accounting system: "Accounting involves so much duplication of effort. First, entries are recorded in a journal, and then the same information is recorded in a ledger. No wonder accountants work such long hours!" Do you agree with this criticism? (Appendix)

13. How does the T account differ from the running balance form for an account? How are they similar? (Appendix)

14. What is the benefit of using a cross-referencing system between a ledger and a journal? (Appendix)

15. How often should a company post entries from the journal to the ledger? (Appendix)

16. What is the purpose of a trial balance? (Appendix)

EXERCISES

LO1

Exercise 3-1 Types of Events

For each of the following events, identify whether it is an external event that would be recorded as a transaction (E), an internal event that would be recorded as a transaction (I), or not recorded (NR):

_____ 1. A supplier of a company's inventory is paid an amount owed on account.

_____ 2. A customer pays its open account.

_____ 3. A new chief executive officer is hired.

_____ 4. The biweekly payroll is paid.

_____ 5. Depreciation on equipment is recognized.

_____ 6. A new advertising agency is hired to develop a series of newspaper ads for the company.

_____ 7. The advertising bill for the first month is paid.

_____ 8. The accountant determines the federal income taxes owed based on the income earned during the period.

LO2

Exercise 3-2 Source Documents Matched with Transactions

Following are a list of source documents and a list of transactions. Indicate by letter next to each transaction the source document that would serve as evidence for the recording of the transaction.

Source Documents

a. Purchase invoice

b. Sales invoice

c. Cash register tape

Transactions

_____ 1. Utilities expense for the month is recorded.

_____ 2. A cash settlement is received from a pending lawsuit.

d. Time cards   _____ 3. Owners contribute cash to start a new corporation.

e. Promissory note

f. Stock certificates   _____ 4. The biweekly payroll is paid.

     _____ 5. Cash sales for the day are recorded.

g. Monthly statement from utility company

h. No standard source document would normally be available   _____ 6. Equipment is acquired on a 30-day open account.

     _____ 7. A sale is made on an open account.

     _____ 8. A building is acquired by signing an agreement to repay a stated amount plus interest in six months.

LO3   **Exercise 3-3** The Effect of Transactions on the Accounting Equation

For each of the following transactions, indicate whether it increases (I), decreases (D), or has no effect (NE) on the total dollar amount of each of the elements of the accounting equation.

Transactions	Assets	= Liabilities +	Stockholders' Equity
Example: Common stock is issued in exchange for cash.	I	NE	I

1. Equipment is purchased for cash.
2. Sales are made on account.
3. Cash sales are made.
4. An account payable is paid off.
5. Cash is collected on an account receivable.
6. Buildings are purchased in exchange for a three-year note payable.
7. Advertising bill for the month is paid.
8. Dividends are paid to stockholders.
9. Land is acquired by issuing shares of stock to the owner of the land.

LO3   **Exercise 3-4** Types of Transactions

There are three elements to the accounting equation: assets, liabilities, and stockholders' equity. Although other possibilities exist, five types of transactions are described here. For *each* of these five types, write out descriptions of at least *two* transactions that illustrate these types of transactions.

Type of Transaction	Assets	= Liabilities +	Stockholders' Equity
1.	Increase	Increase	
2.	Increase		Increase
3.	Decrease	Decrease	
4.	Decrease		Decrease
5.	Increase Decrease		

LO3   **Exercise 3-5** Analyzing Transactions

Prepare a table to summarize the following transactions as they affect the accounting equation. Use the format in Exhibit 3-1.

1. Sales on account of $1,530.
2. Purchases of supplies on account for $1,365.
3. Cash sales of $750.
4. Purchase of equipment for cash of $4,240.
5. Issuance of a promissory note for $2,500.
6. Collections on account for $890.
7. Sale of capital stock in exchange for a parcel of land. The land is appraised at $50,000.
8. Payment of $4,000 in salaries and wages.
9. Payment of open account in the amount of $500.

HOMEWORK

LO4 **Exercise 3-6** Balance Sheet Accounts and Their Use

Choose from the following list of account titles the one that most accurately fits the description of that account or is an example of that account. An account title may be used more than once or not at all.

Cash	Accounts Receivable	Notes Receivable
Prepaid Asset	Land	Buildings
Investments	Accounts Payable	Notes Payable
Taxes Payable	Retained Earnings	Common Stock
Preferred Stock		

_____ 1. A written obligation to repay a fixed amount, with interest, at some time in the future

_____ 2. Twenty acres of land held for speculation

_____ 3. An amount owed by a customer

_____ 4. Corporate income taxes owed to the federal government

_____ 5. Ownership in a company that allows the owner to receive dividends before common shareholders receive any distributions

_____ 6. Five acres of land used as the site for a factory

_____ 7. Amounts owed on an open account to a supplier of inventory, due in 90 days

_____ 8. A checking account at the bank

_____ 9. A warehouse used to store equipment

_____ 10. Claims by the owners on the undistributed net income of a business

_____ 11. Rent paid on an office building in advance of use of the facility

LO5 **Exercise 3-7** Normal Account Balances (Appendix)

Each account has a normal balance. For the following list of accounts, indicate whether the normal balance of each is a debit or a credit.

Account	Normal Balance
1. Cash	_____
2. Prepaid Insurance	_____
3. Retained Earnings	_____
4. Bonds Payable	_____
5. Investments	_____
6. Capital Stock	_____
7. Advertising Fees Earned	_____
8. Wages and Salaries Expense	_____
9. Wages and Salaries Payable	_____
10. Office Supplies	_____
11. Dividends	_____

LO5 **Exercise 3-8** Debits and Credits (Appendix)

The new bookkeeper for Darby Corporation is getting ready to mail the daily cash receipts to the bank for deposit. Because his previous job was at a bank, he is aware that the bank "credits" your account for all deposits and "debits" your account for all checks written. Therefore, he makes the following entry before sending the daily receipts to the bank:

June 5	Accounts Receivable	10,000	
	Sales Revenue	2,450	
	Cash		12,450
	To record cash received on June 5: $10,000 collections on account and $2,450 in cash sales.		

Required

Explain why this entry is wrong, and prepare the correct journal entry. Why does the bank refer to cash received from a customer as a *credit* to that customer's account?

LO7 **Exercise 3-9** Trial Balance (Appendix)

The following list of accounts was taken from the general ledger of Spencer Corporation on December 31, 2007. The bookkeeper thought it would be helpful if the accounts were arranged in alphabetical order. Each account contains the balance normal for that type of account (for example, Cash normally has a debit balance). Prepare a trial balance as of this date, with the accounts arranged in the following order: (1) assets, (2) liabilities, (3) stockholders' equity, (4) revenues, (5) expenses, and (6) dividends.

Account	Balance
Accounts Payable	$ 7,650
Accounts Receivable	5,325
Automobiles	9,200
Buildings	150,000
Capital Stock	100,000
Cash	10,500
Commissions Expense	2,600
Commissions Revenue	12,750
Dividends	2,000
Equipment	85,000
Heat, Light, and Water Expense	1,400
Income Tax Expense	1,700
Income Taxes Payable	2,500
Interest Revenue	1,300
Land	50,000
Notes Payable	90,000
Office Salaries Expense	6,000
Office Supplies	500
Retained Earnings	110,025

MULTI-CONCEPT EXERCISES

LO3,4 **Exercise 3-10** Determining an Ending Account Balance

Jessie's Bead Shop was organized on June 1, 2007. The company received a contribution of $1,000 from each of the two principal owners. During the month, Jessie's Bead Shop had cash sales of $1,400, had sales on account of $450, received $250 from customers in payment of their accounts, purchased supplies on account for $600 and equipment on account for $1,350, received a utility bill for $250 which will not be paid until July, and paid the full amount due on the equipment. Determine the company's cash balance on June 30, 2007.

LO3,4 **Exercise 3-11** Reconstructing a Beginning Account Balance

During the month, services performed for customers on account amounted to $7,500, and collections from customers in payment of their accounts totaled $6,000. At the end of the month, the Accounts Receivable account had a balance of $2,500. What was the Accounts Receivable balance at the beginning of the month?

LO3,4,5 **Exercise 3-12** Journal Entries Recorded Directly in T Accounts (Appendix)

Record each transaction shown below directly in T accounts, using the numbers preceding the transactions to identify them in the accounts. Each account involved needs a separate T account.

1. Received contribution of $6,500 from each of the three principal owners of the We-Go Delivery Service in exchange for shares of stock.
2. Purchased office supplies for cash of $130.

3. Purchased a van for $15,000 on an open account. The company has 25 days to pay for the van.
4. Provided delivery services to residential customers for cash of $125.
5. Billed a local business $200 for delivery services. The customer is to pay the bill within 15 days.
6. Paid the amount due on the van.
7. Received the amount due from the local business billed in transaction (5) above.

LO4,7   **Exercise 3-13** Trial Balance (Appendix)

Refer to the transactions recorded directly in T accounts for the We-Go Delivery Service in Exercise 3-12. Assume that the transactions all took place during December 2007. Prepare a trial balance at December 31, 2007.

LO3,5,6   **Exercise 3-14** Journal Entries (Appendix)

Prepare the journal entry to record each of the following independent transactions (use the number of the transaction in lieu of a date for identification purposes):

1. Sales on account of $1,530
2. Purchases of supplies on account for $1,365
3. Cash sales of $750
4. Purchase of equipment for cash of $4,240
5. Issuance of a promissory note for $2,500
6. Collections on account for $890
7. Sale of capital stock in exchange for a parcel of land; the land is appraised at $50,000
8. Payment of $4,000 in salaries and wages
9. Payment of open account in the amount of $500

LO3,5,6   **Exercise 3-15** Journal Entries (Appendix)

Following is a list of transactions entered into during the first month of operations of Gardener Corporation, a new landscape service. Prepare in journal form the entry to record each transaction.

April 1: Articles of incorporation are filed with the state, and 100,000 shares of common stock are issued for $100,000 in cash.
April 4: A six-month promissory note is signed at the bank. Interest at 9% per annum will be repaid in six months along with the principal amount of the loan of $50,000.
April 8: Land and a storage shed are acquired for a lump sum of $80,000. On the basis of an appraisal, 25% of the value is assigned to the land and the remainder to the building.
April 10: Mowing equipment is purchased from a supplier at a total cost of $25,000. A down payment of $10,000 is made, with the remainder due by the end of the month.
April 18: Customers are billed for services provided during the first half of the month. The total amount billed of $5,500 is due within 10 days.
April 27: The remaining balance due on the mowing equipment is paid to the supplier.
April 28: The total amount of $5,500 due from customers is received.
April 30: Customers are billed for services provided during the second half of the month. The total amount billed is $9,850.
April 30: Salaries and wages of $4,650 for the month of April are paid.

LO5,6   **Exercise 3-16** The Process of Posting Journal Entries to General Ledger Accounts (Appendix)

On June 1, Campbell Corporation purchased 10 acres of land in exchange for a promissory note in the amount of $50,000. Using the formats shown in Exhibit 3-7, prepare the journal entry to record this transaction in a general journal, and post it to the appropriate general ledger accounts. The entry will be recorded on page 7 of the general journal. Use whatever account numbers you would like in the general ledger. Assume that none of the accounts to be debited or credited currently contain a balance.

If at a later date you wanted to review this transaction, would you examine the general ledger or the general journal? Explain your answer.

PROBLEMS

LO1   **Problem 3-1** Events to Be Recorded in Accounts

The following events take place at Dillon's Drive-In:

1. Food is ordered from vendors who will deliver the food within the week.
2. Vendors deliver food on account, payment due in 30 days.
3. Employees take frozen food from the freezers and prepare it for customers.
4. Food is served to customers, and sales are rung up on the cash register; sales will be totaled at the end of the day.
5. Trash is taken to dumpsters, and the floors are cleaned.
6. Cash registers are cleared at the end of the day.
7. Cash is deposited in the bank night depository.
8. Employees are paid weekly paychecks.
9. Vendors noted in item (2) are paid for the food delivered.

Required

Identify each event as internal (I) or external (E), and indicate whether or not each event would be recorded in the *accounts* of the company. For each event that is to be recorded, identify the names of at least two accounts that would be affected.

LO3   **Problem 3-2** Transaction Analysis and Financial Statements

Just Rolling Along Inc. was organized on May 1, 2007, by two college students who recognized an opportunity to make money while spending their days at a beach along Lake Michigan. The two entrepreneurs plan to rent bicycles and in-line skates to weekend visitors to the lakefront. The following transactions occurred during the first month of operations:

May 1: Received contribution of $9,000 from each of the two principal owners of the new business in exchange for shares of stock.

May 1: Purchased 10 bicycles for $300 each on an open account. The company has 30 days to pay for the bicycles.

May 5: Registered as a vendor with the city and paid the $15 monthly fee.

May 9: Purchased 20 pairs of in-line skates at $125 per pair, 20 helmets at $50 each, and 20 sets of protective gear (knee and elbow pads and wrist guards) at $45 per set for cash.

May 10: Purchased $100 in miscellaneous supplies on account. The company has 30 days to pay for the supplies.

May 15: Paid $125 bill from local radio station for advertising for the last two weeks of May.

May 17: Customers rented in-line skates and bicycles for cash of $1,800.

May 24: Billed the local park district $1,200 for in-line skating lessons provided to neighborhood kids. The park district is to pay one-half of the bill within five working days and the rest within 30 days.

May 29: Received 50% of the amount billed to the park district.

May 30: Customers rented in-line skates and bicycles for cash of $3,000.

May 30: Paid wages of $160 to a friend who helped out over the weekend.

May 31: Paid the balance due on the bicycles.

Required

1. Prepare a table to summarize the preceding transactions as they affect the accounting equation. Use the format in Exhibit 3-1. Identify each transaction with the date.
2. Prepare an income statement for the month ended May 31, 2007.
3. Prepare a classified balance sheet at May 31, 2007.
4. Why do you think the two college students decided to incorporate their business rather than operate it as a partnership?

HOMEWORK

Problem 3-3 Transaction Analysis and Financial Statements

Expert Consulting Services Inc. was organized on March 1, 2007, by two former college roommates. The corporation will provide computer consulting services to small businesses. The following transactions occurred during the first month of operations:

March 2: Received contributions of $20,000 from each of the two principal owners of the new business in exchange for shares of stock.

March 7: Signed a two-year promissory note at the bank and received cash of $15,000. Interest, along with the $15,000, will be repaid at the end of the two years.

March 12: Purchased $700 in miscellaneous supplies on account. The company has 30 days to pay for the supplies.

March 19: Billed a client $4,000 for services rendered by Expert in helping to install a new computer system. The client is to pay 25% of the bill upon its receipt and the remaining balance within 30 days.

March 20: Paid $1,300 bill from the local newspaper for advertising for the month of March.

March 22: Received 25% of the amount billed the client on March 19.

March 26: Received cash of $2,800 for services provided in assisting a client in selecting software for its computer.

March 29: Purchased a computer system for $8,000 in cash.

March 30: Paid $3,300 of salaries and wages for March.

March 31: Received and paid $1,400 in gas, electric, and water bills.

Required

1. Prepare a table to summarize the preceding transactions as they affect the accounting equation. Use the format in Exhibit 3-1. Identify each transaction with the date.
2. Prepare an income statement for the month ended March 31, 2007.
3. Prepare a classified balance sheet at March 31, 2007.
4. From reading the balance sheet you prepared in part (3), what events would you expect to take place in April? Explain your answer.

Problem 3-4 Transactions Reconstructed from Financial Statements

The following financial statements are available for Elm Corporation for its first month of operations:

Elm Corporation
Income Statement
For the Month Ended June 30, 2007

Service revenue		$93,600
Expenses:		
Rent	$ 9,000	
Salaries and wages	27,900	
Utilities	13,800	50,700
Net income		$42,900

Elm Corporation
Balance Sheet
June 30, 2007

Assets		Liabilities and Stockholders' Equity	
Cash	$ 22,800	Accounts payable	$ 18,000
Accounts receivable	21,600	Notes payable	90,000
Equipment	18,000	Capital stock	30,000
Building	90,000	Retained earnings	38,400
Land	24,000	Total liabilities and	
Total assets	$176,400	stockholders' equity	$176,400

Required

Using the format illustrated in Exhibit 3-1, prepare a table to summarize the transactions entered into by Elm Corporation during its first month of business. State any assumptions you believe are necessary in reconstructing the transactions.

MULTI-CONCEPT PROBLEMS

LO1,2 **Problem 3-5** Identification of Events with Source Documents

Many events are linked to a source document. The following is a list of events that occurred in an entity:

a. Paid a one-year insurance policy.
b. Paid employee payroll.
c. Sold merchandise to a customer on account.
d. Identified supplies in the storeroom destroyed by fire.
e. Received payment of bills from customers.
f. Purchased land for future expansion.
g. Calculated taxes due.
h. Entered into a car lease agreement and paid the tax, title, and license.

Required

For each item (a) through (h), indicate whether the event should or should not be recorded in the entity's accounts. For each item that should be recorded in the entity's books:

1. Identify one or more source documents that are generated from the event.
2. Identify which source document would be used to record an event when it produces more than one source document.
3. For each document, identify the information that is most useful in recording the event in the accounts.

LO1,3 **Problem 3-6** Transaction Analysis and Financial Statements

Blue Jay Delivery Service is incorporated on January 2, 2007, and enters into the following transactions during its first month of operations:

January 2: Filed articles of incorporation with the state, and issued 100,000 shares of capital stock. Cash of $100,000 is received from the new owners for the shares.
January 3: Purchased a warehouse and land for $80,000 in cash. An appraiser values the land at $20,000 and the warehouse at $60,000.
January 4: Signed a three-year promissory note at the Third State Bank in the amount of $50,000.
January 6: Purchased five new delivery trucks for a total of $45,000 in cash.
January 31: Performed services on account that amounted to $15,900 during the month. Cash amounting to $7,490 was received from customers on account during the month.
January 31: Established an open account at a local service station at the beginning of the month. Purchases of gas and oil during January amounted to $3,230. Blue Jay has until the 10th of the following month to pay its bill.

Required

1. Prepare a table to summarize the preceding transactions as they affect the accounting equation. Ignore depreciation expense and interest expense. Use the format in Exhibit 3-1.
2. Prepare an income statement for the month ended January 31, 2007.
3. Prepare a classified balance sheet at January 31, 2007.
4. Assume that you are considering buying stock in this company. Beginning with the transaction to record the purchase of the property on January 3, list any additional information that you would like to have about each of the transactions during the remainder of the month.

LO1,3 **Problem 3-7** Transaction Analysis and Financial Statements

Neveranerror Inc. was organized on June 2, 2007, by a group of accountants to provide accounting and tax services to small businesses. The following transactions occurred during the first month of business:

June 2: Received contributions of $10,000 from each of the three owners of the business in exchange for shares of stock.
June 5: Purchased a computer system for $12,000. The agreement with the vendor requires a down payment of $2,500 with the balance due in 60 days.

(continued)

June 8: Signed a two-year promissory note at the bank and received cash of $20,000.

June 15: Billed $12,350 to clients for the first half of June. Clients are billed twice a month for services performed during the month, and the bills are payable within 10 days.

June 17: Paid a $900 bill from the local newspaper for advertising for the month of June.

June 23: Received the amounts billed to clients for services performed during the first half of the month.

June 28: Received and paid gas, electric, and water bills. The total amount is $2,700.

June 29: Received the landlord's bill for $2,200 for rent on the office space that Neveran-error leases. The bill is payable by the 10th of the following month.

June 30: Paid salaries and wages for June. The total amount is $5,670.

June 30: Billed $18,400 to clients for the second half of June.

June 30: Declared and paid dividends in the amount of $6,000.

Required

1. Prepare a table to summarize the preceding transactions as they affect the accounting equation. Ignore depreciation expense and interest expense. Use the format in Exhibit 3-1.
2. Prepare the following financial statements:
   a. Income statement for the month ended June 30, 2007.
   b. Statement of retained earnings for the month ended June 30, 2007.
   c. Classified balance sheet at June 30, 2007.
3. Assume that you have just graduated from college and have been approached to join this company as an accountant. From your reading of the financial statements for the first month, would you consider joining the company? Explain your answer. Limit your answer to financial considerations only.

LO3,5   **Problem 3-8** Accounts Used to Record Transactions (Appendix)

A list of accounts, with an identifying number for each, is shown below. Following the list of accounts is a series of transactions entered into by a company during its first year of operations.

Required

For each transaction, indicate the account or accounts that should be debited and credited.

1. Cash	7. Accounts Payable	13. Wage and Salary Expense
2. Accounts Receivable	8. Income Tax Payable	14. Selling Expense
3. Office Supplies	9. Notes Payable	15. Utilities Expense
4. Buildings	10. Capital Stock	16. Income Tax Expense
5. Automobiles	11. Retained Earnings	
6. Land	12. Service Revenue	

	Accounts	
Transactions	**Debited**	**Credited**
Example: Purchased land and building in exchange for a three-year promissory note.	4, 6	9
a. Issued capital stock for cash.	_____	_____
b. Purchased 10 automobiles; paid part in cash and signed a 60-day note for the balance.	_____	_____
c. Purchased land in exchange for a note due in six months.	_____	_____
d. Purchased office supplies; agreed to pay total bill by the 10th of the following month.	_____	_____
e. Billed clients for services performed during the month, and gave them until the 15th of the following month to pay.	_____	_____
f. Received cash on account from clients for services rendered to them in past months.	_____	_____
g. Paid employees salaries and wages earned during the month.	_____	_____
h. Paid newspaper for company ads appearing during the month.	_____	_____
i. Received monthly gas and electric bill from the utility company; payment is due anytime within the first 10 days of the following month.	_____	_____
j. Computed amount of taxes due based on the income of the period; amount will be paid in the following month.	_____	_____

LO3,4,5 **Problem 3-9** Transaction Analysis and Journal Entries Recorded Directly in T Accounts (Appendix)

Four brothers organized Beverly Entertainment Enterprises on October 1, 2007. The following transactions occurred during the first month of operations:

October 1: Received contributions of $10,000 from each of the four principal owners of the new business in exchange for shares of stock.

October 2: Purchased the Arcada Theater for $125,000. The seller agreed to accept a down payment of $12,500 and a seven-year promissory note for the balance. The Arcada property consists of land valued at $35,000 and a building valued at $90,000.

October 3: Purchased new seats for the theater at a cost of $5,000, paying $2,500 down and agreeing to pay the remainder in 60 days.

October 12: Purchased candy, popcorn, cups, and napkins for $3,700 on an open account. The company has 30 days to pay for the concession supplies.

October 13: Sold tickets for the opening-night movie for cash of $1,800, and took in $2,400 at the concession stand.

October 17: Rented out the theater to a local community group for $1,500. The community group is to pay one-half of the bill within five working days and has 30 days to pay the remainder.

October 23: Received 50% of the amount billed to the community group.

October 24: Sold movie tickets for cash of $2,000, and took in $2,800 at the concession stand.

October 26: The four brothers, acting on behalf of Beverly Entertainment, paid a dividend of $750 on the shares of stock owned by each of them, or $3,000 in total.

October 27: Paid $500 for utilities.

October 30: Paid wages and salaries of $2,400 total to the ushers, the projectionist, concession stand workers, and the maintenance crew.

October 31: Sold movie tickets for cash of $1,800, and took in $2,500 at the concession stand.

Required

1. Prepare a table to summarize the preceding transactions as they affect the accounting equation. Use the format in Exhibit 3-1. Identify each transaction with a date.
2. Record each transaction directly in T accounts, using the dates preceding the transactions to identify them in the accounts. Each account involved in the problem needs a separate T account.

LO4,7 **Problem 3-10** Trial Balance and Financial Statements (Appendix)

Refer to the table for Beverly Entertainment Enterprises in part (1) of Problem 3-9.

Required

1. Prepare a trial balance at October 31, 2007.
2. Prepare an income statement for the month ended October 31, 2007.
3. Prepare a statement of retained earnings for the month ended October 31, 2007.
4. Prepare a classified balance sheet at October 31, 2007.

LO3,5,6 **Problem 3-11** Journal Entries (Appendix)

Atkins Advertising Agency began business on January 2, 2007. Listed below are the transactions entered into by Atkins during its first month of operations.

a. Acquired its articles of incorporation from the state, and issued 100,000 shares of capital stock in exchange for $200,000 in cash.

b. Purchased an office building for $150,000 in cash. The building is valued at $110,000, and the remainder of the value is assigned to the land.

c. Signed a three-year promissory note at the bank for $125,000.

d. Purchased office equipment at a cost of $50,000, paying $10,000 down and agreeing to pay the remainder in 10 days.

e. Paid wages and salaries of $13,000 for the first half of the month. Office employees are paid twice a month.

f. Paid the balance due on the office equipment.

(continued)

g. Sold $24,000 of advertising during the first month. Customers have until the 15th of the following month to pay their bills.

h. Paid wages and salaries of $15,000 for the second half of the month.

i. Recorded $3,500 in commissions earned by the salespeople during the month. They will be paid on the fifth of the following month.

Required

Prepare in journal form the entry to record each transaction.

LO3,4,5,7   **Problem 3-12** Journal Entries Recorded Directly in T Accounts (Appendix)

Refer to the transactions for Atkins Advertising Agency in Problem 3-11.

Required

1. Record each transaction directly in T accounts, using the letters preceding the transactions to identify them in the accounts. Each account involved in the problem needs a separate T account.
2. Prepare a trial balance at January 31, 2007.

LO3,5,7   **Problem 3-13** The Detection of Errors in a Trial Balance and Preparation of a Corrected Trial Balance (Appendix)

Malcolm Inc. was incorporated on January 1, 2007, with the issuance of capital stock in return for $90,000 of cash contributed by the owners. The only other transaction entered into prior to beginning operations was the issuance of a $75,300 note payable in exchange for building and equipment. The following trial balance was prepared at the end of the first month by the bookkeeper for Malcolm Inc.

Malcolm Inc.
Trial Balance
January 31, 2007

Account Titles	Debits	Credits
Cash	$ 9,980	
Accounts Receivable	8,640	
Land	80,000	
Building	50,000	
Equipment	23,500	
Notes Payable		$ 75,300
Capital Stock		90,000
Service Revenue		50,340
Wage and Salary Expense	23,700	
Advertising Expense	4,600	
Utilities Expense	8,420	
Dividends		5,000
Totals	$208,840	$220,640

Required

1. Identify the *two* errors in the trial balance. Ignore depreciation expense and interest expense.
2. Prepare a corrected trial balance.

LO3,5,6,7   **Problem 3-14** Journal Entries, Trial Balance, and Financial Statements (Appendix)

Refer to the transactions for Blue Jay Delivery Service in Problem 3-6.

Required:

1. Prepare journal entries on the books of Blue Jay to record the transactions entered into during the month. Ignore depreciation expense and interest expense.
2. Prepare a trial balance at January 31, 2007.
3. Prepare an income statement for the month ended January 31, 2007.
4. Prepare a classified balance sheet at January 31, 2007.
5. Assume that you are considering buying stock in this company. Beginning with the transaction to record the purchase of the property on January 3, list any additional information you would like to have about each of the transactions during the remainder of the month.

LO3,5,6,7 **Problem 3-15** Journal Entries, Trial Balance, and Financial Statements (Appendix)

Refer to the transactions for Neveranerror Inc. in Problem 3-7.

Required:
1. Prepare journal entries on the books of Neveranerror to record the transactions entered into during the month. Ignore depreciation expense and interest expense.
2. Prepare a trial balance at June 30, 2007.
3. Prepare the following financial statements:
   a. Income statement for the month ended June 30, 2007.
   b. Statement of retained earnings for the month ended June 30, 2007.
   c. Classified balance sheet at June 30, 2007.
4. Assume that you have just graduated from college and have been approached to join this company as an accountant. From your reading of the financial statements for the first month, would you consider joining the company? Explain your answer. Limit your answer to financial considerations only.

ALTERNATE PROBLEMS

LO1 **Problem 3-1A** Events to Be Recorded in Accounts

The following events take place at Anaconda Accountants Inc.:

1. Supplies are ordered from vendors who will deliver the supplies within the week.
2. Vendors deliver supplies on account, payment due in 30 days.
3. New computer system is ordered.
4. Old computer system is sold for cash.
5. Services are rendered to customers on account. The invoices are mailed and due in 30 days.
6. Cash received from customer payments is deposited in the bank night depository.
7. Employees are paid weekly paychecks.
8. Vendors noted in item (2) are paid for the supplies delivered.

Required
Identify each event as internal (I) or external (E), and indicate whether each event would be recorded in the *accounts* of the company. For each event that is to be recorded, identify the names of at least two accounts that would be affected.

LO3 **Problem 3-2A** Transaction Analysis and Financial Statements

Beachway Enterprises was organized on June 1, 2007, by two college students who recognized an opportunity to make money while spending their days at a beach in Florida. The two entrepreneurs plan to rent beach umbrellas. The following transactions occurred during the first month of operations:

June 1: Received contributions of $2,000 from each of the two principal owners of the new business in exchange for shares of stock.

June 1: Purchased 25 beach umbrellas for $250 each on account. The company has 30 days to pay for the beach umbrellas.

June 5: Registered as a vendor with the city and paid the $35 monthly fee.

June 10: Purchased $50 in miscellaneous supplies on an open account. The company has 30 days to pay for the supplies.

June 15: Paid $70 bill from a local radio station for advertising for the last two weeks of June.

June 17: Customers rented beach umbrellas for cash of $1,000.

June 24: Billed a local hotel $2,000 for beach umbrellas provided for use during a convention being held at the hotel. The hotel is to pay one-half of the bill in five days and the rest within 30 days.

June 29: Received 50% of the amount billed to the hotel.

June 30: Customers rented beach umbrellas for cash of $1,500.

June 30: Paid wages of $90 to a friend who helped out over the weekend.

June 30: Paid the balance due on the beach umbrellas.

(continued)

Required

1. Prepare a table to summarize the preceding transactions as they affect the accounting equation. Use the format in Exhibit 3-1. Identify each transaction with a date.
2. Prepare an income statement for the month ended June 30, 2007.
3. Prepare a classified balance sheet at June 30, 2007.

LO3

Problem 3-3A Transaction Analysis and Financial Statements

Dynamic Services Inc. was organized on March 1, 2007, by two former college roommates. The corporation will provide computer tax services to small businesses. The following transactions occurred during the first month of operations:

March 2: Received contributions of $10,000 from each of the two principal owners in exchange for shares of stock.

March 7: Signed a two-year promissory note at the bank and received cash of $7,500. Interest, along with the $7,500, will be repaid at the end of the two years.

March 12: Purchased miscellaneous supplies on account for $350, payment due in 30 days.

March 19: Billed a client $2,000 for tax-preparation services. According to an agreement between the two companies, the client is to pay 25% of the bill upon its receipt and the remaining balance within 30 days.

March 20: Paid a $650 bill from the local newspaper for advertising for the month of March.

March 22: Received 25% of the amount billed the client on March 19.

March 26: Received cash of $1,400 for services provided in assisting a client in preparing its tax return.

March 29: Purchased a computer system for $4,000 in cash.

March 30: Paid $1,650 in salaries and wages for March.

March 31: Received and paid $700 of gas, electric, and water bills.

Required

1. Prepare a table to summarize the preceding transactions as they affect the accounting equation. Use the format in Exhibit 3-1. Identify each transaction with the date.
2. Prepare an income statement for the month ended March 31, 2007.
3. Prepare a classified balance sheet at March 31, 2007.
4. From reading the balance sheet you prepared in part (3), what events would you expect to take place in April? Explain your answer.

LO3

Problem 3-4A Transactions Reconstructed from Financial Statements

The following financial statements are available for Oak Corporation for its first month of operations:

Oak Corporation
Income Statement
For the Month Ended July 31, 2007

Service revenue		$75,400
Expenses:		
Rent	$ 6,000	
Salaries and wages	24,600	
Utilities	12,700	43,300
Net income		$32,100

Oak Corporation
Balance Sheet
July 31, 2007

Assets		Liabilities and Stockholders' Equity	
Cash	$ 13,700	Wages payable	$ 6,000
Accounts receivable	25,700	Notes payable	50,000
Equipment	32,000	Unearned service revenue	4,500
Furniture	14,700	Capital stock	30,000
Land	24,000	Retained earnings	19,600
		Total liabilities and	
Total assets	$110,100	stockholders' equity	$110,100

Required

Describe as many transactions as you can that were entered into by Oak Corporation during the first month of business.

ALTERNATE MULTI-CONCEPT PROBLEMS

LO1,2 **Problem 3-5A** Identification of Events with Source Documents

Many events are linked to a source document. The following is a list of events that occurred in an entity:

a. Paid a security deposit and six months' rent on a building.
b. Hired three employees and agreed to pay them $400 per week.
c. Sold merchandise to a customer for cash.
d. Reported a fire that destroyed a billboard that is on the entity's property and is owned and maintained by another entity.
e. Received payment of bills from customers.
f. Purchased stock in another entity to gain some control over it.
g. Signed a note at the bank and received cash.
h. Contracted with a cleaning service to maintain the interior of the building in good repair. No money is paid at this time.

Required

For each item (a) through (h), indicate whether the event should or should not be recorded in the entity's accounts. For each item that should be recorded in the entity's books:

1. Identify one or more source documents that are generated from the event.
2. Identify which source document would be used to record an event when it produces more than one source document.
3. For each document, identify the information that is most useful in recording the event in the accounts.

LO1,3 **Problem 3-6A** Transaction Analysis

Overnight Delivery Inc. is incorporated on January 2, 2007, and enters into the following transactions during its second month of operations:

February 2: Paid $400 for wages earned by employees for the week ending January 31.
February 3: Paid $3,230 for gas and oil billed on an open account in January.
February 4: Declared and paid $2,000 cash dividends to stockholders.
February 15: Received $8,000 cash from customer accounts.
February 26: Provided $16,800 of services on account during the month.
February 27: Received a $3,400 bill from the local service station for gas and oil used during February.

Required

1. Prepare a table to summarize the preceding transactions as they affect the accounting equation. Use the format in Exhibit 3-1.
2. For the transactions on February 2, 3, 4, and 27, indicate whether the amount is an expense of operating in the month of January or February or is not an expense in either month.

LO1,3 **Problem 3-7A** Transaction Analysis and a Balance Sheet

Krittersbegone Inc. was organized on July 1, 2007, by a group of technicians to provide termite inspections and treatment to homeowners and small businesses. The following transactions occurred during the first month of business:

July 2: Received contributions of $3,000 from each of the six owners in exchange for shares of stock.
July 3: Paid $1,000 rent for the month of July.
July 5: Purchased flashlights, tools, spray equipment, and ladders for $18,000, with a down payment of $5,000 and the balance due in 30 days.
July 17: Paid a $200 bill for the distribution of door-to-door advertising.

(continued)

July 28: Paid August rent and July utilities to the landlord in the amounts of $1,000 and $450, respectively.

July 30: Received $8,000 in cash from homeowners for services performed during the month. In addition, billed $7,500 to other customers for services performed during the month. Billings are due in 30 days.

July 30: Paid commissions of $9,500 to the technicians for July.

July 31: Received $600 from a business client to perform services over the next two months.

Required

1. Prepare a table to summarize the preceding transactions as they affect the accounting equation. Ignore depreciation expense. Use the format in Exhibit 3-1.

2. Prepare a classified balance sheet dated July 31, 2007. From the balance sheet, what cash inflow and what cash outflow can you predict in the month of August? Who would be interested in the cash flow information and why?

LO3,5 **Problem 3-8A** Accounts Used to Record Transactions (Appendix)

A list of accounts, with an identifying number for each, is shown below. Following the list of accounts is a series of transactions entered into by a company during its first year of operations.

Required

For each transaction, indicate the account or accounts that should be debited and credited.

1. Cash	6. Land	11. Retained Earnings
2. Accounts Receivable	7. Accounts Payable	12. Service Revenue
3. Prepaid Insurance	8. Income Tax Payable	13. Wage and Salary Expense
4. Office Supplies	9. Notes Payable	14. Utilities Expense
5. Automobiles	10. Capital Stock	15. Income Tax Expense

	Accounts	
Transactions	**Debited**	**Credited**
Example: Purchased office supplies for cash.	4	1
a. Issued capital stock for cash.	___	___
b. Purchased an automobile and signed a 60-day note for the total amount.	___	___
c. Acquired land in exchange for capital stock.	___	___
d. Received cash from clients for services performed during the month.	___	___
e. Paid employees salaries and wages earned during the month.	___	___
f. Purchased flyers and signs from a printer, payment due in 10 days.	___	___
g. Paid for the flyers and signs purchased in part (f).	___	___
h. Received monthly telephone bill; payment is due within 10 days of receipt.	___	___
i. Paid for a six-month liability insurance policy.	___	___
j. Paid monthly telephone bill.	___	___
k. Computed amount of taxes due based on the income of the period and paid the amount.	___	___

LO3,4,5 **Problem 3-9A** Transaction Analysis and Journal Entries Recorded Directly in T Accounts (Appendix)

Three friends organized Rapid City Roller Rink on October 1, 2007. The following transactions occurred during the first month of operations:

October 1: Received contribution of $22,000 from each of the three principal owners of the new business in exchange for shares of stock.

October 2: Purchased land valued at $15,000 and a building valued at $75,000. The seller agreed to accept a down payment of $9,000 and a five-year promissory note for the balance.

October 3: Purchased new tables and chairs for the lounge at the roller rink at a cost of $25,000, paying $5,000 down and agreeing to pay for the remainder in 60 days.

October 9: Purchased 100 pairs of roller skates for cash at $35 per pair.

October 12: Purchased food and drinks for $2,500 on an open account. The company has 30 days to pay for the concession supplies.

October 13: Sold tickets for cash of $400 and took in $750 at the concession stand.

October 17: Rented out the roller rink to a local community group for $750. The community group is to pay one-half of the bill within five working days and has 30 days to pay the remainder.

October 23: Received 50% of the amount billed to the community group.

October 24: Sold tickets for cash of $500, and took in $1,200 at the concession stand.

October 26: The three friends, acting on behalf of Rapid City Roller Rink, paid a dividend of $250 on the shares of stock owned by each of them, or $750 in total.

October 27: Paid $1,275 for utilities.

October 30: Paid wages and salaries of $2,250.

October 31: Sold tickets for cash of $700, and took in $1,300 at the concession stand.

Required

1. Prepare a table to summarize the preceding transactions as they affect the accounting equation. Use the format in Exhibit 3-1. Identify each transaction with a date.
2. Record each transaction directly in T accounts, using the dates preceding the transactions to identify them in the accounts. Each account involved in the problem needs a separate T account.

LO4,7 **Problem 3-10A** Trial Balance and Financial Statements (Appendix)

Refer to the table for Rapid City Roller Rink in part (1) of Problem 3-9A.

Required

1. Prepare a trial balance at October 31, 2007.
2. Prepare an income statement for the month ended October 31, 2007.
3. Prepare a statement of retained earnings for the month ended October 31, 2007.
4. Prepare a classified balance sheet at October 31, 2007.

LO3,5,6 **Problem 3-11A** Journal Entries (Appendix)

Castle Consulting Agency began business in February 2007. Listed below are the transactions entered into by Castle during its first month of operations.

a. Acquired articles of incorporation from the state, and issued 10,000 shares of capital stock in exchange for $150,000 in cash.
b. Paid monthly rent of $400.
c. Signed a five-year promissory note for $100,000 at the bank.
d. Received $5,000 cash from a customer for services to be performed over the next two months.
e. Purchased software to be used on future jobs. The software costs $950 and is expected to be used on five to eight jobs over the next two years.
f. Billed customers $12,500 for work performed during the month.
g. Paid office personnel $3,000 for the month of February.
h. Received a utility bill of $100. The total amount is due in 30 days.

Required

Prepare in journal form the entry to record each transaction.

LO3,4,5,7 **Problem 3-12A** Journal Entries Recorded Directly in T Accounts (Appendix)

Refer to the transactions for Castle Consulting Agency in Problem 3-11A.

Required

1. Record each transaction directly in T accounts, using the letters preceding the transactions to identify them in the accounts. Each account involved in the problem needs a separate T account.
2. Prepare a trial balance at February 28, 2007.

LO3,4,5,7   **Problem 3-13A** Entries Prepared from a Trial Balance and Proof of the Cash Balance (Appendix)

Russell Company was incorporated on January 1, 2007, with the issuance of capital stock in return for $120,000 of cash contributed by the owners. The only other transaction entered into prior to beginning operations was the issuance of a $50,000 note payable in exchange for equipment and fixtures. The following trial balance was prepared at the end of the first month by the bookkeeper for Russell Company:

Russell Company
Trial Balance
January 31, 2007

Account Titles	Debits	Credits
Cash	$???	
Accounts Receivable	30,500	
Equipment and Fixtures	50,000	
Wages Payable		$ 10,000
Notes Payable		50,000
Capital Stock		120,000
Service Revenue		60,500
Wage and Salary Expense	24,600	
Advertising Expense	12,500	
Rent Expense	5,200	

Required
1. Determine the balance in the Cash account.
2. Identify all of the transactions that affected the Cash account during the month. Use a T account to prove what the balance in Cash would be after all transactions are recorded.

LO3,5,6   **Problem 3-14A** Journal Entries (Appendix)

Refer to the transactions for Overnight Delivery Inc. in Problem 3-6A.

Required:
1. Prepare journal entries on the books of Overnight to record the transactions entered into during February.
2. For the transactions on February 2, 3, 4, and 27, indicate whether the amount is an expense of operating in the month of January or February or is not an expense in either month.

LO3,5,6   **Problem 3-15A** Journal Entries and a Balance Sheet (Appendix)

Refer to the transactions for Krittersbegone Inc. in Problem 3-7A.

Required:
1. Prepare journal entries on the books of Krittersbegone to record the transactions entered into during the month. Ignore depreciation expense.
2. Prepare a classified balance sheet dated July 31, 2007. From the balance sheet, what cash inflow and what cash outflow can you predict in the month of August? Who would be interested in the cash flow information and why?

DECISION CASES

READING AND INTERPRETING FINANCIAL STATEMENTS

LO4   **Decision Case 3-1** Comparing Two Companies in the Same Industry: Finish Line and Foot Locker

Refer to the income statements for **Finish Line** and **Foot Locker**, reproduced at the end of the book.

Required
1. Which is the largest expense for each company in the most recent year, and what is its dollar amount? Is it logical that this would be the largest expense, given the nature of each company's business? Explain your answer.

2. One of the accounts on each company's income statement is "Selling, general and administrative expenses." For each of the two most recent years, compute the ratio of this expense to sales for each company. Did this ratio increase or decrease from one year to the next? Which company has the lower ratio in each of the two years?

3. What is the dollar amount of income tax expense that each company reports on its income statement for each of the two most recent years? Compute the ratio of income taxes to income before taxes (use "income from continuing operations, before income taxes" for Foot Locker) for the two most recent years for each company. Is the ratio the same for Finish Line for both years? Is the ratio the same for Foot Locker for both years? Which company has the higher ratio for the each of the two years? What does this ratio information tell you?

LO3 **Decision Case 3-2** Reading and Interpreting Foot Locker's Statement of Cash Flows

Refer to **Foot Locker**'s statement of cash flows for the year ended January 28, 2006, as reproduced at the end of the book.

Required

1. What amount did the company spend on purchases of property and equipment (capital expenditures) during the year? Determine the effect on the accounting equation from these purchases.
2. What amount did the company pay to stockholders in cash dividends during the year? Determine the effect on the accounting equation from these dividends.

LO1,3 **Decision Case 3-3** Reading and Interpreting Southwest Airlines' Balance Sheet

The following item appears in the current liabilities section of **Southwest Airlines'** balance sheet at December 31, 2004.

> Air traffic liability $529 million

In addition, one of Southwest Airlines' notes states: "Tickets sold are initially deferred as 'air traffic liability.' Passenger revenue is recognized when transportation is provided. 'Air traffic liability' primarily represents tickets sold for future travel dates and estimated refunds and exchanges of tickets sold for past travel dates."

Required

1. What economic event caused Southwest Airlines to incur this liability? Was it an external or an internal event?
2. Describe the effect on the accounting equation from the transaction to record the air traffic liability.
3. Assume that one customer purchases a $500 ticket in advance. Determine the effect on the accounting equation from this transaction.
4. What economic event will cause Southwest Airlines to reduce its air traffic liability? Is this an external or an internal event?

MAKING FINANCIAL DECISIONS

LO2,3 **Decision Case 3-4** Cash Flow versus Net Income

Shelia Young started a real estate business at the beginning of January. After approval by the state for a charter to incorporate, she issued 1,000 shares of stock to herself and deposited $20,000 in a bank account under the name Young Properties. Because business was "booming," she spent all of her time during the first month selling properties rather than keeping financial records.

At the end of January, Shelia comes to you with the following plight:

I put $20,000 in to start this business at the beginning of the month. My January 31 bank statement shows a balance of $17,000. After all of my efforts, it appears as if I'm "in the hole" already! On the other hand, that seems impossible—we sold five properties for clients during the month. The total sales value of these properties was $600,000, and I receive a commission of 5% on each sale. Granted, one of the five sellers still owes me an $8,000 commission on the sale, but the other four have been collected in full. Three of the sales, totaling $400,000, were actually made by my assistants. I pay them 4% of the sales value of a property. Sure, I have a few office expenses for my car, utilities, and a secretary, but that's about it. How can I have possibly lost $3,000 this month?

(continued)

You agree to help Shelia figure out how she really did this month. The bank statement is helpful. The total deposits during the month amount to $22,000. Shelia explains that this amount represents the commissions on the four sales collected so far. The canceled checks reveal the following expenditures:

Check No.	Payee—Memo at Bottom of Check	Amount
101	Stevens Office Supply	$ 2,000
102	Why Walk, Let's Talk Motor Co.—new car	3,000
103	City of Westbrook—heat and lights	500
104	Alice Hill—secretary	2,200
105	Ace Property Management—office rent for month	1,200
106	Jerry Hayes (sales assistant)	10,000
107	Joan Harper (sales assistant)	6,000
108	Don's Fillitup—gas and oil for car	100

According to Shelia, the $2,000 check to Stevens Office Supply represents the down payment on a word processor and a copier for the office. The remaining balance is $3,000 and it must be paid to Stevens by February 15. Similarly, the $3,000 check is the down payment on a car for the business. A $12,000 note was given to the car dealer and is due along with interest in one year.

1. Prepare an income statement for the month of January for Young Properties.
2. Prepare a statement of cash flows for the month of January for Young Properties.
3. Draft a memorandum to Shelia Young explaining as simply and as clearly as possible why she *did* in fact have a profitable first month in business but experienced a decrease in her cash account. Support your explanation with any necessary figures.
4. The down payments on the car and the office equipment are reflected on the statement of cash flows. They are assets that will benefit the business for a number of years. Do you think that *any* of the cost associated with the acquisition of these assets should be recognized in some way on the income statement? Explain your answer.

LO1,3,4   **Decision Case 3-5** Loan Request

Simon Fraser started a landscaping and lawn-care business in April 2007 by investing $20,000 cash in the business in exchange for capital stock. Because his business is in the Midwest, the season begins in April and concludes in September. He prepared the following list of accounts (in alphabetical order) at the end of the first season in business.

	Balance
Accounts Payable	$13,000
Accounts Receivable	3,000
Capital Stock	20,000
Cash	1,200
Gas and Oil Expense	15,700
Insurance Expense	2,500
Landscaping Revenue	33,400
Lawn Care Revenue	24,000
Mowing Equipment	5,000
Rent Expense	6,000
Salaries Expense	22,000
Truck	15,000

Simon is pleased with his first year in business. "I paid myself a salary of $22,000 during the year and still have $1,200 in the bank. Sure, I have a few bills outstanding, but my accounts receivable will more than cover those." In fact, Simon is so happy with the first year, that he has come to you in your role as a lending officer at the local bank to ask for a $20,000 loan to allow him to add another truck and mowing equipment for the second season.

Required

1. From your reading of the list of accounts, what does it appear to you that Simon did with the $20,000 in cash he originally contributed to the business? Determine the effect on the accounting equation from the transaction you think took place.
2. Prepare an income statement for the six months ended September 30, 2007.

3. The mowing equipment and truck are assets that will benefit the business for a number of years. Do you think that any of the costs associated with the purchase of these assets should have been recognized as expenses in the first year? How would this have affected the income statement?

4. Prepare a classified balance sheet as of September 30, 2007. As a banker, what two items on the balance sheet concern you the most? Explain your answer.

5. As a banker, would you loan Simon $20,000 to expand his business during the second year? Draft a memo to respond to Simon's request for the loan, indicating whether you will make the loan.

ETHICAL DECISION MAKING

LO1,3   **Decision Case 3-6** Revenue Recognition

You are controller for an architectural firm whose accounting year ends on December 31. As part of the management team, you receive a year-end bonus directly related to the firm's earnings for the year. One of your duties is to review the transactions recorded by the bookkeepers. A new bookkeeper recorded the receipt of $10,000 in cash as an increase in cash and an increase in service revenue.

The $10,000 is a deposit and the bookkeeper explains to you that the firm plans to provide the services to the client in March of the following year.

1. Did the bookkeeper correctly record the client's deposit? Explain your answer.
2. What would you do as controller for the firm? Do you have a responsibility to do anything to correct the books?

LO3,5,6   **Decision Case 3-7** Delay in the Posting of a Journal Entry (Appendix)

As assistant controller for a small consulting firm, you are responsible for recording and posting the daily cash receipts and disbursements to the ledger accounts. After you have posted the entries, your boss, the controller, prepares a trial balance and the financial statements. You make the following entries on June 30, 2007:

2007

June 30	Cash	1,430	
	Accounts Receivable	1,950	
	Service Revenue		3,380
	To record daily cash receipts.		

June 30	Advertising Expense	12,500	
	Utilities Expense	22,600	
	Rent Expense	24,000	
	Salary and Wage Expense	17,400	
	Cash		76,500
	To record daily cash disbursements.		

The daily cash disbursements are much larger on June 30 than any other day because many of the company's major bills are paid on the last day of the month. After you have recorded these two transactions and *before* you have posted them to the ledger accounts, your boss comes to you with the following request:

As you are aware, the first half of the year has been a tough one for the consulting industry and for our business in particular. With first-half bonuses based on net income, I am concerned whether you or I will get any bonus this time around. However, I have a suggestion that should allow us to receive something for our hard work and at the same time will not hurt anyone. Go ahead and post the June 30 cash receipts to the ledger, but don't bother to post that day's cash disbursements. Even though the treasurer writes the checks on the last day of the month and you normally journalize the transaction on the same day, it is pretty silly to bother posting the entry to the ledger, since it takes at least a week for the checks to clear the bank.

(continued)

Required

1. Explain *why* the controller's request will result in an increase in net income.
2. Do you agree with the controller that the omission of the entry on June 30 "will not hurt anyone"? Who might be hurt? Does omitting the entry provide information that is free from bias? Explain your answer.
3. What would you do if the controller had told you to do this? To whom should you talk to about this issue? Is this situation an ethical dilemma? Why?

SOLUTIONS TO KEY TERMS QUIZ

Quiz 1: Processing Accounting Information

2	Event	4	Source document
5	External event	6	Account
3	Internal event	1	Chart of accounts
8	Transaction	7	General ledger

Quiz 2: Appendix

4	Debit	5	Posting
2	Credit	3	Journalizing
8	Double-entry system	7	General journal
6	Journal	1	Trial balance

CHAPTER

4

Income Measurement and Accrual Accounting

Study Links

A Look at the Previous Chapter
Chapter 3 looked at how information is processed. Various tools were introduced as convenient aids in the preparation of periodic financial statements.

A Look at This Chapter
This chapter begins by considering the roles of recognition and measurement in the process of preparing financial statements. The accrual basis of accounting is examined and we see how this basis affects the measurement of income. We look at how revenues and expenses are recognized in an accrual system and at the role of adjustments in this process.

A Look at the Upcoming Chapter
Chapter 4 completes our overview of the accounting model. In the next section, we examine accounting for the various assets of a business. We begin in Chapter 5 by looking at how companies that sell products account for their inventory.

Learning Outcomes

After studying this chapter, you should be able to:

LO1 Explain the significance of recognition and measurement in the preparation and use of financial statements.

LO2 Explain the differences between the cash and accrual bases of accounting.

LO3 Describe the revenue recognition principle and explain its application in various situations.

LO4 Describe the matching principle and the various methods for recognizing expenses.

LO5 Identify the four major types of adjustments and determine their effect on the accounting equation.

LO6 Explain the steps in the accounting cycle and the significance of each step.

© Bob Daemmrich/Photo Edit

Foot Locker, Inc.

MAKING BUSINESS DECISIONS

By now in your study of accounting, you know that companies such as Foot Locker must use the accrual basis in preparing their financial statements. This means that revenues are recorded when they are earned and expenses when they are incurred, regardless of when cash is either received or paid.

Because Foot Locker uses the accrual basis of accounting, certain accounts appear on its balance sheet that would not appear if it used the simpler cash basis. These accounts are important, not just to ensure that the accounting equation is kept in balance, but also because they provide important information to stockholders, bankers, and other users of the statements. Consider two of the accounts that appear on Foot Locker's balance sheet and the notes to the statements that support the amounts contained in these accounts, as shown on the next page.

As we will learn about in this chapter, a company may in certain instances incur an expense either before of after it has paid cash. One of the accounts on

Foot Locker's balance sheet is titled **Other current assets.** According to a note, included in this item are "Prepaid expenses and other current assets." For example, if the company prepays an insurance policy, an asset is created. Over time, the asset expires and is replaced by an expense.

Accrued and other liabilities appear on the liabilities side of Foot Locker's balance sheet. According to another note to the statements, included in this item are "Other payroll and payroll related costs, excluding taxes." Foot Locker operates approximately four thousand stores in malls around the world. Obviously, one of the company's largest costs is its payroll. However, at the date of a balance sheet, the company owes employees for wages they have earned but haven't yet been paid, simply because the last day of the year is not necessarily a payday. Thus, the company has to accrue a liability for salaries and wages earned but not yet paid.

Similar situations arise for companies when they receive cash either before of after it is earned. This chapter will explore all of these situations in more detail and help you to answer important questions about the accrual accounting process, such as:

- What important information does the accrual basis of accounting provide users of the statements that a cash basis does not? (See pp. 157–159)
- What is meant by the revenue recognition principle, and why is it important? (See pp. 160–161)

- What is meant by the matching principle, and how is it applied? (See pp. 161–162)
- What are the various types of adjustments that companies make, and how are they recorded in an accounting system? (See pp. 163–168)

Partial Consolidated Balance Sheets

	2005	2004
	(in millions)	
ASSETS		
Current assets		
Cash and cash equivalents	$ 289	$ 225
Short-term investments	298	267
Total cash, cash equivalents and short-term investments	587	492
Merchandise inventories	1,254	1,151
Other current assets	173	189
LIABILITIES AND SHAREHOLDERS' EQUITY		
Current liabilities		
Accounts payable	$ 361	$ 381
Accrued and other liabilities	305	285
Current portion of long-term debt and obligations under capital leases	51	18
	717	684
8 Other Current Assets		
Net receivables	$ 49	$ 47
Prepaid expenses and other current assets	46	47
Prepaid income taxes	49	40
Deferred taxes	28	53
Current portion of Northern Group note receivable	1	1
Assets of discontinued operations	—	1
	$ 173	$ 189
11 Accrued Liabilities		
Pension and postretirement benefits	$ 72	$ 30
Incentive bonuses	20	34
Other payroll and payroll related costs, excluding taxes	52	51
Taxes other than income taxes	43	45
Property and equipment	16	22
Gift cards and certificates	25	22
Income taxes payable	3	9
Fair value of derivative contracts	1	3
Current deferred tax liabilities	3	1
Sales return reserve	4	3
Liabilities of discontinued operations	2	2
Current portion of repositioning and restructuring reserves	1	1
Current portion of reserve for discontinued operations	8	7
Other operating costs	55	55
	$ 305	$ 285

Source: Foot Locker, Inc.'s 2005 Annual Report, pages 26, 37, and 38.

Recognition and Measurement in Financial Statements

Accounting is a communication process. To successfully communicate information to the users of financial statements, accountants and managers must answer two questions:

1. **What economic events should be communicated, or *recognized*, in the statements?**
2. **How should the effects of these events be *measured* in the statements?**

The dual concepts of recognition and measurement are crucial to the success of accounting as a form of communication.

LO1 Explain the significance of recognition and measurement in the preparation and use of financial statements.

RECOGNITION

"**Recognition** is the process of formally recording or incorporating an item into the financial statements of an entity as an asset, liability, revenue, expense, or the like. Recognition includes depiction of an item in both words and numbers, with the amount included in the totals of the financial statements."[1] We see in this definition the central idea behind general-purpose financial statements. They are a form of communication between the entity and external users. Stockholders, bankers, and other creditors have limited access to relevant information about a company. They depend on the periodic financial statements issued by management to provide the necessary information to make their decisions. Acting on behalf of management, accountants have a moral and ethical responsibility to provide users with financial information that will be useful in making their decisions. The process by which the accountant depicts, or describes, the effects of economic events on the entity is called *recognition*.

The items, such as assets, liabilities, revenues, and expenses, depicted in financial statements are *representations*. Simply stated, the accountant cannot show a stockholder or other user the company's assets, such as cash and buildings. What the user sees in a set of financial statements is a depiction of the real thing. That is, the accountant describes, with words and numbers, the various items in a set of financial statements. The system is imperfect at best and, for that reason, is always in the process of change. As society and the business environment have become more complex, the accounting profession has striven for ways to improve financial statements as a means of communicating with statement users.

Recognition
The process of recording an item in the financial statements as an asset, liability, revenue, expense, or the like.

MEASUREMENT

Accountants depict a financial statement item in both words and *numbers*. The accountant must *quantify* the effects of economic events on the entity. It is not enough to decide that an event is important and thus warrants recognition in the financial statements. To be able to recognize it, the statement preparer must measure the event's financial effects on the company.

Measurement of an item in financial statements requires that two choices be made. First, the accountant must decide on the *attribute* to be measured. Second, a scale of measurement, or *unit of measure*, must be chosen.

The Attribute to Be Measured Assume that a company holds a parcel of real estate as an investment. What attribute—that is, *characteristic*—of the property should be used to measure and thus recognize it as an asset on the balance sheet? The cost of the asset at the time it is acquired is the most logical choice. *Cost* is the amount of cash, or its equivalent, paid to acquire the asset. But how do we report the property on a balance sheet a year from now?

- The simplest approach is to show the property on the balance sheet at its original cost, thus the designation **historical cost**. The use of historical cost is not only simple but also *verifiable*. Assume that two accountants are asked to independently

Historical cost
The amount paid for an asset and used as a basis for recognizing it on the balance sheet and carrying it on later balance sheets.

---

[1] *Statement of Financial Accounting Concepts No. 5*, "Recognition and Measurement in Financial Statements of Business Enterprises" (Stamford, Conn.: Financial Accounting Standards Board, December 1984), par. 6.

Current value
The amount of cash, or its equivalent, that could be received by selling an asset currently.

measure the cost of the asset. After examining the sales contract for the land, they should arrive at the same amount.

- An alternative to historical cost as the attribute to be measured is **current value**. Current value is the amount of cash, or its equivalent, that could be received currently from the sale of the asset. For the company's piece of property, current value is the *estimated* selling price of the land, reduced by any commissions or other fees involved in making the sale. But the amount is only an estimate, not an actual amount. If the company has not yet sold the property, how can we know for certain its selling price? We have to compare it to similar properties that *have* sold recently.

The choice between current value and historical cost as the attribute to be measured is a good example of the trade-off between *relevance* and *reliability*. As indicated earlier, historical cost is verifiable and is thus to a large extent a reliable measure. But is it as relevant to the needs of the decision makers as current value? Put yourself in the position of a banker trying to decide whether to lend money to the company. In evaluating the company's assets as collateral for the loan, is it more relevant to your decision to know what the firm paid for a piece of land 20 years ago or what it could be sold for today? But what *could* the property be sold for today? Two accountants might not necessarily arrive at the same current value for the land. Whereas value or selling price may be more relevant to your decision on the loan, the reliability of this amount is often questionable.

Because of its objective nature, historical cost is the attribute used to measure many of the assets recognized on the balance sheet. However, certain other attributes, such as current value, have increased in popularity in recent years. In other chapters of the book, we will discuss some of the alternatives to historical cost.

The Unit of Measure   Regardless of the attribute of an item to be measured, it is still necessary to choose a yardstick or unit of measure. The yardstick we currently use is units of money. *Money* is something accepted as a medium of exchange or as a means of payment. The unit of money in the United States is the dollar. In Japan the medium of exchange is the yen, and in Great Britain it is the pound.

The use of the dollar as a unit of measure for financial transactions is widely accepted. The *stability* of the dollar as a yardstick is subject to considerable debate, however. Consider an example. You are thinking about buying a certain parcel of land. As part of your decision process, you measure the dimensions of the property and determine that the lot is 80 feet wide and 120 feet deep. Thus, the unit of measure used to determine the lot's size is the square foot. The company that owns the land offers to sell it for $10,000. Although the offer sounds attractive, you decide against the purchase today.

You return in one year to take a second look at the lot. You measure the lot again and, not surprisingly, find the width to still be 80 feet and the depth 120 feet. The owner is still willing to sell the lot for $10,000. This may appear to be the same price as last year. But the *purchasing power* of the unit of measure, the dollar, may very possibly have changed since last year. Even though the foot is a stable measuring unit, the dollar often is not. A *decline* in the purchasing power of the dollar is evidenced by a continuing *rise* in the general level of prices in an economy. For example, rather than paying $10,000 last year to buy the lot, you could have spent the $10,000 on other goods or services. However, a year later, the same $10,000 may very well not buy the same amount of goods and services.

Inflation, or a rise in the general level of prices in the economy, results in a decrease in purchasing power. In the past, the accounting profession has experimented with financial statements adjusted for the changing value of the dollar. As inflation has declined in recent years in the United States, the debate over the use of the dollar as a stable measuring unit has somewhat subsided.[2] It is still important to recognize the inherent weakness in the use of a measuring unit that is subject to change, however.

© Getty Images

What events have economic consequences? The destructive effects of a flood such as caused by hurricanes Katrina or Rita, for example, will result in losses to buildings and other business assets. These losses will surely be reflected in the next year's financial statements of the affected companies—possibly in the income statement, as a downturn or a disruption of revenues due to lost sales. What other financial statements would be affected by a flood?

---

2 The rate of inflation in some countries, most noticeably those in South America, has far exceeded the rate in the United States. Companies operating in some of these countries with hyperinflationary economies are required to make adjustments to their statements.

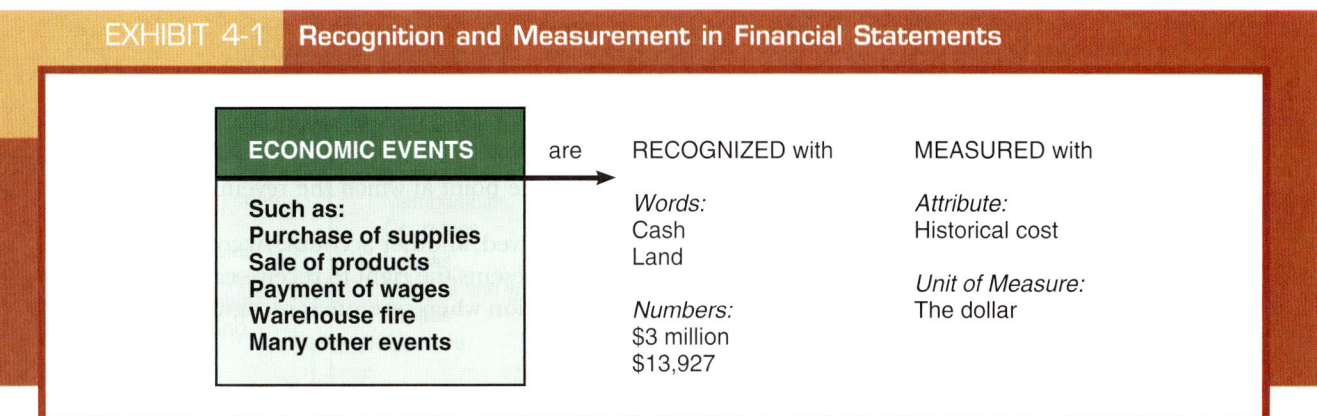

EXHIBIT 4-1 | Recognition and Measurement in Financial Statements

ECONOMIC EVENTS	are	RECOGNIZED with	MEASURED with
Such as: Purchase of supplies Sale of products Payment of wages Warehouse fire Many other events		*Words:* Cash Land *Numbers:* $3 million $13,927	*Attribute:* Historical cost *Unit of Measure:* The dollar

SUMMARY OF RECOGNITION AND MEASUREMENT IN FINANCIAL STATEMENTS

The purpose of financial statements is to communicate various types of economic information about a company. The job of the accountant is to decide which information should be recognized in the financial statements and how the effects of that information on the entity should be measured. Exhibit 4-1 summarizes the role of recognition and measurement in the preparation of financial statements.

The Accrual Basis of Accounting

The accrual basis of accounting is the foundation for the measurement of income in our modern system of accounting. The best way to understand the accrual basis is to compare it with the simpler cash approach.

LO2 Explain the differences between the cash and accrual bases of accounting.

COMPARING THE CASH AND ACCRUAL BASES OF ACCOUNTING

The cash and accrual bases of accounting differ with respect to the *timing* of the recognition of revenues and expenses. For example, assume that on July 24, Barbara White, a salesperson for Spiffy House Painters, contracts with a homeowner to repaint a house for $1,000. A large crew comes in and paints the house the next day, July 25. The customer has 30 days from the day of completion of the job to pay and does, in fact, pay Spiffy on August 25. *When* should Spiffy recognize the $1,000 as revenue? As soon as the contract is signed on July 24? Or on July 25, when the work is done? Or on August 25, when the customer pays the bill?

When Is Revenue Recognized?

July 24	July 25	August 25
Contract is signed.	House is painted.	Customer pays for job.

No Revenue Yet!	**Accrual Basis:** When house is painted	**Cash Basis:** When cash is received

EXHIBIT 4-4 Relationships among Costs, Assets, and Expenses

Various types of **costs** *are incurred:*
Purchases of merchandise
Office space
Heating and lighting

Unexpired costs are called **assets:**
(reported on the balance sheet)
Merchandise Inventory
Office Building

Expired costs are called **expenses:**
(reported on the income statement)
Cost of Goods Sold Expense
Depreciation Expense
Utilities Expense

For example, when a retailer sells a product, the asset sacrificed is Inventory. Cost of Goods Sold is the expense account that is increased, and the Inventory account is decreased. As we will see in the next section, the incurrence of an expense may also result in a liability.

2 minute review

1. Explain the difference between the attribute to be measured and the unit of measure.

2. When is revenue normally recognized?

3. Explain the different ways in which expenses are matched with revenues.

Answers

1. *Accountants must decide whether to use historical cost or another attribute or characteristic of an asset, such as its current value, to measure it. Regardless of the attribute measured, it is necessary to choose a yardstick, or unit of measure. In this country, accountants use the dollar to measure assets and other financial statement items.*

2. *Revenue is normally recognized at the time of sale, regardless of when cash is received. Usually this is when the product is delivered or a service is provided to a customer.*

3. *For certain costs, such as cost of goods sold, it is possible to directly match the expense with revenue generated. For other costs, such as depreciation, an indirect form of matching is necessary in which expenses are allocated to the periods benefited, rather than matched with specific revenues. Finally, the benefits associated with the incurrence of certain costs, such as utilities, expire immediately, and therefore expense is recognized as soon as the cost is incurred.*

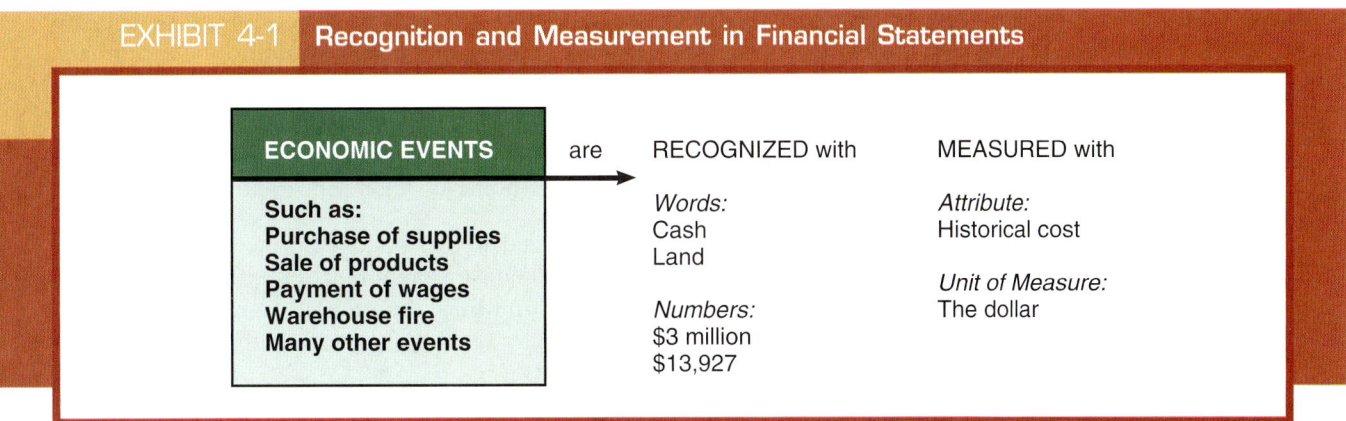

EXHIBIT 4-1 | Recognition and Measurement in Financial Statements

ECONOMIC EVENTS		RECOGNIZED with	MEASURED with
Such as: **Purchase of supplies** **Sale of products** **Payment of wages** **Warehouse fire** **Many other events**	are →	*Words:* Cash Land *Numbers:* $3 million $13,927	*Attribute:* Historical cost *Unit of Measure:* The dollar

SUMMARY OF RECOGNITION AND MEASUREMENT IN FINANCIAL STATEMENTS

The purpose of financial statements is to communicate various types of economic information about a company. The job of the accountant is to decide which information should be recognized in the financial statements and how the effects of that information on the entity should be measured. Exhibit 4-1 summarizes the role of recognition and measurement in the preparation of financial statements.

The Accrual Basis of Accounting

The accrual basis of accounting is the foundation for the measurement of income in our modern system of accounting. The best way to understand the accrual basis is to compare it with the simpler cash approach.

LO2 Explain the differences between the cash and accrual bases of accounting.

COMPARING THE CASH AND ACCRUAL BASES OF ACCOUNTING

The cash and accrual bases of accounting differ with respect to the *timing* of the recognition of revenues and expenses. For example, assume that on July 24, Barbara White, a salesperson for Spiffy House Painters, contracts with a homeowner to repaint a house for $1,000. A large crew comes in and paints the house the next day, July 25. The customer has 30 days from the day of completion of the job to pay and does, in fact, pay Spiffy on August 25. *When* should Spiffy recognize the $1,000 as revenue? As soon as the contract is signed on July 24? Or on July 25, when the work is done? Or on August 25, when the customer pays the bill?

When Is Revenue Recognized?

July 24	**July 25**	**August 25**
Contract is signed.	House is painted.	Customer pays for job.

No Revenue Yet!	**Accrual Basis:** When house is painted	**Cash Basis:** When cash is received

Cash basis
A system of accounting in which revenues are recognized when cash is received and expenses when cash is paid.

Accrual basis
A system of accounting in which revenues are recognized when earned and expenses when incurred.

- In an income statement prepared on the **cash basis**, revenues are recognized when cash is *received*. Thus, on a cash basis, the $1,000 would not be recognized as revenue until the cash is collected, on August 25.

- In an income statement prepared on an **accrual basis**, revenue is recognized when it is *earned*. On this basis, the $1,000 would be recognized as revenue on July 25, when the house is painted. This is the point at which the revenue is earned.

Although cash has not yet been received, another account, Accounts Receivable, is recognized as an asset. This asset represents the right to receive cash in the future. The effect on Spiffy's accounting equation when revenue is recognized before cash is received is as follows:

Balance Sheet			Income Statement	
ASSETS	= LIABILITIES	+ STOCKHOLDERS' EQUITY	+	REVENUES − EXPENSES
Accounts Receivable 1,000			Service Revenue	1,000

At the time cash is collected, accounts receivable is reduced and cash is increased. The effect on the accounting equation from this event is this:

Balance Sheet			Income Statement
ASSETS	= LIABILITIES	+ STOCKHOLDERS' EQUITY	+	REVENUES − EXPENSES
Cash 1,000			
Accounts Receivable (1,000)			

Assume that Barbara White is paid a 10% commission for all contracts and is paid on the 15th of the month following the month a house is painted. Thus, for this job, she will receive a $100 commission check on August 15. When should Spiffy recognize her commission of $100 as an expense? On July 24, when White gets the homeowner to sign a contract? When the work is completed, on July 25? Or on August 15, when she receives the commission check? Again, on a cash basis, commission expense would be recognized on August 15, when cash is *paid* to the salesperson. But on an accrual basis, expenses are recognized when they are *incurred*. In our example, the commission expense is incurred when the house is painted, on July 25.

Exhibit 4-2 summarizes the essential differences between recognition of revenues and expenses on a cash basis and recognition on an accrual basis.

WHAT THE INCOME STATEMENT AND THE STATEMENT OF CASH FLOWS REVEAL

Most business entities, other than the very smallest, use the accrual basis of accounting. Thus, the income statement reflects the accrual basis. Revenues are recognized when they are earned and expenses when they are incurred. At the same time, however, stockholders and creditors are also interested in information concerning the cash flows of an entity. The purpose of a statement of cash flows is to

EXHIBIT 4-2 Comparing the Cash and Accrual Bases of Accounting

	Cash Basis	Accrual Basis
Revenue is recognized	**When Received**	**When Earned**
Expense is recognized	**When Paid**	**When Incurred**

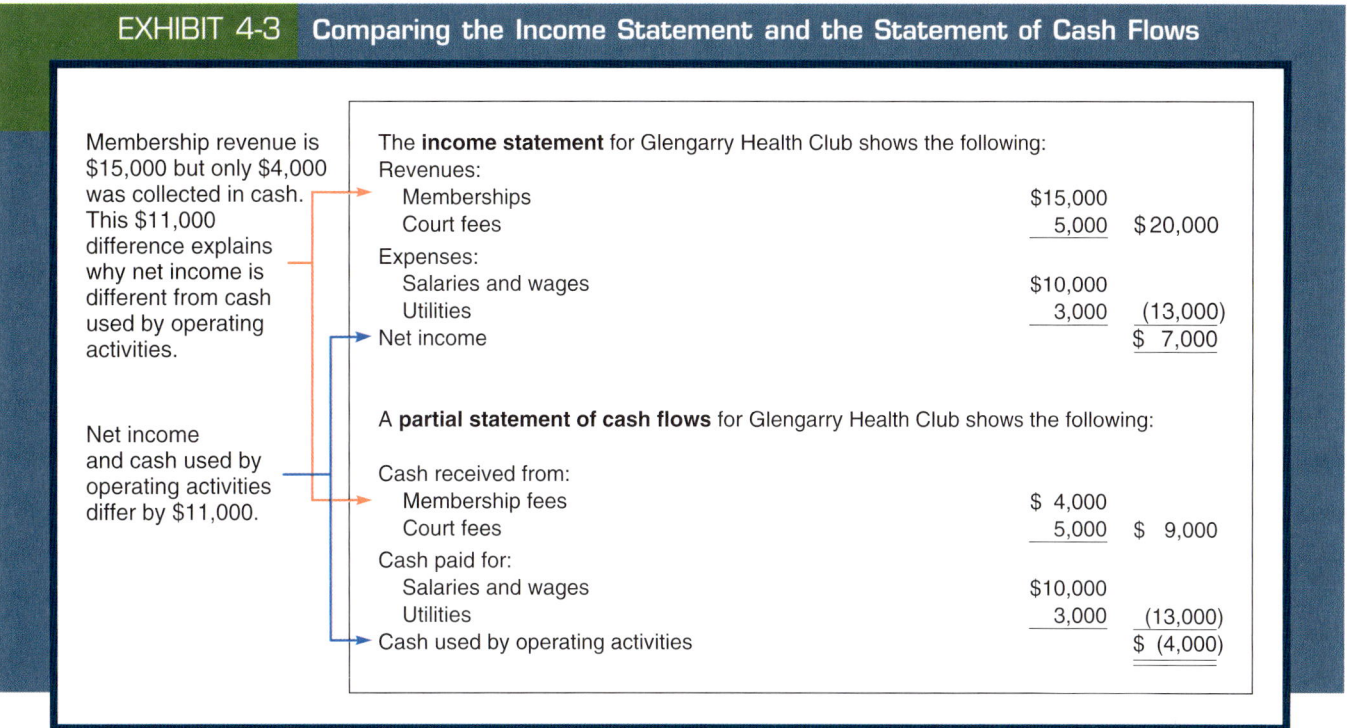

EXHIBIT 4-3   Comparing the Income Statement and the Statement of Cash Flows

Membership revenue is $15,000 but only $4,000 was collected in cash. This $11,000 difference explains why net income is different from cash used by operating activities.

The **income statement** for Glengarry Health Club shows the following:

Revenues:		
Memberships	$15,000	
Court fees	5,000	$20,000
Expenses:		
Salaries and wages	$10,000	
Utilities	3,000	(13,000)
Net income		$ 7,000

Net income and cash used by operating activities differ by $11,000.

A **partial statement of cash flows** for Glengarry Health Club shows the following:

Cash received from:		
Membership fees	$ 4,000	
Court fees	5,000	$ 9,000
Cash paid for:		
Salaries and wages	$10,000	
Utilities	3,000	(13,000)
Cash used by operating activities		$ (4,000)

provide this information. Keep in mind that even though we present a statement of cash flows in a complete set of financial statements, the accrual basis is used for recording transactions and for preparing a balance sheet and an income statement.

Recall the example of Glengarry Health Club in Chapter 3. The club earned revenue from two sources, memberships and court fees. Both of these forms of revenue were recognized on the income statement presented in that chapter and are reproduced in the top portion of Exhibit 4-3. Recall, however, that members have 30 days to pay and that, at the end of the first month of operation, only $4,000 of the membership fees of $15,000 had been collected.

Now consider the statement of cash flows for the first month of operation, partially reproduced in the bottom portion of Exhibit 4-3. Because we want to compare the income statement to the statement of cash flows, only the Operating Activities section of the statement is shown. (The Investing and Financing Activities sections have been omitted from the statement.) Why is net income for the month a *positive* $7,000 but cash from operating activities a *negative* $4,000? Of the membership revenue of $15,000 reflected on the income statement, only $4,000 was collected in cash. Glengarry has accounts receivable for the other $11,000. Thus, cash from operating activities, as reflected on a statement of cash flows, is $11,000 *less* than net income of $7,000, or a negative $4,000.

Each of these two financial statements serves a useful purpose. The income statement reflects the revenues actually earned by the business, regardless of whether cash has been collected. The statement of cash flows tells the reader about the actual cash inflows during a period of time.

ACCRUAL ACCOUNTING AND TIME PERIODS

The *time period* assumption was introduced in Chapter 1. We assume that it is possible to prepare an income statement that fairly reflects the earnings of a business for a specific period of time, such as a month or a year. It is somewhat artificial to divide the operations of a business into periods of time as indicated on a calendar. The conflict arises because earning income is a *process* that takes place *over a period of time* rather than *at any one point in time*.

Consider an alternative to our present system of reporting on the operations of a business on a periodic basis. A new business begins operations with an investment of $50,000. The business operates for 10 years, during which time no records are kept other than a checkbook for the cash on deposit at the bank. At the end of the 10 years, the owners decide to go their separate ways and convert all of their assets to cash. They split among them the balance of $80,000 in the bank account. What is the profit of the business for the 10-year period? The answer is $30,000, the difference between the original cash of $50,000 contributed and the cash of $80,000 available at liquidation.

The point of this simple example is that we could be very precise and accurate in our measurement of the income of a business if it were not necessary to artificially divide operations according to a calendar. Stockholders, bankers, and other interested parties cannot wait until a business liquidates to make decisions, however. They need information on a periodic basis. Thus, the justification for the accrual basis of accounting lies in the needs of financial statement users for periodic information on the financial position and the profitability of the entity.

THE REVENUE RECOGNITION PRINCIPLE

LO3 Describe the revenue recognition principle and explain its application in various situations.

Revenues
Inflows of assets or settlements of liabilities from delivering or producing goods, rendering services, or conducting other activities.

Revenue recognition principle
Revenues are recognized in the income statement when they are realized, or realizable, and earned.

"**Revenues** are inflows or other enhancements of assets of an entity or settlements of its liabilities (or a combination of both) from delivering or producing goods, rendering services, or other activities that constitute the entity's ongoing major or central operations."[3] Two points should be noted about this formal definition of revenues. First, an asset is not always involved when revenue is recognized. The recognition of revenue may result from the settlement of a liability rather than from the acquisition of an asset. Second, entities generate revenue in different ways: some companies produce goods, others distribute or deliver the goods to users, and still others provide some type of service.

On the accrual basis, revenues are recognized when earned. However, the **revenue recognition principle** involves two factors. Revenues are recognized in the income statement when they are both *realized* and *earned*. Revenues are *realized* when goods or services are exchanged for cash or claims to cash, usually at the time of sale. This is normally interpreted to mean at the time of delivery of the product or service to the customer. However, in certain situations it may be necessary either to modify or to interpret the meaning of the revenue recognition principle. The application of the principle to long-term contracts, franchises, commodities, and installment sales are covered in intermediate accounting courses.

In some cases, revenue is earned *continuously* over time. In these cases, a product or service is not delivered at a specific point in time; instead, the earnings process takes place with the passage of time. Rent and interest are two examples. Interest is the cost associated with the use of someone else's money. When should

ETHICS   Bristol-Myers Squibb

Bristol-Myers Squibb, a company that manufactures and sells medicines and healthcare products, had a very difficult year financially in 2002 and the company's stock price dropped more than 50%.

The company's customers are large wholesale companies that buy medicines and other products and then sell the goods to smaller companies, such as local drugstores. Usually, Bristol-Myers sells to its customers the amount of goods the customers can resell quickly. However, in 2001, the manufacturer pushed its customers to order much more than they needed.

As a result, the drug manufacturer recognized much higher sales than usual. In 2002, the SEC investigated this change in selling practice and pressured Bristol-Myers to significantly restate its reported revenue. Overall, the company estimated its aggressive selling tactics had resulted in its reporting excessive sales of $1.5 billion. Bristol-Myers' management claimed its accounting decisions were appropriate.

Why do you think the SEC required the restatements? Did an ethical dilemma exist for anyone involved? If you were an investor in 2001, how might you have benefited or been harmed? Were any investors harmed by the 2002 restatements? If so, how? What responsibility, if any, did Bristol-Myers' accountants owe to its customers? Were any GAAP rules violated?

Source: Gardiner Harris, "SEC is probing Bristol-Myers over sales-incentive accounting," The Wall Street Journal, July 12, 2002.

---

3 *Statement of Financial Accounting Concepts No. 6,* "Elements of Financial Statements" (Stamford, Conn.: Financial Accounting Standards Board, December 1985), par. 78.

a bank recognize the interest earned from granting a 90-day loan? Even though the interest may not be received until the loan itself is repaid, interest is earned every day the loan is outstanding. Later in the chapter, we will look at the process for recognizing interest earned but not yet received. The same procedure is used to recognize revenue from rent that is earned but uncollected.

EXPENSE RECOGNITION AND THE MATCHING PRINCIPLE

Companies incur a variety of costs. A new office building is constructed. Supplies are purchased. Employees perform services. The electric meter is read. In each of these situations, the company incurs a cost, regardless of when it pays cash. Conceptually, **any time a cost is incurred, an asset is acquired**. However, according to the definition in Chapter 1, an asset represents a future economic benefit. An asset ceases being an asset and becomes an expense when the economic benefits from having incurred the cost have expired. Assets are unexpired costs, and expenses are expired costs.

At what point do costs expire and become expenses? The expense recognition principle requires that we recognize expenses in different ways, depending on the nature of the cost. The ideal approach to recognizing expenses is to match them with revenues. Under the **matching principle**, the accountant attempts to associate revenues of a period with the costs necessary to generate those revenues. For certain types of expenses, a direct form of matching is possible; for others, it is necessary to associate costs with a particular period. The classic example of direct matching is cost of goods sold expense with sales revenue. Cost of goods sold is the cost of the inventory associated with a particular sale. A cost is incurred and an asset is recorded when the inventory is purchased. The asset, inventory, becomes an expense when it is sold. Another example of a cost that can be matched directly with revenue is commissions. The commission paid to a salesperson can be matched directly with the sale.

An indirect form of matching is used to recognize the benefits associated with certain types of costs, most noticeably long-term assets, such as buildings and equipment. These costs benefit many periods, but usually it is not possible to match them directly with a specific sale of a product. Instead, they are matched with the periods during which they will provide benefits. For example, an office building may be useful to a company for 30 years. *Depreciation* is the process of allocating the cost of a tangible long-term asset to its useful life. Depreciation Expense is the account used to recognize this type of expense.

The benefits associated with the incurrence of certain other costs are treated in accounting as expiring simultaneously with their acquisition. The justification for this treatment is that no future benefits from the incurrence of the cost are discernible. This is true of most selling and administrative costs. For example, the costs of heat and light in a building benefit only the current period and therefore are recognized as expenses as soon as the costs are incurred. Likewise, income taxes incurred during the period do not benefit any period other than the current period and are thus written off as an expense in the period incurred.

The relationships among costs, assets, and expenses are depicted in Exhibit 4-4 using three examples. First, costs incurred for purchases of merchandise result in an asset, Merchandise Inventory, and are eventually matched with revenue at the time the product is sold. Second, costs incurred for office space result in an asset, Office Building, which is recognized as Depreciation Expense over the useful life of the building. Third, the cost of heating and lighting benefits only the current period and is thus recognized immediately as Utilities Expense.

According to the FASB, **expenses** are "outflows or other using up of assets or incurrences of liabilities (or a combination of both) from delivering or producing goods, rendering services, or carrying out other activities that constitute the entity's ongoing major or central operations."[4] The key point to note about expenses is that they come about in two different ways:

- from the use of an asset or
- from the recognition of a liability.

---

4 SFAC No. 6, par. 80.

LO4 Describe the matching principle and the various methods for recognizing expenses.

Matching principle
The association of revenue of a period with all of the costs necessary to generate that revenue.

Expenses
Outflows of assets or incurrences of liabilities resulting from delivering goods, rendering services, or carrying out other activities.

EXHIBIT 4-4 Relationships among Costs, Assets, and Expenses

For example, when a retailer sells a product, the asset sacrificed is Inventory. Cost of Goods Sold is the expense account that is increased, and the Inventory account is decreased. As we will see in the next section, the incurrence of an expense may also result in a liability.

2 minute review

1. Explain the difference between the attribute to be measured and the unit of measure.

2. When is revenue normally recognized?

3. Explain the different ways in which expenses are matched with revenues.

Answers

1. *Accountants must decide whether to use historical cost or another attribute or characteristic of an asset, such as its current value, to measure it. Regardless of the attribute measured, it is necessary to choose a yardstick, or unit of measure. In this country, accountants use the dollar to measure assets and other financial statement items.*

2. *Revenue is normally recognized at the time of sale, regardless of when cash is received. Usually this is when the product is delivered or a service is provided to a customer.*

3. *For certain costs, such as cost of goods sold, it is possible to directly match the expense with revenue generated. For other costs, such as depreciation, an indirect form of matching is necessary in which expenses are allocated to the periods benefited, rather than matched with specific revenues. Finally, the benefits associated with the incurrence of certain costs, such as utilities, expire immediately, and therefore expense is recognized as soon as the cost is incurred.*

Accrual Accounting and Adjustments

The accrual basis of accounting necessitates a number of adjustments at the end of a period. **Adjusting entries** are the journal entries the accountant makes at the end of a period for a company on the accrual basis of accounting. **Adjusting entries are not needed if a cash basis is used. It is the very nature of the accrual basis that results in the need for adjusting entries.** The frequency of the adjustment process depends on how often financial statements are prepared. Most businesses make adjustments at the end of each month. Recall from Chapter 3 that the emphasis throughout this book is on the *use* of financial statements rather than their preparation. Thus, rather than focus on the adjusting *entries* that the accountant makes, we will concern ourselves with the effect of these adjustments on the accounting equation.

LO5 Identify the four major types of adjustments and determine their effect on the accounting equation.

Adjusting entries
Journal entries made at the end of a period by a company using the accrual basis of accounting.

TYPES OF ADJUSTMENTS

Why are there four basic types, or categories, of adjustments? The answer lies in the distinction between the cash and the accrual bases of accounting. On an accrual basis, *revenue* can be earned either *before* or *after* cash is received. *Expenses* can be incurred either *before* or *after* cash is paid. Each of these four distinct situations requires a different type of adjustment at the end of the period. We will consider each of the four categories and look at some examples of each.

(1) Cash Paid Before Expense Is Incurred (Deferred Expense) Assets are often acquired before their actual use in the business. Insurance policies typically are prepaid, as often is rent. Office supplies are purchased in advance of their use, as are all types of property and equipment. Recall that unexpired costs are assets. As the costs expire and the benefits are used up, the asset must be written off and replaced with an expense.

Assume that on September 1 Foot Locker prepays $2,400 for an insurance policy for the next 12 months. The effect of the prepayment on the accounting equation follows:

	Balance Sheet			Income Statement
ASSETS	**= LIABILITIES**	**+ STOCKHOLDERS' EQUITY**	**+**	**REVENUES − EXPENSES**
Prepaid Insurance	2,400			
Cash	(2,400)			

The asset Prepaid Insurance represents the benefits the company will receive over the next 12 months. Because the insurance is for a 12-month period, $200 of benefits from the asset expires at the end of each month. The adjustment at the end of September to record this expiration accomplishes two purposes: (1) it recognizes the reduction in the asset Prepaid Insurance, and (2) it recognizes the expense associated with using up the benefits for one month. On September 30, the accountant makes an adjustment to recognize the expense and reduce the asset:

	Balance Sheet			Income Statement	
ASSETS	**= LIABILITIES**	**+ STOCKHOLDERS' EQUITY**	**+**	**REVENUES − EXPENSES**	
Prepaid Insurance	(200)			Insurance Expense	(200)

The balance in Prepaid Insurance represents the unexpired benefits from the prepayment of insurance for the remaining 11 months: $200 × 11 = $2,200. The Insurance Expense account reflects the expiration of benefits during the month of September.

Recall that depreciation is the process of allocating the cost of a long-term tangible asset over its estimated useful life. The accountant does not attempt to measure the decline in *value* of the asset but simply tries to allocate its cost over its useful life. Thus, the adjustment for depreciation is similar to the one we made for insurance expense. Assume that on September 1 Foot Locker buys display racks for a new store for which it pays $5,000. The effect of the purchase on the accounting equation is as follows:

			Balance Sheet				Income Statement
ASSETS		**=**	**LIABILITIES**	**+**	**STOCKHOLDERS' EQUITY**	**+**	**REVENUES − EXPENSES**
Furniture	5,000						
Cash	(5,000)						

Real World Practice 4-1

Reading Foot Locker's Balance Sheet and Notes

Refer to Note 8 in the company's annual report that is reproduced at the end of the book. What was the amount of prepaid expenses and other current assets at the end of 2004? at the end of 2005? Given what you know about Foot Locker's business, give some examples of types of prepaid expenses you would expect the company to incur.

Straight-line method
The assignment of an equal amount of depreciation to each period.

Contra account
Any account that is used to offset another account.

Two estimates must be made in depreciating the display racks: (1) the useful life of the asset and (2) the salvage value of the display racks at the end of their useful lives. Estimated salvage value is the amount a company expects to be able to receive when it sells an asset at the end of its estimated useful life. According to the notes to its financial statements, Foot Locker uses an estimated useful life for its furniture, fixtures, and equipment of three to ten years. Assume that for this particular type of furniture that Foot Locker uses an estimated useful life of seven years. Although it is not stated, assume Foot Locker uses an estimated salvage value of $800 at the end of that time. Thus, the *depreciable cost* of the furniture is $5,000 − $800, or $4,200. In a later chapter, we will consider alternative methods for allocating the depreciable cost over the useful life of an asset. For now, we will use the simplest approach, and the one that Foot Locker uses, called the **straight-line method**, which assigns an equal amount of depreciation to each period. The monthly depreciation is found by dividing the depreciable cost of $4,200 over the estimated useful life of 84 months (7 years = 84 months), which equals $50 per month.

The adjustment to recognize depreciation is conceptually the same as the adjustment to write off Prepaid Insurance. That is, the asset account is reduced, and an expense is recognized. However, accountants normally use a contra account to reduce the total amount of long-term tangible assets by the amount of depreciation. A **contra account** is any account that is used to offset another account. For example, Accumulated Depreciation is used to record the decrease in a long-term asset such as the furniture:

			Balance Sheet				Income Statement	
ASSETS		**=**	**LIABILITIES**	**+**	**STOCKHOLDERS' EQUITY**	**+**	**REVENUES − EXPENSES**	
Accumulated							Depreciation Expense	(50)
Depreciation	(50)							

Study Tip

Think of the Accumulated Depreciation account as simply an extension of the related asset account, in this case the Furniture account. Therefore, although the Furniture account is not directly reduced for depreciation, an increase in its companion account, Accumulated Depreciation, has the effect of reducing the asset.

Why do companies use a contra account for depreciation rather than simply reducing the long-term asset directly? If the asset account were reduced each time depreciation is recorded, its original cost would not be readily determinable from the accounting records. Businesses need to know the original cost of each asset, for various reasons. One of the most important of these reasons is the need to know historical cost for computation of depreciation for tax purposes.

On a balance sheet prepared on September 30, the contra account is shown as a reduction in the carrying value of the furniture:

Furniture	$5,000	
Less: Accumulated Depreciation	50	$4,950

(2) Cash Received Before Revenue Is Earned (Deferred Revenue) Recognizing accounting's symmetry will be a great help in your studies. Note that one company's asset is another company's liability. In the earlier example involving the purchase of an insurance policy, a second company, the insurance company, received the cash paid by the first company, Foot Locker. At the time cash is received, the insurance company has a liability because it has taken cash from Foot Locker but has not yet performed the service to earn the revenue. The revenue will be earned with the passage of time. The effect on the accounting equation from the collection of cash on September 1 is as follows:

Balance Sheet						Income Statement
ASSETS	**=**	**LIABILITIES**	**+**	**STOCKHOLDERS' EQUITY**	**+**	**REVENUES − EXPENSES**
Cash 2,400		Insurance Collected in Advance 2,400				

The account Insurance Collected in Advance is a liability. The insurance company is obligated to provide Foot Locker protection for the next 12 months. With the passage of time, the liability is satisfied. The adjustment at the end of each month accomplishes two purposes: it recognizes (1) the reduction in the liability and (2) the revenue earned each month:

Balance Sheet						Income Statement
ASSETS	**=**	**LIABILITIES**	**+**	**STOCKHOLDERS' EQUITY**	**+**	**REVENUES − EXPENSES**
		Insurance Collected in Advance (200)				Insurance Revenue 200

After the adjustment is made, the insurance company's remaining liability is $2,400 − $200, or $2,200, which represents 11 months of insurance collected in advance at $200 per month.

In another example, many magazine subscriptions require the customer to pay in advance. For example, you pay $12 for a one-year subscription to your favorite magazine, and the publisher in turn sends you 12 monthly issues. At the time you send money to the publisher, it incurs a liability. It has taken your money but has not yet done anything to earn it. The publisher has an obligation either to provide you with the magazine over the next 12 months or to refund your $12.

At what point should the publisher recognize revenue from magazine sales? The publisher receives cash at the time the subscription is sold. The revenue has not been *earned* until the company publishes the magazine and mails it to you, however. Thus, a publisher usually recognizes revenue at the time of delivery. An excerpt from page 50 of the 2005 annual report of Meredith Corporation (which publishes *Better Homes and Gardens*) reflects this policy:

> Revenues from magazine subscriptions are deferred and recognized proportionately as products are delivered to subscribers.

Assume that on March 1 Meredith sells 500 one-year subscriptions to a monthly magazine at a price of $12 each. At this point, Meredith has an obligation to deliver magazines over the next 12 months:

© AP/Wide World Photos

A gift card like this is a good example of a deferred revenue. BEST BUY has received the $25 in payment for the card, but because it must wait for the recipient of the gift to pick out a product, it considers the obligation to deliver the product in the future a liability.

Balance Sheet						Income Statement
ASSETS	**=**	**LIABILITIES**	**+**	**STOCKHOLDERS' EQUITY**	**+**	**REVENUES − EXPENSES**
Cash 6,000		Subscriptions Collected in Advance 6,000				

Assuming that each of the subscriptions starts with the March issue of the magazine, at the end of March, Meredith accountants would adjust the records to reflect the revenue earned for the first month:

Balance Sheet						Income Statement
ASSETS	**=**	**LIABILITIES**	**+**	**STOCKHOLDERS' EQUITY**	**+**	**REVENUES − EXPENSES**
		Subscriptions Collected in Advance (500)				Subscription Revenue 500

After the adjustment is made, Meredith's remaining liability is $6,000 − $500, or $5,500, which represents 11 months of unearned revenue at $500 per month.

As you know by now, accounting terminology differs among companies. The account title Subscriptions Collected in Advance is only one of any number of possible titles for the liability related to subscriptions. For example, Meredith's balance sheet does not have this account title, but instead uses the account, Unearned Subscription Revenues.

(3) Expense Incurred Before Cash Is Paid (Accrued Liability) This situation is just the opposite of (1). That is, cash is paid *after* an expense is actually incurred rather than *before* its incurrence, as was the case in (1). Many normal operating costs, such as payroll, various types of taxes, and utilities, fit this situation.

Assume that at one of its stores, Foot Locker pays a total of $28,000 in wages on every other Friday. Assume that the last payday was Friday, May 31. The next two paydays will be Friday, June 14, and Friday, June 28. The effect on the accounting equation on each of these paydays is the same:

		Balance Sheet				Income Statement	
ASSETS	**=**	**LIABILITIES**	**+**	**STOCKHOLDERS' EQUITY**	**+**	**REVENUES − EXPENSES**	
Cash	(28,000)					Wages Expense	(28,000)

On a balance sheet prepared as of June 30, a liability must be recognized. Even though the next payment is not until July 12, Foot Locker *owes* employees wages for the last two days of June and must recognize an expense for the wages earned by employees for these two days. We will assume that the store is open seven days a week and that the daily cost is 1/14th of the biweekly amount of $28,000, or $2,000. In addition to recognizing a liability on June 30, Foot Locker must adjust the records to reflect an expense associated with the cost of wages for the last two days of the month:

		Balance Sheet				Income Statement	
	ASSETS	**=**	**LIABILITIES**	**+**	**STOCKHOLDERS' EQUITY**	**+**	**REVENUES − EXPENSES**
		Wages Payable	4,000			Wages Expense	(4,000)

What adjustment will be made on the next payday, July 12? Foot Locker will need to eliminate the liability of $4,000 for the last two days of wages recorded on June 30 because the amount has now been paid. An additional $24,000 of expense has been incurred for the $2,000 cost per day associated with the first 12 days in July. Finally, cash is reduced for $28,000, which represents the biweekly payroll:

		Balance Sheet				Income Statement	
	ASSETS	**=**	**LIABILITIES**	**+**	**STOCKHOLDERS' EQUITY**	**+**	**REVENUES − EXPENSES**
Cash	(28,000)	Wages Payable	(4,000)			Wages Expense	(24,000)

The following time line illustrates the amount of expense incurred in each of the two months, June and July, for the biweekly payroll:

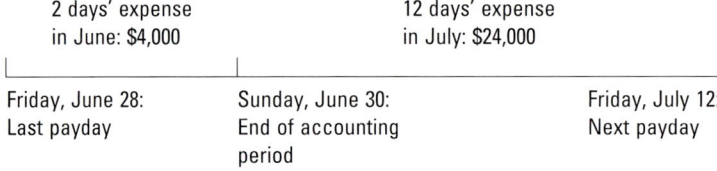

Another typical expense incurred before the payment of cash is interest. In many cases, the interest on a short-term loan is repaid with the amount of the loan, called the *principal,* on the maturity date. For example, assume Granger Company takes out a 9%, 90-day, $20,000 loan with its bank on March 1. The principal and interest will be repaid on May 30. On March 1, both an asset, Cash, and a liability, Notes Payable, are increased:

	Balance Sheet					Income Statement
ASSETS	**=**	**LIABILITIES**	**+**	**STOCKHOLDERS' EQUITY**	**+**	**REVENUES − EXPENSES**
Cash 20,000		Notes Payable 20,000				

The **basic formula for computing interest** follows:

$$I = P \times R \times T$$

where I = the dollar amount of interest
P = the principal amount of the loan
R = the annual rate of interest as a percentage
T = time in years (often stated as a fraction of a year).

The total interest on Granger's loan is as follows:

$$\$20,000 \times 0.09 \times 3/12 = \underline{\$450}$$

Therefore, the amount of interest that must be recognized as expense at the end of March is one-third of $450 because one month of a total of three has passed. Alternatively, the formula for finding the total interest on the loan can be modified to compute the interest for one month:[5]

$$\$20,000 \times 0.09 \times 1/12 = \underline{\$150}$$

On March 31 and April 30, the accountant records adjustments to recognize interest both as an expense and as an obligation. The effect on the accounting equation from the adjustments for the two months combined is as follows:

	Balance Sheet					Income Statement
ASSETS	**=**	**LIABILITIES**	**+**	**STOCKHOLDERS' EQUITY**	**+**	**REVENUES − EXPENSES**
		Interest Payable 300				Interest Expense (300)

The effect on Granger's accounting equation on May 30 when it repays the principal and interest is:

	Balance Sheet					Income Statement
ASSETS	**=**	**LIABILITIES**	**+**	**STOCKHOLDERS' EQUITY**	**+**	**REVENUES − EXPENSES**
Cash (20,450)		Interest Payable (300)				Interest Expense (150)
		Notes Payable (20,000)				

---

5 In practice, interest is calculated on the basis of days rather than months. For example, the interest for March would be $20,000 × 0.09 × 30/365, or $147.95, to reflect 30 days in the month out of a total of 365 days in the year. The reason the number of days in March is 30 rather than 31 is because in computing interest, businesses normally count the day a note matures but not the day it is signed. To simplify the calculations, we will use months, even though the result is slightly inaccurate.

Recognition of this transaction accomplishes three purposes. First, the $20,000 of principal and the total interest of $450 for three months is recognized as a decrease in Cash. Second, Interest Expense of $150 for the month of May is recognized. Finally, the two liabilities remaining on the books, Interest Payable and Notes Payable, are removed.[6]

(4) Revenue Earned Before Cash Is Received (Accrued Asset) Revenue is sometimes earned before the receipt of cash. Rent and interest are both earned with the passage of time and require an adjustment if cash has not yet been received. For example, assume that Grand Management Company rents warehouse space to a number of tenants. Most of its contracts call for prepayment of rent for six months at a time. Its agreement with one tenant, however, allows the tenant to pay Grand $2,500 in monthly rent anytime within the first 10 days of the following month. The adjustment on April 30, the end of the first month of the agreement, is as follows:

Balance Sheet					Income Statement	
ASSETS	**=**	**LIABILITIES**	**+**	**STOCKHOLDERS' EQUITY**	**+**	**REVENUES − EXPENSES**
Rent Receivable 2,500					Rent Revenue	2,500

When the tenant pays its rent on May 7, the effect on Grand's accounting equation is as follows:

Balance Sheet					Income Statement	
ASSETS	**=**	**LIABILITIES**	**+**	**STOCKHOLDERS' EQUITY**	**+**	**REVENUES − EXPENSES**
Cash 2,500						
Rent Receivable (2,500)						

Although we used the example of rent to illustrate this category, the membership revenue of Glengarry Health Club in Chapter 3 also could be used as an example. Whenever a company records revenue before cash is received, some type of receivable is increased and revenue is also increased. In that chapter, the health club earned membership revenue even though members had until the following month to pay their dues.

ACCRUALS AND DEFERRALS

One of the challenges in learning accounting concepts is to gain an understanding of the terminology. Part of the difficulty stems from the alternative terms used by different accountants to mean the same thing. For example, the asset created when insurance is paid for in advance is termed a *prepaid asset* by some and a *prepaid expense* by others. Someone else might refer to it as a *deferred expense*.

We will use the term **deferral** to refer to a situation in which cash has been either paid or received, but the expense or revenue has been deferred to a later time. A **deferred expense** indicates that cash has been paid, but the recognition of expense has been deferred. Because a deferred expense represents a *future benefit* to

Study Tip

Now that we have seen examples of all four types of adjustments, think about a key difference between deferrals (the first two categories) and accruals (the last two categories). When we make adjustments involving deferrals, we must consider any existing balance in a deferred balance sheet account. Conversely, there is no existing account when making an accrual.

Deferral

Cash has either been paid or received, but expense or revenue has not yet been recognized.

---

6 This assumes that Granger did not make an adjustment prior to this to recognize interest expense for the month of May. If a separate adjustment had been made, Interest Payable would be reduced by $450.

a company, it is an asset. An alternative name for deferred expense is *prepaid expense*. Prepaid insurance and office supplies are deferred expenses. An adjustment is made periodically to record the portion of the deferred expense that has expired. A **deferred revenue** means that cash has been received but the recognition of any revenue has been deferred until a later time. Because a deferred revenue represents an *obligation* to a company, it is a liability. An alternative name for deferred revenue is *unearned revenue*. Rent collected in advance is deferred revenue. The periodic adjustment recognizes the portion of the deferred revenue that is earned in that period.

In this chapter, we have discussed in detail the accrual basis of accounting, which involves recognizing changes in resources and obligations as they occur, not simply when cash changes hands. More specifically, we will use the term **accrual** to refer to a situation in which no cash has been paid or received yet, but it is necessary to recognize, or accrue, an expense or a revenue. An **accrued liability** is recognized at the end of the period in cases in which an expense has been incurred but cash has not yet been paid. Wages payable and interest payable are examples of accrued liabilities. An **accrued asset** is recorded when revenue has been earned but cash has not yet been collected. Rent receivable is an accrued asset.

Deferred expense
An asset resulting from the payment of cash before the incurrence of expense.

Deferred revenue
A liability resulting from the receipt of cash before the recognition of revenue.

Accrual
Cash has not yet been paid or received, but expense has been incurred or revenue earned.

Accrued liability
A liability resulting from the recognition of an expense before the payment of cash.

Accrued asset
An asset resulting from the recognition of a revenue before the receipt of cash.

SUMMARY OF ADJUSTMENTS

The four types of adjustments are summarized in Exhibit 4-5. Common examples of each are shown, along with the accounts affected by each. Finally, the following generalizations should help you in gaining a better understanding of adjustments and how they are used:

1. **An adjustment is an internal transaction. It does not involve another entity.**
2. **Because it is an internal transaction, an adjustment never involves an increase or decrease in Cash.**
3. **At least one balance sheet account and one income statement account are involved in an adjustment. It is the nature of the adjustment process that an asset or liability account is adjusted with a corresponding change in either a revenue or an expense account.**

EXHIBIT 4-5 | Accruals and Deferrals

Type	Situation	Examples	Transaction During Period	Adjustment at End of Period
Deferred expense	Cash paid before expense is incurred	Insurance policy Supplies Rent Buildings, equipment	Increase Asset Decrease Cash	Increase Expense Decrease Asset
Deferred revenue	Cash received before revenue is earned	Deposits, rent Subscriptions Gift certificates	Increase Cash Increase Liability	Decrease Liability Increase Revenue
Accrued liability	Expense incurred before cash is paid	Salaries, wages Interest Taxes Rent	No Transaction	Increase Expense Increase Liability
Accrued asset	Revenue earned before cash is received	Interest Rent	No Transaction	Increase Asset Increase Revenue

2 minute review

Assume a company wants to prepare financial statements at the end of its first month of operations. Each of the following transactions were recorded on the company's books on the first day of the month.

1. Purchased a 24-month insurance policy for $3,600.

2. Collected $4,800 from a tenant for office space that the tenant has rented for the next 12 months.

3. Took out a 6%, 180-day, $10,000 loan at the bank.

For each of these transactions, determine the effect on the accounting equation of the adjustment required.

Answers

		Balance Sheet				Income Statement	
ASSETS	**=**	**LIABILITIES**	**+**	**STOCKHOLDERS' EQUITY**	**+**	**REVENUES − EXPENSES**	
1. Prepaid Insurance (150)						Insurance Expense	(150)
2.		Rent Collected in Advance (400)				Rent Revenue	400
3.		Interest Payable 50				Interest Expense	(50)

COMPREHENSIVE EXAMPLE OF ADJUSTMENTS

We will now consider a comprehensive example involving the transactions for the first month of operations and the end-of-period adjustments for a hypothetical business, Duffy Transit Company. A list of accounts and their balances is shown for Duffy Transit at January 31, the end of the first month of business (prior to making any adjustments):

Assets:	
Cash	$ 50,000
Prepaid Insurance	48,000
Land	20,000
Buildings—Garage	160,000
Equipment—Buses	300,000
Liabilities:	
Discount Tickets Sold in Advance	25,000
Notes Payable	150,000
Owners' Equity:	
Capital Stock	400,000
Revenues:	
Daily Ticket Revenue	30,000
Expenses:	
Gas, Oil, and Maintenance	12,000
Wages and Salaries	10,000
Dividends	5,000

Duffy wants to prepare a balance sheet at the end of January and an income statement for its first month of operations. Use of the accrual basis necessitates a number of adjustments to update certain asset and liability accounts and to recognize the correct amounts for the various revenues and expenses.

ADJUSTMENTS AT THE END OF JANUARY

(1) At the beginning of January, Duffy issued an 18-month, 12%, $150,000 promissory note for cash. Although interest will not be repaid until the loan's maturity date, Duffy must accrue interest for the first month. The calculation of interest for one month is $150,000 × 0.12 × 1/12. The adjustment is:

	Balance Sheet					Income Statement	
ASSETS	**=**	**LIABILITIES**	**+**	**STOCKHOLDERS' EQUITY**	**+**	**REVENUES – EXPENSES**	
		Interest Payable 1,500				Interest Expense	(1,500)

(2) Wages and salary expense of $10,000 reflects the amount paid to employees during January. Duffy owes employees an additional $2,800 in salaries and wages at January 31. The effect of the adjustment is as follows:

	Balance Sheet					Income Statement	
ASSETS	**=**	**LIABILITIES**	**+**	**STOCKHOLDERS' EQUITY**	**+**	**REVENUES – EXPENSES**	
		Wages and Salaries Payable 2,800				Wage and Salary Expense	(2,800)

(3) At the beginning of January, Duffy acquired a garage to house the buses at a cost of $160,000. Land is not subject to depreciation. The cost of the land acquired in connection with the purchase of the building will remain on the books until the property is sold. The garage has an estimated useful life of 20 years and an estimated salvage value of $16,000 at the end of its life. The monthly depreciation is found by dividing the depreciable cost of $144,000 by the useful life of 240 months:

$$\frac{\$160,000 - \$16,000}{20 \text{ years} \times 12 \text{ months}} = \frac{\$144,000}{240 \text{ months}} = \underline{\$600} \text{ per month}$$

The adjustment to record the depreciation on the garage for January for a full month is:

	Balance Sheet					Income Statement	
ASSETS	**=**	**LIABILITIES**	**+**	**STOCKHOLDERS' EQUITY**	**+**	**REVENUES – EXPENSES**	
Accumulated Depreciation—Garage (600)						Depreciation Expense— Garage	(600)

(4) Duffy purchased 10 buses for $30,000 each at the beginning of January. The buses have an estimated useful life of five years, at which time the company plans to sell them for $6,000 each. The monthly depreciation on the 10 buses is:

$$10 \times \frac{\$30,000 - \$6,000}{5 \text{ years} \times 12 \text{ months}} = 10 \times \frac{\$24,000}{60 \text{ months}} = \underline{\$4,000} \text{ per month}$$

The adjustment to recognize the depreciation on the buses for the first month is:

	Balance Sheet					Income Statement	
ASSETS	**=**	**LIABILITIES**	**+**	**STOCKHOLDERS' EQUITY**	**+**	**REVENUES – EXPENSES**	
Accumulated Depreciation—Buses (4,000)						Depreciation Expense— Buses	(4,000)

(5) An insurance policy was purchased for $48,000 on January 1. It provides property and liability protection for a 24-month period. The adjustment to allocate the cost to expense for the first month is:

	Balance Sheet					Income Statement	
ASSETS	**=**	**LIABILITIES**	**+**	**STOCKHOLDERS' EQUITY**	**+**	**REVENUES – EXPENSES**	
Prepaid Insurance (2,000)						Insurance Expense	(2,000)

(6) In addition to selling tickets on the bus, Duffy sells discount tickets at the terminal. The tickets are good for a ride anytime within 12 months of purchase. Thus, as these tickets are sold, Duffy increses Cash as well as a liability account, Discount Tickets Sold in Advance. The sale of $25,000 worth of these tickets was recorded during January. At the end of the first month, Duffy counts the number of tickets that have been redeemed. Because $20,400 worth of tickets has been turned in, this is the amount by which the company reduces its liability and recognizes revenue for the month:

		Balance Sheet					Income Statement	
ASSETS	**=**	**LIABILITIES**	**+**	**STOCKHOLDERS' EQUITY**	**+**		**REVENUES − EXPENSES**	
		Discount Tickets Sold					Discount Ticket Revenue	20,400
		in Advance	(20,400)					

(7) Duffy does not need all of the space in its garage and rents a section of it to another company for $2,500 per month. The tenant has until the 10th day of the following month to pay its rent. The adjustment on Duffy's books on the last day of the month is:

		Balance Sheet				Income Statement	
ASSETS		**=**	**LIABILITIES**	**+**	**STOCKHOLDERS' EQUITY**	**+**	**REVENUES − EXPENSES**
Rent Receivable	2,500					Rent Revenue	2,500

(8) Corporations pay estimated taxes on a quarterly basis. Because Duffy is preparing an income statement for the month of January, it must estimate its taxes for the month. We will assume a corporate tax rate of 34% on income before tax. The computation of Income Tax Expense is as follows (the amounts shown for the revenues and expenses reflect the effect of the adjustments):

Revenues:		
Daily Ticket Revenue	$30,000	
Discount Ticket Revenue	20,400	
Rent Revenue	2,500	$52,900
Expenses:		
Gas, Oil, and Maintenance Expense	$12,000	
Wage and Salary Expense	12,800	
Depreciation Expense	4,600	
Insurance Expense	2,000	
Interest Expense	1,500	32,900
Net Income before Tax		$20,000
Times the Corporate Tax Rate		$\times$ 0.34
Income Tax Expense		$ 6,800

Based on this estimate of taxes, the final adjustment Duffy makes is:

		Balance Sheet					Income Statement	
ASSETS	**=**	**LIABILITIES**	**+**	**STOCKHOLDERS' EQUITY**	**+**		**REVENUES − EXPENSES**	
		Income Tax Payable	6,800				Income Tax Expense	(6,800)

INCOME STATEMENT AND BALANCE SHEET FOR DUFFY TRANSIT

Now that the adjustments have been made, financial statements can be prepared. An income statement for January and a balance sheet as of January 31 are shown in Exhibit 4-6. Each of the account balances on the statements was determined by taking the balances in the list of accounts on page 170 and adding or subtracting as appropriate the necessary adjustments. Note the balance in Retained Earnings of $8,200. This amount was found by taking the net income of $13,200 and deducting the dividends of $5,000.

EXHIBIT 4-6 Financial Statements for Duffy Transit Company

DUFFY TRANSIT COMPANY
INCOME STATEMENT
FOR THE MONTH OF JANUARY

Revenues:		
Daily ticket revenue	$30,000	
Discount ticket revenue	20,400	
Rent revenue	2,500	$52,900
Expenses:		
Gas, oil, and maintenance	$12,000	
Wages and salaries	12,800	
Depreciation—garage	600	
Depreciation—buses	4,000	
Insurance	2,000	
Interest	1,500	
Income taxes	6,800	39,700
Net income		$13,200

DUFFY TRANSIT COMPANY
BALANCE SHEET
JANUARY 31

Assets			Liabilities and Stockholders' Equity	
Cash		$ 50,000	Discount tickets	
Rent receivable		2,500	sold in advance	$ 4,600
Prepaid insurance		46,000	Notes payable	150,000
Land		20,000	Interest payable	1,500
Buildings—garage	$160,000		Wages and salaries	
Accumulated			payable	2,800
depreciation	600	159,400	Income tax payable	6,800
Equipment—buses	$300,000		Capital stock	400,000
Accumulated			Retained earnings	8,200
depreciation	4,000	296,000	Total liabilities and	
Total assets		$573,900	stockholders' equity	$573,900

ETHICAL CONSIDERATIONS FOR A COMPANY ON THE ACCRUAL BASIS

The accrual basis requires the recognition of revenues when earned and expenses when incurred regardless of when cash is received or paid. Adjustments are *internal* transactions in that they do not involve an exchange with an outside entity. Because adjustments do not involve another company, accountants may at times feel pressure from others within the organization to either speed or delay the recognition of certain adjustments.

Consider the following two examples for a landscaping company that is concerned about its "bottom line," that is, its net income. A number of jobs are in progress, but because of inclement weather, none of them are very far along. Management asks the accountant to recognize all of the revenue from a job in progress even though no significant work has been done on the job. Further, the accountant has been asked to delay the recognition of various short-term accrued liabilities (and, of course, the accompanying expenses) until the beginning of the new year.

The "correct" response of the accountant to each of these requests may seem obvious: no revenue on the one job should be recognized, and all accrued liabilities should be expensed at year-end. The pressures of the daily work environment make these decisions difficult for the accountant, however. The accountant must always remember that his or her primary responsibility in preparing financial statements is to accurately portray the affairs of the company to the various outside users. Bankers, stockholders, and others rely on the accountant to serve their best interests.

The Accounting Cycle

LO6 Explain the steps in the accounting cycle and the significance of each step.

Accounting cycle
A series of steps performed each period and culminating with the preparation of a set of financial statements.

We have focused our attention in this chapter on accrual accounting and the adjustments it necessitates. The adjustments the accountant makes are one key component in the **accounting cycle**. The accountant for a business follows a series of steps each period. The objective is always the same: **collect the necessary information to prepare a set of financial statements**. Together, these steps make up the accounting cycle. The name comes from the fact that the steps are repeated each period. It is possible that a company performs all of the steps in the accounting cycle once a *month* although in practice certain steps in the cycle may be carried out only once a *year*.

The steps in the accounting cycle are shown in Exhibit 4-7. Note that step 1 involves not only *collecting* information but also *analyzing* it. Transaction analysis is probably the most challenging of all the steps in the accounting cycle. It requires the ability to think logically about an event and its effect on the financial position of the entity. Once the transaction is analyzed, it is recorded in the journal, as indicated by the second step in the exhibit. The first two steps in the cycle take place continuously.

Transactions are posted to the accounts on a periodic basis. The frequency of posting to the accounts depends on two factors: the type of accounting system used by a company and the volume of transactions. In a manual system, entries might be posted daily, weekly, or even monthly, depending on the amount of activity. The larger the number of transactions a company records, the more often it posts.

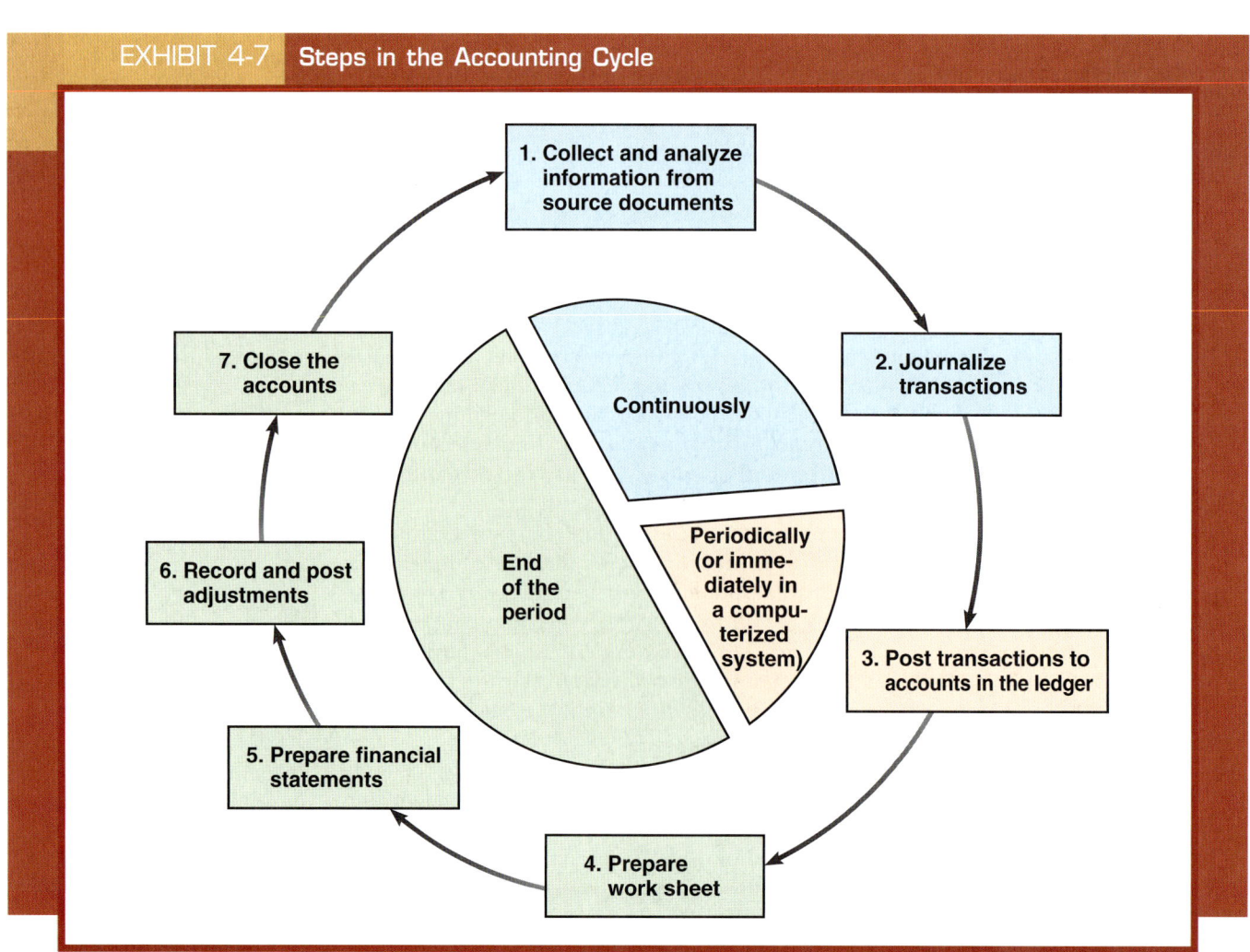

EXHIBIT 4-7   Steps in the Accounting Cycle

In an automated accounting system, posting is likely done automatically by the computer each time a transaction is recorded.

THE USE OF A WORK SHEET

Step 4 in Exhibit 4-7 calls for the preparation of a work sheet. The end of an accounting period is a busy time. In addition to recording daily recurring transactions, the accountant must record adjustments as the basis for preparing financial statements. The time available to prepare the statements is usually very limited. The use of a **work sheet** allows the accountant to gather and organize the information required to adjust the accounts without actually recording and posting the adjustments to the accounts. Recording adjustments and posting them to the accounts can be done after the financial statements are prepared. **A work sheet itself is not a financial statement.** Instead, it is a useful device to *organize* the information needed to prepare the financial statements at the end of the period.

It is not essential that a work sheet be used before preparing financial statements. If it is not used, step 6, recording and posting adjustments, comes before step 5, preparing the financial statements.

THE CLOSING PROCESS

Step 7 in Exhibit 4-7 is the closing process. For purposes of closing the books, accountants categorize accounts into two types.

- Balance sheet accounts are called **real accounts** because they are permanent in nature. For this reason, they are never closed. The balance in each of these accounts is carried over from one period to the next.

- In contrast, revenue, expense, and dividend accounts are *temporary* or **nominal accounts**. The balances in the income statement accounts and the Dividends account are *not* carried forward from one accounting period to the next. For this reason, these accounts are closed at the end of the period.

Closing entries serve two important purposes: (1) to return the balances in all temporary or nominal accounts to zero to start the next accounting period and (2) to transfer the net income (or net loss) and the dividends of the period to the Retained Earnings account.

INTERIM FINANCIAL STATEMENTS

Recall that certain steps in the accounting cycle are sometimes carried out only once a year rather than each month as in our example. For ease of illustration, we assumed a monthly accounting cycle. Many companies adjust and close the accounts only once a year, however. They use a work sheet more frequently than this as the basis for preparing interim statements. Statements prepared monthly, quarterly, or at other intervals less than a year in duration are called **interim statements**. Many companies prepare monthly financial statements for their own internal use. Similarly, corporations whose shares are publicly traded on one of the stock exchanges are required to file quarterly financial statements with the Securities and Exchange Commission.

Suppose that a company prepares monthly financial statements for internal use and completes the accounting cycle in its entirety only once a year. In this case, a work sheet is prepared each month as the basis for interim financial statements. Formal adjusting and closing the books is done only at the end of each year. The adjustments that appear on the monthly work sheet are not posted to the accounts. They are entered on the work sheet simply as a basis for preparing the monthly financial statements.

Work sheet
A device used at the end of the period to gather the information needed to prepare financial statements without actually recording and posting adjustments.

Real accounts
The name given to balance sheet accounts because they are permanent and are not closed at the end of the period.

Nominal accounts
The name given to revenue, expense, and dividend accounts because they are temporary and are closed at the end of the period.

Closing entries
Journal entries made at the end of the period to return the balance in all nominal accounts to zero and transfer the net income or loss and the dividends to Retained Earnings.

Interim statements
Financial statements prepared monthly, quarterly, or at other intervals less than a year in duration.

STUDY HIGHLIGHTS

LO1   **Explain the significance of recognition and measurement in the preparation and use of financial statements (p. 155).**

- Determining which economic events should be recognized and how they should be measured is critical for accounting information to be useful.
  - Recognition drives how and when the effects of economic events are described in the financial statements.
  - Measurement involves deciding on which attribute of an economic event must be measured and the appropriate unit of measure.

LO2   **Explain the differences between the cash and accrual bases of accounting (p. 157).**

- Cash and accrual bases are two alternatives to account for transactions or economic events. They differ in the timing of when revenues and expenses are recognized.
  - Under the accrual method, which is the focus of this text, revenues are recognized when earned, and expenses are recognized when incurred.
  - By contrast, under the cash method, revenues are recognized when cash is received, and expenses are recognized when cash is paid.

LO3   **Describe the revenue recognition principle and explain its application in various situations (p. 160).**

- Revenues are inflows of assets (or reductions of liabilities), generally from providing goods or services to customers.
  - Revenues must be both realized and earned in order to be recognized on the income statement.

LO4   **Describe the matching principle and the various methods for recognizing expenses (p. 161).**

- The matching principle attempts to associate expenses with the time periods in which the expenditures help to generate revenues.
- This principle is particularly important with expenditures for items that last for more than one accounting period. An example would be the depreciation of a building.

LO5   **Identify the four major types of adjustments and determine their effect on the accounting equation (p. 163).**

- Adjustments are made at the end of an accounting period to update revenue or expense accounts in accordance with the revenue recognition and matching principles.
- There are four basic categories of adjustments:
  - Adjustments where cash is paid before expenses are incurred—deferred expenses.
  - Adjustments where cash is received before revenues are earned—deferred revenue.
  - Adjustments where expenses are incurred before cash is paid—accrued liabilities.
  - Adjustments where revenues are recognized before cash is received—accrued assets.

LO6   **Explain the steps in the accounting cycle and the significance of each step (p. 174).**

- The accounting cycle involves seven steps that are repeated each period (see Exhibit 4-7).
  - Collecting and analyzing data, and journalizing transactions occur on a continuous basis.
  - Periodically, transactions are posted to accounts in the ledger.
  - At the end of the period, a work sheet is prepared, financial statements are prepared, adjustments are recorded and posted, and accounts are closed.
- Closing serves two important purposes:
  - It returns the balance of all nominal accounts to zero so that the accounts are ready to record activity for the next accounting period.
  - It transfers net income (loss) and dividends to retained earnings.

ACCOUNTS HIGHLIGHTED

Account Titles	Where It Appears	In What Section	Page Number
Prepaid Insurance	Balance Sheet	Current Assets	163
Accumulated Depreciation	Balance Sheet	Noncurrent Assets (contra)	164
Deferred Revenue	Balance Sheet	Current Liabilities*	164
Wages Payable	Balance Sheet	Current Liabilities	166
Interest Payable	Balance Sheet	Current Liabilities	167
Rent Receivable	Balance Sheet	Current Assets	168

If any part of deferred revenue will not be earned within the next year, it should be classified as a noncurrent liability.

KEY TERMS QUIZ

Read each definition below and then write the number of that definition in the blank beside the appropriate term it defines. The quiz solutions appear at the end of the chapter.

_____	Recognition	_____	Deferral
_____	Historical cost	_____	Deferred expense
_____	Current value	_____	Deferred revenue
_____	Cash basis	_____	Accrual
_____	Accrual basis	_____	Accrued liability
_____	Revenues	_____	Accrued asset
_____	Revenue recognition principle	_____	Accounting cycle
_____	Matching principle	_____	Work sheet
_____	Expenses	_____	Real accounts
_____	Adjusting entries	_____	Nominal accounts
_____	Straight-line method	_____	Closing entries
_____	Contra account	_____	Interim statements

1. A device used at the end of the period to gather the information needed to prepare financial statements without actually recording and posting adjusting entries.

2. Inflows or other enhancements of assets or settlements of liabilities from delivering or producing goods, rendering services, or other activities.

3. Journal entries made at the end of a period by a company using the accrual basis of accounting.

4. Journal entries made at the end of the period to return the balance in all nominal accounts to zero and transfer the net income or loss and the dividends of the period to Retained Earnings.

5. A liability resulting from the receipt of cash before the recognition of revenue.

6. The name given to balance sheet accounts because they are permanent and are not closed at the end of the period.

7. An asset resulting from the recognition of a revenue before the receipt of cash.

8. The amount of cash, or its equivalent, that could be received by selling an asset currently.

9. The assignment of an equal amount of depreciation to each period.

10. Cash has either been paid or received, but expense or revenue has not yet been recognized.

11. A system of accounting in which revenues are recognized when earned and expenses when incurred.

12. Cash has not yet been paid or received, but expense has been incurred or revenue earned.

(continued)

13. Financial statements prepared monthly, quarterly, or at other intervals less than a year in duration.

14. Revenues are recognized in the income statement when they are realized, or realizable, and earned.

15. The process of recording an item in the financial statements as an asset, liability, revenue, expense, or the like.

16. An asset resulting from the payment of cash before the incurrence of expense.

17. The name given to revenue, expense, and dividend accounts because they are temporary and are closed at the end of the period.

18. A system of accounting in which revenues are recognized when cash is received and expenses when cash is paid.

19. A liability resulting from the recognition of an expense before the payment of cash.

20. The association of revenue of a period with all of the costs necessary to generate that revenue.

21. Any account that is used to offset another account.

22. The amount that is paid for an asset and that is used as a basis for recognizing it on the balance sheet and carrying it on later balance sheets.

23. Outflows or other using up of assets or incurrences of liabilities resulting from delivering goods, rendering services, or carrying out other activities.

24. A series of steps performed each period and culminating with the preparation of a set of financial statements.

ALTERNATE TERMS

Historical cost Original cost

Asset Unexpired cost

Deferred expense Prepaid expense, prepaid asset

Deferred revenue Unearned revenue

Expense Expired cost

Nominal account Temporary account

Real account Permanent account

WARMUP EXERCISES & SOLUTIONS

LO5   **Warmup Exercise 4-1** Prepaid Insurance

ABC Corp. purchases a 24-month fire insurance policy on January 1, 2007, for $5,400.

Required
Determine the effect on the accounting equation on January 31, 2007.

Key to the Solution Determine what proportion and therefore what dollar amount of the policy has expired after one month.

LO5   **Warmup Exercise 4-2** Depreciation

DEF Corp. purchased a new car for one of its salespeople on March 1, 2007, for $25,000. The estimated useful life of the car is four years with an estimated salvage value of $1,000.

Required
Determine the effect on the accounting equation on March 31, 2007.

Key to the Solution Determine what dollar amount of the cost of the car should be depreciated and then how much should be depreciated each month.

LO5   **Warmup Exercise 4-3** Interest on a Note

On April 1, 2007, GHI Corp. took out a 12%, 120-day, $10,000 loan at its bank.

Required
Determine the effect on the accounting equation on April 30, 2007.

Key to the Solution Determine the monthly interest cost on a loan that accrues interest at the rate of 12% per year.

SOLUTIONS TO WARMUP EXERCISES

	Balance Sheet						Income Statement	
ASSETS		**=**	**LIABILITIES**	**+**	**STOCKHOLDERS' EQUITY**	**+**	**REVENUES − EXPENSES**	
1. Prepaid Insurance	(225)						Insurance Expense	(225)
2. Accumulated							Depreciation Expense	(500)
Depreciation	(500)							
3.			Interest Payable 100				Interest Expense	(100)

REVIEW PROBLEM & SOLUTION

A list of accounts for Northern Airlines at January 31 is shown below. It reflects the recurring transactions for the month of January, but it does not reflect any month-end adjustments.

Cash	$ 75,000
Parts Inventory	45,000
Land	80,000
Buildings—Hangars	250,000
Accumulated Depreciation—Hangars	24,000
Equipment—Aircraft	650,000
Accumulated Depreciation—Aircraft	120,000
Tickets Sold in Advance	85,000
Capital Stock	500,000
Retained Earnings	368,000
Ticket Revenue	52,000
Maintenance Expense	19,000
Wage and Salary Expense	30,000

The following additional information is available:

a. Airplane parts needed for repairs and maintenance are purchased regularly, and the amounts paid are added to the asset account Parts Inventory. At the end of each month, the inventory is counted. At the end of January, the amount of parts on hand is $36,100. *Hint:* What adjustment is needed to reduce the asset account to its proper carrying value? Any expense involved should be included in Maintenance Expense.

b. The estimated useful life of the hangar is 20 years with an estimated salvage value of $10,000 at the end of its life. The original cost of the hangar was $250,000.

c. The estimated useful life of the aircraft is 10 years with an estimated salvage value of $50,000. The original cost of the aircraft was $650,000.

d. As tickets are sold in advance, the amounts are added to Cash and to the liability account Tickets Sold in Advance. A count of the redeemed tickets reveals that $47,000 worth of tickets were used during January.

e. Wages and salaries owed to employees, but unpaid, at the end of January total $7,600.

f. Northern rents excess hangar space to other companies. The amount owed to Northern, but unpaid, at the end of January is $2,500.

g. Assume a corporate income tax rate of 34%.

Required

1. For each of the preceding items of additional information, determine the effect on the accounting equation at month-end.

2. Prepare an income statement for January and a balance sheet as of January 31.

SOLUTION TO REVIEW PROBLEM

1.

a.

	Balance Sheet						Income Statement	
ASSETS		**=**	**LIABILITIES**	**+**	**STOCKHOLDERS' EQUITY**	**+**	**REVENUES − EXPENSES**	
Parts Inventory	(8,900)						Maintenance Expense	(8,900)

b.

Balance Sheet						Income Statement	
ASSETS	**=**	**LIABILITIES**	**+**	**STOCKHOLDERS' EQUITY**	**+**	**REVENUES − EXPENSES**	
Accumulated Depreciation– Hangars (1,000)						Depreciation Expense— Hangars (1,000)	

c.

Balance Sheet						Income Statement	
ASSETS	**=**	**LIABILITIES**	**+**	**STOCKHOLDERS' EQUITY**	**+**	**REVENUES − EXPENSES**	
Accumulated Depreciation– Aircraft (5,000)						Depreciation Expense— Aircraft (5,000)	

d.

Balance Sheet						Income Statement	
ASSETS	**=**	**LIABILITIES**	**+**	**STOCKHOLDERS' EQUITY**	**+**	**REVENUES − EXPENSES**	
		Tickets Sold in Advance (47,000)				Ticket Revenue 47,000	

e.

Balance Sheet						Income Statement	
ASSETS	**=**	**LIABILITIES**	**+**	**STOCKHOLDERS' EQUITY**	**+**	**REVENUES − EXPENSES**	
		Wages and Salaries Payable 7,600				Wage and Salary Expense (7,600)	

f.

Balance Sheet						Income Statement	
ASSETS	**=**	**LIABILITIES**	**+**	**STOCKHOLDERS' EQUITY**	**+**	**REVENUES − EXPENSES**	
Rent Receivable 2,500						Rent Revenue 2,500	

g.

Balance Sheet						Income Statement	
ASSETS	**=**	**LIABILITIES**	**+**	**STOCKHOLDERS' EQUITY**	**+**	**REVENUES − EXPENSES**	
		Income Tax Payable 10,200				Income Tax Expense (10,200)	

2. Financial statements:

Northern Airlines
Income Statement
For the Month of January

Revenues:		
Ticket revenue	$99,000	
Rent revenue	2,500	$101,500
Expenses:		
Maintenance	$27,900	
Wages and salaries	37,600	
Depreciation—hangars	1,000	
Depreciation—aircraft	5,000	
Income taxes	10,200	81,700
Net income		$ 19,800

REVIEW

Northern Airlines
Balance Sheet
January 31

Assets			Liabilities and Stockholders' Equity	
Cash		$ 75,000	Tickets sold in advance	$ 38,000
Rent receivable		2,500	Wages and Salaries	
Parts inventory		36,100	payable	7,600
Land		80,000	Income tax payable	10,200
Buildings—Hangars	$250,000		Capital stock	500,000
Accumulated			Retained earnings	387,800
depreciation	25,000	225,000		
Aircraft	$650,000			
Accumulated				
depreciation	125,000	525,000	Total liabilities and	
Total assets		$943,600	stockholders' equity	$943,600

QUESTIONS

1. What is meant by the following statement? "The items depicted in financial statements are merely *representations* of the real thing."

2. What is the meaning of the following statement? "The choice between historical cost and current value is a good example of the trade-off in accounting between relevance and reliability."

3. A realtor earns a 10% commission on the sale of a $150,000 home. The realtor lists the home on June 5, the sale occurs on June 12, and the seller pays the realtor the $15,000 commission on July 8. When should the realtor recognize revenue from the sale, assuming (a) the cash basis of accounting and (b) the accrual basis of accounting?

4. What does the following statement mean? "If I want to assess the cash flow prospects for a company down the road, I look at the company's most recent statement of cash flows. An income statement prepared under the accrual basis of accounting is useless for this purpose."

5. What is the relationship between the time period assumption and accrual accounting?

6. Is it necessary for an asset to be acquired when revenue is recognized? Explain your answer.

7. A friend says to you: "I just don't get it. Assets cost money. Expenses reduce income. There must be some relationship among *assets, costs,* and *expenses*—I'm just not sure what it is!" What is the relationship? Can you give an example of it?

8. What is the meaning of *depreciation* to the accountant?

9. What are the four basic types of adjustments? Give an example of each.

10. What is the difference between a real account and a nominal account?

11. What two purposes are served in making closing entries?

EXERCISES

LO3 **Exercise 4-1** Revenue Recognition

The highway department contracted with a private company to collect tolls and maintain facilities on a turnpike. Users of the turnpike can pay cash as they approach the toll booth, or they can purchase a pass. The pass is equipped with an electronic sensor that subtracts the toll fee from the pass balance as the motorist slowly approaches a special toll booth. The passes are issued in $10 increments. Refunds are available to motorists who do not use the pass balance, but these are issued very infrequently. Last year $3,000,000 was collected at the traditional toll booths, $2,000,000 of passes were issued, and $1,700,000 of passes were used at the special toll booth. How much should the company recognize as revenue for the year? Explain how the revenue recognition rule should be applied in this case.

LO4 **Exercise 4-2** The Matching Principle

Three methods of matching costs with revenue were described in the chapter: (a) directly match a specific form of revenue with a cost incurred in generating that revenue, (b) indirectly match a cost with the periods during which it will provide benefits or revenue, and (c) immediately recognize a cost incurred as an expense because no future benefits are expected. For each of the following costs, indicate how it is normally recognized as expense by indicating either (a), (b), or (c). If you think there is more than one possible answer for any of the situations, explain why.

HOMEWORK

_____ 1. New office copier
_____ 2. Monthly bill from the utility company for electricity
_____ 3. Office supplies
_____ 4. Biweekly payroll for office employees
_____ 5. Commissions earned by salespeople
_____ 6. Interest incurred on a six-month loan from the bank
_____ 7. Cost of inventory sold during the current period
_____ 8. Taxes owed on income earned during current period
_____ 9. Cost of three-year insurance policy

LO5

Exercise 4-3 Accruals and Deferrals

For the following situations, indicate whether each involves a deferred expense (DE), a deferred revenue (DR), an accrued liability (AL), or an accrued asset (AA).

Example: ___DE___   Office supplies purchased in advance of their use.

_____ 1. Wages earned by employees but not yet paid
_____ 2. Cash collected from subscriptions in advance of publishing a magazine
_____ 3. Interest earned on a customer loan for which principal and interest have not yet been collected
_____ 4. One year's premium on a life insurance policy paid in advance
_____ 5. Office building purchased for cash
_____ 6. Rent collected in advance from a tenant
_____ 7. State income taxes owed at the end of the year
_____ 8. Rent owed by a tenant but not yet collected

LO5

Exercise 4-4 Office Supplies

Somerville Corp. purchases office supplies once a month and prepares monthly financial statements. The asset account Office Supplies on Hand has a balance of $1,450 on May 1. Purchases of supplies during May amount to $1,100. Supplies on hand at May 31 amount to $920. Determine the effect on the accounting equation of the adjustment necessary on May 31. What would be the effect on net income for May if this adjustment is *not* recorded?

LO5

Exercise 4-5 Prepaid Rent—Quarterly Adjustments

On September 1, Northhampton Industries signed a six-month lease, effective September 1, for office space. Northhampton agreed to prepay the rent and mailed a check for $12,000 to the landlord on September 1. Assume that Northhampton prepares adjusting entries only four times a year, on March 31, June 30, September 30, and December 31.

Required
1. Compute the rental cost for each full month.
2. Determine the effect on the accounting equation of the entry necessary on September 1.
3. Determine the effect on the accounting equation of the adjustment necessary on September 30.
4. Assume that the accountant prepares the adjustments on September 30 but forgets to record an adjustment on December 31. Will net income for the year be understated or overstated? By what amount?

LO5

Exercise 4-6 Depreciation

On July 1, 2007, Red Gate Farm buys a combine for $100,000 in cash. Assume that the combine is expected to have a seven-year life and an estimated salvage value of $16,000 at the end of that time.

Required
1. Determine the effect on the accounting equation of the purchase of the combine on July 1, 2007.
2. Compute the depreciable cost of the combine.
3. Using the straight-line method, compute the monthly depreciation.
4. Determine the effect on the accounting equation of the adjustment necessary to record depreciation at the end of July 2007.
5. Compute the combine's carrying value that will be shown on Red Gate's balance sheet prepared on December 31, 2007.

LO5

Exercise 4-7 Prepaid Insurance—Annual Adjustments

On April 1, 2007, Briggs Corp. purchases a 24-month property insurance policy for $72,000. The policy is effective immediately. Assume that Briggs prepares adjusting entries only once a year, on December 31.

Required

1. Compute the monthly cost of the insurance policy.
2. Determine the effect on the accounting equation of the purchase of the policy on April 1, 2007.
3. Determine the effect on the accounting equation of the adjustment necessary on December 31, 2007.
4. Assume that the accountant forgets to record an adjustment on December 31, 2007. Will net income for the year ended December 31, 2007, be understated or overstated? Explain your answer.

LO5   **Exercise 4-8** Subscriptions

Horse Country Living publishes a monthly magazine for which a 12-month subscription costs $30. All subscriptions require payment of the full $30 in advance. On August 1, 2007, the balance in the Subscriptions Received in Advance account was $40,500. During the month of August, the company sold 900 yearly subscriptions. After the adjustment at the end of August, the balance in the Subscriptions Received in Advance account is $60,000.

Required

1. Determine the effect on the accounting equation of the sale of the 900 yearly subscriptions during the month of August.
2. Determine the effect on the accounting equation of the adjustment necessary on August 31.
3. Assume that the accountant made the correct entry during August to record the sale of the 900 subscriptions but forgot to make the adjustment on August 31. Would net income for August be overstated or understated? Explain your answer.

LO5   **Exercise 4-9** Customer Deposits

Wolfe & Wolfe collected $9,000 from a customer on April 1 and agreed to provide legal services during the next three months. Wolfe & Wolfe expects to provide an equal amount of services each month.

Required

1. Determine the effect on the accounting equation of the receipt of the customer deposit on April 1.
2. Determine the effect on the accounting equation of the adjustment necessary on April 30.
3. What would be the effect on net income for April if the adjustment in (2) is not recorded?

LO5   **Exercise 4-10** Wages Payable

Denton Corporation employs 50 workers in its plant. Each employee is paid $10 per hour and works seven hours per day, Monday through Friday. Employees are paid every Friday. The last payday was Friday, October 20.

Required

1. Compute the dollar amount of the weekly payroll.
2. Determine the effect on the accounting equation of the payment of the weekly payroll on Friday, October 27.
3. Denton prepares monthly financial statements. Determine the effect on the accounting equation of the adjustment necessary on Tuesday, October 31, the last day of the month.
4. Determine the effect on the accounting equation of the payment of the weekly payroll on Friday, November 3.
5. Would net income for the month of October be understated or overstated if Denton doesn't bother with an adjustment on October 31? Explain your answer.

LO5   **Exercise 4-11** Interest Payable

Billings Company takes out a 12%, 90-day, $100,000 loan with First National Bank on March 1, 2007.

Required

1. Determine the effect on the accounting equation on March 1, 2007, when Billings takes out the loan.
2. Determine the effect on the accounting equation of the adjustments necessary for the months of March and April 2007.
3. Determine the effect on the accounting equation on May 30, 2007, when Billings repays the principal and interest to First National.

LO5 **Exercise 4-12** Property Taxes Payable—Annual Adjustments

Lexington Builders owns property in Kaneland County. Lexington's 2006 property taxes amounted to $50,000. Kaneland County will send out the 2007 property tax bills to property owners during April 2008. Taxes must be paid by June 1, 2008. Assume that Lexington prepares adjusting entries only once a year, on December 31, and that property taxes for 2007 are expected to increase by 5% over those for 2006.

Required
1. Determine the effect on the accounting equation of the adjustment necessary to record the property taxes payable on December 31, 2007.
2. Determine the effect on the accounting equation of the payment of the 2007 property taxes on June 1, 2008.

LO5 **Exercise 4-13** Interest Receivable

On June 1, 2007, MicroTel Enterprises lends $60,000 to MaxiDriver Inc. The loan will be repaid in 60 days with interest at 10%.

Required
1. Determine the effect on the accounting equation of the loan on MicroTel's books on June 1, 2007.
2. Determine the effect on the accounting equation of the adjustment necessary on MicroTel's books on June 30, 2007.
3. Determine the effect on the accounting equation on MicroTel's books on July 31, 2007, when MaxiDriver repays the principal and interest.

LO5 **Exercise 4-14** Unbilled Accounts Receivable

Mike and Cary repair computers for small local businesses. Heavy thunderstorms during the last week of June resulted in a record number of service calls. Eager to review the results of operations for the month of June, Mike prepared an income statement and was puzzled by the lower than expected amount of revenues. Cary explained that he had not yet billed the company's customers for $40,000 of work performed during the last week of the month.

Required
1. Should revenue be recorded when services are performed or when customers are billed? Explain your answer.
2. Determine the effect on the accounting equation of the adjustment necessary on June 30.

LO5 **Exercise 4-15** The Effect of Ignoring Adjustments on Net Income

For each of the following independent situations, determine whether the effect of ignoring the required adjustment will result in an understatement (U), an overstatement (O), or no effect (NE) on net income for the period.

Situation	Effect on Net Income
Example: Taxes owed but not yet paid are ignored.	O
1. A company fails to record depreciation on equipment.	
2. Sales made during the last week of the period are not recorded.	
3. A company neglects to record the expired portion of a prepaid insurance policy (its cost was originally recorded in an asset account).	
4. Interest due but not yet paid on a long-term note payable is ignored.	
5. Commissions earned by salespeople but not payable until the 10th of the following month are ignored.	
6. A landlord receives cash on the date a lease is signed for the rent for the first six months and records Unearned Rent Revenue. The landlord fails to make any adjustment at the end of the first month.	

LO5 **Exercise 4-16** The Effect of Adjustments on the Accounting Equation

Determine whether recording each of the following adjustments will increase (I), decrease (D), or have no effect (NE) on each of the three elements of the accounting equation.

	Assets =	Liabilities +	Stockholders' Equity
Example: Wages earned during the period, but not yet paid, are accrued.	NE	I	D
1. Prepaid insurance is reduced for the portion of the policy that has expired during the period.	_____	_____	_____
2. Interest incurred during the period, but not yet paid, is accrued.	_____	_____	_____
3. Depreciation for the period is recorded.	_____	_____	_____
4. Revenue is recorded for the earned portion of a liability for amounts collected in advance from customers.	_____	_____	_____
5. Rent revenue is recorded for amounts owed by a tenant but not yet received.	_____	_____	_____
6. Income taxes owed, but not yet paid, are accrued.	_____	_____	_____

LO6

Exercise 4-17 The Accounting Cycle

The steps in the accounting cycle are listed below in random order. Fill in the blank next to each step to indicate its *order* in the cycle. The first step in the cycle is filled in as an example.

Order	Procedure
_____	Prepare a work sheet.
_____	Close the accounts.
1	Collect and analyze information from source documents.
_____	Prepare financial statements.
_____	Post transactions to accounts in the ledger.
_____	Record and post adjustments.
_____	Journalize daily transactions.

MULTI-CONCEPT EXERCISES

LO1,2,3 ### Exercise 4-18 Revenue Recognition, Cash and Accrual Basis

Hathaway Health Club sold three-year memberships at a reduced rate during its opening promotion. It sold 1,000 three-year, nonrefundable memberships for $366 each. The club expects to sell 100 additional three-year memberships for $900 each over each of the next two years. Membership fees are paid when clients sign up. The club's bookkeeper has prepared the following income statement for the first year of business and projected income statements for Years 2 and 3.

Cash-basis income statements:

	Year 1	Year 2	Year 3
Sales	$366,000	$90,000	$90,000
Equipment*	$100,000	$ 0	$ 0
Salaries and Wages	50,000	50,000	50,000
Advertising	5,000	5,000	5,000
Rent and Utilities	36,000	36,000	36,000
Net income (loss)	$175,000	$(1,000)	$(1,000)

*Equipment was purchased at the beginning of Year 1 for $100,000 and is expected to last for three years and then to be worth $1,000.

Required

1. Convert the income statements for each of the three years to the accrual basis.
2. Describe how the revenue recognition principle applies. Do you believe that the cash-basis or the accrual-basis income statements are more useful to management? to investors? Why?

LO4,5 ### Exercise 4-19 Depreciation Expense

During 2007, Carter Company acquired three assets with the following costs, estimated useful lives, and estimated salvage values:

Date	Asset	Cost	Estimated Useful Life	Estimated Salvage Value
March 28	Truck	$ 18,000	5 years	$ 3,000
June 22	Computer	55,000	10 years	5,000
October 3	Building	250,000	30 years	10,000

The company uses the straight-line method to depreciate all assets and computes depreciation to the nearest month. For example, the computer system will be depreciated for six months in 2007.

Required

1. Compute the depreciation expense that Carter will record on each of the three assets for 2007.
2. Comment on the following statement: "Accountants could save time and money by simply expensing the cost of long-term assets when they are purchased. In addition, this would be more accurate because depreciation requires estimates of useful life and salvage value."

LO4,5 **Exercise 4-20** Accrual of Interest on a Loan

On July 1, 2007, Paxson Corporation takes out a 12%, two-month, $50,000 loan at Friendly National Bank. Principal and interest are to be repaid on August 31.

Required

1. Determine the effects on the accounting equation of each of the following: (a) the borrowing on July 1, (b) the necessary adjustment for the accrual of interest on July 31, and (c) the repayment of the principal and interest.
2. Evaluate the following statement: "It would be much easier not to bother with an adjustment on July 31 and simply record interest expense on August 31 when the loan is repaid."

PROBLEMS

LO5 **Problem 4-1** Adjustments

Water Corporation prepares monthly financial statements and therefore adjusts its accounts at the end of every month. The following information is available for March 2007:

a. Water Corporation takes out a 90-day, 8%, $15,000 note on March 1, 2007, with interest and principal to be paid at maturity.
b. The asset account Office Supplies on Hand has a balance of $1,280 on March 1, 2007. During March, Water adds $750 to the account for the purchases of the period. A count of the supplies on hand at the end of March indicates a balance of $1,370.
c. The company purchased office equipment last year for $62,600. The equipment has an estimated useful life of six years and an estimated salvage value of $5,000.
d. The company's plant operates seven days per week with a daily payroll of $950. Wage earners are paid every Sunday. The last day of the month is Saturday, March 31.
e. The company rented an idle warehouse to a neighboring business on February 1, 2007, at a rate of $2,500 per month. On this date, Water Corporation recorded Rent Collected in Advance for six months' rent received in advance.
f. On March 1, 2007, Water Corporation credited a liability account, Customer Deposits, for $4,800. This sum represents an amount that a customer paid in advance and that will be earned evenly by Water over a four-month period.
g. Based on its income for the month, Water Corporation estimates that federal income taxes for March amount to $3,900.

Required

1. For each of the preceding situations, determine the effect on the accounting equation of the adjustment necessary on March 31, 2007.
2. Assume that Water reports income of $23,000 before any of the adjustments. What net income will Water report for March?

LO5 **Problem 4-2** Annual Adjustments

Palmer Industries prepares annual financial statements and adjusts its accounts only at the end of the year. The following information is available for the year ended December 31, 2007:

a. Palmer purchased computer equipment two years ago for $15,000. The equipment has an estimated useful life of five years and an estimated salvage value of $250.

b. The Office Supplies account had a balance of $3,600 on January 1, 2007. During 2007, Palmer added $17,600 to the account for purchases of office supplies during the year. A count of the supplies on hand at the end of December 2007 indicates a balance of $1,850.

c. On August 1, 2007, Palmer created a liability account, Customer Deposits, for $24,000. This sum represents an amount that a customer paid in advance and that will be earned evenly by Palmer over a six-month period.

d. Palmer rented some office space on November 1, 2007, at a rate of $2,700 per month. On that date, Palmer recorded Prepaid Rent for three months' rent paid in advance.

e. Palmer took out a 120-day, 9%, $200,000 note on November 1, 2007, with interest and principal to be paid at maturity.

f. Palmer operates five days per week with an average daily payroll of $500. Palmer pays its employees every Thursday. December 31, 2007, is a Monday.

Required

1. For each of the preceding situations, determine the effect on the accounting equation of the adjustment necessary on December 31, 2007.

2. Assume that Palmer's accountant forgets to record the adjustments on December 31, 2007. Will net income for the year be understated or overstated? By what amount? (Ignore the effect of income taxes.)

LO5   **Problem 4-3** Recurring Transactions and Adjustments

The following are Butler Realty Corporation's accounts, identified by number. The company has been in the real estate business for 10 years and prepares financial statements monthly. Following the list of accounts is a series of transactions entered into by Butler. For each transaction, enter the number(s) of the account(s) affected.

Accounts

1. Cash	11. Notes Payable
2. Accounts Receivable	12. Capital Stock, $10 par
3. Prepaid Rent	13. Paid-In Capital in Excess of Par
4. Office Supplies	14. Commissions Revenue
5. Automobiles	15. Office Supply Expense
6. Accumulated Depreciation	16. Rent Expense
7. Land	17. Salaries and Wages Expense
8. Accounts Payable	18. Depreciation Expense
9. Salaries and Wages Payable	19. Interest Expense
10. Income Tax Payable	20. Income Tax Expense

Transaction

a. Example: Issued additional shares of stock to owners at amount in excess of par.   1, 12, 13

b. Purchased automobiles for cash.   _____

c. Purchased land; made cash down payment and signed a promissory note for the balance.   _____

d. Paid cash to landlord for rent for the next 12 months.   _____

e. Purchased office supplies on account.   _____

f. Collected cash for commissions from clients for the properties sold during the month.   _____

g. Collected cash for commissions from clients for the properties sold in the prior month.   _____

h. During the month, sold properties for which cash for commissions will be collected from clients next month.   _____

i. Paid for office supplies purchased on account in an earlier month.   _____

j. Recorded an adjustment to recognize wages and salaries incurred but not yet paid.   _____

k. Recorded an adjustment for office supplies used during the month.   _____

l. Recorded an adjustment for the portion of prepaid rent that expired during the month.   _____

m. Made required month-end payment on note taken out in (c); payment is part principal and part interest.   _____

n. Recorded adjustment for monthly depreciation on the autos.   _____

o. Recorded adjustment for income taxes.   _____

HOMEWORK

LO5

Problem 4-4 Use of Account Balances as a Basis for Annual Adjustments

The following account balances are taken from the records of Chauncey Company at December 31, 2007. The Prepaid Insurance account represents the cost of a three-year policy purchased on August 1, 2007. The Rent Collected in Advance account represents the cash received from a tenant on June 1, 2007, for 12 months' rent, beginning on that date. The Note Receivable represents a nine-month promissory note received from a customer on September 1, 2007. Principal and interest at an annual rate of 9% will be received on June 1, 2008.

Prepaid Insurance	$ 7,200
Rent Collected in Advance	6,000
Note Receivable	50,000

Required

1. For each of the three situations described above, determine the effect on the accounting equation of the adjustments necessary on December 31, 2007. Assume that Chauncey records adjustments only once a year, on December 31.
2. Assume that adjustments are made at the end of each month rather than only at the end of the year. What would be the balance in Prepaid Insurance *before* the December adjustment is recorded? Explain your answer.

LO5

Problem 4-5 Use of Account Balances as a Basis for Adjustments

Bob Reynolds operates a real estate business. A list of accounts on April 30, 2007, *before* recording any adjustments, appears as follows:

Cash	$15,700
Prepaid Insurance	450
Office Supplies	250
Office Equipment	50,000
Accumulated Depreciation—Office Equipment	5,000
Automobile	12,000
Accumulated Depreciation—Automobile	1,400
Accounts Payable	6,500
Unearned Commissions	9,500
Notes Payable	2,000
Capital Stock	10,000
Retained Earnings	40,000
Dividends	2,500
Commissions Earned	17,650
Utilities Expense	2,300
Salaries Expense	7,400
Advertising Expense	1,450

Other Data

a. The monthly insurance cost is $50.
b. Office supplies on hand on April 30, 2007, amount to $180.
c. The office equipment was purchased on April 1, 2006. On that date, it had an estimated useful life of 10 years.
d. On September 1, 2006, the automobile was purchased; it had an estimated useful life of five years.
e. A deposit is received in advance of providing any services for first-time customers. Amounts received in advance are recorded initially in the account Unearned Commissions. Based on services provided to these first-time customers, the balance in this account at the end of April should be $5,000.
f. Repeat customers are allowed to pay for services one month after the date of the sale of their property. Services rendered during the month but not yet collected or billed to these customers amount to $1,500.
g. Interest owed on the note payable, but not yet paid, amounts to $20.
h. Salaries owed to employees but unpaid at the end of the month amount to $2,500.

Required

1. For each of the items of other data (**a**) through (**h**), determine the effect on the accounting equation.
2. Compute the net increase or decrease in net income for the month from the recognition of the adjustments in part (**1**). (Ignore income taxes.)
3. Note the balance in Accumulated Depreciation—Office Equipment of $5,000. Explain *why* the account contains a balance of $5,000 on April 30, 2007.

HOMEWORK

LO5 **Problem 4-6** Reconstruction of Adjustments from Account Balances

Taggart Corp. records adjustments each month before preparing monthly financial statements. The following selected account balances on May 31, 2007, and June 30, 2007, reflect month-end adjustments:

Account Title	May 31, 2007	June 30, 2007
Prepaid Insurance	$3,600	$3,450
Equipment	9,600	9,600
Accumulated Depreciation	1,280	1,360
Notes Payable	9,600	9,600
Interest Payable	2,304	2,448

Required

1. The company purchased a 36-month insurance policy on June 1, 2006. Determine the effect on the accounting equation of the adjustment that was made for insurance on June 30, 2007.
2. What was the original cost of the insurance policy? Explain your answer.
3. The equipment was purchased on February 1, 2006, for $9,600. Taggart uses straight-line depreciation and estimates that the equipment will have no salvage value. Determine the effect on the accounting equation of the adjustment that was made for depreciation on June 30, 2007.
4. What is the equipment's estimated useful life in months? Explain your answer.
5. Taggart signed a two-year note payable on February 1, 2006, for the purchase of the equipment. Interest on the note accrues on a monthly basis and will be paid at maturity along with the principal amount of $9,600. Determine the effect on the accounting equation of the adjustment that was made for interest on June 30, 2007.
6. What is the *monthly* interest rate on the loan? Explain your answer.

LO5 **Problem 4-7** Use of Account Balances as a Basis for Adjustments

Four Star Video has been in the video rental business for five years. The following is a list of accounts for Four Star Video at May 31, 2007. It reflects the recurring transactions for the month of May but does not reflect any month-end adjustments.

Cash	$ 4,000
Prepaid Rent	6,600
Video Inventory	25,600
Display Stands	8,900
Accumulated Depreciation	5,180
Accounts Payable	3,260
Customer Subscriptions	4,450
Capital Stock	5,000
Retained Earnings	22,170
Rental Revenue	9,200
Wage and Salary Expense	2,320
Utilities Expense	1,240
Advertising Expense	600

The following additional information is available:

a. Four Star rents a store in a shopping mall and prepays the annual rent of $7,200 on April 1 of each year.
b. The asset account Video Inventory represents the cost of videos purchased from suppliers. When a new title is purchased from a supplier, its cost is added to this account. When a title has served its useful life and can no longer be rented (even at a reduced price), it is removed from the inventory in the store. Based on the monthly count, the cost of titles on hand at the end of May is $23,140.
c. The display stands have an estimated useful life of five years and an estimated salvage value of $500.
d. Wages and salaries owed to employees, but unpaid at the end of May, amount to $1,450.
e. In addition to individual rentals, Four Star operates a popular discount subscription program. Customers pay an annual fee of $120 for an unlimited number of rentals. Based on the $10 per month earned on each of these subscriptions, the amount earned for the month of May is $2,440.
f. Four Star accrues income taxes using an estimated tax rate equal to 30% of the income for the month.

Required

1. For each of the items of additional information, (**a**) through (**f**), determine the effect on the accounting equation.
2. On the basis of the information you have, does Four Star appear to be a profitable business? Explain your answer.

MULTI-CONCEPT PROBLEMS

LO2,3,4   **Problem 4-8** Cash and Accrual Income Statements for a Manufacturer

Drysdale Company was established to manufacture components for the auto industry. The components are shipped the same day they are produced. The following events took place during the first year of operations:

a. Issued common stock for a $50,000 cash investment.
b. Purchased delivery truck at the beginning of the year at a cost of $10,000 cash. The truck is expected to last five years and will be worthless at the end of that time.
c. Manufactured and sold 500,000 components the first year. The costs incurred to manufacture the components are (1) $1,000 monthly rent on a facility that included utilities and insurance, (2) $400,000 of raw materials purchased on account ($100,000 is still unpaid as of year-end, but all materials were used in manufacturing), and (3) $190,000 paid in salaries and wages to employees and supervisors.
d. Paid $100,000 to sales and office staff for salaries and wages.
e. Sold all components on account for $2 each. As of year-end, $150,000 is due from customers.

Required

1. How much revenue will Drysdale recognize under the cash basis and under the accrual basis?
2. Describe how Drysdale should apply the matching principle to recognize expenses.
3. Prepare an income statement under the accrual basis. Ignore income taxes.

LO3,4   **Problem 4-9** Revenue and Expense Recognition

Two years ago, Darlene Darby opened a delivery service. Darby reports the following accounts on her income statement:

Sales	$69,000
Advertising Expense	3,500
Salaries Expense	39,000
Rent Expense	10,000

These amounts represent two years of revenue and expenses. Darby has asked you how she can tell how much of the income is from the first year of business and how much is from the second year. She provides the following additional data:

a. Sales in the second year were double those of the first year.
b. Advertising expense is for a $500 opening promotion and weekly ads in the newspaper.
c. Salaries represent one employee for the first nine months and then two employees for the remainder of the time. Each is paid the same salary. No raises have been granted.
d. Rent has not changed since the business opened.

Required

Prepare income statements for Years 1 and 2.

LO5,6   **Problem 4-10** Monthly Transactions, Adjustments, and Financial Statements

Moonlight Bay Inn is incorporated on January 2, 2007, by its three owners, each of whom contributes $20,000 in cash in exchange for shares of stock in the business. In addition to the sale of stock, the following transactions are entered into during the month of January:

January   2: A Victorian inn is purchased for $50,000 in cash. An appraisal performed on this date indicates that the land is worth $15,000 and the remaining balance of the purchase price is attributable to the house. The owners estimate that the house will have an estimated useful life of 25 years and an estimated salvage value of $5,000.

January   3: A two-year, 12%, $30,000 promissory note was signed at the Second State Bank. Interest and principal will be repaid on the maturity date of January 3, 2009.

January   4: New furniture for the inn is purchased at a cost of $15,000 in cash. The furniture has an estimated useful life of 10 years and no salvage value.

January   5: A 24-month property insurance policy is purchased for $6,000 in cash.

January   6: An advertisement for the inn is placed in the local newspaper. Moonlight Bay pays $450 cash for the ad, which will run in the paper throughout January.

January   7: Cleaning supplies are purchased on account for $950. The bill is payable within 30 days.

January 15: Wages of $4,230 for the first half of the month are paid in cash.

January 16: A guest mails the business $980 in cash as a deposit for a room to be rented for two weeks. The guest plans to stay at the inn during the last week of January and the first week of February.

January 31: Cash receipts from rentals of rooms for the month amount to $8,300.

January 31: Cash receipts from operation of the restaurant for the month amount to $6,600.

January 31: Each stockholder is paid $200 in cash dividends.

Required

1. Determine the effect on the accounting equation of each of the preceding transactions.
2. Prepare a list of accounts and their balances for Moonlight Bay Inn at January 31, 2007. Reflect the recurring transactions for the month of January but not the necessary month-end adjustments.
3. Determine the effect on the accounting equation of the necessary adjustments at January 31, 2007, for each of the following:
   a. Depreciation of the house
   b. Depreciation of the furniture
   c. Interest on the promissory note
   d. Recognition of the expired portion of the insurance
   e. Recognition of the earned portion of the guest's deposit
   f. Wages earned during the second half of January amount to $5,120 and will be paid on February 3.
   g. Cleaning supplies on hand on January 31 amount to $230.
   h. A gas and electric bill that is received from the city amounts to $740 and is payable by February 5.
   i. Income taxes are to be accrued at a rate of 30% of income before taxes.
4. Prepare in good form the following financial statements:
   a. Income statement for the month ended January 31, 2007
   b. Statement of retained earnings for the month ended January 31, 2007
   c. Balance sheet at January 31, 2007
5. Assume that you are the loan officer at Second State Bank (refer to the transaction on January 3). What are your reactions to Moonlight's first month of operations? Are you comfortable with the loan you made?

ALTERNATE PROBLEMS

LO5

Problem 4-1A Adjustments

Flood Relief Inc. prepares monthly financial statements and therefore adjusts its accounts at the end of every month. The following information is available for June 2007:

a. Flood received a $10,000, 4%, two-year note receivable from a customer for services rendered. The principal and interest are due on June 1, 2009. Flood expects to be able to collect the note and interest in full at that time.

b. Office supplies totaling $5,600 were purchased during the month. The asset account Supplies is increased whenever a purchase is made. A count in the storeroom on June 30, 2007, indicated that supplies on hand amount to $507. The supplies on hand at the beginning of the month totaled $475.

c. The company purchased machines last year for $170,000. The machines are expected to be used for four years and have an estimated salvage value of $2,000.

d. On June 1, the company paid $4,650 for rent for June, July, and August, and increased the asset Prepaid Rent. It did not have a balance on June 1.

e. The company operates seven days per week with a weekly payroll of $7,000. Wage earners are paid every Sunday. The last day of the month is Saturday, June 30.

f. Based on its income for the month, Flood estimates that federal income taxes for June amount to $2,900.

Required

1. For each of the preceding situations, determine the effect on the accounting equation of the adjustment necessary on June 30, 2007.
2. Assume that Flood Relief reports income of $35,000 before any of the adjustments. What net income will Flood Relief report for June?

LO5   **Problem 4-2A** Annual Adjustments

Ogonquit Enterprises prepares annual financial statements and adjusts its accounts only at the end of the year. The following information is available for the year ended December 31, 2007:

a. Ogonquit purchased office furniture last year for $25,000. The furniture has an estimated useful life of seven years and an estimated salvage value of $4,000.
b. The Supplies account had a balance of $1,200 on January 1, 2007. During 2007, Ogonquit added $12,900 to the account for purchases of supplies during the year. A count of the supplies on hand at the end of December 2007 indicates a balance of $900.
c. On July 1, 2007, Ogonquit created a liability account, Customer Deposits, for $8,800. This sum represents an amount that a customer paid in advance and that will be earned evenly by Ogonquit over an eight-month period.
d. Ogonquit rented some warehouse space on September 1, 2007, at a rate of $4,000 per month. On that date, Ogonquit recorded Prepaid Rent for six months' rent paid in advance.
e. Ogonquit took out a 90-day, 6%, $30,000 note on November 1, 2007, with interest and principal to be paid at maturity.
f. Ogonquit operates five days per week with an average weekly payroll of $4,150. Ogonquit pays its employees every Thursday. December 31, 2007, is a Monday.

Required

1. For each of the preceding situations, determine the effect on the accounting equation of the adjustment necessary on December 31, 2007.
2. Assume that Ogonquit's accountant forgets to record the adjustments on December 31, 2007. Will net income for the year be understated or overstated? By what amount? (Ignore the effect of income taxes.)

LO5   **Problem 4-3A** Recurring Transactions and Adjustments

The following are the accounts of Dominique Inc., an interior decorator. The company has been in the decorating business for 10 years and prepares quarterly financial statements. Following the list of accounts is a series of transactions entered into by Dominique. For each transaction, enter the number(s) of the account(s) affected.

Accounts

1. Cash	11. Capital Stock, $1 par
2. Accounts Receivable	12. Paid-In Capital in Excess of Par
3. Prepaid Rent	13. Consulting Revenue
4. Office Supplies	14. Office Supply Expense
5. Office Equipment	15. Rent Expense
6. Accumulated Depreciation	16. Salaries and Wages Expense
7. Accounts Payable	17. Depreciation Expense
8. Salaries and Wages Payable	18. Interest Expense
9. Income Tax Payable	19. Income Tax Expense
10. Interim Financing Notes Payable	

Transaction

a. Example: Issued additional shares of stock to owners; shares issued at greater than par.   _1, 11, 12_
b. Purchased office equipment for cash.   _____
c. Collected open accounts receivable from customer.   _____
d. Purchased office supplies on account.   _____
e. Paid office rent for the next six months.   _____
f. Paid interest on an interim financing note.   _____

(continued)

g. Paid salaries and wages.   _____
h. Purchased office equipment; made a down payment in cash
    and signed an interim financing note.   _____
i. Provided services on account.
j. Recorded depreciation on equipment.   _____
k. Recorded income taxes due next month.   _____
l. Recorded the used office supplies.   _____
m. Recorded the used portion of prepaid rent.   _____

LO5

Problem 4-4A Use of Account Balances as a Basis for Annual Adjustments

The following account balances are taken from the records of Laugherty Inc. at December 31, 2007. The Supplies account represents the cost of supplies on hand at the beginning of the year plus all purchases. A physical count on December 31, 2007, shows only $1,520 of supplies on hand. The Unearned Revenue account represents the cash received from a customer on May 1, 2007, for 12 months of service, beginning on that date. The Note Payable represents a six-month promissory note signed with a supplier on September 1, 2007. Principal and interest at an annual rate of 10% will be paid on March 1, 2008.

Supplies	$ 5,790
Unearned Revenue	1,800
Note Payable	60,000

Required

1. For each of the three situations described above, determine the effect on the accounting equation of the adjustments necessary on December 31, 2007. Assume that Laugherty records adjustments only once a year, on December 31.
2. Assume that adjustments are made at the end of each month rather than only at the end of the year. What would be the balance in Unearned Revenue *before* the December adjustment is made? Explain your answer.

LO5

Problem 4-5A Use of Accounting Balances as a Basis for Adjustments

Lori Matlock operates a graphic arts business. A list of accounts on June 30, 2007, *before* recording any adjustments, appears as follows:

Cash	$ 7,000
Prepaid Rent	18,000
Supplies	15,210
Office Equipment	46,120
Accumulated Depreciation—Equipment	4,000
Accounts Payable	1,800
Notes Payable	2,000
Capital Stock	50,000
Retained Earnings	24,350
Dividends	8,400
Revenue	46,850
Utilities Expense	2,850
Salaries Expense	19,420
Advertising Expense	12,000

Other Data

a. The monthly rent cost is $600.
b. Supplies on hand on June 30, 2007, amount to $1,290.
c. The office equipment was purchased on June 1, 2006. On that date, it had an estimated useful life of 10 years and a salvage value of $6,120.
d. Interest owed on the note payable, but not yet paid, amounts to $50.
e. Salaries of $620 are owed to employees but unpaid at the end of the month.

Required

1. For each of the items of other data (**a**) through (**e**), determine the effect on the accounting equation.
2. Compute the net increase or decrease in net income for the month from the recognition of the adjustments you prepared in part (1) (ignore income taxes).
3. Note the balance in Accumulated Depreciation—Equipment of $4,000. Explain *why* the account contains a balance of $4,000 on June 30, 2007.

LO5 **Problem 4-6A** Reconstruction of Adjustments from Account Balances

Zola Corporation records adjustments each month before preparing monthly financial statements. The following selected account balances on May 31, 2007, and June 30, 2007, reflect month-end adjustments:

Account Title	May 31, 2007	June 30, 2007
Prepaid Rent	$4,000	$3,000
Equipment	9,600	9,600
Accumulated Depreciation	800	900
Notes Payable	9,600	9,600
Interest Payable	768	864

Required

1. The company paid for a six-month lease on April 1, 2007. Determine the effect on the accounting equation of the adjustment that was made for rent on June 30, 2007.
2. What amount was prepaid on April 1, 2007? Explain your answer.
3. The equipment was purchased on September 30, 2006, for $9,600. Zola uses straight-line depreciation and estimates that the equipment will have no salvage value. Determine the effect on the accounting equation of the adjustment that was made for depreciation on June 30, 2007.
4. What is the equipment's estimated useful life in months? Explain your answer.
5. Zola signed a two-year note on September 30, 2006, for the purchase of the equipment. Interest on the note accrues on a monthly basis and will be paid at maturity along with the principal amount of $9,600. Determine the effect on the accounting equation of the adjustment that was made for interest expense on June 30, 2007.
6. What is the *monthly* interest rate on the loan? Explain your answer.

LO5 **Problem 4-7A** Use of Account Balances as a Basis for Adjustments

Lewis and Associates has been in the termite inspection and treatment business for five years. The following is a list of accounts for Lewis on June 30, 2007. It reflects the recurring transactions for the month of June but does not reflect any month-end adjustments.

Cash	$ 6,200
Accounts Receivable	10,400
Prepaid Rent	4,400
Chemical Inventory	9,400
Equipment	18,200
Accumulated Depreciation	1,050
Accounts Payable	1,180
Capital Stock	5,000
Retained Earnings	25,370
Treatment Revenue	40,600
Wages and Salary Expense	22,500
Utilities Expense	1,240
Advertising Expense	860

The following additional information is available:

a. Lewis rents a warehouse with office space and prepays the annual rent of $4,800 on May 1 of each year.
b. The asset account Equipment represents the cost of treatment equipment, which has an estimated useful life of 10 years and an estimated salvage value of $200.
c. Chemical inventory on hand equals $1,300.
d. Wages and salaries owed to employees, but unpaid at the end of the month, amount to $1,080.
e. Lewis accrues income taxes using an estimated tax rate equal to 30% of the income for the month.

Required

1. For each of the items of additional information, (**a**) through (**e**), determine the effect on the accounting equation.
2. On the basis of the information you have, does Lewis appear to be a profitable business? Explain your answer.

ALTERNATE MULTI-CONCEPT PROBLEMS

LO2,3,4 **Problem 4-8A** Cash and Accrual Income Statements for a Manufacturer

Marie's Catering makes sandwiches for vending machines. The sandwiches are delivered to the vendor on the same day that they are made. The following events took place during the first year of operations:

a. On the first day of the year, issued common stock for a $20,000 cash investment and a $10,000 investment of equipment. The equipment is expected to last 10 years and will be worthless at the end of that time.
b. Purchased a delivery truck at the beginning of the year at a cost of $14,000 cash. The truck is expected to last five years and will be worthless at the end of that time.
c. Made and sold 50,000 sandwiches during the first year of operations. The costs incurred to make the sandwiches are (1) $800 monthly rent on a facility that included utilities and insurance, (2) $25,000 of meat, cheese, bread, and condiments (all food was purchased on account, and $4,000 is still unpaid at year-end even though all of the food has been used), and (3) $35,000 paid in salaries and wages to employees and supervisors.
d. Paid $12,000 for part-time office staff salaries.
e. Sold all sandwiches on account for $2 each. As of year-end, $25,000 is still due from the vendors.

Required
1. How much revenue will Marie's Catering recognize under the cash basis and under the accrual basis?
2. Explain how accountants apply the revenue recognition principle to Marie's small business. What conditions would allow Marie's to use the cash method to recognize revenue?
3. Prepare an income statement according to the accrual method. Ignore income taxes.

LO3,4 **Problem 4-9A** Revenue and Expense Recognition

Two years ago, Sue Stern opened an audio book rental shop. Sue reports the following accounts on her income statement:

Sales	$84,000
Advertising Expense	10,500
Salaries Expense	12,000
Depreciation on Tapes	5,000
Rent Expense	18,000

These amounts represent two years of revenue and expenses. Sue has asked you how she can tell how much of the income is from the first year and how much is from the second year of business. She provides the following additional data:

a. Sales in the second year are triple those of the first year.
b. Advertising expense is for a $1,500 opening promotion and weekly ads in the newspaper.
c. Salaries represent one employee who was hired eight months ago. No raises have been granted.
d. Rent has not changed since the shop opened.

Required
Prepare income statements for Years 1 and 2.

LO5,6 **Problem 4-10A** Adjustments and Financial Statements

The following account balances are available for Tenfour Trucking Company on January 31, 2007:

Cash	$ 27,340
Accounts Receivable	41,500
Prepaid Insurance	18,000
Warehouse	40,000
Accumulated Depreciation—Warehouse	21,600
Truck Fleet	240,000
Accumulated Depreciation—Truck Fleet	112,500

(continued)

Land	$ 20,000
Accounts Payable	32,880
Notes Payable	50,000
Interest Payable	4,500
Customer Deposits	6,000
Capital Stock	100,000
Retained Earnings	40,470
Freight Revenue	165,670
Gas and Oil Expense	57,330
Maintenance Expense	26,400
Wage and Salary Expense	43,050
Dividends	20,000

Required

1. Determine the effect on the accounting equation of the necessary adjustments at January 31, 2007, for each of the following:
   a. Prepaid insurance represents the cost of a 24-month policy purchased on January 1, 2007.
   b. The warehouse has an estimated useful life of 20 years and an estimated salvage value of $4,000.
   c. The truck fleet has an estimated useful life of six years and an estimated salvage value of $15,000.
   d. The promissory note was signed on January 1, 2006. Interest at an annual rate of 9% and the principal of $50,000 are due on December 31, 2007.
   e. The customer deposits represent amounts paid in advance by new customers. A total of $4,500 of the balance in Customer Deposits was earned during January 2007.
   f. Wages and salaries earned by employees at the end of January but not yet paid amount to $8,200.
   g. Income taxes are accrued at a rate of 30% at the end of each month.
2. Prepare in good form the following financial statements:
   a. Income statement for the month ended January 31, 2007
   b. Statement of retained earnings for the month ended January 31, 2007
   c. Balance sheet at January 31, 2007
3. Compute Tenfour's current ratio. What does this ratio tell you about the company's liquidity?
4. Compute Tenfour's profit margin. What does this ratio tell you about the company's profitability?

DECISION CASES

READING AND INTERPRETING FINANCIAL STATEMENTS

LO1,2,3

Decision Case 4-1 Comparing Two Companies in the Same Industry: Finish Line and Foot Locker

Refer to the financial information for **Finish Line** and **Foot Locker** reproduced at the end of the book for the information needed to answer the following questions.

Required

1. Locate the note in each company's annual report in which they discuss revenue recognition. How does each of them describe the point at which they recognize revenue from store sales? Are there any significant differences in their revenue recognition policies?
2. What dollar amount does Finish Line report for accounts receivable on its most recent balance sheet? What percent of the company's total assets are comprised of accounts receivable? Explain why accounts receivable are such a small percentage of total assets for Finish Line.
3. Note that Foot Locker's balance sheet does not contain an accounts receivable account. Where in the notes to the financial statements does the company report any receivables? What is the dollar amount of Foot Locker's receivables, and what percent of total assets are comprised of receivables?
4. On its balance sheet, Finish Line reports five accounts under "Property and Equipment" and from the total of the five deducts "Accumulated Depreciation." How does this way of presenting the long-term tangible assets differ from the approach used by Foot Locker on its balance sheet? Does Foot Locker disclose the same type of information elsewhere

HOMEWORK

in the annual report? If so, where? Why do you think these companies use different approaches to report this information?

LO3 **Decision Case 4-2** Reading and Interpreting Sears, Roebuck's Notes—Revenue Recognition

The following excerpt is taken from the **Sears, Roebuck and Co.** 2004 annual report: "Additionally, the Company sells extended service contracts with terms of coverage between 12 and 60 months. Revenues from the sale of these contracts are deferred and amortized over the lives of the contracts while the service costs are expensed as incurred." (*Note:* Sears, Roebuck and K-Mart were combined and both are now part of Sears Holdings Corporation.)

Required

1. Why does Sears recognize the revenue over the life of the service contract even though cash is received at the time of the sale?
2. If a product is sold in Year 1 for $2,500, including a $180 service contract that will cover three years, how much revenue is recognized in Years 1, 2, and 3? (Assume a straight-line approach.) What corresponding account can you look for in the financial statements to determine the amount of service contract revenue that will be recognized in the future?

MAKING FINANCIAL DECISIONS

LO2,3,4 **Decision Case 4-3** The Use of Net Income and Cash Flow to Evaluate a Company

After you have gained five years of experience with a large CPA firm, one of your clients, Duke Inc., asks you to take over as chief financial officer for the business. Duke advises its clients on the purchase of software products and assists them in installing the programs on their computer systems. Because the business is relatively new (it began servicing clients in January 2007), its accounting records are somewhat limited. In fact, the only statement available is an income statement for the first year:

Duke Inc.
Income Statement
For the Year Ended December 31, 2007

Revenues		$1,250,000
Expenses:		
Salaries and wages	$480,000	
Supplies	65,000	
Utilities	30,000	
Rent	120,000	
Depreciation	345,000	
Interest	138,000	
Total expenses		1,178,000
Net income		$ 72,000

Based on its relatively modest profit margin of 5.76% (net income of $72,000 divided by revenues of $1,250,000), you are concerned about joining the new business. To alleviate your concerns, the president of the company is able to give you the following additional information:

a. Clients are given 90 days to pay their bills for consulting services provided by Duke. On December 31, 2007, $230,000 of the revenues is yet to be collected in cash.
b. Employees are paid on a monthly basis. Salaries and wages of $480,000 include the December payroll of $40,000, which will be paid on January 5, 2008.
c. The company purchased $100,000 of operating supplies when it began operations in January. The balance of supplies on hand at December 31 amounts to $35,000.
d. Office space is rented in a downtown high-rise building at a monthly rental of $10,000. When the company moved into the office in January, it prepaid its rent for the next 18 months, beginning January 1, 2007.
e. On January 1, 2007, Duke purchased its own computer system and related accessories at a cost of $1,725,000. The estimated useful life of the system is five years.
f. The computer system was purchased by signing a three-year, 8% note payable for $1,725,000 on the date of purchase. The principal amount of the note and interest for the three years are due on January 1, 2010.

Required

1. Based on the income statement and the additional information given, prepare a statement of cash flows for Duke for 2007. (*Hint:* Simply list all of the cash inflows and outflows that relate to operations.)
2. On the basis of the income statement given and the statement of cash flows prepared in part (1), do you think it would be a wise decision on your part to join the company as its chief financial officer? Include in your response any additional questions that you believe are appropriate to ask before joining the company.

LO4

Decision Case 4-4 Depreciation

Jenner Inc., a graphic arts studio, is considering the purchase of computer equipment and software for a total cost of $18,000. Jenner can pay for the equipment and software over three years at the rate of $6,000 per year. The equipment is expected to last 10 to 20 years, but because of changing technology, Jenner believes it may need to replace the system as soon as three to five years. A three-year lease of similar equipment and software is available for $6,000 per year. Jenner's accountant has asked you to recommend whether the company should purchase or lease the equipment and software and to suggest the length of the period over which to depreciate the software and equipment if the company makes the purchase.

Required

Ignoring the effect of taxes, would you recommend the purchase or the lease? Why? Referring to the definition of *depreciation*, what is the appropriate useful life to use for the equipment and software?

ETHICAL DECISION MAKING

LO2,3,4,5

Decision Case 4-5 Revenue Recognition and the Matching Principle

Listum & Sellum Inc. is a medium-size midwestern real estate company. It was founded five years ago by its two principal stockholders, Willie Listum and Dewey Sellum. Willie is president of the company, and Dewey is vice-president of sales. Listum & Sellum has enjoyed tremendous growth since its inception by aggressively seeking out listings for residential real estate and paying a very generous commission to the selling agent.

The company receives a 6% commission for selling a client's property and gives two-thirds of this, or 4% of the selling price, to the selling agent. For example, if a house sells for $100,000, Listum & Sellum receives $6,000 and pays $4,000 of this to the selling agent. At the time of the sale, the company records a debit of $6,000 to Accounts Receivable and a credit of $6,000 to Sales Revenue. The accounts receivable is normally collected within 30 days. Also at the time of sale, the company debits $4,000 to Commissions Expense and credits Commissions Payable for the same amount. Sales agents are paid by the 15th of the month following the month of the sale. In addition to the commissions expense, Listum & Sellum's other two major expenses are advertising of listings in local newspapers and depreciation of the company fleet of Cadillacs (Dewey has always believed that all of the sales agents should drive Cadillacs). The newspaper ads are taken for one month, and the company has until the 10th of the following month to pay that month's bill. The automobiles are depreciated over four years (Dewey doesn't believe that any salesperson should drive a car that is more than four years old).

Due to a downturn in the economy in the Midwest, sales have been sluggish for the first 11 months of the current year, which ends on June 30. Willie is very disturbed by the slow sales this particular year because a large note payable to the local bank is due in July, and the company plans to ask the bank to renew the note for another three years. Dewey seems less concerned by the unfortunate timing of the recession and has some suggestions as to how they can "paint the rosiest possible picture for the banker" when they go for the loan extension in July. In fact, he has some very specific recommendations for you as to how to account for transactions during June, the last month in the fiscal year.

You are the controller for Listum & Sellum and have been treated very well by Willie and Dewey since joining the company two years ago. In fact, Dewey insists that you personally drive the top-of-the-line Cadillac. Following are his suggestions:

First, for any sales made in June, we can record the 6% commission revenue immediately but delay recording the 4% commission expense until July, when the sales agent is paid. We record the sales at the same time we always have, the sales agents get paid when they always have, the bank sees how profitable we have been, we get our loan, and everybody is happy!

HOMEWORK

Second, since we won't be paying our advertising bills for the month of June until July 10, we can just wait until then to record the expense. The timing seems perfect, given that we are to meet with the bank for the loan extension on July 8.

Third, since we will be depreciating the fleet of Caddys for the year ending June 30, how about just changing the estimated useful life on them to eight years instead of four years? We won't say anything to the sales agents; no need to rile them up about having to drive their cars for eight years. Anyhow, the change to eight years would just be for accounting purposes. In fact, we could even switch back to four years for accounting purposes next year. Likewise, the changes in recognizing commission expense and advertising expense don't need to be permanent either; these are just slight bookkeeping changes to help us get over the hump!

Required

1. Explain why each of the three proposed changes in accounting will result in an increase in net income for the year ending June 30.
2. Identify any concerns you have with each of the three proposed changes in accounting from the perspective of generally accepted accounting principles. If these changes are made, do the financial statements faithfully represent what they claim to represent? Are these changes merely bookkeeping changes? Explain your answers.
3. Identify any concerns you have with each of the three proposed changes in accounting from an ethical perspective. Do the proposed changes provide information that is free from bias? Explain your answer.
4. Does the controller benefit by making the proposed changes? Are outsiders harmed? Explain your answers.

LO4   **Decision Case 4-6** Advice to a Potential Investor

Century Company was organized 15 months ago as a management consulting firm. At that time, the owners invested a total of $50,000 cash in exchange for stock. Century purchased equipment for $35,000 cash and supplies to be used in the business. The equipment is expected to last seven years with no salvage value. Supplies are purchased on account and paid for in the month after the purchase. Century normally has about $1,000 of supplies on hand. Its client base has increased so dramatically that the president and chief financial officer have approached an investor to provide additional cash for expansion. The balance sheet and income statement for the first year of business are presented below.

Century Company
Balance Sheet
December 31, 2007

Assets		Liabilities and Stockholders' Equity	
Cash	$10,100	Accounts payable	$ 2,300
Accounts receivable	1,200	Common stock	50,000
Supplies	16,500	Retained earnings	10,500
Equipment	35,000		
Total	$62,800	Total	$62,800

Century Company
Income Statement
For the Year Ended December 31, 2007

Revenues		$82,500
Wages and salaries	$60,000	
Utilities	12,000	72,000
Net income		$10,500

Required

The investor has asked you to look at these financial statements and give an opinion about Century's future profitability. Are the statements prepared in accordance with generally accepted accounting principles? If not, explain why. Based on only these two statements, what would you advise? What additional information would you need in order to give an educated opinion?

H O M E W O R K

SOLUTIONS TO KEY TERMS QUIZ

__15__	Recognition		__10__	Deferral
__22__	Historical cost		__16__	Deferred expense
__8__	Current value		__5__	Deferred revenue
__18__	Cash basis		__12__	Accrual
__11__	Accrual basis		__19__	Accrued liability
__2__	Revenues		__7__	Accrued asset
__14__	Revenue recognition principle		__24__	Accounting cycle
__20__	Matching principle		__1__	Work sheet
__23__	Expenses		__6__	Real accounts
__3__	Adjusting entries		__17__	Nominal accounts
__9__	Straight-line method		__4__	Closing entries
__21__	Contra account		__13__	Interim statements

INTEGRATIVE PROBLEM

Completing Financial Statements, Computing Ratios, Comparing Accrual vs. Cash Income, and Evaluating the Company's Cash Needs

Mountain Home Health Inc. provides home nursing services in the Great Smoky Mountains of Tennessee. When contacted by a client or referred by a physician, nurses visit with the patient and discuss needed services with the physician.

Mountain Home Health earns revenue from patient services. Most of the revenue comes from billing either insurance companies, the state of Tennessee, or the Medicare program. Amounts billed are recorded in the Billings Receivable account. Insurance companies, states, and the federal government do not fully fund all procedures. For example, the state of Tennessee pays an average 78% of billed amounts. Mountain Home Health has already removed the uncollectible amounts from the Billings Receivable account and reports it and Medical Services Revenue at the net amount. Services provided but not yet recorded totaled $16,000, net of allowances for uncollectible amounts. The firm earns a minor portion of its total revenue directly from patients in the form of cash.

Employee salaries, medical supplies, depreciation, and gasoline are the major expenses. Employees are paid every Friday for work performed during the Saturday-to-Friday pay period. Salaries amount to $800 per day. In 2006, December 31 falls on a Sunday. Medical supplies (average use of $1,500 per week) are purchased periodically to support health care coverage. The inventory of supplies on hand on December 31 amounted to $8,653.

The firm owns five automobiles (all purchased at the same time) that average 50,000 miles per year and are replaced every three years. They typically have no residual value. The building has an expected life of 20 years with no residual value. Straight-line depreciation is used on all firm assets. Gasoline costs, which are a cash expenditure, average $375 per day. The firm purchases a three-year, extended warranty contract to cover maintenance costs. The contract costs $9,000 (assume equal use each year).

On December 29, 2006, Mountain Home Health declared a dividend of $10,000, payable on January 15, 2007. The firm makes annual payments of principal and interest each June 30 on the mortgage. The interest rate on the mortgage is 6%.

The following account balances are available for Mountain Home Health on December 31, 2006:

Cash	$ 77,400
Billings Receivable (net)	151,000
Medical Supplies	73,000
Extended Warranty	3,000
Automobiles	90,000
Accumulated Depreciation—Automobiles	60,000
Building	200,000
Accumulated Depreciation—Building	50,000
Accounts Payable	22,000
Dividend Payable	10,000

(continued)

Mortgage Payable	$100,000
Capital Stock	100,000
Additional Paid-In Capital	50,000
Retained Earnings	99,900
Medical Services Revenue	550,000
Salary and Wages Expense	288,000
Gasoline Expense	137,500
Utilities Expense	12,000
Dividends	10,000

Required

1. Determine the effect on the accounting equation of the necessary adjustments on December 31, 2006.
2. Prepare a statement of income and a statement of retained earnings for Mountain Home Health for the year ended December 31, 2006.
3. Prepare a balance sheet for Mountain Home Health as of December 31, 2006.
4. Compute the following as of December 31, 2006:
   a. Working capital
   b. Current ratio
5. Which of the adjustments might cause a difference between cash- and accrual-based income?
6. Mary Francis, controller of Mountain Home, became concerned about the company's cash flow after talking to a local bank loan officer. The firm tries to maintain a seven-week supply of cash to meet the demands of payroll, medical supply purchases, and gasoline. Determine the amount of cash Mountain Home needs to meet the seven-week supply.

5

Inventories and Cost of Goods Sold

Study Links

A Look at the Previous Chapter
Chapter 4 completed our introduction to the accounting model. In that chapter we examined the role of adjustments in an accrual accounting system.

A Look at This Chapter
Starting in this chapter, we move beyond the basic accounting model to consider the accounting for the various elements in the financial statements. We start by looking at how companies that sell a product account for their inventories and the eventual sale of them.

A Look at the Upcoming Chapter
Each of the remaining chapters in this section of the book examine other assets of a company. In Chapter 6 we will consider the most liquid of all assets, cash, and look at the ways in which companies maintain control over it and other valuable assets.

Learning Outcomes

After studying this chapter, you should be able to:

LO1 Identify the forms of inventory held by different types of businesses and the types of costs incurred.

LO2 Show that you understand how wholesalers and retailers account for sales of merchandise.

LO3 Show that you understand how wholesalers and retailers account for cost of goods sold.

LO4 Use the gross profit ratio to analyze a company's ability to cover its operating expenses and earn a profit.

LO5 Explain the relationship between the valuation of inventory and the measurement of income.

LO6 Apply the inventory costing methods of specific identification, weighted average, FIFO, and LIFO using a periodic system.

LO7 Analyze the effects of the different costing methods on inventory, net income, income taxes, and cash flow.

LO8 Analyze the effects of an inventory error on various financial statement items.

LO9 Apply the lower-of-cost-or-market rule to the valuation of inventory.

LO10 Explain why and how the cost of inventory is estimated in certain situations.

LO11 Analyze the management of inventory.

LO12 Explain the effects that inventory transactions have on the statement of cash flows.

LO13 Explain the differences in the accounting for periodic and perpetual inventory systems and apply the inventory costing methods using a perpetual system (Appendix).

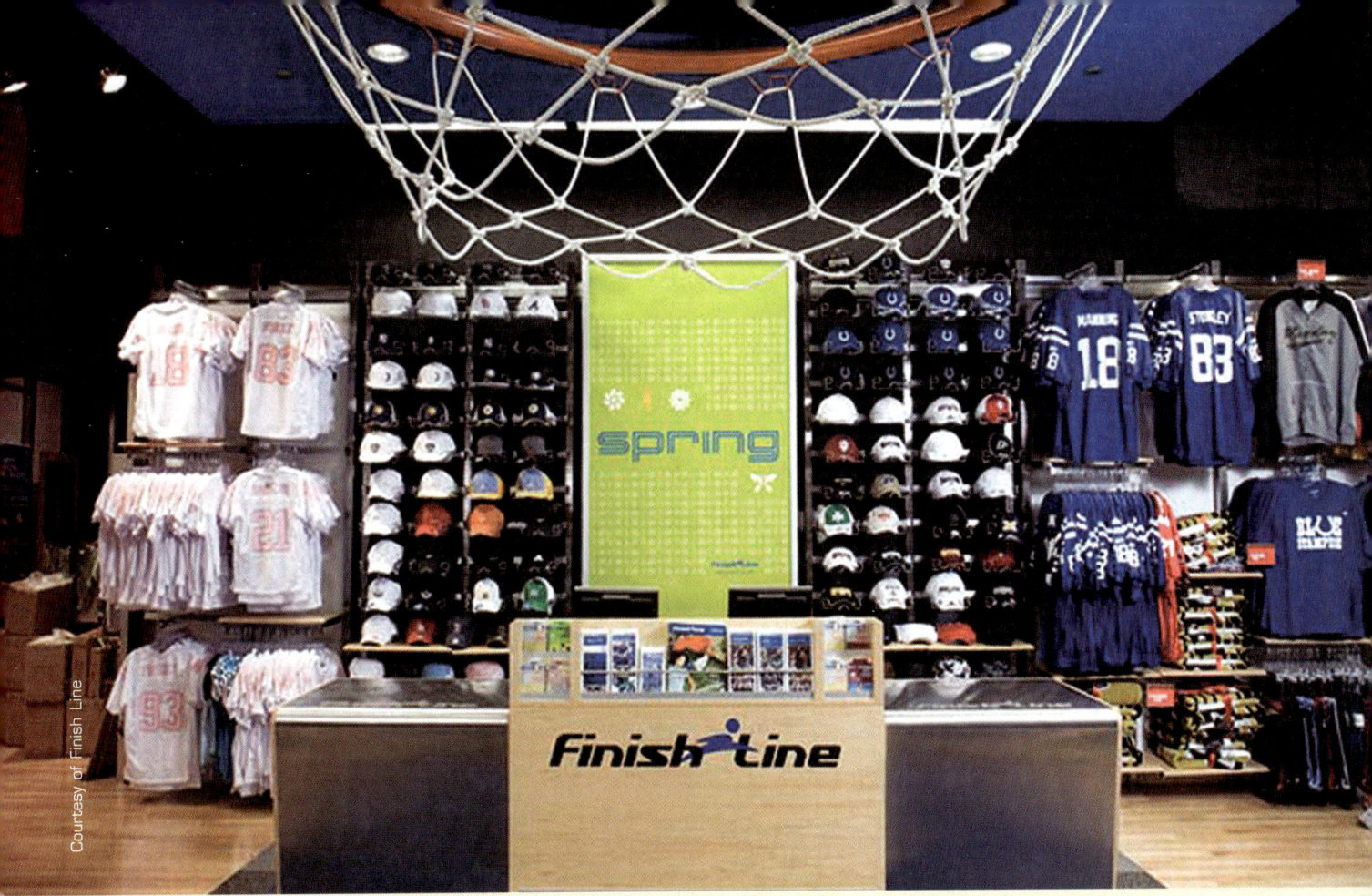

The Finish Line, Inc.

MAKING BUSINESS DECISIONS

The 2006 fiscal year was a record-setting one on many fronts for **Finish Line**, the familiar mall-based merchandiser of athletic shoes and fitness apparel. Sales reached record levels, topping $1.3 billion, an impressive 12% increase over the prior year. The company reported net income of nearly $61 million. And by year-end Finish Line operated 657 stores in the United States, with plans to open 40 new stores in fiscal year 2007.

The income statement on the next page provides evidence of Finish Line's successful year. Of course, an increase in sales is likely to be accompanied by an increase in the cost of the products sold, as indicated by the second line on the income statement titled "Cost of sales." One of the most important tasks facing management of any company is to control the cost of its inventory. Maintaining large stocks of inventory is costly. The more Finish Line can minimize the amount it has tied up in its merchandise of shoes and other apparel, the better off it will be. According to the

partial balance sheet illustrated here, not only did the amount of inventory increase significantly during the year, it is easily the largest of all the company's current assets, accounting for over 70% of the total.

In this chapter, we will look closely at the accounting for inventories and cost of goods sold. We will answer the following important questions:

- How does Finish Line keep track of the cost of its inventory? (See pp. 210–211)
- When the company makes a sale, how does it determine the amount to assign to the cost of the product sold? (See pp. 217–225)
- How can the relationship between the company's sales and the cost of those sales be used to help assess the company's performance? (See pp. 215–216)
- How can the relationship between Finish Line's sales on its income statement and its inventory on the balance sheet be used to help assess how well it is managing its inventory? (See pp. 233–235)

203

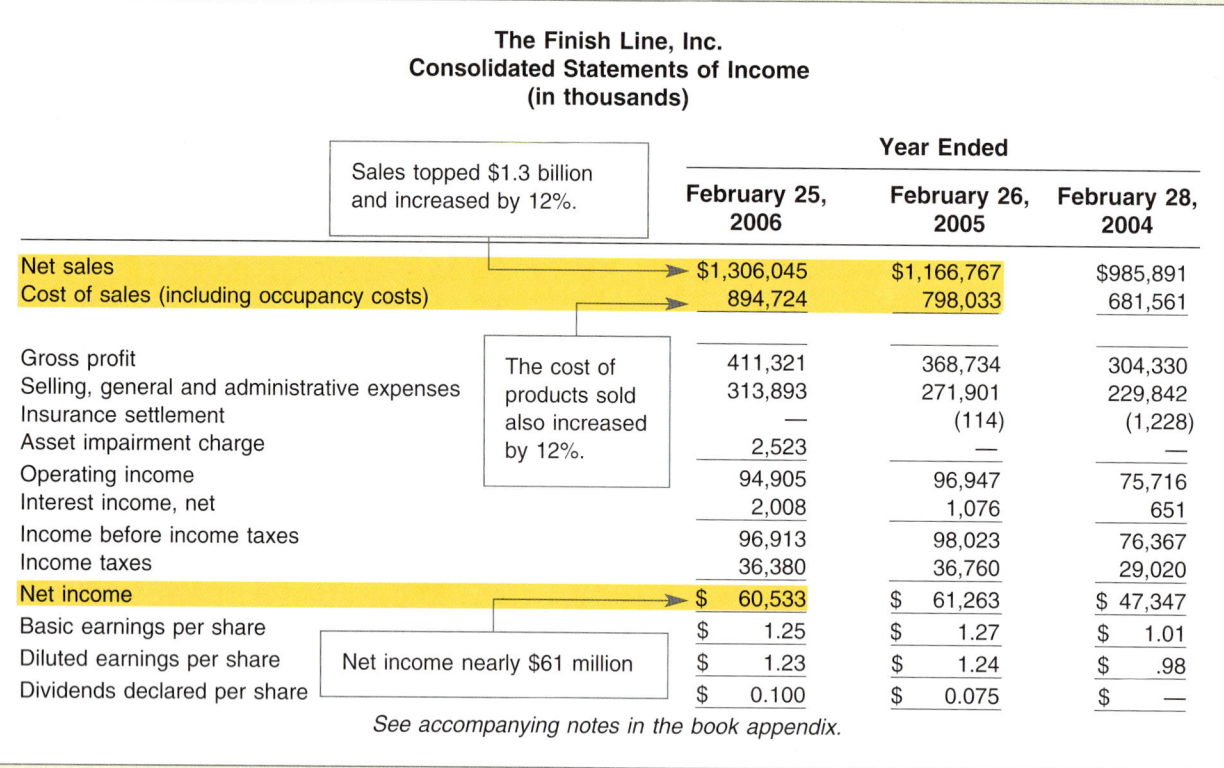

The Finish Line, Inc.
Consolidated Statements of Income
(in thousands)

Sales topped $1.3 billion and increased by 12%.

	Year Ended		
	February 25, 2006	February 26, 2005	February 28, 2004
Net sales	$1,306,045	$1,166,767	$985,891
Cost of sales (including occupancy costs)	894,724	798,033	681,561
Gross profit	411,321	368,734	304,330
Selling, general and administrative expenses	313,893	271,901	229,842
Insurance settlement	—	(114)	(1,228)
Asset impairment charge	2,523	—	—
Operating income	94,905	96,947	75,716
Interest income, net	2,008	1,076	651
Income before income taxes	96,913	98,023	76,367
Income taxes	36,380	36,760	29,020
Net income	$ 60,533	$ 61,263	$ 47,347
Basic earnings per share	$ 1.25	$ 1.27	$ 1.01
Diluted earnings per share	$ 1.23	$ 1.24	$ .98
Dividends declared per share	$ 0.100	$ 0.075	$ —

The cost of products sold also increased by 12%.

Net income nearly $61 million

See accompanying notes in the book appendix.

The Finish Line, Inc.
Consolidated Balance Sheets (Partial)
(in thousands)

	February 25, 2006	February 26, 2005
Assets		
Current Assets		
Cash and cash equivalents	$ 47,488	$ 55,991
Marketable securities	49,075	57,175
Accounts receivable, net	11,999	14,230
Merchandise inventories, net	268,590	241,242
Other	4,375	3,162
Total current assets	381,527	371,800

The company's inventory on hand increased during the year and represents 70% of the current assets.

See accompanying notes in the book appendix.

Source: Finish Line Inc. 2006 Annual Report.

The Nature of Inventory

LO1 Identify the forms of inventory held by different types of businesses and the types of costs incurred.

We have concentrated on the accounting for businesses that sell *services*. Banks, hotels, airlines, health clubs, real estate offices, law firms, and accounting firms are all examples of service companies. In this chapter we turn to accounting by companies that sell products, or what accountants call inventory. Companies that sell inventory can be broadly categorized into two types:

- Retailers and wholesalers purchase inventory in finished form and hold it for resale. For example, as a retailer **Finish Line** buys shoes directly from companies such as **Nike** and **New Balance** and then offers them for sale to consumers.

- In contrast, manufacturers transform raw materials into a finished product prior to sale. A good example of a manufacturing company is **IBM**. It buys all of the various materials that are needed to make computers and then sells the finished product to its customers.

Whether a company is a wholesaler, retailer, or manufacturer, its inventory is an asset that is held for *resale* in the normal course of business. The distinction between inventory and an operating asset is the *intent* of the owner. For example, some of the computers that IBM owns are operating assets because they are used in various activities of the business such as the payroll and accounting functions. Many more of the computers IBM owns are inventory, however, because the company makes them and intends to sell them. This chapter is concerned with the proper valuation of inventory and the related effect on cost of goods sold.

THREE TYPES OF INVENTORY COST AND THREE FORMS OF INVENTORY

It is important to distinguish between the *types* of inventory costs incurred and the *form* the inventory takes. Wholesalers and retailers incur a single type of cost, the *purchase price*, of the inventory they sell. On the balance sheet they use a single account for inventory, titled **Merchandise Inventory**. Wholesalers and retailers buy merchandise in finished form and offer it for resale without transforming the product in any way. Because they do not use factory buildings, assembly lines, or production equipment, merchandise companies have a relatively small dollar amount in operating assets and a large amount in inventory. For example, on its February 25, 2006, balance sheet, Finish Line reported inventory of approximately $269 million and total assets of $628 million. It is not unusual for inventories to account for half of the total assets of a merchandise company.

The cost of inventory to a *merchandiser* is limited to the product's purchase price, which may include other costs we will mention soon. Conversely, three distinct *types* of costs are incurred by a *manufacturer*—direct materials, direct labor, and manufacturing overhead:

- Direct materials, also called **raw materials**, are the ingredients used in making a product. The costs of direct materials used in making a pair of shoes include the costs of fabric, plastic, and rubber.
- Direct labor consists of the amounts paid to workers to manufacture the product. The hourly wage paid to an assembly line worker is a primary ingredient in the cost to make the shoes.
- Manufacturing overhead includes all other costs that are related to the manufacturing process but cannot be directly matched to specific units of output. Depreciation of a factory building and the salary of a supervisor are two examples of overhead costs. Accountants have developed various techniques to assign, or allocate, these manufacturing overhead costs to specific products.

In addition to the three types of costs incurred in a production process, the inventory of a manufacturer takes three distinct *forms*. The three forms or stages in the development of inventory are raw materials, work in process, and finished goods:

- Direct materials or raw materials enter a production process in which they are transformed into a finished product by the addition of direct labor and manufacturing overhead.
- At any point in time, including the end of an accounting period, some of the materials have entered the process and some labor costs have been incurred but the product is not finished. The cost of unfinished products is appropriately called **work in process** or *work in progress*.
- Inventory that has completed the production process and is available for sale is called **finished goods**. Finished goods are the equivalent of merchandise inventory for a retailer or wholesaler in that both represent the inventory of goods held for sale.

Merchandise Inventory
The account wholesalers and retailers use to report inventory held for resale.

Raw materials
The inventory of a manufacturer before the addition of any direct labor or manufacturing overhead. *Alternate term: Direct materials*

Work in process
The cost of unfinished products in a manufacturing company. *Alternate term: Work in progress*

Finished goods
A manufacturer's inventory that is complete and ready for sale.

EXHIBIT 5-1 **Relationships between Types of Businesses and Inventory Costs**

Type of Business	Inventory	Costs Included in Inventory
Retailer/Wholesaler ⟶	Merchandise inventory	Cost to purchase
	Raw materials	Cost of materials before entered into production
Manufacturer ⟨ ⟶	Work in process	Costs of direct materials used, direct labor, and overhead in unfinished items
	Finished goods	Cost of completed, but unsold, items

Many manufacturers disclose the dollar amounts of the various forms of inventory in their annual report. For example, **IBM** disclosed in its online 2005 annual report the following amounts, stated in millions of dollars:

	Millions
Inventories:	
Finished goods	$ 902
Work in process and	
raw materials	1,939
	$2,841

As you can see, finished goods make up less than one-third of IBM's total inventories. However, this may not be the case for other types of businesses, where finished goods are more significant. For example, consider the following excerpt from **Jacuzzi Brands'** 2005 annual report:

	(in millions)
Finished products	$108.7
In-process products	12.9
Raw materials	43.4
	$165.0

As the company that makes whirlpools, showers, and spas, Jacuzzi has nearly two-thirds of its inventory in finished products.

Exhibit 5-1 summarizes the relationships between the types of costs incurred and the forms of inventory for different types of businesses.

The Income Statement for a Merchandiser

A *condensed* multiple-step income statement for Daisy's Running Depot is presented in Exhibit 5-2. First, note the period covered by the statement: for the year ended December 31, 2007. Daisy's ends its fiscal year on December 31; however, many merchandisers end their *fiscal year* on a date other than December 31. Retailers often choose a date toward the end of January because the busy holiday

---

EXHIBIT 5-2 Condensed Income Statement for a Merchandiser

Daisy's Running Depot
Income Statement
For the Year Ended December 31, 2007

Net sales	$100,000
Cost of goods sold	60,000
Gross profit	$ 40,000
Selling and administrative expenses	29,300
Net income before tax	$ 10,700
Income tax expense	4,280
Net income	$ 6,420

---

shopping season is over and time can be devoted to closing the records and preparing financial statements. For example, **Finish Line** ends its fiscal year on the Saturday closest to the end of February.

We will concentrate on the first two items on Daisy's statement: net sales and cost of goods sold. The major difference between this income statement and that for a service company is the inclusion of cost of goods sold. Because a service company does not sell a product, it does not report cost of goods sold. On the income statement of a merchandising company, cost of goods sold is deducted from net sales to arrive at **gross profit** or gross margin.

Gross profit
Net sales less cost of goods sold. *Alternate term: Gross margin*

Net Sales of Merchandise

The first section of Daisy's income statement is presented in Exhibit 5-3. Two deductions—for sales returns and allowances and sales discounts—are made from sales revenue to arrive at **net sales**. **Sales revenue**, or simply sales, is a *representation of the inflow of assets,* either cash or accounts receivable, from the sale of a product during the period.

LO2 Show that you understand how wholesalers and retailers account for sales of merchandise.

SALES RETURNS AND ALLOWANCES

The cornerstone of marketing is to satisfy the customer. Most companies have standard policies that allow the customer to *return* merchandise within a stipulated period of time. **Nordstrom**, the Seattle-based retailer, has a very liberal policy regarding returns. That policy has, in large measure, fueled its growth. A company's policy might be that a customer who is not completely satisfied can return the merchandise anytime within 30 days of purchase for a full refund. Alternatively, the customer may be given an *allowance* for spoiled or damaged merchandise—that is, the customer keeps the merchandise but receives a credit for a certain amount

Net sales
Sales revenue less sales returns and allowances and sales discounts.

Sales revenue
A representation of the inflow of assets. *Alternate term: Sales*

EXHIBIT 5-3 Net Sales Section of the Income Statement

Daisy's Running Depot
Partial Income Statement
For the Year Ended December 31, 2007

Sales revenue	$103,500	
Less: Sales returns and allowances	2,000	
Sales discounts	1,500	
Net sales		$100,000

Sales Returns and Allowances
Contra-revenue account used to record both refunds to customers and reductions of their accounts.

Study Tip

Recall Accumulated Depreciation, a contra account introduced in Chapter 4. It reduces a long-term asset. In other cases, such as this one involving sales, a contra account reduces an income statement account.

in the account balance. Typically, a single account, **Sales Returns and Allowances**, is used to account both for returns and for allowances. If the customer has already paid for the merchandise, either a cash refund is given or the credit amount is applied to future purchases.

CREDIT TERMS AND SALES DISCOUNTS

Most companies have a standard credit policy. Special notation is normally used to indicate a particular firm's policy for granting credit. For example, credit terms of *n/30* mean that the *net* amount of the selling price, that is, the amount determined after deducting any returns or allowances, is due within 30 days of the date of the invoice. *Net, 10 EOM* means that the net amount is due anytime within 10 days after the end of the month in which the sale took place.

Another common element of the credit terms offered to customers is sales discounts, a reduction from the selling price given for early payment. For example, assume that Daisy's offers a customer credit terms of *1/10, n/30*. This means that the customer may deduct 1% from the selling price if the bill is paid within 10 days of the date of the invoice. Normally the discount period begins with the day *after* the invoice date. If the customer does not pay within the first 10 days, the full invoice amount is due within 30 days. Finally, note that the use of *n* for *net* in this notation is really a misnomer. Although the amount due is net of any returns and allowances, it is the *gross* amount that is due within 30 days. That is, no discount is given if the customer does not pay early.

How valuable to the customer is a 1% discount for payment within the first 10 days? Assume that a $1,000 sale is made. If the customer pays at the end of 10 days, the cash paid will be $990, rather than $1,000, a net savings of $10. The customer has saved $10 by paying 20 days earlier than required by the 30-day term. If we assume 360 days in a year, there are 360/20 or 18 periods of 20 days each in a year. Thus, a savings of $10 for 20 days is equivalent to a savings of $10 times 18, or $180 for the year. An annual return of $180/$990, or 18.2%, would be difficult to match with any other type of investment. In fact, a customer might want to consider borrowing the money to pay off the account early.

The **Sales Discounts** account is a *contra-revenue* account and thus reduces sales as shown on the income statement in Exhibit 5-3.

Sales Discounts
Contra-revenue account used to record discounts given customers for early payment of their accounts.

The Cost of Goods Sold

LO3 Show that you understand how wholesalers and retailers account for cost of goods sold.

The cost of goods sold section of the income statement for Daisy's is shown in Exhibit 5-4. Let us take a look at the basic model for cost of goods sold.

THE COST OF GOODS SOLD MODEL

The recognition of cost of goods sold as an expense is an excellent example of the *matching principle*. Sales revenue represents the *inflow* of assets, in the form of cash and accounts receivable, from the sale of products during the period. Likewise, cost of goods sold represents the *outflow* of an asset, inventory, from the sale of those same products. The company needs to match the revenue of the period with one of the most important costs necessary to generate the revenue, the *cost* of the merchandise sold.

It may be helpful in understanding cost of goods sold to realize what it is *not*. *Cost of goods sold is not necessarily equal to the cost of purchases of merchandise during the period*. Except in the case of a new business, a merchandiser starts the year with a certain stock of inventory on hand, called *beginning inventory*. For Daisy's, beginning inventory is the dollar cost of merchandise on hand on January 1, 2007. During the year, Daisy's purchases merchandise. When the cost of goods purchased is added to beginning inventory, the result is **cost of goods available for sale**. Just as the merchandiser starts the period with an inventory of merchandise on hand, a

Cost of goods available for sale
Beginning inventory plus cost of goods purchased.

EXHIBIT 5-4 Cost of Goods Sold Section of the Income Statement

Daisy's Running Depot
Partial Income Statement
For the Year Ended December 31, 2007

Cost of goods sold:		
Inventory, January 1, 2007		$15,000
Purchases	$65,000	
Less: Purchase returns and allowances	1,800	
Purchase discounts	3,700	
Net purchases	$59,500	
Add: Transportation-in	3,500	
Cost of goods purchased		63,000
Cost of goods available for sale		$78,000
Less: Inventory, December 31, 2007		18,000
Cost of goods sold		$60,000

---

certain amount of *ending inventory* is usually on hand at the end of the year. For Daisy's, this is its inventory on December 31, 2007.

As shown in Exhibit 5-5, think of cost of goods available for sale as a "pool" of costs to be distributed between what we sold and what we did not sell. If we subtract from the pool the cost of what we did *not* sell, the *ending inventory,* we will have the amount we *did* sell, the **cost of goods sold**. Cost of goods sold is simply the difference between the cost of goods available for sale and the ending inventory:

Cost of goods sold
Cost of goods available for sale minus ending inventory.

Beginning inventory	What is on hand to start the period
+ Cost of goods purchased	What was acquired for resale during the period
= Cost of goods available for sale	The "pool" of costs to be distributed
− Ending inventory	What was not sold during the period and therefore is on hand to start the next period
= Cost of goods sold	What was sold during the period

The cost of goods sold model for a merchandiser is illustrated in Exhibit 5-6. The amounts used for the illustration are taken from the cost of goods sold section of Daisy's income statement as shown in Exhibit 5-4. Notice that ending inventory exceeds beginning inventory by $3,000. That means that the cost of goods

EXHIBIT 5-5 The Cost of Goods Sold Model

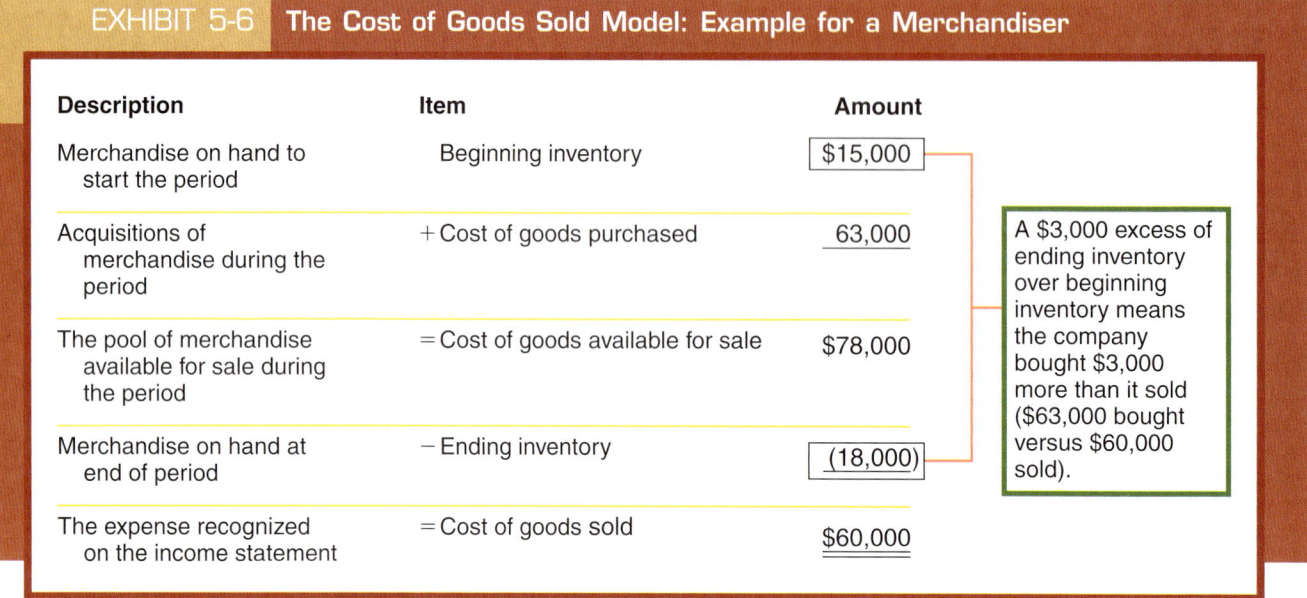

EXHIBIT 5-6   The Cost of Goods Sold Model: Example for a Merchandiser

Description	Item	Amount
Merchandise on hand to start the period	Beginning inventory	$15,000
Acquisitions of merchandise during the period	+ Cost of goods purchased	63,000
The pool of merchandise available for sale during the period	= Cost of goods available for sale	$78,000
Merchandise on hand at end of period	− Ending inventory	(18,000)
The expense recognized on the income statement	= Cost of goods sold	$60,000

A $3,000 excess of ending inventory over beginning inventory means the company bought $3,000 more than it sold ($63,000 bought versus $60,000 sold).

purchased exceeds cost of goods sold by that same amount. Indeed, a key point for stockholders, bankers, and other users is whether inventory is building up, that is, whether a company is not selling as much inventory during the period as it is buying. A buildup may indicate that the company's products are becoming less desirable or that prices are becoming uncompetitive.

Perpetual system
System in which the Inventory account is increased at the time of each purchase and decreased at the time of each sale.

Periodic system
System in which the Inventory account is updated only at the end of the period.

INVENTORY SYSTEMS: PERPETUAL AND PERIODIC

Before we look more closely at the accounting for cost of goods sold, it is necessary to understand the difference between the periodic and the perpetual inventory systems. All businesses use one of these two distinct approaches to account for inventory. With the **perpetual system**, the Inventory account is updated *perpetually*, or after each sale or purchase of merchandise. Conversely, with the **periodic system**, the Inventory account is updated only at the end of the *period*.

In a perpetual system, every time goods are purchased, the Inventory account is increased, with a corresponding increase in Accounts Payable for a credit purchase or a decrease in the Cash account for a cash purchase. In addition to recognizing the increases in Accounts Receivable or Cash and in Sales Revenue when goods are sold, the accountant also records an entry to recognize the *cost* of the goods sold and the decrease in the cost of inventory on hand.

Assume for example that Daisy's sells a pair of running shoes that cost the company $70. In addition to the entry to record the sale, Daisy's would also record an entry that would have the following effect on the accounting equation:

Balance Sheet					Income Statement	
ASSETS	=	LIABILITIES	+	STOCKHOLDERS' EQUITY	+	REVENUES − EXPENSES
Inventory (70)						Cost of Goods Sold (70)

Thus, at any point during the period, the inventory account is up to date. It has been increased for the cost of purchases during the period and reduced for the cost of the sales.

Why don't all companies use the procedure we just described, the perpetual system? Depending on the volume of inventory transactions, that is, purchases and sales of merchandise, a perpetual system can be extremely costly to maintain. Historically, businesses that have a relatively small volume of sales at a high unit price have used perpetual systems. For example, dealers in automobiles, furniture, appliances, and jewelry normally use a perpetual system. Each purchase of a unit of merchandise, such as an automobile, can be easily identified and an increase recorded in the Inventory account. For instance, when an auto is sold, the dealer can easily determine the cost of the particular car sold by looking at a perpetual inventory record.

Can you imagine, however, a similar system for a supermarket or a hardware store? Consider a checkout stand in a grocery store. Through the use of a cash register tape, the sales revenue for that particular stand is recorded at the end of the day. Because of the tremendous volume of sales of various items of inventory, from cans of vegetables to boxes of soap, it may not be feasible to record the cost of goods sold every time a sale takes place. This illustrates a key point in financial information: the cost of the information should never exceed its benefit. If a store manager had to stop and update the records each time a can of **Campbell's** soup was sold, the retailer's business would obviously be disrupted.

To a certain extent, the ability of mass merchandisers to maintain perpetual inventory records has improved with the advent of point-of-sale terminals. When a cashier runs a can of corn over the sensing glass at the checkout stand and the bar code is read, the company's computer receives a message that a can of corn has been sold. In some companies, however, updating the inventory record is in units only and is used as a means to determine when a product needs to be reordered. The company still relies on a periodic system to maintain the *dollar* amount of inventory. In the remainder of this chapter, we limit our discussion to the periodic system. We discuss the perpetual system in more detail in the appendix to this chapter.

BEGINNING AND ENDING INVENTORIES IN A PERIODIC SYSTEM

In a periodic system, the Inventory account is *not* updated each time a sale or purchase is made. Throughout the year, the Inventory account contains the amount of merchandise on hand at the beginning of the year. The account is adjusted only at the end of the year. A company using the periodic system must physically *count* the units of inventory on hand at the end of the period. The number of units of each product is then multiplied by the cost per unit, to determine the dollar amount of ending inventory. Refer to Exhibit 5-4 for Daisy's Running Depot. The procedure just described was used to determine its ending inventory of $18,000. Because one period's ending inventory is the next period's beginning inventory, the beginning inventory of $15,000 was based on the count at the end of the prior year.

In summary, the ending inventory in a periodic system is determined by counting the merchandise, not by looking at the Inventory account at the end of the period. The periodic system results in a trade-off. Use of the periodic system reduces record keeping but at the expense of a certain degree of control. Losses of merchandise due to theft, breakage, spoilage, or other reasons may go undetected in a periodic system because management may assume that all merchandise not on hand at the end of the year was sold. In a retail store, some of the merchandise may have been shoplifted rather than sold. In contrast, with a perpetual inventory system, a count of inventory at the end of the period serves as a *control device*. For example, if the Inventory account shows a balance of $45,000 at the end of the year but only $42,000 of merchandise is counted, management is able to investigate the discrepancy. No such control feature exists in a periodic system.

In addition to the loss of control, the use of a periodic system presents a dilemma when a company wants to prepare *interim* financial statements. Because most companies that use a periodic system find it cost-prohibitive to count the entire inventory more than once a year, they use estimation techniques to determine inventory for monthly or quarterly statements. These techniques are discussed later in this chapter.

THE COST OF GOODS PURCHASED

The cost of goods purchased section of Daisy's income statement is shown in Exhibit 5-7. The company purchased $65,000 of merchandise during the period. Two amounts are deducted from purchases to arrive at net purchases: purchase returns and allowances of $1,800 and purchase discounts of $3,700. The cost of

5-1 **Real World Practice**

Understanding Finish Line's Inventory System

Given the nature of its products, would you expect that **Finish Line** uses a perpetual or a periodic inventory system? Explain your answer.

EXHIBIT 5-7	Cost of Goods Purchased

Daisy's Running Depot
Partial Income Statement
For the Year Ended December 31, 2007

Purchases	$65,000	
Less: Purchase returns and allowances	1,800	
Purchase discounts	3,700	
Net purchases	$59,500	
Add: Transportation-in	3,500	
Cost of goods purchased		$63,000

Transportation-in
Adjunct account used to record freight costs paid by the buyer. *Alternate term: Freight-in*

Purchases
Account used in a periodic inventory system to record acquisitions of merchandise.

$3,500 incurred by Daisy's to ship the goods to its place of business is called **transportation-in** and is added to net purchases of $59,500 to arrive at the cost of goods purchased of $63,000. Another name for transportation-in is *freight-in*.

Purchases   Assume that Daisy's buys shoes on account from Nike at a cost of $4,000. **Purchases** is the temporary account used in a periodic inventory system to record acquisitions of merchandise. The effect of this transaction is to increase liabilities and increase cost of goods sold, which is an expense:

Balance Sheet							Income Statement	
ASSETS	**=**	**LIABILITIES**		**+**	**STOCKHOLDERS' EQUITY**	**+**	**REVENUES – EXPENSES**	
		Accounts Payable	4,000				Purchases	(4,000)

It is important to understand that Purchases is *not* an asset account. It is included in the income statement as an integral part of the calculation of cost of goods sold and is therefore shown as a reduction of stockholders' equity in the accounting equation.

Purchase Returns and Allowances   We discussed returns and allowances earlier in the chapter from the seller's point of view. From the standpoint of the buyer, purchase returns and allowances are reductions in the cost to purchase merchandise. Rather than record these reductions directly in the Purchases account, the accountant uses a separate account. The account, **Purchase Returns and Allowances**, is a *contra account* to Purchases. The use of a contra account allows management to monitor the amount of returns and allowances. For example, a large number of returns during the period relative to the amount purchased may signal that the purchasing department is not buying from reputable sources.

Purchase Returns and Allowances
Contra-purchases account used in a periodic inventory system when a refund is received from a supplier or a reduction given in the balance owed to a supplier.

Suppose that Daisy's returns $850 of merchandise to Nike for credit on its account. The return decreases both liabilities and purchases. Note that because a return reduces purchases, it actually *increases* net income:

Balance Sheet							Income Statement	
ASSETS	**=**	**LIABILITIES**		**+**	**STOCKHOLDERS' EQUITY**	**+**	**REVENUES – EXPENSES**	
		Accounts Payable	(850)				Purchases Returns and Allowances	850

The effect of an allowance for merchandise retained rather than returned is the same as that for a return.

Purchase Discounts   Discounts were discussed earlier in the chapter from the seller's viewpoint. Merchandising companies often purchase inventory on terms that allow for a cash discount for early payment, such as 2/10, net 30. To the buyer, a cash discount is called a *purchase discount* and results in a reduction of the cost to purchase merchandise. Management must monitor the amount of purchase discounts taken as well as those opportunities missed by not taking advantage of the discounts for early payment.

Assume a purchase of merchandise on March 13 for $500, with credit terms of 1/10, net 30. The effect of the purchase is:

	Balance Sheet					Income Statement	
ASSETS	**=**	**LIABILITIES**	**+**	**STOCKHOLDERS' EQUITY**	**+**	**REVENUES − EXPENSES**	
		Accounts Payable	500			Purchases	(500)

Any discount taken by a company is recorded in the Purchase Discounts account and deducted from purchases on the income statement. Assuming that the customer pays on time, the effect of the collection of the open account is as follows:

		Balance Sheet					Income Statement	
ASSETS	**=**	**LIABILITIES**	**+**	**STOCKHOLDERS' EQUITY**	**+**	**REVENUES − EXPENSES**	
Cash	(495)	Accounts Payable	(500)			Purchase Discounts	5

The **Purchase Discounts** account is contra to the Purchases account and thus increases stockholders' equity, as shown in the accounting equation above. Also note in Exhibit 5-7 that purchase discounts are deducted from purchases on the income statement. Finally, note that the effect on the income statement is the same as illustrated earlier for a purchase return: because purchases are reduced, net income is increased.

Purchase Discounts
Contra-purchases account used to record reductions in purchase price for early payment to a supplier.

Shipping Terms and Transportation Costs The *cost principle* governs the recording of all assets. All costs necessary to prepare an asset for its intended use should be included in its cost. The cost of an item to a merchandising company is not necessarily limited to its invoice price. For example, any sales tax paid should be included in computing total cost. Any transportation costs incurred by the buyer should likewise be included in the cost of the merchandise.

The buyer does not always pay to ship the merchandise. This depends on the terms of shipment. Goods are normally shipped either **FOB destination point** or **FOB shipping point**; *FOB* stands for *free on board*. When merchandise is shipped FOB destination point, it is the responsibility of the seller to deliver the products to the buyer. Thus, the seller either delivers the product to the customer or pays a trucking firm, railroad, or other carrier to transport it. Alternatively, the agreement between the buyer and the seller may provide for the goods to be shipped FOB shipping point. In this case, the merchandise is the responsibility of the buyer as soon as it leaves the seller's premises. When the terms of shipment are FOB shipping point, the buyer incurs transportation costs.

Refer to Exhibit 5-7. Transportation-in represents the freight costs Daisy's paid for in-bound merchandise. These costs are added to net purchases, as shown in the exhibit, and increase the cost of goods purchased. Assume that on delivery of a shipment of goods, Daisy's pays an invoice for $300 from Rocky Mountain Railroad. The terms of shipment are FOB shipping point. The effect of the accounting equation is as follows:

FOB destination point
Terms that require the seller to pay for the cost of shipping the merchandise to the buyer.

FOB shipping point
Terms that require the buyer to pay for the shipping costs.

		Balance Sheet					Income Statement	
ASSETS	**=**	**LIABILITIES**	**+**	**STOCKHOLDERS' EQUITY**	**+**	**REVENUES − EXPENSES**	
Cash	(300)					Transportation-in	(300)

The total of net purchases and transportation-in is called the *cost of goods purchased*. Transportation-in will be closed at the end of the period. In summary, cost of goods purchased consists of the following:

Purchases
Less: Purchase returns and allowances
       Purchase discounts
Equals: Net purchases
Add: Transportation-in
Equals: Cost of goods purchased

How should the *seller* account for the freight costs it pays when the goods are shipped FOB destination point? This cost, sometimes called *transportation-out*, is not an addition to the cost of purchases of the seller but is instead one of the costs necessary to *sell* the merchandise. Transportation-out is classified as a *selling expense* on the income statement.

Shipping Terms and Transfer of Title to Inventory Terms of shipment take on additional significance at the end of an accounting period. It is essential that a company establish a proper cutoff at year-end. For example, what if Daisy's purchases merchandise that is in transit at the end of the year? To whom does the inventory belong, Daisy's or the seller? The answer depends on the terms of shipment. If goods are shipped FOB destination point, they remain the legal property of the seller until they reach their destination. Alternatively, legal title to goods shipped FOB shipping point passes to the buyer as soon as the seller turns the goods over to the carrier.

The example in Exhibit 5-8 is intended to summarize our discussion about shipping terms and ownership of merchandise. Assume that Nike sells running shoes to Daisy's towards the end of the year and that the merchandise is in transit at the end of the year. Nike, the seller of the goods, pays the transportation charges only if the terms are FOB destination point. Nike records a sale for goods in transit at year-end, however, only if the terms of shipment are FOB shipping point. If Nike does not record a sale because the goods are shipped FOB destination point, the inventory

---

EXHIBIT 5-8 Shipping Terms and Transfer of Title to Inventory

FACTS Assume that on December 28, 2007, Nike ships running shoes to Daisy's Running Depot. The trucking company delivers the merchandise to Daisy's on January 2, 2008. Daisy's fiscal year-end is December 31.

Company		If Merchandise Is Shipped FOB	
		Destination Point	**Shipping Point**
Nike (seller)	Pay freight costs?	Yes	No
	Record sale in 2007?	No	Yes
	Include inventory on balance sheet at December 31, 2007?	Yes	No
Daisy's (buyer)	Pay freight costs?	No	Yes
	Record purchase in 2007?	No	Yes
	Include inventory on balance sheet at December 31, 2007?	No	Yes

appears on its December 31 balance sheet. Daisy's, the buyer, pays freight costs only if the goods are shipped FOB shipping point. Only in this situation does Daisy's record a purchase of the merchandise and include it as an asset on its December 31 balance sheet.

2 minute review

On April 13, 2004, Bitterroot Distributing sells merchandise to Darby Corp. for $1,000 with credit terms of 2/10, net 30. On April 19, Darby returns $150 of defective merchandise and receives a credit on account from Bitterroot. On April 23, Darby pays the amount due.

1. Determine the effects on Bitterroot's accounting equation from April 13 through April 23. Assume Bitterroot uses a periodic inventory system.

2. Determine the effects on Darby's accounting equation from April 13 through April 23. Assume Darby uses a periodic inventory system.

Answers

	Balance Sheet						Income Statement	
ASSETS	**+**	**LIABILITIES**		**+**	**STOCKHOLDERS' EQUITY**	**+**	**REVENUES – EXPENSES**	
1. April 13:								
Accounts							Sales Revenue	1,000
Receivable	1,000							
April 19:								
Accounts							Sales Returns and	
Receivable	(150)						Allowances	(150)
April 23:								
Cash	833						Sales Discounts	(17)
Accounts								
Receivable	(850)							
2. April 13:		Accounts Payable	1,000				Purchases	(1,000)
April 19:		Accounts Payable	(150)				Purchases Returns	
							and Allowances	150
April 23:								
Cash	(833)	Accounts Payable	(850)				Purchases Discounts	17

THE GROSS PROFIT RATIO

The first three lines on Daisy's income statement in Exhibit 5-2 are:

Net sales	$100,000
Cost of goods sold	60,000
Gross profit	$ 40,000

LO4 Use the gross profit ratio to analyze a company's ability to cover its operating expenses and earn a profit.

The relationship between gross profit and net sales—as measured by the **gross profit ratio**—is one of the most important measures used by managers, investors, and creditors to assess the performance of a company:

Gross profit ratio
Gross profit divided by net sales.

Gross Profit Ratio

Formula	For Daisy Sporting Goods
$\dfrac{\text{Gross Profit}}{\text{Net Sales}}$	$\dfrac{\$40,000}{\$100,000} = 40\%$

A 40% gross profit ratio tells us that for every dollar of sales Daisy has a gross profit of 40 cents. In other words, after deducting 60 cents for the cost of the product, the company has 40 cents on the dollar to cover its operating costs and earn a profit. We will now apply our ratio decision model to analyze this ratio for Finish Line.

USING THE RATIO DECISION MODEL: ANALYZING THE GROSS PROFIT RATIO

Use the following Ratio Decision Process to evaluate the gross profit ratio for Finish Line or any other public company.

1. Formulate the Question

The gross profit ratio tells us how many cents on every dollar are available to cover expenses other than cost of goods sold and to earn a profit.

How much of the sales revenue is used for the cost of the products and thus how much is left to cover other expenses and to earn net income?

2. Gather the Information from the Financial Statements

Both gross profit and sales revenue are reported on Finish Line's income statement for its 2005 fiscal year:

- Sales revenue: From the Income Statement for the Year
- Gross profit: From the Income Statement for the Year

3. Calculate the Ratio

$$\text{Gross Profit Ratio} = \frac{\text{Gross Profit}}{\text{Net Sales}}$$

The Finish Line, Inc.
Partial Consolidated Statements of Income
(in thousands)

	Year Ended		
	February 25, 2006	February 26, 2005	February 28, 2004
Net sales	$1,306,045	$1,166,767	$985,891
Cost of sales (including occupancy costs)	894,724	798,033	681,561
Gross profit	411,321	368,734	304,330

$$\text{Gross Profit Ratio} = \frac{\$411,321}{\$1,306,045} = 31.5\%$$

4. Compare the Ratio with Others

Management and other users compare the gross profit ratio with prior years to see if it has increased, decreased, or remained relatively steady. It is also important to compare the ratio with other companies in the same industry:

Finish Line		Foot Locker	
Year Ended February 25, 2006	Year Ended February 26, 2005	Year Ended January 28, 2006	Year Ended January 29, 2005
31.5%	31.6%	30.2%	30.5%

5. Interpret the Results

For every dollar of sales, Finish Line has approximately 32 cents available after deducting the cost of its products. The ratios for both companies have remained relatively stable over the two-year period. Of course, the gross profit ratio is not enough by itself to determine a company's profitability. Only if all of the expenses other than cost of goods sold are less than a company's gross profit will it report net income on the bottom line of the income statement.

Inventory Valuation and the Measurement of Income

One of the most fundamental concepts in accounting is the relationship between *asset valuation* and the *measurement of income*. Recall a point made in Chapter 4:

Assets are unexpired costs, and expenses are expired costs.

Thus, **the value assigned to an asset on the balance sheet determines the amount eventually recognized as an expense on the income statement.** For example, the amount recorded as the cost of an item of plant and equipment will dictate the amount of depreciation expense recognized on the income statement over the life of the asset. Similarly, the amount recorded as the cost of inventory determines the amount recognized as cost of goods sold on the income statement when the asset is sold. An error in assigning the proper amount to inventory on the balance sheet will affect the amount recognized as cost of goods sold on the income statement. The relationship between inventory as an asset and cost of goods sold can be understood by recalling the cost of goods sold section of the income statement. Assume the following example:

Beginning inventory	$ 500
Add: Purchases	1,200
Cost of goods available for sale	$1,700
Less: Ending inventory	(600)
Cost of goods sold	$1,100

The amount assigned to ending inventory is deducted from cost of goods available for sale to determine cost of goods sold. **If the ending inventory amount is incorrect, cost of goods sold will be wrong, and thus the net income of the period will be in error as well.** (We will look at inventory errors later in the chapter.)

INVENTORY COSTS: WHAT SHOULD BE INCLUDED?

All assets, including inventory, are recorded initially at cost. Cost is defined as "the price paid or consideration given to acquire an asset. As applied to inventories, cost means in principle the sum of the applicable expenditures and charges directly or indirectly incurred in bringing an article to its existing condition and location."[1]

Note the reference to the existing *condition* and *location*. This means that certain costs may also be included in the "price paid." Here are examples:

- As we saw earlier in the chapter, any freight costs incurred by the buyer in shipping inventory to its place of business should be included in the cost of the inventory.

- The cost of insurance taken out during the time that inventory is in transit should be added to the cost of the inventory.

- The cost of storing inventory before the time it is ready to be sold should be included in cost.

- Various types of taxes paid, such as excise and sales taxes, are other examples of costs necessary to put the inventory into a position to be able to sell it.

It is often very difficult, however, to allocate many of these incidental costs among the various items of inventory purchased. For example, consider a $500 freight bill that a supermarket paid on a merchandise shipment that includes 100 different items of inventory. To address the practical difficulty in assigning this type of cost to the different products, many companies have a policy by which transportation costs are charged to expense of the period if they are immaterial in amount. Thus, shipments of merchandise are simply recorded at the net invoice price, that is, after taking any cash discounts for early payment. It is a practical solution to a difficult allocation problem. Once again, the company must apply the cost/benefit test to accounting information.

LO5 Explain the relationship between the valuation of inventory and the measurement of income.

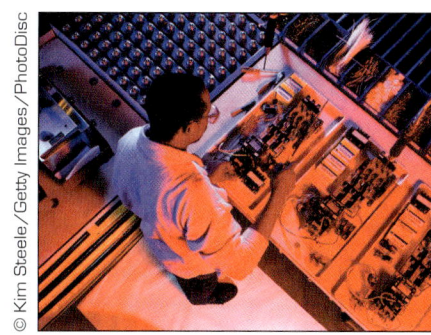

© Kim Steele / Getty Images./PhotoDisc

The inventory of a manufacturer consists of raw material, work in process, and finished goods. The electronic device being built here is part of a firm's work in process inventory. The direct materials probably consist of such items as the individual control knobs purchased from another manufacturer. When the manufacturing process is complete, the inventory of finished goods is ready for sale.

---

1 *Accounting Research Bulletin No. 43,* "Inventory Pricing" (New York: American Institute of Certified Public Accountants, June 1953), Ch. 4, statement 3.

Inventory Costing Methods with a Periodic System

LO6 Apply the inventory costing methods of specific identification, weighted average, FIFO, and LIFO using a periodic system.

To this point, we have assumed that the cost to purchase an item of inventory is constant. For most merchandisers, however, the unit cost of inventory changes frequently. Consider a simple example. Everett Company purchases merchandise twice during the first year of business. The dates, the number of units purchased, and the costs are as follows:

> February 4   200 units purchased at $1.00 per unit = $200
> October 13   200 units purchased at $1.50 per unit = $300

Everett sells 200 units during the first year. Individual sales of the units take place relatively evenly throughout the year. The question is: *which* 200 units did the company sell, the $1.00 units or the $1.50 units or some combination of each? Recall the earlier discussion of the relationship between asset valuation and income measurement. The question is important because the answer determines not only the value assigned to the 200 units of ending inventory *but also* the amount allocated to cost of goods sold for the 200 units sold.

One possible method of assigning amounts to ending inventory and cost of goods sold is to *specifically identify* which 200 units were sold and which 200 units are on hand. This method is feasible for a few types of businesses in which units can be identified by serial numbers, but it is totally impractical in most situations. As an alternative to specific identification, we could make an *assumption* as to which units were sold and which are on hand. Three different answers are possible:

1. **200 units sold at $1.00 each   = $200 cost of goods sold**
   and 200 units on hand at $1.50 each = $300 ending inventory

   or

2. **200 units sold at $1.50 each   = $300 cost of goods sold**
   and 200 units on hand at $1.00 each = $200 ending inventory

   or

3. **200 units sold at $1.25 each   = $250 cost of goods sold**
   and 200 units on hand at $1.25 each = $250 ending inventory

The third alternative assumes an *average cost* for the 200 units on hand and the 200 units sold. The average cost is the cost of the two purchases of $200 and $300, or $500, divided by the 400 units available to sell, or $1.25 per unit.

If we are concerned with the actual *physical flow* of the units of inventory, all of the three methods illustrated may be incorrect. The only approach that will yield a "correct" answer in terms of the actual flow of *units* of inventory is the specific identification method. In the absence of a specific identification approach, it is impossible to say which particular units were *actually* sold. In fact, there may have been sales from each of the two purchases, that is, some of the $1.00 units may have been sold and some of the $1.50 units may have been sold. To solve the problem of assigning costs to identical units, accountants have developed inventory costing assumptions or methods. Each of these methods makes a specific *assumption* about the *flow of costs* rather than the physical flow of units. The only approach that uses the actual flow of the units in assigning costs is the specific identification method.

To take a closer look at specific identification as well as three alternative approaches to valuing inventory, we will use the example at the top of the following page.

The question marks indicate the dilemma. What portion of the cost of goods available for sale of $17,100 should be assigned to the 900 units sold? What portion should be assigned to the 600 units remaining in ending inventory? The purpose of an inventory costing method is to provide a reasonable answer to these two questions.

	Units	Unit Cost	Total Cost
Beginning inventory			
January 1	500	$10	$ 5,000*
Purchases			
January 20	300	11	$ 3,300
April 8	400	12	4,800
September 5	200	13	2,600
December 12	100	14	1,400
Total purchases	1,000 units		$12,100
Available for sale	1,500 units		$17,100
Units sold	900 units		?
Units in ending inventory	600 units		?

*Beginning inventory of $5,000 is carried over as the ending inventory from the prior period. It is highly unlikely that each of the four methods we will illustrate would result in the same dollar amount of inventory at any point in time. It is helpful when first learning the methods, however, to assume the same amount of beginning inventory.

SPECIFIC IDENTIFICATION METHOD

It is not always necessary to make an assumption about the flow of costs. In certain situations, it may be possible to specifically identify which units are sold and which units are on hand. A serial number on an automobile allows a dealer to identify a car on hand and thus its unit cost. An appliance dealer with 15 refrigerators on hand at the end of the year can identify the unit cost of each by matching a tag number with the purchase records. To illustrate the use of the **specific identification method** for our example, assume that the merchandiser is able to identify the specific units in the inventory at the end of the year and their costs as follows:

Specific identification method An inventory costing method that relies on matching unit costs with the actual units sold.

Units on Hand

Date Purchased	Units	Cost	Total Cost
January 20	100	$11	$1,100
April 8	300	12	3,600
September 5	200	13	2,600
Ending inventory	600		$7,300

One of two techniques can be used to find cost of goods sold. We can deduct ending inventory from the cost of goods available for sale:

Cost of goods available for sale	$17,100
Less: Ending inventory	7,300
Equals: Cost of goods sold	$ 9,800

Or we can calculate cost of goods sold independently by matching the units sold with their respective unit costs. By eliminating the units in ending inventory from the original acquisition schedule, the units sold and their costs are as follows:

Units Sold

Date purchased	Units	Cost	Total Cost
Beginning Inventory	500	$10	$5,000
January 20	200	11	2,200
April 8	100	12	1,200
December 12	100	14	1,400
Cost of goods sold	900		$9,800

The practical difficulty in keeping track of individual items of inventory sold is not the only problem with the use of this method. The method also allows management to *manipulate income*. For example, assume that a company is not having a particularly good year. Management may be tempted to do whatever it can to boost net income. One way it can do this is by *selectively selling units with the lowest-possible unit cost*. By doing so, the company can keep cost of goods sold down and net income up. Because of the potential for manipulation with the specific identification method, coupled with the practical difficulty of applying it in most situations, it is not widely used.

WEIGHTED AVERAGE COST METHOD

Weighted average cost method
An inventory costing method that assigns the same unit cost to all units available for sale during the period.

The **weighted average cost method** is a relatively easy approach to costing inventory. It assigns the same unit cost to all units available for sale during the period. The weighted average cost is calculated as follows for our example:

$$\frac{\text{Cost of Goods Available for Sale}}{\text{Units Available for Sale}} = \text{Weighted Average Cost}$$

$$\frac{\$17,100}{1,500} = \$11.40$$

Ending inventory is found by multiplying the weighted average unit cost by the number of units on hand:

$$\frac{\text{Weighted Average}}{\text{Cost}} \times \frac{\text{Number of Units in}}{\text{Ending Inventory}} = \text{Ending Inventory}$$

$$\$11.40 \times 600 = \$6,840$$

Cost of goods sold can be calculated in one of two ways:

Cost of goods available for sale	$17,100
Less: Ending inventory	6,840
Equals: Cost of goods sold	$10,260

or

$$\frac{\text{Weighted Average}}{\text{Cost}} \times \frac{\text{Number of Units}}{\text{Sold}} = \text{Cost of Goods Sold}$$

$$\$11.40 \times 900 = \$10,260$$

Note that the computation of the weighted average cost is based on the cost of *all* units available for sale during the period, not just the beginning inventory or purchases. Also note that the method is called the *weighted* average cost method. As the name indicates, each of the individual unit costs is multiplied by the number of units acquired at each price. The simple arithmetic average of the unit costs for the beginning inventory and the four purchases is ($10 + $11 + $12 + $13 + $14)/5 = $12. The weighted average cost is slightly less than $12 ($11.40), however, because more units were acquired at the lower prices than at the higher prices.

FIRST-IN, FIRST-OUT METHOD (FIFO)

FIFO method
An inventory costing method that assigns the most recent costs to ending inventory.

The **FIFO method** assumes that the first units in, or purchased, are the first units out, or sold. The first units sold during the period are assumed to come from the beginning inventory. After the beginning inventory is sold, the next units sold are assumed to come from the first purchase during the period and so forth. Thus, ending inventory consists of the most recent purchases of the period. In many businesses, this cost-flow assumption is a fairly accurate reflection of the *physical* flow of products. For example, to maintain a fresh stock of products, the physical flow in a grocery store is first-in, first-out.

To calculate *ending inventory*, we start with the *most recent* inventory acquired and work *backward:*

Units on Hand

Date Purchased	Units	Cost	Total Cost
December 12	100	$14	$1,400
September 5	200	13	2,600
April 8	300	12	3,600
Ending inventory	600		$7,600

Cost of goods sold can then be found:

Cost of goods available for sale	$17,100
Less: Ending inventory	7,600
Equals: Cost of goods sold	$ 9,500

Or, because the FIFO method assumes that the first units in are the first ones sold, cost of goods sold can be calculated by starting with the *beginning inventory* and working *forward*:

Units Sold

Date Purchased	Units	Cost	Total Cost
Beginning Inventory	500	$10	$5,000
January 20	300	11	3,300
April 8	100	12	1,200
Units sold	900	Cost of goods sold	$9,500

LAST-IN, FIRST-OUT METHOD (LIFO)

The **LIFO method** assumes that the last units in, or purchased, are the first units out, or sold. The first units sold during the period are assumed to come from the latest purchase made during the period and so forth. Can you think of any businesses where the *physical* flow of products is last-in, first-out? Although this situation is not nearly so common as a first-in, first-out physical flow, a stockpiling operation, such as in a rock quarry, operates on this basis.

To calculate *ending inventory* using LIFO, we start with the *beginning inventory* and work *forward*:

Units on Hand

Date Purchased	Units	Cost	Total Cost
Beginning inventory	500	$10	$5,000
January 20	100	11	1,100
Ending inventory	600		$6,100

Cost of goods sold can then be found:

Cost of goods available for sale	$17,100
Less: Ending inventory	6,100
Equals: Cost of goods sold	$11,000

Or, because the LIFO method assumes that the last units in are the first ones sold, *cost of goods sold* can be calculated by starting with the *most recent* inventory acquired and working *backward*:

Units Sold

Date Purchased	Units	Cost	Total Cost
December 12	100	$14	$ 1,400
September 5	200	13	2,600
April 8	400	12	4,800
January 20	200	11	2,200
Units sold	900	Cost of goods sold	$11,000

LIFO method

An inventory method that assigns the most recent costs to cost of goods sold.

> **Study Tip** There may be cases, such as this illustration of LIFO, in which it is easier to determine ending inventory and then deduct it from cost of goods available for sale to find cost of goods sold. This approach is easier in this example because there are fewer layers in ending inventory than in cost of goods sold. In other cases, it may be quicker to determine cost of goods sold first and then plug in ending inventory.

Selecting an Inventory Costing Method

The mechanics of each of the inventory costing methods are straightforward. But how does a company decide on the best method to use to value its inventory? According to the accounting profession, **the primary determinant in selecting an inventory costing method should be the ability of the method to accurately reflect the net income of the period.** But how and why does a particular costing method

L07 Analyze the effects of the different costing methods on inventory, net income, income taxes, and cash flow.

accurately reflect the net income of the period? Because there is no easy answer to this question, a number of arguments have been raised by accountants to justify the use of one method over the others. We turn now to some of these arguments.

COSTING METHODS AND CASH FLOW

Comparative income statements for our example are presented in Exhibit 5-9. Note that with the use of the weighted average method, net income is between the amounts for FIFO and LIFO. Because the weighted average method normally yields results between the other two methods, we concentrate on the two extremes, LIFO and FIFO. The major advantage of using the weighted average method is its simplicity.

The original data for our example involved a situation in which prices were *rising* throughout the period: beginning inventory cost $10 per unit, and the last purchase during the year was at $14. With LIFO, the most recent costs are assigned to cost of goods sold; with FIFO, the older costs are assigned to expense. Thus, in a period of rising prices, the assignment of the *higher* prices to cost of goods sold under LIFO results in a *lower gross profit* under LIFO than under FIFO ($7,000 for LIFO and $8,500 for FIFO). Because operating expenses are not affected by the choice of inventory method, the lower gross profit under LIFO results in lower income before tax, which in turn leads to lower taxes. If we assume a 40% tax rate, income tax expense under LIFO is only $2,000, compared with $2,600 under FIFO, a savings of $600 in taxes. Another way to look at the taxes saved by using LIFO is to focus on the difference in the expense under each method:

LIFO cost of goods sold	$11,000
− FIFO cost of goods sold	9,500
Additional expense from use of LIFO	$ 1,500
× Tax rate	0.40
Tax savings from the use of LIFO	$ 600

> **Study Tip**
>
> During a period of falling prices, all of the effects shown here would be just the opposite. For example, cost of goods sold would be lower under LIFO than under FIFO.

To summarize, *during a period of rising prices*, the two methods result in the following:

Item	LIFO	Relative To	FIFO
Cost of goods sold	Higher		Lower
Gross profit	Lower		Higher
Income before taxes	Lower		Higher
Taxes	Lower		Higher

In conclusion, lower taxes with the use of LIFO result in cash savings.

EXHIBIT 5-9 **Income Statements for the Inventory Costing Methods**

	Weighted Average	FIFO	LIFO
Sales revenue—$20 each	$18,000	$18,000	$18,000
Beginning inventory	$ 5,000	$ 5,000	$ 5,000
Purchases	12,100	12,100	12,100
Cost of goods available for sale	$17,100	$17,100	$17,100
Ending inventory	**6,840**	**7,600**	**6,100**
Cost of goods sold	**$10,260**	**$ 9,500**	**$11,000**
Gross profit	**$ 7,740**	**$ 8,500**	**$ 7,000**
Operating expenses	2,000	2,000	2,000
Net income before tax	**$ 5,740**	**$ 6,500**	**$ 5,000**
Income tax expense (40%)	**2,296**	**2,600**	**2,000**
Net income	**$ 3,444**	**$ 3,900**	**$ 3,000**

NOTE: Figures that differ among the three methods are in bold.

The tax savings available from the use of LIFO during a period of rising prices is largely responsible for its popularity. Keep in mind, however, that the cash saved from a lower tax bill with LIFO is only a temporary savings, or what is normally called a *tax deferral*. At some point in the life of the business, the inventory that is carried at the older, lower-priced amounts will be sold. This will result in a tax bill higher than that under FIFO. Yet even a tax deferral is beneficial; given the opportunity, it is better to pay less tax today and more in the future because today's tax savings can be invested.

2 *minute review*

1. Which of the inventory methods will result in the least amount of income before taxes, assuming a period of rising prices?

2. What is the easiest way to calculate the tax savings from using one method versus another?

Answers

1. *LIFO*

2. *The easiest approach to calculating the tax savings is to multiply the tax rate times the difference in cost of goods sold between the two methods.*

LIFO LIQUIDATION

Recall the assumption made about which costs remain in inventory when LIFO is used. The costs of the oldest units remain in inventory, and if prices are rising, the costs of these units will be lower than the costs of more recent purchases. Now assume that the company *sells more units than it buys during the period*. When a company using LIFO experiences a liquidation, some of the units assumed to be sold will come from the older layers, with a relatively low unit cost. This situation, called a **LIFO liquidation**, presents a dilemma for the company.

A partial or complete liquidation of the older, lower-priced units will result in a low cost of goods sold figure and a correspondingly high gross profit for the period. In turn, the company faces a large tax bill because of the relatively high gross profit. In fact, a liquidation causes the tax advantages of using LIFO to reverse on the company, which is faced with paying off some of the taxes that were deferred in earlier periods. Should a company facing this situation buy inventory at the end of the year to avoid the consequences of a liquidation? This is a difficult question to answer and depends on many factors, including the company's cash position. At the least, the accountant must be aware of the potential for a large tax bill if a liquidation occurs.

Of course, a LIFO liquidation also benefits—and may even distort—reported earnings if the liquidation is large enough. For this reason and the tax problem, many companies are reluctant to liquidate their LIFO inventory. The problem often festers, and companies find themselves with inventory costed at decade-old price levels.

LIFO liquidation
The result of selling more units than are purchased during the period, which can have negative tax consequences if a company is using LIFO.

THE LIFO CONFORMITY RULE

Would it be possible for a company to have the best of both worlds? That is, could it use FIFO to report its income to stockholders, thus maximizing the amount of net income reported to this group, and use LIFO to report to the IRS, minimizing its taxable income and the amount paid to the government? Unfortunately, the IRS says that if a company chooses LIFO for reporting cost of goods sold on its tax return, then it must also use LIFO on its books, that is, in preparing its income statement. This is called the **LIFO conformity rule**. Note that the rule applies only to the use of LIFO on the tax return. A company is free to use different methods in preparing its tax return and its income statement as long as the method used for the tax return is *not* LIFO.

LIFO conformity rule
The IRS requirement that if LIFO is used on the tax return, it must also be used in reporting income to stockholders.

THE LIFO RESERVE: ESTIMATING LIFO'S EFFECT ON INCOME AND ON TAXES PAID

If a company decides to use LIFO, an investor can still determine how much more income the company would have reported had it used FIFO. In addition, he or she can approximate the tax savings to the company from the use of LIFO. Consider Note 3 from the 2004 annual report for **Winnebago Industries**, the RV maker:

Note 3: Inventories

Inventories consist of the following: (dollars in thousands)	August 28, 2004	August 30, 2003
Finished goods	$ 58,913	$ 36,140
Work-in-process	47,337	47,098
Raw materials	51,675	56,382
	$157,925	$139,620
LIFO reserve	(27,192)	(25,338)
	$130,733	$114,282

The above value of inventories, before reduction for the LIFO reserve, approximates replacement cost at the respective dates.

The following steps explain the logic for using the information in the inventory note to estimate LIFO's effect on income and on taxes:

1. The excess of the value of a company's inventory stated at FIFO over the value stated at LIFO is called the **LIFO reserve.** The cumulative excess of the value of Winnebago Industries' inventory on a FIFO basis over the value on a LIFO basis is $27,192,000 at the end of 2004.

2. Because Winnebago Industries reports inventory at a lower value on its balance sheet using LIFO, it will report a higher cost of goods sold amount on the income statement. Thus, the LIFO reserve not only represents the excess of the inventory balance on a FIFO basis over that on a LIFO basis but also represents the cumulative amount by which cost of goods sold on a LIFO basis exceeds cost of goods sold on a FIFO basis.

3. The increase in Winnebago Industries' LIFO reserve in 2004 was $1,854,000 ($27,192,000 − $25,338,000). This means that the increase in cost of goods sold for 2004 from using LIFO instead of FIFO was also this amount. Thus, income before tax for 2004 was $1,854,000 lower because the company used LIFO.

4. If we assume a corporate tax rate of 35%, the tax savings from using LIFO amounted to $1,854,000 × 0.35, or $648,900.

> **LIFO reserve**
> The excess of the value of a company's inventory stated at FIFO over the value stated at LIFO.

COSTING METHODS AND INVENTORY PROFITS

FIFO, LIFO, and weighted average are all cost-based methods to value inventory. They vary in terms of which costs are assigned to inventory and which to cost of goods sold, but all three assign *historical costs* to inventory. In our previous example, the unit cost for inventory purchases gradually increased during the year from $10 for the beginning inventory to a high of $14 on the date of the last purchase.

An alternative to assigning any of the historical costs incurred during the year to ending inventory and cost of goods sold would be to use **replacement cost** to value each of these. Assume that the cost to replace a unit of inventory at the end of the year is $15. Use of a replacement cost system results in the following:

> **Replacement cost**
> The current cost of a unit of inventory.

Ending inventory = 600 units × $15 per unit = $ 9,000

Cost of goods sold = 900 units × $15 per unit = $13,500

A replacement cost approach is not acceptable under the profession's current standards, but many believe that it provides more relevant information to users. Inventory must be replaced if a company is to remain in business. Many accountants argue that the use of historical cost in valuing inventory leads to what is called **inventory profit**, particularly if FIFO is used in a period of rising prices. For example, cost of goods sold in our illustration was only $9,500 on a FIFO basis, compared with $13,500 if the replacement cost of $15 per unit is used. The $4,000 difference between the two cost of goods sold figures is a profit from holding the inventory during a period of rising prices and is called *inventory profit*. To look at this another way, assume that the units are sold for $20 each. The following analysis reconciles the difference between gross profit on a FIFO basis and on a replacement cost basis:

Sales revenue—900 units × $20 =		$18,000
Cost of goods sold—FIFO basis		9,500
Gross profit—FIFO basis		$ 8,500
Cost of goods sold—replacement cost basis	$13,500	
Cost of goods sold—FIFO basis	9,500	
Profit from holding inventory during a period of inflation		4,000
Gross profit on a replacement cost basis		$ 4,500

Inventory profit
The portion of the gross profit that results from holding inventory during a period of rising prices.

Those who argue in favor of a replacement cost approach would report only $4,500 of gross profit. They believe that the additional $4,000 of profit reported on a FIFO basis is simply due to holding the inventory during a period of rising prices. According to this viewpoint, if the 900 units sold during the period are to be replaced, a necessity if the company is to continue operating, the use of replacement cost in calculating cost of goods sold results in a better measure of gross profit than if it is calculated using FIFO.

Given that our current standards require the use of historical costs rather than replacement costs, does any one of the costing methods result in a better approximation of replacement cost of goods sold than the others? Because LIFO assigns the cost of the most recent purchases to cost of goods sold, it most nearly approximates the results with a replacement cost system. The other side of the argument, however, is that whereas LIFO results in the best approximation of *replacement cost of goods sold* on the *income statement*, FIFO most nearly approximates replacement cost of the *inventory* on the *balance sheet*. A comparison of the amounts from our example verifies this:

	Ending Inventory	Cost of Goods Sold
Weighted average	$6,840	$10,260
FIFO	7,600	9,500
LIFO	6,100	11,000
Replacement cost	9,000	13,500

CHANGING INVENTORY METHODS

The purpose of each of the inventory costing methods is to *match costs with revenues*. If a company believes that a different method will result in a better matching than that being provided by the method currently being used, it should change methods. A company must be able to justify a change in methods, however. Taking advantage of the tax breaks offered by LIFO is *not* a valid justification for a change in methods.

INVENTORY VALUATION IN OTHER COUNTRIES

The acceptable methods of valuing inventory differ considerably around the world. Although FIFO is the most popular method in the United States, LIFO continues to be widely used, as is the average cost method. Many countries prohibit the use of LIFO for either tax or financial reporting purposes. In Chapter 1 we mentioned the attempts by the International Accounting Standards Board (IASB) to develop worldwide accounting standards. This group does not allow the use of LIFO by companies that follow its standards.

LO8 Analyze the effects of an inventory error on various financial statement items.

INVENTORY ERRORS

Earlier in the chapter we considered the inherent tie between the valuation of assets, such as inventory, and the measurement of income, such as cost of goods sold. The importance of inventory valuation to the measurement of income can be illustrated by considering inventory errors. Many different types of inventory errors exist. Some errors are mathematical; for example, a bookkeeper may incorrectly add a column total. Other errors relate specifically to the physical count of inventory at year-end. For example, the count might inadvertently omit one section of a warehouse. Other errors arise from cutoff problems at year-end.

For example, assume that merchandise in transit at the end of the year is shipped FOB (free on board) shipping point. Under these shipment terms, the inventory belongs to the buyer at the time it is shipped. Because the shipment has not arrived at the end of the year, however, it cannot be included in the physical count. Unless some type of control is in place, the amount in transit may be erroneously omitted from the valuation of inventory at year-end.

To demonstrate the effect of an inventory error on the income statement, consider the following example. Through a scheduling error, two different inventory teams were assigned to count the inventory in the same warehouse on December 31, 2007. The correct amount of ending inventory is $250,000, but because two different teams counted the same inventory in one warehouse, the amount recorded is $300,000. The effect of this error on net income is analyzed in the left half of Exhibit 5-10.

The *overstatement* of *ending inventory* in 2007 leads to an *understatement* of the 2007 cost of goods sold *expense*. Because cost of goods sold is understated, *gross profit* for the year is *overstated*. Operating expenses are unaffected by an inventory error. Thus, *net income* is *overstated* by the same amount of overstatement of gross profit.[2] The most important conclusion from the exhibit is that an overstatement of ending inventory leads to a corresponding overstatement of net income.

Unfortunately, the effect of a misstatement of the year-end inventory is not limited to the net income for that year. As indicated in the right-hand portion of Exhibit 5-10, the error also affects the income statement for the following year. This happens simply because *the ending inventory of one period is the beginning inventory of the following period.* The *overstatement* of the 2008 *beginning inventory* leads

EXHIBIT 5-10 **Effects of Inventory Error on the Income Statement**

	2007			2008		
	Reported	**Corrected**	**Effect of Error**	**Reported**	**Corrected**	**Effect of Error**
Sales	$1,000*	$1,000		$1,500	$1,500	
Cost of goods sold:						
Beginning inventory	$ 200	$ 200		**$ 300**	**$ 250**	$50 OS
Add: Purchases	700	700		1,100	1,100	
Cost of goods available for sale	$ 900	$ 900		**$1,400**	**$1,350**	50 OS
Less: Ending inventory	**300**	**250**	$50 OS†	350	350	
Cost of goods sold	**$ 600**	**$ 650**	50 US‡	**$1,050**	**$1,000**	50 OS
Gross profit	**$ 400**	**$ 350**	50 OS	**$ 450**	**$ 500**	50 US
Operating expenses	100	100		120	120	
Net income	**$ 300**	**$ 250**	50 OS	**$ 330**	**$ 380**	50 US

NOTE: *Figures that differ as a result of the error are in bold.*
*All amounts are in thousands of dollars.

†OS = *Overstatement*
‡US = *Understatement*

---

2 An overstatement of gross profit also results in an overstatement of income tax expense. Thus, because tax expense is overstated, the overstatement of net income is not so large as the overstatement of gross profit. For now we will ignore the effect of taxes, however.

to an *overstatement* of *cost of goods available for sale.* Because cost of goods available for sale is overstated, *cost of goods sold* is also *overstated.* The *overstatement* of cost of goods sold *expense* results in an *understatement* of *gross profit* and thus an *understatement* of *net income.*

Exhibit 5-10 illustrates the nature of a *counterbalancing error.* The effect of the overstatement of net income in the first year, 2007, is offset or counterbalanced by the understatement of net income by the same dollar amount in the following year. If the net incomes of two successive years are misstated in the opposite direction by the same amount, what is the effect on retained earnings? Assume that retained earnings at the beginning of 2007 is correctly stated at $300,000. The counter balancing nature of the error is seen by analyzing retained earnings. For 2007 the analysis would indicate the following (OS = overstated and US = understated):

	2007 Reported	2007 Corrected	Effect of Error
Beginning retained earnings	$300,000	$300,000	Correct
Add: Net income	300,000	250,000	$50,000 OS
Ending retained earnings	$600,000	$550,000	$50,000 OS

An analysis for 2008 would show the following:

	2008 Reported	2008 Corrected	Effect of Error
Beginning retained earnings	$600,000	$550,000	$50,000 OS
Add: Net income	330,000	380,000	$50,000 US
Ending retained earnings	$930,000	$930,000	Correct

Thus, even though retained earnings is overstated at the end of the first year, it is correctly stated at the end of the second year. This is the nature of a counterbalancing error.

The effect of the error on the balance sheet is shown in Exhibit 5-11. The only accounts affected by the error are Inventory and Retained Earnings. The overstatement of the 2007 ending inventory results in an overstatement of total assets at the end of the first year. Similarly, as our earlier analysis indicates, the overstatement of 2007 net income leads to an overstatement of retained earnings by the same amount. Because the error is counterbalancing, the 2008 year-end balance sheet is correct; that is, ending inventory is not affected by the error, and thus the amount for total assets at the end of 2008 is also correct. The effect of the error

EXHIBIT 5-11 Effects of Inventory Error on the Balance Sheet

	2007 Reported	2007 Corrected	2008 Reported	2008 Corrected
Inventory	$ 300*	$ 250	$ 350	$ 350
All other assets	1,700	1,700	2,080	2,080
Total assets	$2,000	$1,950	$2,430	$2,430
Total liabilities	$ 400	$ 400	$ 500	$ 500
Capital stock	1,000	1,000	1,000	1,000
Retained earnings	600	550	930	930
Total liabilities and stockholders' equity	$2,000	$1,950	$2,430	$2,430

NOTE: Figures that differ as a result of the error are in bold.
*All amounts are in thousands of dollars.

EXHIBIT 5-12	Summary of the Effects of Inventory Errors

	Effect of Overstatement of Ending Inventory on	
	Current Year	Following Year
Cost of goods sold	Understated	Overstated
Gross profit	Overstated	Understated
Net income	Overstated	Understated
Retained earnings, end of year	Overstated	Correctly stated
Total assets, end of year	Overstated	Correctly stated

	Effect of Understatement of Ending Inventory on	
	Current Year	Following Year
Cost of goods sold	Overstated	Understated
Gross profit	Understated	Overstated
Net income	Understated	Overstated
Retained earnings, end of year	Understated	Correctly stated
Total assets, end of year	Understated	Correctly stated

Study Tip

Note the logic behind the notion that an overstatement of ending inventory leads to overstatements of both total assets and retained earnings at the end of the year. This is logical because a balance sheet must balance; that is, the left side must equal the right side. If the left side (inventory) is overstated, then the right side (retained earnings) will also be overstated.

on retained earnings is limited to the first year because of the counterbalancing nature of the error.

The effects of inventory errors on various financial statement items are summarized in Exhibit 5-12. Our analysis focused on the effects of an overstatement of inventory. The effects of an understatement are just the opposite and are summarized in the bottom portion of the exhibit.

Not all errors are counterbalancing. For example, if a section of a warehouse *continues* to be omitted from the physical count every year, both the beginning and the ending inventory will be incorrect each year and the error will not counter balance.

Part of the auditor's job is to perform the necessary tests to obtain reasonable assurance that inventory has not been overstated or understated. If there is an error and inventory is wrong, however, the balance sheet and the income statement will both be distorted. For example, if ending inventory is overstated, inflating total assets, then cost of goods sold will be understated, boosting profits. Thus, such an error overstates the financial health of the organization in two ways. A lender or an investor must make a decision based on the current year's statement and cannot wait until the next accounting cycle, when this error is reversed. This is one reason that investors and creditors insist on audited financial statements.

2 minute review

Skipper Corp. omits one section of its warehouse in the year-end inventory count.

1. Will the omission understate or overstate cost of goods sold on the income statement in the year the error is made?

2. Will the omission understate or overstate retained earnings on the balance sheet at the end of the year the error is made?

3. Will the omission affect retained earnings on the balance sheet at the end of the following year after the error is made? Explain your answer.

A n s w e r s

1. *Cost of goods sold will be overstated because the ending inventory is understated.*

2. *Retained earnings at the end of the year in which the error is made will be understated because cost of goods sold is overstated, and thus net income, which goes into retained earnings, is understated.*

3. *Retained earnings at the end of the following year will not be affected because of the counterbalancing nature of this error. Net income in the year of the error is understated, as described above. However, net income of the following year is overstated because cost of goods sold is understated as the result of an understatement of that year's beginning inventory.*

Valuing Inventory at Lower of Cost or Market

One of the components sold by an electronics firm has become economically obsolete. A particular style of suit sold by a retailer is outdated and can no longer be sold at regular price. In each of these instances, it is likely that the retailer will have to sell the merchandise for less than the normal selling price. In these situations, a departure from the cost basis of accounting may be necessary because the *market value* of the inventory may be less than its *cost* to the company. The departure is called the **lower-of-cost-or-market (LCM) rule**.

At the end of each accounting period, the original cost, as determined using one of the costing methods such as FIFO, is compared with the market price of the inventory. If market is less than cost, the inventory is written down to the lower amount.

For example, if cost is $100,000 and market value is $85,000, the accountant makes an adjustment, which has the following effect:

LO9 Apply the lower-of-cost-or-market rule to the valuation of inventory.

Lower-of-cost-or-market (LCM) rule
A conservative inventory valuation approach that is an attempt to anticipate declines in the value of inventory before its actual sale.

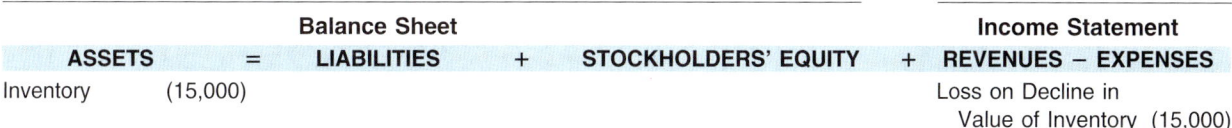

Balance Sheet						Income Statement
ASSETS	**=**	**LIABILITIES**	**+**	**STOCKHOLDERS' EQUITY**	**+**	**REVENUES − EXPENSES**
Inventory	(15,000)					Loss on Decline in Value of Inventory (15,000)

Note that the adjustment reduces both assets, in the form of inventory, and net income. The reduction in net income is the result of reporting the Loss on Decline in Value of Inventory on the income statement as an item of Other Expense.

WHY REPLACEMENT COST IS USED AS A MEASURE OF MARKET

A better name for the lower-of-cost-or-market rule would be the lower-of-cost-or-replacement-cost rule because accountants define *market* as *replacement cost*.[3] To understand why replacement cost is used as a basis to compare with original cost, consider the following example. Assume that Finish Line pays $75 for a pair of running shoes and normally sells them for $100. Thus, the normal markup on selling price is $25/$100, or 25%, as indicated in the column Before Price Change in Exhibit 5-13. Now assume that this style of running shoes becomes less popular. The retailer checks with Nike and finds that because of the style change, the cost to the retailer to replace the pair of running shoes is now only $60. The retailer realizes that if the shoes are to be sold at all, they will have to be offered at a reduced price. The selling price is dropped from $100 to $80. If the retailer now buys a pair of shoes for $60 and sells them for $80, the gross profit will be $20 and

---

3 Technically, the use of replacement cost as a measure of market value is subject to two constraints. First, market cannot be more than the net realizable value of the inventory. Second, inventory should not be recorded at less than net realizable value less a normal profit margin. The rationale for these two constraints is covered in intermediate accounting texts. For our purposes, we assume that replacement cost falls between the two constraints.

EXHIBIT 5-13 Gross Profit Percentage Before and After Price Change

	Before Price Change	After Price Change
Selling price	$100	$80
Cost	75	60
Gross profit	$ 25	$20
Gross profit percentage	25%	25%

the gross profit percentage will be maintained at 25%, as indicated in the right-hand column of Exhibit 5-13.

To compare the results with and without the use of the LCM rule, assume that the facts are the same as before and that the retailer has 10 pairs of those shoes in inventory on December 31, 2007. In addition, assume that all 10 pair are sold at a clearance sale in January 2008 at the reduced price of $80 each. If the lower-of-cost-or-market rule is not used, the results for the two years will be as follows:

LCM Rule Not Used	2007	2008	Total
Sales revenue ($80 per unit)	$ 0	$800	$800
Cost of goods sold			
(original cost of $75 per unit)	0	(750)	(750)
Gross profit	$ 0	$ 50	$ 50

If the LCM rule is not applied, the gross profit is distorted. Instead of the normal 25%, a gross profit percentage of $50/$800, or 6.25%, is reported in 2008 when the 10 pairs of shoes are sold. If the LCM rule is applied, however, the results for the two years are as follows:

LCM Rule Used	2007	2008	Total
Sales revenue ($80 per unit)	$ 0	$800	$800
Cost of goods sold			
(replacement cost of $60 per unit)	0	(600)	(600)
Loss on decline in value of inventory:			
10 units × ($75 − $60)	(150)	0	(150)
Gross profit	$(150)	$200	$ 50

The use of the LCM rule serves two important functions: (1) to report the loss in value of the inventory, $15 per pair of running shoes or $150 in total, in the year the loss occurs and (2) to report in the year the shoes are actually sold the normal gross profit of $200/$800, or 25%, which is not affected by a change in the selling price.

CONSERVATISM IS THE BASIS FOR THE LOWER-OF-COST-OR-MARKET RULE

The departure from the cost basis is normally justified on the basis of *conservatism*. According to the accounting profession, conservatism is "a prudent reaction to uncertainties to try to insure that uncertainties and risks inherent in business situations are adequately considered."[4] In our example, the future selling price of a pair of shoes is uncertain because of the style changes. The use of the LCM rule serves two purposes. First, the inventory of shoes is written down from $75 to $60 each. Second, the decline in value of the inventory is recognized at the time it is first observed rather than waiting until the shoes are sold. An investor in a company with deteriorating inventory has good reason to be alarmed. Merchandisers who

---

4 *Statement of Financial Accounting Concepts No. 2*, "Qualitative Characteristics of Accounting Information" (Stamford, Conn.: Financial Accounting Standards Board, May 1980), par. 95.

do not make the proper adjustments to their product lines go out of business as they compete with the lower prices of warehouse clubs and the lower overhead of e-business and home shopping networks.

You should realize that the write-down of the shoes violates the historical cost principle, which says that assets should be carried on the balance sheet at their original cost. But the LCM rule is considered a valid exception to the principle because it is a prudent reaction to the uncertainty involved and, thus, an application of conservatism in accounting.

APPLICATION OF THE LCM RULE

We have yet to consider how the LCM rule is applied to the entire inventory of a company. Three different interpretations of the rule are possible:

1. **The lower of total cost or total market value for the entire inventory could be reported.**

2. **The lower of cost or market value for each individual product or item could be reported.**

3. **The lower of cost or market value for groups of items could be reported. A company is free to choose any one of these approaches in applying the lower-of-cost-or-market rule. Three different answers are possible, depending on the approach selected.**

The item-by-item (No. 2 above) approach is the most popular of the three approaches, for two reasons. First, it produces the most conservative result. The reason is that with either a group-by-group or a total approach, increases in the values of some items of inventory will offset declines in the values of other items. The item-by-item approach, however, ignores increases in value and recognizes all declines in value. Second, the item-by-item approach is the method required for tax purposes, although unlike LIFO, it is not required for book purposes merely because it is used for tax computations.

Consistency is important in deciding which of these approaches to use in applying the LCM rule. As is the case with the selection of one of the inventory costing methods discussed earlier in the chapter, the approach chosen to apply the rule should be used consistently from one period to the next.

5-2 Real World Practice

Reading Finish Line's Notes

A note to Finish Line's financial statements states, "Merchandise inventories are valued at the lower of cost or market using a weighted-average cost method, which approximates the first-in, first-out method." Why do you think the application of the lower-of-cost-or-market rule would be important to a business like Finish Line? In applying the rule, how does the company define "cost"?

Methods for Estimating Inventory Value

Situations arise in which it may not be practicable or even possible to measure inventory at cost. At times it may be necessary to *estimate* the amount of inventory. Two similar methods are used for very different purposes to estimate the amount of inventory. They are the gross profit method and the retail inventory method.

LO10 Explain why and how the cost of inventory is estimated in certain situations.

GROSS PROFIT METHOD

A company that uses a periodic inventory system may experience a problem if inventory is stolen or destroyed by fire, flooding, or some other type of damage. Without a perpetual inventory record, what is the cost of the inventory stolen or destroyed? The **gross profit method** is a useful technique to estimate the cost of inventory lost in these situations. The method relies *entirely* on the ability to reliably estimate the *ratio of gross profit to sales*.

Exhibit 5-14 illustrates how the normal income statement model that we use to find cost of goods sold can be rearranged to estimate inventory. The model on the left shows the components of cost of goods sold as they appear on the income statement. Assuming a periodic system, the inventory on hand at the end of the period is counted and is subtracted from cost of goods available for sale to determine cost of goods sold. The model is rearranged on the right as a basis for estimating inventory under the gross profit method. The only difference in the two models is in the reversal of the last two components: ending inventory and cost of goods sold.

Gross profit method
A technique used to establish an estimate of the cost of inventory stolen, destroyed, or otherwise damaged or of the amount of inventory on hand at an interim date.

EXHIBIT 5-14	The Gross Profit Method for Estimating Inventory

Income Statement Model	Gross Profit Method Model
Beginning Inventory	Beginning Inventory
+ Purchases	+ Purchases
= Cost of Goods Available for Sale	= Cost of Goods Available for Sale
– Ending Inventory (per count)	– Estimated Cost of Goods Sold
= Cost of Goods Sold	= Estimated Inventory

Rather than attempting to estimate *ending* inventory, we are trying to estimate the amount of inventory that should be on hand at a specific date, such as the date of a fire or flood. The estimate of cost of goods sold is found by estimating gross profit and deducting this estimate from sales revenue.

To understand this method, assume that on March 12, 2007, a portion of Hardluck Company's inventory is destroyed in a fire. The company determines, by a physical count, that the cost of the merchandise not destroyed is $200. Hardluck needs to estimate the cost of the inventory lost for purposes of insurance reimbursement. If the insurance company pays Hardluck an amount equivalent to the cost of the inventory destroyed, no loss will be recognized. If the cost of the inventory destroyed exceeds the amount reimbursed by the insurance company, a loss will be recorded for the excess amount.

Assume that the insurance company agrees to pay Hardluck $250 as full settlement for the inventory lost in the fire. From its records, Hardluck is able to determine the following amounts for the period from January 1 to the date of the fire, March 12:

Net sales from January 1 to March 12	$6,000
Beginning inventory—January 1	1,200
Purchases from January 1 to March 12	3,500

Assume that based on recent years' experience, Hardluck estimates its gross profit ratio as 30% of net sales. The steps it will take to estimate the lost inventory follow:

1. Determine gross profit:

Net Sales	×	Gross Profit Ratio	=	Gross Profit
$6,000	×	30%	=	$1,800

2. Determine cost of goods sold:

Net Sales	–	Gross Profit	=	Cost of Goods Sold
$6,000	–	$1,800	=	$4,200

3. Determine cost of goods available for sale at time of fire:

Beginning Inventory	+	Purchases	=	Cost of Goods Available for Sale
$1,200	+	$3,500	=	$4,700

4. Determine inventory at time of the fire:

Cost of Goods Available for Sale	–	Cost of Goods Sold	=	Inventory
$4,700	–	$4,200	=	$500

5. Determine the amount of inventory destroyed:

Inventory at Time of Fire	–	Inventory Not Destroyed	=	Inventory Destroyed
$500	–	$200	=	$300

Hardluck would make an adjustment to recognize a loss for the excess of the cost of the lost inventory over the amount of reimbursement from the insurance company. The effect of the adjustment is as follows:

Balance Sheet							Income Statement	
ASSETS		**=**	**LIABILITIES**	**+**	**STOCKHOLDERS' EQUITY**	**+**	**REVENUES − EXPENSES**	
Cash	250						Loss on Insurance	
Inventory	(300)						Settlement	(50)

Another situation in which the gross profit method is used is for *interim financial statements*. Most companies prepare financial statements at least once every three months. In fact, the **Securities and Exchange Commission** requires a quarterly report from corporations whose stock is publicly traded. Companies using the periodic inventory system, however, find it cost-prohibitive to count the inventory every three months. The gross profit method is used to estimate the cost of the inventory at these interim dates. A company is allowed to use the method only in interim reports. Inventory reported in the annual report must be based on actual, not estimated, cost.

RETAIL INVENTORY METHOD

The counting of inventory in most retail businesses is an enormous undertaking. Imagine the time involved to count all of the various items stocked in a hardware store. Because of the time and cost involved in counting inventory, most retail businesses take a physical inventory only once a year. The **retail inventory method** is used to estimate inventory for interim statements, typically prepared monthly.

The retail inventory method has another important use. Consider the year-end inventory count in a large supermarket. One employee counts the number of tubes of toothpaste on the shelf and relays the relevant information either to another employee or to a tape-recording device: "16 tubes of 8-ounce ABC brand toothpaste at $1.69." The key is that the price recorded is the *selling price* or *retail price* of the product, not its cost. It is much quicker to count the inventory at retail than it would be to trace the cost of each item to purchase invoices. The retail method can then be used to convert the inventory from retail to cost. The methodology used with the retail inventory method, whether for interim statements or at year-end, is similar to the approach used with the gross profit method and is covered in detail in intermediate accounting textbooks.

Retail inventory method
A technique used by retailers to convert the retail value of inventory to a cost basis.

Analyzing the Management of Inventory

Inventory is the lifeblood of a company that sells a product. Finish Line must strike a balance between maintaining a sufficient variety of shoes to meet customers' needs and incurring the high cost of carrying inventory. The cost of storage and the lost income from the money tied up in inventory make it very expensive to keep on hand. Thus, the more quickly a company can sell—that is, turn over—its inventory the better. The **inventory turnover ratio** is calculated as follows:

LO11 Analyze the management of inventory.

Inventory turnover ratio
A measure of the number of times inventory is sold during the period.

$$\text{Inventory Turnover Ratio} = \frac{\text{Cost of Goods Sold}}{\text{Average Inventory}}$$

It is a measure of the number of times inventory is sold during the period.

Use the Ratio Decision Process on pages 234–235 to compute and analyze the inventory turnover ratio for Finish Line.

USING THE RATIO DECISION MODEL: ANALYZING THE MANAGEMENT OF INVENTORY

Use the following Ratio Decision Process to analyze the inventory of Finish Line or any other public company.

1. Formulate the Question

Managers, investors, and creditors are all interested in how well a company manages its inventory. The quicker inventory can be sold, the sooner the money will be available to invest in more inventory or to use for other purposes. Those interested must be able to answer the following question:

How many times a year does a company turn over its inventory?

2. Gather the Information from the Financial Statements

Cost of goods sold is reported on the income statement, representing a flow for a period of time. On the other hand, inventory is an asset, representing a balance at a point in time. Thus, a comparison of the two requires the cost of goods sold for the year and an average of the balance in inventory:

- Cost of goods sold: From the income statement for the year
- Average inventory: From the balance sheets at the end of the two most recent years

3. Calculate the Ratio

Average merchandise inventories =
($241,242,000 + $268,590,000)/2 =
$254,916,000

$$\text{Inventory Turnover Ratio} = \frac{\text{Cost of Goods Sold}}{\text{Average Inventory}}$$

The Finish Line, Inc.
Partial Consolidated Statements of Income
(in thousands)

	Year Ended		
	February 25, 2006	February 26, 2005	February 28, 2004
Net sales	$1,306,045	$1,166,767	$985,891
Cost of sales (including occupancy costs)	894,724	798,033	681,561

The Finish Line, Inc.
Partial Consolidated Balance Sheets
(in thousands)

	February 25, 2006	February 26, 2005
Assets		
Current Assets:		
Merchandise inventories, net	$268,590	$241,242

$$\text{Inventory Turnover} = \frac{\$894,724,000}{\$254,916,000} = 3.5 \text{ times}$$

4. Compare the Ratio with Others

Management compares the current year's turnover rate with prior years to see if the company is experiencing slower or faster turns of its inventory. It is also important to compare the rate with other companies in the same industry:

Finish Line		Foot Locker	
Year Ended February 25, 2006	Year Ended February 26, 2005	Year Ended January 28, 2006	Year Ended January 29, 2005
3.5 times	3.7 times	3.3 times	3.6 times

5. Interpret the Results

This ratio tells us that in fiscal year 2006, Finish Line turned over its inventory an average of 3.5 times. In fact, both companies turned over their inventory in excess of three times in both years. An alternative way to look at a company's efficiency in managing its inventory is to calculate the number of days, on average, that inventory is on hand before it is sold. This measure is called the **number of days' sales in inventory** and is calculated as follows for Finish Line in 2006 (we will assume 360 days in a year):

$$\text{Number of Days' Sales in Inventory} = \frac{\text{Number of Days in the Period}}{\text{Inventory Turnover Ratio}}$$

$$= \frac{360}{3.5}$$

$$= 103 \text{ days}$$

This measure tells us that it took Finish Line 103 days, or just over three months, on the average to sell its inventory.

> **Number of days' sales in inventory**
> A measure of how long it takes to sell inventory.

How Inventories Affect the Cash Flows Statement

The effects on the income statement and the statement of cash flows from inventory-related transactions differ significantly. We have focused our attention in this chapter on how the purchase and the sale of inventory are reported on the income statement. We found that the cost of the inventory sold during the period is deducted on the income statement as cost of goods sold.

The appropriate reporting on a statement of cash flows for inventory transactions depends on whether the direct or indirect method is used. If the direct method is used to prepare the Operating Activities category of the statement, the amount of cash paid to suppliers of inventory is shown as a deduction in this section of the statement.

If the more popular indirect method is used, it is necessary to make adjustments to net income for the changes in two accounts: Inventories and Accounts Payable. These adjustments are summarized in Exhibit 5-15. An increase in inventory is deducted because it indicates that the company is building up its stock of inventory and thus expending cash. A decrease in inventory is added to net income. An increase in accounts payable is added because it indicates that during the period, the company has increased the amount it owes suppliers and has therefore conserved its cash. A decrease in accounts payable is deducted because the company actually reduced the amount owed suppliers during the period.

LO12 Explain the effects that inventory transactions have on the statement of cash flows.

EXHIBIT 5-15 Inventories and the Statement of Cash Flows

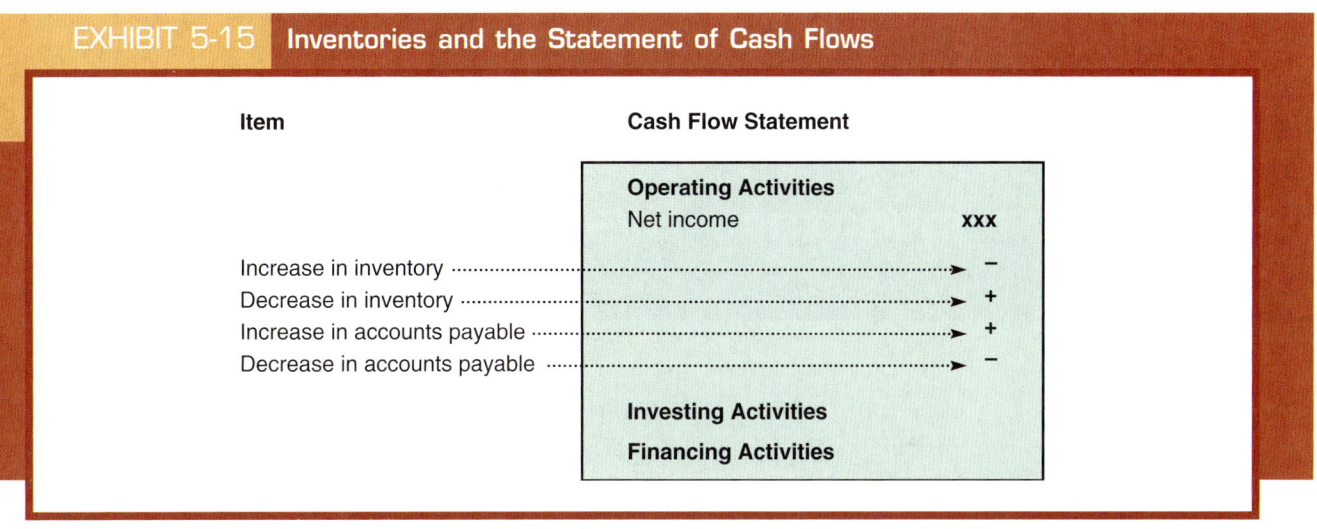

Item	Cash Flow Statement	
	Operating Activities	
	Net income	**xxx**
Increase in inventory		−
Decrease in inventory		+
Increase in accounts payable		+
Decrease in accounts payable		−
	Investing Activities	
	Financing Activities	

The Operating Activities category of the statement of cash flows for Finish Line is presented in Exhibit 5-16. The increase in inventory is deducted because the increase in this asset uses the company's cash. A decrease in accounts payable also uses Finish Line's cash. Thus, the decrease in this item in 2006 is deducted from net income.

EXHIBIT 5-16 Partial Consolidated Statement of Cash Flows for Finish Line

The Finish Line, Inc.
Consolidated Statements of Cash Flows
(in thousands)

	Year Ended		
	February 25, 2006	February 26, 2005	February 28, 2004
Operating activities			
Net income	$60,533	$61,263	$47,347
Adjustments to reconcile net income to net cash provided by operating activities:			
Asset impairment charge	2,523	—	—
Depreciation and amortization	34,633	27,169	23,732
Deferred income taxes	(5,024)	5,123	2,413
Loss on disposal of property and equipment	262	508	200
Tax benefit from exercise of stock options	2,646	3,341	6,258
Changes in operating assets and liabilities, net of effects of acquisition			
Accounts receivable	2,231	(7,661)	(407)
Merchandise inventories	(27,348)	(44,374)	(33,819)
Other current assets	(1,213)	(304)	5,867
Accounts payable	(8,372)	34,534	1,562
Employee compensation	(857)	1,019	3,373
Other liabilities and accrued expenses	7,686	2,752	6,699
Deferred credits from landlords	6,327	3,777	4,011
Net cash provided by operating activities	74,027	87,147	67,236

Increase here uses cash and thus is deducted

Decrease here uses cash and thus is deducted

See accompanying notes in the book appendix.

Accounting Tools: Inventory Costing Methods with the Use of a Perpetual Inventory System

APPENDIX

The illustrations of the inventory costing methods in the chapter assumed the use of a periodic inventory system. In this appendix, we will see how the methods are applied when a company maintains a perpetual inventory system. It is important to understand the difference between inventory *costing systems* and inventory *methods*. The two inventory systems differ in terms of how often the inventory account is updated: periodically or perpetually. However, when a company sells identical units of product and the cost to purchase each unit is subject to change, it also must choose an inventory costing method, such as FIFO, LIFO, or weighted average.

Earlier in the chapter, we illustrated the various costing methods with a periodic system. We now use the same data to illustrate how the methods differ when a perpetual system is used. Keep in mind that if a company uses specific identification, the results will be the same regardless of whether it uses the periodic or the perpetual system. To compare the periodic and perpetual systems for the other methods, we must add one important piece of information: the date of each of the sales. The original data as well as number of units sold on the various dates are summarized below:

Date	Purchases	Sales	Balance
Beginning inventory			500 units @ $10
January 20	300 units @ $11		800 units
February 18		450 units	350 units
April 8	400 units @ $12		750 units
June 19		300 units	450 units
September 5	200 units @ $13		650 units
October 20		150 units	500 units
December 12	100 units @ $14		600 units

FIFO Costing with a Perpetual System

Exhibit 5-17 illustrates the FIFO method on a perpetual basis. The basic premise of FIFO applies whether a periodic or a perpetual system is used: the first units purchased are assumed to be the first units sold. With a perpetual system, however,

EXHIBIT 5-17 Perpetual System: FIFO Cost-Flow Assumption

Date	Purchases Units	Unit Cost	Total Cost	Sales Units	Unit Cost	Total Cost	Balance Units	Unit Cost	Balance
1/1							500	$10	$5,000
1/20	300	$11	$3,300				500	10	
							300	11	8,300
2/18				450	$10	$4,500	50	10	
							300	11	3,800
4/8	400	12	4,800				50	10	
							300	11	
							400	12	8,600
6/19				50	10	500	50	11	
				250	11	2,750	400	12	5,350
9/5	200	13	2,600				50	11	
							400	12	
							200	13	7,950
10/20				50	11	550	300	12	
				100	12	1,200	200	13	6,200
12/12	100	14	1,400				300	12	
							200	13	
							100	14	7,600

LO13 Explain the differences in the accounting for periodic and perpetual inventory systems and apply the inventory costing methods using a perpetual system.

this concept is applied *at the time of each sale.* For example, note in the exhibit which 450 units are assumed to be sold on February 18. The 450 units sold are taken from the beginning inventory of 500 units with a unit cost of $10. Thus, the inventory or balance after this sale as shown in the last three columns is 50 units at $10 and 300 units at $11, for a total of $3,800. The purchase on April 8 of 400 units at $12 is added to the running balance. On a FIFO basis, the sale of 300 units on June 19 comes from the remainder of the beginning inventory of 50 units and another 250 units from the first purchase at $11 on January 20. The balance after this sale is 50 units at $11 and 400 units at $12. You should follow through the last three transactions in the exhibit to make sure that you understand the application of FIFO on a perpetual basis. An important point to note about the ending inventory of $7,600 is that it is the same amount that we calculated for FIFO periodic earlier in the chapter:

FIFO periodic (Exhibit 5-9)	$7,600
FIFO perpetual (Exhibit 5-17)	$7,600

Whether the method is applied each time a sale is made or only at the end of the period, the earliest units in are the first units out, and the two systems will yield the same ending inventory under FIFO.

LIFO Costing with a Perpetual System

A LIFO cost flow with the use of a perpetual system is illustrated in Exhibit 5-18. First, note which 450 units are assumed to be sold on February 18. The sale consists of the most recent units acquired, 300 units at $11, and then 150 units from the beginning inventory at $10. Thus, the balance after this sale is simply the remaining 350 units from the beginning inventory priced at $10. The purchase on April 8 results in a balance of 350 units at $10 and 400 units at $12.

EXHIBIT 5-18   **Perpetual System: LIFO Cost-Flow Assumption**

	Purchases			Sales			Balance		
Date	Units	Unit Cost	Total Cost	Units	Unit Cost	Total Cost	Units	Unit Cost	Balance
1/1							500	$10	$5,000
1/20	300	$11	$3,300				500	10	
							300	11	8,300
2/18				300	$11	$3,300			
				150	10	1,500	350	10	3,500
4/8	400	12	4,800				350	10	
							400	12	8,300
6/19				300	12	3,600	350	10	
							100	12	4,700
9/5	200	13	2,600				350	10	
							100	12	
							200	13	7,300
10/20				150	13	1,950	350	10	
							100	12	
							50	13	5,350
12/12	100	14	1,400				350	10	
							100	12	
							50	13	
							100	14	6,750

Note what happens with LIFO when it is applied on a perpetual basis. In essence, a gap is created. Units acquired at the earliest price of $10 and units acquired at the most recent price of $12 are on hand, but none of those at the middle price of $11 remain. This situation arises because LIFO is applied every time a sale is made rather than only at the end of the year. Because of this difference, the amount of ending inventory differs, depending on which system is used:

LIFO periodic (Exhibit 5-9)	$6,100
LIFO perpetual (Exhibit 5-18)	$6,750

Moving Average with a Perpetual System

When a weighted average cost assumption is applied with a perpetual system, it is sometimes called a **moving average**. As indicated in Exhibit 5-19, each time a purchase is made, a new weighted average cost must be computed, thus the name *moving average*. For example, the goods available for sale after the January 20 purchase consist of 500 units at $10 and 300 units at $11, which results in an average cost of $10.38. This is the unit cost applied to the 450 units sold on February 18. The 400 units purchased on April 8 require the computation of a new unit cost, as indicated in the second footnote to the exhibit. As you might have suspected, the ending inventory with an average cost flow differs, depending on whether a periodic or a perpetual system is used:

Moving average
The name given to an average cost method when it is used with a perpetual inventory system.

Weighted average periodic (Exhibit 5-9)	$6,840
Moving average perpetual (Exhibit 5-19)	$7,290

EXHIBIT 5-19 Perpetual System: Moving Average Cost-Flow Assumption

Date	Purchases Units	Unit Cost	Total Cost	Sales Units	Unit Cost	Total Cost	Balance Units	Unit Cost	Balance
1/1							500	$10.00	$5,000
1/20	300	$11	$3,300				800	10.38*	8,304
2/18				450	$10.38	$4,671	350	10.38	3,633
4/8	400	12	4,800				750	11.24†	8,430
6/19				300	11.24	3,372	450	11.24	5,058
9/5	200	13	2,600				650	11.78‡	7,657
10/20				150	11.78	1,767	500	11.78	5,890
12/12	100	14	1,400				600	12.15§	7,290

The moving average prices per unit are calculated as follows:
*($5,000 + $3,300)/800 units = $10.38 (rounded to nearest cent)
†($3,633 + $4,800)/750 units = $11.24
‡($5,058 + $2,600)/650 units = $11.78
§($5,890 + $1,400)/600 units = $12.15

STUDY HIGHLIGHTS

LO1 **Identify the forms of inventory held by different types of businesses and the types of costs incurred (p. 204).**

- Inventory is a current asset held for resale in the normal course of business. The nature of inventory held depends upon whether a business is a reseller of goods (wholesaler or retailer) or a manufacturer.
  - Resellers incur a single cost to purchase inventory held for sale.
  - Manufacturers incur costs that can be classified as raw materials, direct labor, and manufacturing overhead.

LO2 **Show that you understand how wholesalers and retailers account for sales of merchandise (p. 207).**

- Net sales represents sales less deductions for discounts and merchandise returned (returns and allowances) and is a key figure on the income statement.
  - Sales discounts are given to customers who pay their bills promptly.
  - Returns and allowances have the same effect on sales as do sales discounts; that is, they reduce sales.

LO3 **Show that you understand how wholesalers and retailers account for cost of goods sold (p. 208).**

- The cost of goods sold represents goods sold, as opposed to the inventory purchased during the year. Cost of goods sold is matched with the sales of the period.
  - The cost of goods sold in any one period is equal to:
    Beginning inventory + Purchases − Ending inventory
  - Under the perpetual method, the inventory account is updated after each sale or purchase of merchandise.
  - In contrast, under the periodic method, the inventory account is updated only at the end of the period.
- The cost of goods purchased includes any costs necessary to acquire the goods less any purchase discounts, returns, and allowances.
  - Transportation-in is the cost to ship goods to a company and is typically classified as part of cost of goods purchased.

LO4 **Use the gross profit ratio to analyze a company's ability to cover its operating expenses and earn a profit (p. 215).**

- The gross profit ratio is the relationship between gross profit and net sales. Managers, investors, and creditors use this important ratio to measure one aspect of profitability.
  - The ratio is calculated as follows: $\dfrac{\text{Gross profit}}{\text{Net sales}}$

LO5 **Explain the relationship between the valuation of inventory and the measurement of income (p. 217).**

- Inventory costs ultimately become the cost of goods sold reflected in the income statement.
  - Since inventory is not expensed as the cost of goods sold until merchandise is sold, determining which costs belong in inventory affects the timing of when these expenses are reflected in net income.

LO6 **Apply the inventory costing methods of specific identification, weighted average, FIFO, and LIFO using a periodic system (p. 218).**

- The purchase price of inventory items may change frequently, and several alternatives are available to assign costs to the goods sold and those that remain in ending inventory.
  - Specific identification assigns the actual costs of acquisition to items of inventory. In some circumstances, it is not practical to do this.
  - The three other methods involve making assumptions about the cost of inventory:
    - Weighted average assigns the same unit cost to all units available for sale during the period.
    - The FIFO method assumes that the first units purchased are the first units sold.
    - The LIFO method assumes that the last units purchased are the first units sold.

Analyze the effects of the different costing methods on inventory, net income, income taxes, and cash flow (p. 221).

- The ability to accurately measure net income for a period should be the driving force behind selecting an inventory costing method.
  - Inventory costing methods impact the cost of goods sold and, therefore, net income.
  - If a company uses LIFO for tax purposes, it must also use it for financial reporting purposes.

Analyze the effects of an inventory error on various financial statement items (p. 226).

- The link between the balance sheet and the income statement can be seen through the effect of errors in inventory valuation.
  - Overstatement of ending inventory results in an understatement of the cost of goods sold and therefore an overstatement of net income.
  - The effects of errors in inventory may offset themselves over time. These are known as counterbalancing errors.

Apply the lower-of-cost-or-market rule to the valuation of inventory (p. 229).

- The principle of conservatism in accounting may warrant a departure from historical cost. This departure is known as the lower-of-cost-or-market rule (LCM).
  - Under LCM, the historical cost of inventory is compared with its replacement cost. If the replacement cost is lower, the Inventory account is reduced and a loss is recognized.

Explain why and how the cost of inventory is estimated in certain situations (p. 231).

- Certain circumstances arise that prohibit an accurate accounting of inventory, such as floods or fires that destroy merchandise.
  - Under these circumstances, the gross profit method may be used to estimate the cost of inventory.

Analyze the management of inventory (p. 233).

- Inventory turnover is a measure of how efficiently inventory is managed. The ratio measures how quickly inventory is sold and is calculated as follows:

$$\frac{\text{Cost of goods sold}}{\text{Average inventory}}$$

The higher the ratio, the less time inventory resides in storage (i.e., the more quickly it turns over).

- The average length of time that it takes to sell inventory can be derived from the inventory turnover ratio:

$$\text{Number of days' sales in inventory} = \frac{\text{Number of days in the period}}{\text{Inventory turnover ratio}}$$

Explain the effects that inventory transactions have on the statement of cash flows (p. 235).

- Under the indirect method of calculating cash flows from operating activities, both the changes in the Inventory account and the Accounts Payable account must be taken into consideration.

Explain the differences in the accounting for periodic and perpetual inventory systems and apply the inventory costing methods using a perpetual system (Appendix p. 237).

- The three inventory costing methods, FIFO, LIFO, and weighted average, may be used in combination with a perpetual inventory system.
  - The inventory costing method is applied after each sale of merchandise to update the Inventory account.
  - The results from using LIFO differ depending on whether a periodic or perpetual system is used. The same is true with weighted average, which is called moving average in a perpetual system.

RATIO REVIEW

$$\text{Gross Profit Ratio} = \frac{\text{Gross Profit (Income Statement)}}{\text{Net Sales (Income Statement)}}$$

$$\text{Inventory Turnover Ratio} = \frac{\text{Cost of Goods Sold (Income Statement)}}{\text{Average Inventory* (Balance Sheet)}}$$

*Average inventory can be estimated using the following calculation:

$$\frac{\text{Beginning Inventory} + \text{Ending Inventory}}{2}$$

$$\text{Number of Days' Sales in Inventory} = \frac{\text{Number of Days in the Period**}}{\text{Inventory Turnover Ratio}}$$

**Usually assume 360 days unless some other number is a better estimate of the number of days in the period.

ACCOUNTS HIGHLIGHTED

Account Titles	Where It Appears	In What Section	Page Number
Merchandise Inventory	Balance Sheet	Current Assets	205
Sales Revenue	Income Statement	Sales	207
Sales Returns and Allowances	Income Statement	Contra to Sales Revenue	208
Sales Discounts	Income Statement	Contra to Sales Revenue	208
Cost of Goods Sold	Income Statement	Expenses	209
Purchases	Income Statement	Cost of Goods Sold	212
Purchase Returns and Allowances	Income Statement	Contra to Purchases	212
Purchase Discounts	Income Statement	Contra to Purchases	213
Transportation-in	Income Statement	Added to Purchases	212
Transportation-out	Income Statement	Selling Expense	214
Loss on Decline in Value of Inventory	Income Statement	Other Expenses	229

KEY TERMS QUIZ

Because of the large number of terms introduced in this chapter, there are two key terms quizzes. Read each definition below and then write the number of the definition in the blank beside the appropriate term it defines. The quiz solutions appear at the end of the chapter.

Quiz 1: Merchandise Accounting

_____	Merchandise Inventory	_____	Cost of goods sold
_____	Raw materials	_____	Perpetual system
_____	Work in process	_____	Periodic system
_____	Finished goods	_____	Transportation-in
_____	Gross profit	_____	Purchases
_____	Net sales	_____	Purchase Returns and Allowances
_____	Sales revenue	_____	Purchase Discounts
_____	Sales Returns and Allowances	_____	FOB destination point
_____	Sales Discounts	_____	FOB shipping point
_____	Cost of goods available for sale	_____	Gross profit ratio

1. The contra-revenue account used to record both refunds to customers and reductions of their accounts.
2. The adjunct account used to record freight costs paid by the buyer.

3. The system in which the Inventory account is increased at the time of each purchase of merchandise and decreased at the time of each sale.
4. The contra-purchases account used in a periodic inventory system when a refund is received from a supplier or a reduction given in the balance owed to the supplier.
5. The contra-revenue account used to record discounts given customers for early payment of their accounts.
6. Terms that require the seller to pay for the cost of shipping the merchandise to the buyer.
7. Terms that require the buyer to pay the shipping costs.
8. The system in which the Inventory account is updated only at the end of the period.
9. Beginning inventory plus cost of goods purchased.
10. The contra-purchases account used to record reductions in purchase price for early payment to the supplier.
11. The account used in a periodic inventory system to record acquisitions of merchandise.
12. Sales revenue less sales returns and allowances and sales discounts.
13. Cost of goods available for sale minus ending inventory.
14. Gross profit divided by net sales.
15. Sales less cost of goods sold.
16. The cost of unfinished products in a manufacturing company.
17. The account that wholesalers and retailers use to report inventory held for sale.
18. The inventory of a manufacturer before the addition of any direct labor or manufacturing overhead.
19. A manufacturer's inventory that is complete and ready for sale.
20. A representation of the inflow of assets from the sale of a product.

Quiz 2: Inventory Valuation

_____ Specific identification method	_____ Inventory profit
_____ Weighted average cost method	_____ Lower-of-cost-or-market (LCM) rule
_____ FIFO method	_____ Gross profit method
_____ LIFO method	_____ Retail inventory method
_____ LIFO liquidation	_____ Inventory turnover ratio
_____ LIFO conformity rule	_____ Number of days' sales in inventory
_____ LIFO reserve	_____ Moving average (Appendix)
_____ Replacement cost	

1. The name given to an average cost method when it is used with a perpetual inventory system.
2. An inventory costing method that assigns the same unit cost to all units available for sale during the period.
3. A conservative inventory valuation approach that is an attempt to anticipate declines in the value of inventory before its actual sale.
4. An inventory costing method that assigns the most recent costs to ending inventory.
5. The current cost of a unit of inventory.
6. An inventory costing method that assigns the most recent costs to cost of goods sold.
7. A measure of how long it takes to sell inventory.
8. A technique used to establish an estimate of the cost of inventory stolen, destroyed, or otherwise damaged or of the amount of inventory on hand at an interim date.
9. A technique used by retailers to convert the retail value of inventory to a cost basis.
10. The IRS requirement that if LIFO is used on the tax return, it must also be used in reporting income to stockholders.
11. An inventory costing method that relies on matching unit costs with the actual units sold.
12. The portion of the gross profit that results from holding inventory during a period of rising prices.
13. The result of selling more units than are purchased during the period, which can have negative tax consequences if a company is using LIFO.
14. The excess of the value of a company's inventory stated at FIFO over the value stated at LIFO.
15. A measure of the number of times inventory is sold during a period.

ALTERNATE TERMS

Gross profit Gross margin

Interim statements Quarterly or monthly statements

Market (value for inventory) Replacement cost

Merchandiser Wholesaler, retailer

Raw materials Direct materials

Retail price Selling price

Sales revenue Sales

Transportation-in Freight-in

Work in process Work in progress

WARMUP EXERCISES & SOLUTIONS

LO2

Warmup Exercise 5-1 Net Sales

McDowell Merchandising reported sales revenue, sales returns and allowances, and sales discounts of $57,000, $1,500, and $900, respectively, in 2007.

Required

Prepare the net sales section of McDowell's 2007 income statement.

Key to the Solution Refer to Exhibit 5-3.

LO3

Warmup Exercise 5-2 Cost of Goods Sold

The following amounts are taken from White Wholesaler's records (all amounts are for 2007):

Inventory, January 1	$14,200
Inventory, December 31	10,300
Purchases	87,500
Purchase Discounts	4,200
Purchase Returns and Allowances	1,800
Transportation-in	4,500

Required

Prepare the cost of goods sold section of White's 2007 income statement.

Key to the Solution Refer to Exhibit 5-4.

LO6

Warmup Exercise 5-3 Inventory Valuation

Busby Corp. began the year with 75 units of inventory that it paid $2 each to acquire. During the year it purchased an additional 100 units for $3 each. Busby sold 150 units during the year.

Required

1. Compute cost of goods sold and ending inventory assuming Busby uses FIFO.
2. Compute cost of goods sold and ending inventory assuming Busby uses LIFO.

Key to the Solution Review the mechanics of the methods, beginning on page 220.

LO9

Warmup Exercise 5-4 Lower of Cost or Market

Glendive reports its inventory on a FIFO basis and has inventory with a cost of $78,000 on December 31. The cost to replace the inventory on this date would be only $71,000.

Required

Determine the effect on the accounting equation from any adjustment necessary on December 31.

Key to the Solution Recall the need to write down inventory when market is less than cost.

LO11

Warmup Exercise 5-5 Inventory Turnover

Sidney began the year with $130,000 in merchandise inventory and ended the year with $190,000. Sales and cost of goods sold for the year were $900,000 and $640,000, respectively.

Required

1. Compute Sidney's inventory turnover ratio.
2. Compute the number of days' sales in inventory.

Key to the Solution Review how these two statistics are computed on pages 233–235.

SOLUTIONS TO WARMUP EXERCISES

Warmup Exercise 5-1

McDowell Merchandising
Partial Income Statement
For the Year Ended December 31, 2007

Sales revenue	$57,000	
Less: Sales returns and allowances	1,500	
Sales discounts	900	
Net sales		$54,600

Warmup Exercise 5-2

White Wholesalers
Partial Income Statement
For the Year Ended December 31, 2007

Inventory, January 1, 2007		$ 14,200	
Purchases	$87,500		
Less: Purchase returns and allowances	1,800		
Purchase discounts	4,200		
Net purchases	$81,500		
Add: Transportation-in	4,500		
Cost of goods purchased		86,000	
Cost of goods available for sale		$100,200	
Less: Inventory, December 31, 2007		10,300	
Cost of goods sold			$89,900

Warmup Exercise 5-3

1. Cost of goods sold: $(75 \times \$2) + (75 \times \$3) = \underline{\underline{\$375}}$

   Ending inventory: $25 \times \$3 = \underline{\underline{\$\ 75}}$

2. Cost of goods sold: $(100 \times \$3) + (50 \times \$2) = \underline{\underline{\$400}}$

   Ending inventory: $25 \times \$2 = \underline{\underline{\$\ 50}}$

Warmup Exercise 5-4

	Balance Sheet				Income Statement
ASSETS	**=**	**LIABILITIES**	**+**	**STOCKHOLDERS' EQUITY**	**+ REVENUES − EXPENSES**
Inventory (7,000)					Loss on Decline in
					Value of Inventory (7,000)

Warmup Exercise 5-5

1. $\text{Inventory Turnover Ratio} = \dfrac{\text{Cost of Goods Sold}}{\text{Average Inventory}}$

   $= \dfrac{\$640,000}{(\$130,000 + \$190,000)/2}$

   $= \dfrac{\$640,000}{\$160,000} = 4 \text{ times}$

2. $\dfrac{\text{Number of Days'}}{\text{Sales in Inventory}} = \dfrac{\text{Number of Days in the Period}}{\text{Inventory Turnover Ratio}}$

   $= \dfrac{360}{4} = 90 \text{ days}$

REVIEW PROBLEM & SOLUTION

Stewart Distributing Company sells a single product for $2 per unit and uses a periodic inventory system. The following data are available for the year:

Date	Transaction	Number of Units	Unit Cost	Total
1/1	Beginning inventory	500	$1.00	$500.00
2/5	Purchase	350	1.10	385.00
4/12	Sale	(550)		
7/17	Sale	(200)		
9/23	Purchase	400	1.30	520.00
11/5	Sale	(300)		

Required

1. Compute cost of goods sold, assuming the use of the weighted average costing method.
2. Compute the dollar amount of ending inventory, assuming the FIFO costing method.
3. Compute gross profit, assuming the LIFO costing method.
4. Assume a 40% tax rate. Compute the amount of taxes saved if Stewart uses the LIFO method rather than the FIFO method.

SOLUTION TO REVIEW PROBLEM

1. Cost of goods sold, weighted average cost method:

Cost of goods available for sale	
$500 + $385 + $520 =	$1,405
Divided by:	
Units available for sale:	
500 + 350 + 400 =	÷ 1,250 units
Weighted average cost	$1.124 per unit
× Number of units sold:	
550 + 200 + 300 =	× 1,050 units
Cost of goods sold	$1,180.20

2. Ending inventory, FIFO cost method:

Units available for sale	1,250
− Units sold	− 1,050
= Units in ending inventory	200
× Most recent purchase price of	× $ 1.30
= Ending inventory	$ 260

3. Gross profit, LIFO cost method:

Sales revenue: 1,050 units × $2 each	$2,100
Cost of goods sold	
400 units × $1.30 = $520	
350 units × $1.10 = 385	
300 units × $1.00 = 300	− 1,205
Gross profit	$ 895

4. Taxes saved from using LIFO instead of FIFO:

LIFO Cost of goods sold		$1,205
− FIFO Cost of goods sold:		
Cost of goods available for sale	$1,405	
Ending inventory from part (2)	260	
Cost of goods sold		− 1,145
= Additional expense from use of LIFO		$ 60
× Tax rate		× 0.40
= Tax savings from the use of LIFO		$ 24

QUESTIONS

1. What are three distinct types of costs that manufacturers incur? Describe each of them.

2. When a company gives a cash refund on returned merchandise, why doesn't it just reduce Sales Revenue instead of using a contra-revenue account?

3. What do credit terms of *3/20, n/60* mean? How valuable to the customer is the discount offered in these terms?

4. What is the difference between a periodic inventory system and a perpetual inventory system?

5. How have point-of-sale terminals improved the ability of mass merchandisers to use a perpetual inventory system?

6. In a periodic inventory system, what kind of account is Purchases? Is it an asset or an expense or neither?

7. Why are shipping terms, such as FOB shipping point or FOB destination point, important in deciding ownership of inventory at the end of the year?

8. How and why are transportation-in and transportation-out recorded differently?

9. How is a company's gross profit determined? What does the gross profit ratio tell you about a company's performance during the year?

10. What is the relationship between the valuation of inventory as an asset on the balance sheet and the measurement of income?

11. What is the justification for including freight costs incurred in acquiring incoming goods in the cost of the inventory rather than simply treating the cost as an expense of the period? What is the significance of this decision for accounting purposes?

12. What are the inventory characteristics that would allow a company to use the specific identification method? Give at least two examples of inventory for which the method is appropriate.

13. How can the specific identification method allow management to manipulate income?

14. What is the significance of the adjective *weighted* in the weighted average cost method? Use an example to illustrate your answer.

15. Which inventory method, FIFO or LIFO, more nearly approximates the physical flow of products in most businesses? Explain your answer.

16. York Inc. manufactures notebook computers and has experienced noticeable declines in the purchase price of many of the components it uses, including computer chips. Which inventory costing method should York use if it wants to maximize net income? Explain your answer.

17. Which inventory costing method should a company use if it wants to minimize taxes? Does your response depend on whether prices are rising or falling? Explain your answers.

18. The president of Ace Retail is commenting on the company's new controller: "The woman is brilliant! She has shown us how we can maximize our income and at the same time minimize the amount of taxes we have to pay the government. Because the cost to purchase our inventory constantly goes up, we will use FIFO to calculate cost of goods sold on the income statement to minimize the amount charged to cost of goods sold and thus maximize net income. For tax purposes, however, we will use LIFO because this will minimize taxable income and thus minimize the amount we have to pay in taxes." Should the president be enthralled with the new controller? Explain your answer.

19. What does the term *LIFO liquidation* mean? How can it lead to poor buying habits?

20. Historical-based costing methods are sometimes criticized for leading to inventory profits. In a period of rising prices, which inventory costing method will lead to the most "inventory profit"? Explain your answer.

21. Is it acceptable for a company to disclose in its annual report that it is switching from some other inventory costing method to LIFO *to save on taxes?*

22. Delevan Corp. uses a periodic inventory system and is counting its year-end inventory. Due to a lack of communication, two different teams count the same section of the warehouse. What effect will this error have on net income?

23. What is the rationale for valuing inventory at the lower of cost or market?

24. Why is it likely that the result from applying the lower-of-cost-or-market rule using a total approach, that is, by comparing total cost to total market value, and the result from applying the rule on an item-by-item basis will differ?

25. Patterson's controller makes the following suggestion: "I have a brilliant way to save us money. Because we are already using the gross profit method for our quarterly statements, we can start using it to estimate the year-end inventory for the annual report and save the money normally spent to have the inventory counted on December 31." What do you think of his suggestion?

26. Why does a company save time and money by using the retail inventory method at the end of the year?

27. Ralston Corp.'s cost of sales has remained steady over the last two years. During this same time period, however, its inventory has increased considerably. What does this information tell you about the company's inventory turnover? Explain your answer.

28. Why is the weighted average cost method called a *moving* average when a company uses a perpetual inventory system? (Appendix)

HOMEWORK

EXERCISES

LO1 **Exercise 5-1** Classification of Inventory Costs

Put an X in the appropriate column next to the inventory item to indicate its most likely classification on the books of a company that manufactures furniture and then sells it in retail company stores.

	Classification			
Inventory Item	**Raw Material**	**Work in Process**	**Finished Goods**	**Merchandise Inventory**
Fabric				
Lumber				
Unvarnished tables				
Chairs on the showroom floor				
Cushions				
Decorative knobs				
Drawers				
Sofa frames				
Chairs in the plant warehouse				
Chairs in the retail storeroom				

LO1 **Exercise 5-2** Inventoriable Costs

During the first month of operations, ABC Company incurred the following costs in ordering and receiving merchandise for resale. No inventory has been sold.

List price, $100, 200 units purchased
Volume discount, 10% off list price
Paid freight costs, $56
Insurance cost while goods were in transit, $32
Long-distance phone charge to place orders, $4.35
Purchasing department salary, $1,000
Supplies used to label goods at retail price, $9.75
Interest paid to supplier, $46

Required

What amount do you recommend the company record as merchandise inventory on its balance sheet? Explain your answer. For any items not to be included in inventory, indicate their appropriate treatment in the financial statements.

LO2 **Exercise 5-3** Perpetual and Periodic Inventory Systems

Following is a partial list of account balances for two different merchandising companies. The amounts in the accounts represent the balances at the end of the year *before* any adjustments are made or the books are closed.

Company A		**Company B**	
Sales Revenue	$50,000	Sales Revenue	$85,000
Sales Discounts	3,000	Sales Discounts	2,000
Merchandise Inventory	12,000	Merchandise Inventory	9,000
Cost of Goods Sold	38,000	Purchases	41,000
		Purchase Discounts	4,000
		Purchases Returns and Allowances	1,000

Required

1. Identify which inventory system, perpetual or periodic, each of the two companies uses. Explain how you know which system each uses by looking at the types of accounts on their books.
2. How much inventory does Company A have on hand at the end of the year? What is its cost of goods sold for the year?
3. Explain why you cannot determine Company B's cost of goods sold for the year from the information available.

LO2   **Exercise 5-4** Perpetual and Periodic Inventory Systems

From the following list, identify whether the merchandisers described would most likely use a perpetual or periodic inventory system.

    _____   Appliance store
    _____   Car dealership
    _____   Drugstore
    _____   Furniture store
    _____   Grocery store
    _____   Hardware store
    _____   Jewelry store

How might changes in technology affect the ability of merchandisers to use perpetual inventory systems?

LO3   **Exercise 5-5** Missing Amounts in Cost of Goods Sold Model

For each of the following independent cases, fill in the missing amounts:

	Case 1	Case 2	Case 3
Beginning inventory	$ (a)	$2,350	$1,890
Purchases (gross)	6,230	5,720	(e)
Purchase returns and allowances	470	800	550
Purchase discounts	200	(c)	310
Transportation-in	150	500	420
Cost of goods available for sale	7,110	(d)	8,790
Ending inventory	(b)	1,750	1,200
Cost of goods sold	5,220	5,570	(f)

LO3   **Exercise 5-6** Purchase Discounts

For each of the following transactions of Buckeye Corporation, determine the effect on the accounting equation (all purchases on credit are made with terms of 1/10, net 30, and Buckeye uses the periodic system of inventory):

July   3: Purchased merchandise on credit from Wildcat Corp. for $3,500.
July   6: Purchased merchandise on credit from Cyclone Company for $7,000.
July 12: Paid amount owed to Wildcat Corp.
August 5: Paid amount owed to Cyclone Company.

LO3   **Exercise 5-7** Purchases—Periodic System

For each of the following transactions of Wolverine Corporation, determine the effect on the accounting equation. The company uses the periodic system.

March   3: Purchased merchandise from Spartan Corp. for $2,500 with terms of 2/10, net/30. Shipping costs of $250 were paid to Neverlate Transit Company.
March   7: Purchased merchandise from Boilermaker Company for $1,400 with terms of net/30.
March 12: Paid amount owed to Spartan Corp.
March 15: Received a credit of $500 on defective merchandise purchased from Boilermaker Company. The merchandise was kept.
March 18: Purchased merchandise from Gopher Corp. for $1,600 with terms of 2/10, net 30.
March 22: Received a credit of $400 from Gopher Corp. for spoiled merchandise returned to them. This is the amount of credit exclusive of any discount.
April   6: Paid amount owed to Boilermaker Company.
April 18: Paid amount owed to Gopher Corp.

LO3   **Exercise 5-8** Shipping Terms and Transfer of Title

On December 23, 2007, Miller Wholesalers ships merchandise to Michael Retailers with terms of FOB destination point. The merchandise arrives at Michael's warehouse on January 3, 2008.

HOMEWORK

Required

1. Identify who pays to ship the merchandise.
2. Determine whether or not the inventory should be included as an asset on Michael's December 31, 2007, balance sheet. Should the sale be included on Miller's 2007 income statement?
3. Explain how your answers to part (2) would have been different if the terms of shipment had been FOB shipping point.

LO3 **Exercise 5-9** Transfer of Title to Inventory

From the following list, identify whether the transactions described should be recorded by Cameron Companies during December 2007 or January 2008.

Purchases of merchandise that are in transit from vendors to Cameron Companies on December 31, 2007:

_____ Shipped FOB shipping point
_____ Shipped FOB destination point

Sales of merchandise that are in transit to customers of Cameron Companies on December 31, 2007:

_____ Shipped FOB shipping point
_____ Shipped FOB destination point

LO5 **Exercise 5-10** Inventory and Income Manipulation

The president of SOS Inc. is concerned that the net income at year-end will not reach the expected figure. When the sales manager receives a large order on the last day of the fiscal year, the president tells the accountant to record the sale but to ignore any inventory adjustment because the physical inventory has already been taken. How will this affect the current year's net income? next year's income? What would you do if you were the accountant? Assume that SOS uses a periodic inventory system.

LO6 **Exercise 5-11** Inventory Costing Methods

VanderMeer Inc. reported the following information for the month of February:

Inventory, February 1	65 units @ $20
Purchases:	
February 7	50 units @ $22
February 18	60 units @ $23
February 27	45 units @ $24

During February, VanderMeer sold 140 units. The company uses a periodic inventory system.

Required
What is the value of ending inventory and cost of goods sold for February under the following assumptions:

1. Of the 140 units sold, 55 cost $20, 35 cost $22, 45 cost $23, and 5 cost $24.
2. FIFO
3. LIFO
4. Weighted average

LO7 **Exercise 5-12** Evaluation of Inventory Costing Methods

Write the letter of the method that is most applicable to each statement.

a. Specific identification
b. Average cost
c. First-in, first-out (FIFO)
d. Last-in, first-out (LIFO)

_____ 1. Is the most realistic ending inventory.
_____ 2. Results in cost of goods sold being closest to current product costs.
_____ 3. Results in highest income during periods of inflation.
_____ 4. Results in highest ending inventory during periods of inflation.

_____ 5. Smooths out costs during periods of inflation.

_____ 6. Is not practical for most businesses.

_____ 7. Puts more weight on the cost of the larger number of units purchased.

_____ 8. Is an assumption that most closely reflects the physical flow of goods for most businesses.

LO8   **Exercise 5-13** Inventory Errors

For each of the following independent situations, fill in the blanks to indicate the effect of the error on each of the various financial statement items. Indicate an understatement (U), an overstatement (O), or no effect (NE). Assume that each of the companies uses a periodic inventory system.

	Balance Sheet		Income Statement	
Error	Inventory	Retained Earnings	Cost of Goods Sold	Net Income
1. Goods in transit at year-end are not included in the physical count; they were shipped FOB shipping point.	_____	_____	_____	_____
2. One section of a warehouse is counted twice during the year-end count of inventory.	_____	_____	_____	_____
3. During the count at year-end, the inventory sheets for one of the stores of a discount retailer are lost.	_____	_____	_____	_____

LO8   **Exercise 5-14** Transfer of Title to Inventory

For each of the following transactions, indicate which company should include the inventory on its December 31, 2007, balance sheet:

1. Michelson Supplies Inc. shipped merchandise to PJ Sales on December 28, 2007, terms FOB destination. The merchandise arrives at PJ's on January 4, 2008.
2. Quarton Inc. shipped merchandise to Filbrandt on December 25, 2007, FOB destination. Filbrandt received the merchandise on December 31, 2007.
3. James Bros. Inc. shipped merchandise to Randall Company on December 27, 2007, FOB shipping point. Randall Company received the merchandise on January 3, 2008.
4. Hinz Company shipped merchandise to Barner Inc. on December 24, 2007, FOB shipping point. The merchandise arrived at Barner's on December 29, 2007.

LO10   **Exercise 5-15** Gross Profit Method

On February 12, a hurricane destroys the entire inventory of Suncoast Corporation. An estimate of the amount of inventory lost is needed for insurance purposes. The following information is available:

Inventory on January 1	$ 15,400
Net sales from January 1 to February 12	105,300
Purchases from January 1 to February 12	84,230

Suncoast estimates its gross profit ratio as 25% of net sales. The insurance company has agreed to pay Suncoast $10,000 as a settlement for the inventory destroyed.

Required

Determine the effect on the accounting equation of the adjustment to recognize the inventory lost and the insurance reimbursement.

LO11   **Exercise 5-16** Inventory Turnover for Best Buy

The following amounts are available from the 2005 annual report of **Best Buy Inc.** (all amounts are in millions of dollars):

Cost of goods sold	$20,938
Merchandise inventories, February 26, 2005	2,851
Merchandise inventories, February 28, 2004	2,607

HOMEWORK

Required
1. Compute Best Buy's inventory turnover ratio for 2005.
2. What is the average length of time it takes to sell an item of inventory? Explain your answer.
3. Do you think the average length of time it took Best Buy to sell inventory in 2005 is reasonable? What other information do you need to fully answer this question?

LO12

Exercise 5-17 Impact of Transactions Involving Inventories on Statement of Cash Flows

From the following list, identify whether the change in the account balance during the year would be added to (A) or deducted from (D) net income when the indirect method is used to determine cash flows from operating activities.

_____ Increase in accounts payable	_____ Increase in inventories
_____ Decrease in accounts payable	_____ Decrease in inventories

LO12

Exercise 5-18 Effects of Transactions Involving Inventories on the Statement of Cash Flows—Direct Method

Masthead Company's comparative balance sheets included inventory of $180,400 at December 31, 2006, and $241,200 at December 31, 2007. Masthead's comparative balance sheets also included accounts payable of $85,400 at December 31, 2006, and $78,400 at December 31, 2007. Masthead's accounts payable balances are composed solely of amounts due to suppliers for purchases of inventory on account. Cost of goods sold, as reported by Masthead on its 2007 income statement, amounted to $1,200,000.

Required
What is the amount of cash payments for inventory that Masthead will report in the Operating Activities category of its 2007 statement of cash flows assuming that the direct method is used?

LO12

Exercise 5-19 Effects of Transactions Involving Inventories on the Statement of Cash Flows—Indirect Method

Refer to all of the facts in Exercise 5-18.

Required
Assume instead that Masthead uses the indirect method to prepare its statement of cash flows. Indicate how each item will be reflected as an adjustment to net income in the Operating Activities category of the statement of cash flows.

MULTI-CONCEPT EXERCISES

LO2,3

Exercise 5-20 Income Statement for a Merchandiser

Fill in the missing amounts in the following income statement for Carpenters Department Store Inc.:

Sales revenue		$125,600
Less: Sales returns and allowances		(a)
Net sales		$122,040
Cost of goods sold:		
Beginning inventory		$ 23,400
Purchases	$ (b)	
Less: Purchase discounts	1,300	
Net purchases	$ (c)	
Add: Transportation-in	6,550	
Cost of goods purchased		81,150
Cost of goods available for sale		$104,550
Less: Ending inventory		(e)
Cost of goods sold		(d)
Gross profit		$ 38,600
Operating expenses		(f)
Income before tax		$ 26,300
Income tax expense		10,300
Net income		$ (g)

LO2,3 **Exercise 5-21** Partial Income Statement—Periodic System

LaPine Company has the following account balances as of December 31, 2007:

Purchase returns and allowances	$ 400
Inventory, January 1	4,000
Sales	80,000
Transportation-in	1,000
Sales returns and allowances	500
Purchase discounts	800
Inventory, December 31	3,800
Purchases	30,000
Sales discounts	1,200

Required
Prepare a partial income statement for LaPine Company for 2007 through gross profit. Calculate LaPine's gross profit ratio for 2007.

LO6,7 **Exercise 5-22** Inventory Costing Methods—Periodic System

The following information is available concerning the inventory of Carter Inc.:

	Units	Unit Cost
Beginning inventory	200	$10
Purchases:		
March 5	300	11
June 12	400	12
August 23	250	13
October 2	150	15

During the year, Carter sold 1,000 units. It uses a periodic inventory system.

Required
1. Calculate ending inventory and cost of goods sold for each of the following three methods:
   a. Weighted average
   b. FIFO
   c. LIFO
2. Assume an estimated tax rate of 30%. How much more or less (indicate which) will Carter pay in taxes by using FIFO instead of LIFO? Explain your answer.

LO5,9 **Exercise 5-23** Lower-of-Cost-or-Market Rule

Awards Etc. carries an inventory of trophies and ribbons for local sports teams and school clubs. The cost of trophies has dropped in the past year, which pleases the company except for the fact that it has on hand considerable inventory that was purchased at the higher prices. The president is not pleased with the lower profit margin the company is earning. "The lower profit margin will continue until we sell all of this old inventory," he grumbled to the new staff accountant. "Not really," replied the accountant. "Let's write down the inventory to the replacement cost this year, and then next year our profit margin will be in line with the competition."

Required
Explain why the inventory can be carried at an amount less than its cost. Which accounts will be affected by the write-down? What will be the effect on income in the current year and future years?

LO7,13 **Exercise 5-24** Inventory Costing Methods—Perpetual System (Appendix)

The following information is available concerning Stillwater Inc.:

	Units	Unit Cost
Beginning inventory	200	$10
Purchases:		
March 5	300	11
June 12	400	12
August 23	250	13
October 2	150	15

Stillwater, which uses a perpetual system, sold 1,000 units for $22 each during the year. Sales occurred on the following dates:

	Units
February 12	150
April 30	200
July 7	200
September 6	300
December 3	150

Required

1. Calculate ending inventory and cost of goods sold for each of the following three methods:
   a. Moving average
   b. FIFO
   c. LIFO
2. For each of the three methods, compare the results with those for Carter in Exercise 5-22. Which of the methods gives a different answer depending on whether a company uses a periodic or a perpetual inventory system?
3. Assume the use of the perpetual system and an estimated tax rate of 30%. How much more or less (indicate which) will Stillwater pay in taxes by using LIFO instead of FIFO? Explain your answer.

PROBLEMS

LO1 **Problem 5-1** Inventory Costs in Various Businesses

Businesses incur various costs in selling goods and services. Each business must decide which costs are expenses of the period and which should be included in the cost of the inventory. Various types of businesses are listed below, along with certain types of costs they incur:

		Accounting Treatment		
Business	Types of Costs	Expense of the Period	Inventory Cost	Other Treatment
Retail shoe store	Shoes for sale			
	Shoe boxes			
	Advertising signs			
Grocery store	Canned goods on the shelves			
	Produce			
	Cleaning supplies			
	Cash registers			
Frame shop	Wooden frame supplies			
	Nails			
	Glass			
Walk-in print shop	Paper			
	Copy machines			
	Toner cartridges			
Restaurant	Frozen food			
	China and silverware			
	Prepared food			
	Spices			

Required

Fill in the table to indicate the correct accounting for each of these types of costs by placing an X in the appropriate column. For any costs that receive other treatment, explain what the appropriate treatment is for accounting purposes.

LO4 **Problem 5-2** Calculation of Gross Profit for Wal-Mart and Target

The following information was summarized from the consolidated statements of income of **Wal-Mart Stores Inc. and Subsidiaries** for the years ended January 31, 2005, and 2004, and the consolidated statements of operations of **Target Corporation** for the years ended January 29, 2005, and January 31, 2004 (for each company, years are labeled as 2004 and 2003, respectively):

(in Millions)	2004		2003	
	Sales*	Cost of Sales	Sales*	Cost of Sales
Wal-Mart	$285,222	$219,793	$256,329	$198,747
Target	45,682	31,445	40,928	28,389

Described as net sales by Wal-Mart.

Required

1. Calculate the gross profit ratios for Wal-Mart and Target for 2004 and 2003.
2. Which company appears to be performing better? What factors might cause the difference in the gross profit ratios of the two companies? What other information should you consider to determine how these companies are performing in this regard?

LO7   **Problem 5-3** Evaluation of Inventory Costing Methods

Users of financial statements rely on the information available to them to decide whether or not to invest in a company or lend it money. As an investor, you are comparing three companies in the same industry. The cost to purchase inventory is rising in the industry. Assume that all expenses incurred by the three companies are the same except for cost of goods sold. The companies use the following methods to value ending inventory:

> Company A—weighted average cost
> Company B—first-in, first-out (FIFO)
> Company C—last-in, first-out (LIFO)

Required

1. Which of the three companies will report the highest net income? Explain your answer.
2. Which of the three companies will pay the least in income taxes? Explain your answer.
3. Which method of inventory costing do you believe is superior to the others in providing information to potential investors? Explain.
4. Explain how your answers to (1), (2), and (3) would change if the costs to purchase inventory had been falling instead of rising.

LO8   **Problem 5-4** Inventory Error

The following highly condensed income statements and balance sheets are available for Budget Stores for a two-year period (all amounts are stated in thousands of dollars):

Income Statements	2007	2006
Revenues	$20,000	$15,000
Cost of goods sold	13,000	10,000
Gross profit	$ 7,000	$ 5,000
Operating expenses	3,000	2,000
Net income	$ 4,000	$ 3,000

Balance Sheets	December 31, 2007	December 31, 2006
Cash	$ 1,700	$ 1,500
Inventory	4,200	3,500
Other current assets	2,500	2,000
Long-term assets	15,000	14,000
Total assets	$23,400	$21,000
Liabilities	$ 8,500	$ 7,000
Capital stock	5,000	5,000
Retained earnings	9,900	9,000
Total liabilities and stockholders' equity	$23,400	$21,000

Before releasing the 2007 annual report, Budget's controller learns that the inventory of one of the stores (amounting to $600,000) was inadvertently omitted from the count on December 31, 2006. The inventory of the store was correctly included in the December 31, 2007, count.

Required

1. Prepare revised income statements and balance sheets for Budget Stores for each of the two years. Ignore the effect of income taxes.
2. If Budget did not prepare revised statements before releasing the 2007 annual report, what would be the amount of overstatement or understatement of net income for the two-year period? What would be the overstatement or understatement of retained earnings at December 31, 2007, if revised statements were not prepared?
3. Given your answers in (2), does it matter if Budget bothers to restate the financial statements of the two years to rectify the error? Explain your answer.

LO10   **Problem 5-5** Gross Profit Method of Estimating Inventory Losses

On August 1, an office supply store was destroyed by an explosion in its basement. A small amount of inventory valued at $4,500 was saved. An estimate of the amount of inventory lost is needed for insurance purposes. The following information is available:

Inventory, January 1	$ 3,200
Purchases, January–July	164,000
Sales, January–July	113,500

The normal gross profit ratio is 40%. The insurance company will pay the store $65,000.

Required

1. Using the gross profit method, estimate the amount of inventory lost in the explosion.
2. An adjustment will be made to recognize the inventory loss and the insurance reimbursement. Determine the effect on the accounting equation.

LO11   **Problem 5-6** Inventory Turnover for Apple Computer and Dell Computer

The following information was summarized from the 2004 annual report of **Apple Computer Inc.:**

	(in millions)
Cost of sales for the year ended:	
September 25, 2004	$6,020
September 27, 2003	4,499
Inventories:	
September 25, 2004	101
September 27, 2003	56
Net sales for the year ended:	
September 25, 2004	8,279
September 27, 2003	6,207

The following information was summarized from the fiscal year 2005 annual report of **Dell Computer Corporation:**

	(in millions)
Cost of sales* for the year ended:	
January 28, 2005	$40,190
January 30, 2004	33,892
Inventories:	
January 28, 2005	459
January 30, 2004	327
Net revenue for the year ended:	
January 28, 2005	49,205
January 30, 2004	41,444

Described as "cost of revenue" by Dell.

Required

1. Calculate the gross profit ratios for Apple Computer and Dell for each of the two years presented.
2. Calculate the inventory turnover ratios for both companies for the most recent year.
3. Which company appears to be performing better? What other information should you consider to determine how these companies are performing in this regard?

LO12   **Problem 5-7** Effects of Changes in Inventory and Accounts Payable Balances on Statement of Cash Flows

Copeland Antiques reported a net loss of $33,200 for the year ended December 31, 2007. The following items were included on Copeland's balance sheets at December 31, 2007 and 2006:

	12/31/07	12/31/06
Cash	$ 65,300	$ 46,100
Trade accounts payable	123,900	93,700
Inventories	192,600	214,800

Copeland uses the indirect method to prepare its statement of cash flows. Copeland does not have any other current assets or current liabilities and did not enter into any investing or financing activities during 2007.

Required

1. Prepare Copeland's 2007 statement of cash flows.
2. Draft a brief memo to the president to explain why cash increased during such an unprofitable year.

MULTI-CONCEPT PROBLEMS

LO2,3, 12   **Problem 5-8** Purchases and Sales of Merchandise, Cash Flows

Two Wheeler, a bike shop, opened for business on April 1. It uses a periodic inventory system. The following transactions occurred during the first month of business:

April 1: Purchased five units from Duhan Co. for $500 total, with terms 3/10, net 30, FOB destination.
April 10: Paid for the April 1 purchase.
April 15: Sold one unit for $200 cash.
April 18: Purchased 10 units from Clinton Inc. for $900 total, with terms 3/10, net/30, FOB destination.
April 25: Sold three units for $200 each, cash.
April 28: Paid for the April 18 purchase.

Required

1. For each of the preceding transactions of Two Wheeler, determine the effect on the accounting equation.
2. Determine net income for the month of April. Two Wheeler incurred and paid $100 for rent and $50 for miscellaneous expenses during April. Ending inventory is $967 (ignore income taxes).
3. Assuming that these are the only transactions during April (including rent and miscellaneous expenses), compute net cash flow from operating activities.
4. Explain why cash outflow is so much larger than expenses on the income statement.

LO2,3,4 **Problem 5-9** Gap Inc.'s Sales, Cost of Goods Sold, and Gross Profit

The consolidated balance sheets of **Gap Inc.** included merchandise inventory in the amount of $1,814,000,000 as of January 29, 2005 (the end of fiscal year 2004), and $1,704,000,000 as of January 31, 2004 (the end of fiscal year 2003). Net sales were $16,267,000,000 and $15,854,000,000 at the end of fiscal years 2004 and 2003, respectively. Cost of goods sold and occupancy expenses were $9,886,000,000 and $9,885,000,000 at the end of fiscal years 2004 and 2003, respectively.

Required

1. Unlike most other merchandisers, Gap Inc. doesn't include accounts receivable on its balance sheet. Why doesn't Gap Inc.'s balance sheet include this account?
2. Determine the effect on the accounting equation for sales during the year ended January 29, 2005.
3. Gap Inc. sets forth net sales but not gross sales on its income statement. What type(s) of deduction(s) would be made from gross sales to arrive at the amount of net sales reported? Why might the company decide not to report the amount(s) of the deduction(s) separately?

HOMEWORK

4. Reconstruct the cost of goods sold section of Gap Inc.'s 2004 income statement.
5. Calculate the gross profit ratios for Gap Inc. for 2004 and 2003, and comment on the change noted, if any. Is the company's performance improving? What factors might have caused the change in the gross profit ratio?

LO2,3

Problem 5-10 Financial Statements

A list of accounts for Maple Inc. at 12/31/07 follows:

Accounts Receivable	$ 2,359
Advertising Expense	4,510
Buildings and Equipment, Net	55,550
Capital Stock	50,000
Cash	590
Depreciation Expense	2,300
Dividends	6,000
Income Tax Expense	3,200
Income Tax Payable	3,200
Interest Receivable	100
Inventory:	
January 1, 2007	6,400
December 31, 2007	7,500
Land	20,000
Purchase Discounts	800
Purchases	40,200
Retained Earnings, January 1, 2007	32,550
Salaries Expense	25,600
Salaries Payable	650
Sales	84,364
Sales Returns	780
Transportation-in	375
Utilities Expense	3,600

Required
1. Determine cost of goods sold for 2007.
2. Determine net income for 2007.
3. Prepare a balance sheet dated December 31, 2007.

LO5,6,7

Problem 5-11 Comparison of Inventory Costing Methods—Periodic System

Bitten Company's inventory records show 600 units on hand on October 1 with a unit cost of $5 each. The following transactions occurred during the month of October:

Date	Unit Purchases	Unit Sales
October 4		500 @ $10.00
8	800 @ $5.40	
9		700 @ $10.00
18	700 @ $5.76	
20		800 @ $11.00
29	800 @ $5.90	

All expenses other than cost of goods sold amount to $3,000 for the month. The company uses an estimated tax rate of 30% to accrue monthly income taxes.

Required
1. Prepare a chart comparing cost of goods sold and ending inventory using the periodic system and the following costing methods:

	Cost of Goods Sold	Ending Inventory	Total
Weighted average			
FIFO			
LIFO			

2. What does the Total column represent?
3. Prepare income statements for each of the three methods.
4. Will the company pay more or less tax if it uses FIFO rather than LIFO? How much more or less?

LO5,7, 13   **Problem 5-12** Comparison of Inventory Costing Methods—Perpetual System (Appendix)

Repeat Problem 5-11 using the perpetual system.

LO5,6,7   **Problem 5-13** Inventory Costing Methods—Periodic System

Oxendine Company's inventory records for the month of November reveal the following:

Inventory, November 1	200 units @ $18.00
November 4, purchase	250 units @ $18.50
November 7, sale	300 units @ $42.00
November 13, purchase	220 units @ $18.90
November 18, purchase	150 units @ $19.00
November 22, sale	380 units @ $42.50
November 24, purchase	200 units @ $19.20
November 28, sale	110 units @ $43.00

Selling and administrative expenses for the month were $10,800. Depreciation expense was $4,000. Oxendine's tax rate is 35%.

Required

1. Calculate the cost of goods sold and ending inventory under each of the following three methods (assume a periodic inventory system): (a) FIFO, (b) LIFO, and (c) weighted average.
2. Calculate the gross profit and net income under each costing assumption.
3. Under which costing method will Oxendine pay the least taxes? Explain your answer.

LO5,6,7   **Problem 5-14** Inventory Costing Methods—Periodic System

Following is an inventory acquisition schedule for Weaver Corp. for 2007:

	Units	Unit Cost
Beginning inventory	5,000	$10
Purchases:		
February 4	3,000	9
April 12	4,000	8
September 10	2,000	7
December 5	1,000	6

During the year, Weaver sold 12,500 units at $12 each. All expenses except cost of goods sold and taxes amounted to $20,000. The tax rate is 30%.

Required

1. Compute cost of goods sold and ending inventory under each of the following three methods (assume a periodic inventory system): (a) weighted average, (b) FIFO, and (c) LIFO.
2. Prepare income statements under each of the three methods.
3. Which method do you recommend so that Weaver pays the least amount of taxes during 2007? Explain your answer.
4. Weaver anticipates that unit costs for inventory will increase throughout 2008. Will it be able to switch from the method you recommended it use in 2007 to another method to take advantage for tax purposes of the increase in prices? Explain your answer.

LO1,7,9   **Problem 5-15** Interpreting Tribune Company's Inventory Accounting Policy

The 2004 annual report of **Tribune Company and Subsidiaries** includes the following in the note that summarizes its accounting policies:

> **Inventories** Inventories are stated at the lower of cost or market. Cost is determined on the last-in, first-out ("LIFO") basis for newsprint and on the first-in, first-out ("FIFO") or average basis for all other inventories.

Required

1. What *types* of inventory cost does Tribune Company carry? What about newspapers? Are newspapers considered inventory?
2. Why would the company choose three different methods to value its inventory?

HOMEWORK

LO7,9

Problem 5-16 Interpreting Sears' Inventory Accounting Policy

The 2004 annual report of **Sears, Roebuck and Co.** includes the following information in the note that describes its accounting policies relating to merchandise inventories:

> Approximately 86% of merchandise inventories are valued at the lower of cost or market, with cost determined using the retail inventory method ("RIM") under the last-in, first-out ("LIFO") cost flow assumption. To estimate the effects of inflation on inventories, the Company utilizes internally developed price indices.

Your grandfather knows you are studying accounting and asks you what this information means.

Required

1. Sears uses the LIFO cost flow assumption. Does this mean it sells its newest merchandise first? Explain your answer.
2. Does Sears report merchandise inventories on its balance sheet at their retail value? Explain your answer.

ALTERNATE PROBLEMS

LO1

Problem 5-1A Inventory Costs in Various Businesses

Sound Traxs Inc. sells and rents DVDs to retail customers. The accountant is aware that at the end of the year she must account for inventory but is unsure what DVDs are considered inventory and how to value them. DVDs purchased by the company are placed on the shelf for rental. Every three weeks the company performs a detailed analysis of the rental income from each DVD and decides whether to keep it as a rental or to offer it for sale in the re-sale section of the store. Resale DVDs sell for $10 each regardless of the price Sound Traxs paid for the tape.

Required

1. How should Sound Traxs account for each of the two types of DVDs—rentals and resales— on its balance sheet?
2. How would you suggest Sound Traxs account for the DVDs as they are transferred from one department to another?

LO4

Problem 5-2A Calculation of Gross Profit for Best Buy and Circuit City

The following information was summarized from the 2005 and 2004 consolidated statements of income of **Best Buy, Inc.** (for the years ended February 26, 2005, and February 28, 2004) and **Circuit City** (for the years ended February 28, 2005, and February 29, 2004). For each company, years are labeled as 2005 and 2004, respectively.

	2005		2004	
(in Millions)	**Sales***	**Cost of Goods Sold****	**Sales***	**Cost of Goods Sold****
Best Buy	$27,433	$20,938	$24,548	$18,677
Circuit City	10,472	7,904	9,857	7,573

*Described as "Revenue" by Best Buy and as "Net Sales and Operating Revenues" by Circuit City.
**Described as "cost of sales, buying and warehousing" by Circuit City.

Required

1. Calculate the gross profit ratios for Best Buy and Circuit City for 2005 and 2004.
2. Which company appears to be performing better? What factors might cause the difference in the gross profit ratios of the two companies? What other information should you consider to determine how these companies are performing in this regard?

LO7

Problem 5-3A Evaluation of Inventory Costing Methods

Three large mass merchandisers use the following methods to value ending inventory:

Company X—weighted average cost
Company Y—first-in, first-out (FIFO)
Company Z—last-in, first-out (LIFO)

The cost of inventory has steadily increased over the past 10 years of the product life. Recently, however, prices have started to decline slightly due to foreign competition.

Required

1. Will the effect on net income of the decline in cost of goods sold be the same for all three companies? Explain your answer.
2. Company Z would like to change its inventory costing method from LIFO to FIFO. Write an acceptable note for its annual report to justify the change.

LO8

Problem 5-4A Inventory Error

The following condensed income statements and balance sheets are available for Planter Stores for a two-year period (all amounts are stated in thousands of dollars):

Income Statements	2007	2006
Revenues	$35,982	$26,890
Cost of goods sold	12,594	9,912
Gross profit	$23,388	$16,978
Operating expenses	13,488	10,578
Net income	$ 9,900	$ 6,400

Balance Sheets	December 31, 2007	December 31, 2006
Cash	$ 9,400	$ 4,100
Inventory	4,500	5,400
Other current assets	1,600	1,250
Long-term assets, net	24,500	24,600
Total assets	$40,000	$35,350
Current liabilities	$ 9,380	$10,600
Capital stock	18,000	18,000
Retained earnings	12,620	6,750
Total liabilities and stockholders' equity	$40,000	$35,350

Before releasing the 2007 annual report, Planter's controller learns that the inventory of one of the stores (amounting to $500,000) was counted twice in the December 31, 2006, inventory. The inventory was correctly counted in the December 31, 2007, inventory count.

Required

1. Prepare revised income statements and balance sheets for Planter Stores for each of the two years. Ignore the effect of income taxes.
2. Compute the current ratio at December 31, 2006, before the statements are revised, and then compute the current ratio at the same date after the statements are revised. If Planter applied for a loan in early 2007 and the lender required a current ratio of at least 1-to-1, would the error have affected the loan? Explain your answer.
3. If Planter did not prepare revised statements before releasing the 2007 annual report, what would be the amount of overstatement or understatement of net income for the two-year period? What would be the overstatement or understatement of retained earnings at December 31, 2007, if revised statements were not prepared?
4. Given your answers to (2) and (3), does it matter if Planter bothers to restate the financial statements of the two years to correct the error? Explain your answer.

LO10

Problem 5-5A Gross Profit Method of Estimating Inventory Losses

On July 1, an explosion destroyed a fireworks supply company. A small amount of inventory valued at $4,500 was saved. An estimate of the amount of inventory lost is needed for insurance purposes. The following information is available:

Inventory, January 1	$14,200
Purchases, January–June	77,000
Sales, January–June	93,500

The normal gross profit ratio is 70%. The insurance company will pay the supply company $50,000.

Required

1. Using the gross profit method, estimate the amount of inventory lost in the explosion.
2. An adjustment will be made to recognize the inventory loss and the insurance reimbursement. Determine the effect on the accounting equation.

LO11

Problem 5-6A Inventory Turnover for Wal-Mart and Target

The following information was summarized from the 2005 annual report of **Wal-Mart Stores, Inc.:**

	(in millions)
Cost of sales for the year ended January 31:	
2005	$219,793
2004	198,747
Inventories, January 31:	
2005	29,447
2004	26,612

The following information was summarized from the 2004 annual report of **Target Corporation:**

	(in millions)
Cost of sales for the year ended:	
January 29, 2005	$31,445
January 31, 2004	28,389
Inventory:	
January 29, 2005	5,384
January 31, 2004	4,531

Required

1. Calculate the inventory turnover ratios for Wal-Mart for the year ending January 31, 2005, and Target for the year ending January 29, 2005.
2. Which company appears to be performing better? What other information should you consider to determine how these companies are performing in this regard?

LO12

Problem 5-7A Effects of Changes in Inventory and Accounts Payable Balances on Statement of Cash Flows

Carpetland City reported net income of $78,500 for the year ended December 31, 2007. The following items were included on Carpetland's balance sheet at December 31, 2007 and 2006:

	12/31/07	12/31/06
Cash	$ 14,400	$26,300
Trade accounts payable	23,900	93,700
Inventories	105,500	84,900

Carpetland uses the indirect method to prepare its statement of cash flows. Carpetland does not have any other current assets or current liabilities and did not enter into any investing or financing activities during 2007.

Required

1. Prepare Carpetland's 2007 statement of cash flows.
2. Draft a brief memo to the president to explain why cash decreased during a profitable year.

ALTERNATE MULTI-CONCEPT PROBLEMS

LO2,3,12

Problem 5-8A Purchases and Sales of Merchandise, Cash Flows

Chestnut Corp., a ski shop, opened for business on October 1. It uses a periodic inventory system. The following transactions occurred during the first month of business:

October   1: Purchased three units from Elm Inc. for $249 total, terms 2/10, net 30, FOB destination.
October 10: Paid for the October 1 purchase.

October 15: Sold one unit for $200 cash.

October 18: Purchased 10 units from Wausau Company for $800 total, with terms 2/10, net/30, FOB destination.

October 25: Sold three units for $200 each, cash.

October 30: Paid for the October 18 purchase.

Required

1. For each of the preceding transactions of Chestnut, determine the effect on the accounting equation.
2. Determine the number of units on hand on October 31.
3. If Chestnut started the month with $2,000, determine its balance in cash at the end of the month, assuming that these are the only transactions that occurred during October. Why has the cash balance decreased when the company reported net income?

LO2,3,4 **Problem 5-9A** Walgreen's Sales, Cost of Goods Sold, and Gross Profit

The following information was summarized from the consolidated balance sheets of **Walgreen Co. and Subsidiaries** as of August 31, 2004, and August 31, 2003, and the consolidated statements of income for the years ended August 31, 2004, and August 31, 2003.

(in millions)	2004	2003
Accounts receivable, net	$ 1,169.1	$ 1,017.8
Cost of sales	27,310.4	23,706.2
Inventories	4,738.6	4,202.7
Net sales	37,508.2	32,505.4

Required

1. Determine the effect on the accounting equation related to the collection of accounts receivable and sales during 2004. Assume hypothetically that all of Walgreen's sales are on account.
2. Walgreen Co. sets forth net sales but not gross sales on its income statement. What type(s) of deduction(s) would be made from gross sales to arrive at the amount of net sales reported? Why might the company decide not to report the amount(s) of the deduction(s) separately?
3. Reconstruct the cost of goods sold section of Walgreen's 2004 income statement.
4. Calculate the gross profit ratios for Walgreen Co. for 2004 and 2003 and comment on the change noted, if any. Is the company's performance improving? What factors might have caused the change in the gross profit ratio?

LO2,3 **Problem 5-10A** Financial Statements

A list of accounts for Lloyd Inc. at December 31, 2007, follows:

Accounts Receivable	$ 56,359
Advertising Expense	12,900
Capital Stock	50,000
Cash	22,340
Dividends	6,000
Income Tax Expense	1,450
Income Tax Payable	1,450
Inventory	
January 1, 2007	6,400
December 31, 2007	5,900
Purchase Discounts	1,237
Purchases	62,845
Retained Earnings, January 1, 2007	28,252
Salaries Payable	650
Sales	112,768
Sales Returns	1,008
Transportation-in	375
Utilities Expense	1,800
Wages and Salaries Expense	23,000
Wages Payable	120

Required

1. Determine cost of goods sold for 2007.
2. Determine net income for 2007.
3. Prepare a balance sheet dated December 31, 2007.

LO5,6,7

Problem 5-11A Comparison of Inventory Costing Methods—Periodic System

Stellar Inc.'s inventory records show 300 units on hand on November 1 with a unit cost of $4 each. The following transactions occurred during the month of November:

Date	Unit Purchases	Unit Sales
November 4		200 @ $9.00
8	500 @ $4.50	
9		500 @ $9.00
18	700 @ $4.75	
20		400 @ $9.50
29	600 @ $5.00	

All expenses other than cost of goods sold amount to $2,000 for the month. The company uses an estimated tax rate of 25% to accrue monthly income taxes.

Required

1. Prepare a chart comparing cost of goods sold and ending inventory using the periodic system and the following costing methods:

	Cost of Goods Sold	Ending Inventory	Total
Weighted average			
FIFO			
LIFO			

2. What does the Total column represent?
3. Prepare income statements for each of the three methods.
4. Will the company pay more or less tax if it uses FIFO rather than LIFO? How much more or less?

LO5,7,13

Problem 5-12A Comparison of Inventory Costing Methods—Perpetual System (Appendix)

Repeat Problem 5-11A, using the perpetual system.

LO5,6,7

Problem 5-13A Inventory Costing Methods—Periodic System

Story Company's inventory records for the month of November reveal the following:

Inventory, November 1	300 units @ $27.00
November 4, purchase	375 units @ $26.50
November 7, sale	450 units @ $63.00
November 13, purchase	330 units @ $26.00
November 18, purchase	225 units @ $25.40
November 22, sale	570 units @ $63.75
November 24, purchase	300 units @ $25.00
November 28, sale	165 units @ $64.50

Selling and administrative expenses for the month were $16,200. Depreciation expense was $6,000. Story's tax rate is 35%.

Required

1. Calculate the cost of goods sold and ending inventory under each of the following three methods (assume a periodic inventory system): (a) FIFO, (b) LIFO, and (c) weighted average.
2. Calculate the gross profit and net income under each costing assumption.
3. Under which costing method will Story pay the least taxes? Explain your answer.

LO5,6,7

Problem 5-14A Inventory Costing Methods—Periodic System

Following is an inventory acquisition schedule for Fees Corp. for 2007:

	Units	Unit Cost
Beginning inventory	4,000	$20
Purchases:		
February 4	2,000	18
April 12	3,000	16
September 10	1,000	14
December 5	2,500	12

During the year, Fees sold 11,000 units at $30 each. All expenses except cost of goods sold and taxes amounted to $60,000. The tax rate is 30%.

Required

1. Compute cost of goods sold and ending inventory under each of the following three methods (assume a periodic inventory system): (a) weighted average, (b) FIFO, and (c) LIFO.
2. Prepare income statements under each of the three methods.
3. Which method do you recommend so that Fees pays the least amount of taxes during 2007? Explain your answer.
4. Fees anticipates that unit costs for inventory will increase throughout 2008. Will it be able to switch from the method you recommended it use in 2007 to another method to take advantage for tax purposes of the increase in prices? Explain your answer.

LO1,7,9 **Problem 5-15A** Interpreting the New York Times Company's Financial Statements

The 2004 annual report of the **New York Times Company** includes the following note:

> Inventories. Inventories are stated at the lower of cost or current market value. Inventory cost is generally based on the last-in, first-out ("LIFO") method for newsprint and the first-in, first-out ("FIFO") method for other inventories.

Required

1. What *types* of inventory costs does the New York Times Company have? What about newspapers? Aren't these considered inventory?
2. Why did the company choose two different methods to value its inventory?

LO7,9 **Problem 5-16A** Interpreting Home Depot's Financial Statements

The 2004 annual report for **Home Depot** includes the following in the note that summarizes its accounting policies:

> Merchandise Inventories. The majority of the Company's Merchandise Inventories are stated at the lower of cost (first-in, first-out) or market, as determined by the retail inventory method.

A friend knows that you are studying accounting and asks you what this note means.

Required

1. Home Depot uses the first-in, first-out method. Does this mean that it always sells its oldest merchandise first?
2. Does Home Depot report inventories on its balance sheet at their retail value?

DECISION CASES

READING AND INTERPRETING FINANCIAL STATEMENTS

LO1,3 **Decision Case 5-1** Comparing Two Companies in the Same Industry: Finish Line and Foot Locker

Refer to the financial information for **Finish Line** and **Foot Locker** reproduced at the end of this book and answer the following questions:

Required

1. Are Finish Line and Foot Locker merchandisers, manufacturers, or service providers?
2. What is the dollar amount of inventories that each company reports on its balance sheet at the end of the most recent year? What percentage of total assets do inventories represent for each company?
3. Refer to Note 1 in Finish Line's annual report. What inventory valuation method does the company use? What is the advantage to the company of using this method?
4. Refer to Note 1 in Foot Locker's annual report. What inventory valuation method, or methods, does the company use? Does the fact that Foot Locker and Finish Line use different methods make it difficult to compare the two companies?
5. Given the nature of their businesses, which inventory system, periodic or perpetual, would you expect both Finish Line and Foot Locker to use? Explain your answer.

HOMEWORK

LO7

Decision Case 5-2 Reading and Interpreting J.C.Penney's Financial Statements

J.C.Penney reports merchandise inventory in the Current Assets section of the balance sheet in its 2004 annual report as follows (amounts in millions of dollars):

	2004	2003
Merchandise inventory (net of LIFO reserves of $25 and $43)	$3,169	$3,156

Required

1. What method does J.C.Penney use to report the value of its inventory?
2. What is the amount of the LIFO reserve at the end of each of the two years?
3. Explain the meaning of the increase or decrease in the LIFO reserve during 2004. What does this tell you about inventory costs for the company? Are they rising or falling? Explain your answer.

LO1,6,9

Decision Case 5-3 Reading and Interpreting Circuit City's Inventory Note

Note 1M in **Circuit City**'s 2005 annual report is titled "Merchandise Inventory" and reads as follows:

> Inventory is comprised of finished goods held for sale and is stated at the lower of cost or market. Cost is determined by the average cost method. The company estimates the realizable value of inventory based on assumptions about forecasted consumer demand, market conditions and obsolescence. If the estimated realizable value is less than cost, the inventory value is reduced to its estimated realizable value. If estimates regarding consumer demand and market conditions are inaccurate or unexpected changes in technology affect demand, the company could be exposed to losses in excess of amounts recorded.

Required

1. What inventory costing method does Circuit City use to value its inventory? Does this method seem appropriate for the type of business that the company operates? Explain your answer.
2. Circuit City states its inventory at the lower-of-cost-or-market value. How does the company define "market"? What factors does it take into account in estimating the market value of its inventory?
3. Why do you think the company included the last sentence above, which concludes with "the company could be exposed to losses in excess of amounts recorded"?

MAKING FINANCIAL DECISIONS

LO2,3,4

Decision Case 5-4 Gross Profit for a Merchandiser

Emblems For You sells specialty sweatshirts. The purchase price is $10 per unit, plus 10% tax and a shipping cost of 50¢ per unit. When the units arrive, they must be labeled, at an additional cost of 75¢ per unit. Emblems purchased, received, and labeled 1,500 units, of which 750 units were sold during the month for $20 each. The controller has prepared the following income statement:

Sales	$15,000
Cost of sales ($11 × 750)	8,250
Gross profit	$ 6,750
Shipping expense	750
Labeling expense	1,125
Net income	$ 4,875

Emblems is aware that a gross profit of 40% is standard for the industry. The marketing manager believes that Emblems should lower the price because the gross profit is higher than the industry average.

Required

1. Calculate Emblems' gross profit ratio.
2. Explain why you believe that Emblems should or should not lower its selling price.

LO2,3,4 **Decision Case 5-5** Pricing Decision

Caroline's Candy Corner sells gourmet chocolates. The company buys chocolates in bulk for $5.00 per pound plus 5% sales tax. Credit terms are 2/10, net 25, and the company always pays promptly in order to take advantage of the discount. The chocolates are shipped to Caroline FOB shipping point. Shipping costs are $0.05 per pound. When the chocolates arrive at the shop, Caroline's Candy repackages them into one-pound boxes labeled with the store name. Boxes cost $0.70 each. The company pays its employees an hourly wage of $5.25 plus a commission of $0.10 per pound.

Required

1. What is the cost per one-pound box of chocolates?
2. What price must Caroline's Candy charge in order to have a 40% gross profit?
3. Do you believe this is a sufficient gross profit for this kind of business? What other costs might the company still incur?

LO3 **Decision Case 5-6** Use of a Perpetual Inventory System

Darrell Keith is starting a new business. He would like to keep a tight control over it. Therefore, he wants to know *exactly* how much gross profit he earns on each unit he sells. Darrell has set up an elaborate numbering system to identify each item as it is purchased and then to match the item with a sales price. Each unit is assigned a number as follows:

0000-000-00-000

a. The first four numbers represent the month and day an item was received.
b. The second set of numbers is the last three numbers of the purchase order that authorized the purchase of the item.
c. The third set of numbers is the two-number department code assigned to different types of products.
d. The last three numbers are a chronological code assigned to units as they are received during a given day.

Required

1. Write a short memo to Darrell explaining the benefits and costs involved in a perpetual inventory system in conjunction with his quest to know exactly how much he will earn on each unit.
2. Comment on Darrell's inventory system, assuming that he is selling (a) automobiles or (b)trees, shrubs, and plants.

LO6,7 **Decision Case 5-7** Inventory Costing Methods

You are the controller for Georgetown Company. At the end of its first year of operations, the company is experiencing cash flow problems. The following information has been accumulated during the year:

Purchases	
January	1,000 units @ $8
March	1,200 units @ 8
October	1,500 units @ 9

During the year, Georgetown sold 3,000 units at $15 each. The expected tax rate is 35%. The president doesn't understand how to report inventory in the financial statements because no record of the cost of the units sold was kept as each sale was made.

Required

1. What inventory *system* must Georgetown use?
2. Determine the number of units on hand at the end of the year.
3. Explain cost-flow assumptions to the president and the method you recommend. Prepare income statements to justify your position, comparing your recommended method with at least one other method.

LO8 **Decision Case 5-8** Inventory Errors

You are the controller of a rapidly growing mass merchandiser. The company uses a periodic inventory system. As the company has grown and accounting systems have developed, errors have occurred in both the physical count of inventory and the valuation of inventory on the balance sheet. You have been able to identify the following errors as of December 2007:

- In 2005 one section of the warehouse was counted twice. The error resulted in inventory overstated on December 31, 2005, by approximately $45,600.
- In 2006 the replacement cost of some inventory was less than the FIFO value used on the balance sheet. The inventory would have been $6,000 less on the balance sheet dated December 31, 2006.
- In 2007 the company used the gross profit method to estimate inventory for its quarterly financial statements. At the end of the second quarter, the controller made a math error and understated the inventory by $20,000 on the quarterly report. The error was not discovered until the end of the year.

Required

What, if anything, should you do to correct each of these errors? Explain your answers.

ETHICAL DECISION MAKING

LO2

Decision Case 5-9 Sales Returns and Allowances

You are the controller for a large chain of discount merchandise stores. You receive a memorandum from the sales manager for the midwestern region. He raises an issue regarding the proper treatment of sales returns. The manager urges you to discontinue the "silly practice" of recording Sales Returns and Allowances each time a customer returns a product. In the manager's mind, this is a waste of time and unduly complicates the financial statements. The manager recommends, "Things could be kept a lot simpler by just reducing Sales Revenue when a product is returned."

Required
1. What do you think the sales manager's *motivation* might be for writing you the memo? Is it that he believes the present practice is a waste of time and unduly complicates the financial statements?
2. Do you agree with the sales manager's recommendation? Explain why you agree or disagree.
3. Write a brief memo to the sales manager outlining your position on this matter.

LO7

Decision Case 5-10 Selection of an Inventory Method

As controller of a widely held public company, you are concerned with making the best decisions for the stockholders. At the end of its first year of operations, you are faced with the choice of method to value inventory. Specific identification is out of the question because the company sells a large quantity of diversified products. You are trying to decide between FIFO and LIFO. Inventory costs have increased 33% over the year. The chief executive officer has instructed you to do whatever it takes in all areas to report the highest income possible.

Required
1. Which method will satisfy the CEO?
2. Which method do you believe is in the best interest of the stockholders? Explain your answer.
3. Write a brief memo to the CEO to convince him that reporting the highest income is not always the best approach for the shareholders.

LO9

Decision Case 5-11 Write-Down of Obsolete Inventory

As a newly hired staff accountant, you are assigned the responsibility of physically counting inventory at the end of the year. The inventory count proceeds in a timely fashion. The inventory is outdated, however. You suggest that the inventory could not be sold for the cost at which it is carried and that the inventory should be written down to a much lower level. The controller replies that experience has taught her how the market changes and she knows that the units in the warehouse will be more marketable again. The company plans to keep the goods until they are back in style.

Required
1. What effect will writing off the inventory have on the current year's income?
2. What effect does not writing off the inventory have on the year-end balance sheet?
3. What factors should you consider in deciding whether to persist in your argument that the inventory should be written down?
4. If you fail to write down the inventory, do outside readers of the statements have reliable information? Explain your answer.

SOLUTIONS TO KEY TERMS QUIZ

Quiz 1: Merchandise Accounting

17	Merchandise Inventory	13	Cost of goods sold
18	Raw materials	3	Perpetual system
16	Work in process	8	Periodic system
19	Finished goods	2	Transportation-in
15	Gross profit	11	Purchases
12	Net sales	4	Purchase Returns and Allowances
20	Sales revenue	10	Purchase Discounts
1	Sales Returns and Allowances	6	FOB destination point
5	Sales Discounts	7	FOB shipping point
9	Cost of goods available for sale	14	Gross profit ratio

Quiz 2: Inventory Valuation

11	Specific identification method	12	Inventory profit
2	Weighted average cost method	3	Lower-of-cost-or-market (LCM) rule
4	FIFO method	8	Gross profit method
6	LIFO method	9	Retail inventory method
13	LIFO liquidation	15	Inventory turnover ratio
10	LIFO conformity rule	7	Number of days' sales in inventory
14	LIFO reserve	1	Moving average (Appendix)
5	Replacement cost		

HOMEWORK

6

Cash and Internal Control

Study Links

A Look at the Previous Chapter
In Chapter 5 we examined companies that sell a product and how they account for purchases and sales of their merchandise. We also considered how they track their product costs and value their inventory according to one of the cost flow methods.

A Look at This Chapter
Sale of merchandise results in the collection of cash at some point from the customer. In this chapter, we consider this most liquid of all assets and the ways in which companies try to maintain control over cash as well as other valuable assets.

A Look at the Upcoming Chapter
Two other liquid assets appear towards the top of a balance sheet. In the next chapter we will consider how companies account for the receivables that result from sales on credit as well as how they account for investments that are made with available cash.

Learning Outcomes

After studying this chapter, you should be able to:

LO1 Identify and describe the various forms of cash reported on a balance sheet.

LO2 Show that you understand various techniques that companies use to control cash.

LO3 Explain the importance of internal control to a business and the significance of the Sarbanes-Oxley Act of 2002.

LO4 Describe the basic internal control procedures.

LO5 Describe the various documents used in recording purchases and their role in controlling cash disbursements.

The Finish Line, Inc.

MAKING BUSINESS DECISIONS

Finish Line, like all businesses, relies on a steady flow of cash to function smoothly. Cash is needed to buy shoes and other apparel the retailer sells in its over 650 stores located in malls across the United States. More cash will be needed to open the 40 new Finish Line stores that are planned for fiscal year 2007. Although all stores are leased—holding down the upfront costs when a store is opened—the company still spends significant amounts for furniture, fixtures, and the initial stock of inventory.

Cash was also needed recently to make Finish Line's first acquisition of another company. In January of 2005 it acquired **The Hang-Up Shoppes, Inc.**, a company doing business under the trade name **Man Alive** with 51 stores in thirteen states. Finish Line spent about $12 million for this purchase, paying $10.5 million up front with the remainder due later.

The acquisition of the Man Alive stores certainly used some of Finish Line's cash. Still, as shown on the accompanying partial sheet, Finish Line's cash amounted to over $47 million at the end of the 2006 fiscal year and represented over 7.5% of the company's total assets. With such a significant balance in cash at any point in time, control over this most liquid of all assets is crucial to Finish Line. In this chapter, we will look closely at both the accounting for cash and cash equivalents and at the ways companies maintain effective control over all valuable assets, including cash. Following are some important questions we will answer:

- What does the first line on Finish Line's balance sheet represent, that is, what is included in cash and cash equivalents? (See pp. 272–273)

- What are some of the techniques that companies use to control cash? (See pp. 273–279)

- Why is it essential for a company to maintain an effective internal control system, and what are some of the basic procedures that help make a system effective? (See pp. 279–285)

- How can the use of business documents add to the effectiveness of an internal control system? (See pp. 285–293)

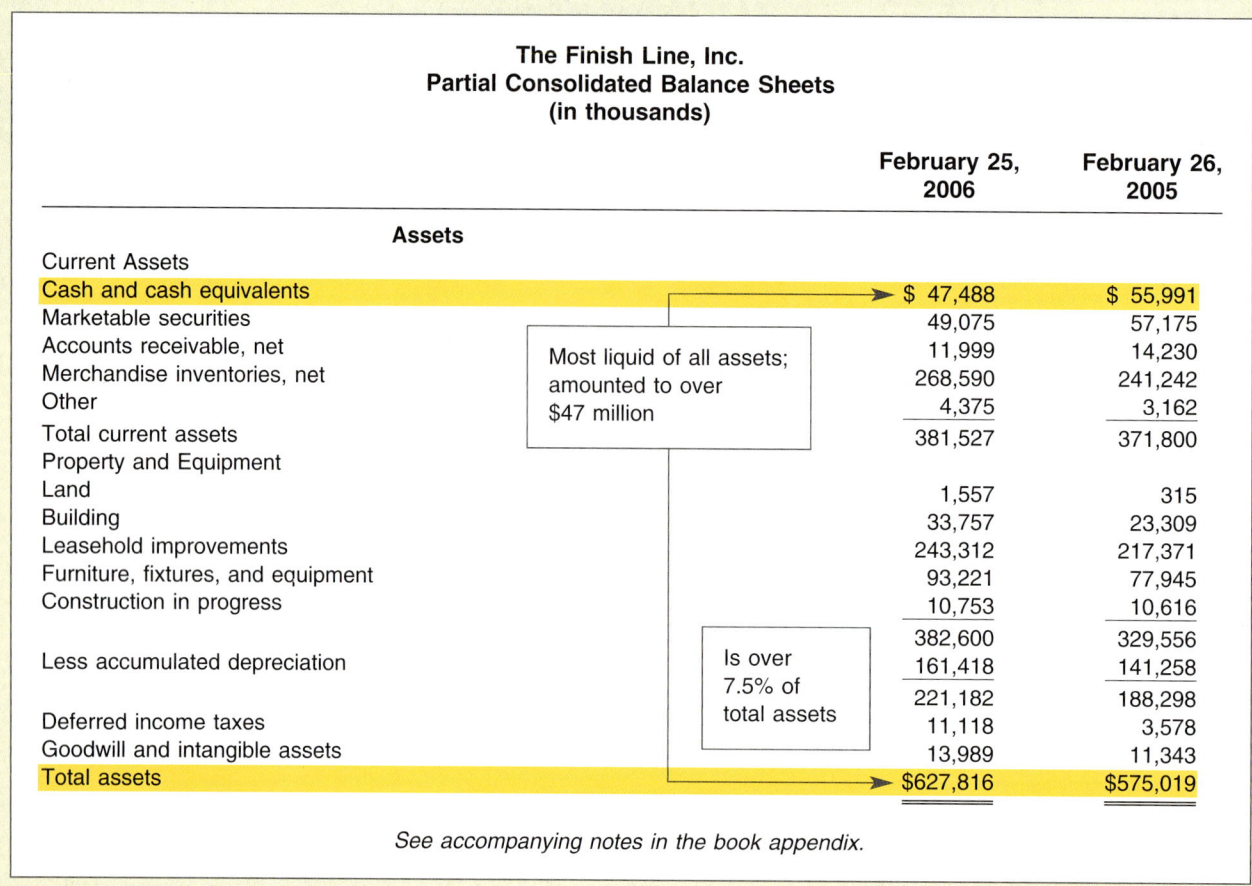

The Finish Line, Inc.
Partial Consolidated Balance Sheets
(in thousands)

	February 25, 2006	February 26, 2005
Assets		
Current Assets		
Cash and cash equivalents	$ 47,488	$ 55,991
Marketable securities	49,075	57,175
Accounts receivable, net	11,999	14,230
Merchandise inventories, net	268,590	241,242
Other	4,375	3,162
Total current assets	381,527	371,800
Property and Equipment		
Land	1,557	315
Building	33,757	23,309
Leasehold improvements	243,312	217,371
Furniture, fixtures, and equipment	93,221	77,945
Construction in progress	10,753	10,616
	382,600	329,556
Less accumulated depreciation	161,418	141,258
	221,182	188,298
Deferred income taxes	11,118	3,578
Goodwill and intangible assets	13,989	11,343
Total assets	$627,816	$575,019

Most liquid of all assets; amounted to over $47 million

Is over 7.5% of total assets

See accompanying notes in the book appendix.

Source: Finish Line's 2006 Annual Report.

What Constitutes Cash?

LO1 Identify and describe the various forms of cash reported on a balance sheet.

Cash takes many different forms. Coin and currency on hand and cash on deposit in the form of checking, savings, and money market accounts are the most obvious forms of cash. Also included in cash are various forms of checks, including undeposited checks from customers, cashier's checks, and certified checks. The proliferation of different types of financial instruments on the market today makes it very difficult to decide on the appropriate classification of these various items. The key to the classification of an amount as cash is that it be *readily available to pay debts.* Technically, a bank has the legal right to demand that a customer notify it before making withdrawals from savings accounts, or time deposits, as they are often called. Because this right is rarely exercised, however, savings accounts are normally classified as cash. In contrast, a certificate of deposit has a specific maturity date and carries a penalty for early withdrawal and is therefore not included in cash.

CASH EQUIVALENTS AND THE STATEMENT OF CASH FLOWS

Cash equivalent
An investment that is readily convertible to a known amount of cash and has an original maturity to the investor of three months or less.

Note that the first item on Finish Line's balance sheet in the chapter opener is titled Cash and cash equivalents. Examples of items normally classified as cash equivalents are commercial paper issued by corporations, treasury bills issued by the federal government, and money market funds offered by financial institutions. According to current accounting standards, classification as a **cash equivalent** is

EXHIBIT 6-2 | Bank Statement

Mt. Etna State Bank
Chicago, Illinois
Statement of Account

Mickey's Marathon Sports
502 Dodge St.
Chicago, IL 66666

FOR THE MONTH ENDING **June 30, 2007**
ACCOUNT **0371-22-514**

Date	Description	Subtractions	Additions	Balance
6-01	Previous balance			3,236.41
6-01	Check 497	723.40		2,513.01
6-02	Check 495	125.60		2,387.41
6-06	Check 491	500.00		1,887.41
6-07	Deposit		1,423.16	3,310.57
6-10	Check 494	185.16		3,125.41
6-13	NSF check	245.72		2,879.69
6-15	Deposit		755.50	3,635.19
6-18	Check 499	623.17		3,012.02
6-20	Check 492	125.00		2,887.02
6-22	Deposit		1,875.62	4,762.64
6-23	Service charge	20.00		4,742.64
6-24	Check 493	875.75		3,866.89
6-24	Check 503	402.10		3,464.79
6-26	Customer note, interest		550.00	4,014.79
6-26	Service fee on note	16.50		3,998.29
6-27	Check 500	1,235.40		2,762.89
6-28	Deposit		947.50	3,710.39
6-30	Check 498	417.25		3,293.14
6-30	Interest earned		15.45	3,308.59
6-30	Statement Totals	5,495.05	5,567.23	

The following types of items appear on Mickey's bank statement:

Canceled checks—Mickey's checks that cleared the bank during the month of June are listed with the corresponding check number and the date paid. Keep in mind that some of these checks may have been written by Mickey's in a previous month but were not presented for payment to the bank until June. You also should realize that during June, Mickey's may have written some checks that do not yet appear on the bank statement because they have not been presented for payment. A check written by a company but not yet presented to the bank for payment is called an **outstanding check**.

Deposits—In keeping with the internal control principle calling for the deposit of all cash receipts intact, most companies deposit all checks, coin, and currency on a daily basis. For the sake of brevity, we have limited to four the number of deposits that Mickey's made during the month. Keep in mind that Mickey's also may have made a deposit on the last day or two of the month and that this deposit may not yet be reflected on the bank statement. This type of deposit is called a **deposit in transit**.

NSF check—NSF is an abbreviation for not sufficient funds. The NSF check listed on the bank statement on June 13 is a customer's check that Mickey's recorded on its books, deposited, and thus included in its cash account. When Mt. Etna State Bank learned that the check was not good because the customer did not have sufficient funds on hand in its bank account to cover the check, the bank deducted the amount from Mickey's account. Mickey's needs to contact its customer to collect the amount due; ideally, the customer will issue a new check once it has sufficient funds in its account.

Outstanding check
A check written by a company but not yet presented to the bank for payment.

Deposit in transit
A deposit recorded on the books but not yet reflected on the bank statement.

Service charge—Banks charge for various services they provide to customers. Among the most common bank service charges are monthly activity fees, fees charged for new checks, for the rental of a lockbox at the bank in which to store valuable company documents, and for the collection of customer notes by the bank.

Customer note and interest—It is often convenient to have customers pay amounts owed to a company directly to that company's bank. The bank simply acts as a collection agency for the company.

Interest earned—Most checking accounts pay interest on the average daily balance in the account. Rates paid on checking accounts are usually significantly less than could be earned on most other forms of investment.

THE BANK RECONCILIATION

For a company such as Finish Line with its over 650 stores, you can imagine the large number of bank accounts it maintains. A **bank reconciliation** should be prepared for each individual bank account as soon as the bank statement is received. Ideally, the reconciliation should be performed or, at a minimum, thoroughly reviewed by someone independent of custody, record-keeping, and authorization responsibilities relating to cash. As the name implies, the purpose of a bank reconciliation is to *reconcile* or resolve any differences between the balance that the bank shows for an account with the balance that appears on the company's books. Differences between the two amounts are investigated, and if necessary, adjustments are made. The following are the steps in preparing a bank reconciliation:

Bank reconciliation
A form used by the accountant to reconcile or resolve any differences between the balance shown on the bank statement for a particular account with the balance shown in the accounting records.

1. Trace deposits listed on the bank statement to the books. Any deposits recorded on the books but not yet shown on the bank statement are deposits in transit. Prepare a list of the deposits in transit.

2. Arrange the canceled checks in numerical order, and trace each of them to the books. Any checks recorded on the books but not yet listed on the bank statement are outstanding. Prepare a list of the outstanding checks.

3. List all items, other than deposits, shown as additions on the bank statement, such as interest paid by the bank for the month and amounts collected by the bank from one of the company's customers. When the bank pays interest or collects an amount owed to a company by one of the company's customers, the bank increases or *credits* its liability to the company on its own books. For this reason, these items are called **credit memoranda**. Prepare a list of credit memoranda.

Credit memoranda
Additions on a bank statement for such items as interest paid on the account and notes collected by the bank for the customer.

4. List all amounts, other than canceled checks, shown as subtractions on the bank statement, such as any NSF checks and the various service charges mentioned earlier. When a company deposits money in a bank, a liability is created on the books of the bank. Therefore, when the bank reduces the amount of its liability for these various items, it *debits* the liability on its own books. For this reason, these items are called **debit memoranda**. Prepare a list of debit memoranda.

Debit memoranda
Deductions on a bank statement for such items as NSF checks and various service charges.

5. Identify any errors made by the bank or by the company in recording the various cash transactions.

6. Use the information collected in steps 1 through 5 to prepare a bank reconciliation.

Companies use a number of different *formats* in preparing bank reconciliations. For example, some companies take the balance shown on the bank statement and reconcile this amount to the balance shown on the books. Another approach, which we will illustrate for Mickey's, involves reconciling the bank balance and the book balance to an adjusted balance, rather than one to the other. As we will see, the advantage of this approach is that it yields the correct balance and makes it easy for the company to make any necessary adjustments to its books. A bank reconciliation for Mickey's Marathon Sports is shown in Exhibit 6-3.

EXHIBIT 6-3   Bank Reconciliation

Mickey's Marathon Sports
Bank Reconciliation
June 30, 2007

Balance per bank statement, June 30			$3,308.59
Add:	Deposit in transit		642.30
Deduct:	Outstanding checks:		
	No. 496	$ 79.89	
	No. 501	213.20	
	No. 502	424.75	(717.84)
Adjusted balance, June 30			$3,233.05
Balance per books, June 30			$2,895.82
Add:	Customer note collected	$500.00	
	Interest on customer note	50.00	
	Interest earned during June	15.45	
	Error in recording check 498	54.00	619.45
Deduct:	NSF check	$245.72	
	Collection fee on note	16.50	
	Service charge for lockbox	20.00	(282.22)
Adjusted balance, June 30			$3,233.05

The following are explanations for the various items on the reconciliation:

1. The balance per bank statement of $3,308.59 is taken from the June statement as shown in Exhibit 6-2.

2. Mickey's records showed a deposit for $642.30 made on June 30 that is not reflected on the bank statement. The deposit in transit is listed as an addition to the bank statement balance.

3. The accounting records indicate three checks written but not yet reflected on the bank statement. The three outstanding checks are as follows:

496   $ 79.89
501   $213.20
502   $424.75

Outstanding checks are the opposite of deposits in transit and therefore are deducted from the bank statement balance.

4. The adjusted balance of $3,233.05 is found by adding the deposit in transit and deducting the outstanding checks from the bank statement balance.

5. The $2,895.82 book balance on June 30 is taken from the company's records as of that date.

6. According to the bank statement, $550 was added to the account on June 26 for the collection of a note with interest. We assume that the repayment of the note itself accounted for $500 of this amount and that the other $50 was for interest. The bank statement notifies Mickey's that the note with interest has been collected. Therefore, Mickey's must add $550 to the book balance.

7. An entry on June 30 on the bank statement shows an increase of $15.45 for interest earned on the bank account during June. This amount is added to the book balance.

8. A review of the canceled checks returned with the bank statement detected an error made by Mickey's. The company records indicated that check 498 was recorded incorrectly as $471.25; the check was actually written for $417.25 and

reflected as such on the bank statement. This error, referred to as a *transposition error*, resulted from transposing the 7 and the 1 in recording the check in the books. The error is the difference between the amount of $471.25 recorded and the amount of $417.25 that should have been recorded, or $54.00. Because Mickey's recorded the cash payment at too large an amount, $54.00 must be added back to the book balance.

9. In addition to canceled checks, three other deductions appear on the bank statement. Each of these must be deducted from the book balance:

   a. A customer's NSF check for $245.72 (see June 13 entry on bank statement)

   b. A $16.50 fee charged by the bank to collect the customer's note discussed in item (6) (see June 26 entry on bank statement)

   c. A service fee of $20.00 charged by the bank for rental of a lockbox (see June 23 entry on bank statement)

10. The additions of $619.45 and deductions of $282.22 resulted in an adjusted cash balance of $3,233.05. Note that this adjusted balance agrees with the adjusted bank statement balance on the bank reconciliation [see item (4)]. Thus, all differences between the two balances have been explained.

THE BANK RECONCILIATION AND THE NEED FOR ADJUSTMENTS TO THE RECORDS

After it completes the bank reconciliation, Mickey's must prepare a number of adjustments to its records. In fact, all of the information for these adjustments will be from one section of the bank reconciliation. Do you think that the additions and deductions made to the bank balance or the ones made to the book balance are the basis for the adjustments? It is logical that the additions and deductions to the Cash account *on the books* should be the basis for the adjustments because these are items that Mickey's was unaware of before receiving the bank statement. Conversely, the additions and deductions to the bank's balance, that is, the deposits in transit and the outstanding checks, are items that Mickey's has already recorded on its books.

ESTABLISHING A PETTY CASH FUND

Recall one of the fundamental rules in controlling cash: all disbursements should be made by check. Most businesses make an exception to this rule in the case of minor expenditures, for which they use a **petty cash fund**. This fund consists of coin and currency kept on hand to make minor disbursements. The necessary steps in setting up and maintaining a petty cash fund follow:

Petty cash fund
Money kept on hand for making minor disbursements in coin and currency rather than by writing checks.

1. A check is written for a lump-sum amount, such as $100 or $500. The check is cashed, and the coin and currency are entrusted to a petty cash custodian.

2. A journal entry is made to record the establishment of the fund.

3. Upon presentation of the necessary documentation, employees receive minor disbursements from the fund. In essence, cash is traded from the fund in exchange for a receipt.

4. Periodically, the fund is replenished by writing and cashing a check in the amount necessary to bring the fund back to its original balance.

5. At the time the fund is replenished, an adjustment is made both to record its replenishment (by decreasing cash) and to recognize the various expenses incurred.

The use of this fund is normally warranted on the basis of cost versus benefits. That is, the benefits in time saved in making minor disbursements from cash are thought to outweigh the cost associated with the risk of loss from decreased control over cash disbursements. The fund also serves a practical purpose for certain expenditures such as taxi fares and messengers which often must be paid in cash.

Now that we have considered the importance of control over cash, we turn to the broader topic of internal control systems.

🕐 2 minute review

1. What are the most common additions and deductions to the balance per the bank statement on a reconciliation that adjusts both the bank statement and balance per the books to the adjusted balance? Specify whether each is added or deducted.

2. What are the most common additions and deductions to the balance per the books on a reconciliation that adjusts both the bank statement and balance per the books to the adjusted balance? Specify whether each is added or deducted.

3. Describe the adjustment needed when a petty cash fund is replenished.

Answers

1. *The most common additions to the balance per the bank statement are deposits-in-transit and the most common deductions are outstanding checks.*

2. *The most common additions to the balance per the books are collections on customers' notes and interest earned on the bank account. The most common deductions are for NSF checks and various fees charged by the bank.*

3. *When the petty cash fund is replenished, cash is decreased and the various expenses are recognized by recording increases in each of them.*

An Introduction to Internal Control

An employee of a large auto parts warehouse routinely takes spare parts home for personal use. A payroll clerk writes and signs two checks for an employee and then splits the amount of the second check with the worker. Through human error, an invoice is paid for merchandise never received from the supplier. These cases sound quite different from one another, but they share one important characteristic. They all point to a deficiency in a company's internal control system. An **internal control system** consists of the policies and procedures necessary to ensure the safeguarding of an entity's assets, the reliability of its accounting records, and the accomplishment of its overall objectives.

Three assets are especially critical to the operation of a merchandising company such as Finish Line: cash, accounts receivable, and inventory. Activities related to these three assets compose the operating cycle of a business. Cash is used to buy inventory, the inventory is eventually sold, and assuming a sale on credit, the account receivable from the customer is collected. After considering an important congressional act, we turn to the ways in which a company attempts to *control* the assets at its disposal, a subject which is explored further at appropriate points in the book.

THE SARBANES-OXLEY ACT OF 2002

As briefly described in Chapter 1, the **Sarbanes-Oxley Act** of 2002 (commonly referred to as SOX) was a direct response by Congress to the numerous corporate scandals that surfaced in the first few years of the new millennium. High-profile cases involving questionable accounting practices by companies such as **Enron** and **WorldCom** caused the federal government to step in and attempt to restore the public's confidence in the financial reporting system. The various provisions of SOX are very far reaching, including provisions designed to ensure the independence of a company's auditors. For example, external auditors can no longer provide bookkeeping, human resource, information system design, and brokerage services for clients that they audit.

LO3 Explain the importance of internal control to a business and the significance of the Sarbanes-Oxley Act of 2002.

Internal control system
Policies and procedures necessary to ensure the safeguarding of an entity's assets, the reliability of its accounting records, and the accomplishment of overall company objectives.

Sarbanes-Oxley Act
An act of Congress in 2002 intended to bring reform to corporate accountability and stewardship in the wake of a number of major corporate scandals.

EXHIBIT 6-4	Management Report on Internal Control—Finish Line

Management Report on Internal Control over Financial Reporting

Management states its responsibility for the internal control system. →

The management of The Finish Line, Inc. (the "Company") is responsible for establishing and maintaining adequate internal control over financial reporting (as defined in Rule 13a–15(f) and 15d–15(f) under the Securities Exchange Act of 1934, as amended). The company's internal control system was designed to provide reasonable assurance to the Company's management and Board of Directors regarding the preparation and fair presentation of published financial statements.

Internal control over financial reporting is defined in Rule 13a–15(f) and 15d–15(f) under the Securities Exchange Act of 1934 as a process designed by, or under the supervision of, the company's principal executive and principal financial officers and effected by the company's board of directors, management and other personnel, to provide reasonable assurance regarding the reliability of financial reporting and the preparation of financial statements for external purposes in accordance with U.S. generally accepted accounting principles and includes those policies and procedures that: (1) pertain to the maintenance of records that in reasonable detail accurately and fairly reflect the transactions and dispositions of the assets of the company; (2) provide reasonable assurance that transactions are recorded as necessary to permit preparation of financial statements in accordance with U.S. generally accepted accounting principles, and that receipts and expenditures of the company are being made only in accordance with authorizations of management and directors of the company; and (3) provide reasonable assurance regarding prevention or timely detection of unauthorized acquisition, use or disposition of the company's assets that could have a material effect on the financial statements.

All internal control systems, no matter how well designed, have inherent limitations. Therefore, even those systems determined to be effective can provide only reasonable assurance with respect to financial statement preparation and presentation.

Management's assessment of the effectiveness of the internal control system. →

The Company's management assessed the effectiveness of the company's internal control over financial reporting as of February 25, 2006. In making this assessment, it used the criteria set forth by the Committee of Sponsoring Organizations of the Treadway Commission (COSO) in *Internal Control—Integrated Framework*. Based on our assessment we believe that, as of February 25, 2006, the Company's internal control over financial reporting is effective based on those criteria.

Auditors have issued a report on management's assessment. →

The company's independent registered public accounting firm, Ernst & Young LLP, has issued an audit report on our assessment of the Company's internal control over financial reporting. This report appears on the following page.

Internal control report
A report, required by Section 404 of the Sarbanes-Oxley Act, to be included in a company's annual report, in which management assesses the effectiveness of the internal control structure.

Public Company Accounting Oversight Board
The five-member body created by the Sarbanes-Oxley Act that was given the authority to set auditing standards in the United States.

Another major part of SOX, specifically Section 404, deals directly with a company's internal control system. Among the more important of the provisions in Section 404 is the one that requires the annual report to include an **internal control report**. In the report management is required to:

1. **State its responsibility to establish and maintain an adequate internal control structure and procedures for financial reporting.**

2. **Assess the effectiveness of its internal control structure and procedures for financial reporting.**

Finish Line's Report on Internal Control over Financial Reporting is shown in Exhibit 6-4. The first paragraph states management's *responsibility* for its system of internal control, and the fourth paragraph indicates that management believes internal control over financial reporting is effective.

Note also the last paragraph in Exhibit 6-4. Another important provision in SOX is that a company's outside auditors must also issue a report on their assessment of the company's internal control. The statement in the last paragraph calls attention to this report. **Ernst & Young LLP** is Finish Line's independent auditor

EXHIBIT 6-5	Auditor's Report on Internal Control

REPORT OF INDEPENDENT REGISTERED PUBLIC ACCOUNTING FIRM
ON INTERNAL CONTROL OVER FINANCIAL REPORTING

The Board of Directors and Shareholders of The Finish Line, Inc.

We have audited management's assessment, included in the accompanying Management Report on Internal Control over Financial Reporting (included in Item 8), that The Finish Line, Inc. maintained effective internal control over financial reporting as of February 25, 2006, based on criteria established in Internal Control—Integrated Framework issued by the Committee of Sponsoring Organizations of the Treadway Commission (the COSO criteria). The Finish Line, Inc.'s management is responsible for maintaining effective internal control over financial reporting and for its assessment of the effectiveness of internal control over financial reporting. Our responsibility is to express an opinion on management's assessment and an opinion on the effectiveness of the Company's internal control over financial reporting based on our audit.

Audit followed the standards of the Public Company Accounting Oversight Board. → We conducted our audit in accordance with the standards of the Public Company Accounting Oversight Board (United States). Those standards require that we plan and perform the audit to obtain reasonable assurance about whether effective internal control over financial reporting was maintained in all material respects. Our audit included obtaining an understanding of internal control over financial reporting, evaluating management's assessment, testing and evaluating the design and operating effectiveness of internal control, and performing such other procedures as we considered necessary in the circumstances. We believe that our audit provides a reasonable basis for our opinion.

A company's internal control over financial reporting is a process designed to provide reasonable assurance regarding the reliability of financial reporting and the preparation of financial statements for external purposes in accordance with generally accepted accounting principles. A company's internal control over financial reporting includes those policies and procedures that (1) pertain to the maintenance of records that, in reasonable detail, accurately and fairly reflect the transactions and dispositions of the assets of the company; (2) provide reasonable assurance that transactions are recorded as necessary to permit preparation of financial statements in accordance with generally accepted accounting principles, and that receipts and expenditures of the company are being made only in accordance with authorizations of management and directors of the company; and (3) provide reasonable assurance regarding prevention or timely detection of unauthorized acquisition, use, or disposition of the company's assets that could have a material effect on the financial statements.

Because of its inherent limitations, internal control over financial reporting may not prevent or detect misstatements. Also, projections of any evaluation of effectiveness to future periods are subject to the risk that controls may become inadequate because of changes in conditions, or that the degree of compliance with the policies or procedures may deteriorate.

Auditors' opinions → In our opinion, management's assessment that The Finish Line, Inc. maintained effective internal control over financial reporting as of February 25, 2006, is fairly stated, in all material respects, based on the COSO criteria. Also, in our opinion, The Finish Line, Inc. maintained, in all material respects, effective internal control over financial reporting as of February 25, 2006, based on the COSO criteria.

We also have audited, in accordance with the standards of the Public Company Accounting Oversight Board (United States), the consolidated balance sheets of The Finish Line, Inc. as of February 25, 2006 and February 26, 2005, and the related consolidated statements of income, changes in shareholders' equity and cash flows for each of the three years in the period ended February 25, 2006 of The Finish Line, Inc., and our report dated May 4, 2006 expressed an unqualified opinion thereon.

ERNST & YOUNG LLP

Indianapolis, Indiana
May 4, 2006

and its report is shown in Exhibit 6-5. Note the reference in the second paragraph to the **Public Company Accounting Oversight Board (PCAOB)**. The PCAOB is the five-member body created by SOX and given the authority to set auditing standards in the United States.

The fifth paragraph in Ernst & Young's report contains two important statements, namely, that in their opinion:

1. **Management's assessment that the company maintained effective internal control over financial reporting is fairly stated.**

2. **Finish Line has maintained effective internal control over financial reporting.**

Note at the top of the independent auditors' report in Exhibit 6-5 that it is directed to the board of directors and shareholders of Finish Line. The **board of directors** usually consists of key officers of the corporation as well as a number of directors whom it does not directly employ. For example, Finish Line's board of eight directors consists of three insiders and five outsiders. Another key provision in SOX was one requiring that the audit committee be made up entirely of outside directors. The **audit committee** is a subset of the board of directors that provides direct contact between stockholders and the independent accounting firm.

One of the most frequently debated issues in many of the high profile cases involving financial reporting scandals was the behavior of the key officers of the companies. Many stockholders and others affected by these scandals felt that top management should have taken more responsibility for the accuracy of the information presented in the financial statements. Another provision in SOX directly addressed this issue. For the first time ever, the Chief Executive Officer (CEO) and the Chief Financial Officer (CFO) for a company must sign a statement certifying that the information in the financial statements fairly presents the financial condition and results of operations of the company. This provision places the responsibility for the information in the financial statements directly in the hands of the company's CEO and CFO.

THE CONTROL ENVIRONMENT

The success of an internal control system begins with the competence of the people in charge of it. Management's operating style will have a determinable impact on the effectiveness of various policies. An autocratic style in which a few key officers tightly control operations will result in an environment different from that of a decentralized organization in which departments have more freedom to make decisions. Personnel policies and practices form another factor in the internal control of a business. An appropriate system for hiring competent employees and firing incompetent ones is crucial to an efficient operation. After all, no internal control system will work very well if employees who are dishonest or poorly trained are on the payroll. On the other hand, too few people doing too many tasks defeats the purpose of an internal control system. Finally, the effectiveness of internal control in a business is influenced by the board of directors, particularly its audit committee.

THE ACCOUNTING SYSTEM

An **accounting system** consists of all the methods and records used to accurately report an entity's transactions and to maintain accountability for its assets and liabilities. Regardless of the degree of computer automation, the use of a journal to record transactions is an integral part of all accounting systems. Refinements are sometimes made to the basic components of the system, depending on the company's needs. For example, most companies use specialized journals to record recurring transactions, such as sales of merchandise on credit.

An accounting system can be completely manual, fully computerized, or as is often the case, a mixture of the two. Internal controls are important to all businesses, regardless of the degree of automation of the accounting system. The system must be capable of handling both the volume and the complexity of transactions entered into by a business. Most businesses use computers because of the sheer volume of transactions. The computer is ideally suited to the task of processing large numbers of repetitive transactions efficiently and quickly.

Board of directors
Group composed of key officers of a corporation and outside members responsible for general oversight of the affairs of the entity.

Audit committee
Board of directors subset that acts as a direct contact between the stockholders and the independent accounting firm.

Real World Practice 6-2

Reading Foot Locker's Annual Report

Locate in Foot Locker's annual report, the auditors' report on internal control. Who wrote the report? To whom is the report addressed? What did the auditors conclude in their report?

Accounting system
Methods and records used to accurately report an entity's transactions and to maintain accountability for its assets and liabilities.

The cost of computing has dropped so substantially that virtually every business can now afford a system. Today, some computer software programs that are designed for home-based businesses cost under $100 and are meant to run on machines that cost less than $1,000. Inexpensive software programs that categorize expenses and print checks, produce financial statements, and analyze financial ratios are available.

INTERNAL CONTROL PROCEDURES

Management establishes policies and procedures on a number of different levels to ensure that corporate objectives will be met. Some procedures are formalized in writing. Others may not be written but are just as important. Certain **administrative controls** within a company are more concerned with the efficient operation of the business and adherence to managerial policies than with the accurate reporting of financial information. For example, a company policy that requires all prospective employees to be interviewed by the personnel department is an administrative control. Other **accounting controls** primarily concern safeguarding assets and ensuring the reliability of the financial statements. We now turn to a discussion of some of the most important internal control procedures:

Proper authorizations
Segregation of duties
Independent verification
Safeguarding assets and records
Independent review and appraisal
The design and use of business documents

Proper Authorizations   Management grants specific departments the authority to perform various activities. Along with the *authority* goes *responsibility*. Most large organizations give the authority to hire new employees to the personnel department. Management authorizes the purchasing department to order goods and services for the company and the credit department to establish specific policies for granting credit to customers. By specifically authorizing certain individuals to carry out specific tasks for the business, management is able to hold these same people responsible for the outcome of their actions.

The authorizations for some transactions are general in nature; others are specific. For example, a cashier authorizes the sale of a book in a bookstore by ringing up the transaction (a general authorization). It is likely, however, that the bookstore manager's approval is required before a book can be returned (a specific authorization).

Segregation of Duties   What might happen if one employee is given the authority both to prepare checks and to sign them? What could happen if a single employee is allowed to order inventory and receive it from the shipper? Or what if the cashier at a checkout stand also records the daily receipts in the journal? If the employee in each of these situations is honest and never makes mistakes, nothing bad will happen. However, if the employee is dishonest or makes human errors, the company can experience losses. These situations all point to the need for the segregation of duties, which is one of the most fundamental of all internal control procedures. Without segregation of duties, an employee is able not only to perpetrate a fraud but also to conceal it. A good system of internal control requires that the *physical custody* of assets be separated from the *accounting* for those same assets.

Like most internal control principles, the concept of segregation of duties is an ideal that is not always completely attainable. For example, many smaller businesses simply do not have adequate personnel to achieve complete segregation of key functions. In certain instances, these businesses need to rely on the direct involvement of the owners in the business and on independent verification.

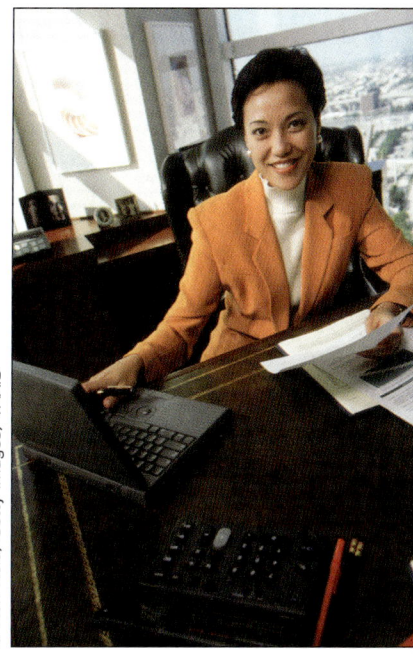

© Ken Reid/Getty Images/TAXIS

This woman is using the paper source document in her hand as a reference for entering data into the accounting system. For proper internal control, should she be able to order inventory and receive it and then enter the information into the system? Is she authorized to make journal entries? If so, does her laptop have safeguards against access by unauthorized personnel? These and other internal control procedures are part of the control environment within every company.

LO4 Describe the basic internal control procedures.

Administrative controls
Procedures concerned with efficient operation of the business and adherence to managerial policies.

Accounting controls
Procedures concerned with safeguarding the assets or the reliability of the financial statements.

Independent Verification   Related to the principle of segregation of duties is the idea of independent verification. The work of one department should act as a check on the work of another. For example, the physical count of the inventory in a perpetual inventory system provides such a check. The accounting department maintains the general ledger card for inventory and updates it as sales and purchases are made. The physical count of the inventory by an independent department acts as the check on the work of the accounting department. As another example, consider the bank reconciliation that we saw earlier in the chapter (Exhibit 6-3) as a control device. The reconciliation of a company's bank account with the bank statement by someone not responsible for either the physical custody of cash or the cash records acts as an independent check on the work of these parties.

Safeguarding Assets and Records   Adequate safeguards must be in place to protect assets and the accounting records from losses of various kinds. Cash registers, safes, and lockboxes are important safeguards for cash. Secured storage areas with limited access are essential for the safekeeping of inventory. Protection of the accounting records against misuse is equally important. For example, access to a computerized accounting record should be limited to those employees authorized to prepare journal entries. This can be done with the use of a personal identification number and a password to access the system.

Independent Review and Appraisal   A well-designed system of internal control provides for periodic review and appraisal of the accounting system as well as the people operating it. The group primarily responsible for review and appraisal of the system is the **internal audit staff**. Most large corporations today have a full-time staff of internal auditors. They provide management with periodic reports on the effectiveness of the control system and the efficiency of operations.

Internal audit staff Department responsible for monitoring and evaluating the internal control system.

The primary concern of the independent public accountants, or external auditors, is whether or not the financial statements have been presented fairly. Internal auditors focus more on the efficiency with which the organization is run. They are responsible for periodically reviewing both accounting and administrative controls. The internal audit staff also helps to ensure that the company's policies and procedures are followed.

The Design and Use of Business Documents   *Business documents* are the crucial link between economic transactions entered into by an entity and the accounting record of these events. They are often called *source documents*. Many of these are generated by the computer, but a few may be completed manually. The source document for the recognition of the expense of an employee's wages is the time card. The source documents for a sale include the sales order, the sales invoice, and the related shipping document. Business documents must be designed so that they capture all relevant information about an economic event. They are also designed to ensure that related transactions are properly classified.

Business documents themselves must be properly controlled. For example, a key feature for documents is a *sequential numbering system* just like you have for your personal checks. This system results in a complete accounting for all documents in the series and negates the opportunity for an employee to misdirect one. Another key feature of well-designed business documents is the use of *multiple copies*. The various departments involved in a particular activity, such as sales or purchasing, are kept informed of the status of outstanding orders through the use of copies of documents.

LIMITATIONS ON INTERNAL CONTROL

Internal control is a relative term. No system of internal control is totally foolproof. An entity's size affects the degree of control that it can obtain. In general, large organizations are able to devote a substantial amount of resources to safeguarding assets and records because these companies have the assets to justify the cost. Because the installation and maintenance of controls can be costly, an internal audit staff is a luxury that many small businesses cannot afford. The mere segregation of duties can result in added costs if two employees must be involved in a task previously performed by only one.

Segregation of duties can be effective in preventing collusion, but no system of internal control can ensure that it will not happen. It does no good to have one employee count the cash at the end of the day and another to record it if the two act in concert to steal from the company. Rotation of duties can help to lessen the likelihood for problems of this sort. An employee is less likely to collude with someone to steal if the assignment is a temporary one. Another control feature, a system of authorizations, is meaningless if management continually overrides it. Management must believe in a system of internal control enough to support it.

Intentional acts to misappropriate company assets are not the only problem. All sorts of human errors can weaken a system of internal control. Misunderstood instructions, carelessness, fatigue, and distraction can all lead to errors. A well-designed system of internal control should result in the best-possible people being hired to perform the various tasks, but no one is perfect.

⏱ *2 minute review*

1. Explain why an internal control system is important to the operation of a company that sells a product.

2. Explain the difference between administrative controls and accounting controls.

3. Explain how the concept of segregation of duties involves an evaluation of costs versus benefits.

Answers

1. An effective system of internal control is critical to protecting a company's investment in three of its major assets: cash, accounts receivable, and inventory. Without an effective system, these assets are subject to misuse.

2. Administrative controls are concerned with the efficient operation of a business and adherence to managerial policies. Alternatively, accounting controls deal with safeguarding assets and ensuring the reliability of the financial statements.

3. Involving more than one employee in a specific function reduces the likelihood of theft or other misuse of company assets. However, all businesses must decide whether the benefit of segregation of duties outweighs the additional cost of involving more than one employee in a specific function such as the preparation and distribution of the payroll.

Computerized Business Documents and Internal Control

Specific internal controls are necessary to control cash receipts and cash disbursements in a merchandising company such as Finish Line. In addition to the separation of the custodianship of cash from the recording of it in the accounts, two other fundamental principles apply to its control. First, all cash receipts should be deposited *intact* in the bank on a *daily* basis. *Intact* means that no disbursements should be made from the cash received from customers. The second basic principle is related to the first: all cash disbursements should be made by check. The use of sequentially numbered checks results in a clear record of all disbursements. The only exception to this rule is the use of a petty cash fund to make cash disbursements for minor expenditures such as postage stamps and repairs.

LO5 Describe the various documents used in recording purchases and their role in controlling cash disbursements.

CONTROL OVER CASH RECEIPTS

Most merchandisers receive checks and currency from customers in two distinct ways: (1) cash received over the counter, that is, from cash sales and (2) cash received in the mail, that is, cash collections from credit sales. Each of these types of cash receipts poses its own particular control problems.

Cash Received over the Counter   Several control mechanisms are used to handle these cash payments. First, cash registers allow the customer to see the display, which deters the salesclerk from ringing up a sale for less than the amount received from the customer and pocketing the difference. A locked-in cash register tape is another control feature. At various times during the day, an employee other than the clerk unlocks the register, removes the tape, and forwards it to the accounting department. At the end of the shift, the salesclerk remits the coin and currency from the register to a central cashier. Any difference between the amount of cash remitted to the cashier and the amount on the tape submitted to the accounting department is investigated.

Finally, prenumbered customer receipts, prepared in duplicate, are a useful control mechanism. The customer is given a copy, and the salesclerk retains another. The salesclerk is accountable for all numbers in a specific series of receipts and must be able to explain any differences between the amount of cash remitted to the cashier and the amount collected per the receipts.

Cash Received in the Mail   Most customers send checks rather than currency through the mail. Any form of cash received in the mail from customers should be applied to their account balances. The customer wants assurance that the account is appropriately reduced for the amount of the payment. The company must be assured that all cash received is deposited in the bank and that the account receivable is reduced accordingly.

To achieve a reasonable degree of control, two employees should be present when the mail is opened.[1] The first employee opens the mail in the presence of the second employee, counts the money received, and prepares a control list of the amount received on that particular day. The list is often called a *prelist* and is prepared in triplicate. The second employee takes the original to the cashier along with the total cash received on that day. The cashier is the person who makes the bank deposit. One copy of the prelist is forwarded to the accounting department to be used as the basis for recording the increase in Cash and the decrease in Accounts Receivable. The other copy is retained by one of the two persons opening the mail. A comparison of the prelist to the bank deposit slip is a timely way to detect receipts that do not make it to the bank. Because the two employees acting in concert could circumvent the control process, rotation of duties is important.

Monthly customer statements act as an additional control device for customer payments received in the mail. Assume that the two employees responsible for opening the mail and remitting checks to the cashier decide to pocket a check received from a customer. Checks made payable to a company *can* be stolen and cashed. The customer provides the control element. Because the check is not remitted to the cashier, the accounting department will not be notified to reduce the customer's account for the payment. The monthly statement, however, should alert the customer to the problem. The amount the customer thought was owed will be smaller than the balance due on the statement. At this point, the customer should ask the company to investigate the discrepancy. As evidence of its payment on account, the customer will be able to point to a canceled check—which was cashed by the unscrupulous employees.

Finally, keep in mind that the use of customer statements as a control device will be effective only if the employees responsible for the custody of cash received

---

1 In some companies, this control procedure may be omitted because of the cost of having two employees present when the mail is opened.

through the mail, for record keeping, and for authorization of adjustments to customers' accounts are not allowed to prepare and mail statements to customers. Employees allowed to do so are in a position to alter customers' statements.

Cash Discrepancies   Discrepancies occur occasionally due to theft by dishonest employees and to human error. For example, if a salesclerk either intentionally or unintentionally gives the wrong amount of change, the amount remitted to the cashier will not agree with the cash register tape. Any material differences should be investigated. Of particular significance are *recurring* differences between the amount remitted by any one cashier and the amount on the cash register tape.

THE ROLE OF COMPUTERIZED BUSINESS DOCUMENTS IN CONTROLLING CASH DISBURSEMENTS

A company makes cash payments for a variety of purposes: to purchase merchandise, supplies, plant, and equipment; to pay operating expenditures; and to cover payroll expenses, to name a few. We will concentrate on the disbursement of cash to purchase goods for resale, focusing particularly on the role of business documents in the process. Merchandising companies rely on a smooth and orderly inflow of quality goods for resale to customers. It is imperative that suppliers be paid on time so that they will continue to make goods available.

Business documents play a vital role in the purchasing function. The example that follows begins with a requisition for merchandise by the shoe department of Mickey's Marathon Sports. The example continues through the receipt of the goods and the eventual payment to the supplier. The entire process is summarized in Exhibit 6-6. You will want to refer to this exhibit throughout the remainder of this section.

Purchase Requisition   The shoe department at Mickey's Marathon Sports weekly reviews its stock to determine if any items need replenishing. On the basis of its needs, the supervisor of the shoe department fills out the **purchase requisition form** shown in Exhibit 6-7 on page 289. The form indicates the supplier or vendor, Fleet Foot.

The purchasing department has the responsibility for making the final decision on a vendor. Giving the purchasing department this responsibility means that it is held accountable for acquiring the goods at the lowest price, given certain standards for merchandise quality. Mickey's assigns a separate item number to each of the thousands of individual items of merchandise it stocks. Note that the requisition also indicates the vendor's number for each item. The unit of measure for each item is indicated in the quantity column. For example, "24 PR" means 24 pairs of shoes. The original and a copy of the purchase requisition are sent to the purchasing department. The shoe department keeps one copy for its records.

Purchase requisition form
Form a department uses to initiate a request to order merchandise.

Purchase Order   Like many other businesses, Mickey's uses a computerized purchasing system. Most companies either have purchased software or have developed software internally to perform such functions as purchasing, sales, and payroll. The software is capable not only of increasing the speed and accuracy of the process but also of generating the necessary documents.

A computer-generated **purchase order** is shown in Exhibit 6-8. Purchase orders are usually prenumbered; a company should periodically investigate any missing numbers. The purchasing department uses its copy of the purchase requisition as a basis for preparing the purchase order. An employee in the purchasing department keys in the relevant information from the purchase requisition and adds the unit cost for each item gathered from the vendor's price guide. The software program generates the purchase order as shown in Exhibit 6-8. You should trace all of the information for at least one of the three items ordered from the purchase requisition to the purchase order.

Purchase order
Form sent by the purchasing department to the supplier.

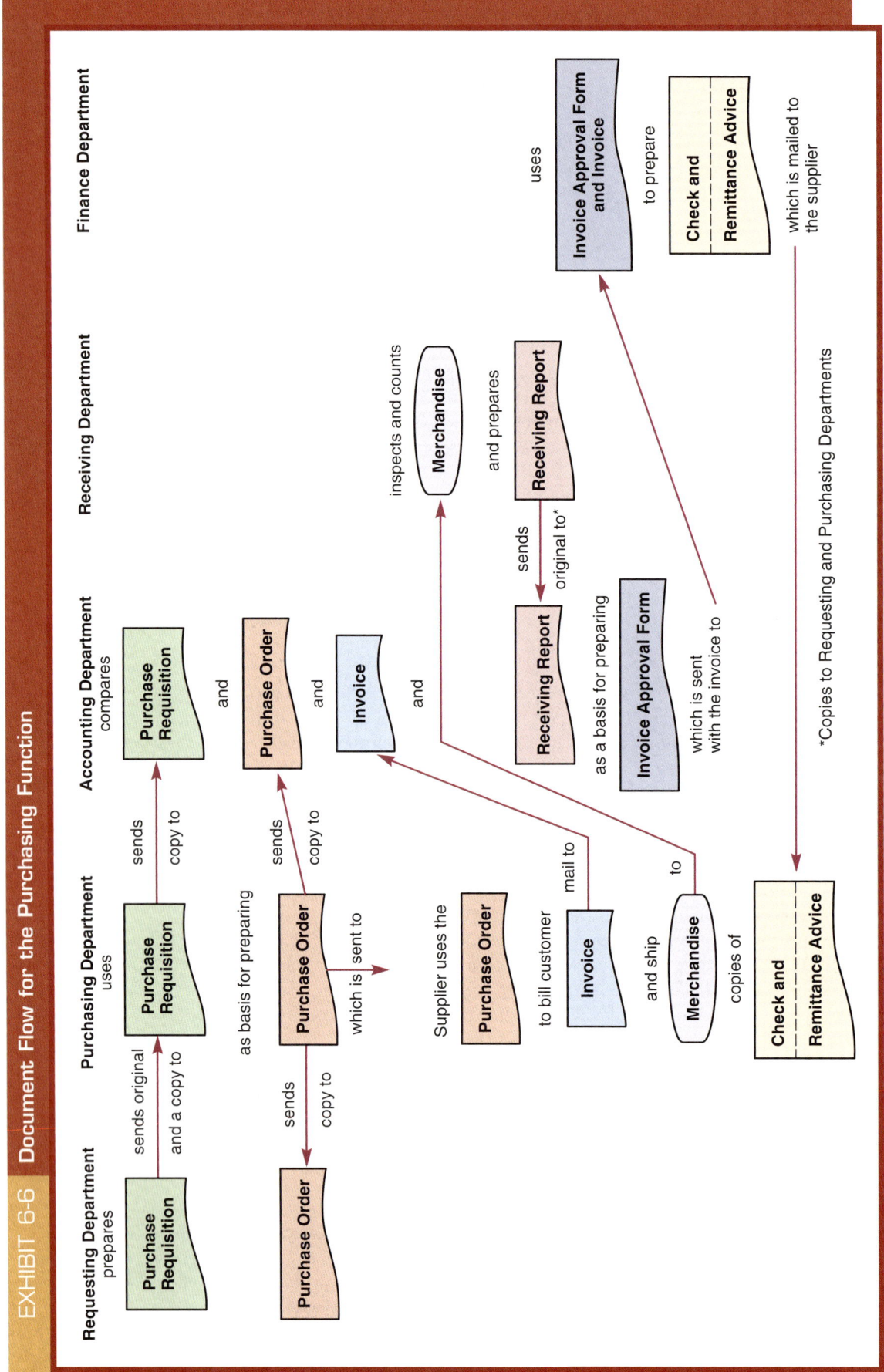

EXHIBIT 6-6 Document Flow for the Purchasing Function

EXHIBIT 6-7 Purchase Requisition

Mickey's Marathon Sports
502 Dodge St.
Chicago, IL 66666

PURCHASE REQUISITION

Date 5/28/07   **PR 75638**

Preferred vendor Fleet Foot

Date needed by 6/5/07

The following items are requested for   weekly dept. order

Item No.	Quantity	Description/Vendor No.
314627	24 PR	Sprinter/5265
323515	12 PR	Blazer/7512
323682	6 PR	Enduros/1580

Requested by *Joe Smith*   **Department** Shoe department

The system generates the original purchase order and three copies. As indicated in Exhibit 6-6, the original is sent to the supplier after a supervisor in the purchasing department approves it. One copy is sent to the accounting department, where it will be matched with the original requisition. A second copy is sent to the shoe department as confirmation that its request for the items has been attended

EXHIBIT 6-8 Computer-Generated Purchase Order

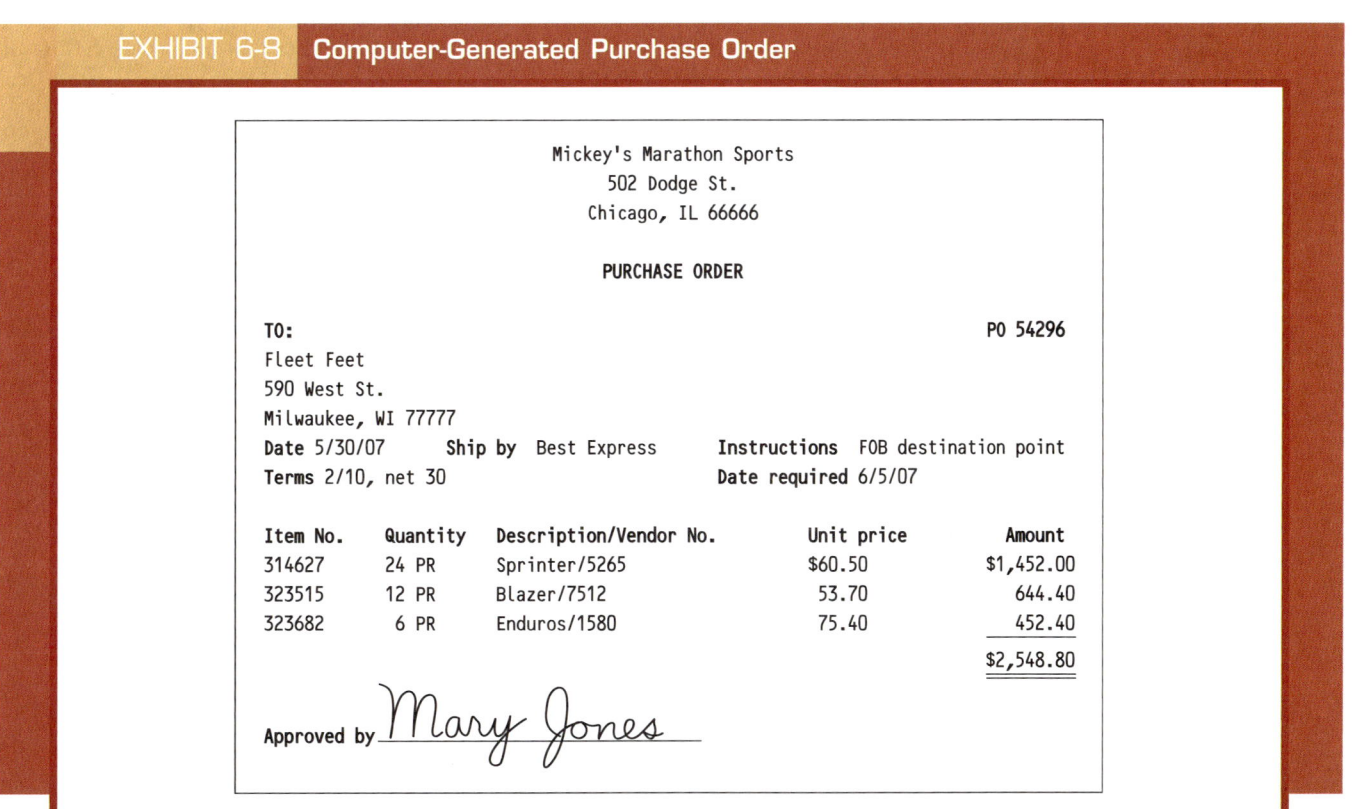

Mickey's Marathon Sports
502 Dodge St.
Chicago, IL 66666

PURCHASE ORDER

TO: PO 54296
Fleet Feet
590 West St.
Milwaukee, WI 77777

Date 5/30/07   Ship by Best Express   Instructions FOB destination point
Terms 2/10, net 30   Date required 6/5/07

Item No.	Quantity	Description/Vendor No.	Unit price	Amount
314627	24 PR	Sprinter/5265	$60.50	$1,452.00
323515	12 PR	Blazer/7512	53.70	644.40
323682	6 PR	Enduros/1580	75.40	452.40
				$2,548.80

Approved by *Mary Jones*

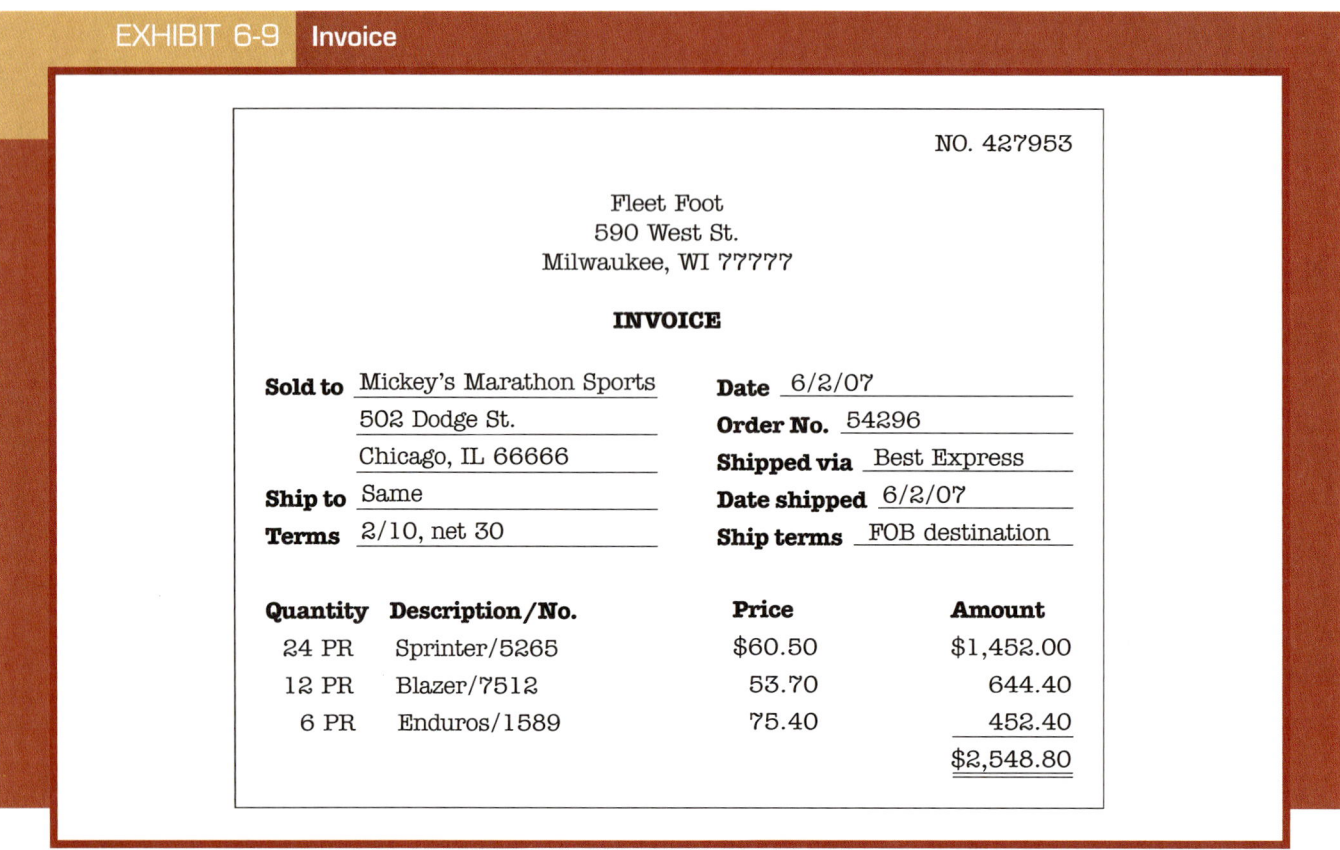

EXHIBIT 6-9   Invoice

NO. 427953

Fleet Foot
590 West St.
Milwaukee, WI 77777

INVOICE

Sold to Mickey's Marathon Sports   **Date** 6/2/07
502 Dodge St.   **Order No.** 54296
Chicago, IL 66666   **Shipped via** Best Express
Ship to Same   **Date shipped** 6/2/07
Terms 2/10, net 30   **Ship terms** FOB destination

Quantity	Description/No.	Price	Amount
24 PR	Sprinter/5265	$60.50	$1,452.00
12 PR	Blazer/7512	53.70	644.40
6 PR	Enduros/1589	75.40	452.40
			$2,548.80

to by the purchasing department. The purchasing department keeps the third copy for its records.

A purchase order is not the basis for recording a purchase and a liability. Legally, the order is merely an offer by the company to purchase goods from the supplier. Technically, the receipt of goods from the supplier is the basis for the purchaser's recognition of a liability. As a matter of practice, however, most companies record the payable upon receipt of the invoice.

Invoice   When Fleet Foot ships the merchandise, it also mails an invoice to Mickey's, requesting payment according to the agreed-upon terms, in this case 2/10, net 30. Recall from Chapter 5 that this means the customer (Mickey's) receives a 2% discount by paying within ten days of purchase; if not, the full amount is due within thirty days of purchase. The **invoice** may be mailed separately or included with the shipment of merchandise. Fleet Foot, the seller, calls this document a *sales invoice;* it is the basis for recording a sale and an account receivable. Mickey's, the buyer, calls the same document a *purchase invoice,* which is the basis for recording a purchase and an account payable. The invoice that Fleet Foot sent to Mickey's accounting department is shown in Exhibit 6-9.

Receiving Report   The accounting department receives the invoice for the three items ordered. Within a few days before or after the receipt of the invoice, the merchandise arrives at Mickey's warehouse. As soon as the items are unpacked, the receiving department inspects and counts them. The same software program that generated the purchase order also generates a receiving report, as shown in Exhibit 6-10.

Mickey's uses a **blind receiving report**. The column for the quantity received is left blank and is filled in by the receiving department. Rather than being able simply to indicate that the number ordered was received, an employee must count the pairs of shoes to determine that the number ordered is actually received. You should trace all of the relevant information for one of the three items ordered from the purchase order to the receiving report. The accounting system generates an

Invoice
Form sent by the seller to the buyer as evidence of a sale.

Blind receiving report
Form used by the receiving department to account for the quantity and condition of merchandise received from a supplier.

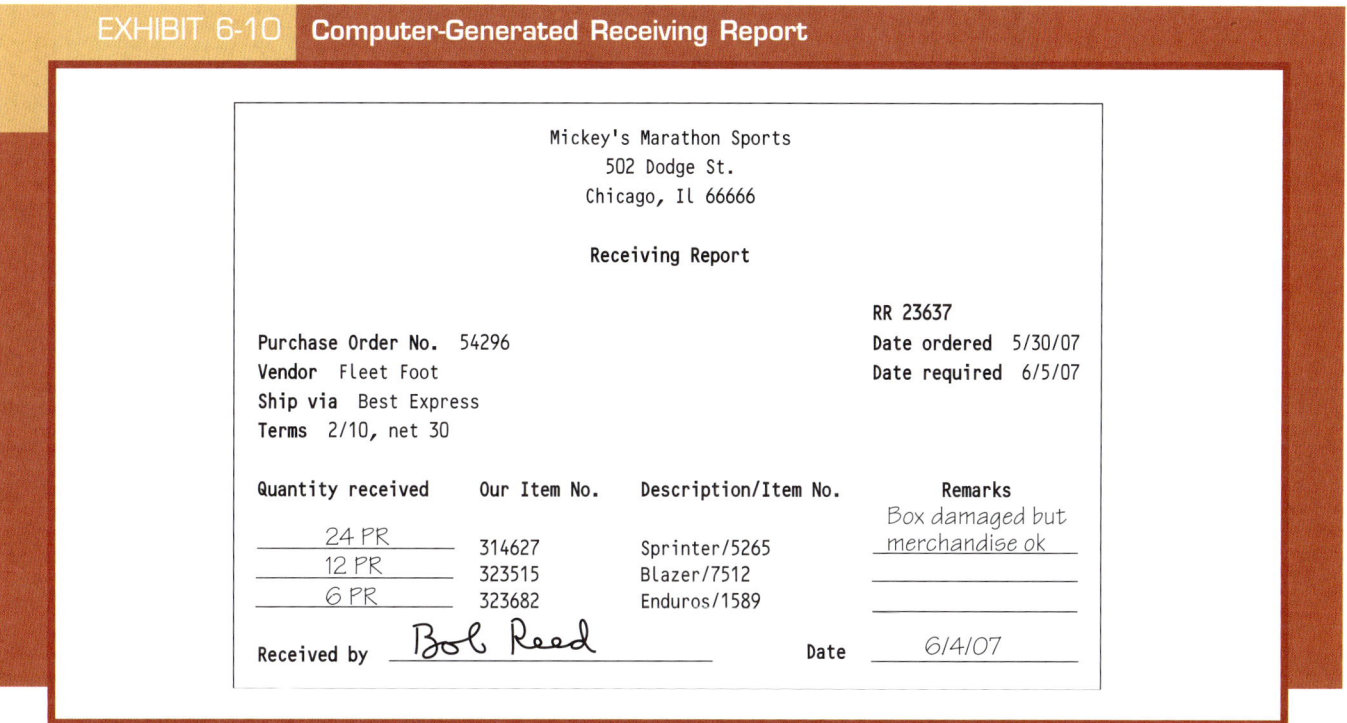

EXHIBIT 6-10 **Computer-Generated Receiving Report**

Mickey's Marathon Sports
502 Dodge St.
Chicago, Il 66666

Receiving Report

RR 23637

Purchase Order No. 54296
Vendor Fleet Foot
Ship via Best Express
Terms 2/10, net 30

Date ordered 5/30/07
Date required 6/5/07

Quantity received	Our Item No.	Description/Item No.	Remarks
24 PR	314627	Sprinter/5265	Box damaged but merchandise ok
12 PR	323515	Blazer/7512	
6 PR	323682	Enduros/1589	

Received by Bob Reed **Date** 6/4/07

original receiving report and three copies. The receiving department keeps one copy for its records and sends the original to the accounting department. One copy is sent to the purchasing department to be matched with the purchase order, and the other copy is sent to the shoe department as verification that the items it originally requested have been received.

Invoice Approval Form At this point, Mickey's accounting department has copies of the purchase requisition from the shoe department, the purchase order from the purchasing department, the invoice from the supplier, and the receiving report from the warehouse. The accounting department uses an **invoice approval form** to document the accuracy of the information on each of these other forms. The invoice approval form for Mickey's Marathon Sports is shown in Exhibit 6-11.

The invoice is compared to the purchase requisition to ensure that the company is billed for goods that it requested. A comparison of the invoice with the purchase order ensures that the goods were in fact ordered. Finally, the receiving report is compared with the invoice to verify that all goods it is being billed for were received. An accounting department employee must also verify the mathematical accuracy of the amounts that appear on the invoice. The date the invoice must be paid to take advantage of the discount is noted so that the finance department will be sure to send the check by this date. At this point, the accounting department prepares the journal entry to increase the Inventory and Accounts Payable accounts. The invoice approval form and the invoice are then sent to the finance department. Some businesses call the invoice approval form a *voucher;* it is used for all expenditures, not just for purchases of merchandise. Finally, it is worth noting that some businesses do not use a separate invoice approval form but simply note approval directly on the invoice itself.

Check with Remittance Advice Mickey's finance department is responsible for issuing checks. This results from the need to segregate custody of cash (the signed check) from record keeping (the updating of the ledger). On receipt of the invoice approval form from the accounting department, a clerk in the finance department types a check with a remittance advice attached, as shown in Exhibit 6-12.[2]

Invoice approval form
Form the accounting department uses before making payment to document the accuracy of all the information about a purchase. *Alternate term: Voucher*

---

2 In some companies, an employee in the accounting department prepares checks and sends them to the finance department for review and signature. Also, many companies use computer-generated checks, rather than manually typed ones.

EXHIBIT 6-11	Invoice Approval Form

Mickey's Marathon Sports
502 Dodge St.
Chicago, IL 66666

Invoice Approval Form

	No.	**Check**
Purchase Requisition	PR 75638	✓
Purchase Order	PO 54296	✓
Receiving Report	RR 23637	✓

Invoice:

No.	427953
Date	6/2/07
Price	✓
Extensions	✓
Footings	✓

Last Day to Pay for Discount 6/12/07

Approved for Payment by *Alice Johnson*

EXHIBIT 6-12	Check with Remittance Advice

3690

Mickey's Marathon Sports
502 Dodge St.
Chicago, IL 66666

June 12 20 07

PAY TO THE
ORDER OF ____ Fleet Foot ____ $2,497.82

Two thousand four hundred ninety seven and 82/100   DOLLARS

Second National Bank
Missoula, MT
3690 035932 9321

John B. Martin

Purchase Order No.	Invoice No.	Invoice Date	Description	Amount
PO 54296	427953	6/2/07	24 PR Sprinter	$1,452.00
			12 PR Blazer	644.40
			6 PR Enduros	452.40
			Total	$2,548.80
			Less: 2% discount	50.98
			Net remitted	$2,497.82

Before the check is signed, the documents referred to on the invoice approval form are reviewed and canceled to prevent reuse. The clerk then forwards the check to one of the company officers authorized to sign checks. According to one of Mickey's internal control policies, only the treasurer and the assistant treasurer are authorized to sign checks. Both officers must sign check amounts above a specified dollar limit. To maintain separation of duties, the finance department should mail the check. The remittance advice informs the supplier as to the nature of the payment and is torn off by the supplier before cashing the check.

STUDY HIGHLIGHTS

Identify and describe the various forms of cash reported on a balance sheet (p. 272).

LO1

- Cash can take many forms; however, the key attribute is that the asset is readily available to pay debts.
  - Cash equivalents are those investments that are readily convertible to a known amount of cash. "Readily" has been interpreted to be three months or less.

Show that you understand various techniques that companies use to control cash (p. 273).

LO2

- The liquidity of cash makes controls over it very important to have in place.
  - Cash management—managing the need to have on hand enough cash to ensure cash flow needs, but not so much that excess funds earn little return and may be more vulnerable to misappropriation.
  - Bank reconciliations use third-party documents (bank statement) to reconcile differences between the amount in the bank and on the books. Done by an independent party, bank reconciliations are effective control procedures.
  - Petty cash funds are an effective way to minimize access to large cash accounts in order to pay for relatively small expenditures.

Explain the importance of internal control to a business and the significance of the Sarbanes-Oxley Act of 2002 (p. 279).

LO3

- The Sarbanes-Oxley Act of 2002 required publicly traded companies to improve the documentation and functioning of their internal controls.
  - Management must now render an opinion on the efficiency of the internal control system in place at its company. A strong control environment is a must for companies.
  - Auditors must also increase their documentation and understanding of the internal controls of their clients.
  - Significant amounts of resources have been devoted to comply with the provisions of Sarbanes-Oxley.

Describe the basic internal control procedures (p. 283).

LO4

- Control procedures are actions taken by company personnel to make sure policies set forth by management are followed.
- Important accounting controls are concerned with safeguarding assets and producing accurate and timely financial statements. They include:
  - Proper authorizations—only certain personnel may authorize transactions.
  - Segregation of duties—physical custody of assets must not be combined with the ability to account for those assets.
  - Independent verification—for example, an inventory count.
  - Safeguarding assets and records—both must be adequately protected.
  - Independent review and appraisal—primarily done by internal audit.
  - Design and use of business documents—source document control.

HIGHLIGHTS

LO5 **Describe the various documents used in recording purchases and their role in controlling cash disbursement (p. 285).**

- The documents used to record purchase transactions are instrumental in controlling both cash and inventory.
- The document flow diagram in Exhibit 6-6 provides an excellent summary of documents in the purchasing process. Some of the key documents include:
  - Purchase order
  - Vendor invoice
  - Receiving report
  - Check

ACCOUNTS HIGHLIGHTED

Account Titles	Where It Appears	In What Section	Page Number
Cash and Cash Equivalents	Balance Sheet	Current Assets	272
Petty Cash Fund	Balance Sheet	Current Assets	278

KEY TERMS QUIZ

Read each definition below and then write the number of the definition in the blank beside the appropriate term it defines. The quiz solutions appear at the end of the chapter.

_____ Cash equivalent

_____ Bank statement

_____ Outstanding check

_____ Deposit in transit

_____ Bank reconciliation

_____ Credit memoranda

_____ Debit memoranda

_____ Petty cash fund

_____ Internal control system

_____ Sarbanes-Oxley Act

_____ Internal control report

_____ Public Company Accounting Oversight Board

_____ Board of directors

_____ Audit committee

_____ Accounting system

_____ Administrative controls

_____ Accounting controls

_____ Internal audit staff

_____ Purchase requisition form

_____ Purchase order

_____ Invoice

_____ Blind receiving report

_____ Invoice approval form

1. The form sent by the seller to the buyer as evidence of a sale.

2. The group composed of key officers of a corporation and outside members responsible for the general oversight of the affairs of the entity.

3. Policies and procedures necessary to ensure the safeguarding of an entity's assets, the reliability of its accounting records, and the accomplishment of overall company objectives.

4. Procedures concerned with safeguarding the assets or the reliability of the financial statements.

5. The form a department uses to initiate a request to order merchandise.

6. A form the accounting department uses before making payment to document the accuracy of all the information about a purchase.

7. A form used by the accountant to reconcile or resolve any differences between the balance shown on the bank statement for a particular account with the balance shown in the accounting records.

8. An investment that is readily convertible to a known amount of cash and has an original maturity to the investor of three months or less.

9. Deductions on a bank statement for such items as NSF checks and various service charges.

10. A check written by a company but not yet presented to the bank for payment.

11. A detailed list, prepared by the bank, of all the activity for a particular account during the month.

12. A report required by Section 404 of SOX, to be included in a company's annual report, in which management assesses the effectiveness of the internal control structure.

13. A deposit recorded on the books but not yet reflected on the bank statement.

14. The methods and records used to accurately report an entity's transactions and to maintain accountability for its assets and liabilities.

15. Additions on a bank statement for such items as interest paid on the account and notes collected by the bank.

16. The board of directors subset that acts as a direct contact between the stockholders and the independent accounting firm.

17. Money kept on hand for making minor disbursements in coin and currency rather than by writing checks.

18. The five-member body created by the Sarbanes-Oxley Act that was given the authority to set auditing standards in the United States.

19. A form used by the receiving department to account for the quantity and condition of merchandise received from a supplier.

20. Procedures concerned with efficient operation of the business and adherence to managerial policies.

21. The form sent by the purchasing department to the supplier.

22. An act of Congress in 2002 intended to bring reform to corporate accountability and stewardship in the wake of a number of major corporate scandals.

23. Department responsible for monitoring and evaluating the internal control system.

ALTERNATE TERMS

Invoice Purchase invoice, sales invoice   **Invoice approval form** Voucher

WARMUP EXERCISES & SOLUTIONS

Warmup Exercise 6-1 Composition of Cash   **LO1**

For the following items, indicate whether each should be included (I) or excluded (E) from the line item titled Cash and cash equivalents on the balance sheet.

_____ 1. Certificate of deposit maturing in 60 days
_____ 2. Checking account
_____ 3. Certificate of deposit maturing in six months
_____ 4. Savings account
_____ 5. Shares of GM stock
_____ 6. Petty cash
_____ 7. Corporate bonds maturing in 30 days
_____ 8. Certified check

Key to the Solution Recall the key to classification as part of cash: the amount must be readily available to pay debts, and cash equivalents must have an original maturity to the investor of three months or less.

REVIEW

LO4 **Warmup Exercise 6-2** Internal Control

List the internal control procedures discussed in the text.

Key to the Solution Refer to the section in the chapter that discusses internal control procedures.

SOLUTIONS TO WARMUP EXERCISES

Warmup Exercise 6-1
1. I 2. I 3. E 4. I 5. E 6. I 7. E 8. I

Warmup Exercise 6-2
1. Proper authorizations
2. Segregation of duties
3. Independent verification
4. Safeguarding assets and records
5. Independent review and appraisal
6. Design and use of business documents

REVIEW PROBLEM & SOLUTION

The following information is available for Woodbury Corp. on June 30, 2007:

a. The balance in cash as reported on the June 30, 2007, bank statement is $5,654.98.
b. Woodbury made a deposit of $865.00 on June 30 that is not included on the bank statement.
c. A comparison between the canceled checks returned with the bank statement and Woodbury's records indicated that two checks had not yet been returned to the bank for payment. The amounts of the two checks were $236.77 and $116.80.
d. The Cash account on the company's books reported a balance on June 30 of $4,165.66.
e. Woodbury rents some excess storage space in one of its warehouses and the tenant pays its monthly rent directly to the bank for deposit in Woodbury's account. The bank statement indicates that a deposit of $1,500.00 was made during the month of June.
f. Interest earned on the checking account and added to Woodbury's account during June was $11.75.
g. Bank services charges were $15.00 for the month of June as reported on the bank statement.
h. A comparison between the checks returned with the bank statement and the company's records revealed that a check written by the company in the amount of $56.00 was recorded by the company erroneously as a check for $560.00.

Required
Prepare a bank reconciliation for the month of June in good form.

SOLUTION TO REVIEW PROBLEM

Woodbury Corp.
Bank Reconciliation
June 30, 2007

Balance per bank statement, June 30		$5,654.98
Add: Deposit in transit		865.00
Deduct: Outstanding checks:		
	$ 236.77	
	116.80	(353.57)
Adjusted balance, June 30		$6,166.41
Balance per books, June 30		$4,165.66
Add: Tenant's rent collected by bank	$1,500.00	
Interest earned on checking account	11.75	
Error in recording check	504.00	2,015.75
Deduct: Bank service charges		(15.00)
Adjusted balance, June 30		$6,166.41

REVIEW

QUESTIONS

1. What is a cash equivalent? Why is it included with cash on the balance sheet?

2. Why does the purchase of an item classified as a cash equivalent *not* appear on the statement of cash flows as an investing activity?

3. A friend says to you: "I understand why it is important to deposit all receipts intact and not keep coin and currency sitting around the business. Beyond this control feature, however, I believe that a company should strive to keep the maximum amount possible in checking accounts to always be able to pay bills on time." How would you evaluate your friend's statement?

4. A friends says to you: "I'm confused. I have a memo included with my bank statement indicating a $20 service charge for printing new checks. If the bank is deducting this amount from my account, why do they call it a 'debit memorandum'? I thought a decrease in a cash account would be a credit, not a debit." How can you explain this?

5. Different formats for bank reconciliations are possible. What is the format for a bank reconciliation in which a service charge for a lockbox is *added* to the balance per the bank statement? Explain your answer.

6. What circumstances led to the passage of the Sarbanes-Oxley Act in 2002?

7. What is the typical composition of a board of directors of a publicly held corporation?

8. An order clerk fills out a purchase requisition for an expensive item of inventory and the receiving report when the merchandise arrives. The clerk takes the inventory home and then sends the invoice to the accounting department so that the supplier will be paid. What basic internal control procedure could have prevented this misuse of company assets?

9. What are some of the limitations on a company's effective system of internal control?

10. What two basic procedures are essential to an effective system of internal control over cash?

11. How would you evaluate the following statement? "The only reason a company positions its cash register so that customers can see the display is so customers feel comfortable they are being charged the correct amount for the purchase."

12. Which document, a purchase order or an invoice, is the basis for recording a purchase and a corresponding liability? Explain your answer.

13. What is a blind receiving report and how does it act as a control device?

14. What is the purpose of comparing a purchase invoice with a purchase order? Of comparing a receiving report with a purchase invoice?

EXERCISES

LO1

Exercise 6-1 Cash Equivalents

Systematic Enterprises invested its excess cash in the following instruments during December 2007:

Certificate of deposit, due January 31, 2010	$ 75,000
Certificate of deposit, due March 30, 2008	150,000
Commercial paper, original maturity date February 28, 2008	125,000
Deposit into a money market fund	25,000
Investment in stock	65,000
90-day Treasury bills	100,000
Treasury note, due December 1, 2037	500,000

Required

Determine the amount of cash equivalents which should be combined with cash on the company's balance sheet at December 31, 2007, and for purposes of preparing a statement of cash flows for the year ended December 31, 2007.

LO2

Exercise 6-2 Items on a Bank Reconciliation

Assume that a company is preparing a bank reconciliation for the month of June. It reconciles the bank balance and the book balance to the correct balance. For each of the following items, indicate whether the item is an addition to the bank balance (A-Bank), an addition to the book balance (A-Book), a deduction from the bank balance (D-Bank), a deduction from the book balance (D-Book), or would not appear on the June reconciliation (NA).

_____ 1. Check written in June but not yet returned to the bank for payment

_____ 2. Customer's NSF check

HOMEWORK

_____ 3. Customer's check written in the amount of $54 but recorded on the books in the amount of $45*

_____ 4. Service charge for new checks

_____ 5. Principal and interest on a customer's note collected for the company by the bank

_____ 6. Customer's check deposited on June 30 but not reflected on the bank statement

_____ 7. Check written on the company's account, paid by the bank, and returned with the bank statement

_____ 8. Check written on the company's account for $123 but recorded on the books as $132*

_____ 9. Interest on the checking account for the month of June

*Answer in terms of the adjustment needed to correct for the error.

LO4 **Exercise 6-3** Internal Control

The university drama club is planning a raffle. The president overheard you talking about internal control to another accounting student, so she has asked you to set up some guidelines to "be sure" that all money collected for the raffle is accounted for by the club.

Required

1. Describe guidelines that the club should follow to achieve an acceptable level of internal control.
2. Comment on the president's request that she "be sure" all money is collected and recorded.

LO4 **Exercise 6-4** Segregation of Duties

The following tasks are performed by three employees, each of whom is capable of performing all of them. Do not concern yourself with the time required to perform the tasks but with the need to provide for segregation of duties. Assign the duties by using a check mark to indicate which employee should perform each task. Remember that you may assign any one of the tasks to any of the employees.

	Employee		
Task	Mary	Sue	John
Prepare invoices			
Mail invoices			
Pick up mail from post office			
Open mail, separate checks			
List checks on deposit slip in triplicate			
Post payment to customer's account			
Deposit checks			
Prepare monthly schedule of accounts receivable			
Reconcile bank statements			

MULTI-CONCEPT EXERCISE

LO1,2 **Exercise 6-5** Composition of Cash

Using a Y for yes or an N for no, indicate whether or not each of the following items should be included in cash and cash equivalents on the balance sheet. If an item should not be included in cash and cash equivalents, indicate where it should appear on the balance sheet.

_____ 1. Checking account at Third County Bank

_____ 2. Petty cash fund

_____ 3. Coin and currency

_____ 4. Postage stamps

_____ 5. An IOU from an employee

_____ 6. Savings account at the Ft. Worth Savings & Loan

_____ 7. A six-month CD

(continued)

_____ 8. Undeposited customer checks

_____ 9. A customer's check returned by the bank and marked NSF

_____ 10. Sixty-day U.S. Treasury bills

_____ 11. A cashier's check

PROBLEMS

LO2 **Problem 6-1** Bank Reconciliation

The following information is available to assist you in preparing a bank reconciliation for Calico Corners on May 31, 2007:

a. The balance on the May 31, 2007, bank statement is $8,432.11.

b. Not included on the bank statement is a $1,250.00 deposit made by Calico Corners late on May 31.

c. A comparison between the canceled checks returned with the bank statement and the company records indicated that the following checks are outstanding at May 31:

No. 123	$ 23.40
No. 127	145.00
No. 128	210.80
No. 130	67.32

d. The Cash account on the company's books shows a balance of $9,965.34.

e. The bank acts as a collection agency for interest earned on some municipal bonds held by Calico Corners. The May bank statement indicates interest of $465.00 earned during the month.

f. Interest earned on the checking account and added to Calico Corners' account during May was $54.60. Miscellaneous bank service charges amounted to $50.00.

g. A customer's NSF check in the amount of $166.00 was returned with the May bank statement.

h. A comparison between the deposits listed on the bank statement and the company's books revealed that a customer's check in the amount of $123.45 was recorded on the books during May but was never added to the company's account. The bank erroneously added the check to the account of Calico Closet, which has an account at the same bank.

i. The comparison of deposits per the bank statement with those per the books revealed that another customer's check in the amount of $101.10 was correctly added to the company's account. In recording the check on the company's books, however, the accountant erroneously increased the Cash account $1,011.00.

Required

1. Prepare a bank reconciliation in good form.

2. A friend says to you: "I don't know why companies bother to prepare bank reconciliations—it seems a waste of time. Why don't they just do like I do and adjust the Cash account for any difference between what the bank shows as a balance and what shows up in the books?" Explain to your friend *why* a bank reconciliation should be prepared as soon as a bank statement is received.

LO4 **Problem 6-2** Internal Control Procedures

You are opening a summer business, a chain of three drive-thru snow-cone stands. You have hired other college students to work and have purchased a cash register with locked-in tapes. You retain one key, and the other is available to the lead person on each shift.

Required

1. Write a list of the procedures for all employees to follow when ringing up sales and giving change.

2. Write a list of the procedures for the lead person to follow in closing out at the end of the day. Be as specific as you can so that employees will have few if any questions.

3. What is your main concern in the design of internal control for the snow-cone stands? How did you address that concern? Be specific.

LO5 **Problem 6-3** The Design of Internal Control Documents

Motel $49.99 has purchased a large warehouse to store all supplies used by housekeeping departments in the company's expanding chain of motels. In the past, each motel bought supplies from local distributors and paid for the supplies from cash receipts.

Required

1. Name some potential problems with the old system.
2. Design a purchase requisition form and a receiving report to be used by the housekeeping departments and the warehouse. Indicate how many copies of each form should be used and who should receive each copy.

MULTI-CONCEPT PROBLEMS

LO1,2 **Problem 6-4** Cash and Liquid Assets on the Balance Sheet

The following accounts are listed in a company's general ledger. The accountant wants to place the items in order of liquidity on the balance sheet.

> Accounts receivable
> Certificates of deposit (six months)
> Investment in stock
> Prepaid rent
> Money market fund
> Petty cash fund

Required

Rank the accounts in terms of liquidity. Identify items to be included in the total of cash, and explain why the items not included in cash on the balance sheet are not as liquid as cash. Explain how these items should be classified.

LO3,4 **Problem 6-5** Internal Control

At Morris Mart Inc. all sales are on account. Mary Morris-Manning is responsible for mailing invoices to customers, recording the amount billed, opening mail, and recording the payment. Mary is very devoted to the family business and never takes off more than one or two days for a long weekend. The customers know Mary and sometimes send personal notes with their payments. Another clerk handles all aspects of accounts payable. Mary's brother, who is president of Morris Mart, has hired an accountant to help with expansion.

Required

1. List some problems with the current accounts receivable system.
2. What suggestions would you make to improve internal control?
3. How would you explain to Mary that she personally is not the problem?

ALTERNATE PROBLEMS

LO2 **Problem 6-1A** Bank Reconciliation

The following information is available to assist you in preparing a bank reconciliation for Karen's Catering on March 31, 2007:

a. The balance on the March 31, 2007, bank statement is $6,506.10.
b. Not included on the bank statement is a deposit made by Karen's late on March 31 in the amount of $423.00.
c. A comparison between the canceled checks listed on the bank statement and the company records indicated that the following checks are outstanding at March 31:

No. 112	$ 42.92
No. 117	307.00
No. 120	10.58
No. 122	75.67

d. The bank acts as a collection agency for checks returned for insufficient funds. The March bank statement indicates that one such check in the amount of $45.00 was collected and deposited and a collection fee of $4.50 was charged.

(continued)

e. Interest earned on the checking account and credited to Karen's account during March was $4.30. Miscellaneous bank service charges amounted to $22.00.

f. A comparison between the deposits listed on the bank statement and the company's books revealed that a customer's check in the amount of $1,250.00 appears on the bank statement in March but was never credited to the customer's account on the company's books.

g. The comparison of checks cleared per the bank statement with those per the books revealed that the wrong amount was charged to the company's account for a check. The amount of the check was $990.00. The proof machine encoded the check in the amount of $909.00, the amount charged against the company's account.

Required

1. Determine the balance on the books before any adjustments as well as the corrected balance to be reported on the balance sheet.
2. What would you recommend Karen do as a result of the bank error in item (g) above? Why?

LO4   **Problem 6-2A** Internal Control Procedures

The loan department in a bank is subject to regulation. Internal auditors work for the bank to ensure that the loan department complies with requirements. The internal auditors must verify that each car loan file has a note signed by the maker, verification of insurance, and a title issued by the state that names the bank as co-owner.

Required

1. Explain why the bank and the regulatory agency are concerned with these documents.
2. Describe the internal control procedures that should be in place to ensure that these documents are obtained and safeguarded.

LO5   **Problem 6-3A** The Design of Internal Control Documents

Tiger's Group is a newly formed company that produces and sells children's movies about an imaginary character. The movies are in such great demand that they are shipped to retail outlets as soon as they are produced. The company must pay a royalty to several actors for each movie that it sold to retail outlets.

Required

1. Describe some internal control features that should be in place to ensure that all royalties are paid to the actors.
2. Design the shipping form that Tiger's Group should use for the movies. Be sure to include authorizations and indicate the number of copies and the routing of the copies.

ALTERNATE MULTI-CONCEPT PROBLEMS

LO1,2   **Problem 6-4A** Cash and Liquid Assets on the Balance Sheet

The following accounts are listed in a company's general ledger:

	December 31, 2007	December 31, 2006
Accounts receivable	$12,300	$10,000
Certificates of deposit (three months)	10,000	10,000
Marketable securities	4,500	4,000
Petty cash fund	1,200	1,500
Money market fund	25,800	28,000
Cash in checking account	6,000	6,000

Required

1. Which items are cash equivalents?
2. Explain where items that are not cash equivalents should be classified on the balance sheet.
3. What are the amount and the direction of change in cash and cash equivalents for 2007? Is the company as liquid at the end of 2007 as it was at the end of 2006? Explain your answer.

LO3,4   **Problem 6-5A** Internal Control

Abbott Inc. is expanding and needs to hire more personnel in the accounting office. Barbara Barker, the chief accounting clerk, knew that her cousin Cheryl was looking for a job. Barbara and Cheryl are also roommates. Barbara offered Cheryl a job as her assistant. Barbara will be responsible for Cheryl's performance reviews and training.

Required

1. List some problems with the proposed personnel situations in the accounting department.
2. Explain why accountants are concerned with the hiring of personnel. What suggestions would you make to improve internal control at Abbott?
3. How would you explain to Barbara and Cheryl that they personally are not the problem?

DECISION CASES

READING AND INTERPRETING FINANCIAL STATEMENTS

LO1   **Decision Case 6-1** Comparing Two Companies in the Same Industry: Finish Line and Foot Locker

Refer to the financial information for **Finish Line** and **Foot Locker** reproduced at the end of this book.

Required:

1. What is the balance in "Cash and cash equivalents" on the balance sheet of each company at the end of the most recent year? What is the amount of increase or decrease in this balance from the end of the prior year?
2. On what other statement in each company's annual report does the increase or decrease in cash and cash equivalents appear? Explain why it appears on this statement.
3. According to the notes to their financial statements, how does each company define "Cash and cash equivalents"? Are there any differences in their definitions?

LO3   **Decision Case 6-2** Reading and Interpreting IBM's Report of Management

IBM's 2004 annual report includes the following selected paragraphs from its Report of Management found on page 9:

> IBM maintains an effective internal control structure. It consists, in part, of organizational arrangements with clearly defined lines of responsibility and delegation of authority, and comprehensive systems and control procedures. An important element of the control environment is an ongoing internal audit program. Our system contains self-monitoring mechanisms, and actions are taken to correct deficiencies as they are identified. . . .
>
> PricewaterhouseCoopers LLP, an independent registered public accounting firm, is retained to audit IBM's consolidated financial statements and management's assessment of the effectiveness of the company's internal control over financial reporting. Its accompanying report is based on audits conducted in accordance with the standards of the Public Company Accounting Oversight Board (United States). . . .
>
> The Audit Committee of the Board of Directors is composed solely of independent, nonmanagement directors, and is responsible for recommending to the Board the independent registered public accounting firm to be retained for the coming year, subject to stockholder ratification. The Audit Committee meets periodically and privately with the independent registered public accounting firm, with the company's internal auditors, as well as with IBM management, to review accounting, auditing, internal control structure and financial reporting matters.

Required:

1. Describe the main components of IBM's internal control structure.
2. Who is IBM's external auditor? In addition to auditing IBM's financial statements, what else does this firm audit? What body's standards does the firm follow in conducting its audit?
3. What is the composition of IBM's Audit Committee? Describe its role.

MAKING FINANCIAL DECISIONS

LO1 **Decision Case 6-3** Liquidity

R Montague and J Capulet both distribute films to movie theaters. The following are the current assets for each at the end of the year (all amounts are in millions of dollars):

	R Montague	J Capulet
Cash	$10	$ 5
Six-month certificates of deposit	9	0
Short-term investments in stock	0	6
Accounts receivable	15	23
Allowance for doubtful accounts	(1)	(1)
Total current assets	$33	$33

Required

As a loan officer for the First National Bank of Verona Heights, assume that both companies have come to you asking for a $10 million, six-month loan. If you could lend money to only one of the two, which one would it be? Justify your answer by writing a brief memo to the president of the bank.

ETHICAL DECISION MAKING

LO3,4 **Decision Case 6-4** Cash Receipts in a Bookstore

You were recently hired by a large retail bookstore chain. Your training involved spending a week at the largest and most profitable store in the district. The store manager assigned the head cashier to train you on the cash register and closing procedures required by the company's home office. In the process, the head cashier instructed you to keep an envelope for cash over and short that would include cash or IOUs equal to the net amount of overages or shortages in the cash drawer. "It is impossible to balance exactly, so just put extra cash in this envelope and use the cash when you are short." You studied accounting for one semester in college and remembered your professor saying that "all deposits should be made intact, daily."

Required

Draft a memorandum to the store manager detailing any problems you see with the current system. This memo should address the issue of the reliability of the cash receipts number. It should also answer the following question, "Does this method provide information to the company that would enable someone to detect whether or not theft has occurred during the particular day in question?" Your memo should suggest an alternative method of internal control for cash receipts.

SOLUTIONS TO KEY TERMS QUIZ

8	Cash equivalent	2	Board of directors
11	Bank statement	16	Audit committee
10	Outstanding check	14	Accounting system
13	Deposit in transit	20	Administrative controls
7	Bank reconciliation	4	Accounting controls
15	Credit memoranda	23	Internal audit staff
9	Debit memoranda	5	Purchase requisition form
17	Petty cash fund	21	Purchase order
3	Internal control system	1	Invoice
22	Sarbanes-Oxley Act	19	Blind receiving report
12	Internal control report	6	Invoice approval form
18	Public Company Accounting Oversight Board		

HOMEWORK

CHAPTER

7

Investments and Receivables

Study Links

A Look at the Previous Chapter
Chapter 6 looked at the various forms cash can take and the importance of cash control to a business.

A Look at This Chapter
Many companies invest their cash in various types of financial instruments, as well as in the stocks and bonds of other companies. This chapter illustrates the accounting for these investments. In many instances the cash available to invest comes from the collection of receivables. The chapter also examines the accounting for both accounts receivable and notes receivable.

A Look at the Upcoming Chapters
This chapter concludes our look at a company's most liquid assets, that is, its current assets. Chapter 8 focuses on the long-term operational assets, such as property, plant and equipment and intangibles, necessary to run a business. In Chapters 9 and 10, we explore the use of liabilities to finance the purchase of assets.

Learning Outcomes

After studying this chapter, you should be able to:

LO1 Show that you understand the accounting for and disclosure of various types of investments companies make.

LO2 Show that you understand how to account for accounts receivable, including bad debts.

LO3 Explain how information about sales and receivables can be combined to evaluate how efficient a company is in collecting its receivables.

LO4 Show that you understand how to account for interest-bearing notes receivable.

LO5 Explain various techniques that companies use to accelerate the inflow of cash from sales.

LO6 Explain the effects of transactions involving liquid assets on the statement of cash flows.

LO7 Show that you understand the accounting for and disclosure of investments in the stocks and bonds of other companies (Appendix).

Apple Computer Company

MAKING BUSINESS DECISIONS

For years, the names **Apple Computer Company** and Macintosh have been synonymous. Incorporated in the state of California in 1977, the company made a name for itself by carving out a niche in the personal computer market and developing its own operating system to run its "Mac" desktops and laptops. In fact, it proudly makes the claim that it is the only company in the personal computer industry that designs and manufactures the entire PC.

A few years ago, however, Apple broadened its horizons and in the process revolutionized the music business by introducing the "iPod." Apple's version of the digital music player is lighter than two CDs, yet it can hold up to 10,000 songs and thousands of digital photographs. Apple touts that this amounts to one new song a day for the next 27 years! To provide synergies between its Mac PCs and the new iPods, Apple has developed its iTunes Music Store. Customers are able to build that collection of 10,000 tunes to listen to on their iPod by downloading the songs from the iTunes Music Store, which is available on either a Mac or Windows PC.

The expansion of its product base was just one of the strategic moves made by Apple in recent years. It added another important new initiative in 2001 with the introduction of retail stores in shopping malls and urban shopping districts. By the end of its 2004 fiscal year, Apple had opened 84 retail stores in the United States and two international stores in Japan. The company hopes the stores will bring new customers to it and allow it to better control the customer retail experience.

Have Apple's key business decisions to get into the digital music business and to open retail stores paid off for it and its stockholders? The tools learned in previous chapters, as well as those presented in this chapter, will help you answer this question. Recall that a company's comparative income statements show the reader whether sales have increased and, if so, whether that increase has translated to an improved bottom line, that is, an increase in net income. As reported in its 2004 annual report, Apple's sales rose steadily from $5.7 billion in 2002 to $8.3 billion in 2004. Even more dramatic was the improvement of the bottom line: from a meager $65 million in net income in 2002 to $276 million in 2004!

What company wouldn't be envious of Apple's steady sales climb over recent years? Keep in mind, though, that sales and cash are not the same. As with most companies, Apple makes many of its sales on credit, and it must collect the resulting accounts receivable to add cash to its balance sheet. And, as you know from personal experience, idle cash does not earn a very good return—most bank accounts these days barely pay 2% interest. So it becomes equally important to understand what Apple does with its cash. Investments on the balance sheet indicate what the company does with idle cash, cash that is not immediately needed to buy more inventory or plant and equipment or to repay loans.

The accompanying partial balance sheet gives you an idea of the importance of Apple's three most liquid assets: cash and cash equivalents, short-term investments, and accounts receivable. But beyond the absolute dollar amounts and their relative size, what else would you want to know about each of these assets? In the last chapter, we looked at cash and cash equivalents.

This chapter will answer some important questions about receivables and investments, such as:

* How does a company report accounts receivable on its balance sheet? (See pp. 310–311)
* What is the purpose of subtracting an allowance from the balance of accounts receivable? (See p. 311)
* Can the relationship between sales on the income statement and accounts receivable on the balance sheet be of any value in assessing a company's performance? (See p. 316)
* How does a company report short-term investments on its balance sheet? (See pp. 307–309)
* What types of investments do companies make? (See pp. 307–309)
* How does a company earn income from these investments? (See pp. 328–329)

Answers to these questions are found in the text. They can help you decide whether Apple's forays into the digital music business and retail outlets were wise business decisions.

Apple's Consolidated Balance Sheets

(in millions)	September 25, 2004	September 27, 2003
ASSETS		
Current assets:		
Cash and cash equivalents	$2,969	$3,396
Short-term investments	2,495	1,170
Accounts receivable, less allowances of $47 and $49, respectively	774	766
Inventories	101	56
Deferred tax assets	231	190
Other current assets	485	309
Total current assets	$7,055	$5,887

Apple's three most important liquid assets →

Source: Apple Computer Company's 2004 Annual Report.

Accounting for Investments

LO1 Show that you understand the accounting for and disclosure of various types of investments companies make.

The investments that companies make take a variety of forms and are made for various reasons. Some corporations find themselves with excess cash during certain times of the year and invest this idle cash in various highly liquid financial instruments, such as certificates of deposit and money market funds. Chapter 6 pointed out that these investments are included with cash and are called cash equivalents if they have an original maturity to the investor of three months or less. Otherwise, they are accounted for as short-term investments.

In addition to investments in highly liquid financial instruments, some companies invest in the stocks and bonds of other corporations, as well as bonds issued by various government agencies. Securities issued by corporations as a form of ownership in the business, such as common stock and preferred stock, are called **equity securities**. Because these securities are a form of ownership, they do not have a maturity date. As we will see later, investments in equity securities can be classified as either current or long-term, depending on the company's intent. Alternatively, securities issued by corporations and governmental bodies as a form of borrowing are called **debt securities** and often take the form of bonds. The term of a bond can be relatively short, such as 5 years, or much longer, such as 20 or 30 years. Regardless of the term, classification as a current or noncurrent asset by the investor depends on whether it plans to sell or redeem the debt securities within the next year.

Equity securities
Securities issued by corporations as a form of ownership in the business.
Alternate term: Stocks

Debt securities
Securities issued by corporations and governmental bodies as a form of borrowing.
Alternate term: Bonds

Investments in Highly Liquid Financial Instruments

We now turn to the appropriate accounting for these various types of investments. We begin by considering the accounting for highly liquid financial instruments such as certificates of deposit and then turn to the accounting for investments in the stocks and bonds of other companies.

INVESTING IDLE CASH

The seasonal nature of most businesses leads to a potential cash shortage during certain times of the year and an excess of cash during other times. Companies typically deal with cash shortages by borrowing on a short-term basis, either from a bank in the form of notes or from other entities in the form of commercial paper. The maturities of the bank notes or the commercial paper generally range anywhere from 30 days to six months. These same companies use various financial instruments as a way to invest excess cash during other times of the year. We will present the accounting for the most common type of highly liquid financial instrument, a certificate of deposit (CD).

ACCOUNTING FOR AN INVESTMENT IN A CERTIFICATE OF DEPOSIT (CD)

Assume that on October 2, 2007, Creston Corp. invests $100,000 of excess cash in a 120-day certificate of deposit. The CD matures on January 30, 2008, at which time Creston receives the $100,000 invested and interest at an annual rate of 6%. On October 2, 2007, the company has simply traded one asset for another:

Balance Sheet						Income Statement	
ASSETS	**=**	**LIABILITIES**	**+**	**STOCKHOLDERS' EQUITY**	**+**	**REVENUES − EXPENSES**	
Short-Term							
Investments—CD 100,000							
Cash (100,000)							

Assuming December 31 is the end of Creston's fiscal year, an adjustment is needed on this date to record interest earned during 2007, even though no cash will be received until the CD matures in 2008. The adjustment recognizes a new asset as well as an addition on the income statement:

Balance Sheet						Income Statement	
ASSETS	**=**	**LIABILITIES**	**+**	**STOCKHOLDERS' EQUITY**	**+**	**REVENUES − EXPENSES**	
Interest Receivable 1,500						Interest Revenue 1,500	

The basic formula to compute interest is as follows:

Interest (I) = Principal (P) × Interest Rate (R) × Time (T)

Because interest rates are normally stated on an annual basis, time is interpreted to mean the fraction of a year that the investment is outstanding. The amount

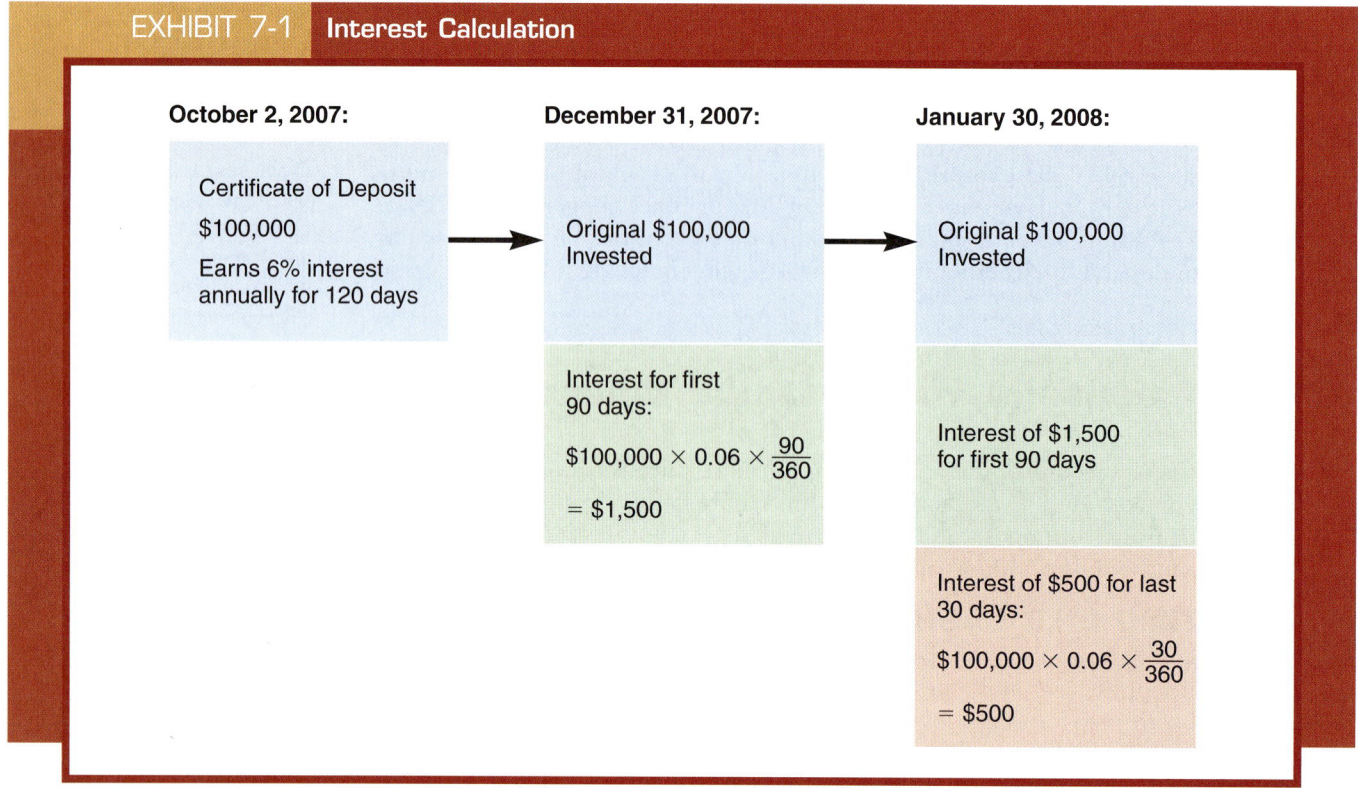

EXHIBIT 7-1   Interest Calculation

October 2, 2007:

Certificate of Deposit
$100,000

Earns 6% interest annually for 120 days

December 31, 2007:

Original $100,000 Invested

Interest for first 90 days:

$100,000 × 0.06 × $\frac{90}{360}$

= $1,500

January 30, 2008:

Original $100,000 Invested

Interest of $1,500 for first 90 days

Interest of $500 for last 30 days:

$100,000 × 0.06 × $\frac{30}{360}$

= $500

of interest is based on the principal or amount invested ($100,000), times the rate of interest (6%), times the fraction of a year the CD was outstanding in 2007 (29 days in October + 30 days in November + 31 days in December = 90 days). To simplify interest calculations, it is easiest to assume 360 days in a year. With the availability of computers to do the work, however, most businesses now use 365 days in a year to calculate interest. Throughout this book, we assume 360 days in a year to allow us to focus on concepts rather than detailed calculations. Thus, in our example, the fraction of a year that the CD is outstanding during 2007 is 90/360.

The effect of the receipt of the principal amount of the CD of $100,000 and interest for 120 days is:

		Balance Sheet				Income Statement	
ASSETS		**=**	**LIABILITIES**	**+**	**STOCKHOLDERS' EQUITY**	**+**	**REVENUES − EXPENSES**
Cash	102,000					Interest Revenue	500
Short-Term							
Investment—CD	(100,000)						
Interest Receivable	(1,500)						

This transaction results in the removal of both the CD and the interest receivable from the records and recognizes $500 in interest earned during the first 30 days of 2008: $100,000 × 0.06 × 30/360 = $500. Exhibit 7-1 summarizes the calculation of interest in each of the two accounting periods.

Investments in Stocks and Bonds

Corporations frequently invest in the securities of other businesses. These investments take two forms: debt securities and equity securities.

No Significant Influence Corporations have varying motivations for investing in the stocks and bonds of other companies. We will refer to the company that invests as the *investor* and the company whose stocks or bonds are purchased as the *investee*. In addition to buying certificates of deposit and other financial instruments, companies invest excess funds in stocks and bonds over the short run. For example, Apple invests primarily in bonds of other companies. The seasonality of certain businesses may result in otherwise idle cash being available during certain times of the year. In other cases, stocks and bonds are purchased as a way to invest cash over the long run. Often these types of investments are made in anticipation of a need for cash at some distant point in the future. For example, a company may invest today in a combination of stocks and bonds because it will need cash 10 years from now to build a new plant. The investor may be primarily interested in periodic income in the form of interest and dividends, in appreciation in the value of the securities, or in some combination of the two.

Significant Influence Sometimes shares of stock in another company are bought with a different purpose in mind. If a company buys a relatively large percentage of the common stock of the investee, it may be able to secure significant influence over the policies of this company. For example, a company might buy 30% of the common stock of a supplier of its raw materials to ensure a steady source of inventory. When an investor is able to secure influence over the investee, the equity method of accounting is used. According to current accounting standards, this method is appropriate when an investor owns at least 20% of the common stock of the investee.

Control Finally, a corporation may buy stock in another company with the purpose of obtaining control over that other entity. Normally, this requires an investment in excess of 50% of the common stock of the investee. When an investor owns more than half the stock of another company, accountants normally prepare a set of consolidated financial statements. This involves combining the financial statements of the individual entities into a single set of statements. An investor with an interest of more than 50% in another company is called the parent, and the investee in these situations is called the subsidiary.

In the appendix to this chapter we will discuss how companies account for investments that do not give them any significant influence over the other company. (Accounting for investments in which there is either significant influence or control is covered in advanced accounting textbooks.) The following chart summarizes the accounting by an investor for investments in the common stock of another company:

Accounts Receivable

Account receivable
A receivable arising from the sale of goods or services with a verbal promise to pay.

Receivables can result from a variety of transactions. The most common type of receivable is the one that arises from the sale of goods or services to customers with a verbal promise to pay within a specified period of time. This type of receivable is called an **account receivable**. Accounts receivable do not bear interest. Apple or any other company would rather not sell on credit, preferring to make all sales for cash. Selling on credit causes two problems: it slows down the inflow of cash to the company, and it raises the possibility that the customer may not pay its bill on time or possibly ever. To remain competitive, however, Apple and most other businesses must sell their products and services on credit.

THE USE OF A SUBSIDIARY LEDGER

Apple states on page 74 of its 2004 annual report that it "distributes its products through third-party resellers and directly to certain education, consumer, and commercial customers." Accounts receivable is the asset that arises from a sale on credit to any of these customers. For example, assume Apple sells $25,000 of hardware to a school. The sale results in the recognition of an asset and additional revenue:

		Balance Sheet					Income Statement	
ASSETS	**=**	**LIABILITIES**	**+**	**STOCKHOLDERS' EQUITY**	**+**	**REVENUES − EXPENSES**	
Accounts Receivable	25,000					Sales Revenue	25,000

It is important for control purposes that Apple keep a record of to whom the sale was and include this amount on a periodic statement or bill sent to the customer (in this case, a school). What if a company has a hundred or a thousand different customers? Some mechanism is needed to track the balance owed by each of these customers. The mechanism companies use is called a **subsidiary ledger**.

Subsidiary ledger
The detail for a number of individual items that collectively make up a single general ledger account.

Control account
The general ledger account that is supported by a subsidiary ledger.

A subsidiary ledger contains the necessary detail on each of a number of items that collectively make up a single general ledger account, called the **control account**. This detail is shown in the following example for accounts receivable:

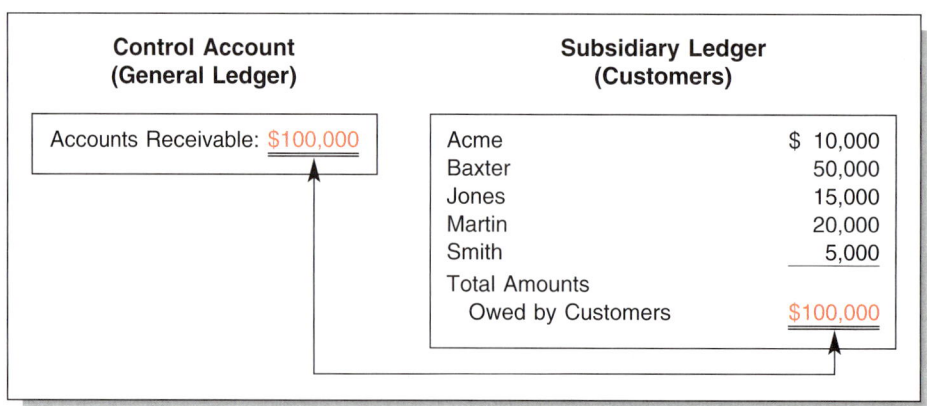

In theory, any one of the accounts in the general ledger could be supported by a subsidiary ledger. In addition to Accounts Receivable, two other common accounts supported by subsidiary ledgers are Plant and Equipment and Accounts Payable. An accounts payable subsidiary ledger contains a separate account for each of the suppliers or vendors from which a company purchases inventory. A plant and equipment subsidiary ledger consists of individual accounts, along with their balances, for each of the various long-term tangible assets the company owns.

It is important to understand that a subsidiary ledger does not take the place of the control account in the general ledger. Instead, at any point in time, the balances of the accounts that make up the subsidiary ledger should total to the single balance in the related control account. In the remainder of this chapter, we will illustrate the use of only the control account. However, whenever a specific customer's account is increased or decreased, we will note the name of the customer next to the control account in the journal entry.

THE VALUATION OF ACCOUNTS RECEIVABLE

Apple's 2004 annual report revealed the following receivables on the balance sheet:

(amounts in millions)	2004	2003
Accounts receivables, less allowances of $47 and $49, respectively	$774	$766

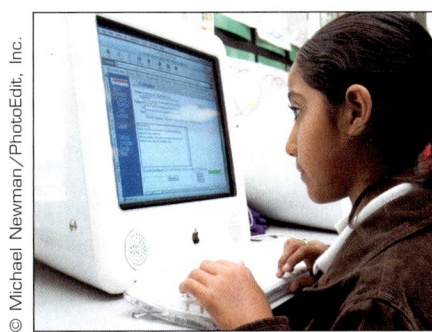

Apple does not sell its products under the assumption that any particular customer will not pay its bill. In fact, the credit department of a business is responsible for performing a credit check on all potential customers before granting them credit. Management of Apple is not naive enough, however, to believe that all customers will be able always to pay their accounts when due. This would be the case only if (1) all customers were completely trustworthy and (2) customers never experience unforeseen financial difficulties that make it impossible to pay on time.

The reduction in Apple's receivables for an allowance is how most companies deal with bad debts in their accounting records. Bad debts are unpaid customer accounts that a company gives up trying to collect. Some companies describe the allowance more fully as the allowance for doubtful accounts or the allowance for uncollectible accounts. Using the end of 2004 as an example, Apple believes that the net recoverable amount of its receivables is $774 million, even though the gross amount of receivables is $47 million higher than this amount. The company has reduced the gross receivables for an amount it believes necessary to reflect the asset on the books at the net recoverable amount or net realizable value. We now take a closer look at how a company accounts for bad debts.

Apple's extensive collaboration with education includes discounts for college or university students, faculty, staff or administration, K-12 students and teachers—even home-schooled students. From online purchases or by way of an Apple store, accounts receivable is the asset that arises from a sale on credit through the educational channel.

TWO METHODS TO ACCOUNT FOR BAD DEBTS

Assume that Roberts Corp. makes a $500 sale to Dexter Inc. on November 10, 2007, with credit terms of 2/10, net 60. (Credit terms were explained in Chapter 5.) The effect on the accounting equation of the sale is as follows:

Balance Sheet						Income Statement	
ASSETS	**=**	**LIABILITIES**	**+**	**STOCKHOLDERS' EQUITY**	**+**	**REVENUES – EXPENSES**	
Accounts Receivable—						Sales Revenue	500
Dexter	500						

Assume further that Dexter not only misses taking advantage of the discount for early payment but also is unable to pay within 60 days. After pursuing the account for four months into 2008, the credit department of Roberts informs the accounting department that it has given up on collecting the $500 from Dexter and advises that the account should be written off. To do so, the accounting department makes an adjustment:

Balance Sheet						Income Statement	
ASSETS	**=**	**LIABILITIES**	**+**	**STOCKHOLDERS' EQUITY**	**+**	**REVENUES – EXPENSES**	
Accounts Receivable—						Bad Debts Expense	(500)
Dexter	(500)						

Direct write-off method
The recognition of bad debts expense at the point an account is written off as uncollectible.

This approach to accounting for bad debts is called the **direct write-off method**. Do you see any problems with its use?

- What about Roberts' balance sheet at the end of 2007? By ignoring the possibility that not all of its outstanding accounts receivable will be collected, Roberts is overstating the value of this asset at December 31, 2007.
- What about the income statement for 2007? By ignoring the possibility of bad debts on sales made during 2007, Roberts has violated the matching principle. This principle requires that all costs associated with making sales in a period be matched with the sales of that period. Roberts has overstated net income for 2007 by ignoring bad debts as expense. The problem is one of timing: even though any one particular account may not prove to be uncollectible until a later period (e.g., the Dexter account), the cost associated with making sales on credit (bad debts) should be recognized in the period of sale.

Allowance method
A method of estimating bad debts on the basis of either the net credit sales of the period or the accounts receivable at the end of the period.

Accountants use the **allowance method** to overcome the deficiencies of the direct write-off method. They estimate the amount of bad debts before these debts actually occur. For example, assume that Roberts' total sales during 2007 amount to $600,000 and that at the end of the year, the outstanding accounts receivable total $250,000. Also assume that Roberts estimates from past experience that 1% of the sales of the period, or $6,000, will prove to be uncollectible. Under the allowance method, Roberts makes the following adjustment at the end of 2007.

Balance Sheet				Income Statement	
ASSETS	=	**LIABILITIES**	+	**STOCKHOLDERS' EQUITY**	+	**REVENUES – EXPENSES**
Allowance for Doubtful Accounts (6,000)					Bad Debts Expense (6,000)

Allowance for doubtful accounts
A contra-asset account used to reduce accounts receivable to its net realizable value. *Alternate term: Allowance for uncollectible accounts*

Bad Debts Expense recognizes the cost associated with the reduction in value of the asset Accounts Receivable. A contra-asset account is used to reduce the asset to its net realizable value. This is accomplished by using an allowance account, **Allowance for Doubtful Accounts**. Roberts presents accounts receivable on its December 31, 2007, balance sheet as follows:

Accounts receivable	$250,000
Less: Allowance for doubtful accounts	(6,000)
Net accounts receivable	$244,000

Study Tip

Note the similarities between the Allowance for Doubtful Accounts contra account and another contra account, Accumulated Depreciation. Both are used to reduce an asset account to a lower carrying or book value.

WRITE-OFFS OF UNCOLLECTIBLE ACCOUNTS WITH THE ALLOWANCE METHOD

Like the direct write-off method, the allowance method reduces Accounts Receivable to write off a specific customer's account. If the account receivable no longer exists, there is no need for the related allowance account; thus, this account is reduced as well. For example, assume, as we did earlier, that Dexter's $500 account is written off on May 1, 2008. Under the allowance method, the effect of the write-off is as follows:

Balance Sheet				Income Statement	
ASSETS	=	**LIABILITIES**	+	**STOCKHOLDERS' EQUITY**	+	**REVENUES – EXPENSES**
Allowance for Doubtful Accounts 500					
Accounts Receivable— Dexter (500)					

To summarize, whether the direct write-off method or the allowance method is used, the entry to write off a specific customer's account reduces the gross amount of Accounts Receivable. It is the other side of the transaction that differs between the two methods:

- Under the direct write-off method, an *expense* is increased.
- Under the allowance method, the *allowance* account is reduced.

TWO APPROACHES TO THE ALLOWANCE METHOD OF ACCOUNTING FOR BAD DEBTS

Because the allowance method results in a better matching, accounting standards require the use of it rather than the direct write-off method unless bad debts are immaterial in amount. Accountants use one of two different variations of the allowance method to estimate bad debts. One approach emphasizes matching bad debts expense with revenue on the income statement and bases bad debts on a percentage of the sales of the period. This was the method we illustrated earlier for Roberts Corp. The other approach emphasizes the net realizable amount (value) of accounts receivable on the balance sheet and bases bad debts on a percentage of the accounts receivable balance at the end of the period.

Percentage of Net Credit Sales Approach If a company has been in business for enough years, it may be able to use the past relationship between bad debts and net credit sales to predict bad debt amounts. Net means that credit sales have been adjusted for sales discounts and returns and allowances. Assume that the accounting records for Bosco Corp. reveal the following:

Year	Net Credit Sales	Bad Debts
2002	$1,250,000	$ 26,400
2003	1,340,000	29,350
2004	1,200,000	23,100
2005	1,650,000	32,150
2006	2,120,000	42,700
	$7,560,000	$153,700

Although the exact percentage varied slightly over the five-year period, the average percentage of bad debts to net credit sales is very close to 2% ($153,700/ $7,560,000 = 0.02033). Bosco needs to determine whether this estimate is realistic for the current period. For example, are current economic conditions considerably different from those in the prior years? Has the company made sales to any new customers with significantly different credit terms? If the answers to these types of questions are yes, Bosco should consider adjusting the 2% experience rate to estimate future bad debts. Otherwise, it should proceed with this estimate. Assuming that it uses the 2% rate and that its net credit sales during 2007 are $2,340,000, Bosco makes the following adjustment:

Balance Sheet						Income Statement
ASSETS	**=**	**LIABILITIES**	**+**	**STOCKHOLDERS' EQUITY**	**+**	**REVENUES − EXPENSES**
Allowance for Doubtful						Bad Debts Expense (46,800)
Accounts (46,800)						

Thus, Bosco matches bad debt expense of $46,800 with sales revenue of $2,340,000.

Percentage of Accounts Receivable Approach Some companies believe they can more accurately estimate bad debts by relating them to the balance in the Accounts Receivable account at the end of the period rather than to the sales of the period. The objective with both approaches is the same, however: to use past experience with bad debts to predict future amounts. Assume that the records for Cougar Corp. reveal the following:

Year	Balance in Accounts Receivable December 31	Bad Debts
2002	$ 650,000	$ 5,250
2003	785,000	6,230
2004	854,000	6,950
2005	824,000	6,450
2006	925,000	7,450
	$4,038,000	$32,330

The ratio of bad debts to the ending balance in Accounts Receivable over the past five years is $32,330/$4,038,000, or approximately 0.008 (0.8%). Assuming balances in Accounts Receivable and the Allowance for Doubtful Accounts on December 31, 2007, of $865,000 and $2,100, respectively, Cougar adjusts its records as follows:

	Balance Sheet			Income Statement
ASSETS	**= LIABILITIES + STOCKHOLDERS' EQUITY +**			**REVENUES – EXPENSES**
Allowance for Doubtful Accounts (4,820)				Bad Debts Expense (4,820)

The logic for the amount recognized as bad debts is as follows:

Balance required in allowance account after adjustment	$6,920
Less: Balance in allowance account before adjustment	2,100
Amount of adjustment	$4,820

Note the one major difference between this approach and the percentage of sales approach:

- Under the percentage of net credit sales approach, the balance in the allowance account is ignored, and the bad debts expense is simply a percentage of the sales of the period.

- Under the percentage of accounts receivable approach, however, the balance in the allowance account must be considered.

The net realizable value of Accounts Receivable is determined as follows:

Accounts receivable	$865,000
Less: Allowance for doubtful accounts	(6,920)
Net realizable value	$858,080

Aging of Accounts Receivable Some companies use a variation of the percentage of accounts receivable approach to estimate bad debts. This variation is actually a refinement of the approach because it considers the length of time that the receivables have been outstanding. It stands to reason that the older an account receivable is, the less likely it is to be collected. An **aging schedule** categorizes the various accounts by length of time outstanding. An example of an aging schedule is shown in Exhibit 7-2. We assume that the company's policy is to allow 30 days for payment of an outstanding account. After that time, the account is past due. An alphabetical list of customers appears in the first column, with the balance in each account shown in the appropriate column to the right. The dotted lines after A. Matt's account indicate that many more accounts appear in the records; we have included just a few to show the format of the schedule. The totals on the aging schedule are used as the basis for estimating bad debts, as shown in Exhibit 7-3.

Note that the estimated percentage of uncollectibles increases as the period of time the accounts have been outstanding lengthens. If we assume that Allowance

Aging schedule
A form used to categorize the various individual accounts receivable according to the length of time each has been outstanding.

EXHIBIT 7-2 **Aging Schedule**

| | | Number of Days Past Due | | | |
Customer	Current	1–30	31–60	61–90	Over 90
L. Ash	$ 4,400				
B. Budd	3,200				
C. Cox		$ 6,500			
E. Fudd					$6,300
G. Hoff			$ 900		
A. Matt	5,500				
......					
......					
......					
T. West		3,100			
M. Young				$ 4,200	
Totals*	$85,600	$31,200	$24,500	$18,000	$9,200

*Only a few of the customer accounts are illustrated; thus, the column totals are higher than the amounts for the accounts illustrated.

---

for Doubtful Accounts has a balance of $1,230 before adjustment, the accountant makes the following adjustments:

Balance Sheet					Income Statement
ASSETS	**=**	**LIABILITIES**	**+**	**STOCKHOLDERS' EQUITY**	**+ REVENUES – EXPENSES**
Allowance for Doubtful					Bad Debts Expense (13,324)
Accounts (13,324)					

The logic for the amount recognized as bad debts is as follows:

Balance required in allowance account after adjustment	$14,554
Less: Balance in allowance account before adjustment	1,230
Amount of adjustment	$13,324

The net realizable value of accounts receivable would be determined as follows:

Accounts receivable	$168,500
Less: Allowance for doubtful accounts	14,554
Net realizable value	$153,946

EXHIBIT 7-3 **Use of an Aging Schedule to Estimate Bad Debts**

Category	Amount	Estimated Percent Uncollectible	Estimated Amount Uncollectible
Current	$ 85,600	1%	$ 856
Past due:			
1–30 days	31,200	4%	1,248
31–60 days	24,500	10%	2,450
61–90 days	18,000	30%	5,400
Over 90 days	9,200	50%	4,600
Totals	$168,500		$14,554

⏱ *2 minute review*

1. What is the theoretical justification for recognizing bad debts under the allowance method?

2. What accounts are used at the end of the period to recognize bad debts?

3. Two approaches are available to recognize bad debts. What are they? Which one of the two takes into account any existing balance in Allowance for Doubtful Accounts when the adjustment is made to recognize bad debts for the period?

Answers

1. Use of the allowance method is an attempt by accountants to match bad debts as an expense with the revenue of the period in which a sale on credit took place.

2. Bad Debts Expense and Allowance for Doubtful Accounts are the two accounts used at the end of the period to recognize bad debts.

3. The two approaches are the percentage of net credit sales approach and the percentage of accounts receivable approach. Only the latter takes into account the balance in Allowance for Doubtful Accounts.

The Accounts Receivable Turnover Ratio

LO3 Explain how information about sales and receivables can be combined to evaluate how efficient a company is in collecting its receivables.

Managers, investors, and creditors are keenly interested in how well a company manages its accounts receivable. One simple measure is to compare a company's sales to its accounts receivable. The result is the accounts receivable turnover ratio:

$$\text{Accounts Receivable Turnover} = \frac{\text{Net Credit Sales}}{\text{Average Accounts Receivable}}$$

Typically, the faster the turnover is, the better. For example, if a company has sales of $10 million and an average accounts receivable of $1 million, it turns over its accounts receivable 10 times per year. If we assume 360 days in a year, that is once every 36 days. An observer would compare that figure with historical figures to see if the company is experiencing slower or faster collections. A comparison could also be made to other companies in the same industry. If receivables are turning over too slowly, that could mean that the company's credit department is not operating effectively and the company therefore is missing opportunities with the cash that isn't available. On the other hand, a turnover rate that is too fast might mean that the company's credit policies are too stringent and that sales are being lost as a result.

USING THE RATIO DECISION MODEL: ANALYZING THE ACCOUNTS RECEIVABLE RATE OF COLLECTION

Use the following Ratio Decision Process to evaluate the accounts receivable rate of collection of Apple or any public company:

1. Formulate the Question
Managers, investors, and creditors are interested in how well a company manages its accounts receivable. Each dollar of sales on credit produces a dollar of accounts receivable. And the quicker each dollar of accounts receivable can be collected, the sooner the money will be available for other purposes. *So, how quickly is a company like Apple able to collect its accounts receivable?*

2. Gather the Information from the Financial Statements

Recall from earlier chapters that sales are recorded on an income statement, representing a *flow* for a period of time. Accounts receivable, an asset, represents a *balance* at a point in time. Thus, a comparison of the two requires the amount of net credit sales for the year and an average of the balance in accounts receivable:

- Net credit sales: From the income statement for the year
- Average accounts receivable: From the beginning and ending balance sheets

3. Calculate the Ratio

$$\text{Accounts Receivable Turnover} = \frac{\text{Net Credit Sales}}{\text{Average Accounts Receivable}}$$

Apple's Consolidated Statements of Operations (Partial)
(In millions, except share and per share amounts)

Three fiscal years ended September 25, 2004	2004	2003	2002
Net sales	$8,279	$6,207	$5,742
Cost of sales	6,020	4,499	4,139
Gross margin	2,259	1,708	1,603

Apple's Consolidated Balance Sheets (Partial)
(in millions)

	September 25, 2004	September 27, 2003
ASSETS		
Current assets:		
Cash and cash equivalents	$2,969	$3,396
Short-term investments	2,495	1,170
Accounts receivable, less allowances of $47 and $49, respectively	774	766

$$\text{Accounts Receivable Turnover} = \frac{\$8,279^*}{\$770} = 10.8 \text{ times}$$

*Assuming all sales are on credit.

Average accounts receivable less allowances = ($774 + $766)/2 = $770

4. Compare the Ratio with Others

Management compares the current year's turnover rate with prior years to see if the company is experiencing slower or faster collections. It is also important to compare the rate with other companies in the same industry:

Apple Computer		Dell Computer	
Year Ended September 25, 2004	Year Ended September 27, 2003	Year Ended January 28, 2005	Year Ended January 30, 2004
10.8 times	9.3 times	12.2 times	13.3 times

5. Interpret the Results

Typically, the more times a company turns over its receivables each year, the better. For example, Apple improved its turnover, from 9.3 times in 2003 to 10.8 times in 2004. If we assume 360 days in a year, a turnover of just over 10 times means receivables are collected on the average every 36 days (360/10). Dell's turnover is slightly faster than Apple's, resulting in a few less days that it takes to collect receivables.

Notes Receivable

LO4 Show that you understand how to account for interest-bearing notes receivable.

A **promissory note** is a written promise to repay a definite sum of money on demand or at a fixed or determinable date in the future. Promissory notes normally require the payment of interest for the use of someone else's money. The party that agrees to repay money is the **maker** of the note, and the party that receives money in the future is the **payee**. A company that holds a promissory note received from another company has an asset, called a **note receivable**; the company that makes or gives a promissory note to another company has a liability, a **note payable**. Over the life of the note, the maker incurs interest expense on its note payable, and the payee earns interest revenue on its note receivable. The following summarizes this relationship:

Promissory note
A written promise to repay a definite sum of money on demand or at a fixed or determinable date in the future.

Maker
The party that agrees to repay the money for a promissory note at some future date.

Payee
The party that will receive the money from a promissory note at some future date.

Note receivable
An asset resulting from the acceptance of a promissory note from another company.

Note payable
A liability resulting from the signing of a promissory note.

Party	Recognizes on Balance Sheet	Recognizes on Income Statement
Maker	Note payable	Interest expense
Payee	Note receivable	Interest revenue

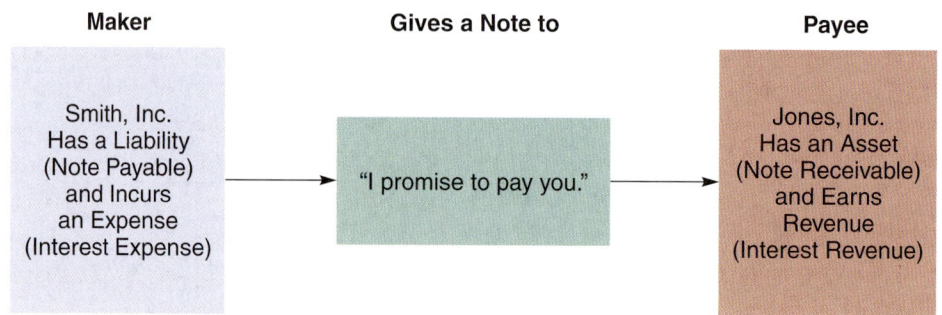

Promissory notes are used for a variety of purposes. Banks normally require a company to sign a promissory note to borrow money. They are often used in the sale of consumer durables with relatively high purchase prices, such as appliances and automobiles. At times a promissory note is issued to replace an existing overdue account receivable.

IMPORTANT TERMS CONNECTED WITH PROMISSORY NOTES

It is important to understand the following terms when dealing with promissory notes:

Key terms for promissory notes
These terms, with their definitions in the text, are important for your understanding.

Principal—the amount of cash received, or the fair value of the products or services received, by the maker when a promissory note is issued.

Maturity date—the date that the promissory note is due.

Term—the length of time a note is outstanding; that is, the period of time between the date it is issued and the date it matures.

Maturity value—the amount of cash the maker is to pay the payee on the maturity date of the note.

Interest—the difference between the principal amount of the note and its maturity value.

Assume that on December 13, 2007, HighTec sells a computer to Baker Corp. at an invoice price of $15,000. Because Baker is short of cash, it gives HighTec a 90-day,

12% promissory note. The total amount of interest due on the maturity date is determined as follows:

$$\$15,000 \times 0.12 \times 90/360 = \$450$$

The effect of the receipt of the note by HighTec is as follows:

	Balance Sheet						Income Statement	
ASSETS		=	**LIABILITIES**	+	**STOCKHOLDERS' EQUITY**	+	**REVENUES − EXPENSES**	
Notes Receivable	15,000						Sales Revenue	15,000

If we assume that December 31 is the end of HighTec's accounting year, an adjustment is needed to recognize interest earned but not yet received. It is required when a company uses the accrual basis of accounting. The question is: how many days of interest have been earned during December? *It is normal practice to count the day a note matures, but not the day it is signed, in computing interest.* Thus, in our example, interest would be earned for 18 days (December 14 to December 31) during 2007 and for 72 days in 2008:

Month	Number of Days Outstanding
December 2004	18 days
January 2005	31 days
February 2005	28 days
March 2005	13 days (matures on March 13, 2008)
Total days	90 days

Thus, the amount of interest earned during 2007 is $\$15,000 \times 0.12 \times 18/360$, or $90. An adjustment is made on December 31 to record interest earned during 2007:

	Balance Sheet						Income Statement	
ASSETS		=	**LIABILITIES**	+	**STOCKHOLDERS' EQUITY**	+	**REVENUES − EXPENSES**	
Interest Receivable	90						Interest Revenue	90

On March 13, 2008, HighTec collects the principal amount of the note and interest from Baker:

	Balance Sheet						Income Statement	
ASSETS		=	**LIABILITIES**	+	**STOCKHOLDERS' EQUITY**	+	**REVENUES − EXPENSES**	
Cash	15,450						Interest Revenue	360
Notes Receivable	(15,000)							
Interest Receivable	(90)							

This adjustment accomplishes a number of purposes. First, it removes the amount of $15,000 originally recorded in the Notes Receivable account. Second, it recognizes interest earned during the 72 days in 2008 that the note was outstanding. The calculation of interest earned during 2008 is as follows:

$$\$15,000 \times 0.12 \times 72/360 = \$360$$

Third, Interest Receivable for $90 is removed from the records now that the note has been collected. Finally, cash of $15,450 is collected, which represents the principal amount of the note, $15,000, plus interest of $450 for 90 days.

Accelerating the Inflow of Cash from Sales

LO5 Explain various techniques that companies use to accelerate the inflow of cash from sales.

Earlier in the chapter we pointed out why cash sales are preferable to credit sales: credit sales slow down the inflow of cash to the company and create the potential for bad debts. To remain competitive, most businesses find it necessary to grant credit to customers. That is, if one company won't grant credit to a customer, the customer may find another company that will. Companies have found it possible, however, to circumvent the problems inherent in credit sales. We now consider some approaches that companies use to speed up the flow of cash from sales.

CREDIT CARD SALES

Most retail establishments, as well as many service businesses, accept one or more major credit cards. Among the most common cards are MasterCard®, VISA®, American Express®, Carte Blanche®, Discover Card®, and Diners Club®. Most merchants find that they must honor at least one or more of these credit cards to remain competitive. In return for a fee, the merchant passes the responsibility for collection on to the credit card company. Thus, the credit card issuer assumes the risk of nonpayment. The basic relationships among the three parties—the customer, the merchant, and the credit company—are illustrated in Exhibit 7-4. Assume that Joe Smith buys an iPod in an Apple store and charges the $200 cost to his VISA credit card. When Joe is presented with his bill, he is asked to sign a multiple-copy **credit card draft** or invoice. Joe keeps one copy of the draft and leaves the other two copies at the Apple store. The store keeps one copy as the basis for recording its sales of the day and sends the other copy to VISA for payment. VISA uses the copy of the draft it gets for two purposes: to reimburse Apple $190 (keeping $10, or 5% of the original sale, as a collection fee) and to include Joe Smith's $200 purchase on the monthly bill it mails him.

Credit card draft
A multiple-copy document used by a company that accepts a credit card for a sale. *Alternate term: Invoice*

Assume that total credit card sales on June 5 amount to $8,000. The effect on the accounting equations is as follows:

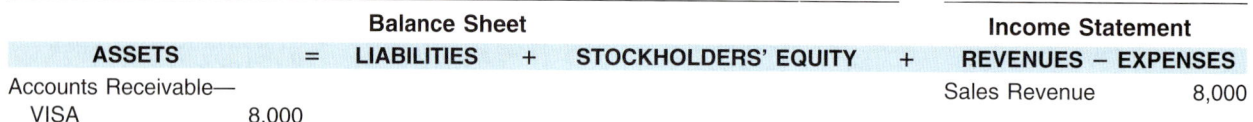

Balance Sheet						Income Statement	
ASSETS	=	**LIABILITIES**	+	**STOCKHOLDERS' EQUITY**	+	**REVENUES − EXPENSES**	
Accounts Receivable—VISA 8,000						Sales Revenue	8,000

EXHIBIT 7-4 Basic Relationships among Parties with Credit Card Sales

Assume that Apple remits the credit card draft to VISA once a week and that the total sales for the week ending June 11 amount to $50,000. Further assume that on June 13 VISA pays the amount due to Apple, after deducting a 5% collection fee. The adjustment is as follows:

Balance Sheet							Income Statement
ASSETS		=	**LIABILITIES**	+	**STOCKHOLDERS' EQUITY**	+	**REVENUES − EXPENSES**
Cash	47,500						Collection Fee Expense (2,500)
Accounts Receivable—							
VISA	(50,000)						

Some credit cards, such as MasterCard and VISA, allow a merchant to present a credit card draft directly for deposit in a bank account, in much the same way the merchant deposits checks, coins, and currency. Obviously, this type of arrangement is even more advantageous for the merchant because the funds are available as soon as the drafts are credited to the bank account. Assume that on July 9 Apple presents VISA credit card drafts to its bank for payment in the amount of $20,000 and that the collection charge is 4%. The effect of the collection is as follows:

Balance Sheet							Income Statement
ASSETS		=	**LIABILITIES**	+	**STOCKHOLDERS' EQUITY**	+	**REVENUES − EXPENSES**
Cash	19,200						Collection Fee Expense (800)
							Sales Revenue 20,000

DISCOUNTING NOTES RECEIVABLE

Promissory notes are negotiable, which means that they can be endorsed and given to someone else for collection. In other words, a company can sign the back of a note, just as it would a check, sell it to a bank, and receive cash before the note's maturity date. This process is called **discounting** and is another way for companies to speed the collection of cash from receivables. A note can be sold immediately to a bank on the date it is issued, or it can be sold after it has been outstanding but before the due date.

When a note is discounted at a bank, it is normally done "with recourse." This means that if the original customer fails to pay the bank the total amount due on the maturity date of the note, the company that transferred the note to the bank is liable for the full amount. Because there is uncertainty as to whether the company will have to make good on any particular note that it discounts at the bank, a contingent liability exists from the time the note is discounted until its maturity date. The accounting profession has adopted guidelines to decide whether a particular uncertainty requires that the company record a contingent liability on its balance sheet. Under these guidelines, the contingency created by the discounting of a note with recourse is not recorded as a liability. However, a note in the financial statements is used to inform the reader of the existing uncertainty.

Discounting
The process of selling a promissory note.

How Liquid Assets Affect the Statement of Cash Flows

As we discussed in Chapter 6, cash equivalents are combined with cash on the balance sheet. These items are very near maturity and do not present any significant risk of collectibility. Because of this, any purchases or redemptions of cash equivalents are not considered significant activities to be reported on a statement of cash flows.

The purchase and the sale of investments are considered significant activities and are therefore reported on the statement of cash flows. Cash flows from purchases,

LO6 Explain the effects of transactions involving liquid assets on the statement of cash flows.

sales, and maturities of investments are usually classified as investing activities. The following excerpt from **Apple**'s 2004 statement of cash flows illustrates the reporting for these activities (all amounts in millions of dollars):

Investing Activities	2004	2003	2002
Purchases of short-term investments	(3,270)	(2,648)	(4,144)
Proceeds from maturities of short-term investments	1,141	2,446	2,846
Proceeds from sales of short-term investments	801	1,116	1,254
Proceeds from sales of noncurrent investments	5	45	25

The collection of either accounts receivable or notes receivable generates cash for a business and affects the operating activities section of the statement of cash flows. Most companies use the indirect method of reporting cash flows and begin the statement of cash flows with the net income of the period. Net income includes the sales revenue for the period. Therefore, a decrease in accounts receivable or notes receivable during the period indicates that the company collected more cash than it recorded in sales revenue. Thus, a decrease in accounts receivable or notes receivable must be added back to net income because more cash was collected than is reflected in the sales revenue number. Alternatively, an increase in accounts receivable or notes receivable indicates that the company recorded more sales revenue than cash collected during the period. Therefore, an increase in accounts receivable or notes receivable requires deduction from the net income of the period to arrive at cash flow from operating activities. The following excerpt from Apple's 2004 statement of cash flows illustrates how it reports the change in accounts receivable on its statement of cash flows:

Operating Activities	2004	2003	2002
Changes in operating assets and liabilities:			
Accounts receivable	(8)	(201)	(99)

These adjustments, as well as the cash flows from buying and selling investments, are summarized in Exhibit 7-5. We present a complete discussion of the statement of cash flows, including the reporting of investments, in Chapter 12.

EXHIBIT 7-5 **How Investments and Receivables Affect the Statement of Cash Flows**

Accounting for Investments in Stocks and Bonds

Companies face a number of major issues in deciding how to account for and report on investments in the stocks and bonds of other companies:

1. **What should be the basis for the recognition of periodic income from an investment? That is, what event causes income to be recognized?**

2. **How should an investment be valued and thus reported at the end of an accounting period? At original cost? At fair value?**

3. **How should an investment be classified on a balance sheet? As a current asset? As a noncurrent asset?**

The answer to each of these questions depends on the type of investment. Accountants classify investments in the securities of other companies into one of three categories.[1]

Held-to-maturity securities: Investments in the bonds of other companies when the investor has the positive intent and the ability to hold the securities to maturity. Note that only bonds can qualify as held-to-maturity securities, because shares of stock do not have a maturity date.

Trading securities: Stocks and bonds that are bought and held for the purpose of selling them in the near term. These securities are usually held for only a short period of time with the objective of generating profits on short-term appreciation in the market price of the stocks and bonds.

Available-for-sale securities: Stocks and bonds that are not classified as either held-to-maturity or trading securities.

INVESTMENTS IN HELD-TO-MATURITY SECURITIES

By their nature, only bonds—not stock—can qualify as held-to-maturity securities. A bond is categorized as a held-to-maturity security if the investor plans to hold it until it matures. An investor may buy the bonds either on the original issuance date or later. If the investor buys them on the date they are originally issued, the purchase is from the issuer. It is also possible for an investor to buy bonds on the open market after they have been outstanding for a period of time.

Consider the following example. On January 1, 2007, ABC issues $10,000,000 of bonds that will mature in ten years. Assume that Atlantic buys $100,000 of these bonds at face value, which is the amount that will be repaid to the investor when the bonds mature. In many instances, bonds are purchased at an amount more or less than face value. We will limit our discussion, however, to the simpler case in which bonds are purchased for face value. The bonds pay 10% interest semiannually on June 30 and December 31. This means Atlantic will receive 5% of $100,000, or $5,000, on each of these dates. The effect of the purchase on the accounting equation is as follows:

L07 Show that you understand the accounting for and disclosure of investments in the stocks and bonds of other companies.

Held-to-maturity securities
Investments in bonds of other companies in which the investor has the positive intent and the ability to hold the securities to maturity.

Trading securities
Stocks and bonds of other companies bought and held for the purpose of selling them in the near term to generate profits on appreciation in their price.

Available-for-sale securities
Stocks and bonds that are not classified as either held-to-maturity or trading securities.

---

1 Statement of Financial Accounting Standards No. 115, "Accounting for Certain Investments in Debt and Equity Securities" (Stamford, Conn.: Financial Accounting Standards Board, May 1993), pars. 7–12.

Balance Sheet					Income Statement
ASSETS	=	LIABILITIES	+	STOCKHOLDERS' EQUITY	+	REVENUES – EXPENSES
Investment in Bonds 100,000					
Cash (100,000)					

On June 30, Atlantic must record the receipt of semiannual interest. The effect of the receipt of interest on this date is as follows:

Balance Sheet					Income Statement
ASSETS	=	LIABILITIES	+	STOCKHOLDERS' EQUITY	=	REVENUES – EXPENSES
Cash 5,000					Interest Revenue 5,000

Note that income was recognized when interest was received. If interest is not received at the end of an accounting period, a company should accrue interest earned but not yet received. Also note that an investment in held-to-maturity bonds is normally classified as a *noncurrent asset*. Any held-to-maturity bonds that are one year or less from maturity, however, are classified in the Current Assets section of a balance sheet.

Assume that before the maturity date, Atlantic needs cash and decides to sell the bonds. Keep in mind that this is a definite change in Atlantic's plans, since the bonds were initially categorized as held-to-maturity securities. Any difference between the proceeds received from the sale of the bonds and the amount paid for the bonds is recognized as either a gain or a loss.

Assume that on January 1, 2008, Atlantic sells all its ABC bonds at 99. This means that the amount of cash received is 0.99 × $100,000, or $99,000. The effect on the accounting equations from the sale of the bonds is as follows:

Balance Sheet					Income Statement
ASSETS	=	LIABILITIES	+	STOCKHOLDERS' EQUITY	+	REVENUES – EXPENSES
Cash 99,000					Loss on Sale of Bonds (1,000)
Investment in Bonds (100,000)					

The $1,000 loss on the sale of the bonds is the excess of the amount paid for the purchase of the bonds of $100,000 over the cash proceeds from the sale of $99,000. The loss is reported in the Other Income and Expenses section on the 2008 income statement.

INVESTMENTS IN TRADING SECURITIES

A company invests in trading securities as a way to profit from increases in the market prices of these securities over the short term. Because the intent is to hold them for the short term, trading securities are classified as current assets. All trading securities are recorded initially at cost, including any brokerage fees, commissions, or other fees paid to acquire the shares. Assume that Dexter Corp. invests in the following securities on November 30, 2007:

Security	Cost
Stuart common stock	$50,000
Menlo preferred stock	25,000
Total cost	$75,000

When Dexter buys the stocks, investments are increased and cash is reduced:

Balance Sheet					Income Statement
ASSETS	=	LIABILITIES	+	STOCKHOLDERS' EQUITY	+	REVENUES – EXPENSES
Investment in Stuart Common Stock 50,000					
Investment in Menlo Preferred Stock 25,000					
Cash (75,000)					

Many companies attempt to pay dividends every year as a signal of overall financial strength and profitability.[2] Assume that on December 10, 2007, Dexter received dividends of $1,000 from Stuart and $600 from Menlo. The dividends received from trading securities are recognized as income as shown in the accounting equation:

Balance Sheet							Income Statement	
ASSETS		**=**	**LIABILITIES**	**+**	**STOCKHOLDERS' EQUITY**	**+**	**REVENUES − EXPENSES**	
Cash	1,600						Dividend Income	1,600

Unlike interest on a bond or a note, dividends do not accrue over time. In fact, a company has no legal obligation to pay dividends until its board of directors declares them. Up to that point, the investor has no guarantee that dividends will ever be paid.

As noted earlier, trading securities are purchased with the intention of holding them for a short period of time. Assume that Dexter sells the Stuart stock on December 15, 2007, for $53,000. In this case, Dexter recognizes a gain for the excess of the cash proceeds, $53,000, over the amount recorded on the books, $50,000:

Balance Sheet							Income Statement	
ASSETS		**=**	**LIABILITIES**	**+**	**STOCKHOLDERS' EQUITY**	**+**	**REVENUES − EXPENSES**	
Cash	53,000						Gain on Sale of Stock	3,000
Investment in Stuart								
Common Stock	(50,000)							

The gain is considered realized and is classified on the income statement as other income.

Assume that on December 22, 2007, Dexter replaces the Stuart stock in its portfolio by purchasing Canby common stock for $40,000:

Balance Sheet							Income Statement	
ASSETS		**=**	**LIABILITIES**	**+**	**STOCKHOLDERS' EQUITY**	**+**	**REVENUES − EXPENSES**	
Investment in Canby								
Common Stock	40,000							
Cash	(40,000)							

Now assume that Dexter ends its accounting period on December 31. Should it adjust the carrying value of its investments to reflect their fair values or market prices on this date? According to the accounting profession, fair values should be used to report investments in trading securities on a balance sheet. The fair values are thought to be relevant information to the various users of financial statements. Assume the following information for Dexter on December 31, 2007:

Security	Total Cost	Total Fair Value on December 31, 2007	Gain (Loss)
Menlo preferred stock	$25,000	$27,500	$2,500
Canby common stock	40,000	39,000	(1,000)
Totals	$65,000	$66,500	$1,500

---

2 IBM's September 2006 dividend continued a string of consecutive quarterly dividends that started in 1916.

On December 31, Dexter will make an adjustment in its records that has the following effect on the accounting equation:

Balance Sheet				Income Statement	
ASSETS	=	**LIABILITIES** +	**STOCKHOLDERS' EQUITY** +	**REVENUES – EXPENSES**	
Investment in Menlo				Unrealized Gain—Trading	
Preferred Stock	2,500			Securities	1,500
Investment in Canby					
Common Stock	(1,000)				

Note that this adjustment results in each security being written up or down so that it will appear on the December 31 balance sheet at its market or fair value. This type of fair value accounting for trading securities is often referred to as a *mark-to-market* approach because at the end of each period, the value of each security is adjusted or "marked" to its current market value. It is important to realize that for trading securities, the changes in value are recognized on the income statement. The difference of $1,500 between the original cost of the two securities, $65,000, and their fair value, $66,500, is recorded in the account Unrealized Gain—Trading Securities to call attention to the fact that the securities have not been sold. Even though the gain or loss is *unrealized*, it is recognized on the income statement as a form of other income or loss.

Assume one final transaction in our Dexter example. On January 20, 2008, Dexter sells the Menlo stock for $27,000. The effect on the accounting equation of the sale is as follows:

Balance Sheet				Income Statement	
ASSETS	=	**LIABILITIES** +	**STOCKHOLDERS' EQUITY** +	**REVENUES – EXPENSES**	
Cash	27,000			Loss on Sale Stock	(500)
Investment in Menlo					
Preferred Stock	(27,500)				

The important point to note about this entry is that the $500 loss represents the difference between the cash proceeds of $27,000 and the fair value of the stock at the most recent reporting date, $27,500. Because the Menlo stock was adjusted to a fair value of $27,500 on December 31, the excess of this amount over the cash proceeds of $27,000 results in a loss of $500. Keep in mind that a gain of $2,500 was recognized last year when the stock was adjusted to its fair value at the end of the year. Thus, the net gain from the Menlo stock is the excess of the sales price of $27,000 over the cost of $25,000, or $2,000. The result is that this net amount is recognized in two periods:

- As a $2,500 holding gain in 2007.
- As a $500 loss on sale in 2008.

This is summarized as follows:

Date	Event	Amount	
November 30, 2007	Purchase	$25,000	Gain of $2,500 in 2007
December 31, 2007	Year-End	$27,500	
January 20, 2008	Sale	$27,000	Loss of ___500 in 2008
			Net Gain of $2,000

INVESTMENTS IN AVAILABLE-FOR-SALE SECURITIES

Stocks and bonds that do not qualify as trading securities and bonds that are not intended to be held to maturity are categorized as *available-for-sale securities*. The accounting for these securities is similar to the accounting for trading securities, with one major exception: even though fair value accounting is used to report available-for-sale securities at the end of an accounting period, any gains or losses resulting from marking to market are not reported on the income statement but instead are accumulated in a stockholders' equity account. This inconsistency is justified by the accounting profession on the grounds that the inclusion in income of fluctuations in the value of securities that are available for sale but that are not necessarily being actively traded could lead to volatility in reported earnings. Regardless, reporting gains and losses on the income statement for one class of securities but not for others is a subject of considerable debate. Investments in available-for-sale securities may be classified as either current or noncurrent assets.

To understand the use of fair value accounting for available-for-sale securities, assume that Lenox Corp. purchases two different stocks late in 2007. The costs and fair values at the end of 2007 are as follows:

Security	Total Cost	Total Fair Value on December 31, 2007	Gain (Loss)
Adair preferred stock	$15,000	$16,000	$ 1,000
Casey common stock	35,000	32,500	(2,500)
Totals	$50,000	$48,500	$(1,500)

On December 31, Lenox adjusts its record to reflect the changes in value of the two securities:

Balance Sheet							Income Statement
ASSETS		**=**	**LIABILITIES**	**+**	**STOCKHOLDERS' EQUITY**	**+**	**REVENUES − EXPENSES**
Investment in Adair					Unrealized Gain/Loss—		
Preferred Stock	1,000				Available-for-Sale		
Investment in Casey					Securities (1,500)		
Common Stock	(2,500)						

Note the similarity between this adjustment and the one we made at the end of the period in the example for trading securities on page 326. In both instances, the individual investments are adjusted to their fair values for purposes of presenting them on the year-end balance sheet. The unrealized loss of $1,500 does not, however, affect income in this case. Instead, the loss is shown as a reduction of stockholders' equity on the balance sheet.

Now assume that Lenox sells its Casey stock for $34,500 on June 30, 2008. The effect of the sale on the accounting equation is as follows:

Balance Sheet							Income Statement
ASSETS		**=**	**LIABILITIES**	**+**	**STOCKHOLDERS' EQUITY**	**+**	**REVENUES − EXPENSES**
Cash	34,500				Unrealized Gain/Loss—		Loss on Sale on Stock (500)
Investment in Casey					Available-for-Sale		
Common Stock	(32,500)				Securities 2,500		

Lenox recognizes a realized loss on the income statement of $500, which represents the excess of the cost of the stock of $35,000 over the cash proceeds of $34,500. Note, however, that the Investment in Casey Common Stock is removed from the books at $32,500, the fair value at the end of the prior period. Thus, it is also necessary to adjust the Unrealized Gain/Loss account for $2,500, the difference between the original cost of $35,000 and the fair value at the end of 2007 of $32,500.

Finally, assume that Lenox does not buy any additional securities during the remainder of 2008 and that the fair value of the one investment it holds, the Adair preferred stock, is $19,000 on December 31, 2008.

The adjustment on this date is as follows:

Balance Sheet							Income Statement
ASSETS		**=**	**LIABILITIES**	**+**	**STOCKHOLDERS' EQUITY**	**+**	**REVENUES − EXPENSES**
Investment in Adair					Unrealized Gain/Loss—		
Preferred Stock	3,000				Available-for-Sale		
					Securities 3,000		

EXHIBIT 7-6 **Accounting for Investments without Significant Influence**

Categories	Types	Asset Classified on Balance Sheet as	Recognize as Income	Report on Balance Sheet at	Report Changes in Fair Value on
Held-to-maturity	Bonds	Noncurrent*	Interest	Cost**	Not applicable
Trading	Bonds, stock	Current	Interest, dividends	Fair value	Income statement
Available-for-sale	Bonds, stock	Current or noncurrent	Interest, dividends	Fair value	Balance sheet (in stockholders' equity)

*Reclassified as current if they mature within one year of the balance sheet date.

**As mentioned earlier, bonds are often purchased at an amount more or less than face value. When this is the case, the bond account must be adjusted periodically, and the asset is reported on the balance sheet at amortized cost.

The increase in Investment in Adair Preferred Stock results in a balance of $19,000 in this account, the fair value of the stock. The stockholders' equity account now has a *positive* balance of $4,000, as follows:

Adjustment on December 31, 2007	$(1,500)
Adjustment on June 30, 2008	2,500
Adjustment on December 31, 2008	3,000
Balance on December 31, 2008	$ 4,000

The balance of $4,000 in this account represents the excess of the $19,000 fair value of the one security now held over its original cost of $15,000.

SUMMARY OF ACCOUNTING AND REPORTING REQUIREMENTS

A summary of the accounting and reporting requirements for each of the three categories of investments is shown in Exhibit 7-6.

- **Periodic income from each of these types of investments is recognized in the form of interest and dividends.**

- **Held-to-maturity bonds are reported on the balance sheet at amortized cost** (see second footnote in Exhibit 7-6).

- **Both trading securities and available-for-sale securities are reported on the balance sheet at fair value.**

- **Unrealized gains and losses from holding trading securities are recognized on the income statement, whereas these same gains and losses for available-for-sale securities are accumulated in a stockholders' equity account.**

THE CONTROVERSY OVER FAIR VALUE ACCOUNTING

Only recently have accounting standards changed to require that certain investments be reported at fair value. Before the change, the lower-of-cost-or-market rule was followed when accounting for these investments. The use of market or fair values is clearly an exception to the cost principle as first introduced in Chapter 1. Whether the exception is justified has been, and will continue to be, a matter of debate.

One concern of financial statement users is the hybrid system now used to report assets on a balance sheet. Consider the following types of assets and how we report them on the balance sheet:

Asset	Reported on the Balance Sheet at
Inventories	Lower of cost or market
Investments	Either cost or fair value
Property, plant, and equipment	Original cost, less accumulated depreciation

It is difficult to justify so many different valuation methods to report the assets of a single company. The lower-of-cost-or-market approach to valuing inventory is based on conservatism. Why should it be used for inventories while fair value is used for investments? Proponents of fair values believe that the information provided to the reader of the statements is more relevant, and they argue that the subjectivity inherent in valuing other types of assets is not an issue when dealing with securities that have a ready market. The controversy surrounding the valuation of assets on a balance sheet is likely to continue.

2 minute review

1. What are the three categories of investments?

2. Two of the three categories of investments may contain either stocks or bonds. Which one of the three contains only bonds? Explain your answer.

3. What is the one major distinction between the reporting requirements for trading securities and for available-for sale securities?

Answers

1. *Held-to-maturity, trading, and available-for-sale.*

2. *Bonds are the only securities that can be held to maturity. Stocks do not have a maturity date.*

3. *Any changes in fair value of trading securities are reported on the income statement. Changes in fair value of available-for-sale securities are reported in stockholders' equity on the balance sheet.*

STUDY HIGHLIGHTS

Show that you understand the accounting for and disclosure of various types of investments that companies make (p. 306).   **LO1**

- Typically, excess cash expected to last for short periods of time is invested in highly liquid financial instruments, such as CDs.
- Sometimes cash is also invested in securities of other corporations:
  - Equity securities—securities issued by corporations as a form of ownership in the business.
  - Debt securities—securities issued by corporation as a form of borrowing.
- At times, a company may wish to purchase a relatively large portion of another firm's stock to acquire influence over that firm.

Show that you understand how to account for accounts receivable, including bad debts (p. 310).   **LO2**

- Accounts receivable arise from sales on credit. Companies with many customers may keep detailed records of accounts receivable in a separate subsidiary ledger.
- Because not all customers pay their accounts receivable, an estimate of the accounts receivable less any doubtful accounts must be presented on the balance sheet.
- Bad debts are estimated under the allowance method by one of two approaches:
  - Percentage of net credit sales
  - Percentage of net receivables

Explain how information about sales and receivables can be combined to evaluate how efficient a company is in collecting its receivables (p. 316).   **LO3**

- Information about net credit sales and the average accounts receivable balance may be combined to calculate the accounts receivable turnover to see how well a company is managing its collections on account.

HIGHLIGHTS

LO4 **Show that you understand how to account for interest-bearing notes receivable (p. 318).**

- Notes receivable ultimately result in the receipt of both interest and principal to the holder of the notes.
- Because interest receipts may not coincide with the end of the period, adjusting entries may need to be made to accrue interest receivable and interest revenue.

LO5 **Explain various techniques that companies use to accelerate the inflow of cash from sales (p. 320).**

- To be competitive, companies must make sales on credit to customers.
- One way to avoid bad debts associated with extending credit directly to the customer, and to accelerate cash collections from sales, is by accepting credit cards for payment of goods and services.

LO6 **Explain the effects of transactions involving liquid assets on the statement of cash flows (p. 321).**

- Changes in cash equivalents are not shown on the statement.
- Cash flows related to the purchase and sale of investments are classified as Investing Activities in the statement of cash flows.
- Under the indirect method, increases in accounts and notes receivable are deducted and decreases in these accounts are added back in the Operating Activities section of the statement.

LO7 **Show that you understand the accounting for and disclosure of investments in the stocks and bonds of other companies (Appendix p. 323).**

- Held-to-Maturity Securities
  - These are bonds that the investor plans to hold until they mature. Interest is earned on the bonds while they are held.
- Trading Securities
  - These are held for the short term.
  - Interest or dividends are recognized as income.
  - They are adjusted to fair value at the end of an accounting period.
  - Any increase or decrease in value is recognized on the income statement.
- Available-for-Sale Securities
  - Those securities not classified as either held-to-maturity or trading.
  - Rules are similar to those for trading securities.
  - Primary difference is that changes in fair values are not recognized on the income statement; instead, they are reported as a separate component of stockholders' equity.

RATIO REVIEW

$$\text{Accounts Receivable Turnover} = \frac{\text{Net Credit Sales (Income Statement)}}{\text{Average Accounts Receivable (Balance Sheet)}}$$

ACCOUNTS HIGHLIGHTED

Account Titles	Where It Appears	In What Section	Page Number
Short-term investments	Balance Sheet	Current Assets	307
Long-term investments	Balance Sheet	Noncurrent Assets	324
Accounts receivable	Balance Sheet	Current Assets	310
Allowance for doubtful accounts	Balance Sheet	Current Assets	312

(continued)

Bad debts expense	Income Statement	Operating Expenses	312
Notes receivable	Balance Sheet	Current or Noncurrent Assets	319
Interest receivable	Balance Sheet	Current Assets	319
Interest revenue	Income Statement	Other Income	319
Unrealized gain/loss— available-for-sale securities	Balance Sheet	Stockholders' Equity	327
Unrealized gain/loss— trading securities	Income Statement	Other Income	326
Gain/loss on sale of investments	Income Statement	Other Income	324

KEY TERMS QUIZ

Read each definition below and then write the number of the definition in the blank beside the appropriate term it defines. The quiz solutions appear at the end of the chapter.

_____	Equity securities	_____	Note receivable
_____	Debt securities	_____	Note payable
_____	Account receivable	_____	Principal
_____	Subsidiary ledger	_____	Maturity date
_____	Control account	_____	Term
_____	Direct write-off method	_____	Maturity value
_____	Allowance method	_____	Interest
_____	Allowance for doubtful accounts	_____	Credit card draft
_____	Aging schedule	_____	Discounting
_____	Promissory note	_____	Held-to-maturity securities
_____	Maker	_____	Trading securities
_____	Payee	_____	Available-for-sale securities

1. Securities issued by corporations as a form of ownership in the business.
2. Securities issued by corporations and governmental bodies as a form of borrowing.
3. Stocks and bonds of other companies bought and held for the purpose of selling them in the near term to generate profits on appreciation in their price.
4. Stocks and bonds that are not classified as either held-to-maturity or trading securities.
5. Investments in bonds of other companies in which the investor has the positive intent and the ability to hold the securities to maturity.
6. A method of estimating bad debts on the basis of either the net credit sales of the period or the accounts receivable at the end of the period.
7. The party that will receive the money from a promissory note at some future date.
8. A written promise to repay a definite sum of money on demand or at a fixed or determinable date in the future.
9. A liability resulting from the signing of a promissory note.
10. A multiple-copy document used by a company that accepts a credit card for a sale.
11. An asset resulting from the acceptance of a promissory note from another company.
12. The process of selling a promissory note.
13. The party that agrees to repay the money for a promissory note at some future date.
14. A form used to categorize the various individual accounts receivable according to the length of time each has been outstanding.
15. The detail for a number of individual items that collectively make up a single general ledger account.
16. The recognition of bad debts expense at the point an account is written off as uncollectible.
17. The general ledger account that is supported by a subsidiary ledger.
18. The difference between the principal amount of the note and its maturity value.
19. The amount of cash received, or the fair value of the products or services received, by the maker when a promissory note is issued.

20. The amount of cash the maker is to pay the payee on the maturity date of the note.
21. The length of time a note is outstanding; that is, the period of time between the date it is issued and the date it matures.
22. The date that the promissory note is due.
23. A contra-asset account used to reduce accounts receivable to its net realizable value.
24. A receivable arising from the sale of goods or services with a verbal promise to pay.

ALTERNATE TERMS

Allowance for doubtful accounts Allowance for uncollectible accounts

Credit card draft Invoice

Debt securities Bonds

Equity securities Stocks

Net realizable value Net recoverable amount

Short-term investments Marketable securities

WARMUP EXERCISES

Warmup Exercise 7-1 Accounting for Bad Debts

Brown Corp. ended the year with balances in Accounts Receivable of $60,000 and in Allowance for Doubtful Accounts of $800 (credit balance before adjustment). Net sales for the year amounted to $200,000. Determine the effect on the accounting equation, assuming the following:

1. Estimated percentage of net sales uncollectible is 1%.
2. Estimated percentage of year-end accounts receivable uncollectible is 4%.

Key to the Solution Recall that the percentage of net sales approach does not take into account any existing balance in the allowance account, but the percentage of receivables approach does.

Warmup Exercise 7-2 Investments (Appendix)

Indicate whether each of the following events will result in an increase (I), decrease (D), or have no effect (NE) on net income for the period.

1. Trading securities are sold for more than their carrying value.
2. An interest check is received for held-to-maturity securities.
3. Available-for-sale securities increase in value during the period.
4. Available-for-sale securities are sold for less than their carrying value.
5. Trading securities decrease in value during the period.
6. Held-to-maturity securities are redeemed on their maturity date at face value.

Key to the Solution Recall from earlier in the chapter the differences in accounting for the various types of investments.

SOLUTIONS TO WARMUP EXERCISES

Warmup Exercise 7-1

	Balance Sheet				Income Statement	
ASSETS	=	LIABILITIES	+	STOCKHOLDERS' EQUITY +	REVENUES − EXPENSES	
1. Allowance for Doubtful Accounts (2,000)					Bad Debts Expense	(2,000)
2. Allowance for Doubtful Accounts (1,600)					Bad Debts Expense	(1,600)

Warmup Exercise 7-2

1. I 2. I 3. NE 4. D 5. D 6. NE

REVIEW

REVIEW PROBLEM

The following items pertain to the current assets section of the balance sheet for Jackson Corp. at the end of its accounting year, December 31, 2007. Each item must be considered and any necessary adjustment recognized. Additionally, the accountant for Jackson wants to develop the current assets section of the balance sheet as of the end of 2007.

a. Cash and cash equivalents amount to $19,375.
b. A 9%, 120-day certificate of deposit was purchased on December 1, 2007, for $10,000.
c. Gross accounts receivable at December 31, 2007, amount to $44,000. Before adjustment, the balance in Allowance for Doubtful Accounts is $340. Based on past experience, the accountant estimates that 3% of the gross accounts receivable outstanding at December 31, 2007, will prove to be uncollectible.
d. A customer's 12%, 90-day promissory note in the amount of $6,000 is held at the end of the year. The note has been held for 45 days during 2007.

Required

1. Determine the effect on the accounting equation from the adjustments in parts (b),(c), and (d).
2. Prepare the current assets section of Jackson's balance sheet as of December 31, 2007. In addition to items a–d, the balances in Inventory and Prepaid Insurance on this date are $65,000 and $4,800, respectively.

SOLUTION TO REVIEW PROBLEM

1. The effect on the accounting equation from each item is as follows:
   b. Jackson needs an adjustment to record interest earned on the certificate of deposit. The CD has been outstanding for 30 days during 2007; therefore, the amount of interest earned is calculated as follows:

$$\$10,000 \times 0.09 \times 30/360 = \$75$$

The effect of the adjustment is as follows:

	Balance Sheet					Income Statement	
ASSETS	**=**	**LIABILITIES**	**+**	**STOCKHOLDERS' EQUITY**	**+**	**REVENUES − EXPENSES**	
Interest Receivable 75						Interest Revenue	75

   c. Based on gross accounts receivable of $44,000 at year-end and an estimate that 3% of this amount will be uncollectible, the balance in Allowance for Doubtful Accounts should be $1,320 ($44,000 × 3%). Given a current balance of $340, an adjustment for $980 ($1,320 − $340) is needed to bring the balance to the desired amount of $1,320:

	Balance Sheet					Income Statement	
ASSETS	**=**	**LIABILITIES**	**+**	**STOCKHOLDERS' EQUITY**	**+**	**REVENUES − EXPENSES**	
Allowance for Doubtful Accounts (980)						Bad Debts Expense	(980)

   d. An adjustment is needed to accrue interest on the promissory note ($6,000 × 0.12 × 45/360 = $90):

	Balance Sheet					Income Statement	
ASSETS	**=**	**LIABILITIES**	**+**	**STOCKHOLDERS' EQUITY**	**+**	**REVENUES − EXPENSES**	
Interest Receivable 90						Interest Revenue	90

REVIEW

2. The current assets section of Jackson's balance sheet appears as follows:

Jackson Corp.
Partial Balance Sheet
December 31, 2007

Current assets:		
Cash and cash equivalents		$ 19,375
Certificate of deposit		10,000
Accounts receivable	$44,000	
Less: Allowance for doubtful accounts	1,320	42,680
Notes receivable		6,000
Interest receivable		165*
Inventory		65,000
Prepaid insurance		4,800
Total current assets		$148,020

*$75 from CD and $90 from promissory note

QUESTIONS

1. On December 31, Stockton Inc. invests idle cash in two different certificates of deposit. The first is an 8%, 90-day CD, and the second has an interest rate of 9% and matures in 120 days. How is each of these CDs classified on the December 31 balance sheet?

2. What is the theoretical justification for the allowance method of accounting for bad debts?

3. In estimating bad debts, why is the balance in Allowance for Doubtful Accounts considered when the percentage of accounts receivable approach is used but not when the percentage of net credit sales approach is used?

4. When estimating bad debts on the basis of a percentage of accounts receivable, what is the advantage of using an aging schedule?

5. What is the distinction between an account receivable and a note receivable?

6. Why does the discounting of a note receivable with recourse result in a contingent liability? Should the liability be reported on the balance sheet?

7. Stanzel Corp. purchased 1,000 shares of IBM common stock. What will determine whether the shares are classified as trading securities or available-for-sale securities? (Appendix)

8. What is the primary difference in the accounting requirements for trading securities and available-for-sale securities? How is this difference justified? (Appendix)

9. Why are changes in the fair value of trading securities reported in the account Unrealized Gains/Losses—Trading Securities even though the gains and losses are reported on the income statement? (Appendix)

EXERCISES

LO1   **Exercise 7-1** Certificate of Deposit

On May 31, 2007, Elmer Corp. purchased a 120-day, 9% certificate of deposit for $50,000. The CD was redeemed on September 28, 2007. Determine the effect on the accounting equation of:

a. The purchase of the CD.
b. The accrual of interest adjustment for interest earned through June 30, the end of the company's fiscal year.
c. The redemption of the CD.

Assume 360 days in a year.

LO1   **Exercise 7-2** Classification of Cash Equivalents and Investments on a Balance Sheet

Classify each of the following items as either a cash equivalent (CE), a short-term investment (STI), or a long-term investment (LTI).

1. A 120-day certificate of deposit.
2. Three hundred shares of GM common stock. The company plans on selling the stock in six months.

3. A six-month U.S Treasury bill.
4. A 60-day certificate of deposit.
5. Ford Motor Co. bonds maturing in 15 years. The company intends to hold the bonds until maturity.
6. Commercial paper issued by ABC Corp., maturing in four months.
7. 500 shares of Chrysler common stock. The company plans to sell the stock in 60 days to help pay for a note due at that time at the bank.
8. 200 shares of GE preferred stock. The company intends to hold the stock for 10 years and then sell it to help finance construction of a new factory.
9. Ten-year U.S. Treasury bonds. The company plans to sell the bonds on the open market in six months.
10. A 90-day U.S. Treasury bill.

LO2

Exercise 7-3 Comparison of the Direct Write-Off and Allowance Methods of Accounting for Bad Debts

In its first year of business, Rideaway Bikes has net income of $145,000, exclusive of any adjustment for bad debt expense. The president of the company has asked you to calculate net income under each of two alternatives of accounting for bad debts: the direct write-off method and the allowance method. The president would like to use the method that will result in the higher net income. So far, no adjustments have been made to write off uncollectible accounts or to estimate bad debts. The relevant data are as follows:

Write-offs of uncollectible accounts during the year	$10,500
Net credit sales	$650,000
Estimated percentage of net credit sales that will be uncollectible	2%

Required

Compute net income under each of the two alternatives. Does Rideaway have a choice as to which method to use? If so, should it base its choice on which method will result in the higher net income? (Ignore income taxes.)

LO2

Exercise 7-4 Allowance Method of Accounting for Bad Debts—Comparison of the Two Approaches

Kandel Company had the following data available for 2007 (before making any adjustments):

Accounts receivable, 12/31/07	$320,100
Allowance for doubtful accounts	2,600
Net credit sales, 2007	834,000

Required

Determine the effect on the accounting equation of the adjustment to recognize bad debts under the following assumptions: (a) bad debts expense is expected to be 2% of net credit sales for the year, and (b) Kandel expects it will not be able to collect 6% of the balance in accounts receivable at year-end.

LO3

Exercise 7-5 Accounts Receivable Turnover for General Mills

The 2004 annual report of **General Mills** (the maker of Cheerios® and Wheaties®) reported the following amounts (in millions of dollars).

Net sales, for the year ended May 30, 2004	$11,070
Receivables, less allowance for doubtful accounts of $19, May 30, 2004	1,010
Receivable, less allowance for doubtful accounts of $28, May 25, 2003	980

Required

1. Compute General Mills' accounts receivable turnover ratio for 2004. (Assume that all sales are on credit.)
2. What is the average collection period, in days, for an account receivable? Explain your answer.
3. Give some examples of the types of customers you would expect General Mills to have. Do you think the average collection period for sales to these customers is reasonable? What other information do you need to fully answer this question?

HOMEWORK

LO4

Exercise 7-6 Notes Receivable

On September 1, 2007, Dougherty Corp. accepted a six-month, 7%, $45,000 interest-bearing note from Rozelle Company in payment of an accounts receivable. Dougherty's year-end is December 31. Rozelle paid the note and interest on the due date.

Required

1. Who is the maker and who is the payee of the note?
2. What is the maturity date of the note?
3. Determine the effect on Dougherty's accounting equation of:
   a. The acceptance of the note.
   b. The accrual of interest earned through December 31, 2007, the end of the company's year.
   c. Receipt of payment of the note and interest.

LO5

Exercise 7-7 Credit Card Sales

Darlene's Diner accepts American Express® credit cards from its customers. Darlene's is closed on Sundays and on that day records the weekly sales and remits the credit card drafts to American Express. For the week ending on Sunday, June 12, cash sales totaled $2,430, and credit card sales amounted to $3,500. On June 15, Darlene's received $3,360 from American Express as payment for the credit card drafts. Determine the effect on the accounting equation on June 12 and June 15. As a percentage, what collection fee is American Express charging Darlene?

LO6

Exercise 7-8 Impact of Transactions Involving Receivables on Statement of Cash Flows

From the following list, identify whether the change in the account balance during the year would be added to or deducted from net income when the indirect method is used to determine cash flows from operating activities.

Increase in accounts receivable
Decrease in accounts receivable
Increase in notes receivable
Decrease in notes receivable

LO6

Exercise 7-9 Cash Collections—Direct Method

Emily Enterprises' comparative balance sheets included accounts receivable of $224,600 at December 31, 2006, and $205,700 at December 31, 2007. Sales reported on Emily's 2007 income statement amounted to $2,250,000. What is the amount of cash collections that Emily will report in the operating activities category of its 2007 statement of cash flows assuming that the direct method is used?

LO7

Exercise 7-10 Classification of Investments (Appendix)

Red Oak makes the following investments in the stock of other companies during 2007. For each investment, indicate how it would be accounted for and where it would be reported. Use the following designations: trading security (T), available-for-sale security (AS), equity investee (E), or a subsidiary included in consolidated statements (S).

1. 500 shares of ABC common stock to be held for short-term share appreciation.
2. 20,000 shares of the 50,000 shares of Ace common stock to be held for the long term.
3. 100 shares of Creston preferred stock to be held for an indefinite period of time.
4. 80,000 of the 100,000 shares of Orient common stock.
5. 10,000 of the 40,000 shares of Omaha preferred stock to be held for the long term.

LO7

Exercise 7-11 Classification of Investments (Appendix)

Indicate whether each of the following investments should be classified as a held-to-maturity security (HM), a trading security (T), or an available-for-sale security (AS):

1. Shares of IBM stock to be held indefinitely.
2. GM bonds due in 10 years. The intent is to hold them until they mature.
3. Shares of Motorola stock. Plans are to hold the stock until the price goes up by 10% and then sell it.
4. Ford Motor Company bonds due in 15 years. The bonds are part of a portfolio that turns over an average of every 60 days.
5. Chrysler bonds due in 10 years. Plans are to hold them indefinitely.

LO7   **Exercise 7-12** Purchase and Sale of Bonds (Appendix)

Starship Enterprises enters into the following transactions during 2007 and 2008:

2007
Jan.   1:   Purchased $100,000 face value of Northern Lights Inc. bonds at face value. The newly issued bonds have an inerest rate of 8% paid semiannually on June 30 and December 31. The bonds mature in five years.
June 30:   Received interest on the Northern Lights bonds.
Dec. 31:   Received interest on the Northern Lights bonds.

2008
Jan.   1:   Sold the Northern Lights Inc. bonds for $102,000.

Assume Starship classifies all bonds as held to maturity.

Required
1. Determine the effect on Starship's accounting equation on each of the preceding dates.
2. Why was Starship able to sell its Northern Lights bonds for $102,000?

LO7   **Exercise 7-13** Investment in Stock (Appendix)

On December 1, 2007, Chicago Corp. purchases 1,000 shares of the preferred stock of Denver Corp. for $40 per share. Chicago expects the price of the stock to increase over the next few months and plans to sell it for a profit. On December 20, 2007, Denver declares a dividend of $1 per share to be paid on January 15, 2008. On December 31, 2007, Chicago's accounting year-end, the Denver stock is trading on the market at $42 per share. Chicago sells the stock on February 12, 2008, at a price of $45 per share.

Required
1. Should Chicago classify its investments as held-to-maturity, trading, or available-for-sale securities? Explain your answer.
2. Determine the effects on the accounting equation of Chicago's purchase of the preferred stock on December 1, 2007; the dividend declared on December 20, 2007; the change in market value at December 31, 2007; the receipt of the dividend on January 15, 2008; and the sale on February 12, 2008.
3. In what category of the balance sheet should Chicago classify its investment on its December 31, 2007, balance sheet?

LO7   **Exercise 7-14** Investment in Stock (Appendix)

On August 15, 2007, Cubs Corp. purchases 5,000 shares of common stock in Sox Inc. at a market price of $15 per share. In addition, Cubs' pays brokerage fees of $1,000. Cubs plans to hold the stock indefinitely rather than as a part of its active trading portfolio. The market value of the stock is $13 per share on December 31, 2007, the end of Cubs' accounting year. On July 8, 2008, Cubs sells the Sox stock for $10 per share.

Required
1. Should Cubs classify its investment as held-to-maturity, trading, or available-for-sale securities? Explain your answer.
2. Determine the effects on the accounting equation of Cubs' purchase of the common stock on August 15, 2007; the change in market value at December 31, 2007; and the sale on July 8, 2008.
3. In what category of the balance sheet should Cubs classify its investment on its December 31, 2007, balance sheet?

MULTI-CONCEPT EXERCISE

LO1,2,6   **Exercise 7-15** Impact of Transactions Involving Cash, Securities, and Receivables on Statement of Cash Flows

From the following list, identify each item as operating (O), investing (I), financing (F), or not separately reported on the statement of cash flows (N). Assume that the indirect method is used to determine the cash flows from operating activities.

     Purchase of cash equivalents
     Redemption of cash equivalents

Purchase of investments
Sale of investments
Write-off of customer account (under the allowance method)

PROBLEMS

LO2

Problem 7-1 Allowance Method for Accounting for Bad Debts

At the beginning of 2007, EZ Tech Company's accounts receivable balance was $140,000, and the balance in Allowance for Doubtful Accounts was $2,350. EZ Tech's sales in 2007 were $1,050,000, 80% of which were on credit. Collections on account during the year were $670,000. The company wrote off $4,000 of uncollectible accounts during the year.

Required
1. Determine the effect on EZ's accounting equation relative to the sale, collections, and write-offs of accounts receivable during 2007.
2. Determine the effect on EZ's accounting equation of the estimate of bad debts, assuming (a) bad debt expense is 3% of credit sales and (b) amounts expected to be uncollectible are 6% of the year-end accounts receivable.
3. What is the net realizable value of accounts receivable on December 31, 2007, under each assumption in part (2)?
4. What effect does the recognition of bad debt expense have on the net realizable value? What effect does the write-off of accounts have on the net realizable value?

LO2

Problem 7-2 Aging Schedule to Account for Bad Debts

Sparkle Jewels distributes fine stones. It sells on credit to retail jewelry stores and extends terms that require the stores to pay in 60 days. For accounts that are not overdue, Sparkle has found that there is a 95% probability of collection. For accounts up to one month past due, the likelihood of collection decreases to 80%. If accounts are between one and two months past due, the probability of collection is 60%, and if an account is over two months past due, Sparkle Jewels estimates that there is only a 40% chance of collecting the receivable.

On December 31, 2007, the balance in Allowance for Doubtful Accounts is $12,300. The amounts of gross receivables, by age, on this date are as follows:

Category	Amount
Current	$200,000
Past due:	
Less than one month	45,000
One to two months	25,000
Over two months	10,000

Required
1. Prepare a schedule to estimate the amount of uncollectible accounts at December 31, 2007.
2. On the basis of the schedule in part (1), determine the effect on the accounting equation of the estimate of bad debts at December 31, 2007.
3. Show how accounts receivable would be presented on the December 31, 2007, balance sheet.

LO3

Problem 7-3 Accounts Receivable Turnover for Whirlpool and Maytag

The following information was summarized from the 2004 annual report of **Whirlpool Corporation**:

	(in millions)
Trade receivables, less allowances (2004: $107; 2003: $113)	
December 31, 2004	$ 2,032
December 31, 2003	1,913
Net sales for the year ended December 31:	
2004	13,220
2003	12,176

The following information was summarized from the 2004 annual report of **Maytag Corporation**:

	(in thousands)
Accounts receivable, less allowance for doubtful accounts (2004—$9,678; 2003—$15,752)	
January 1, 2005	$ 629,901
January 3, 2004	596,832
Net sales for the year ended:	
January 1, 2005	4,721,538
January 3, 2004	4,791,866

Required

1. Calculate the accounts receivable turnover ratios for Whirlpool and Maytag for 2004.
2. Calculate the average collection period, in days, for both companies for 2004. Comment on the reasonableness of the collection periods for these companies considering the nature of their business.
3. Which company appears to be performing better? What other information should you consider in determining how these companies are performing?

LO5

Problem 7-4 Credit Card Sales

Gas stations sometimes sell gasoline at a lower price to customers who pay cash than to customers who use a charge card. A local gas station owner pays 2% of the sales price to the credit card company when customers pay with a credit card. The owner pays $0.75 per gallon of gasoline and must earn at least $0.25 per gallon of gross profit to stay competitive.

Required

1. Determine the price the owner must charge credit card customers to maintain the station's gross profit.
2. How much discount could the owner offer to cash customers and still maintain the same gross profit?

LO6

Problem 7-5 Effects of Changes in Receivable Balances on Statement of Cash Flows

Stegner Inc. reported net income of $130,000 for the year ended December 31, 2007. The following items were included on Stegner's balance sheets at December 31, 2007 and 2006:

	12/31/07	12/31/06
Cash	$105,000	$110,000
Accounts receivable	223,000	83,000
Notes receivable	95,000	100,000

Stegner uses the indirect method to prepare its statement of cash flows. Stegner does not have any other current assets or current liabilities and did not enter into any investing or financing activities during 2007.

Required

1. Prepare Stegner's 2007 statement of cash flows.
2. Draft a brief memo to the owner to explain why cash decreased during a profitable year.

LO7

Problem 7-6 Investments in Bonds and Stock (Appendix)

Swartz Inc. enters into the following transactions during 2007:

July   1: Paid $10,000 to acquire on the open market $10,000 face value of Gallatin bonds. The bonds have a stated annual interest rate of 6% with interest paid semiannually on June 30 and December 31. The bonds mature in 5½ years.
Oct. 23: Purchased 600 shares of Eagle Rock common stock at $20 per share.
Nov. 21: Purchased 200 shares of Montana preferred stock at $30 per share.
Dec. 10: Received dividends of $1.50 per share on the Eagle Rock stock and $2.00 per share on the Montana stock.
Dec. 28: Sold 400 shares of Eagle Rock common stock at $25 per share.
Dec. 31: Received interest from the Gallatin bonds.
Dec. 31: Noted market price of $29 per share for the Eagle Rock stock and $26 per share for the Montana stock.

Required

1. Determine the effect on the accounting equation of each of the preceding transactions. Swartz classifies the bonds as held-to-maturity securities and all stock investments as trading securities.
2. Prepare a partial balance sheet as of December 31, 2007, to indicate the proper presentation of the investments.
3. Indicate the items, and the amount of each, that will appear on the 2007 income statement relative to the investments.

LO7 **Problem 7-7** Investments in Stock (Appendix)

Atlas Superstores occasionally finds itself with excess cash to invest and consequently entered into the following transactions during 2007:

Jan. 15: Purchased 200 shares of Sears common stock at $50 per share, plus $500 in commissions.
May 23: Received dividends of $2 per share on the Sears stock.
June 1: Purchased 100 shares of Ford Motor Co. stock at $74 per share, plus $300 in commissions.
Oct. 20: Sold all the Sears stock at $42 per share, less commissions of $400.
Dec. 15: Received notification from Ford Motor Co. that a $1.50 per share dividend had been declared. The checks will be mailed to stockholders on January 10, 2008.
Dec. 31: Noted that the Ford Motor Co. stock was quoted on the stock exchange at $85 per share.

Required

1. Determine the effect on Atlas's accounting equation of each of the preceding transactions. Assume that Atlas categorizes all investments as available-for-sale securities.
2. What is the total amount that Atlas should report on its income statement from its investments during 2007?
3. Assume all the same facts except that Atlas categorizes all investments as trading securities. How would your answer to part (2) change? Explain why your answer would change.

MULTI-CONCEPT PROBLEM

LO2,4 **Problem 7-8** Accounts and Notes Receivable

Linus Corp. sold merchandise for $5,000 to C. Brown on May 15, 2007, with payment due in 30 days. Subsequent to this, Brown experienced cash flow problems and was unable to pay its debt. On August 10, 2007, Linus stopped trying to collect the outstanding receivable from Brown and wrote off the account as uncollectible. On December 1, 2007, Brown sent Linus a check for $1,000 and offered to sign a two-month, 9%, $4,000 promissory note to satisfy the remaining obligation. Brown paid the entire amount due Linus, with interest, on January 31, 2008. Linus ends its accounting year on December 31 each year, and uses the allowance method to account for bad debts.

Required

1. For each of the transactions during the period from May 15, 2007, to January 31, 2008, determine the effect on Linus's accounting equation.
2. Why would Brown bother to send Linus a check for $1,000 on December 1 and agree to sign a note for the balance, given that such a long period of time had passed since the original purchase?

ALTERNATE PROBLEMS

LO2 **Problem 7-1A** Allowance Method for Accounting for Bad Debts

At the beginning of 2007, Miyazaki Company's accounts receivable balance was $105,000, and the balance in Allowance for Doubtful Accounts was $1,950. Miyazaki's sales in 2007 were $787,500, 80% of which were on credit. Collections on account during the year were $502,500. The company wrote off $3,000 of uncollectible accounts during the year.

Required

1. Determine the effect on Miyazaki's accounting equation of the sales, collections, and write-offs of accounts receivable during 2007.
2. Determine the effect on Miyazaki's accounting equation of the estimate of bad debts, assuming (a) bad debt expense is 3% of credit sales or (b) amounts expected to be uncollectible are 6% of the year-end accounts receivable.
3. What is the net realizable value of accounts receivable on December 31, 2007, under each assumption in part (2)?
4. What effect does the recognition of bad debt expense have on the net realizable value? What effect does the write-off of accounts have on the net realizable value?

LO2

Problem 7-2A Aging Schedule to Account for Bad Debts

Rough Stuff is a distributor of large rocks. It sells on credit to commercial landscaping companies and extends terms that require customers to pay in 60 days. For accounts that are not overdue, Rough Stuff has found that there is a 90% probability of collection. For accounts up to one month past due, the likelihood of collection decreases to 75%. If accounts are between one and two months past due, the probability of collection is 65%, and if an account is over two months past due, Rough Stuff estimates that there is only a 25% chance of collecting the receivable.

On December 31, 2007, the credit balance in Allowance for Doubtful Accounts is $34,590. The amounts of gross receivables, by age, on this date are as follows:

Category	Amount
Current	$200,000
Past due:	
Less than one month	60,300
One to two months	35,000
Over two months	45,000

Required

1. Prepare a schedule to estimate the amount of uncollectible accounts at December 31, 2007.
2. Rough Stuff knows that $40,000 of the $45,000 amount that is more than two months overdue is due from one customer that is in severe financial trouble. It is rumored that the customer will be filing for bankruptcy in the near future. As controller for Rough Stuff, how would you handle this situation?
3. Show how accounts receivable would be presented on the December 31, 2007, balance sheet.

LO3

Problem 7-3A Accounts Receivable Turnover for Best Buy and Circuit City

The following information was summarized from a recent annual report of **Best Buy Co. Inc.**:

	(in millions)
Receivables:	
February 28, 2004	$ 343
March 1, 2003	312
Revenues for the year ended:	
February 28, 2004	24,547
March 1, 2003	20,946

The following information was summarized from a recent annual report of **Circuit City Stores, Inc.** (receivables are net of allowances):

	(in thousands)
Accounts receivable:	
February 29, 2004	$ 154,039
February 28, 2003	140,385
Net sales and operating revenues for the year ended:	
February 29, 2004	9,745,445
February 28, 2003	9,953,530

Required

1. Calculate the accounts receivable turnover ratios for Best Buy and Circuit City for the years ending in 2004.

2. Calculate the average collection period, in days, for both companies for 2004. Comment on the reasonableness of the collection periods for these companies considering the nature of their business.
3. Which company appears to be performing better? What other information should you consider in determining how these companies are performing?

LO5

Problem 7-4A Credit Card Sales

A local fast-food restaurant is considering accepting major credit cards in its outlets. Current annual sales are $800,000 per outlet. The company can purchase the equipment needed to handle credit cards and have an additional phone line installed in each outlet for approximately $800 per outlet. The equipment will be an expense in the year it is installed. The employee training time is minimal. The credit card company will charge a fee equal to 1.5% of sales for the use of credit cards. The company is unable to determine by how much, if any, sales will increase and whether cash customers will use a credit card rather than cash. No other fast-food restaurants in the local area accept credit cards for sales payment.

Required
1. Assuming only 5% of existing cash customers will use a credit card, what increase in sales is necessary to pay for the credit card equipment in the first year?
2. What other factors might the company consider in addition to an increase in sales dollars?

LO6

Problem 7-5A Effects of Changes in Receivable Balances on Statement of Cash Flows

St. Charles Antiques Market reported a net loss of $6,000 for the year ended December 31, 2007. The following items were included on St. Charles Antiques Market's balance sheets at December 31, 2007 and 2006:

	12/31/07	12/31/06
Cash	$ 36,300	$ 3,100
Accounts receivable	79,000	126,000
Notes receivable	112,600	104,800

St. Charles Antiques Market uses the indirect method to prepare its statement of cash flows. It does not have any other current assets or current liabilities and did not enter into any investing or financing activities during 2007.

Required
1. Prepare St. Charles Antiques Market's 2007 statement of cash flows.
2. Draft a brief memo to the owner to explain why cash increased during such an unprofitable year.

LO7

Problem 7-6A Investments in Bonds and Stock (Appendix)

Vermont Corp. enters into the following transactions during 2007:

July 1: Paid $10,000 to acquire on the open market $10,000 face value of Maine bonds. The bonds have a stated annual interest rate of 8% with interest paid semiannually on June 30 and December 31. The remaining life of the bonds on the date of purchase is $3\frac{1}{2}$ years.
Oct. 23: Purchased 1,000 shares of Virginia common stock at $15 per share.
Nov. 21: Purchased 600 shares of Carolina preferred stock at $8 per share.
Dec. 10: Received dividends of $0.50 per share on the Virginia stock and $1.00 per share on the Carolina stock.
Dec. 28: Sold 700 shares of Virginia common stock at $19 per share.
Dec. 31: Received interest from the Maine bonds.
Dec. 31: The Virginia stock and the Carolina stock have market prices of $20 per share and $11 per share, respectively.

Required
1 Determine the effect on Vermont's accounting equation of each of the preceding transactions. Vermont classifies the bonds as held-to-maturity securities and all stock investments as trading securities.
2. Prepare a partial balance sheet as of December 31, 2007, to indicate the proper presentation of the investments.
3. Indicate the items, and the amount of each, that will appear on the 2007 income statement relative to the investments.

LO7 **Problem 7-7A** Investments in Stock (Appendix)

Trendy Supercenter occasionally finds itself with excess cash to invest and consequently entered into the following transactions during 2007:

Jan. 15: Purchased 100 shares of IBM common stock at $130 per share, plus $250 in commissions.

May 23: Received dividends of $1 per share on the IBM stock.

June 1: Purchased 200 shares of General Motors stock at $60 per share, plus $300 in commissions.

Oct. 20: Sold all of the IBM stock at $140 per share, less commissions of $400.

Dec. 15: Received notification from General Motors that a $0.75 per share dividend had been declared. The checks will be mailed to stockholders on January 10, 2008.

Dec. 31: Noted that the General Motors stock was quoted on the stock exchange at $45 per share.

Required

1. Determine the effect on Trendy's accounting equation of each of the preceding transactions. Assume that Trendy categorizes all investments as available-for-sale securities.
2. What is the total amount of income that Trendy should recognize from its investments during 2007?
3. Assume all of the same facts except that Trendy categorizes all investments as trading securities. How would your answer to part (2) change? Explain why your answer would change.

ALTERNATE MULTI-CONCEPT PROBLEM

LO2.4 **Problem 7-8A** Accounts and Notes Receivable

Tweety Inc. sold merchandise for $6,000 to P.D. Cat on July 31, 2007, with payment due in 30 days. Subsequent to this, Cat experienced cash flow problems and was unable to pay its debt. On December 24, 2007, Tweety stopped trying to collect the outstanding receivable from Cat and wrote off the account as uncollectible. On January 15, 2008, Cat sent Tweety a check for $1,500 and offered to sign a two-month, 8%, $4,500 promissory note to satisfy the remaining obligation. Cat paid the entire amount on the note due Tweety, with interest, on March 15, 2008. Tweety ends its accounting year on December 31 each year.

Required

1. For each of the transactions during the period from July 31, 2007, to March 15, 2008, determine the effect on Tweety's accounting equation.
2. Why would Cat bother to send Tweety a check for $1,500 on January 15 and agree to sign a note for the balance, given that such a long period of time had passed since the original purchase?

DECISION CASES

READING AND INTERPRETING FINANCIAL STATEMENTS

LO2 **Decision Case 7-1** Reading Apple's Balance Sheet and Notes to the Statements

Following is information available in **Apple Computer**'s 2004 annual report in Note 2 to the financial statements:

The following table summarizes the activity in the allowance for doubtful accounts (in millions):

	2004	2003	2002
Beginning allowance balance	$ 49	$ 51	$ 51
Charged to costs and expenses	3	4	10
Deductions (a)	(5)	(6)	(10)
Ending allowance balance	$ 47	$ 49	$ 51

(a) Represents amounts written off against the allowance, net recoveries.

HOMEWORK

Use this information and that provided in the chapter opener to answer each of the following questions:

Required

1. What is the balance in Apple's Allowance for Doubtful Accounts at the end of 2004 and 2003?
2. What is the net realizable value of accounts receivable at the end of each of these two years?
3. What was the amount of bad debts expense for 2004 and 2003?
4. What was the amount of accounts receivable written off in 2004 and in 2003?
5. Compare the amounts of accounts written off in 2004 and 2003 to the amounts written off in 2002. Why do you think the amounts written off have decreased significantly in the two most recent years?

LO1,6   **Decision Case 7-2** Reading Apple Computer's Statement of Cash Flows

The following items appeared in the Investing Activities section of **Apple Computer**'s 2004 statement of cash flows (all amounts are in millions of dollars):

	2004	2003	2002
Purchases of short-term investments	$(3,270)	$(2,648)	$(4,144)
Proceeds from maturities of short-term investments	1,141	2,446	2,846
Proceeds from sales of short-term investments	801	1,116	1,254
Proceeds from sales of noncurrent investments	5	45	25

Required

1. What amount did Apple spend in 2004 to purchase short-term investments? How does this amount compare to the amounts spent in the two prior years?
2. What amount did Apple receive from investments that matured in 2004? How does this amount compare to the amounts received in the two prior years?
3. The third line in the excerpt above reports proceeds from sales, rather than maturities, of short-term investments. Why would certain types of investments mature while others would be sold?

LO3   **Decision Case 7-3** Comparing Two Companies in the Same Industry: Foot Locker and Finish Line

Refer to the financial statement information of **Foot Locker** and **Finish Line** reproduced at the end of this book.
1. Calculate the account receivables turnover ratios for both companies for the most recent year.
2. Calculate the average length of time it takes each company to collect its accounts receivable.
3. Compare the two companies on the basis of your calculations in (1) and (2).

MAKING FINANCIAL DECISIONS

LO1,2   **Decision Case 7-4** Liquidity

Oak and Maple both provide computer consulting services to their clients. The following are the current assets for each at the end of the year (all amounts are in millions of dollars):

	Oak	Maple
Cash	$10	$ 5
Six-month certificates of deposit	9	0
Short-term investments in stock	0	6
Accounts receivable	15	23
Allowance for doubtful accounts	(1)	(1)
Total current assets	$33	$33

Required

As a loan officer for the First National Bank of Verona Heights, assume that both companies have come to you asking for a $10 million, six-month loan. If you could lend money to only one of the two, which one would it be? Justify your answer by writing a brief memo to the president of the bank.

ETHICAL DECISION MAKING

LO5   **Decision Case 7-5** Notes Receivable

Patterson Company is a large diversified business with a unit that sells commercial real estate. As a company, Patterson has been profitable in recent years with the exception of the real estate business, where economic conditions have resulted in weak sales. The vice president of the real estate division is aware of the poor performance of his group and needs to find ways to "show a profit."

During the current year the division is successful in selling a 100-acre tract of land for a new shopping center. The original cost of the property to Patterson was $4 million. The buyer has agreed to sign a $10 million note with payments of $2 million due at the end of each of the next five years. The property was appraised late last year at a market value of $7.5 million. The vice president has come to you, the controller, and asked that you record a sale for $10 million with a corresponding increase in Notes Receivable for $10 million.

Required

1. Does the suggestion by the vice president as to how to record the sale violate any accounting principle? If so, explain the principle it violates.
2. What would you do? Write a brief memo to the vice president explaining the proper accounting for the sale.

LO7   **Decision Case 7-6** Fair Market Values for Investments (Appendix)

Kennedy Corp. operates a chain of discount stores. The company regularly holds stock of various companies in a trading securities portfolio. One of these investments is 10,000 shares of Clean Air Inc. stock purchased for $100 per share during December 2007.

Clean Air manufactures highly specialized equipment used to test automobile emissions. Unfortunately, the market price of Clean Air's stock dropped during December 2007 and closed the year trading at $75 per share. Kennedy expects the Clean Air stock to experience a turnaround, however, as states pass legislation to require an emissions test on all automobiles.

As controller for Kennedy, you have followed the fortunes of Clean Air with particular interest. You and the company's treasurer are both concerned by the negative impact that a write-down of the stock to fair value would have on Kennedy's earnings for 2007. You have calculated net income for 2007 to be $400,000, exclusive of the recognition of any loss on the stock.

The treasurer comes to you on January 31, 2008, with the following idea:

"Since you haven't closed the books yet for 2007, and we haven't yet released the 2007 financials, let's think carefully about how Clean Air should be classified. I realize that we normally treat these types of investments as trading securities, but if we categorize the Clean Air stock on the balance sheet as available-for-sale rather than a trading security, we won't need to report the adjustment to fair value on the income statement. I don't see anything wrong with this since we would still report the stock at its fair value on the balance sheet."

Required

1. Compute Kennedy's net income for 2007, under two different assumptions: (a) the stock is classified as a trading security, and (b) the stock is classified as an available-for-sale security.
2. Which classification do you believe is appropriate, according to accounting standards? Explain your answer.
3. Would you have any ethical concerns in following the treasurer's advice? Explain your answer. If the investment is listed as available-for-sale, does the information faithfully represent what it claims to represent? Who benefits and who is harmed by the decision to reclassify? Explain your answer.

SOLUTIONS TO KEY TERMS QUIZ

1	Equity securities		11	Note receivable
2	Debt securities		9	Note payable
24	Account receivable		19	Principal
15	Subsidiary ledger		22	Maturity date
17	Control account		21	Term
16	Direct write-off method		20	Maturity value
6	Allowance method		18	Interest
23	Allowance for doubtful accounts		10	Credit card draft
14	Aging schedule		12	Discounting
8	Promissory note		5	Held-to-maturity securities
13	Maker		3	Trading securities
7	Payee		4	Available-for-sale securities

Operating Assets: Property, Plant, and Equipment, Natural Resources, and Intangibles

Study Links

A Look at Previous Chapters
Chapter 7 presented the accounting for a company's current assets of accounts receivable, notes receivable, and investments. These assets are important aspects of short-term liquidity.

A Look at This Chapter
In this chapter we will examine a company's operating assets of property, plant, and equipment as well as natural resources and intangibles. These assets are an important indicator of a company's ability to produce revenue in the long term.

A Look at Upcoming Chapters
Later chapters discuss the financing of long-term assets. Chapter 10 presents long-term liabilities as a source of financing. Chapter 11 describes the use of stock as a source of funds for financing long-term assets.

Learning Outcomes

After studying this chapter, you should be able to:

LO1 Understand balance sheet disclosures for operating assets.

LO2 Determine the acquisition cost of an operating asset.

LO3 Explain how to calculate the acquisition cost of assets purchased for a lump sum.

LO4 Describe the impact of capitalizing interest as part of the acquisition cost of an asset.

LO5 Compare depreciation methods and understand the factors affecting the choice of method.

LO6 Understand the impact of a change in the estimate of the asset life or residual value.

LO7 Determine which expenditures should be capitalized as asset costs and which should be treated as expenses.

LO8 Analyze the effect of the disposal of an asset at a gain or loss.

LO9 Understand the balance sheet presentation of intangible assets.

LO10 Describe the proper amortization of intangible assets.

LO11 Explain the impact that long-term assets have on the statement of cash flows.

LO12 Understand how investors can analyze a company's operating assets.

Nike

Nike is the largest seller of athletic footwear, athletic apparel, equipment, and accessories in the world. To achieve this position of dominance requires a large investment in property, plant, and equipment. The Nike World Campus, owned by Nike and located in Beaverton, Oregon, is a 176-acre facility of 16 buildings which functions as the world headquarters and is occupied by almost 6,000 employees. The company has distribution and customer service facilities in Tennessee, Oregon, and New Hampshire as well as in Japan and Europe. At May 31, 2004, the company's balance sheet indicates nearly $1.6 billion of property, plant, and equipment. The company's decisions to continually invest in new plant and equipment are very important and a key to the company's future. Investors and others who read Nike's financial statements must analyze the company's tangible assets in order to gauge the company's ability to generate profits in future periods.

But Nike's intangible assets are equally important. The Nike brand name and company logo are some of the most recognizable in the world. During the second quarter ended November 30, 2003, Nike completed the acquisition of Converse Inc. The purchase price was $310 million, and the majority of the purchase represented identifiable intangible assets such as trademarks and copyrights. Nearly all of the remainder represented the intangible asset known as goodwill. The acquisition of Converse further strengthens Nike and grants it an even more dominant position in the athletic footwear business.

Accountants have had to consider carefully the accounting for all long-lived assets but especially for intangible assets. Investors must be able to read Nike's financial statements and understand how their assets influence the value of the company. Hopefully, the stock price accurately reflects the value of those assets and the company's ability to use the assets wisely.

The accompanying partial balance sheet presents Nike's property, plant, and equipment and its intangible assets. In this chapter we will consider the following:

- What financial statement disclosures are available for a company's operating assets? (See pp. 350–351)
- How should a company depreciate or amortize such assets? (See pp. 365–366)

- How can an investor analyze the operating assets portion of the balance sheet when evaluating a company? (See pp. 368–370)

Answers to these questions are found in the text. They can help you evaluate Nike's assets using its financial statements.

NIKE, INC.
CONSOLIDATED BALANCE SHEETS

	May 31,	
	2004	2003
ASSETS	(in millions)	
Current Assets:		
Cash and equivalents	$ 828.0	$ 634.0
Short-term investments	400.8	—
Accounts receivable, less allowance for doubtful accounts of $95.3 and $81.9	2,120.2	2,083.9
Inventories (Note 2)	1,633.6	1,514.9
Deferred income taxes (Note 8)	165.0	221.8
Prepaid expenses and other current assets	364.4	332.5
Total current assets	5,512.0	4,787.1
Property, plant and equipment, net (Note 3)	1,586.9	1,620.8
Identifiable intangible assets, net (Note 4)	366.3	118.2
Goodwill (Note 4)	135.4	65.6
Deferred income taxes and other assets (Note 8)	291.0	229.4
Total assets	$7,891.6	$6,821.1

Operating Assets: Property, Plant, and Equipment

LO1 Understand balance sheet disclosures for operating assets.

BALANCE SHEET PRESENTATION

Operating assets constitute the major productive assets of many companies. Current assets are important to a company's short-term liquidity; operating assets are absolutely essential to its long-term future. These assets must be used to produce the goods or services the company sells to customers. The dollar amount invested in operating assets may be very large, as is the case with most manufacturing companies. On the other hand, operating assets on the balance sheet may be insignificant to a company's value, as is the case with a computer software firm or many of the so-called Internet firms. Users of financial statements must assess the operating assets to make important decisions. For example, lenders are interested in the value of the operating assets as collateral when making lending decisions. Investors must evaluate whether the operating assets indicate long-term potential and can provide a return to the stockholders.

The terms used to describe the operating assets and the balance sheet presentation of those assets vary somewhat by company. Some firms refer to this category of assets as *fixed* or *plant assets*. Other firms prefer to present operating assets in

Note 3—Property, Plant and Equipment
Property, plant and equipment includes the following:

	May 31,	
	2004	2003
	(in millions)	
Land	$ 179.5	$ 191.1
Buildings	813.6	785.0
Machinery and equipment	1,608.6	1,538.7
Leasehold improvements	470.2	433.4
Construction in process	60.4	40.6
	3,132.3	2,988.8
Less accumulated depreciation	1,545.4	1,368.0
	$1,586.9	$1,620.8

two categories: *tangible assets* and *intangible assets*. The balance sheet of **Nike, Inc.,** uses one line item for *property, plant, and equipment* and presents the details in the notes. Because the latter term can encompass a variety of items, we will use the more descriptive term *intangible assets* for the second category. We begin by examining the accounting issues concerned with the first category: property, plant, and equipment.

The May 31, 2004, notes of Nike, Inc., present property, plant, and equipment shown at the top of the page (in millions). Note that the acquisition costs of the land, buildings, machinery and equipment, leasehold improvements, and construction in process are stated, and the amount of accumulated depreciation is deducted to determine the net amount. The accumulated depreciation is related to the last four assets, since land is not a depreciable item.

ACQUISITION OF PROPERTY, PLANT, AND EQUIPMENT

Assets classified as property, plant, and equipment are initially recorded at acquisition cost (also referred to as *historical cost*). As indicated in Nike's notes, these assets are normally presented on the balance sheet at original acquisition cost minus accumulated depreciation. It is important, however, to define the term acquisition cost (also known as original cost) in a more exact manner. What items should be included as part of the original acquisition? **Acquisition cost** should include all of the costs that are normal and necessary to acquire the asset and prepare it for its intended use. Items included in acquisition cost would generally include the following:

LO2 Determine the acquisition cost of an operating asset.

Acquisition cost
The amount that includes all of the cost normally necessary to acquire an asset and prepare it for its intended use. *Alternate terms: Historical cost; Original cost*

Purchase price

Taxes paid at time of purchase (for example, sales tax)

Transportation charges

Installation costs

An accountant must exercise careful judgment to determine which costs are "normal" and "necessary" and should be included in the calculation of the acquisition cost of operating assets. Acquisition cost should not include expenditures unrelated to the acquisition (for example, repair costs if an asset is damaged during installation) or costs incurred after the asset was installed and use begun.

Group Purchase Quite often a firm purchases several assets as a group and pays a lump-sum amount. This is most common when a company purchases land and a building situated on it and pays a lump-sum amount for both. It is important to

LO3 Explain how to calculate the acquisition cost of assets purchased for a lump sum.

measure separately the acquisition cost of the land and of the building. Land is not a depreciable asset, but the amount allocated to the building is subject to depreciation. In cases such as this, the purchase price should be allocated between land and building on the basis of the proportion of the *fair market values* of each.

For example, assume that on January 1, ExerCo purchased a building and the land that it is situated on for $100,000. The accountant was able to establish that the fair market values of the two assets on January 1 were as follows:

Land	$ 30,000
Building	90,000
Total	$120,000

On the basis of the estimated market values, the purchase price should be allocated as follows:

To land	$100,000 × $30,000/$120,000 = $25,000
To building	$100,000 × $90,000/$120,000 = $75,000

The impact on the accounting equation would be as follows:

		Balance Sheet				Income Statement
ASSETS	**=**	**LIABILITIES**	**+**	**STOCKHOLDERS' EQUITY**	**+**	**REVENUES – EXPENSES**
Land	25,000					
Building	75,000					
Cash	(100,000)					

Market value is best established by an independent appraisal of the property. If such appraisal is not possible, the accountant must rely on the market value of other similar assets, on the value of the assets in tax records, or on other available evidence.

These efforts to allocate dollars between land and buildings will permit the appropriate allocation for depreciation. But when an investor or lender views the balance sheet, he or she is often more interested in the current market value. The best things that can be said about historical cost are that it is a verifiable number and that it is conservative. But it is still up to the lender or the investor to determine the appropriate value for these assets.

LO4 Describe the impact of capitalizing interest as part of the acquisition cost of an asset.

Capitalization of Interest We have seen that acquisition cost may include several items. But should the acquisition cost of an asset include the interest cost necessary to finance the asset? That is, should interest be treated as an asset, or should it be treated as an expense of the period?

Generally, the interest on borrowed money should be treated as an expense of the period. If a company buys an asset and borrows money to finance the purchase, the interest on the borrowed money is not considered part of the asset's cost. Financial statements generally treat investing and financing as separate decisions. Purchase of an asset, an investing activity, is treated as a business decision that is separate from the decision concerning the financing of the asset. Therefore, interest is treated as a period cost and should appear on the income statement as interest expense in the period incurred.

There is one exception to this general guideline, however. If a company constructs an asset over a period of time and borrows money to finance the construction, the amount of interest incurred during the construction period is not treated as interest expense. Instead, the interest must be included as part of the acquisition cost of the asset. This is referred to as **capitalization of interest**. The amount of interest that is capitalized (treated as an asset) is based on the *average accumulated expenditures*. The logic of using the average accumulated expenditure is that

Capitalization of interest
Interest on constructed assets is added to the asset account.

this number represents an average amount of money tied up in the project over a year. If it takes $400,000 to construct a building, the interest should not be figured on the full $400,000 because there were times during the year when less than the full amount was being used.

When it costs $400,000 to build an asset and the amount of interest to be capitalized is $10,000, the acquisition cost of the asset is $410,000. The asset should appear on the balance sheet at that amount. Depreciation of the asset should be based on $410,000, less any residual value.

Land Improvements It is important to distinguish between land and other costs associated with it. The acquisition cost of land should be kept in a separate account because land has an unlimited life and is not subject to depreciation. Other costs associated with land should be recorded in an account such as Land Improvements. For example, the costs of paving a parking lot are properly treated as **land improvements**, which have a limited life. Some landscaping costs also have a limited life. Therefore, the acquisition costs of land improvements should be depreciated over their useful lives.

USE AND DEPRECIATION OF PROPERTY, PLANT, AND EQUIPMENT

All property, plant, and equipment, except land, have a limited life and decline in usefulness over time. The accrual accounting process requires a proper *matching* of expenses and revenue to accurately measure income. Therefore, the accountant must estimate the decline in usefulness of operating assets and allocate the acquisition cost in a manner consistent with the decline in usefulness. This allocation is the process generally referred to as **depreciation**.

Unfortunately, proper matching for operating assets is not easy because of the many factors involved. An asset's decline in usefulness is related to *physical deterioration* factors such as wear and tear. In some cases, the physical deterioration results from heavy use of the asset in the production process, but it may also result from the passage of time or exposure to the elements.

The decline in an asset's usefulness is also related to *obsolescence* factors. Some operating assets, such as computers, decline in usefulness simply because they have been surpassed by a newer model or newer technology. Finally, the decline in an asset's usefulness is related to a company's *repair and maintenance* policy. A company with an aggressive and extensive repair and maintenance program will not experience a decline in usefulness of operating assets as rapidly as one without such a policy.

Because the decline in an asset's usefulness is related to a variety of factors, several depreciation methods have been developed. In theory, a company should use a depreciation method that allocates the original cost of the asset to the periods benefited and that allows the company to accurately match the expense to the revenue generated by the asset. We will present three methods of depreciation: *straight line*, *units of production*, and *double declining balance*.

All depreciation methods are based on the asset's original acquisition cost. In addition, all methods require an estimate of two additional factors: the asset's *life* and its *residual value*. The residual value (also referred to as *salvage value*) should represent the amount that could be obtained from selling or disposing of the asset at the end of its useful life. Often, this may be a small amount or even zero.

Straight-Line Method The **straight-line method** of depreciation allocates the cost of the asset evenly over time. This method calculates the annual depreciation as follows:

Depreciation = (Acquisition Cost − Residual Value)/Life

For example, assume that on January 1, 2007, ExerCo, a manufacturer of exercise equipment, purchased a machine for $20,000. The company estimated that the machine's life would be five years and its residual value at the end of 2011 would be $2,000. The annual depreciation should be calculated as follows:

Land improvements
Costs that are related to land but that have a limited life.

LO5 Compare depreciation methods and understand the factors affecting the choice of method.

Depreciation
The allocation of the original cost of an asset to the periods benefited by its use.

8-1 Real World Practice

Reading Foot Locker's Balance Sheet

What amount did Foot Locker report as depreciation in 2005? Where is it disclosed? What depreciation method was used?

Straight-line method
A method by which the same dollar amount of depreciation is recorded in each year of asset use.

$$\text{Depreciation} = (\text{Acquisition Cost} - \text{Residual Value})/\text{Life}$$
$$\text{Depreciation} = (\$20{,}000 - \$2{,}000)/5$$
$$= \$3{,}600$$

Book value
The original cost of an asset minus the amount of accumulated depreciation.

An asset's **book value** is defined as its acquisition cost minus its total amount of accumulated depreciation. Thus, the book value of the machine in this example is $16,400 at the end of 2007:

$$\text{Book Value} = \text{Acquisition Cost} - \text{Accumulated Depreciation}$$
$$\text{Book Value} = \$20{,}000 - \$3{,}600$$
$$= \$16{,}400$$

The book value at the end of 2008 is $12,800:

$$\text{Book Value} = \text{Acquisition Cost} - \text{Accumulated Depreciation}$$
$$\text{Book Value} = \$20{,}000 - (2 \times \$3{,}600)$$
$$= \$12{,}800$$

The most attractive features of the straight-line method are its ease and its simplicity. It is the most popular method for presenting depreciation in the annual report to stockholders.

Units-of-Production Method In some cases, the decline in an asset's usefulness is directly related to wear and tear as a result of the number of units it produces. In those cases, depreciation should be calculated by the **units-of-production method**. With this method, the asset's life is expressed in terms of the number of units that the asset can produce. The depreciation *per unit* can be calculated as follows:

Units-of-production method
Depreciation is determined as a function of the number of units the asset produces.

$$\text{Depreciation per Unit} = (\text{Acquisition Cost} - \text{Residual Value})/$$
$$\text{Total Number of Units in Asset's Life}$$

The annual depreciation for a given year can be calculated based on the number of units produced during that year, as follows:

$$\text{Annual Depreciation} = \text{Depreciation per Unit} \times \text{Units Produced in Current Year}$$

For example, assume that ExerCo in the previous example wanted to use the units-of-production method for 2007. Also assume that ExerCo has been able to estimate that the total number of units that will be produced during the asset's five-year life is 18,000. During 2007 ExerCo produced 4,000 units. The depreciation per unit for ExerCo's machine can be calculated as follows:

$$\text{Depreciation per Unit} = (\text{Acquisition Cost} - \text{Residual Value})/\text{Life in Units}$$
$$\text{Depreciation per Unit} = (\$20{,}000 - \$2{,}000)/18{,}000$$
$$= \$1 \text{ per Unit}$$

The amount of depreciation that should be recorded as an expense for 2007 is $4,000:

$$\text{Annual Depreciation} = \text{Depreciation per Unit} \times \text{Units Produced in 2007}$$
$$\text{Annual Depreciation} = \$1 \text{ per Unit} \times 4{,}000 \text{ Units}$$
$$= \$4{,}000$$

Depreciation will be recorded until the asset produces 18,000 units. The machine cannot be depreciated below its residual value of $2,000.

The units-of-production method is most appropriate when the accountant is able to estimate the total number of units that will be produced over the asset's life. For example, if a factory machine is used to produce a particular item, the life of the asset may be expressed in terms of the number of units produced. Further, the units produced must be related to particular time periods so that depreciation expense can be matched accurately with the related revenue. A variation of the units-of-production method can be used when the life of the asset is expensed in other factors such as miles driven or hours of use.

Accelerated depreciation
A higher amount of depreciation is recorded in the early years and a lower amount in the later years. *Alternate term:*
Allowance for depreciation

Accelerated Depreciation Methods In some cases, more cost should be allocated to the early years of an asset's use and less to the later years. For those assets, an accelerated method of depreciation is appropriate. The term **accelerated depreciation** refers to several depreciation methods by which a higher amount of depreciation is recorded in the early years than in later ones.

One form of accelerated depreciation is the **double-declining-balance method**. Under this method, depreciation is calculated at double the straight-line rate but on a declining amount. The first step is to calculate the straight-line rate as a percentage. The straight-line rate for the ExerCo asset with a five-year life is

$$100\%/5 \text{ Years} = 20\%$$

The second step is to double the straight-line rate:

$$2 \times 20\% = 40\%$$

This rate will be applied in all years to the asset's book value at the beginning of each year. As depreciation is recorded, the book value declines. Thus, a constant rate is applied to a declining amount. This constant rate is applied to the full cost or initial book value, not to cost minus residual value as in the other methods. However, the machine cannot be depreciated below its residual value.

The amount of depreciation for 2007 would be calculated as follows:

$$\text{Depreciation} = \text{Beginning Book Value} \times \text{Rate}$$
$$\text{Depreciation} = \$20,000 \times 40\%$$
$$= \$8,000$$

The amount of depreciation for 2008 would be calculated as follows:

$$\text{Depreciation} = \text{Beginning Book Value} \times \text{Rate}$$
$$\text{Depreciation} = (\$20,000 - \$8,000) \times 40\%$$
$$= \$4,800$$

The complete depreciation schedule for ExerCo for all five years of the machine's life would be as follows:

Year	Rate	Book Value at Beginning of Year	Depreciation	Book Value at End of Year
2007	40%	$20,000	$ 8,000	$12,000
2008	40	12,000	4,800	7,200
2009	40	7,200	2,880	4,320
2010	40	4,320	1,728	2,592
2011	40	2,592	592	2,000
Total			$18,000	

In the ExerCo example, the depreciation for 2011 cannot be calculated as $2,592 × 40% because this would result in an accumulated depreciation amount of more than $18,000. The total amount of depreciation recorded in Years 1 through 4 is $17,408. The accountant should record only $592 depreciation ($18,000 − $17,408) in 2011 so that the remaining value of the machine is $2,000 at the end of 2011.

The double-declining-balance method of depreciation results in an accelerated depreciation pattern. It is most appropriate for assets subject to a rapid decline in usefulness as a result of technical or obsolescence factors. Double-declining-balance depreciation is not widely used for financial statement purposes but may be appropriate for certain assets. As discussed earlier, most companies use straight-line depreciation for financial statement purposes because it generally produces the highest net income, especially in growing companies that have a stable or expanding base of assets.

Comparison of Depreciation Methods In this section, you have learned about several methods of depreciating operating assets. Exhibit 8-1 presents a comparison of the depreciation and book values of the ExerCo asset for 2007–2011 using the straight-line and double-declining-balance methods (we have excluded the units-of-production method). Note that both methods result in a depreciation total of $18,000 over the five-year period. The amount of depreciation per year depends, however, on the method of depreciation chosen.

Nonaccountants often misunderstand the accountant's concept of depreciation. Accountants do not consider depreciation to be a process of *valuing* the asset. That

Double-declining-balance method
Depreciation is recorded at twice the straight-line rate, but the balance is reduced each period.

Study Tip Residual value is deducted for all depreciation methods except for the declining-balance methods.

EXHIBIT 8-1	Comparison of Depreciation and Book Values of Straight-Line and Double-Declining-Balance Methods

	Straight-Line		Double-Declining-Balance	
Year	Depreciation	Book Value	Depreciation	Book Value
2007	$ 3,600	$16,400	$ 8,000	$12,000
2008	3,600	12,800	4,800	7,200
2009	3,600	9,200	2,880	4,320
2010	3,600	5,600	1,728	2,592
2011	3,600	2,000	592	2,000
Totals	$18,000		$18,000	

is, depreciation does not describe the increase or decrease in the market value of the asset. Accountants consider depreciation to be a process of *cost allocation*. The purpose is to allocate the original acquisition cost to the periods benefited by the asset. The depreciation method chosen should be based on the decline in the asset's usefulness. A company can choose a different depreciation method for each individual fixed asset or for each class or category of fixed assets.

The choice of depreciation method can have a significant impact on the bottom line. If two companies are essentially identical in every other respect, a different depreciation method for fixed assets can make one company look more profitable than another. Or a company that uses accelerated depreciation for one year can find that its otherwise declining earnings are no longer declining if it switches to straight-line depreciation. Investors should pay some attention to depreciation methods when comparing companies. Statement users must be aware of the different depreciation methods to understand the calculation of income and to compare companies that may not use the same methods.

Some investors ignore depreciation altogether when evaluating a company, not because they do not know that assets depreciate but because they want to focus on cash flow instead of earnings. Depreciation is a "noncash" charge that reduces net income.

Depreciation and Income Taxes Financial accounting involves the presentation of financial statements to external users of accounting information, users such as investors and creditors. When depreciating an asset for financial accounting purposes, the accountant should choose a depreciation method that is consistent with the asset's decline in usefulness and that properly allocates its cost to the periods that benefit from its use.

Depreciation is also deducted for income tax purposes. Sometimes depreciation is referred to as a *tax shield* because it reduces (as do other expenses) the amount of income tax that would otherwise have to be paid. When depreciating an asset for tax purposes, a company should generally choose a depreciation method that reduces the present value of its tax burden to the lowest possible amount over the life of the asset. Normally, this is best accomplished with an accelerated depreciation method, which allows a company to save more income tax in the early years of the asset. This happens because the higher depreciation charges reduce taxable income more than the straight-line method does. The method allowed for tax purposes is referred to as MACRS, which stands for Modified Accelerated Cost Recovery System. As a form of accelerated depreciation, it results in a larger amount of depreciation in the early years of asset life and a smaller amount in later years.

Choice of Depreciation Method As we have stated, in theory a company should choose the depreciation method that best allocates the original cost of the asset to the periods benefited by the use of the asset. Theory aside, it is important to examine the other factors that affect a company's decision in choosing a depreciation method or methods. Exhibit 8-2 presents the factors that affect this decision and the likely choice that arises from each factor. Usually, the factors that are the most important are whether depreciation is calculated for presentation on the financial statements to stockholders or is calculated for income tax purposes.

When depreciation is calculated for financial statement purposes, a company generally wants to present the most favorable impression (the highest income) possible. Therefore, most companies choose the straight-line method of depreciation. In fact, more than 90% of large companies use the straight-line method for financial statement purposes.

If the objective of the company's management is to minimize its income tax liability, then the company will generally not choose the straight-line method for tax purposes. As discussed in the preceding section, accelerated depreciation allows the company to save more on income taxes because depreciation is a tax shield.

Therefore, it is not unusual for a company to use *two* depreciation methods for the same asset, one for financial reporting purposes and another for tax purposes. This may seem somewhat confusing, but it is the direct result of the differing goals of financial and tax accounting. See Chapter 10 for more about this issue.

Change in Depreciation Estimate An asset's acquisition cost is known at the time it is purchased, but its life and its residual value must be estimated. These estimates are then used as the basis for depreciating it. Occasionally, an estimate of the asset's life or residual value must be altered after the depreciation process has begun. This is an example of an accounting change that is referred to as a **change in estimate**.

Assume the same facts as in the ExerCo example. The company purchased a machine on January 1, 2007, for $20,000. ExerCo estimated that the machine's life would be five years and its residual value at the end of five years would be $2,000. Assume that ExerCo has depreciated the machine using the straight-line method for two years. At the beginning of 2009, ExerCo believes that the total machine life

LO6 Understand the impact of a change in the estimate of the asset life or residual value.

Change in estimate
A change in the life of the asset or in its residual value.

EXHIBIT 8-2   Management's Choice of Depreciation Method

Factor	Likely Choice
Simplicity	The straight-line method is easiest to compute and record.
Reporting to stockholders	Usually firms wish to maximize net income in reporting to stockholders and will use the straight-line method.
Comparability	Usually firms use the same depreciation method as other firms in the same industry or line of business.
Management bonus plans	If management is paid a bonus based on net income, they are likely to use the straight-line method.
Technological competitiveness	If technology is changing rapidly, a firm should consider an accelerated method of depreciation.
Reporting to the Internal Revenue Service	Firms will usually use an accelerated method of depreciation to minimize taxable income in reporting to the IRS.

will be seven years, or another five years beyond the two years the machine has been used. Thus, depreciation must be adjusted to reflect the new estimate of the asset's life.

A change in estimate should be recorded *prospectively*, meaning that the depreciation recorded in prior years is not corrected or restated. Instead, the new estimate should affect the current year and future years. ExerCo should depreciate the remaining depreciable amount during 2009 through 2013. The amount to be depreciated over that time period should be calculated as follows:

Acquisition Cost, January 1, 2007	$20,000
Less: Accumulated Depreciation	
(2 years at $3,600 per year)	7,200
Book Value, January 1, 2009	$12,800
Less: Residual Value	2,000
Remaining Depreciable Amount	$10,800

The remaining depreciable amount should be recorded as depreciation over the remaining life of the machine. In the ExerCo case, the depreciation amount for 2009 and the following four years would be $2,160:

Depreciation = Remaining Depreciable Amount/Remaining Life
Depreciation = $10,800/5 Years
  = $2,160

If the change in estimate is a material amount, the company should disclose in the footnotes to the 2009 financial statements that depreciation has changed as a result of a change in estimate. The company's auditors have to be very careful that management's decision to change its estimate of the depreciable life of the asset is not simply an attempt to manipulate earnings. Particularly in capital-intensive manufacturing concerns, lengthening the useful life of equipment can have a material impact on earnings.

A change in estimate of an asset's residual value is treated in a manner similar to a change in an asset's life. There should be no attempt to correct or restate the income statements of past periods that were based on the original estimate. Instead, the accountant should use the new estimate of residual value to calculate depreciation for the current and future years.

2 *minute review*

1. What items should be included when calculating the acquisition cost of an asset?

2. Which will be higher in the early years of an asset's life—straight-line depreciation or accelerated depreciation? Which will be higher in the later years? Which will be higher in total over the entire life of the asset?

Answers

1. *The general rule for calculating the acquisition cost of an asset is to include all of the costs that were necessary to acquire the asset and prepare it for use. Normally, that would include the purchase price, but it would also include costs such as freight costs, taxes, and installation costs if they were necessary to prepare the asset for use.*

2. *Accelerated depreciation will be higher in the early years of the asset, and straight-line will be higher in the later years. Over the life of the asset, the total amount of depreciation will be the same under all of the methods, assuming that the same amount of salvage value is estimated for each of the methods.*

LO7 Determine which expenditures should be capitalized as asset costs and which should be treated as expenses.

CAPITAL VERSUS REVENUE EXPENDITURES

Accountants must often decide whether certain expenditures related to operating assets should be treated as an addition to the cost of the asset or as an expense. One of the most common examples involving this decision concerns repairs to an asset. Should the repairs constitute capital expenditures or revenue expenditures? A **capital expenditure** is a cost that is added to the acquisition cost of the asset. A **revenue expenditure** is not treated as part of the cost of the asset but as an expense on the income statement. Thus, the company must decide whether to treat an item as an asset (balance sheet) and depreciate its cost over its life or to treat it as an expense (income statement) of a single period.

The distinction between capital and revenue expenditures is a matter of judgment. Generally, the guideline that should be followed is that if an expenditure increases the life of the asset or its productivity, it should be treated as a capital expenditure and added to the asset account. If an expenditure simply maintains an asset in its normal operating condition, however, it should be treated as an expense. The *materiality* of the expenditure must also be considered. Most companies establish a policy of treating an expenditure smaller than a specified amount as a revenue expenditure (an expense on the income statement).

It is very important that a company not improperly capitalize a material expenditure that should have been written off right away. The capitalization policies of companies are closely watched by Wall Street analysts who try to assess the value of these companies. When a company is capitalizing rather than expensing certain items to artificially boost earnings, that revelation can be very damaging to the stock price.

Expenditures related to operating assets may be classified in several categories. For each type of expenditure, its treatment as capital or revenue should be as follows:

Category	Example	Asset or Expense
Normal maintenance	Repainting	Expense
Minor repair	Replace spark plugs	Expense
Major repair	Replace a vehicle's engine	Asset, if life or productivity is enhanced
Addition	Add a wing to a building	Asset

An item treated as a capital expenditure affects the amount of depreciation that should be recorded over the asset's remaining life. We return to the ExerCo example to illustrate. Assume again that ExerCo purchased a machine on January 1, 2007, for $20,000. ExerCo estimated that its residual value at the end of five years would be $2,000 and has depreciated the machine using the straight-line method for 2007 and 2008. At the beginning of 2009, ExerCo made a $3,000 overhaul to the machine, extending its life by three years. Because the expenditure qualifies as a capital expenditure, the cost of overhauling the machine should be added to the asset account. The impact on the accounting equation is as follows:

	Balance Sheet						Income Statement
ASSETS		**=**	**LIABILITIES**	**+**	**STOCKHOLDERS' EQUITY**	**+**	**REVENUES – EXPENSES**
Machine	3,000						
Cash	(3,000)						

For the years 2007 and 2008, ExerCo recorded depreciation of $3,600 per year:

Depreciation = (Acquisition Cost – Residual Value)/Life
Depreciation = ($20,000 – $2,000)/5
= $3,600

Beginning in 2009, the company should record depreciation of $2,300 per year, computed as follows:

Original Cost, January 1, 2007	$20,000
Less: Accumulated Depreciation (2 years × $3,600)	7,200
Book Value, January 1, 2009	$12,800
Plus: Major Overhaul	3,000
Less: Residual Value	(2,000)
Remaining Depreciable Amount	$13,800

Capital expenditure
A cost that improves the asset and is added to the asset account. *Alternate term:* Item treated as asset

Revenue expenditure
A cost that keeps an asset in its normal operating condition and is treated as an expense. *Alternate term:* Item treated as an expense of the period

Should the costs of cleaning up a flood-contaminated factory be considered an expense of one period or a capital expenditure added to the cost of the plant asset? To make the best decision, management should gather all the facts about the extent of the cleanup and its environmental impact.

Depreciation = Remaining Depreciable Amount/Remaining Life
Depreciation per year = $13,800/6 Years
= $2,300

ENVIRONMENTAL ASPECTS OF OPERATING ASSETS

As the number of the government's environmental regulations has increased, businesses have been required to expend more money complying with them. A common example involves costs to comply with federal requirements to clean up contaminated soil surrounding plant facilities. In some cases, the costs are very large and may exceed the value of the property. Should such costs be considered an expense and recorded entirely in one accounting period, or should they be treated as a capital expenditure and added to the cost of the asset? If there is a legal obligation to clean up the property or to restore the property to its original condition, companies are required to record the cost of asset retirement obligations as part of the cost of the asset. For example, if a company owns a factory and has made a binding promise to restore the property that is used by the factory to its original condition, then the costs of restoring the property must be added to the asset account. Of course, it is sometimes difficult to determine whether a legal obligation exists. It is important, however, for companies at least to conduct a thorough investigation to determine the potential environmental considerations that may affect the value of operating assets and to ponder carefully the accounting implications of new environmental regulations.

DISPOSAL OF PROPERTY, PLANT, AND EQUIPMENT

An asset may be disposed of in any of several different ways. One common method is to sell the asset for cash. Sale of an asset involves two important considerations. First, depreciation must be recorded up to the date of sale. If the sale does not occur at the fiscal year-end, usually December 31, depreciation must be recorded for a partial period from the beginning of the year to the date of sale. Second, the company selling the asset must calculate and record the gain or loss on its sale.

Refer again to the ExerCo example. Assume that ExerCo purchased a machine on January 1, 2007, for $20,000, estimating its life to be five years and the residual value to be $2,000. ExerCo used the straight-line method of depreciation. Assume that ExerCo sold the machine on July 1, 2009, for $12,400. Depreciation for the six-month time period from January 1 to July 1, 2009, is $1,800 ($3,600 per year × 1/2 year = $1,800).

After the July 1 entry, the balance of the Acumulated Depreciation—Machine account is $9,000, which reflects depreciation for the 2½ years from the date of purchase to the date of sale. The impact on the accounting equation is as follows:

LO8 Analyze the effect of the disposal of an asset at a gain or loss.

Balance Sheet					Income Statement	
ASSETS	**=**	**LIABILITIES**	**+**	**STOCKHOLDERS' EQUITY**	**+ REVENUES**	**− EXPENSES**
Accumulated					Gain on Sale	
Depreciation—Machine 9,000					of Asset	1,400
Cash 12,400						
Machine (20,000)						

Gain on Sale of Asset
The excess of the selling price over the asset's book value.

When an asset is sold, all accounts related to it must be removed. In the preceding entry, the Machine account is reduced to eliminate the account, and the Accumulated Depreciation—Machine account is reduced to eliminate it. The **Gain on Sale of Asset** indicates the amount by which the sale price of the machine *exceeds* the book value. Thus, the gain can be calculated as follows:

Asset cost	$20,000
Less: Accumulated depreciation	9,000
Book value	$11,000
Sale price	12,400
Gain on sale of asset	$ 1,400

© EPA/DAN ANDERSON/Landov

The account Gain on Sale of Asset is an income statement account and should appear in the Other Income/Expense category of the statement. The Gain on Sale of Asset account is not treated as revenue because it does not constitute the company's ongoing or central activity. Instead, it appears as income but in a separate category to denote its incidental nature.

The calculation of a loss on the sale of an asset is similar to that of a gain. Assume in the above example that ExerCo had sold the machine on July 1, 2009, for $10,000 cash. As in the previous example, depreciation must be recorded to the date of sale, July 1. The impact on the accounting equation from the sale of the asset is as follows:

Balance Sheet					Income Statement	
ASSETS	**=**	**LIABILITIES**	**+**	**STOCKHOLDERS' EQUITY +**	**REVENUES –**	**EXPENSES**
Accumulated					Loss on Sale	
Depreciation—Machine 9,000					of Asset	(1,000)
Cash 10,000						
Machine (20,000)						

The **Loss on Sale of Asset** indicates the amount by which the asset's sales price is *less than* its book value. Thus, the loss could be calculated as follows:

Loss on Sale of Asset
The amount by which selling price is less than book value.

Asset cost	$20,000
Less: Accumulated depreciation	9,000
Book value	$11,000
Sale price	10,000
Loss on sale of asset	$ 1,000

The Loss on Sale of Asset account is an income statement account and should appear in the Other Income/Expense category of the income statement.

Operating Assets: Natural Resources

BALANCE SHEET PRESENTATION

Important operating assets for some companies consist of **natural resources** such as coalfields, oil wells, other mineral deposits, and timberlands. Natural resources share one characteristic: the resource is consumed as it is used. For example, the coal a utility company uses to make electricity is consumed in the process. Most natural resources cannot be replenished in the foreseeable future. Coal and oil, for example, can be replenished only by nature over millions of years. Timberlands may be replenished in a shorter time period, but even trees must grow for many years to be usable for lumber.

Natural resources
Assets that are consumed during their use.

Natural resources should be carried in the Property, Plant, and Equipment category of the balance sheet as an operating asset. Like other assets in the category, natural resources should initially be recorded at *acquisition cost*. Acquisition cost should include the cost of acquiring the natural resource and the costs necessary to prepare the asset for use. The preparation costs for natural resources may often be very large; for example, a utility may spend large sums to remove layers of dirt before the coal can be mined. These preparation costs should be added to the cost of the asset.

DEPLETION OF NATURAL RESOURCES

When a natural resource is used or consumed, it should be treated as an expense. The process of recording the expense is similar to the depreciation or amortization process but is usually referred to as *depletion*. The amount of depletion expense each period should reflect the portion of the natural resource that was used up during the current year.

EXHIBIT 8-3	Weyerhauser Company 2004 Assets Section and Natural Resources Note

	(Dollar amounts in millions)	
ASSETS	**DECEMBER 26, 2004**	**DECEMBER 28, 2003**
Property and equipment, net (Note 8)	11,843	12,243
Construction in progress	269	403
Timber and timberlands at cost, less depletion charged to disposals	4,212	4,287
Investments in and advances to equity affiliates (Note 3)	489	546
Goodwill (Note 4)	3,244	3,237

Depletion rates used to relieve timber inventory are determined with reference to the net carrying value of timber and the related volume of timber estimated to be available over the the growth cycle. The growth cycle volume considers regulatory and environmental constraints affecting operable acres, management strategies to be applied, inventory data improvements, growth rate revisions and recalibrations, and the exclusion of known dispositions and inoperable acreage.

Assume, for example, that Local Coal Company purchased a coalfield on January 1, 2007, for $1 million. The company employed a team of engineering experts who estimated the total coal in the field to be 200,000 tons and who determined that the field's residual value after removal of the coal would be zero. Local Coal should calculate the depletion per ton as follows:

$$\text{Depletion per Ton} = (\text{Acquisition Cost} - \text{Residual Value}) / \text{Total Number of Tons in Asset's Life}$$
$$= (\$1,000,000 - 0)/200,000 \text{ tons}$$
$$= \$5 \text{ per ton}$$

Depletion expense for each year should be calculated as follows:

$$\text{Depletion Expense} = \text{Depletion per Ton} \times \text{Tons Mined during Year}$$

Assume that Local Coal Company mined 10,000 tons of coal during 2007. The depletion expense for 2007 for Local Coal follows:

$$\$5 \times 10,000 \text{ tons} = \$50,000$$

Local Coal should record the depletion in an Accumulated Depletion—Coalfield account, which would appear as a contra-asset on the balance sheet. Rather than using an accumulated depletion account, some companies may decrease the asset account directly.

There is an interesting parallel between depletion of natural resources and depreciation of plant and equipment. That is, depletion is very similar to depreciation using the units-of-production method. Both require an estimate of the useful life of the asset in terms of the total amount that can be produced (for units-of-production method) or consumed (for depletion) over the asset's life.

Natural resources may be important assets for some companies. For example, Exhibit 8-3 highlights the asset portion of the 2004 balance sheet and the accompanying note of **Weyerhauser**. The company had timber and timberlands, net of depletion, of $4,212 million as of December 26, 2004. The note indicates that the company records the depletion of timber on the basis of annual amount of timber cut in relation to the total amount of recoverable timber.

Operating Assets: Intangible Assets

Intangible assets
Assets with no physical properties.

Intangible assets are long-term assets with no physical properties. Because one cannot see or touch most intangible assets, it is easy to overlook their importance. Intangibles are recorded as assets, however, because they provide future economic

---

EXHIBIT 8-4 | Most Common Intangible Assets

Intangible Asset	Description
Patent	Right to use, manufacture, or sell a product; granted by the U.S. Patent Office. Patents have a legal life of 20 years.
Copyright	Right to reproduce or sell a published work. Copyrights are granted for 50 years plus the life of the creator.
Trademark	A symbol or name that allows a product or service to be identified; provides legal protection for 20 years plus an indefinite number of renewal periods.
Goodwill	The excess of the purchase price to acquire a business over the value of the individual net assets acquired.

---

benefits to the company. In fact, an intangible asset may be the most important asset a company owns or controls. For example, a pharmaceutical company may own some property, plant, and equipment, but its most important asset may be its patent for a particular drug or process. Likewise, the company that publishes this textbook may consider the copyrights to textbooks to be among its most important revenue-producing assets.

The balance sheet includes the intangible assets that meet the accounting definition of assets. Patents, copyrights, and brand names are included because they are owned by the company and will produce a future benefit that can be identified and measured. The balance sheet, however, would indicate only the acquisition cost of those assets, not the value of the assets to the company or the sales value of the assets.

Of course, the balance sheet does not include all of the items that may produce future benefit to the company. A company's employees, its management team, its location, or the intellectual capital of a few key researchers may well provide important future benefits and value. They are not recorded on the balance sheet, however, because they do not meet the accountant's definition of *assets* and cannot be easily identified or measured.

BALANCE SHEET PRESENTATION

Intangible assets are long-term assets and should be shown separately from property, plant, and equipment. Exhibit 8-4 contains a list of the most common intangible assets. Some companies develop a separate category, Intangible Assets, for the various types of intangibles. Nike presents only two lines for intangible assets: one for Identifiable Intangible Assets and another for Goodwill. Exhibit 8-5 presents the note that indicates the company's intangible assets consist of patents, trademarks, and goodwill. The presentation of intangible assets varies widely, however.

The nature of many intangibles is fairly evident, but goodwill is not so easily understood. **Goodwill** represents the amount of the purchase price paid in excess of the market value of the individual net assets when a business is purchased. Goodwill is recorded only when a business is purchased. It is not recorded when a company engages in activities that do not involve the purchase of another business entity. For example, customer loyalty or a good management team may represent "goodwill," but neither meets the accountants' criteria to be recorded as an asset on a firm's financial statements.

Some investors in U.S. companies believe that goodwill is not an asset because it is difficult to determine the factors that caused this asset. They prefer to focus their attention on a company's tangible assets. These investors simply reduce the amount shown on the balance sheet by the amount of goodwill, deducting it from total assets and reducing stockholders' equity by the same amount. That approach ignores the fact that goodwill can be important for many companies. Goodwill meets the accounting definition of an asset and should be recognized on the balance sheet.

LO9 Understand the balance sheet presentation of intangible assets.

Goodwill
The excess of the purchase price to acquire a business over the value of the individual net assets acquired. *Alternate term: Purchase price in excess of the market value of the assets*

EXHIBIT 8-5 The Nike, Inc., Consolidated Assets Section and Intangibles Note

The following table summarizes the Company's identifiable intangible assets balances as of May 31, 2004 and May 31, 2003:

(In millions)	Gross Carrying Amount	Accumulated Amortization	Net Carrying Amount
	May 31, 2004		
Amortized intangible assets:			
Patents	$27.9	$(11.9)	$ 16.0
Trademarks	14.1	(11.5)	2.6
Other	17.0	(10.8)	6.2
Total	$59.0	$(34.2)	$ 24.8
Unamortized intangible assets:			
Trademarks			$341.5
Total			$366.3

The change in the book value of goodwill, which relates to the Company's Other operating segment, is as follows (in millions).

Goodwill—May 31, 2003	$ 65.6
Acquisition of Subsidiaries	69.8
Goodwill—May 31, 2004	$135.4

ACQUISITION COST OF INTANGIBLE ASSETS

As was the case with property, plant, and equipment, the acquisition cost of an intangible asset includes all of the costs to acquire the asset and prepare it for its intended use. This should include all necessary costs such as legal costs incurred at the time of acquisition. Acquisition cost also should include those costs that are incurred after acquisition and that are necessary to the existence of the asset. For example, if a firm must pay legal fees to protect a patent from infringement, the costs should be considered part of the acquisition cost and should be included in the Patent account.

You should also be aware of one item that is similar to intangible assets but is *not* on the balance sheet. **Research and development costs** are expenditures incurred in the discovery of new knowledge and the translation of research into a design or plan for a new product or service or in a significant improvement to an existing product or service. Firms that engage in research and development do so because they believe such activities provide future benefit to the company. In fact, many firms have become leaders in an industry by engaging in research and development and the discovery of new products or technology. It is often very difficult, however, to identify the amount of future benefits of research and development and to associate those benefits with specific time periods. Because of the difficulty in predicting future benefits, the FASB has ruled that firms are not allowed to treat research and development costs as assets; all such expenditures must be treated as expenses in the period incurred. Many firms, especially high-technology ones, argue that this accounting rule results in seriously understated balance sheets. In their view, an important "asset" is not portrayed on their balance sheet. They also argue that they are at a competitive disadvantage when compared with foreign companies that are allowed to treat at least a portion of research

Research and development costs
Costs incurred in the discovery of new knowledge.

and development as an asset. Users of financial statements somehow need to be aware of those "hidden assets" when analyzing the balance sheets of companies that must expense research and development costs.

It is important to distinguish between patent costs and research and development costs. Patent costs include legal and filing fees necessary to acquire a patent. Such costs are capitalized as an intangible asset, Patent. However, the Patent account should not include the costs of research and development of a new product. Those costs are not capitalized but are treated as an expense, Research and Development.

AMORTIZATION OF INTANGIBLES

There has been considerable discussion over the past few years about whether intangible assets should be amortized and, if so, over what period of time. The term *amortization* is very similar to depreciation of property, plant, and equipment. Amortization involves allocating the acquistion cost of an intangible asset to the periods benefited by the use of the asset. If an intangible asset is amortized, most companies use the straight-line method of amortization, and we will use that method for illustration purposes. Occasionally, however, you may see instances of an accelerated form of amortization if the decline in usefulness of the intangible asset does not occur evenly over time.

LO10 Describe the proper amortization of intangible assets.

If an intangible asset has a finite life, amortization must be recognized. A finite life exists when an intangible asset is legally valid only for a certain length of time. For example, a patent is granted for a time period of 20 years and gives the patent holder the legal right to exclusive use of the patented design or invention. A copyright is likewise granted for a specified legal life. A finite life also exists when there is no legal life but the management of the company knows for certain that they will only be able to use the intangible asset for a specified period of time. For example, a company may have purchased the right to use a list of names and addresses of customers for a two-year time period. In that case, the intangible asset can only be used for two years and has a finite life.

When an intangible asset with a finite life is amortized, the time period over which amortization should be recorded must be considered carefully. The general guideline that should be followed is that **amortization should be recorded over the legal life or the useful life, whichever is shorter**. For example, patents may have a legal life of 20 years, but many are not useful for that long because new products and technology make the patent obsolete. The patent should be amortized over the number of years in which the firm receives benefits, which may be a period shorter than the legal life.

Assume that Nike developed a patent for a new shoe product on January 1, 2007. The costs involved with patent approval were $10,000, and the company wants to record amortization on the straight-line basis over a five-year life with no residual value. The effect on the accounting equation of the amortization for 2007 is as follows:

Balance Sheet				Income Statement	
ASSETS	**= LIABILITIES**	**+**	**STOCKHOLDERS' EQUITY**	**+ REVENUES − EXPENSES**	
Accumulated Amortization	(2,000)			Patent Expense	(2,000)

Rather than use an accumulated amortization account, some companies decrease (credit) the intangible asset account directly. The asset should be reported on the balance sheet at acquisition cost ($10,000) less accumulated amortization ($2,000), or $8,000, as of December 31, 2007.

While intangibles such as patents and copyrights have a finite life, many others do not. **If an intangible asset has an indefinite life, amortization should not be recognized.** For example, a television or radio station may have paid to acquire a broadcast license. A broadcast license is usually for a certain time period but can be renewed at the end of that time period. In that case, the life of the asset is indefinite, and amortization of the intangible asset representing the broadcast rights should not be recognized. A second example would be a trademark. For many companies, such as **Nike** or **Coca-Cola**, a trademark is a very valuable asset that provides name recognition and enhances sales. A trademark is granted for a certain time period but can be renewed at the end of that period so the life may be quite indefinite. The value of some trademarks may continue for a long time. If the life of an intangible asset represented by trademarks is indefinite, amortization should not be recorded. Note in Exhibit 8-5 that Nike has considered some trademarks to have an indefinite life and has not amortized them. Others have been amortized because they have a limited life.

Goodwill is an important intangible asset on the balance sheet of many companies. Until 2001, accounting rules had required companies to record amortization of goodwill over a time period not to exceed 40 years. However, in 2001, the FASB ruled that goodwill should be treated as an intangible asset with an *indefinite* life and companies should no longer record amortization expense related to goodwill. Companies have generally favored the new accounting stance. Hopefully, it will allow companies to more accurately inform statement users of their true value.

While companies should not record amortization of intangible assets with an indefinite life, they are required each year to determine whether the asset has been *impaired*. A discussion of asset impairment is beyond the scope of this text, but generally, it means a loss should be recorded when the value of the asset has declined. For example, some trademarks, such as Xerox and Polaroid, that were quite powerful in the past have declined in value over time. By recognizing an impairment of the asset, the loss is recorded in the time period that the value declines rather than when the asset is sold. It requires a great deal of judgment to determine when intangible assets have been impaired because the true value of an intangible asset is often difficult to determine. A rather drastic example of impairment occurs when a company realizes that an intangible asset has become completely worthless and should be written off.

Assume that Nike learns on January 1, 2008, when accumulated amortization is $2,000 (or the book value of the patent is $8,000), that a competing company has developed a new product that renders Nike's patent worthless. Nike has a loss of $8,000. The effect on the accounting equation of the patent write-off is as follows:

	Balance Sheet				Income Statement
ASSETS	**=**	**LIABILITIES**	**+**	**STOCKHOLDERS' EQUITY**	**+**	**REVENUES − EXPENSES**
Accumulated					Loss on Patent (8,000)
Amortization 2,000					
Patent (10,000)					

2 minute review

1. What are some examples of intangible assets?

2. Over what time period should intangibles with a finite life be amortized? What method is generally used?

Answers

1. *Intangibles are assets that have no physical properties. Examples are copyrights, trademarks, patents, franchises, and goodwill.*

2. *Intangibles with a finite life should be amortized over the legal life of the asset or the useful life, whichever is shorter. Most companies use the straight-line method of amortization. Accelerated methods of amortization are allowed but are not often used.*

EXHIBIT 8-6   Long-Term Assets and the Statement of Cash Flows

How Long-Term Assets Affect the Statement of Cash Flows

Determining the impact that acquisition, depreciation, and sale of long-term assets have on the statement of cash flows is important. Each of these business activities influences the statement of cash flows. Exhibit 8-6 illustrates the items discussed in this chapter and their effect on the statement of cash flows.

The acquisition of a long-term asset is an investing activity and should be reflected in the Investing Activities category of the statement of cash flows. The acquisition should appear as a deduction or negative item in that section because it requires the use of cash to purchase the asset. This applies whether the long-term asset is property, plant, and equipment or an intangible asset.

The depreciation or amortization of a long-term asset is not a cash item. It was referred to earlier as a noncash charge to earnings. Nevertheless, it must be presented on the statement of cash flows (if the indirect method is used for the statement). The reason is that it was deducted from earnings in calculating the net income figure. Therefore, it must be eliminated or "added back" if the net income amount is used to indicate the amount of cash generated from operations. Thus, depreciation and amortization should be presented in the Operating Activities category of the statement of cash flows as an addition to net income.

The sale or disposition of long-term assets is an investing activity. When an asset is sold, the amount of cash received should be reflected as an addition or plus amount in the Investing Activities category of the statement of cash flows. If the asset was sold at a gain or loss, however, one additional aspect should be reflected. Because the gain or loss was reflected on the income statement, it should be eliminated from the net income amount presented in the Operating Activities category (if the indirect method is used). A sale of an asset is not an activity related to normal, ongoing operations, and all amounts involved with the sale should be removed from the Operating Activities category. Exhibit 8-7 indicates the Operating and Investing categories of the 2004 statement of cash flows of **Nike, Inc.** The company had a net income of $945.6 million during 2004. Nike's performance is an excellent example of the difference between net income and actual cash flow. Note that the company generated a positive cash flow from operating activities of $1,514.4 million. One of the primary reasons was that depreciation of $252.1 million and amortization of $58.3 million affected the income statement but do not involve a cash outflow and are therefore added back on the statement of cash flows. Also note that the Investing Activities category indicates major outlays of cash for new property, plant, and equipment of $213.9 million and for the purchase of a subsidiary of $289.1 million. These cash outflows are indications of Nike's need for cash that must be generated from its operating activities.

LO11 Explain the impact that long-term assets have on the statement of cash flows.

8-2   Real World Practice

Reading Finish Line's Statement of Cash Flows

What amount of cash was used by Finish Line to purchase property and equipment in 2005? How much depreciation was recognized by the company during the year?

EXHIBIT 8-7 **Nike, Inc.'s Consolidated Partial Statement of Cash Flows**

Year ended May 31, (millions)	2004
Cash provided (used) by operations:	
Net income	$ 945.6
Income charges not affecting cash:	
Cumulative effect of accounting change	—
Depreciation	252.1
Deferred income taxes	19.0
Amortization and other	58.3
Income tax benefit from exercise of stock options	47.2
Changes in certain working capital components:	
Decrease (increase) in accounts receivable	82.5
(Increase) decrease in inventories	(55.9)
(Increase) decrease in prepaids and other current assets	(103.5)
Increase in accounts payable, accrued liabilities and income taxes payable	269.1
Cash provided by operations	1,514.4
Cash provided (used) by investing activities:	
Purchases of short-term investments	(400.8)
Additions to property, plant and equipment and other	(213.9)
Disposals of property, plant and equipment	11.6
Increase in other assets	(53.4)
(Decrease) increase in other liabilities	(0.9)
Acquisition of subsidiary, net of cash acquired	(289.1)
Cash used by investing activities	(946.5)

Analyzing Long-Term Assets for Average Life and Asset Turnover

LO12 Understand how investors can analyze a company's operating assets.

Because long-term assets constitute the major productive assets of most companies, it is important to analyze the age and composition of these assets. Analysis of the age of the assets can be accomplished fairly easily for those companies that use the straight-line method of depreciation. A rough measure of the average life of the assets can be calculated as:

$$\text{Average Life} = \frac{\text{Property, Plant and Equipment}}{\text{Depreciation Expense}}$$

The average age of the assets can be calculated as follows:

$$\text{Average Age} = \frac{\text{Accumulated Depreciation}}{\text{Depreciation Expense}}$$

The asset category of the balance sheet is also important in analyzing a company's profitability. The asset turnover is a measure of the productivity of the assets and is measured as follows:

$$\text{Asset Turnover} = \frac{\text{Net Sales}}{\text{Average Total Assets}}$$

This ratio is a measure of how many dollars of assets are necessary for every dollar of sales. If a company is using its assets efficiently, each dollar of assets will create a high amount of sales. Technically, a ratio is based on average total assets, but long-term assets often constitute the largest portion of a company's total assets.

For more on these measures of the age, life, and performance of the assets of Nike, Inc., and how they are used, see the Ratio Decision Model on the next page.

USING THE RATIO DECISION MODEL: ANALYZING AVERAGE LIFE AND ASSET TURNOVER

Use the following Ratio Decision Process to evaluate the average life and asset turnover for Nike or any other public company.

1. Formulate the Question

Long-term assets constitute the major productive assets of most companies. Investors and others who read financial statements must determine the age and composition of the operating assets. Two important questions are:

What is the average *life* of the assets?
What is the average *age* of the assets?

The operating asset category is also important in analyzing whether the operating assets will allow the company to be profitable in future periods. Therefore, a third question is:

How *productive* are the operating assets?

The productivity of assets can be calculated using the asset turnover ratio.

2. Gather the Information from the Financial Statements

Average Life and Average Age
For companies that use the straight-line method of depreciation:

- Total property, plant, and equipment: From the balance sheet (see Nike's Note 3)
- Total accumulated depreciation: From the balance sheet (see Nike's Note 3)
- Annual depreciation expense: From the statement of cash flows

Asset Turnover

- Average total assets: From the income statement

3. Calculate the Ratio

$$\text{Average Life} = \frac{\text{Property, Plant and Equipment}}{\text{Depreciation Expense}}$$

Nike, Inc.
Note 3—Property, Plant and Equipment

	May 31,	
	2004	2003
	(in millions)	
Land	$ 179.5	$ 191.1
Buildings	813.6	755.0
Machinery and equipment	1,608.6	1,538.7
Leasehold improvements	470.2	433.4
Construction in process	60.4	40.6
	3,132.3	2,988.8
Less accumulated depreciation	1,545.4	1,368.0
	$1,586.9	$1,620.8

Nike, Inc.
Partial Consolidated Statements of Cash Flows

	Year Ended May 31,	
	2004	2003
	(in millions)	
Depreciation	$252.1	$239.3

$$\text{Average Life} = \frac{\$3,132.3}{\$252.1} = 12.4 \text{ years}$$

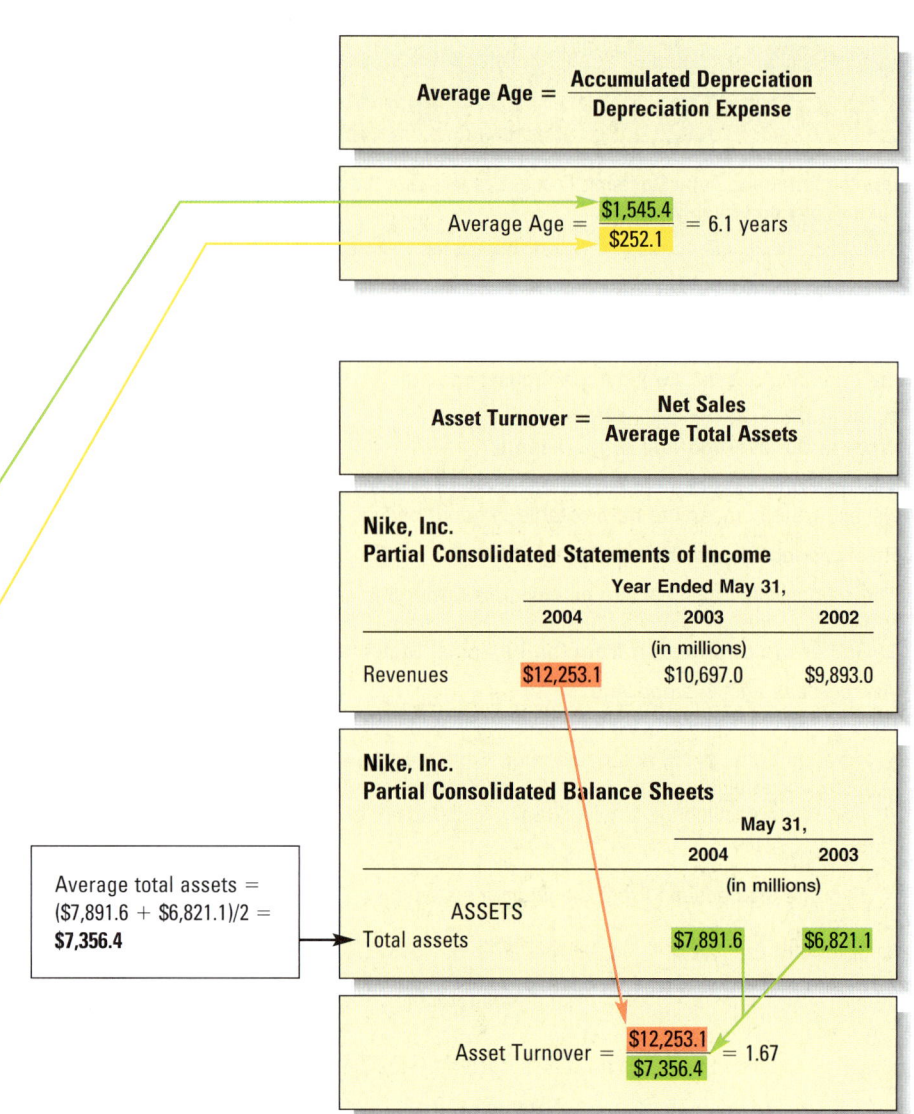

$$\text{Average Age} = \frac{\text{Accumulated Depreciation}}{\text{Depreciation Expense}}$$

$$\text{Average Age} = \frac{\$1,545.4}{\$252.1} = 6.1 \text{ years}$$

$$\text{Asset Turnover} = \frac{\text{Net Sales}}{\text{Average Total Assets}}$$

Nike, Inc.
Partial Consolidated Statements of Income

	Year Ended May 31,		
	2004	2003	2002
	(in millions)		
Revenues	$12,253.1	$10,697.0	$9,893.0

Nike, Inc.
Partial Consolidated Balance Sheets

	May 31,	
	2004	2003
	(in millions)	
ASSETS		
Total assets	$7,891.6	$6,821.1

Average total assets =
($7,891.6 + $6,821.1)/2 =
$7,356.4

$$\text{Asset Turnover} = \frac{\$12,253.1}{\$7,356.4} = 1.67$$

4. Compare the Ratio with Others

Nike's age, composition, and productivity of operating assets should be compared to prior years and to companies in the same industry.

	Nike		Foot Locker	
	2004	2003	2004	2003
Average life of assets	12.4	12.5	9.5	9.0
Average age of assets	6.1	5.7	4.9	4.6
Asset turnover	1.7	1.6	1.8	1.8

5. Interpret the Results

The average life and age of Nike's assets have been consistent from year to year and are in line with other companies in the industry. The asset turnover ratio is a measure of how many dollars of assets are necessary for every dollar of sales. If a company uses its assets efficiently, each dollar of asset will create a high amount of sales. Technically, this ratio is based on average *total* assets, but operating assets constitute the largest portion of a company's total assets. Nike's asset turnover ratio indicates that each dollar of assets in 2004 produced $1.67 of sales. It is an indication that the assets are currently productive and will be able to provide a profit in future periods.

STUDY HIGHLIGHTS

Understand balance sheet disclosures for operating assets (p. 350).   **LO1**

- Operating assets are the major productive assets of many companies, and investors must be able to evaluate the long-term potential of these assets for a return on their investments.
  - Operating assets may be classified as being either tangible or intangible assets.
  - Tangible assets are referred to as property, plant, and equipment or alternately fixed assets.
  - Intangible assets include goodwill, patents, copyrights, and various types of intellectual property.

Determine the acquisition cost of an operating asset (p. 351).   **LO2**

- Assets classified as property, plant, and equipment (or fixed assets) are initially recorded at the cost to acquire the assets, also referred to as historical cost.
  - Acquisition costs include those that are normal and necessary to acquire the asset and prepare it for its intended use. Generally, acquisition costs would include purchase price, taxes paid at time of purchase, transportation charges, and installation costs.

Explain how to calculate the acquisition cost of assets purchased for a lump sum (p. 351).   **LO3**

- Sometimes more than one asset is purchased for a single sum of money and the acquisition costs must be allocated between the assets.
  - In these cases, the purchase price should be allocated between the assets acquired based on the proportion of the fair market value each asset represents of the total purchase price.

Describe the impact of capitalizing interest as a part of the acquisition cost of an asset (p. 352).   **LO4**

- Generally, the interest on borrowed money used to acquire assets should not be capitalized, and instead should be treated as an expense of the period.
- One important exception to this general guideline exists for interest incurred from money borrowed to construct assets. This interest must be capitalized as part of the acquisition cost of the asset.

Compare depreciation methods and understand factors affecting the choice of method (p. 353).   **LO5**

- All property, plant, and equipment (except land) have a limited life, and a proper matching of expenses through depreciation is required. Several depreciation methods are available, including straight-line, units-of-production, and accelerated depreciation methods.
- In theory, the depreciation method that best allocates the original cost of the asset to the periods benefited by the use of the asset should be chosen. However, depreciation method choices are often influenced by tax and shareholder perceptions.

Understand the impact of a change in the estimate of the asset life or residual value (p. 357).   **LO6**

- Occasionally, an estimate of the asset's life or residual value must be modified after the depreciation process has begun. This is an example of an accounting change that is referred to as a change in estimate.

Determine which expenditures should be capitalized as asset costs and which should be treated as expenses (p. 358).   **LO7**

- The nature of some expenditures related to a capital asset, such as repairs or replacement parts, must be determined for the proper financial accounting treatment.
  - Capital expenditures are added to the acquisition cost of an asset and depreciated over time.
  - Revenue expenditures are not treated as part of the cost of the asset, but as an expense on the income statement in the period incurred.

HIGHLIGHTS

LO8   **Analyze the effect of the disposal of an asset at a gain or loss (p. 360).**

- Assets are usually disposed of through sales, which are exchange transactions that result in a gain or loss.
  - The gain or loss on an asset is the difference between the sales (or exchange) price and the book value of the asset, where book value is the acquisition cost less any accumulated depreciation on the asset.

LO9   **Understand the balance sheet presentation of intangible assets (p. 363).**

- Intangible assets are long-term assets that should be shown separately from property, plant, and equipment on the balance sheet.

LO10   **Describe the proper amortization of intangible assets (p. 365).**

- The amortization of intangibles is a process similar to that of depreciating capital assets.
- If an intangible asset has a finite useful life, amortization expense must be taken on the asset over the legal life or useful life, whichever is shorter.

LO11   **Explain the impact that long-term assets have on the statement of cash flows (p. 367).**

- Long-term assets impact the statement of cash flows when they are acquired, depreciated, and sold.
  - Cash used to acquire long-term assets or cash received on the sale of long-term assets is reflected in the Investing Activities section of the statement of cash flows.
  - Depreciation and amortization are noncash expenses recorded on the accrual income statement. Accordingly, net income on a cash basis must be arrived at by adding depreciation and amortization back to accrual net income.

LO12   **Understand how investors can analyze a company's operating assets (p. 368).**

- Investors are interested in how productive a company's operating assets are.
- The Ratio Decision Process is a valuable tool that can be used to examine the productivity of operating assets with the asset turnover ratio.

HIGHLIGHTS

RATIO REVIEW

$$\text{Average Life} = \frac{\text{Property, Plant and Equipment}}{\text{Depreciation Expense}}$$

$$\text{Average Age} = \frac{\text{Accumulated Depreciation}}{\text{Depreciation Expense}}$$

$$\text{Asset Turnover} = \frac{\text{Net Sales}}{\text{Average Total Assets}}$$

ACCOUNTS HIGHLIGHTED

Account Title	Appears on the	In the Section of	Page Number
Land	Balance Sheet	Operating Assets	352
Buildings	Balance Sheet	Operating Assets	352
Machinery	Balance Sheet	Operating Assets	359
Accumulated depreciation (a contra account)	Balance Sheet	Operating Assets	358
Depreciation expense	Income Statement	Operating Expenses	358
Gain on sale of asset	Income Statement	Other Income	360
Loss on sale of asset	Income Statement	Other Expense	360
Depletion expense	Income Statement	Operating Expenses	362
Copyright	Balance Sheet	Intangible Assets	363
Trademark	Balance Sheet	Intangible Assets	363
Goodwill	Balance Sheet	Intangible Assets	363
Amortization expense	Income Statement	Operating Expenses	365
Accumulated amortization (a contra account)	Balance Sheet	Intangible Assets	365

KEY TERMS QUIZ

Read each definition below and then write the number of the definition in the blank beside the appropriate term it defines. The quiz solutions appear at the end of the chapter.

_____ Acquisition cost	_____ Change in estimate
_____ Capitalization of interest	_____ Capital expenditure
_____ Land improvements	_____ Revenue expenditure
_____ Depreciation	_____ Gain on Sale of Asset
_____ Straight-line method	_____ Loss on Sale of Asset
_____ Book value	_____ Natural resources
_____ Units-of-production method	_____ Intangible assets
_____ Accelerated depreciation	_____ Goodwill
_____ Double-declining-balance method	_____ Research and development costs

1. This amount includes all of the costs normally necessary to acquire an asset and prepare it for its intended use.

2. Additions made to a piece of property such as paving or landscaping a parking lot. The costs are treated separately from land for purposes of recording depreciation.

3. A method by which the same dollar amount of depreciation is recorded in each year of asset use.

4. A method by which depreciation is determined as a function of the number of units the asset produces.

5. The process of treating the cost of interest on constructed assets as a part of the asset cost rather than as an expense.

6. A change in the life of an asset or in its expected residual value.

7. The allocation of the original acquisition cost of an asset to the periods benefited by its use.

8. A cost that improves an operating asset and is added to the asset account.

9. The original acquisition cost of an asset minus the amount of accumulated depreciation.

10. A cost that keeps an operating asset in its normal operating condition and is treated as an expense of the period.

11. An account whose amount indicates that the selling price received on an asset's disposal exceeds its book value.

12. An account whose amount indicates that the book value of an asset exceeds the selling price received on its disposal.

13. A term that refers to several methods by which a higher amount of depreciation is recorded in the early years of an asset's life and a lower amount is recorded in the later years.

14. Long-term assets that have no physical properties; for example, patents, copyrights, and goodwill.

15. A method by which depreciation is recorded at twice the straight-line rate, but the depreciable balance is reduced in each period.

16. The amount indicating that the purchase price of a business exceeded the total fair market value of the identifiable net assets at the time the business was acquired.

17. Expenditures incurred in the discovery of new knowledge and the translation of research into a design or plan for a new product.

18. Assets that are consumed during their use; for example, coal or oil.

ALTERNATE TERMS

Accumulated depreciation Allowance for depreciation

Acquisition cost Historical cost

Capitalize Treat as asset

Construction in progress Construction in process

Goodwill Purchase price in excess of the market value of assets

Hidden assets Unrecorded or off-balance-sheet assets

Property, Plant, and Equipment Fixed assets

Prospective Current and future years

Residual value Salvage value

Revenue expenditure An expense of the period

WARMUP EXERCISES

LO5 **Warmup Exercise 8-1** Depreciation Methods

Assume that a company purchases a depreciable asset on January 1 for $10,000. The asset has a four-year life and will have zero residual value at the end of the fourth year.

Required
Calculate depreciation expense for each of the four years using the straight-line method and the double-declining-balance method.

LO5 **Warmup Exercise 8-2** Depreciation and Cash Flow

Use the information from Exercise 8-1. Assume that the double-declining-balance method will be used for tax purposes and the straight-line method will be used for the financial statement to be given to the stockholders. Also assume that the tax rate is 40%.

Required
How much will the tax savings be in the first year as a result of using the accelerated method of depreciation?

REVIEW

SOLUTIONS TO WARMUP EXERCISES

Warmup Exercise 8-1

	Straight-Line	Double-Declining-Balance	
Year 1	$2,500*	$10,000 × 0.50**	= $5,000
2	2,500	($10,000 − $5,000) × 0.50	= $2,500
3	2,500	($10,000 − $7,500) × 0.50	= $1,250
4	2,500	($10,000 − $8,750) × 0.50	= $625

*$10,000/4 years
**Straight-line rate as a percentage is 1 year/4 years, or 25%. Double the rate is 25% × 2, or 50%.

Warmup Exercise 8-2

The tax savings is equal to the difference in depreciation between the two methods times the tax rate. Therefore, the tax savings is ($5,000 − $2,500) × 0.40 = $1,000.

REVIEW PROBLEM

The accountant for Becker Company wants to develop a balance sheet as of December 31, 2007. A review of the asset records has revealed the following information:

a. Asset A was purchased on July 1, 2005, for $40,000 and has been depreciated on the straight-line basis using an estimated life of six years and a residual value of $4,000.
b. Asset B was purchased on January 1, 2006, for $66,000. The straight-line method has been used for depreciation purposes. Originally, the estimated life of the asset was projected to be six years with a residual value of $6,000; however, at the beginning of 2007, the accountant learned that the remaining life of the asset was only three years with a residual value of $2,000.
c. Asset C was purchased on January 1, 2006, for $50,000. The double-declining-balance method has been used for depreciation purposes, with a four-year life and a residual value estimate of $5,000.

Required

1. Assume that these assets represent pieces of equipment. Calculate the acquisition cost, accumulated depreciation, and book value of each asset as of December 31, 2007.
2. How would the assets appear on the balance sheet on December 31, 2007?
3. Assume that Becker Company sold Asset B on January 2, 2008, for $25,000. Calculate the amount of the resulting gain or loss, and determine the effect on the accounting equation of the sale. Where would the gain or loss appear on the income statement?

SOLUTION TO REVIEW PROBLEM

1.

Asset A

2005	Depreciation	($40,000 − $4,000)/6 × 1/2 Year	= $ 3,000
2006		($40,000 − $4,000)/6	= 6,000
2007		($40,000 − $4,000)/6	= 6,000
	Accumulated Depreciation		$15,000

Asset B

2006	Depreciation	($66,000 − $6,000)/6	= $10,000
2007		($66,000 − $10,000 − $2,000)/3	= 18,000
	Accumulated Depreciation		$28,000

Note the impact of the change in estimate on 2007 depreciation.

Asset C

2006	Depreciation	$50,000 × 25% × 2	= $25,000
2007		($50,000 − $25,000) × (25% × 2)	= 12,500
	Accumulated Depreciation		$37,500

Becker Company
Summary of Asset Cost and Accumulated Depreciation
As of December 31, 2007

Asset	Acquisition Cost	Accumulated Depreciation	Book Value
A	$ 40,000	$15,000	$25,000
B	66,000	28,000	38,000
C	50,000	37,500	12,500
Totals	$156,000	$80,500	$75,500

2. The assets would appear in the Long-Term Assets category of the balance sheet as follows:

Equipment	$156,000	
Less: Accumulated depreciation	80,500	
Equipment (net)		$75,500

3.

Asset B book value	$ 38,000
Selling price	25,000
Loss on sale of asset	$ 13,000

Balance Sheet						Income Statement
ASSETS		=	**LIABILITIES**	+	**STOCKHOLDERS' EQUITY** +	**REVENUES − EXPENSES**
Cash	25,000					Loss on Sale of Asset (13,000)
Asset B	(66,000)					
Accumulated Depreciation	28,000					

The Loss on Sale of Asset account should appear in the Other Income/Other Expense category of the income statement. It is similar to an expense but is not the company's major activity.

QUESTIONS

1. What are several examples of operating assets? Why are operating assets essential to a company's long-term future?

2. What is the meaning of the term acquisition cost of operating assets? Give some examples of costs that should be included in the acquisition cost.

3. When assets are purchased as a group, how should the acquisition cost of the individual assets be determined?

4. Why is it important to account separately for the cost of land and building, even when the two assets are purchased together?

5. Under what circumstances should interest be capitalized as part of the cost of an asset?

6. What factors may contribute to the decline in usefulness of operating assets? Should the choice of depreciation method be related to these factors? Must a company choose just one method of depreciation for all assets?

7. Why do you think that most companies use the straight-line method of depreciation?

8. How should the residual value of an operating asset be treated when using the straight-line method? How should it be treated when using the double-declining-balance method?

9. Why do many companies use one method to calculate depreciation for the income statement developed for stockholders and another method for income tax purposes?

10. What should a company do if it finds that the original estimate of the life of an asset or the residual value of the asset must be changed?

11. What are the meanings of the terms capital expenditures and revenue expenditures? What determines whether an item is a capital or revenue expenditure?

12. How is the gain or loss on the sale of an operating asset calculated? Where would the Gain on Sale of Asset account appear on the financial statements?

REVIEW

13. What are several examples of items that constitute intangible assets? In what category of the balance sheet should intangible assets appear?

14. What is the meaning of the term goodwill? Give an example of a transaction that would result in the recording of goodwill on the balance sheet.

15. Do you agree with the FASB's ruling that all research and development costs should be treated as an expense on the income statement? Why or why not?

16. Do you agree with some accountants who argue that intangible assets have an indefinite life and therefore should not be subject to amortization?

17. When an intangible asset is amortized, should the asset's amortization occur over its legal life or over its useful life? Give an example in which the legal life exceeds the useful life.

18. Suppose that an intangible asset is being amortized over a 10-year time period but a competitor has just introduced a new product that will have a serious negative impact on the asset's value. Should the company continue to amortize the intangible asset over the 10-year life?

EXERCISES

LO2

Exercise 8-1 Acquisition Cost

Ruby Company purchased a piece of equipment with a list price of $60,000 on January 1, 2007. The following amounts were related to the equipment purchase:

- Terms of the purchase were 2/10, net 30. Ruby paid for the purchase on January 8.
- Freight costs of $1,000 were incurred.
- A state agency required that a pollution-control device be installed on the equipment at a cost of $2,500.
- During installation, the equipment was damaged and repair costs of $4,000 were incurred.
- Architect's fees of $6,000 were paid to redesign the work space to accommodate the new equipment.
- Ruby purchased liability insurance to cover possible damage to the asset. The three-year policy cost $8,000.
- Ruby financed the purchase with a bank loan. Interest of $3,000 was paid on the loan during 2007.

Required
Determine the acquisition cost of the equipment.

LO2

Exercise 8-2 Lump-Sum Purchase

To add to his growing chain of grocery stores, on January 1, 2007, Danny Marks bought a grocery store of a small competitor for $520,000. An appraiser, hired to assess the value of the assets acquired, determined that the land had a market value of $200,000, the building a market value of $150,000, and the equipment a market value of $250,000.

Required
1. What is the acquisition cost of each asset?
2. Danny plans to depreciate the operating assets on a straight-line basis for 20 years. Determine the amount of depreciation expense for 2007 on these newly acquired assets. You may assume zero residual value for all assets.
3. How would the assets appear on the balance sheet as of December 31, 2007?

LO2

Exercise 8-3 Straight-Line and Units-of-Production Methods

Assume that Sample Company purchased factory equipment on January 1, 2007, for $60,000. The equipment has an estimated life of five years and an estimated residual value of $6,000. Sample's accountant is considering whether to use the straight-line or the units-of-production method to depreciate the asset. Because the company is beginning a new production process, the equipment will be used to produce 10,000 units in 2007, but production subsequent to 2007 will increase by 10,000 units each year.

Required

Calculate the depreciation expense, the accumulated depreciation, and the book value of the equipment under both methods for each of the five years of the asset's life. Do you think that the units-of-production method yields reasonable results in this situation?

LO5   **Exercise 8-4** Accelerated Depreciation

Koffman's Warehouse purchased a forklift on January 1, 2007, for $6,000. It is expected to last for five years and have a residual value of $600. Koffman's uses the double-declining-balance method for depreciation.

Required

1. Calculate the depreciation expense, the accumulated depreciation, and the book value for each year of the forklift's life.
2. Determine the effect on the accounting equation of the depreciation expense for 2007.
3. Refer to Exhibit 8-2. What factors may have influenced Koffman to use the double-declining-balance method?

LO6   **Exercise 8-5** Change in Estimate

Assume that Bloomer Company purchased a new machine on January 1, 2007, for $80,000. The machine has an estimated useful life of nine years and a residual value of $8,000. Bloomer has chosen to use the straight-line method of depreciation. On January 1, 2009, Bloomer discovered that the machine would not be useful beyond December 31, 2012, and estimated its value at that time to be $2,000.

Required

1. Calculate the depreciation expense, the accumulated depreciation, and the book value of the asset for each year, 2007 to 2012.
2. Was the depreciation recorded in 2007 and 2008 wrong? If so, why was it not corrected?

LO8   **Exercise 8-6** Asset Disposal

Assume that Gonzalez Company purchased an asset on January 1, 2005, for $60,000. The asset had an estimated life of six years and an estimated residual value of $6,000. The company used the straight-line method to depreciate the asset. On July 1, 2007, the asset was sold for $40,000 cash.

Required

1. Determine the amount of depreciation for 2007. Also determine the effect on the accounting equation of the sale of the asset.
2. How should the gain or loss on the sale of the asset be presented on the income statement?

LO8   **Exercise 8-7** Asset Disposal

Refer to Exercise 8-6. Assume that Gonzalez Company sold the asset on July 1, 2007, and received $15,000 cash and a note for an additional $15,000.

Required

1. Determine the amount of depreciation for 2007. Also determine the effect on the accounting equation of the sale of the asset.
2. How should the gain or loss on the sale of the asset be presented on the income statement?

LO10   **Exercise 8-8** Amortization of Intangibles

For each of the following intangible assets, indicate the amount of amortization expense that should be recorded for the year 2007 and the amount of accumulated amortization on the balance sheet as of December 31, 2007.

	Trademark	**Patent**	**Copyright**
Cost	$40,000	$50,000	$80,000
Date of purchase	1/1/00	1/1/02	1/1/05
Useful life	indefinite	10 yrs.	20 yrs.
Legal life	undefined	20 yrs.	50 yrs.
Method	SL*	SL	SL

*Represents the straight-line method.

LO11   **Exercise 8-9** Impact of Transactions Involving Operating Assets on Statement of Cash Flows

From the following list, identify each item as operating (O), investing (I), financing (F), or not separately reported on the statement of cash flows (N).

_____ Purchase of land

_____ Proceeds from sale of land

_____ Gain on sale of land

_____ Purchase of equipment

_____ Depreciation expense

_____ Proceeds from sale of equipment

_____ Loss on sale of equipment

LO11   **Exercise 8-10** Impact of Transactions Involving Intangible Assets on Statement of Cash Flows

From the following list, identify each item as operating (O), investing (I), financing (F), or not separately reported on the statement of cash flows (N).

_____ Cost incurred to acquire copyright

_____ Proceeds from sale of patent

_____ Gain on sale of patent

_____ Research and development costs

_____ Amortization of patent

MULTI-CONCEPT EXERCISES

LO1,7   **Exercise 8-11** Capital versus Revenue Expenditures

On January 1, 2005, Jose Company purchased a building for $200,000 and a delivery truck for $20,000. The following expenditures have been incurred during 2007, related to the building and the truck:

- The building was painted at a cost of $5,000.
- To prevent leaking, new windows were installed in the building at a cost of $10,000.
- To allow an improved flow of production, a new conveyor system was installed at a cost of $40,000.
- The delivery truck was repainted with a new company logo at a cost of $1,000.
- To allow better handling of large loads, a hydraulic lift system was installed on the truck at a cost of $5,000.
- The truck's engine was overhauled at a cost of $4,000.

Required

1. Determine which of these costs should be capitalized. Also, determine the effect on the accounting equation for the capitalized costs. Assume that all costs were incurred on January 1, 2007.
2. Determine the amount of depreciation for the year 2007. The company uses the straight-line method and depreciates the building over 25 years and the truck over six years. Assume zero residual value for all assets.
3. How would the assets appear on the balance sheet of December 31, 2007?

LO4,5   **Exercise 8-12** Capitalization of Interest and Depreciation

During 2007, Mercator Company borrowed $80,000 from a local bank and, in addition, used $120,000 of cash to construct a new corporate office building. Based on average accumulated expenditures, the amount of interest capitalized during 2007 was $8,000. Construction was completed and the building was occupied on January 1, 2008.

Required

1. Determine the acquisition cost of the new building.
2. The building has an estimated useful life of 20 years and a $5,000 salvage value. Assuming that Mercator uses the straight-line basis to depreciate its operating assets, determine the amount of depreciation expense for 2007 and 2008.

LO9,10 **Exercise 8-13** Research and Development and Patents

Erin Company incurred the following costs during 2007:

a. Research and development costs of $20,000 were incurred. The research was conducted to discover a new product to sell to customers in future years. A product was successfully developed, and a patent for the new product was granted during 2007. Erin is unsure of the period benefited by the research but believes the product will result in increased sales over the next five years.

b. Legal costs and application fees of $10,000 for the patent were incurred on January 1, 2007. The patent was granted for a life of 20 years.

c. A patent infringement suit was successfully defended at a cost of $8,000. Assume that all costs were incurred on January 1, 2008.

Required

Determine how the costs in parts (a) and (b) should be presented on Erin's financial statements as of December 31, 2007. Also determine the amount of amortization of intangible assets that Erin should record in 2007 and 2008.

PROBLEMS

LO3 **Problem 8-1** Lump-Sum Purchase of Assets and Subsequent Events

Carter Development Company purchased, for cash, a large tract of land that was immediately platted and deeded into smaller sections:

Section 1, retail development with highway frontage

Section 2, multifamily apartment development

Section 3, single-family homes in the largest section

Based on recent sales of similar property, the fair market values of the three sections are as follows:

Section 1, $630,000

Section 2, $378,000

Section 3, $252,000

Required

1. What value is assigned to each section of land if the tract was purchased for (a) $1,260,000, (b) $1,560,000, or (c) $1,000,000?

2. How does the purchase of the tract affect the balance sheet?

3. Why would Carter be concerned with the value assigned to each section? Would Carter be more concerned with the values assigned if instead of purchasing three sections of land, it purchased land with buildings? Why or why not?

LO5 **Problem 8-2** Depreciation as a Tax Shield

The term *tax shield* refers to the amount of income tax saved by deducting depreciation for income tax purposes. Assume that Supreme Company is considering the purchase of an asset as of January 1, 2007. The cost of the asset with a five-year life and zero residual value is $100,000. The company will use the straight-line method of depreciation.

Supreme's income for tax purposes before recording depreciation on the asset will be $50,000 per year for the next five years. The corporation is currently in the 35% tax bracket.

Required

Calculate the amount of income tax that Supreme must pay each year if the asset is not purchased. Calculate the amount of income tax that Supreme must pay each year if the asset is purchased. What is the amount of the depreciation tax shield?

LO5 **Problem 8-3** Book versus Tax Depreciation

Griffith Delivery Service purchased a delivery truck for $33,600. The truck has an estimated useful life of six years and no salvage value. For the purpose of preparing financial statements, Griffith is planning to use straight-line depreciation. For tax purposes, Griffith follows

MACRS. Depreciation expense using MACRS is $6,720 in Year 1, $10,750 in Year 2, $6,450 in Year 3, $3,870 in each of Years 4 and 5, and $1,940 in Year 6.

Required

1. What is the difference between straight-line and MACRS depreciation expense for each of the six years?
2. Griffith's president has asked why you have used one method for the books and another for calculating taxes. "Can you do this? Is it legal? Don't we take the same total depreciation either way?" he asked. Write a brief memo answering his questions and explaining the benefits of using two methods for depreciation.

LO11   **Problem 8-4** Depreciation and Cash Flow

O'hare Company's only asset as of January 1, 2007, was a limousine. During 2007, only three transactions occurred:

Provided services of $100,000 on account.

Collected all accounts receivable.

Depreciation on the limousine was $15,000.

Required

1. Develop an income statement for O'hare for 2007.
2. Determine the amount of the net cash inflow for O'hare for 2007.
3. Explain in one or more sentences why the amount of the net income on O'hare's income statement does not equal the amount of the net cash inflow.
4. If O'hare developed a cash flow statement for 2007 using the indirect method, what amount would appear in the category titled Cash Flow from Operating Activities?

LO11   **Problem 8-5** Reconstruct Net Book Values Using Statement of Cash Flows

Centralia Stores Inc. had property, plant, and equipment, net of accumulated depreciation of $4,459,000; and intangible assets, net of accumulated amortization, of $673,000 at December 31, 2007. The company's 2007 statement of cash flows, prepared using the indirect method, included the following items.

The Cash Flows from Operating Activities section included three additions to net income: (1) depreciation expense in the amount of $672,000, (2) amortization expense in the amount of $33,000, and (3) the loss on the sale of equipment in the amount of $35,000. The Cash Flows from Operating Activities section also included a subtraction from net income for the gain on the sale of a copyright of $55,000. The Cash Flows from Investing Activities section included outflows for the purchase of a building in the amount of $292,000 and $15,000 for the payment of legal fees to protect a patent from infringement. The Cash Flows from Investing Activities section also included inflows from the sale of equipment in the amount of $315,000 and the sale of a copyright in the amount of $75,000.

Required

1. Determine the book values of the assets that were sold during 2007.
2. Reconstruct the amount of property, plant, and equipment, net of accumulated depreciation, that was reported on the company's balance sheet at December 31, 2006.
3. Reconstruct the amount of intangibles, net of accumulated amortization, that was reported on the company's balance sheet at December 31, 2006.

MULTI-CONCEPT PROBLEMS

LO1,3, **Problem 8-6** Cost of Assets, Subsequent Book Values, and Balance Sheet Presentation
5,7,8

The following events took place at Pete's Painting Company during 2007:

a. On January 1, Pete bought a used truck for $14,000. He added a tool chest and side racks for ladders for $4,800. The truck is expected to last four years and then be sold for $800. Pete uses straight-line depreciation.
b. On January 1, he purchased several items at an auction for $2,400. These items had fair market values as follows:

10 cases of paint trays and roller covers	$ 200
Storage cabinets	600
Ladders & scaffolding	2,400

Pete will use all the paint trays and roller covers this year. The storage cabinets are expected to last nine years, and the ladders and scaffolding for four years.

c. On February 1, Pete paid the city $1,500 for a three-year license to operate the business.

d. On September 1, Pete sold an old truck for $4,800. The truck had cost $12,000 when it was purchased on September 1, 2002. It had been expected to last eight years and have a salvage value of $800.

Required

1. For each situation, explain the value assigned to the asset when it is purchased [or for part (d), the book value when sold].
2. Determine the amount of depreciation or other expense to be recorded for each asset for 2007.
3. How would these assets appear on the balance sheet as of December 31, 2007?

LO2,5 **Problem 8-7** Cost of Assets and the Effect on Depreciation

Early in its first year of business, Toner Company, a fitness and training center, purchased new workout equipment. The acquisition included the following costs:

Purchase price	$150,000
Tax	15,000
Transportation	4,000
Setup*	25,000
Painting*	3,000

The equipment was adjusted to Toner's specific needs and painted to match the other equipment in the gym.

The bookkeeper recorded an asset, Equipment, $165,000 (purchase price and tax). The remaining costs were expensed for the year. Toner used straight-line depreciation. The equipment was expected to last 10 years with zero salvage value.

Required

1. How much depreciation did Toner report on its income statement related to this equipment in Year 1? What do you believe is the correct amount of depreciation to report in Year 1 related to this equipment?
2. Income is $100,000, before costs related to the equipment are reported. How much income will Toner report in Year 1? What amount of income should it report? You may ignore income tax.
3. Using the equipment as an example, explain the difference between a cost and an expense.

LO5,7,8 **Problem 8-8** Capital Expenditures, Depreciation, and Disposal

Merton Company purchased a building at a cost of $364,000 on January 1, 2006. Merton estimated that the building's life would be 25 years and the residual value at the end of 25 years would be $14,000.

On January 1, 2007, the company made several expenditures related to the building. The entire building was painted and floors were refinished at a cost of $21,000. A federal agency required Merton to install additional pollution-control devices in the building at a cost of $42,000. With the new devices, Merton believed it was possible to extend the life of the building by an additional six years.

In 2008 Merton altered its corporate strategy dramatically. The company sold the building on April 1, 2008, for $392,000 in cash and relocated all operations in another state.

Required

1. Determine the amount of depreciation that should be reflected on the income statement for 2006 and 2007.
2. Explain why the cost of the pollution-control equipment was not expensed in 2007. What conditions would have allowed Merton to expense the equipment? If Merton has a choice, would it prefer to expense or capitalize the equipment?
3. What amount of gain or loss did Merton record when it sold the building? What amount of gain or loss would have been reported if the pollution-control equipment had been expensed in 2009?

LO6,10 **Problem 8-9** Amortization of Intangible, Revision of Rate

During 2002, Reynosa Inc.'s R&D department developed a new manufacturing process. R&D costs were $85,000. The process was patented on October 1, 2002. Legal costs to acquire the patent were $11,900. Reynosa decided to expense the patent over a 20-year time period. Reynosa's fiscal year ends on September 30.

On October 1, 2007, Reynosa's competition announced that it had obtained a patent on a new process that would make Reynosa's patent completely worthless.

Required
1. How should Reynosa record the $85,000 and $11,900 costs?
2. How much amortization expense should Reynosa report in each year through the year ended September 30, 2007?
3. What amount of loss should Reynosa report in the year ended September 30, 2008?

LO8,11 **Problem 8-10** Purchase and Disposal of Operating Asset and Effects on Statement of Cash Flows

On January 1, 2007, Castlewood Company purchased some machinery for its production line for $104,000. Using an estimated useful life of eight years and a residual value of $8,000, the annual straight-line depreciation of the machinery was calculated to be $12,000. Castlewood used the machinery during 2007 and 2008 but then decided to automate its production process. On December 31, 2008, Castlewood sold the machinery at a loss of $5,000 and purchased new, fully automated machinery for $205,000.

Required
1. How would the transactions described above be presented on Castlewood's statements of cash flows for the years ended December 31, 2007 and 2008?
2. Why would Castlewood sell at a loss machinery that had a remaining useful life of six years and purchase new machinery with a cost almost twice that of the old?

LO9,10, 11 **Problem 8-11** Amortization of Intangibles and Effects on Statement of Cash Flows

Tableleaf Inc. purchased a patent a number of years ago. The patent is being amortized on a straight-line basis over its estimated useful life. The company's comparative balance sheets as of December 31, 2007 and 2006, included the following line item:

	12/31/07	12/31/06
Patent, less accumulated amortization of $119,000 (2007) and $102,000 (2006)	$170,000	$187,000

Required
1. How much amortization expense was recorded during 2007?
2. What was the patent's acquisition cost? When was it acquired? What is its estimated useful life? How was the acquisition of the patent reported on that year's statement of cash flows?
3. Assume that Tableleaf uses the indirect method to prepare its statement of cash flows. How is the amortization of the patent reported annually on the statement of cash flows?
4. How would the sale of the patent on January 1, 2008, for $200,000 be reported on the 2008 statement of cash flows?

ALTERNATE PROBLEMS

LO3 **Problem 8-1A** Lump-Sum Purchase of Assets and Subsequent Events

Dixon Manufacturing purchased, for cash, three large pieces of equipment. Based on recent sales of similar equipment, the fair market values are as follows:

Piece 1	$200,000
Piece 2	$200,000
Piece 3	$440,000

Required

1. What value is assigned to each piece of equipment if the equipment was purchased for (a) $480,000, (b) $680,000, or (c) $800,000?
2. How does the purchase of the equipment affect total assets?

LO5   **Problem 8-2A** Depreciation as a Tax Shield

The term *tax shield* refers to the amount of income tax saved by deducting depreciation for income tax purposes. Assume that Rummy Company is considering the purchase of an asset as of January 1, 2007. The cost of the asset with a five-year life and zero residual value is $60,000. The company will use the double-declining-balance method of depreciation.

Rummy's income for tax purposes before recording depreciation on the asset will be $62,000 per year for the next five years. The corporation is currently in the 30% tax bracket.

Required

Calculate the amount of income tax that Rummy must pay each year if the asset is not purchased and then the amount of income tax that Rummy must pay each year if the asset is purchased. What is the amount of tax shield over the life of the asset? What is the amount of tax shield for Rummy if it uses the straight-line method over the life of the asset? Why would Rummy choose to use the accelerated method?

LO5   **Problem 8-3A** Book versus Tax Depreciation

Payton Delivery Service purchased a delivery truck for $28,200. The truck will have a useful life of six years and zero salvage value. For the purposes of preparing financial statements, Payton is planning to use straight-line depreciation. For tax purposes, Payton follows MACRS. Depreciation expense using MACRS is $5,650 in Year 1, $9,025 in Year 2, $5,400 in Year 3, $3,250 in each of Years 4 and 5, and $1,625 in Year 6.

Required

1. What would be the difference between straight-line and MACRS depreciation expense for each of the six years?
2. Payton's president has asked why you have used one method for the books and another for calculating taxes. "Can you do this? Is it legal? Don't we take the same total depreciation either way?" he asked. Write a brief memo answering his questions and explaining the benefits of using two methods for depreciation.

LO11   **Problem 8-4A** Amortization and Cash Flow

Book Company's only asset as of January 1, 2007, was a copyright. During 2007, only three transactions occurred:

    Royalties earned from copyright use, $500,000 in cash

    Cash paid for advertising and salaries, $62,500

    Depreciation, $50,000

Required

1. What amount of income will Book report in 2007?
2. What is the amount of cash on hand at December 31, 2007?
3. Explain how the cash balance increased from zero at the beginning of the year to its end-of-year balance. Why does the increase in cash not equal the income?

LO11   **Problem 8-5A** Reconstruct Net Book Values Using Statement of Cash Flows

E-Gen Enterprises Inc. had property, plant, and equipment, net of accumulated depreciation, of $1,555,000; and intangible assets, net of accumulated amortization, of $34,000 at December 31, 2007. The company's 2007 statement of cash flows, prepared using the indirect method, included the following items.

The Cash Flows from Operating Activities section included three additions to net income: (1) depreciation expense in the amount of $205,000, (2) amortization expense in the amount of $3,000, and (3) the loss on the sale of land in the amount of $17,000. The Cash Flows from Operating Activities section also included a subtraction from net income for the gain on the sale of a trademark of $7,000. The Cash Flows from Investing Activities section included outflows for the purchase of equipment in the amount of $277,000 and $6,000 for the payment of legal fees to protect a copyright from infringement. The Cash Flows from Investing Activities section also included inflows from the sale of land in the amount of $187,000 and the sale of a trademark in the amount of $121,000.

Required

1. Determine the book values of the assets that were sold during 2007.
2. Reconstruct the amount of property, plant, and equipment, net of accumulated depreciation, that was reported on the company's balance sheet at December 31, 2006.
3. Reconstruct the amount of intangibles, net of accumulated amortization, that was reported on the company's balance sheet at December 31, 2006.

ALTERNATE MULTI-CONCEPT PROBLEMS

LO1,5, 8,9,10 **Problem 8-6A** Cost of Assets, Subsequent Book Values, and Balance Sheet Presentation

The following events took place at Tasty-Toppins Inc., a pizza shop that specializes in home delivery, during 2007:

a January 1, purchased a truck for $16,000 and added a cab and oven at a cost of $10,900. The truck is expected to last five years and be sold for $300 at the end of that time. The company uses straight-line depreciation for its trucks.
b. January 1, purchased equipment for $2,700 from a competitor who was retiring. The equipment is expected to last three years with zero salvage value. The company uses the double declining-balance method to depreciate its equipment.
c. April 1, sold a truck for $1,500. The truck had been purchased for $8,000 exactly five years earlier, had an expected salvage value of $1,000, and was depreciated over an eight-year life using the straight-line method.
d. July 1, purchased a $14,000 patent for a unique baking process to produce a new product. The patent is valid for 15 more years; however, the company expects to produce and market the product for only four years. The patent's value at the end of the four years will be zero.

Required

For each situation, explain the amount of depreciation or amortization recorded for each asset in the current year and the book value of each asset at the end of the year. For part (c), indicate the accumulated depreciation and book value at the time of sale.

LO2,5 **Problem 8-7A** Cost of Assets and the Effect on Depreciation

Early in its first year of business, Key Inc., a locksmith and security consultant, purchased new equipment. The acquisition included the following costs:

Purchase price	$168,000
Tax	16,500
Transportation	4,400
Setup*	1,100
Operating cost for first year	26,400

The equipment was adjusted to Key's specific needs.

The bookkeeper recorded the asset, Equipment, at $216,400. Key used straight-line depreciation. The equipment was expected to last 10 years with zero residual value.

Required

1. Was $216,400 the proper amount to record for the acquisition cost? If not, explain how each expenditure should be recorded.
2. How much depreciation did Key report on its income statement related to this equipment in Year 1? How much should have been reported?
3. If Key's income before the costs associated with the equipment is $55,000, what amount of income did Key report? What amount should it have reported? You may ignore income tax.
4. Explain how Key should determine the amount to capitalize when recording an asset. What is the effect on the income statement and balance sheet of Key's error?

LO7,8 **Problem 8-8A** Capital Expenditures, Depreciation, and Disposal

Wagner Company purchased a retail shopping center at a cost of $612,000 on January 1, 2006. Wagner estimated that the life of the building would be 25 years and the residual value at the end of 25 years would be $12,000.

On January 1, 2007, the company made several expenditures related to the building. The entire building was painted and floors were refinished at a cost of $115,200. A local zoning agency required Wagner to install additional fire-protection equipment, including sprinklers and built-in alarms, at a cost of $87,600. With the new protection, Wagner believed it was possible to increase the residual value of the building to $30,000.

In 2008 Wagner altered its corporate strategy dramatically. The company sold the retail shopping center on January 1, 2008, for $360,000 cash.

Required

1. Determine the amount of depreciation that should be reflected on the income statement for 2006 and 2007.
2. Explain why the cost of the fire-protection equipment was not expensed in 2007. What conditions would have allowed Wagner to expense it? If Wagner has a choice, would it prefer to expense or capitalize the improvement?
3. What amount of gain or loss did Wagner record when it sold the building? What amount of gain or loss would have been reported if the fire-protection equipment had been expensed in 2007?

LO6,10

Problem 8-9A Amortization of Intangible, Revision of Rate

During 2002, Maciel Inc.'s R&D department developed a new manufacturing process. R&D costs were $350,000. The process was patented on October 1, 2002. Legal costs to acquire the patent were $23,800. Maciel decided to expense the patent over a 20-year time period using the straight-line method. Maciel's fiscal year ends on September 30.

On October 1, 2007, Maciel's competition announced that it had obtained a patent on a new process that would make Maciel's patent completely worthless.

Required

1. How should Maciel record the $350,000 and $23,800 costs?
2. How much amortization expense should Maciel report in each year through the year ended September 30, 2007?
3. What amount of loss should Maciel report in the year ended September 30, 2008?

LO8,11

Problem 8-10A Purchase and Disposal of Operating Asset and Effects on Statement of Cash Flows

On January 1, 2007, Mansfield Inc. purchased a medium-sized delivery truck for $45,000. Using an estimated useful life of five years and a residual value of $5,000, the annual straight-line depreciation of the trucks was calculated to be $8,000. Mansfield used the truck during 2007 and 2008 but then decided to purchase a much larger delivery truck. On December 31, 2008, Mansfield sold the delivery truck at a loss of $12,000 and purchased a new, larger delivery truck for $80,000.

Required

1. How would the transactions described above be presented on Mansfield's statements of cash flows for the years ended December 31, 2007 and 2008?
2. Why would Mansfield sell a truck that had a remaining useful life of three years at a loss and purchase a new truck with a cost almost twice that of the old?

LO9,10,11

Problem 8-11A Amortization of Intangibles and Effects on Statement of Cash Flows

Quickster Inc. acquired a patent a number of years ago. The patent is being amortized on a straight-line basis over its estimated useful life. The company's comparative balance sheets as of December 31, 2007 and 2006, included the following line item:

	12/31/07	12/31/06
Patent, less accumulated amortization of $1,661,000 (2007) and $1,510,000 (2006)	$1,357,000	$1,508,000

Required

1. How much amortization expense was recorded during 2007?
2. What was the patent's acquisition cost? When was it acquired? What is its estimated useful life? How was the acquisition of the patent reported on that year's statement of cash flows?
3. Assume that Quickster uses the indirect method to prepare its statement of cash flows. How is the amortization of the patent reported annually on the statement of cash flows?
4. How would the sale of the patent on January 1, 2008, for $1,700,000 be reported on the 2008 statement of cash flows?

DECISION CASES

READING AND INTERPRETING FINANCIAL STATEMENTS

LO1,9

Decision Case 8-1 Foot Locker

Refer to **Foot Locker**'s financial statements and notes included in the 2005 annual report excerpts reprinted at the back of this book.

Required
1. What items does Foot Locker list in the Property and Equipment category?
2. What method is used to depreciate the operating assets?
3. What is the estimated useful life of the operating assets?
4. What are the accumulated depreciation and book values of property and equipment for the most recent fiscal year?
5. Were any assets purchased or sold during the most recent fiscal year?

LO11

Decision Case 8-2 Foot Locker's Statement of Cash Flows

Refer to the statement of cash flows in **Foot Locker**'s 2005 annual report reprinted in the appendix at the back of the book and answer the following questions:

Required
1. What amount of cash was used to purchase property and equipment during 2005?
2. Did the company sell any property and equipment during 2005?
3. What amount was reported for depreciation and amortization during 2005? Does the fact that depreciation and amortization are listed in the Cash Flows from Operating Activities section mean that Foot Locker created cash by reporting depreciation?

LO1, 9,12

Decision Case 8-3 Comparing Two Companies in the Same Industry: Foot Locker and Finish Line

Refer to the financial information of **Foot Locker** and **Finish Line** reprinted in the appendix at the back of this book.

Required
1. Compare the list of property, plant, and equipment represented in the Foot Locker note to the list of property and equipment on the Finish Line balance sheet. How are these lists similar? Note the differences between these lists and provide a logical reason for the differences.
2. What method is used by each company to depreciate the assets? Why do you think each company has chosen the method it uses?
3. What are the accumulated depreciation and book values of the property and equipment for each company? What does this information tell you about these competitors?
4. What is the estimated life of the Foot Locker assets? How does this compare to the estimated life of Finish Line's assets?
5. Refer to the Investing Activities portion of the cash flow statements of the two companies. Were any assets purchased or sold by either company during the year? This section of the statements does not tell if there was a gain or loss on the sale of long-term assets. Where would you find that information?
6. Do you think these two companies are investing in their future? Are their operating assets adding value to the company? Explain your answers.

MAKING FINANCIAL DECISIONS

LO1, 5,12

Decision Case 8-4 Comparing Companies

Assume that you are a financial analyst attempting to compare the financial results of two companies. The 2007 income statement of Straight Company is as follows:

Sales		$720,000
Cost of goods sold		360,000
Gross profit		$360,000
Administrative costs	$ 96,000	
Depreciation expense	120,000	216,000
Income before tax		$144,000
Tax expense (40%)		57,600
Net income		$ 86,400

Straight Company depreciates all operating assets using the straight-line method for tax purposes and for the annual report provided to stockholders. All operating assets were purchased on the same date, and all assets had an estimated life of five years when purchased. Straight Company's balance sheet reveals that on December 31, 2007, the balance of the Accumulated Depreciation account was $240,000.

You want to compare the annual report of Straight Company to that of Accelerated Company. Both companies are in the same industry, and both have exactly the same assets, sales, and expenses except that Accelerated uses the double-declining-balance method for depreciation for income tax purposes and for the annual report provided to stockholders.

Required

Develop Accelerated Company's 2007 income statement. As a financial analyst interested in investing in one of the companies, do you find Straight or Accelerated more attractive? Because depreciation is a "noncash" expense, should you be indifferent between the two companies? Explain your answer.

LO5   **Decision Case 8-5** Depreciation Alternatives

Medsupply Inc. produces supplies used in hospitals and nursing homes. Its sales, production, and costs to produce are expected to remain constant over the next five years. The corporate income tax rate is expected to increase over the next three years. The current rate, 15%, is expected to increase to 20% next year and then to 25% and continue at that rate indefinitely.

Medsupply is considering the purchase of new equipment that is expected to last for five years and to cost $150,000 with zero salvage value. As the controller, you are aware that the company can use one method of depreciation for accounting purposes and another method for tax purposes. You are trying to decide between the straight-line and the double-declining-balance methods.

Required

Recommend which method to use for accounting purposes and which to use for tax purposes. Be able to justify your answer on both a numerical and a theoretical basis. How does a noncash adjustment to income, such as depreciation, affect cash flow?

ETHICAL DECISION MAKING

LO3   **Decision Case 8-6** Valuing Assets

Denver Company recently hired Terry Davis as an accountant. He was given responsibility for all accounting functions related to fixed asset accounting. Tammy Sharp, Terry's boss, asked him to review all transactions involving the current year's acquisition of fixed assets and to take necessary action to ensure that acquired assets were recorded at proper values. Terry is satisfied that all transactions are proper except for an April 15 purchase of an office building and the land on which it is situated. The purchase price of the acquisition was $200,000. Denver Company has not separately reported the land and building, however.

Terry hired an appraiser to determine the market values of the land and the building. The appraiser reported that his best estimates of the values were $150,000 for the building and $70,000 for the land. When Terry proposed that these values be used to determine the acquisition cost of the assets, Tammy disagreed. She told Terry to request another appraisal of the property and asked him to stress to the appraiser that the land component of the acquisition could not be depreciated for tax purposes. The second appraiser estimated that the values were $180,000 for the building and $40,000 for the land. Terry and Tammy agreed that the second appraisal should be used to determine the acquisition cost of the assets.

Required

Did Terry and Tammy act ethically in this situation? Explain your answer.

LO5   **Decision Case 8-7** Depreciation Estimates

Langsom's Mfg. is planning for a new project. Usually Langsom's depreciates long-term equipment for 10 years. The equipment for this project is specialized and will have no further use at the end of the project in three years. The manager of the project wants to depreciate the equipment over the usual 10 years and plans on writing off the remaining book value at the end of Year 3 as a loss. You believe that the equipment should be depreciated over the three-year life.

Required

Which method do you think is conceptually better? What should you do if the manager insists on depreciating the equipment over 10 years?

SOLUTIONS TO KEY TERMS QUIZ

1	Acquisition cost	6	Change in estimate
5	Capitalization of interest	8	Capital expenditure
2	Land improvements	10	Revenue expenditure
7	Depreciation	11	Gain on Sale of Asset
3	Straight-line method	12	Loss on Sale of Asset
9	Book value	18	Natural resources
4	Units-of-production method	14	Intangible assets
13	Accelerated depreciation	16	Goodwill
15	Double-declining-balance method	17	Research and development costs

INTEGRATIVE PROBLEM

Correct an income statement and statement of cash flows and assess the impact of a change in inventory method; compute the effect of a bad-debt recognition.

The following income statement, statement of cash flows, and additional information are available for PEK Company:

Pek Company
Income Statement
For the Year Ended December 31, 2007

Sales revenue		$1,250,000
Cost of goods sold		636,500
Gross profit		$ 613,500
Depreciation on plant equipment	$58,400	
Depreciation on buildings	12,000	
Interest expense	33,800	
Other expenses	83,800	188,000
Income before taxes		$ 425,500
Income tax expense (30% rate)		127,650
Net income		$ 297,850

Pek Company
Statement of Cash Flows
For the Year Ended December 31, 2007

Cash flows from operating activities:	
Net income	$297,850
Adjustments to reconcile net income to net cash provided by operating activities (includes depreciation expense)	83,200
Net cash provided by operating activities	$381,050
Cash flows from financing activities:	
Dividends	(35,000)
Net increase in cash	$346,050

Additional information:

a. Beginning inventory and purchases for the one product the company sells are as follows:

	Units	Unit Cost
Beginning inventory	50,000	$2.00
Purchases:		
February 5	25,000	2.10
March 10	30,000	2.20
April 15	40,000	2.50
June 16	75,000	3.00
September 5	60,000	3.10
October 3	40,000	3.25

b. During the year, the company sold 250,000 units at $5 each.

c. PEK uses the periodic FIFO method to value its inventory and the straight-line method to depreciate all of its long-term assets.

d. During the year-end audit, it was discovered that a January 3, 2007, transaction for the lump-sum purchase of a mixing machine and a boiler was not recorded. The fair market values of the mixing machine and the boiler were $200,000 and $100,000, respectively. Each asset has an estimated useful life of 10 years with no residual value expected. The purchase of the assets was financed by issuing a $270,000 five-year promissory note directly to the seller. Interest of 8% is paid annually on December 31.

Required

1. Prepare a revised income statement and a revised statement of cash flows to take into account the omission of the entry to record the purchase of the two assets. (*Hint:* You will need to take into account any change in income taxes as a result of changes in any income statement items. Assume that income taxes are paid on December 31 of each year.)

2. Assume the same facts as above, except that the company is considering the use of an accelerated method rather than the straight-line method for the assets purchased on January 3, 2007. All other assets would continue to be depreciated on a straight-line basis. Prepare a revised income statement and a revised statement of cash flows, assuming the company decides to use the accelerated method for these two assets rather than the straight-line method resulting in depreciation of $49,091 for 2007.

Treat the answers in requirements (3) and (4) as independent of the other parts.

3. Assume PEK decides to use the LIFO method rather than the FIFO method to value its inventory and recognize cost of goods sold for 2007. Compute the effect (amount of increase or decrease) this would have on cost of goods sold, income tax expense, and net income.

4. Assume PEK failed to record an estimate of bad debts for 2007 (bad debt expense is normally included in "other expenses"). Before any adjustment, the balance in Allowance for Doubtful Accounts is $8,200. The credit manager estimates that 3% of the $800,000 of sales on account will prove to be uncollectible. Based on this information, compute the effect (amount of increase or decrease) of recognition of the bad-debt estimate on other expenses, income tax expense, and net income.

CHAPTER

9

Current Liabilities, Contingencies, and the Time Value of Money

Study Links

A Look at Previous Chapters
The previous chapters have been concerned with the asset portion of the balance sheet. We have examined the accounting for current assets such as inventory as well as long-term assets such as property, plant, and equipment.

A Look at This Chapter
In this chapter we will examine the accounting for current liabilities that are an important aspect of a company's liquidity. We will also study how contingent liabilities should be treated on the financial statement. Finally, we will introduce the concept of the time value of money. This important concept will be used extensively in future chapters.

A Look at the Upcoming Chapter
Chapter 10 presents the accounting for long-term liabilities. The time value of money concept developed in Chapter 9 will be applied to several long-term liability issues in Chapter 10.

Learning Outcomes

After studying this chapter, you should be able to:

LO1 Identify the components of the current liability category of the balance sheet.

LO2 Examine how accruals affect the current liability category.

LO3 Show that you understand how changes in current liabilities affect the statement of cash flows.

LO4 Determine when contingent liabilities should be presented on the balance sheet or disclosed in notes and how to calculate their amounts.

LO5 Explain the difference between simple and compound interest.

LO6 Calculate amounts using the future value and present value concepts.

LO7 Apply the compound interest concepts to some common accounting situations.

LO8 Show that you understand the deductions and expenses for payroll accounting (Appendix A).

LO9 Determine when compensated absences must be accrued as a liability (Appendix A).

© AP/Wide World Photos

Jacuzzi

Jacuzzi is one of the most recognizable product names in the world. The company that produces whirlpools, Jacuzzi Brands, Inc., is the leading manufacturer and distributor of branded bath and plumbing products for the residential, commercial, and institutional markets. These include whirlpool baths, spas, showers, sanitary ware, and bathtubs. The company also produces professional grade drainage, water control, commercial faucets, and other plumbing products, as well as premium vacuum cleaner systems.

Competition is intense within the markets that Jacuzzi Brands operates in. Demand for the products is primarily driven by new home starts, remodeling, and commercial construction activity. Many external factors affect their business, including weather and the impact of interest rates in the broader economy. That means the company's business is somewhat seasonal, with more sales in spring and summer months. The business is also volatile since the housing market and construction activity fluctuate a great deal.

As a result, the company must monitor its liquidity very carefully. An important aspect of liquidity management is attention to its current liabilities. During the past few years, Jacuzzi Brands has taken important steps to improve its efficiency and reduce inventory levels. But the company must also have enough current assets on hand to pay current liabilities, such as suppliers' bills, on time. The company must be able to borrow money on a short-term basis to meet its cyclical needs for resources. Maintaining a good relationship with lenders and suppliers is key. The company cannot achieve its profitability goals without effective management of its liquidity, including its current liabilities.

The accompanying balance sheet presents Jucuzzi Brands' current assets and liabilities. In this chapter we will consider the following:

- What accounts should be presented in the current liabilities section of the balance sheet? (See pp. 395–400)

- How are changes in the current liability accounts related to the amount of cash available to the company? (See pp. 399–400)
- What is the proper recording and disclosure of liabilities that are contingent on future events? (See pp. 401–404)

Answers to these questions and additional information related to current liabilities are found in this text. They can help you evaluate the current liabilities section of the balance sheet of Jacuzzi Brands.

Jacuzzi Brands Consolidated Balance Sheets
(in millions, except share data)

	At September 30,	
	2004	**2003**
Current assets:		
Cash and cash equivalents	$ 39.6	$ 31.2
Trade receivables, net of allowances of $9.0 in 2004 and 2003	247.7	229.6
Inventories	195.4	165.0
Deferred income taxes	30.3	15.5
Assets held for sale	3.6	16.8
Other current assets	23.7	30.1
Total current assets	540.3	488.2
Property, plant and equipment, net	124.9	129.7
Pension assets	150.3	148.3
Insurance for asbestos claims	171.0	160.0
Goodwill	281.7	283.1
Other intangibles, net	59.7	60.8
Other non-current assets	43.9	66.7
Total assets	$1,371.8	$1,336.8
Liabilities and stockholders' equity		
Current liabilities:		
Notes payable	$ 21.1	$ 23.5
Current maturities of long-term debt	3.9	25.2
Trade accounts payable	123.7	102.3
Income taxes payable	18.3	10.8
Liabilities associated with assets held for sale	—	8.7
Accrued expenses and other current liabilities	134.4	128.2
Total current liabilities	301.4	298.7
Long-term debt	446.8	451.4
Deferred income taxes	25.1	26.2
Asbestos claims	171.0	160.0
Other liabilities	138.4	144.8
Total liabilities	1,082.7	1,081.1
Commitments and contingencies		
Stockholders' equity:		
Common stock (par value $.01 per share, authorized 300,000,000 shares; issued 99,096,734 shares; outstanding 76,103,459 and 74,986,982 shares in 2004 and 2003, respectively)	1.0	1.0
Paid-in capital	639.7	650.1
Accumulated deficit	(5.2)	(33.7)
Unearned restricted stock	(4.6)	(0.8)
Accumulated other comprehensive loss	(8.2)	(8.7)
Treasury stock (22,993,275 and 24,109,752 shares in 2004 and 2003, respectively), at cost	(333.6)	(352.2)
Total stockholders' equity	289.1	255.7
Total liabilities and stockholders' equity	$1,371.8	$1,336.8

This chapter looks at what accounts should be presented in the current liabilities section.

Current Liabilities

A classified balance sheet presents financial statement items by category in order to provide more information to financial statement users. The balance sheet generally presents two categories of liabilities, current and long-term.

Current liabilities finance the working capital of the company. At any given time during the year, current liabilities may fluctuate substantially. It is important that the company generates sufficient cash flow to retire these debts as they come due. As long as the company's ratio of current assets to current liabilities stays fairly constant from quarter to quarter or year to year, financial statement users are not going to be too concerned.

The current liability portion of the 2004 balance sheet of **Jacuzzi Brands, Inc.**, is presented in the chapter opener. Some companies list the accounts in the current liability category in the order of payment due date. That is, the account that requires payment first is listed first, the account requiring payment next is listed second, and so forth. This allows users of the statement to assess the cash flow implications of each account. Jacuzzi Brands uses a different approach and lists Notes Payable as the first account.

Current liabilities were first introduced in Chapter 2. In general, a **current liability** is an obligation that will be satisfied within one year. Although current liabilities are not due immediately, they are still recorded at face value; that is, the time until payment is not taken into account. If it were, current liabilities would be recorded at a slight discount to reflect interest that would be earned between now and the due date. The face value amount is generally used for all current liabilities because the time period involved is short enough that it is not necessary to record or calculate an interest factor. In addition, when interest rates are low, one need not worry about the interest that could be earned in this short period of time. In Chapter 10 we will find that many long-term liabilities must be stated at their present value on the balance sheet.

The current liability classification is important because it is closely tied to the concept of *liquidity*. Management of the firm must be prepared to pay current liabilities within a very short time period. Therefore, management must have access to liquid assets, cash, or other assets that can be converted to cash in amounts sufficient to pay the current liabilities. Firms that do not have sufficient resources to pay their current liabilities are often said to have a liquidity problem.

A handy ratio to help creditors or potential creditors determine a company's liquidity is the current ratio. (See Chapter 2 for an introduction to the current ratio.) A current ratio of current assets to current liabilities of 2:1 is usually a very comfortable margin. If the firm has a large amount of inventory, it is sometimes useful to exclude inventory (prepayments are also excluded) when computing the ratio. That provides the "quick" ratio. Usually, one would want a quick ratio of at least 1.5:1 to feel secure that the company could pay its bills on time. Of course, the guidelines given for the current ratio, 2:1, and the quick ratio, 1.5:1, are only

LO1 Identify the components of the current liability category of the balance sheet.

Current liability
Accounts that will be satisfied within one year or the current operating cycle. *Alternate term: Short-term liability*

9-1 Real World Practice

Reading Jacuzzi Brands' Balance Sheet

Refer to Jacuzzi Brands' September 30, 2004, balance sheet in the chapter opener. What accounts are listed as current liabilities? How much did Trade Accounts Payable change from 2003 to 2004?

ETHICS Rent-Way

Rent-Way, the nation's second-largest company of rent-to-own stores, was started in 1981. In 1993, it began selling its stock on the stock exchange. In 2001, when the company was operating more than 1,000 stores, it was determined that company expenses had been improperly understated by an estimated $25 to $35 million. Two months later, the company raised its estimate of the understatement to $55 to $65 million, and six months after that the estimate of understatement was more than doubled to about $127 million over a two-year period. During that time, the company's new chief financial officer, William McDonnell, discovered that several weeks before each year-end, the company stopped recording accounts payable to reduce its reported expenses.

What is the company doing that is an ethical concern? Why is this an issue? Why would understating expenses also affect current liabilities? What responsibility does management have to design, detect, or prevent errors in the financial statements?

Source: Queena Sook Kim, "Rent-Way details improper bookkeeping," The Wall Street Journal, June 8, 2001.

rules of thumb. The actual current and quick ratios of companies vary widely and depend on the company, the management policies, and the type of industry. Exhibit 9-1 presents the current and quick ratios for several companies that you will see in this chapter. The ratios do vary from company to company, yet all are solid companies without liquidity problems.

Accounting for current liabilities is an area in which U.S. accounting standards are very similar to those of most other countries. Nearly all countries encourage firms to provide a breakdown of liabilities into current and long-term in order to allow users to evaluate liquidity.

ACCOUNTS PAYABLE

Accounts payable

Amounts owed for inventory, goods, or services acquired in the normal course of business.

Accounts payable represent amounts owed for the purchase of inventory, goods, or services acquired in the normal course of business. Often, Accounts Payable is the first account listed in the current liability category because it requires the payment of cash before other current liabilities. **Jacuzzi Brands** is different from most other companies because it lists Notes Payable before Accounts Payable.

Normally, a firm has an established relationship with several suppliers, and formal contractual arrangements with those suppliers are unnecessary. Accounts payable usually do not require the payment of interest, but terms may be given to encourage early payment. For example, terms may be stated as 2/10, n/30, which means that a 2% discount is available if payment occurs within the first 10 days and that if payment is not made within 10 days, the full amount must be paid within 30 days.

Timely payment of accounts payable is an important aspect of the management of cash flow. Generally, it is to the company's benefit to take advantage of discounts when they are available. After all, if your supplier is going to give you a 2% discount for paying on Day 10 instead of Day 30, that means you are earning 2% on your money over 20/360 of a year. If you took the 2% discount throughout the year, you would be getting a 36% annual return on your money, since there are 18 periods of 20 days each in a year. It is essential, therefore, that the accounts payable system be established in a manner that alerts management to take advantage of offered discounts.

NOTES PAYABLE

Notes payable

Amounts owed that are represented by a formal contract.

The first current liability on Jacuzzi Brands' 2004 balance sheet is notes payable of $21.1 million. **How is a note payable different from an account payable?** The most important difference is that an account payable is not a formal contractual arrangement, whereas a **note payable** is represented by a formal agreement or note signed by the parties to the transaction. Notes payable may arise from dealing with a supplier or from acquiring a cash loan from a bank or creditor. Those notes that are expected to be paid within one year of the balance sheet date should be classified as current liabilities.

The accounting for notes payable depends on whether the interest is paid on the note's due date or is deducted before the borrower receives the loan proceeds. With the first type of note, the terms stipulate that the borrower receives a short-term loan and agrees to repay the principal and interest at the note's due date.

EXHIBIT 9-1	Current and Quick Ratios of Selected Companies for 2004

Company	Industry	Current Ratio	Quick Ratio
Jacuzzi Brands	Leisure Equipment	1.79	1.04
Sara Lee	Food Products	1.06	0.55
Tommy Hilfiger	Clothing	3.87	2.77
Boeing	Aerospace	0.72	0.42
Nike	Footwear	2.50	1.67

For example, assume that Ballys receives a one-year loan from First National Bank on January 1. The face amount of the note of $1,000 must be repaid on December 31 along with interest at the rate of 12%. The effect on the financial statements as of January 1 is as follows:

Balance Sheet						Income Statement	
ASSETS	**=**	**LIABILITIES**		**+ STOCKHOLDERS' EQUITY**	**+**	**REVENUES – EXPENSES**	
Cash	1,000	Notes Payable	1,000				

When the loan is repaid on December 31, Ballys must pay $1,120 ($1,000 of principal and $120 of interest) and must eliminate the Notes Payable account. The effect of the repayment is as follows:

Balance Sheet						Income Statement	
ASSETS	**=**	**LIABILITIES**		**+ STOCKHOLDERS' EQUITY**	**+**	**REVENUES – EXPENSES**	
Cash	(1,120)	Notes Payable	(1,000)			Interest Expense	(120)

Banks also use another form of note, one in which the interest is deducted in advance. Suppose that on January 1, 2007, First National Bank granted to Ballys a $1,000 loan, due on December 31, 2007, but deducted the interest in advance and gave Ballys the remaining amount of $880 ($1,000 face amount of the note less interest of $120). This is sometimes referred to as *discounting a note* because a Discount on Notes Payable account is established when the loan is recorded. The effect is as follows:

Balance Sheet						Income Statement	
ASSETS	**=**	**LIABILITIES**		**+ STOCKHOLDERS' EQUITY**	**+**	**REVENUES – EXPENSES**	
Cash	880	Notes Payable	1,000				
		Discount on Notes Payable	(120)				

The **Discount on Notes Payable** account should be treated as a reduction of Notes Payable. If a balance sheet was developed immediately after the January 1 loan, the note would appear in the current liability category as follows:

Notes Payable	$1,000
Less: Discount on Notes Payable	120
Net Liability	$ 880

The original balance in the Discount on Notes Payable account represents interest that must be transferred to interest expense over the life of the note. Before Ballys presents its year-end financial statements, it must make an adjustment to transfer the discount to interest expense. The effect of the adjustment on December 31 is as follows:

Discount on notes payable
A contra liability that represents interest deducted from a loan in advance.

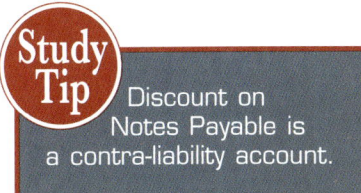
Study Tip Discount on Notes Payable is a contra-liability account.

Balance Sheet						Income Statement	
ASSETS	**=**	**LIABILITIES**		**+ STOCKHOLDERS' EQUITY**	**+**	**REVENUES – EXPENSES**	
		Discount on Notes Payable	120			Interest Expense	(120)

Thus, the balance of the Discount on Notes Payable account is zero, and $120 has been transferred to interest expense. When the note is repaid on December 31, 2007, Ballys must repay the full amount of the note.

It is important to compare the two types of notes payable. In the previous two examples, the stated interest rate on each note was 12%. The dollar amount of interest incurred in each case was $120. However, the interest *rate* on a discounted note, the second example, is always higher than it appears. Ballys received the use of only $880, yet it was required to repay $1,000. Therefore, the interest rate incurred on the note was actually $120/$880, or approximately 13.6%.

CURRENT MATURITIES OF LONG-TERM DEBT

Current maturities of long-term debt
The portion of a long-term liability that will be paid within one year. *Alternate terms: Long-term debt, current portion*

Another account that appears in the current liability category of Jacuzzi Brands' balance sheet is **Current Maturities of Long-Term Debt**. On other companies' balance sheets, this item may appear as Long-Term Debt, Current Portion. This account should appear when a firm has a liability and must make periodic payments. For example, assume that on January 1, 2007, your firm obtained a $10,000 loan from the bank. The terms of the loan require you to make payments in the amount of $1,000 per year for 10 years, payable each January 1, beginning January 1, 2008.

The December 31, 2007, balance sheet should indicate that the liability for the note payable is classified into two portions: a $1,000 current liability that must be repaid within one year and a $9,000 long-term liability.

On January 1, 2008, the company must pay $1,000 and should eliminate the current liability of $1,000.

On December 31, 2008, the company should again record the current portion of the liability. Therefore, the 2008 year-end balance sheet should indicate that the liability is classified into two portions: a $1,000 current liability and an $8,000 long-term liability. The process should be repeated each year until the bank loan has been fully paid. When an investor or creditor reads a balance sheet, he or she wants to distinguish between debt that is long-term and debt that is short-term. Therefore, it is important to segregate that portion of the debt that becomes due within one year.

The balance sheet account labeled Current Maturities of Long-Term Debt should include only the amount of principal to be paid. The amount of interest that has been incurred but is unpaid should be listed separately in an account such as Interest Payable.

TAXES PAYABLE

LO2 Examine how accruals affect the current liability category.

Corporations pay a variety of taxes, including federal and state income taxes, property taxes, and other taxes. Usually, the largest dollar amount is incurred for state and federal income taxes. Taxes are an expense of the business and should be accrued in the same manner as any other business expense. A company that ends its accounting year on December 31 is not required to calculate the amount of tax owed to the government until the following March 15 or April 15, depending on the type of business. Therefore, year-end financial statements should reflect the amount of taxes incurred as an expense on the income statement and the amount of taxes that will be paid on March 15 or April 15 as a current liability on the balance sheet.

The calculation of the amount of tax a business owes is very complex. For now, the important point is that taxes are an expense when incurred (not when they are paid) and must be recorded as a liability as incurred.

Some analysts prefer to measure a company's profits before it pays taxes for several reasons. For one thing, tax rates change from year to year. A small change in the tax rate may drastically change a firm's profitability. Also, investors should realize that taxes occur in every year but that tax changes are not a recurring element of a business. Additionally, taxes are somewhat beyond the control of a company's management. For these reasons, **it is important to consider a firm's operations *before* taxes to better evaluate management's ability to control operations**.

OTHER ACCRUED LIABILITIES

Jacuzzi Brands' 2004 balance sheet listed an amount of $134.4 million as current liability under the category of Accrued Expenses. What items might be included in this category?

In previous chapters, especially Chapter 4, we covered many examples of accrued liabilities. **Accrued liabilities** include any amount that has been incurred due to the passage of time but has not been paid as of the balance sheet date. A common example is salary or wages payable. Suppose that your firm has a payroll of $1,000 per day, Monday through Friday, and that employees are paid at the close of work each Friday. Also suppose that December 31 is the end of your accounting year and falls on a Tuesday. Your firm should reflect the $2,000 of salary incurred but unpaid as an expense on the income statement and as a current liability on the balance sheet.

The amount of the salary payable would be classified as a current liability and could appear in a category such as Other Accrued Liabilities.

Interest is another item that often must be accrued at year-end. Assume that you received a one-year loan of $10,000 on December 1. The loan carries a 12% interest rate.

The income statement developed for the year ending December 31 should reflect one month's interest ($100) as expense even though it may not actually be due. The interest has been incurred and is therefore an expense. The balance sheet should reflect $100 as interest payable. An Interest Payable account representing one month's interest ($100) should be classified as a current liability, assuming that it is to be paid within one year of the December 31 date.

Accrued liability
A liability that has been incurred but not yet paid.

READING THE STATEMENT OF CASH FLOWS FOR CHANGES IN CURRENT LIABILITIES

It is important to understand the impact that current liabilities have on a company's cash flows. Exhibit 9-2 illustrates the placement of current liabilities on the statement of cash flows (using the indirect method) and their effect. Most current liabilities are directly related to a firm's ongoing operations. Therefore, the change in the balance of each current liability account should be reflected in the Operating Activities category of the statement of cash flows. A decrease in a current liability account indicates that cash has been used to pay the liability and should appear as a deduction on the cash flow statement. An increase in a current liability account indicates a recognized expense that has not yet been paid. Look for it as an increase in the Operating Activities category of the cash flow statement.

A partial cash flow statement of **Jacuzzi Brands** is presented in Exhibit 9-3. Note that one of the items in the 2004 Operating Activities category is listed as ❶ Other Liabilities of $7.5 million. This means that the balance of those current liabilities increased by $7.5 million, resulting in an increase of cash.

Almost all current liabilities appear in the Operating Activities category of the statement of cash flows, but there are exceptions. If a current liability is not directly

LO3 Show that you understand how changes in current liabilities affect the statement of cash flows.

| EXHIBIT 9-2 | Current Liabilities on the Statement of Cash Flows |

Item	Cash Flow Statement
	Operating Activities
	Net income xxx
Increase in current liability	+
Decrease in current liability	−
	Investing Activities
	Financing Activities
Increase in notes payable	+
Decrease in notes payable	−

EXHIBIT 9-3	Jacuzzi Brands' 2004 Partial Consolidated Statement of Cash Flows

Jacuzzi Brands, Inc
CONSOLIDATED STATEMENTS OF CASH FLOWS

(in millions)	For the Fiscal Years Ended September 30,		
	2004	2003	2002
OPERATING ACTIVITIES:			
Earnings from continuing operations	$ 29.1	$ 10.1	$ 31.9
Adjustments to reconcile earnings from continuing operations to net cash provided by operating activities of continuing operations:			
Depreciation and amortization	26.4	24.6	26.1
Amortization of debt issuance costs and other financing costs	3.7	8.9	6.9
Charges for debt restructuring and refinancing costs	—	21.5	9.2
Provision for (benefit from) deferred income taxes	2.2	(8.7)	(34.8)
Provision for doubtful accounts	5.4	5.8	3.3
Gain on sale of real estate	(0.8)	(3.5)	(0.8)
Stock-based compensation expense, net	1.4	1.4	0.7
Loss on sale of property, plant, and equipment	0.7	0.2	1.7
Impairment, restructuring, and non-cash charges	8.0	12.5	0.8
Changes in operating assets and liabilities, excluding the effects of acquisition and dispositions:			
Trade receivables	(18.2)	(15.4)	(15.1)
Inventories	(27.5)	0.6	1.7
Other current assets	0.8	(2.4)	3.9
Other assets	(4.9)	(4.3)	(3.1)
Trade accounts payable	17.6	3.2	2.0
Income taxes payable	2.8	46.7	(1.0)
Accrued expenses and other current liabilities	7.2	(12.1)	(2.0)
① Other liabilities	(7.5)	(8.1)	8.7
Other, net	—	(1.1)	(1.1)
Net cash provided by operating activities of continuing operations	46.4	79.9	39.0

related to operating activities, it should not appear in that category. For example, if Jacuzzi Brands uses some notes payable as a means of financing, distinct from operating activities, those borrowings and repayments are reflected in the Financing Activities rather than the Operating Activities category.

2 minute review

1. What is the definition of current liabilities? Give some examples of items that are typically in the current liability category.

2. How is the current ratio calculated? What is it intended to measure?

3. In which category of the cash flow statement do most current liability items appear?

Answers

1. Current liabilities are defined as items that will be paid within one year of the balance sheet date. Examples of current liabilities include accounts payable, notes payable if due within one year, taxes payable, and other accrued liabilities. Also, if a portion of a long-term debt will be paid within one year, that portion should be reported as a current liability.

2. *The current ratio is calculated as total current assets divide by total current liabilities. It is a measure of the liquidity of the company, or the ability of the company to pay its short-term obligations.*

3. *Most current liabilities are reported in the Operating Activities category of the cash flow statement. You should note that it is the change in the balance of the current liability that is reported.*

Contingent Liabilities

We have seen that accountants must exercise a great deal of expertise and judgment in deciding what to record and in determining the amount to record. This is certainly true regarding contingent liabilities. A **contingent liability** is an obligation that involves an existing condition for which the outcome is not known with certainty and depends on some event that will occur in the future. The actual amount of the liability must be estimated because we cannot clearly predict the future. The important accounting issues are whether contingent liabilities should be recorded and, if so, in what amounts.

This is a judgment call that is usually resolved through discussions among the company's management and its outside auditors. Management usually would rather not disclose contingent liabilities until they come due. The reason is that investors' and creditors' judgment of management is based on the company's earnings, and the recording of a contingent liability must be accompanied by a charge to (reduction in) earnings. Auditors, on the other hand, want management to disclose as much as possible because the auditors are essentially representing the interests of investors and creditors who want to have as much information as possible.

CONTINGENT LIABILITIES THAT ARE RECORDED

A contingent liability should be accrued and presented on the balance sheet if it is probable and if the amount can be reasonably estimated. But when is an event *probable*, and what does *reasonably estimated* mean? The terms must be defined based on the facts of each situation. A financial statement user would want the company to err on the side of full disclosure. On the other hand, the company should not be required to disclose every remote possibility.

Product Warranties and Guarantees: Common Contingent Liabilities that Are Recorded A common contingent liability that must be presented as a liability by firms involves product warranties or guarantees. Many firms sell products for which they provide the customer a warranty against defects that may develop in the products. If a product becomes defective within the warranty period, the selling firm ensures that it will repair or replace the item. This is an example of a contingent liability because the expense of fixing a product depends on some of the products becoming defective—an uncertain, although likely, event.

At the end of each period, the selling firm must estimate how many of the products sold in the current year will become defective in the future and the cost of repair or replacement. This type of contingent liability is often referred to as an **estimated liability** to emphasize that the costs are not known at year-end and must be estimated.

As an example, assume that Quickkey Computer sells a computer product for $5,000. When the customer buys the product, Quickkey provides a one-year warranty in case it must be repaired. Assume that in 2007 Quickkey sold 100 computers for a total sales revenue of $500,000. At the end of 2007, Quickkey must record an estimate of the warranty costs that will occur on 2007 sales. Using an analysis of past warranty records, Quickkey estimates that repairs will average 2% of total sales. The 2007 balance sheet should indicate a liability of $10,000 in the account Estimated Liability for Warranty. This liability is classified as a current liability because Quickkey provides a one-year warranty. Quickkey's income statement should reflect a warranty expense of $10,000 to accrue the estimated amount of expense incurred.

LO4 Determine when contingent liabilities should be presented on the balance sheet or disclosed in notes and how to calculate their amounts.

Contingent liability
An existing condition for which the outcome is not known but depends on some future event. *Alternate term: Contingent loss*

> **Study Tip** Contingent liabilities are recorded only if they are probable and if the amount can be reasonably estimated.

Estimated liability
A contingent liability that is accrued and reflected on the balance sheet.

The amount of warranty costs that a company presents as an expense is of interest to investors and potential creditors. If the expense as a percentage of sales begins to rise, one might conclude that the product is becoming less reliable.

Warranties are an excellent example of the matching principle. In our Quickkey example, the warranty costs related to 2007 sales were estimated and recorded in 2007. This was done to match the 2007 sales with the expenses related to those sales. If actual repairs of the computers occurred in 2008, they do not result in an expense. The repair costs incurred in 2008 should be treated as a reduction in the liability that had previously been estimated.

Because items such as warranties involve estimation, you may wonder what happens if the amount estimated is not accurate. The company must analyze past warranty records carefully and incorporate any changes in customer buying habits, usage, technological changes, and other changes. Still, even with careful analysis, the actual amount of the expense is not likely to equal the estimated amount. Generally, firms do not change the amount of the expense recorded in past periods for such differences. They may adjust the amount recorded in future periods, however.

Premiums or Coupons: Other Contingent Liabilities that Are Recorded

Warranties provide an example of a contingent liability that must be estimated and recorded. Another example is premium or coupon offers that accompany many products. Cereal boxes are an everyday example of premium offers. The boxes often allow customers to purchase a toy or game at a reduced price if the purchase is accompanied by cereal box tops or proof of purchase. The offer given to cereal customers represents a contingent liability. At the end of each year, the cereal company must estimate the number of premium offers that will be redeemed and the cost involved and must report a contingent liability for that amount.

Some Lawsuits and Legal Claims Are Contingent Liabilities that Must Be Recorded

Legal claims that have been filed against a firm are also examples of contingent liabilities. In today's business environment, lawsuits and legal claims are a fact of life. They represent a contingent liability because an event has occurred but the outcome of that event, the resolution of the lawsuit, is not known. The defendant in the lawsuit must make a judgment about the lawsuit's outcome in order to decide whether the item should be recorded on the balance sheet or should be disclosed in the notes. If it is probable the legal claim's outcome will be unfavorable, then an amount should be recorded as a contingent liability on the balance sheet. Exhibit 9-4 provides portions of a note disclosure that accompanied the 2004 financial statements of **Jacuzzi Brands, Inc.** The note concerned litigation over environmental damage that is alleged to have occurred as a result of the company's activities. Environmental remediation claims are very common for companies in many industries. In this case, Jacuzzi Brands believed that an unfavorable outcome was probable and, as a result, recorded a contingent liability of $2.1 million current liability and 2.0 million long-term liability as an estimate of the amount that will be owed at the eventual outcome of this claim.

As you might imagine, firms are not usually eager to record contingent lawsuits as liabilities because the amount of loss is often difficult to estimate. Also, some may view the accountant's decision as an admission of guilt if a lawsuit is recorded as a liability before the courts have finalized a decision. Accountants must often consult with lawyers or other legal experts to determine the probability of the loss of a lawsuit. In cases involving contingencies, it is especially important that the accountant make an independent judgment based on the facts and not be swayed by the desires of other parties.

CONTINGENT LIABILITIES THAT ARE DISCLOSED

Any contingent liability that both is probable and can be reasonably estimated must be reported as a liability. We now must consider contingent liabilities that do not meet the probable criterion or cannot be reasonably estimated. In either

EXHIBIT 9-4　Note Disclosure for Contingent Liability from Jacuzzi Brands' 2004 Financial Statements

Environmental Regulations

We are subject to numerous foreign, federal, state and local laws and regulations concerning such matters as zoning, health and safety and protection of the environment. . . .

　　We are investigating and remediating contamination at a number of present and former operating sites under the federal Comprehensive Environmental Response, compensation and Liability Act of 1980 ("CERCLA" or "Superfund"), the federal Resource Conservation and Recovery Act or comparable state statutes or agreements with third parties. These proceedings are in various stages ranging from initial investigations to active settlement negotiations to the cleanup of sites. We have been named as a potentially responsible party at a number of Superfund sites under CERCLA or comparable state statutes. Under these statutes, responsibility for the entire cost of cleanup of a contaminated site can be imposed upon any current or former site owners or operators, or upon any party who sent waste to the site, regardless of the lawfulness of the original activities of the original activities that led to the contamination. . . .

　　As of September 30, 2004, we had accrued approximately $2.1 million ($0.1 million accrued as current liabilities and $2.0 million as non-current liabilities) for environmental liabilities recorded on an undiscounted basis. We accrue an amount for each case when the likelihood of an unfavorable outcome is probable and the amount of loss associated with such an unfavorable outcome is reasonably estimable. We believe that the range of liability for these matters could reach $15.0 million if it included cases where the likelihood of an unfavorable outcome is only reasonably possible.

case, **a contingent liability must be disclosed in the financial statement notes but not reported on the balance sheet if the contingent liability is at least reasonably possible**.

Although information in the notes to the financial statements contains very important data on which investors base decisions, some accountants believe that note disclosure does not have the same impact as does recording a contingent liability on the balance sheet. For one thing, note disclosure does not affect the important financial ratios that investors use to make decisions.

In the previous section, we presented a legal claim involving Jacuzzi Brands as an example of a contingent liability that was probable and therefore was recorded on the balance sheet as a liability. Most lawsuits, however, are not recorded as liabilities either because the risk of loss is not considered probable or because the amount of the loss cannot be reasonably estimated. If a company does not record a lawsuit as a liability, it must still consider whether the lawsuit should be disclosed in the notes to the financial statements. If the risk of loss is at least *reasonably possible,* then the company should provide note disclosure. This is the course of action taken for most contingent liabilities involving lawsuits.

Exhibit 9-5 contains additional excerpts from the notes to the 2004 financial statements of **Jacuzzi Brands**. The note indicates that Jacuzzi Brands is subject to a variety of lawsuits and legal actions, which arise from the normal course of business.

The note also indicates that the company does not believe the lawsuits will have a "material adverse effect" on the company's condition. You should note that the excerpt in Exhibit 9-5 is an example of contingent liabilities that have been disclosed in the notes to the financial statements *but have not been recorded as liabilities on the balance sheet.* Readers of the financial statements, and analysts, must carefully read the notes to determine the impact of such contingent liabilities.

EXHIBIT 9-5　Note Disclosure for Contingencies from Jacuzzi Brands' 2004 Annual Report

Certain of our subsidiaries are defendants or plaintiffs in lawsuits that have arisen in the normal course of business. While certain of these matters involve substantial amounts, it is management's opinion, based on the advice of counsel, that the ultimate resolution of such litigation and environmental matters will not have a material adverse effect on the Company's financial condition, results of operations or cash flows.

EXHIBIT 9-6	Note Disclosure for Contingent Asset from Jacuzzi Brands' Financial Statements

Litigation resulting from a dispute with the former owners of the Sundance Spas business has resulted in a judgment of approximately $5.1 million in our favor. The gain of $3.9 million resulting from the judgment is not included in the results of our operations in fiscal 2004 as it is still subject to appeal.

The amount and the timing of the cash outlays associated with contingent liabilities are especially difficult to determine. Lawsuits, for example, may extend several years into the future, and the dollar amount of possible loss may be subject to great uncertainty.

CONTINGENT LIABILITIES VERSUS CONTINGENT ASSETS

Contingent asset
An existing condition for which the outcome is not known but by which the company stands to gain. *Alternate term: Contingent gain*

Contingent liabilities that are probable and can be reasonably estimated must be presented on the balance sheet before the outcome of the future events is known. This accounting rule applies only to contingent losses or liabilities. It does not apply to contingencies by which the firm may *gain*. Generally, contingent gains or **contingent assets** are not reported until the gain actually occurs. **That is, contingent liabilities may be accrued, but contingent assets are not accrued.** Exhibit 9-6 contains another portion of the notes from the 2004 financial statements of **Jacuzzi Brands, Inc.** This is an example of a contingent asset because the company may receive some amounts at a future time. The financial statements reveal that Jacuzzi Brands has won a legal settlement but has not recorded any of the potential recoveries from the lawsuit even though it appears quite likely that some amount will be received. This may seem inconsistent—it is. Contingent liabilities may be recorded in some cases but contingent assets are not. Remember that accounting is a discipline based on a conservative set of principles. It is prudent and conservative to delay the recording of a gain until an asset is actually received but to record contingent liabilities in advance.

Of course, even though the contingent assets are not reported, the information may still be important to investors. Wall Street analysts make their living trying to place a value on contingent assets that they believe will result in future benefits. By buying stock of a company that has unrecorded assets, or advising their clients to do so, investment analysts hope to make money when those assets become a reality.

2 *minute review*

1. Under what circumstances should contingent liabilities be reported in the financial statements?

2. Under what circumstances should contingent liabilities be disclosed in the notes and not recorded in the financial statements?

3. Are contingent assets treated the same as contingent liabilities?

Answers

1. Contingent liabilities should be reported in the financial statements if they are probable and the amount of the liability can be reasonably estimated.

2. Contingent liabilities should be disclosed in the notes if they are reasonably possible.

3. Contingent assets are generally not recorded until the amount is received. They are not treated in the same manner as contingent liabilities. This indicates the conservative nature of accounting.

Time Value of Money Concepts

In this section we will study the impact that interest has on decision making because of the time value of money. The **time value of money** concept means that people prefer a payment at the present time rather than in the future because of the interest factor. If an amount is received at the present time, it can be invested, and the resulting accumulation will be larger than if the same amount is received in the future. Thus, there is a *time value* to cash receipts and payments. This time value concept is important to every student for two reasons: it affects your personal financial decisions, and it affects accounting valuation decisions.

Exhibit 9-7 indicates some of the personal and accounting decisions affected by the time value of money concept. In your personal life, you make decisions based on the time value of money concept nearly every day. When you invest money, you are interested in how much will be accumulated, and you must determine the *future value* based on the amount of interest that will be compounded. When you borrow money, you must determine the amount of the loan payments. You may not always realize it, but the amount of the loan payment is based on the *present value* of the loan, another time value of money concept.

Time value of money is also important because of its implications for accounting valuations. We will discover in Chapter 10 that the issue price of a bond is based on the present value of the cash flows that the bond will produce. The valuation of the bond and the recording of the bond on the balance sheet are based on this concept. Further, the amount that is considered interest expense on the financial statements is also based on time value of money concepts. The bottom portion of Exhibit 9-7 indicates that the valuations of many other accounts, including Notes Receivable and Leases, are based on compound interest calculations.

The time value of money concept is used in virtually every advanced business course. Investment courses, marketing courses, and many other business courses will

Time value of money
An immediate amount should be preferred over an amount in the future.

EXHIBIT 9-7 | **Importance of the Time Value of Money**

Personal Financial Decision	Action
■ How much money will accumulate if you invest in a CD or money market account? →	Calculate the future value based on compound interest.
■ If you take out an auto loan, what will be the monthly loan payments? →	Calculate the payments based on the present value of the loan.
■ If you invest in the bond market, what should you pay for a bond? →	Calculate the present value of the bond based on compound interest.
■ If you win the lottery, should you take an immediate payment or payment over time? →	Calculate the present value of the alternatives based on compound interest.

Valuation Decisions on the Financial Statements	Valuation
■ Long-term assets ⟶	Historical cost, but not higher than present value of the cash flows
■ Notes receivable ⟶	Present value of the cash flows
■ Loan payments ⟶	Based on the present value of the loan
■ Bond issue price ⟶	Present value of the cash flows
■ Leases ⟶	Present value of the cash flows

use the time value of money concept. **In fact, it is probably the most important decision-making tool to master in preparation for the business world.** This section of the text begins with an explanation of how simple interest and compound interest differ and then proceeds to the concepts of present values and future values.

SIMPLE INTEREST

LO5 Explain the difference between simple and compound interest.

Simple interest is interest earned on the principal amount. If the amount of principal is unchanged from year to year, the interest per year will remain the same. Interest can be calculated by the following formula:

$$I = P \times R \times T$$

where

Simple interest
Interest is calculated on the principal amount only.

I = Dollar amount of interest per year
P = Principal
R = Interest rate as a percentage
T = Time in years

For example, assume that our firm has signed a two-year note payable for $3,000. Interest and principal are to be paid at the due date with simple interest at the rate of 10% per year. The amount of interest on the note would be $600, calculated as $3,000 × 0.10 × 2. We would be required to pay $3,600 on the due date: $3,000 principal and $600 interest.

COMPOUND INTEREST

Compound interest
Interest is calculated on the principal plus previous amounts of interest.
Alternate term: Interest on interest

Compound interest means that interest is calculated on the principal plus previous amounts of accumulated interest. Thus, interest is compounded, or there is interest on interest. For example, assume a $3,000 note payable for which interest and principal are due in two years with interest compounded annually at 10% per year. Interest would be calculated as follows:

Year	Principal Amount at Beginning of Year	Interest at 10%	Accumulated at Year-End
1	$3,000	$300	$3,300
2	3,300	330	3,630

We would be required to pay $3,630 at the end of two years, $3,000 principal and $630 interest. A comparison of the note payable with 10% simple interest in the first example with the note payable with 10% compound interest in the second example clearly indicates that the amount accumulated with compound interest is always a higher amount because of the interest-on-interest feature.

INTEREST COMPOUNDING

LO6 Calculate amounts using the future value and present value concepts.

For most accounting problems, we will assume that compound interest is compounded annually. In actual business practice, compounding usually occurs over much shorter intervals. This can be confusing because the interest rate is often stated as an annual rate even though it is compounded over a shorter period. If compounding is not done annually, you must adjust the interest rate by dividing the annual rate by the number of compounding periods per year.

For example, assume that the note payable from the previous example carried a 10% interest rate compounded semiannually for two years. The 10% annual rate should be converted to 5% per period for four semiannual periods. The amount of interest would be compounded, as in the previous example, but for four periods instead of two. The compounding process is shown at the top of the following page. The example illustrates that compounding more frequently results in a larger amount accumulated. In fact, many banks and financial institutions now compound interest on savings accounts on a daily basis.

Period	Principal Amount at Beginning of Year	Interest at 5% per Period	Accumulated at End of Period
1	$3,000	$150	$3,150
2	3,150	158	3,308
3	3,308	165	3,473
4	3,473	174	3,647

In the remainder of this section, we will assume that compound interest is applicable. Four compound interest calculations must be understood:

1. **Future value of a single amount**
2. **Present value of a single amount**
3. **Future value of an annuity**
4. **Present value of an annuity**

FUTURE VALUE OF A SINGLE AMOUNT

We are often interested in the amount of interest plus principal that will be accumulated at a future time. This is called a *future amount* or *future value*. The future amount is always larger than the principal amount (payment) because of the interest that accumulates. The formula to calculate the **future value of a single amount** is as follows:

$$FV = p(1 + i)^n$$

where

FV = Future value to be calculated
p = Present value or principal amount
i = Interest rate
n = Number of periods of compounding

Future value of a single amount
Amount accumulated at a future time from a single payment or investment.

Example 1: Your three-year-old son, Robert, just inherited $50,000 in cash and securities from his grandfather. If the funds were left in the bank and in the stock market and received an annual return of 10%, how much would be there in 15 years when Robert starts college?

Solution:

$FV = \$50,000(1 + 0.10)^{15}$
$= \$50,000(4.177)$
$= \$208,850$

In some cases, we will use time diagrams to illustrate the relationships. A time diagram to illustrate a future value would be of the following form:

Payment ——————— Interest ——————— FV

Known Amount   Future Value = ?
of Payment
(Present Value)

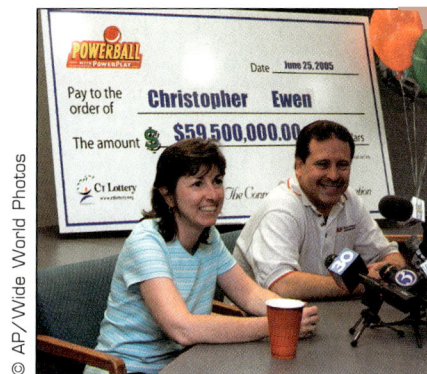

Assume you won the lottery and this check is yours. Which payment option would you take—a lump sum or an amount every year for 10 years? Only by understanding time value of money concepts could you make an intelligent choice.

Example 2: Consider a $2,000 note payable that carries interest at the rate of 10% compounded annually. The note is due in two years, and the principal and interest must be paid at that time. The amount that must be paid in two years is the future value. The future value can be calculated in the manner we have used in the previous examples:

Year	Principal Amount at Beginning of Year	Interest at 10%	Accumulated at Year-End
1	$2,000	$200	$2,200
2	2,200	220	2,420

The future value can also be calculated by using the following formula:

$$FV = \$2,000(1 + 0.10)^2$$
$$= \$2,000(1.21)$$
$$= \$2,420$$

Rather than using a formula, there are other methods to calculate future value. Tables can be constructed to assist in the calculations. Table 9-1, on page 415, indicates the future value of $1 at various interest rates and for various time periods. To find the future value of a two-year note at 10% compounded annually, you read across the line for two periods and down the 10% column and see an interest rate factor of 1.210. Because the table has been constructed for future values of $1, we would determine the future value of $2,000 as follows:

$$FV = \$2,000 \times 1.210$$
$$= \$2,420$$

Many financial calculators are also available to perform future value calculations. We will illustrate the calculations with a widely used calculator, **Texas Instruments'** Advanced Business Analyst®. All financial calculators perform the calculations in the same manner, but the methods to enter the data, the keystrokes, might vary somewhat from one calculator to another.[1]

To calculate the future value in our example, you should perform the following steps:

ENTER	DISPLAY
2 N	N = 2
10 I/Y	I/Y = 10
0 PMT	PMT = 0
2000 PV	PV = 2,000
CPT FV	FV = 2,420

A third method used to perform the calculations is to use the built-in functions of a computerized spreadsheet. In Appendix B, we will illustrate how to use a common spreadsheet, Microsoft® Excel, to perform the same calculations. *Note that the numbers produced by each method may differ by a few dollars because of rounding differences. You should ignore those small differences and concentrate on the methods used to perform the interest rate calculations.*

Remember that compounding does not always occur annually. How does this affect the calculation of future value amounts?

Example 3: Suppose we want to find the future value of a $2,000 note payable due in two years. The note payable requires interest to be compounded quarterly at the rate of 12% per year. To calculate the future value, we must adjust the interest rate to a quarterly basis by dividing the 12% rate by the number of compounding periods per year, which in the case of quarterly compounding is four:

12%/4 quarters = 3% per quarter

Also, the number of compounding periods is eight—four per year times two years.

---

[1] Some preliminary steps are necessary before using the calculator for the calculations we will illustrate. First, your calculator likely is set to accommodate annual payments, rather than monthly payments. See your calculator instruction manual to set it to annual payments if necessary. Second, when calculating the present value or future value of an annuity of payments, assume that the payments constitute an ordinary annuity, also called an annuity in arrears. That is, assume the payments occur at the end of each period. Your calculator should be set to end-of-period payments. Again, refer to your instruction manual to make sure it is set correctly.

The future value of the note can be found in two ways. First, we can insert the proper values into the future value formula:

$$FV = \$2,000(1 + 0.03)^8$$
$$= \$2,000(1.267)$$
$$= \$2,534$$

We can arrive at the same future value amount with the use of Table 9-1. Refer to the interest factor in the table indicated for 8 periods and 3%. The future value would be calculated as follows:

$$FV = \$2,000\text{(interest factor)}$$
$$= \$2,000(1.267)$$
$$= \$2,534$$

The steps using the calculator are as follows:

ENTER	DISPLAY
8 N	N = 8
3 I/Y	I/Y = 3
0 PMT	PMT = 0
2000 PV	PV = 2,000
CPT FV	FV = 2,534

PRESENT VALUE OF A SINGLE AMOUNT

In many situations, we do not want to calculate how much will be accumulated at a future time. Rather, we want to determine the present amount that is equivalent to an amount at a future time. This is the present value concept. The **present value of a single amount** represents the value today of a single amount to be received or paid at a future time. This can be portrayed in a time diagram as follows:

Present value of a single amount
Amount at a present time that is equivalent to a payment or investment at a future time.

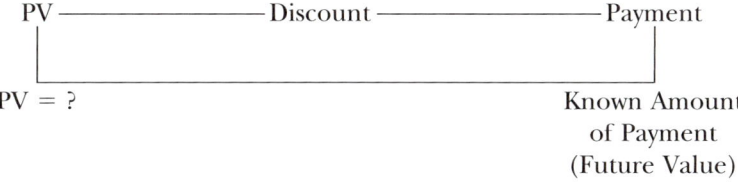

The time diagram portrays discount, rather than interest, because we often speak of "discounting" the future payment back to the present time.

Example 4: Suppose you know that you will receive $2,000 in two years. You also know that if you had the money now, it could be invested at 10% compounded annually. What is the present value of the $2,000? Another way to ask the same question is, What amount must be invested today at 10% compounded annually in order to have $2,000 accumulated in two years?

The formula used to calculate present value is as follows:

$$PV = \text{Future value} \times (1 + i)^{-n}$$

where

$$PV = \text{Present value amount in dollars}$$
$$\text{Future value} = \text{Amount to be received in the future}$$
$$i = \text{Interest rate or discount rate}$$
$$n = \text{Number of periods}$$

We can use the present value formula to solve for the present value of the $2,000 note as follows:

$$PV = \$2,000 \times (1 + 0.10)^{-2}$$
$$= \$2,000 \times (0.826)$$
$$= \$1,652$$

Tables have also been developed to determine the present value of $1 at various interest rates and number of periods. Table 9-2, on page 416, presents the present value or discount factors for an amount of $1 to be received at a future time. To use the table for our two-year note example, you must read across the line for two periods and down the 10% column to the discount factor of 0.826. The present value of $2,000 would be calculated as follows:

$$PV = \$2,000 \, (\text{discount factor})$$
$$= \$2,000 \, (0.826)$$
$$= \$1,652$$

The steps using the calculator are as follows:

ENTER	DISPLAY
2 N	N = 2
10 I/Y	I/Y = 10
0 PMT	PMT = 0
2000 FV	FV = 2,000
CPT PV	PV = 1,653

Two other points are important. First, the example illustrates that the present value amount is always less than the future payment. This happens because of the discount factor. In other words, if we had a smaller amount at the present (the present value), we could invest it and earn interest that would accumulate to an amount equal to the larger amount (the future payment). Second, study of the present value and future value formulas indicates that each is the reciprocal of the other. When we want to calculate a present value amount, we normally use Table 9-2 and multiply a discount factor times the payment. However, we could also use Table 9-1 and divide by the interest factor. Thus, the present value of the $2,000 to be received in the future could also be calculated as follows:

$$PV = \$2,000/1.210$$
$$= \$1,652$$

Example 5: A recent magazine article projects that it will cost $120,000 to attend a four-year college 10 years from now. If that is true, how much money would you have to put into an account today to fund that education, assuming a 5% rate of return?

$$PV = \$120,000 \, (1 + 0.05)^{-10}$$
$$= \$120,000 \, (0.614) \ (\text{Table } 9\text{–}4, \, n = 10, \, i = 5\%)$$
$$= \$73,680$$

FUTURE VALUE OF AN ANNUITY

Annuity
A series of payments of equal amounts.

The present value and future value amounts are useful when a single amount is involved. Many accounting situations involve an annuity, however. **Annuity** means a series of payments of equal amounts. Consider the calculation of the future value when a series of payments is involved.

Example 6: Suppose that you are to receive $3,000 per year at the end of each of the next four years. Also assume that each payment could be invested at an interest rate of 10% compounded annually. How much would be accumulated in principal and interest by the end of the fourth year? This is an example of an annuity of payments of equal amounts. A time diagram would portray the payments as follows:

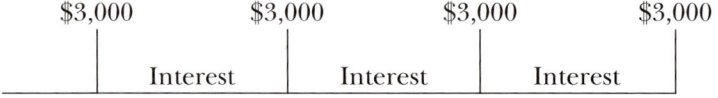

$3,000 $3,000 $3,000 $3,000

Interest   Interest   Interest

FV = ?

Because we are interested in calculating the future value, we could use the future value of $1 concept and calculate the future value of each $3,000 payment using Table 9-1 as follows:

$3,000 × 1.331 Interest for 3 Periods	$ 3,993
3,000 × 1.210 Interest for 2 Periods	3,630
3,000 × 1.100 Interest for 1 Period	3,300
3,000 × 1.000 Interest for 0 Periods	3,000
Total Future Value	$13,923

Note that four payments would be received but that only three of them would draw interest because the payments are received at the end of each period.

Fortunately, there is an easier method to calculate the **future value of an annuity**. Table 9-3, on page 417, has been constructed to indicate the future value of a series of payments of $1 per period at various interest rates and number of periods. The table can be used for the previous example by reading across the four-period line and down the 10% column to a table factor of 4.641. The future value of an annuity of $3,000 per year can be calculated as follows:

$$FV = \$3,000 \text{(table factor)}$$
$$= \$3,000(4.641)$$
$$= \$13,923$$

Future value of an annuity
Amount accumulated in the future when a series of payments is invested and accrues interest.
Alternate term: *Amount of an annuity*

The steps using the calculator are as follows:

ENTER	DISPLAY
4 N	N = 4
10 I/Y	I/Y = 10
3000 PMT	PMT = 3,000
0 PV	PV = 0
CPT FV	FV = 13,923

Example 7: Your cousin just had a baby girl two weeks ago and is already thinking about sending her to college. When the girl is 15, how much money would be in her college account if your cousin deposits $2,000 into it on each of her 15 birthdays? The interest rate is 10%.

$$FV = \$2,000 \text{(table factor)}$$
$$= \$2,000(31.772)$$
$$= \$63,544$$

The steps using the calculator are as follows:

ENTER	DISPLAY
15 N	N = 15
10 I/Y	I/Y = 10
2000 PMT	PMT = 2,000
0 PV	PV = 0
CPT FV	FV = 63,545

When compounding occurs more frequently than annually, adjustments must be made to the interest rate and number of periods, adjustments similar to those discussed previously for single amounts.

Example 8: How would the future value be calculated if the previous example was modified so that we deposited $1,000 semiannually and the interest rate was 10% compounded semiannually (or 5% per period) for 15 years? Table 9-3 could be used by reading across the line for 30 periods and down the column for 5% to obtain a table factor of 66.439. The future value would be calculated as follows:

$$FV = \$1,000 \text{(table factor)}$$
$$= \$1,000 \text{(66.439)}$$
$$= \$66,439$$

The steps using the calculator are as follows:

ENTER	DISPLAY
30 N	**N = 30**
5 I/Y	**I/Y = 5**
1000 PMT	**PMT = 1,000**
0 PV	**PV = 0**
CPT FV	**FV = 66,439**

Comparing the two examples illustrates once again that more frequent compounding results in larger accumulated amounts.

PRESENT VALUE OF AN ANNUITY

Many accounting applications of the time value of money concept concern situations for which we want to know the present value of a series of payments that will occur in the future. This involves calculating the present value of an annuity. An annuity is a series of payments of equal amounts.

Example 9: Suppose that you will receive an annuity of $4,000 per year for four years, with the first received one year from today. The amounts received can be invested at a rate of 10% compounded annually. What amount would you need at the present time to have an amount equivalent to the series of payments and interest in the future? To answer this question, you must calculate the **present value of an annuity**. A time diagram of the series of payments would appear as follows:

Present value of an annuity
The amount at a present time that is equivalent to a series of payments and interest in the future.

$4,000	$4,000	$4,000	$4,000
Discount	Discount	Discount	Discount

PV = ?

Because you are interested in calculating the present value, you could refer to the present value of $1 concept and discount each of the $4,000 payments individually using table factors from Table 9-2 as follows:

$4,000 × 0.683 Factor for 4 Periods	$ 2,732
4,000 × 0.751 Factor for 3 Periods	3,004
4,000 × 0.826 Factor for 2 Periods	3,304
4,000 × 0.909 Factor for 1 Period	3,636
Total Present Value	$12,676

For a problem of any size, it is very cumbersome to calculate the present value of each payment individually. Therefore, tables have been constructed to ease the computational burden. Table 9-4, on page 418, provides table factors to calculate the present value of an annuity of $1 per year at various interest rates and number of periods. The previous example can be solved by reading across the four-year line and down the 10% column to obtain a table factor of 3.170. The present value would then be calculated as follows:

$$PV = \$4,000 \text{(table factor)}$$
$$= \$4,000 \text{(3.170)}$$
$$= \$12,680$$

Note that there is a $4 difference in the present value calculated by the first and second methods. This difference is caused by a small amount of rounding in the table factors that were used.

The steps using the calculator are as follows:

ENTER	DISPLAY
4 N	N = 4
10 I/Y	I/Y = 10
4000 PMT	PMT = 4,000
0 FV	FV = 0
CPT PV	PV = 12,680

Example 10: You just won the lottery. You can take your $1 million in a lump sum today, or you can receive $100,000 per year over the next 12 years. Assuming a 5% interest rate, which would you prefer, ignoring tax considerations?

Solution:

$$PV = \$100,000 \text{(table factor)}$$
$$= \$100,000 \text{(8.863)}$$
$$= \$886,300$$

The steps using the calculator are as follows:

ENTER	DISPLAY
12 N	N = 12
5 I/Y	I/Y = 5
100,000 PMT	PMT = 100,000
0 FV	FV = 0
CPT PV	PV = 886,325

Because the present value of the payments over 12 years is less than the $1 million immediate payment, you should prefer the immediate payment.

SOLVING FOR UNKNOWNS

In some cases, the present value or future value amounts will be known but the interest rate or the number of payments must be calculated. The formulas that have been presented thus far can be used for such calculations, but you must be careful to analyze each problem to be sure that you have chosen the correct relationship. We will use two examples to illustrate the power of the time value of money concepts.

LO7 Apply the compound interest concepts to some common accounting situations.

Assume that you have just purchased a new automobile for $14,420 and must decide how to pay for it. Your local bank has graciously granted you a five-year loan. Because you are a good credit risk, the bank will allow you to make annual payments on the loan at the end of each year. The amount of the loan payments, which include principal and interest, is $4,000 per year. You are concerned that your total payments will be $20,000 ($4,000 per year for five years) and want to calculate the interest rate that is being charged on the loan.

Because the market or present value of the car, as well as the loan, is $14,420, a time diagram of our example would appear as follows:

$4,000	$4,000	$4,000	$4,000	$4,000
Discount	Discount	Discount	Discount	Discount

$PV = 14,420$

The interest rate that we must solve for represents the discount rate that was applied to the $4,000 payments to result in a present value of $14,420. Therefore, the applicable formula is the following:

$$PV = \$4,000(\text{table factor})$$

In this case, *PV* is known, so the formula can be rearranged as follows:

$$\text{Table factor} = PV/\$4,000$$
$$= \$14,420/\$4,000$$
$$= 3.605$$

The value of 3.605 represents a table factor in Table 9-4. We must read across the five-year line until we find a table factor of 3.605. In this case, that table factor is found in the 12% column. Therefore, the rate of interest being paid on the auto loan is 12%.

The steps using the calculator are as follows:

ENTER	DISPLAY
5 N	N = 5
14420 PV	PV = 14,420
4000 PMT +/−	PMT = −4,000
0 FV	FV = 0
CPT I/Y	I/Y = 11.99

[*Note:* On many calculators, including **Texas Instruments**, the payment amount (PMT) must be entered as a negative value in order to calculate I/Y.]

The second example involves solving for the number of interest periods. Assume that you want to accumulate $12,000 as a down payment on a home. You believe that you can save $1,000 per semiannual period, and your bank will pay interest of 8% per year, or 4% per semiannual period. How long will it take you to accumulate the desired amount?

The accumulated amount of $12,000 represents the future value of an annuity of $1,000 per semiannual period. Therefore, we can use the interest factors of Table 9-3 to assist in the solution. The applicable formula in this case is the following:

$$FV = \$1,000(\text{table factor})$$

The future value is known to be $12,000, and we must solve for the interest factor or table factor. Therefore, we can rearrange the formula as follows:

$$\text{Table factor} = FV/\$1,000$$
$$= \$12,000/\$1,000$$
$$= 12.00$$

Using Table 9-3, we must scan down the 4% column until we find a table value that is near 12.00. The closest table value we find is 12.006. That table value corresponds to 10 periods. Therefore, if we deposit $1,000 per semiannual period and invest the money at 4% per semiannual period, it will take 10 semiannual periods (five years) to accumulate $12,000.

The steps using the calculator are as follows:

ENTER	DISPLAY
4 I/Y	I/Y = 4
1000 PMT +/−	PMT = −1,000
12,000 FV	FV = 12,000
CPT N	N = 10

[*Note:* On many calculators, including **Texas Instruments**, the payment amount (PMT) must be entered as a negative value in order to calculate N.]

TABLE 9-1 Future Value of $1

(N) PERIODS	Rate of Interest in %											
	2	**3**	**4**	**5**	**6**	**7**	**8**	**9**	**10**	**11**	**12**	**15**
1	1.020	1.030	1.040	1.050	1.060	1.070	1.080	1.090	1.100	1.110	1.120	1.150
2	1.040	1.061	1.082	1.103	1.124	1.145	1.166	1.188	1.210	1.232	1.254	1.323
3	1.061	1.093	1.125	1.158	1.191	1.225	1.260	1.295	1.331	1.368	1.405	1.521
4	1.082	1.126	1.170	1.216	1.262	1.311	1.360	1.412	1.464	1.518	1.574	1.749
5	1.104	1.159	1.217	1.276	1.338	1.403	1.469	1.539	1.611	1.685	1.762	2.011
6	1.126	1.194	1.265	1.340	1.419	1.501	1.587	1.677	1.772	1.870	1.974	2.313
7	1.149	1.230	1.316	1.407	1.504	1.606	1.714	1.828	1.949	2.076	2.211	2.660
8	1.172	1.267	1.369	1.477	1.594	1.718	1.851	1.993	2.144	2.305	2.476	3.059
9	1.195	1.305	1.423	1.551	1.689	1.838	1.999	2.172	2.358	2.558	2.773	3.518
10	1.219	1.344	1.480	1.629	1.791	1.967	2.159	2.367	2.594	2.839	3.106	4.046
11	1.243	1.384	1.539	1.710	1.898	2.105	2.332	2.580	2.853	3.152	3.479	4.652
12	1.268	1.426	1.601	1.796	2.012	2.252	2.518	2.813	3.138	3.498	3.896	5.350
13	1.294	1.469	1.665	1.886	2.133	2.410	2.720	3.066	3.452	3.883	4.363	6.153
14	1.319	1.513	1.732	1.980	2.261	2.579	2.937	3.342	3.797	4.310	4.887	7.076
15	1.346	1.558	1.801	2.079	2.397	2.759	3.172	3.642	4.177	4.785	5.474	8.137
16	1.373	1.605	1.873	2.183	2.540	2.952	3.426	3.970	4.595	5.311	6.130	9.358
17	1.400	1.653	1.948	2.292	2.693	3.159	3.700	4.328	5.054	5.895	6.866	10.761
18	1.428	1.702	2.026	2.407	2.854	3.380	3.996	4.717	5.560	6.544	7.690	12.375
19	1.457	1.754	2.07	2.527	3.026	3.617	4.316	5.142	6.116	7.263	8.613	14.232
20	1.486	1.806	2.191	2.653	3.207	3.870	4.661	5.604	6.727	8.062	9.646	16.367
21	1.516	1.860	2.279	2.786	3.400	4.141	5.034	6.109	7.40	8.949	10.804	18.822
22	1.546	1.916	2.370	2.925	3.604	4.430	5.437	6.659	8.140	9.934	12.100	21.645
23	1.577	1.974	2.465	3.072	3.820	4.741	5.871	7.258	8.954	11.026	13.552	24.891
24	1.608	2.033	2.563	3.225	4.049	5.072	6.341	7.911	9.850	12.239	15.179	28.625
25	1.641	2.094	2.666	3.386	4.292	5.427	6.848	8.623	10.835	13.585	17.000	32.919
26	1.673	2.157	2.772	3.556	4.549	5.807	7.396	9.399	11.918	15.080	19.040	37.857
27	1.707	2.221	2.883	3.733	4.822	6.214	7.988	10.245	13.110	16.739	21.325	43.535
28	1.741	2.288	2.999	3.920	5.112	6.649	8.627	11.167	14.421	18.580	23.884	50.066
29	1.776	2.357	3.119	4.116	5.418	7.114	9.317	12.172	15.863	20.624	26.750	57.575
30	1.811	2.427	3.243	4.322	5.743	7.612	10.063	13.268	17.449	22.892	29.960	66.212

TABLE 9-2 Present Value of $1

(N) PERIODS	Rate of Interest in %											
	2	3	4	5	6	7	8	9	10	11	12	15
1	0.980	0.971	0.962	0.952	0.943	0.935	0.926	0.917	0.909	0.901	0.893	0.870
2	0.961	0.943	0.925	0.907	0.890	0.873	0.857	0.842	0.826	0.812	0.797	0.756
3	0.942	0.915	0.889	0.864	0.840	0.816	0.794	0.772	0.751	0.731	0.712	0.658
4	0.924	0.888	0.855	0.823	0.792	0.763	0.735	0.708	0.683	0.659	0.636	0.572
5	0.906	0.863	0.822	0.784	0.747	0.713	0.681	0.650	0.621	0.593	0.567	0.497
6	0.888	0.837	0.790	0.746	0.705	0.666	0.630	0.596	0.564	0.535	0.507	0.432
7	0.871	0.813	0.760	0.711	0.665	0.623	0.583	0.547	0.513	0.482	0.452	0.376
8	0.853	0.789	0.731	0.677	0.627	0.582	0.540	0.502	0.467	0.434	0.404	0.327
9	0.837	0.766	0.703	0.645	0.592	0.544	0.500	0.460	0.424	0.391	0.361	0.284
10	0.820	0.744	0.676	0.614	0.558	0.508	0.463	0.422	0.386	0.352	0.322	0.247
11	0.804	0.722	0.650	0.585	0.527	0.475	0.429	0.388	0.350	0.317	0.287	0.215
12	0.788	0.701	0.625	0.557	0.497	0.444	0.397	0.356	0.319	0.286	0.257	0.187
13	0.773	0.681	0.601	0.530	0.469	0.415	0.368	0.326	0.290	0.258	0.229	0.163
14	0.758	0.661	0.577	0.505	0.442	0.388	0.340	0.299	0.263	0.232	0.205	0.141
15	0.743	0.642	0.555	0.481	0.417	0.362	0.315	0.275	0.239	0.209	0.183	0.123
16	0.728	0.623	0.534	0.458	0.394	0.339	0.292	0.252	0.218	0.188	0.163	0.107
17	0.714	0.605	0.513	0.436	0.371	0.317	0.270	0.231	0.198	0.170	0.146	0.093
18	0.700	0.587	0.494	0.416	0.350	0.296	0.250	0.212	0.180	0.153	0.130	0.081
19	0.686	0.570	0.475	0.396	0.331	0.277	0.232	0.194	0.164	0.138	0.116	0.070
20	0.673	0.554	0.456	0.377	0.312	0.258	0.215	0.178	0.149	0.124	0.104	0.061
21	0.660	0.538	0.439	0.359	0.294	0.242	0.199	0.164	0.135	0.112	0.093	0.053
22	0.647	0.522	0.422	0.342	0.278	0.226	0.184	0.150	0.123	0.101	0.083	0.046
23	0.634	0.507	0.406	0.326	0.262	0.211	0.170	0.138	0.112	0.091	0.074	0.040
24	0.622	0.492	0.390	0.310	0.247	0.197	0.158	0.126	0.102	0.082	0.066	0.035
25	0.610	0.478	0.375	0.295	0.233	0.184	0.146	0.116	0.092	0.074	0.059	0.030
26	0.598	0.464	0.361	0.281	0.220	0.172	0.135	0.106	0.084	0.066	0.053	0.026
27	0.586	0.450	0.347	0.268	0.207	0.161	0.125	0.098	0.076	0.060	0.047	0.023
28	0.574	0.437	0.333	0.255	0.196	0.150	0.116	0.090	0.069	0.054	0.042	0.020
29	0.563	0.424	0.321	0.243	0.185	0.141	0.107	0.082	0.063	0.048	0.037	0.017
30	0.552	0.412	0.308	0.231	0.174	0.131	0.099	0.075	0.057	0.044	0.033	0.015

TABLE 9-3 Future Value of Annuity of $1

(N) PERIODS	Rate of Interest in %											
	2	3	4	5	6	7	8	9	10	11	12	15
1	1.000	1.000	1.000	1.000	1.000	1.000	1.000	1.000	1.000	1.000	1.000	1.000
2	2.020	2.030	2.040	2.050	2.060	2.070	2.080	2.090	2.100	2.110	2.120	2.150
3	3.060	3.091	3.122	3.153	3.184	3.215	3.246	3.278	3.310	3.342	3.374	3.473
4	4.122	4.184	4.246	4.310	4.375	4.440	4.506	4.573	4.641	4.710	4.779	4.993
5	5.204	5.309	5.416	5.526	5.637	5.751	5.867	5.985	6.105	6.228	6.353	6.742
6	6.308	6.468	6.633	6.802	6.975	7.153	7.336	7.523	7.716	7.913	8.115	8.754
7	7.434	7.662	7.898	8.142	8.394	8.654	8.923	9.200	9.487	9.783	10.089	11.067
8	8.583	8.892	9.214	9.549	9.897	10.260	10.637	11.028	11.436	11.859	12.300	13.727
9	9.755	10.159	10.583	11.027	11.491	11.978	12.488	13.021	13.579	14.164	14.776	16.786
10	10.950	11.464	12.006	12.578	13.181	13.816	14.487	15.193	15.937	16.722	17.549	20.304
11	12.169	12.808	13.486	14.207	14.972	15.784	16.645	17.560	18.531	19.561	20.655	24.349
12	13.412	14.192	15.026	15.917	16.870	17.888	18.977	20.141	21.384	22.713	24.133	29.002
13	14.680	15.618	16.627	17.713	18.882	20.141	21.495	22.953	24.523	26.212	28.029	34.352
14	15.974	17.086	18.292	19.599	21.015	22.550	24.215	26.019	27.975	30.095	32.393	40.505
15	17.293	18.599	20.024	21.579	23.276	25.129	27.152	29.361	31.772	34.405	37.280	47.580
16	18.639	20.157	21.825	23.657	25.673	27.888	30.324	33.003	35.950	39.190	42.753	55.717
17	20.012	21.762	23.698	25.840	28.213	30.840	33.750	36.974	40.545	44.501	48.884	65.075
18	21.412	23.414	25.645	28.132	30.906	33.999	37.450	41.301	45.599	50.396	55.750	75.836
19	22.841	25.117	27.671	30.539	33.760	37.379	41.446	46.018	51.159	56.939	63.440	88.212
20	24.297	26.870	29.778	33.066	36.786	40.995	45.762	51.160	57.275	64.203	72.052	102.444
21	25.783	28.676	31.969	35.719	39.993	44.865	50.423	56.765	64.002	72.265	81.699	118.810
22	27.299	30.537	34.248	38.505	43.392	49.006	55.457	62.873	71.403	81.214	92.503	137.632
23	28.845	32.453	36.618	41.430	46.996	53.436	60.893	69.532	79.543	91.148	104.603	159.276
24	30.422	34.426	39.083	44.502	50.816	58.177	66.765	76.790	88.497	102.174	118.155	184.168
25	32.030	36.459	41.646	47.727	54.865	63.249	73.106	84.701	98.347	114.413	133.334	212.793
26	33.671	38.553	44.312	51.113	59.156	68.676	79.954	93.324	109.182	127.999	150.334	245.712
27	35.344	40.710	47.084	54.669	63.706	74.484	87.351	102.723	121.100	143.079	169.374	283.569
28	37.051	42.931	49.968	58.403	68.528	80.698	95.339	112.968	134.210	159.817	190.699	327.104
29	38.792	45.219	52.966	62.323	73.640	87.347	103.966	124.135	148.631	178.397	214.583	377.170
30	40.568	47.575	56.085	66.439	79.058	94.461	113.283	136.308	164.494	199.021	241.333	434.745

TABLE 9-4 Present Value of Annuity of $1

(N) PERIODS	Rate of Interest in %											
	2	3	4	5	6	7	8	9	10	11	12	15
1	0.980	0.971	0.962	0.952	0.943	0.935	0.926	0.917	0.909	0.901	0.893	0.870
2	1.942	1.913	1.886	1.859	1.833	1.808	1.783	1.759	1.736	1.713	1.690	1.626
3	2.884	2.829	2.775	2.723	2.673	2.624	2.577	2.531	2.487	2.444	2.402	2.283
4	3.808	3.717	3.630	3.546	3.465	3.387	3.312	3.240	3.170	3.102	3.037	2.855
5	4.713	4.580	4.452	4.329	4.212	4.100	3.993	3.890	3.791	3.696	3.605	3.352
6	5.601	5.417	5.242	5.076	4.917	4.767	4.623	4.486	4.355	4.231	4.111	3.784
7	6.472	6.230	6.002	5.786	5.582	5.389	5.206	5.033	4.868	4.712	4.564	4.160
8	7.325	7.020	6.733	6.463	6.210	5.971	5.747	5.535	5.335	5.146	4.968	4.487
9	8.162	7.786	7.435	7.108	6.802	6.515	6.247	5.995	5.759	5.537	5.328	4.772
10	8.983	8.530	8.111	7.722	7.360	7.024	6.710	6.418	6.145	5.889	5.650	5.019
11	9.787	9.253	8.760	8.306	7.887	7.499	7.139	6.805	6.495	6.207	5.938	5.234
12	10.575	9.954	9.385	8.863	8.384	7.943	7.536	7.161	6.814	6.492	6.194	5.421
13	11.348	10.635	9.986	9.394	8.853	8.358	7.904	7.487	7.103	6.750	6.424	5.583
14	12.106	11.296	10.563	9.899	9.295	8.745	8.244	7.786	7.367	6.982	6.628	5.724
15	12.849	11.938	11.118	10.380	9.712	9.108	8.559	8.061	7.606	7.191	6.811	5.847
16	13.578	12.561	11.652	10.838	10.106	9.447	8.851	8.313	7.824	7.379	6.974	5.954
17	14.292	13.166	12.166	11.274	10.477	9.763	9.122	8.544	8.022	7.549	7.120	6.047
18	14.992	13.754	12.659	11.690	10.828	10.059	9.372	8.756	8.201	7.702	7.250	6.128
19	15.678	14.324	13.134	12.085	11.158	10.336	9.604	8.950	8.365	7.839	7.366	6.198
20	16.351	14.877	13.590	12.462	11.470	10.594	9.818	9.129	8.514	7.963	7.469	6.259
21	17.011	15.415	14.029	12.821	11.764	10.836	10.017	9.292	8.649	8.075	7.562	6.312
22	17.658	15.937	14.451	13.163	12.042	11.061	10.201	9.442	8.772	8.176	7.645	6.359
23	18.292	16.444	14.857	13.489	12.303	11.272	10.371	9.580	8.883	8.266	7.718	6.399
24	18.914	16.936	15.247	13.799	12.550	11.469	10.529	9.707	8.985	8.348	7.784	6.434
25	19.523	17.413	15.622	14.094	12.783	11.654	10.675	9.823	9.077	8.422	7.843	6.464
26	20.121	17.877	15.983	14.375	13.003	11.826	10.810	9.929	9.161	8.488	7.896	6.491
27	20.707	18.327	16.330	14.643	13.211	11.987	10.935	10.027	9.237	8.548	7.943	6.514
28	21.281	18.764	16.663	14.898	13.406	12.137	11.051	10.116	9.307	8.602	7.984	6.534
29	21.844	19.188	16.984	15.141	13.591	12.278	11.158	10.198	9.370	8.650	8.022	6.551
30	22.396	19.600	17.292	15.372	13.765	12.409	11.258	10.274	9.427	8.694	8.055	6.566

Accounting Tools: Payroll Accounting

Salaries payable was one of the current liabilities discussed in Chapter 2. At the end of each accounting period, the accountant must accrue salaries that have been earned by the employees but have not yet been paid. To this point, we have not considered the accounting that must be done for payroll deductions and other payroll expenses.

LO8 Show that you understand the deductions and expenses for payroll accounting.

Payroll deductions and expenses occur not only at year-end but every time, throughout the year, that employees are paid. The amount of cash paid for salaries and wages is the largest cash outflow for many firms. It is imperative that sufficient cash be available not only to meet the weekly or monthly payroll but also to remit the payroll taxes to the appropriate government agencies when required. The purpose of this appendix is to introduce the calculations and the accounting entries that are necessary when payroll is recorded.

The issue of payroll expenses is of great concern to businesses, particularly small entrepreneurial ones. One of the large issues facing companies is how to meet the increasing cost of hiring people. Salary is just one component. How are these companies going to pay salaries plus benefits such as health insurance, life insurance, disability, unemployment benefits, workers' compensation, and so on? More and more companies are trying to keep their payrolls as small as possible in order to avoid these costs. Unfortunately, this has been a contributing factor in the trends of using more part-time employees and of outsourcing some business functions. Outsourcing, or hiring independent contractors, allows the company to reduce salary expense and the expenses related to fringe benefits. However, it does not necessarily improve the company's profitability. The expenses that are increased as a result of hiring outside contractors must also be considered. A manager must carefully consider all of the costs that are affected before deciding whether to hire more employees or to go with an independent contractor.

Calculation of Gross Wages

Consider the basic steps that must be performed in the payroll process. The first step is to calculate the **gross wages** of all employees. The gross wage represents the wage amount before deductions. Companies often have two general classes of employees, hourly and salaried. The gross wage of each hourly employee is calculated by multiplying the number of hours worked times his or her hourly wage rate. Salaried employees are not paid on a per-hour basis but at a flat rate per week, month, or year. For both hourly and salaried employees, the payroll accountant must also consider any overtime, bonus, or other salary supplement that may affect gross wages.

Gross wages
The amount of wages before deductions.
Alternate term: Gross pay

Calculation of Net Pay

The second step in the payroll process is to calculate the deductions from each employee's paycheck to determine **net pay**. Deductions from the employees' checks

Net pay
The amount of wages after deductions.

represent a current liability to the employer because the employer must remit the amounts at a future time to the proper agencies or government offices, for example to the U.S. Treasury Service. The deductions that are made depend on the type of company and the employee. The most important deductions are indicated in the following sections.

INCOME TAX

The employer must withhold federal income tax from most employees' paychecks. The amount withheld depends on the employee's earnings and the number of *exemptions* claimed by that employee. An exemption reflects the number of dependents a taxpayer can claim. The more exemptions, the lower is the withholding amount required by the government. Tables are available from the Internal Revenue Service to calculate the proper amount that should be withheld. This amount must be remitted to the U.S. Treasury Service periodically; the frequency depends on the company's size and its payroll. Income tax withheld represents a liability to the employer and is normally classified as a current liability.

Many states also have an income tax, and the employer must often withhold additional amounts for the state tax.

FICA—EMPLOYEES' SHARE

FICA stands for Federal Insurance Contributions Act; it is commonly called the *social security tax.* The FICA tax is assessed on both the employee and the employer. The employees' portion must be withheld from paychecks at the applicable rate. The FICA taxes support Social Security and Medicare. Social Security benefits include old-age, survivors, and disability insurance or OASDI. Medicare is the hospital insurance portion. Currently, the Social Security portion is assessed at 6.2% of wages up to $94,200. The employee's share of the Medicare portion is 1.45% of wages with no limit. Thus, the total amount assessed is 7.65%, which we will refer to as the FICA tax. Other rates and special rules apply to certain types of workers and to self-employed individuals. The amounts withheld from the employees' checks must be remitted to the federal government periodically.

FICA taxes withheld from employees' checks represent a liability to the employer until remitted. It is important to remember that the employees' portion of the FICA tax does not represent an expense to the employer.

VOLUNTARY DEDUCTIONS

If you have ever received a paycheck, you are probably aware that a variety of items was deducted from the amount you earned. Many of these are voluntary deductions chosen by the employee. They may include health insurance, pension or retirement contributions, savings plans, contributions to charities, union dues, and others. Each of these items is deducted from the employees' paychecks, is held by the employer, and is remitted at a future time. Therefore, each represents a current liability to the employer until remitted.

Employer Payroll Taxes

The payroll items discussed thus far do not represent expenses to the employer because they are assessed on the employees and deducted from their paychecks. However, there are taxes that the employer must pay. The two most important are FICA and unemployment taxes.

FICA—EMPLOYER'S SHARE

The FICA tax is assessed on both the employee and the employer. The employee amount is withheld from the employees' paychecks and represents a liability but is not an expense to the employer. Normally, an equal amount is assessed on the employer. Therefore, the employer must pay an additional 7.65% of employee wages to the federal government. The employer's portion represents an expense to the employer and should be reflected in a Payroll Tax Expense account or similar type of account. This portion is a liability to the employer until it is remitted.

UNEMPLOYMENT TAX

Most employers must also pay unemployment taxes. The state and federal governments jointly sponsor a program to collect unemployment tax from employers and to pay workers who lose their jobs. The maximum rate of unemployment taxes is 3.4%, of which 2.7% is the state portion and 0.7% the federal portion, on an employee's first $7,000 of wages earned each year. The rate is adjusted according to a company's employment history, however. If a company has been fairly stable and few of its employees have filed for unemployment benefits, the rate is adjusted downward.

Unemployment taxes are levied against the employer, not the employee. Therefore, the tax represents an expense to the employer and should be reflected in a Payroll Tax Expense account or similar type of account. The tax also represents a liability to the employer until it is remitted.

Payroll Example

Assume that Kori Company has calculated the gross wages of all employees for the month of July to be $100,000. Also assume that the following amounts have been withheld from the employees' paychecks:

Income Tax	$20,000
FICA	7,650
United Way Contributions	5,000
Union Dues	3,000

In addition, assume that Kori's unemployment tax rate is 3%, that no employees have reached the $7,000 limit, and that Kori's portion of FICA matches the employees' share. The transactions to record payroll, to pay the employees, and to record the employer's payroll expenses have the following effects on the accounting equation:

Balance Sheet						Income Statement
ASSETS	**=**	**LIABILITIES**	**+**	**STOCKHOLDERS' EQUITY**	**+**	**REVENUES − EXPENSES**
		Salaries Payable	64,350			Salaries Expense (100,000)
		Income Tax Payable	20,000			
		FICA Payable	7,650			
		United Way Payable	5,000			
		Union Dues Payable	3,000			

Balance Sheet						Income Statement
ASSETS	**=**	**LIABILITIES**	**+**	**STOCKHOLDERS' EQUITY**	**+**	**REVENUES − EXPENSES**
Cash (64,350)		Salaries Payable	(64,350)			

Balance Sheet						Income Statement
ASSETS	**=**	**LIABILITIES**	**+**	**STOCKHOLDERS' EQUITY**	**+**	**REVENUES − EXPENSES**
		FICA Payable	7,650			Payroll Tax Expense (10,650)
		Unemployment Tax Payable	3,000			

Periodically, Kori must remit amounts to the appropriate government body or agency. The effect on the accounting equation to record remittance, assuming remittance at the end of July, is as follows:

Balance Sheet						Income Statement
ASSETS	**=**	**LIABILITIES**		**+**	**STOCKHOLDERS' EQUITY**	**+**	**REVENUES − EXPENSES**
Cash (46,300)		Income Tax Payable	(20,000)			
		FICA Payable	(15,300)			
		United Way Payable	(5,000)			
		Union Dues Payable	(3,000)			
		Unemployment				
		Tax Payable	(3,000)			

Compensated Absences

LO9 Determine when compensated absences must be accrued as a liability.

Compensated absences
Employee absences for which the employee will be paid. *Alternate terms: Vacation pay* and *sick pay*

Most employers allow employees to accumulate a certain number of sick days and to take a certain number of paid vacation days each year. This causes an accounting question when recording payroll amounts. When should the sick days and vacation days be treated as an expense—in the period they are earned or in the period they are taken by the employee?

The FASB has coined the term **compensated absences.** These are absences from employment, such as vacation, illness, and holidays, for which it is expected that employees will be paid. The FASB has ruled that an expense should be accrued if certain conditions are met: the services have been rendered, the rights (days) accumulate, and payment is probable and can be reasonably estimated. The result of the FASB ruling is that most employers are required to record a liability and expense for vacation days when earned, but sick days are not recorded until employees are actually absent.

Compensated absence is another example of the matching principle at work, and so it is consistent with good accounting theory. Unfortunately, it has also resulted in some complex calculations and additional work for payroll accountants. Part of the complexity is due to unresolved legal issues about compensated absences.

U.S. accounting standards on this issue are much more detailed and extensive than the standards of many foreign countries. As a result, U.S. companies may believe that they are subject to higher record-keeping costs than their foreign competitors.

Accounting Tools: Using Excel for Problems Involving Interest Calculations

The purpose of Appendix B is to illustrate how the functions built in to the Excel® spreadsheet can be used to calculate future value and present value amounts. We will illustrate the use of Excel with the same examples that are used in the body of Chapter 9.

To view the Excel functions, click on the PASTE function of the Excel toolbar (the paste function is on the top of the Excel toolbar and is noted by the symbol *fx*) and then choose the FINANCIAL option. Several different calculations are available. We will illustrate two of them: FV and PV.

Example 1: Your three-year-old son, Robert, just inherited $50,000 in cash and securities from his grandfather. If the funds were left in the bank and in the stock market and received an annual return of 10%, how much would be there in 15 years when Robert starts college?

Solution: In Excel, use the FV function and enter the values as follows:

Note that the future value of $208,862 is slightly different than that given in the body of the text because of rounding when using the table factors.

Example 2: Consider a $2,000 note payable that carries interest at the rate of 10% compounded annually. The note is due in two years, and the principal and interest must be paid at that time. What amount must be paid in two years?

Solution: In Excel, use the FV function and enter the values as follows:

The future value is $2,420.

Example 3: Suppose we want to find the future value of a $2,000 note payable due in two years. The note payable requires interest to be compounded quarterly at the rate of 12% per year. What future amount must be paid in two years?

Solution: In Excel, use the FV function and enter the values as follows:

The future value is $2,534 (rounded to the nearest dollar).

Example 4: Suppose you know that you will receive $2,000 in two years. You also know that if you had the money now, it could be invested at 10% compounded annually. What is the present value of the $2,000?

Solution: Since this problem requires the calculation of a present value, the PV function of Excel should be chosen and used as follows:

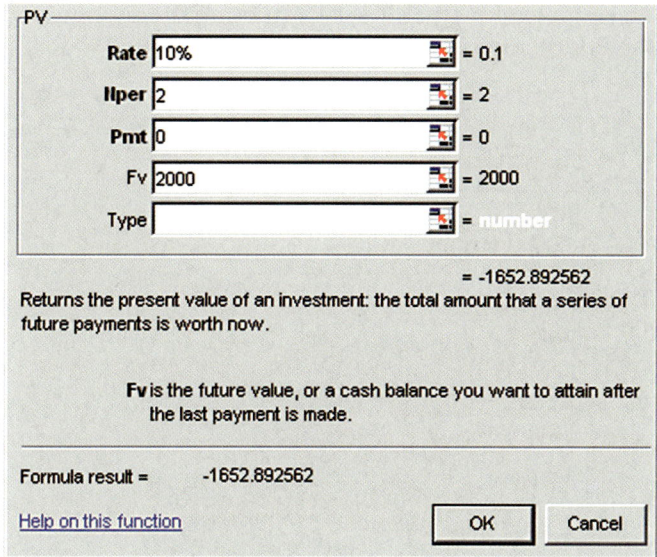

The present value is $1,653 (rounded to the nearest dollar).

Example 5: A recent magazine article projects that it will cost $120,000 to attend a four-year college 10 years from now. If that is true, how much money would you have to put into an account today to fund that education, assuming a 5% rate of return?

Solution: The PV function of Excel should again be used as follows:

The present value calculated ($73,670—rounded to the nearest dollar) differs slightly from that derived when using the table factors because of rounding in the tables.

Example 6: Suppose that you are to receive $3,000 per year at the end of each of the next four years. Also assume that each payment could be invested at an interest rate of 10% compounded annually. How much would be accumulated in principal and interest by the end of the fourth year?

Solution: This problem involves the calculation of the future value of an annuity, and you should use the FV function of Excel as follows:

The future value of the series of payments is $13,923. Note that the payments are simply entered as the Pmt variable in the spreadsheet.

Example 7: Your cousin just had a baby girl two weeks ago and is already thinking about sending her to college. When the girl is 15, how much money would be in her college account if your cousin deposits $2,000 into it on each of her 15 birthdays? The interest rate is 10%.

Solution: Use the Excel FV function as follows:

The future value amount is $63,545 (rounded to the nearest dollar).

Example 8: How would the future value be calculated if the previous example was modified so that we deposited $1,000 semiannually and the interest rate was 10% compounded semiannually (or 5% per period) for 15 years?

Solution: Because the compounding is semiannually, use the FV function of Excel as follows:

The future value is $66,439 (rounded to the nearest dollar).

Example 9: Suppose that you will receive an annuity of $4,000 per year for four years, with the first received one year from today. The amounts received can be invested at a rate of 10% compounded annually. What amount would you need at the present time to have an amount equivalent to the series of payments and interest in the future?

Solution: This problem involves the calculation of the present value of an annuity, so use the PV function of Excel as follows:

The present value of $12,679 (rounded to the nearest dollar) differs slightly from that derived when using the tables because of rounding in the table factors.

Example 10: You just won the lottery. You can take your $1 million in a lump sum today, or you can receive $100,000 per year over the next 12 years. Assuming a 5% interest rate, which would you prefer, ignoring tax considerations?

Solution: Use the PV function of Excel as follows:

Because the present value of the payments over 12 years is $886,325 (rounded to the nearest dollar) and is less than the $1 million available immediately, you should choose the immediate payment.

STUDY HIGHLIGHTS

LO1   **Identify the components of the current liability category of the balance sheet (p. 395).**

- Current liabilities are obligations of a company that generally must be satisfied within one year. Some companies list them in the balance sheet in order of the account that requires payment first.
- Current liability accounts include accounts payable, notes payable, the current portion of long-term debt, taxes payable, and accrued liabilities.

LO2   **Examine how accruals affect the current liability category (p. 398).**

- Accrued liabilities result from expenses that are incurred but have not yet been paid.
- Common accrued liabilities include taxes payable, salaries payable, and interest payable.

LO3   **Show that you understand how changes in current liabilities affect the statement of cash flows (p. 399).**

- Most current liabilities are directly related to the ongoing operations of a company.
  - Decreases in current liabilities indicate that cash has been used to satisfy obligations and are cash outflows not represented by some expenses in the income statement.
  - Increases in current liabilities indicate that some expenses in the income statement have not been paid in cash and are not cash outflows represented by some expenses on the income statement.

Determine when contingent liabilities should be presented on the balance sheet or disclosed in notes and how to calculate their amounts (p. 401).

LO4

- Contingent liabilities should be accrued and disclosed only when the event that they depend upon is probable and the amount can reasonably be estimated.
- The amount of a contingent liability is often an estimate made by experts both inside the firm (managers for amounts of warranty expenses) and outside the firm (e.g., attorneys for amounts in a lawsuit).

Explain the difference between simple and compound interest (p. 406).

LO5

- Simple interest is earned only on the principal amount, whereas compound interest is earned on the principal plus previous amounts of accumulated interest.

Calculate amounts using the future value and present value concepts (p. 406).

LO6

- Present and future value calculations are made for four different scenarios:
  - Future value of a single amount
  - Present value of a single amount
  - Future value of an annuity
  - Present value of an annuity

Apply the compound interest concepts to some common accounting situations (p. 413).

LO7

- Often all of the variables necessary to calculate amounts related to present and future value concepts will be available except for one unknown amount that can be solved for.
- Financial calculators allow for these situations and easily solve for unknown values such as present or future value, payments, and interest rate.

Show that you understand the deduction and expenses for payroll accounting (Appendix A p. 419).

LO8

- Payroll-related expenses must often be accrued at the end of the period, and the accounting involves some specialized accounts.
  - Net pay is the cash disbursed to employees, less income tax withheld for the employee, FICA, and any voluntary deductions specified by the employee.
  - The employer has expenses for salaries and wages beyond those amounts themselves. Two of the most important are FICA (same amount as employee) and unemployment taxes.

Determine when compensated absences must be accrued as a liability (Appendix A p. 422).

LO9

- Most employers allow employees to take paid vacation and to accumulate a certain number of sick days per year. These represent compensated absences.
- Normally the expense and related liability for vacation days are recorded when earned, but sick days are not recorded until actually taken.

HIGHLIGHTS

RATIO REVIEW

Working Capital* = Current Assets − Current Liabilities

Current Ratio = Current Assets/Current Liabilities

Quick Ratio = Quick Assets**/Current Liabilities

*Working capital is defined and discussed in Chapter 2.
**Quick assets are those assets that can be converted into cash quickly. It may be measured differently by different companies but generally is measured as Total Current Assets − Inventory − Prepaid Expenses.

ACCOUNTS HIGHLIGHTED

Account Titles	Where It Appears	In What Section	Page Number
Accounts Payable	Balance Sheet	Current Liabilities	396
Notes Payable	Balance Sheet	Current Liabilities	396
Current Maturities of Long-Term Debt	Balance Sheet	Current Liabilities	398
Taxes Payable	Balance Sheet	Current Liabilities	398
Accrued Liabilities	Balance Sheet	Current Liabilities	398
Contingent Liabilities	Balance Sheet	Current Liabilities or Long-term (depending upon when it will be paid)	401

KEY TERMS QUIZ

Read each definition below, and then write the number of the definition in the blank beside the appropriate term it defines. The quiz solutions appear at the end of the chapter.

_____ Current liability	_____ Simple interest
_____ Accounts payable	_____ Compound interest
_____ Notes payable	_____ Future value of a single amount
_____ Discount on notes payable	_____ Present value of a single amount
_____ Current maturities of long-term debt	_____ Annuity
_____ Accrued liability	_____ Future value of an annuity
_____ Contingent liability	_____ Present value of an annuity
_____ Estimated liability	_____ Gross wages (Appendix A)
_____ Contingent asset	_____ Net pay (Appendix A)
_____ Time value of money	_____ Compensated absences (Appendix A)

1. Accounts that will be satisfied within one year or the next operating cycle.

2. The amount needed at the present time to be equivalent to a series of payments and interest in the future.

3. Amounts owed for the purchase of inventory, goods, or services acquired in the normal course of business.

4. A contra-liability account that represents interest deducted from a loan or note in advance.

5. A series of payments of equal amount.

6. The portion of a long-term liability that will be paid within one year of the balance sheet date.

7. A liability that has been incurred but has not been paid as of the balance sheet date.

8. Amounts owed that are represented by a formal contractual agreement. These amounts usually require the payment of interest.

9. A liability that involves an existing condition for which the outcome is not known with certainty and depends on some future event.

10. Interest that is earned or paid on the principal amount only.

11. A contingent liability that is accrued and is reflected on the balance sheet. Common examples are warranties, guarantees, and premium offers.

12. An amount that involves an existing condition dependent on some future event by which the company stands to gain. These amounts are not normally reported.

13. Interest calculated on the principal plus previous amounts of interest accumulated.

14. The concept that indicates that people should prefer to receive an immediate amount at the present time over an equal amount in the future.

15. The amount that will be accumulated in the future when one amount is invested at the present time and accrues interest until the future time.

16. The amount that will be accumulated in the future when a series of payments is invested and accrues interest until the future time.

17. The present amount that is equivalent to an amount at a future time.

18. The amount of an employee's wages before deductions.

19. Employment absences, such as sick days and vacation days, for which it is expected that employees will be paid.

20. The amount of an employee's paycheck after deductions.

ALTERNATE TERMS

Accrued Interest Interest payable

Compensated Absences Accrued vacation or sick pay

Compound Interest Interest on interest

Contingent Asset Contingent gain

Contingent Liability Contingent loss

Current Liability Short-term liability

Current Maturities of Long-Term Debt Long-term debt, current portion

Discounting a Note Interest in advance

FICA Social Security

Future Value of an Annuity Amount of an annuity

Gross Wages Gross pay

Income Tax Liability Income tax payable

Warranties Guarantees

WARMUP EXERCISES

LO1   **Warmup Exercise 9-1**

A company has the following current assets: Cash, $10,000; Accounts Receivable, $70,000; and Inventory, $20,000. The company also has current liabilities of $40,000. Calculate the company's current ratio and quick ratio.

LO3   **Warmup Exercise 9-2**

A company has the following current liabilities at the beginning of the period: Accounts Payable, $30,000; Taxes Payable $10,000. At the end of the period the balances of the account are as follows: Accounts Payable, $20,000; Taxes Payable, $15,000. What amounts will appear in the cash flow statement, and in what category of the statement will they appear?

LO6   **Warmup Exercise 9-3**

A. You invest $1,000 at the beginning of the year. How much will be accumulated in five years if you earn 10% interest compounded annually?

B. You invest $1,000 *per year* at the end of each year for five years. How much will be accumulated in five years if you earn 10% interest compounded annually?

C. You will receive $1,000 in five years. What is the present value of that amount if you can earn 10% interest compounded annually?

D. You will receive $1,000 *per year* at the end of each year for five years. What is the present value of that amount if you can earn 10% interest compounded annually?

SOLUTIONS TO WARMUP EXERCISES

Warmup Exercise 9-1

Current Ratio: Current Assets/Current Liabilities

Cash ($10,000) + Accounts Receivable ($70,000) + Inventory ($20,000) = $100,000

$$\$100,000/\$40,000 = 2.5 \text{ Current Ratio}$$

Quick Ratio: Quick Assets/Current Liabilities

Cash ($10,000) + Accounts Receivable ($70,000) = $80,000

$$\$80,000/\$40,000 = 2.0 \text{ Quick Ratio}$$

Warmup Exercise 9-2

The amounts appearing in the cash flow statement should be in the Operating Activities category of the statement. The amounts shown should be the *changes* in the balances of the accounts.

Accounts Payable decreased by $10,000 and should appear as a decrease in the cash flow statement.

Taxes Payable increased by $5,000 and should appear as an increase in the cash flow statement.

Warmup Exercise 9-3

A.

ENTER	DISPLAY
5 N	N = 5
10 I/Y	I/Y = 10
0 PMT	PMT = 0
1000 PV	PV = 1,000
CPT FV	FV = 1,611

A. $FV = \$1,000$(table factor)   using Table 9-1
   $= \$1,000(1.611)$ where $i = 10\%$, $n = 5$
   $= \$1,611$

B.

ENTER	DISPLAY
5 N	N = 5
10 I/Y	I/Y = 10
0 PMT	PMT = 1,000
1000 PV	PV = 0
CPT FV	FV = 6,105

B. $FV = \$1,000$(table factor)   using Table 9-3
   $= \$1,000(6.105)$ where $i = 10\%$, $n = 5$
   $= \$6,105$

C.

ENTER	DISPLAY
5 N	N = 5
10 I/Y	I/Y = 10
0 PMT	PMT = 0
1000 PV	FV = 1,000
CPT FV	PV = 621

C. $PV = \$1,000$(table factor)   using Table 9-2
   $= \$1,000(0.621)$ where $i = 10\%$, $n = 5$
   $= \$621$

D.

ENTER	DISPLAY
5 N	N = 5
10 I/Y	I/Y = 10
0 PMT	PMT = 1,000
1000 PV	FV = 0
CPT FV	PV = 3,791

D. $PV = \$1,000$(table factor)   using Table 9-4
   $= \$1,000(3.791)$ where $i = 10\%$, $n = 5$
   $= \$3,791$

REVIEW

REVIEW PROBLEM

Part A

The accountant for Lunn Express wants to develop a balance sheet as of December 31, 2007. The following items pertain to the liability category and must be considered in order to determine the items that should be reported in the Current Liabilities section of the balance sheet. You may assume that Lunn began business on January 1, 2007, and therefore the beginning balance of all accounts was zero.

a. During 2007 Lunn purchased $100,000 of inventory on account from suppliers. By year-end, $40,000 of the balance has been eliminated as a result of payments. All items were purchased on terms of 2/10, n/30. Lunn uses the gross method of recording payables.

b. On April 1, 2007, Lunn borrowed $10,000 on a one-year note payable from Philips Bank. Terms of the loan indicate that Lunn must repay the principal and 12% interest at the due date of the note.

c. On October 1, 2007, Lunn also borrowed $8,000 from Dove Bank on a one-year note payable. Dove Bank deducted 10% interest in advance and gave to Lunn the net amount. At the due date, Lunn must repay the principal of $8,000.

d. On January 1, 2007, Lunn borrowed $20,000 from Owens Bank by signing a 10-year note payable. Terms of the note indicate that Lunn must make annual payments of principal each January 1 beginning in 2008 and also must pay interest each January 1 in the amount of 8% of the outstanding balance of the loan.

e. The accountant for Lunn has completed an income statement for 2007 that indicates that income before taxes was $10,000. Lunn must pay tax at the rate of 40% and must remit the tax to the Internal Revenue Service by April 15, 2008.

f. As of December 31, 2007, Lunn owes to employees salaries of $3,000 for work performed in 2007. The employees will be paid on the first payday of 2008.

g. During 2007 two lawsuits were filed against Lunn. In the first lawsuit, a customer sued for damages because of an injury that occurred on Lunn's premises. Lunn's legal counsel advised that it is probable that the lawsuit will be settled in 2008 at an amount of $7,000. The second lawsuit involves a patent infringement suit of $14,000 filed against Lunn by a competitor. The legal counsel has advised that there is some possibility that Lunn may be at fault but that a loss does not appear probable at this time.

Part B

a. What amount will be accumulated by January 1, 2011, if $5,000 is invested on January 1, 2007, at 10% interest compounded semiannually?

b. Assume that we are to receive $5,000 on January 1, 2011. What amount at January 1, 2007, is equivalent to the $5,000 that is to be received in 2011? Assume that interest is compounded annually at 10%.

c. What amount will be accumulated by January 1, 2011, if $5,000 is invested each semiannual period for eight periods beginning with June 30, 2007, and ending December 31, 2010? Interest will accumulate at 10% compounded semiannually.

d. Assume that we are to receive $5,000 each semiannual period for eight periods beginning on June 30, 2007. What amount at January 1, 2011, is equivalent to the future series of payments? Assume that interest will accrue at 10% compounded semiannually.

e. Assume that a new bank has begun a promotional campaign to attract savings accounts. The bank advertisement indicates that customers who invest $1,000 will double their money in 10 years. Assuming annual compounding of interest, what rate of interest is the bank offering?

Required

1. Consider all items in Part A. Develop the Current Liabilities section of Lunn's balance sheet as of December 31, 2007. To make investment decisions about this company, what additional data would you need? You do not need to consider the notes that accompany the balance sheet.

2. Answer the five questions in Part B.

SOLUTION TO REVIEW PROBLEM PART A

The accountant's decisions for items (a) through (g) of Part A should be as follows:

a. The balance of the Accounts Payable account should be $60,000. The payables should be reported at the gross amount, and discounts would not be reported until the time of payment.

b. The note payable to Philips Bank of $10,000 should be included as a current liability. Also, interest payable of $900 ($10,000 × 12% × 9/12) should be considered a current liability.

c. The note payable to Dove Bank should be considered a current liability and listed at $8,000 minus the contra account Discount on Note Payable of $600 ($8,000 × 10% × 9/12 remaining).

d. The debt to Owens Bank should be split between current liability and long-term liability with the current portion shown as $2,000. Also, interest payable of $1,600 ($20,000 × 8% × 1 year) should be considered a current liability.

e. Income taxes payable of $4,000 ($10,000 × 40%) is a current liability.

f. Salaries payable of $3,000 represent a current liability.

g. The lawsuit involving the customer must be reported as a current liability of $7,000 because the possibility of loss is probable. The second lawsuit should not be reported but should be disclosed as a note to the balance sheet.

Lunn Express
Partial Balance Sheet
As of December 31, 2007

Current Liabilities		
Accounts payable		$60,000
Interest payable ($900 + $1,600)		2,500
Salaries payable		3,000
Taxes payable		4,000
Note payable to Philips Bank		10,000
Note payable to Dove Bank	$8,000	
Less: Discount on note payable	(600)	7,400
Current maturity of long-term debt		2,000
Contingent liability for pending lawsuit		7,000
Total Current Liabilities		**$95,900**

Other data necessary to make an investment decision might include current assets and total assets as of December 31, 2007. If current assets are significantly larger than current liabilities, you can be comfortable that the company is capable of paying its short-term debt. The dollar amount of current assets and liabilities must be evaluated with regard to the size of the company. The larger the company, the less significant $95,900 in current liabilities would be.

SOLUTION TO PART B

a.

ENTER	DISPLAY
8 N	N = 8
5 I/Y	I/Y = 5
0 PMT	PMT = 0
5000 PV	PV = 5,000
CPT FV	FV = 7,387

a. $FV = \$5,000$(table factor)   using Table 9-1
   $= \$5,000(1.477)$ where $i = 5\%$, $n = 8$
   $= \$7,385$

b.

ENTER	DISPLAY
4 N	N = 4
10 I/Y	I/Y = 10
0 PMT	PMT = 0
5000 FV	FV = 5,000
CPT PV	PV = 3,415

b. $PV = \$5,000$(table factor)   using Table 9-2
   $= \$5,000(0.683)$ where $i = 10\%$, $n = 4$
   $= \$3,415$

(continued)

REVIEW

c. *FV* annuity = $5,000(table factor)   using Table 9-3
       = $5,000(9.549)   where $i = 5\%$, $n = 8$
       = $47,745

c.

ENTER	DISPLAY
8 N	N = 8
5 I/Y	I/Y = 5
5000 PMT	PMT = 5,000
0 PV	PV = 0
CPT FV	FV = 47,746

d. *PV* annuity = $5,000(table factor)   using Table 9-4
       = $5,000(6.463)   where $i = 5\%$, $n = 8$
       = $32,315

d.

ENTER	DISPLAY
8 N	N = 8
5 I/Y	I/Y = 5
5000 PMT	PMT = 5,000
0 PV	FV = 0
CPT FV	PV = 32,316

e.   *FV* = $1,000(table factor)   using Table 9-1

Because the future value is known to be $2,000, the formula can be written as

     $2,000 = $1,000(table factor)

and rearranged as

Table factor = $2,000/$1,000 = 2.0.

In Table 9-1, the table factor of 2.0 and 10 years corresponds with an interest rate of between 7% and 8%.

e.

ENTER	DISPLAY
10 N	N = 10
0 PMT	PMT = 0
1000 PV +/−	PV = −1,000
2000 FV	FV = 2,000
CPT I/Y	I/Y = 7.177

(*Note:* In this case, the present value must be entered as a negative amount.)

QUESTIONS

1. What is the definition of *current liabilities*? Why is it important to distinguish between current and long-term liabilities?

2. Most firms attempt to pay their accounts payable within the discount period to take advantage of the discount. Why is that normally a sound financial move?

3. Assume that your local bank gives you a $1,000 loan at 10% per year but deducts the interest in advance. Is 10% the "real" rate of interest that you will pay? How could the true interest rate be calculated?

4. Is the account Discount on Notes Payable an income statement or balance sheet account?

5. A firm's year ends on December 31. Its tax is computed and submitted to the U.S. Treasury on March 15 of the following year. When should the taxes be reported as a liability?

6. What is a contingent liability? Why are contingent liabilities accounted for differently than contingent assets?

7. Many firms believe that it is very difficult to estimate the amount of a possible future contingency. Should a contingent liability be reported even if the dollar amount of the loss is not known? Should it be disclosed in the notes to financial statements?

8. Assume that a lawsuit has been filed against your firm. Your legal counsel has assured you that a loss is not probable. How should the lawsuit be disclosed on the financial statements?

9. What is the difference between simple interest and compound interest? Would the amount of interest be higher or lower if the interest is simple rather than compound?

10. What is the effect if interest is compounded quarterly versus annually?

11. What is the meaning of the terms *present value* and *future value*? How can you determine whether to calculate the present value of an amount or the future value?

12. What is the meaning of the word *annuity*? Could the present value of an annuity be calculated as a series of single amounts? If so, how?

13. Assume that you know the total dollar amount of a loan and the amount of the monthly payments. How could you determine the interest rate as a percentage of the loan?

14. The present value and future value concepts are applied to measure the amount of several accounts common in accounting. What are some accounts that are valued in this manner?

HOMEWORK

15. Your employer withholds federal income tax from your paycheck and remits it to the U.S. Treasury. How is the federal tax treated on the employer's financial statements? (Appendix A)

16. Unemployment tax is a tax on the employer rather than on the employee. How should unemployment taxes be treated on the employer's financial statements? (Appendix A)

17. What is the meaning of the term *compensated absences*? Give some examples. (Appendix A)

18. Do you agree or disagree with the following statement: "Vacation pay should be reported as an expense when the employee takes the vacation"? (Appendix A)

EXERCISES

LO1 **Exercise 9-1** Current Liabilities

The items listed below are accounts on Smith's balance sheet of December 31, 2007.

Taxes Payable
Accounts Receivable
Notes Payable, 9%, due in 90 days
Investment in Bonds
Capital Stock
Accounts Payable
Estimated Warranty Payable in 2008
Retained Earnings
Trademark
Mortgage Payable ($10,000 due every year until 2024)

Required

Identify which of the above accounts should be classified as a current liability on Smith's balance sheet. For each item that is not a current liability, indicate the category of the balance sheet in which it would be classified.

LO1 **Exercise 9-2** Current Liabilities

The following items all represent liabilities on a firm's balance sheet.

a. An amount of money owed to a supplier based on the terms 2/20, n/40, for which *no* note was executed.
b. An amount of money owed to a creditor on a note due April 30, 2008.
c. An amount of money owed to a creditor on a note due August 15, 2009.
d. An amount of money owed to employees for work performed during the last week in December.
e. An amount of money owed to a bank for the use of borrowed funds due on March 1, 2008.
f. An amount of money owed to a creditor as an annual installment payment on a 10-year note.
g. An amount of money owed to the federal government, based on the company's annual income.

Required

1. For each lettered item, state whether it should be classified as a current liability on the December 31, 2007, balance sheet. Assume that the operating cycle is shorter than one year. If the item should not be classified as a current liability, indicate where on the balance sheet it should be presented.
2. For each item identified as a current liability in part (1), state the account title that is normally used to report the item on the balance sheet.
3. Why would an investor or creditor be interested in whether an item is a current or a long-term liability?

LO1 **Exercise 9-3** Current Liabilities Section

Jackie Company had the following accounts and balances on December 31, 2007:

Income Taxes Payable	$61,250	Notes Payable, 10%, due June 2, 2008	$ 1,000
Allowance for Doubtful Accounts	17,800	Accounts Receivable	67,500
Accounts Payable	24,400	Discount on Notes Payable	150
Interest Receivable	5,000	Current Maturities of Long-Term Debt	6,900
Unearned Revenue	4,320	Interest Payable	3,010
Wages Payable	6,000		

Required

Prepare the current liabilities section of Jackie Company's balance sheet as of December 31, 2007.

LO2   **Exercise 9-4** Transaction Analysis

Polly's Cards & Gifts Shop had the following transactions during the year:

a. Polly's purchased inventory on account from a supplier for $8,000. Assume that Polly's uses a periodic inventory system.
b. On May 1, land was purchased for $44,500. A 20% down payment was made, and an 18-month, 8% note was signed for the remainder.
c. Polly's returned $450 worth of inventory purchased in item (a), which was found broken when the inventory was received.
d. Polly's paid the balance due on the purchase of inventory.
e. On June 1, Polly signed a one-year, $15,000 note to First State Bank and received $13,800.
f. Polly's sold 200 gift certificates for $25 each for cash. Sales of gift certificates are recorded as a liability. At year-end, 35% of the gift certificates had been redeemed.
g. Sales for the year were $120,000, of which 90% were for cash. State sales tax of 6% applied to all sales and must be remitted to the state by January 31.

Required

1. Determine the effect on the accounting equation of items (a) through (g).
2. Assume that Polly's accounting year ends on December 31. Determine the effect on the accounting equation of any year-end adjustments.
3. What is the total of the current liabilities at the end of the year?

LO2   **Exercise 9-5** Current Liabilities and Ratios

Listed below are several accounts that appeared on Kruse's 2007 balance sheet.

Accounts Payable	$ 55,000	Equipment	$950,000
Marketable Securities	40,000	Taxes Payable	15,000
Accounts Receivable	180,000	Retained Earnings	250,000
Notes Payable, 12%, due in 60 days	20,000	Inventory	85,000
Capital Stock	1,150,000	Allowance for Doubtful Accounts	20,000
Salaries Payable	10,000	Land	600,000
Cash	15,000		

Required

1. Prepare the current liabilities section of Kruse's 2007 balance sheet.
2. Compute Kruse's working capital.
3. Compute Kruse's current ratio. What does this ratio indicate about Kruse's condition?

LO2   **Exercise 9-6** Discounts

Each of the following situations involves the use of discounts.

1. How much discount may Seals Inc. take in each of the following transactions? What was the annualized interest rate?
   a. Seals purchases inventory costing $450, 2/10, n/40.
   b. Seals purchases new office furniture costing $1,500, terms 1/10, n/30.
2. Calculate the discount rate Croft Co. received in each of these transactions.
   a. Croft purchased office supplies costing $200 and paid within the discount period with a check for $196.
   b. Croft purchased merchandise for $2,800. It paid within the discount period with a check for $2,674.

LO2 **Exercise 9-7** Notes Payable and Interest

On July 1, 2007, Jo's Flower Shop borrowed $25,000 from the bank. Jo signed a 10-month, 8% promissory note for the entire amount. Jo's uses a calendar year-end.

Required
1. Determine the effect on the accounting equation of the issuance of the promissory note on July 1.
2. Determine the effect on the accounting equation of any year-end adjustments.
3. Determine the effect on the accounting equation of the payment of principal and interest on July 1.

LO2 **Exercise 9-8** Non-Interest-Bearing Notes Payable

On October 1, 2007, Ratkowski Inc. borrowed $18,000 from Second National Bank by issuing a 12-month note. The bank discounted the note at 9%.

Required
1. Determine the effect on the accounting equation of the issuance of the note.
2. What is the effect of the accrual of interest on December 31?
3. What is the effect of the payment of the note on October 1, 2008?
4. What effective rate of interest did Ratkowski pay?

LO3 **Exercise 9-9** Impact of Transactions Involving Current Liabilities on Statement of Cash Flows

From the following list, identify whether the change in the account balance during the year would be reported as an operating (O), investing (I), or financing (F) activity, or not separately reported on the statement of cash flows (N). Assume that the indirect method is used to determine the cash flows from operating activities.

_____ Accounts payable

_____ Current maturities of long-term debt

_____ Notes payable

_____ Other accrued liabilities

_____ Salaries and wages payable

_____ Taxes payable

LO3 **Exercise 9-10** Impact of Transactions Involving Contingent Liabilities on Statement of Cash Flows

From the following list, identify whether the change in the account balance during the year would be reported as an operating (O), investing (I), or financing (F) activity, or not separately reported on the statement of cash flows (N). Assume that the indirect method is used to determine the cash flows from operating activities.

_____ Estimated liability for warranties

_____ Estimated liability for product premiums

_____ Estimated liability for probable loss relating to litigation

LO3 **Exercise 9-11** Impact of Transactions Involving Payroll Liabilities on Statement of Cash Flows (Appendix A)

From the following list, identify whether the change in the account balance during the year would be reported as an operating (O), investing (I), or financing (F) activity, or not separately reported on the statement of cash flows (N). Assume that the indirect method is used to determine the cash flows from operating activities.

_____ Accrued vacation days (compensated absences)

_____ Health insurance premiums payable

_____ FICA payable

_____ Union dues payable

_____ Salary payable

_____ Unemployment taxes payable

LO4

Exercise 9-12 Warranties

Clean Corporation manufactures and sells dishwashers. Clean provides all customers with a two-year warranty guaranteeing to repair, free of charge, any defects reported during this time period. During the year, it sold 100,000 dishwashers, for $325 each. Analysis of past warranty records indicates that 12% of all sales will be returned for repair within the warranty period. Clean expects to incur expenditures of $14 to repair each dishwasher. The account Estimated Liability for Warranties had a balance of $120,000 on January 1. Clean incurred $150,000 in actual expenditures during the year.

Required

Determine the effect on the accounting equation of the events related to the warranty transactions during the year. Determine the adjusted ending balance in the Estimated Liability for Warranties account.

LO5

Exercise 9-13 Simple Versus Compound Interest

Part 1. For each of the following notes, calculate the simple interest due at the end of the term.

Note	Face Value (Principal)	Rate	Term
1	$20,000	4%	6 years
2	20,000	6%	4 years
3	20,000	8%	3 years

Part 2. Now assume that the interest on the notes is compounded annually. Calculate the amount of interest due at the end of the term for each note.

Part 3. Now assume that the interest on the notes is compounded semiannually. Calculate the amount of interest due at the end of the term for each note.

What conclusion can you draw from a comparison of your results in parts (1), (2), and (3)?

LO6

Exercise 9-14 Present Value, Future Value

Brian Inc. estimates it will need $150,000 in 10 years to expand its manufacturing facilities. A bank has agreed to pay Brian 5% interest, compounded annually, if the company deposits the entire amount now needed to accumulate $150,000 in 10 years. How much money does Brian need to deposit now?

LO6

Exercise 9-15 Effect of Compounding Period

Kern Company deposited $1,000 in the bank on January 1, 2007, earning 8% interest. Kern Company withdraws the deposit plus accumulated interest on January 1, 2009. Compute the amount of money Kern withdraws from the bank, assuming that interest is compounded (a) annually, (b) semiannually, and (c) quarterly.

LO6

Exercise 9-16 Present Value, Future Value

The following situations involve time value of money calculations:

1. A deposit of $7,000 is made on January 1, 2007. The deposit will earn interest at a rate of 8%. How much will be accumulated on January 1, 2012, assuming that interest is compounded (a) annually, (b) semiannually, and (c) quarterly?
2. A deposit is made on January 1, 2007, to earn interest at an annual rate of 8%. The deposit will accumulate to $15,000 by January 1, 2012. How much money was originally deposited, assuming that interest is compounded (a) annually, (b) semiannually, and (c) quarterly?

LO6

Exercise 9-17 Present Value, Future Value

The following are situations requiring the application of the time value of money:

1. On January 1, 2007, $16,000 is deposited. Assuming an 8% interest rate, calculate the amount accumulated on January 1, 2012, if interest is compounded (a) annually, (b) semiannually, and (c) quarterly.
2. Assume that a deposit made on January 1, 2007, earns 8% interest. The deposit plus interest accumulated to $20,000 on January 1, 2012. How much was invested on January 1, 2007, if interest was compounded (a) annually, (b) semiannually, and (c) quarterly?

HOMEWORK

LO7   **Exercise 9-18** Annuity

Steve Jones has decided to start saving for his son's college education by depositing $2,000 at the end of every year for 15 years. A bank has agreed to pay interest at the rate of 4% compounded annually. How much will Steve have in the bank immediately after his 15th deposit?

LO7   **Exercise 9-19** Calculation of Years

Kelly Seaver has decided to start saving for her daughter's college education. She wants to accumulate $41,000. The bank will pay interest at the rate of 4% compounded annually. If Kelly plans to make payments of $1,600 at the end of each year, how long will it take her to accumulate $41,000?

LO7   **Exercise 9-20** Value of Payments

On graduation from college, Susana Lopez signed an agreement to buy a used car. Her annual payments, due at the end of each year for two years, are $1,480. The car dealer used a 12% rate compounded annually to determine the amount of the payments.

Required
1. What should Susana consider the value of the car to be?
2. If she had wanted to make quarterly payments, what would her payments have been, based on the value of the car as determined in part (1)? How much less interest would she have had to pay if she had been making quarterly payments instead of annual payments? What do you think would have happened to the payment amount and the interest if she had asked for monthly payments?

LO8   **Exercise 9-21** Payroll Transactions (Appendix A)

During the month of January, VanderSalm Company's employees earned $385,000. The following rates apply to VanderSalm's gross payroll:

Federal Income Tax Rate	28%
State Income Tax Rate	5%
FICA Tax Rate	7.65%
Federal Unemployment Tax Rate	0.8%
State Unemployment Tax Rate	3.2%

In addition, employee deductions were $7,000 for health insurance and $980 for union dues.

Required
1. Calculate the withholdings and net pay for wages for the company. You may assume the FICA tax applies to all employees.
2. Calculate the employer's portion of payroll taxes for January.
3. If the company paid fringe benefits, such as employees' health insurance coverage, how would these contributions affect the payroll entries?

LO8   **Exercise 9-22** Payroll, Employer's Portion (Appendix A)

Tasty Bakery Shop has six employees on its payroll. Payroll records include the following information on employee earnings for each employee:

Name	Earnings from 1/1 to 6/30/2007	Earnings for 3rd Quarter 2007
Dell	$ 23,490	$11,710
Fin	4,240	2,660
Hook	34,100	15,660
Patty	38,400	26,200
Tuss	30,050	19,350
Woo	6,300	3,900
Totals	$136,580	$79,480

FICA taxes are levied at 7.65% on the first $94,200 of each employee's current year's earnings. The unemployment tax rates are 0.8% for federal and 2.6% for state unemployment.

Assume that unemployment taxes are levied on the first $7,000 of each employee's current year's earnings.

Required

1. Calculate the employer's portion of payroll taxes incurred by Tasty Bakery for each employee for the third quarter of 2007. Round your answers to the nearest dollar.
2. Determine the effect on the accounting equation of the employer's portion of payroll taxes.

LO9   **Exercise 9-23** Compensated Absences (Appendix A)

Wonder Inc. has a monthly payroll of $72,000 for its 24 employees. In addition to their salary, employees earn one day of vacation and one sick day for each month that they work. There are 20 workdays in a month.

Required

1. Determine the effect on the accounting equation, if any, of recording (a) vacation benefits and (b) sick days.
2. From the owner's perspective, should the company offer the employees vacation and sick pay that accumulates year to year?

MULTI-CONCEPT EXERCISES

LO6,7   **Exercise 9-24** Compare Alternatives

Jane Bauer has won the lottery and has four options for receiving her winnings:

1. Receive $100,000 at the beginning of the current year
2. Receive $108,000 at the end of the year
3. Receive $20,000 at the end of each year for 8 years
4. Receive $10,000 at the end of each year for 30 years

Jane can invest her winnings at an interest rate of 8% compounded annually at a major bank. Which of the payment options should Jane choose?

LO6,7   **Exercise 9-25** Two Situations

The following situations involve the application of the time value of money concepts:

1. Sampson Company just purchased a piece of equipment with a value of $53,300. Sampson financed this purchase with a loan from the bank and must make annual loan payments of $13,000 at the end of each year for the next five years. Interest is compounded annually on the loan. What is the interest rate on the bank loan?
2. Simon Company needs to accumulate $200,000 to repay bonds due in six years. Simon estimates it can save $13,300 at the end of each semiannual period at a local bank offering an annual interest rate of 8% compounded semiannually. Will Simon have enough money saved at the end of six years to repay the bonds?

PROBLEMS

LO2   **Problem 9-1** Notes and Interest

Glencoe Inc. operates with a June 30 year-end. During 2007, the following transactions occurred:

a. January 1: Signed a one-year, 10% loan for $25,000. Interest and principal are to be paid at maturity.
b. January 10: Signed a line of credit with the Little Local Bank to establish a $400,000 line of credit. Interest of 9% will be charged on all borrowed funds.
c. February 1: Issued a $20,000 non-interest-bearing, six-month note to pay for a new machine. Interest on the note, at 12%, was deducted in advance.
d. March 1: Borrowed $150,000 on the line of credit.

e. June 1: Repaid $100,000 on the line of credit, plus accrued interest.

f. June 30: Made all necessary adjusting entries.

g. August 1: Repaid the non-interest-bearing note.

h. September 1: Borrowed $200,000 on the line of credit.

i. November 1: Issued a three-month, 8%, $12,000 note in payment of an overdue open account.

j. December 31: Repaid the one-year loan [from item (a)] plus accrued interest.

Required

1. Determine the effect on the accounting equation of items (a) through (j).

2. As of December 31, which notes are outstanding, and how much interest is due on each?

LO3   **Problem 9-2** Effects of Sara Lee's Current Liabilities on Its Statement of Cash Flows

The following items are classified as current liabilities on **Sara Lee Corporation**'s consolidated balance sheet at July 3, 2004, and June 28, 2003 (in millions):

	2004	2003
Notes payable	$ 54	$ 75
Accounts payable	1,325	1,346
Accrued liabilities:		
Payroll and employee benefits	1,162	1,195
Advertising and promotions	540	440
Taxes other than payroll and income	123	112
Income taxes	257	11
Other	892	945
Current maturities of long-term debt	1,070	1,004

Required

1. Sara Lee uses the indirect method to prepare its statement of cash flows. Prepare the Operating Activities section of the cash flow statement, which indicates how each item will be reflected as an adjustment to net income. If you did not include any of the items set forth above, explain why not.

2. How would you decide if Sara Lee has the ability to pay these liabilities as they become due?

LO3   **Problem 9-3** Effects of Tommy Hilfiger's Changes in Current Assets and Liabilities on Statement of Cash Flows

The following items, listed in alphabetical order, are included in the Current Assets and Current Liabilities categories on the consolidated balance sheet of **Tommy Hilfiger Corporation** at March 31, 2004 and 2003 (in thousands):

	2004	2003
Accounts payable	$ 32,718	$ 47,753
Accounts receivable	188,514	185,309
Accrued expenses and other liabilities	207,190	185,923
Short-term borrowings	-0-	19,380
Inventories	206,302	229,654
Other current assets	36,342	28,183

Required

1. Tommy Hilfiger uses the indirect method to prepare its statement of cash flows. Prepare the Operating Activities section of the cash flow statement, which indicates how each item will be reflected as an adjustment to net income.

2. If you did not include any of the items set forth above in your answer to part (1), explain how these items would be reported on the statement of cash flows.

LO4   **Problem 9-4** Warranties

Clearview Company manufactures and sells high-quality television sets. The most popular line sells for $1,000 each and is accompanied by a three-year warranty to repair, free of charge, any defective unit. Average costs to repair each defective unit will be $90 for replacement parts and $60 for labor. Clearview estimates that warranty costs of $12,600 will be incurred during 2007. The company actually sold 600 television sets and incurred replacement part costs of $3,600 and labor costs of $5,400 during the year. The adjusted 2007 ending balance in the Estimated Liability for Warranties account is $10,200.

Required
1. How many defective units from this year's sales does Clearview Company estimate will be returned for repair?
2. What percentage of sales does Clearview Company estimate will be returned for repair?
3. What steps should Clearview take if actual warranty costs incurred during 2008 are significantly higher than the estimated liability recorded at the end of 2007?

LO4   **Problem 9-5** Warranties

Bombeck Company sells a product for $1,500. When the customer buys it, Bombeck provides a one-year warranty. Bombeck sold 120 products during 2007. Based on analysis of past warranty records, Bombeck estimates that repairs will average 3% of total sales.

Required
1. Determine the effect on the accounting equation of the estimated liability.
2. Assume that products under warranty must be repaired during 2007 using repair parts from inventory costing $4,950. What is the effect of the entry to record the repair of products?

LO5   **Problem 9-6** Comparison of Simple and Compound Interest

On June 30, 2007, Rolf Inc. borrowed $25,000 from its bank, signing an 8%, two-year note.

Required
1. Assuming that the bank charges simple interest on the note, determine the effect on the accounting equation on each of the following dates:

   December 31, 2007
   December 31, 2008
   June 30, 2009

2. Assume instead that the bank charges 8% on the note, which is compounded semi-annually. Determine the effect on the accounting equation on the dates in part (1).
3. How much additional interest expense will Rolf have in part (2) than in part (1)?

LO6   **Problem 9-7** Investment with Varying Interest Rate

Shari Thompson invested $1,000 in a financial institution on January 1, 2007. She leaves her investment in the institution until December 31, 2011. How much money does Shari accumulate if she earned interest, compounded annually, at the following rates?

2007	4%
2008	5
2009	6
2010	7
2011	8

LO6   **Problem 9-8** Comparison of Alternatives

On January 1, 2007, Chen Yu's Office Supply Store plans to remodel the store and install new display cases. Chen has the following options of payment. Chen's interest rate is 8%.

a. Pay $180,000 on January 1, 2007.
b. Pay $196,200 on January 1, 2008.
c. Pay $220,500 on January 1, 2009.
d. Make four annual payments of $55,000 beginning on December 31, 2007.

Required
Which option should he choose? (*Hint:* Calculate the present value of each option as of January 1, 2007.)

LO8   **Problem 9-9** Payroll Transactions (Appendix A)

Vivian Company has calculated the gross wages of all employees for the month of August to be $210,000. The following amounts have been withheld from the employees' paychecks:

HOMEWORK

Income Tax	$42,500
FICA	16,000
Heart Fund Contributions	5,800
Union Dues	3,150

Vivian's unemployment tax rate is 3%, and its portion of FICA matches the employees' share.

Required

1. Determine the effect on the accounting equation of accruing the amount payable to employees.
2. Determine the effect on the accounting equation when the employees are paid.
3. Determine the effect on the accounting equation of recording the employer's payroll costs.
4. Determine the effect on the accounting equation when the withholdings were remitted.

LO9

Problem 9-10 Compensated Absences (Appendix A)

Hetzel Inc. pays its employees every Friday. For every four weeks that employees work, they earn one vacation day. For every six weeks that they work without calling in sick, they earn one sick day. If employees quit or retire, they can receive a lump-sum payment for their unused vacation days and unused sick days.

Required

Write a short memo to the bookkeeper to explain how and when he should report vacation and sick days. Explain how the matching principle applies and why you believe that the timing you recommend is appropriate.

MULTI-CONCEPT PROBLEMS

LO2,5

Problem 9-11 Interest in Advance versus Interest Paid When Loan Is Due

On July 1, 2007, Leach Company needs exactly $103,200 in cash to pay an existing obligation. Leach has decided to borrow from State Bank, which charges 14% interest on loans. The loan will be due in one year. Leach is unsure, however, whether to ask the bank for (a) an interest-bearing loan with interest and principal payable at the end of the year or (b) a loan due in one year but with interest deducted in advance.

Required

1. What will be the face value of the note assuming that
   a. interest is paid when the loan is due?
   b. interest is deducted in advance?
2. Calculate the effective interest rate on the note assuming that
   a. interest is paid when the loan is due.
   b. interest is deducted in advance.
3. Assume that Leach negotiates and signs the one-year note with the bank on July 1, 2007. Also assume that Leach's accounting year ends December 31. Determine the effect on the accounting equation of the issuance of the note and the interest on the note, assuming that
   a. interest is paid when the loan is due.
   b. interest is deducted in advance.
4. Prepare the appropriate balance sheet presentation for July 1, 2007, immediately after the note has been issued, assuming that
   a. interest is paid when the loan is due.
   b. interest is deducted in advance.

LO1,4

Problem 9-12 Contingent Liabilities

Listed below are several items for which the outcome of events is unknown at year-end.

a. A company offers a two-year warranty on sales of new computers. It believes that 4% of the computers will require repairs.
b. The company is involved in a trademark infringement suit. The company's legal experts believe an award of $500,000 in the company's favor will be made.
c. A company is involved in an environmental clean-up lawsuit. The company's legal counsel believes it is possible the outcome will be unfavorable but has not been able to estimate the costs of the possible loss.

d. A soap manufacturer has included a coupon offer in the Sunday newspaper supplements. The manufacturer estimates that 25% of the 50-cent coupons will be redeemed.

e. A company has been sued by the federal government for price fixing. The company's legal counsel believes there will be an unfavorable verdict and has made an estimate of the probable loss.

Required

1. Identify which of the items (a) through (e) should be recorded at year-end.
2. Identify which of the items (a) through (e) should not be recorded but should be disclosed in the year-end financial statements.

LO6,7   **Problem 9-13** Time Value of Money Concepts

The following situations involve the application of the time value of money concept.

1. Janelle Carter deposited $9,750 in the bank on January 1, 1990, at an interest rate of 11% compounded annually. How much has accumulated in the account by January 1, 2007?
2. Mike Smith deposited $21,600 in the bank on January 1, 1997. On January 2, 2007, this deposit has accumulated to $42,487. Interest is compounded annually on the account. What is the rate of interest that Mike earned on the deposit?
3. Lee Spony made a deposit in the bank on January 1, 2000. The bank pays interest at the rate of 8% compounded annually. On January 1, 2007, the deposit has accumulated to $15,000. How much money did Lee originally deposit on January 1, 2000?
4. Nancy Holmes deposited $5,800 in the bank on January 1 a few years ago. The bank pays an interest rate of 10% compounded annually, and the deposit is now worth $15,026. How many years has the deposit been invested?

LO6,7   **Problem 9-14** Comparison of Alternatives

Brian Imhoff's grandparents want to give him some money when he graduates from high school. They have offered Brian three choices:

a. Receive $15,000 immediately. Assume that interest is compounded annually.
b. Receive $2,250 at the end of each six months for four years. The first check will be received in six months.
c. Receive $4,350 at the end of each year for four years. Assume interest is compounded annually.

Required

Brian wants to have money for a new car when he graduates from college in four years. Assuming an interest rate of 8%, what option should he choose to have the most money in four years?

ALTERNATE PROBLEMS

LO2   **Problem 9-1A** Notes and Interest

McLaughlin Inc. operates with a June 30 year-end. During 2007, the following transactions occurred:

a. January 1: Signed a one-year, 10% loan for $35,000. Interest and principal are to be paid at maturity.
b. January 10: Signed a line of credit with the Little Local Bank to establish a $560,000 line of credit. Interest of 9% will be charged on all borrowed funds.
c. February 1: Issued a $28,000 non-interest-bearing, six-month note to pay for a new machine. Interest on the note, at 12%, was deducted in advance.
d. March 1: Borrowed $210,000 on the line of credit.
e. June 1: Repaid $140,000 on the line of credit, plus accrued interest.
f. June 30: Made all necessary adjustments.
g. August 1: Repaid the non-interest-bearing note.
h. September 1: Borrowed $280,000 on the line of credit.
i. November 1: Issued a three-month, 8%, $16,800 note in payment of an overdue open account.
j. December 31: Repaid the one-year loan [from item (a)] plus accrued interest.

Required

1. Determine the effect on the accounting equation of items (a) through (g).
2. As of December 31, which notes are outstanding, and how much interest is due on each?

LO3

Problem 9-2A Effects of Boeing's Current Liabilities on Its Statement of Cash Flows

The following items are classified as current liabilities on **Boeing Company**'s consolidated statements of financial condition (or balance sheet) at December 31 (in millions):

	2004	2003
Accounts payable and other liabilities	$14,869	$13,514
Advances in excess of related costs	4,123	3,464
Income taxes payable	522	277
Short-term debt and current portion of long-term debt	1,321	1,144

Required

1. Boeing uses the indirect method to prepare its statement of cash flows. Prepare the Operating Activities section of the cash flow statement, which indicates how each item will be reflected as an adjustment to net income. If you did not include any of the items set forth above, explain why not.
2. How would you decide if Boeing has the ability to pay these liabilities as they become due?

LO3

Problem 9-3A Effects of Nike's Changes in Current Assets and Liabilities on Its Statement of Cash Flows

The following items, listed in alphabetical order, are included in the Current Assets and Current Liabilities categories on the consolidated balance sheet of **Nike Inc.** at May 31, 2004 and 2003 (in millions):

	2004	2003
Accounts payable	$ 763.8	$ 572.7
Accounts receivable	2,120.2	2,083.9
Accrued liabilities	974.4	1,036.2
Current portion of long-term debt	6.6	205.7
Income taxes payable	118.2	130.6
Inventories	1,633.6	1,514.9
Notes payable	146.0	75.4
Prepaid expenses and other current assets	364.4	332.5

Required

1. Nike uses the indirect method to prepare its statement of cash flows. Prepare the Operating Activities section of the cash flow statement, which indicates how each item will be reflected as an adjustment to net income.
2. If you did not include any of the items set forth above in your answer to part (1), explain how these items would be reported on the statement of cash flows.

LO4

Problem 9-4A Warranties

Sound Company manufactures and sells high-quality stereo sets. The most popular line sells for $2,000 each and is accompanied by a three-year warranty to repair, free of charge, any defective unit. Average costs to repair each defective unit will be $180 for replacement parts and $120 for labor. Sound estimates that warranty costs of $25,200 will be incurred during 2007. The company actually sold 600 sets and incurred replacement part costs of $7,200 and labor costs of $10,800 during the year. The adjusted 2007 ending balance in the Estimated Liability for Warranties account is $20,400.

Required

1. How many defective units from this year's sales does Sound Company estimate will be returned for repair?
2. What percent of sales does Sound Company estimate will be returned for repair?

LO4 **Problem 9-5A** Warranties

Beck Company sells a product for $3,200. When the customer buys it, Beck provides a one-year warranty. Beck sold 120 products during 2007. Based on analysis of past warranty records, Beck estimates that repairs will average 4% of total sales.

Required
1. Determine the effect on the accounting equation of the estimated liability.
2. Assume that during 2007, products under warranty must be repaired using repair parts from inventory costing $10,200. Determine the effect on the accounting equation of the repair of products.
3. Assume that the balance of the Estimated Liabilities for Warranties account as of the beginning of 2007 was $1,100. Calculate the balance of the account as of the end of 2007.

LO5 **Problem 9-6A** Comparison of Simple and Compound Interest

On June 30, 2007, Rolloff Inc. borrowed $25,000 from its bank, signing a 6% note. Principal and interest are due at the end of two years.

Required
1. Assuming that the note earns simple interest for the bank, calculate the amount of interest accrued on each of the following dates:

   December 31, 2007
   December 31, 2008
   June 30, 2009

2. Assume instead that the note earns 6% for the bank but is compounded semiannually. Calculate the amount of interest accrued on the same dates as in part (1).
3. How much additional interest expense will Rolloff have to pay with semiannual interest?

LO6 **Problem 9-7A** Investment with Varying Interest Rate

Trena Thompson invested $2,000 in a financial institution on January 1, 2007. She leaves her investment in the institution until December 31, 2011. How much money does Trena accumulate if she earned interest, compounded annually, at the following rates?

2007	4%
2008	5
2009	6
2010	7
2011	8

LO6 **Problem 9-8A** Comparison of Alternatives

On January 1, 2007, Chen Yu's Office Supply Store plans to remodel the store and install new display cases. Chen has the following options of payment. Chen's interest rate is 8%.

a. Pay $270,000 on January 1, 2007.
b. Pay $294,300 on January 1, 2008.
c. Pay $334,750 on January 1, 2009.
d. Make four annual payments of $82,500 beginning on December 31, 2007.

Required
Which option should he choose? (*Hint:* Calculate the present value of each option as of January 1, 2007.)

LO8 **Problem 9-9A** Payroll Transactions (Appendix A)

Calvin Company has calculated the gross wages of all employees for the month of August to be $336,000. The following amounts have been withheld from the employees' paychecks:

Income Tax	$68,000
FICA	25,600
Heart Fund Contributions	9,280
Union Dues	5,040

Calvin's unemployment tax rate is 3%, and its portion of FICA matches the employees' share.

HOMEWORK

Required
1. Determine the effect on the accounting equation of accruing the amount payable to employees.
2. Determine the effect on the accounting equation when the employees are paid.
3. Determine the effect on the accounting equation of recording the employer's payroll costs.
4. Determine the effect on the accounting equation when the withholdings were remitted.

LO9   **Problem 9-10A** Compensated Absences (Appendix A)

Assume that you are the accountant for a large company with several divisions. The manager of Division B has contacted you with a concern. During 2007, several employees retired from Division B. the company's policy is that employees can be paid for days of sick leave accrued at the time they retire. Payment occurs in the year following retirement. The manager has been told by corporate headquarters that she cannot replace the employees in 2008 because the payment of the accrued sick pay will be deducted from Division B's budget in that year.

Required
In a memo to the manager of Division B, explain the proper accounting for accrued sick pay. Do you think that the policies of corporate headquarters should be revised?

ALTERNATE MULTI-CONCEPT PROBLEMS

LO2,5   **Problem 9-11A** Interest in Advance versus Interest Paid When Loan Is Due

On July 1, 2007, Moton Company needs exactly $206,400 in cash to pay an existing obligation. Moton has decided to borrow from State Bank, which charges 14% interest on loans. The loan will be due in one year. Moton is unsure, however, whether to ask the bank for (a) an interest-bearing loan with interest and principal payable at the end of the year or (b) a non-interest-bearing loan due in one year but with interest deducted in advance.

Required
1. What will be the face value of the note assuming that
   a. interest is paid when the loan is due?
   b. interest is deducted in advance?
2. Calculate the effective interest rate on the note assuming that
   a. interest is paid when the loan is due.
   b. interest is deducted in advance.
3. Assume that Moton negotiates and signs the one-year note with the bank on July 1, 2007. Also assume that Moton's accounting year ends December 31. Determine the effect on the accounting equation of the issuance of the note and the interest on the note, assuming that
   a. interest is paid when the loan is due.
   b. interest is deducted in advance.
4. Prepare the appropriate balance sheet presentation for July 1, 2007, immediately after the note has been issued, assuming that
   a. interest is paid when the loan is due.
   b. interest is deducted in advance.

LO1,4   **Problem 9-12A** Contingent Liabilities

Listed below are several items for which the outcome of events is unknown at year-end.

a. A company has been sued by the federal government for price fixing. The company's legal counsel believes there will be an unfavorable verdict and has made an estimate of the probable loss.
b. A company is involved in an environmental clean-up lawsuit. The company's legal counsel believes it is possible the outcome will be unfavorable but has not been able to estimate the costs of the possible loss.
c. The company is involved in a trademark infringement suit. The company's legal experts believe an award of $750,000 in the company's favor will be made.
d. A company offers a three-year warranty on sales of new computers. It believes that 6% of the computers will require repairs.
e. A snack food manufacturer has included a coupon offer in the Sunday newspaper supplements. The manufacturer estimates that 30% of the 40-cent coupons will be redeemed.

Required

1. Identify which of the items (a) through (e) should be recorded at year-end.
2. Identify which of the items (a) through (e) should not be recorded but should be disclosed in the year-end financial statements.

LO6,7 **Problem 9-13A** Time Value of Money Concepts

The following situations involve the application of the time value of money concept:

1. Jan Cain deposited $19,500 in the bank on January 1, 1990, at an interest rate of 11% compounded annually. How much has accumulated in the account by January 1, 2007?
2. Mark Schultz deposited $43,200 in the bank on January 1, 1997. On January 2, 2007, this deposit has accumulated to $84,974. Interest is compounded annually on the account. What is the rate of interest that Mark earned on the deposit?
3. Les Hinckle made a deposit in the bank on January 1, 2000. The bank pays interest at the rate of 8% compounded annually. On January 1, 2007, the deposit has accumulated to $30,000. How much money did Lee originally deposit on January 1, 2000?
4. Val Hooper deposited $11,600 in the bank on January 1 a few years ago. The bank pays an interest rate of 10% compounded annually, and the deposit is now worth $30,052. For how many years has the deposit been invested?

LO6,7 **Problem 9-14A** Comparison of Alternatives

Darlene Page's grandparents want to give her some money when she graduates from high school. They have offered Darlene three choices:

a. Receive $16,000 immediately. Assume that interest is compounded annually.
b. Receive $2,400 at the end of each six months for four years. The first check will be received in six months.
c. Receive $4,640 at the end of each year for four years. Assume interest is compounded annually.

Required

Darlene wants to have money for a new car when she graduates from college in four years. Assuming an interest rate of 8%, what option should she choose to have the most money in four years?

DECISION CASES

READING AND INTERPRETING FINANCIAL STATEMENTS

LO1,2 **Decision Case 9-1** Finish Line's Current Liabilities

Refer to **Finish Line**'s financial information as reprinted in the appendix at the end of the book. Using the company balance sheet and accompanying notes, write a response to the following questions:

Required

1. Determine the company's current ratio for fiscal years 2006 and 2005. What do the ratios indicate about the liquidity of the company?
2. Explain why accrued property and sales tax is considered a current liability on the company's balance sheet.
3. Refer to the company's notes. Does the company have any contingent liabilities for lawsuits or litigation? If so, how were these contingent liabilities treated on the financial statements?

LO3,4 **Decision Case 9-2** Comparing Two Companies in the Same Industry: Foot Locker and Finish Line

Refer to the most recent statements of cash flow of **Foot Locker** and **Finish Line** as reprinted in the appendix at the end of this book.

Required

1. Compare the Operating Activities category of each company's statement of cash flows. What company was able to generate more cash from its operating activities? What were the most important ways the companies were able to generate cash from their operating activities?

2. Both companies have a negative amount in the operating category related to inventories. What does that indicate about the companies' activities?
3. Finish Line has a large positive amount in the operating category related to accounts payable in the prior year (year ended February 26, 2005). Does this indicate that the Accounts Payable account has increased or decreased? What does this indicate about the company's liquidity in future periods?
4. Foot Locker was able to generate more cash from operating activities in 2005 than in 2004, in spite of a lower net income. What factors allowed it to generate more cash?

LO3,4   **Decision Case 9-3** Microsoft Corporation's Contingent Liabilities

Microsoft Corporation has a fiscal year ending on June 30 and uses the indirect method to prepare its statement of cash flows. The notes to the 2004 financial statements include the following information about contingencies:

> European Commission competition law matter. On March 25, 2004, the European Commission announced a decision in its competition law investigation of Microsoft. The Commission concluded that we infringed European competition law by refusing to provide our competitors with licenses to certain protocol technology in the Windows server operating systems and by including streaming media playback functionality in Windows desktop operating systems. The Commission ordered us to make the relevant licenses to our technology available to our competitors and to develop and make available a version of the Windows desktop operating system that does not include specified software relating to media playback. The decision also imposed a fine of 497 million, which resulted in a charge of 497 million. We filed an appeal of the decision to the Court of First Instance on June 6, 2004, and will seek interim measures suspending the operation of certain provisions of the decision. We contest the conclusion that European competition law was infringed and will defend our position vigorously. A hearing on our petition for interim measures will be held on September 30–October 1, 2004. In other ongoing investigations, various foreign governments and several state Attorneys General have requested information from us concerning competition, privacy, and security issues.

> RealNetworks litigation. On December 18, 2003, RealNetworks, Inc. filed suit against us alleging violations of federal and state antitrust and unfair competition laws, related to streaming media features of Windows and related technologies. RealNetworks seeks damages and injunctive relief, including a permanent injunction requiring us to offer a version of Windows products with no streaming media features. We deny the allegation and will vigorously defend the action. RealNetworks filed the case in federal court in San Jose, California. It has been consolidated for pretrial purposes with other cases pending in the U.S. District Court in Baltimore.

Required
1. Regarding the first paragraph of the contingency note, is disclosure of the settlement in the notes to the financial statements all that is required of Microsoft, or is accrual required? At what point should accrual occur? If you decide that accrual is required, how would this contingent liability be reported on Microsoft's balance sheet at June 30, 2004?
2. If accrual is required, how would it affect the statement of cash flows for the year ended June 30, 2004?
3. Regarding the second paragraph of the contingency note, is disclosure of the legal dispute in the notes to the financial statements all that is required of Microsoft, or is accrual required? If so, at what point should accrual occur?

LO4   **Decision Case 9-4** Ford Motor Company's Contingent Liability

The following is an excerpt from **Ford Motor Company**'s notes that accompanied its financial statements for the year ended December 31, 2000.

> In the United States, the recall of certain **Firestone** tires, most of which were installed as original equipment on Ford Explorers, has led to a significant number of personal injury and class action lawsuits against Ford and Firestone. Plaintiffs in the personal injury cases typically allege that their injuries were caused by defects in the tire that caused it to lose its tread and/or by defects in the Explorer that caused the vehicle to roll over. For those cases involving Explorer rollovers in which damages have been specified, the damages specified by the plaintiffs, including both actual and punitive damages, aggregated approximately $590 million. However, in most of the actions

described above, no dollar amount of damages is specified or the specific amount referred to is only the jurisdictional minimum. It has been our experience that in cases that allege a specific amount of damages in excess of the jurisdictional mini-mum, such amounts, on average, bear little relation to the actual amounts of dam-ages, if any, paid by Ford in resolving such cases.

Required

1. Based on this excerpt, how do you think Ford should have treated the contingency on its financial statements for the year ended December 31, 2000?
2. Find more recent financial statements of Ford Motor Company. At what point did the company record amounts related to the Firestone tire legal issues?

MAKING FINANCIAL DECISIONS

LO1,2 **Decision Case 9-5** Current Ratio Loan Provision

Assume that you are the controller of a small, growing sporting goods company. The prospects for your firm in the future are quite good, but like most other firms, it has been experiencing some cash flow difficulties because all available funds have been used to pur-chase inventory and finance start-up costs associated with a new business. At the beginning of the current year, your local bank advanced a loan to your company. Included in the loan is the following provision:

> The company is obligated to pay interest payments each month for the next five years. Principal is due and must be paid at the end of Year 5. The company is further ob-ligated to maintain a current assets to current liabilities ratio of 2:1 as indicated on quarterly statements to be submitted to the bank. If the company fails to meet any loan provisions, all amounts of interest and principal are due immediately upon no-tification by the bank.

You, as controller, have just gathered the following information as of the end of the first month of the current quarter:

Current liabilities:	
Accounts payable	$400,000
Taxes payable	100,000
Accrued expenses	50,000
Total current liabilities	$550,000

You are concerned about the loan provision that requires a 2:1 ratio of current assets to cur-rent liabilities.

Required

1. Indicate what actions could be taken during the next two months to meet the loan pro-vision. Which of the available actions should be recommended?
2. Could management take short-term actions to artificially make the company's liquidity appear to be better? What are the long-run implications of such actions?

LO7 **Decision Case 9-6** Alternative Payment Options

Kathy Clark owns a small company that makes ice machines for restaurants and food-service facilities. Kathy knows a lot about producing ice machines but is less familiar with the best terms to extend to her customers. One customer is opening a new business and has asked Kathy to consider any of the following options to pay for his new $20,000 ice machine:

a. Term 1: 10% down, the remainder paid at the end of the year plus 8% simple interest.
b. Term 2: 10% down, the remainder paid at the end of the year plus 8% interest, com-pounded quarterly.
c. Term 3: $0 down, but $21,600 due at the end of the year.

Required

Make a recommendation to Kathy. She believes that 8% is a fair return on her money at this time. Should she accept option (a), (b), or (c), or take the $20,000 cash at the time of the sale? Justify your recommendation with calculations. What factors, other than the actual amount of cash received from the sale, should be considered?

HOMEWORK

ETHICAL DECISION MAKING

LO4   **Decision Case 9-7** Warranty Cost Estimate

John Walton is an accountant for ABC Auto Dealers, a large auto dealership in a metropolitan area. ABC sells both new and used cars. New cars are sold with a five-year warranty, the cost of which is carried by the manufacturer. For several years, however, ABC has offered a two-year warranty on used cars. The cost of the warranty is an expense to ABC, and John has been asked by his boss, Mr. Sawyer, to review warranty costs and recommend the amount to accrue on the year-end financial statements.

For the past several years, ABC has recorded as warranty expense 5% of used car sales. John has analyzed past repair records and found that repairs, although fluctuating somewhat from year to year, have averaged near the 5% level. John is convinced, however, that 5% is inadequate for the coming year. He bases his judgment on industry reports of increased repair costs and on the fact that several cars that were recently sold on warranty have experienced very high repair costs. John believes that the current-year repair accrual will be at least 10%. He discussed the higher expense amount with Mr. Sawyer, who is the controller of ABC.

Mr. Sawyer was not happy with John's decision concerning warranty expense. He reminded John of the need to control expenses during the recent sales downturn. He also reminded John that ABC is seeking a large loan from the bank and that the bank loan officers may not be happy with recent operating results, especially if ABC begins to accrue larger amounts for future estimated amounts such as warranties. Finally, Mr. Sawyer reminded John that most of the employees of ABC, including Mr. Sawyer, were members of the company's profit-sharing plan and would not be happy with the reduced share of profits. Mr. Sawyer thanked John for his judgment concerning warranty cost but told him that the accrual for the current year would remain at 5%.

John left the meeting with Mr. Sawyer somewhat frustrated. He was convinced that his judgment concerning the warranty costs was correct. He knew that the owner of ABC would be visiting the office next week and wondered whether he should discuss the matter with him personally at that time. John also had met one of the loan officers from the bank several times and considered calling her to discuss his concern about the warranty expense amount on the year-end statements.

Required

Discuss the courses of action available to John. What should John do concerning his judgment of warranty costs?

LO4   **Decision Case 9-8** Retainer Fees as Sales

Bunch o' Balloons markets balloon arrangements to companies who want to thank clients and employees. Bunch o' Balloons has a unique style that has put it in high demand. Consequently, Bunch o' Balloons has asked clients to establish an account. Clients are asked to pay a retainer fee equal to about three months of client purchases. The fee will be used to cover the cost of arrangements delivered and will be reevaluated at the end of each month. At the end of the current month Bunch o' Balloons has $43,900 of retainer fees in its possession. The controller is eager to show this amount as sales because "it represents certain sales for the company."

Required

Do you agree with the controller? When should the sales be reported? Why would the controller be eager to report the cash receipts as sales?

SOLUTIONS TO KEY TERMS QUIZ

#	Term	#	Term
1	Current liability	10	Simple interest
3	Accounts payable	13	Compound interest
8	Notes payable	15	Future value of a single amount
4	Discount on notes payable	17	Present value of a single amount
6	Current maturities of long-term debt	5	Annuity
7	Accrued liability	16	Future value of an annuity
9	Contingent liability	2	Present value of an annuity
11	Estimated liability	18	Gross wages (Appendix A)
12	Contingent asset	20	Net pay (Appendix A)
14	Time value of money	19	Compensated absences (Appendix A)

HOMEWORK

10

Long-Term Liabilities

Study Links

A Look at Previous Chapters
Chapter 9 was concerned with current liabilities and short-term liquidity. We also introduced the concept of the time value of money.

A Look at This Chapter
In this chapter we examine the use of long-term liabilities as an important source of financing a company's needs. We will utilize the time value of money concept because it is the basis for the valuation of all long-term liabilities.

A Look at Upcoming Chapters
Chapter 11 will examine the presentation of stockholders' equity, the other major category on the right-hand side of the balance sheet.

Learning Outcomes

After studying this chapter, you should be able to:

LO1 Identify the components of the long-term liability category of the balance sheet.

LO2 Define the important characteristics of bonds payable.

LO3 Determine the issue price of a bond using compound interest techniques.

LO4 Show that you understand the effect on the balance sheet of the issuance of bonds.

LO5 Find the amortization of premium or discount using the effective interest method.

LO6 Find the gain or loss on retirement of bonds.

LO7 Determine whether or not a lease agreement must be reported as a liability on the balance sheet.

LO8 Explain the effects that transactions involving long-term liabilities have on the statement of cash flows.

LO9 Explain deferred taxes and calculate the deferred tax liability. (Appendix)

Coca-Cola

MAKING BUSINESS DECISIONS

Coca-Cola® is one of the world's foremost brands with worldwide sales of nearly $22 billion in 2004. The company is truly a global corporation with nearly 300 brands in almost 200 countries. While it began many years ago in the United States, now more than 70% of Coca-Cola Company's income comes from business outside the United States. Recently, the growth in company sales has slowed to 4% or less per year, and the company has faced new challenges in the beverage industry. Despite continued turbulence in worldwide markets and challenges from competitors, the firm maintains its focus on growth.

To meet long-term growth objectives, Coca-Cola must make significant investments to support its products. The process also involves investment to develop new global brands and to acquire local or global brands, when appropriate. In addition, the company makes significant marketing investments to encourage consumer loyalty. Coca-Cola has developed relationships with many sports organizations, including the **NBA** and **NASCAR**, to enhance consumer awareness and promote sales of its products. Outside the United States, there is a strong push to sell in many other markets, including those in India and Brazil.

To expand profitably, Coca-Cola requires more money than it generates in profits. Therefore, it uses a common financing tool: *long-term debt*. In fact, the balance sheet of December 31, 2004, indicates the company has over $4 billion of long-term debt, other liabilities, and deferred income taxes. The 2004 annual report states, "Our company maintains debt levels we consider prudent based on our cash flow, interest coverage ratio, and percentage of debt to capital.[1] The company monitors interest rate conditions carefully and in 2004 retired nearly $600 million in long-term debt and replaced it with other debt. Because it is a global company, Coca-Cola has access to key financial markets around the world, which allows it to borrow at the lowest possible rates. While most of its loans are in U.S. dollars, management continually adjusts the

---

1 Coca-Cola's 2004 annual report, p. 31.

composition of the debt to accommodate shifting interest rates and currency exchange rates to minimize the overall cost.

The accompanying balance sheet presents the liabilities and shareowner's equity portion of the balance sheet for The Coca-Cola Company and its subsidiaries. This chapter answers the following questions:

- What are the components of the long-term liability of the balance sheet? (See pp. 457–458)

- What is the proper accounting and reporting of bonds payable? (See pp. 458–469)

- What is the importance of financial arrangements such as leases as a means of financing a company? (See pp. 469–473)

Other issues related to long-term liabilities are also found in this text. This information can help you evaluate the Long-Term Liabilities section of the balance sheet of The Coca-Cola Company.

Coca-Cola's 2004 Annual Report

The Coca-Cola Company and Subsidiaries
December 31,
(In millions except share data)

	2004	2003
LIABILITIES AND SHAREOWNERS' EQUITY		
CURRENT		
Accounts payable and accrued expenses	$ 4,283	$ 4,058
Loans and notes payable	4,531	2,583
Current maturities of long-term debt	1,490	323
Accrued income taxes	667	922
TOTAL CURRENT LIABILITIES	10,971	7,886
LONG-TERM DEBT (Coca-Cola's long-term debt)	1,157	2,517
OTHER LIABILITIES	2,814	2,512
DEFERRED INCOME TAXES	450	337
SHAREOWNERS' EQUITY		
Common stock, $0.25 par value Authorized: 5,600,000,000 shares; issued: 3,500,489,544 shares in 2004 and 3,494,799,258 shares in 2003	875	874
Capital surplus	4,928	4,395
Reinvested earnings	29,105	26,687
Accumulated other comprehensive income (loss)	(1,348)	(1,995)
	33,560	29,961
Less treasury stock, at cost (1,091,150,977 shares in 2004; 1,053,267,474 shares in 2003)	(17,625)	(15,871)
	15,935	14,090
TOTAL LIABILITIES AND SHAREOWNERS' EQUITY	$ 31,327	$ 27,342

NET OPERATING REVENUES AND OPERATING INCOME BY OPERATING SEGMENT*

The Coca-Cola Company and Subsidiaries

2004 Net Operating Revenues

2004 Operating Income

*Charts and percentages are calculated excluding Corporate.

Balance Sheet Presentation

In general, **long-term liabilities** are obligations that will not be satisfied within one year. Essentially, all liabilities that are not classified as current liabilities are classified as long-term. We will concentrate on the long-term liabilities of bonds or notes, leases, and deferred taxes. On the balance sheet, the items are listed after current liabilities. For example, the Noncurrent Liabilities section of **PepsiCo, Inc.**'s balance sheet is highlighted in Exhibit 10-1. PepsiCo has acquired financing through a combination of long-term debt, stock issuance, and internal growth or retained earnings. Exhibit 10-1 indicates that long-term debt is one portion of the long-term liability category of the balance sheet. But the balance sheet also reveals two other items that must be considered part of the long-term liability category: deferred income taxes and other liabilities. We begin by looking at a particular type of long-term debt, bonds payable. We will concentrate on these long-term liabilities:

- Bonds or notes
- Leases
- Deferred taxes

LO1 Identify the components of the long-term liability category of the balance sheet.

Long-term liability
An obligation that will not be satisfied within one year or the current operating cycle.

EXHIBIT 10-1 | **PepsiCo's Balance Sheet**

Consolidated Partial Balance Sheet

PepsiCo, Inc. and Subsidiaries

December 25, 2004 and December 27, 2003

(In millions except per share amounts)	2004	2003
LIABILITIES AND SHAREHOLDERS' EQUITY		
Current Liabilities		
Short-term obligations	$ 1,054	$ 591
Accounts payable and other current liabilities	5,599	5,213
Income taxes payable	99	611
Total Current Liabilities	6,752	6,415
Long-Term Debt Obligations	2,397	1,702
Other Liabilities	4,099	4,075
Deferred Income Taxes	1,216	1,261
Total Liabilities	14,464	13,453
Preferred Stock, no par value	41	41
Repurchased Preferred Stock	(90)	(63)
Common Shareholders' Equity		
Common stock, par value 1 2/3 per share (issued 1,782 shares)	30	30
Capital in excess of par value	618	548
Retained earnings	18,730	15,961
Accumulated other comprehensive loss	(886)	(1,267)
	18,443	15,250
Less: repurchased common stock, at cost (103 and 77 shares, respectively)	(4,920)	(3,376)
Total Common Shareholders' Equity	13,523	11,874
Total Liabilities and Shareholders' Equity	$ 27,987	$ 25,327

(Annotation: PepsiCo's long-term debt)

See accompanying notes to consolidated financial statements.

In late 2001, Enron, the nation's largest marketer of electricity and natural gas, reported massive losses and reductions in shareholder equity. At that time, the company issued a major restatement of their previously issued financial statements that covered a four-year period and then filed for bankruptcy.

Enron management, working closely with its chief consultant and auditor, Arthur Andersen, had set up several partnerships. These were owned by the Enron Corporation. Then, Enron accountants recorded a significant amount of Enron's long-term debt on the books of the partnerships rather than on the corporation's books. By doing this, Enron avoided reporting billions of dollars of debt on its own balance sheets.

During the period of these transactions, Enron executives were paid large bonuses that were based on Enron's earnings performance and increases in its stock price.

What did the company do that was of ethical concern? Why should Enron have disclosed the debt on its balance sheet instead of on that of the partnerships? How did not having the debt on Enron's books affect the company's earnings and its executives' bonuses?

Sources: Mitchell Pacelle, "Enron report gives details of deals that masked debt," The Wall Street Journal, *September 23, 2002; "The Fall of Enron,"* Business News Online, *December 17, 2001.*

Bonds Payable

LO2 Define the important characteristics of bonds payable.

CHARACTERISTICS OF BONDS

A bond is a security or financial instrument that allows firms to borrow money and repay the loan over a long period of time. The bonds are sold, or *issued*, to investors who have amounts to invest and want a return on their investment. The *borrower* (issuing firm) promises to pay interest on specified dates, usually annually or semiannually. The borrower also promises to repay the principal on a specified date, the *due date* or maturity date.

A bond certificate, illustrated in Exhibit 10-2, is issued at the time of purchase and indicates the *terms* of the bond. Generally, bonds are issued in denominations of $1,000. The denomination of the bond is usually referred to as the **face value** or par value. This is the amount that the firm must pay at the maturity date of the bond.

Firms issue bonds in very large amounts, often in millions in a single issue. After bonds are issued, they may be traded on a bond exchange in the same way that stocks are sold on the stock exchanges. Therefore, bonds are not always held until maturity by the initial investor but may change hands several times before their eventual due date. Because bond maturities are as long as 30 years, the "secondary" market in bonds—the market for bonds already issued—is a critical factor in a company's ability to raise money. Investors in bonds may want to sell them if interest rates paid by competing investments become more attractive or if the issuer becomes less creditworthy. Buyers of these bonds may be betting that interest rates will reverse course or that the company will get back on its feet. Trading in the secondary market does not affect the financial statements of the issuing company.

We have described the general nature of bonds, but all bonds do not have the same terms and features. Following are some important features that often appear in the bond certificate.

Collateral The bond certificate should indicate the *collateral* of the loan. Collateral represents the assets that back the bonds in case the issuer cannot make the interest and principal payments and must default on the loan. **Debenture bonds** are not backed by specific collateral of the issuing company. Rather, the investor must examine the general creditworthiness of the issuer. If a bond is a *secured bond*, the certificate indicates specific assets that serve as collateral in case of default.

Due Date The bond certificate specifies the date that the bond principal must be repaid. Normally, bonds are *term bonds*, meaning that the entire principal amount is due on a single date. Alternatively, bonds may be issued as **serial bonds**, meaning

---

Face value
The principal amount of the bond as stated on the bond certificate. *Alternate term: Par value*

Debenture bonds
Bonds that are not backed by specific collateral.

Serial bonds
Bonds that do not all have the same due date; a portion of the bonds comes due each time period.

EXHIBIT 10-2 Bond Certificate

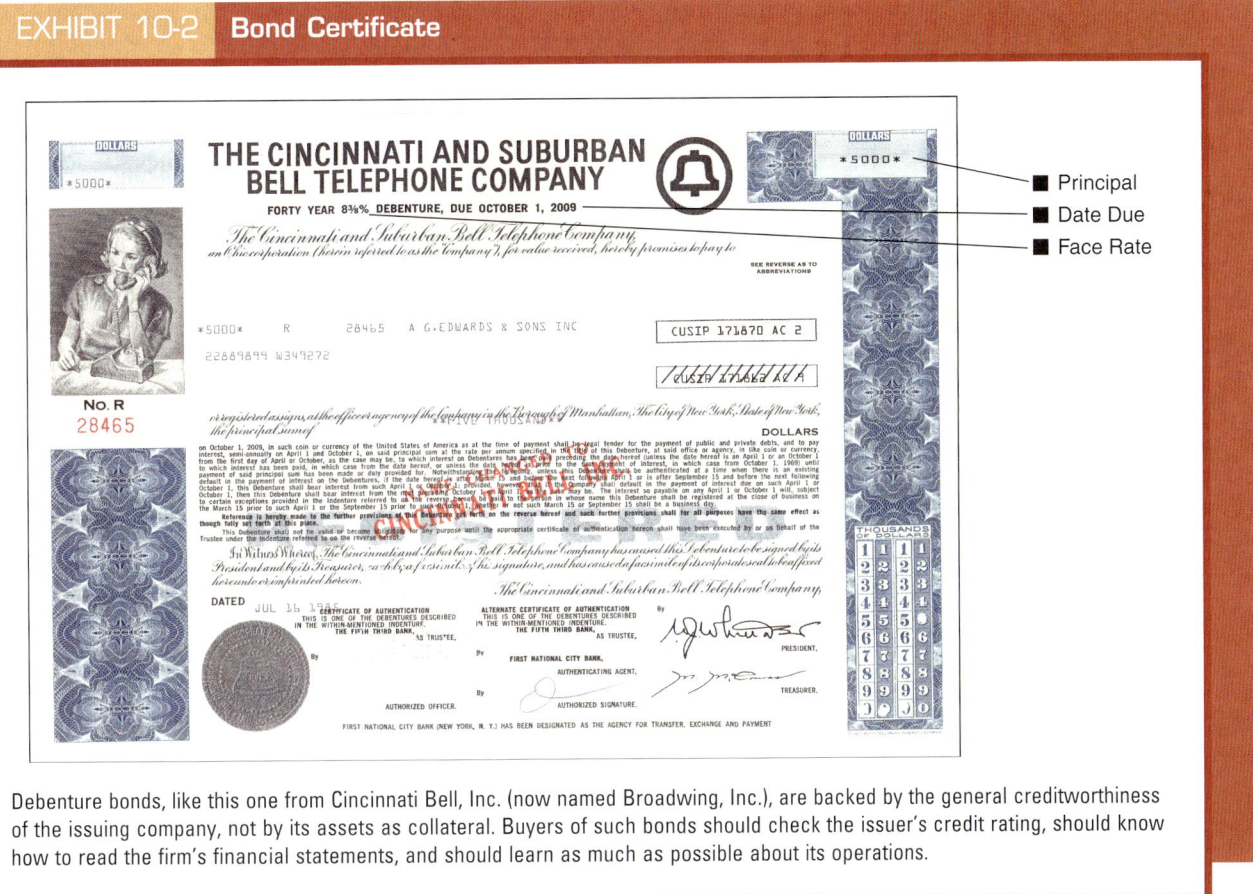

■ Principal
■ Date Due
■ Face Rate

Debenture bonds, like this one from Cincinnati Bell, Inc. (now named Broadwing, Inc.), are backed by the general creditworthiness of the issuing company, not by its assets as collateral. Buyers of such bonds should check the issuer's credit rating, should know how to read the firm's financial statements, and should learn as much as possible about its operations.

that not all of the principal is due on the same date. For example, a firm may issue serial bonds that have a portion of the principal due each year for the next 10 years. Issuing firms may prefer serial bonds because a firm does not need to accumulate the entire amount for principal repayment at one time.

Other Features Some bonds are issued as convertible or callable bonds. *Convertible bonds* can be converted into common stock at a future time. This feature allows the investor to buy a security that pays a fixed interest rate but that can be converted at a future date into an equity security (stock) if the issuing firm is growing and profitable. The conversion feature is also advantageous to the issuing firm because convertible bonds normally carry a lower rate of interest.

Callable bonds may be retired before their specified due date. *Callable* generally refers to the issuer's right to retire the bonds. If the buyer or investor has the right to retire the bonds, they are referred to as *redeemable bonds*. Usually, callable bonds stipulate the price to be paid at redemption; this price is referred to as the *redemption price* or the *reacquisition price*. The callable feature is like an insurance policy for the company. Say a bond pays 10%, but interest rates plummet to 6%. Rather than continuing to pay 10%, the company is willing to offer a slight premium over face value for the right to retire those 10% bonds so that it can borrow at 6%. Of course, the investor is invariably disappointed when the company invokes its call privilege.

As you can see, bonds have various terms and features. Each firm seeks to structure the bond agreement in the manner that best meets its financial needs and will attract investors at the most favorable rates.

Bonds are a popular source of financing because of the tax advantages when compared with the issuance of stock. Interest paid on bonds is deductible for tax purposes, but dividends paid on stock are not. This may explain why the amount

Callable bonds
Bonds that may be redeemed or retired before their specified due date.

of debt on many firms' balance sheets has increased in recent years. Debt became popular in the 1980s to finance mergers and again in recent years when interest rates reached 20-year lows. Still, investors and creditors tend to downgrade a company when the amount of debt it has on the balance sheet is deemed to be excessive.

ISSUANCE OF BONDS

When bonds are issued, the issuing firm must recognize the incurrence of a liability in exchange for cash. If bonds are issued at their face amount, the accounting entry is straightforward. For example, assume that on April 1 a firm issues bonds with a face amount of $10,000 and receives $10,000. In this case, the asset Cash and the liability Bonds Payable are both increased by $10,000.

FACTORS AFFECTING BOND PRICE

LO3 Determine the issue price of a bond using compound interest techniques.

Face rate of interest
The rate of interest on the bond certificate. *Alternate terms: Stated rate, normal rate, coupon rate*

Market rate of interest
The rate that investors could obtain by investing in other bonds that are similar to the issuing firm's bonds. *Alternate terms: Yield, effective rate*

Study Tip
Calculating the issue price of a bond always involves a calculation of the present value of the cash flows.

Bond issue price
The present value of the annuity of interest payments plus the present value of the principal.

With bonds payable, two interest rates are always involved. The **face rate of interest** (also called the *stated rate, nominal rate, contract rate, or coupon rate*) is the rate specified on the bond certificate. It is the amount of interest that will be paid each interest period. For example, if $10,000 worth of bonds is issued with an 8% annual face rate of interest, then interest of $800 ($10,000 × 8% × 1 year) would be paid at the end of each annual period. Alternatively, bonds often require the payment of interest semiannually. If the bonds in our example required the 8% annual face rate to be paid semiannually (at 4%), then interest of $400 ($10,000 × 8% × ½ year) would be paid each semiannual period.

The second important interest rate is the **market rate of interest** (also called the *effective rate* or *bond yield*). The market rate of interest is the rate that bondholders could obtain by investing in other bonds that are similar to the issuing firm's bonds. The issuing firm does not set the market rate of interest. That rate is determined by the bond market on the basis of many transactions for similar bonds. The market rate incorporates all of the "market's" knowledge about economic conditions and all its expectations about future conditions. Normally, issuing firms try to set a face rate that is equal to the market rate. However, because the market rate changes daily, there are almost always small differences between the face rate and the market rate at the time bonds are issued.

In addition to the number of interest payments and the maturity length of the bond, the face rate and the market rate of interest must both be known in order to calculate the issue price of a bond. The **bond issue price** equals the *present value* of the cash flows that the bond will produce. Bonds produce two types of cash flows for the investor: interest receipts and repayment of principal (face value). The interest receipts constitute an annuity of payments each interest period over the life of the bonds. The repayment of principal (face value) is a one-time receipt that occurs at the end of the term of the bonds. We must calculate the present value of the interest receipts (using Table 9-4 on page 418) and the present value of the principal amount (using Table 9-2 on page 416). The total of the two present-value calculations represents the issue price of the bond.

An Example Suppose that on January 1, 2007, Discount Firm wants to issue bonds with a face value of $10,000. The face or coupon rate of interest has been set at 8%. The bonds will pay interest annually, and the principal amount is due in four years. Also suppose that the market rate of interest for other similar bonds is currently 10%. Because the market rate of interest exceeds the coupon rate, investors will not be willing to pay $10,000 but something less. We want to calculate the amount that will be obtained from the issuance of Discount Firm's bonds.

Discount's bond will produce two sets of cash flows for the investor: an annual interest payment of $800 ($10,000 × 8%) per year for four years and repayment of the principal of $10,000 at the end of the fourth year. To calculate the issue price, we must calculate the present value of the two sets of cash flows. A time diagram portrays the cash flows as follows:

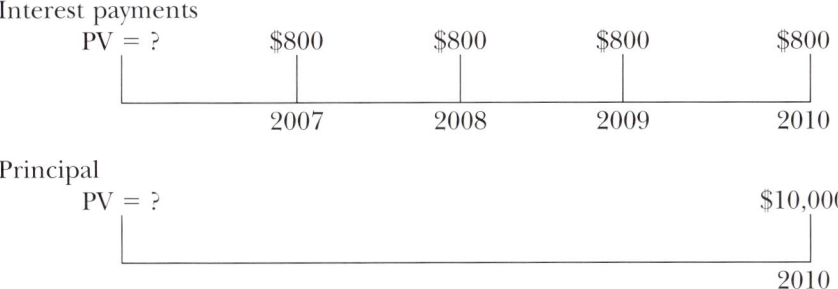

Interest payments
PV = ? $800 $800 $800 $800
                2007   2008   2009   2010

Principal
PV = ? $10,000
                                          2010

We can calculate the issue price by using the compound-interest tables found in Chapter 9, as follows:

$800 × 3.170 (factor from Table 9-4 for 4 periods, 10%)	$2,536
$10,000 × 0.683 (factor from Table 9-2 for 4 periods, 10%)	6,830
Issue price	$9,366

Perform the following steps when using a calculator to determine the present value in our example:

ENTER	DISPLAY
4 N	N = 4
10 I/Y	I/Y = 10
800 PMT	PMT = 800
10000 FV	FV = 10,000
CPT PV	PV = 9,366

The factors used to calculate the present value represent four periods and 10% interest. This is a key point. The issue price of a bond is always calculated using the market rate of interest. The face rate of interest determines the amount of the interest payments, but the market rate determines the present value of the payments and the present value of the principal (and therefore the issue price).

Our example of Discount Firm reveals that the bonds with a $10,000 face value amount would be issued for $9,366. The bond markets and the financial press often state the issue price as a percentage of the face amount. The percentage for Discount's bonds can be calculated as ($9,366/$10,000) × 100, or 93.66%.

Exhibit 10-3 illustrates how bonds are actually listed in the reporting of the bond markets. The exhibit lists two types of **IBM** bonds that were traded on a particular day. The portion immediately after the company name, for example "6⅜ 09," indicates that the face rate of interest is 6⅜% and the due date of the bonds is the year 2009. The next column, for example "6.5," indicates that the bond investor who purchased the bonds on that day will receive a yield of 6.5%. The column labeled "vol" indicates the number of bonds, in thousands, that were bought and sold during the day. The column labeled "close" indicates the market price of the bonds at the end of the day. For example, the first issue of IBM bonds closed at 98¾, which means

10-1 Real World Practice

Reading Coca-Cola's Balance Sheet

Coca-Cola lists three items as long-term liabilities on its 2004 balance sheet. What are those items? Did they increase or decrease?

EXHIBIT 10-3   Listing of Bonds on the Bond Market

Bonds	Cur Yld	Vol	Close	Net Chg
IBM 6⅜09	6.5	280	98¾	−¼
IBM 7¼10	7.1	68	101½	+¼

that the price was 98¾% of the face value of the bonds. These bonds are trading at a discount because the face rate (6⅜%) is less than the market rate of 6.5%. The bonds in the second issue—"7¼ 10"—have a face rate of 7¼%, will become due in the year 2010, and closed at 101½, or at a premium. The net change column indicates the change in the bond price that occurred for the day's trading.

PREMIUM OR DISCOUNT ON BONDS

LO4 Show that you understand the effect on the balance sheet of the issuance of bonds.

Premium
The excess of the issue price over the face value of the bonds.

Discount
The excess of the face value of bonds over the issue price.

Premium or **discount** represents the difference between the face value and the issue price of a bond. We may state the relationship as follows:

Premium = Issue Price − Face Value
Discount = Face Value − Issue Price

In other words, when issue price exceeds face value, the bonds have sold at a premium, and when the face value exceeds the issue price, the bonds have sold at a discount.

We will continue with the Discount Firm example to illustrate the accounting for bonds sold at a discount. Discount Firm's bonds sold at a discount calculated as follows:

Discount = $10,000 − $9,366
= $634

The effect on Discount Firm's accounting equation as a result of the issuance of the bonds is as follows:

Balance Sheet					Income Statement	
ASSETS	=	LIABILITIES	+	STOCKHOLDERS' EQUITY	+	REVENUES − EXPENSES
Cash 9,366		Bonds Payable 10,000				
		Discount on Bonds				
		Payable (634)				

The Discount on Bonds Payable account is shown as a contra liability on the balance sheet in conjunction with the Bonds Payable account and is a deduction from that account. If Discount Firm prepared a balance sheet immediately after the bond issuance, the following would appear in the Long-Term Liabilities category of the balance sheet:

Long-term liabilities:	
Bonds payable	$10,000
Less: Discount on bonds payable	634
	$ 9,366

The Discount Firm example has illustrated a situation in which the market rate of a bond issue is higher than the face rate. Now we will examine the opposite situation, when the face rate exceeds the market rate. Again, we are interested in calculating the issue price of the bonds.

Issuing at a Premium Suppose that on January 1, 2007, Premium Firm wants to issue the same bonds as in the previous example: $10,000 face value bonds, with an 8% face rate of interest and with interest paid annually each year for four years. Assume, however, that the market rate of interest is 6% for similar bonds. The issue price is calculated as the present value of the annuity of interest payments plus the present value of the principal at the market rate of interest. The calculations are as follows:

$800 × 3.465 (factor from Table 9-4 for 4 periods, 6%)	$ 2,772
$10,000 × 0.792 (factor from Table 9-2 for 4 periods, 6%)	7,920
Issue price	$10,692

Perform the following steps when using a calculator to determine the present value in our example:

ENTER	DISPLAY
4 N	N = 4
6 I/Y	I/Y = 6
800 PMT	PMT = 800
10000 FV	FV = 10,000
CPT PV	PV = 10,693*
*(rounded)	

We have calculated that the bonds would be issued for $10,692. Because the bonds would be issued at an amount that is higher than the face value amount, they would be issued at a premium. The amount of the premium is calculated as follows:

$$\text{Premium} = \$10,692 - \$10,000$$
$$= \$692$$

The effect on the accounting equation of the isuance of the bonds at a premium is as follows:

Balance Sheet						Income Statement
ASSETS	=	LIABILITIES		+	STOCKHOLDERS' EQUITY +	REVENUES – EXPENSES
Cash 10,692		Bonds Payable	10,000			
		Discount on Bonds				
		Payable	692			

The account Premium on Bonds Payable is an addition to the Bonds Payable account. If Premium Firm presented a balance sheet immediately after the bond issuance, the Long-Term Liabilities category of the balance sheet would appear as follows:

Long-term liabilities:
Bonds payable	$10,000
Plus: Premium on bonds payable	692
	$10,692

Study Tip When interest rates increase, present values decrease. This is called an inverse relationship.

You should learn two important points from the Discount Firm and Premium Firm examples:

- **You should be able to determine whether a bond will sell at a premium or discount by the relationship that exists between the face rate and the market rate of interest.** *Premium* and *discount* do not mean "good" and "bad." Premium or discount arises solely because of the difference that exists between the face rate and the market rate of interest for a bond issue. The same relationship always exists, so that the following statements hold true:

    If Market Rate = Face Rate, THEN bonds are issued at face value amount.
    If Market Rate > Face Rate, THEN bonds are issued at a discount.
    If Market Rate < Face Rate, THEN bonds are issued at a premium.

- **The relationship between interest rates and bond prices is always inverse.** To understand the term *inverse relationship*, refer to the Discount Firm and Premium Firm examples. The bonds of the two firms are identical in all respects except for the market rate of interest. When the market rate was 10%, the bond issue price was $9,366 (the Discount Firm example). When the market rate was 6%, the bond issue price increased to $10,692 (the Premium Firm example). The examples illustrate that as interest rates decrease, prices on the bond markets increase and that as interest rates increase, bond prices decrease.

Many investors in the stock market perceive that they are taking a great deal of risk with their capital. In truth, bond investors are taking substantial risks too. The most obvious risk is that the company will fail and not be able to pay its debts. But another risk is that interest rates on comparable investments will rise. Interest rate risk can have a devastating impact on the current market value of bonds. One way to minimize interest rate risk is to hold the bond to maturity, at which point the company must pay the face amount.

BOND AMORTIZATION

LO5 Find the amortization of premium or discount using the effective interest method.

Purpose of Amortization The amount of interest expense that should be reflected on a firm's income statement for bonds payable is the true, or effective, interest. The effective interest should reflect the face rate of interest as well as interest that results from issuing the bond at a premium or discount. To reflect that interest component, the amount initially recorded in the Premium on Bonds Payable or the Discount on Bonds Payable account must be amortized or spread over the life of the bond.

Amortization refers to the process of transferring an amount from the discount or premium account to interest expense each time period to adjust interest expense. One commonly used method of amortization is the effective interest method. We will illustrate how to amortize a discount amount and then how to amortize a premium amount.

To illustrate amortization of a discount, we need to return to our Discount Firm example introduced earlier. We have seen that the issue price of the bond could be calculated as $9,366, resulting in a contra-liability balance of $634 in the Discount on Bonds Payable account (see the accounting equation on page 462). But what does the initial balance of the Discount account really represent? The discount should be thought of as additional interest that Discount Firm must pay over and above the 8% face rate. Remember that Discount received only $9,366 but must repay the full principal of $10,000 at the bond due date. For that reason, the $634 discount is an additional interest cost that must be reflected as interest expense. It is reflected as interest expense by the process of amortization. In other words, interest expense is made up of two components: cash interest and amortization. We will now consider how to amortize premium or discount.

Effective interest method of amortization
The process of transferring a portion of the premium or discount to interest expense; this method results in a constant effective interest rate. *Alternate term: Interest method*

Carrying value
The face value of a bond plus the amount of unamortized premium or minus the amount of unamortized discount. *Alternate term: Book value*

Effective Interest Method: Impact on Expense The **effective interest method of amortization** amortizes discount or premium in a manner that produces a constant effective interest rate from period to period. The *dollar amount* of interest expense will vary from period to period, but the rate of interest will be constant. This interest rate is referred to as the *effective interest rate* and is equal to the market rate of interest at the time the bonds are issued.

To illustrate this point, we introduce two new terms. The **carrying value** of bonds is represented by the following:

$$\text{Carrying Value} = \text{Face Value} - \text{Unamortized Discount}$$

For example, the carrying value of the bonds for our Discount Firm example, as of the date of issuance of January 1, 2007, could be calculated as follows:

$$\$10,000 - \$634 = \$9,366$$

In those situations in which there is a premium instead of a discount, carrying value is represented by the following:

$$\text{Carrying Value} = \text{Face Value} + \text{Unamortized Premium}$$

For example, the carrying value of the bonds for our Premium Firm example, as of the date of issuance of January 1, 2007, could be calculated as follows:

$$\$10,000 + \$692 = \$10,692$$

The second term has been suggested earlier. The *effective rate of interest* is represented by the following:

$$\text{Effective Rate} = \text{Annual Interest Expense/Carrying Value}$$

EXHIBIT 10-4	Discount Amortization: Effective Interest Method of Amortization

Date	Column 1 Cash Interest	Column 2 Interest Expense	Column 3 Discount Amortized	Column 4 Carrying Value
	8%	10%	Col. 2 − Col. 1	
1/1/2007	—	—	—	$ 9,366
12/31/2007	$800	$937	$137	9,503
12/31/2008	800	950	150	9,653
12/31/2009	800	965	165	9,818
12/31/2010	800	982	182	10,000

Effective Interest Method: An Example The amortization table in Exhibit 10-4 illustrates effective interest amortization of the bond discount for our Discount Firm example.

As illustrated in Exhibit 10-4, the effective interest method of amortization is based on several important concepts. The relationships can be stated in equation form as follows:

Cash Interest (in Column 1) = Bond Face Value × Face Rate
Interest Expense (in Column 2) = Carrying Value × Effective Rate
Discount Amortized (in Column 3) = Interest Expense − Cash Interest

The first column of the exhibit indicates that the cash interest to be paid is $800 ($10,000 × 8%). The second column indicates the annual interest expense at the effective rate of interest (market rate at the time of issuance). This is a constant rate of interest (10% in our example) and is calculated by multiplying the carrying value *as of the beginning of the period* by the market rate of interest. In 2007, the interest expense is $937 ($9,366 × 10%). Note that the amount of interest expense changes each year because the carrying value changes as discount is amortized. The amount of discount amortized each year in Column 3 is the difference between the cash interest in Column 1 and the interest expense in Column 2. Again, note that the amount of discount amortized changes in each of the four years. Finally, the carrying value in Column 4 is the previous year's carrying value plus the discount amortized in Column 3. When bonds are issued at a discount, the carrying value starts at an amount less than face value and increases each period until it reaches the face value amount.

Exhibit 10-4 is the basis for determining the effect of amortization on the firm's financial statements. The effect of the interest payment and the amortization of discount for 2007 (note the December 31, 2007, line of the table) is as follows:

Balance Sheet					Income Statement	
ASSETS	**=**	**LIABILITIES**	**+ STOCKHOLDERS' EQUITY**	**+**	**REVENUES − EXPENSES**	
Cash (800)		Discount on Bonds Payable 137			Interest Expense	(937)

The balance of the Discount on Bonds Payable account as of December 31, 2007, would be calculated as follows:

Beginning balance, January 1, 2007	$634
Less: Amount amortized	137
Ending balance, December 31, 2007	$497

The December 31, 2007, balance represents the amount *unamortized*, or the amount that will be amortized in future time periods. On the balance sheet presented as

EXHIBIT 10-5	Premium Amortization: Effective Interest Method of Amortization

Date	Column 1 Cash Interest	Column 2 Interest Expense	Column 3 Premium Amortized	Column 4 Carrying Value
	8%	6%	Col. 1 − Col. 2	
1/1/2007	—	—	—	$10,692
12/31/2007	$800	$642	$158	10,534
12/31/2008	800	632	168	10,366
12/31/2009	800	622	178	10,188
12/31/2010	800	612	188	10,000

of December 31, 2007, the unamortized portion of the discount appears as the balance of the Discount on Bonds Payable account as follows:

Long-term liabilities	
Bonds payable	$10,000
Less: Discount on bonds payable	497
	$ 9,503

The process of amortization would continue for four years, until the balance of the Discount on Bonds Payable account has been reduced to zero. By the end of 2010, all of the balance of the Discount on Bonds Payable account will have been transferred to the Interest Expense account and represents an increase in interest expense each period.

The amortization of a premium has an impact opposite that of the amortization of a discount. We will use our Premium Firm example to illustrate. Recall that on January 1, 2007, Premium Firm issued $10,000 face value bonds with a face rate of interest of 8%. At the time the bonds were issued, the market rate was 6%, resulting in an issue price of $10,692 and a credit balance in the Premium on Bonds Payable account of $692.

The amortization table in Exhibit 10-5 illustrates effective interest amortization of the bond premium for Premium Firm. As the exhibit illustrates, effective interest amortization of a premium is based on the same concepts as amortization of a discount. The following relationships still hold true:

Cash Interest (in Column 1) = Bond Face Value × Face Rate
Interest Expense (in Column 2) = Carrying Value × Effective Rate

The first column of the exhibit indicates that the cash interest to be paid is $800 ($10,000 × 8%). The second column indicates the annual interest expense at the effective rate. In 2007 the interest expense is $642 ($10,692 × 6%). Note, however, two differences between Exhibit 10-4 and Exhibit 10-5. In the amortization of a premium, the cash interest in Column 1 exceeds the interest expense in Column 2. Therefore, the premium amortized is defined as follows:

Premium Amortized (in Column 3) = Cash Interest − Interest Expense

Also note that the carrying value in Column 4 starts at an amount higher than the face value of $10,000 ($10,692) and is amortized downward until it reaches face value. Therefore, the carrying value at the end of each year is the carrying value at the beginning of the period minus the premium amortized for that year. For example, the carrying value in Exhibit 10-5 at the end of 2007 ($10,534) was calculated by subtracting the premium amortized for 2007 ($158 in Column 3) from the carrying value at the beginning of 2007 ($10,692).

Exhibit 10-5 is the basis for determining the effect of amortization of a premium on the firm's financial statements. The effect of the interest payment and the amortization of premium for 2007 (note the December 31, 2007, line of the table) is as follows:

Study Tip

Amortization of a discount increases interest expense. Amortization of a premium reduces interest expense.

Balance Sheet						Income Statement	
ASSETS	**=**	**LIABILITIES**	**+**	**STOCKHOLDERS' EQUITY**	**+**	**REVENUES − EXPENSES**	
Cash (800)		Premium on Bonds Payable (158)				Interest Expense	(642)

The balance of the Premium on Bonds Payable account as of December 31, 2007, would be calculated as follows:

Beginning balance, January 1, 2007	$692
Less: Amount amortized	158
Ending balance, December 31, 2007	$534

The December 31, 2007, balance represents the amount *unamortized*, or the amount that will be amortized in future time periods. On the balance sheet presented as of December 31, 2007, the unamortized portion of the premium appears as the balance of the Premium on Bonds Payable account as follows:

Long-term liabilities:	
Bonds payable	$10,000
Plus: Premium on bonds payable	534
	$10,534

The process of amortization would continue for four years, until the balance of the Premium on Bonds Payable account has been reduced to zero. By the end of 2010, all of the balance of the Premium on Bonds Payable account will have been transferred to the Interest Expense account and represents a reduction of interest expense each period.

2 minute review

1. How do you calculate the issue price of a bond?

2. What effect does amortizing a premium have on the amount of interest expense for the bond? What effect does amortizing a discount have?

Answers

1. *To calculate the issue price of a bond, you must calculate the present value of the annuity of interest payments and add to it the present value of the principal to be repaid, using the market rate of interest as the rate in the calculations.*

2. *When a premium is amortized, it decreases the amount of interest on the bond, and when a discount is amortized, it increases the amount of interest expense on the bond.*

REDEMPTION OF BONDS

Redemption at Maturity The term *redemption* refers to retirement of bonds by repayment of the principal. If bonds are retired on their due date, the accounting entry is not difficult. Refer again to the Discount Firm example. If Discount Firm retires its bonds on the due date of December 31, 2010, it must repay the principal of $10,000, and Cash is reduced by $10,000. Notice that no gain or loss is incurred because the carrying value of the bond at that point is $10,000.

Retired Early at a Gain A firm may want to retire bonds before their due date for several reasons. A firm may simply have excess cash and may determine that the best use of those funds is to repay outstanding bond obligations. Bonds may also be retired early because of changing interest rate conditions. If interest rates in the economy decline, firms may find it advantageous to retire bonds that have been issued at higher rates. Of course, what is advantageous to the issuer is not necessarily so for the investor. Early retirement of callable bonds is always a possibility that must be anticipated. Large institutional investors expect such a development and merely reinvest the money elsewhere. Many individual investors are more seriously inconvenienced when a bond issue is called.

LO6 Find the gain or loss on retirement of bonds.

Gain or loss on redemption
The difference between the carrying value and the redemption price at the time bonds are redeemed.

Bond terms generally specify that if bonds are retired before their due date, they are not retired at the face value amount but at a call price or redemption price indicated on the bond certificate. Also, the amount of unamortized premium or discount on the bonds must be considered when bonds are retired early. The retirement results in a **gain or loss on redemption** that must be calculated as follows:

Gain = Carrying Value − Redemption Price
Loss = Redemption Price − Carrying Value

In other words, the issuing firm must calculate the carrying value of the bonds at the time of redemption and compare it with the total redemption price. If the carrying value is higher than the redemption price, the issuing firm must record a gain. If the carrying value is lower than the redemption price, the issuing firm must record a loss.

We will use the Premium Firm example to illustrate the calculation of gain or loss. Assume that on December 31, 2007, Premium Firm wants to retire its bonds due in 2010. Assume, as in the previous section, that the bonds were issued at a premium of $692 at the beginning of 2007. Premium Firm has used the effective interest method of amortization and has recorded the interest and amortization entries for the year (see page 467). This has resulted in a balance of $534 in the Premium on Bonds Payable account as of December 31, 2007. Assume also that Premium Firm's bond certificates indicate that the bonds may be retired early at a call price of 102 (meaning 102% of face value). Thus, the redemption price is 102% of $10,000, or $10,200.

Premium Firm's retirement of bonds would result in a gain. The gain can be calculated using two steps.

1. **Calculate the carrying value of the bonds as of the date they are retired.** The carrying value of Premium Firm's bonds at that date is calculated as follows:

Carrying Value = Face Value + Unamortized Premium
= $10,000 + $534
= $10,534

Note that the carrying value we have calculated is the same amount indicated for December 31, 2007, in Column 4 of the effective interest amortization table of Exhibit 10-5.

2. **Calculate the gain:**

Gain = Carrying Value − Redemption Price
= $10,534 − ($10,000 × 1.02)
= $10,534 − $10,200
= $334

It is important to remember that when bonds are retired, the balance of the Bonds Payable account and the remaining balance of the Premium on Bonds Payable account must be eliminated from the balance sheet.

Retired Early at a Loss To illustrate retirement of bonds at a loss, assume that Premium Firm retires bonds at December 31, 2007, as in the previous section. However, assume that the call price for the bonds is 107 (or 107% of face value).

We can again perform the calculations in two steps.

1. **Calculate the carrying value:**

Carrying Value = Face Value + Unamortized Premium
= $10,000 + $534
= $10,534

2. **Compare the carrying value with the redemption price to calculate the amount of the loss:**

Loss = Redemption Price − Carrying Value
= ($10,000 × 1.07) − $10,534
= $10,700 − $10,534
= $166

In this case, a loss of $166 has resulted from the retirement of Premium Firm bonds. A loss means that the company paid more to retire the bonds than the amount at which the bonds were recorded on the balance sheet.

Financial Statement Presentation of Gain or Loss The accounts Gain on Bond Redemption and Loss on Bond Redemption are income statement accounts. A gain on bond redemption increases Premium Firm's income; a loss decreases its income. In most cases, a gain or loss should not be considered "unusual" or "infrequent" and therefore should not be placed in the section of the income statement where extraordinary items are presented. While gains and losses should be treated as part of the company's operating income, some statement users may consider them as "one-time" events and wish to exclude them when predicting a company's future income. For that reason, it would be very helpful if companies would present their gains and losses separately on the income statement so that readers could determine whether or not such amounts will affect future periods.

Liability for Leases

Long-term bonds and notes payable are important sources of financing for many large corporations and are quite prominent in the long-term liability category of the balance sheet for many firms. But other important elements of that category of the balance sheet also represent long-term obligations. We will introduce you to leases because they are a major source of financing for many companies. We will introduce another liability, deferred taxes, in the appendix at the end of this chapter. In some cases, these liabilities are required to be reported on the financial statements and are important components of the Long-Term Liabilities section of the balance sheet. In other cases, the items are not required to be presented in the financial statements and can be discerned only by a careful reading of the notes to the financial statements.

LEASES

A *lease*, a contractual arrangement between two parties, allows one party, the *lessee*, the right to use an asset in exchange for making payments to its owner, the *lessor*. A common example of a lease arrangement is the rental of an apartment. The tenant is the lessee and the landlord is the lessor.

Lease agreements are a form of financing. In some cases, it is more advantageous to lease an asset than to borrow money to purchase it. The lessee can conserve cash because a lease does not require a large initial cash outlay. A wide variety of lease arrangements exists, ranging from simple agreements to complex ones that span a long time period. Lease arrangements are popular because of their flexibility. The terms of a lease can be structured in many ways to meet the needs of the lessee and lessor. This results in difficult accounting questions:

1. **Should the right to use property be reported as an asset by the lessee?**
2. **Should the obligation to make payments be reported as a liability by the lessee?**
3. **Should all leases be accounted for in the same manner regardless of the terms of the lease agreement?**

The answers are that some leases should be reported as an asset and a liability by the lessee and some should not. The accountant must examine the terms of the lease agreement and compare those terms with an established set of criteria.

Lease Criteria From the viewpoint of the lessee, there are two types of lease agreements: operating and capital. In an **operating lease**, the lessee acquires the right to use an asset for a limited period of time. The lessee is *not* required to record the right to use the property as an asset or to record the obligation for payments as a liability. Therefore, the lessee is able to attain a form of *off-balance-sheet financing*. That is, the lessee has attained the right to use property but has not recorded that

LO7 Determine whether or not a lease agreement must be reported as a liability on the balance sheet.

Operating lease
A lease that does not meet any of the four criteria and is not recorded as an asset by the lessee.

right, or the accompanying obligation, on the balance sheet. By escaping the balance sheet, the lease does not add to debt or impair the debt-to-equity ratio that investors usually calculate. Management has a responsibility to make sure that such off-balance-sheet financing is not in fact a long-term obligation. The company's auditors are supposed to analyze the terms of the lease carefully to make sure that management has exercised its responsibility.

Capital lease
A lease that is recorded as an asset by the lessee.

The second type of lease agreement is a **capital lease**. In this type of lease, the lessee has acquired sufficient rights of ownership and control of the property to be considered its owner. The lease is called a *capital lease* because it is capitalized (recorded) on the balance sheet by the lessee.

A lease should be considered a capital lease by the lessee if one or more of the following criteria are met:[2]

1. **The lease transfers ownership of the property to the lessee at the end of the lease term.**

2. **The lease contains a bargain-purchase option to purchase the asset at an amount lower than its fair market value.**

3. **The lease term is 75% or more of the property's economic life.**

4. **The present value of the minimum lease payments is 90% or more of the fair market value of the property at the inception of the lease.**

If none of the criteria are met, the lease agreement is accounted for as an operating lease. This is an area in which it is important for the accountant to exercise professional judgment. In some cases, firms may take elaborate measures to evade or manipulate the criteria that would require lease capitalization. The accountant should determine what is full and fair disclosure based on an unbiased evaluation of the substance of the transaction.

Operating Leases You have already accounted for operating leases in previous chapters when recording rent expense and prepaid rent. A rental agreement for a limited time period is also a lease agreement.

Suppose, for example, that Lessee Firm wants to lease a car for a new salesperson. A lease agreement is signed with Lessor Dealer on January 1, 2007, to lease a car for the year for $4,000, payable on December 31, 2007. Typically, a car lease does not transfer title at the end of the term, does not include a bargain-purchase price, and does not last for more than 75% of the car's life. In addition, the present value of the lease payments is not 90% of the car's value. Because the lease does not meet any of the specified criteria, it should be presented as an operating lease. Lessee Firm would simply record lease expense, or rent expense, of $4,000 for the year.

Although operating leases are not recorded on the balance sheet by the lessee, they are mentioned in financial statement notes. The FASB requires note disclosure of the amount of future lease obligations for leases that are considered operating leases. Exhibit 10-6 provides a portion of the note from **Tommy Hilfiger Corporation**'s 2004 annual report. The note reveals that Tommy Hilfiger has used operating leases as an important source of financing and has significant off-balance-sheet commitments in future periods as a result. An investor might want to add this off-balance-sheet item to the debt on the balance sheet to get a conservative view of the company's obligations.

Capital Leases Capital leases are presented as assets and liabilities by the lessee because they meet one or more of the lease criteria. Suppose that Lessee Firm in the previous example wanted to lease a car for a longer period of time. Assume that on January 1, 2007, Lessee signs a lease agreement with Lessor Dealer to lease a car. The terms of the agreement specify that Lessee will make annual lease payments of $4,000 per year for five years, payable each December 31. Assume also

---

2 *Statement of Financial Accounting Standards No. 13*, "Accounting for Leases" (Stamford, Conn.: FASB, 1976).

EXHIBIT 10-6	Tommy Hilfiger Corporation's 2004 Note Disclosure of Leases

Operating leases can be used as an important source of financing.

Commitments and Contingencies
Leases (in millions)
The Company leases office, warehouse and showroom space, retail stores and office equipment under operating leases, which expire not later than 2022. The Company normalizes fixed escalations in rental expense under its operating leases. Minimum annual rentals under non-cancelable operating leases, excluding operating cost escalations and contingent rental amounts based upon retail sales, are payable as follows:

Fiscal Year Ending March 31,

2005	$ 48,847
2006	45,247
2007	40,897
2008	34,610
2009	30,641
Thereafter	$120,602

Rent expense was $46,640, $46,306, and $34,781 for the years ended March 31, 2004, 2003, and 2002, respectively.

that the lease specifies that at the end of the lease agreement, the title to the car is transferred to Lessee Firm. Lessee must decide how to account for the lease agreement.

The contractual arrangement between Lessee Firm and Lessor Dealer is called a lease agreement, but clearly the agreement is much different from a year-to-year lease arrangement. Essentially, Lessee Firm has acquired the right to use the asset for its entire life and does not need to return it to Lessor Dealer. You may call this agreement a lease, but it actually represents a purchase of the asset by Lessee with payments made over time.

The lease should be treated as a capital lease by Lessee because it meets at least one of the four criteria (it meets the first criteria concerning transfer of title). A capital lease must be recorded at its present value by Lessee as an asset and as an obligation. As of January 1, 2007, we must calculate the present value of the annual payments. If we assume an interest rate of 8%, the present value of the payments is $15,972 ($4,000 × an annuity factor of 3.993 from Table 9-4 on page 418).

Perform the following steps when using a calculator to determine the present value in our example:

> **Study Tip** It is called a *capital lease* because the lease is capitalized or put on the books of the lessee as an asset.

ENTER	DISPLAY
5 N	N = 5
8 I/Y	I/Y = 8
4000 PMT	PMT = 4,000
0 FV	FV = 0
CPT PV	PV = 15,971*
*(rounded)	

The effect on Lessee Firm's accounting equation of treating the lease as a capital lease is as follows:

Balance Sheet					Income Statement	
ASSETS	**=**	**LIABILITIES**	**+**	**STOCKHOLDERS' EQUITY**	**+**	**REVENUES − EXPENSES**
Leased Asset 15,972		Lease Obligation 15,972				

The Leased Asset account is a long-term asset similar to plant and equipment and represents the fact that Lessee has acquired the right to use and retain the asset.

EXHIBIT 10-7	Lease Amortization: Effective Interest Method of Amortization

Date	Column 1 Lease Payment	Column 2 Interest Expense	Column 3 Reduction of Obligation	Column 4 Lease Obligation
		8%	Col. 1 − Col. 2	
1/1/2007	—	—	—	$15,972
12/31/2007	$4,000	$1,278	$2,722	13,250
12/31/2008	4,000	1,060	2,940	10,310
12/31/2009	4,000	825	3,175	7,135
12/31/2010	4,000	571	3,429	3,706
12/31/2011	4,000	294	3,706	–0–

Because the leased asset represents depreciable property, depreciation must be reported for each of the five years of asset use. On December 31, 2007, Lessee records depreciation of $3,194 ($15,972/5 years), assuming that the straight-line method is adopted. The effect of the depreciation is as follows:

	Balance Sheet				Income Statement
ASSETS	=	**LIABILITIES**	+	**STOCKHOLDERS' EQUITY** +	**REVENUES − EXPENSES**
Accumulated Depreciation— Leased Asset (3,194)					Depreciation Expense (3,194)

Depreciation of leased assets is referred to as *amortization* by some firms.

On December 31, Lessee Firm also must make a payment of $4,000 to Lessor Dealer. A portion of each payment represents interest on the obligation (loan), and the remainder represents a reduction of the principal amount. Each payment must be separated into its principal and interest components. Generally, the effective interest method is used for that purpose. An effective interest table can be established using the same concepts as were used to amortize a premium or discount on bonds payable.

Exhibit 10-7 illustrates the effective interest method applied to the Lessee Firm example. Note that the table begins with an obligation amount equal to the present value of the payments of $15,972. Each payment is separated into principal and interest amounts so that the amount of the loan obligation at the end of the lease agreement equals zero. The amortization table is the basis for the amounts that are reflected on the financial statement. Exhibit 10-7 indicates that the $4,000 payment in 2007 should be considered as interest of $1,278 (8% of $15,972) and reduction of principal of $2,722. The effect on the accounting equation of the December 31, 2007, payment is as follows:

	Balance Sheet				Income Statement
ASSETS	=	**LIABILITIES**	+	**STOCKHOLDERS' EQUITY** +	**REVENUES − EXPENSES**
Cash (4,000)		Lease Obligation (2,722)			Interest Expense (1,278)

Therefore, for a capital lease, Lessee Firm must record both an asset and a liability. The asset is reduced by the process of depreciation. The liability is reduced by reductions of principal using the effective interest method. According to Exhibit 10-7, the total lease obligation as of December 31, 2007, is $13,250. This amount must be separated into current and long-term categories. The portion of the liability that will be paid within one year of the balance sheet should be considered a current liability. Reference to Exhibit 10-7 indicates that the liability will be reduced by $2,940 in 2008, and that amount should be considered a current liability. The remaining amount of the liability, $10,310 ($13,250 − $2,940), should be considered long-term. On the balance sheet as of December 31, 2007, Lessee Firm reports the following balances related to the lease obligation:

Assets:		
Leased assets	$15,972	
Less: Accumulated depreciation	3,194	
		$12,778
Current liabilities:		
Lease obligation		$ 2,940
Long-term liabilities:		
Lease obligation		$10,310

Notice that the depreciated asset does not equal the present value of the lease obligation. This is not unusual. For example, an automobile often may be completely depreciated but still have payments due on it.

The criteria used to determine whether a lease is an operating or a capital lease have provided a standard accounting treatment for all leases. The accounting for leases in foreign countries generally follows guidelines similar to those used in the United States. The criteria used in foreign countries to determine whether or not a lease is a capital lease are usually less detailed and less specific, however. As a result, capitalization of leases occurs less frequently in foreign countries than in the United States because of the increased use of judgment necessary in applying the accounting rules.

⏱ *2 minute review*

1. When a lease is considered a capital lease to the lessee, what entry is made to initially record the lease agreement?

2. When the lessee makes a lease payment on a capital lease, how is the payment recorded?

Answers

1. *A capital lease is recorded as an asset, in an account such as Leased Asset, and as a liability, in an account such as Lease Obligation. The lease is recorded at the amount of the present value of the lease payments.*

2. *When a lease payment is made, the portion of the payment that is interest is recorded to the Interest Expense account, and the portion of the payment that is principal is considered a reduction in the Lease Obligation account.*

Analyzing Debt to Assess a Firm's Ability to Pay Its Liabilities

Long-term liabilities are a component of the "capital structure" of the company and are included in the calculation of the debt-to-equity ratio:

$$\text{Debt-to-Equity Ratio} = \frac{\text{Total Liabilities}}{\text{Total Stockholders' Equity}}$$

Most investors would prefer to see equity rather than debt on the balance sheet. Debt, and its interest charges, make up a fixed obligation that must be repaid in a finite period of time. In contrast, equity never has to be repaid, and the dividends that are declared on it are optional. Stock investors view debt as a claim against the company that must be satisfied before they get a return on their money.

Other ratios used to measure the degree of debt obligation include the times interest earned ratio and the debt service coverage ratio:

$$\text{Times Interest Earned Ratio} = \frac{\text{Income Before Interest and Tax}}{\text{Interest Expense}}$$

$$\text{Debt Service Coverage Ratio} = \frac{\text{Cash Flow from Operations Before Interest and Tax}}{\text{Interest and Principal Payments}}$$

10-2 | **Real World Practice**

Reading Finish Line's Balance Sheet

Calculate the 2005 and 2006 debt-to-equity ratios for Finish Line. Did the 2006 ratio go up or down from the previous year?

Lenders want to be sure that borrowers can pay the interest and repay the principal on a loan. Both of the preceding ratios reflect the degree to which a company can make its debt payment out of current cash flow.

For more on these ratios for **PepsiCo, Inc.**, and how they are used, see the Ratio Decision Model at the bottom of this page.

How Long-Term Liabilities Affect the Statement of Cash Flows

LO8 Explain the effects that transactions involving long-term liabilities have on the statement of cash flows.

Exhibit 10-8 indicates the impact that long-term liabilities have on a company's cash flow and their placement on the cash flow statement.

Most long-term liabilities are related to a firm's financing activities. Therefore, the change in the balance of each long-term liability account should be reflected in the Financing Activities category of the statement of cash flows. The decrease in a long-term liability account indicates that cash has been used to pay the liability. Therefore, in the statement of cash flows, a decrease in a long-term liability account should appear as a subtraction or reduction. The increase in a long-term liability account indicates that the firm has obtained additional cash via a long-term obligation. Therefore, an increase in a long-term liability account should appear in the statement of cash flows as an addition.

USING THE RATIO DECISION MODEL: ANALYZING THE DEBT-TO-EQUITY AND TIMES INTEREST EARNED RATIOS

Use the following Ratio Decision Process to evaluate the debt for PepsiCo or any other public company.

1. Formulate the Question
Long-term debt is an important element of the financing of a company. Most companies use a combination of debt and equity (stock) to finance their operations, achieve a profit, and provide a return to their investors. Investors and creditors must carefully review the financial statements to determine whether or not a company will be able to meet its obligations. The use of debt is a good management strategy, but sometimes a company may have too much debt. The important question to ask is:

What is the amount of debt in relation to the total equity of the company?

A second important question to ask is:

Will the company be able to meet its obligations related to the debt? That is, when an interest payment comes due, will the company have the ability to make the payment?

2. Gather the Information Needed
In order to address the questions above, information from the balance sheet and the income statement needs to be collected and analyzed.

- Total debt and total equity: From the balance sheet.
- Income before interest and tax: From the income statement. (Go online to get this statement from PepsiCo.)
- Interest expense: From the income statement.

(continued)

3. Calculate the Ratio

$$\text{Debt-to-Equity Ratio} = \frac{\text{Total Liabilities}}{\text{Total Stockholders' Equity}}$$

PepsiCo, Inc. and Subsidiaries
Partial Consolidated Balance Sheet
December 25, 2004 and December 27, 2003

(in millions except per share amounts)	2004	2003
LIABILITIES AND SHAREHOLDERS' EQUITY		
Total Liabilities	14,464	13,453
. . .		
Total Common Shareholders' Equity	13,523	11,896

$$\text{Debt-to-Equity Ratio} = \frac{\$14,464}{\$13,523} = 1.07$$

$$\text{Times Interest Earned Ratio} = \frac{\text{Income Before Interest and Tax}}{\text{Interest Expense}}$$

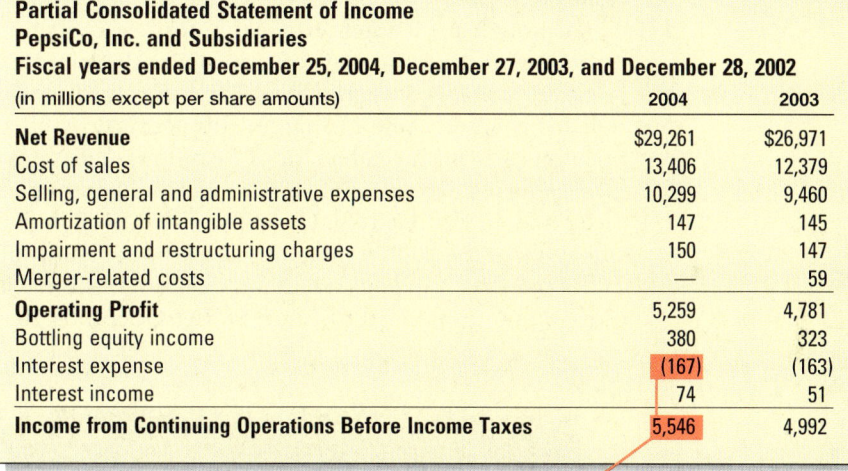

Partial Consolidated Statement of Income
PepsiCo, Inc. and Subsidiaries
Fiscal years ended December 25, 2004, December 27, 2003, and December 28, 2002

(in millions except per share amounts)	2004	2003
Net Revenue	$29,261	$26,971
Cost of sales	13,406	12,379
Selling, general and administrative expenses	10,299	9,460
Amortization of intangible assets	147	145
Impairment and restructuring charges	150	147
Merger-related costs	—	59
Operating Profit	5,259	4,781
Bottling equity income	380	323
Interest expense	(167)	(163)
Interest income	74	51
Income from Continuing Operations Before Income Taxes	5,546	4,992

Since the ratio concerns income BEFORE interest and income tax, you must add the amount of interest, $167, to the $5,546 to get $5,713.

$$\text{Times Interest Earned Ratio} = \frac{\$5,713}{\$167} = 34.20$$

4. Compare the Ratio with Others

PepsiCo's debt-to-equity ratio and times interest earned ratio should be compared to prior years and to companies in the same industry.

	PepsiCo		Coca-Cola	
	2004	2003	2004	2003
Debt-to-equity ratio	1.07	1.13	0.97	0.94
Times interest earned ratio	34.20	31.63	32.74	31.87

5. Interpret the Results

Both PepsiCo and Coca-Cola are very strong companies with a very safe balance of debt to equity. PepsiCo has slightly more debt than stockholders' equity in both 2004 and 2003, while Coca-Cola has slightly less debt than stockholders' equity. Both companies have a small amount of interest obligations compared to their income available to meet those obligations. PepsiCo has 34.20 times more income than its interest expense for 2004, while Coca-Cola has 32.74. These ratios indicate that the creditors for both companies are confident that each company will be able to meet its interest obligations on its long-term debt.

EXHIBIT 10-8   Long-Term Liabilities on the Statement of Cash Flows

Item	Statement of Cash Flows
	Operating Activities
	Net income **xxx**
Increase in current liability ··········	➤ **+**
Decrease in current liability ··········	➤ **−**
	Investing Activities
	Financing Activities
Increase in long-term liability ··········	➤ **+**
Decrease in long-term liability ··········	➤ **−**

The statement of cash flows of Coca-Cola Company is presented in Exhibit 10-9. Note that the Financing Activities category contains two items related to long-term liabilities. In 2004, long-term debt was issued for $3,030 million and is an addition to cash. This indicates that Coca-Cola increased its cash position by borrowings. Second, the payment of debt is listed as a deduction of $1,316 million. This indicates that Coca-Cola paid long-term liabilities, resulting in a reduction of cash.

Although most long-term liabilities are reflected in the Financing Activities category of the statement of cash flows, there are exceptions. The most notable exception involves the Deferred Tax account (discussed in the appendix at the end of this chapter). The change in this account is reflected in the Operating Activities category of the statement of cash flows. This presentation is necessary because the Deferred Tax account is related to an operating item, income tax expense. For example, in Exhibit 10-9, **Coca-Cola** listed $162 million in the Operating Activities category of the 2004 statement of cash flows. This indicates that $162 million more was recorded as expense than was paid out in cash. Therefore, the amount is a positive amount in, or an addition to, the Operating Activities category.

APPENDIX

Accounting Tools: Other Liabilities

In this appendix we will discuss another item found in the long-term liabilities category of many companies, deferred taxes. Our purpose here is to make you aware of its existence when reading financial statements.

LO9 Explain deferred taxes and calculate the deferred tax liability.

DEFERRED TAX

The financial statements of most major firms include an item titled Deferred Income Taxes or Deferred Tax (see PepsiCo's deferred taxes in Exhibit 10-1 and Coca-Cola's in the chapter opening). In most cases, the account appears in the Long-Term Liabilities section of the balance sheet, and the dollar amount might

EXHIBIT 10-9 **The Coca-Cola Company and Subsidiaries' 2004 Consolidated Statements of Cash Flows**

CONSOLIDATED STATEMENTS OF CASH FLOWS

The Coca-Cola Company and Subsidiaries

Year Ended December 31,	2004	2003	2002
(In millions)			
OPERATING ACTIVITIES			
Net income	$ 4,847	$ 4,347	$ 3,050
Depreciation and amortization	893	850	806
Stock-based compensation expense	345	422	365
Deferred income taxes	162	(188)	40
Equity income (loss), net of dividends	(476)	(294)	(256)
Foreign currency adjustments	(59)	(79)	(76)
Gains on issuances of stock by equity investees	(24)	(8)	—
(Gains) losses on sales of assets, including bottling interests	(20)	(5)	3
Cumulative effect of accounting changes	—	—	926
Other operating charges	480	330	—
Other items	437	249	291
Net change in operating assets and liabilities	(617)	(168)	(407)
Net cash provided by operating activities	5,968	5,456	4,742
INVESTING ACTIVITIES			
Acquisitions and investments, principally trademarks and bottling companies	(267)	(359)	(544)
Purchases of investments and other assets	(46)	(177)	(141)
Proceeds from disposals of investments and other assets	161	147	243
Purchases of property, plant, and equipment	(755)	(812)	(851)
Proceeds from disposals of property, plant, and equipment	341	87	69
Other investing activities	63	178	159
Net cash used in investing activities	(503)	(936)	(1,065)
FINANCING ACTIVITIES			
Issuances of debt	3,030	1,026	1,622
Payments of debt	(1,316)	(1,119)	(2,378)
Issuances of stock	193	98	107
Purchases of stock for treasury	(1,739)	(1,440)	(691)
Dividends	(2,429)	(2,166)	(1,987)
Net cash used in financing activities	(2,261)	(3,601)	(3,327)
EFFECT OF EXCHANGE RATE CHANGES ON CASH AND CASH EQUIVALENTS	141	183	44
CASH AND CASH EQUIVALENTS			
Net increase during the year	3,345	1,102	394
Balance at beginning of year	3,362	2,260	1,866
Balance at end of year	$ 6,707	$ 3,362	$ 2,260

> Changes in long-term debt generally affect the financing activities category.

be large enough to catch the user's attention. In fact, deferred income taxes represent one of the most misunderstood aspects of financial statements. In this section, we address some of the questions concerning deferred taxes.

Deferred tax is an amount that reconciles the differences between the accounting done for purposes of financial reporting to stockholders ("book" purposes) and the accounting done for tax purposes. It may surprise you that U.S. firms are allowed to use accounting methods for financial reporting that differ from those used for tax calculations. The reason is that the Internal Revenue Service defines income and expense differently than does the Financial Accounting Standards Board. As a result, companies tend to use accounting methods that minimize income for tax purposes but maximize income in the annual report to

Deferred tax
The account used to reconcile the difference between the amount recorded as income tax expense and the amount that is payable as income tax.

stockholders. This is not true in some foreign countries where financial accounting and tax accounting are more closely aligned. Firms in those countries do not report deferred tax, because the difference between methods is not significant.

When differences between financial and tax reporting do occur, we can classify them into two types: permanent and temporary. **Permanent differences** occur when an item is included in the tax calculation and is never included for book purposes—or vice versa, when an item is included for book purposes but not for tax purposes.

For example, the tax laws allow taxpayers to exclude interest on certain investments, usually state and municipal bonds, from their income. These are generally called *tax-exempt bonds.* If a corporation buys tax-exempt bonds, it does not have to declare the interest as income for tax purposes. When the corporation develops its income statement for stockholders (book purposes), however, the interest is included and appears in the Interest Income account. Therefore, tax-exempt interest represents a permanent difference between tax and book calculations.

Temporary differences occur when an item affects both the book and the tax calculations but not in the same time period. A difference caused by depreciation methods is the most common type of temporary difference. In previous chapters you have learned that depreciation may be calculated using a straight-line method or an accelerated method such as the double-declining-balance method. Most firms do not use the same depreciation method for book and tax purposes, however. Generally, straight-line depreciation is used for book purposes and an accelerated method is used for tax purposes because accelerated depreciation lowers taxable income—at least in early years—and therefore reduces the tax due. The IRS refers to this accelerated method as the *Modified Accelerated Cost Recovery System (MACRS).* It is similar to other accelerated depreciation methods in that it allows the firm to take larger depreciation deductions for tax purposes in the early years of the asset and smaller deductions in the later years. Over the life of the depreciable asset, the total depreciation using straight-line is equal to that using MACRS. Therefore, this difference is an example of a temporary difference between book and tax reporting.

The Deferred Tax account is used to reconcile the differences between the accounting for book purposes and for tax purposes. It is important to distinguish between permanent and temporary differences because the FASB has ruled that not all differences should affect the Deferred Tax account. The Deferred Tax account should reflect temporary differences but not items that are permanent differences between book accounting and tax reporting.[3]

Example of Deferred Tax Assume that Startup Firm begins business on January 1, 2007. During 2007 the firm has sales of $6,000 and has no expenses other than depreciation and income tax at the rate of 40%. Startup has depreciation on only one asset. That asset was purchased on January 1, 2007, for $10,000 and has a four-year life. Startup has decided to use the straight-line depreciation method for financial reporting purposes. Startup's accountants have chosen to use MACRS for tax purposes, however, resulting in $4,000 depreciation in 2007 and a decline of $1,000 per year thereafter.

The depreciation amounts for each of the four years for Startup's asset are as follows:

Year	Tax Depreciation	Book Depreciation	Difference
2007	$ 4,000	$ 2,500	$1,500
2008	3,000	2,500	500
2009	2,000	2,500	(500)
2010	1,000	2,500	(1,500)
Totals	$10,000	$10,000	$ 0

---

3 *Statement of Financial Accounting Standards No. 109,* "Accounting for Income Taxes" (Stamford, Conn.: FASB, 1992).

Startup's tax calculation for 2007 is based on the accelerated depreciation of $4,000, as follows:

Sales	$6,000
Depreciation Expense	4,000
Taxable Income	$2,000
× Tax Rate	40%
Tax Payable to IRS	$ 800

For the year 2007, Startup owes $800 of tax to the Internal Revenue Service. This amount is ordinarily recorded as tax payable until the time it is remitted.

Startup wants also to develop an income statement to send to the stockholders. What amount should be shown as tax expense on the income statement? You may guess that the Tax Expense account on the income statement should reflect $800 because that is the amount to be paid to the IRS. That guess is not accurate in this case, however. Remember that the tax payable amount was calculated using the depreciation method that Startup chose for tax purposes. The income statement must be calculated using the straight-line method, which Startup uses for book purposes. Therefore, Startup's income statement for 2007 appears as follows:

Sales	$6,000
Depreciation Expense	2,500
Income before Tax	$3,500
Tax Expense (40%)	1,400
Net Income	$2,100

The effect on Startup's financial statements is as follows:

Balance Sheet						Income Statement	
ASSETS	**=**	**LIABILITIES**	**+**	**STOCKHOLDERS' EQUITY**	**+**	**REVENUES − EXPENSES**	
		Tax Payable	800			Tax Expense	(1,400)
		Deferred Tax	600				

The Deferred Tax account is a balance sheet account. A balance in it reflects the fact that Startup has received a tax benefit by recording accelerated depreciation, in effect delaying the ultimate obligation to the IRS. To be sure, the amount of deferred tax still represents a liability of Startup. The Deferred Tax account balance of $600 represents the amount of the 2007 temporary difference of $1,500 times the tax rate of 40% ($1,500 × 40% = $600).

What can we learn from the Startup example? First, when you see a firm's income statement, the amount listed as tax expense does not represent the amount of cash paid to the government for taxes. Accrual accounting procedures require that the tax expense amount be calculated using the accounting methods chosen for book purposes.

Second, when you see a firm's balance sheet, the amount in the Deferred Tax account reflects all of the temporary differences between the accounting methods chosen for tax and book purposes. The accounting and financial communities are severely divided on whether the Deferred Tax account represents a "true" liability. For one thing, many investment analysts do not view it as a real liability because they have noticed that it continues to grow year after year. Others look at it as a bookkeeping item that is simply there to balance the books. The FASB has taken the stance that deferred tax is an amount that results in a future obligation and meets the definition of a liability. The controversy concerning deferred taxes is likely to continue for many years.

STUDY HIGHLIGHTS

LO1   **Identify the components of the long-term liability category of the balance sheet (p. 457).**

- Long-term liabilities are generally obligations of a company that will not be satisfied within one year. On the balance sheet, they are listed after current liabilities.

LO2   **Define the important characteristics of bonds payable (p. 458).**

- Bonds payable result from borrowing funds and are generally issued in denominations of $1,000.
- Important characteristics of bonds payable include par value, due date, interest rate, whether the bonds are convertible or callable, and any property collateralizing the bonds.

LO3   **Determine the issue price of a bond using compound interest techniques (p. 460).**

- Bonds are issued at a price which reflects the market rate of interest on the day the bond is purchased. The actual issue price of a bond represents the present value of all future cash flows related to the bond.

LO4   **Show that you understand the effect on the balance sheet of the issuance of bonds (p. 462).**

- Bonds are recorded on the balance sheet at an amount which takes into account the premium or discount associated with bonds on the date they are issued.
  - Bond premiums represent amounts paid in excess of par and bond discounts represent amounts paid below par.

LO5   **Find the amortization of premium or discount using the effective interest method (p. 464).**

- The premium or discount on bonds must be amortized over the life of the bond to accurately reflect the interest expense.
- The effective interest method amortizes discounts or premiums in a way that produces a constant interest rate from one period to the next.

LO6   **Find the gain or loss on retirement of bonds (p. 467).**

- Bonds are retired for various reasons, and if they are retired before their due date, the amount is different from the face value. Unamortized bond premiums or discounts may result in a gain or loss.
  - If the redemption price is less than the carrying value, a gain results. If the redemption price is greater than the carrying value, a loss results.

LO7   **Determine whether or not a lease agreement must be reported as a liability on the balance sheet (p. 469).**

- Leases can be classified as two types: operating leases and capital leases. Capital leases imply more rights of ownership. The accounting for these two types of leases is as follows:
  - Under an operating lease, the lessee does not record either the right to use the leased asset or any related obligation to make lease payments on the balance sheet.
  - Under a capital lease, the lessee records both the right to use the property and the lease payments that are obligated to be paid on the balance sheet.

LO8   **Explain the effects that transactions involving long-term liabilities have on the statement of cash flows (p. 474).**

- Cash flows related to long-term liabilities are generally related to a firm's financing activities.

LO9   **Explain deferred taxes and calculate the deferred tax liability (Appendix p. 476).**

- Differences arise between the tax treatment of revenue and expense items for financial accounting (book) and tax accounting methods. Deferred taxes are those amounts that reconcile these differences.

- Permanent differences occur when an item is included for tax purposes, but not book, or vice versa.
- Temporary differences occur when there are differences between the time an item is recognized for tax purposes and the time it is recognized for book purposes.

RATIO REVIEW

$$\text{Debt-to-Equity Ratio} = \frac{\text{Total Liabilities}}{\text{Total Stockholders' Equity}}$$

$$\text{Times Interest Earned Ratio} = \frac{\text{Income Before Interest and Tax}}{\text{Interest Expense}}$$

ACCOUNTS HIGHLIGHTED

Account Title	Where It Appears	In What Section	Page Number
Bonds Payable	Balance Sheet	Long-Term Liabilities	460
Premium on Bonds Payable	Balance Sheet	Long-Term Liabilities	462
Discount on Bonds Payable	Balance Sheet	Long-Term Liabilities as a contra account	462
Gain on Bond Redemption	Income Statement	Other Income/Expense	468
Loss on Bond Redemption	Income Statement	Other Income/Expense	468
Leased Asset	Balance Sheet	Property, Plant, and Equipment	471
Lease Obligation	Balance Sheet	Long-Term Liabilities	471
Deferred Income Tax	Balance Sheet	May be Asset or Liability	476

KEY TERMS QUIZ

Read each definition below and then write the number of that definition in the blank beside the appropriate term it defines. The quiz solutions appear at the end of the chapter.

_____ Long-term liability	_____ Discount
_____ Face value	_____ Effective interest method of amortization
_____ Debenture bonds	_____ Carrying value
_____ Serial bonds	_____ Gain or loss on redemption
_____ Callable bonds	_____ Operating lease
_____ Face rate of interest	_____ Capital lease
_____ Market rate of interest	_____ Deferred tax (Appendix)
_____ Bond issue price	_____ Permanent difference (Appendix)
_____ Premium	_____ Temporary difference (Appendix)

1. The principal amount of the bond as stated on the bond certificate.
2. Bonds that do not all have the same due date. A portion of the bonds comes due each time period.
3. The interest rate stated on the bond certificate. It is also called the _nominal_ or _coupon rate._
4. The total of the present value of the cash flows produced by a bond. It is calculated as the present value of the annuity of interest payments plus the present value of the principal.
5. An obligation that will not be satisfied within one year.

6. The excess of the issue price over the face value of bonds. It occurs when the face rate on the bonds exceeds the market rate.

7. Bonds that are backed by the general creditworthiness of the issuer and are not backed by specific collateral.

8. The excess of the face value of bonds over the issue price. It occurs when the market rate on the bonds exceeds the face rate.

9. Bonds that may be redeemed or retired before their specified due date.

10. The process of transferring a portion of premium or discount to interest expense. This method transfers an amount resulting in a constant effective interest rate.

11. The face value of a bond plus the amount of unamortized premium or minus the amount of unamortized discount.

12. The interest rate that bondholders could obtain by investing in other bonds that are similar to the issuing firm's bonds.

13. The difference between the carrying value and the redemption price at the time bonds are redeemed. This amount is presented as an income statement account.

14. A lease that does not meet any of four criteria and is not recorded by the lessee.

15. A lease that meets one or more of four criteria and is recorded as an asset by the lessee.

16. A difference between the accounting for tax purposes and the accounting for financial reporting purposes. This type of difference affects both book and tax calculations but not in the same time period.

17. The account used to reconcile the difference between the amount recorded as income tax expense and the amount that is payable as income tax.

18. A difference between the accounting for tax purposes and the accounting for financial reporting purposes. This type of difference occurs when an item affects one set of calculations but never affects the other set.

ALTERNATE TERMS

Bond Face Value Bond par value

Bonds Payable Notes payable

Bond Retirement Extinguishment of bonds

Carrying Value of Bond Book value of bond

Effective Interest Amortization Interest method of amortization

Face Rate of Interest Stated rate or nominal rate or coupon rate of interest

Long-Term Liabilities Noncurrent liabilities

Market Rate of Interest Yield or effective rate of interest

Redemption Price Reacquisition price

Temporary Difference Timing difference

WARMUP EXERCISES & SOLUTIONS

Warmup Exercise 10-1

A bond due in 10 years, with face value of $1,000 and face rate of interest of 8%, is issued when the market rate of interest is 6%.

Required

1. What is the issue price of the bond?
2. What is the amount of premium or discount on the bond at the time of issuance?
3. What amount of interest expense will be shown on the income statement for the first year of the bond?
4. What amount of the premium or discount will be amortized during the first year of the bond?

Warmup Exercise 10-2

You have signed an agreement to lease a car for four years and will make annual payments of $4,000 at the end of each year. (Assume that the lease meets the criteria for a capital lease.)

Required
1. Calculate the present value of the lease payments, assuming an 8% interest rate.
2. What is the effect on the accounting equation of the signing of the lease?
3. When the first lease payment is made, what portion of the payment will be considered interest?

SOLUTIONS TO WARMUP EXERCISES

Warmup Exercise 10-1

1. The issue price of the bond would be calculated at the present value:

$80 (7.360) = $ 588.80   using Table 9-4, where i = 6% and n = 10
$1,000 (0.558) =   558.00   using Table 9-2, where i = 6% and n = 10
Issue price $1,146.80

Perform the following steps when using a calculator to determine the present value:

ENTER	DISPLAY
10 N	N = 10
6 I/Y	I/Y = 8
80 PMT	PMT = 80
1000 FV	FV = 1000
CPT PV	PV = 1,147*
*(rounded)	

2. The amount of the premium is the difference between the issue price and the face value:

Premium = $1,146.80 − $1,000
= $146.80

3. The amount of interest expense can be calculated as follows:

Interest Expense = $1,146.80 × 0.06
= $68.81

4. The amount that will be amortized can be calculated as follows:

Amortized = Cash Interest − Interest Expense
= ($1,000 × 0.08) − ($1,146.80 × 0.06)
= $80.00 − $68.81
= $11.19

Warmup Exercise 10-2

1. The present value of the lease payments can be calculated as follows:

Present Value = $4,000 (3.312) using Table 9-4, where i = 8%, n = 4
= $13,248

Perform the following steps when using a calculator to determine the present value:

ENTER	DISPLAY
4 N	N = 4
8 I/Y	I/Y = 8
4000 PMT	PMT = 4,000
0 FV	FV = 0
CPT PV	PV = 13,248*
*(rounded)	

REVIEW

2.

		Balance Sheet				Income Statement
ASSETS	**=**	**LIABILITIES**	**+**	**STOCKHOLDERS' EQUITY**	**+**	**REVENUES − EXPENSES**
Leased Asset	13,248	Lease Obligation	13,248			

3. The amount of interest can be calculated as follows:

$$\text{Interest} = \$13{,}248 \times 0.08$$
$$= \$1{,}059.84$$

REVIEW PROBLEM & SOLUTION

The following items pertain to the liabilities of Brent Foods. You may assume that Brent Foods began business on January 1, 2007, and therefore the beginning balance of all accounts was zero.

a. On January 1, 2007, Brent Foods issued bonds with a face value of $50,000. The bonds are due in five years and have a face interest rate of 10%. The market rate on January 1 for similar bonds was 12%. The bonds pay interest annually each December 31. Brent has chosen to use the effective interest method of amortization for any premium or discount on the bonds.
b. On December 31, 2007, Brent Foods signed a lease agreement with Cordova Leasing. The agreement requires Brent to make annual lease payments of $3,000 per year for four years, with the first payment due on January 1, 2009. The agreement stipulates that ownership of the property is transferred to Brent at the end of the four-year lease. Assume that an 8% interest rate is used for the leasing transaction.
c. On January 1, 2008, Brent redeems its bonds payable at the specified redemption price of 101. Because this item occurs in 2008, it does not affect the balance sheet prepared for year-end 2007.

Required
1. Determine the effect on the accounting equation of the December 31, 2007, interest adjustment in item (a) and the signing of the lease in item (b).
2. Develop the Long-Term Liabilities section of Brent Foods' balance sheet as of December 31, 2007, based on items (a) and (b). You do not need to consider the notes that accompany the balance sheet.
3. Would the company prefer to treat the lease in item (b) as an operating lease? Why or why not?
4. Calculate the gain or loss on the bond redemption for item (c).

SOLUTION TO REVIEW PROBLEM

1. a. The issue price of the bonds on January 1 must be calculated at the present value of the interest payments and the present value of the principal, as follows:

$5,000 × 3.605	$18,025
$50,000 × 0.567	28,350
Issue price	$46,375

Perform the following steps when using a calculator to determine the present value:

ENTER	DISPLAY
5 N	N = 5
12 I/Y	I/Y = 12
5000 PMT	PMT = 5,000
50000 FV	FV = 50,000
CPT PV	PV = 46,395

Note: The difference is caused by rounding that occurs when using the factors from Tables 9-2 and 9-4.

The amount of the discount is calculated as follows:

$$\$50{,}000 - \$46{,}375 = \$3{,}625$$

The effect of the interest and amortization as of December 31, 2007, is as follows:

Balance Sheet					Income Statement	
ASSETS	**=**	**LIABILITIES**	**+**	**STOCKHOLDERS' EQUITY**	**+**	**REVENUES − EXPENSES**
Cash	(5,000)	Discount on Bonds Payable 565				Interest Expense (5,565)

The interest expense is calculated using the effective interest method by multiplying the carrying value of the bonds times the market rate of interest ($46,375 × 12%).

Brent must show two accounts in the Long-Term Liabilities section of the balance sheet: Bonds Payable of $50,000 and Discount on Bonds Payable of $3,060 ($3,625 less $565 amortized).

b. The lease meets the criteria to be a capital lease. Brent must report the lease as an asset and report the obligation for lease payments as a liability. The transaction should be reported at the present value of the lease payments, $9,936 (computed by multiplying $3,000 by the annuity factor of 3.312). The effect of treating the lease as a capital lease is as follows:

Balance Sheet					Income Statement	
ASSETS	**=**	**LIABILITIES**	**+**	**STOCKHOLDERS' EQUITY**	**+**	**REVENUES − EXPENSES**
Leased Asset	9,936	Lease Obligation	9,936			

Because the lease agreement was signed on December 31, 2007, it is not necessary to amortize the Lease Obligation account in 2007. The account should be stated in the Long-Term Liabilities section of Brent's balance sheet at $9,936.

2. The Long-Term Liabilities section of Brent's balance sheet for December 31, 2007, on the basis of items (a) and (b) is as follows:

Brent Foods
Partial Balance Sheet
As of December 31, 2007

Long-term liabilities:		
Bonds payable	$50,000	
Less: Unamortized discount on bonds payable	3,060	$46,940
Lease obligation		9,936
Total long-term liabilities		$56,876

3. The company would prefer that the lease be an operating lease because it would not have to report the asset or liability on the balance sheet. This off-balance-sheet financing may give a more favorable impression of the company.

4. Brent must calculate the loss on the bond redemption as the difference between the carrying value of the bonds ($46,940) and the redemption price ($50,000 × 1.01). The amount of the loss is calculated as follows:

$50,500 − $46,940 = $3,560 loss on redemption

QUESTIONS

1. Which interest rate, the face rate or the market rate, should be used when calculating the issue price of a bond? Why?

2. What is the tax advantage that companies experience when bonds are issued instead of stock?

3. Does the issuance of bonds at a premium indicate that the face rate is higher or lower than the market rate of interest?

4. How does the effective interest method of amortization result in a constant rate of interest?

5. What is the meaning of the following sentence: "Amortization affects the amount of interest expense"? How does amortization of premium affect the amount of interest expense? How does amortization of discount affect the amount of interest expense?

6. Does amortization of a premium increase or decrease the bond carrying value? Does amortization of a discount increase or decrease the bond carrying value?

7. Is there always a gain or loss when bonds are redeemed? How is the gain or loss calculated?

HOMEWORK

8. What are the reasons that not all leases are accounted for in the same manner? Do you think it would be possible to develop a new accounting rule that would treat all leases in the same manner?

9. What is the meaning of the term *off-balance-sheet financing?* Why do some firms want to engage in off-balance-sheet transactions?

10. What are the effects on the financial statements if a lease is considered an operating lease rather than a capital lease?

11. Should depreciation be reported on leased assets? If so, over what period of time should depreciation occur?

12. Why do firms have a Deferred Tax account? Where should that account be shown on the financial statements? (Appendix)

13. How can you determine whether an item should reflect a permanent or a temporary difference when calculating the deferred tax amount? (Appendix)

14. Does the amount of income tax expense presented on the income statement represent the amount of tax actually paid? Why or why not? (Appendix)

15. Do you agree with this statement: "All liabilities could be legally enforced in a court of law"? (Appendix)

EXERCISES

LO2 **Exercise 10-1** Relationships

The following components are computed annually when a bond is issued for other than its face value:

- Cash interest payment
- Interest expense
- Amortization of discount/premium
- Carrying value of bond

Required
State whether each component will increase (I), decrease (D), or remain constant (C) as the bond approaches maturity, given the following situations:

1. Issued at a discount.
2. Issued at a premium.

LO3 **Exercise 10-2** Issue Price

Youngblood Inc. plans to issue $500,000 face value bonds with a stated interest rate of 8%. They will mature in 10 years. Interest will be paid semiannually. At the date of issuance, assume the market rate is (a) 8%, (b) 6%, and (c) 10%.

Required
For each market interest rate, answer the following questions:

1. What is the amount due at maturity?
2. How much cash interest will be paid every six months?
3. At what price will the bond be issued?

LO3 **Exercise 10-3** Issue Price

The following terms relate to independent bond issues:

a. 500 bonds; $1,000 face value; 8% stated rate; 5 years; annual interest payments
b. 500 bonds; $1,000 face value; 8% stated rate; 5 years; semiannual interest payments
c. 800 bonds; $1,000 face value; 8% stated rate; 10 years; semiannual interest payments
d. 2,000 bonds; $500 face value; 12% stated rate; 15 years; semiannual interest payments

Required
Assuming the market rate of interest is 10%, calculate the selling price for each bond issue.

LO4 **Exercise 10-4** Impact of Two Bond Alternatives

Yung Chong Company wants to issue 100 bonds, $1,000 face value, in January. The bonds will have a 10-year life and pay interest annually. The market rate of interest on January 1 will be 9%. Yung Chong is considering two alternative bond issues: (a) bonds with a face rate of 8% and (b) bonds with a face rate of 10%.

Required
1. Could the company save money by issuing bonds with an 8% face rate? If it chooses alternative (a), what would be the interest cost as a percentage?
2. Could the company benefit by issuing bonds with a 10% face rate? If it chooses alternative (b), what would be the interest cost as a percentage?

LO6   **Exercise 10-5** Redemption of Bonds

Reynolds Corporation issued $75,000 face value bonds at a discount of $2,500. The bonds contain a call price of 103. Reynolds decides to redeem the bonds early when the unamortized discount is $1,750.

Required
1. Calculate Reynolds Corporation's gain or loss on the early redemption of the bonds.
2. Describe how the gain or loss would be reported on the income statement and in the notes to the financial statements.

LO6   **Exercise 10-6** Redemption of a Bond at Maturity

On March 31, 2007, Sammonds Inc. issued $250,000 face value bonds at a discount of $7,000. The bonds were retired at their maturity date, March 31, 2017.

Required
Assuming the last interest payment and the amortization of the discount have already been recorded, calculate the gain or loss on the redemption of the bonds on March 31, 2017. Indicate the effect on the accounting equation of the redemption of the bonds.

LO7   **Exercise 10-7** Leased Asset

Hopper Corporation signed a 10-year capital lease on January 1, 2007. The lease requires annual payments of $8,000 every December 31.

Required
1. Assuming an interest rate of 9%, calculate the present value of the minimum lease payments.
2. Explain why the value of the leased asset and the accompanying lease obligation are not initially reported on the balance sheet at $80,000.

LO7   **Exercise 10-8** Financial Statement Impact of a Lease

Benjamin's Warehouse signed a six-year capital lease on January 1, 2007, with payments due every December 31. Interest is calculated annually at 10%, and the present value of the minimum lease payments is $13,065.

Required
1. Calculate the amount of the annual payment that Benjamin's must make every December 31.
2. Calculate the amount of the lease obligation that would be presented on the December 31, 2008, balance sheet (after two lease payments have been made).

LO7   **Exercise 10-9** Leased Assets

Koffman and Sons signed a four-year lease for a forklift on January 1, 2007. Annual lease payments of $1,510, based on an interest rate of 8%, are to be made every December 31, beginning with December 31, 2007.

Required
1. Assume the lease is treated as an operating lease.
   a. Will the value of the forklift appear on Koffman's balance sheet?
   b. What account will indicate lease payments have been made?
2. Assume the lease is treated as a capital lease.
   a. Indicate the effect on the accounting equation when the lease is signed. Explain why the value of the leased asset is not recorded at $6,040 ($1,510 × 4).
   b. Indicate the effect on the accounting equation of the first lease payment on December 31, 2007.
   c. Calculate the amount of depreciation expense on December 31, 2007.
   d. At what amount would the lease obligation be presented on the balance sheet as of December 31, 2007?

LO8 **Exercise 10-10** Impact of Transactions Involving Bonds on Statement of Cash Flows

From the following list, identify each item as operating (O), investing (I), financing (F), or not separately reported on the statement of cash flows (N).

_____ Proceeds from issuance of bonds payable

_____ Interest expense

_____ Redemption of bonds payable at maturity

LO8 **Exercise 10-11** Impact of Transactions Involving Capital Leases on Statement of Cash Flows

Assume that Garnett Corporation signs a lease agreement with Duncan Company to lease a piece of equipment and determines that the lease should be treated as a capital lease. Garnett records a leased asset in the amount of $53,400 and a lease obligation in the same amount on its balance sheet.

Required
1. Indicate how this transaction would be reported on Garnett's statement of cash flows.
2. From the following list of transactions relating to this lease, identify each item as operating (O), investing (I), financing (F), or not separately reported on the statement of cash flows (N).

_____ Reduction of lease obligation (principal portion of lease payment)

_____ Interest expense

_____ Depreciation expense—leased assets

LO8 **Exercise 10-12** Impact of Transactions Involving Tax Liabilities on Statement of Cash Flows

From the following list, identify each item as operating (O), investing (I), financing (F), or not separately reported on the statement of cash flows (N). For items identified as operating, indicate whether the related amount would be added to or deducted from net income in determining the cash flows from operating activities.

_____ Decrease in taxes payable

_____ Increase in deferred taxes

LO9 **Exercise 10-13** Temporary and Permanent Differences (Appendix)

Madden Corporation wants to determine the amount of deferred tax that should be reported on its 2007 financial statements. It has compiled a list of differences between the accounting conducted for tax purposes and the accounting used for financial reporting (book) purposes.

Required
For each of the following items, indicate whether the difference should be classified as a permanent or a temporary difference.

1. During 2007, Madden received interest on state bonds purchased as an investment. The interest can be treated as tax-exempt interest for tax purposes.
2. During 2007, Madden paid for a life insurance premium on two key executives. Madden's accountant has indicated that the amount of the premium cannot be deducted for income tax purposes.
3. During December 2007, Madden received money for renting a building to a tenant. Madden must report the rent as income on its 2007 tax form. For book purposes, however, the rent will be considered income on the 2008 income statement.
4. Madden owns several pieces of equipment that it depreciates using the straight-line method for book purposes. An accelerated method of depreciation is used for tax purposes, however.
5. Madden offers a warranty on the product it sells. The corporation records the expense of the warranty repair costs in the year the product is sold (the accrual method) for book purposes. For tax purposes, however, Madden is not allowed to deduct the expense until the period when the product is repaired.
6. During 2007, Madden was assessed a large fine by the federal government for polluting the environment. Madden's accountant has indicated that the fine cannot be deducted as an expense for income tax purposes.

LO9 **Exercise 10-14** Deferred Tax (Appendix)

On January 1, 2007, Kunkel Corporation purchased an asset for $32,000. Assume this is the only asset owned by the corporation. Kunkel has decided to use the straight-line method to depreciate it. For tax purposes, it will be depreciated over three years. It will be depreciated over five years, however, for the financial statements provided to stockholders. Assume that Kunkel Corporation is subject to a 40% tax rate.

Required

Calculate the balance to be reflected in the Deferred Tax account for Kunkel Corporation for each year 2007 through 2011.

MULTI-CONCEPT EXERCISES

LO4,5 **Exercise 10-15** Issuance of a Bond at Face Value

On January 1, 2007, Whitefeather Industries issued 300, $1,000 face value bonds. The bonds have a five-year life and pay interest at the rate of 10%. Interest is paid semiannually on July 1 and January 1. The market rate of interest on January 1 was 10%.

Required

1. Calculate the issue price of the bonds and record the issuance of the bonds on January 1, 2007.
2. Explain how the issue price would have been affected if the market rate of interest had been higher than 10%.
3. Determine the effect on the accounting equation of the payment of interest on July 1, 2007.
4. Calculate the amount of interest accrued on December 31, 2007.

LO4,5 **Exercise 10-16** Impact of a Discount

Berol Corporation sold 20-year bonds on January 1, 2007. The face value of the bonds was $100,000, and they carry a 9% stated rate of interest, which is paid on December 31 of every year. Berol received $91,526 in return for the issuance of the bonds when the market rate was 10%. Any premium or discount is amortized using the effective interest method.

Required

1. Determine the effect on the accounting equation of the sale of the bonds on January 1, 2007, and the proper balance sheet presentation on this date.
2. Determine the effect on the accounting equation of the payment of interest on December 31, 2007, and the proper balance sheet presentation on this date.
3. Explain why it was necessary for Berol to issue the bonds for only $91,526 rather than $100,000.

LO4,5 **Exercise 10-17** Impact of a Premium

Assume the same set of facts for Berol Corporation as in Exercise 10-17 except that it received $109,862 in return for the issuance of the bonds when the market rate was 8%.

Required

1. Determine the effect on the accounting equation of the sale of the bonds on January 1, 2007, and the proper balance sheet presentation on this date.
2. Determine the effect on the accounting equation of the payment of interest on December 31, 2007, and the proper balance sheet presentation on this date.
3. Explain why the company was able to issue the bonds for $109,862 rather than for the face amount.

PROBLEMS

LO3 **Problem 10-1** Factors That Affect the Bond Issue Price

Becca Company is considering the issue of $100,000 face value, 10-year term bonds. The bonds will pay 6% interest each December 31. The current market rate is 6%; therefore, the bonds will be issued at face value.

(continued)

HOMEWORK

Required

1. For each of the following independent situations, indicate whether you believe that the company will receive a premium on the bonds or will issue them at a discount or at face value. Without using numbers, explain your position.
   a. Interest is paid semiannually instead of annually.
   b. Assume instead that the market rate of interest is 7%; the nominal rate is still 6%.
2. For each situation in part (1), prove your statement by determining the issue price of the bonds given the changes in parts (a) and (b).

LO5

Problem 10-2 Amortization of Discount

Stacy Company issued five-year, 10% bonds with a face value of $10,000 on January 1, 2007. Interest is paid annually on December 31. The market rate of interest on this date is 12%, and Stacy Company receives proceeds of $9,275 on the bond issuance.

Required

1. Prepare a five-year table (similar to Exhibit 10-4) to amortize the discount using the effective interest method.
2. What is the total interest expense over the life of the bonds? cash interest payment? discount amortization?
3. Determine the effect on the accounting equation of the payment of interest and the amortization of discount on December 31, 2009 (the third year), and determine the balance sheet presentation of the bonds on that date.

LO5

Problem 10-3 Amortization of Premium

Assume the same set of facts for Stacy Company as in Problem 10-2 except that the market rate of interest of January 1, 2007, is 8% and the proceeds from the bond issuance equal $10,803.

Required

1. Prepare a five-year table (similar to Exhibit 10-5) to amortize the premium using the effective interest method.
2. What is the total interest expense over the life of the bonds? cash interest payment? premium amortization?
3. Determine the effect on the accounting equation of the payment of interest and the amortization of premium on December 31, 2009 (the third year), and determine the balance sheet presentation of the bonds on that date.

LO6

Problem 10-4 Redemption of Bonds

McGee Company issued $200,000 face value bonds at a premium of $4,500. The bonds contain a call provision of 101. McGee decides to redeem the bonds, due to a significant decline in interest rates. On that date, McGee had amortized only $1,000 of the premium.

Required

1. Calculate the gain or loss on the early redemption of the bonds.
2. Calculate the gain or loss on the redemption, assuming that the call provision is 103 instead of 101.
3. Indicate where the gain or loss should be presented on the financial statements.
4. Why do you suppose the call price is normally higher than 100?

LO7

Problem 10-5 Financial Statement Impact of a Lease

On January 1, 2007, Muske Trucking Company leased a semitractor and trailer for five years. Annual payments of $28,300 are to be made every December 31, beginning December 31, 2007. Interest expense is based on a rate of 8%. The present value of the minimum lease payments is $113,000 and has been determined to be greater than 90% of the fair market value of the asset on January 1, 2007. Muske uses straight-line depreciation on all assets.

Required

1. Prepare a table similar to Exhibit 10-7 to show the five-year amortization of the lease obligation.
2. Determine the effect on the accounting equation of the lease transaction on January 1, 2007.

3. Determine the effect on the accounting equation of the annual payment, interest expense, and depreciation on December 31, 2008 (the second year of the lease).
4. Prepare the balance sheet presentation as of December 31, 2008, for the leased asset and the lease obligation.

LO9   **Problem 10-6** Deferred Tax (Appendix)

Erinn Corporation has compiled its 2007 financial statements. Included in the Long-Term Liabilities category of the balance sheet are the following amounts:

	2007	2006
Deferred tax	$180	$100

Included in the income statement are the following amounts related to income taxes:

	2007	2006
Income before tax	$500	$400
Tax expense	200	160
Net income	$300	$240

In the notes that accompany the 2007 statement are the following amounts:

	2007
Current provision for tax	$120
Deferred portion	80

Required
1. Prepare the journal entry in 2007 for income tax expense, deferred tax, and income tax payable.
2. Assume that a stockholder has inquired about the meaning of the numbers recorded and disclosed about deferred tax. Explain why the Deferred Tax liability account exists. Also, what do the terms *current provision* and *deferred portion* mean? Why is the deferred amount in the note $80 when the deferred amount on the 2007 balance sheet is $180?

LO9   **Problem 10-7** Deferred Tax Calculations (Appendix)

Wyhowski Inc. reported income from operations, before taxes, for 2005–2007 as follows:

2005	$210,000
2006	240,000
2007	280,000

When calculating income, Wyhowski deducted depreciation on plant equipment. The equipment was purchased January 1, 2005, at a cost of $88,000. The equipment is expected to last three years and have an $8,000 salvage value. Wyhowski uses straight-line depreciation for book purposes. For tax purposes, depreciation on the equipment is $50,000 in 2005, $20,000 in 2006, and $10,000 in 2007. Wyhowski's tax rate is 35%.

Required
1. How much did Wyhowski pay in income tax each year?
2. How much income tax expense did Wyhowski record each year?
3. What is the balance in the Deferred Income Tax account at the end of 2005, 2006, and 2007?

MULTI-CONCEPT PROBLEMS

LO4,5   **Problem 10-8** Bond Transactions

Brand Company issued $1,000,000 face value, 8-year, 12% bonds on April 1, 2007, when the market rate of interest was 12%. Interest payments are due every October 1 and April 1. Brand uses a calendar year-end.

Required
1. Determine the effect on the accounting equation of the issuance of the bonds on April 1, 2007.

(continued)

2. Determine the effect on the accounting equation of the interest payment on October 1, 2007.

3. Explain why additional interest must be recorded on December 31, 2007. What impact does this have on the amounts paid on April 1, 2008?

4. Determine the total cash inflows and outflows that occurred on the bonds over the eight-year life.

LO1,9   **Problem 10-9** Partial Classified Balance Sheet for Walgreens

The following items, listed alphabetically, appear on **Walgreens**' consolidated balance sheet at August 31, 2004 (in millions):

Accrued expenses and other liabilities	$1,370.5
Deferred income tax (long-term)	274.1
Income taxes payable	65.9
Other noncurrent liabilities	850.4
Trade accounts payable	2,641.5

Required

1. Prepare the Current Liabilities and Long-Term Liabilities sections of Walgreens' classified balance sheet at August 31, 2004.

2. Walgreens' had total liabilities of $4,539.0 million and total shareholders' equity of $7,117.8 at August 31, 2003. Total shareholders' equity at August 31, 2004, amounted to $8,139.7. Compute the company's debt-to-equity ratio at August 31, 2004 and 2003, respectively. As an investor, how would you react to the changes in this ratio?

3. What other related ratios would the company's lenders use to assess the company? What do these ratios measure?

ALTERNATE PROBLEMS

LO3   **Problem 10-1A** Factors That Affect The Bond Issue Price

Rivera Inc. is considering the issuance of $500,000 face value, 10-year term bonds. The bonds will pay 5% interest each December 31. The current market rate is 5%; therefore, the bonds will be issued at face value.

Required

1. For each of the following independent situations, indicate whether you believe that the company will receive a premium on the bonds or will issue them at a discount or at face value. Without using numbers, explain your position.
   a. Interest is paid semiannually instead of annually.
   b. Assume instead that the market rate of interest is 4%; the nominal rate is still 5%.

2. For each situation in part (1), prove your statement by determining the issue price of the bonds given the changes in parts (a) and (b).

LO5   **Problem 10-2A** Amortization of Discount

Ortega Company issued five-year, 5% bonds with a face value of $50,000 on January 1, 2007. Interest is paid annually on December 31. The market rate of interest on this date is 8%, and Ortega Company receives proceeds of $44,011 on the bond issuance.

Required

1. Prepare a five-year table (similar to Exhibit 10-4) to amortize the discount using the effective interest method.

2. What is the total interest expense over the life of the bonds? cash interest payment? discount amortization?

3. Determine the effect on the accounting equation of the payment of interest on December 31, 2009 (the third year), and the balance sheet presentation of the bonds on that date.

LO5   **Problem 10-3A** Amortization of Premium

Assume the same set of facts for Ortega Company as in Problem 10-2A except that the market rate of interest of January 1, 2007, is 4% and the proceeds from the bond issuance equal $52,230.

Required

1. Prepare a five-year table (similar to Exhibit 10-5) to amortize the premium using the effective interest method.
2. What is the total interest expense over the life of the bonds? cash interest payment? premium amortization?
3. Determine effect on the accounting equation of the payment of interest on December 31, 2009 (the third year), and the balance sheet presentation of the bonds on that date.

LO6   **Problem 10-4A** Redemption of Bonds

Elliot Company issued $100,000 face value bonds at a premium of $5,500. The bonds contain a call provision of 101. Elliot decides to redeem the bonds, due to a significant decline in interest rates. On that date, Elliot has amortized only $2,000 of the premium.

Required

1. Calculate the gain or loss on the early redemption of the bonds.
2. Calculate the gain or loss on the redemption, assuming that the call provision is 104 instead of 101.
3. Indicate how the gain or loss would be reported on the income statement and in the notes to the financial statements.
4. Why do you suppose that the call price of the bonds is normally an amount higher than 100?

LO7   **Problem 10-5A** Financial Statement Impact of a Lease

On January 1, 2007, Kiger Manufacturing Company leased a factory machine for six years. Annual payments of $21,980 are to be made every December 31, beginning December 31, 2007. Interest expense is based on a rate of 9%. The present value of the minimum lease payments is $98,600 and has been determined to be greater than 90% of the fair market value of the machine on January 1, 2007. Kiger uses straight-line depreciation on all assets.

Required

1. Prepare a table similar to Exhibit 10-7 to show the six-year amortization of the lease obligation.
2. Determine the effect on the accounting equation of the lease on January 1, 2007.
3. Determine the effect on the accounting equation of the annual payment, interest expense, and depreciation on December 31, 2008 (the second year of the lease).
4. Prepare the balance sheet presentation as of December 31, 2008, for the leased asset and the lease obligation.

LO9   **Problem 10-6A** Deferred Tax (Appendix)

Thad Corporation has compiled its 2007 financial statements. Included in the Long-Term Liabilities category of the balance sheet are the following amounts:

	2007	2006
Deferred tax	$180	$200

Included in the income statement are the following amounts related to income taxes:

	2007	2006
Income before tax	$500	$400
Tax expense	100	150
Net income	$400	$250

Required

1. Determine the effect on the accounting equation in 2007 for income tax expense, deferred tax, and income tax payable.
2. Assume that a stockholder has inquired about the meaning of the numbers recorded. Explain why the Deferred Tax liability account exists.

LO9   **Problem 10-7A** Deferred Tax Calculations (Appendix)

Clemente Inc. has reported income for book purposes as follows for the past three years:

(in thousands)	Year 1	Year 2	Year 3
Income before taxes	$120	$120	$120

(continued)

Clemente has identified two items that are treated differently in the financial records and in the tax records. The first one is interest income on municipal bonds, which is recognized on the financial reports to the extent of $5,000 each year but does not show up as a revenue item on the company's tax return. The other item is equipment that is depreciated using the straight-line method, at the rate of $20,000 each year, for financial accounting but is depreciated for tax purposes at the rate of $30,000 in Year 1, $20,000 in Year 2, and $10,000 in Year 3.

Required

1. Determine the amount of cash paid for income taxes each year by Clemente. Assume that a 40% tax rate applies to all three years.
2. Calculate the balance in the Deferred Tax account at the end of Years 1, 2, and 3. How does this account appear on the balance sheet?

ALTERNATE MULTI-CONCEPT PROBLEMS

LO4,6   **Problem 10-8A** Financial Statement Impact of a Bond

Worthington Company issued $1,000,000 face value, six-year, 10% bonds on July 1, 2007, when the market rate of interest was 12%. Interest payments are due every July 1 and January 1. Worthington uses a calendar year-end.

Required

1. Determine the effect on the accounting equation of the issuance of the bonds on July 1, 2007.
2. Determine the effect on the accounting equation of accrual of interest on December 31, 2007.
3. Determine the effect on the accounting equation of the interest payment on January 1, 2008.
4. Calculate the amount of cash that will be paid for the retirement of the bonds on the maturity date.

LO1,9   **Problem 10-9A** Partial Classified Balance Sheet for Boeing

The following items appear on the consolidated balance sheet of **Boeing Inc.** at December 31, 2004 (in millions). The information in parentheses was added to aid in your understanding.

Accounts payable and other liabilities	$14,869
Accrued retiree healthcare	5,959
Advances in excess of related costs	4,123
Short-term debt and current portion of long-term debt	1,321
Income tax payable	522
Long-term debt	10,879
Deferred income taxes (long-term)	1,090
Deferred lease income (long-term)	745

Required

1. Prepare the Current Liabilities and Long-Term Liabilities sections of Boeing's classified balance sheet at December 31, 2004.
2. Boeing had total liabilities of $44,847 and total shareholders' equity of $8,139 at December 31, 2003. Total shareholders' equity amounted to $11,286 at December 31, 2004. (All amounts are in millions.) Compute Boeing's debt-to-equity ratio at December 31, 2004 and 2003. As an investor, how would you react to the change in this ratio?
3. What other related ratios would the company's lenders use to assess the company? What do these ratios measure?

DECISION CASES

READING AND INTERPRETING FINANCIAL STATEMENTS

LO1,7   **Decision Case 10-1** Evaluating the Liabilities of Foot Locker

Refer to the **Foot Locker** balance sheet of 2005 and answer the following questions:

1. What are the items listed as long-term liabilities by Foot Locker? How did those liabilities change from 2004 to 2005?

2. Calculate the debt-to-equity ratio and the times interest earned ratio of the company for 2004 and 2005. What do those ratios reveal about the company and its ability to meet its obligations on its long-term liabilities?

LO8 **Decision Case 10-2** Reading Finish Line's and Foot Locker's Statement of Cash Flows

Refer to the **Finish Line** Statement of Cash Flows for the period ended February 25, 2006, and the **Foot Locker** statement for the period ended January 28, 2006, and answer the following questions:

1. What were the major sources and uses of cash disclosed in the financing activities portion of the statement of cash flows for each company?
2. Explain why a negative amount related to debt is shown for Foot Locker.
3. What does the statement of cash flow reveal about the use of debt by Finish Line?

LO8,9 **Decision Case 10-3** Reading PepsiCo's Statement of Cash Flows

A portion of the Financing Activities section of **PepsiCo**'s statement of cash flows for the year ended December 25, 2004, follows (in millions):

Financing Activities:	
Proceeds from the issuance of long-term debt	$ 504
Payment of long-term debt	(512)
Short-term borrowings by original maturity:	
More than three months—proceeds	153
More than three months—payments	(160)
Three months or less, net	1,119

Required

1. Explain why proceeds from debt is shown as a positive amount and payment of debt is shown as a negative amount.
2. During 2004, interest rates had declined to low levels. Explain why the company paid off debt during such conditions.
3. PepsiCo has a Deferred Income Tax account listed in the asset category of its balance sheet. Would an increase in that account result in an addition or a subtraction on the statement of cash flows? In which category?

MAKING FINANCIAL DECISIONS

LO1 **Decision Case 10-4** Making a Loan Decision

Assume that you are a loan officer in charge of reviewing loan applications from potential new clients at a major bank. You are considering an application from Molitor Corporation, which is a fairly new company with a limited credit history. It has provided a balance sheet for its most recent fiscal year as follows:

Molitor Corporation
Balance Sheet
December 31, 2007

Assets		Liabilities	
Cash	$ 10,000	Accounts payable	$100,000
Receivables	50,000	Notes payable	200,000
Inventory	100,000		
Equipment	500,000	**Stockholders' Equity**	
		Common stock	80,000
		Retained earnings	280,000
		Total liabilities and	
Total assets	$660,000	stockholders' equity	$660,000

Your bank has established certain guidelines that must be met before making a favorable loan recommendation. These include minimum levels for several financial ratios. You are particularly concerned about the bank's policy that loan applicants must have a total-assets-to-debt ratio of at least 2-to-1 to be acceptable. Your initial analysis of Molitor's balance sheet has indicated that the firm has met the minimum total-assets-to-debt ratio requirement. On reading the notes that accompany the financial statements, however, you discover the statement at the top of the following page:

(continued)

Molitor has engaged in a variety of innovative financial techniques resulting in the acquisition of $200,000 of assets at very favorable rates. The company is obligated to make a series of payments over the next five years to fulfill its commitments in conjunction with these financial instruments. Current generally accepted accounting principles do not require the assets acquired or the related obligations to be reflected on the financial statements.

Required

1. How should this note affect your evaluation of Molitor's loan application? Calculate a revised total-assets-to-debt ratio for Molitor.
2. Do you believe that the bank's policy concerning a minimum total-assets-to-debt ratio can be modified to consider financing techniques that are not reflected on the financial statements? Write a statement that expresses your position on this issue.

LO6   ### Decision Case 10-5 Bond Redemption Decision

Armstrong Areo Ace, a flight training school, issued $100,000 of 20-year bonds at face value when the market rate was 10%. The bonds have been outstanding for 10 years. The company pays annual interest on January 1. The current rate for similar bonds is 4%. On January 1, the controller would like to purchase the bonds on the open market, retire the bonds, then issue $100,000 of 10-year bonds to pay 4% annual interest.

Required

Draft a memo to the controller advising him to retire the outstanding bonds and issue new debt. Ignore taxes. (*Hint:* Find the selling price of bonds that pay 10% when the market rate is 4%.)

ACCOUNTING AND ETHICS: WHAT WOULD YOU DO?

LO7   ### Decision Case 10-6 Determination of Asset Life

Jen Latke is an accountant for Hale's Manufacturing Company. Hale's has entered into an agreement to lease a piece of equipment from EZ Leasing. Jen must decide how to report the lease agreement on Hale's financial statements.

Jen has reviewed the lease contract carefully. She has also reviewed the four lease criteria specified in the accounting rules. She has been able to determine that the lease does not meet three of the criteria. However, she is concerned about the criterion that indicates that if the term of the lease is 75% or more of the life of the property, the lease should be classified as a capital lease. Jen is fully aware that Hale's does not want to record the lease agreement as a capital lease but prefers to show it as a type of off-balance-sheet financing.

Jen's reading of the lease contract indicates that the asset has been leased for seven years. She is unsure of the life of such assets, however, and has consulted two sources to determine it. One of them states that equipment similar to that owned by Hale's is depreciated over nine years. The other, a trade publication of the equipment industry, indicates that equipment of this type will usually last for 12 years.

Required

1. How should Jen report the lease agreement in the financial statements?
2. If Jen decides to present the lease as an off-balance-sheet arrangement, has she acted ethically?

SOLUTIONS TO KEY TERMS QUIZ

5	Long-term liability		3	Face rate of interest
1	Face value		12	Market rate of interest
7	Debenture bonds		4	Bond issue price
2	Serial bonds		6	Premium
9	Callable bonds		8	Discount

__10__	Effective interest method of amortization		__15__	Capital lease
__11__	Carrying value		__17__	Deferred tax
__13__	Gain or loss on redemption		__18__	Permanent difference
__14__	Operating lease		__16__	Temporary difference

CHAPTER

11

Stockholders' Equity

Study Links

A Look at Previous Chapters
The previous chapter indicated how companies use long-term debt as a means of financing the company.

A Look at This Chapter
In this chapter we will concentrate on the issues concerned with the stockholders' equity section of the balance sheet. The use of equity is an important source of financing for all corporations. The chapter also considers the various types of dividends paid to stockholders.

A Look at the Upcoming Chapter
In Chapter 12 we turn our attention to an expanded discussion of the preparation and use of the statement of cash flows.

Learning Outcomes

After studying this chapter, you should be able to:

LO1 Identify the components of the Stockholders' Equity category of the balance sheet and the accounts found in each component.

LO2 Show that you understand the characteristics of common and preferred stock and the differences between the classes of stock.

LO3 Determine the financial statement impact when stock is issued for cash or for other consideration.

LO4 Describe the financial statement impact of stock treated as treasury stock.

LO5 Compute the amount of cash dividends when a firm has issued both preferred and common stock.

LO6 Show that you understand the difference between cash and stock dividends and the effect of stock dividends.

LO7 Determine the difference between stock dividends and stock splits.

LO8 Show that you understand the statement of stockholders' equity and comprehensive income.

LO9 Understand how investors use ratios to evaluate stockholders' equity.

LO10 Explain the effects that transactions involving stockholders' equity have on the statement of cash flows.

LO11 Describe the important differences between the sole proprietorship and partnership forms of organization versus the corporate form (Appendix).

© Timothy A. Clary/AFP/Getty Images

Jacuzzi

This chapter will discuss a company that was introduced previously: **Jacuzzi Brands, Inc.** The company is a leader in its industry with a very recognizable name and product line. However, like all companies, Jacuzzi must constantly consider how to finance its operations. The company's need for funds has been considerable. During 2004 it used over $30 million to repay outstanding debt. Additionally, during 2005 the company expected total capital expenditures for fiscal 2005 to be approximately $28.0 million for new business requirements, system upgrades, and initiatives involving the improvement of manufacturing efficiencies.

Jacuzzi has always used both debt and equity as a means of financing but has tended to rely more heavily on debt. There are downsides, however, to the use of debt. The company's 2004 annual report indicates "We have substantial indebtedness and servicing our indebtedness could reduce funds available to operate our business." It also indicates that the debt instruments have covenants or restrictions which might limit the company's ability to operate in certain ways.

Because debt is a fixed obligation, the company might choose to obtain financing by the use of equity. The stockholders' equity portion is important because it indicates the ability of the company to raise money that may be vital to the success of the company. One of the significant items in the Stockholders' Equity section of the balance sheet for Jacuzzi Brands is the amount of treasury stock, which will be discussed in this chapter.

The accompanying balance sheet presents the Stockholders' Equity portion of the balance sheet for Jacuzzi Brands, Inc. This chapter will consider the following:

- What are the components of the Stockholders' Equity section of the balance sheet? (See pp. 502–504)
- What is the meaning and importance of treasury stock? (See pp. 507–508)

- What are the types of dividends that a company might pay? (See pp. 508–513)
- Why is comprehensive income different from net income? (See pp. 513–514)

Answers to these questions and other issues related to stockholders' equity are found in this text. They can help you evaluate the long-term Stockholders' Equity section of the balance sheet of Jacuzzi Brands, Inc., and other companies.

Jacuzzi Brands, Inc.
Consolidated Balance Sheets
(in millions, except share data)

	At September 30,	
	2004	2003
Stockholders' Equity:		
Common stock (par value $.01 per share, authorized 300,000,000 shares; issued 99,096,734 shares; outstanding 76,103,459 and 74,986,982 shares in 2004 and 2003, respectively)	$ 1.0	$ 1.0
Paid-in capital	639.7	650.1
Accumulated deficit	(5.2)	(33.7)
Unearned restricted stock	(4.6)	(0.8)
Accumulated other comprehensive loss	(8.2)	(8.7)
Treasury stock (22,993,275) and 24,109,752 shares in 2004 and 2003, respectively), at cost	(333.6)	(352.2)
Total stockholders' equity	289.1	255.7
TOTAL LIABILITIES AND STOCKHOLDERS' EQUITY	$ 1,371.8	$ 1,336.8

An Overview of Stockholders' Equity

EQUITY AS A SOURCE OF FINANCING

Whenever a company needs to raise money, it must choose from the alternative financing sources that are available. Financing can be divided into two general categories: debt (borrowing from banks or other creditors) and equity (issuing stock). The company's management must consider the advantages and disadvantages of each alternative. Exhibit 11-1 indicates a few of the factors that must be considered.

Issuing stock is a very popular method of financing because of its flexibility. It provides advantages for the issuing company and the investors (stockholders). Investors are primarily concerned with the return on their investment. With stock, the return might be in the form of dividends paid to the investors but might also be the price appreciation of the stock. Stock is popular because it generally provides a higher rate of return (but also a higher degree of risk) than can be obtained by creditors who receive interest from lending money. Stock is popular with issuing companies because dividends on stock can be adjusted according to the company's profitability; higher dividends can be paid when the firm is profitable and lower dividends when it is not. Interest on debt financing, on the other

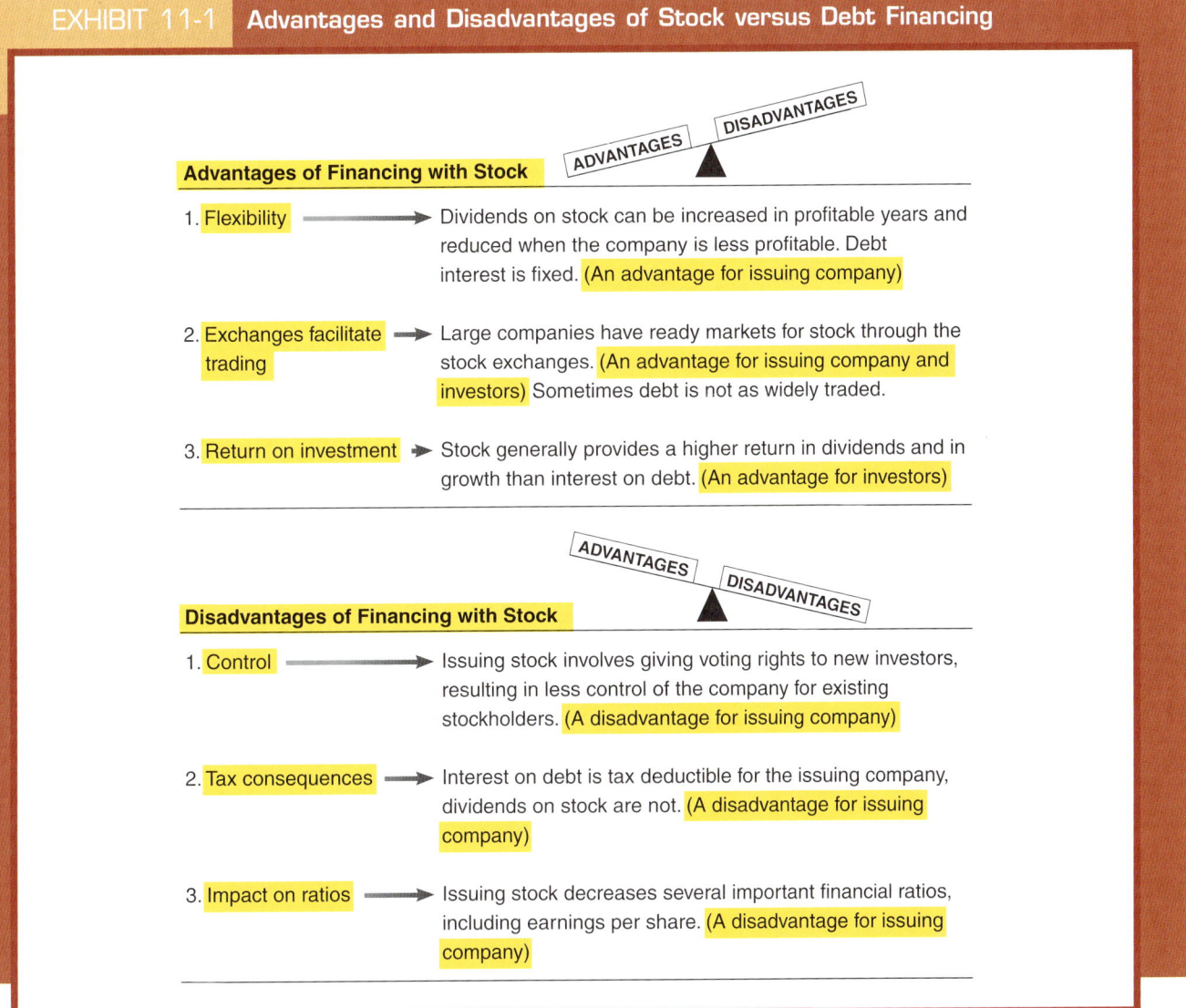

EXHIBIT 11-1   Advantages and Disadvantages of Stock versus Debt Financing

Advantages of Financing with Stock

1. Flexibility — Dividends on stock can be increased in profitable years and reduced when the company is less profitable. Debt interest is fixed. (An advantage for issuing company)

2. Exchanges facilitate trading — Large companies have ready markets for stock through the stock exchanges. (An advantage for issuing company and investors) Sometimes debt is not as widely traded.

3. Return on investment — Stock generally provides a higher return in dividends and in growth than interest on debt. (An advantage for investors)

Disadvantages of Financing with Stock

1. Control — Issuing stock involves giving voting rights to new investors, resulting in less control of the company for existing stockholders. (A disadvantage for issuing company)

2. Tax consequences — Interest on debt is tax deductible for the issuing company, dividends on stock are not. (A disadvantage for issuing company)

3. Impact on ratios — Issuing stock decreases several important financial ratios, including earnings per share. (A disadvantage for issuing company)

hand, is generally fixed and is a legal liability that cannot be adjusted when a company experiences lower profitability.

There are several disadvantages in issuing stock. Stock usually has voting rights, and issuing stock allows new investors to vote. Existing investors may not want to share the control of the company with new stockholders. From the issuing company's viewpoint, there is also a serious tax disadvantage to stock versus debt. As indicated in Chapter 10, interest on debt is tax deductible and results in lower taxes. Dividends on stock, on the other hand, are not tax deductible and do not result in tax savings to the issuing company. Finally, issuing stock has an impact on the company's financial statements. Issuing stock decreases several important financial ratios, such as earnings per share. Issuing debt does not have a similar effect on the earnings per share ratio.

Management must consider many other factors in deciding between debt and equity financing. The company's goal should be financing the company in a manner that results in the lowest overall cost of capital to the firm. Usually, companies attain that goal by having a reasonable balance of both debt and equity financing.

STOCKHOLDERS' EQUITY ON THE BALANCE SHEET

The basic accounting equation is often stated as follows:

Assets = Liabilities + Owners' Equity

Owners' equity is viewed as a residual amount. That is, the owners of a corporation have a claim to all assets after the claims represented by liabilities to creditors have been satisfied.

In this text, we concentrate on the corporate form of organization and refer to the owners' equity as *stockholders' equity*. As in past chapters, we restate the basic accounting equation for a corporation as follows:

Assets = Liabilities + Stockholders' Equity

The stockholders are the owners of a corporation. They have a residual interest in its assets after the claims of all creditors have been satisfied.

The stockholders' equity category of all corporations has two major components or subcategories:

Total Stockholders' Equity = Contributed Capital
+
Retained Earnings

Contributed capital represents the amount the corporation has received from the sale of stock to stockholders. Retained earnings is the amount of net income that the corporation has earned but not paid as dividends. Instead, the corporation retains and reinvests the income.

Although all corporations maintain the two primary categories of contributed capital and retained earnings, within these categories they use a variety of accounts that have several alternative titles. The next section examines two important items: income and dividends, and their impact on the Retained Earnings account.

HOW INCOME AND DIVIDENDS AFFECT RETAINED EARNINGS

The Retained Earnings account plays an important role because it serves as a link between the income statement and the balance sheet. The term *articulated statements* refers to the fact that the information on the income statement is related to the information on the balance sheet. The bridge (or link) between the two statements is the Retained Earnings account. Exhibit 11-2 presents this relationship graphically. As the exhibit indicates, the income statement is used to calculate a company's net income for a given period of time. The amount of the net income is transferred to the statement of retained earnings and is added to the beginning balance of retained earnings (with dividends deducted) to calculate the ending balance of retained earnings. The ending balance of retained earnings is the amount that is portrayed on the balance sheet in the Stockholders' Equity category. That is why you must always prepare the income statement before you prepare the balance sheet, as you have discovered when developing financial statements in previous chapters of the text.

IDENTIFYING THE COMPONENTS OF THE STOCKHOLDERS' EQUITY SECTION OF THE BALANCE SHEET

The liabilities and stockholders' equity portion of the balance sheet of Jacuzzi Brands, Inc., was presented in the chapter opener. We will focus on the Stockholders' (Shareholders') Equity category of the balance sheet. All corporations begin the Stockholders' Equity category with a list of the firm's contributed capital. In some cases, there are two categories of stock: common stock and preferred stock (the latter is discussed later in this chapter). Common stock normally carries voting rights. The common stockholders elect the officers of the corporation and establish its by-laws and governing rules. It is not unusual for corporations to have more than one type of common stock, each with different rights or terms.

Number of Shares It is important to determine the number of shares of stock for each stock account. Corporate balance sheets report the number of shares in three categories: **authorized**, **issued**, and **outstanding shares**.

LO1 Identify the components of the Stockholders' Equity category of the balance sheet and the accounts found in each component.

Authorized shares
The maximum number of shares a corporation may issue as indicated in the corporate charter.

EXHIBIT 11-2	Retained Earnings Connects the Income Statement and the Balance Sheet

To become incorporated, a business must develop articles of incorporation and apply to the proper state authorities for a corporate charter. The corporation must specify the maximum number of shares that it will be allowed to issue. This maximum number of shares is called the *authorized stock*. A corporation applies for authorization to issue many more shares than it will issue immediately, to allow for future growth and other events that may occur over its long life. For example, Jacuzzi Brands, Inc., indicates that it has 300,000,000 shares of common stock authorized but that only 99,096,734 shares had been issued as of September 30, 2004.

The number of shares *issued* indicates the number of shares that have been sold or transferred to stockholders. The number of shares issued does not necessarily mean, however, that those shares are currently outstanding. The term *outstanding* indicates shares actually in the hands of the stockholders. Shares that have been issued by the corporation and then repurchased are counted as shares issued but not as shares outstanding. Quite often corporations repurchase their own stock as treasury stock (explained in more detail later in this chapter). Treasury stock reduces the number of shares outstanding. The number of Jacuzzi Brands' shares of common stock outstanding at September 30, 2004, is given on the balance sheet on page 500 but could be calculated as follows:

Number of shares issued	99,096,734
Less: Treasury stock	22,993,275
Number of shares outstanding	76,103,459

Par Value: The Firm's "Legal Capital" The Stockholders' Equity category of many balance sheets refers to an amount as the *par value* of the stock. For example, Jacuzzi Brands' common stock has a par value of $8.01 per share. **Par value** is an arbitrary amount stated on the face of the stock certificate and represents the legal capital of the corporation. Most corporations set the par value of the stock at very low amounts because there are legal difficulties if stock is sold at less than par. Therefore, par value does not indicate the stock's value or the amount that is obtained when it is sold on the stock exchange; it is simply an arbitrary amount that exists to fulfill legal requirements. A company's legal requirement depends on its state of incorporation. Some states do not require corporations to indicate a par value; others require them to designate the *stated value* of the stock. A stated value is accounted for in the same manner as a par value and appears in the Stockholders' Equity category in the same manner as a par value.

Issued shares
The number of shares sold or distributed to stockholders.

Outstanding shares
The number of shares issued less the number of shares held as treasury stock.

Study Tip Treasury stock is included in the number of shares issued. It is not part of the number of shares outstanding.

Par value
An arbitrary amount that represents the legal capital of the firm.

The amount of the par value is the amount that is presented in the stock account. That is, the dollar amount in a firm's stock account can be calculated as its par value per share times number of shares issued. For Jacuzzi Brands, the dollar amount appearing in the common stock account can be calculated as follows:

$0.01 Par Value per Share × 99,096,734 Shares Issued = $0.99 million
(rounded to $1.0 million on the balance sheet) Balance in the Common Stock Account

Additional paid-in capital

The amount received for the issuance of stock in excess of the par value of the stock. *Alternate term: Paid-in capital in excess of par*

Additional Paid-in Capital The dollar amounts of the stock accounts in the Stockholders' Equity category do not indicate the amount that was received when the stock was sold to stockholders. The Common Stock and Preferred Stock accounts indicate only the par value of the stock. When stock is issued for an amount higher than the par value, the excess is reported as **additional paid-in capital**. Several alternative titles are used for this account, including Paid-in Capital in Excess of Par, Capital Surplus (an old term that should no longer be used), and Premium on Stock. Regardless of the title, the account represents the amount received in excess of par when stock was issued.

Jacuzzi Brands' balance sheet indicates paid-in capital of $639.7 million at September 30, 2004. The company, like many other corporations, presents only one amount for additional paid-in capital for all stock transactions. Therefore, we are unable to determine whether the amount resulted from the issuance of common stock or other stock transactions. As a result, it is often impossible to determine the issue price of each category of stock even with a careful analysis of the balance sheet and the accompanying notes.

Retained earnings

Net income that has been made by the corporation but not paid out as dividends. *Alternate term: Retained income*

Retained Earnings: The Amount Not Paid as Dividends **Retained earnings** represents net income that the firm has earned but has *not* paid as dividends. Remember that retained earnings is an amount that is accumulated over the entire life of the corporation and does not represent the income or dividends for a specific year. It is important to note that a balance in retained earnings does not indicate that the company had a net income of this amount in the current year; it simply means that over the life of the corporation, the company has retained more net income than it paid out as dividends to stockholders. Jacuzzi Brands is somewhat unique because it has an "accumulated deficit," indicating the company has had net losses (rather than net income) in the past.

It is also important to remember that the balance of the Retained Earnings account does not mean that liquid assets of that amount are available to the stockholders. Corporations decide to retain income because they have needs other than paying dividends to stockholders. The needs may include the purchase of assets, the retirement of debt, or other financial needs. Money spent for those needs usually benefits the stockholders in the long run, but liquid assets equal to the balance of the Retained Earnings account are not necessarily available to stockholders. In theory, income should be retained whenever the company can reinvest the money and get a better return within the business than the shareholders can get on their own. In summary, retained earnings is a stockholders' equity account. Although the company's assets have increased, retained earnings does not represent a pool of liquid assets.

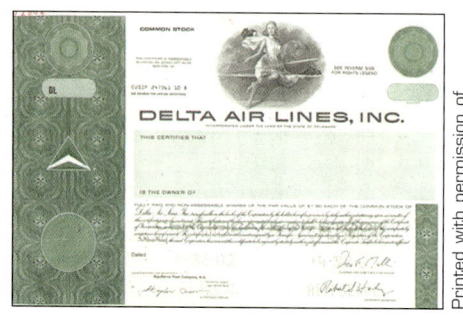

A prospective stockholder may purchase shares and receive certificates, like this one, either directly from the company or through a stockbroker. Usually, a broker purchases shares in its own name for the investor's account—and the investor never sees a certificate.

Printed with permission of Delta Air Lines, Inc.

What Is Preferred Stock?

Many companies have a class of stock called *preferred stock*. One of the advantages of preferred stock is the flexibility it provides because its terms and provisions can be tailored to meet the firm's needs. These terms and provisions are detailed in the stock certificate. Generally, preferred stock offers holders a preference to dividends declared by the corporation. That is, if dividends are declared, the preferred stockholders must receive dividends first, before the holders of common stock.

The dividend rate on preferred stock may be stated in two ways. First, it may be stated as a percentage of the stock's par value. For example, if a stock is presented on the balance sheet as $100 par, 7% preferred stock, its dividend rate is $7 per share ($100 times 7%). Second, the dividend may be stated as a per-share amount. For example, a stock may appear on the balance sheet as $100 par, $7 preferred stock, meaning that the dividend rate is $7 per share. Investors in common stock should note the dividend requirements of the preferred shareholder. The greater the obligation to the preferred shareholder, the less desirable the common stock becomes.

Several important provisions of preferred stock relate to the payment of dividends. Some preferred stock issues have a **cumulative feature**, which means that if a dividend is not declared to the preferred stockholders in one year, dividends are considered to be *in arrears*. Before a dividend can be declared to common stockholders in a subsequent period, the preferred stockholders must be paid all dividends in arrears as well as the current year's dividend. The cumulative feature ensures that the preferred stockholders will receive a dividend before one is paid to common stockholders. It does not guarantee a dividend to preferred stockholders, however. There is no legal requirement mandating that a corporation declare a dividend, and preferred stockholders have a legal right to receive a dividend only when it has been declared.

Some preferred stocks have a **participating feature**. Its purpose is to allow the preferred stockholders to receive a dividend in excess of the regular rate when a firm has been particularly profitable and declares an abnormally large dividend. When the participating feature is present and a firm declares a dividend, the preferred stockholders first have a right to the current year's dividend, and then the common stockholders must receive an equal portion (usually based on the par or stated value of the stocks) of the dividend. The participating feature then applies to any dividend declared in excess of the amounts in the first two steps. The preferred stockholders are allowed to share in the excess, normally on the basis of the total par value of the preferred and common stock. The participating feature is explained in more detail in the section of this chapter concerning dividends.

Preferred stock may also be convertible or callable. The **convertible feature** allows the preferred stockholders to convert their stockholdings to common stock. Convertible preferred stock offers stockholders the advantages of the low risk generally associated with preferred stock and the possibility of the higher return that is associated with common stock. The **callable feature** allows the issuing firm to retire the stock after it has been issued. Normally, the call price is specified as a fixed dollar amount. Firms may exercise the call option to eliminate a certain class of preferred stock so that control of the corporation is maintained in the hands of fewer stockholders. The call option also may be exercised when the dividend rate on the preferred stock is too high and other, more cost-effective financing alternatives are available.

Preferred stock is attractive to many investors because it offers a return in the form of a dividend at a level of risk that is lower than that of most common stocks. Usually, the dividend available on preferred stock is more stable from year to year, and as a result, the market price of the stock is also more stable. In fact, if preferred stock carries certain provisions, the stock is very similar to bonds or notes payable. Management must evaluate whether such securities really represent debt and should be presented in the liability category of the balance sheet or whether

LO2 Show that you understand the characteristics of common and preferred stock and the differences between the classes of stock.

11-2 **Real World Practice**

Reading Finish Line's Annual Report
Refer to the Finish Line balance sheet of February 25, 2006. Did the company have any preferred stock during the most recent year? How many classes of common stock did the company have?

Cumulative feature
The right to dividends in arrears before the current-year dividend is distributed.

Participating feature
Allows preferred stockholders to share on a percentage basis in the distribution of an abnormally large dividend.

Convertible feature
Allows preferred stock to be exchanged for common stock.

Callable feature
Allows the firm to eliminate a class of stock by paying the stockholders a specified amount.
Alternate term: Redeemable

they represent equity and should be presented in the equity category. Such a decision involves the concept of *substance over form*. That is, a company must look not only at the legal form but also at the economic substance of the security to decide whether it is debt or equity.

Issuance of Stock

LO3 Determine the financial statement impact when stock is issued for cash or for other consideration.

STOCK ISSUED FOR CASH

Stock may be issued in several different ways. It may be issued for cash or for non-cash assets. When stock is issued for cash, the amount of its par value should be reported in the stock account and the amount in excess of par should be reported in an additional paid-in capital account. For example, assume that on July 1 a firm issued 1,000 shares of $10 par common stock for $15 per share. The effect on the balance sheet is as follows:

		Balance Sheet					Income Statement	
ASSETS	**=**	**LIABILITIES**	**+**	**STOCKHOLDERS' EQUITY**		**+**	**REVENUES – EXPENSES**	
Cash	15,000			Common Stock	10,000			
				Additional Paid-in				
				Capital—Common	5,000			

As noted earlier, the Common Stock account and the Additional Paid-in Capital account are both presented in the Stockholders' Equity category of the balance sheet and represent the contributed capital component of the corporation.

If no-par stock is issued, the corporation does not distinguish between common stock and additional paid-in capital. If the firm in the previous example had issued no-par stock on July 1 for $15 per share, the entire amount of $15,000 would be presented in the Common Stock account.

STOCK ISSUED FOR NONCASH CONSIDERATION

Occasionally, stock is issued in return for something other than cash. For example, a corporation may issue stock to obtain land or buildings. When such a transaction occurs, the company faces the difficult task of deciding what value to place on the transaction. This is especially difficult when the market values of the elements of the transaction are not known with complete certainty. According to the general guideline, the transaction should be reported at fair market value. Market value may be indicated by the value of the consideration given (stock) or the value of the consideration received (property), whichever can be most readily determined.

Assume that on July 1 a firm issued 500 shares of $10 par preferred stock to acquire a building. The stock is not widely traded, and the current market value of the stock is not evident. The building has recently been appraised by an independent firm as having a market value of $12,000. In this case, the issuance of the stock affects the balance sheet as follows:

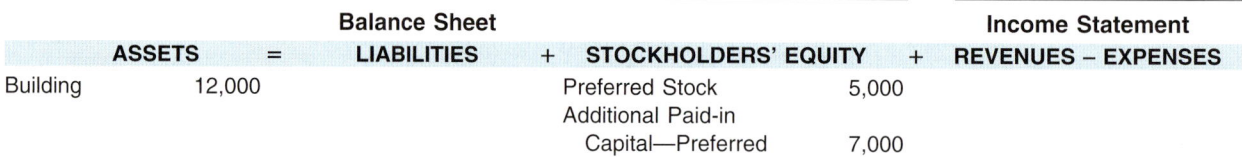

		Balance Sheet					Income Statement	
ASSETS	**=**	**LIABILITIES**	**+**	**STOCKHOLDERS' EQUITY**		**+**	**REVENUES – EXPENSES**	
Building	12,000			Preferred Stock	5,000			
				Additional Paid-in				
				Capital—Preferred	7,000			

In other situations, the market value of the stock might be more readily determined and should be used as the best measure of the value of the transaction. Market value may be represented by the current stock market quotation or by a recent cash sale of the stock. The company should attempt to develop the best estimate of the market value of the noncash transaction and should neither intentionally overstate nor intentionally understate the assets received by the issuance of stock.

What Is Treasury Stock?

The Stockholders' Equity category of Jacuzzi Brands' balance sheet in the chapter opener includes **treasury stock** in the amount of $333.6 million. The Treasury Stock account is created when a corporation buys its own stock sometime after issuing it. For an amount to be treated as treasury stock, (1) it must be the corporation's own stock, (2) it must have been issued to the stockholders at some point, (3) it must have been repurchased from the stockholders, and (4) it must not be retired but must be held for some purpose. Treasury stock is not considered outstanding stock and does not have voting rights.

A corporation might repurchase stock as treasury stock for several reasons. The most common is to have stock available to distribute to employees for bonuses or as part of an employee-benefit plan. Firms also might buy treasury stock to maintain a favorable market price for the stock or to improve the appearance of the firm's financial ratios. More recently, firms have purchased their stock to maintain control of the ownership and to prevent unwanted takeover or buyout attempts. Of course, the lower the stock price, the more likely a company is to buy back its own stock and wait for the shares to rise in value before reissuing them.

The two methods to account for treasury stock transactions are the cost method and the par value method. We will present the more commonly used cost method. Assume that the Stockholders' Equity section of Rezin Company's balance sheet on December 31, 2006, appears as follows:

Common stock, $10 par value,	
1,000 shares issued and outstanding	$10,000
Additional paid-in capital—Common	12,000
Retained earnings	15,000
Total stockholders' equity	$37,000

Assume that on February 1, 2007, Rezin buys 100 of its shares as treasury stock at $25 per share. The effect on Rezin's balance sheet is as follows:

	Balance Sheet						Income Statement	
ASSETS		**=**	**LIABILITIES**	**+**	**STOCKHOLDERS' EQUITY**	**+**	**REVENUES − EXPENSES**	
Cash	(2,500)				Treasury Stock	(2,500)		

The purchase of treasury stock does not directly affect the Common Stock account itself. The Treasury Stock account is considered a contra account and is subtracted from the total of contributed capital and retained earnings in the Stockholders' Equity section. Treasury Stock is *not* an asset account. When a company buys its own stock, it is contracting its size and reducing the equity of stockholders. Therefore, Treasury Stock is a contra-equity account, not an asset.

The Stockholders' Equity section of Rezin's balance sheet on February 1, 2007, after the purchase of the treasury stock, appears as follows:

Common stock, $10 par value,	
1,000 shares issued, 900 outstanding	$10,000
Additional paid-in capital—Common	12,000
Retained earnings	15,000
Total contributed capital and retained earnings	$37,000
Less: Treasury stock, 100 shares at cost	2,500
Total stockholders' equity	$34,500

LO4 Describe the financial statement impact of stock treated as treasury stock.

Treasury stock
Stock issued by the firm and then repurchased but not retired.

Corporations may choose to reissue stock to investors after it has been held as treasury stock. When treasury stock is resold for more than it cost, the difference between the sales price and the cost appears in the Additional Paid-in Capital—Treasury Stock account. For example, if Rezin resold 100 shares of treasury stock on May 1, 2007, for $30 per share, the Treasury Stock account would be reduced by $2,500 (100 shares times $25 per share), and the Additional Paid-in Capital—Treasury Stock account would be increased by $500 (100 shares times the difference between the purchase price of $25 and the reissue price of $30).

When treasury stock is resold for an amount less than its cost, the difference between the sales price and the cost is deducted from the Additional Paid-in Capital—Treasury Stock account. If that account does not exist, the difference should be deducted from the Retained Earnings account. For example, assume that Rezin Company had resold 100 shares of treasury stock on May 1, 2007, for $20 per share, instead of $30 as in the previous example. In this example, Rezin has had no other treasury stock transactions, and therefore, no balance existed in the Additional Paid-in Capital—Treasury Stock account. Rezin would then reduce the Treasury Stock account by $2,500 (100 shares times $25 per share) and would reduce Retained Earnings by $500 (100 shares times the difference between the purchase price of $25 and the reissue price of $20 per share). Thus, the Additional Paid-in Capital—Treasury Stock account may have a positive balance, but entries that result in a negative balance in the account should not be made.

Note that **income statement accounts are never involved** in treasury stock transactions. Regardless of whether treasury stock is reissued for more or less than its cost, the effect is reflected in the stockholders' equity accounts. It is simply not possible for a firm to engage in transactions involving its own stock and have the result affect the performance of the firm as reflected on the income statement.

2 minute review

1. Where does the Treasury Stock account appear on the balance sheet?

2. What is the effect on stockholders' equity when stock is purchased as treasury stock?

3. How does treasury stock affect the number of shares issued and outstanding?

Answers

1. *Treasury Stock is a contra-equity account, and the balance should appear as a reduction in the Stockholders' Equity category of the balance sheet.*

2. *When treasury stock is purchased, it reduces total stockholders' equity.*

3. *Treasury stock is still stock that has been issued and so does not affect the number of shares issued. But it is stock that is held by the company, rather than the stockholders, and the purchase of treasury stock reduces the number of shares of stock outstanding.*

Retirement of Stock

Retirement of stock
When the stock is repurchased with no intention to reissue at a later date.

Retirement of stock occurs when a corporation buys back stock after it has been issued to investors and does not intend to reissue the stock. Retirement often occurs because the corporation wants to eliminate a particular class of stock or a particular group of stockholders. When stock is repurchased and retired, the balances of the stock account and the paid-in capital account that were created when the stock was issued must be eliminated. When the original issue price is higher than the repurchase price of the stock, the difference is reflected in the Paid-in

Capital from Stock Retirement account. When the repurchase price of the stock is more than the original issue price, the difference reduces the Retained Earnings account. The general principle for retirement of stock is the same as for treasury stock transactions. No income statement accounts are affected by the retirement. The effect is reflected in the Cash account and the stockholders' equity accounts.

Dividends: Distribution of Income to Shareholders

CASH DIVIDENDS

Corporations may declare and issue several different types of dividends, the most common of which is a cash dividend to stockholders. Cash dividends may be declared quarterly, annually, or at other intervals. Normally, cash dividends are declared on one date, referred to as the *date of declaration,* and are paid out on a later date, referred to as the *payment date.* The dividend is paid to the stockholders that own the stock as of a particular date, the *date of record.*

Generally, two requirements must be met before the board of directors can declare a cash dividend. First, sufficient cash must be available by the payment date to pay to the stockholders. Second, the Retained Earnings account must have a sufficient positive balance. Dividends reduce the balance of the account, and therefore Retained Earnings must have a balance before the dividend declaration. Most firms have an established policy concerning the portion of income that will be declared as dividends. The **dividend payout ratio** is calculated as the annual dividend amount divided by the annual net income. The dividend payout ratio for many firms is 50% or 60% and seldom exceeds 70%. Typically, utilities pay a high proportion of their earnings. In contrast, fast-growing companies in technology often pay nothing to shareholders. Some investors want and need the current income of a high-dividend payout, but others would rather not receive dividend income and prefer to gamble that the stock price will appreciate.

Cash dividends become a liability on the date they are declared. An accounting entry should be recorded on that date to acknowledge the liability and reduce the balance of the Retained Earnings account. For example, assume that on July 1 the board of directors of Grant Company declared a cash dividend of $7,000 to be paid on September 1. Grant reflects the declaration as a reduction of Retained Earnings and an increase in Cash Dividend Payable.

The Cash Dividend Payable account is a liability and is normally shown in the Current Liabilities section of the balance sheet.

The important point to remember is that dividends reduce the amount of retained earnings *when declared.* When dividends are paid, the company reduces the liability to stockholders reflected in the Cash Dividend Payable account.

Dividend payout ratio
The annual dividend amount divided by the annual net income.

> **Study Tip** A dividend is not an expense on the income statement. It is a reduction of retained earnings and appears on the retained earnings statement. If it is a cash dividend, it also reduces the cash balance when paid.

CASH DIVIDENDS FOR PREFERRED AND COMMON STOCK

When cash dividends involving more than one class of stock are declared, the corporation must determine the proper amount to allocate to each class of stock. As indicated earlier, the amount of dividends that preferred stockholders have rights to depends on the terms and provisions of the preferred stock. The proper allocation of cash dividends is illustrated with an example of a firm that has two classes of stock, preferred and common.

Assume that on December 31, 2007, Stricker Company has outstanding 10,000 shares of $10 par, 8% preferred stock and 40,000 shares of $5 par common stock. Stricker was unable to declare a dividend in 2005 or 2006 but wants to declare a $70,000 dividend for 2007. The dividend is to be allocated to preferred and common stockholders in accordance with the terms of the stock agreements.

LO5 Compute the amount of cash dividends when a firm has issued both preferred and common stock.

Noncumulative Preferred Stock If the terms of the stock agreement indicate that the preferred stock is not cumulative, the preferred stockholders do not have a right to dividends in arrears. The dividends that were not declared in 2005 and 2006 are simply lost and do not affect the distribution of the dividend in 2007. Therefore, the cash dividend declared in 2007 is allocated between preferred and common stockholders as follows:

	To Preferred	To Common
Step 1: Distribute current-year dividend to preferred		
(10,000 shares × $10 par × 8% × 1 year)	$8,000	
Step 2: Distribute remaining dividend to common ($70,000 − $8,000)		$62,000
Total allocated	$8,000	$62,000
Dividend per share		
Preferred: $8,000/10,000 shares	$0.80	
Common: $62,000/40,000 shares		$1.55

Cumulative Preferred Stock If the terms of the stock agreement indicate that the preferred stock is cumulative, the preferred stockholders have a right to dividends in arrears before the current year's dividend is distributed. Therefore, Stricker performs the following steps:

	To Preferred	To Common
Step 1: Distribute dividends in arrears to preferred		
(10,000 shares × $10 par × 8% × 2 years)	$16,000	
Step 2: Distribute current-year dividend to preferred		
(10,000 shares × $10 par × 8% × 1 year)	8,000	
Step 3: Distribute remainder to common ($70,000 − $24,000)		$46,000
Total allocated	$24,000	$46,000
Dividend per share		
Preferred: $24,000/10,000 shares	$2.40	
Common: $46,000/40,000 shares		$1.15

STOCK DIVIDENDS

LO6 Show that you understand the difference between cash and stock dividends and the effect of stock dividends.

Stock dividend
The issuance of additional shares of stock to existing stockholders.

Cash dividends are the most popular and widely used form of dividend, but corporations may at times use stock dividends instead of, or in addition to, cash dividends. A **stock dividend** occurs when a corporation declares and issues additional shares of its own stock to its existing stockholders. Firms use stock dividends for several reasons. First, a corporation may simply not have sufficient cash available to declare a cash dividend. Stock dividends do not require the use of the corporation's resources and allow cash to be retained for other purposes. Second, stock dividends result in additional shares of stock outstanding and may decrease the market price per share of stock if the dividend is large (small stock dividends tend to have little effect on market price). The lower price may make the stock more attractive to a wider range of investors and allow enhanced financing opportunities. Finally, stock dividends normally do not represent taxable income to the recipients and may be attractive to some wealthy stockholders.

Similar to cash dividends, stock dividends are normally declared by the board of directors on a specific date, and the stock is distributed to the stockholders at a later date. The corporation recognizes the stock dividend on the date of declaration. Assume that Shah Company's Stockholders' Equity category of the balance sheet appears as follows as of January 1, 2007:

Common stock, $10 par,	
5,000 shares issued and outstanding	$ 50,000
Additional paid-in capital—Common	30,000
Retained earnings	70,000
Total stockholders' equity	$150,000

Assume that on January 2, 2007, Shah declares a 10% stock dividend to common stockholders to be distributed on April 1, 2007. Small stock dividends (usually those of 20% to 25% or less) normally are recorded at the *market value* of the stock as of the date of declaration. Assume that Shah's common stock is selling at $40 per share on that date. Therefore, the total market value of the stock dividend is $20,000 (10% of 5,000 shares outstanding, or 500 shares, times $40 per share). The effect of the stock dividend on January 2, the date of declaration, is as follows:

	Balance Sheet				Income Statement
ASSETS	**=**	**LIABILITIES**	**+ STOCKHOLDERS' EQUITY**	**+**	**REVENUES – EXPENSES**
			Retained Earnings (20,000)		
			Common Stock		
			Dividend Distributable 5,000		
			Additional Paid-in		
			Capital—Common 15,000		

The Common Stock Dividend Distributable account represents shares of stock to be issued; it is not a liability account because no cash or assets are to be distributed to the stockholders. Thus, it should be treated as an account in the Stockholders' Equity section of the balance sheet and is a part of the contributed capital component of equity.

Note that the declaration of a stock dividend does not affect the total stockholders' equity of the corporation, although the retained earnings are reduced. That is, the Stockholders' Equity section of Shah's balance sheet on January 2, 2007, is as follows after the declaration of the dividend:

Common stock, $10 par,	
5,000 shares issued and outstanding	$ 50,000
Common stock dividend distributable, 500 shares	5,000
Additional paid-in capital—Common	45,000
Retained earnings	50,000
Total stockholders' equity	$150,000

The account balances are different, but total stockholders' equity is $150,000 both before and after the declaration of the stock dividend. In effect, retained earnings has been capitalized (transferred permanently to the contributed capital accounts). When a corporation actually issues a stock dividend, it is necessary to transfer an amount from the Stock Dividend Distributable account to the appropriate stock account.

Our stock dividend example has illustrated the general rule that stock dividends should be reported at fair market value. That is, in the transaction to reflect the stock dividend, retained earnings is decreased in the amount of the fair market value per share of the stock times the number of shares to be distributed. When a large stock dividend is declared, however, accountants do not follow the general rule we have illustrated. A large stock dividend is a stock dividend of more than 20% to 25% of the number of shares of stock outstanding. In that case, the stock dividend is reported at *par value* rather than at fair market value. That is, Retained Earnings is decreased in the amount of the par value per share times the number of shares to be distributed.

Refer again to the Shah Company example. Assume that instead of a 10% dividend, on January 2, 2007, Shah declares a 100% stock dividend to be distributed on April 1, 2007. The stock dividend results in 5,000 additional shares being issued and certainly meets the definition of a large stock dividend. The effect on the accounting equation on the declaration date is:

Balance Sheet					Income Statement
ASSETS	**=**	**LIABILITIES**	**+**	**STOCKHOLDERS' EQUITY**	**+** **REVENUES – EXPENSES**
				Retained Earnings (50,000)	
				Common Stock	
				Dividend Distributable 50,000	

When the stock is actually distributed, the amount of $50,000 is transferred from the Common Stock Dividend Distributable account to the Common Stock account. The Stockholders' Equity category of Shah's balance sheet as of April 1 after the stock dividend is as follows:

Common stock, $10 par,	
10,000 shares issued and outstanding	$100,000
Additional paid-in capital—Common	30,000
Retained earnings	20,000
Total stockholders' equity	$150,000

Again, note that the stock dividend has not affected total stockholders' equity. Shah has $150,000 of stockholders' equity both before and after the stock dividend. The difference between large and small stock dividends is the amount transferred from retained earnings to the contributed capital portion of equity.

STOCK SPLITS

LO7 Determine the difference between stock dividends and stock splits.

Stock split
The creation of additional shares of stock with a reduction of the par value of the stock.

A **stock split** is similar to a stock dividend in that it results in additional shares of stock outstanding and is nontaxable. In fact, firms may use a stock split for nearly the same reasons as a stock dividend: to increase the number of shares, reduce the market price per share, and make the stock more accessible to a wider range of investors. There is an important legal difference, however. Stock dividends do not affect the par value per share of the stock, whereas stock splits reduce the par value per share. There also is an important accounting difference. An accounting transaction is *not recorded* when a corporation declares and executes a stock split. None of the stockholders' equity accounts are affected by the split. Rather, the note information accompanying the balance sheet must disclose the additional shares and the reduction of the par value per share.

Return to the Shah Company example. Assume that on January 2, 2007, Shah issued a 2-for-1 stock split instead of a stock dividend. The split results in an additional 5,000 shares of stock outstanding but is not recorded in a formal accounting transaction. Therefore, the Stockholders' Equity section of Shah Company immediately after the stock split on January 2, 2007, is as follows:

Common stock, $5 par,	
10,000 shares issued and outstanding	$ 50,000
Additional paid-in capital—Common	30,000
Retained earnings	70,000
Total stockholders' equity	$150,000

Note that the par value per share has been reduced from $10 to $5 per share of stock as a result of the split. Like a stock dividend, the split does not affect total

EXHIBIT 11-3	Nordstrom's Partial Stockholders' Equity Section

Condensed Consolidated Partial Balance Sheets
(amounts in thousands)

	April 30, 2005	January 29, 2005	May 1, 2004
Shareholders' Equity:			
Common stock, no par:			
500,000 shares authorized;			
136,632, 135,665 and 139,816			
shares issued and outstanding	619,640	552,655	466,573
Unearned stock compensation	(593)	(299)	(522)
Retained earnings	1,266,337	1,227,303	1,254,566
Accumulated other comprehensive			
earnings	7,568	9,335	11,013
Total shareholders' equity	1,892,952	1,788,994	1,731,630

Shares outstanding before stock split →

stockholders' equity because no assets have been transferred. Therefore, the split simply results in more shares of stock with claims to the same net assets of the firm.

Exhibit 11-3 presents the Stockholders' Equity category of **Nordstrom, Inc.**'s balance sheets as of April 30, 2005. At that time, the company had 136,632 shares of common stock outstanding. After the balance sheet date, the company declared a 2-for-1 stock split. That means that every stockholder that was holding one share of stock before the stock split had two shares after the split. The effect of the split was to double the number of shares of stock. Thus, the number of shares of stock after the split was 136,632 × 2, or 273,264. However, each stockholder still had the same *proportional* ownership of the company. When a company has a stock split, it restates the number of shares for all previous years also. Although a stock split does not increase the wealth of the shareholder, it is usually a good sign. Companies with rising stock prices declare a stock split to make the stock more marketable to the small investor, who would be more likely to buy a stock at $50 per share than at $100.

Statement of Stockholders' Equity

In addition to a balance sheet, an income statement, and a cash flow statement, many annual reports contain a **statement of stockholders' equity**. The purpose of this statement is to explain all the reasons for the difference between the beginning and the ending balance of each of the accounts in the Stockholders' Equity category of the balance sheet. Of course, if the only changes are the result of income and dividends, a statement of retained earnings is sufficient. When other changes have occurred in stockholders' equity accounts, this more complete statement is necessary.

The statement of stockholders' equity of Fun Fitness, Inc., is presented in Exhibit 11-4 for the year 2007. The statement starts with the beginning balances of each of the accounts as of December 31, 2007. Fun Fitness's stockholders' equity is presented in four categories (the columns on the statement) as of December 31, 2007, as follows (in millions):

LO8 Show that you understand the statement of stockholders' equity and comprehensive income.

Statement of stockholders' equity
Reflects the differences between beginning and ending balances for all accounts in the Stockholders' Equity category of the balance sheet.

Number of shares	1,000,000
Common stock	$50.0
Paid-in capital	$350.0
Retained earnings	$400.0

EXHIBIT 11-4 **Fun Fitness's Statement of Stockholders' Equity, 2007**

Fun Fitness, Inc.
Statement of Stockholders' Equity
For the Year Ended December 31, 2007

(dollar amounts in millions)

| Stockholders' Equity | Common Stock | | Paid-In Capital | Retained Earnings |
	Shares	Amount		
Balance, December 31, 2006	1,000,000	$50.0	$350.0	$400.0
Net earnings				64.0
Cash dividend declared				(25.0)
Issuance of stock	100,000	5.0	39.0	
Balance, December 31, 2007	1,100,000	$55.0	$389.0	$439.0

The statement of stockholders' equity indicates the items or events that affected stockholders' equity during 2007. The items or events were as follows:

Item or Event	Effect on Stockholders' Equity
Net earnings ⟶	Increased retained earnings by $64.0 million
Dividends ⟶	Decreased retained earnings by $25.0 million
Shares issued ⟶	Increased common stock by $5.0 million and Increased paid-in capital by $39.0 million

The last line of the statement of stockholders' equity indicates the ending balances of the stockholders' equity accounts as of the balance sheet date, December 31, 2007. Note that each of the stockholders' equity accounts increased during 2007. The statement of stockholders' equity is useful in explaining the reasons for the changes that occurred.

What Is Comprehensive Income?

There has always been some question about which items or transactions should be shown on the income statement and should be included in the calculation of net income. Generally, the accounting rule-making bodies have held that the income statement should reflect an *all-inclusive* approach. That is, all events and transactions that affect income should be shown on the income statement. This approach prevents the manipulation of the income figure by those who would like to show "good news" on the income statement and "bad news" directly on the retained earnings statement or the statement of stockholders' equity. The result of the all-inclusive approach is that the income statement includes items that are not necessarily under management's control, such as losses from natural disasters, and thus the income statement may not be a true reflection of a company's future potential.

The FASB has accepted certain exceptions to the all-inclusive approach and has allowed items to be recorded directly to the Stockholders' Equity category. This text has discussed one such item: unrealized gains and losses on investment securities. Exhibit 11-5 presents several additional items that are beyond the scope of this text. Items such as these have been excluded from the income statement for various reasons. Quite often, the justification is a concern for the volatility of the net income number. The items we have cited are often large dollar amounts; if included in the income statement, they would cause income to fluctuate widely from period to period. Therefore, the income statement is deemed to be more useful if the items are excluded.

A new term has been coined to incorporate the "income-type" items that escape the income statement. **Comprehensive income** is the net assets increase resulting from all transactions during a time period (except for investments by owners and distributions to owners). Exhibit 11-5 presents the statement of comprehensive income and its relationship to the traditional income statement. It illustrates that comprehensive income encompasses all the revenues and expenses that are presented on the income statement to calculate net income and also includes items that are not presented on the income statement but affect total stockholders' equity.[1] The comprehensive income measure is truly

Comprehensive income
The total change in net assets from all sources except investments by or distributions to the owners.

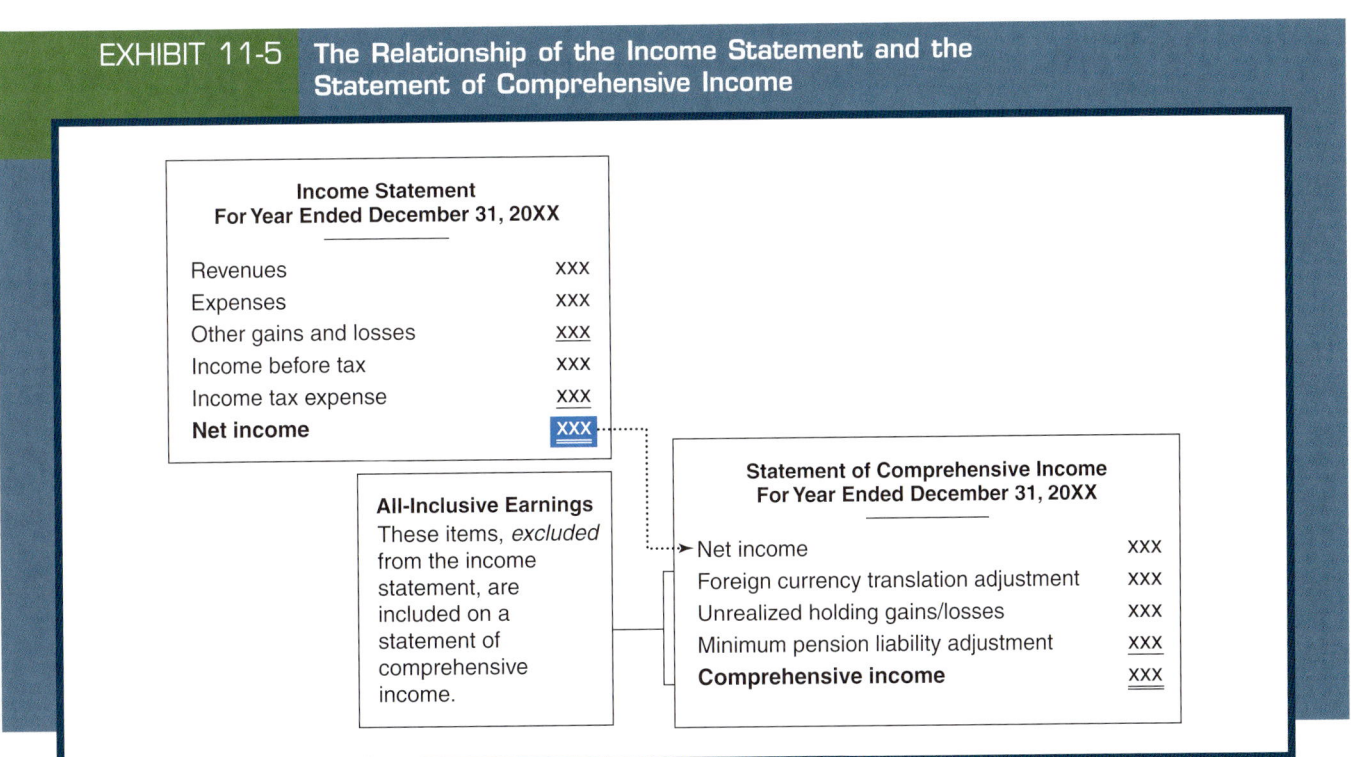

EXHIBIT 11-5 **The Relationship of the Income Statement and the Statement of Comprehensive Income**

Income Statement
For Year Ended December 31, 20XX

Revenues	XXX
Expenses	XXX
Other gains and losses	XXX
Income before tax	XXX
Income tax expense	XXX
Net income	XXX

All-Inclusive Earnings
These items, *excluded* from the income statement, are included on a statement of comprehensive income.

Statement of Comprehensive Income
For Year Ended December 31, 20XX

Net income	XXX
Foreign currency translation adjustment	XXX
Unrealized holding gains/losses	XXX
Minimum pension liability adjustment	XXX
Comprehensive income	XXX

---

1 The format of Exhibit 11-5 is suggested by the FASB. The FASB also allows other possible formats of the statement of comprehensive income.

all-inclusive because it includes such transactions as unrealized gains and prior-period adjustments that affect stockholders' equity. Firms are required to disclose comprehensive income because it provides a more complete measure of performance.

What Analyzing Stockholders' Equity Reveals About a Firm's Value

LO9 Understand how investors use ratios to evaluate stockholders' equity.

BOOK VALUE PER SHARE

Users of financial statements are often interested in computing the value of a corporation's stock. This is a difficult task because *value* is not a well-defined term and means different things to different users. One measure of value is the book value of the stock. **Book value per share** of common stock represents the rights that each share of common stock has to the net assets of the corporation. The term *net assets* refers to the total assets of the firm minus total liabilities. In other words, net assets equal the total stockholders' equity of the corporation. Therefore, when only common stock is present, book value per share is measured as follows:

Book value per share
Total stockholders' equity divided by the number of shares of common stock outstanding.

$$\text{Book Value per Share} = \frac{\text{Total Stockholders' Equity}}{\text{Number of Shares of Stock Outstanding}}$$

The book value per share is the amount per share of net assets to which the company's common stockholders have the rights. It does not indicate the market value of the common stock. That is, book value per share does not indicate the price that should be paid by those who want to buy or sell the stock on the stock exchange. Book value is also an incomplete measure of value because the corporation's net assets are normally measured on the balance sheet at the original cost, not at the current value of the assets.

For more on how investors use book value per share, and what this measure means, see the Ratio Decision Model that follows.

USING THE RATIO DECISION MODEL: ANALYZING BOOK VALUE PER SHARE

Use the following Ratio Decision Process to evaluate the book value per common share of Jacuzzi Brands or any other public company.

1. Formulate the Question

Investors realize that there are several measures of the value of a company that impact the stock price of a company. Investors in common stock also realize that they have a right to the company's assets only after the rights of creditors and preferred stockholders are satisfied. Investors can determine their rights by calculating the book value per share of the stock. Normally, a company will not be liquidated, but investors still need to understand how the book value per share relates to the actual stock price for the company. The important questions are:

What price per share does an investor want to pay for a company's stock? Should it be above or below book value per share?

2. Gather the Information from the Financial Statements

- Total stockholders' equity: From the statement of stockholders' equity
- Number of shares of stock outstanding: From the statement of stockholders' equity

3. Calculate the Ratio

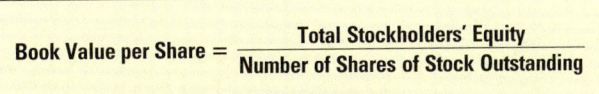

$$\text{Book Value per Share} = \frac{\text{Total Stockholders' Equity}}{\text{Number of Shares of Stock Outstanding}}$$

Jacuzzi Brands, Inc.
CONSOLIDATED BALANCE SHEETS
(in millions, except share data)

	At September 30,	
	2004	**2003**
Stockholders' Equity:		
Common stock (par value $.01 per share, authorized 300,000,000 shares; issued 99,096,734 shares; outstanding 76,103,459 and 74,986,982 shares in 2004 and 2003, respectively)	$ 1.0	$ 1.0
Paid-in capital	639.7	650.1
Accumulated deficit	(5.2)	(33.7)
Unearned restricted stock	(4.6)	(0.8)
Accumulated other comprehensive loss	(8.2)	(8.7)
Treasury stock (22,993,275 and 24,109,752 shares in 2004 and 2003, respectively), at cost	(333.6)	(352.2)
Total stockholders' equity	289.1	255.7
TOTAL LIABILITIES AND STOCKHOLDERS' EQUITY	$1,371.8	$1,336.8

$$\text{Book Value per Share} = \frac{\$289,100,000}{76,103,459} = \$3.80$$

4. Compare the Ratio with Others

Jacuzzi's book value per share of common stock may be compared to prior years and to companies in the same industry.

	Jacuzzi		American Standard	
	2004	2003	2004	2003
Book value per share	$3.80	$3.41	$4.33	$3.27

5. Interpret the Results

For 2004, Jacuzzi Brands, Inc.'s common stockholders have the right to $3.80 per share of net assets in the corporation. That has increased from the $3.41 per share in 2003.

The book value per share indicates the recorded minimum value per share of the stock, but it is not a very accurate measure of the price that an investor would be willing to pay for a share of stock. The book value of a stock is often thought to be the "floor" of a stock price. If any company has a stock price that is less than its book value, it may be an indication that the stockholders would be better off if the company were liquidated, rather than continue in business.

EXHIBIT 11-6 | **Workout Wonders' Stockholders' Equity Section**

Stockholders' Equity Section of Balance Sheet
December 31, 2007, and December 31, 2006

(in millions)	2007	2006
Preferred stock, no par value (liquidation value, $500)	400	400
Common stock, par value 1 2/3 per share (issued 1,782 shares)	30	30
Capital in excess of par value	618	548
Retained earnings	18,730	15,961
Accumulated other comprehensive loss	(886)	(1,267)
Less: Repurchased common stock, at cost (103 and 77 shares, respectively)	(4,920)	(3,376)
Total shareholders' equity	13,972	12,296

CALCULATING BOOK VALUE WHEN PREFERRED STOCK IS PRESENT

The focus of the computation of book value per share is always on the value per share of the *common* stock. Therefore, the computation must be adjusted for corporations that have both preferred and common stock. The numerator of the fraction, total stockholders' equity, should be reduced by the rights that preferred stockholders have to the corporation's net assets. Normally, this can be accomplished by deducting the redemption value or liquidation value of the preferred stock along with any dividends in arrears on cumulative preferred stock. The denominator should not include the number of shares of preferred stock.

To illustrate the computation of book value per share when both common and preferred stock are present, we refer to the Stockholders' Equity category of Workout Wonders, presented in Exhibit 11-6. When calculating book value per share, we want to consider only the *common* stockholders' equity. Exhibit 11-6 indicates that the company had total stockholders' equity in 2007 of $13,972 million but also that preferred stockholders had a right to $500 million in the event of liquidation. Therefore, $500 million must be deducted to calculate the rights of the common stockholders:

$$\$13,972 - \$500 = \$13,472 \text{ million common stockholders' equity}$$

The number of shares of common stock *outstanding* for the company is 1,782 million issued less 103 million of treasury stock. Therefore, the computation of book value per share is as follows:

$$\$13,472/1,679 = \$8.02 \text{ Book Value per Share}$$

This indicates that if the company was liquidated and the assets sold at their recorded values, the common stockholders would receive $8.02 per share. Of course, if the company went bankrupt and had to liquidate assets at distressed values, stockholders would receive something less than book value.

⏱ *2 minute review*

1. What effect does a stock dividend have on a firm's stockholders' equity?

2. What effect does a stock split have on a firm's stockholders' equity?

3. How is book value per share calculated?

Accounting Tools: Unincorporated Businesses

The focus of Chapter 11, as with the rest of the text, has been on the corporate form of organization. Most of the large, influential companies in the United States are organized as corporations. They have a legal and economic existence that is separate from that of the owners of the business, the stockholders. Yet many other companies in the economy are organized as sole proprietorships or partnerships. The purpose of this appendix is to show briefly how the characteristics of such organizations affect the accounting, particularly the accounting for the Owners' Equity category of the balance sheet.

LO11 Describe the important differences between the sole proprietorship and partnership forms of organization versus the corporate form.

SOLE PROPRIETORSHIPS

A **sole proprietorship** is a business owned by one person. Most sole proprietorships are small in size, with the owner serving as the operator or manager of the company. The primary advantage of the sole proprietorship form of organization is its simplicity. The Owner's Equity category of the balance sheet consists of one account, the owner's capital account. The owner answers to no one but himself or herself. A disadvantage of the sole proprietorship is that all the responsibility for the success or failure of the venture attaches to the owner, who often has limited resources.

Sole proprietorship
A business with a single owner.

There are three important points to remember about this form of organization. First, a sole proprietorship is not a separate entity for legal purposes. This means that the law does not distinguish between the assets of the business and those of its owner. If an owner loses a lawsuit, for example, the law does not limit an owner's liability to the amount of assets of the business but extends liability to the owner's personal assets. Thus, the owner is said to have *unlimited liability*.

Second, accountants adhere to the *entity principle* and maintain a distinction between the owner's personal assets and the assets of the sole proprietorship. The balance sheet of a sole proprietorship should reflect only the "business" assets and liabilities, with the difference reflected as owner's capital.

Third, a sole proprietorship is not treated as a separate entity for federal income tax purposes. That is, the sole proprietorship does not pay tax on its income. Rather, the business income must be declared as income on the owner's personal tax return, and income tax is assessed at the personal tax rate rather than the rate that applies to companies organized as corporations. This may or may not be advantageous, depending on the amount of income involved and the owner's tax situation.

Typical Transactions When the owners of a corporation, the stockholders, invest in the corporation, they normally do so by purchasing stock. When investing in a sole proprietorship, the owner simply contributes cash, or other assets, into the business. For example, assume that on January 1, 2007, Peter Tom began a new business by investing $10,000 cash. The effect on the accounting equation of Peter Tom Company is as follows:

Balance Sheet							Income Statement	
ASSETS		**=**	**LIABILITIES**	**+**	**OWNER'S EQUITY**		**+**	**REVENUES − EXPENSES**
Cash	10,000				Peter Tom, Capital	10,000		

The Peter Tom, Capital account is an owner's equity account and reflects the rights of the owner to the business assets.

An owner's withdrawal of assets from the business is recorded as a reduction of owner's equity. Assume that on July 1, 2007, Peter Tom took an auto valued at $6,000 from the business to use as his personal auto. The effect on the accounting equation is as follows:

			Balance Sheet				Income Statement
ASSETS	**=**	**LIABILITIES**	**+**	**OWNER'S EQUITY**	**+**	**REVENUES – EXPENSES**
Equipment (6,000)				Peter Tom, Drawing (6,000)		

The Peter Tom, Drawing account is a contra-equity account. Sometimes a drawing account is referred to as a *withdrawals account*, as in Peter Tom, Withdrawals. An increase in the account reduces the owner's equity. At the end of the fiscal year, the drawing account should be closed to the capital account and the effect is as follows:

			Balance Sheet				Income Statement
ASSETS	**=**	**LIABILITIES**	**+**	**OWNER'S EQUITY**	**+**	**REVENUES – EXPENSES**
				Peter Tom, Capital (6,000)		
				Peter Tom, Drawing 6,000		

The amount of the net income of the business should also be reflected in the capital account. Assume that all revenue and expense accounts of Peter Tom Company have been closed to the Income Summary account, resulting in a balance of $4,000, the net income for the year. The Income Summary account is closed to capital and the capital amount is increased.

The Owner's Equity section of the balance sheet for Peter Tom Company consists of one account, the capital account, calculated as follows:

Beginning balance, Jan. 1, 2007	$ 0
Plus: Investments	10,000
Net income	4,000
Less: Withdrawals	(6,000)
Ending balance, Dec. 31, 2007	$ 8,000

PARTNERSHIPS

Partnership
A business owned by two or more individuals and with the characteristic of unlimited liability.

A **partnership** is a company owned by two or more persons. Like sole proprietorships, most partnerships are fairly small businesses formed when individuals combine their capital and managerial talents for a common business purpose. Other partnerships are large, national organizations. For example, the major public accounting firms are very large, national companies but are organized in most states as partnerships.

Partnerships have characteristics similar to those of sole proprietorships. The following are the most important characteristics of partnerships:

1. *Unlimited liability.* **Legally, the assets of the business are not separate from the partners' personal assets. Each partner is personally liable for the debts of the partnership. Creditors have a legal claim first to the assets of the partnership and then to the assets of the individual partners.**

2. *Limited life.* **Corporations have a separate legal existence and an unlimited life; partnerships do not. The life of a partnership is limited; it exists as long as the contract between the partners is valid. The partnership ends when a partner withdraws or a new partner is added. A new partnership must be created for the business to continue.**

3. *Not taxed as a separate entity.* **Partnerships are subject to the same tax features as sole proprietorships. The partnership itself does not pay federal income**

tax. Rather, the income of the partnership is treated as personal income on each of the partners' individual tax returns and is taxed as personal income. All partnership income is subject to federal income tax on the individual partners' returns even if it is not distributed to the partners. A variety of other factors affects the tax consequences of partnerships versus the corporate form of organization. These aspects are quite complex and beyond the scope of this text.

A partnership is based on a **partnership agreement**. It is very important that the partners agree, in writing, about all aspects of the partnership. The agreement should detail items such as how much capital each partner is to invest, the time each is expected to devote to the business, the salary of each, and how income of the partnership is to be divided. If a partnership agreement is not present, the courts may be forced to settle disputes among partners. Therefore, the partners should develop a partnership agreement when the firm is first established and should review the agreement periodically to determine if changes are necessary.

Partnership agreement
Specifies how much the owners will invest, their salaries, and how profits will be shared.

Investments and Withdrawals In a partnership, it is important to account separately for the capital of each of the partners. A capital account should be established in the Owners' Equity section of the balance sheet for each partner of the company. Investments into the company should be credited to the partner making the investment. For example, assume that on January 1, 2007, Paige Thoms and Amy Rebec begin a partnership named AP Company. Page contributes $10,000 cash, and Amy contributes equipment valued at $5,000. The effect on the accounting equation is as follows:

	Balance Sheet						Income Statement
ASSETS		=	**LIABILITIES**	+	**OWNERS' EQUITY**	+	**REVENUES – EXPENSES**
Cash	10,000				Page Thoms, Capital	10,000	
Equipment	5,000				Amy Rebec, Capital	5,000	

A drawing account also should be established for each owner of the company to account for withdrawals of assets. Assume that on April 1, 2007, each owner withdraws $2,000 of cash from AP Company. The effect is as follows:

	Balance Sheet						Income Statement
ASSETS		=	**LIABILITIES**	+	**OWNERS' EQUITY**	+	**REVENUES – EXPENSES**
Cash	(4,000)				Page Thoms, Drawing	(2,000)	
					Amy Rebec, Drawing	(2,000)	

Distribution of Income The partnership agreement governs the manner in which income should be allocated to partners. The distribution may recognize the partners' relative investment in the business, their time and effort, their expertise and talents, or other factors. We will illustrate three methods of income allocation, but be aware that partnerships use many other allocation methods. Although these allocation methods are straightforward, partnerships dissolve often because one or more of the partners believes that the allocation is unfair. It is very difficult to devise a method that will make all partners happy.

One way to allocate income is to divide it evenly between or among the partners. In fact, when a partnership agreement is not present, the courts specify that an equal allocation must be applied, regardless of the relative contributions or efforts of the partners. For example, assume that AP Company has $30,000 of net income for the period and has established an agreement that income should be allocated evenly between the two partners, Paige and Amy. Each capital account would be increased by $15,000.

An equal distribution of income to all partners is easy to apply but is not fair to those partners who have contributed more in money or time to the partnership.

Another way to allocate income is to specify in the partnership agreement that income be allocated according to a *stated ratio*. For example, Paige and Amy may specify that all income of AP Company should be allocated on a 2-to-1 ratio, with Paige receiving the larger portion. If that allocation method is applied to the preceding example, Paige Thoms, Capital would be increased by $20,000 and Amy Rebec, Capital would be increased by $10,000.

Finally, we illustrate an allocation method that more accurately reflects the partners' input. It is based on salaries, interest on invested capital, and a stated ratio. Assume that the partnership agreement of AP Company specifies that Paige and Amy be allowed a salary of $6,000 and $4,000, respectively, that each partner receive 10% on her capital balance, and that any remaining income be allocated equally. Assume that AP Company has been in operation for several years and the capital balances of the owners at the end of 2007, before the income distribution, are as follows:

Paige Thoms, Capital	$40,000
Amy Rebec, Capital	50,000

If AP Company calculated that its 2007 net income (before partner salaries) was $30,000, income would be allocated between the partners as follows:

	Paige	Amy
Distributed for salaries:	$ 6,000	$ 4,000
Distributed for interest:		
Paige: ($40,000 × 10%)	4,000	
Amy: ($50,000 × 10%)		5,000
Remainder = $30,000 − $10,000 − $9,000 = $11,000		
Remainder distributed equally:		
Paige: ($11,000/2)	5,500	
Amy: ($11,000/2)		5,500
Total distributed	$15,500	$14,500

Paige Thoms, Capital would be increased by $15,500 and Amy Rebec, Capital by $14,500. This indicates that the amounts of $15,500 and $14,500 were allocated to Paige and Amy, respectively. It does not indicate the amount actually paid to (or withdrawn by) the partners. However, for tax purposes, the income of the partnership is treated as personal income on the partners' individual tax returns regardless of whether or not the income is actually paid in cash to the partners. This aspect often encourages partners to withdraw income from the business and makes it difficult to retain sufficient capital for the business to operate profitably.

STUDY HIGHLIGHTS

LO1 **Identify the components of the Stockholders' Equity category of the balance sheet and the accounts found in each component (p. 502).**

- Stockholders' equity consists of contributed capital from stockholders and retained earnings from the current and prior periods of operation that have not been paid as dividends.
  - Disclosure for stocks must include the number of shares authorized, issued, and outstanding, along with the par value.

LO2 **Show that you understand the characteristics of common and preferred stock and the differences between the classes of stock (p. 505).**

- The types of stock issued by a firm are common stock and preferred stock.
  - Preferred stock receives first preference for dividends and generally provides a more stable dividend stream to stockholders than common stock.

- Common stockholders have a claim to the residual interest in a company after all debtors' and preferred stockholders' claims are satisfied. Generally, only common stockholders are allowed voting rights.

Determine the financial statement impact when stock is issued for cash or for other consideration (p. 506).

LO3

- When stock is issued for cash or other consideration, the number of outstanding shares is increased, the par value of stock is recorded along with any amount in excess of par being recorded to the Additional Paid-in Capital account.
  - When stock is sold for cash, the asset Cash is increased. When issued for non-cash consideration, other asset accounts are increased.

Describe the financial statement impact of stock treated as treasury stock (p. 507).

LO4

- Treasury stock results when a corporation buys back its own stock.
  - Treasury stock is accounted for as a contra-equity account and is a reduction of stockholders' equity.

Compute the amount of cash dividends when a firm has issued both preferred and common stock (p. 509).

LO5

- The amount of a preferred stock dividend will depend on the terms of the stock agreement: cumulative, noncumulative, or cumulative and participating.

Show that you understand the difference between cash and stock dividends and the effect of stock dividends (p. 510).

LO6

- Stock dividends are given in lieu of cash dividends. Stockholders receive shares of stock which does not require a current use of cash resources by the corporation.
  - Stock dividends do not affect total stockholders' equity. They reduce retained earnings and increase the amount of common stock and additional paid-in capital.

Determine the difference between stock dividends and stock splits (p. 512).

LO7

- Both stock splits and stock dividends increase the number of shares of stock outstanding though they are fundamentally different transactions.
  - Stock splits do not require an accounting transaction to be recorded, reduce the par value of the stock, and have no effect on retained earnings or additional paid-in capital.

Show that you understand the statement of stockholders' equity and comprehensive income (p. 513).

LO8

- The statement of stockholders' equity shows how all the equity accounts changed for a particular accounting period or specific periods.
- Comprehensive income is based on the notion that the income statement be inclusive of all items affecting the wealth of an entity. The calculation of comprehensive income takes into account the increase in net assets during a time period.

Understand how investors use ratios to evaluate stockholders' equity (p. 516).

LO9

- Ratios used to analyze stockholders' equity are designed to measure some aspect of the value of the firm held by stockholders. Some common measures include:
  - Book value per share—a measure based on balance sheet accounting amounts recorded.
  - Market value per share—a measure aimed at assessing fair market value based on the current price of stock.

Explain the effects that transactions involving stockholders' equity have on the statement of cash flows (p. 519).

LO10

- Transactions involving stockholders' equity accounts are classified as financing activities. Issuing stock produces cash inflows. Dividends and the retirement or repurchase of stock produce cash outflows.

Describe the important differences between the sole proprietorship and partnership forms of organization versus the corporate form (Appendix p. 521).

LO11

- Sole proprietorships are businesses that are not incorporated and are owned by one individual. The business entity and individual are not distinguished from one another for legal and tax purposes.

HIGHLIGHTS

- Partnerships are also unincorporated entities but are owned by two or more individuals. The partners and their respective shares of the business are not distinguished from one another for legal purposes. The partnership itself is not taxed on earnings but individual partners are for their share.
- Corporations, unlike partnerships, have some of the following distinguishing characteristics: they are generally taxable entities and have an unlimited life. The corporate form has been adopted by most larger businesses and is therefore emphasized in this text.

RATIO REVIEW

$$\text{Book Value per Share} = \frac{\text{Total Stockholders' Equity*}}{\text{Number of Shares of Common Stock Outstanding}}$$

*When there is preferred stock outstanding, the redemption value or liquidation value (disclosed on the preferred stock line or in the notes) of the preferred stock must be subtracted from total stockholders' equity.

ACCOUNTS HIGHLIGHTED

Account Title	Where It Appears	In What Section	Page Number
Common Stock	Balance Sheet	Contributed Capital	502
Preferred Stock	Balance Sheet	Contributed Capital	502
Additional Paid-in Capital	Balance Sheet	Contributed Capital	502
Retained Earnings	Balance Sheet	Retained Earnings	502
Treasury Stock	Balance Sheet	(bottom portion of stockholders' equity as a contra account)	507
Cash Dividend Payable	Balance Sheet	Current Liabilities	509
Stock Dividend Distributable	Balance Sheet	Contributed Capital	511

KEY TERMS QUIZ

Read each definition below and then write the number of the definition in the blank beside the appropriate term it defines. The quiz solutions appear at the end of the chapter.

_____ Authorized shares		_____ Retirement of stock	
_____ Issued shares		_____ Dividend payout ratio	
_____ Outstanding shares		_____ Stock dividend	
_____ Par value		_____ Stock split	
_____ Additional paid-in capital		_____ Statement of stockholders' equity	
_____ Retained earnings		_____ Comprehensive income	
_____ Cumulative feature		_____ Book value per share	
_____ Participating feature		_____ Market value per share	
_____ Convertible feature		_____ Sole proprietorship (Appendix)	
_____ Callable feature		_____ Partnership (Appendix)	
_____ Treasury stock		_____ Partnership agreement (Appendix)	

1. The number of shares sold or distributed to stockholders.
2. An arbitrary amount that is stated on the face of the stock certificate and that represents the legal capital of the firm.
3. Net income that has been made by the corporation but not paid out as dividends.

4. The right to dividends in arrears before the current-year dividend is distributed.

5. Allows preferred stock to be returned to the corporation in exchange for common stock.

6. Stock issued by the firm and then repurchased but not retired.

7. The annual dividend amount divided by the annual net income.

8. A statement that reflects the differences between beginning and ending balances for all accounts in the Stockholders' Equity category.

9. Creation of additional shares of stock and reduction of the par value of the stock.

10. Total stockholders' equity divided by the number of shares of common stock outstanding.

11. The total change in net assets from all sources except investments by or distributions to the owners.

12. The selling price of the stock as indicated by the most recent stock transactions on, for example, the stock exchange.

13. The maximum number of shares a corporation may issue as indicated in the corporate charter.

14. The number of shares issued less the number of shares held as treasury stock.

15. The amount received for the issuance of stock in excess of the par value of the stock.

16. A provision allowing the preferred stockholders to share, on a percentage basis, in the distribution of an abnormally large dividend.

17. Allows the issuing firm to eliminate a class of stock by paying the stockholders a fixed amount.

18. When the stock of a corporation is repurchased with no intention to reissue at a later date.

19. A corporation's declaration and issuance of additional shares of its own stock to existing stockholders.

20. A business owned by two or more individuals with the characteristic of unlimited liability.

21. A document that specifies how much each owner should invest, the salary of each owner, and how profits are to be shared.

22. A business with a single owner.

ALTERNATE TERMS

Additional paid-in capital Paid-in capital in excess of par value

Additional paid-in capital—treasury stock Paid-in capital from treasury stock transactions

Callable Redeemable

Capital account Owners' equity account

Contributed capital Paid-in capital

Retained earnings Retained income

Small stock dividend Stock dividend less than 20%

Stockholders' equity Owners' equity

WARMUP EXERCISES & SOLUTIONS

Warmup Exercise 11-1

A company has a Retained Earnings account with a January 1 balance of $500,000. The accountant has reviewed the following information for the current year:

Increase in cash balance	$50,000
Net income	80,000
Dividends declared	30,000
Dividends paid	20,000
Decrease in accounts receivable balance	10,000

Required

Calculate the ending balance of the Retained Earnings account.

Key to the Solution Cash and accounts receivable do not affect retained earnings. Also note that dividends are deducted from retained earnings at the time they are declared rather than when they are paid.

Warmup Exercise 11-2

A company begins business on January 1 and issues 100,000 shares of common stock. On July 1, the company declares and issues a 2-for-1 stock split. On October 15, the company purchases 20,000 shares of stock as treasury stock and reissues 5,000 shares by the end of the month.

Required

Calculate the number of shares issued and the number of shares outstanding as of the end of the first year of operations.

Warmup Exercise 11-3

A. Company A has total stockholders' equity at year-end of $500,000 and has 10,000 shares of stock.
B. Company B has total stockholders' equity at year-end of $500,000 and has 10,000 shares of stock. The company also has 50,000 shares of preferred stock, which has a $1 par value and a liquidation value of $3 per share.

Required

Calculate the book value per share for Company A and Company B.

Key to the Solution Book value per share is calculated for the common stockholder. If preferred stock is present, an amount must be deducted that represents the amount the preferred stockholder would receive at liquidation.

SOLUTION TO WARMUP EXERCISES

Warmup Exercise 11-1

The ending balance of the Retained Earnings account should be calculated as follows:

Beginning balance	$500,000
Plus: Net income	80,000
Less: Dividends declared	(30,000)
Ending balance	$550,000

Warmup Exercise 11-2

The number of shares of stock issued is 200,000, or 100,000 times 2 because of the stock split. The number of shares outstanding is 185,000, calculated as follows:

Number of shares after split	100,000 × 2 = 200,000
Less purchase of treasury stock	(20,000)
Plus stock reissued	5,000
Total outstanding	185,000 shares

Warmup Exercise 11-3

A. Book value per share is $50, or $500,000/10,000.
B. Book value per share is $35, or ($500,000 − $150,000)/10,000.

REVIEW PROBLEM & SOLUTION

Andrew Company was incorporated on January 1, 2007, under a corporate charter that authorized the issuance of 50,000 shares of $5 par common stock and 20,000 shares of $100 par, 8% preferred stock. The following events occurred during 2007. Andrew wants to record the events and develop financial statements on December 31, 2007.

a. Issued for cash 10,000 shares of common stock at $25 per share and 1,000 shares of preferred stock at $110 per share on January 15, 2007.
b. Acquired a patent on April 1 in exchange for 2,000 shares of common stock. At the time of the exchange, the common stock was selling on the local stock exchange for $30 per share.

c. Repurchased 500 shares of common stock on May 1 at $20 per share. The corporation is holding the stock to be used for an employee bonus plan.

d. Declared a cash dividend of $1 per share to common stockholders and an 8% dividend to preferred stockholders on July 1. The preferred stock is noncumulative, nonpartici-pating. The dividend will be distributed on August 1.

e. Distributed the cash dividend on August 1.

f. Declared and distributed to preferred stockholders a 10% stock dividend on September 1. At the time of the dividend declaration, preferred stock was valued at $130 per share.

g. On December 31, calculated the annual net income for the year to be $200,000.

Required

1. Indicate the effect on the accounting equation for items (a) through (f).
2. Develop the Stockholders' Equity section of Andrew Company's balance sheet at December 31, 2007. You do not need to consider the notes that accompany the balance sheet.
3. Determine the book value per share of the common stock. Assume that the preferred stock can be redeemed at par.

SOLUTION TO REVIEW PROBLEM

1. The effects of items (a) through (f) on the accounting equation are as follows:

a.

			Balance Sheet					**Income Statement**
	ASSETS	**=**	**LIABILITIES**	**+**	**STOCKHOLDERS' EQUITY**	**+**	**REVENUES − EXPENSES**
Cash	360,000				Common Stock	50,000		
					Additional Paid-in			
					Capital—Common	200,000		
					Preferred Stock	100,000		
					Additional Paid-in			
					Capital—Preferred	10,000		

b. The patent received for stock should be recorded at the value of the stock:

			Balance Sheet					**Income Statement**
	ASSETS	**=**	**LIABILITIES**	**+**	**STOCKHOLDERS' EQUITY**	**+**	**REVENUES − EXPENSES**
Patent	60,000				Common Stock	10,000		
					Additional Paid-in			
					Capital—Common	50,000		

c. Stock reacquired constitutes treasury stock and should be recorded as follows:

			Balance Sheet					**Income Statement**
	ASSETS	**=**	**LIABILITIES**	**+**	**STOCKHOLDERS' EQUITY**	**+**	**REVENUES − EXPENSES**
Cash	(10,000)				Treasury Stock	(10,000)		

d. A cash dividend should be declared on the number of shares of stock outstanding as of July 1. The effect is as follows:

			Balance Sheet					**Income Statement**
	ASSETS	**=**	**LIABILITIES**	**+**	**STOCKHOLDERS' EQUITY**	**+**	**REVENUES − EXPENSES**
			Dividends Payable—		Retained Earnings	(19,500)		
			Common	11,500				
			Dividends Payable—					
			Preferred	8,000				

The number of common shares outstanding should be calculated as the number of shares issued (12,000) less the number of shares of treasury stock (500). The preferred stock dividend should be calculated as 1,000 shares times $100 par times 8%.

e.

	Balance Sheet				Income Statement
ASSETS	**=**	**LIABILITIES**	**+**	**STOCKHOLDERS' EQUITY**	**+**	**REVENUES – EXPENSES**
Cash (19,500)		Dividends Payable— Common (11,500)			
		Dividends Payable— Preferred (8,000)			

f. A stock dividend should be based on the number of shares of stock outstanding and should be declared and recorded at the market value of the stock. The impact is as follows:

	Balance Sheet				Income Statement
ASSETS	**=**	**LIABILITIES**	**+**	**STOCKHOLDERS' EQUITY**	**+**	**REVENUES – EXPENSES**
				Retained Earnings (13,000)	
				Preferred Stock 10,000	
				Additional Paid-in Capital—Preferred 3,000	

2. The Stockholders' Equity for Andrew Company after completing these transactions appears as follows:

Preferred stock, $100 par, 8%,	
20,000 shares authorized, 1,100 issued	$110,000
Common stock, $5 par,	
50,000 shares authorized, 12,000 issued	60,000
Additional paid-in capital—Preferred	13,000
Additional paid-in capital—Common	250,000
Retained earnings	167,500*
Total contributed capital and retained earnings	$600,500
Less: Treasury stock, 500 shares, common	(10,000)
Total stockholders' equity	$590,500

*$200,000 − $19,500 − $13,000 = $167,500

3. The book value per share of the common stock is calculated as follows:

($590,500 − $110,000)/11,500 shares = $41.78

QUESTIONS

1. What are the two major components of stockholders' equity? Which accounts generally appear in each component?

2. Corporations disclose the number of shares authorized, issued, and outstanding. What is the meaning of each of these terms? What causes a difference between the number of shares issued and the number outstanding?

3. Why do firms designate an amount as the par value of stock? Does par value indicate the selling price or market value of the stock?

4. If a firm has a net income for the year, will the balance in the Retained Earnings account equal the net income? What is the meaning of the balance of the account?

5. What is the meaning of the statement that preferred stock has a preference to dividends declared by the corporation? Do preferred stockholders have the right to dividends in arrears on preferred stock?

6. Why might some stockholders be inclined to buy preferred stock rather than common stock? What are the advantages of investing in preferred stock?

7. Why are common shareholders sometimes called *residual owners* when a company has both common and preferred stock outstanding?

8. When stock is issued in exchange for an asset, at what amount should the asset be reported? How could the fair market value be determined?

(continued)

9. What is treasury stock? Why do firms use it? Where does it appear on a corporation's financial statements?

10. When treasury stock is bought and sold, the transactions do not result in gains or losses reported on the income statement. What account or accounts are used instead? Why are no income statement amounts recorded?

11. Many firms operate at a dividend payout ratio of less than 50%. Why do firms not pay a larger percentage of income as dividends?

12. What is a *stock dividend*? How should it be recorded?

13. Would you rather receive a cash dividend or a stock dividend from a company? Explain.

14. What is the difference between stock dividends and stock splits? How should stock splits be recorded?

15. How is the book value per share calculated? Does the amount calculated as book value per share mean that stockholders will receive a dividend equal to the book value?

16. Can the market value per share of stock be determined by the information on the income statement?

17. What is the difference between a statement of stockholders' equity and a retained earnings statement?

18. What is an advantage of organizing a company as a corporation rather than a partnership? Why don't all companies incorporate? (Appendix)

19. What are some ways that partnerships could share income among the partners? (Appendix)

EXERCISES

LO1   **Exercise 11-1** Stockholders' Equity Accounts

MJ Company has identified the following items. Indicate whether or not each item is included in an account in the Stockholders' Equity category of the balance sheet and identify the account title. Also indicate whether the item would increase or decrease stockholders' equity.

1. Preferred stock issued by MJ
2. Amount received by MJ in excess of par value when preferred stock was issued
3. Dividends in arrears on MJ preferred stock
4. Cash dividend declared but unpaid on MJ stock
5. Stock dividend declared but unissued by MJ
6. Treasury stock
7. Amount received in excess of cost when treasury stock is reissued by MJ
8. Retained earnings

LO1   **Exercise 11-2** Solve for Unknowns

The Stockholders' Equity category of Zache Company's balance sheet appears below.

Common stock, $10 par, 10,000 shares issued,	
9,200 outstanding	$??
Additional paid-in capital	??
Total contributed capital	$350,000
Retained earnings	100,000
Treasury stock, ?? shares at cost	10,000
Total stockholders' equity	$??

Required
1. Determine the missing values that are indicated by question marks.
2. What was the cost per share of the treasury stock?

LO3   **Exercise 11-3** Stock Issuance

Horace Company had the following transactions during 2007, its first year of business.

a. Issued 5,000 shares of $5 par common stock for cash at $15 per share.
b. Issued 7,000 shares of common stock on May 1 to acquire a factory building from Barkley Company. Barkley had acquired the building in 2003 at a price of $150,000. Horace estimated that the building was worth $175,000 on May 1, 2007.
c. Issued 2,000 shares of stock on June 1 to acquire a patent. The accountant has been unable to estimate the value of the patent but has determined that Horace's common stock was selling at $25 per share on June 1.

Required

1. Determine the effect on the accounting equation of the events.
2. Determine the balance sheet amounts for common stock and additional paid-in capital.

LO3   **Exercise 11-4** Stock Issuances

The following transactions are for Weber Corporation in 2007:

a. On March 1, the corporation was organized and received authorization to issue 5,000 shares of 8%, $100 par value preferred stock and 2,000,000 shares of $10 par value common stock.
b. On March 10, Weber issued 5,000 shares of common stock at $35 per share.
c. On March 18, Weber issued 100 shares of preferred stock at $120 per share.
d. On April 12, Weber issued another 10,000 shares of common stock at $45 per share.

Required

1. Determine the effect on the accounting equation of each of the events.
2. Prepare the Stockholders' Equity section of the balance sheet as of December 31, 2007.
3. Does the balance sheet indicate the market value of the stock at year-end? Explain.

LO5   **Exercise 11-5** Treasury Stock

The Stockholders' Equity category of Bradford Company's balance sheet on January 1, 2007, appeared as follows:

Common stock, $10 par, 10,000 shares issued and outstanding	$100,000
Additional paid-in capital	50,000
Retained earnings	80,000
Total stockholders' equity	$230,000

The following transactions occurred during 2007:

a. Reacquired 2,000 shares of common stock at $20 per share on July 1.
b. Reacquired 400 shares of common stock at $18 per share on August 1.

Required

1. Determine the effect on the accounting equation of the events.
2. Assume the company resold the shares of treasury stock at $28 per share on October 1. Did the company benefit from the treasury stock transaction? If so, where is the "gain" presented on the balance sheet?

LO4   **Exercise 11-6** Treasury Stock Transactions

The Stockholders' Equity category of Little Joe's balance sheet on January 1, 2007, appeared as follows:

Common stock, $5 par, 40,000 shares issued and outstanding	$200,000
Additional paid-in capital	90,000
Retained earnings	100,000
Total stockholders' equity	$390,000

The following transactions occurred during 2007:

a. Reacquired 5,000 shares of common stock at $20 per share on February 1.
b. Reacquired 1,200 shares of common stock at $13 per share on March 1.

Required

1. Determine each event's effect on the accounting equation.
2. Assume that the treasury stock was reissued on October 1 at $12 per share. Did the company benefit from the treasury stock reissuance? Where is the "gain" or "loss" presented on the financial statements?
3. What effect did the two transactions to purchase treasury stock and the later reissuance of that stock have on the Stockholders' Equity section of the balance sheet?

LO5   **Exercise 11-7** Cash Dividends

Kerry Company has 1,000 shares of $100 par value, 9% preferred stock and 10,000 shares of $10 par value common stock outstanding. The preferred stock is cumulative and non-participating. Dividends were paid in 2003. Since 2003, Kerry has declared and paid dividends as follows:

2004	$ 0
2005	10,000
2006	20,000
2007	25,000

Required

1. Determine the amount of the dividends to be allocated to preferred and common stockholders for each year, 2005 to 2007.
2. If the preferred stock had been noncumulative, how much would have been allocated to the preferred and common stockholders each year?

LO5   **Exercise 11-8** Cash Dividends

The Stockholders' Equity category of Jackson Company's balance sheet as of January 1, 2007, appeared as follows:

Preferred stock, $100 par, 8%,	
2,000 shares issued and outstanding	$200,000
Common stock, $10 par,	
5,000 shares issued and outstanding	50,000
Additional paid-in capital	300,000
Total contributed capital	$550,000
Retained earnings	400,000
Total stockholders' equity	$950,000

The notes that accompany the financial statements indicate that Jackson has not paid dividends for the two years prior to 2007. On July 1, 2007, Jackson declares a dividend of $100,000 to be paid to preferred and common stockholders on August 1.

Required

1. Determine the amounts of the dividend to be allocated to preferred and common stockholders, assuming that the preferred stock is noncumulative, nonparticipating stock.
2. Determine the effect on the accounting equation of the July 1 and August 1, 2007, events.
3. Determine the amounts of the dividend to be allocated to preferred and common stockholders, assuming instead that the preferred stock is cumulative, nonparticipating stock.

LO6   **Exercise 11-9** Stock Dividends

The Stockholders' Equity category of Worthy Company's balance sheet as of January 1, 2007, appeared as follows:

Common stock, $10 par,	
40,000 shares issued and outstanding	$400,000
Additional paid-in capital	100,000
Retained earnings	400,000
Total stockholders' equity	$900,000

The following transactions occurred during 2007:

a. Declared a 10% stock dividend to common stockholders on January 15. At the time of the dividend, the common stock was selling for $30 per share. The stock dividend was to be issued to stockholders on January 30, 2007.
b. Distributed the stock dividend to the stockholders on January 30, 2007.

Required

1. Determine the effect on the accounting equation of the 2007 events.
2. Develop the Stockholders' Equity category of Worthy Company's balance sheet as of January 31, 2007, after the stock dividend was issued. What effect did these transactions have on total stockholders' equity?

HOMEWORK

LO7 **Exercise 11-10** Stock Dividends versus Stock Splits

Campbell Company wants to increase the number of shares of its common stock outstanding and is considering a stock dividend versus a stock split. The Stockholders' Equity of the firm on its most recent balance sheet appeared as follows:

Common stock, $10 par,	
50,000 shares issued and outstanding	$ 500,000
Additional paid-in capital	750,000
Retained earnings	880,000
Total stockholders' equity	$2,130,000

If a stock dividend is chosen, the firm wants to declare a 100% stock dividend. Because the stock dividend qualifies as a "large stock dividend," it must be recorded at par value. If a stock split is chosen, Campbell will declare a 2-for-1 split.

Required

1. Compare the effects of the stock dividends and stock splits on the accounting equation.
2. Develop the Stockholders' Equity category of Campbell's balance sheet (a) after the stock dividend and (b) after the stock split.

LO7 **Exercise 11-11** Stock Dividends and Stock Splits

Whitacre Company's Stockholders' Equity section of the balance sheet on December 31, 2006, was as follows:

Common stock, $10 par value,	
60,000 shares issued and outstanding	$ 600,000
Additional paid-in capital	480,000
Retained earnings	1,240,000
Total stockholders' equity	$2,320,000

On May 1, 2007, Whitacre declared and issued a 15% stock dividend, when the stock was selling for $20 per share. Then on November 1, it declared and issued a 2-for-1 stock split.

Required

1. How many shares of stock are outstanding at year-end?
2. What is the par value per share of these shares?
3. Develop the Stockholders' Equity category of Whitacre's balance sheet as of December 31, 2007.

LO8 **Exercise 11-12** Reporting Changes in Stockholders' Equity Items

On May 1, 2006, Ryde Inc. had common stock of $345,000, additional paid-in capital of $1,298,000 and retained earnings of $3,013,000. Ryde did not purchase or sell any common stock during the year. The company reported net income of $556,000 and declared dividends in the amount of $78,000 during the year ended April 30, 2007.

Required

Prepare a financial statement that explains all the reasons for the differences between the beginning and ending balances for the accounts in the Stockholders' Equity category of the balance sheet.

LO8 **Exercise 11-13** Comprehensive Income

Assume that you are the accountant for Ellis Corporation, which has issued its 2007 annual report. You have received an inquiry from a stockholder who has questions about several items in the annual report, including why Ellis has not shown certain transactions on the income statement. In particular, Ellis's 2007 balance sheet revealed two accounts in Stockholders' Equity (Unrealized Gain/Loss—Available-for-Sale Securities and Loss on Foreign Currency Translation Adjustments) for which the dollar amounts involved were not reported on the income statement.

Required

Draft a written response to the stockholder's inquiry that explains the nature of the two accounts and the reason that the amounts involved were not recorded on the 2007 income statement. Do you think the concept of comprehensive income would be useful to explain the impact of all events for Ellis Corporation?

LO9 **Exercise 11-14** Payout Ratio and Book Value per Share

Divac Company has developed a statement of stockholders' equity for the year 2007 as follows:

	Preferred Stock	Paid-In Capital— Preferred	Common Stock	Paid-In Capital— Common	Retained Earnings
Balance, Jan. 1	$100,000	$50,000	$400,000	$40,000	$200,000
Stock issued			100,000	10,000	
Net income					80,000
Cash dividend					−45,000
Stock dividend	10,000	5,000			−15,000
Balance, Dec. 31	$110,000	$55,000	$500,000	$50,000	$220,000

Divac's preferred stock is $100 par, 8% stock. If the stock is liquidated or redeemed, stockholders are entitled to $120 per share. There are no dividends in arrears on the stock. The common stock has a par value of $5 per share.

Required
1. Determine the dividend payout ratio for the common stock.
2. Determine the book value per share of Divac's common stock.

LO10 **Exercise 11-15** Impact of Transactions Involving Issuance of Stock on Statement of Cash Flows

From the following list, identify each item as operating (O), investing (I), financing (F), or not separately reported on the statement of cash flows (N).

_____ Issuance of common stock for cash
_____ Issuance of preferred stock for cash
_____ Issuance of common stock for equipment
_____ Issuance of preferred stock for land and building
_____ Conversion of preferred stock into common stock

LO10 **Exercise 11-16** Impact of Transactions Involving Treasury Stock on Statement of Cash Flows

From the following list, identify each item as operating (O), investing (I), financing (F), or not separately reported on the statement of cash flows (N).

_____ Repurchase of common stock as treasury stock
_____ Reissuance of common stock (held as treasury stock)
_____ Retirement of treasury stock

LO10 **Exercise 11-17** Impact of Transactions Involving Dividends on Statement of Cash Flows

From the following list, identify each item as operating (O), investing (I), financing (F), or not separately reported on the statement of cash flows (N).

_____ Payment of cash dividend on common stock
_____ Payment of cash dividend on preferred stock
_____ Distribution of stock dividend
_____ Declaration of stock split

LO10 **Exercise 11-18** Determining Dividends Paid on Statement of Cash Flows

Clifford Company's comparative balance sheet included dividends payable of $80,000 at December 31, 2006, and $100,000 at December 31, 2007. Dividends declared by Clifford during 2007 amounted to $400,000.

Required
1. Calculate the amount of dividends actually paid to stockholders during 2007.
2. How will Clifford report the dividend payments on its 2007 statement of cash flows?

HOMEWORK

LO11 **Exercise 11-19** Sole Proprietorship (Appendix)

Terry Woods opened Par Golf as a sole proprietor by investing $50,000 cash on January 1, 2007. Because the business was new, it operated at a net loss of $10,000 for 2007. During the year, Terry withdrew $20,000 from the business for living expenses. Terry also had $4,000 of interest income from sources unrelated to the business.

Required
Present the Owner's Equity category of Par Golf's balance sheet as of December 31, 2007.

LO11 **Exercise 11-20** Partnerships (Appendix)

Sports Central is a sporting goods store owned by Lewis, Jamal, and Lapin in partnership. On January 1, 2007, their capital balances were as follows:

Lewis, Capital	$20,000
Jamal, Capital	50,000
Lapin, Capital	30,000

During 2007, Lewis withdrew $5,000; Jamal, $12,000; and Lapin, $9,000. Income for the partnership for 2007 was $50,000.

Required
If the partners agreed to allocate income equally, what was the ending balance in each of their capital accounts on December 31, 2007?

PROBLEMS

LO1 **Problem 11-1** Stockholders' Equity Category

Peeler Company was incorporated as a new business on January 1, 2007. The corporate charter approved on that date authorized the issuance of 1,000 shares of $100 par, 7% cumulative, nonparticipating preferred stock and 10,000 shares of $5 par common stock. On January 10, Peeler issued for cash 500 shares of preferred stock at $120 per share and 4,000 shares of common at $80 per share. On January 20, it issued 1,000 shares of common stock to acquire a building site, at a time when the stock was selling for $70 per share.

During 2007, Peeler established an employee benefit plan and acquired 500 shares of common stock at $60 per share as treasury stock for that purpose. Later in 2007, it resold 100 shares of the stock at $65 per share.

On December 31, 2007, Peeler determined its net income for the year to be $40,000. The firm declared the annual cash dividend to preferred stockholders and a cash dividend of $5 per share to the common stockholders. The dividends will be paid in 2008.

Required
Develop the Stockholders' Equity category of Peeler's balance sheet as of December 31, 2007. Indicate on the statement the number of shares authorized, issued, and outstanding for both preferred and common stock.

LO2 **Problem 11-2** Evaluating Alternative Investments

Ellen Hays received a windfall from one of her investments. She would like to invest $100,000 of the money in Linwood Inc., which is offering common stock, preferred stock, and bonds on the open market. The common stock has paid $8 per share in dividends for the past three years and the company expects to be able to perform as well in the current year. The current market price of the common stock is $100 per share. The preferred stock has an 8% dividend rate, cumulative and nonparticipating. The bonds are selling at par with an 8% stated rate.

1. What are the advantages and disadvantages of each type of investment?
2. Recommend one type of investment over the others to Ellen, and justify your reason.

LO5

Problem 11-3 Dividends for Preferred and Common Stock

The Stockholders' Equity category of Greenbaum Company's balance sheet as of December 31, 2007, appeared as follows:

Preferred stock, $100 par, 8%,	
1,000 shares issued and outstanding	$ 100,000
Common stock, $10 par,	
20,000 shares issued and outstanding	200,000
Additional paid-in capital	250,000
Total contributed capital	$ 550,000
Retained earnings	450,000
Total stockholders' equity	$1,000,000

The notes to the financial statements indicate that dividends were not declared or paid for 2005 or 2006. Greenbaum wants to declare a dividend of $59,000 for 2007.

Required

Determine the total and the per-share amounts that should be declared to the preferred and common stockholders under the following assumptions:

1. The preferred stock is noncumulative, nonparticipating.
2. The preferred stock is cumulative, nonparticipating.

LO6

Problem 11-4 Effect of Stock Dividend

Favre Company has a history of paying cash dividends on its common stock. The firm did not have a particularly profitable year, however, in 2007. At the end of the year, Favre found itself without the necessary cash for a dividend and therefore declared a stock dividend to its common stockholders. A 50% stock dividend was declared to stockholders on December 31, 2007. The board of directors is unclear about a stock dividend's effect on Favre's balance sheet and has requested your assistance.

Required

1. Write a statement to indicate the effect that the stock dividend has on the financial statements of Favre Company.
2. A group of common stockholders has contacted the firm to express its concern about the effect of the stock dividend and to question the effect the stock dividend may have on the market price of the stock. Write a statement to address the stockholders' concerns.

LO7

Problem 11-5 Dividends and Stock Splits

On January 1, 2007, Frederiksen Inc.'s Stockholders' Equity category appeared as follows:

Preferred stock, $80 par value, 7%,	
3,000 shares issued and outstanding	$ 240,000
Common stock, $10 par value,	
15,000 shares issued and outstanding	150,000
Additional paid-in capital—Preferred	60,000
Additional paid-in capital—Common	225,000
Total contributed capital	$ 675,000
Retained earnings	2,100,000
Total stockholders' equity	$2,775,000

The preferred stock is noncumulative and nonparticipating. During 2007, the following transactions occurred:

a. On March 1, declared a cash dividend of $16,800 on preferred stock. Paid the dividend on April 1.
b. On June 1, declared a 5% stock dividend on common stock. The current market price of the common stock was $18. The stock was issued on July 1.
c. On September 1, declared a cash dividend of $0.50 per share on the common stock; paid the dividend on October 1.
d. On December 1, issued a 2-for-1 stock split of common stock, when the stock was selling for $50 per share.

Required

1. Explain each transaction's effect on the stockholders' equity accounts and the total stockholders' equity.
2. Develop the Stockholders' Equity category of the December 31, 2007, balance sheet. Assume the net income for the year was $650,000.
3. Write a paragraph that explains the difference between a stock dividend and a stock split.

LO8 **Problem 11-6** Statement of Stockholders' Equity

Refer to all the facts in Problem 11-1.

Required

Develop a statement of stockholders' equity for Peeler Company for 2007. The statement should start with the beginning balance of each stockholders' equity account and explain the changes that occurred in each account to arrive at the 2007 ending balances.

LO8 **Problem 11-7** Wal-Mart's Comprehensive Income

The consolidated statement of shareholders' equity of **Wal-Mart Stores, Inc.,** for the year ended January 31, 2005, appears below.

Consolidated Statement of Shareholders' Equity
(amounts in millions)

	Number of Shares	Common Stock	Capital in Excess of Par Value	Retained Earnings	Accumulated Comprehensive Income	Total
Balance, January 31, 2004	4,311	$431	$2,135	$40,206	$ 851	$43,623
Comprehensive Income						
Net income				10,267		10,267
Other accumulated comprehensive income						
Foreign currency translation adjustment					2,130	2,130
Hedge accounting adjustment					(194)	(194)
Minimum pension liability adjustment					(93)	(93)
Total Comprehensive Income						$12,110
Cash dividends ($0.28 per share)				(2,214)		(2,214)
Purchase of Company stock	(81)	(8)	(136)	(4,405)		(4,549)
Stock options exercised and other	4		426			426
Balance, January 31, 2005	4,234	$423	$2,425	$43,854	$2,694	$49,396

Required

1. Which items were included in comprehensive income? If these items had been included on the income statement as part of net income, what would have been the effect?
2. Do you think that the concept of comprehensive income would be useful to explain the impact of all the events that took place during 2004 to the stockholders of Wal-Mart?

LO10 **Problem 11-8** Effects of Stockholders' Equity Transactions on Statement of Cash Flows

Refer to all the facts in Problem 11-1.

Required

Indicate how each of the transactions affects the cash flows of Peeler Company by preparing the Financing Activities section of the 2007 statement of cash flows. Provide an explanation for the exclusion of any of these transactions from the Financing Activities section of the statement.

LO11 **Problem 11-9** Income Distribution of a Partnership (Appendix)

Louise Abbott and Buddie Costello are partners in a comedy club business. The partnership agreement specifies the manner in which income of the business is to be distributed. Louise is to receive a salary of $20,000 for managing the club, and Buddie is to receive interest at the rate of 10% on her capital balance of $300,000. Remaining income is to be distributed on a 2-to-1 ratio.

Required

Determine the amount that should be distributed to each partner, assuming the following business net incomes:

1. $15,000
2. $50,000
3. $80,000

LO11   **Problem 11-10** Sole Proprietorships (Appendix)

On May 1, Chong Yu deposited $120,000 of his own savings in a separate bank account to start a printing business. He purchased copy machines for $42,000. Expenses for the year, including depreciation on the copy machines, were $84,000. Sales for the year, all in cash, were $108,000. Chong withdrew $12,000 during the year.

Required

1. What is the balance in Chong's capital account at the end of the year?
2. Explain why the balance in Chong's capital account is different from the amount of cash on hand.

LO11   **Problem 11-11** Partnerships (Appendix)

Kirin Nerise and Milt O'Brien agreed to form a partnership to operate a sandwich shop. Kirin contributed $25,000 cash and will manage the store. Milt contributed computer equipment worth $8,000 and $92,000 cash. Milt will keep the financial records. During the year, sales were $90,000 and expenses (including a salary to Kirin) were $76,000. Kirin withdrew $500 per month. Milt withdrew $4,000 (total). Their partnership agreement specified that Kirin would receive a salary of $7,200 for the year. Milt would receive 6% interest on his initial capital investment. All remaining income or loss would be equally divided.

Required

Calculate the ending balance in each of the partners' equity accounts.

MULTI-CONCEPT PROBLEMS

LO1,4   **Problem 11-12** Analysis of Stockholders' Equity

The Stockholders' Equity section of the December 31, 2007, balance sheet of Eldon Company appeared as follows:

Preferred stock, $30 par value,	
5,000 shares authorized, ? shares issued	$120,000
Common stock, ? par,	
10,000 shares authorized, 7,000 shares issued	70,000
Additional paid-in capital—Preferred	6,000
Additional paid-in capital—Common	560,000
Additional paid-in capital—Treasury stock	1,000
Total contributed capital	$757,000
Retained earnings	40,000
Less: Treasury stock, preferred, 100 shares	(3,200)
Total stockholders' equity	$??

Required

Determine the following items, based on Eldon's balance sheet:

1. The number of shares of preferred stock issued
2. The number of shares of preferred stock outstanding
3. The average per-share sales price of the preferred stock when issued
4. The par value of the common stock
5. The average per-share sales price of the common stock when issued
6. The cost of the treasury stock per share
7. The total stockholders' equity
8. The per-share book value of the common stock, assuming that there are no dividends in arrears and that the preferred stock can be redeemed at its par value

HOMEWORK

LO3,4,7

Problem 11-13 Effects of Stockholders' Equity Transactions on the Balance Sheet

The following transactions occurred at Horton Inc. during its first year of operation:

a. Issued 100,000 shares of common stock at $5 each; 1,000,000 shares are authorized at $1 par value.
b. Issued 10,000 shares of common stock for a building and land. The building was appraised for $20,000, but the value of the land is undeterminable. The stock is selling for $10 on the open market.
c. Purchased 1,000 shares of its own common stock on the open market for $16 per share.
d. Declared a dividend of $0.10 per share on outstanding common stock. The dividend is to be paid after the end of the first year of operations. Market value of the stock is $26.
e. Declared a 2-for-1 stock split. The market value of the stock was $37 before the stock split.
f. Reported $180,000 of income for the year.

Required

1. Indicate each transaction's effect on the assets, liabilities, and stockholders' equity of Horton Inc.
2. Prepare the Stockholders' Equity section of the balance sheet.
3. Write a paragraph that explains the number of shares of stock issued and outstanding at the end of the year.

LO1,4

Problem 11-14 Stockholders' Equity Section of the Balance Sheet

The newly hired accountant at Ives Inc. prepared the following balance sheet:

Assets	
Cash	$ 3,500
Accounts receivable	5,000
Treasury stock	500
Plant, property, and equipment	108,000
Retained earnings	1,000
Total assets	$118,000

Liabilities	
Accounts payable	$ 5,500
Dividends payable	1,500

Owners' Equity	
Common stock, $1 par,	
100,000 shares issued	100,000
Additional paid-in capital	11,000
Total liabilities and owners' equity	$118,000

Required

1. Prepare a corrected balance sheet. Write a short explanation for each correction.
2. Why does the Retained Earnings account have a negative balance?

ALTERNATE PROBLEMS

LO1

Problem 11-1A Stockholders' Equity Category

Kebler Company was incorporated as a new business on January 1, 2007. The corporate charter approved on that date authorized the issuance of 2,000 shares of $100 par 7% cumulative, nonparticipating preferred stock and 20,000 shares of $5 par common stock. On January 10, Kebler issued for cash 1,000 shares of preferred stock at $120 per share and 8,000 shares of common at $80 per share. On January 20, it issued 2,000 shares of common stock to acquire a building site, at a time when the stock was selling for $70 per share.

During 2007 Kebler established an employee benefit plan and acquired 1,000 shares of common stock at $60 per share as treasury stock for that purpose. Later in 2007, it resold 100 shares of the stock at $65 per share.

On December 31, 2007, Kebler determined its net income for the year to be $80,000. The firm declared the annual cash dividend to preferred stockholders and a cash dividend of $5 per share to the common stockholders. The dividend will be paid in 2008.

Required

Develop the Stockholders' Equity category of Kebler's balance sheet as of December 31, 2007. Indicate on the statement the number of shares authorized, issued, and outstanding for both preferred and common stock.

LO2   **Problem 11-2A** Evaluating Alternative Investments

Rob Lowe would like to invest $100,000 in Franklin Inc., which is offering common stock, preferred stock, and bonds on the open market. The common stock has paid $1 per share in dividends for the past three years, and the company expects to be able to double the dividend in the current year. The current market price of the common stock is $10 per share. The preferred stock has an 8% dividend rate. The bonds are selling at par with a 5% stated rate.

Required

1. Explain Franklin's obligation to pay dividends or interest on each instrument.
2. Recommend one type of investment over the others to Rob, and justify your reason.

LO5   **Problem 11-3A** Dividends for Preferred and Common Stock

The Stockholders' Equity category of Rausch Company's balance sheet as of December 31, 2007, appeared as follows:

Preferred stock, $100 par, 8%,	
2,000 shares issued and outstanding	$ 200,000
Common stock, $10 par,	
40,000 shares issued and outstanding	400,000
Additional paid-in capital	500,000
Total contributed capital	$1,100,000
Retained earnings	900,000
Total stockholders' equity	$2,000,000

The notes to the financial statements indicate that dividends were not declared or paid for 2005 or 2006. Rausch wants to declare a dividend of $118,000 for 2007.

Required

Determine the total and the per-share amounts that should be declared to the preferred and common stockholders under the following assumptions:

1. The preferred stock is noncumulative, nonparticipating.
2. The preferred stock is cumulative, nonparticipating.

LO6   **Problem 11-4A** Effect of Stock Dividend

Travanti Company has a history of paying cash dividends on its common stock. Although the firm has been profitable this year, the board of directors has been planning construction of a second manufacturing plant. To reduce the amount that they must borrow to finance the expansion, the directors are contemplating replacing their usual cash dividend with a 40% stock dividend. The board is unsure what the effect of a stock dividend will be on the company's balance sheet and has requested your assistance.

Required

1. Write a statement to indicate the effect that the stock dividend has on the financial statements of Travanti Company.
2. A group of common stockholders has contacted the firm to express its concern about the effect of the stock dividend and to question the effect that the stock dividend may have on the market price of the stock. Write a statement to address the stockholders' concerns.

LO7   **Problem 11-5A** Dividends and Stock Splits

On January 1, 2007, Svenberg Inc.'s Stockholders' Equity category appeared as follows:

Preferred stock, $80 par value, 8%,	
1,000 shares issued and outstanding	$ 80,000
Common stock, $10 par value,	
10,000 shares issued and outstanding	100,000
Additional paid-in capital—Preferred	60,000
Additional paid-in capital—Common	225,000
Total contributed capital	$ 465,000
Retained earnings	1,980,000
Total stockholders' equity	$2,445,000

The preferred stock is noncumulative and nonparticipating. During 2007, the following transactions occurred:

a. On March 1, declared a cash dividend of $6,400 on preferred stock. Paid the dividend on April 1.
b. On June 1, declared an 8% stock dividend on common stock. The current market price of the common stock was $26. The stock was issued on July 1.
c. On September 1, declared a cash dividend of $0.70 per share on the common stock; paid the dividend on October 1.
d. On December 1, issued a 3-for-1 stock split of common stock, when the stock was selling for $30 per share.

Required

1. Explain each transaction's effect on the stockholders' equity accounts and the total stockholders' equity.
2. Develop the Stockholders' Equity category of the balance sheet. Assume the net income for the year was $720,000.
3. Write a paragraph that explains the difference between a stock dividend and a stock split.

LO8

Problem 11-6A Statement of Stockholders' Equity

Refer to all the facts in Problem 11-1A.

Required

Develop a statement of stockholders' equity for Kebler Company for 2007. The statement should start with the beginning balance of each stockholders' equity account and explain the changes that occurred in each account to arrive at the 2007 ending balances.

LO8

Problem 11-7A Costco's Comprehensive Income

The consolidated statement of stockholders' equity of **Costco Wholesale Corporation** for the year ended August 29, 2004, appears as follows:

CONSOLIDATED STATEMENTS OF STOCKHOLDERS' EQUITY AND COMPREHENSIVE INCOME
For the 52 weeks ended August 29, 2004 (in thousands)

	Common Stock		Additional Paid-In Capital	Other Accumulated Comprehensive Income/(Loss)	Retained Earnings	Total
	Shares	Amount				
Balance at August 31, 2003	457,479	$2,287	$1,280,942	$(77,980)	$5,349,731	$6,554,980
Comprehensive Income						
Net Income	—	—	—	—	882,393	882,393
Other accumulated comprehensive income	—	—	—	94,124	—	94,124
Stock options exercised including income tax benefits and other	5,153	26	148,785	—	—	148,811
Conversion of convertible debentures	5	—	131	—	—	131
Stock-based compensation	—	—	36,508	—	—	36,508
Cash dividends	—	—	—	—	(92,137)	(92,137)
Balance at August 29, 2004	462,637	$2,313	$1,466,366	$ 16,144	$6,139,987	$7,624,810

Required

1. Costco has an item in the statement of stockholders' equity that is Other Accumulated Comprehensive Income. What are the possible sources of other comprehensive income as discussed in your text?
2. Besides Net Income and Other Accumulated Comprehensive Income, what other items affected stockholders' equity during the period?
3. How do cash dividends affect stockholders' equity? How would a stock dividend affect stockholders' equity?

Problem 11-8A Effects of Stockholders' Equity Transactions on the Statement of Cash Flows

Refer to all the facts in Problem 11-1A.

Required

Indicate how each of the transactions affects the cash flows of Kebler Company, by preparing the Financing Activities section of the 2007 statement of cash flows. Provide an explanation for the exclusion of any of these transactions from the Financing Activities section of the statement.

Problem 11-9A Income Distribution of a Partnership (Appendix)

Kay Katz and Doris Kan are partners in a dry-cleaning business. The partnership agreement specifies the manner in which income of the business is to be distributed. Kay is to receive a salary of $40,000 for managing the business. Doris is to receive interest at the rate of 10% on her capital balance of $600,000. Remaining income is to be distributed on a 2-to-1 ratio.

Required

Determine the amount that should be distributed to each partner, assuming the following business net incomes:

1. $30,000
2. $100,000
3. $160,000

Problem 11-10A Sole Proprietorships (Appendix)

On May 1, Chen Chien Lao deposited $150,000 of her own savings in a separate bank account to start a printing business. She purchased copy machines for $52,500. Expenses for the year, including depreciation on the copy machines, were $105,000. Sales for the year, all in cash, were $135,000. Chen withdrew $15,000 during the year.

Required

1. What is the balance in Chen's capital account at the end of the year?
2. Explain why the balance in Chen's capital account is different from the amount of cash on hand.

Problem 11-11A Partnerships (Appendix)

Karen Locke and Gina Keyes agreed to form a partnership to operate a sandwich shop. Karen contributed $35,000 cash and will manage the store. Gina contributed computer equipment worth $11,200 and $128,800 cash. Gina will keep the financial records. During the year, sales were $126,000 and expenses (including a salary for Karen) were $106,400. Karen withdrew $700 per month. Gina withdrew $5,600 (total). Their partnership agreement specified that Karen would receive a salary of $10,800 for the year. Gina would receive 6% interest on her initial capital investment. All remaining income or loss would be equally divided.

Required

Calculate the ending balance in the equity account of each of the partners.

ALTERNATE MULTI-CONCEPT PROBLEMS

LO1,4   **Problem 11-12A** Analysis of Stockholders' Equity

The Stockholders' Equity section of the December 31, 2007, balance sheet of Carter Company appeared as follows:

Preferred stock, $50 par value,	
10,000 shares authorized, ? shares issued	$ 400,000
Common stock, ? par value,	
20,000 shares authorized, 14,000 shares issued	280,000
Additional paid-in capital—Preferred	12,000
Additional paid-in capital—Common	980,000
Additional paid-in capital—Treasury stock	2,000
Total contributed capital	$1,674,000
Retained earnings	80,000
Less: Treasury stock, preferred, 200 shares	(12,800)
Total stockholders' equity	$??

Determine the following items, based on Carter's balance sheet.

1. The number of shares of preferred stock issued
2. The number of shares of preferred stock outstanding
3. The average per-share sales price of the preferred stock when issued
4. The par value of the common stock
5. The average per-share sales price of the common stock when issued
6. The cost of the treasury stock per share
7. The total stockholders' equity
8. The per-share book value of the common stock, assuming that there are no dividends in arrears and that the preferred stock can be redeemed at its par value

LO3,4,7   **Problem 11-13A** Effects of Stockholders' Equity Transactions on Balance Sheet

The following transactions occurred at Hilton Inc. during its first year of operation:

a. Issued 10,000 shares of common stock at $10 each; 100,000 shares are authorized at $1 par value.
b. Issued 10,000 shares of common stock for a patent, which is expected to be effective for the next 15 years. The value of the patent is undeterminable. The stock is selling for $10 on the open market.
c. Purchased 1,000 shares of its own common stock on the open market for $10 per share.
d. Declared a dividend of $0.50 per share of outstanding common stock. The dividend is to be paid after the end of the first year of operations. Market value of the stock is $10.
e. Income for the year is reported as $340,000.

Required

1. Indicate each transaction's effect on the assets, liabilities, and stockholders' equity of Hilton Inc.
2. Hilton's president has asked you to explain the difference between contributed capital and retained earnings. Discuss these terms as they relate to Hilton.
3. Determine the book value per share of the stock at the end of the year.

Problem 11-14A Stockholders' Equity Section of the Balance Sheet

The newly hired accountant at Grainfield Inc. is considering the following list of accounts as he prepares the balance sheet. All of the accounts have positive balances. The company is authorized to issue 1,000,000 shares of common stock and 10,000 shares of preferred stock. The treasury stock was purchased at $5 per share.

Treasury stock (common)	$ 15,000
Retained earnings	54,900
Dividends payable	1,500
Common stock, $1 par	100,000
Additional paid-in capital	68,400
Preferred stock, $10 par, 5%	50,000

Required

1. Prepare the Stockholders' Equity section of the balance sheet for Grainfield.
2. Explain why some of the listed accounts are not shown in the Stockholders' Equity section.

DECISION CASES

READING AND INTERPRETING FINANCIAL STATEMENTS

LO1,8   **Decision Case 11-1** Comparing Two Companies in the Same Industry: Foot Locker and Finish Line

Refer to the Stockholders' Equity section of the balance sheets of **Foot Locker** as of January 28, 2006, and of **Finish Line** as of February 25, 2006.

Required

1. For each company, what are the numbers of shares of common stock authorized, issued, and outstanding as of the balance sheet date?

2. Did the balance of the Retained Earnings account of each company increase or decrease during the year? What are the possible factors that affect the Retained Earnings balance?
3. How does the total stockholders' equity of each company compare to the other company? Does the difference mean that one company's stock is more valuable than the other's? Explain your answer.

LO10   **Decision Case 11-2**   Reading Finish Line's Statement of Cash Flows

Refer to **Finish Line**'s statement of cash flows for the year ending February 25, 2006.

Required:
1. What sources of cash are revealed in the Financing Activities category of the statement of cash flows?
2. What was the amount of dividends paid to stockholders during the period?
3. The Financing Activities section indicates a large negative amount for the purchase of treasury stock. When treasury stock is purchased, what is the effect on the accounts of the balance sheet?

MAKING FINANCIAL DECISIONS

LO1,2   **Decision Case 11-3** Debt versus Preferred Stock

Assume that you are an analyst attempting to compare the financial structures of two companies. In particular, you must analyze the debt and equity categories of the two firms and calculate a debt-to-equity ratio for each firm. The liability and equity categories of First Company at year-end appeared as follows:

Liabilities	
Accounts payable	$ 500,000
Loan payable	800,000
Stockholders' Equity	
Common stock	300,000
Retained earnings	600,000
Total liabilities and equity	$2,200,000

First Company's loan payable bears interest at 8%, which is paid annually. The principal is due in five years.

The liability and equity categories of Second Company at year-end appeared as follows:

Liabilities	
Accounts payable	$ 500,000
Stockholders' Equity	
Common stock	300,000
Preferred stock	800,000
Retained earnings	600,000
Total liabilities and equity	$2,200,000

Second Company's preferred stock is 8%, cumulative stock. A provision of the stock agreement specifies that the stock must be redeemed at face value in five years.

Required
1. It appears that the loan payable of First Company and the preferred stock of Second Company are very similar. What are the differences between the two securities?
2. When calculating the debt-to-equity ratio, do you believe that the Second Company preferred stock should be treated as debt or as stockholders' equity? Write a statement expressing your position on this issue.

LO2   **Decision Case 11-4** Preferred versus Common Stock

Rohnan Inc. needs to raise $500,000. It is considering two options:

a. Issue preferred stock, $100 par, 8%, cumulative, nonparticipating, callable at $110. The stock could be issued at par.

b. Issue common stock, $1 par, market $10. Currently, the company has 400,000 shares outstanding equally in the hands of five owners. The company has never paid a dividend.

Required

Rohnan has asked you to consider both options and make a recommendation. It is equally concerned with cash flow and company control. Write your recommendations.

ETHICAL DECISION MAKING

LO9

Decision Case 11-5 Inside Information

Jim Brock was an accountant with Hubbard Inc., a large corporation with stock that was publicly traded on the New York Stock Exchange. One of Jim's duties was to manage the corporate reporting department, which was responsible for developing and issuing Hubbard's annual report. At the end of 2007, Hubbard closed its accounting records, and initial calculations indicated a very profitable year. In fact, the net income exceeded the amount that had been projected during the year by the financial analysts who followed Hubbard's stock.

Jim was very pleased with the company's financial performance. In January 2008, he suggested that his father buy Hubbard's stock because he was sure the stock price would increase when the company announced its 2007 results. Jim's father followed the advice and bought a block of stock at $25 per share.

On February 15, 2008, Hubbard announced its 2007 results and issued the annual report. The company received favorable press coverage about its performance, and the stock price on the stock exchange increased to $32 per share.

Required

What was Jim's professional responsibility to Hubbard Inc. concerning the issuance of the 2007 annual report? Did Jim act ethically in this situation?

LO5

Decision Case 11-6 Dividend Policy

Hancock Inc. is owned by nearly 100 shareholders. Judith Stitch owns 48% of the stock. She needs cash to fulfill her commitment to donate the funds to construct a new art gallery. Some of her friends have agreed to vote for Hancock to pay a larger-than-normal dividend to shareholders. Judith has asked you to vote for the large dividend because she knows that you also support the arts. When informed that the dividend may create a working capital hardship on Hancock, Judith responded: "There is plenty of money in Retained Earnings. The dividend will not affect the cash of the company." Respond to her comment. What ethical questions do you and Judith face? How would you vote?

SOLUTIONS TO KEY TERMS QUIZ

13	Authorized shares	18	Retirement of stock
1	Issued shares	7	Dividend payout ratio
14	Outstanding shares	19	Stock dividend
2	Par value	9	Stock split
15	Additional paid-in capital	8	Statement of stockholders' equity
3	Retained earnings	11	Comprehensive income
4	Cumulative feature	10	Book value per share
16	Participating feature	12	Market value per share
5	Convertible feature	22	Sole proprietorship
17	Callable feature	20	Partnership
6	Treasury stock	21	Partnership agreement

INTEGRATIVE PROBLEM

Evaluating financing options for asset acquisition and their impact on financial statements

Following are the financial statements for Griffin Inc. for the year 2007.

Griffin Inc.
Balance Sheet
December 31, 2007
(in millions)

Assets		Liabilities	
Cash	$ 1.6	Current portion of lease	
Other current assets	6.4	obligation	$ 1.0
Leased assets (net of		Other current liabilities	3.0
accumulated depreciation)	7.0	Lease obligation—Long-term	6.0
Other long-term assets	45.0	Other long-term liabilities	6.0
		Total liabilities	$16.0
		Stockholders' Equity	
		Preferred stock	$ 1.0
		Additional paid-in capital—Preferred	2.0
		Common stock	4.0
		Additional paid-in capital—Common	16.0
		Retained earnings	21.0
		Total stockholders' equity	$44.0
		Total liabilities and	
Total assets	$60.0	stockholders' equity	$60.0

Griffin Inc.
Income Statement
For the Year Ended December 31, 2007
(in millions)

Revenues		$ 50.0
Expenses:		
Depreciation of leased asset	$ 1.0	
Depreciation—Other assets	3.2	
Interest on leased asset	0.5	
Other expenses	27.4	
Income tax (30% rate)	5.4	
Total expenses		(37.5)
Income before extraordinary loss		$ 12.5
Extraordinary loss (net of $0.9 taxes)		(2.1)
Net income		$ 10.4
EPS before extraordinary loss		$ 3.10
EPS extraordinary loss		(0.53)
EPS—Net income		$ 2.57

Additional information:

Griffin Inc. has authorized 500,000 shares of 10%, $10 par value cumulative preferred stock. There were 100,000 shares issued and outstanding at all times during 2007. The firm has also authorized 5 million shares of $1 par common stock, with 4 million shares issued and outstanding.

On January 1, 2007, Griffin Inc. acquired an asset, a piece of specialized heavy equipment, for $8 million with a capital lease. The lease contract indicates that the term of the lease is eight years. Payments of $1.5 million are to be made each December 31. The first lease payment was made December 31, 2007, and consisted of $1 million principal and $0.5 million of interest expense. The capital lease is depreciated using the straight-line method over eight years with zero salvage value.

Required

1. Assuming the equipment was acquired using a capital lease, indicate the effect on the accounting equation of the acquisition, depreciation, and lease payment.

2. The management of Griffin Inc. is considering the financial statement impact of methods of financing, other than the capital lease, that could have been used to acquire the equipment. For each alternative (a), (b), and (c), indicate the effect on the accounting equation and prepare revised 2007 financial statements. Calculate, as revised, the following amounts or ratios:

> Current ratio
> Debt-to-equity ratio
> Net income
> EPS—Net income

Assume that the following alternative actions would have taken place on January 1, 2007.

a. Instead of acquiring the equipment with a capital lease, the company negotiated an operating lease to use the asset. The lease requires annual year-end payments of $1.5 million and results in "off-balance-sheet" financing. (*Hint:* The $1.5 million should be treated as rental expense.)

b. Instead of acquiring the equipment with a capital lease, Griffin Inc. issued bonds for $8 million and purchased the equipment with the proceeds of the bond issue. Assume the bond interest of $0.5 million was accrued and paid on December 31, 2007. A portion of the principal also is paid each year for eight years. On December 31, 2007, the company paid $1 million of principal and anticipated another $1 million of principal to be paid in 2008. Assume the equipment would have an eight-year life and would be depreciated on a straight-line basis with zero salvage value.

c. Instead of acquiring the equipment with a capital lease, Griffin Inc. issued 200,000 additional shares of 10% preferred stock to raise $8 million and purchased the equipment for $8 million with the proceeds from the stock issue. Dividends on the stock are declared and paid annually. Assume that a dividend payment was made on December 31, 2007. Assume the equipment would have an eight-year life and would be depreciated on a straight-line basis with zero salvage value.

12

The Statement of Cash Flows

Study Links

A Look at Previous Chapters
In previous chapters, we have seen that assets and liabilities involve important cash flows to a business at one time or another. In Chapter 2, we introduced the statement of cash flows along with the other financial statements.

Chapter 11 completed our examination of the accounting and reporting issues for a company's various assets, liabilities, and equities. Specifically, in that chapter, we considered how companies account for stockholders' equity.

A Look at This Chapter
Now that we have a fuller appreciation of how to account for the various assets and liabilities of a business, we turn our attention in this chapter to an in-depth examination of the *statement of cash flows*.

A Look at the Upcoming Chapter
Stockholders, creditors, and other groups use financial statements, including the statement of cash flows, to analyze a company. We called attention in earlier chapters to various ratios often used to aid in these analyses. In the final chapter, we discuss the use of ratios and other types of analysis to better understand the financial strength and health of companies.

Learning Outcomes

After studying this chapter, you should be able to:

LO1 Explain the purpose of a statement of cash flows.

LO2 Explain what cash equivalents are and how they are treated on the statement of cash flows.

LO3 Describe operating, investing, and financing activities, and give examples of each.

LO4 Describe the difference between the direct and the indirect methods of computing cash flow from operating activities.

LO5 Prepare a statement of cash flows, using the direct method to determine cash flow from operating activities.

LO6 Prepare a statement of cash flows, using the indirect method to determine cash flow from operating activities.

LO7 Use cash flow information to help analyze a company.

LO8 Use a work sheet to prepare a statement of cash flows, using the indirect method to determine cash flow from operating activities (Appendix).

Best Buy

"Cash is king" is an expression that you have undoubtedly heard. After learning the basics of accounting in this course, you now have a good idea of the meaning of this expression. Cash is the one universally recognized medium of exchange in today's world. Currencies vary—from the dollar in this country to the peso in Mexico to the euro in the European community of countries—but regardless, cash is what bankers and other creditors expect when it comes time to settle outstanding obligations. And its what stockholders expect if dividends are going to be paid.

Best Buy, North America's leading specialty retailer for a wide variety of consumer electronics, computers, and appliances, understands the supremacy of cash as well as any company does. A glance at the company's statement of cash flows, on the next page, shows a business that not only achieved record earnings that approached one billion dollars in fiscal 2005, but one that also nearly doubled its cash and cash equivalents to a year-end balance of $470 million.

What a company *does* with its cash is central to its long-term success. And a statement of cash flows gives us a clear picture of what the company has done historically with this most liquid of all assets. When you examine Best Buy's statement, one of the first items to get your attention is that as impressive as its net earnings of $984 million are, the cash provided by its operations was almost double this amount.

So what did the company do with nearly $2 billion of cash that its operations generated during the year? The remaining two sections of the statement provide the answers. First, as any successful company does, Best Buy invested in its future by adding to its property and equipment, which for a merchandiser means expansion of its retail stores. The statement shows us that the company used over half of that $1.8 billion of cash from operations in its various investing activities. It then used another $459 million of cash in its financing activities. These activities included repaying $371 million of debt and returning $137 million to its stockholders in the form of dividends.

In this chapter, we will take a close look at the relationship between earnings on a company's income statement and its cash activities as reported on a

(continued on page 553)

Best Buy
Consolidated Statements of Cash Flows
$ in millions

For the Fiscal Years Ended	February 26, 2005	February 28, 2004	March 1, 2003
Operating Activities			
Net earnings	$ 984	$ 705	$ 99
(Gain) loss from and disposal of discontinued operations, net of tax	(50)	95	441
Cumulative effect of change in accounting principles, net of tax	—	—	82
Earnings from continuing operations	934	800	622
Adjustments to reconcile earnings from continuing operations to total cash provided by operating activities from continuing operations:			
Depreciation	459	385	310
Asset impairment charges	22	22	11
Deferred income taxes	(28)	(14)	(37)
Other	23	16	15
Changes in operating assets and liabilities, net of acquired assets and liabilities:			
Receivables	(30)	(27)	(89)
Merchandise inventories	(240)	(507)	(256)
Other assets	(190)	(25)	(21)
Accounts payable	347	272	(5)
Other liabilities	243	250	117
Accrued income taxes	301	197	111
Total cash provided by operating activities from continuing operations	1,841	1,369	778
Investing Activities			
Additions to property and equipment	(502)	(545)	(725)
Purchases of available-for-sale securities	(7,789)	(2,989)	(1,844)
Sales of available-for-sale securities	7,118	2,175	1,610
Other, net	7	1	49
Total cash used in investing activities from continuing operations	(1,166)	(1,358)	(910)
Financing Activities			
Long-term debt payments	(371)	(17)	(13)
Issuance of common stock under employee stock purchase plan and for the exercise of stock options	256	114	40
Repurchase of common stock	(200)	(100)	—
Dividends paid	(137)	(130)	—
Net proceeds from issuance of long-term debt	—	—	18
Other, net	(7)	46	(15)
Total cash (used in) provided by financing activities from continuing operations	(459)	(87)	30
Effect of Exchange Rate Changes on Cash	9	1	—
Net Cash Used in Discontinued Operations	—	(53)	(79)
Increase (Decrease) in Cash and Cash Equivalents	225	(128)	(181)
Cash and Cash Equivalents at Beginning of Year	245	373	554
Cash and Cash Equivalents at End of Year	$ 470	$ 245	$ 373
Supplemental Disclosure of Cash Flow Information			
Income tax paid	$ 241	$ 306	$ 283
Interest paid	35	22	24
Capital and financing lease obligations incurred	117	26	—

See Notes to Consolidated Financial Statements.

Record earnings of almost $1 billion

Cash from operations about twice net earnings

Includes cost to open new stores

Over half of cash generated from operations used to invest

Another $.5 billion used in financing activities

Balance nearly doubled

statement of cash flows. Management of a company, creditors, and stockholders are all interested in not only a company's bottom line, but also where its cash comes from and where it goes. This chapter answers these key questions for Best Buy and for all companies:

- Why are net earnings not the same as cash provided by operating activities? (See pp. 553–555)

- How do accountants reconcile the difference between these two amounts? (See pp. 560–562)

- What are the various sources and uses of cash in a company's investing and financing activities? (See pp. 558–559)

- How can information about a company's cash flows be used to analyze its performance? (See pp. 577–580)

All external parties have an interest in a company's cash flows.

- Stockholders need some assurance that enough cash is being generated from operations to pay dividends and invest in the company's future.
- Creditors want to know if cash from operations is sufficient to repay their loans along with interest.

This chapter will show you how to read, understand, and prepare the statement of cash flows, which is perhaps the key financial statement for the survival of every business.

Cash Flows and Accrual Accounting

The *bottom line* is a phrase used in many different ways in today's society. "I wish politicians would cut out all of the rhetoric and get to the bottom line." "The bottom line is that the manager was fired because the team wasn't winning." "Our company's bottom line is twice what it was last year." This last use of the phrase, in reference to a company's net income, is probably the way in which *bottom line* was first used. In recent years, managers, stockholders, creditors, analysts, and other users of financial statements have become more and more wary of focusing on any one number as an indicator of a company's overall performance. Most experts now agree that there has been a tendency to rely far too heavily on net income and its companion, earnings per share, and in many cases to ignore a company's cash flows. As you know by now from your study of accounting, you can't pay bills with net income; you need cash!

To understand the difference between a company's bottom line and its cash flow, consider the case of **Best Buy** in its 2005 fiscal year. Best Buy reported net earnings (income) of $984 million. However, as shown in the chapter opener, during this same time period its cash increased by only $225 million. How is this possible? First, net income is computed on an accrual basis, not a cash basis. Second, the income statement primarily reflects events related to the operating activities of a business, that is, selling products or providing services.

A company's cash position can increase or decrease over a period, and it can report a net profit or a net loss. If you think about it, one of four combinations is possible:

1. **A company can report an increase in cash and a net profit.**
2. **A company can report a decrease in cash and a net profit.**
3. **A company can report an increase in cash and a net loss.**
4. **A company can report a decrease in cash and a net loss.**

Exhibit 12-1 illustrates this point by showing the performance of four well-known companies, including Best Buy. Best Buy is the only one of the four companies that both improved its cash position and reported a net profit. **Radio Shack** reported a net profit but saw its cash decline in 2004. **Gateway** reported a net loss in 2004 but improved its cash position. Finally, **Northwest Airlines** experienced both a net loss in 2004 and saw its cash decline. To summarize, **a company with a profitable year does not necessarily increase its cash position, nor does a company with an unprofitable year always experience a decrease in cash.**

EXHIBIT 12-1	Cash Flows and Net Income for Four Companies (all amounts in millions of dollars—years ending December 31, 2004, unless otherwise noted)

Company	Beginning Balance in Cash	Ending Balance in Cash	Increase (Decrease) in Cash	Net Income (Loss)
Best Buy (fiscal year ended February 26, 2005)	$ 245	$470	$ 225	$ 984
Radio Shack	634.7	437.9	(196.8)	337.2
Gateway	349.1	383.0	33.9	(567.6)
Northwest Airlines	1,146	707	(439)	(862)

Purpose of the Statement of Cash Flows

LO1 Explain the purpose of a statement of cash flows.

Statement of cash flows

The financial statement that summarizes an entity's cash receipts and cash payments during the period from operating, investing, and financing activities.

The **statement of cash flows** is an important complement to the other major financial statements. It summarizes the operating, investing, and financing activities of a business over a period of time. The balance sheet summarizes the cash on hand and the balances in other assets, liabilities, and owners' equity accounts, providing a snapshot at a specific point in time. **The statement of cash flows reports the changes in cash over a period of time and, most important,** *explains these changes.*

The income statement summarizes performance on an accrual basis. Income on this basis is considered a better indicator of *future* cash inflows and outflows than is a statement limited to current cash flows. The statement of cash flows complements the accrual-based income statement by allowing users to assess a company's performance on a cash basis. As we will see in the following simple example, however, it also goes beyond presenting data related to operating performance and looks at other activities that affect a company's cash position.

AN EXAMPLE

Consider the following discussion between the owner of Fox River Realty and the company accountant. After a successful first year in business in 2006, in which it earned a profit of $100,000, the owner reviews the income statement for the second year, as presented in Exhibit 12-2.

The owner is pleased with the results and asks to see the balance sheet. Comparative balance sheets for the first two years are presented in Exhibit 12-3.

Where Did the Cash Go? At first glance, the owner is surprised to see the significant decline in the Cash account. She immediately presses the accountant for answers. With such a profitable year, where has the cash gone? Specifically, why has cash decreased from $150,000 to $50,000, even though income rose from $100,000 in the first year to $250,000 in the second year?

EXHIBIT 12-2	Income Statement for Fox River Realty

Fox River Realty
Income Statement
For the Year Ended December 31, 2007

Revenues	$400,000
Depreciation expense	$ 50,000
All other expenses	100,000
Total expenses	$150,000
Net income	$250,000

EXHIBIT 12-3 **Comparative Balance Sheets for Fox River Realty**

Fox River Realty
Comparative Balance Sheets
December 31

	2007	2006
Cash	$ 50,000	$150,000
Plant and equipment	600,000	350,000
Accumulated depreciation	(150,000)	(100,000)
Total assets	$500,000	$400,000
Notes payable	$100,000	$150,000
Common stock	250,000	200,000
Retained earnings	150,000	50,000
Total equities	$500,000	$400,000

The accountant begins his explanation to the owner by pointing out that income on a cash basis is even *higher* than the reported $250,000. Because depreciation expense is an expense that does not use cash (cash is used when the plant and equipment are purchased, not when they are depreciated), cash provided from operating activities is calculated as follows:

Net income	$250,000
Add back: Depreciation expense	50,000
Cash provided by operating activities	$300,000

Further, the accountant reminds the owner of the additional $50,000 that she invested in the business during the year. Now the owner is even more bewildered: with cash from operations of $300,000 and her own infusion of $50,000, why did cash *decrease* by $100,000? The accountant refreshes the owner's memory on three major outflows of cash during the year. First, even though the business earned $250,000, she withdrew $150,000 in dividends during the year. Second, the comparative balance sheets indicate that notes payable with the bank were reduced from $150,000 to $100,000, requiring the use of $50,000 in cash. Finally, the comparative balance sheets show an increase in plant and equipment for the year from $350,000 to $600,000—a sizable investment of $250,000 in new long-term assets.

Statement of Cash Flows To summarize what happened to the cash, the accountant prepares a statement of cash flows as shown in Exhibit 12-4. Although the owner is not particularly happy with the decrease in cash for the year, she is at least satisfied with the statement as an explanation of where the cash came from and how it was used. The statement summarizes the important cash activities for the year and fills a void created with the presentation of just an income statement and a balance sheet.

Reporting Requirements for a Statement of Cash Flows

Accounting standards specify both the basis for preparing the statement of cash flows and the classification of items on the statement.[1] First, the statement must

---

1 *Statement of Financial Accounting Standards No. 95*, "Statement of Cash Flows" (Stamford, Conn.: Financial Accounting Standards Board, November 1987).

EXHIBIT 12-4 **Statement of Cash Flows for Fox River Realty**

Fox River Realty
Statement of Cash Flows
For the Year Ended December 31, 2007

Cash provided (used) by operating activities:	
Net income	$ 250,000
Add back: Depreciation expense	50,000
Net cash provided (used) by operating activities	$ 300,000
Cash provided (used) by investing activities:	
Purchase of new plant and equipment	$(250,000)
Cash provided (used) by financing activities:	
Additional investment by owner	$ 50,000
Cash dividends paid to owner	(150,000)
Repayment of notes payable to bank	(50,000)
Net cash provided (used) by financing activities	$(150,000)
Net increase (decrease) in cash	$(100,000)
Cash balance at beginning of year	150,000
Cash balance at end of year	$ 50,000

be prepared on a cash basis. Second, the cash flows must be classified into three categories:

- Operating activities
- Investing activities
- Financing activities

We now take a closer look at each of these important requirements in preparing a statement of cash flows.

THE DEFINITION OF CASH: CASH AND CASH EQUIVALENTS

LO2 Explain what cash equivalents are and how they are treated on the statement of cash flows.

The purpose of the statement of cash flows is to provide information about a company's cash inflows and outflows. Thus, it is essential to have a clear understanding of what the definition of *cash* includes. According to accounting standards, certain items are recognized as being equivalent to cash and are combined with cash on the balance sheet and the statement of cash flows.

Commercial paper (short-term notes issued by corporations), money market funds, and Treasury bills are examples of cash equivalents. To be classified as a **cash equivalent**, an item must be readily convertible to a known amount of cash and have a maturity *to the investor* of three months or less. For example, a three-year Treasury note purchased two months before its maturity is classified as a cash equivalent. The same note purchased two years before maturity would be classified as an investment instead.

Cash equivalent
An item readily convertible to a known amount of cash and with a maturity to the investor of three months or less.

To understand why cash equivalents are combined with cash when preparing a statement of cash flows, assume that a company has a cash balance of $10,000 and no assets that qualify as cash equivalents. Further assume that the $10,000 is used to purchase 90-day Treasury bills. The effect on the accounting equation of the purchase is as follows:

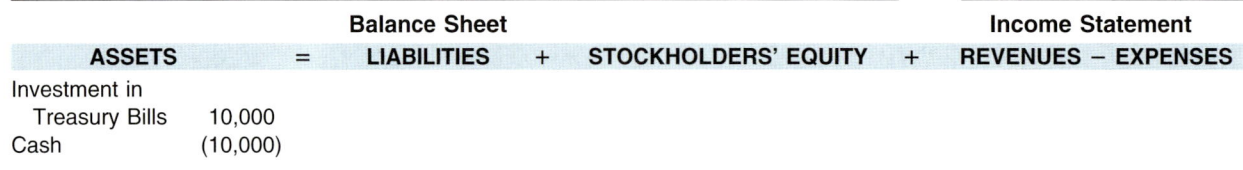

	Balance Sheet				Income Statement
ASSETS	**=**	**LIABILITIES**	**+**	**STOCKHOLDERS' EQUITY**	**+**	**REVENUES − EXPENSES**
Investment in					
Treasury Bills 10,000					
Cash (10,000)					

For record-keeping purposes, it is important to recognize this transaction as a transfer between cash in the bank and an investment in a government security. In the strictest sense, the investment represents an outflow of cash. The purchase of a security with such a short maturity does not, however, involve any significant degree of risk in terms of price changes and thus is not reported on the statement of cash flows as an outflow. Instead, for purposes of classification on the balance sheet and the statement of cash flows, this is merely a transfer *within* the cash and cash equivalents category. The point is that before the purchase of the Treasury bills the company had $10,000 in cash and cash equivalents, and after the purchase it still had $10,000 in cash and cash equivalents. *Because nothing changed, the transaction is not reported on the statement of cash flows.*

Now, assume a different transaction in which a company purchases shares of GM common stock for cash. The effect on the accounting equation of this purchase is as follows:

Balance Sheet					Income Statement
ASSETS	**=**	**LIABILITIES**	**+**	**STOCKHOLDERS' EQUITY**	**+**	**REVENUES − EXPENSES**
Investment in GM					
Common Stock 10,000					
Cash (10,000)					

This purchase involves a certain amount of risk for the company making the investment. The GM stock is not convertible to a known amount of cash because its market value is subject to change. Thus, for balance sheet purposes, the investment is not considered a cash equivalent and is not therefore combined with cash but is classified as either a short-term or long-term investment, depending on the company's intent in holding the stock. In the preparation of a statement of cash flows, the *investment in stock of another company is considered a significant activity and thus is reported on the statement of cash flows.*

CLASSIFICATION OF CASH FLOWS

For the statement of cash flows, companies are required to classify activities into three categories: operating, investing, or financing. These categories represent the major functions of an entity, and classifying activities in this way allows users to look at important relationships. For example, one important financing activity for many businesses is borrowing money. Grouping the cash inflows from borrowing money during the period with the cash outflows from repayments of loans during the period makes it easier for analysts and other users of the statements to evaluate the company.

Each of the three types of activities can result both in cash inflows and in cash outflows to the company. Thus, the general format for the statement is as shown in Exhibit 12-5. Note the direct tie between the bottom portion of this statement and the balance sheet. The beginning and ending balances in cash and cash equivalents, shown as the last two lines on the statement of cash flows, are taken directly from the comparative balance sheets. Some companies end their statement of cash flows with the figure for the net increase or decrease in cash and cash equivalents and do not report the beginning and ending balances in cash and cash equivalents directly on the statement of cash flows. Instead, the reader must turn to the balance sheet for these amounts.

Operating Activities   Operating activities involve acquiring and selling products and services. The specific activities of a business depend on its type. For example, the purchase of raw materials is an important operating activity for a manufacturer. For a retailer, the purchase of inventory from a distributor constitutes an operating activity. For a realty company, the payment of a commission to a salesperson is an operating activity. All three types of businesses sell either products or services, and their sales are important operating activities.

A statement of cash flows reflects the cash effects, either inflows or outflows, associated with each of these activities. For example, the manufacturer's payment for purchases of raw materials results in a cash outflow. The receipt of cash from

LO3 Describe operating, investing, and financing activities, and give examples of each.

Operating activities
Activities concerned with the acquisition and sale of products and services.

EXHIBIT 12-5   Format for the Statement of Cash Flows

The Smith Corporation
Statement of Cash Flows
For the Year Ended December 31, 2007

Cash flows from operating activities:		
Inflows	$ xxx	
Outflows	(xxx)	
Net cash provided (used) by operating activities		$xxx
Cash flows from investing activities:		
Inflows	$ xxx	
Outflows	(xxx)	
Net cash provided (used) by investing activities		xxx
Cash flows from financing activities:		
Inflows	$ xxx	
Outflows	(xxx)	
Net cash provided (used) by financing activities		xxx
Net increase (decrease) in cash and cash equivalents		$xxx
Cash and cash equivalents at beginning of year		xxx
Cash and cash equivalents at end of year		$xxx

---

collecting an account receivable results in a cash inflow. The income statement reports operating activities on an accrual basis. The statement of cash flows reflects a company's operating activities on a cash basis.

Investing activities
Activities concerned with the acquisition and disposal of long-term assets.

Investing Activities   **Investing activities** involve acquiring and disposing of long-term assets. Replacing worn-out plant and equipment and expanding the existing base of long-term assets are essential to all businesses. Cash is paid for these acquisitions, often called *capital expenditures*. The following excerpt from **Best Buy**'s 2005 statement of cash flows (also shown in the chapter opener) indicates that the company spent $502 million for ❶ additions to property and equipment during fiscal 2005 (all amounts are in millions of dollars):

Investing activities:	
❶ Additions to property and equipment	(502)
❷ Purchases of available-for-sale securities	(7,789)
❸ Sales of available-for-sale securities	7,118
Other, net	7
Total cash used in investing activities from continuing operations	(1,166)

Sales of long-term assets, such as plant and equipment, are not generally a significant source of cash. These assets are acquired to be used in producing goods and services, or to support this function, rather than to be resold, as is true for inventory. Occasionally, however, plant and equipment may wear out or no longer be needed and are offered for sale. Best Buy does not separately report any sales of property and equipment during 2005.

In Chapter 7, we explained why companies sometimes invest in the stocks and bonds of other companies. During 2005, Best Buy spent $7,789 million to ❷ buy the securities of other companies and generated $7,118 million from ❸ selling those investments. Finally, the acquisition of one company by another is an important investing activity, although no such acquisitions are reported on Best Buy's statement.

Financing Activities   All businesses rely on internal financing, external financing, or a combination of the two in meeting their needs for cash. Initially, a new business must have a certain amount of investment by the owners to begin operations.

After this, many companies use notes, bonds, and other forms of debt to provide financing.[2] Issuing stock and various forms of debt results in cash inflows that appear as **financing activities** on the statement of cash flows. On the other side, the repurchase of a company's own stock and the repayment of borrowings are important cash outflows to be reported in the Financing Activities section of the statement. Another important activity often listed in the Financing Activities section of the statement is the payment of cash dividends. Best Buy's 2005 statement of cash flows lists many of the common cash inflows and outflows from financing activities (amounts in millions of dollars):

Financing activities
Activities concerned with the raising and repayment of funds in the form of debt and equity.

Financing Activities

❶ Long-term debt payments		(371)
❸ Issuance of common stock under employee stock purchase plan and for the exercise of stock options		256
❹ Repurchase of common stock		(200)
❷ Dividends paid		(137)
Net proceeds from the issuance of long-term debt		—
Other, net		(7)
Total cash used in financing activities from continuing operations		(459)

In 2005, Best Buy did not issue any new debt but paid $371 million to ❶ retire existing long-term debt. Another $137 million was paid in ❷ dividends to stockholders. Also, during the year, the company raised $256 million by ❸ issuing common stock and paid $200 million to ❹ buy back some of its stock.

Summary of the Three Types of Activities To summarize the categorization of the activities of a business as operating, investing, and financing, refer to Exhibit 12-6. The exhibit lists examples of each of the three activities along with the related balance sheet accounts and the account classifications on the balance sheet.

EXHIBIT 12-6	**Classification of Items on the Statement of Cash Flows**

Activity	Examples	Effect on Cash	Related Balance Sheet Account	Classification on Balance Sheet
Operating	Collection of customer accounts	Inflow	Accounts receivable	Current asset
	Payment to suppliers for inventory	Outflow	Accounts payable Inventory	Current liability Current asset
	Payment of wages	Outflow	Wages payable	Current liability
	Payment of taxes	Outflow	Taxes payable	Current liability
Investing	Capital expenditures	Outflow	Plant and equipment	Long-term asset
	Purchase of another company	Outflow	Long-term investment	Long-term asset
	Sale of plant and equipment	Inflow	Plant and equipment	Long-term asset
	Sale of another company	Inflow	Long-term investment	Long-term asset
Financing	Issuance of capital stock	Inflow	Capital stock	Stockholders' equity
	Issuance of bonds	Inflow	Bonds payable	Long-term liability
	Issuance of bank note	Inflow	Notes payable	Long-term liability
	Repurchase of stock	Outflow	Treasury stock	Stockholders' equity
	Retirement of bonds	Outflow	Bonds payable	Long-term liability
	Repayment of notes	Outflow	Notes payable	Long-term liability
	Payment of dividends	Outflow	Retained earnings	Stockholders' equity

2 **Wm. Wrigley Jr. Company** is unusual in this regard in that it relies almost solely on funds generated from stockholders, in the form of common stock, for financing. On December 31, 2004, total long-term liabilities accounted for less than 9% of the total liabilities and stockholders' equity on the balance sheet on that date.

In the exhibit, operating activities center on the acquisition and sale of products and services and related costs, such as wages and taxes. Two important observations can be made about the cash flow effects from the operating activities of a business. **First, the cash flows from these activities are the cash effects of transactions that enter into the determination of net income.** For example, the sale of a product enters into the calculation of net income. The cash effect of this transaction—that is, the collection of the account receivable—results in a cash inflow from operating activities. **Second, cash flows from operating activities usually relate to an increase or decrease in either a current asset or a current liability.** For example, the payment of taxes to the government results in a decrease in taxes payable, which is a current liability on the balance sheet.

Note that investing activities normally relate to long-term assets on the balance sheet. For example, the purchase of new plant and equipment increases long-term assets, and the sale of these same assets reduces long-term assets on the balance sheet.

Finally, **note that financing activities usually relate to either long-term liabilities or stockholders' equity accounts.** There are exceptions to these observations about the type of balance sheet account involved with each of the three types of activities, but these rules of thumb are useful as we begin to analyze transactions and attempt to determine their classification on the statement of cash flows.

TWO METHODS OF REPORTING CASH FLOW FROM OPERATING ACTIVITIES

LO4 Describe the difference between the direct and the indirect methods of computing cash flow from operating activities.

Direct method
For preparing the Operating Activities section of the statement of cash flows, the approach in which cash receipts and cash payments are reported.

Indirect method
For preparing the Operating Activities section of the statement of cash flows, the approach in which net income is reconciled to net cash flow from operations.

Companies use one of two different methods to report the amount of cash flow from operating activities. The first approach, called the **direct method**, involves reporting major classes of gross cash receipts and cash payments. For example, cash collected from customers is reported separately from any interest and dividends received. Each of the major types of cash payments related to the company's operations follows, such as cash paid for inventory, for salaries and wages, for interest, and for taxes. An acceptable alternative to this approach is the **indirect method**. Under the indirect method, net cash flow from operating activities is computed by adjusting net income to remove the effect of all deferrals of past operating cash receipts and payments and all accruals of future operating cash receipts and payments.

Although the direct method is preferred by the Financial Accounting Standards Board, it is used much less frequently than the indirect method in practice. To compare and contrast the two methods, assume that Boulder Company begins operations as a corporation on January 1, 2007, with the owners' investment of $10,000 in cash. An income statement for 2007 and a balance sheet as of December 31, 2007, are presented in Exhibits 12-7 and 12-8, respectively.

EXHIBIT 12-7 Boulder Company's Income Statement

Boulder Company
Income Statement
For the Year Ended December 31, 2007

Revenues	$80,000
Operating expenses	(64,000)
Income before tax	$16,000
Income tax expense	(4,000)
Net income	$12,000

EXHIBIT 12-8   Boulder Company's Balance Sheet

Boulder Company
Balance Sheet
As of December 31, 2007

Assets		Liabilities and Stockholders' Equity	
Cash	$15,000	Accounts payable	$ 6,000
Accounts receivable	13,000	Capital stock	10,000
		Retained earnings	12,000
Total	$28,000	Total	$28,000

Direct Method   To report cash flow from operating activities under the direct method, we look at each of the items on the income statement and determine how much cash each of these activities either generated or used. For example, revenues for the period were $80,000. Since the balance sheet at the end of the period shows a balance in Accounts Receivable of $13,000, however, Boulder collected only $80,000 − $13,000, or $67,000, from its sales of the period. Thus, the first line on the statement of cash flows in Exhibit 12-9 reports $67,000 in cash collected from customers. Remember that the *net increase* in Accounts Receivable must be deducted from sales to find cash collected. For a new company, this is the same as the ending balance because the company starts the year without a balance in Accounts Receivable.

The same logic can be applied to determine the amount of cash expended for operating purposes. Operating expenses on the income statement are reported at $64,000. According to the balance sheet, however, $6,000 of the expense is unpaid at the end of the period as evidenced by the balance in Accounts Payable. Thus, the amount of cash expended for operating purposes as reported on the statement of cash flows in Exhibit 12-9 is $64,000 − $6,000, or $58,000. The other cash payment in the Operating Activities section of the statement is $4,000 for income taxes. Because no liability for income taxes is reported on the balance sheet, we know that $4,000 represents both the income tax expense of the period and the amount paid to the government. The only other item on the statement of cash flows in Exhibit 12-9 is the cash inflow from financing activities for the amount of cash invested by the owner in return for capital stock.

EXHIBIT 12-9   Statement of Cash Flows Using the Direct Method

Boulder Company
Statement of Cash Flows
For the Year Ended December 31, 2007

Cash flows from operating activities

Cash collected from customers	$ 67,000
Cash payments for operating purposes	(58,000)
Cash payments for taxes	(4,000)
Net cash inflow from operating activities	$ 5,000

Cash flows from financing activities

Issuance of capital stock	$ 10,000
Net increase in cash	$ 15,000
Cash balance, beginning of period	–0–
Cash balance, end of period	$ 15,000

EXHIBIT 12-10	Statement of Cash Flows Using the Indirect Method

Boulder Company
Statement of Cash Flows
For the Year Ended December 31, 2007

Cash flows from operating activities		
Net income		$12,000
Adjustments to reconcile net income to net cash from operating activities:		
Increase in accounts receivable		(13,000)
Increase in accounts payable		6,000
Net cash inflow from operating activities		$ 5,000
Cash flows from financing activities		
Issuance of capital stock		$10,000
Net increase in cash		$15,000
Cash balance, beginning of period		–0–
Cash balance, end of period		$15,000

Indirect Method When the indirect method is used, the first line in the Operating Activities section of the statement of cash flows as shown in Exhibit 12-10 is the net income of the period. Net income is then *adjusted* to reconcile it to the amount of cash provided by operating activities. As reported on the income statement, this net income figure includes the sales of $80,000 for the period. As we know, however, the amount of cash collected was $13,000 less than this because not all customers paid Boulder the amount due. **The increase in Accounts Receivable for the period is deducted from net income on the statement because the increase indicates that the company sold more during the period than it collected in cash.**

The logic for the addition of the increase in Accounts Payable is similar, although the effect is the opposite. The amount of operating expenses deducted on the income statement was $64,000. We know, however, that the amount of cash paid was $6,000 less than this, as the balance in Accounts Payable indicates. **The increase in Accounts Payable for the period is added back to net income on the statement because the increase indicates that the company paid less during the period than it recognized in expense on the income statement.** One observation can be noted about this example. Because this is the first year of operations for Boulder, we wouldn't be too concerned that accounts receivable is increasing faster than accounts payable. If this becomes a trend, however, we would try to improve the accounts receivable collections process.

Two important observations should be made in comparing the two methods illustrated in Exhibits 12-9 and 12-10. First, the amount of cash provided by operating activities is the same under the two methods: $5,000; the two methods are simply different computational approaches to arrive at the cash generated from operations. Second, the remainder of the statement of cash flows is the same, regardless of which method is used. The only difference between the two methods is in the Operating Activities section of the statement.

Real World Practice 12-1

Reading Best Buy's Statement of Cash Flows

Does Best Buy use the direct or the indirect method in the Operating Activities section of its statement of cash flows? How can you tell which it is?

NONCASH INVESTING AND FINANCING ACTIVITIES

Occasionally, companies engage in important investing and financing activities that do not affect cash. For example, assume that at the end of the year Wolk Corp. issues capital stock to an inventor in return for the exclusive rights to a patent. Although the patent has no ready market value, the stock could have been sold on the open market for $25,000. The effect on the accounting equation of this transaction is as follows:

Balance Sheet						Income Statement
ASSETS	**=**	**LIABILITIES**	**+**	**STOCKHOLDERS' EQUITY**	**+**	**REVENUES − EXPENSES**
Patent	25,000			Capital Stock	25,000	

This transaction does not involve cash and is therefore not reported on the statement of cash flows. However, what if we changed the scenario slightly? Assume that Wolk wants the patent but the inventor is not willing to accept stock in return for it. So instead Wolk sells stock on the open market for $25,000 and then pays this amount in cash to the inventor for the rights to the patent. Consider the effects on the accounting equation of these two transactions. First, the sale of stock increases Cash and Stockholders' Equity:

Balance Sheet						Income Statement
ASSETS	**=**	**LIABILITIES**	**+**	**STOCKHOLDERS' EQUITY**	**+**	**REVENUES − EXPENSES**
Cash	25,000			Capital Stock	25,000	

Next, the acquisition of the patent has the following effect:

Balance Sheet						Income Statement
ASSETS	**=**	**LIABILITIES**	**+**	**STOCKHOLDERS' EQUITY**	**+**	**REVENUES − EXPENSES**
Patent	25,000					
Cash	(25,000)					

How would each of these two transactions be reported on a statement of cash flows? The first transaction appears as a cash inflow in the Financing Activities section of the statement; the second is reported as a cash outflow in the Investing Activities section. The point is that even though the *form* of this arrangement (with stock sold for cash and then the cash paid to the inventor) differs from the form of the first arrangement (with stock exchanged directly for the patent), the *substance* of the two arrangements is the same. That is, both involve a significant financing activity, the issuance of stock, and an important investing activity, the acquisition of a patent. Because the substance is what matters, accounting standards require that any significant noncash transactions be reported either in a separate schedule or in a note to the financial statements. For our transaction in which stock was issued directly to the inventor, presentation in a schedule is as follows:

Supplemental schedule of noncash investing and financing activities
Acquisition of patent in exchange for capital stock $25,000

To this point, we have concentrated on the purpose of a statement of cash flows and the major reporting requirements related to it. We turn next to a methodology to use in actually preparing the statement.

2 minute review

1. What are cash equivalents, and why are any increases or decreases in them not reported on a statement of cash flows?

2. What are the three types of activities reported on a statement of cash flows?

3. What are the two methods of reporting cash flow from operating activities, and how do they differ?

Answers

1. *A cash equivalent is an item readily convertible to a known amount of cash and with an original maturity to the investor of three months or less. Because the maturity date of these items, such as a 60-day certificate of deposit, is so near, they are not considered to carry any significant risks in terms of price changes. Thus, any changes in cash equivalents are not reported on the statement of cash flows.*

2. *Operating, investing, and financing activities.*

3. *Direct and indirect methods. The direct method involves reporting major classes of gross cash receipts and cash payments. Under the indirect method, net cash flow from operating activities is computed by adjusting net income to remove the effect of all deferrals of past operating cash receipts and payments and all accruals of future operating cash receipts and payments.*

How the Statement of Cash Flows Is Put Together

Two interesting observations can be made about the statement of cash flows. First, the "answer" to a statement of cash flows is known before we start to prepare it. That is, the change in cash for the period is known by comparing two successive balance sheets. Thus, it is not the change in cash itself that is emphasized on the statement of cash flows but the *explanations* for the change in cash. That is, each item on a statement of cash flows helps to explain why cash changed by the amount it did during the period. The second important observation about the statement of cash flows relates even more specifically to how we prepare it. Both an income statement and a balance sheet are prepared simply by taking the balances in each of the various accounts in the general ledger and putting them in the right place on the right statement. This is not true for the statement of cash flows. Instead, it is necessary to analyze the transactions during the period and attempt to (1) determine which of these affected cash and (2) classify each of the cash effects into one of the three categories.

In the simple examples presented so far in the chapter, we prepared the statement of cash flows without the use of any special tools. In more complex situations, however, some type of methodology is needed. We first will review the basic accounting equation and then illustrate a systematic approach for preparing the statement. The chapter appendix presents a work-sheet approach to the preparation of the statement of cash flows.

THE ACCOUNTING EQUATION AND THE STATEMENT OF CASH FLOWS

The basic accounting equation is as follows:

Assets = Liabilities + Owners' Equity

or, for corporations:

Assets = Liabilities + Stockholders' Equity

Next, consider this refinement of the equation:

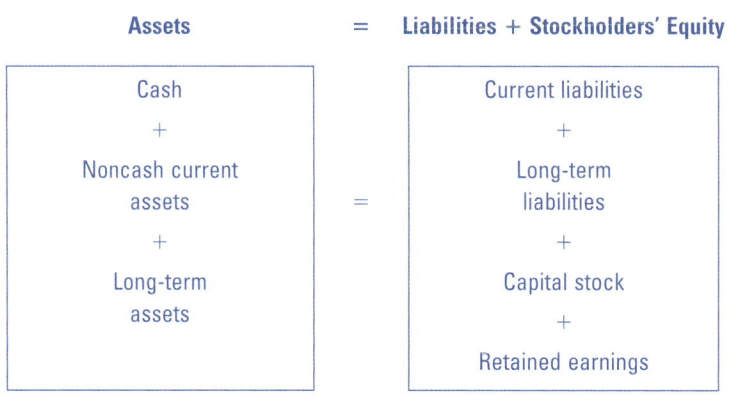

Assets	=	**Liabilities + Stockholders' Equity**
Cash		Current liabilities
+		+
Noncash current assets	=	Long-term liabilities
+		+
Long-term assets		Capital stock
		+
		Retained earnings

The equation can be rearranged so that only cash is on the left side and all other items are on the right side:

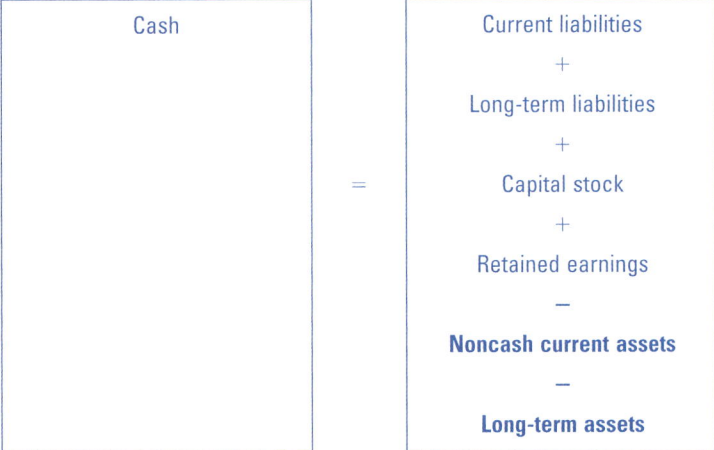

Therefore, any changes in cash must be accompanied by a corresponding change in the right side of the equation. For example, an increase or inflow of cash could result from an *increase* in long-term liabilities in the form of issuing bonds payable, an important financing activity for many companies. Or an increase in cash could come from a *decrease* in long-term assets in the form of a sale of fixed assets. The various possibilities for inflows (+) and outflows (−) of cash can be summarized by activity as follows:

Activity	Left Side	Right Side	Example
Operating			
	+ Cash	− Noncash current assets	Collect accounts receivable
	− Cash	+ Noncash current assets	Prepay insurance
	+ Cash	+ Current liabilities	Collect customer's deposit
	− Cash	− Current liabilities	Pay suppliers
	+ Cash	+ Retained earnings	Make a cash sale
Investing			
	+ Cash	− Long-term assets	Sell equipment
	− Cash	+ Long-term assets	Buy equipment
Financing			
	+ Cash	+ Long-term liabilities	Issue bonds
	− Cash	− Long-term liabilities	Retire bonds
	+ Cash	+ Capital stock	Issue capital stock
	− Cash	− Capital stock	Buy capital stock
	− Cash	− Retained earnings	Pay dividends

By considering these examples we see that inflows and outflows of cash relate to increases and decreases in the various balance sheet accounts. We now turn to analyzing these accounts as a way to assemble a statement of cash flows.

AN APPROACH TO PREPARING THE STATEMENT OF CASH FLOWS: DIRECT METHOD

The following steps can be used to prepare a statement of cash flows:

1. Set up three schedules with the following headings:

   a. Cash Flows from Operating Activities

   b. Cash Flows from Investing Activities

   c. Cash Flows from Financing Activities

As we analyze the transactions that affect each of the noncash balance sheet accounts, any cash effects are entered on the appropriate master account. When

LO5 Prepare a statement of cash flows, using the direct method to determine cash flow from operating activities.

completed, the three master schedules contain all of the information needed to prepare a statement of cash flows.

2. **Determine the cash flows from operating activities.** Generally, this requires analyzing each item on the *income statement* and the *current asset* and *current liability* accounts. As cash flows are identified in this analysis, they are entered on the schedule of cash flows from operating activities.

3. **Determine the cash flows from investing activities.** Generally, this requires analyzing the *long-term asset* accounts and any additional information provided. As cash flows are identified in this analysis, they are entered on the schedule of cash flows from investing activities. Any significant noncash activities are entered on a supplemental schedule.

4. **Determine the cash flows from financing activities.** Generally, this requires analyzing the *long-term liability* and *stockholders' equity* accounts and any additional information provided. As cash flows are identified in this analysis, they are entered on the schedule of cash flows from financing activities. Any significant noncash activities are entered on a supplemental schedule.

Remember that these are general rules that the cash effects of changes in current accounts are reported in the operating section, those relating to long-term asset accounts in the investing section, and those relating to long-term liabilities and stockholders' equity in the financing section. The general rules for classification of activities have a few exceptions, but we will not concern ourselves with them.

To illustrate this approach, we will refer to the income statement in Exhibit 12-11 and to the comparative balance sheets and the additional information provided for Julian Corp. in Exhibit 12-12.

Determine the Cash Flows from Operating Activities To do this, we need to consider each of the items on the income statement and any related current assets or liabilities from the balance sheet.

Sales Revenue and Accounts Receivable Sales as reported on the income statement in Exhibit 12-11 amounted to $670,000.

Based on the beginning and ending balances in Exhibit 12–12, Accounts Receivable increased by $6,000, from $57,000 to $63,000. **This indicates that Julian**

EXHIBIT 12-11 **Julian Corp.'s Income Statement**

Julian Corp.
Income Statement
For the Year Ended December 31, 2007

Revenues and gains:		
Sales revenue	$670,000	
Interest revenue	15,000	
Gain on sale of machine	5,000	
Total revenues and gains		$690,000
Expenses and losses:		
Cost of goods sold	$390,000	
Salaries and wages	60,000	
Depreciation	40,000	
Insurance	12,000	
Interest	15,000	
Income taxes	50,000	
Loss on retirement of bonds	3,000	
Total expenses and losses		570,000
Net income		$120,000

EXHIBIT 12-12   Julian Corp.'s Comparative Balance Sheets

Julian Corp.
Comparative Balance Sheets

	December 31	
	2007	**2006**
Cash	$ 35,000	$ 46,000
Accounts receivable	63,000	57,000
Inventory	84,000	92,000
Prepaid insurance	12,000	18,000
Total current assets	$194,000	$213,000
Long-term investments	$120,000	$ 90,000
Land	150,000	100,000
Property and equipment	320,000	280,000
Accumulated depreciation	(100,000)	(75,000)
Total long-term assets	$490,000	$395,000
Total assets	$684,000	$608,000
Accounts payable	$ 38,000	$ 31,000
Salaries and wages payable	7,000	9,000
Income taxes payable	8,000	5,000
Total current liabilities	$ 53,000	$ 45,000
Notes payable	$ 85,000	$ 35,000
Bonds payable	200,000	260,000
Total long-term liabilities	$285,000	$295,000
Capital stock	$100,000	$ 75,000
Retained earnings	246,000	193,000
Total stockholders' equity	$346,000	$268,000
Total liabilities and stockholders' equity	$684,000	$608,000

Additional Information
1. Long-term investments were purchased for $30,000. The securities are classified as available for sale.
2. Land was purchased by issuing a $50,000 note payable.
3. Equipment was purchased for $75,000.
4. A machine with an original cost of $35,000 and a book value of $20,000 was sold for $25,000.
5. Bonds with a face value of $60,000 were retired by paying $63,000 in cash.
6. Capital stock was issued in exchange for $25,000 in cash.
7. Dividends of $67,000 were paid.

had **$6,000 more in sales to its customers than it collected in cash from them** (assuming that all sales are on credit). Thus, cash collections must have been $670,000 − $6,000, or $664,000. Another way to look at this is as follows:

Beginning accounts receivable	$ 57,000
+ Sales revenue	670,000
− Cash collections	(X)
= Ending accounts receivable	$ 63,000

Solving for X, we can find cash collections:

$$57,000 + 670,000 - X = 63,000$$
$$X = 664,000$$

At this point, note the inflow of Cash for $664,000 as shown in the Schedule of Cash Flows from Operating Activities, in Exhibit 12-13.

EXHIBIT 12-13	Schedule of Cash Flows from Operating Activities

Cash Flows from Operating Activities

Cash receipts from:	
Sales on account	664,000
Interest	15,000
Cash payments for:	
Inventory purchases	(375,000)
Salaries and wages	(62,000)
Insurance	(6,000)
Interest	(15,000)
Taxes	(47,000)

Interest Revenue Julian reported interest revenue on the income statement of $15,000. Did the company actually receive this amount of cash, or was it merely an accrual of revenue earned but not yet received? The answer can be found by examining the Current Assets section of the balance sheet. **Because there is no Interest Receivable account, the amount of interest earned was the amount of cash received.**

The cash received should be entered in the Schedule of Cash Flows from Operating Activities, as shown in Exhibit 12-13.

Gain on Sale of Machine A gain on the sale of a machine of $5,000 is reported as the next line on the income statement. Any cash received from the sale of a long-term asset is reported in the Investing Activities section of the statement of cash flows. Thus, we ignore the gain when reporting cash flows from operating activities under the direct method.

Cost of Goods Sold, Inventory, and Accounts Payable Cost of goods sold, as reported on the income statement, amounts to $390,000. Recall that $390,000 is not the amount of cash expended to pay suppliers of inventory. First, cost of goods sold represents the cost of the inventory sold during the period, not the amount purchased. Thus, we must analyze the Inventory account to determine the purchases of the period. Second, the amount of purchases is not the same as the cash paid to suppliers, because purchases are normally on account. Thus, we must analyze the Accounts Payable account to determine the cash payments.

Based on the beginning and ending balances from Exhibit 12-12, inventory decreased during the year by $8,000, from $92,000 to $84,000. **This means that the cost of inventory sold was $8,000 more than the purchases of the period.** Thus, purchases must have been $390,000 − $8,000, or $382,000. Another way to look at this is as follows:

Beginning inventory	$ 92,000
+ Purchases	X
− Cost of goods sold	(390,000)
= Ending inventory	$ 84,000

Solving for X, we can find purchases:

$$92,000 + X - 390,000 = 84,000$$
$$X = 382,000$$

Note from Exhibit 12-12 that Accounts Payable increased during the year by $7,000, from $31,000 to $38,000. **This means that Julian's purchases were $7,000 more during the period than its cash payments.** Also, recall that we determined earlier that purchases were $382,000. Thus, cash payments must have been $382,000 − $7,000, or $375,000. Another way to look at this is as follows:

Beginning accounts payable	$ 31,000
+ Purchases	382,000
− Cash payments	(X)
= Ending accounts payable	$ 38,000

Solving for *X*, we can find cash payments:

$$31,000 + 382,000 - X = 38,000$$
$$X = \underline{375,000}$$

At this point, we indicate in the schedule in Exhibit 12-13 that the cash payments for inventory total $375,000.

Salaries and Wages Expense and Salaries and Wages Payable The second expense listed on the income statement in Exhibit 12-11 is salaries and wages of $60,000. However, did Julian *pay* this amount to employees during the year? The answer can be found by examining the Salaries and Wages Payable account in the balance sheet in Exhibit 12-12. From the balance sheet, we note that the liability account decreased by $2,000, from $9,000 to $7,000.

This means that the amount of cash paid to employees was $2,000 more than the amount of expense accrued. Another way to look at the cash payments of $60,000 + $2,000, or $62,000, is as follows:

Beginning salaries and wages payable	$ 9,000
+ Salaries and wages expense	60,000
− Cash payments to employees	(X)
= Ending salaries and wages payable	$ 7,000

Solving for *X*, we can find cash payments:

$$9,000 + 60,000 - X = 7,000$$
$$X = \underline{62,000}$$

As you see in Exhibit 12-13, cash paid of $62,000 appears as a cash outflow in the Schedule of Cash Flows from Operating Activities.

Depreciation Expense The next item on the income statement is depreciation of $40,000. Depreciation of tangible long-term assets, amortization of intangible assets, and depletion of natural resources are different from most other expenses in that they have no effect on cash flow. The only related cash flows are from the purchase and the sale of these long-term assets, and these are reported in the Investing Activities section of the statement of cash flows. Thus, depreciation is not reflected on the Schedule of Cash Flows from Operating Activities when the direct method is used as in Exhibit 12-13.

Insurance Expense and Prepaid Insurance According to the income statement in Exhibit 12-11, Julian recorded Insurance Expense of $12,000 during 2007. This amount is not the cash payments for insurance, however, because Julian has a Prepaid Insurance account on the balance sheet. Recall from Chapter 4 that as a company buys insurance, it increases its Prepaid Insurance account. As the insurance expires, this account is reduced and an expense is recognized. Note from the balance sheets in Exhibit 12-12 that the Prepaid Insurance account decreased during the year by $6,000, from $18,000 to $12,000. **This means that the amount of cash paid for insurance was $6,000 less than the amount of expense recognized.** Thus, the cash payments must have been $12,000 − $6,000, or $6,000. Another way to look at the cash payments is as follows:

Beginning prepaid insurance	$18,000
+ Cash payments for insurance	X
− Insurance expense	(12,000)
= Ending prepaid insurance	$12,000

Solving for *X*, we can find the amount of cash paid:

$$18,000 + X - 12,000 = 12,000$$
$$X = \underline{6,000}$$

Note the cash outflow of $6,000 as entered in Exhibit 12-13 of the Schedule of Cash Flows from Operating Activities.

Interest Expense The amount of interest expense reported on the income statement is $15,000. Because the balance sheet does not report an accrual of interest owed but not yet paid (an Interest Payable account), we know that $15,000 is also the amount of cash paid. The schedule in Exhibit 12-13 reflects the cash outflow of $15,000 for interest. Whether interest paid is properly classified as an operating activity is subject to considerable debate. The Financial Accounting Standards Board decided in favor of classification of *interest* as an *operating* activity because, unlike dividends, it appears on the income statement. This, it was argued, provides a direct link between the statement of cash flows and the income statement. Many argue, however, that it is inconsistent to classify dividends paid as a financing activity but interest paid as an operating activity. After all, both represent returns paid to providers of capital: interest to creditors and dividends to stockholders.

Income Tax Expense and Income Taxes Payable The income statement in Exhibit 12-11 reports income tax expense of $50,000. We know, however, that this is not necessarily the amount paid to the government during the year. In fact, note the increase in the Income Taxes Payable account on the balance sheets in Exhibit 12-12. The liability increased by $3,000, from $5,000 to $8,000. **This means that the amount of cash paid to the government in taxes was $3,000 less than the amount of expense accrued.** Another way to look at the cash payments of $50,000 − $3,000, or $47,000, is as follows:

Beginning income taxes payable	$ 5,000
+ Income tax expense	50,000
− Cash payments for taxes	(X)
= Ending income taxes payable	$ 8,000

Solving for *X*, we can find the amount of cash paid:

$$5,000 + 50,000 - X = 8,000$$
$$X = \underline{47,000}$$

As you see by examining Exhibit 12-13, the cash payments for taxes is the last item on the Schedule of Cash Flows from Operating Activities.

Loss on Retirement of Bonds A $3,000 loss on the retirement of bonds is reported as the last item under expenses and losses on the income statement in Exhibit 12-11. Any cash paid to retire a long-term liability is reported in the Financing Activities section of the statement of cash flows. Thus, we ignore the loss when reporting cash flows from operating activities under the direct method.

Compare Net Income with Net Cash Flow from Operating Activities At this point, all of the items on the income statement have been analyzed, as have all of the current asset and current liability accounts. All of the information needed to prepare the Operating Activities section of your statement of cash flows has been gathered.

To summarize, the preparation of the Operating Activities section of the statement of cash flows requires the conversion of each item on the income statement to a cash basis. The current asset and current liability accounts are analyzed to discover the cash effects of each item on the income statement. Exhibit 12-14 summarizes this conversion process.

Note in the exhibit the various adjustments made to put each income statement item on a cash basis. For example, the $6,000 increase in accounts receivable for the period is deducted from sales revenue of $670,000 to arrive at cash collected from customers. Similar adjustments are made to each of the other income statement items with the exception of depreciation, the gain, and the loss. Depreciation is ignored because it does not have an effect on cash flow. The gain relates to the sale of a long-term asset, and any cash effect is reflected in the Investing Activities section of the statement of cash flows. Similarly, the loss resulted from the retirement of bonds, and any cash flow effect is reported in the Financing Activities section. The bottom of the exhibit highlights an important point: Julian reported net income of $120,000 but actually generated $174,000 in cash from operations.

EXHIBIT 12-14 **Conversion of Income Statement Items to Cash Basis**

Income Statement	Amount	Adjustments	Cash Flows
Sales revenue	$670,000		$670,000
		+ Decreases in accounts receivable	–0–
		– Increases in accounts receivable	(6,000)
		Cash collected from customers	$664,000
Interest revenue	15,000		$ 15,000
		+ Decreases in interest receivable	–0–
		– Increases in interest receivable	–0–
		Cash collected in interest	$ 15,000
Gain on sale of machine	5,000	*Not an operating activity*	$ –0–
Cost of goods sold	390,000		$390,000
		+ Increases in inventory	–0–
		– Decreases in inventory	(8,000)
		+ Decreases in accounts payable	–0–
		– Increases in accounts payable	(7,000)
		Cash paid to suppliers	$375,000
Salaries and wages	60,000		$ 60,000
		+ Decreases in salaries/wages payable	2,000
		– Increases in salaries/wages payable	–0–
		Cash paid to employees	$ 62,000
Depreciation	40,000	*No cash flow effect*	$ –0–
Insurance	12,000		$ 12,000
		+ Increases in prepaid insurance	–0–
		– Decreases in prepaid insurance	(6,000)
		Cash paid for insurance	$ 6,000
Interest	15,000		$ 15,000
		+ Decreases in interest payable	–0–
		– Increases in interest payable	–0–
		Cash paid for interest	$ 15,000
Income taxes	50,000		$ 50,000
		+ Decreases in income taxes payable	–0–
		– Increases in income taxes payable	(3,000)
		Cash paid for taxes	$ 47,000
Loss on retirement of bonds	3,000	*Not an operating activity*	$ –0–
Net income	$120,000	Net cash flow from operating activities	$174,000

Determine the Cash Flows from Investing Activities At this point, we turn our attention to the long-term asset accounts and any additional information available about these accounts. Julian has three long-term assets on its balance sheet: Long-Term Investments, Land, and Property and Equipment.

Long-Term Investments Item 1 in the additional information in Exhibit 12-12 indicates that Julian purchased $30,000 of investments during the year. The $30,000 net increase in the Long-Term Investments account confirms this (no mention is made of the sale of any investments during 2007). The purchase of investments requires the use of $30,000 of cash, as indicated on the Schedule of Cash Flows from Investing Activities in Exhibit 12-15 on page 578.

Land Note from the balance sheets in Exhibit 12-12 the $50,000 net increase in land, from $100,000 to $150,000. Item 2 in the additional information indicates that Julian purchased land by issuing a $50,000 note payable. This transaction obviously does not involve cash. It does have both an important financing element and an investing component, however. The issuance of the note is a financing activity, and the acquisition of land is an investing activity. Because no cash was

EXHIBIT 12-15 **Schedule of Cash Flows from Investing Activities**

Cash Flows from Investing Activities

Cash inflows from:	
Sale of machine	25,000
Cash outflows for:	
Purchase of investments	(30,000)
Purchase of property and equipment	(75,000)

involved, the transaction is reported in a separate schedule instead of directly on the statement of cash flows:

Supplemental schedule of noncash investing and financing activities
Acquisition of land in exchange for note payable $50,000

Property and Equipment Property and equipment increased by $40,000 during 2007. However, Julian both acquired equipment and sold a machine (items 3 and 4 in the additional information). As we discussed earlier in the chapter, acquisitions of new plant and equipment are important investing activities for most businesses. Thus, the $75,000 expended to acquire new property and equipment appears in the schedule in Exhibit 12-15 as a cash outflow.

As reported in the balance sheets in Exhibit 12-12, the Property and Equipment account increased during the year by only $40,000, from $280,000 to $320,000. Since Julian *added* to this account $75,000, however, we know it must have *disposed* of some assets as well. In fact, item 4 in the additional information in Exhibit 12-12 reports the sale of a machine with an original cost of $35,000. An analysis of the Property and Equipment account at this point confirms this amount:

Beginning property and equipment	$280,000
+ Acquisitions	75,000
− Disposals	(X)
= Ending property and equipment	$320,000

Solving for X, we can find the *cost* of the fixed assets sold during the year:

$$280,000 + 75,000 - X = 320,000$$
$$X = 35,000$$

The additional information also indicates that the book value of the machine sold was $20,000. This means that if the original cost was $35,000 and the book value was $20,000, the Accumulated Depreciation on the machine sold must have been $35,000 − $20,000, or $15,000. An analysis similar to the one we just looked at for Property and Equipment confirms this amount:

Beginning accumulated depreciation	$ 75,000
+ Depreciation expense	40,000
− Accumulated depreciation on assets sold	(X)
= Ending accumulated depreciation	$100,000

Solving for X, we can find the accumulated depreciation on the assets disposed of during the year:

$$75,000 + 40,000 - X = 100,000$$
$$X = 15,000$$

Finally, we are told in the additional information that the machine was sold for $25,000. **If the selling price was $25,000 and the book value was $20,000, Julian reports a gain on sale of $5,000, an amount that is confirmed on the income statement in Exhibit 12-11.** To summarize, the machine was sold for $25,000, an amount that

EXHIBIT 12-16	Schedule of Cash Flows from Financing Activities

Cash Flows from Financing Activities

Cash inflows from:	
Issuance of stock	25,000
Cash outflows for:	
Retirement of bonds	(63,000)
Payment of cash dividends	(67,000)

exceeded its book value of $20,000, thus generating a gain of $5,000. The cash inflow of $25,000 is entered on the Schedule of Cash Flows from Investing Activities in Exhibit 12-15.

Determine the Cash Flows from Financing Activities These activities generally involve long-term liabilities and stockholders' equity. We first consider Julian's two long-term liabilities, Notes Payable and Bonds Payable, and then the two stockholders' equity accounts: Capital Stock and Retained Earnings.

Notes Payable Recall that item 2 in the additional information reported that Julian purchased land in exchange for a $50,000 note payable. This amount is confirmed on the balance sheets, which show an increase in notes payable of $50,000, from $35,000 to $85,000. In our discussion of investing activities, we already entered this transaction on a supplemental schedule of noncash activities because it was a significant financing activity but did not involve cash.

Bonds Payable The balance sheets in Exhibit 12-12 report a decrease in bonds payable of $60,000, from $260,000 to $200,000. Item 5 in the additional information in Exhibit 12-12 indicates that bonds with a face value of $60,000 were retired by paying $63,000 in cash. The book value of the bonds retired is the same as the face value of $60,000 because there is no unamortized discount or premium on the records. **When a company has to pay more in cash ($63,000) to settle a debt than the book value of the debt ($60,000), it reports a loss.** Recall the $3,000 loss reported on the income statement in Exhibit 12-11. For purposes of preparing a statement of cash flows with the direct method, however, the important amount is the $63,000 in cash paid to retire the bonds. This amount appears as a cash outflow in the Schedule of Cash Flows from Financing Activities, as shown in Exhibit 12-16.

Capital Stock Exhibit 12-12 indicates an increase in capital stock of $25,000, from $75,000 to $100,000. Julian issued capital stock in exchange for $25,000 in cash, according to item 6 in the additional information in Exhibit 12-12. Some companies issue additional stock after the initial formation of a corporation to raise needed capital. The increase in Cash from this issuance is presented as a cash inflow in the Schedule of Cash Flows from Financing Activities, as shown in Exhibit 12-16.

Retained Earnings This account increased during the year by $53,000, from $193,000 to $246,000. Because we know from Exhibit 12-11 that net income was $120,000, however, the company must have declared some dividends. We can determine the amount of cash dividends for 2007 in the following manner:

Beginning retained earnings	$193,000
+ Net income	120,000
− Cash dividends	(X)
= Ending retained earnings	$246,000

Solving for *X*, we can find the amount of cash dividends paid during the year:[3]

$$193{,}000 + 120{,}000 - X = 246{,}000$$
$$X = \underline{67{,}000}$$

---

3 Any decrease in Retained Earnings represents the dividends *declared* during the period rather than the amount paid. If there had been a Dividends Payable account, we would analyze it to find the amount of dividends paid. The lack of a balance in such an account at either the beginning or the end of the period tells us that Julian paid the same amount of dividends that it declared during the period.

Item 7 in the additional information confirms that this was in fact the amount of dividends paid during the year. The dividends paid appear in the Schedule of Cash Flows from Financing Activities, as presented in Exhibit 12-16.

Using the Three Schedules to Prepare a Statement of Cash Flows All of the information needed to prepare a statement of cash flows is now available in the three schedules along with the supplemental schedule prepared earlier. From the information gathered in Exhibits 12-13, 12-15, and 12-16, a completed statement of cash flows appears in Exhibit 12-17.

What does Julian's statement of cash flows tell us? Cash flow from operations totaled $174,000. Cash used to acquire investments and equipment amounted to $80,000, after receiving $25,000 from the sale of a machine. A net amount of $105,000 was used for financing activities. Thus, Julian used more cash than it generated, and that's why the cash balance declined. That's okay for a year or two, but if this continues, the company won't be able to pay its bills.

EXHIBIT 12-17 **Completed Statement of Cash Flows for Julian Corp.**

Julian Corp.
Statement of Cash Flows
For the Year Ended December 31, 2007

Cash flows from operating activities

Cash receipts from:

Sales on account	$ 664,000
Interest	15,000
Total cash receipts	$ 679,000

Cash payments for:

Inventory purchases	$(375,000)
Salaries and wages	(62,000)
Insurance	(6,000)
Interest	(15,000)
Taxes	(47,000)
Total cash payments	$(505,000)
Net cash provided by operating activities	$ 174,000

Cash flows from investing activities

Purchase of investments	$ (30,000)
Purchase of property and equipment	(75,000)
Sale of machine	25,000
Net cash used by investing activities	$ (80,000)

Cash flows from financing activities

Retirement of bonds	$ (63,000)
Issuance of stock	25,000
Payment of cash dividends	(67,000)
Net cash used by financing activities	$(105,000)
Net decrease in cash	$ (11,000)
Cash balance, December 31, 2006	46,000
Cash balance, December 31, 2007	$ 35,000

Supplemental schedule of noncash investing and financing activities

Acquisition of land in exchange for note payable	$ 50,000

AN APPROACH TO PREPARING THE STATEMENT OF CASH FLOWS: INDIRECT METHOD

The purpose of the Operating Activities section of the statement changes when we use the indirect method. Instead of reporting cash receipts and cash payments, **the objective is to reconcile net income to net cash flow from operating activities.** The other two sections of the completed statement in Exhibit 12-17, the investing and financing sections, are unchanged. The use of the indirect or the direct method for presenting cash flow from operating activities does not affect these two sections.

An approach similar to that used for the direct method can be used to prepare the Operating Activities section of the statement of cash flows under the indirect method.

Net Income Recall that the first line in the Operating Activities section of the statement under the indirect method is net income. That is, we start with the assumptions that all revenues and gains reported on the income statement increase cash flow and that all expenses and losses decrease cash flow. Julian's net income of $120,000, as reported on its income statement in Exhibit 12-11, is reported as the first item in the Operating Activities section of the statement of cash flows as shown in Exhibit 12-18.

Increase in Accounts Receivable Recall from the balance sheets in Exhibit 12-12 the net increase in Accounts Receivable of $6,000. Because net income includes sales, as opposed to cash collections, the $6,000 *net increase* must be *deducted* to adjust net income to cash from operations as shown in Exhibit 12-18.

Gain on Sale of Machine The gain itself did not generate any cash, but the *sale* of the machine did. And as we found earlier, the cash generated by selling the machine was reported in the Investing Activities section of the statement. The cash proceeds included the gain. Because the gain is included in the net income figure, it must be *deducted* to determine cash from operations. Also note that the gain is included twice in cash inflows if it is not deducted from the net income figure in the Operating Activities section. Note the deduction of $5,000 in Exhibit 12-18.

Decrease in Inventory As the $8,000 net decrease in the Inventory account indicates, Julian liquidated a portion of its stock of inventory during the year. A net decrease in this account indicates that the company sold more products than it purchased during the year. As shown in Exhibit 12-18, the *net decrease* of $8,000 is *added back* to net income.

Increase in Accounts Payable According to Exhibit 12-12, Julian owed suppliers $31,000 at the start of the year. By the end of the year, the balance had grown to $38,000. Effectively, the company saved cash by delaying the payment of some of its outstanding accounts payable. The *net increase* of $7,000 in this account is *added back* to net income, as shown in Exhibit 12-18.

LO6 Prepare a statement of cash flows, using the indirect method to determine cash flow from operating activities.

12-2 Real World Practice

Reading Best Buy's Statement of Cash Flows

Did Best Buy's Receivables increase or decrease during the most recent year? Why is the change in this account deducted on the statement of cash flows?

EXHIBIT 12-18 Indirect Method for Reporting Cash Flows from Operating Activities

Julian Corp.
Partial Statement of Cash Flows
For the Year Ended December 31, 2007

Net cash flows from operating activities

Net income	$120,000
Adjustments to reconcile net income to net cash provided by operating activities:	
Increase in accounts receivable	(6,000)
Gain on sale of machine	(5,000)
Decrease in inventory	8,000
Increase in accounts payable	7,000
Decrease in salaries and wages payable	(2,000)
Depreciation expense	40,000
Decrease in prepaid insurance	6,000
Increase in income taxes payable	3,000
Loss on retirement of bonds	3,000
Net cash provided by operating activities	$174,000

Real World Practice **12-3**

Reading Best Buy's Statement of Cash Flows

According to the supplemental disclosure at the bottom of Best Buy's statement of cash flows, what amount did the company pay in income taxes in the most recent year? Would this necessarily be the same amount that the company reported as income tax expense on its income statement? Explain your answer.

Decrease in Salaries and Wages Payable Salaries and Wages Payable decreased during the year by $2,000. The rationale for *deducting* the $2,000 *net decrease* in this liability in Exhibit 12-18 follows from what we just said about an increase in Accounts Payable. The payment to employees of $2,000 more than the amount included in expense on the income statement requires an additional deduction under the indirect method.

Depreciation Expense Depreciation is a noncash expense. Because it was deducted to arrive at net income, we must *add back* $40,000, the amount of depreciation, to find cash from operations. The same holds true for amortization of intangible assets and depletion of natural resources.

Decrease in Prepaid Insurance This account decreased by $6,000, according to Exhibit 12-12. A decrease in this account indicates that Julian deducted more on the income statement for the insurance expense of the period than it paid in cash for new policies. That is, the cash outlay for insurance protection was not as large as the amount of expense reported on the income statement. Thus, the *net decrease* in the account is *added back* to net income in Exhibit 12-18.

Increase in Income Taxes Payable Exhibit 12-12 reports a net increase of $3,000 in Income Taxes Payable. The *net increase* of $3,000 in this liability is *added back* to net income in Exhibit 12-18 because the payments to the government were $3,000 less than the amount included on the income statement.

Loss on Retirement of Bonds The $3,000 loss from retiring bonds was reported on the income statement as a deduction. There are two parts to the explanation for *adding back* the loss to net income to eliminate its effect in the Operating Activities section of the statement. First, any cash outflow from retiring bonds is properly classified as a financing activity, not an operating activity. The entire cash outflow should be reported in one classification rather than being allocated between two classifications. Second, the amount of the cash outflow is $63,000, not $3,000. To summarize, to convert net income to a cash basis, we add the loss back in the Operating Activities section to eliminate its effect. The actual use of cash to retire the bonds is shown in the financing section of the statement.

Summary of Adjustments to Net Income under the Indirect Method The following is a list of the most common adjustments to net income when the indirect method is used to prepare the Operating Activities section of the statement of cash flows:

Additions to Net Income	Deductions from Net Income
Decrease in accounts receivable	Increase in accounts receivable
Decrease in inventory	Increase in inventory
Decrease in prepayments	Increase in prepayments
Increase in accounts payable	Decrease in accounts payable
Increase in accrued liabilities	Decrease in accrued liabilities
Losses on sales of long-term assets	Gains on sales of long-term assets
Losses on retirements of bonds	Gains on retirements of bonds
Depreciation, amortization, and depletion	

COMPARISON OF THE INDIRECT AND DIRECT METHODS

The amount of cash provided by operating activities is the same under the direct and the indirect methods. The relative merits of the two methods, however, have stirred considerable debate in the accounting profession. The Financial Accounting Standards Board has expressed a strong preference for the direct method but allows companies to use the indirect method.

If a company uses the indirect method, it must separately disclose two important cash payments: income taxes paid and interest paid. Thus, if Julian uses the indirect method, it reports the following either at the bottom of the statement of cash flows or in a note to the financial statements:

Income taxes paid	$47,000
Interest paid	15,000

Advocates of the direct method believe that the information provided with this approach is valuable in evaluating a company's operating efficiency. For example, the use of the direct method allows the analyst to follow any trends in cash receipts from customers and compare them with cash payments to suppliers. The information presented in the Operating Activities section of the statement under the direct method is certainly user-friendly. Someone without a technical background in accounting can easily tell where cash came from and where it went during the period.

Advocates of the indirect method argue two major points. Many companies believe that the use of the direct method reveals too much about their business by telling readers exactly the amount of cash receipts and cash payments from operations. Whether or not the use of the direct method tells the competition too much about a company is subject to debate. The other argument made for the indirect method is that it focuses attention on the differences between income on an accrual basis and a cash basis. In fact, this reconciliation of net income and cash provided by operating activities is considered to be important enough that **if a company uses the direct method, it must present a separate schedule to reconcile net income to net cash from operating activities.** This schedule, in effect, is the same as the Operating Activities section for the indirect method.

The Use of Cash Flow Information

The statement of cash flows is a critical disclosure to a company's investors and creditors. Many investors focus on cash flow from operations, rather than net income, as their key statistic. Similarly, many bankers are as concerned with cash flow from operations as they are with net income because they care about a company's ability to pay its bills. There is the concern that accrual accounting can mask cash flow problems. For example, a company with smooth earnings could be building up accounts receivable and inventory. This may not become evident until the company is in deep trouble.

The statement of cash flows provides investors, analysts, bankers, and other users with a valuable starting point as they attempt to evaluate a company's financial health. From this point, these groups must decide *how* to use the information presented on the statement. They pay particular attention to the *relationships* among various items on the statement, as well as to other financial statement items. In fact, many large banks have their own cash flow models, which typically involve a rearrangement of the items on the statement of cash flows to suit their needs. We now consider two examples of how various groups use cash flow information.

CREDITORS AND CASH FLOW ADEQUACY

Bankers and other creditors are especially concerned with a company's ability to meet its principal and interest obligations. *Cash flow adequacy* is a measure intended to help in this regard.[4] It gauges the cash available to meet future debt obligations after paying taxes and interest costs and making capital expenditures. Because capital expenditures on new plant and equipment are a necessity for most companies, analysts are concerned with the cash available to repay debt *after* the company has replaced and updated its existing base of long-term assets.

Cash flow adequacy can be computed as follows:

$$\text{Cash Flow Adequacy} = \frac{\text{Cash Flow from Operating Activities} - \text{Capital Expenditures}}{\text{Average Amount of Debt Maturing over Next Five Years}}$$

LO7 Use cash flow information to help analyze a company.

© AP/Wide World Photos

Managers, investors, and brokers gauge the relative strengths of retailers like Best Buy by observing which stores are the most popular. Of course, they also study the financial statements, particularly the statement of cash flows and its indicators of cash flow adequacy, as the most fundamental way to measure a firm's strength.

---

4 An article appearing in the January 10, 1994, edition of *The Wall Street Journal* reported that **Fitch Investors Service Inc.** has published a rating system to compare the cash flow adequacy of companies that it rates single-A in its credit ratings. The rating system is intended to help corporate bond investors assess the ability of these companies to meet their maturing debt obligations. Lee Berton, "Investors Have a New Tool for Judging Issuers' Health: 'Cash-Flow Adequacy,'" p. C1.

How could you use the information in an annual report to measure a company's cash flow adequacy? First, whether a company uses the direct or indirect method to report cash flow from operating activities, this number represents cash flow after paying interest and taxes. The numerator of the ratio is determined by deducting capital expenditures, as they appear in the Investing Activities section of the statement, from cash flow from operating activities. A disclosure required by the Securities and Exchange Commission provides the information needed to calculate the denominator of the ratio. This regulatory body requires companies to report the annual amount of long-term debt maturing over each of the next five years. For more on the cash flow adequacy of **Best Buy**, see the Ratio Decision Process below.

Best Buy's Cash Flow Adequacy As an example of the calculation of this ratio, consider the following amounts from Best Buy's statement of cash flows for the year ended February 26, 2005 (amounts in millions of dollars):

Total cash provided by operating activities from continuing operations	$1,841
Additions to property and equipment	502

Note 4 in Best Buy's 2005 annual report provides the following information:

The future maturities of long-term debt, including master and capitalized leases, consist of the following:

Fiscal Year

2006	$ 72
2007 (1)	415
2008	14
2009	14
2010	20
Thereafter	65
	$600[5]

(1) Holders of our debentures due in 2022 may require us to purchase all or a portion of their debentures on January 15, 2007. The table assumes that all holders of our debentures exercise their redemption options.

---

5 Best Buy 2005 Annual Report, p. 74.

USING THE RATIO DECISION MODEL: ANALYZING CASH FLOW ADEQUACY

Use the following Ratio Decision Process to evaluate the cash flow adequacy of Best Buy or any other public company.

1. Formulate the Question
Managers, investors, and creditors are all interested in a company's cash flows. They must be able to answer the following question:

Did the company generate enough cash this year from its operations to pay for its capital expenditures and meet its maturing debt obligations?

2. Gather the Information from the Financial Statements

- Total cash from operating activities: From the statement of cash flows
- Necessary capital expenditures: From the statement of cash flows
- Average debt maturing over next five years: From the note disclosures

(continued)

3. Calculate the Ratio

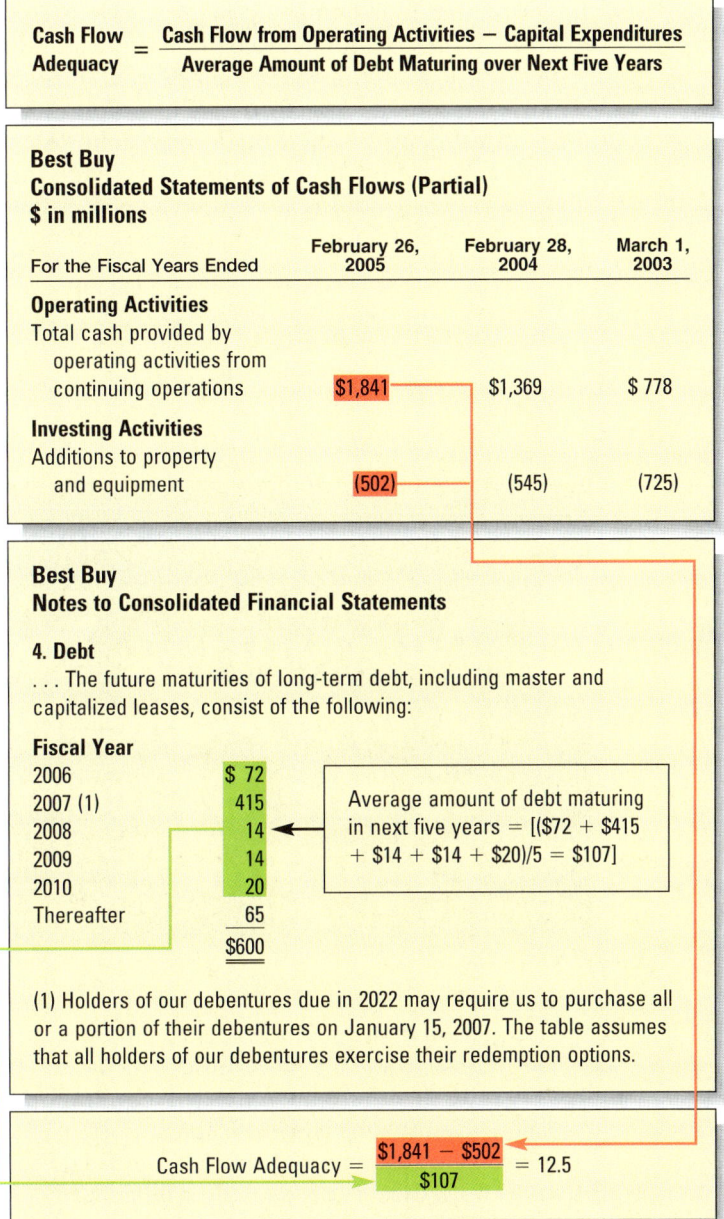

$$\frac{\text{Cash Flow}}{\text{Adequacy}} = \frac{\text{Cash Flow from Operating Activities} - \text{Capital Expenditures}}{\text{Average Amount of Debt Maturing over Next Five Years}}$$

Best Buy
Consolidated Statements of Cash Flows (Partial)
$ in millions

For the Fiscal Years Ended	February 26, 2005	February 28, 2004	March 1, 2003
Operating Activities			
Total cash provided by operating activities from continuing operations	$1,841	$1,369	$ 778
Investing Activities			
Additions to property and equipment	(502)	(545)	(725)

Best Buy
Notes to Consolidated Financial Statements

4. Debt

. . . The future maturities of long-term debt, including master and capitalized leases, consist of the following:

Fiscal Year

2006	$ 72
2007 (1)	415
2008	14
2009	14
2010	20
Thereafter	65
	$600

Average amount of debt maturing in next five years = [($72 + $415 + $14 + $14 + $20)/5 = $107]

(1) Holders of our debentures due in 2022 may require us to purchase all or a portion of their debentures on January 15, 2007. The table assumes that all holders of our debentures exercise their redemption options.

$$\text{Cash Flow Adequacy} = \frac{\$1,841 - \$502}{\$107} = 12.5$$

4. Compare the Ratio with Others

Best Buy's cash flow adequacy may be compared to prior years and to companies of similar size in the same industry.

	Best Buy		Circuit City	
	Year Ended February 26, 2005	Year Ended February 28, 2004	Year Ended February 28, 2005	Year Ended February 29, 2004
Cash Flow Adequacy	12.5	5.2	158.2	(83.7)

5. Interpret the Results

Best Buy's ratio of 12.5 is an improvement over the prior year and indicates that its 2005 cash flow was more than sufficient to repay its average annual debt over the next five years. The unusually high cash flow adequacy for Circuit City in 2005 is partly due to relatively low amounts of debt maturing in the near future, and the negative ratio in 2004 is partly due to a negative amount of cash provided by operating activities from continuing operations in that year.

STOCKHOLDERS AND CASH FLOW PER SHARE

One measure of the relative worth of an investment in a company is the ratio of the stock's market price per share to the company's earnings per share (that is, the price/earnings ratio). But many stockholders and Wall Street analysts are even more interested in the price of the stock in relation to the company's cash flow per share. Cash flow for purposes of this ratio is normally limited to cash flow from operating activities. This ratio has been used by these groups to evaluate investments—even though the accounting profession has expressly forbidden the reporting of cash flow per share information in the financial statements. The accounting profession's belief is that this type of information is not an acceptable alternative to earnings per share as an indicator of company performance.

APPENDIX

Accounting Tools: A Work-Sheet Approach to the Statement of Cash Flows

LO8 Use a work sheet to prepare a statement of cash flows, using the indirect method to determine cash flow from operating activities.

In the chapter, we illustrated a systematic approach to aid in the preparation of a statement of cash flows. We now consider the use of a work sheet as an alternative tool to organize the information needed to prepare the statement. We will use the information given in the chapter for Julian Corp. (refer to Exhibits 12-11 and 12-12 for the income statements and comparative balance sheets). Although it is possible to use a work sheet to prepare the statement when the Operating Activities section is prepared under the direct method, we illustrate the use of a work sheet using the more popular *indirect* method.

A work sheet for Julian Corp. is presented in Exhibit 12-19. The following steps were taken to prepare the work sheet:

Step 1: The balances in each account at the end and at the beginning of the period are entered in the first two columns of the work sheet. For Julian, these balances can be found in its comparative balance sheets in Exhibit 12-12. Note that contra assets, liabilities, and stockholders' equity accounts are bracketed on the work sheet. Because the work sheet lists all balance sheet accounts, the total of the asset balances must equal the total of the liability and stockholders' equity balances, and thus, the totals at the bottom for these first two columns equal $0.

Step 2: The additional information listed at the bottom of Exhibit 12-12 is used to record the various investing and financing activities on the work sheet (the item numbers discussed below correspond to the superscript numbers on the work sheet in Exhibit 12-19):

| EXHIBIT 12-19 | Julian Corp. Statement of Cash Flows Work Sheet |

Julian Corp.
Statement of Cash Flows Work Sheet (Indirect Method)
(all amounts in thousands of dollars)

| | Balances | | | Cash Inflows (Outflows) | | | Noncash |
| | 12/31/07 | 12/31/06 | Changes | Operating | Investing | Financing | Activities |
Accounts							
Cash	35	46	$(11)^{16}$				
Accounts Receivable	63	57	6^{10}	$(6)^{10}$			
Inventory	84	92	$(8)^{11}$	8^{11}			
Prepaid Insurance	12	18	$(6)^{12}$	6^{12}			
Long-Term Investments	120	90	30^{1}		$(30)^{1}$		
Land	150	100	50^{2}				$(50)^{2}$
Property and Equipment	320	280	75^{3}		$(75)^{3}$		
			$(35)^{4}$		25^{4}		
Accumulated Depreciation	(100)	(75)	15^{4}				
			$(40)^{9}$	40^{9}			
Accounts Payable	(38)	(31)	$(7)^{13}$	7^{13}			
Salaries and Wages Payable	(7)	(9)	2^{14}	$(2)^{14}$			
Income Taxes Payable	(8)	(5)	$(3)^{15}$	3^{15}			
Notes Payable	(85)	(35)	$(50)^{2}$				50^{2}
Bonds Payable	(200)	(260)	60^{5}			$(63)^{5}$	
Capital Stock	(100)	(75)	$(25)^{6}$			25^{6}	
Retained Earnings	(246)	(193)	67^{7}	$(5)^{4}$		$(67)^{7}$	
				3^{5}			
			$(120)^{8}$	120^{8}			
Totals	–0–	–0–	–0–	174	(80)	(105)	–0–
Net decrease in cash				$(11)^{16}$			

Source: *The authors are grateful to Jeannie Folk for the development of this work sheet.*

1. Long-term investments were purchased for $30,000. Because this transaction required the use of cash, it is entered as a bracketed amount in the Investing column and as an addition to the Long-Term Investments account in the Changes column.

2. Land was acquired by issuing a $50,000 note payable. This transaction is entered on two lines on the work sheet. First, $50,000 is added to the Changes column for Land and as a corresponding deduction in the Noncash column (the last column on the work sheet). Likewise, $50,000 is added for Notes Payable to the Changes column and to the Noncash column.

3. Item 3 in the additional information indicates the acquisition of equipment for $75,000. This amount appears on the work sheet as an addition to Property and Equipment in the Changes column and as a deduction (cash outflow) in the Investing column.

4. A machine with an original cost of $35,000 and a book value of $20,000 was sold for $25,000, resulting in four entries on the work sheet. First, the amount of cash received, $25,000, is entered as an addition in the Investing column on the line for property and equipment. On the same line, the cost of the

machine, $35,000, is entered as a deduction in the Changes column. The difference between the cost of the machine, $35,000, and its book value, $20,000, is its accumulated depreciation of $15,000. This amount is shown as a deduction from this account in the Changes column. Because the gain of $5,000 is included in net income, it is deducted in the Operating column (on the Retained Earnings line).

5. Bonds with a face value of $60,000 were retired by paying $63,000 in cash, resulting in the entry of three amounts on the work sheet. The face value of the bonds, $60,000, is entered as a reduction of Bonds Payable in the Changes column. The amount paid to retire the bonds, $63,000, is entered on the same line in the Financing column. The loss of $3,000 is added in the Operating column because it was a deduction to arrive at net income.

6. Capital stock was issued for $25,000. This amount is entered on the Capital Stock line under the Changes column (as an increase in the account) and under the Financing column as an inflow.

7. Dividends of $67,000 were paid. This amount is entered as a reduction in Retained Earnings in the Changes column and as a cash outflow in the Financing Activities column.

Step 3: Because the indirect method is being used, net income of $120,000 for the period is entered as an addition to Retained Earnings in the Operating column of the work sheet (entry 8). The amount is also entered as an increase (bracketed) in the Changes column.

Step 4: Any noncash revenues or expenses are entered on the work sheet on the appropriate lines. For Julian, depreciation expense of $40,000 is added (bracketed) to Accumulated Depreciation in the Changes column and in the Operating column. This entry is identified on the work sheet as entry 9.

Step 5: Each of the changes in the noncash current asset and current liability accounts is entered in the Changes column and in the Operating column. These entries are identified on the work sheet as entries 10 through 15.

Step 6: Totals are determined for the Operating, Investing, and Financing columns and entered at the bottom of the work sheet. The total for the final column, Noncash Activities, of $0, is also entered.

Step 7: The net cash inflow (outflow) for the period is determined by adding the totals of the operating, investing, and financing columns. For Julian, the net cash *outflow* is $11,000, shown as entry 16 at the bottom of the statement. This same amount is then transferred to the line for Cash in the Changes column. Finally, the total of the Changes column at this point should net to $0.

STUDY HIGHLIGHTS

Explain the purpose of a statement of cash flows (p. 554). **LO1**

- The statement of cash flows helps investors to understand cash inflows and outflows of an entity based on its operating, investing, and financing activities. It provides complementary information to the accrual-based income statement.

Explain what cash equivalents are and how they are treated on the statement of cash flows (p. 556). **LO2**

- Cash equivalents are assets that are readily convertible to a determinable amount of cash, having a maturity date of three months or less.
- The term "cash" in the statement of cash flows includes cash and cash equivalents.

Describe operating, investing, and financing activities, and give examples of each (p. 557). **LO3**

- Activities that generate or consume cash are classified into three categories for the statement of cash flows.
  - Operating activities usually involve cash flows related to the production of goods or services for customers.
  - Investing activities are those related to acquiring and disposing of long-term assets.
  - Financing activities are those related to raising funds through debt and equity securities and making payments related to those securities.

Describe the difference between the direct and the indirect methods of computing cash flow from operating activities (p. 560). **LO4**

- The indirect method derives cash flows from operating activities by starting with net income, and then making adjustments for the effects of accruals and deferrals resulting from accrual-based accounting.
- The direct method reports cash receipts and cash disbursements related to operations.

Prepare a statement of cash flows, using the direct method to determine cash flow from operating activities (p. 565). **LO5**

- Using a systematic approach, it is possible to determine the cash flow from the major operating activities, such as sales, purchases, salaries and wages, and operating expenses, and also from investing and financing activities.

Prepare a statement of cash flows, using the indirect method to determine cash flow from operating activities (p. 575). **LO6**

- This approach uses the changes in current asset and liability accounts related to accruals and deferrals to adjust net income to cash flows from operating activities.

Use cash flow information to help analyze a company (p. 577). **LO7**

- Cash flow per share and cash flow adequacy are two measures investors and creditors can use to evaluate the financial health of an entity.

Use a work sheet to prepare a statement of cash flows, using the indirect method to determine cash flow from operating activities (Appendix p. 580). **LO8**

- A work sheet can be used to help in the preparation of a statement of cash flows.

HIGHLIGHTS

RATIO REVIEW

$$\text{Cash Flow Adequacy} = \frac{\text{Cash Flow from Operating Activities} - \text{Capital Expenditures (Statement of Cash Flows)}}{\text{Average Amount of Debt Maturing over Next Five Years (Notes to the Financial Statements)}}$$

KEY TERMS QUIZ

Read each definition below and then write the number of that definition in the blank beside the appropriate term it defines. The quiz solutions appear at the end of the chapter.

_____ Statement of cash flows   _____ Financing activities

_____ Cash equivalent   _____ Direct method

_____ Operating activities   _____ Indirect method

_____ Investing activities

1. Activities concerned with the acquisition and sale of products and services.

2. For preparing the Operating Activities section of the statement of cash flows, the approach in which net income is reconciled to net cash flow from operations.

3. The financial statement that summarizes an entity's cash receipts and cash payments during the period from operating, investing, and financing activities.

4. An item readily convertible to a known amount of cash and with a maturity to the investor of three months or less.

5. Activities concerned with the acquisition and disposal of long-term assets.

6. For preparing the Operating Activities section of the statement of cash flows, the approach in which cash receipts and cash payments are reported.

7. Activities concerned with the raising and repayment of funds in the form of debt and equity.

ALTERNATE TERMS

Bottom line Net income

Cash flow from operating activities Cash flow from operations

Statement of cash flows Cash flows statement

WARMUP EXERCISES & SOLUTIONS

LO1   **Warmup Exercise 12-1** Purpose of the Statement of Cash Flows

Most companies begin the statement of cash flows by indicating the amount of net income and ending it with the beginning and ending cash balances. Why is the statement necessary if net income already appears on the income statement and the cash balances can be found on the balance sheet?

Key to the Solution Recall the *purpose* of the statement of cash flows as described in the beginning of the chapter.

LO3   **Warmup Exercise 12-2** Classification of Activities

For each of the following activities, indicate whether it should appear on the statement of cash flows as an operating (O), investing (I), or financing (F) activity. Assume the company uses the direct method of reporting in the Operating Activities section.

_____ 1. New equipment is acquired for cash.

_____ 2. Thirty-year bonds are issued.

(continued)

3. Cash receipts from the cash register are recorded.
_____ 4. The bi-weekly payroll is paid.
_____ 5. Common stock is issued for cash.
_____ 6. Land that was being held for future expansion is sold at book value.

Key to the Solution Recall the general rules for each of the categories: operating activities involve acquiring and selling products and services; investing activities deal with acquiring and disposing of long-term assets; and financing activities are concerned with the raising and repayment of funds in the form of debt and equity.

Warmup Exercise 12-3 Adjustments to Net Income with the Indirect Method LO6

Assume that a company uses the indirect method to prepare the Operating Activities section of the statement of cash flows. For each of the following items, indicate whether it would be added to net income (A), deducted from net income (D), or not reported in this section of the statement under the indirect method (NR).

_____ 1. Decrease in accounts payable
_____ 2. Increase in accounts receivable
_____ 3. Decrease in prepaid insurance
_____ 4. Purchase of new factory equipment
_____ 5. Depreciation expense
_____ 6. Gain on retirement of bonds

Key to the Solution Refer to the summary of adjustments to net income under the indirect method on page 576.

SOLUTIONS TO WARMUP EXERCISES

Warmup Exercise 12-1
The statement of cash flows is a complement to the other statements in that it summarizes the operating, investing, and financing activities over a period of time. Even though the net income and cash balances are available on other statements, the statement of cash flows explains to the reader *why* net income is different from cash flow from operations and *why* cash changed by the amount it did during the period.

Warmup Exercise 12-2
1. I 2. F 3. O 4. O 5. F 6. I

Warmup Exercise 12-3
1. D 2. D 3. A 4. NR 5. A 6. D

REVIEW PROBLEM & SOLUTION

An income statement and comparative balance sheets for Dexter Company are shown below and on the following page.

Dexter Company
Income Statement
For the Year Ended December 31, 2007

Sales revenue	$89,000
Cost of goods sold	57,000
Gross profit	$32,000
Depreciation expense	$ 6,500
Advertising expense	3,200
Salaries expense	12,000
Total operating expenses	$21,700
Operating income	$10,300
Loss on sale of land	2,500
Income before tax	$ 7,800
Income tax expense	2,600
Net income	$ 5,200

REVIEW

Dexter Company
Comparative Balance Sheets

	December 31	
	2007	**2006**
Cash	$ 12,000	$ 9,500
Accounts receivable	22,000	18,400
Inventory	25,400	20,500
Prepaid advertising	10,000	8,600
Total current assets	$ 69,400	$ 57,000
Land	$120,000	$ 80,000
Equipment	190,000	130,000
Accumulated depreciation	(70,000)	(63,500)
Total long-term assets	$240,000	$146,500
Total assets	$309,400	$203,500
Accounts payable	$ 15,300	$ 12,100
Salaries payable	14,000	16,400
Income taxes payable	1,200	700
Total current liabilities	$ 30,500	$ 29,200
Capital stock	$200,000	$100,000
Retained earnings	78,900	74,300
Total stockholders' equity	$278,900	$174,300
Total liabilities and stockholders' equity	$309,400	$203,500

Additional Information

1. Land was acquired during the year for $70,000.
2. An unimproved parcel of land was sold during the year for $27,500. Its original cost to Dexter was $30,000.
3. A specialized piece of equipment was acquired in exchange for capital stock in the company. The value of the capital stock was $60,000.
4. In addition to the capital stock issued in item (3), stock was sold for $40,000.
5. Dividends of $600 were paid.

Required

Prepare a statement of cash flows for 2007 using the direct method in the Operating Activities section of the statement. Include supplemental schedules to report any noncash investing and financing activities and to reconcile net income to net cash provided by operating activities.

SOLUTION TO REVIEW PROBLEM

Dexter Company
Statement of Cash Flows
For the Year Ended December 31, 2007

Cash flows from operating activities		
Cash collections from customers		$ 85,400
Cash payments:		
To suppliers	$(58,700)	
For advertising	(4,600)	
To employees	(14,400)	
For income taxes	(2,100)	
Total cash payments		$(79,800)
Net cash provided by operating activities		$ 5,600
Cash flows from investing activities		
Purchase of land		$(70,000)
Sale of land		27,500
Net cash used by investing activities		$(42,500)
Cash flows from financing activities		
Issuance of capital stock		$ 40,000
Payment of cash dividends		(600)
Net cash provided by financing activities		$ 39,400
Net increase in cash		$ 2,500
Cash balance, December 31, 2006		9,500
Cash balance, December 31, 2007		$ 12,000

(continued)

Supplemental schedule of noncash investing and financing activities	
Acquisition of specialized equipment in exchange for capital stock	$ 60,000
Reconciliation of net income to net cash provided by operating activities	
Net income	$ 5,200
Adjustments to reconcile net income to net cash provided by operating activities:	
Increase in accounts receivable	(3,600)
Increase in inventory	(4,900)
Increase in prepaid advertising	(1,400)
Increase in accounts payable	3,200
Decrease in salaries payable	(2,400)
Increase in income taxes payable	500
Depreciation expense	6,500
Loss on sale of land	2,500
Net cash provided by operating activities	$ 5,600

QUESTIONS

1. What is the purpose of the statement of cash flows? As a flows statement, explain how it differs from the income statement.

2. What is a cash equivalent? Why is it included with cash for purposes of preparing a statement of cash flows?

3. Preston Corp. acquires a piece of land by signing a $60,000 promissory note and making a down payment of $20,000. How should this transaction be reported on the statement of cash flows?

4. Hansen Inc. made two purchases during December. One was a $10,000 Treasury bill that matures in 60 days from the date of purchase. The other was a $20,000 investment in Motorola common stock that will be held indefinitely. How should each of these be treated for purposes of preparing a statement of cash flows?

5. Companies are required to classify cash flows as operating, investing, or financing. Which of these three categories do you think will most likely have a net cash *outflow* over a number of years? Explain your answer.

6. A fellow student says to you: "The statement of cash flows is the easiest of the basic financial statements to prepare because you know the answer before you start. You compare the beginning and ending balances in cash on the balance sheet and compute the net inflow or outflow of cash. What could be easier?" Do you agree? Explain your answer.

7. What is your evaluation of the following statement? "Depreciation is responsible for providing some of the highest amounts of cash for capital-intensive businesses. This is obvious by examining the Operating Activities section of the statement of cash flows. Other than the net income of the period, depreciation is often the largest amount reported in this section of the statement."

8. Which method for preparing the Operating Activities section of the statement of cash flows, the direct or the indirect method, do you believe provides more information to users of the statement? Explain your answer.

9. Assume that a company uses the indirect method to prepare the Operating Activities section of the statement of cash flows. Why would a decrease in accounts receivable during the period be added back to net income?

10. Why is it necessary to analyze both inventory and accounts payable in trying to determine cash payments to suppliers when the direct method is used?

11. A company has a very profitable year. What explanations might there be for a decrease in cash?

12. A company reports a net loss for the year. Is it possible that cash could increase during the year? Explain your answer.

13. What effect does a decrease in income taxes payable for the period have on cash generated from operating activities? Does it matter whether the direct or the indirect method is used?

14. Why do accounting standards require a company to separately disclose income taxes paid and interest paid if it uses the indirect method?

15. Is it logical that interest paid is classified as a cash outflow in the *Operating* Activities section of the statement of cash flows but that dividends paid are included in the *Financing* Activities section? Explain your answer.

16. Jackson Company prepays the rent on various office facilities. The beginning balance in Prepaid Rent was $9,600, and the ending balance was $7,300. The income statement reports Rent Expense of $45,900. Under the direct method, what amount would appear for cash paid in rent in the Operating Activities section of the statement of cash flows?

17. Baxter Inc. buys 2,000 shares of its own common stock at $20 per share as treasury stock. How is this transaction reported on the statement of cash flows?

18. Duke Corp. sold a delivery truck for $9,000. Its original cost was $25,000, and the book value at the time of the sale was $11,000. How does the transaction to record

the sale appear on a statement of cash flows prepared under the indirect method?

19. Billings Company has a patent on its books with a balance at the beginning of the year of $24,000. The ending balance for the asset was $20,000. The company neither bought nor sold any patents during the year, nor does it use an Accumulated Amortization account. Assuming that the company uses the indirect method in

preparing a statement of cash flows, how is the decrease in the Patents account reported on the statement?

20. Ace Inc. declared and distributed a 10% stock dividend during the year. Explain how, if at all, you think this transaction should be reported on a statement of cash flows.

21. Explain where the information comes from in order to determine a company's cash flow adequacy.

EXERCISES

LO2

Exercise 12-1 Cash Equivalents

Metropolis Industries invested its excess cash in the following instruments during December 2007:

Certificate of deposit, due January 31, 2008	$ 35,000
Certificate of deposit, due June 30, 2008	95,000
Investment in City of Elgin bonds, due May 1, 2009	15,000
Investment in Quantum Data stock	66,000
Money Market Fund	105,000
90-day Treasury bills	75,000
Treasury note, due December 1, 2008	200,000

Required

Determine the amount of cash equivalents that should be combined with cash on the company's balance sheet at December 31, 2007, and for purposes of preparing a statement of cash flows for the year ended December 31, 2007.

LO3

Exercise 12-2 Classification of Activities

For each of the following transactions reported on a statement of cash flows, fill in the blank to indicate if it would appear in the Operating Activities section (O), in the Investing Activities section (I), or in the Financing Activities section (F). Put an *S* in the blank if the transaction does not affect cash but is reported in a supplemental schedule of noncash activities. Assume the company uses the direct method in the Operating Activities section.

_____ 1. A company purchases its own common stock in the open market and immediately retires it.

_____ 2. A company issues preferred stock in exchange for land.

_____ 3. A six-month bank loan is obtained.

_____ 4. Twenty-year bonds are issued.

_____ 5. A customer's open account is collected.

_____ 6. Income taxes are paid.

_____ 7. Cash sales for the day are recorded.

_____ 8. Cash dividends are declared and paid.

_____ 9. A creditor is given shares of common stock in the company in return for cancellation of a long-term loan.

_____ 10. A new piece of machinery is acquired for cash.

_____ 11. Stock of another company is acquired as an investment.

_____ 12. Interest is paid on a bank loan.

_____ 13. Factory workers are paid.

LO3

Exercise 12-3 Retirement of Bonds Payable on the Statement of Cash Flows—Indirect Method

Redstone Inc. has the following debt outstanding on December 31, 2007:

10% bonds payable, due 12/31/11	$500,000	
Discount on bonds payable	(40,000)	$460,000

On this date, Redstone retired the entire bond issue by paying cash of $510,000.

Required

1. Determine the effect on the accounting equation of the bond retirement.
2. Describe how the bond retirement would be reported on the statement of cash flows, assuming that Redstone uses the indirect method.

LO5 **Exercise 12-4** Cash Collections—Direct Method

Stanley Company's comparative balance sheets included accounts receivable of $80,800 at December 31, 2006, and $101,100 at December 31, 2007. Sales reported by Stanley on its 2007 income statement amounted to $1,450,000. What is the amount of cash collections that Stanley will report in the Operating Activities section of its 2007 statement of cash flows assuming that the direct method is used?

LO5 **Exercise 12-5** Cash Payments—Direct Method

Lester Enterprises' comparative balance sheets included inventory of $90,200 at December 31, 2006, and $70,600 at December 31, 2007. Lester's comparative balance sheets also included accounts payable of $57,700 at December 31, 2006, and $39,200 at December 31, 2007. Lester's accounts payable balances are composed solely of amounts due to suppliers for purchases of inventory on account. Cost of goods sold, as reported by Lester on its 2007 income statement, amounted to $770,900. What is the amount of cash payments for inventory that Lester will report in the Operating Activities section of its 2007 statement of cash flows assuming that the direct method is used?

LO5 **Exercise 12-6** Operating Activities Section—Direct Method

The following account balances for the noncash current assets and current liabilities of Labrador Company are available:

	December 31	
	2007	**2006**
Accounts receivable	$ 4,000	$ 6,000
Inventory	32,000	25,000
Office supplies	7,000	10,000
Accounts payable	7,500	4,500
Salaries and wages payable	1,500	2,500
Interest payable	500	1,000
Income taxes payable	4,500	3,000

In addition, the income statement for 2007 is as follows:

	2007
Sales revenue	$100,000
Cost of goods sold	75,000
Gross profit	$ 25,000
General and administrative expense	$ 8,000
Depreciation expense	3,000
Total operating expenses	$ 11,000
Income before interest and taxes	$ 14,000
Interest expense	3,000
Income before tax	$ 11,000
Income tax expense	5,000
Net income	$ 6,000

Required

1. Prepare the Operating Activities section of the statement of cash flows using the direct method.
2. What does the use of the direct method reveal about a company that the indirect method does not?

LO5   **Exercise 12-7** Determination of Missing Amounts—Cash Flow from Operating Activities

The computation of cash provided by operating activities requires analysis of the noncash current asset and current liability accounts. Determine the missing amounts for each of the following independent cases:

Case 1

Accounts receivable, beginning of year	$150,000
Accounts receivable, end of year	100,000
Credit sales for the year	175,000
Cash sales for the year	60,000
Write-offs of uncollectible accounts	35,000
Total cash collections for the year (from cash sales and collections on account)	?

Case 2

Inventory, beginning of year	$ 80,000
Inventory, end of year	55,000
Accounts payable, beginning of year	25,000
Accounts payable, end of year	15,000
Cost of goods sold	175,000
Cash payments for inventory (assume all purchases of inventory are on account)	?

Case 3

Prepaid insurance, beginning of year	$ 17,000
Prepaid insurance, end of year	20,000
Insurance expense	15,000
Cash paid for new insurance policies	?

Case 4

Income taxes payable, beginning of year	$ 95,000
Income taxes payable, end of year	115,000
Income tax expense	300,000
Cash payments for taxes	?

LO5   **Exercise 12-8** Dividends on the Statement of Cash Flows

The following selected account balances are available from the records of Lewistown Company:

	December 31	
	2007	**2006**
Dividends payable	$ 30,000	$ 20,000
Retained earnings	375,000	250,000

Other information available for 2007 follows:

a. Lewistown reported $285,000 of net income for the year.
b. It declared and distributed a stock dividend of $50,000 during the year.
c. It declared cash dividends at the end of each quarter and paid them within the next 30 days of the following quarter.

Required

1. Determine the amount of cash dividends *paid* during the year for presentation in the Financing Activities section of the statement of cash flows.
2. Should the stock dividend described in part (b) appear on a statement of cash flows? Explain your answer.

LO6   **Exercise 12-9** Adjustments to Net Income with the Indirect Method

Assume that a company uses the indirect method to prepare the Operating Activities section of the statement of cash flows. For each of the following items, fill in the blank to indicate whether it would be added to net income (A), deducted from net income (D), or not reported in this section of the statement under the indirect method (NR).

  _____   1. Depreciation expense
  _____   2. Gain on sale of used delivery truck
  _____   3. Bad debts expense

(continued)

———— 4. Increase in accounts payable
———— 5. Purchase of new delivery truck
———— 6. Loss on retirement of bonds
———— 7. Increase in prepaid rent
———— 8. Decrease in inventory
———— 9. Issuance of note payable due in three years
———— 10. Amortization of patents

LO6

Exercise 12-10 Operating Activities Section—Indirect Method

The following account balances for the noncash current assets and current liabilities of Suffolk Company are available:

	December 31	
	2007	2006
Accounts receivable	$43,000	$35,000
Inventory	30,000	40,000
Prepaid rent	17,000	15,000
Totals	$90,000	$90,000
Accounts payable	$26,000	$19,000
Income taxes payable	6,000	10,000
Interest payable	15,000	12,000
Totals	$47,000	$41,000

Net income for 2007 is $40,000. Depreciation expense is $20,000. Assume that all sales and all purchases are on account.

Required
1. Prepare the Operating Activities section of the statement of cash flows using the indirect method.
2. Provide a brief explanation as to why cash flow from operating activities is more or less than the net income of the period.

LO7

Exercise 12-11 Cash Flow Adequacy

On its most recent statement of cash flows, a company reported net cash provided by operating activities of $12,000,000. Its capital expenditures for the same year were $2,000,000. A note to the financial statements indicated that the total amount of debt that would mature over the next five years was $20,000,000.

Required
1. Compute the company's cash flow adequacy ratio.
2. If you were a banker and were considering loaning money to this company, why would you be interested in knowing its cash flow adequacy ratio? Would you feel comfortable making a loan based on the ratio you computed in (1) above? Explain your answer.

MULTI-CONCEPT EXERCISES

LO2,3

Exercise 12-12 Classification of Activities

Use the following legend to indicate how each of the following transactions would be reported on the statement of cash flows (assume that the stocks and bonds of other companies are classified as long-term investments):

II = Inflow from investing activities
OI = Outflow from investing activities
IF = Inflow from financing activities
OF = Outflow from financing activities
CE = Classified as a cash equivalent and included with cash for purposes of preparing the statement of cash flows

HOMEWORK

_____ 1. Purchased a six-month certificate of deposit.
_____ 2. Purchased a 60-day Treasury bill.
_____ 3. Issued 1,000 shares of common stock.
_____ 4. Purchased 1,000 shares of stock in another company.
_____ 5. Purchased 1,000 shares of its own stock to be held in the treasury.
_____ 6. Invested $1,000 in a money market fund.
_____ 7. Sold 500 shares of stock of another company.
_____ 8. Purchased 20-year bonds of another company.
_____ 9. Issued 30-year bonds.
_____ 10. Repaid a six-month bank loan.

LO3,5 **Exercise 12-13** Classification of Activities

Use the following legend to indicate how each of the following transactions would be reported on the statement of cash flows (assume that the company uses the direct method in the Operating Activities section):

IO = Inflow from operating activities
OO = Outflow from operating activities
II = Inflow from investing activities
OI = Outflow from investing activities
IF = Inflow from financing activities
OF = Outflow from financing activities
NR = Not reported in the body of the statement of cash flows but included in a supplemental schedule

_____ 1. Collected $10,000 in cash from customers' open accounts for the period.
_____ 2. Paid one of the company's inventory suppliers $500 in settlement of an open account.
_____ 3. Purchased a new copier for $6,000; signed a 90-day note payable.
_____ 4. Issued bonds at face value of $100,000.
_____ 5. Made $23,200 in cash sales for the week.
_____ 6. Purchased an empty lot adjacent to the factory for $50,000. The seller of the land agrees to accept a five-year promissory note as consideration.
_____ 7. Renewed the property insurance policy for another six months. Cash of $1,000 is paid for the renewal.
_____ 8. Purchased a machine for $10,000.
_____ 9. Paid cash dividends of $2,500.
_____ 10. Reclassified as short-term a long-term note payable of $5,000 that is due within the next year.
_____ 11. Purchased 500 shares of the company's own stock on the open market for $4,000.
_____ 12. Sold 500 shares of Nike stock for book value of $10,000 (they had been classified as long-term investments).

LO3,6 **Exercise 12-14** Long-Term Assets on the Statement of Cash Flows—Indirect Method

The following account balances are taken from the records of Martin Corp. for the past two years:

	December 31	
	2007	**2006**
Plant and equipment	$750,000	$500,000
Accumulated depreciation	160,000	200,000
Patents	92,000	80,000
Retained earnings	825,000	675,000

Other information available for 2007 follows:

a. Net income for the year was $200,000.
b. Depreciation expense on plant and equipment was $50,000.
c. Plant and equipment with an original cost of $150,000 were sold for $64,000 (you will need to determine the book value of the assets sold).
d. Amortization expense on patents was $8,000.
e. Both new plant and equipment and patents were purchased for cash during the year.

Required

Indicate, with amounts, how all items related to these long-term assets would be reported in the 2007 statement of cash flows, including any adjustments in the Operating Activities section of the statement. Assume that Martin uses the indirect method.

LO1,5   **Exercise 12-15** Income Statement, Statement of Cash Flows (Direct Method), and Balance Sheet

The following events occurred at Handsome Hounds Grooming Company during its first year of business:

a. To establish the company, the two owners contributed a total of $50,000 in exchange for common stock.
b. Grooming service revenue for the first year amounted to $150,000, of which $40,000 was on account.
c. Customers owe $10,000 at the end of the year from the services provided on account.
d. At the beginning of the year, a storage building was rented. The company was required to sign a three-year lease for $12,000 per year and make a $2,000 refundable security deposit. The first year's lease payment and the security deposit were paid at the beginning of the year.
e. At the beginning of the year, the company purchased a patent at a cost of $100,000 for a revolutionary system to be used for dog grooming. The patent is expected to be useful for 10 years. The company paid 20% down in cash and signed a four-year note at the bank for the remainder.
f. Operating expenses, including amortization of the patent and rent on the storage building, totaled $80,000 for the first year. No expenses were accrued or unpaid at the end of the year.
g. The company declared and paid a $20,000 cash dividend at the end of the first year.

Required

1. Prepare an income statement for the first year.
2. Prepare a statement of cash flows for the first year, using the direct method in the Operating Activities section.
3. Did the company generate more or less cash flow from operations than it earned in net income? Explain why there is a difference.
4. Prepare a balance sheet as of the end of the first year.

PROBLEMS

LO6   **Problem 12-1** Statement of Cash Flows—Indirect Method

The following balances are available for Chrisman Company:

	December 31	
	2007	**2006**
Cash	$ 8,000	$ 10,000
Accounts receivable	20,000	15,000
Inventory	15,000	25,000
Prepaid rent	9,000	6,000
Land	75,000	75,000
Plant and equipment	400,000	300,000
Accumulated depreciation	(65,000)	(30,000)
Totals	$462,000	$401,000
Accounts payable	$ 12,000	$ 10,000
Income taxes payable	3,000	5,000
Short-term notes payable	35,000	25,000
Bonds payable	75,000	100,000
Common stock	200,000	150,000
Retained earnings	137,000	111,000
Totals	$462,000	$401,000

Bonds were retired during 2007 at face value, plant and equipment were acquired for cash, and common stock was issued for cash. Depreciation expense for the year was $35,000. Net income was reported at $26,000.

Required

1. Prepare a statement of cash flows for 2007, using the indirect method in the Operating Activities section.
2. Did Chrisman generate sufficient cash from operations to pay for its investing activities? How did it generate cash other than from operations? Explain your answers.

LO8 **Problem 12-2** Statement of Cash Flows Using a Work Sheet—Indirect Method (Appendix)

Refer to all of the facts in Problem 12-1.

Required

1. Using the format in the chapter's appendix, prepare a statement of cash flows work sheet.
2. Prepare a statement of cash flows for 2007, using the indirect method in the Operating Activities section.
3. Did Chrisman generate sufficient cash from operations to pay for its investing activities? How did it generate cash other than from operations? Explain your answers.

LO5 **Problem 12-3** Statement of Cash Flows—Direct Method

Peoria Corp. has just completed another very successful year, as indicated by the following income statement:

	For the Year Ended December 31, 2007
Sales revenue	$1,250,000
Cost of goods sold	700,000
Gross profit	$ 550,000
Operating expenses	150,000
Income before interest and taxes	$ 400,000
Interest expense	25,000
Income before taxes	$ 375,000
Income tax expense	150,000
Net income	$ 225,000

Presented below are comparative balance sheets:

	December 31	
	2007	2006
Cash	$ 52,000	$ 90,000
Accounts receivable	180,000	130,000
Inventory	230,000	200,000
Prepayments	15,000	25,000
Total current assets	$ 477,000	$ 445,000
Land	$ 750,000	$ 600,000
Plant and equipment	700,000	500,000
Accumulated depreciation	(250,000)	(200,000)
Total long-term assets	$1,200,000	$ 900,000
Total assets	$1,677,000	$1,345,000
Accounts payable	$ 130,000	$ 148,000
Other accrued liabilities	68,000	63,000
Income taxes payable	90,000	110,000
Total current liabilities	$ 288,000	$ 321,000
Long-term bank loan payable	$ 350,000	$ 300,000
Common stock	$ 550,000	$ 400,000
Retained earnings	489,000	324,000
Total stockholders' equity	$1,039,000	$ 724,000
Total liabilities and stockholders' equity	$1,677,000	$1,345,000

Other information follows:

a. Dividends of $60,000 were declared and paid during the year.
b. Operating expenses include $50,000 of depreciation.
c. Land and plant and equipment were acquired for cash, and additional stock was issued for cash. Cash was also received from additional bank loans.

The president has asked you some questions about the year's results. She is very impressed with the profit margin of 18% (net income divided by sales revenue). She is bothered, however, by the decline in the cash balance during the year. One of the conditions of the existing bank loan is that the company maintain a minimum cash balance of $50,000.

Required
1. Prepare a statement of cash flows for 2007, using the direct method in the Operating Activities section.
2. On the basis of your statement in requirement (1), draft a brief memo to the president to explain why cash decreased during such a profitable year. Include in your explanation any recommendations for improving the company's cash flow in future years.

LO6   **Problem 12-4** Statement of Cash Flows—Indirect Method

Refer to all of the facts in Problem 12-3.

Required
1. Prepare a statement of cash flows for 2007, using the indirect method in the Operating Activities section.
2. On the basis of your statement in requirement (1), draft a brief memo to the president to explain why cash decreased during such a profitable year. Include in your explanation any recommendations for improving the company's cash flow in future years.

LO8   **Problem 12-5** Statement of Cash Flows Using a Work Sheet—Indirect Method (Appendix)

Refer to all of the facts in Problem 12-3.

Required
1. Using the format in the chapter's appendix, prepare a statement of cash flows work sheet.
2. Prepare a statement of cash flows for 2007, using the indirect method in the Operating Activities section.
3. On the basis of your statement in requirement (2), draft a brief memo to the president to explain why cash decreased during such a profitable year. Include in your explanation any recommendations for improving the company's cash flow in future years.

LO5   **Problem 12-6** Statement of Cash Flows—Direct Method

The income statement for Astro Inc. for 2007 follows:

	For the Year Ended December 31, 2007
Sales revenue	$ 500,000
Cost of goods sold	400,000
Gross profit	$ 100,000
Operating expenses	180,000
Loss before interest and taxes	$ (80,000)
Interest expense	20,000
Net loss	$(100,000)

Presented below are comparative balance sheets:

	December 31	
	2007	2006
Cash	$ 95,000	$ 80,000
Accounts receivable	50,000	75,000
Inventory	100,000	150,000
Prepayments	55,000	45,000
Total current assets	$ 300,000	$ 350,000

	December 31	
	2007	**2006**
Land	$ 475,000	$ 400,000
Plant and equipment	870,000	800,000
Accumulated depreciation	(370,000)	(300,000)
Total long-term assets	$ 975,000	$ 900,000
Total assets	$1,275,000	$1,250,000
Accounts payable	$ 125,000	$ 100,000
Other accrued liabilities	35,000	45,000
Interest payable	15,000	10,000
Total current liabilities	$ 175,000	$ 155,000
Long-term bank loan payable	$ 340,000	$ 250,000
Common stock	$ 450,000	$ 400,000
Retained earnings	310,000	445,000
Total stockholders' equity	$ 760,000	$ 845,000
Total liabilities and stockholders' equity	$1,275,000	$1,250,000

Other information follows:

a. Dividends of $35,000 were declared and paid during the year.
b. Operating expenses include $70,000 of depreciation.
c. Land and plant and equipment were acquired for cash, and additional stock was issued for cash. Cash was also received from additional bank loans.

The president has asked you some questions about the year's results. He is disturbed with the $100,000 net loss for the year. He notes, however, that the cash position at the end of the year is improved. He is confused about what appear to be conflicting signals: "How could we have possibly added to our bank accounts during such a terrible year of operations?"

Required
1. Prepare a statement of cash flows for 2007, using the direct method in the Operating Activities section.
2. On the basis of your statement in requirement (1), draft a brief memo to the president to explain why cash increased during such an unprofitable year. Include in your memo your recommendations for improving the company's bottom line.

LO6   **Problem 12-7** Statement of Cash Flows—Indirect Method

Refer to all of the facts in Problem 12-6.

Required
1. Prepare a statement of cash flows for 2007, using the indirect method in the Operating Activities section.
2. On the basis of your statement in requirement (1), draft a brief memo to the president to explain why cash increased during such an unprofitable year. Include in your memo your recommendations for improving the company's bottom line.

LO8   **Problem 12-8** Statement of Cash Flows Using a Work Sheet—Indirect Method (Appendix)

Refer to all of the facts in Problem 12-6.

Required
1. Using the format in the chapter's appendix, prepare a statement of cash flows work sheet.
2. Prepare a statement of cash flows for 2007, using the indirect method in the Operating Activities section.
3. On the basis of your statement in requirement (2), draft a brief memo to the president to explain why cash increased during such an unprofitable year. Include in your memo your recommendations for improving the company's bottom line.

LO6   **Problem 12-9** Year-End Balance Sheet and Statement of Cash Flows—Indirect Method

The balance sheet of Terrier Company at the end of 2006 is presented here, along with certain other information for 2007:

	December 31, 2006
Cash	$ 140,000
Accounts receivable	155,000
Total current assets	$ 295,000
Land	$ 300,000
Plant and equipment	500,000
Accumulated depreciation	(150,000)
Investments	100,000
Total long-term assets	$ 750,000
Total assets	$1,045,000
Current liabilities	$ 205,000
Bonds payable	$ 300,000
Common stock	$ 400,000
Retained earnings	140,000
Total stockholders' equity	$ 540,000
Total liabilities and stockholders' equity	$1,045,000

Other information follows:

a. Net income for 2007 was $70,000.
b. Included in operating expenses was $20,000 in depreciation.
c. Cash dividends of $25,000 were declared and paid.
d. An additional $150,000 of bonds was issued for cash.
e. Common stock of $50,000 was purchased for cash and retired.
f. Cash purchases of plant and equipment during the year were $200,000.
g. An additional $100,000 of bonds was issued in exchange for land.
h. Sales exceeded cash collections on account during the year by $10,000. All sales are on account.
i. The amount of current liabilities remained unchanged during the year.

Required

1. Prepare a statement of cash flows for 2007, using the indirect method in the Operating Activities section. Include a supplemental schedule for noncash activities.
2. Prepare a balance sheet at December 31, 2007.
3. Provide a possible explanation as to why Terrier decided to issue additional bonds for cash during 2007.

LO8   **Problem 12-10** Statement of Cash Flows Using a Work Sheet—Indirect Method (Appendix)

Refer to all of the facts in Problem 12-9.

Required

1. Prepare a balance sheet at December 31, 2007.
2. Using the format in the chapter's appendix, prepare a statement of cash flows work sheet.
3. Prepare a statement of cash flows for 2007, using the indirect method in the Operating Activities section.
4. Provide a possible explanation as to why Terrier decided to issue additional bonds for cash during 2007.

MULTI-CONCEPT PROBLEMS

LO4,5

Problem 12-11 Statement of Cash Flows—Direct Method

Glendive Corp. is in the process of preparing its statement of cash flows for the year ended June 30, 2007. An income statement for the year and comparative balance sheets follow:

	For the Year Ended June 30, 2007
Sales revenue	$550,000
Cost of goods sold	350,000
Gross profit	$200,000
General and administrative expenses	$ 55,000
Depreciation expense	75,000
Loss on sale of plant assets	5,000
Total expenses and losses	$135,000
Income before interest and taxes	$ 65,000
Interest expense	15,000
Income before taxes	$ 50,000
Income tax expense	17,000
Net income	$ 33,000

	June 30 2007	2006
Cash	$ 31,000	$ 40,000
Accounts receivable	90,000	75,000
Inventory	80,000	95,000
Prepaid rent	12,000	16,000
Total current assets	$213,000	$226,000
Land	$250,000	$170,000
Plant and equipment	750,000	600,000
Accumulated depreciation	(310,000)	(250,000)
Total long-term assets	$690,000	$520,000
Total assets	$903,000	$746,000
Accounts payable	$155,000	$148,000
Other accrued liabilities	32,000	26,000
Income taxes payable	8,000	10,000
Total current liabilities	$195,000	$184,000
Long-term bank loan payable	$100,000	$130,000
Common stock	$350,000	$200,000
Retained earnings	258,000	232,000
Total stockholders' equity	$608,000	$432,000
Total liabilities and stockholders' equity	$903,000	$746,000

Dividends of $7,000 were declared and paid during the year. New plant assets were purchased for $195,000 in cash during the year. Also, land was purchased for cash. Plant assets were sold during the year for $25,000 in cash. The original cost of the assets sold was $45,000, and their book value was $30,000. Additional stock was issued for cash, and a portion of the bank loan was repaid.

Required
1. Prepare a statement of cash flows, using the direct method in the Operating Activities section.
2. Evaluate the following statement: "Whether a company uses the direct or the indirect method to report cash flows from operations is irrelevant because the amount of cash flow from operating activities is the same regardless of which method is used."

LO4,6

Problem 12-12 Statement of Cash Flows—Indirect Method

Refer to all of the facts in Problem 12-11.

Required
1. Prepare a statement of cash flows for 2007, using the indirect method in the Operating Activities section.
2. Evaluate the following statement: "Whether a company uses the direct or indirect method to report cash flows from operations is irrelevant because the amount of cash flow from operating activities is the same regardless of which method is used."

LO2,5 **Problem 12-13** Statement of Cash Flows—Direct Method

Lang Company has not yet prepared a formal statement of cash flows for 2007. Comparative balance sheets as of December 31, 2007 and 2006, and a statement of income and retained earnings for the year ended December 31, 2007, follow:

Lang Company
Balance Sheet
December 31

(thousands omitted)

Assets	2007	2006
Current assets:		
Cash	$ 60	$ 100
U.S. Treasury bills (six-month)	–0–	50
Accounts receivable	610	500
Inventory	720	600
Total current assets	$1,390	$1,250
Long-term assets:		
Land	$ 80	$ 70
Buildings and equipment	710	600
Accumulated depreciation	(180)	(120)
Patents (less amortization)	105	130
Total long-term assets	$ 715	$ 680
Total assets	$2,105	$1,930

Liabilities and Owners' Equity	2007	2006
Current liabilities:		
Accounts payable	$ 360	$ 300
Taxes payable	25	20
Notes payable	400	400
Total current liabilities	$ 785	$ 720
Term notes payable—due 2011	200	200
Total liabilities	$ 985	$ 920
Owners' equity:		
Common stock outstanding	$ 830	$ 700
Retained earnings	290	310
Total owners' equity	$1,120	$1,010
Total liabilities and owners' equity	$2,105	$1,930

Lang Company
Statement of Income and Retained Earnings
For the Year Ended December 31, 2007

(thousands omitted)

Sales		$2,408
Less expenses and interest:		
Cost of goods sold	$1,100	
Salaries and benefits	850	
Heat, light, and power	75	
Depreciation	60	
Property taxes	18	
Patent amortization	25	
Miscellaneous expense	10	
Interest	55	2,193
Net income before income taxes		$ 215
Income taxes		105
Net income		$ 110
Retained earnings—January 1, 2007		310
		$ 420
Stock dividend distributed		130
Retained earnings—December 31, 2007		$ 290

Required

1. For purposes of a statement of cash flows, are the U.S. Treasury bills cash equivalents? If not, how should they be classified? Explain your answers.

2. Prepare a statement of cash flows for 2007, using the direct method in the Operating Activities section.   (CMA adapted)

ALTERNATE PROBLEMS

LO6   **Problem 12-1A** Statement of Cash Flows—Indirect Method

The following balances are available for Madison Company:

	December 31	
	2007	**2006**
Cash	$ 12,000	$ 10,000
Accounts receivable	10,000	12,000
Inventory	8,000	7,000
Prepaid rent	1,200	1,000
Land	75,000	75,000
Plant and equipment	200,000	150,000
Accumulated depreciation	(75,000)	(25,000)
Totals	$231,200	$230,000
Accounts payable	$ 15,000	$ 15,000
Income taxes payable	2,500	2,000
Short-term notes payable	20,000	22,500
Bonds payable	75,000	50,000
Common stock	100,000	100,000
Retained earnings	18,700	40,500
Totals	$231,200	$230,000

Bonds were issued during 2007 at face value, and plant and equipment were acquired for cash. Depreciation expense for the year was $50,000. A net loss of $21,800 was reported.

Required
1. Prepare a statement of cash flows for 2007, using the indirect method in the Operating Activities section.
2. Explain briefly how Madison was able to increase its cash balance during a year in which it incurred a net loss.

LO8   **Problem 12-2A** Statement of Cash Flows Using a Work Sheet—Indirect Method (Appendix)

Refer to all of the facts in Problem 12-1A.

Required
1. Using the format in the chapter's appendix, prepare a statement of cash flows work sheet.
2. Prepare a statement of cash flows for 2007, using the indirect method in the Operating Activities section.
3. Explain briefly how Madison was able to increase its cash balance during a year in which it incurred a net loss.

LO5   **Problem 12-3A** Statement of Cash Flows—Direct Method

Wabash Corp. has just completed another very successful year, as indicated by the following income statement:

	For the Year Ended December 31, 2007
Sales revenue	$2,460,000
Cost of goods sold	1,400,000
Gross profit	$1,060,000
Operating expenses	460,000
Income before interest and taxes	$ 600,000
Interest expense	100,000
Income before taxes	$ 500,000
Income tax expense	150,000
Net income	$ 350,000

The following are comparative balance sheets:

	December 31	
	2007	**2006**
Cash	$ 140,000	$ 210,000
Accounts receivable	60,000	145,000
Inventory	200,000	180,000
Prepayments	15,000	25,000
Total current assets	$ 415,000	$ 560,000
Land	$ 600,000	$ 700,000
Plant and equipment	850,000	600,000
Accumulated depreciation	(225,000)	(200,000)
Total long-term assets	$1,225,000	$1,100,000
Total assets	$1,640,000	$1,660,000
Accounts payable	$ 140,000	$ 120,000
Other accrued liabilities	50,000	55,000
Income taxes payable	80,000	115,000
Total current liabilities	$ 270,000	$ 290,000
Long-term bank loan payable	$ 200,000	$ 250,000
Common stock	$ 450,000	$ 400,000
Retained earnings	720,000	720,000
Total stockholders' equity	$1,170,000	$1,120,000
Total liabilities and stockholders' equity	$1,640,000	$1,660,000

Other information follows:

a. Dividends of $350,000 were declared and paid during the year.
b. Operating expenses include $25,000 of depreciation.
c. Land was sold for its book value, and new plant and equipment was acquired for cash.
d. Part of the bank loan was repaid, and additional common stock was issued for cash.

The president has asked you some questions about the year's results. She is very impressed with the profit margin of 14% (net income divided by sales revenue). She is bothered, however, by the decline in the company's cash balance during the year. One of the conditions of the existing bank loan is that the company maintain a minimum cash balance of $100,000.

Required

1. Prepare a statement of cash flows for 2007, using the direct method in the Operating Activities section.
2. On the basis of your statement in requirement (1), draft a brief memo to the president to explain why cash decreased during such a profitable year. Include in your explanation any recommendations for improving the company's cash flow in future years.

LO6   **Problem 12-4A** Statement of Cash Flows—Indirect Method

Refer to all of the facts in Problem 12-3A.

Required

1. Prepare a statement of cash flows for 2007, using the indirect method in the Operating Activities section.
2. On the basis of your statement in requirement (1), draft a brief memo to the president to explain why cash decreased during such a profitable year. Include in your explanation any recommendations for improving the company's cash flow in future years.

LO8   **Problem 12-5A** Statement of Cash Flows Using a Work Sheet—Indirect Method (Appendix)

Refer to all of the facts in Problem 12-3A.

Required

1. Using the format in the chapter's appendix, prepare a statement of cash flows work sheet.
2. Prepare a statement of cash flows for 2007, using the indirect method in the Operating Activities section.
3. On the basis of your statement in requirement (2), draft a brief memo to the president to explain why cash decreased during such a profitable year. Include in your explanation any recommendations for improving the company's cash flow in future years.

HOMEWORK

LO5 **Problem 12-6A** Statement of Cash Flows—Direct Method

The income statement for Pluto Inc. for 2007 follows:

	For the Year Ended December 31, 2007
Sales revenue	$350,000
Cost of goods sold	150,000
Gross profit	$200,000
Operating expenses	250,000
Loss before interest and taxes	$(50,000)
Interest expense	10,000
Net loss	$(60,000)

Presented below are comparative balance sheets:

	December 31	
	2007	2006
Cash	$ 25,000	$ 10,000
Accounts receivable	30,000	80,000
Inventory	100,000	100,000
Prepayments	36,000	35,000
Total current assets	$191,000	$225,000
Land	$300,000	$200,000
Plant and equipment	500,000	250,000
Accumulated depreciation	(90,000)	(50,000)
Total long-term assets	$710,000	$400,000
Total assets	$901,000	$625,000
Accounts payable	$ 50,000	$ 10,000
Other accrued liabilities	40,000	20,000
Interest payable	22,000	12,000
Total current liabilities	$112,000	$ 42,000
Long-term bank loan payable	$450,000	$100,000
Common stock	$300,000	$300,000
Retained earnings	39,000	183,000
Total stockholders' equity	$339,000	$483,000
Total liabilities and stockholders' equity	$901,000	$625,000

Other information follows:

a. Dividends of $84,000 were declared and paid during the year.
b. Operating expenses include $40,000 of depreciation.
c. Land and plant and equipment were acquired for cash. Cash was received from additional bank loans.

The president has asked you some questions about the year's results. He is disturbed with the net loss of $60,000 for the year. He notes, however, that the cash position at the end of the year is improved. He is confused about what appear to be conflicting signals: "How could we have possibly added to our bank accounts during such a terrible year of operations?"

Required

1. Prepare a statement of cash flows for 2007, using the direct method in the Operating Activities section.
2. On the basis of your statement in requirement (1), draft a brief memo to the president to explain why cash increased during such an unprofitable year. Include in your memo your recommendations for improving the company's bottom line.

LO6 **Problem 12-7A** Statement of Cash Flows—Indirect Method

Refer to all of the facts in Problem 12-6A.

Required

1. Prepare a statement of cash flows for 2007, using the indirect method in the Operating Activities section.

(continued)

2. On the basis of your statement in requirement (1), draft a brief memo to the president to explain why cash increased during such an unprofitable year. Include in your memo your recommendations for improving the company's bottom line.

LO8   **Problem 12-8A** Statement of Cash Flows Using a Work Sheet—Indirect Method (Appendix)

Refer to all of the facts in Problem 12-6A.

Required

1. Using the format in the chapter's appendix, prepare a statement of cash flows work sheet.
2. Prepare a statement of cash flows for 2007, using the indirect method in the Operating Activities section.
3. On the basis of your statement in requirement (2), draft a brief memo to the president to explain why cash increased during such an unprofitable year. Include in your memo your recommendations for improving the company's bottom line.

LO6   **Problem 12-9A** Year-End Balance Sheet and Statement of Cash Flows—Indirect Method

The balance sheet of Poodle Company at the end of 2006 is presented below along with certain other information for 2007:

	December 31, 2006
Cash	$ 155,000
Accounts receivable	140,000
Total current assets	$ 295,000
Land	$ 100,000
Plant and equipment	700,000
Accumulated depreciation	(175,000)
Investments	125,000
Total long-term assets	$ 750,000
Total assets	$1,045,000
Current liabilities	$ 325,000
Bonds payable	$ 100,000
Common stock	$ 500,000
Retained earnings	120,000
Total stockholders' equity	$ 620,000
Total liabilities and stockholders' equity	$1,045,000

Other information follows:

a. Net income for 2007 was $50,000.
b. Included in operating expenses was $25,000 in depreciation.
c. Cash dividends of $40,000 were declared and paid.
d. An additional $50,000 of common stock was issued for cash.
e. Bonds payable of $100,000 were purchased for cash and retired at no gain or loss.
f. Cash purchases of plant and equipment during the year were $60,000.
g. An additional $200,000 of land was acquired in exchange for a long-term note payable.
h. Sales exceeded cash collections on account during the year by $15,000. All sales are on account.
i. The amount of current liabilities decreased by $20,000 during the year.

Required

1. Prepare a statement of cash flows for 2007, using the indirect method in the Operating Activities section. Include a supplemental schedule for noncash activities.
2. Prepare a balance sheet at December 31, 2007.
3. What primary uses did Poodle make of the cash it generated from operating activities?

LO8   **Problem 12-10A** Statement of Cash Flows Using a Work Sheet—Indirect Method (Appendix)

Refer to all of the facts in Problem 12-9A.

Required

1. Prepare a balance sheet at December 31, 2007.
2. Using the format in the chapter's appendix, prepare a statement of cash flows work sheet.

3. Prepare a statement of cash flows for 2007, using the indirect method in the Operating Activities section.
4. Provide a possible explanation as to why Poodle decided to purchase and retire bonds during 2007.

ALTERNATE MULTI-CONCEPT PROBLEMS

LO4,5

Problem 12-11A Statement of Cash Flows—Direct Method

Bannack Corp. is in the process of preparing its statement of cash flows for the year ended June 30, 2007. An income statement for the year and comparative balance sheets follow:

	For the Year Ended June 30, 2007
Sales revenue	$400,000
Cost of goods sold	240,000
Gross profit	$160,000
General and administrative expenses	$ 40,000
Depreciation expense	80,000
Loss on sale of plant assets	10,000
Total expenses and losses	$130,000
Income before interest and taxes	$ 30,000
Interest expense	15,000
Income before taxes	$ 15,000
Income tax expense	5,000
Net income	$ 10,000

	June 30	
	2007	2006
Cash	$ 25,000	$ 40,000
Accounts receivable	80,000	69,000
Inventory	75,000	50,000
Prepaid rent	2,000	18,000
Total current assets	$182,000	$177,000
Land	$ 60,000	$150,000
Plant and equipment	575,000	500,000
Accumulated depreciation	(310,000)	(250,000)
Total long-term assets	$325,000	$400,000
Total assets	$507,000	$577,000
Accounts payable	$145,000	$140,000
Other accrued liabilities	50,000	45,000
Income taxes payable	5,000	15,000
Total current liabilities	$200,000	$200,000
Long-term bank loan payable	$ 75,000	$150,000
Common stock	$100,000	$100,000
Retained earnings	132,000	127,000
Total stockholders' equity	$232,000	$227,000
Total liabilities and stockholders' equity	$507,000	$577,000

Dividends of $5,000 were declared and paid during the year. New plant assets were purchased for $125,000 in cash during the year. Also, land was sold for cash at its book value. Plant assets were sold during the year for $20,000 in cash. The original cost of the assets sold was $50,000, and their book value was $30,000. A portion of the bank loan was repaid.

Required

1. Prepare a statement of cash flows for 2007, using the direct method in the Operating Activities section.

(continued)

2. Evaluate the following statement: "Whether a company uses the direct or the indirect method to report cash flows from operations is irrelevant because the amount of cash flow from operating activities is the same regardless of which method is used."

LO4,6　**Problem 12-12A** Statement of Cash Flows—Indirect Method

Refer to all of the facts in Problem 12-11A.

Required

1. Prepare a statement of cash flows for 2007, using the indirect method in the Operating Activities section.
2. Evaluate the following statement: "Whether a company uses the direct or the indirect method to report cash flows from operations is irrelevant because the amount of cash flow from operating activities is the same regardless of which method is used."

LO2,5　**Problem 12-13A** Statement of Cash Flows—Direct Method

Shepard Company has not yet prepared a formal statement of cash flows for 2007. Comparative balance sheets as of December 31, 2007 and 2006, and a statement of income and retained earnings for the year ended December 31, 2007, appear below and on the following page.

Shepard Company
Balance Sheet
December 31

(thousands omitted)

Assets	2007	2006
Current assets:		
Cash	$ 50	$ 75
U.S. Treasury bills (six-month)	25	0
Accounts receivable	125	200
Inventory	525	500
Total current assets	$ 725	$ 775
Long-term assets:		
Land	$ 100	$ 80
Buildings and equipment	510	450
Accumulated depreciation	(190)	(150)
Patents (less amortization)	90	110
Total long-term assets	$ 510	$ 490
Total assets	$1,235	$1,265

Liabilities and Owners' Equity		
Current liabilities:		
Accounts payable	$ 370	$ 330
Taxes payable	10	20
Notes payable	300	400
Total current liabilities	$ 680	$ 750
Term notes payable—due 2011	200	200
Total liabilities	$ 880	$ 950
Owners' equity:		
Common stock outstanding	$ 220	$ 200
Retained earnings	135	115
Total owners' equity	$ 355	$ 315
Total liabilities and owners' equity	$1,235	$1,265

(continued)

HOMEWORK

Shepard Company
Statement of Income and Retained Earnings
Year Ended December 31, 2007

(thousands omitted)

Sales		$1,416
Less expenses and interest:		
Cost of goods sold	$990	
Salaries and benefits	195	
Heat, light, and power	70	
Depreciation	40	
Property taxes	2	
Patent amortization	20	
Miscellaneous expense	2	
Interest	45	1,364
Net income before income taxes		$ 52
Income taxes		12
Net income		$ 40
Retained earnings—January 1, 2007		115
		$ 155
Stock dividend distributed		20
Retained earnings—December 31, 2007		$ 135

Required

1. For purposes of a statement of cash flows, are the U.S. Treasury bills cash equivalents? If not, how should they be classified? Explain your answers.
2. Prepare a statement of cash flows for 2007, using the direct method in the Operating Activities section. (CMA adapted)

DECISION CASES

LO3,4 **Decision Case 12-1** Comparing Two Companies in the Same Industry: Finish Line and Foot Locker

Refer to the statement of cash flows for both **Finish Line** and **Foot Locker** for the most recent year and any other pertinent information, reproduced at the back of this book.

Required

1. Which method, direct or indirect, does each company use in preparing the Operating Activities section of their statements of cash flows? Explain.
2. By what amount did net cash provided by operating activities increase or decrease from the prior year for each company? What is the largest adjustment to reconcile net income to net cash provided by operating activities for each company?
3. Did merchandise inventories increase or decrease during the most recent year for each company? What are logical reasons for those changes in inventory levels?
4. What amount did each company spend during the most recent year to acquire property and equipment? How does this amount compare with the amount each company spent in the prior year?
5. What is the primary source of financing for each of the two companies? Did either or both companies buy back some of their own shares during the most recent year? If so, what might be some of the reasons for doing this?

LO7 **Decision Case 12-2** Computing and Interpreting Foot Locker's Cash Flow Adequacy

Refer to **Foot Locker**'s statement of cash flows for the most recent year and any other pertinent information, reproduced at the back of this book.

Required

1. Compute the company's cash flow adequacy ratio for the most recent year.
2. What does the ratio computed in (1) above tell you?

MAKING FINANCIAL DECISIONS

LO1,5   **Decision Case 12-3** Dividend Decision and the Statement of Cash Flows—Direct Method

Bailey Corp. just completed the most profitable year in its 25-year history. Reported earnings of $1,020,000 on sales of $8,000,000 resulted in a very healthy profit margin of 12.75%. Each year before releasing the financial statements, the board of directors meets to decide on the amount of dividends to declare for the year. For each of the past nine years, the company has declared a dividend of $1 per share of common stock, which has been paid on January 15 of the following year.

Presented below are the income statement for the year and comparative balance sheets as of the end of the last two years.

	For the Year Ended December 31, 2007
Sales revenue	$8,000,000
Cost of goods sold	4,500,000
Gross profit	$3,500,000
Operating expenses	1,450,000
Income before interest and taxes	$2,050,000
Interest expense	350,000
Income before taxes	$1,700,000
Income tax expense (40%)	680,000
Net income	$1,020,000

	December 31	
	2007	2006
Cash	$ 480,000	$ 450,000
Accounts receivable	250,000	200,000
Inventory	750,000	600,000
Prepayments	60,000	75,000
Total current assets	$1,540,000	$1,325,000
Land	$3,255,000	$2,200,000
Plant and equipment	4,200,000	2,500,000
Accumulated depreciation	(1,250,000)	(1,000,000)
Long-term investments	500,000	900,000
Patents	650,000	750,000
Total long-term assets	$7,355,000	$5,350,000
Total assets	$8,895,000	$6,675,000
Accounts payable	$ 350,000	$ 280,000
Other accrued liabilities	285,000	225,000
Income taxes payable	170,000	100,000
Dividends payable	0	200,000
Notes payable due within next year	200,000	0
Total current liabilities	$1,005,000	$ 805,000
Long-term notes payable	$ 300,000	$ 500,000
Bonds payable	2,200,000	1,500,000
Total long-term liabilities	$2,500,000	$2,000,000
Common stock, $10 par	$2,500,000	$2,000,000
Retained earnings	2,890,000	1,870,000
Total stockholders' equity	$5,390,000	$3,870,000
Total liabilities and stockholders' equity	$8,895,000	$6,675,000

Additional information follows:

a. All sales are on account, as are all purchases.
b. Land was purchased through the issuance of bonds. Additional land (beyond the amount purchased through the issuance of bonds) was purchased for cash.
c. New plant and equipment were acquired during the year for cash. No plant assets were retired during the year. Depreciation expense is included in operating expenses.

HOMEWORK

d. Long-term investments were sold for cash during the year.

e. No new patents were acquired, and none were disposed of during the year. Amortization expense is included in operating expenses.

f. Notes payable due within the next year represents the amount reclassified from long-term to short-term.

g. Fifty thousand shares of common stock were issued during the year at par value.

As Bailey's controller, you have been asked to recommend to the board whether or not to declare a dividend this year and, if so, if the precedent of paying a $1 per share dividend can be maintained. The president is eager to keep the dividend at $1 in view of the successful year just completed. He is also concerned, however, about the effect of a dividend on the company's cash position. He is particularly concerned about the large amount of notes payable that comes due next year. He further notes the aggressive growth pattern in recent years, as evidenced this year by large increases in land and plant and equipment.

Required

1. Using the format in Exhibit 12-14, convert the income statement from an accrual basis to a cash basis.

2. Prepare a statement of cash flows, using the direct method in the Operating Activities section.

3. What do you recommend to the board of directors concerning the declaration of a cash dividend? Should the $1 per share dividend be declared? Should a smaller amount be declared? Should no dividend be declared? Support your answer with any necessary computations. Include in your response your concerns, from a cash flow perspective, about the following year.

LO1,6   **Decision Case 12-4** Equipment Replacement Decision and Cash Flows from Operations

Conrad Company has been in operation for four years. The company is pleased with the continued improvement in net income but is concerned about a lack of cash available to replace existing equipment. Land, buildings, and equipment were purchased at the beginning of Year 1. No subsequent fixed asset purchases have been made, but the president believes that equipment will need to be replaced in the near future. The following information is available (all amounts are in millions of dollars):

	Year of Operation			
	Year 1	**Year 2**	**Year 3**	**Year 4**
Net income (loss)	$(10)	$ (2)	$15	$20
Depreciation expense	30	25	15	14
Increase (decrease) in:				
Accounts receivable	32	5	12	20
Inventories	26	8	5	9
Prepayments	0	0	10	5
Accounts payable	15	3	(5)	(4)

Required

1. Compute the cash flow from operations for each of Conrad's first four years of operation.

2. Write a memo to the president explaining why the company is not generating sufficient cash from operations to pay for the replacement of equipment.

ETHICAL DECISION MAKING

LO1,6   **Decision Case 12-5** Loan Decision and the Statement of Cash Flows—Indirect Method

Mega Enterprises is in the process of negotiating an extension of its existing loan agreements with a major bank. The bank is particularly concerned with Mega's ability to generate sufficient cash flow from operating activities to meet the periodic principal and interest payments. In conjunction with the negotiations, the controller prepared the following statement of cash flows to present to the bank:

Mega Enterprises
Statement of Cash Flows
For the Year Ended December 31, 2007

(all amounts in millions of dollars)

Cash flows from operating activities

Net income	$ 65
Adjustments to reconcile net income to net cash provided by operating activities:	
Depreciation and amortization	56
Increase in accounts receivable	(19)
Decrease in inventory	27
Decrease in accounts payable	(42)
Increase in other accrued liabilities	18
Net cash provided by operating activities	$ 105

Cash flows from investing activities

Acquisitions of other businesses	$(234)
Acquisitions of plant and equipment	(125)
Sale of other businesses	300
Net cash used by investing activities	$ (59)

Cash flows from financing activities

Additional borrowings	$ 150
Repayments of borrowings	(180)
Cash dividends paid	(50)
Net cash used by financing activities	$ (80)
Net decrease in cash	$ (34)
Cash balance, January 1, 2007	42
Cash balance, December 31, 2007	$ 8

During 2007, Mega sold one of its businesses in California. A gain of $150 million was included in 2007 income as the difference between the proceeds from the sale of $450 million and the book value of the business of $300 million. The effect on the accounting equation of the transaction to record the sale is as follows (in millions of dollars):

Balance Sheet						Income Statement	
ASSETS		**=**	**LIABILITIES**	**+**	**STOCKHOLDERS' EQUITY**	**+**	**REVENUES − EXPENSES**
Cash	450						
California Properties	(300)					Gain on Sale	150

Required

1. Comment on the presentation of the sale of the California business on the statement of cash flows. Does the way in which the sale was reported violate generally accepted accounting principles? Regardless of whether it violates GAAP, does the way in which the transaction was reported on the statement result in a misstatement of the net decrease in cash for the period? Explain your answers.

2. Prepare a revised statement of cash flows for 2007, with the proper presentation of the sale of the California business.

3. Has the controller acted in an unethical manner in the way the sale was reported on the statement of cash flows? Explain your answer.

LO2,3   Decision Case 12-6 Cash Equivalents and the Statement of Cash Flows

In December 2007, Rangers Inc. invested $100,000 of idle cash in U.S. Treasury notes. The notes mature on October 1, 2008, at which time Rangers expects to redeem them at face value of $100,000. The treasurer believes that the notes should be classified as cash equivalents because of the plans to hold them to maturity and receive face value. He would also like to avoid presentation of the purchase as an investing activity because the company has made sizable capital expenditures during the year. The treasurer realizes that the decision about classification of the Treasury notes rests with you as controller.

HOMEWORK

Required

1. According to generally accepted accounting principles, how should the investment in U.S. Treasury notes be classified for purposes of preparing a statement of cash flows for the year ended December 31, 2007? Explain your answer.
2. If the notes are classified as an operating rather than an investing activity, is the information provided to outside readers free from bias? Explain.
3. As controller for Rangers, what would you do in this situation? What would you tell the treasurer?

SOLUTIONS TO KEY TERMS QUIZ

3	Statement of cash flows		7	Financing activities
4	Cash equivalent		6	Direct method
1	Operating activities		2	Indirect method
5	Investing activities			

CHAPTER

13

Financial Statement Analysis

Study Links

A Look at Previous Chapters
In Chapter 2, we introduced a few key financial ratios and saw the way that investors and creditors use them to better understand a company's financial statements. In many of the subsequent chapters, we introduced ratios relevant to the particular topic being discussed.

A Look at This Chapter
Ratio analysis is one important type of *analysis used to interpret financial statements*. In this chapter, we expand our discussion of ratio analysis and introduce other valuable techniques used by investors, creditors, and analysts in reaching informed decisions. We will find that ratios and other forms of analyses can provide additional insight beyond that available from merely reading the financial statements.

Learning Outcomes

After studying this chapter, you should be able to:

LO1 Explain the various limitations and considerations in financial statement analysis.

LO2 Use comparative financial statements to analyze a company over time (horizontal analysis).

LO3 Use common-size financial statements to compare various financial statement items (vertical analysis).

LO4 Compute and use various ratios to assess liquidity.

LO5 Compute and use various ratios to assess solvency.

LO6 Compute and use various ratios to assess profitability.

LO7 Explain how to report on and analyze other income statement items (Appendix).

© Michael Newman/PhotoEdit, Inc.

Wm. Wrigley Jr. Company

MAKING BUSINESS DECISIONS

Turn to the outside to grow the business. That was the decision the world's largest manufacturer of chewing and bubble gum made in 2005. Two of **Wrigley**'s brand names, Juicy Fruit® and Spearmint®, are among the most recognizable in the world and have heritages that go back more than 100 years. Wrigley did not stray too far from its core business in adding certain of the confectionary assets of **Kraft Foods** to its list of top performers. With the acquisition, Wrigley picked up brand names such as Altoids® and Life Savers®. One need look no further than the purchase price of $1.46 billion to know that Wrigley is serious about expanding its reach and capturing more of the world's market for confectionary products.

Undoubtedly, investors will closely scrutinize Wrigley's financial statements after this major acquisition. Will the 114-year-old company be able to improve upon its already impressive track record in recent years? Sales and earnings have grown steadily, with both reaching record levels in 2004. Most companies, and their stockholders, would be envious of this solid performance indicated by Wrigley's Financial Highlights reproduced here. A quick calculation shows a profit margin of around 14% in each of the last two years. Over 40% of those profits were returned to stockholders in the form of dividends. Few companies are able to report a return on equity of the 25% or more that Wrigley has consistently achieved in recent years.

What are the tools that investors will use to measure the success of Wrigley in the years after the Kraft acquisition? In earlier chapters, we looked at various ratios; in this last chapter, we will examine additional tools available to judge the financial health of a company. This chapter will answer these questions:

- What tools can be used to assess the performance of a company over time? (See pp. 616–620)
- How can common-size financial statements be used to assess a company's performance in any one period? (See pp. 621–622)
- What ratios are available to judge a company's liquidity, solvency, and profitability? (See pp. 623–637)

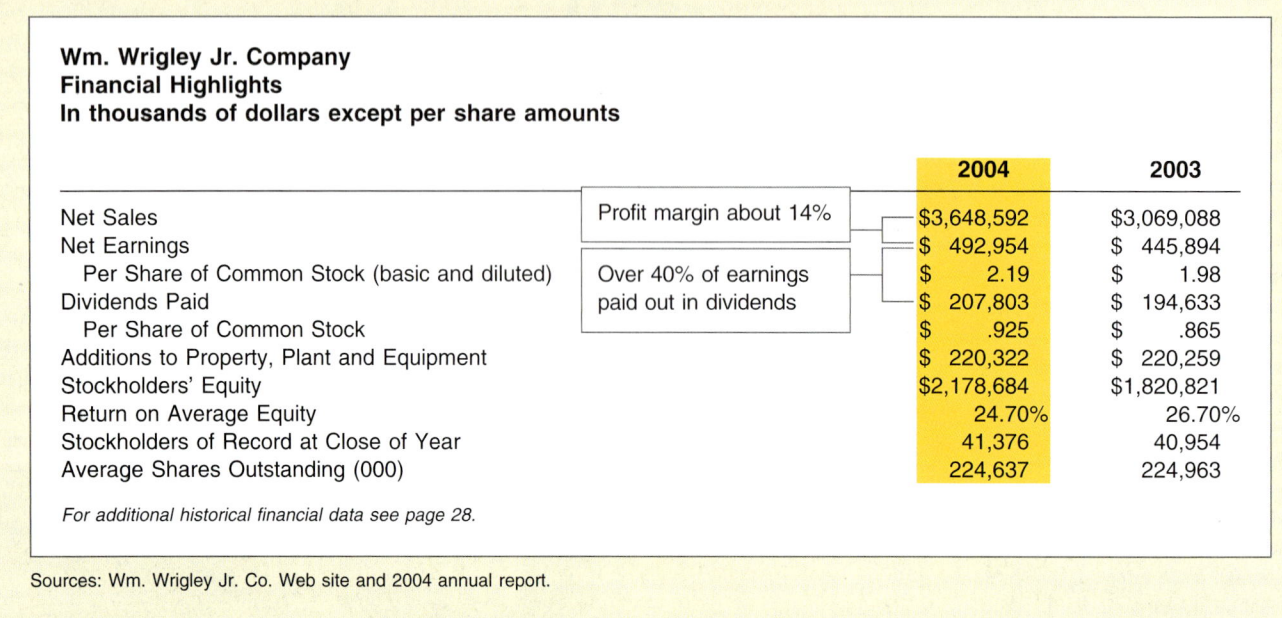

Wm. Wrigley Jr. Company
Financial Highlights
In thousands of dollars except per share amounts

			2004	2003
Net Sales	Profit margin about 14%		$3,648,592	$3,069,088
Net Earnings			$ 492,954	$ 445,894
Per Share of Common Stock (basic and diluted)	Over 40% of earnings paid out in dividends		$ 2.19	$ 1.98
Dividends Paid			$ 207,803	$ 194,633
Per Share of Common Stock			$ .925	$ .865
Additions to Property, Plant and Equipment			$ 220,322	$ 220,259
Stockholders' Equity			$2,178,684	$1,820,821
Return on Average Equity			24.70%	26.70%
Stockholders of Record at Close of Year			41,376	40,954
Average Shares Outstanding (000)			224,637	224,963

For additional historical financial data see page 28.

Sources: Wm. Wrigley Jr. Co. Web site and 2004 annual report.

Precautions in Statement Analysis

Various groups have different purposes for analyzing a company's financial statements. For example, a banker is primarily interested in the likelihood that a loan will be repaid. Certain ratios indicate the ability to repay principal and interest. A stockholder, on the other hand, is concerned with a fair return on the amount invested in the company. Again, certain ratios are helpful in assessing the return to the stockholder. The managers of a business are also interested in the tools of financial statement analysis because various outside groups judge managers by using certain key ratios. Fortunately, most financial statements provide information about financial performance. Publicly held corporations are required to include in their annual reports a section that reviews the past year, with management's comments on its performance as measured by selected ratios and other forms of analysis.

Before we turn to various techniques commonly used in the financial analysis of a company, it is important to understand some of the limitations and other considerations in statement analysis.

WATCH FOR ALTERNATIVE ACCOUNTING PRINCIPLES

LO1 Explain the various limitations and considerations in financial statement analysis.

Every set of financial statements is based on various assumptions. For example, a cost-flow method must be assumed in valuing inventory and recognizing cost of goods sold. The accountant chooses FIFO, LIFO, or one of the other acceptable methods. The analyst or other user finds this type of information in the notes to the financial statements. The selection of a particular inventory valuation method has a significant effect on certain key ratios. Recognition of the acceptable alternatives is especially important in comparing two or more companies. *Changes* in accounting methods, such as a change in the depreciation method, also make comparing results for a given company over time more difficult. Again, the reader must turn to the notes for information regarding these changes.

TAKE CARE WHEN MAKING COMPARISONS

Users of financial statements often place too much emphasis on summary indicators and key ratios, such as the current ratio and the earnings per share amount.

No single ratio is capable of telling the user everything there is to know about a particular company. The calculation of various ratios for a company is only a starting point. One technique we discuss is the comparison of ratios for different periods of time. Has the ratio gone up or down from last year? What is the percentage of increase or decrease in the ratio over the last five years? Recognizing trends in ratios is important in analyzing any company.

The potential investor must also recognize the need to compare one company with others in the same industry. For example, a particular measure of performance may cause an investor to conclude that the company is not operating efficiently. Comparison with an industry standard, however, might indicate that the ratio is normal for companies in that industry. Various organizations publish summaries of selected ratios for a sample of companies in the United States. The ratios are usually organized by industry. Dun & Bradstreet's *Industry Norms and Key Business Ratios,* for example, is an annual review that organizes companies into major industry segments and approximately 800 specific lines of business.

Although industry comparisons are useful, caution is necessary in interpreting the results of such analyses. Few companies in today's economy operate in a single industry. Exceptions exist, but most companies cross the boundaries of a single industry. *Conglomerates,* companies operating in more than one industry, present a special challenge to the analyst. Keep in mind also the point made earlier about alternative accounting methods. It is not unusual to find companies in the same industry using different inventory valuation techniques or depreciation methods.

Finally, many corporate income statements contain nonoperating items, such as extraordinary items, cumulative effects from accounting changes, and gains and losses from discontinued operations. When these items exist, the reader must exercise extra caution in making comparisons. To assess the future prospects of a group of companies, you may want to compare income statements *before* taking into account the effects these items have on income.

UNDERSTAND THE POSSIBLE EFFECTS OF INFLATION

Inflation, or an increase in the level of prices, is another important consideration in analyzing financial statements. The statements, to be used by outsiders, are based on historical costs and are not adjusted for the effects of increasing prices. For example, consider the following trend in a company's sales for the past three years:

	2007	2006	2005
Net sales	$121,000	$110,000	$100,000

As measured by the actual dollars of sales, sales have increased by 10% each year. Caution is necessary in concluding that the company is better off in each succeeding year because of the increase in sales *dollars.* Assume, for example, that 2005 sales of $100,000 are the result of selling 100,000 units at $1 each. Are 2006 sales of $110,000 the result of selling 110,000 units at $1 each or of selling 100,000 units at $1.10 each? Although on the surface it may seem unimportant which result accounts for the sales increase, the answer can have significant ramifications. If the company found it necessary to increase selling price to $1.10 in the face of increasing *costs,* it may be no better off than it was in 2005 in terms of gross profit. On the other hand, if the company is able to increase sales revenue by 10% primarily based on growth in unit sales, then its performance would be considered stronger than if the increase is merely due to a price increase. The point to be made is one of caution: published financial statements are stated in historical costs and therefore have not been adjusted for the effects of inflation.

Fortunately, inflation has been relatively subdued in the past several years. During the late 1970s, the FASB actually required a separate note in the financial statements to calculate the effects of inflation. The requirement was abandoned in the mid-1980s when inflation had subsided and the profession decided that the cost of providing inflation-adjusted information exceeded the benefits to the users.

Analysis of Comparative and Common-Size Statements

Horizontal analysis
A comparison of financial statement items over a period of time.

Vertical analysis
A comparison of various financial statement items within a single period with the use of common-size statements.

LO2 Use comparative financial statements to analyze a company over time (horizontal analysis).

We are now ready to analyze a set of financial statements. We will begin by looking at the comparative statements of a company for a two-year period. The analysis of the statements over a series of years is often called **horizontal analysis**. We will then see how the statements can be recast in what are referred to as *common-size statements*. The analysis of common-size statements is called **vertical analysis**. Finally, we will consider the use of a variety of ratios to analyze a company.

HORIZONTAL ANALYSIS

Comparative balance sheets for a hypothetical entity, Henderson Company, are presented in Exhibit 13-1. The increase or decrease in each of the major accounts on the balance sheet is shown in both absolute dollars and as a percentage. The base year for computing the percentage increase or decrease in each account is the first year, 2006, and is normally shown on the right side. By reading across from right to left (thus the term *horizontal analysis*), the analyst can quickly spot any unusual changes in accounts from the previous year. Three accounts stand out: ❶ Cash decreased by 76%, ❷ Inventory increased by 73%, and ❸ Accounts Payable increased by 70%. (These lines are also boldfaced for convenience.) Individually,

---

EXHIBIT 13-1 Comparative Balance Sheets—Horizontal Analysis

Read from earlier year to later year. Usually this is from right to left.

Henderson Company
Comparative Balance Sheets
December 31, 2007 and 2006
(all amounts In thousands of dollars)

The base year is normally on the right.

Dollar change from year to year.

Percentage change from one year to the next year.

In **horizontal analysis**, read right to left to compare one year's results with the next as a dollar amount of change and as a percentage of change from year to year.

	December 31 2007	December 31 2006	Increase (Decrease) Dollars	Increase (Decrease) Percent
Cash	$ 320	$ 1,350	$ (1,030) ❶	(76)%
Accounts receivable	5,500	4,500	1,000	22
Inventory	**4,750**	**2,750**	**2,000** ❷	**73**
Prepaid insurance	150	200	(50)	(25)
Total current assets	$10,720	$ 8,800	$ 1,920	22
Land	$ 2,000	$ 2,000	$ –0–	–0–
Buildings and equipment	6,000	4,500	1,500	33
Accumulated depreciation	(1,850)	(1,500)	(350)	(23)
Total long-term assets	$ 6,150	$ 5,000	$ 1,150	23
Total assets	$16,870	$13,800	$ 3,070	22
Accounts payable	$ 4,250	$ 2,500	$ 1,750 ❸	70
Taxes payable	2,300	2,100	200	10
Notes payable	600	800	(200)	(25)
Current portion of bonds	100	100	–0–	–0–
Total current liabilities	$ 7,250	$ 5,500	$ 1,750	32
Bonds payable	700	800	(100)	(13)
Total liabilities	$ 7,950	$ 6,300	$ 1,650	26
Preferred stock, $5 par	$ 500	$ 500	$ –0–	–0–
Common stock, $1 par	1,000	1,000	–0–	–0–
Retained earnings	7,420	6,000	1,420	24
Total stockholders' equity	$ 8,920	$ 7,500	$ 1,420	19
Total liabilities and stockholders' equity	$16,870	$13,800	$ 3,070	22

NOTE: Referenced amounts boldfaced for convenience.

each of these large changes is a red flag. Taken together, these changes send the financial statement user the warning that the business may be deteriorating. Each of these large changes should be investigated further.

Exhibit 13-2 shows comparative statements of income and retained earnings for Henderson for 2007 and 2006. At first glance, ❶ the 20% increase in sales to $24 million appears promising, but management was not able to limit the increase in either ❷ cost of goods sold or ❸ selling, general, and administrative expense to 20%. The analysis indicates that cost of goods sold increased by 29% and selling, general, and administrative expense increased by 50%. The increases in these two expenses more than offset the increase in sales and resulted in a ❹ decrease in operating income of 25%.

Companies that experience sales growth often become lax about controlling expenses. Their managements sometimes forget that it is the bottom line that counts, not the top line. Perhaps the salespeople are given incentives to increase sales without considering the costs of the sales. Maybe management is spending too much on overhead, including its own salaries. The owners of the business will have to address these concerns if they want to get a reasonable return on their investment.

Horizontal analysis can be extended to include more than two years of results. At a minimum, publicly held companies are required to include income statements and statements of cash flows for the three most recent years and balance sheets as of the end of the two most recent years. Many annual reports include, as supplementary information, financial summaries of operations for extended periods of time. As illustrated in Exhibit 13-3, for example, **Wrigley** includes an 11-year summary of selected financial data, such as net sales, dividends paid, return on average equity, and total assets. Note the increase in net sales in every year over the 11-year period. Also note, however, that Wrigley does not include

13-1 Real World Practice

Reading Finish Line's Annual Report

Refer to Finish Line's comparative balance sheets as reproduced at the end of the book. Compute the percentage increase or decrease in the following accounts: Merchandise inventories, net; Leasehold improvements; and Furniture, fixtures, and equipment. Why do you think all three of these accounts increased during the year?

EXHIBIT 13-2 Comparative Statements of Income and Retained Earnings—Horizontal Analysis

Henderson Company
Comparative Statements of Income and Retained Earnings
For the Years Ended December 31, 2007 and 2006
(all amounts in thousands of dollars)

	December 31		Increase (Decrease)		
	2007	2006	Dollars		Percent
Net sales	$24,000	$20,000	$ 4,000	❶	20%
Cost of goods sold	18,000	14,000	4,000	❷	29
Gross profit	$ 6,000	$ 6,000	$ –0–		–0–
Selling, general, and administrative					
expense	3,000	2,000	1,000	❸	50
Operating income	$ 3,000	$ 4,000	$(1,000)	❹	(25)
Interest expense	140	160	(20)		(13)
Income before tax	$ 2,860	$ 3,840	$ (980)		(26)
Income tax expense	1,140	1,540	(400)		(26)
Net income	$ 1,720	$ 2,300	$ (580)		(25)
Preferred dividends	50	50			
Income available to common	$ 1,670	$ 2,250			
Common dividends	250	250			
To retained earnings	$ 1,420	$ 2,000			
Retained earnings, 1/1	6,000	4,000			
Retained earnings, 12/31	$ 7,420	$ 6,000			

These three increases in revenue and expenses resulted in an operating income *decrease* of 25%.

NOTE: Referenced amounts boldfaced for convenience.

EXHIBIT 13-3	Wrigley Financial Summary

Selected Financial Data

In thousands of dollars and shares, except per share amounts, stockholders of record and employees

	2004	2003	2002	2001
OPERATING DATA				
Net Sales	$ 3,648,592	3,069,088	2,746,318	2,401,419
Cost of Sales	1,609,978	1,317,416	1,186,685	1,030,129
Income Taxes	227,542	205,647	181,896	164,380
Net Earnings*	492,954	445,894	401,525	362,986
Per Share of Common Stock (basic and diluted)	2.19	1.98	1.78	1.61
Dividends Paid	207,803	194,633	181,232	167,922
Per Share of Common Stock	.925	.865	.805	.745
As a Percent of Net Earnings	42%	44%	45%	46%
Dividends Declared Per Share of Common Stock	.940	.880	.820	.760
Average Shares Outstanding	224,637	224,963	225,145	225,349
OTHER FINANCIAL DATA				
Net Property, Plant and Equipment	$ 1,142,620	956,180	836,110	684,379
Total Assets	3,166,703	2,527,371	2,108,296	1,777,793
Working Capital	787,940	825,797	620,205	581,519
Stockholder's Equity	2,178,684	1,820,821	1,522,576	1,276,197
Return on Average Equity	24.7%	26.7%	28.7%	30.1%
Stockholders of Record at Close of Year	41,376	40,954	40,534	38,701
Employees at Close of Year	14,800	12,000	11,250	10,800
Market Price of Stock				
High	69.73	58.90	58.90	53.30
Low	55.23	51.05	44.21	42.94

> Net sales has increased each year for ten consecutive years.

*includes amounts related to factory closure — net gain of $6,763 or $.03 per share in 1998, and net costs of $2,145 or $.01 per share and $12,990 or $.06 per share in 1997 and 1996, respectively; and nonrecurring net gain on sale of Singapore property in 1994 of $24,766 or $.11 per share

in the summary the gross profit ratio (gross profit divided by net sales). A comparison of the trend in this ratio would help to determine if the company has effectively controlled the cost to manufacture its products. The summary does show that Wrigley has reported an increase in net earnings for nine consecutive years, an enviable record for any company.

Tracking items over a series of years, a practice called *trend analysis,* can be a very powerful tool for the analyst. Advanced statistical techniques are available for analyzing trends in financial data and, most important, for projecting those trends to future periods. Some of the techniques, such as time series analysis, have been used extensively in forecasting sales trends.

EXHIBIT 13-3	Wrigley Financial Summary (continued)

2000	1999	1998	1997	1996	1995	1994
2,126,114	2,045,227	1,990,286	1,923,963	1,835,987	1,754,931	1,596,551
932,802	923,631	894,988	892,751	859,414	820,478	737,239
150,370	136,247	136,378	122,614	128,840	126,492	122,746
328,942	308,183	304,501	271,626	230,272	223,739	230,533
1.45	1.33	1.31	1.17	.99	.96	.99
159,138	153,812	150,835	135,680	118,308	111,401	104,694
.701	.664	.650	.585	.510	.480	.450
48%	50%	50%	50%	51%	50%	45%
.701	.740	.655	.595	.510	.495	.470
227,037	231,722	231,928	231,928	231,966	232,132	232,716
607,034	599,140	520,090	430,474	388,149	347,491	289,420
1,574,740	1,547,745	1,520,855	1,343,126	1,233,543	1,099,219	978,834
540,505	551,921	624,546	571,857	511,272	458,683	413,414
1,132,897	1,138,775	1,157,032	985,379	897,431	796,852	688,470
29.0%	26.8%	28.4%	28.9%	27.2%	30.1%	36.5%
37,781	38,626	38,052	36,587	34,951	28,959	24,078
9,800	9,300	9,200	8,200	7,800	7,300	7,000
48.31	50.31	52.16	41.03	31.44	27.00	26.94
29.94	33.25	35.47	27.28	24.19	21.44	19.06

13-2 Real World Practice

Reading Wrigley's Annual Report

Refer to Wrigley's financial highlights in Exhibit 13-3 on pages 618–619. Compute the company's gross profit ratio for each of the 11 years. Is there a noticeable upward or downward trend in the ratio over this time period?

Historically, attention has focused on the balance sheet and income statement in analyzing a company's position and results of operation. Only recently have analysts and other users begun to appreciate the value in incorporating the statement of cash flows into their analyses.

Comparative statements of cash flows for Henderson appear in Exhibit 13-4. Henderson's financing activities remained constant over the two-year period, as indicated in that section of the statements. Each year the company paid $200,000 on notes, another $100,000 to retire bonds, and $300,000 to stockholders in dividends. Cash outflow from investing activities slowed down somewhat in 2007, with the purchase of $1,500,000 in new buildings, compared with $2,000,000 the year before.

The most noticeable difference between Henderson's statements of cash flows for the two years is in the Operating Activities section. Operations ❶ generated almost $2 million less in cash in 2007 than in 2006 ($1.07 million in 2007 versus $2.95 million in 2006). The decrease in ❷ net income was partially responsible for this reduction in cash from operations. However, the increases in ❸ accounts receivable and ❹ inventories in 2007 had a significant impact on the decrease in cash generated from operating activities.

EXHIBIT 13-4   Comparative Statements of Cash Flow—Horizontal Analysis

Henderson Company
Comparative Statements of Cash Flows
For the Years Ended December 31, 2007 and 2006
(all amounts in thousands of dollars)

	2007	2006	Increase (Decrease) Dollars	Increase (Decrease) Percent
Net Cash Flows from Operating Activities				
❷ Net income	$1,720	$2,300	$ (580)	(25)%
Adjustments:				
Depreciation expense	350	300		
Changes in:				
❸ Accounts receivable	(1,000)	500		
❹ Inventory	(2,000)	(300)		
Prepaid insurance	50	50		
Accounts payable	1,750	(200)		
Taxes payable	200	300		
Net cash provided by operating activities ❶ Unfavorable	$1,070	$2,950	$(1,880)	(64)%
Net Cash Flows from Investing Activities				
Purchase of buildings	$(1,500)	$(2,000)	$ (500)	(25)%
Net Cash Flows from Financing Activities				
Repayment of notes	$ (200)	$ (200)	–0–	–0–
Retirement of bonds	(100)	(100)	–0–	–0–
Cash dividends—preferred	(50)	(50)	–0–	–0–
Cash dividends—common	(250)	(250)	–0–	–0–
Net cash used by financing activities	$ (600)	$ (600)	–0–	–0–
Net increase (decrease) in cash	$(1,030)	$ 350		
Beginning cash balance	1,350	1,000		
Ending cash balance	$ 320	$ 1,350		
Supplemental Information				
Interest paid	$ 140	$ 160		
Income taxes paid	$ 940	$ 1,440		

NOTE: Referenced amounts boldfaced for convenience.

VERTICAL ANALYSIS

Often it is easier to examine comparative financial statements if they have been standardized. *Common-size statements* recast all items on the statement as a percentage of a selected item on the statement. This excludes size as a relevant variable in the analysis. One could use this type of analysis to compare **Wal-Mart** with the smaller **Kmart** or to compare **IBM** with the much smaller **Apple Computer**. It is also a convenient way to compare the same company from year to year.

Vertical analysis involves looking at the relative size and composition of various items on a particular financial statement. Common-size comparative balance sheets for Henderson Company are presented in Exhibit 13-5. Note that all asset accounts are stated as a percentage of total assets. Similarly, all liability and stockholders' equity accounts are stated as a percentage of total liabilities and stockholders' equity. The combination of the comparative balance sheets for the two years and the common-size feature allows the analyst to spot critical changes in the composition of the assets. We noted in Exhibit 13-1 that cash had decreased by 76% over the two years. The decrease of ❶ cash from 9.8% of total assets to only 1.9% is highlighted in Exhibit 13-5.

LO3 Use common-size financial statements to compare various financial statement items (vertical analysis).

EXHIBIT 13-5 **Common-Size Comparative Balance Sheets—Vertical Analysis**

Henderson Company
Common-Size Comparative Balance Sheets
December 31, 2007 and 2006
(all amounts in thousands of dollars)

	December 31, 2007		December 31, 2006	
	Dollars	**Percent**	**Dollars**	**Percent**
Cash	$ 320	**1.9%** ←	$ 1,350 ❶	**9.8%**
Accounts receivable	5,500	32.6	4,500	32.6
Inventory	4,750	**28.1**	2,750 ❸	**19.9**
Prepaid insurance	150	0.9	200	1.5
Total current assets	$ 10,720	❷ **63.5%**	$ 8,800	63.8%
Land	$ 2,000	11.9%	$ 2,000	14.5%
Buildings and equipment, net	4,150	24.6	3,000	21.7
Total long-term assets	$ 6,150	36.5%	$ 5,000	36.2%
Total assets	$16,870	100.0%	$13,800	100.0%
Accounts payable	$ 4,250	25.2%	$ 2,500	18.1%
Taxes payable	2,300	13.6	2,100	15.2
Notes payable	600	3.6	800	5.8
Current portion of bonds	100	0.6	100	0.7
Total current liabilities	$ 7,250	❹ **43.0%**	$ 5,500	39.8%
Bonds payable	700	❺ 4.1	800	5.8
Total liabilities	$ 7,950	47.1%	$ 6,300	45.6%
Preferred stock, $5 par	$ 500	3.0%	$ 500	3.6%
Common stock, $1 par	1,000	5.9	1,000	7.3
Retained earnings	7,420	44.0	6,000	43.5
Total stockholders' equity	$ 8,920	❻ **52.9%**	$ 7,500	54.4%
Total liabilities and stockholders' equity	$16,870	100.0%	$13,800	100.0%

Compare percentages across years to spot year-to-year trends.

In **vertical analysis**, compare each line item as a percentage of total (100%) to highlight a company's overall condition.

NOTE: Referenced amounts boldfaced for convenience.

One can also observe in the exhibit that ❷ total current assets have continued to represent just under two-thirds (63.5%) of total assets. If cash has decreased significantly in terms of the percentage of total assets, what accounts have increased to maintain current assets at two-thirds of total assets? We can quickly determine from the data in Exhibit 13-5 that although ❸ inventory represented 19.9% of total assets at the end of 2006, the percentage is up to 28.1% at the end of 2007. This change in the relative composition of current assets between cash and inventory may have important implications. The change, for instance, may signal that the company is having trouble selling inventory.

Total ❹ current liabilities represent a slightly higher percentage of total liabilities and stockholders' equity at the end of 2007 than at the end of 2006. The increase is balanced by a slight decrease in the relative percentages of ❺ long-term debt (the bonds) and of ❻ stockholders' equity. We will return later to further analysis of the composition of both the current and the noncurrent accounts.

Common-size comparative income statements for Henderson are presented in Exhibit 13-6. The *base,* or benchmark, on which all other items in the income statement are compared is ❶ net sales. Again, observations from the comparative statements alone are further confirmed by examining the common-size statements. Although the **gross profit ratio**—*gross profit as a percentage of net sales*—was 30% in 2006, the same ratio for 2007 is only 25% ❷. Recall the earlier observation that although sales increased by 20% from one year to the next, ❸ cost of goods sold increased by 29%.

In addition to the gross profit ratio, an important relationship from Exhibit 13-6 is the *ratio of net income to net sales,* or **profit margin ratio**. The ratio, an overall indicator of management's ability to control expenses, reflects the amount of income for each dollar of sales. Some analysts prefer to look at income before tax, rather than final net income, because taxes are not typically an expense that can be controlled. Further, if the company does not earn a profit before tax, it will incur no tax expense. Note the decrease in Henderson's ❹ profit margin: from 11.5% in 2006 to 7.1% in 2007 (or from 19.2% to 11.9% on a before-tax basis).

Gross profit ratio
Gross profit to net sales.

Profit margin ratio
Net income to net sales.

EXHIBIT 13-6 Common-Size Comparative Income Statements—Vertical Analysis

Henderson Company
Common-Size Comparative Income Statements
For the Years Ended December 31, 2007 and 2006
(all amounts in thousands of dollars)

	2007		2006	
	Dollars	**Percent**	**Dollars**	**Percent**
Net sales	$24,000	❶ 100.0%	$20,000	100.0%
Cost of goods sold	❸ 18,000	75.0	14,000	70.0
Gross profit	$ 6,000	❷ 25.0%	$ 6,000	30.0%
Selling, general, and administrative expense	3,000	12.5	2,000	10.0
Operating income	$ 3,000	12.5%	$ 4,000	20.0%
Interest expense	140	0.6	160	0.8
Income before tax	$ 2,860	11.9%	$ 3,840	19.2%
Income tax expense	1,140	4.8	1,540	7.7
Net income	$ 1,720	❹ 7.1%	$ 2,300	11.5%

Gross profit as a percentage of sales is the **gross profit ratio.**

The ratio of net income to net sales is the **profit margin ratio.**

NOTE: Referenced amounts boldfaced for convenience.

2 minute review

1. Explain the basic difference between horizontal and vertical analysis.

2. Assume that you are concerned about whether or not accounts receivable has been increasing over the last few years. Which type of analysis, horizontal or vertical, would you perform to help address your concern?

3. Assume that you are concerned about whether or not selling and administrative expenses were unreasonable this past year given the level of sales. Which type of analysis, horizontal or vertical, would you perform to help address your concern?

Answers

1. *Horizontal analysis is used to compare a particular financial statement item over a period of time, whereas vertical analysis allows someone to compare various financial statement items within a single period. With vertical analysis, all of the items are stated as a percentage of a specific item on that statement, such as sales on the income statement or total assets on the balance sheet.*

2. *Horizontal analysis could be used to examine the trend in accounts receivable over recent years.*

3. *Vertical analysis could be used to examine the relationship between selling and administrative expenses and sales. However, you may also want to compare this percentage with the ratio in prior years (thus, you would be performing horizontal analysis as well).*

Liquidity Analysis and the Management of Working Capital

Two ratios were discussed in the last section: the *gross profit ratio* and the *profit margin ratio*. A ratio is simply the relationship, normally stated as a percentage, between two financial statement amounts. In this section, we consider a wide range of ratios used by management, analysts, and others for a variety of purposes. We classify the ratios in three main categories according to their use in performing (1) liquidity analysis, (2) solvency analysis, and (3) profitability analysis.

Liquidity is a relative measure of the nearness to cash of the assets and liabilities of a company. Nearness to cash deals with the length of time before cash is realized. Various ratios are used to measure liquidity, and they basically concern the company's ability to pay its debts as they come due. Recall the distinction between the current and long-term classifications on the balance sheet. Current assets are assets that will be either converted into cash or consumed within one year or the operating cycle, if the cycle is longer than one year. The operating cycle for a manufacturing company is the length of time between the purchase of raw materials and the eventual collection of any outstanding account receivable from the sale of the product. Current liabilities are a company's obligations that require the use of current assets or the creation of other current liabilities to satisfy them.

The nearness to cash of the current assets is indicated by their placement on the balance sheet. Current assets are listed on the balance sheet in descending order of their nearness to cash. Liquidity is, of course, a matter of degree, with cash being the most liquid of all assets. With few exceptions, such as prepaid insurance, most current assets are convertible into cash. However, accounts receivable is closer to being converted into cash than is inventory. An account receivable need only be collected to be converted to cash. An item of inventory must first be sold, and then, assuming that sales of inventory are on account, the account must be collected before cash is realized.

LO4 Compute and use various ratios to assess liquidity.

Liquidity
The nearness to cash of the assets and liabilities.

WORKING CAPITAL

Working capital is the excess of current assets over current liabilities at a point in time:

Working Capital = Current Assets − Current Liabilities

Working capital
Current assets minus current liabilities.

Reference to Henderson's comparative balance sheets in Exhibit 13-1 indicates the following:

	December 31	
	2007	**2006**
Current assets	$10,720,000	$8,800,000
Current liabilities	7,250,000	5,500,000
Working capital	$ 3,470,000	$3,300,000

The management of working capital is an extremely important task for any business. A comparison of Henderson's working capital at the end of each of the two years indicates a slight increase in the degree of protection for short-term creditors of the company. Management must always strive for the ideal balance of current assets and current liabilities. The amount of working capital is limited in its informational value, however. For example, it tells us nothing about the composition of the current accounts. Also, the dollar amount of working capital may not be useful for comparison with other companies of different sizes in the same industry. Working capital of $3,470,000 may be adequate for Henderson Company, but it might signal impending bankruptcy for a company much larger than Henderson.

CURRENT RATIO

Current ratio
The ratio of current assets to current liabilities.

The **current ratio** is one of the most widely used of all financial statement ratios and is calculated as follows:

$$\text{Current Ratio} = \frac{\text{Current Assets}}{\text{Current Liabilities}}$$

For Henderson Company, the ratio at each year-end is as follows:

December 31	
2007	**2006**
$\dfrac{\$10,720,000}{\$7,250,000} = 1.48 \text{ to } 1$	$\dfrac{\$8,800,000}{\$5,500,000} = 1.60 \text{ to } 1$

At the end of 2007, Henderson had $1.48 of current assets for every $1 of current liabilities. Is this current ratio adequate? Or is it a sign of impending financial difficulties? There is no definitive answer to either of these questions. Some analysts use a general rule of thumb of 2:1 for the current ratio as a sign of short-term financial health. The answer depends first on the industry. Companies in certain industries have historically operated with current ratios much less than 2:1.

A second concern in interpreting the current ratio involves the composition of the current assets. Cash is usually the only acceptable means of payment for most liabilities. Therefore, it is important to consider the makeup, or *composition*, of the current assets. Refer to Exhibit 13-5 and Henderson's common-size balance sheets. Not only did the current ratio decline during 2007 but also the proportion of the total current assets made up by inventory increased, whereas the proportion made up by accounts receivable remained the same. Recall that accounts receivable is only one step removed from cash, whereas inventory requires both sale and collection of the subsequent account.

ACID-TEST RATIO

Acid-test or quick ratio
A stricter test of liquidity than the current ratio; excludes inventory and prepayments from the numerator.

The **acid-test or quick ratio** is a stricter test of a company's ability to pay its current debts as they are due. Specifically, it is intended to deal with the composition problem because it *excludes* inventories and prepaid assets from the numerator of the fraction:

$$\text{Acid-Test or Quick Ratio} = \frac{\text{Quick Assets}}{\text{Current Liabilities}}$$

where

$$\text{Quick Assets} = \text{Cash} + \text{Marketable Securities} + \text{Current Receivables}$$

Henderson's quick assets consist of only cash and accounts receivable, and its quick ratios are as follows:

December 31	
2007	**2006**
$\dfrac{\$320{,}000 + \$5{,}500{,}000}{\$7{,}250{,}000} = 0.80 \text{ to } 1$	$\dfrac{\$1{,}350{,}000 + \$4{,}500{,}000}{\$5{,}500{,}000} = 1.06 \text{ to } 1$

Does the quick ratio of less than 1:1 at the end of 2007 mean that Henderson will be unable to pay creditors on time? **For many companies, an acid-test ratio below 1 is not desirable because it may signal the need to liquidate marketable securities to pay bills, regardless of the current trading price of the securities.** (Recall that Henderson has no marketable securities.) Although the quick ratio is a better indication of short-term debt-paying ability than the current ratio, it is still not perfect. For example, we would want to know the normal credit terms that Henderson extends to its customers, as well as the credit terms that the company receives from its suppliers.

Assume that Henderson requires its customers to pay their accounts within 30 days and that the normal credit terms extended by Henderson's suppliers allow payment anytime within 60 days. The relatively longer credit terms extended by Henderson's suppliers give it some cushion in meeting its obligations. The due date of the $2,300,000 in taxes payable could also have a significant effect on the company's ability to remain in business.

CASH FLOW FROM OPERATIONS TO CURRENT LIABILITIES

Two limitations exist with either the current ratio or the quick ratio as a measure of liquidity. First, almost all debts require the payment of cash. Thus, a ratio that focuses on cash is more useful. Second, both ratios focus on liquid assets at a *point in time.* Cash flow from operating activities, as reported on the statement of cash flows, can be used to indicate the flow of cash during the year to cover the debts due.[1] The **cash flow from operations to current liabilities ratio** is computed as follows:

Cash flow from operations to current liabilities ratio
A measure of the ability to pay current debts from operating cash flows.

$$\frac{\text{Cash Flow from Operations}}{\text{to Current Liabilities Ratio}} = \frac{\text{Net Cash Provided by Operating Activities}}{\text{Average Current Liabilities}}$$

Note the use of *average* current liabilities in the denominator. This results in a denominator that is consistent with the numerator, which reports the cash flow over a period of time. Because we need to calculate the *average* current liabilities for both years, it is necessary to add the ending balance sheet for 2005 for use in the analysis. The balance sheet for Henderson on December 31, 2005, is given in Exhibit 13-7. The ratio for Henderson for each year is as follows:

2007	**2006**
$\dfrac{\$1{,}070{,}000}{(\$7{,}250{,}000 + \$5{,}500{,}000)/2} = 16.8\%$	$\dfrac{\$2{,}950{,}000}{(\$5{,}500{,}000 + \$5{,}600{,}000)/2} = 53.2\%$

Two factors are responsible for the large decrease in this ratio from 2006 to 2007. First, cash generated from operations during 2007 was less than half what it was during 2006 (the numerator). Second, average current liabilities were smaller in 2006 than in 2007 (the denominator). In examining the health of the company

---

[1] For a detailed discussion on the use of information contained in the statement of cash flows in performing ratio analysis, see Charles A. Carslaw and John R. Mills, "Developing Ratios for Effective Cash Flow Statement Analysis," *Journal of Accountancy* (November 1991), pp. 63–70.

EXHIBIT 13-7	Henderson Company's Balance Sheet, End of 2005

Henderson Company
Balance Sheet
December 31, 2005
(all amounts in thousands of dollars)

Cash	$ 1,000
Accounts receivable	5,000
Inventory	2,450
Prepaid insurance	250
Total current assets	$ 8,700
Land	$ 2,000
Buildings and equipment, net	1,300
Total long-term assets	$ 3,300
Total assets	$12,000
Accounts payable	$ 2,700
Taxes payable	1,800
Notes payable	1,000
Current portion of bonds	100
Total current liabilities	$ 5,600
Bonds payable	900
Total liabilities	$ 6,500
Preferred stock, $5 par	$ 500
Common stock, $1 par	1,000
Retained earnings	4,000
Total stockholders' equity	$ 5,500
Total liabilities and stockholders' equity	$12,000

in terms of its liquidity, an analyst would concentrate on the reason for these decreases.

ACCOUNTS RECEIVABLE ANALYSIS

The analysis of accounts receivable is an important component in the management of working capital. A company must be willing to extend credit terms that are liberal enough to attract and maintain customers, but at the same time, management must continually monitor the accounts to ensure collection on a timely basis. One measure of the efficiency of the collection process is the **accounts receivable turnover ratio**:

Accounts receivable turnover ratio
A measure of the number of times accounts receivable are collected in a period.

$$\text{Accounts Receivable Turnover Ratio} = \frac{\text{Net Credit Sales}}{\text{Average Accounts Receivable}}$$

Note an important distinction between this ratio and either the current or the quick ratio. Although both of those ratios measure liquidity at a point in time and all numbers come from the balance sheet, a turnover ratio is an *activity* ratio and consists of an activity (sales, in this case) divided by a base to which it is naturally related (accounts receivable). Because an activity such as sales is for a period of time (a year, in this case), the base should be stated as an average for that same period of time.

The accounts receivable turnover ratios for both years can now be calculated (we assume that all sales are on account):

2007	**2006**
$\dfrac{\$24,000,000}{(\$5,500,000 + \$4,500,000)/2} = 4.8 \text{ times}$	$\dfrac{\$20,000,000}{(\$4,500,000 + \$5,000,000)/2} = 4.2 \text{ times}$

Accounts turned over, on average, 4.2 times in 2006, compared with 4.8 times in 2007. This means that the average number of times accounts were collected during each year was between four and five times. What does this mean about the average length of time that an account was outstanding? Another way to measure efficiency in the collection process is to calculate the **number of days' sales in receivables**:

$$\text{Number of Days' Sales in Receivables} = \frac{\text{Number of Days in the Period}}{\text{Accounts Receivable Turnover}}$$

Number of days' sales in receivables
A measure of the average age of accounts receivable.

For simplicity, we assume 360 days in a year:

2007	2006
$\frac{360 \text{ days}}{4.8 \text{ times}} = 75 \text{ days}$	$\frac{360 \text{ days}}{4.2 \text{ times}} = 86 \text{ days}$

The average number of days an account is outstanding, or the average collection period, is 75 days in 2007, down from 86 days in 2006. Is this acceptable? The answer depends on the company's credit policy. If Henderson's normal credit terms require payment within 60 days, further investigation is needed, even though the number of days outstanding has decreased from the previous year.

Management needs to be concerned with both the collectibility of an account as it ages and the cost of funds tied up in receivables. For example, a $1 million average receivable balance that requires an additional month to collect suggests that the company is forgoing $10,000 in lost profits if we assume that the money could be reinvested in the business to earn 1% per month, or 12% per year.

INVENTORY ANALYSIS

A similar set of ratios can be calculated to analyze the efficiency in managing inventory. The **inventory turnover ratio** is as follows:

$$\text{Inventory Turnover Ratio} = \frac{\text{Cost of Goods Sold}}{\text{Average Inventory}}$$

Due to the perishable nature of their products, grocery chains have high inventory turnovers and short cash to cash operating cycles. Firms in other segments have relatively longer cycles.

Inventory turnover ratio
A measure of the number of times inventory is sold during a period.

The ratio for each of the two years follows:

2007	2006
$\frac{\$18,000,000}{(\$4,750,000 + \$2,750,000)/2} = 4.8 \text{ times}$	$\frac{\$14,000,000}{(\$2,750,000 + \$2,450,000)/2} = 5.4 \text{ times}$

Henderson was slightly more efficient in 2006 in moving its inventory. The number of "turns" each year varies widely for different industries. For example, a wholesaler of perishable fruits and vegetables may turn over inventory at least 50 times per year. An airplane manufacturer, however, may turn over its inventory once or twice a year. What does the number of turns per year tell us about the average length of time it takes to sell an item of inventory? The **number of days' sales in inventory** is an alternative measure of the company's efficiency in managing inventory. It is the number of days between the date an item of inventory is purchased and the date it is sold:

Number of days' sales in inventory
A measure of how long it takes to sell inventory.

$$\text{Number of Days' Sales in Inventory} = \frac{\text{Number of Days in the Period}}{\text{Inventory Turnover}}$$

The number of days' sales in inventory for Henderson is as follows:

2007	2006
$\frac{360 \text{ days}}{4.8 \text{ times}} = 75 \text{ days}$	$\frac{360 \text{ days}}{5.4 \text{ times}} = 67 \text{ days}$

This measure can reveal a great deal about inventory management. For example, an unusually low turnover (and, of course, high number of days in inventory) may signal a large amount of obsolete inventory or problems in the sales department. Or, it may indicate that the company is pricing its products too high and the market is reacting by reducing demand for the company's products.

CASH OPERATING CYCLE

Cash to cash operating cycle
The length of time from the purchase of inventory to the collection of any receivable from the sale.

The **cash to cash operating cycle** is the length of time between the purchase of merchandise for sale, assuming a retailer or wholesaler, and the eventual collection of the cash from the sale. One method to approximate the number of days in a company's operating cycle involves combining two measures:

Cash to Cash Operating Cycle = Number of Days' Sales in Inventory
+ Number of Days' Sales in Receivables

Henderson's operating cycles for 2007 and 2006 are as follows:

2007	2006
75 days + 75 days = 150 days	67 days + 86 days = 153 days

The average length of time between the purchase of inventory and the collection of cash from sale of the inventory was 150 days in 2007. Note that although the length of the operating cycle did not change significantly from 2006 to 2007, the composition did change: the increase in the average number of days in inventory was offset by the decrease in the average number of days in receivables.

Solvency Analysis

LO5 Compute and use various ratios to assess solvency.

Solvency
The ability of a company to remain in business over the long term.

Solvency refers to a company's ability to remain in business over the long term. It is related to liquidity but differs in time. Although liquidity relates to the firm's ability to pay next year's debts as they come due, solvency concerns the ability of the firm to stay financially healthy over the period of time that existing debt (short- and long-term) will be outstanding.

DEBT-TO-EQUITY RATIO

Debt-to-equity ratio
The ratio of total liabilities to total stockholders' equity.

Capital structure is the focal point in solvency analysis. This refers to the composition of the right side of the balance sheet and the mix between debt and stockholders' equity. The composition of debt and equity in the capital structure is an important determinant of the cost of capital to a company. We will have more to say later about the effects that the mix of debt and equity has on profitability. For now, consider the **debt-to-equity ratio**:

$$\text{Debt-to-Equity Ratio} = \frac{\text{Total Liabilities}}{\text{Total Stockholders' Equity}}$$

Henderson's debt-to-equity ratio at each year-end is as follows:

December 31	
2007	**2006**
$\frac{\$7,950,000}{\$8,920,000} = 0.89$ to 1	$\frac{\$6,300,000}{\$7,500,000} = 0.84$ to 1

The 2007 ratio indicates that for every $1 of capital that stockholders provided, creditors provided $0.89. Variations of the debt-to-equity ratio are sometimes used to assess solvency. For example, an analyst might calculate the ratio of total liabilities to the sum of total liabilities and stockholders' equity. This results in a ratio that differs from the debt-to-equity ratio, but the objective of the measure is the same—to determine the degree to which the company relies on outsiders for funds.

What is an *acceptable* ratio of debt to equity? As with all ratios, the answer depends on the company, the industry, and many other factors. **You should not assume that a lower debt-to-equity ratio is better.** Certainly, taking on additional debt is risky. Many companies are able to benefit from borrowing money, however, by putting the cash raised to good uses in their businesses. Later in the chapter, we discuss the concept of leverage: using borrowed money to benefit the company and its stockholders.

In the 1980s, investors and creditors tolerated a much higher debt-to-equity ratio than is considered prudent today. The savings and loan crisis in the 1980s prompted the federal government to enact regulations requiring financial institutions to have a lower proportion of debt-to-equity. By the mid-1990s, investors and creditors were demanding that all types of companies display lower debt-to-equity ratios.

> **Study Tip** The elements in many ratios are intuitive and should not require memorization to remember. For example, it is logical that the debt-to-equity ratio is computed by dividing total liabilities by total stockholders' equity.

TIMES INTEREST EARNED

The debt-to-equity ratio is a measure of the company's overall long-term financial health. Management must also be aware of its ability to meet current interest payments to creditors. The **times interest earned ratio** indicates the company's ability to meet current-year interest payments out of current-year earnings:

$$\text{Times Interest Earned Ratio} = \frac{\text{Net Income} + \text{Interest Expense} + \text{Income Tax Expense}}{\text{Interest Expense}}$$

Times interest earned ratio
An income statement measure of the ability of a company to meet its interest payments.

Both interest expense and income tax expense are added back to net income in the numerator because interest is a deduction in arriving at the amount of income subject to tax. Stated slightly differently, if a company had just enough income to cover the payment of interest, tax expense would be zero. The greater the interest coverage is, the better, as far as lenders are concerned. Bankers often place more importance on the times interest earned ratio than even on earnings per share. The ratio for Henderson for each of the two years indicates a great deal of protection in this regard:

2007	2006
$\dfrac{\$1,720,000 + \$140,000 + \$1,140,000}{\$140,000}$	$\dfrac{\$2,300,000 + \$160,000 + \$1,540,000}{\$160,000}$
= 21.4 to 1	= 25 to 1

DEBT SERVICE COVERAGE

Two problems exist with the times interest earned ratio as a measure of the ability to pay creditors. First, the denominator of the fraction considers only *interest*. Management must also be concerned with the *principal* amount of loans maturing in the next year. The second problem deals with the difference between the cash and the accrual bases of accounting. The numerator of the times interest earned ratio is not a measure of the *cash* available to repay loans. Keep in mind the various non-cash adjustments, such as depreciation, that enter into the determination of net income. Also, recall that the denominator of the times interest earned ratio is a measure of interest expense, not interest payments. The **debt service coverage ratio** is a measure of the amount of cash that is generated from operating activities during the year and that is available to repay interest due and any maturing principal amounts (that is, the amount available to "service" the debt):

Debt service coverage ratio
A statement of cash flows measure of the ability of a company to meet its interest and principal payments.

$$\text{Debt Service Coverage Ratio} = \frac{\text{Cash Flow from Operations Before Interest and Tax Payments}}{\text{Interest and Principal Payments}}$$

Some analysts use an alternative measure in the numerator of this ratio, as well as for other purposes. The alternative is referred to as EBITDA, which stands for earnings before interest, taxes, depreciation, and amortization. Whether or not EBITDA is a good substitute for cash flow from operations before interest and tax payments depends on whether or not there were significant changes in current assets and current liabilities during the period. If significant changes in these accounts occurred during the period, cash flow from operations before interest and tax payments is a better measure of a company's ability to cover interest and debt payments.

Cash flow from operations is available on the comparative statement of cash flows in Exhibit 13-4. As was the case with the times interest earned ratio, the net cash provided by operating activities is adjusted to reflect the amount available *before* paying interest and taxes.

Keep in mind that the income statement in Exhibit 13-2 reflects the *expense* for interest and taxes each year. The amounts of interest and taxes *paid* each year are shown as supplemental information at the bottom of the statement of cash flows in Exhibit 13-4 and are relevant in computing the debt service coverage ratio.

We must include any principal payments with interest paid in the denominator of the debt service coverage ratio. According to the Financing Activities section of the statements of cash flows in Exhibit 13-4, Henderson repaid $200,000 each year on the notes payable and $100,000 each year on the bonds. The debt service coverage ratios for the two years are calculated as follows:

2007

$$\frac{\$1,070,000 + \$140,000 + \$940,000}{\$140,000 + \$200,000 + \$100,000} = 4.89 \text{ times}$$

2006

$$\frac{\$2,950,000 + \$160,000 + \$1,440,000}{\$160,000 + \$200,000 + \$100,000} = 9.89 \text{ times}$$

Like Henderson's times interest earned ratio, its debt service coverage ratio decreased during 2007. According to the calculations, however, Henderson still generated almost $5 of cash from operations during 2007 to "cover" every $1 of required interest and principal payments.

CASH FLOW FROM OPERATIONS TO CAPITAL EXPENDITURES RATIO

Cash flow from operations to capital expenditures ratio
A measure of the ability of a company to finance long-term asset acquisitions with cash from operations.

One final measure is useful in assessing the solvency of a business. The **cash flow from operations to capital expenditures ratio** measures a company's ability to use operations to finance its acquisitions of productive assets. To the extent that a company is able to do this, it should rely less on external financing or additional contributions by the owners to replace and add to the existing capital base. The ratio is computed as follows:

$$\text{Cash Flow from Operations to Capital Expenditures Ratio} = \frac{\text{Cash Flow from Operations} - \text{Total Dividends Paid}}{\text{Cash Paid for Acquisitions}}$$

Note that the numerator of the ratio measures the cash flow *after* meeting all dividend payments.[2] The calculation of the ratios for Henderson follows:

2007	**2006**
$\dfrac{\$1,070,000 - \$300,000}{\$1,500,000} = 51.3\%$	$\dfrac{\$2,950,000 - \$300,000}{\$2,000,000} = 132.5\%$

Although the amount of capital expenditures was less in 2007 than in 2006, the company generated considerably less cash from operations in 2007 to cover these acquisitions. In fact, the ratio of less than 100% in 2007 indicates that Henderson was not able to finance all of its capital expenditures from operations *and* cover its dividend payments.

---

2 Dividends paid are reported on the statement of cash flows in the Financing Activities section. The amount *paid* should be used for this calculation rather than the amount declared, which appears on the statement of retained earnings.

⏱ *2 minute review*

1. Explain the difference between liquidity and solvency as it relates to a company's financial position.

2. Assume that you are a supplier and are considering whether to sell to a company on account. Which of the two, liquidity or solvency, are you more concerned with?

Answers

1. *Liquidity is a relative measure of the nearness to cash of the assets and liabilities of a company. Measures of liquidity are intended to determine the company's ability to pay its debts as they come due. Solvency refers to a company's ability to remain in business over the long term. Liquidity and solvency are certainly related, but the latter takes a much more long-term view of the financial health of the company.*

2. *Because you need to assess the ability of the company to pay its account on a timely basis, you would be more concerned with the liquidity of the company over the short term.*

Profitability Analysis

Liquidity analysis and solvency analysis deal with management's ability to repay short- and long-term creditors. Creditors are concerned with a company's profitability because a profitable company is more likely to be able to make principal and interest payments. Of course, stockholders care about a company's profitability because it affects the market price of the stock and the ability of the company to pay dividends. Various measures of **profitability** indicate how well management is using the resources at its disposal to earn a return on the funds invested by various groups. Two frequently used profitability measures, the gross profit ratio and the profit margin ratio, were discussed earlier in the chapter. We now turn to other measures of profitability.

LO6 Compute and use various ratios to assess profitability.

Profitability
How well management is using company resources to earn a return on the funds invested by various groups.

RATE OF RETURN ON ASSETS

Before computing the rate of return, we must answer an important question: *return to whom?* **Every return ratio is a measure of the relationship between the income earned by the company and the investment made in the company by various groups.** The broadest rate of return ratio is the **return on assets ratio** because it considers the investment made by *all* providers of capital, from short-term creditors to bondholders to stockholders. Therefore, the denominator, or base, for the return on assets ratio is average total liabilities and stockholders' equity—which of course is the same as average total assets.

The numerator of a return ratio will be some measure of the company's income for the period. The income selected for the numerator must match the investment or base in the denominator. For example, if average total assets is the base in the denominator, it is necessary to use an income number that is applicable to all providers of capital. Therefore, the income number used in the rate of return on assets is income *after* adding back interest expense. This adjustment considers creditors as one of the groups that have provided funds to the company. In other words, we want the amount of income before either creditors or stockholders have been given any distributions (that is, interest to creditors or dividends to stockholders). Interest expense must be added back on a net-of-tax basis. Because net income is on an after-tax basis, for consistency purposes interest must also be placed on a net, or after-tax, basis.

The return on assets ratio is as follows:

Return on assets ratio
A measure of a company's success in earning a return for all providers of capital.

$$\text{Return on Assets Ratio} = \frac{\text{Net Income} + \text{Interest Expense, Net of Tax}}{\text{Average Total Assets}}$$

If we assume a 40% tax rate (which *is* the actual ratio of income tax expense to income before tax for Henderson), its return on assets ratios are as follows:

		2007		2006
Net income		$ 1,720,000		$ 2,300,000
Add back:				
Interest expense	$140,000		$160,000	
× (1 − tax rate)	× 0.6	84,000	× 0.6	96,000
Numerator		$ 1,804,000		$ 2,396,000
Assets, beginning of year		$13,800,000		$12,000,000
Assets, end of year		16,870,000		13,800,000
Total		$30,670,000		$25,800,000
Denominator:				
Average total assets				
(total above divided by 2)		$15,335,000		$12,900,000
		$1,804,000		$2,396,000
		$15,335,000		$12,900,000
Return on assets ratio		= 11.76%		= 18.57%

COMPONENTS OF RETURN ON ASSETS

Return on sales ratio
A variation of the profit margin ratio; measures earnings before payments to creditors.

What caused Henderson's return on assets to decrease so dramatically from the previous year? The answer can be found by considering the two individual components that make up the return on assets ratio. The first of these components is the **return on sales ratio** and is calculated as follows:

$$\text{Return on Sales Ratio} = \frac{\text{Net Income} + \text{Interest Expense, Net of Tax}}{\text{Net Sales}}$$

The return on sales ratios for Henderson for the two years follow:

2007	2006
$\dfrac{\$1,720,000 + \$84,000}{\$24,000,000} = 7.52\%$	$\dfrac{\$2,300,000 + \$96,000}{\$20,000,000} = 11.98\%$

The ratio for 2007 indicates that for every $1 of sales, the company was able to earn a profit, before the payment of interest, of between 7 and 8 cents, as compared with a return of almost 12 cents on the dollar in 2006.

Asset turnover ratio
The relationship between net sales and average total assets.

The other component of the rate of return on assets is the **asset turnover ratio**. The ratio is similar to both the inventory turnover and the accounts receivable turnover ratios because it is a measure of the relationship between some activity (net sales, in this case) and some investment base (average total assets):

$$\text{Asset Turnover Ratio} = \frac{\text{Net Sales}}{\text{Average Total Assets}}$$

For Henderson, the ratio for each of the two years follows:

2007	2006
$\dfrac{\$24,000,000}{\$15,335,000} = 1.57 \text{ times}$	$\dfrac{\$20,000,000}{\$12,900,000} = 1.55 \text{ times}$

It now becomes evident that the explanation for the decrease in Henderson's return on assets lies in the drop in the return on sales, since the asset turnover ratio was almost the same. To summarize, note the relationship among the three ratios:

Return on Assets = Return on Sales × Asset Turnover

For 2007, Henderson's return on assets consists of the following:

$$\frac{\$1,804,000}{\$24,000,000} \times \frac{\$24,000,000}{\$15,335,000} = 7.52\% \times 1.57 = 11.8\%$$

Finally, notice that net sales cancels out of both ratios, leaving the net income adjusted for interest divided by average assets as the return on assets ratio.

RETURN ON COMMON STOCKHOLDERS' EQUITY

Reasoning similar to that used to calculate return on assets can be used to calculate the return on capital provided by the common stockholder. Because we are interested in the return to the common stockholder, our base is no longer average total assets but average common stockholders' equity. Similarly, the appropriate income figure for the numerator is net income less preferred dividends because we are interested in the return to the common stockholder after all claims have been settled. Income taxes and interest expense have already been deducted in arriving at net income, but preferred dividends have not been because dividends are a distribution of profits, not an expense.

The **return on common stockholders' equity ratio** is computed as follows:

> **Return on common stockholders' equity ratio**
> A measure of a company's success in earning a return for the common stockholders.

$$\text{Return on Common Stockholders' Equity Ratio} = \frac{\text{Net Income} - \text{Preferred Dividends}}{\text{Average Common Stockholders' Equity}}$$

The average common stockholders' equity for Henderson is calculated using information from Exhibits 13-1 and 13-7:

	Account Balances at December 31		
	2007	**2006**	**2005**
Common stock, $1 par	$1,000,000	$1,000,000	$1,000,000
Retained earnings	7,420,000	6,000,000	4,000,000
Total common equity	$8,420,000	$7,000,000	$5,000,000

Average common equity:
2006: ($7,000,000 + $5,000,000)/2 = $6,000,000
2007: ($8,420,000 + $7,000,000)/2 = $7,710,000

Net income less preferred dividends—or "income available to common," as it is called—can be found by referring to net income on the income statement and to preferred dividends on the statement of retained earnings. The combined statement of income and retained earnings in Exhibit 13-2 gives the relevant amounts for the numerator. Henderson's return on equity for the two years is as follows:

2007	2006
$\dfrac{\$1,720,000 - \$50,000}{\$7,710,000} = 21.66\%$	$\dfrac{\$2,300,000 - \$50,000}{\$6,000,000} = 37.50\%$

Even though Henderson's return on stockholders' equity ratio decreased significantly from one year to the next, most stockholders would be very happy to achieve these returns on their money. Very few investments offer much more than 10% return unless substantial risk is involved.

RETURN ON ASSETS, RETURN ON EQUITY, AND LEVERAGE

The return on assets for 2007 was 11.8%. But the return to the common stockholders was much higher: 21.7%. How do you explain this phenomenon? Why are the stockholders receiving a higher return on their money than all of the providers of money combined are getting? A partial answer to these questions can be found by reviewing the cost to Henderson of the various sources of capital.

Exhibit 13-1 indicates that notes, bonds, and preferred stock are the primary sources of capital other than common stock (accounts payable and taxes payable are *not* included because they represent interest-free loans to the company from suppliers and the government). These sources and the average amount of each outstanding during 2007 follow:

	Account Balances at December 31		
	2007	**2006**	**Average**
Notes payable	$ 600,000	$ 800,000	$ 700,000
Current portion of bonds	100,000	100,000	100,000
Bonds payable—Long-term	700,000	800,000	750,000
Total liabilities	$1,400,000	$1,700,000	$1,550,000
Preferred stock	$ 500,000	$ 500,000	$ 500,000

What was the cost to Henderson of each of these sources? The cost of the money provided by the preferred stockholders is clearly the amount of dividends of $50,000. The cost as a percentage is $50,000/$500,000, or 10%. The average cost of the borrowed money can be approximated by dividing the 2007 interest expense of $140,000 by the average of the notes payable and bonds payable of $1,550,000. The result is an average cost of these two sources of $140,000/$1,550,000, or approximately 9%.

Leverage
The use of borrowed funds and amounts contributed by preferred stockholders to earn an overall return higher than the cost of these funds.

The concept of **leverage** refers to the practice of using borrowed funds and amounts received from preferred stockholders in an attempt to earn an overall return that is higher than the cost of these funds. Recall the rate of return on assets for 2007: 11.8%. Because this return is on an after-tax basis, it is necessary, for comparative purposes, to convert the average cost of borrowed funds to an after-tax basis. Although we computed an average cost for borrowed money of 9%, the actual cost of the borrowed money is 5.4% [9% × (100% − 40%)] after taxes. Because dividends are *not* tax-deductible, the cost of the money provided by preferred stockholders is 10%, as calculated earlier.

Has Henderson successfully employed favorable leverage? That is, has it been able to earn an overall rate of return on assets that is higher than the amounts that it must pay creditors and preferred stockholders? Henderson has been successful in using outside money: neither of the sources must be paid a rate in excess of the 11.8% overall rate on assets used. Also keep in mind that Henderson has been able to borrow some amounts on an interest-free basis. As mentioned earlier, the accounts payable and taxes payable represent interest-free loans from suppliers and the government, although the loans are typically for a short period of time, such as 30 days.

In summary, the excess of the 21.7% return on equity over the 11.8% return on assets indicates that the Henderson management has been successful in employing leverage; that is, there is favorable leverage. Is it possible to be unsuccessful in this pursuit; that is, can there be unfavorable leverage? If the company must pay more for the amounts provided by creditors and preferred stockholders than it can earn overall, as indicated by the return on assets, there will, in fact, be unfavorable leverage. This may occur when interest requirements are high and net income is low. A company would likely have a high debt-to-equity ratio as well when there is unfavorable leverage.

EARNINGS PER SHARE

Earnings per share
A company's bottom line stated on a per-share basis.

Earnings per share is one of the most quoted statistics for publicly traded companies. Stockholders and potential investors want to know what their share of profits is, not just the total dollar amount. Presentation of profits on a per-share basis also allows the stockholder to relate earnings to what he or she paid for a share of stock or to the current trading price of a share of stock.

In simple situations, such as our Henderson Company example, earnings per share (EPS) is calculated as follows:

$$\text{Earnings per Share} = \frac{\text{Net Income} - \text{Preferred Dividends}}{\text{Weighted Average Number of Common Shares Outstanding}}$$

Because Henderson had 1,000,000 shares of common stock outstanding throughout both 2006 and 2007, its EPS for each of the two years is as follows:

2007	2006
$\dfrac{\$1,720,000 - \$50,000}{1,000,000 \text{ shares}} = \$1.67$ per share	$\dfrac{\$2,300,000 - \$50,000}{1,000,000 \text{ shares}} = \$2.25$ per share

A number of complications can arise in the computation of EPS, and the calculations can become exceedingly complex for a company with many different types of securities in its capital structure. These complications are beyond the scope of this book and are discussed in more advanced accounting courses.

PRICE/EARNINGS RATIO

Earnings per share is an important ratio for an investor because of its relationship to dividends and market price. Stockholders hope to earn a return by receiving periodic dividends or eventually selling the stock for more than they paid for it, or both. Although earnings are related to dividends and market price, the latter two are of primary interest to the stockholder.

We mentioned earlier the desire of investors to relate the earnings of the company to the market price of the stock. Now that we have stated Henderson's earnings on a per-share basis, we can calculate the **price/earnings (P/E) ratio**. What market price is relevant? Should we use the market price that the investor paid for a share of stock, or should we use the current market price? Because earnings are based on the most recent evaluation of the company for accounting purposes, it seems logical to use current market price, which is based on the stock market's current assessment of the company. Therefore, the ratio is computed as follows:

Price/earnings (P/E) ratio
The relationship between a company's performance according to the income statement and its performance in the stock market.

$$\text{Price/Earnings Ratio} = \frac{\text{Current Market Price}}{\text{Earnings per Share}}$$

Assume that the current market price for Henderson's common stock is $15 per share at the end of 2007 and $18 per share at the end of 2006. The price/earnings ratio for each of the two years is as follows:

2007	2006
$\dfrac{\$15 \text{ per share}}{\$1.67 \text{ per share}} = 9 \text{ to } 1$	$\dfrac{\$18 \text{ per share}}{\$2.25 \text{ per share}} = 8 \text{ to } 1$

What is normal for a P/E ratio? As is the case for all other ratios, it is difficult to generalize as to what is good or bad. The P/E ratio compares the stock market's assessment of a company's performance with its success as reflected on the income statement. A relatively high P/E ratio may indicate that a stock is overpriced by the market; one that is relatively low could indicate that it is underpriced.

The P/E ratio is often thought to indicate the "quality" of a company's earnings. For example, assume that two companies have identical EPS ratios of $2 per share. Why should investors be willing to pay $20 per share (or 10 times earnings) for the stock of one company but only $14 per share (or 7 times earnings) for the stock of the other company? First, we must realize that many factors in addition to the reported earnings of the company affect market prices. General economic conditions, the outlook for the particular industry, and pending lawsuits are just three examples of the various factors that can affect the trading price of a company's stock. The difference in P/E ratios for the two companies may reflect the market's assessment of the accounting practices of the companies, however. Assume that the company with a market price of $20 per share uses LIFO in valuing inventory and that the company trading at $14 per share uses FIFO. The difference in prices may indicate that investors believe that even though the companies have the same EPS, the LIFO company is "better off" because it will have a lower amount of taxes to pay. (Recall that in a period of inflation, the use of LIFO results in more cost of goods sold, less income, and therefore less income taxes.) Finally, aside from the way investors view the accounting practices of different companies, they also consider the fact that, to a large extent, earnings reflect the use of historical costs, as opposed to fair market values, in assigning values to assets. Investors must consider the extent to which a company's assets are worth more than what was paid for them.

DIVIDEND RATIOS

Dividend payout ratio
The percentage of earnings paid out as dividends.

Dividend yield ratio
The relationship between dividends and the market price of a company's stock.

Two ratios are used to evaluate a company's dividend policies: the **dividend payout ratio** and the **dividend yield ratio**. The dividend payout ratio is the ratio of the common dividends per share to the earnings per share:

$$\text{Dividend Payout Ratio} = \frac{\text{Common Dividends per Share}}{\text{Earnings per Share}}$$

Exhibit 13-2 indicates that Henderson paid $250,000 in common dividends each year, or with 1 million shares outstanding, $0.25 per share. The two payout ratios are as follows:

2007	2006
$\frac{\$0.25}{\$1.67} = 15.0\%$	$\frac{\$0.25}{\$2.25} = 11.1\%$

Henderson management was faced with an important financial policy decision in 2007. Should the company maintain the same dividend of $0.25 per share, even though EPS dropped significantly? Many companies prefer to maintain a level dividend pattern, hoping that a drop in earnings is only temporary.

The second dividend ratio of interest to stockholders is the dividend yield ratio:

$$\text{Dividend Yield Ratio} = \frac{\text{Common Dividends per Share}}{\text{Market Price per Share}}$$

The yield to Henderson's stockholders would be calculated as follows:

2007	2006
$\frac{\$0.25}{\$15} = 1.7\%$	$\frac{\$0.25}{\$18} = 1.4\%$

As we see, Henderson common stock does not provide a high yield to its investors. The relationship between the dividends and the market price indicates that investors buy the stock for reasons other than the periodic dividend return.

The dividend yield is very important to investors who depend on dividend checks to pay their living expenses. Utility stocks are popular among retirees because these shares have dividend yields as high as 5%. That is considered a good investment with relatively low risk and some opportunity for gains in the stock price. On the other hand, investors who want to put money into growing companies are willing to forgo dividends if it means the potential for greater price appreciation.

SUMMARY OF SELECTED FINANCIAL RATIOS

We have completed our review of the various ratios used to assess a company's liquidity, solvency, and profitability. For ease of reference, Exhibit 13-8 summarizes the ratios discussed in this chapter. Keep in mind that this list is not all-inclusive and that certain ratios used by analysts and others may be specific to a particular industry or type of business.

EXHIBIT 13-8   Summary of Selected Financial Ratios

Liquidity Analysis

Working capital

$$\text{Current Assets} - \text{Current Liabilities}$$

Current ratio

$$\frac{\text{Current Assets}}{\text{Current Liabilities}}$$

Acid-test ratio (quick ratio)

$$\frac{\text{Cash} + \text{Marketable Securities} + \text{Current Receivables}}{\text{Current Liabilities}}$$

Cash flow from operations to current liabilities ratio

$$\frac{\text{Net Cash Provided by Operating Activities}}{\text{Average Current Liabilities}}$$

Accounts receivable turnover ratio

$$\frac{\text{Net Credit Sales}}{\text{Average Accounts Receivable}}$$

Number of days' sales in receivables

$$\frac{\text{Number of Days in the Period}}{\text{Accounts Receivable Turnover}}$$

Inventory turnover ratio

$$\frac{\text{Cost of Goods Sold}}{\text{Average Inventory}}$$

Number of days' sales in inventory

$$\frac{\text{Number of Days in the Period}}{\text{Inventory Turnover}}$$

Cash to cash operating cycle

$$\text{Number of Days' Sales in Inventory} + \text{Number of Days' Sales in Receivables}$$

Solvency Analysis

Debt-to-equity ratio

$$\frac{\text{Total Liabilities}}{\text{Total Stockholders' Equity}}$$

Times interest earned ratio

$$\frac{\text{Net Income} + \text{Interest Expense} + \text{Income Tax Expense}}{\text{Interest Expense}}$$

Debt service coverage ratio

$$\frac{\text{Cash Flow from Operations before Interest and Tax Payments}}{\text{Interest and Principal Payments}}$$

Cash flow from operations to capital expenditures ratio

$$\frac{\text{Cash Flow from Operations} - \text{Total Dividends Paid}}{\text{Cash Paid for Acquisitions}}$$

Profitability Analysis

Gross profit ratio

$$\frac{\text{Gross Profit}}{\text{Net Sales}}$$

Profit margin ratio

$$\frac{\text{Net Income}}{\text{Net Sales}}$$

Return on assets ratio

$$\frac{\text{Net Income} + \text{Interest Expense, Net of Tax}}{\text{Average Total Assets}}$$

Return on sales ratio

$$\frac{\text{Net Income} + \text{Interest Expense, Net of Tax}}{\text{Net Sales}}$$

Asset turnover ratio

$$\frac{\text{Net Sales}}{\text{Average Total Assets}}$$

Return on common stockholders' equity ratio

$$\frac{\text{Net Income} - \text{Preferred Dividends}}{\text{Average Common Stockholders' Equity}}$$

Earnings per share

$$\frac{\text{Net Income} - \text{Preferred Dividends}}{\text{Weighted Average Number of Common Shares Outstanding}}$$

Price/earnings ratio

$$\frac{\text{Current Market Price}}{\text{Earnings per Share}}$$

Dividend payout ratio

$$\frac{\text{Common Dividends per Share}}{\text{Earnings per Share}}$$

Dividend yield ratio

$$\frac{\text{Common Dividends per Share}}{\text{Market Price per Share}}$$

Accounting Tools: Reporting and Analyzing Other Income Statement Items

LO7 Explain how to report on and analyze other income statement items.

Not all companies have income statements that are as easy to understand and interpret as **Wrigley**'s statement. Some companies report any one or some combination of the following three items on their income statements: discontinued operations, extraordinary items, and cumulative effect of a change in accounting principle. Although the nature of each of these items is very distinct, the three do share some common characteristics. First, they are all reported near the end of the income statement, after income from continuing operations. Second, they are reported separately on the income statement to call the reader's attention to their unique nature and to the fact that any additions to, or deductions from, income that they give rise to may not necessarily reoccur in future periods. Finally, each of these items is shown net of their tax effects. This means that any additional taxes due because of them, or any tax benefits from them, are deducted from the items themselves. Following is a brief description of each item.

DISCONTINUED OPERATIONS

When a company decides to either sell or otherwise dispose of one of its operations, it must separately report on that division or segment of the business on its income statement. This includes any gain or loss from the disposal of the business as well as any net income or loss from operating the business until the date of disposal. Because the discontinued segment of the business will not be part of the company's operations in the future, **discontinued operations** are separately disclosed on the income statement. Analysts and other users would normally consider only income from continuing operations in making their decisions.

EXTRAORDINARY ITEMS

According to accounting standards, certain events that give rise to gains or losses are deemed to be extraordinary and are thus separately disclosed on the income statement. To qualify for extraordinary treatment, the gain or loss must be due to an event that is both unusual in nature and infrequent in occurrence.[3] Under current accounting standards, an **extraordinary item** is relatively rare, such as when a natural catastrophe like a tornado destroys a plant in an area not known for tornadoes. As is the case for discontinued operations, analysts and others often ignore the amount of such gains and losses in reaching their decisions since they are aware that these items are not likely to reoccur in the future.

CUMULATIVE EFFECT OF A CHANGE IN ACCOUNTING PRINCIPLE

This line item on the income statement arises when a company makes a change in one of its accounting principles, practices, or methods. For example, when a company changes its depreciation from straight-line to accelerated or its method of valuing inventory from FIFO to average cost, it must report a separate line item on its income statement called **cumulative effect of a change in accounting principle**. The amount of this line item represents the difference in income in all prior years

Discontinued operations
A line item on the income statement to reflect any gains or losses from the disposal of a segment of the business as well as any net income or loss from operating that segment.

Extraordinary item
A line item on the income statement to reflect any gains or losses that arise from an event that is both unusual in nature and infrequent in occurrence.

Cumulative effect of a change in accounting principle
A line item on the income statement to reflect the effect on prior years' income from a change in accounting principle.

3 *APB Opinion No. 30,* "Reporting the Results of Operations," Accounting Principles Board, 1973.

between the old method and the new method. Sometimes, a change in accounting principle is dictated by a new accounting standard. An analyst trying to predict the future profitability of a company might very well ignore a cumulative effect reported as part of net income knowing that this item will not likely reoccur in the future.

STUDY HIGHLIGHTS

Explain the various limitations and considerations in financial statement analysis (p. 614).

LO1

- Financial statement analysis can be a powerful and useful tool in assessing various characteristics of a firm's operations, but the following factors should be considered when conducting this analysis:
  - Alternative accounting principles may sometimes be used.
  - Comparisons must consider inflation, trends over time, and industry norms, among many other variables that influence a business.
  - Ratios from financial statements tell only part of the story about a firm's performance.

Use comparative financial statements to analyze a company over time (horizontal analysis) (p. 616).

LO2

- Amounts appearing on comparative financial statements may be used to perform what is known as horizontal analysis.

Use common-size financial statements to compare various financial statement items (vertical analysis) (p. 621).

LO3

- Common-size statements recast all items as a percentage of a selected item on the statement, such as sales on the income statement.
- The use of common-size financial statements, also known as vertical analysis, facilitates comparisons between companies in addition to comparisons between different periods for the same company.

Compute and use various ratios to assess liquidity (p. 623).

LO4

- Liquidity is a measure of the relative ease with which assets can be converted to cash. Several ratios may be used to assess different aspects of liquidity, including:
  - Current, acid-test (quick), cash from operations to current liabilities, accounts receivable turnover, and inventory turnover ratios.
  - The cash to cash operating cycle measures the average length of time between the purchase of inventory and collection of cash after a sale takes place.

Compute and use various ratios to assess solvency (p. 628).

LO5

- Solvency measures a company's ability to maintain its financial health over the long term. Several ratios may be used to assess different aspects of solvency, including:
  - Debt-to-equity, times interest earned, debt service coverage, and cash flow from operations to capital expenditures ratios.

Compute and use various ratios to assess profitability (p. 631).

LO6

- Profitability concerns the ability of management to use a company's resources to earn a return on funds invested. Measures of profitability include:
  - Return on assets, return on common stockholders' equity, earnings per share, price/earnings, dividend payout, and dividend yield ratios.

Explain how to report on and analyze other income statement items (Appendix p. 638).

LO7

- Some components of the income statement are reported after income from operations or are reported separately because of their unique nature. These items include:
  - Discontinued operations, extraordinary items, and the cumulative effect of a change in accounting principle.

HIGHLIGHTS

KEY TERMS QUIZ

Because of the number of terms introduced in this chapter, there are two key terms quizzes. For each quiz, read each definition below and then write the number of that definition in the blank beside the appropriate term it defines. The quiz solutions appear at the end of the chapter.

Quiz 1:

_____ Horizontal analysis

_____ Vertical analysis

_____ Gross profit ratio

_____ Profit margin ratio

_____ Liquidity

_____ Working capital

_____ Current ratio

_____ Acid-test or quick ratio

_____ Cash flow from operations to current liabilities ratio

_____ Accounts receivable turnover ratio

_____ Number of days' sales in receivables

_____ Inventory turnover ratio

_____ Number of days' sales in inventory

_____ Cash to cash operating cycle

1. A stricter test of liquidity than the current ratio; excludes inventory and prepayments from the numerator.
2. Current assets minus current liabilities.
3. The ratio of current assets to current liabilities.
4. A measure of the average age of accounts receivable.
5. A measure of the ability to pay current debts from operating cash flows.
6. A measure of the number of times accounts receivable are collected in a period.
7. A measure of how long it takes to sell inventory.
8. The length of time from the purchase of inventory to the collection of any receivable from the sale.
9. A measure of the number of times inventory is sold during a period.
10. Gross profit to net sales.
11. A comparison of various financial statement items within a single period with the use of common-size statements.
12. Net income to net sales.
13. The nearness to cash of the assets and liabilities.
14. A comparison of financial statement items over a period of time.

Quiz 2:

_____ Solvency

_____ Debt-to-equity ratio

_____ Times interest earned ratio

_____ Debt service coverage ratio

_____ Cash flow from operations to capital expenditures ratio

_____ Profitability

_____ Return on assets ratio

_____ Return on sales ratio

_____ Asset turnover ratio

_____ Return on common stockholders' equity ratio

_____ Leverage

_____ Earnings per share

_____ Price/earnings (P/E) ratio

_____ Dividend payout ratio

_____ Dividend yield ratio

_____ Discontinued operations (Appendix)

_____ Extraordinary item (Appendix)

_____ Cumulative effect of a change in accounting principle (Appendix)

1. A measure of a company's success in earning a return for the common stockholders.
2. The relationship between a company's performance according to the income statement and its performance in the stock market.
3. The ability of a company to remain in business over the long term.

4. A variation of the profit margin ratio; measures earnings before payments to creditors.

5. A company's bottom line stated on a per-share basis.

6. The percentage of earnings paid out as dividends.

7. The ratio of total liabilities to total stockholders' equity.

8. A measure of the ability of a company to finance long-term asset acquisitions with cash from operations.

9. A measure of a company's success in earning a return for all providers of capital.

10. The relationship between net sales and average total assets.

11. The relationship between dividends and the market price of a company's stock.

12. The use of borrowed funds and amounts contributed by preferred stockholders to earn an overall return higher than the cost of these funds.

13. An income statement measure of the ability of a company to meet its interest payments.

14. A statement of cash flows measure of the ability of a company to meet its interest and principal payments.

15. How well management is using company resources to earn a return on the funds invested by various groups.

16. A line item on the income statement to reflect any gains or losses that arise from an event that is both unusual in nature and infrequent in occurrence.

17. A line item on the income statement to reflect the effect on prior years' income from a change in accounting principle.

18. A line item on the income statement to reflect any gains or losses from the disposal of a segment of the business as well as any net income or loss from operating that segment.

ALTERNATE TERMS

Acid-test ratio Quick ratio

Horizontal analysis Trend analysis

Number of days' sales in receivables Average collection period

Price/earnings ratio P/E ratio

WARMUP EXERCISES & SOLUTIONS

LO4,5,6 **Warmup Exercise 13-1** Types of Ratios

Fill in the blanks that follow to indicate whether each of the following ratios is concerned with a company's liquidity (L), its solvency (S), or its profitability (P).

_____ 1. Return on assets ratio

_____ 2. Current ratio

_____ 3. Debt-to-equity ratio

_____ 4. Earnings per share

_____ 5. Inventory turnover ratio

_____ 6. Gross profit ratio

Key to the Solution Review the summary of selected ratios in Exhibit 13-8.

LO4 **Warmup Exercise 13-2** Accounts Receivable Turnover

Company A reported sales during the year of $1,000,000. Its average accounts receivable balance during the year was $250,000. Company B reported sales during the same year of $400,000 and had an average accounts receivable balance of $40,000.

Required

1. Compute the accounts receivable turnover for both companies.

2. What is the average length of time each company takes to collect its receivables?

Key to the Solution Review the summary of selected ratios in Exhibit 13-8.

LO6 **Warmup Exercise 13-3** Earnings per Share

A company reported net income during the year of $90,000 and paid dividends of $15,000 to its common stockholders and $10,000 to its preferred stockholders. During the year, 20,000 shares of common stock were outstanding and 10,000 shares of preferred stock were outstanding.

Required

Compute earnings per share for the year.

Key to the Solution Recall that earnings per share only has relevance to the common stockholders and therefore it is a measure of the earnings per common share outstanding, after taking into account any claims of preferred stockholders.

SOLUTIONS TO WARMUP EXERCISES

Warmup Exercise 13-1

1. P   2. L   3. S   4. P   5. L   6. P

Warmup Exercise 13-2

1. Company A turns over its accounts receivable, on the average, 4 times during the year ($1,000,000/$250,000) and Company B 10 times during the year ($400,000/$40,000).
2. Assuming 360 days in a year, Company A takes, on the average, 90 days to collect its accounts receivable, and Company B takes, on the average, 36 days.

Warmup Exercise 13-3

Earnings per share: ($90,000 − $10,000)/20,000 shares = $4 per share.

REVIEW PROBLEM & SOLUTION

On pages 642–644 are the comparative financial statements for **Wm. Wrigley Jr. Company**, the chewing gum manufacturer, as shown in its 2004 annual report.

Required

1. Compute the following ratios for the two years 2004 and 2003, either for each year or as of the end of each of the years, as appropriate. Beginning balances for 2003 are not available; that is, you do not have a balance sheet as of the end of 2002. Therefore, to be consistent, use year-end balances for both years where you would normally use average

---

Wm. Wrigley Jr. Company
Consolidated Statement of Earnings
In thousands of dollars except per share amounts

	2004	2003	2002
EARNINGS			
Net sales	$3,648,592	3,069,088	2,746,318
Cost of sales	1,609,978	1,317,416	1,186,685
Gross profit	2,038,614	1,751,672	1,559,633
Selling, general and administrative expense	1,318,395	1,102,310	974,559
Operating income	720,219	649,362	585,074
Investment income	11,871	9,608	8,918
Other expense	(11,594)	(7,429)	(10,571)
Earnings before income taxes	720,496	651,541	583,421
Income taxes	227,542	205,647	181,896
Net earnings	$ 492,954	445,894	401,525
PER SHARE AMOUNTS			
Net earnings per share of Common Stock (basic and diluted)	$ 2.19	1.98	1.78
Dividends paid per share of Common Stock	.925	.865	.805

See accompanying accounting policies and notes.

REVIEW

amounts for the year. To compute the return on assets ratio, you will need to find the tax rate. Use the relationship between income taxes and earnings before taxes to find the rate for each year.

a. Current ratio
b. Quick ratio
c. Cash flow from operations to current liabilities ratio
d. Number of days' sales in receivables
e. Number of days' sales in inventory
f. Debt-to-equity ratio
g. Debt service coverage ratio
h. Cash flow from operations to capital expenditures ratio
i. Return on assets ratio
j. Return on common stockholders' equity ratio

(continued)

Wm. Wrigley Jr. Company
Consolidated Statement of Cash Flows
In thousands of dollars

	2004	2003	2002
OPERATING ACTIVITIES			
Net earnings	$ 492,954	445,894	401,525
Adjustments to reconcile net earnings to net cash provided by operating activities:			
Depreciation	141,851	120,040	85,568
Loss on retirements of property, plant and equipment	12,417	15,510	1,014
(Increase) Decrease in:			
Accounts receivable	25,706	9,718	(55,288)
Inventories	(3,213)	(11,426)	(31,858)
Other current assets	8,937	(16,195)	1,304
Deferred charges and other assets	(48,911)	(2,244)	(78,585)
Increase (Decrease) in:			
Accounts payable	43,013	27,442	756
Accrued expenses	43,595	23,972	33,416
Income and other taxes payable	(6,070)	9,011	(3,715)
Deferred income taxes	(7,014)	7,947	19,082
Other noncurrent liabilities	21,242	15,826	1,216
Net cash provided by operating activities	724,507	645,495	374,435
INVESTING ACTIVITIES			
Additions to property, plant and equipment	(220,322)	(220,259)	(216,872)
Proceeds from retirements of property, plant and equipment	2,468	8,581	5,017
Acquisition, net of cash acquired	(264,477)	—	—
Purchases of short-term investments	(40,464)	(43,369)	(41,177)
Maturities of short-term investments	40,453	48,077	44,858
Net cash used in investing activities	(482,342)	(206,970)	(208,174)
FINANCING ACTIVITIES			
Dividends paid	(207,803)	(194,633)	(181,232)
Common Stock purchased, net	(28,409)	(22,532)	(16,402)
Borrowings under the line of credit, net	90,000	—	—
Net cash used in financing activities	(146,212)	(217,165)	(197,634)
Effect of exchange rate changes on cash and cash equivalents	27,383	4,581	2,864
Net increase (decrease) in cash and cash equivalents	123,336	225,941	(28,509)
Cash and cash equivalents at beginning of year	505,217	279,276	307,785
Cash and cash equivalents at end of year	$ 628,553	505,217	279,276
SUPPLEMENTAL CASH FLOW INFORMATION			
Income taxes paid	$ 234,800	192,646	173,010
Interest paid	$ 3,879	1,724	1,636
Interest and dividends received	$ 11,871	9,621	8,974

See accompanying accounting policies and notes.

Wm. Wrigley Jr. Company
Consolidated Balance Sheet
In thousands of dollars

	2004	2003
ASSETS		
Current assets:		
Cash and cash equivalents	$ 628,553	505,217
Short-term investments, at amortized cost	22,764	22,509
Accounts receivable (less allowance for doubtful accounts: 2004–$11,682; 2003–$9,232)	356,389	328,862
Inventories:		
Finished goods	135,527	127,839
Raw materials, work in process and supplies	262,580	222,129
	398,107	349,968
Other current assets	65,336	67,170
Deferred income taxes—current	34,761	23,826
Total current assets	1,505,910	1,297,552
Marketable equity securities, at fair value	16,970	16,239
Deferred charges and other assets	250,158	186,770
Goodwill and other intangibles	210,806	37,482
Deferred income taxes—noncurrent	40,239	33,148
Property, plant and equipment, at cost:		
Land	53,209	50,499
Buildings and building equipment	555,375	422,468
Machinery and equipment	1,464,903	1,272,226
	2,073,487	1,745,193
Less accumulated depreciation	930,867	789,013
Net property, plant and equipment	1,142,620	956,180
TOTAL ASSETS	$3,166,703	2,527,371
LIABILITIES AND STOCKHOLDERS' EQUITY		
Current liabilities:		
Line of credit	$ 90,000	—
Accounts payable	216,764	134,888
Accrued expenses	271,236	206,360
Dividends payable	52,821	49,469
Income and other taxes payable	76,554	75,611
Deferred income taxes—current	10,595	5,427
Total current liabilities	717,970	471,755
Deferred income taxes—noncurrent	88,112	82,919
Other noncurrent liabilities	181,937	151,876
Stockholders' equity:		
Preferred Stock—no par value		
Authorized: 20,000 shares		
Issued: None		
Common Stock—no par value		
Common Stock		
Authorized: 400,000 shares		
Issued: 2004–198,930 shares; 2003–191,964 shares	13,254	12,790
Class B Common Stock—convertible		
Authorized: 80,000 shares		
Issued and outstanding: 2004–33,511 shares; 2003–40,477 shares	2,242	2,706
Additional paid-in capital	17,764	8,342
Retained earnings	2,435,838	2,152,566
Common Stock in treasury, at cost (2004–7,670 shares; 2003–7,581 shares)	(346,087)	(320,450)
Accumulated other comprehensive income:		
Foreign currency translation adjustment	44,936	(42,692)
Gain (loss) on derivative contracts	758	(1,902)
Unrealized holding gains on marketable equity securities	9,979	9,461
	55,673	(35,133)
Total stockholders' equity	2,178,684	1,820,821
TOTAL LIABILITIES AND STOCKHOLDERS' EQUITY	$3,166,703	2,527,371

See accompanying accounting policies and notes.

2. Comment on Wrigley's liquidity. Has it improved or declined over the two-year period?
3. Does Wrigley appear to be solvent to you? Does there appear to be anything unusual about its capital structure?
4. Comment on Wrigley's profitability. Would you buy stock in the company?

SOLUTION TO REVIEW PROBLEM

1. Ratios:
   a. 2004: $\$1,505,910/\$717,970 = \underline{2.10}$

   2003: $\$1,297,552/\$471,755 = \underline{2.75}$

   b. 2004: $(\$628,553 + \$22,764 + \$356,389)/\$717,970 = \underline{1.40}$

   2003: $(\$505,217 + \$22,509 + \$328,862)/\$471,755 = \underline{1.82}$

   c. 2004: $\$724,507/\$717,970 = \underline{1.01}$

   2003: $\$645,495/\$471,755 = \underline{1.37}$

   d. 2004: 360 days$/[(\$3,648,592/\$356,389)] = 360/10.24 = \underline{35 \text{ days}}$

   2003: 360 days$/[(\$3,069,088/\$328,862)] = 360/9.33 = \underline{39 \text{ days}}$

   e. 2004: 360 days$/[(\$1,609,978/\$398,107)] = 360/4.04 = \underline{89 \text{ days}}$

   2003: 360 days$/[(\$1,317,416/\$349,968)] = 360/3.76 = \underline{96 \text{ days}}$

   f. 2004: $(\$717,970 + \$88,112 + \$181,937)/\$2,178,684 = \underline{0.45}$

   2003: $(\$471,755 + \$82,919 + \$151,876)/\$1,820,821 = \underline{0.39}$

   g. 2004: $(\$724,507 + \$234,800 + \$3,879)/\$3,879 = \underline{248}$

   2003: $(\$645,495 + \$192,646 + \$1,724)/\$1,724 = \underline{487}$

   h. 2004: $(\$724,507 - \$207,803)/\$220,322 = \underline{2.35}$

   2003: $(\$645,495 - \$194,633)/\$220,259 = \underline{2.05}$

   i. 2004: $\{\$492,954 + [\$3,879^{a}(1 - 0.32^{b})]\}/\$3,166,703 = \underline{15.7\%}$

   2003: $\{\$445,894 + [\$1,724^{a}(1 - 0.32^{b})]\}/\$2,527,371 = \underline{17.7\%}$

   j. 2004: $\$492,954/\$2,178,684^{c} = \underline{22.6\%}$

   2003: $\$445,894/\$1,820,821^{c} = \underline{24.5\%}$

2. Although both the current ratio and the quick ratio declined during 2004, the current ratio is still over 2 to 1 and the quick ratio is 1.4 to 1. Cash flow from operations to current liabilities also declined, although the ratio at the end of 2004 was still greater than 1 to 1 overall. Wrigley appears to be quite liquid and should have no problems meeting its short-term obligations.

3. Wrigley is extremely solvent. Its capital structure reveals that it does not rely in any significant way on long-term debt to finance its business. The amount of noncurrent liabilities is only about 9% of total liabilities and stockholders' equity at the end of each year. In fact, a majority of Wrigley's debt is in the form of interest-free current liabilities. Most revealing is the debt service coverage ratio of 248 times in 2004 and 487 times in 2003. The total interest expense each year is insignificant.

4. The return on assets for 2004 is 15.7%, and the return on common stockholders' equity is 22.6%. Although these return ratios are down slightly from the prior year, they indicate a very profitable company. It should be noted that the company paid nearly half of its 2004 earnings in dividends. Wrigley appears to be a very sound investment, but many other factors, including information on the current market price of the stock, should be considered before making a decision.

---

[a]Wrigley does not separately disclose interest expense on its income statement; the amounts of interest paid that are reported at the bottom of statements of cash flows have been used for the calculations.
[b]Tax rate for each of the two years:
  2004: $\$227,542/\$720,496 = 0.32$
  2003: $\$205,647/\$651,541 = 0.32$

[c]In addition to its common stock, Wrigley has outstanding Class B common stock. Because this is a second class of stock (similar in many respects to preferred stock), the contributed capital attributable to it should be deducted from total stockholders' equity in the denominator. Similarly, any dividends paid on the Class B common stock should be deducted from net income in the numerator to find the return to the regular common stockholders. We have ignored the difficulties involved in determining these adjustments in our calculations of return on equity.

REVIEW

QUESTIONS

1. Two companies are in the same industry. Company A uses the LIFO method of inventory valuation, and Company B uses FIFO. What difficulties does this present when comparing the two companies?

2. You are told to compare the company's results for the year, as measured by various ratios, with one of the published surveys that arranges information by industry classification. What are some of the difficulties you may encounter when making comparisons using industry standards?

3. What types of problems does inflation cause in analyzing financial statements?

4. Distinguish between horizontal and vertical analysis. Why is the analysis of common-size statements called *vertical* analysis? Why is horizontal analysis sometimes called *trend* analysis?

5. A company experiences a 15% increase in sales over the previous year. However, gross profit actually decreased by 5% from the previous year. What are some of the possible causes for an increase in sales but a decline in gross profit?

6. A company's total current assets have increased by 5% over the prior year. Management is concerned, however, about the composition of the current assets. Why is the composition of current assets important?

7. Ratios were categorized in the chapter according to their use in performing three different types of analysis. What are the three types of ratios?

8. Describe the operating cycle for a manufacturing company. How would the cycle differ for a retailer?

9. What accounts for the order in which current assets are presented on a balance sheet?

10. A company has a current ratio of 1.25 but an acid-test or quick ratio of only 0.65. How can this difference in the two ratios be explained? What are some concerns that you would have about this company?

11. Explain the basic concept underlying all turnover ratios. Why is it advisable in computing a turnover ratio to use an average in the denominator (for example, average inventory)?

12. Sanders Company's accounts receivable turned over nine times during the year. The credit department extends terms of 2/10, net 30. Does the turnover ratio indicate any problems that management should investigate?

13. The turnover of inventory for Ace Company has slowed from 6.0 times per year to 4.5 times. What are some of the possible explanations for this decrease?

14. How does the operating cycle for a manufacturer differ from the operating cycle for a service company, for example, an airline?

15. What is the difference between liquidity analysis and solvency analysis?

16. Why is the debt service coverage ratio a better measure of solvency than the times interest earned ratio?

17. A friend tells you that the best way to assess solvency is by comparing total debt to total assets. Another friend says that solvency is measured by comparing total debt to total stockholders' equity. Which one is right?

18. A company is in the process of negotiating with a bank for an additional loan. Why will the bank be very interested in the company's debt service coverage ratio?

19. What is the rationale for deducting dividends when computing the ratio of cash flow from operations to capital expenditures?

20. The rate of return on assets ratio is computed by dividing net income and interest expense, net of tax, by average total assets. Why is the numerator net income and interest expense, net of tax, rather than just net income?

21. A company has a return on assets of 14% and a return on common stockholders' equity of 11%. The president of the company has asked you to explain the reason for this difference. What causes the difference? How is the concept of financial leverage involved?

22. What is meant by the "quality" of a company's earnings? Explain why the price/earnings ratio for a company may indicate the quality of earnings.

23. Some ratios are more useful for management, whereas others are better suited to the needs of outsiders, such as stockholders and bankers. What is an example of a ratio that is primarily suited to management use? What is one that is more suited to use by outsiders?

24. The needs of service-oriented companies in analyzing financial statements differ from those of product-oriented companies. Why is this true? Give an example of a ratio that is meaningless to a service business.

25. What is the reason for reporting discontinued operations, extraordinary items, and the cumulative effect of a change in accounting principle separately on an income statement? (Appendix)

EXERCISES

LO4   **Exercise 13-1** Accounts Receivable Analysis

The following account balances are taken from the records of the Faraway Travel Agency:

	December 31		
	2007	**2006**	**2005**
Accounts receivable	$150,000	$100,000	$80,000

	2007	**2006**
Net credit sales	$600,000	$540,000

Faraway extends credit terms requiring full payment in 60 days, with no discount for early payment.

Required
1. Compute Faraway's accounts receivable turnover ratio for 2007 and 2006.
2. Compute the number of days' sales in receivables for 2007 and 2006. Assume 360 days in a year.
3. Comment on the efficiency of Faraway's collection efforts over the two-year period.

LO4 **Exercise 13-2** Inventory Analysis

The following account balances are taken from the records of Lewis Inc., a wholesaler of fresh fruits and vegetables:

	December 31		
	2007	**2006**	**2005**
Merchandise inventory	$ 200,000	$ 150,000	$120,000

	2007	**2006**
Cost of goods sold	$7,100,000	$8,100,000

Required
1. Compute Lewis's inventory turnover ratio for 2007 and 2006.
2. Compute the number of days' sales in inventory for 2007 and 2006. Assume 360 days in a year.
3. Comment on your answers in parts (1) and (2) relative to the company's management of inventory over the two years. What problems do you see in its inventory management?

LO4 **Exercise 13-3** Accounts Receivable and Inventory Analyses for Coca-Cola and PepsiCo

The following information was obtained from the 2004 and 2003 financial statements of **Coca-Cola Company and Subsidiaries** and **PepsiCo Inc. and Subsidiaries** (year-ends for PepsiCo are December 25, 2004 and December 27, 2003):

(in millions)		Coca-Cola	PepsiCo
Accounts and notes receivable, net[a]	12/31/04	$ 2,171	$ 2,999
	12/31/03	2,091	2,830
Inventories	12/31/04	1,420	1,541
	12/31/03	1,252	1,412
Net revenue[b]	2004	21,962	29,261
	2003	21,044	26,971
Cost of goods sold[c]	2004	7,638	13,406
	2003	7,762	12,379

[a]*Described as "trade accounts receivable" by Coca-Cola.*
[b]*Described as "net operating revenues" by Coca-Cola.*
[c]*Described as "cost of sales" by PepsiCo.*

Required
1. Using the information provided above, compute the following for each company for 2004:
   a. Accounts receivable turnover ratio
   b. Number of days' sales in receivables
   c. Inventory turnover ratio
   d. Number of days' sales in inventory
   e. Cash to cash operating cycle
2. Comment briefly on the liquidity of each of these two companies.

LO4

Exercise 13-4 Liquidity Analyses for Coca-Cola and PepsiCo

The following information was summarized from the balance sheets of the **Coca-Cola Company and Subsidiaries** at December 31, 2004, and **PepsiCo Inc. and Subsidiaries** at December 25, 2004:

(in millions)	Coca-Cola	PepsiCo
Cash and cash equivalents	$ 6,707	$ 1,280
Short-term investments/marketable securities	61	2,165
Accounts and notes receivables, net*	2,171	2,999
Inventories	1,420	1,541
Prepaid expenses and other current assets	1,735	654
Total current assets	$12,094	$ 8,639
Current liabilities	$10,971	$ 6,752
Other liabilities	4,421	7,712
Stockholders' equity	15,935	13,523

Described as "trade accounts receivable" by Coca-Cola.

Required

1. Using the information provided above, compute the following for each company at the end of 2004:
   a. Current ratio
   b. Quick ratio
2. Comment briefly on the liquidity of each of these two companies. Which appears to be more liquid?
3. What other ratios would help you to more fully assess the liquidity of these companies?

LO4

Exercise 13-5 Liquidity Analyses for McDonald's and Wendy's

The following information was summarized from the balance sheets of **McDonald's Corporation** and **Wendy's International Inc.** at December 31, 2004, and January 2, 2005, respectively:

	McDonald's (in millions)	Wendy's (in thousands)
Current Assets:		
Cash and cash equivalents	$ 1,379.8	$ 176,749
Accounts receivable, net*	745.5	127,158
Notes receivable, net	—	11,626
Deferred income taxes	0	27,280
Inventories**	147.5	56,010
Other current assets	585.0	—
Advertising fund restricted assets	0	60,021
Total current assets	$ 2,857.8	$ 458,844
Current liabilities	$ 3,520.5	$ 688,387
Other liabilities	$10,115.5	$ 793,468
Stockholders' equity	$14,201.5	$1,715,689

McDonald's combines accounts and notes receivable.
**Inventories and other for Wendy's.*

Required

1. Using the information provided above, compute the following for each company at year end:
   a. Working capital
   b. Current ratio
   c. Quick ratio
2. Comment briefly on the liquidity of each of these two companies. Which appears to be more liquid?
3. McDonald's reported cash flows from operations of $3,903.6 million during 2004. Wendy's reported cash flows from operations of $502,352 thousand. Current liabilities reported by McDonald's at December 31, 2003, and Wendy's at December 28, 2003, were $2,748.5 million and $528,473 thousand, respectively. Calculate the cash flow from operations to current liabilities ratio for each company. Does the information provided by this ratio change your opinion as to the relative liquidity of each of these two companies?
4. What steps might be taken by McDonald's to cover its short-term cash requirements?

LO5 **Exercise 13-6** Solvency Analyses for IBM

The following information was obtained from the comparative financial statements included in **IBM**'s 2004 annual report (all amounts are in millions of dollars):

	December 31, 2004	December 31, 2003
Total liabilities	$79,436	$76,593
Total shareholders' equity	29,747	27,864

	For the Years Ended December 31	
	2004	2003
Interest expense	$ 139	$ 145
Provision for income taxes	3,580	3,261
Net income	8,430	7,583
Net cash provided by operating activities from continuing operations	15,406	14,569
Cash dividends paid	1,174	1,085
Payments for plant, rental machines and other property	4,368	4,393
Payments to settle debt	4,538	5,831

Required

1. Using the information provided above, compute the following for 2004 and 2003:
   a. Debt-to-equity ratio (at each year-end)
   b. Times interest earned ratio
   c. Debt service coverage ratio
   d. Cash flow from operations to capital expenditures ratio
2. Comment briefly on the company's solvency.

LO5 **Exercise 13-7** Solvency Analysis

The following information is available from the balance sheets at the ends of the two most recent years and the income statement for the most recent year of Impact Company:

	December 31	
	2007	2006
Accounts payable	$ 65,000	$ 50,000
Accrued liabilities	25,000	35,000
Taxes payable	60,000	45,000
Short-term notes payable	0	75,000
Bonds payable due within next year	200,000	200,000
Total current liabilities	$ 350,000	$ 405,000
Bonds payable	$ 600,000	$ 800,000
Common stock, $10 par	$1,000,000	$1,000,000
Retained earnings	650,000	500,000
Total stockholders' equity	$1,650,000	$1,500,000
Total liabilities and stockholders' equity	$2,600,000	$2,705,000

	2007
Sales revenue	$1,600,000
Cost of goods sold	950,000
Gross profit	$ 650,000
Selling and administrative expense	300,000
Operating income	$ 350,000
Interest expense	89,000
Income before tax	$ 261,000
Income tax expense	111,000
Net income	$ 150,000

(continued)

Other Information

a. Short-term notes payable represents a 12-month loan that matured in November 2007. Interest of 12% was paid at maturity.

b. One million dollars of serial bonds had been issued 10 years earlier. The first series of $200,000 matured at the end of 2007, with interest of 8% payable annually.

c. Cash flow from operations was $185,000 in 2007. The amounts of interest and taxes paid during 2007 were $89,000 and $96,000, respectively.

Required

1. Compute the following for Impact Company:
   a. The debt-to-equity ratio at December 31, 2007, and December 31, 2006
   b. The times interest earned ratio for 2007
   c. The debt service coverage ratio for 2007
2. Comment on Impact's solvency at the end of 2007. Do the times interest earned ratio and the debt service coverage ratio differ in their indication of Impact's ability to pay its debts?

LO6

Exercise 13-8 Return Ratios and Leverage

The following selected data are taken from the financial statements of Evergreen Company:

Sales revenue	$ 650,000
Cost of goods sold	400,000
Gross profit	$ 250,000
Selling and administrative expense	100,000
Operating income	$ 150,000
Interest expense	50,000
Income before tax	$ 100,000
Income tax expense (40%)	40,000
Net income	$ 60,000
Accounts payable	$ 45,000
Accrued liabilities	70,000
Income taxes payable	10,000
Interest payable	25,000
Short-term loans payable	150,000
Total current liabilities	$ 300,000
Long-term bonds payable	$ 500,000
Preferred stock, 10%, $100 par	$ 250,000
Common stock, no par	600,000
Retained earnings	350,000
Total stockholders' equity	$1,200,000
Total liabilities and stockholders' equity	$2,000,000

Required

1. Compute the following ratios for Evergreen Company:
   a. Return on sales
   b. Asset turnover (Assume that total assets at the beginning of the year were $1,600,000.)
   c. Return on assets
   d. Return on common stockholders' equity (Assume that the only changes in stockholders' equity during the year were from the net income for the year and dividends on the preferred stock.)
2. Comment on Evergreen's use of leverage. Has it successfully employed leverage? Explain.

LO6

Exercise 13-9 Relationships among Return on Assets, Return on Sales, and Asset Turnover

A company's return on assets is a function of its ability to turn over its investment (asset turnover) and earn a profit on each dollar of sales (return on sales). For each of the *independent* cases below, determine the missing amounts. (*Note:* Assume in each case that the company has no interest expense; that is, net income is used as the definition of income in all calculations.)

Case 1	
Net income	$10,000
Net sales	$80,000
Average total assets	$60,000
Return on assets	?

Case 2

Net income	$25,000
Average total assets	$250,000
Return on sales	2%
Net sales	?

Case 3

Average total assets	$80,000
Asset turnover	1.5 times
Return on sales	6%
Return on assets	?

Case 4

Return on assets	10%
Net sales	$50,000
Asset turnover	1.25 times
Net income	?

Case 5

Return on assets	15%
Net income	$20,000
Return on sales	5%
Average total assets	?

LO6

Exercise 13-10 EPS, P/E Ratio, and Dividend Ratios

The stockholders' equity section of the balance sheet for Cooperstown Corp. at the end of 2007 appears as follows:

8%, $100 par, cumulative preferred stock, 200,000 shares authorized,	
50,000 shares issued and outstanding	$ 5,000,000
Additional paid-in capital on preferred	2,500,000
Common stock, $5 par, 500,000 shares authorized,	
400,000 shares issued and outstanding	2,000,000
Additional paid-in capital on common	18,000,000
Retained earnings	37,500,000
Total stockholders' equity	$65,000,000

Net income for the year was $1,300,000. Dividends were declared and paid on the preferred shares during the year, and a quarterly dividend of $0.40 per share was declared and paid each quarter on the common shares. The closing market price for the common shares on December 31, 2007, was $24.75 per share.

Required

1. Compute the following ratios for the common stock:
   a. Earnings per share
   b. Price/earnings ratio
   c. Dividend payout ratio
   d. Dividend yield ratio
2. Assume that you are an investment adviser. What other information would you want to have before advising a client regarding the purchase of Cooperstown stock?

LO6

Exercise 13-11 Earnings per Share and Extraordinary Items

The stockholders' equity section of the balance sheet for Lahey Construction Company at the end of 2007 follows:

9%, $10 par, cumulative preferred stock, 500,000 shares authorized,	
200,000 shares issued and outstanding	$ 2,000,000
Additional paid-in capital on preferred	7,500,000
Common stock, $1 par, 2,500,000 shares authorized,	
1,500,000 shares issued and outstanding	1,500,000
Additional paid-in capital on common	21,000,000
Retained earnings	25,500,000
Total stockholders' equity	$57,500,000

(continued)

HOMEWORK

The lower portion of the 2007 income statement indicates the following:

Net income before tax		$ 9,750,000
Income tax expense (40%)		(3,900,000)
Income before extraordinary items		$ 5,850,000
Extraordinary loss from flood	$(6,200,000)	
Less related tax effect (40%)	2,480,000	(3,720,000)
Net income		$ 2,130,000

Assume the number of shares outstanding did not change during the year.

Required

1. Compute earnings per share *before* extraordinary items.
2. Compute earnings per share *after* the extraordinary loss.
3. Which of the two EPS ratios is more useful to management? Explain your answer. Would your answer be different if the ratios were to be used by an outsider, for example, by a potential stockholder? Why?

MULTI-CONCEPT EXERCISES

LO2,3   **Exercise 13-12** Common-Size Balance Sheets and Horizontal Analysis

Comparative balance sheets for Farinet Company for the past two years are as follows:

	December 31	
	2007	**2006**
Cash	$ 16,000	$ 20,000
Accounts receivable	40,000	30,000
Inventory	30,000	50,000
Prepaid rent	18,000	12,000
Total current assets	$104,000	$112,000
Land	$150,000	$150,000
Plant and equipment	800,000	600,000
Accumulated depreciation	(130,000)	(60,000)
Total long-term assets	$820,000	$690,000
Total assets	$924,000	$802,000
Accounts payable	$ 24,000	$ 20,000
Income taxes payable	6,000	10,000
Short-term notes payable	70,000	50,000
Total current liabilities	$100,000	$ 80,000
Bonds payable	$150,000	$200,000
Common stock	$400,000	$300,000
Retained earnings	274,000	222,000
Total stockholders' equity	$674,000	$522,000
Total liabilities and stockholders' equity	$924,000	$802,000

Required

1. Using the format in Exhibit 13-5, prepare common-size comparative balance sheets for the two years for Farinet Company.
2. What observations can you make about the changes in the relative composition of Farinet's accounts from the common-size balance sheets? List at least five observations.
3. Using the format in Exhibit 13-1, prepare comparative balance sheets for Farinet Company, including columns both for the dollars and for the percentage increase or decrease in each item on the statement.
4. Identify the five items on the balance sheet that experienced the largest change from one year to the next. For each of these, explain where you would look to find additional information about the change.

LO2,3   **Exercise 13-13** Common-Size Income Statements and Horizontal Analysis

Income statements for Mariners Corp. for the past two years follow:

	(amounts in thousands of dollars)	
	2007	**2006**
Sales revenue	$60,000	$50,000
Cost of goods sold	42,000	30,000
Gross profit	$18,000	$20,000
Selling and administrative expense	9,000	5,000
Operating income	$ 9,000	$15,000
Interest expense	2,000	2,000
Income before tax	$ 7,000	$13,000
Income tax expense	2,000	4,000
Net income	$ 5,000	$ 9,000

Required

1. Using the format in Exhibit 13-6, prepare common-size comparative income statements for the two years for Mariners Corp.
2. What observations can you make about the common-size statements? List at least four observations.
3. Using the format in Exhibit 13-2, prepare comparative income statements for Mariners Corp., including columns both for the dollars and for the percentage increase or decrease in each item on the statement.
4. Identify the two items on the income statement that experienced the largest change from one year to the next. For each of these, explain where you would look to find additional information about the change.

PROBLEMS

LO4   **Problem 13-1** Effect of Transactions on Working Capital, Current Ratio, and Quick Ratio

(*Note:* Consider completing Problem 13-2 after this problem to ensure that you obtain a clear understanding of the effect of various transactions on these measures of liquidity.) The following account balances are taken from the records of Liquiform Inc.:

Cash	$ 70,000
Short-term investments	60,000
Accounts receivable	80,000
Inventory	100,000
Prepaid insurance	10,000
Accounts payable	75,000
Taxes payable	25,000
Salaries and wages payable	40,000
Short-term loans payable	60,000

Required

1. Use the information provided above to compute the amount of working capital and Liquiform's current and quick ratios (round to three decimal points).
2. Determine the effect that each of the following transactions will have on Liquiform's working capital, current ratio, and quick ratio by recalculating each and then indicating whether the measure is increased, decreased, or not affected by the transaction. (For the ratios, round to three decimal points.) Consider each transaction independently; that is, assume that it is the *only* transaction that takes place.

(continued)

| | Effect of Transaction on | | |
Transaction	Working Capital	Current Ratio	Quick Ratio
a. Purchased inventory on account for $20,000.			
b. Purchased inventory for cash, $15,000.			
c. Paid suppliers on account, $30,000.			
d. Received cash on account, $40,000.			
e. Paid insurance for next year, $20,000.			
f. Made sales on account, $60,000.			
g. Repaid short-term loans at bank, $25,000.			
h. Borrowed $40,000 at bank for 90 days.			
i. Declared and paid $45,000 cash dividend.			
j. Purchased $20,000 of short-term investments.			
k. Paid $30,000 in salaries.			
l. Accrued additional $15,000 in taxes.			

LO4

Problem 13-2 Effect of Transactions on Working Capital, Current Ratio, and Quick Ratio

(*Note:* Consider completing this problem after Problem 13-1 to ensure that you obtain a clear understanding of the effect of various transactions on these measures of liquidity.) The following account balances are taken from the records of Veriform Inc.:

Cash	$ 70,000
Short-term investments	60,000
Accounts receivable	80,000
Inventory	100,000
Prepaid insurance	10,000
Accounts payable	75,000
Taxes payable	25,000
Salaries and wages payable	40,000
Short-term loans payable	210,000

Required

1. Use the information provided above to compute the amount of working capital and Veriform's current and quick ratios (round to three decimal points).
2. Determine the effect that each of the following transactions will have on Veriform's working capital, current ratio, and quick ratio by recalculating each and then indicating whether the measure is increased, decreased, or not affected by the transaction. (For the ratios, round to three decimal points.) Consider each transaction independently; that is, assume that it is the *only* transaction that takes place.

| | Effect of Transaction on | | |
Transaction	Working Capital	Current Ratio	Quick Ratio
a. Purchased inventory on account for $20,000.			
b. Purchased inventory for cash, $15,000.			
c. Paid suppliers on account, $30,000.			
d. Received cash on account, $40,000.			
e. Paid insurance for next year, $20,000.			
f. Made sales on account, $60,000.			
g. Repaid short-term loans at bank, $25,000.			
h. Borrowed $40,000 at bank for 90 days.			
i. Declared and paid $45,000 cash dividend.			
j. Purchased $20,000 of short-term investments.			
k. Paid $30,000 in salaries.			
l. Accrued additional $15,000 in taxes.			

LO6

Problem 13-3 Goals for Sales and Return on Assets

The president of Blue Skies Corp. is reviewing with his vice presidents the operating results of the year just completed. Sales increased by 15% from the previous year to $60,000,000. Average total assets for the year were $40,000,000. Net income, after adding back interest expense, net of tax, was $5,000,000.

The president is happy with the performance over the past year but is never satisfied with the status quo. He has set two specific goals for next year: (1) a 20% growth in sales and (2) a return on assets of 15%.

To achieve the second goal, the president has stated his intention to increase the total asset base by 12.5% over the base for the year just completed.

Required

1. For the year just completed, compute the following ratios:
   a. Return on sales
   b. Asset turnover
   c. Return on assets
2. Compute the necessary asset turnover for next year to achieve the president's goal of a 20% increase in sales.
3. Calculate the income needed next year to achieve the goal of a 15% return on total assets. (*Note:* Assume that *income* is defined as net income plus interest, net of tax.)
4. Based on your answers to parts (2) and (3), comment on the reasonableness of the president's goals. What must the company focus on to attain these goals?

LO6   **Problem 13-4** Goals for Sales and Income Growth

Sunrise Corp. is a major regional retailer. The chief executive officer (CEO) is concerned with the slow growth both of sales and of net income and the subsequent effect on the trading price of the common stock. Selected financial data for the past three years follow.

Sunrise Corp.
(in millions)

	2007	2006	2005
1. Sales	$200.0	$192.5	$187.0
2. Net income	6.0	5.8	5.6
3. Dividends declared and paid	2.5	2.5	2.5
December 31 balances:			
4. Owners' equity	70.0	66.5	63.2
5. Debt	30.0	29.8	30.3
Selected year-end financial ratios			
Net income to sales	3.0%	3.0%	3.0%
Asset turnover	2 times	2 times	2 times
6. Return on owners' equity*	8.6%	8.7%	8.9%
7. Debt to total assets	30.0%	30.9%	32.4%

*Based on year-end balances in owners' equity.

The CEO believes that the price of the stock has been adversely affected by the downward trend of the return on equity, the relatively low dividend payout ratio, and the lack of dividend increases. To improve the price of the stock, she wants to improve the return on equity and dividends. She believes that the company should be able to meet these objectives by (1) increasing sales and net income at an annual rate of 10% a year and (2) establishing a new dividend policy that calls for a dividend payout of 50% of earnings or $3,000,000, whichever is larger.

The 10% annual sales increase will be accomplished through a new promotional program. The president believes that the present net income to sales ratio of 3% will be unchanged by the cost of this new program and any interest paid on new debt. She expects that the company can accomplish this sales and income growth while maintaining the current relationship of total assets to sales. Any capital that is needed to maintain this relationship and that is not generated internally would be acquired through long-term debt financing. The CEO hopes that debt would not exceed 35% of total liabilities and owners' equity.

Required

1. Using the CEO's program, prepare a schedule that shows the appropriate data for the years 2008, 2009, and 2010 for the items numbered 1 through 7 on the preceding schedule.
2. Can the CEO meet all of her requirements if a 10% per year growth in income and sales is achieved? Explain your answer.
3. What alternative actions should the CEO consider to improve the return on equity and to support increased dividend payments?
4. Explain the reasons that the CEO might have for wanting to limit debt to 35% of total liabilities and owners' equity.

(CMA adapted)

MULTI-CONCEPT PROBLEMS

LO4,5,6 | **Problem 13-5** Basic Financial Ratios

The accounting staff of CCB Enterprises has completed the financial statements for the 2007 calendar year. The statement of income for the current year and the comparative statements of financial position for 2007 and 2006 follow.

CCB Enterprises
Statement of Income
For the Year Ended December 31, 2007
(thousands omitted)

Revenue:		
Net sales	$800,000	
Other	60,000	
Total revenue	$860,000	
Expenses:		
Cost of goods sold	$540,000	
Research and development	25,000	
Selling and administrative	155,000	
Interest	20,000	
Total expenses	$740,000	
Income before income taxes	$120,000	
Income taxes	48,000	
Net income	$ 72,000	

CCB Enterprises
Comparative Statements of Financial Position
December 31, 2007 and 2006
(thousands omitted)

	2007	2006
Assets		
Current assets:		
Cash and short-term investments	$ 26,000	$ 21,000
Receivables, less allowance for doubtful accounts		
($1,100 in 2007 and $1,400 in 2006)	48,000	50,000
Inventories, at lower of FIFO cost or market	65,000	62,000
Prepaid items and other current assets	5,000	3,000
Total current assets	$144,000	$136,000
Other assets:		
Investments, at cost	$106,000	$106,000
Deposits	10,000	8,000
Total other assets	$116,000	$114,000
Property, plant, and equipment:		
Land	$ 12,000	$ 12,000
Buildings and equipment, less accumulated depreciation		
($126,000 in 2007 and $122,000 in 2006)	268,000	248,000
Total property, plant, and equipment	$280,000	$260,000
Total assets	$540,000	$510,000
Liabilities and Stockholders' Equity		
Current liabilities:		
Short-term loans	$ 22,000	$ 24,000
Accounts payable	72,000	71,000
Salaries, wages, and other	26,000	27,000
Total current liabilities	$120,000	$122,000
Long-term debt	160,000	171,000
Total liabilities	$280,000	$293,000
Stockholders' equity:		
Common stock, at par	$ 44,000	$ 42,000
Paid-in capital in excess of par	64,000	61,000
Total paid-in capital	$108,000	$103,000
Retained earnings	152,000	114,000
Total stockholders' equity	$260,000	$217,000
Total liabilities and stockholders' equity	$540,000	$510,000

Required

1. Calculate the following financial ratios for 2007 for CCB Enterprises:
   a. Times interest earned
   b. Return on total assets
   c. Return on common stockholders' equity
   d. Debt-equity ratio (at December 31, 2007)
   e. Current ratio (at December 31, 2007)
   f. Quick (acid-test) ratio (at December 31, 2007)
   g. Accounts receivable turnover ratio (Assume that all sales are on credit.)
   h. Number of days' sales in receivables
   i. Inventory turnover ratio (Assume that all purchases are on credit.)
   j. Number of days' sales in inventory
   k. Number of days in cash operating cycle
2. Prepare a few brief comments on the overall financial health of CCB Enterprises. For each comment, indicate any information that is not provided in the problem and that you would need to fully evaluate the company's financial health.

(CMA adapted)

LO5,6   **Problem 13-6**   Projected Results to Meet Corporate Objectives

Tablon Inc. is a wholly owned subsidiary of Marbel Co. The philosophy of Marbel's management is to allow the subsidiaries to operate as independent units. Corporate control is exercised through the establishment of minimum objectives for each subsidiary, accompanied by substantial rewards for success and penalties for failure. The time period for performance review is long enough for competent managers to display their abilities.

Each quarter the subsidiary is required to submit financial statements. The statements are accompanied by a letter from the subsidiary president explaining the results to date, a forecast for the remainder of the year, and the actions to be taken to achieve the objectives if the forecast indicates that the objectives will not be met.

Marbel management, in conjunction with Tablon management, had set the objectives listed below for the year ending May 31, 2008. These objectives are similar to those set in previous years.

- Sales growth of 20%
- Return on stockholders' equity of 15%
- A long-term debt-to-equity ratio of not more than 1.0
- Payment of a cash dividend of 50% of net income, with a minimum payment of at least $400,000

Tablon's controller has just completed the financial statements for the six months ended November 30, 2007, and the forecast for the year ending May 31, 2008. The statements follow.

After a cursory glance at the financial statements, Tablon's president concluded that not all objectives would be met. At a staff meeting of the Tablon management, the president asked the controller to review the projected results and recommend possible actions that could be taken during the remainder of the year so that Tablon would be more likely to meet the objectives.

Tablon Inc.
Income Statement
(thousands omitted)

	Year Ended May 31, 2007	Six Months Ended November 30, 2007	Forecast for Year Ending May 31, 2008
Sales	$25,000	$15,000	$30,000
Cost of goods sold	$13,000	$ 8,000	$16,000
Selling expenses	5,000	3,500	7,000
Administrative expenses and interest	4,000	2,500	5,000
Income taxes (40%)	1,200	400	800
Total expenses and taxes	$23,200	$14,400	$28,800
Net income	$ 1,800	$ 600	$ 1,200
Dividends declared and paid	600	0	600
Income retained	$ 1,200	$ 600	$ 600

Tablon Inc.
Statement of Financial Position
(thousands omitted)

	May 31, 2007	November 30, 2007	Forecast for May 31, 2008
Assets			
Cash	$ 400	$ 500	$ 500
Accounts receivable (net)	4,100	6,500	7,100
Inventory	7,000	8,500	8,600
Plant and equipment (net)	6,500	7,000	7,300
Total assets	$18,000	$22,500	$23,500
Liabilities and Equities			
Accounts payable	$ 3,000	$ 4,000	$ 4,000
Accrued taxes	300	200	200
Long-term borrowing	6,000	9,000	10,000
Common stock	5,000	5,000	5,000
Retained earnings	3,700	4,300	4,300
Total liabilities and equities	$18,000	$22,500	$23,500

Required

1. Calculate the projected results for each of the four objectives established for Tablon Inc. State which results will not meet the objectives by year-end.
2. From the data presented, identify the factors that seem to contribute to the failure of Tablon Inc. to meet all of its objectives.
3. Explain the possible actions that the controller could recommend in response to the president's request.

(CMA adapted)

LO4,5,6   **Problem 13-7** Comparison with Industry Averages

Heartland Inc. is a medium-size company that has been in business for 20 years. The industry has become very competitive in the last few years, and Heartland has decided that it must grow if it is going to survive. It has approached the bank for a sizable five-year loan, and the bank has requested its most recent financial statements as part of the loan package.

The industry in which Heartland operates consists of approximately 20 companies relatively equal in size. The trade association to which all of the competitors belong publishes an annual survey of the industry, including industry averages for selected ratios for the competitors. All companies voluntarily submit their statements to the association for this purpose.

Heartland's controller is aware that the bank has access to this survey and is very concerned about how the company fared this past year compared with the rest of the industry. The ratios included in the publication, and the averages for the past year, are as follows:

Ratio	Industry Average
Current ratio	1.23
Acid-test (quick) ratio	0.75
Accounts receivable turnover	33 times
Inventory turnover	29 times
Debt-to-equity ratio	0.53
Times interest earned	8.65 times
Return on sales	6.57%
Asset turnover	1.95 times
Return on assets	12.81%
Return on common stockholders' equity	17.67%

The financial statements to be submitted to the bank in connection with the loan follow:

Heartland Inc.
Statement of Income and Retained Earnings
For the Year Ended December 31, 2007
(thousands omitted)

Sales revenue	$542,750
Cost of goods sold	(435,650)
Gross profit	$107,100
Selling, general, and administrative expenses	$(65,780)
Loss on sales of securities	(220)
Income before interest and taxes	$ 41,100
Interest expense	(9,275)
Income before taxes	$ 31,825
Income tax expense	(12,730)
Net income	$ 19,095
Retained earnings, January 1, 2007	58,485
	$ 77,580
Dividends paid on common stock	(12,000)
Retained earnings, December 31, 2007	$ 65,580

Heartland Inc.
Comparative Statements of Financial Position
(thousands omitted)

	December 31, 2007	December 31, 2006
Assets		
Current assets:		
Cash	$ 1,135	$ 750
Marketable securities	1,250	2,250
Accounts receivable, net of allowances	15,650	12,380
Inventories	12,680	15,870
Prepaid items	385	420
Total current assets	$ 31,100	$ 31,670
Long-term investments	$ 425	$ 425
Property, plant, and equipment:		
Land	$ 32,000	$ 32,000
Buildings and equipment, net of accumulated depreciation	216,000	206,000
Total property, plant, and equipment	$248,000	$238,000
Total assets	$279,525	$270,095
Liabilities and Stockholders' Equity		
Current liabilities:		
Short-term notes	$ 8,750	$ 12,750
Accounts payable	20,090	14,380
Salaries and wages payable	1,975	2,430
Income taxes payable	3,130	2,050
Total current liabilities	$ 33,945	$ 31,610
Long-term bonds payable	$ 80,000	$ 80,000
Stockholders' equity:		
Common stock, no par	$100,000	$100,000
Retained earnings	65,580	58,485
Total stockholders' equity	$165,580	$158,485
Total liabilities and stockholders' equity	$279,525	$270,095

Required

1. Prepare a columnar report for the controller of Heartland Inc., comparing the industry averages for the ratios published by the trade association with the comparable ratios for Heartland. For Heartland, compute the ratios as of December 31, 2007, or for the year ending December 31, 2007, whichever is appropriate.
2. Briefly evaluate Heartland's ratios relative to the industry averages.
3. Do you think that the bank will approve the loan? Explain your answer.

HOMEWORK

ALTERNATE PROBLEMS

LO5

Problem 13-1A Effect of Transactions on Debt-to-Equity Ratio

(*Note:* Consider completing Problem 13-2A after this problem to ensure that you obtain a clear understanding of the effect of various transactions on this measure of solvency.)
The following account balances are taken from the records of Monet's Garden Inc.:

Current liabilities	$150,000
Long-term liabilities	375,000
Stockholders' equity	400,000

Required

1. Use the information provided above to compute Monet's debt-to-equity ratio (round to three decimal points).
2. Determine the effect that each of the following transactions will have on Monet's debt-to-equity ratio by recalculating the ratio and then indicating whether the ratio is increased, decreased, or not affected by the transaction. (Round to three decimal points.) Consider each transaction independently; that is, assume that it is the *only* transaction that takes place.

Transaction	Effect of Transaction on Debt-to-Equity Ratio
a. Purchased inventory on account for $20,000.	
b. Purchased inventory for cash, $15,000.	
c. Paid suppliers on account, $30,000.	
d. Received cash on account, $40,000.	
e. Paid insurance for next year, $20,000.	
f. Made sales on account, $60,000.	
g. Repaid short-term loans at bank, $25,000.	
h. Borrowed $40,000 at bank for 90 days.	
i. Declared and paid $45,000 cash dividend.	
j. Purchased $20,000 of short-term investments.	
k. Paid $30,000 in salaries.	
l. Accrued additional $15,000 in taxes.	

LO5

Problem 13-2A Effect of Transactions on Debt-to-Equity Ratio

(*Note:* Consider completing this problem after Problem 13-1A to ensure that you obtain a clear understanding of the effect of various transactions on this measure of solvency.)
The following account balances are taken from the records of Degas Inc.:

Current liabilities	$ 25,000
Long-term liabilities	125,000
Stockholders' equity	400,000

Required

1. Use the information provided above to compute Degas' debt-to-equity ratio (round to three decimal points).
2. Determine the effect that each of the following transactions will have on Degas' debt-to-equity ratio by recalculating the ratio and then indicating whether the ratio is increased, decreased, or not affected by the transaction. (Round to three decimal points.) Consider each transaction independently; that is, assume that it is the *only* transaction that takes place.

Transaction	Effect of Transaction on Debt-to-Equity Ratio
a. Purchased inventory on account for $20,000.	
b. Purchased inventory for cash, $15,000.	
c. Paid suppliers on account, $30,000.	
d. Received cash on account, $40,000.	
e. Paid insurance for next year, $20,000.	
f. Made sales on account, $60,000.	
g. Repaid short-term loans at bank, $25,000.	

h. Borrowed $40,000 at bank for 90 days.
i. Declared and paid $45,000 cash dividend.
j. Purchased $20,000 of short-term investments.
k. Paid $30,000 in salaries.
l. Accrued additional $15,000 in taxes.

LO6

Problem 13-3A Goals for Sales and Return on Assets

The president of Blue Moon Corp. is reviewing with her department managers the operating results of the year just completed. Sales increased by 12% from the previous year to $750,000. Average total assets for the year were $400,000. Net income, after adding back interest expense, net of tax, was $60,000.

The president is happy with the performance over the past year but is never satisfied with the status quo. She has set two specific goals for next year: (1) a 15% growth in sales and (2) a return on assets of 20%.

To achieve the second goal, the president has stated her intention to increase the total asset base by 10% over the base for the year just completed.

Required

1. For the year just completed, compute the following ratios:
   a. Return on sales
   b. Asset turnover
   c. Return on assets
2. Compute the necessary asset turnover for next year to achieve the president's goal of a 15% increase in sales.
3. Calculate the income needed next year to achieve the goal of a 20% return on total assets. (*Note:* Assume that *income* is defined as net income plus interest, net of tax.)
4. Based on your answers to parts (2) and (3), comment on the reasonableness of the president's goals. What must the company focus on to attain these goals?

LO6

Problem 13-4A Goals for Sales and Income Growth

Sunset Corp. is a major regional retailer. The chief executive officer (CEO) is concerned with the slow growth both of sales and of net income and the subsequent effect on the trading price of the common stock. Selected financial data for the past three years follow.

Sunset Corp.
(in millions)

	2007	2006	2005
1. Sales	$100.0	$96.7	$93.3
2. Net income	3.0	2.9	2.8
3. Dividends declared and paid	1.2	1.2	1.2
December 31 balances:			
4. Owners' equity	40.0	38.2	36.5
5. Debt	10.0	10.2	10.2
Selected year-end financial ratios			
Net income to sales	3.0%	3.0%	3.0%
Asset turnover	2 times	2 times	2 times
6. Return on owners' equity*	7.5%	7.6%	7.7%
7. Debt to total assets	20.0%	21.1%	21.8%

Based on year-end balances in owners' equity.

The CEO believes that the price of the stock has been adversely affected by the downward trend of the return on equity, the relatively low dividend payout ratio, and the lack of dividend increases. To improve the price of the stock, he wants to improve the return on equity and dividends.

He believes that the company should be able to meet these objectives by (1) increasing sales and net income at an annual rate of 10% a year and (2) establishing a new dividend policy that calls for a dividend payout of 60% of earnings or $2,000,000, whichever is larger.

The 10% annual sales increase will be accomplished through a product enhancement program. The president believes that the present net income to sales ratio of 3% will be unchanged by the cost of this new program and any interest paid on new debt. He expects that the company can accomplish this sales and income growth while maintaining the current relationship of total assets to sales. Any capital that is needed to maintain this relationship and that is not generated internally would be acquired through long-term debt financing. The CEO hopes that debt would not exceed 25% of total liabilities and owners' equity.

Required

1. Using the CEO's program, prepare a schedule that shows the appropriate data for the years 2008, 2009, and 2010 for the items numbered 1 through 7 on the preceding schedule.
2. Can the CEO meet all of his requirements if a 10% per-year growth in income and sales is achieved? Explain your answers.
3. What alternative actions should the CEO consider to improve the return on equity and to support increased dividend payments?

(CMA adapted)

ALTERNATE MULTI-CONCEPT PROBLEMS

LO4,5,6   **Problem 13-5A** Basic Financial Ratios

The accounting staff of SST Enterprises has completed the financial statements for the 2007 calendar year. The statement of income for the current year and the comparative statements of financial position for 2007 and 2006 follow.

SST Enterprises
Statement of Income
Year Ended December 31, 2007
(thousands omitted)

Revenue:	
Net sales	$600,000
Other	45,000
Total revenue	$645,000
Expenses:	
Cost of goods sold	$405,000
Research and development	18,000
Selling and administrative	120,000
Interest	15,000
Total expenses	$558,000
Income before income taxes	$ 87,000
Income taxes	27,000
Net income	$ 60,000

SST Enterprises
Comparative Statements of Financial Position
December 31, 2007 and 2006
(thousands omitted)

	2007	2006
Assets		
Current assets:		
Cash and short-term investments	$ 27,000	$ 20,000
Receivables, less allowance for doubtful accounts		
($1,100 in 2007 and $1,400 in 2006)	36,000	37,000
Inventories, at lower of FIFO cost or market	35,000	42,000
Prepaid items and other current assets	2,000	1,000
Total current assets	$100,000	$100,000
Property, plant, and equipment:		
Land	$ 9,000	$ 9,000
Buildings and equipment, less accumulated depreciation		
($74,000 in 2007 and $62,000 in 2006)	191,000	186,000
Total property, plant, and equipment	$200,000	$195,000
Total assets	$300,000	$295,000

	2007	2006
Liabilities and Stockholders' Equity		
Current liabilities:		
Short-term loans	$ 20,000	$ 15,000
Accounts payable	80,000	68,000
Salaries, wages, and other	5,000	7,000
Total current liabilities	$105,000	$ 90,000
Long-term debt	15,000	40,000
Total liabilities	$120,000	$130,000
Stockholders' equity:		
Common stock, at par	$ 50,000	$ 50,000
Paid-in capital in excess of par	25,000	25,000
Total paid-in capital	$ 75,000	$ 75,000
Retained earnings	105,000	90,000
Total stockholders' equity	$180,000	$165,000
Total liabilities and stockholders' equity	$300,000	$295,000

Required

1. Calculate the following financial ratios for 2007 for SST Enterprises:
   a. Times interest earned
   b. Return on total assets
   c. Return on common stockholders' equity
   d. Debt-equity ratio (at December 31, 2007)
   e. Current ratio (at December 31, 2007)
   f. Quick (acid-test) ratio (at December 31, 2007)
   g. Accounts receivable turnover ratio (assume that all sales are on credit)
   h. Number of days' sales in receivables
   i. Inventory turnover ratio (assume that all purchases are on credit)
   j. Number of days' sales in inventory
   k. Number of days in cash operating cycle
2. Prepare a few brief comments on the overall financial health of SST Enterprises. For each comment, indicate any information that is not provided in the problem and that you would need to fully evaluate the company's financial health.

(CMA adapted)

LO5,6   **Problem 13-6A** Projected Results to Meet Corporate Objectives

Grout Inc. is a wholly owned subsidiary of Slait Co. The philosophy of Slait's management is to allow the subsidiaries to operate as independent units. Corporate control is exercised through the establishment of minimum objectives for each subsidiary, accompanied by substantial rewards for success and penalties for failure. The time period for performance review is long enough for competent managers to display their abilities.

Each quarter the subsidiary is required to submit financial statements. The statements are accompanied by a letter from the subsidiary president explaining the results to date, a forecast for the remainder of the year, and the actions to be taken to achieve the objectives if the forecast indicates that the objectives will not be met.

Slait management, in conjunction with Grout management, had set the objectives listed below for the year ending September 30, 2008. These objectives are similar to those set in previous years.

- Sales growth of 10%
- Return on stockholders' equity of 20%
- A long-term debt-to-equity ratio of not more than 1.0
- Payment of a cash dividend of 50% of net income, with a minimum payment of at least $500,000

Grout's controller has just completed preparing the financial statements for the six months ended March 31, 2008, and the forecast for the year ending September 30, 2008. The statements are presented below.

After a cursory glance at the financial statements, Grout's president concluded that not all objectives would be met. At a staff meeting of the Grout management, the president asked the controller to review the projected results and recommend possible actions that could be taken during the remainder of the year so that Grout would be more likely to meet the objectives.

Grout Inc.
Income Statement
(thousands omitted)

	Year Ended September 30, 2007	Six Months Ended March 31, 2008	Forecast for Year Ending September 30, 2008
Sales	$10,000	$6,000	$12,000
Cost of goods sold	$ 6,000	$4,000	$ 8,000
Selling expenses	1,500	900	1,800
Administrative expenses and interest	1,000	600	1,200
Income taxes	500	300	600
Total expenses and taxes	$ 9,000	$5,800	$11,600
Net income	$ 1,000	$ 200	$ 400
Dividends declared and paid	500	0	400
Income retained	$ 500	$ 200	$ 0

Grout Inc.
Statement of Financial Position
(thousands omitted)

	September 30, 2007	March 31, 2008	Forecast for September 30, 2008
Assets			
Cash	$ 400	$ 500	$ 500
Accounts receivable (net)	2,100	3,400	2,600
Inventory	7,000	8,500	8,400
Plant and equipment (net)	2,800	2,500	3,200
Total assets	$12,300	$14,900	$14,700
Liabilities and Equities			
Accounts payable	$ 3,000	$ 4,000	$ 4,000
Accrued taxes	300	200	200
Long-term borrowing	4,000	5,500	5,500
Common stock	4,000	4,000	4,000
Retained earnings	1,000	1,200	1,000
Total liabilities and equities	$12,300	$14,900	$14,700

Required

1. Calculate the projected results for each of the four objectives established for Grout Inc. State which results will not meet the objectives by year-end.
2. From the data presented, identify the factors that seem to contribute to the failure of Grout Inc. to meet all of its objectives.
3. Explain the possible actions that the controller could recommend in response to the president's request.

(CMA adapted)

LO4,5,6   **Problem 13-7A** A Comparison with Industry Averages

Midwest Inc. is a medium-size company that has been in business for 20 years. The industry has become very competitive in the last few years, and Midwest has decided that it must grow if it is going to survive. It has approached the bank for a sizable five-year loan, and the bank has requested its most recent financial statements as part of the loan package.

The industry in which Midwest operates consists of approximately 20 companies relatively equal in size. The trade association to which all of the competitors belong publishes an annual survey of the industry, including industry averages for selected ratios for the competitors. All companies voluntarily submit their statements to the association for this purpose.

Midwest's controller is aware that the bank has access to this survey and is very concerned about how the company fared this past year compared with the rest of the industry. The ratios included in the publication, and the averages for the past year, are as follows:

Ratio	Industry Average
Current ratio	1.20
Acid-test (quick) ratio	0.50
Inventory turnover	35 times
Debt-to-equity ratio	0.50
Times interest earned	25 times
Return on sales	3%
Asset turnover	3.5 times
Return on common stockholders' equity	20%

The financial statements to be submitted to the bank in connection with the loan follow:

Midwest Inc.
Statement of Income and Retained Earnings
For the Year Ended December 31, 2007
(thousands omitted)

Sales revenue	$420,500
Cost of goods sold	(300,000)
Gross profit	$120,500
Selling, general, and administrative expenses	(85,000)
Income before interest and taxes	$ 35,500
Interest expense	(8,600)
Income before taxes	$ 26,900
Income tax expense	(12,000)
Net income	$ 14,900
Retained earnings, January 1, 2007	12,400
	$ 27,300
Dividends paid on common stock	(11,200)
Retained earnings, December 31, 2007	$ 16,100

Midwest Inc.
Comparative Statements of Financial Position
(thousands omitted)

	December 31, 2007	December 31, 2006
Assets		
Current assets:		
Cash	$ 1,790	$ 2,600
Marketable securities	1,200	1,700
Accounts receivable, net of allowances	400	600
Inventories	8,700	7,400
Prepaid items	350	400
Total current assets	$ 12,440	$ 12,700
Long-term investments	$ 560	$ 400
Property, plant, and equipment:		
Land	$ 12,000	$ 12,000
Buildings and equipment, net of accumulated depreciation	87,000	82,900
Total property, plant, and equipment	$ 99,000	$ 94,900
Total assets	$112,000	$108,000
Liabilities and Stockholders' Equity		
Current liabilities:		
Short-term notes	$ 800	$ 600
Accounts payable	6,040	6,775
Salaries and wages payable	1,500	1,200
Income taxes payable	1,560	1,025
Total current liabilities	$ 9,900	$ 9,600
Long-term bonds payable	$ 36,000	$ 36,000
Stockholders' equity:		
Common stock, no par	$ 50,000	$ 50,000
Retained earnings	16,100	12,400
Total stockholders' equity	$ 66,100	$ 62,400
Total liabilities and stockholders' equity	$112,000	$108,000

Required

1. Prepare a columnar report for the controller of Midwest Inc., comparing the industry averages for the ratios published by the trade association with the comparable ratios for Midwest. For Midwest, compute the ratios as of December 31, 2007, or for the year ending December 31, 2007, whichever is appropriate.
2. Briefly evaluate Midwest's ratios relative to the industry.
3. Do you think that the bank will approve the loan? Explain your answer.

DECISION CASES

READING AND INTERPRETING FINANCIAL STATEMENTS

LO2   **Decision Case 13-1** Horizontal Analysis for Finish Line

Refer to **Finish Line**'s financial statements included in its 2006 annual report reprinted at the back of the book.

Required

1. Prepare a work sheet with the following headings:

	Increase (Decrease) from			
	2005 to 2006		2004 to 2005	
Income Statement Accounts	**Dollars**	**Percent**	**Dollars**	**Percent**

2. Complete the work sheet using each of the account titles on Finish Line's income statement. Round dollar amounts to the nearest one-tenth of $1 million and percentages to the nearest one-tenth of a percent.
3. What observations can you make from this horizontal analysis? What is your overall analysis of operations? Have the company's operations improved over the three-year period?

LO3   **Decision Case 13-2** Vertical Analysis for Finish Line

Refer to **Finish Line**'s financial statements included in its 2006 annual report reprinted at the back of the book.

Required

1. Using the format in Exhibit 13-6, prepare common-size comparative income statements for 2006 and 2005. Use as the base "Net sales." Round dollar amounts to the nearest one-tenth of $1 million and percentages to the nearest one-tenth of a percent.
2. What changes do you detect in the income statement relationships from 2005 to 2006?
3. Using the format in Exhibit 13-5, prepare common-size comparative balance sheets on February 25, 2006, and February 26, 2005. Round dollar amounts to the nearest one-tenth of $1 million and percentages to the nearest one-tenth of a percent.
4. What observations can you make about the relative composition of Finish Line's assets from the common-size statements? What observations can be made about the changes in the relative composition of liabilities and stockholders' equity accounts?

LO3   **Decision Case 13-3** Comparing Two Companies in the Same Industry: Finish Line and Foot Locker

This case should be completed after responding to the requirements in Case 13-2. Refer to the financial statement information of **Finish Line** and **Foot Locker** reprinted at the back of the book.

Required:

1. Using the format in Exhibit 13-6, prepare common-size comparative income statements for the years ending January 28, 2006, and January 29, 2005, for Foot Locker. Show all dollar amounts in millions of dollars and round all percentages to the nearest one-tenth of a percent.
2. The common-size comparative income statements indicates the relative importance of items on the statement. Compare the common-size income statements of Foot Locker

and Finish Line. What are the most important differences between the two companies' income statements?

3. Using the format in Exhibit 13-5, prepare common-size comparative balance sheets on January 28, 2006, and January 29, 2005, for Foot Locker. Show all dollar amounts in millions of dollars and round all percentages to the nearest one-tenth of a percent.

4. The common-size comparative balance sheets indicates the relative importance of items on the statement. Compare the common-size balance sheets of Foot Locker and Finish Line. What are the most important differences between the two companies' balance sheets?

LO4,5,6 **Decision Case 13-4** Ratio Analysis for Finish Line

Refer to **Finish Line**'s financial statements included in its 2006 annual report reprinted at the back of the book.

Required

1. Compute the following ratios and other amounts for each of the two years, 2006 and 2005. Because only two years of data are given on the balance sheets, to be consistent, you should use year-end balances for each year in lieu of average balances. Assume 360 days to a year. State any other necessary assumptions in making the calculations. Round all ratios to the nearest one-tenth of a percent.
   a. Working capital
   b. Current ratio
   c. Acid-test ratio
   d. Cash flow from operations to current liabilities
   e. Number of days' sales in receivables
   f. Number of days' sales in inventory
   g. Debt-to-equity ratio
   h. Cash flow from operations to capital expenditures
   i. Asset turnover
   j. Return on sales
   k. Return on assets
   l. Return on common stockholders' equity
2. What is your overall analysis of the financial health of Finish Line?

MAKING FINANCIAL DECISIONS

LO4,5,6 **Decision Case 13-5** Acquisition Decision

Diversified Industries is a large conglomerate and is continually in the market for new acquisitions. The company has grown rapidly over the last 10 years through buyouts of medium-size companies. Diversified does not limit itself to companies in any one industry but looks for firms with a sound financial base and the ability to stand on their own financially.

The president of Diversified recently told a meeting of the company's officers: "I want to impress two points on all of you. First, we are not in the business of looking for bargains. Diversified has achieved success in the past by acquiring companies with the ability to be a permanent member of the corporate family. We don't want companies that may appear to be a bargain on paper but can't survive in the long run. Second, a new member of our family must be able to come in and make it on its own—the parent is not organized to be a funding agency for struggling subsidiaries."

Ron Dixon is the vice president of acquisitions for Diversified, a position he has held for five years. He is responsible for making recommendations to the board of directors on potential acquisitions. Because you are one of his assistants, he recently brought you a set of financials for a manufacturer, Heavy-Duty Tractors, Inc. Dixon believes that Heavy-Duty is a "can't-miss" opportunity for Diversified and asks you to confirm his hunch by performing basic financial statement analysis on the company. The most recent comparative balance sheets and income statement for the company follow:

Heavy-Duty Tractors Inc.
Comparative Statements of Financial Position
(thousands omitted)

	December 31, 2007	December 31, 2006
Assets		
Current assets:		
Cash	$ 48,500	$ 24,980
Marketable securities	3,750	0
Accounts receivable, net of allowances	128,420	84,120
Inventories	135,850	96,780
Prepaid items	7,600	9,300
Total current assets	$324,120	$215,180
Long-term investments	$ 55,890	$ 55,890
Property, plant, and equipment:		
Land	$ 45,000	$ 45,000
Buildings and equipment, less accumulated depreciation of $385,000 in 2007 and $325,000 in 2006	545,000	605,000
Total property, plant, and equipment	$590,000	$650,000
Total assets	$970,010	$921,070
Liabilities and Stockholders' Equity		
Current liabilities:		
Short-term notes	$ 80,000	$ 60,000
Accounts payable	65,350	48,760
Salaries and wages payable	14,360	13,840
Income taxes payable	2,590	3,650
Total current liabilities	$162,300	$126,250
Long-term bonds payable, due 2014	$275,000	$275,000
Stockholders' equity:		
Common stock, no par	$350,000	$350,000
Retained earnings	182,710	169,820
Total stockholders' equity	$532,710	$519,820
Total liabilities and stockholders' equity	$970,010	$921,070

Heavy-Duty Tractors Inc.
Statement of Income and Retained Earnings
For the Year Ended December 31, 2007
(thousands omitted)

Sales revenue	$875,250
Cost of goods sold	542,750
Gross profit	$332,500
Selling, general, and administrative expenses	264,360
Operating income	$ 68,140
Interest expense	45,000
Net income before taxes and extraordinary items	$ 23,140
Income tax expense	9,250
Income before extraordinary items	$ 13,890
Extraordinary gain, less taxes of $6,000	9,000
Net income	$ 22,890
Retained earnings, January 1, 2007	169,820
	$192,710
Dividends paid on common stock	10,000
Retained earnings, December 31, 2007	$182,710

Required

1. How liquid is Heavy-Duty Tractors? Support your answer with any ratios that you believe are necessary to justify your conclusion. Also indicate any other information that you would want to have in making a final determination on its liquidity.

2. In light of the president's comments, should you be concerned about the solvency of Heavy-Duty Tractors? Support your answer with the necessary ratios. How does the maturity date of the outstanding debt affect your answer?

3. Has Heavy-Duty demonstrated the ability to be a profitable member of the Diversified family? Support your answer with the necessary ratios.

4. What will you tell your boss? Should he recommend to the board of directors that Diversified put in a bid for Heavy-Duty Tractors?

LO3

Decision Case 13-6 Pricing Decision

BPO's management believes that the company has been successful at increasing sales because it has not increased the selling price of the products, even though its competition has increased prices and costs have increased. Price and cost relationships in Year 1 were established because they represented industry averages. The following income statements are available for BPO's first three years of operation:

	Year 3	Year 2	Year 1
Sales	$125,000	$110,000	$100,000
Cost of goods sold	62,000	49,000	40,000
Gross profit	$ 63,000	$ 61,000	$ 60,000
Operating expenses	53,000	49,000	45,000
Net income	$ 10,000	$ 12,000	$ 15,000

Required

1. Using the format in Exhibit 13-6, prepare common-size comparative income statements for the three years.
2. Explain why net income has decreased while sales have increased.
3. Prepare an income statement for Year 4. Sales volume in units is expected to increase by 10%, and costs are expected to increase by 8%.
4. Do you think BPO should raise its prices or maintain the same selling prices? Explain your answer.

ETHICAL DECISION MAKING

LO4,5

Decision Case 13-7 Provisions in a Loan Agreement

As controller of Midwest Construction Company, you are reviewing with your assistant, Dave Jackson, the financial statements for the year just ended. During the review, Jackson reminds you of an existing loan agreement with Southern National Bank. Midwest has agreed to the following conditions:

- The current ratio will be maintained at a minimum level of 1.5 to 1.0 at all times.
- The debt-to-equity ratio will not exceed 0.5 to 1.0 at any time.

Jackson has drawn up the following preliminary, condensed balance sheet for the year just ended:

Midwest Construction Company
Balance Sheet
December 31
(in millions of dollars)

Current assets	$16		Current liabilities	$10
Long-term assets	64		Long-term debt	15
			Stockholders' equity	55
Total	$80		Total	$80

Jackson wants to discuss two items with you. First, long-term debt currently includes a $5 million note payable, to Eastern State Bank, that is due in six months. The plan is to go to Eastern before the note is due and ask it to extend the maturity date of the note for five years. Jackson doesn't believe that Midwest needs to include the $5 million in current liabilities because the plan is to roll over the note.

Second, in December of this year, Midwest received a $2 million deposit from the state for a major road project. The contract calls for the work to be performed over the next 18 months. Jackson recorded the $2 million as revenue this year because the contract is with the state; there shouldn't be any question about being able to collect.

LO4

Required

1. Based on the balance sheet Jackson prepared, is Midwest in compliance with its loan agreement with Southern? Support your answer with any necessary computations.

2. What would you do with the two items in question? Do you see anything wrong with the way Jackson has handled each of them? Explain your answer.
3. Prepare a revised balance sheet based on your answer to part (2). Also, compute a revised current ratio and debt-to-equity ratio. Based on the revised ratios, is Midwest in compliance with its loan agreement?

Decision Case 13-8 Inventory Turnover

Garden Fresh Inc. is a wholesaler of fresh fruits and vegetables. Each year it submits a set of financial ratios to a trade association. Even though the association doesn't publish the individual ratios for each company, the president of Garden Fresh thinks it is important for public relations that his company look as good as possible. Due to the nature of the fresh fruits and vegetables business, one of the major ratios tracked by the association is inventory turnover. Garden Fresh's inventory stated at FIFO cost was as follows:

	Year Ending December 31	
	2007	**2006**
Fruits	$10,000	$ 9,000
Vegetables	30,000	33,000
Totals	$40,000	$42,000

Sales revenue for the year ending December 31, 2007, is $3,690,000. The company's gross profit ratio is normally 40%.

Based on these data, the president thinks the company should report an inventory turnover ratio of 90 times per year.

Required
1. Explain, using the necessary calculations, how the president came up with an inventory turnover ratio of 90 times.
2. Do you think the company should report a turnover ratio of 90 times? If not, explain why you disagree and explain, with calculations, what you think the ratio should be.
3. Assume you are the controller for Garden Fresh. What will you tell the president?

SOLUTIONS TO KEY TERMS QUIZ

Quiz 1:

14	Horizontal analysis		5	Cash flow from operations to current liabilities ratio
11	Vertical analysis			
10	Gross profit ratio		6	Accounts receivable turnover ratio
12	Profit margin ratio		4	Number of days' sales in receivables
13	Liquidity		9	Inventory turnover ratio
2	Working capital		7	Number of days' sales in inventory
3	Current ratio		8	Cash to cash operating cycle
1	Acid-test or quick ratio			

Quiz 2:

3	Solvency		4	Return on sales ratio
7	Debt-to-equity ratio		10	Asset turnover ratio
13	Times interest earned ratio		1	Return on common stockholders' equity ratio
14	Debt service coverage ratio			
8	Cash flow from operations to capital expenditures ratio		12	Leverage
			5	Earnings per share
15	Profitability		2	Price/earnings (P/E) ratio
9	Return on assets ratio		6	Dividend payout ratio

HOMEWORK

__11__	Dividend yield ratio	__17__	Cumulative effect of a change in accounting principle
__18__	Discontinued operations		
__16__	Extraordinary item		

INTEGRATIVE PROBLEM

Presented below are a statement of income and retained earnings and comparative balance sheets for Gallagher, Inc., which operates a national chain of sporting goods stores:

Gallagher, Inc.
Statement of Income and Retained Earnings
For the Year Ended December 31, 2007
(all amounts in thousands of dollars)

Net sales	$48,000
Cost of goods sold	36,000
Gross profit	$12,000
Selling, general, and administrative expense	6,000
Operating income	$ 6,000
Interest expense	280
Income before tax	$ 5,720
Income tax expense	2,280
Net income	$ 3,440
Preferred dividends	100
Income available to common	$ 3,340
Common dividends	500
To retained earnings	$ 2,840
Retained earnings, 1/1	12,000
Retained earnings, 12/31	$14,840

Gallagher, Inc.
Comparative Balance Sheets
December 31, 2007 and 2006
(all amounts in thousands of dollars)

	December 31	
	2007	**2006**
Cash	$ 840	$ 2,700
Accounts receivable	12,500	9,000
Inventory	8,000	5,500
Prepaid insurance	100	400
Total current assets	$21,440	$17,600
Land	$ 4,000	$ 4,000
Buildings and equipment	12,000	9,000
Accumulated depreciation	(3,700)	(3,000)
Total long-term assets	$12,300	$10,000
Total assets	$33,740	$27,600
Accounts payable	$ 7,300	$ 5,000
Taxes payable	4,600	4,200
Notes payable	2,400	1,600
Current portion of bonds	200	200
Total current liabilities	$14,500	$11,000
Bonds payable	1,400	1,600
Total liabilities	$15,900	$12,600
Preferred stock, $5 par	$ 1,000	$ 1,000
Common stock, $1 par	2,000	2,000
Retained earnings	14,840	12,000
Total stockholders' equity	$17,840	$15,000
Total liabilities and stockholders' equity	$33,740	$27,600

Required

1. Prepare a statement of cash flows for Gallagher, Inc., for the year ended December 31, 2007, using the **indirect** method in the Operating Activities section of the statement.

2. Gallagher's management is concerned with both its short-term liquidity and its solvency over the long run. To help it evaluate these, compute the following ratios, rounding all answers to the nearest one-tenth of a percent:
   a.   Current ratio
   b.   Acid-test ratio
   c.   Cash flow from operations to current liabilities ratio
   d.   Accounts receivable turnover ratio
   e.   Number of days' sales in receivables
   f.   Inventory turnover ratio
   g.   Number of days' sales in inventory
   h.   Debt-to-equity ratio
   i.   Debt service coverage ratio
   j.   Cash flow from operations to capital expenditures ratio

3. Comment on Gallagher's liquidity and its solvency. What additional information do you need to fully evaluate the company?

Excerpts from The Finish Line, Inc., Form 10-K for 2006

A-1 to A-22

Excerpts from Foot Locker, Inc., Form 10-K for 2005

B-1 to B-37

APPENDIXES A AND B

These excerpts consist of Item 8, which are the financial statements and supplementary data for each company. For full annual reports for these companies, please see the links at the company Web sites or go to http://www.thomsonedu.com/accounting/porter and select this text.

SECURITIES AND EXCHANGE COMMISSION
Washington, D.C. 20549

FORM 10-K

(Mark One)

☒   **Annual report pursuant to Section 13 or 15(d) of the Securities Exchange Act of 1934**
For the fiscal year ended February 25, 2006
or

☐   **Transition report pursuant to Section 13 or 15(d) of the Securities Exchange Act of 1934**
For the transition period from   to
Commission File Number 0-20184

THE FINISH LINE, INC.
(Exact name of registrant as specified in its charter)

Indiana	**35-1537210**
(State of Incorporation)	(I.R.S. Employer ID No.)

3308 N. Mitthoeffer Road, Indianapolis, Indiana 46235
Registrant's telephone number, including area code: (317) 899-1022

Securities registered pursuant to Section 12(b) of the Act:

(Title of Each Class)	(Name of each exchange on which registered)
None	**None**

Securities registered pursuant to Section 12(g) of the Act:
Class A Common Stock, $.01 par value

Indicate by check mark if the registrant is a well-known seasoned issuer, as defined in Rule 405 of the Securities Act.   Yes ☒   No ☐

Indicate by check mark if the registrant is not required to file reports pursuant to Section 13 or Section 15(d) of the Act.   Yes ☐   No ☒

Indicate by check mark whether Registrant (1) has filed all reports required to be filed by Section 13 or 15(d) of the Securities Exchange Act of 1934 during the preceding 12 months (or for such shorter period that the registrant was required to file such reports) and (2) has been subject to such filing requirements for the past 90 days.   Yes ☒   No ☐

Indicate by check mark if disclosure of delinquent filers pursuant to Item 405 of Regulation S-K (§229.405 of this chapter) is not contained herein, and will not be contained, to the best of registrant's knowledge, in definitive proxy or information statements incorporated by reference in Part III of this Form 10-K or any amendment to this form 10-K.   ☒

Indicate by check mark whether the registrant is a large accelerated filer, an accelerated filer, or a non-accelerated filer. See definition of "accelerated filer and large accelerated filer" in Rule 12b-2 of the Securities Exchange Act of 1934.

Large accelerated filer ☐   Accelerated filer ☒   Non-accelerated filer ☐

Indicate by check mark whether the registrant is a shell company (as defined in Rule 12b-2 of the Act).   Yes ☒   No ☐

The aggregate market value of the voting stock held by non-affiliates of the Registrant as of August 26, 2005, the last business day of the registrant's most recently completed second fiscal quarter, was approximately $696,972,000, which was based on the last sale price reported for such date by NASDAQ.

The number of shares of the Registrant's Common Stock outstanding on April 21, 2006 was:

Class A Common Stock: 43,137,813
Class B Common Stock: 5,141,336
DOCUMENTS INCORPORATED BY REFERENCE

Portions of the Registrant's Proxy Statement (to be filed within 120 days after February 25, 2006) for the Annual Meeting of Shareholders to be held on July 20, 2006 (hereinafter referred to as the "2006 Proxy Statement") are incorporated into Part III.

Item 8—Financial Statements and Supplementary Data

Management Report on Internal Control Over Financial Reporting

The management of The Finish Line, Inc. (the "Company") is responsible for establishing and maintaining adequate internal control over financial reporting (as defined in Rule 13a-15(f) and 15d-15(f) under the Securities Exchange Act of 1934, as amended). The Company's internal control system was designed to provide reasonable assurance to the Company's management and Board of Directors regarding the preparation and fair presentation of published financial statements.

Internal control over financial reporting is defined in Rule 13a-15(f) and 15d-15(f) under the Securities Exchange Act of 1934 as a process designed by, or under the supervision of, the company's principal executive and principal financial officers and effected by the company's board of directors, management and other personnel, to provide reasonable assurance regarding the reliability of financial reporting and the preparation of financial statements for external purposes in accordance with U.S. generally accepted accounting principles and includes those policies and procedures that: (1) pertain to the maintenance of records that in reasonable detail accurately and fairly reflect the transactions and dispositions of the assets of the company; (2) provide reasonable assurance that transactions are recorded as necessary to permit preparation of financial statements in accordance with U.S. generally accepted accounting principles, and that receipts and expenditures of the company are being made only in accordance with authorizations of management and directors of the company; and (3) provide reasonable assurance regarding prevention or timely detection of unauthorized acquisition, use or disposition of the company's assets that could have a material effect on the financial statements.

All internal control systems, no matter how well designed, have inherent limitations. Therefore, even those systems determined to be effective can provide only reasonable assurance with respect to financial statement preparation and presentation.

The Company's management assessed the effectiveness of the Company's internal control over financial reporting as of February 25, 2006. In making this assessment, it used the criteria set forth by the Committee of Sponsoring Organizations of the Treadway Commission (COSO) in *Internal Control—Integrated Framework*. Based on our assessment we believe that, as of February 25, 2006, the Company's internal control over financial reporting is effective based on those criteria.

The Company's independent registered public accounting firm, Ernst & Young LLP, has issued an audit report on our assessment of the Company's internal control over financial reporting. This report appears on the following page.

25

REPORT OF INDEPENDENT REGISTERED PUBLIC ACCOUNTING FIRM ON
INTERNAL CONTROL OVER FINANCIAL REPORTING

The Board of Directors and Shareholders of The Finish Line, Inc.

We have audited management's assessment, included in the accompanying Management Report on Internal Control over Financial Reporting (included in Item 8), that The Finish Line, Inc. maintained effective internal control over financial reporting as of February 25, 2006, based on criteria established in Internal Control—Integrated Framework issued by the Committee of Sponsoring Organizations of the Treadway Commission (the COSO criteria). The Finish Line, Inc.'s management is responsible for maintaining effective internal control over financial reporting and for its assessment of the effectiveness of internal control over financial reporting. Our responsibility is to express an opinion on management's assessment and an opinion on the effectiveness of the Company's internal control over financial reporting based on our audit.

We conducted our audit in accordance with the standards of the Public Company Accounting Oversight Board (United States). Those standards require that we plan and perform the audit to obtain reasonable assurance about whether effective internal control over financial reporting was maintained in all material respects. Our audit included obtaining an understanding of internal control over financial reporting, evaluating management's assessment, testing and evaluating the design and operating effectiveness of internal control, and performing such other procedures as we considered necessary in the circumstances. We believe that our audit provides a reasonable basis for our opinion.

A company's internal control over financial reporting is a process designed to provide reasonable assurance regarding the reliability of financial reporting and the preparation of financial statements for external purposes in accordance with generally accepted accounting principles. A company's internal control over financial reporting includes those policies and procedures that (1) pertain to the maintenance of records that, in reasonable detail, accurately and fairly reflect the transactions and dispositions of the assets of the company; (2) provide reasonable assurance that transactions are recorded as necessary to permit preparation of financial statements in accordance with generally accepted accounting principles, and that receipts and expenditures of the company are being made only in accordance with authorizations of management and directors of the company; and (3) provide reasonable assurance regarding prevention or timely detection of unauthorized acquisition, use, or disposition of the company's assets that could have a material effect on the financial statements.

Because of its inherent limitations, internal control over financial reporting may not prevent or detect misstatements. Also, projections of any evaluation of effectiveness to future periods are subject to the risk that controls may become inadequate because of changes in conditions, or that the degree of compliance with the policies or procedures may deteriorate.

In our opinion, management's assessment that The Finish Line, Inc. maintained effective internal control over financial reporting as of February 25, 2006, is fairly stated, in all material respects, based on the COSO criteria. Also, in our opinion, The Finish Line, Inc. maintained, in all material respects, effective internal control over financial reporting as of February 25, 2006, based on the COSO criteria.

We also have audited, in accordance with the standards of the Public Company Accounting Oversight Board (United States), the consolidated balance sheets of The Finish Line, Inc. as of February 25, 2006 and February 26, 2005, and the related consolidated statements of income, changes in shareholders' equity and cash flows for each of the three years in the period ended February 25, 2006 of The Finish Line, Inc., and our report dated May 4, 2006 expressed an unqualified opinion thereon.

Ernst & Young LLP

Indianapolis, Indiana
May 4, 2006

26

REPORT OF INDEPENDENT REGISTERED PUBLIC ACCOUNTING FIRM

The Board of Directors and Shareholders of The Finish Line, Inc.

We have audited the accompanying consolidated balance sheets of The Finish Line, Inc. as of February 25, 2006 and February 26, 2005, and the related consolidated statements of income, changes in shareholders' equity and cash flows for each of the three years in the period ended February 25, 2006. These financial statements are the responsibility of the Company's management. Our responsibility is to express an opinion on these financial statements based on our audits.

We conducted our audits in accordance with the standards of the Public Company Accounting Oversight Board (United States). Those standards require that we plan and perform the audit to obtain reasonable assurance about whether the financial statements are free of material misstatement. An audit includes examining, on a test basis, evidence supporting the amounts and disclosures in the financial statements. An audit also includes assessing the accounting principles used and significant estimates made by management, as well as evaluating the overall financial statement presentation. We believe that our audits provide a reasonable basis for our opinion.

In our opinion, the consolidated financial statements referred to above present fairly, in all material respects, the consolidated financial position of The Finish Line, Inc. at February 25, 2006 and February 26, 2005, and the consolidated results of its operations and its cash flows for each of the three years in the period ended February 25, 2006, in conformity with U.S. generally accepted accounting principles.

We also have audited, in accordance with the standards of the Public Company Accounting Oversight Board (United States), the effectiveness of The Finish Line, Inc.'s. internal control over financial reporting as of February 25, 2006, based on criteria established in Internal Control—Integrated Framework issued by the Committee of Sponsoring Organizations of the Treadway Commission and our report dated May 4, 2006, expressed an unqualified opinion thereon.

Ernst & Young LLP

Indianapolis, Indiana
May 4, 2006

27

THE FINISH LINE, INC.
CONSOLIDATED BALANCE SHEETS
(in thousands)

	February 25, 2006	February 26, 2005
Assets		
Current Assets		
Cash and cash equivalents	$ 47,488	$ 55,991
Marketable securities	49,075	57,175
Accounts receivable, net	11,999	14,230
Merchandise inventories, net	268,590	241,242
Other	4,375	3,162
Total current assets	381,527	371,800
Property and Equipment		
Land	1,557	315
Building	33,757	23,309
Leasehold improvements	243,312	217,371
Furniture, fixtures, and equipment	93,221	77,945
Construction in progress	10,753	10,616
	382,600	329,556
Less accumulated depreciation	161,418	141,258
	221,182	188,298
Deferred income taxes	11,118	3,578
Goodwill and intangible assets	13,989	11,343
Total assets	$ 627,816	$ 575,019
Liabilities and Shareholder's Equity		
Current Liabilities		
Accounts payable	$ 84,006	$ 92,378
Employee compensation	12,026	12,883
Accrued property and sales tax	8,254	6,914
Deferred income taxes	12,429	7,645
Other liabilities and accrued expenses	25,700	17,196
Total current liabilities	142,415	137,016
Commitments and contingencies		
Deferred credits from landlords	56,859	50,532
Other long-term liabilities	—	1,500
Shareholders' Equity		
Preferred stock, $.01 par value; 1,000 shares authorized; none issued	—	—
Common stock, $.01 par value		
Class A:		
Shares authorized—100,000		
Shares issued—47,649		
Shares outstanding (2006—42,865; 2005—43,578)	476	476
Class B:		
Shares authorized—10,000		
Shares issued and outstanding—5,141	52	52
Additional paid-in capital	142,645	138,130
Retained earnings	319,656	263,971
Treasury stock (2006—4,784, 2005—4,071)	(34,287)	(16,658)
Total shareholders' equity	428,542	385,971
Total liabilities and shareholders' equity	$ 627,816	$ 575,019

See accompanying notes

THE FINISH LINE, INC.
CONSOLIDATED STATEMENTS OF INCOME
(in thousands)

	Year Ended		
	February 25, 2006	February 26, 2005	February 28, 2004
Net sales	$1,306,045	$1,166,767	$ 985,891
Cost of sales (including occupancy costs)	894,724	798,033	681,561
Gross profit	411,321	368,734	304,330
Selling, general and administrative expenses	313,893	271,901	229,842
Insurance settlement	—	(114)	(1,228)
Asset impairment charge	2,523	—	—
Operating income	94,905	96,947	75,716
Interest income, net	2,008	1,076	651
Income before income taxes	96,913	98,023	76,367
Income taxes	36,380	36,760	29,020
Net income	$ 60,533	$ 61,263	$ 47,347
Basic earnings per share	$ 1.25	$ 1.27	$ 1.01
Diluted earnings per share	$ 1.23	$ 1.24	$ .98
Dividends declared per share	$ 0.100	$ 0.075	$ —

See accompanying notes

29

THE FINISH LINE, INC.
CONSOLIDATED STATEMENTS OF CASH FLOWS
(in thousands)

	Year Ended		
	February 25, 2006	February 26, 2005	February 28, 2004
Operating activities			
Net income	$ 60,533	$ 61,263	$ 47,347
Adjustments to reconcile net income to net cash provided by operating activities:			
Asset impairment charge	2,523	—	—
Depreciation and amortization	34,633	27,169	23,732
Deferred income taxes	(5,024)	5,123	2,413
Loss on disposal of property and equipment	262	508	200
Tax benefit from exercise of stock options	2,646	3,341	6,258
Changes in operating assets and liabilities, net of effects of acquisition			
Accounts receivable	2,231	(7,661)	(407)
Merchandise inventories	(27,348)	(44,374)	(33,819)
Other current assets	(1,213)	(304)	5,867
Accounts payable	(8,372)	34,534	1,562
Employee compensation	(857)	1,019	3,373
Other liabilities and accrued expenses	7,686	2,752	6,699
Deferred credits from landlords	6,327	3,777	4,011
Net cash provided by operating activities	74,027	87,147	67,236
Investing activities			
Purchases of property and equipment	(70,126)	(58,172)	(55,619)
Proceeds from disposals of property and equipment	137	513	33
Purchases of available-for-sale marketable securities	(283,100)	(170,124)	(41,975)
Proceeds from sale of available-for-sale marketable securities	291,200	131,724	43,704
Acquisitions, net of cash acquired	—	(10,247)	—
Lease acquisition costs	(17)	(2,358)	—
Net cash used in investing activities	(61,906)	(108,664)	(53,857)
Financing activities			
Principal payments on assumed debt	—	(1,499)	—
Dividends paid to shareholders	(4,864)	(2,415)	—
Proceeds from issuance of common stock	4,105	4,345	10,299
Purchase of treasury stock	(19,865)	—	—
Net cash (used in) provided by financing activities	(20,624)	431	10,299
Net (decrease) increase in cash and cash equivalents	(8,503)	(21,086)	23,678
Cash and cash equivalents at beginning of year	55,991	77,077	53,399
Cash and cash equivalents at end of year	$ 47,488	$ 55,991	$ 77,077

See accompanying notes

THE FINISH LINE, INC.
CONSOLIDATED STATEMENTS OF CHANGES IN SHAREHOLDERS' EQUITY
(in thousands)

	Number of Shares			Amount		Additional Paid-in Capital	Retained Earnings	Accumulated Other Comprehensive Income	Treasury Stock	Totals
	Class A	Class B	Treasury	Class A	Class B					
Balance at March 1, 2003	18,695	4,348	3,353	$ 220	$ 44	$ 124,347	$158,992	$ 2	$ (26,854)	$256,751
Comprehensive income:										
Net income for 2004							47,347			47,347
Other comprehensive income-Net unrealized loss on available-for-sale securities, net of tax benefit of $1								(2)		(2)
Total comprehensive income										47,345
Non-qualified Class A Common Stock options exercised	979		(979)			7,816			8,302	16,118
Share based compensation						439				439
Conversion of Class B Common Stock to Class A Common Stock	1,483	(1,483)		15	(15)					—
Balance at February 28, 2004	21,157	2,865	2,374	235	29	132,602	206,339	—	(18,552)	320,653
Comprehensive income—net income for 2005							61,263			61,263
Cash dividends declared ($.075 per share)							(3,631)			(3,631)
Two-for-one stock split	21,157	2,865	2,372	235	29	(264)				—
Non-qualified Class A Common Stock options exercised	664		(664)			5,240			1,860	7,100
Share based compensation						408				408
Shares issued under employee stock purchase plan	11		(11)			144			34	178
Conversion of Class B Common Stock to Class A Common Stock	589	(589)		6	(6)					—
Balance at February 26, 2005	43,578	5,141	4,071	476	52	138,130	263,971	—	(16,658)	385,971
Comprehensive income—net income for 2006							60,533			60,533
Cash dividends declared ($.10 per share)							(4,848)			(4,848)
Non-qualified Class A Common Stock options exercised	480		(480)			3,824			1,717	5,541
Share based compensation	101		(101)			329			406	735
Shares issued under employee stock purchase plan	31		(31)			362			113	475
Treasury Stock purchased	(1,325)		1,325						(19,865)	(19,865)
Balance at February 25, 2006	42,865	5,141	4,784	$ 476	$ 52	$ 142,645	$319,656	$ —	$ (34,287)	$428,542

See accompanying notes

THE FINISH LINE, INC.
NOTES TO CONSOLIDATED FINANCIAL STATEMENTS

1. Significant Accounting Policies

Basis of Presentation. The consolidated financial statements include the accounts of The Finish Line, Inc. ("Finish Line") and its wholly-owned subsidiaries The Finish Line Man Alive, Inc. ("Man Alive"), The Finish Line USA, Inc., The Finish Line Distribution, Inc., Spike's Holding, LLC (a wholly-owned subsidiary of The Finish Line USA, Inc.), Finish Line Transportation Co., Inc. and Paiva, Inc. (collectively, the "Company"). All significant intercompany transactions and balances have been eliminated. Throughout these notes to the consolidated financial statements, the fiscal years ended February 25, 2006, February 26, 2005 and February 28, 2004 are referred to as 2006, 2005 and 2004, respectively.

The Company uses a "Retail" calendar. The Company's fiscal year ends on the Saturday closest to the last day of February and included 52 weeks in 2006, 2005, and 2004.

Nature of Operations. Finish Line is a specialty retailer of men's, women's and children's brand-name athletic, lifestyle and outdoor footwear, activewear and accessories. Man Alive is a hip-hop fashion retailer offering men's and ladies' name brand fashions from the industry's leading designers. Paiva, Inc. is the Company's new concept for the active woman, which premiered with its first store opening on April 14, 2006. The Company manages its business on the basis of one reportable segment. Finish Line stores average approximately 5,641 square feet, Man Alive stores average approximately 3,110 square feet, and Paiva, Inc. stores will average approximately 4,000 square feet in size and all are primarily located in enclosed malls throughout most of the United States.

In 2006, the Company purchased approximately 80% of its merchandise from its five largest suppliers. The largest supplier, Nike, accounted for approximately 59%, 58% and 56% of merchandise purchases in 2006, 2005 and 2004, respectively.

Use of Estimates. Preparation of the financial statements requires management to make estimates and assumptions that affect the amounts reported in the financial statements and accompanying notes. Actual results could differ from those estimates.

Reclassifications. Certain reclassifications have been made to prior years' consolidated financial statements to conform to the 2006 presentation. These reclassifications had no effect on net income.

Cash and Cash Equivalents. Cash and cash equivalents are primarily invested in tax-exempt instruments with high liquidity, less than 90 days when purchased.

Marketable Securities. The Company accounts for its marketable securities in accordance with Statement of Financial Accounting Standards ("SFAS") No. 115, "Accounting for Certain Investments in Debt and Equity Securities." As of February 25, 2006 and February 26, 2005, all of the Company's marketable securities were classified as available-for-sale, and accordingly reported at fair value. Marketable Securities consist of Market Auction Preferred Stock ("MAPS"). MAPS are securities, which generally have maturities extending well beyond one year; however, the dividend rate resets periodically through a Dutch auction process and there is an active market through which the Company can readily liquidate its holdings. Therefore, these amounts have been classified as current. A Dutch auction is a competitive bidding process to set a dividend rate for the next term. All sellers and buyers sell and buy at par and therefore there are no realized or unrealized gains or losses related to these securities.

Merchandise Inventories. Merchandise inventories are valued at the lower of cost or market using a weighted-average cost method, which approximates the first-in, first-out method. Merchandise inventories are

32

THE FINISH LINE, INC.
NOTES TO CONSOLIDATED FINANCIAL STATEMENTS—(Continued)

recorded net of markdown and shrink reserves. Vendor rebates are accounted for in accordance with Emerging Issues Task Force ("EITF") 02-16 "Accounting by a Customer (Including a Reseller) for Certain Consideration Received from a Vendor" ("EITF 02-16") and are applied as a reduction to the cost of merchandise inventories.

Property and Equipment. Property and equipment are stated at cost and depreciated on a straight-line basis over the estimated useful lives of the assets: 30 years for buildings and 3 to 10 years for furniture, fixtures and equipment. Improvements to leased premises are amortized on a straight-line basis over the shorter of the estimated useful life of the asset, generally 10 years, or the remaining lease term. Significant additions and improvements that extend the useful life of an asset are capitalized. Maintenance and repairs are charged to current operations as incurred. Depreciation expense for the years ended 2006, 2005 and 2004 was $34,320,000, $27,169,000 and $23,732,000, respectively.

Impairment of Long-Lived Assets. The Company accounts for long-lived assets in accordance with the provisions of SFAS No. 144 ("FAS 144"), "Accounting for the Impairment or Disposal of Long-Lived Assets." The Company reviews long-lived assets for impairment, after a start-up phase, whenever events or changes in circumstances indicate that the carrying amount of an asset may not be recoverable. Recoverability of assets to be held and used is determined by a comparison of the carrying amount of an asset to future undiscounted net cash flows expected to be generated by the asset. If such assets are considered to be impaired, the impairment recognized is measured by comparing projected individual store discounted cash flows to the asset carrying values.

Goodwill and Intangible Assets. The Company accounts for goodwill and other intangible assets in accordance with SFAS No. 142 ("FAS 142"), "Goodwill and Other Intangible Assets." FAS 142 requires that goodwill and intangible assets with indefinite lives are not amortized but reviewed for impairment if impairment indicators arise and, at a minimum, annually. Intangible assets with indefinite lives include the goodwill and tradename recorded in connection with the acquisition of Man Alive (See Note 2). The Company's goodwill and tradename are not amortizable for tax purposes. Intangible assets that are deemed to have finite lives are amortized over their estimated useful lives. Intangible assets with finite lives relate to lease acquisition costs and are amortized over the lease term, which range from 4 to 10 years. The gross cost of the intangible assets with finite lives is $2,575,000 with accumulated amortization of $313,000 as of February 25, 2006. Amortization expense for the year ended February 25, 2006 was $313,000.

Deferred Credits From Landlords. Deferred credits from landlords consist of step rent and allowances from landlords related to the Company's retail stores. Step rent represents the difference between actual operating lease payments due and straight-line rent expense, which is recorded by the Company over the term of the lease, including the build-out period. This amount is generally recorded as a deferred credit in the early years of the lease, when cash payments are generally lower than the straight-line rent expense, and reduced in the later years of the lease, when payments begin to exceed the straight-line expense. During 2006, the Company concluded that rent payments required by certain fixed rental lease agreements were not being recognized over the proper lease term. As a result, the Company has increased "Deferred credits from landlords" on the consolidated balance sheets by $2,100,000, and has increased "Cost of sales (including occupancy costs)" on the consolidated statements of income by the same amount. The after-tax impact of this non-cash adjustment was $1,312,000. Landlord allowances are generally comprised of amounts promised to the Company by landlords in the form of cash or rent abatements. These allowances are part of the negotiated terms of the lease. In situations where cash is to be received, the Company records a receivable for the full amount of the allowance when certain performance criteria articulated in the lease are met, typically when the store opens, and a liability is concurrently established. This deferred credit from landlords is amortized into income (through lower rent expense) over the term (including the pre-opening build-out period) of the applicable lease and the receivable is reduced as amounts are received from the landlord.

33

THE FINISH LINE, INC.
NOTES TO CONSOLIDATED FINANCIAL STATEMENTS—(Continued)

Revenue Recognition.   Revenues are recognized at the time the customer receives the merchandise. Sales include merchandise, net of returns and exclude all taxes. Revenue from gift certificates and layaway sales is recognized when the customer receives the merchandise.

Costs of Sales.   Costs of sales include the cost associated with acquiring merchandise from vendors, occupancy costs, provision for inventory shortages, and credits and allowances from our merchandise vendors following EITF 02-16 guidance.

Because the Company does not include the costs associated with operating the distribution facility and freight within cost of sales, the Company's gross profit may not be comparable to those of other retailers that may include all costs related to their distribution facilities in costs of sales and in the calculation of gross profit.

Selling, General, and Administrative Expenses.   Selling, general and administrative expenses include store payroll and related payroll benefits, store operating expenses, advertising, cooperative advertising allowances following EITF 02-16 guidance, costs associated with operating our distribution facility and freight, including moving merchandise from our distribution center to stores, and other corporate related expenses.

Advertising.   The Company expenses the cost of advertising as incurred, net of reimbursements for cooperative advertising. The reimbursements for cooperative advertising are agreed upon with vendors and are recorded in the same period as the associated expenses are incurred following EITF 02-16 guidance. Advertising expense net of cooperative credits for 2006, 2005 and 2004 amounted to $21,232,000, $21,766,000 and $14,660,000, respectively.

Store Pre-opening and Closing Costs.   Store pre-opening costs and other non-capitalized expenditures, including payroll, training costs and straight-line rent expense, are expensed as incurred. In the event a store is closed before its lease has expired, any estimated post-closing lease obligations, less sublease rental income, is provided for when the leased space is no longer in use as required by SFAS No. 146 "Accounting for Costs Associated with Exit or Disposal Activities."

Income Taxes.   Deferred income taxes reflect the impact of temporary differences between the amounts of assets and liabilities recognized for financial reporting purposes and such amounts recognized for income tax purposes.

Earnings Per Share.   Earnings per share are calculated based on the weighted-average number of outstanding common shares. Diluted earnings per share are calculated based on the weighted-average number of outstanding common shares, plus the effect of dilutive stock options and restrictive stock. All per share amounts, unless otherwise noted, are presented on a diluted basis, that is, based on the weighted-average number of outstanding common shares and the effect of all potentially dilutive common shares (primarily unexercised stock options and restrictive stock).

Financial Instruments.   Financial instruments consist of cash and cash equivalents, accounts receivable, marketable securities and accounts payable. The carrying value of cash and cash equivalents, marketable securities, accounts receivable, and accounts payable approximate fair value.

At February 25, 2006 and February 26, 2005, the Company had not invested in, nor did it have, any derivative financial instruments.

Stock-Based Compensation.   As allowed by SFAS Statement No. 148, "Accounting for Stock-Based Compensation—Transition and Disclosure," which amends SFAS Statement No. 123 ("FAS 123"), "Accounting

34

The change in the additional minimum liability was a decrease of $15 million after-tax in 2005 and an increase of $14 million after-tax in 2004 to accumulated other comprehensive loss.

As of January 28, 2006 and January 29, 2005, the accumulated benefit obligation for all pension plans, totaling $688 million and $702 million, respectively, exceeded plan assets.

The following weighted-average assumptions were used to determine the benefit obligations under the plans:

	Pension Benefits		Postretirement Benefits	
	2005	2004	2005	2004
Discount rate	5.43%	5.50%	5.50%	5.50%
Rate of compensation increase	3.77%	3.79%		

The components of net benefit expense (income) are:

	Pension Benefits			Postretirement Benefits		
	2005	2004	2003	2005	2004	2003
	(in millions)					
Service cost	$ 9	$ 9	$ 8	$ —	$ —	$ —
Interest cost	36	39	43	1	1	2
Expected return on plan assets	(49)	(48)	(46)	—	—	—
Amortization of prior service cost (benefit)	1	1	—	(1)	(1)	(1)
Amortization of net (gain) loss	13	11	9	(12)	(13)	(16)
Net benefit expense (income)	$ 10	$ 12	$ 14	$(12)	$(13)	$(15)

The following weighted-average assumptions were used to determine net benefit cost:

	Pension Benefits			Postretirement Benefits		
	2005	2004	2003	2005	2004	2003
Discount rate	5.50%	5.90%	6.50%	5.50%	5.90%	6.50%
Rate of compensation increase	3.77%	3.79%	3.72%			
Expected long-term rate of return on assets	8.88%	8.89%	8.88%			

The expected long-term rate of return on invested plan assets is based on historical long-term performance and future expected performance of those assets based upon current asset allocations.

Beginning with 2001, new retirees were charged the expected full cost of the medical plan and existing retirees will incur 100 percent of the expected future increase in medical plan costs. Any changes in the health care cost trend rates assumed would not affect the accumulated benefit obligation or net benefit income since retirees will incur 100 percent of such expected future increases.

In December 2003, the United States enacted into law the Medicare Prescription Drug, Improvement and Modernization Act of 2003 (the "Act"). The Act establishes a prescription drug benefit under Medicare, known as "Medicare Part D," and a Federal subsidy to sponsors of retiree health care benefit plans that provide a benefit that is at least actuarially equivalent to Medicare Part D. In May 2004, the FASB issued FASB Staff Position No. 106-2, "Accounting and Disclosure Requirements Related to the Medicare Prescription Drug, Improvement and Modernization Act of 2003" ("FSP 106-2"). FSP 106-2 requires companies to account for the effect of the subsidy on benefits attributable to past service as an actuarial experience gain and as a reduction of the service cost component of net postretirement health care costs for amounts attributable to current service, if the benefit provided is at least actuarially equivalent to Medicare Part D. During 2005, the Company reviewed its retiree health care benefit plans in light of the final regulations for implementing Medicare Part D by the Centers for Medicare and Medicaid Services. The Company has determined that it will qualify for the subsidy, however the effect of the subsidy will not be significant to either the benefit obligation or net benefit income.

The Company's pension plan weighted-average asset allocations at January 28, 2006 and January 29, 2005, by asset category are as follows:

Asset Category	2005	2004
Equity securities	62%	63%
Foot Locker, Inc. common stock	2%	2%
Debt securities	34%	33%
Real estate	1%	1%
Other	1%	1%
Total	**100%**	**100%**

The U.S. defined benefit plan held 396,000 shares of Foot Locker, Inc. common stock as of January 28, 2006 and January 29, 2005. Currently, the target composition of the weighted-average plan assets is 64 percent equity and 36 percent fixed income securities, although the Company may alter the targets from time to time depending on market conditions and the funding requirements of the pension plans. The Company believes that plan assets are invested in a prudent manner with an objective of providing a total return that, over the long term, provides sufficient assets to fund benefit obligations, taking into account the Company's expected contributions and the level of risk deemed appropriate. The Company's investment strategy is to utilize asset classes with differing rates of return, volatility and correlation to reduce risk by providing diversification relative to equities. Diversification within asset classes is also utilized to reduce the effect that the return of any single investment may have on the entire portfolio. The Company contributed $68 million to its pension plans in February 2006.

Estimated future benefit payments for each of the next five years and the five years thereafter are as follows:

	Pension Benefits	Postretirement Benefits
	(in millions)	
2006	$ 64	$2
2007	62	3
2008	60	3
2009	60	2
2010	58	2
2011–2015	263	6

Savings Plans

The Company has two qualified savings plans, a 401(k) Plan that is available to employees whose primary place of employment is the U.S., and an 1165 (e) Plan, which began during 2004 that is available to employees whose primary place of employment is in Puerto Rico. Both plans require that the employees have attained at least the age of twenty-one and have completed one year of service consisting of at least 1,000 hours. The savings plans allow eligible employees to contribute up to 25 percent and 10 percent, for the U.S. and Puerto Rico plans, respectively, of their compensation on a pre-tax basis. The Company matches 25 percent of the first 4 percent of the employees' contributions with Company stock and such matching Company contributions are vested incrementally over 5 years for both plans. The charge to operations for the Company's matching contribution for the U.S. plan was $1.6 million, $1.3 million and $1.5 million in 2005, 2004 and 2003, respectively.

21   Stock Plans

In 2003, the Company adopted the 2003 Stock Option and Award Plan (the "2003 Stock Option Plan") and the 2003 Employees Stock Purchase Plan (the "2003 Stock Purchase Plan"). Under the 2003 Stock Option Plan, options, restricted stock, stock appreciation rights (SARs), or other stock-based awards may be granted to officers and other employees at not less than the market price on the date of the grant. Unless a longer or shorter period is established at the time of the option grant, generally, one-third of each stock option grant becomes exercisable on each of the first three anniversary dates of the date of grant. The maximum number of shares of stock reserved for issuance pursuant to the 2003 Stock Option Plan is 4,000,000 shares. The number of shares reserved for issuance as restricted stock and other stock-based awards cannot exceed 1,000,000 shares. The Company adopted the 2003 Stock Purchase Plan whose terms are substantially the same as the 1994 Employees Stock Purchase Plan (the "1994 Stock Purchase Plan"), which expired in June 2004. Under the 2003 Stock Purchase Plan, 3,000,000 shares of common stock became available for purchase beginning June 2005.

Under the Company's 2003 Stock Purchase Plan participating employees are able to contribute up to 10 percent of their annual compensation to acquire shares of common stock at 85 percent of the lower market price on one of two specified dates in each plan year. Of the 3,000,000 shares of common stock authorized for purchase under this plan, 1,191 participating employees purchased 237,353 shares in 2005.

Under the Company's 1998 Stock Option and Award Plan (the "1998 Plan"), options to purchase shares of common stock may be granted to officers and other employees at not less than the market price on the date of grant. Under the plan, the Company may grant officers and other employees, including those at the subsidiary level, stock options, SARs, restricted stock or other stock-based awards. Generally, one-third of each stock option grant becomes exercisable on each of the first three anniversary dates of the date of grant. The options terminate up to 10 years from the date of grant. In 2000, the Company amended the 1998 Plan to provide for awards of up to 12,000,000 shares of the Company's common stock. The number of shares reserved for issuance as restricted stock and other stock-based awards, as amended, cannot exceed 3,000,000 shares.

In addition, options to purchase shares of common stock remain outstanding under the Company's 1995 and 1986 stock option plans. The 1995 Stock Option and Award Plan (the "1995 Plan") is substantially the same as the 1998 Plan. The number of shares authorized for awards under the 1995 Plan is 6,000,000 shares. The number of shares reserved for issuance as restricted stock under the 1995 Plan is limited to 1,500,000 shares. No further awards may be made under the 1995 Plan as of March 8, 2005. Options granted under the 1986 Stock Option Plan (the "1986 Plan") generally become exercisable in two equal installments on the first and the second anniversaries of the date of grant. No further options may be granted under the 1986 Plan.

The 2002 Foot Locker Directors' Stock Plan replaced both the Directors' Stock Plan, which was adopted in 1996, and the Directors' Stock Option Plan, which was adopted in 2000. There are 500,000 shares authorized under the 2002 Plan. No further grants or awards may be made under either of the prior plans. Options granted prior to 2003 have a three-year vesting schedule. Options granted beginning in 2003 become exercisable one year from the date of grant.

When common stock is issued under these plans, the proceeds from options exercised or shares purchased are credited to common stock to the extent of the par value of the shares issued and the excess is credited to additional paid-in capital. When treasury common stock is issued, the difference between the average cost of treasury stock used and the proceeds from options exercised or shares awarded or purchased is charged or credited, as appropriate, to either additional paid-in capital or retained earnings. The tax benefits relating to amounts deductible for federal income tax purposes, which are not included in income for financial reporting purposes, have been credited to additional paid-in capital.

The fair values of the issuance of the stock-based compensation pursuant to the Company's various stock option and purchase plans were estimated at the grant date using a Black-Scholes option-pricing model.

	Stock Option Plans			Stock Purchase Plan		
	2005	2004	2003	2005	2004	2003
Weighted-average risk free rate of interest	3.99%	2.57%	2.26%	4.19%	1.33%	1.11%
Expected volatility	28%	33%	37%	25%	32%	31%
Weighted-average expected award life......................	3.8 years	3.7 years	3.4 years	.7 years	.7 years	.7 years
Dividend yield	1.1%	1.1%	1.2%	—	—	—
Weighted-average fair value	$6.69	$6.51	$2.90	$5.54	$11.44	$14.15

The Black-Scholes option valuation model was developed for estimating the fair value of traded options that have no vesting restrictions and are fully transferable. Because option valuation models require the use of subjective assumptions, changes in these assumptions can materially affect the fair value of the options, and because the Company's options do not have the characteristics of traded options, the option valuation models do not necessarily provide a reliable measure of the fair value of its options.

The information set forth in the following table covers options granted under the Company's stock option plans:

	2005		2004		2003	
	Number of Shares	Weighted-Average Exercise Price	Number of Shares	Weighted-Average Exercise Price	Number of Shares	Weighted-Average Exercise Price
	(in thousands, except prices per share)					
Options outstanding at beginning of year ...	5,909	$16.69	6,886	$14.73	7,676	$15.18
Granted	1,014	$27.42	1,183	$25.20	1,439	$10.81
Exercised	682	$15.03	1,853	$14.43	1,830	$12.50
Expired or canceled	279	$22.11	307	$19.13	399	$19.55
Options outstanding at end of year	5,962	$18.45	5,909	$16.69	6,886	$14.73
Options exercisable at end of year	4,042	$16.00	3,441	$15.34	4,075	$15.99
Options available for future grant at end of year	5,768		7,464		8,780	

The following table summarizes information about stock options outstanding and exercisable at January 28, 2006:

	Options Outstanding			Options Exercisable	
Range of Exercise Prices	Shares	Weighted-Average Remaining Contractual Life	Weighted-Average Exercise Price	Shares	Weighted-Average Exercise Price
	(in thousands, except prices per share)				
$ 4.53 to $10.89	1,012	6.6	$ 9.79	702	$ 9.59
$11.31 to $12.99	1,158	5.0	12.24	1,154	12.24
$13.34 to $16.02	1,047	6.0	15.83	1,043	15.84
$16.19 to $25.37	1,016	4.1	22.93	799	23.15
$25.39 to $27.01	1,032	8.3	25.65	327	25.39
$27.10 to $28.50	697	9.1	28.04	17	28.15
$ 4.53 to $28.50	5,962	6.4	$18.45	4,042	$16.00

22 Restricted Stock

Restricted shares of the Company's common stock may be awarded to certain officers and key employees of the Company. There were 225,000, 330,000, and 845,000 restricted shares of common stock granted in 2005, 2004 and 2003, respectively. In 2005 and 2004, 20,000 and 72,005 restricted stock units, respectively, were granted to certain executives located outside of the United States; each restricted unit represents the right to receive one share of the Company's common stock provided that the vesting conditions are satisfied. The market values of the shares and units at the date of grant amounted to $6.5 million in 2005, $10.2 million in 2004 and $9.8 million in 2003. The market values are recorded within shareholders' equity and are amortized as compensation expense over the related vesting periods. These awards fully vest after the passage of a restriction period, generally three years, except for certain grants in 2005, 2004 and 2003. The Company granted 105,000 shares of restricted stock in 2005, which vest in three equal installments on approximately each of the next three years grant date anniversary, 75,000 shares of restricted stock in 2004, which vest over 13 months and in 2003 granted 200,000 shares of restricted stock that vested 50 percent one year following the date of grant and 50 percent that will vest two years from the date of grant. During 2005, 2004 and 2003, respectively, 176,135, 30,000 and 80,000 restricted shares and units were forfeited. The deferred compensation balance, reflected as a reduction to shareholders' equity, was $6.2 million, $9.0 million and $7.1 million as of January 28, 2006, January 29, 2005 and January 31, 2004, respectively. The Company recorded compensation expense related to restricted shares, net of forfeitures, of $6.1 million in 2005, $8.0 million in 2004 and $4.1 million in 2003.

23 Legal Proceedings

Legal proceedings pending against the Company or its consolidated subsidiaries consist of ordinary, routine litigation, including administrative proceedings, incidental to the business of the Company, as well as litigation incidental to the sale and disposition of businesses that have occurred in past years. These legal proceedings include commercial, intellectual property, customer, and labor-and-employment-related claims, including class action lawsuits in which plaintiffs allege violations by the Company of state wage and hour and other laws. Management does not believe that the outcome of such proceedings would have a material adverse effect on the Company's consolidated financial position, liquidity, or results of operations, taken as a whole.

24 Commitments

In connection with the sale of various businesses and assets, the Company may be obligated for certain lease commitments transferred to third parties and pursuant to certain normal representations, warranties, or indemnifications entered into with the purchasers of such businesses or assets. Although the maximum potential amounts for such obligations cannot be readily determined, management believes that the resolution of such contingencies will not have a material effect on the Company's consolidated financial position, liquidity, or results of operations. The Company is also operating certain stores and making rental payments for which lease agreements are in the process of being negotiated with landlords. Although there is no contractual commitment to make these payments, it is likely that a lease will be executed.

The Company does not have any off-balance sheet financing, other than operating leases entered into in the normal course of business and disclosed above or unconsolidated special purpose entities. The Company does not participate in transactions that generate relationships with unconsolidated entities or financial partnerships, including variable interest entities.

25 Shareholder Information and Market Prices (Unaudited)

Foot Locker, Inc. common stock is listed on The New York Stock Exchange as well as on the böerse-stuttgart stock exchange in Germany and the Elektronische Börse Schweiz (EBS) stock exchange in Switzerland. In addition, the stock is traded on the Cincinnati stock exchange.

As of January 28, 2006, the Company had 24,933 shareholders of record owning 155,503,606 common shares.

Market prices for the Company's common stock were as follows:

	2005		2004	
	High	Low	High	Low
Common Stock				
Quarter				
1st Q	$29.95	$25.88	$27.59	$21.75
2nd Q	27.65	24.31	25.03	19.97
3rd Q	25.37	18.75	24.80	19.98
4th Q	24.07	18.74	27.26	22.75

During 2005, the Company declared quarterly dividends of $0.075 per share during the first, second and third quarters. On November 16, 2005, the Company increased the quarterly dividend per share by 20 percent to $0.09, beginning in the fourth quarter of 2005.

During 2004, the Company declared quarterly dividends of $0.06 per share during the first, second and third quarters. On November 17, 2004, the Company increased the quarterly dividend per share to $0.075, beginning in the fourth quarter of 2004.

26   Quarterly Results (Unaudited)

	1st Q	2nd Q	3rd Q	4th Q	Year
		(in millions, except per share amounts)			
Sales					
2005	$1,377	1,304	1,408	1,564	5,653
2004	1,186	1,268	1,366	1,535	5,355
Gross margin [a]					
2005	$ 418	377	430	484[c]	1,709
2004	361	369	426	477	1,633
Operating profit [b]					
2005	$ 94	71	104	140	409
2004	78	61	117	133	389
Income from continuing operations					
2005	$ 58	44	65	96	263
2004	47	45	74	89	255
Net income					
2005	$ 58	44	66	96	264
2004	48	82	74	89	293
Basic earnings per share:					
2005					
Income from continuing operations	$ 0.37	0.29	0.42	0.62	1.70
Income from discontinued operations	—	—	0.01	—	0.01
Net income	0.37	0.29	0.43	0.62	1.71
2004					
Income from continuing operations	$ 0.33	0.30	0.47	0.58	1.69
Loss from discontinued operations	—	0.25	—	—	0.25
Net income	0.33	0.55	0.47	0.58	1.94
Diluted earnings per share:					
2005					
Income from continuing operations	$ 0.37	0.28	0.41	0.61	1.67
Income from discontinued operations	—	—	0.01	—	0.01
Net income	0.37	0.28	0.42	0.61	1.68
2004					
Income from continuing operations	$ 0.31	0.29	0.47	0.57	1.64
Loss from discontinued operations	—	0.24	—	—	0.24
Net income	0.31	0.53	0.47	0.57	1.88

(a)   Gross margin represents sales less cost of sales. Includes the effects of the reclassification of tenant allowances as deferred credits, which are amortized as a reduction of rent expense as a component of costs of sales. Costs of sales was reduced by $1 million in each of the first three quarters of 2004 and by $2 million for the fourth quarter of 2004.

(b)   Operating profit represents income from continuing operations before income taxes, interest expense, net and non-operating income.

(c)   The fourth quarter of 2005 includes permanent markdowns of $7 million.

FIVE-YEAR SUMMARY OF SELECTED FINANCIAL DATA

The selected financial data below should be read in conjunction with the Consolidated Financial Statements and the notes thereto and other information contained elsewhere in this report. All selected financial data have been restated for discontinued operations and the reclassification of tenant allowances as deferred rent credits.

($ in millions, except per share amounts)	2005	2004	2003	2002	2001
Summary of Continuing Operations					
Sales	$5,653	5,355	4,779	4,509	4,379
Gross margin [1]	1,709	1,633	1,482	1,348	1,312
Selling, general and administrative expenses	1,129	1,088	987	928	923
Restructuring charges (income)	—	2	1	(2)	34
Depreciation and amortization [1]	171	154	152	153	158
Interest expense, net	10	15	18	26	24
Other (income) expense	(6)	—	—	(3)	(2)
Income from continuing operations	263	255	209	162	111[3]
Cumulative effect of accounting change [2]	—	—	(1)	—	—
Basic earnings per share from continuing operations	1.70	1.69	1.47	1.15	0.79[3]
Basic earnings per share from cumulative effect of accounting change	—	—	—	—	—
Diluted earnings per share from continuing operations	1.67	1.64	1.40	1.10	0.77[3]
Diluted earnings per share from cumulative effect of accounting change	—	—	—	—	—
Common stock dividends declared	0.32	0.26	0.15	0.03	—
Weighted-average common shares outstanding (in millions)	155.1	150.9	141.6	140.7	139.4
Weighted-average common shares outstanding assuming dilution (in millions)	157.6	157.1	152.9	150.8	146.9
Financial Condition					
Cash, cash equivalents and short-term investments	$ 587	492	448	357	215
Merchandise inventories	1,254	1,151	920	835	793
Property and equipment, net [4]	675	715	668	664	665
Total assets [4]	3,312	3,237	2,713	2,514	2,328
Short-term debt	—	—	—	—	—
Long-term debt and obligations under capital leases	326	365	335	357	399
Total shareholders' equity	2,027	1,830	1,375	1,110	992
Financial Ratios					
Return on equity (ROE)	13.6%	15.9	16.8	15.4	11.1
Operating profit margin	7.2%	7.3	7.2	6.0	4.5
Income from continuing operations as a percentage of sales	4.7%	4.8	4.4	3.6	2.5[3]
Net debt capitalization percent [5]	45.2%	50.4	53.3	58.6	61.1
Net debt capitalization percent (without present value of operating leases) [5]	—	—	—	—	15.6
Current ratio	2.8	2.7	2.8	2.2	2.0
Other Data					
Capital expenditures	$ 155	156	144	150	116
Number of stores at year end	3,921	3,967	3,610	3,625	3,590
Total selling square footage at year end (in millions)	8.71	8.89	7.92	8.04	7.94
Total gross square footage at year end (in millions)	14.48	14.78	13.14	13.22	13.14

(1) Gross margin and depreciation expense include the effects of the reclassification of tenant allowances as deferred credits, which are amortized as a reduction of rent expense as a component of costs of sales. Gross margin was reduced by $5 million in 2004 and 2003, $4 million in 2002 and 2001 and accordingly, depreciation expense was increased by the corresponding amount.

(2) 2003 relates to adoption of SFAS No. 143 "Accounting for Asset Retirement Obligations."

(3) In applying the provisions of EITF 90-16, income from continuing operations for 2001 would have been reclassified to include the results of the Northern Group. Accordingly, income from continuing operations would have been $91 million. As such basic earnings per share would have been $0.65 for fiscal 2001. Diluted earnings per share would have been $0.64 for fiscal 2001. However, upon achieving divestiture accounting in the fourth quarter of 2002, the results would have been reclassified to reflect the results as shown above and as originally reported by the Company.

(4) Property and equipment, net and total assets include the reclassification of tenant allowances as deferred credits, which were previously recorded as a reduction to the cost of property and equipment, and are now classified as part of the deferred rent liability. Property and equipment, net and total assets were increased by $22 million in 2004, $24 million in 2003 and $28 million in each of 2002 and 2001.

(5) Represents total debt, net of cash, cash equivalents and short-term investments and includes the effect of interest rate swaps of $1 million that decreased long-term debt at January 28, 2006, $4 million that increased long-term debt at January 29, 2005 and $1 million that reduced long-term debt at January 31, 2004.

GLOSSARY

Accelerated depreciation A higher amount of depreciation is recorded in the early years and a lower amount in the later years; also called *allowance for depreciation.* (p. 354)

Account Record used to accumulate amounts for each individual asset, liability, revenue, expense, and component of owners' equity. (p. 113)

Account receivable A receivable arising from the sale of goods or services with a verbal promise to pay. (p. 310)

Accounting The process of identifying, measuring, and communicating economic information to various users. (p. 14)

Accounting controls Procedures concerned with safeguarding the assets or the reliability of the financial statements. (p. 283)

Accounting cycle A series of steps performed each period and culminating with the preparation of a set of financial statements. (p. 174)

Accounting system Methods and records used to accurately report an entity's transactions and to maintain accountability for its assets and liabilities. (p. 282)

Accounts payable Amounts owed for inventory, goods, or services acquired in the normal course of business. (p. 396)

Accounts receivable turnover ratio A measure of the number of times accounts receivable are collected in a period. (p. 626)

Accrual Cash has not yet been paid or received, but expense has been incurred or revenue earned. (p. 169)

Accrual basis A system of accounting in which revenues are recognized when earned and expenses when incurred. (p. 158)

Accrued asset An asset resulting from the recognition of a revenue before the receipt of cash. (p. 169)

Accrued liability A liability resulting from the recognition of an expense before the payment of cash. (pp. 169, 399)

Acid-test or quick ratio A stricter test of liquidity than the current ratio; excludes inventory and prepayments from the numerator. (p. 624)

Acquisition cost The amount that includes all of the cost normally necessary to acquire an asset and prepare it for its intended use; also called *historical cost* or *original cost.* (p. 351)

Additional paid-in capital The amount received for the issuance of stock in excess of the par value of the stock; also called *paid-in capital in excess of par.* (p. 504)

Adjusting entries Journal entries made at the end of a period by a company using the accrual basis of accounting. (p. 163)

Administrative controls Procedures concerned with efficient operation of the business and adherence to managerial policies. (p. 283)

Aging schedule A form used to categorize the various individual accounts receivable according to the length of time each has been outstanding. (p. 314)

Allowance for doubtful accounts A contra-asset account used to reduce accounts receivable to its net realizable value; also called *allowance for uncollectible accounts.* (p. 312)

Allowance method A method of estimating bad debts on the basis of either the net credit sales of the period or the accounts receivable at the end of the period. (p. 312)

American Accounting Association The professional organization for accounting educators. (p. 35)

American Institute of Certified Public Accountants (AICPA) The professional organization for certified public accountants. (p. 28)

Annuity A series of payments of equal amounts. (p. 410)

Asset A future economic benefit. (p. 8)

Asset turnover ratio The relationship between net sales and average total assets. (p. 632)

Audit committee Board of directors subset that acts as a direct contact between stockholders and the independent accounting firm. (p. 282)

Auditing The process of examining the financial statements and the underlying records of a company in order to render an opinion as to whether the statements are fairly represented. (p. 33)

Auditors' report The opinion rendered by a public accounting firm concerning the fairness of the presentation of the financial statements; also called the *report of independent accountants.* (p. 33)

Authorized shares The maximum number of shares a corporation may issue as indicated in the corporate charter. (p. 502)

Available-for-sale securities Stocks and bonds that are not classified as either held-to-maturity or trading securities. (p. 323)

Balance sheet The financial statement that summarizes the assets, liabilities, and owners' equity at a specific point in time; also called the *statement of financial position.* (p. 18)

Bank reconciliation A form used by the accountant to reconcile or resolve any differences between the balance shown on the bank statement for a particular account with the balance shown in the accounting records. (p. 276)

Bank statement A detailed list, provided by the bank, of all the activity for a particular account during the month. (p. 273)

Blind receiving report Form used by the receiving department to account for the quantity and condition of merchandise received from a supplier. (p. 290)

Board of directors Group composed of key officers of a corporation and outside members responsible for general oversight of the affairs of the entity. (p. 282)

Bond A certificate that represents a corporation's promise to repay a certain amount of money and interest in the future. (p. 6)

Bond issue price The present value of the annuity of interest payments plus the present value of the principal. (p. 460)

Book value The original cost of an asset minus the amount of accumulated depreciation. (p. 354)

Book value per share Total stockholders equity divided by the number of shares of common stock outstanding. (p. 516)

Business All the activities necessary to provide the members of an economic system with goods and services. (p. 4)

Business entity An organization operated to earn a profit. (p. 5)

Callable bonds Bonds that may be redeemed or retired before their specified due date. (p. 459)

Callable feature Allows the firm to eliminate a class of stock by paying the stockholders a specified amount; also referred to as *redeemable*. (p. 505)

Capital expenditure A cost that improves the asset and is added to the asset account; also called *an item treated as an asset*. (p. 359)

Capital lease A lease that is recorded as an asset by the lessee. (p. 470)

Capital stock Indicates the owners' contributions to a corporation. (p. 7)

Capitalization of interest Interest on constructed assets is added to the asset account. (p. 352)

Carrying value The face value of a bond plus the amount of unamortized premium or minus the amount of unamortized discount; also known as *book value*. (p.464)

Cash basis A system of accounting in which revenues are recognized when cash is received and expenses when cash is paid. (p. 158)

Cash equivalent An investment that is readily convertible to a known amount of cash and a maturity to the investor of three months or less. (pp. 272, 556)

Cash flow from operations to capital expenditures ratio A measure of the ability of a company to finance long-term asset acquisitions with cash from operations. (p. 630)

Cash flow from operations to current liabilities ratio A measure of the ability to pay current debts from operating cash flows. (p. 625)

Cash to cash operating cycle The length of time from the purchase of inventory to the collection of any receivable from the sale. (p. 628)

Certified Public Accountant (CPA) The designation for an individual who has passed a uniform exam administered by the AICPA and met other requirements as determined by individual states. (p. 28)

Change in estimate A change in the life of the asset or in its residual value. (p. 357)

Chart of accounts A numerical list of all the accounts used by a company. (p. 113)

Closing entries Journal entries made at the end of the period to return the balance in all nominal accounts to zero and transfer the net income or loss and the dividends to Retained Earnings. (p. 175)

Comparability For accounting information, the quality that allows a user to analyze two or more companies and look for similarities and differences. (p. 64)

Compensated absences Employee absences for which the employee will be paid. (p. 422)

Compound interest Interest calculated on the principal plus previous amounts of interest; also called *interest on interest*. (p. 406)

Comprehensive income The total change in net assets from all sources except investments by or distributions to the owners. (p. 515)

Conservatism The practice of using the least optimistic estimate when two estimates of amounts are about equally likely. (p. 65)

Consistency For accounting information, the quality that allows a user to compare two or more accounting periods for a single company. (p. 64)

Contingent asset An existing condition for which the outcome is not known but by which the company stands to gain. (p. 404)

Contingent liability An existing condition for which the outcome is not known but depends on some future even; also known as *contingent loss*. (p. 401)

Contra account Any account that is used to offset another account. (p. 164)

Control account The general ledger account that is supported by a subsidiary ledger. (p. 310)

Controller The chief accounting officer for a company. (p. 33)

Convertible feature Allows preferred stock to be exchanged for common stock. (p. 505)

Corporation A form of entity organized under the laws of a particular state; ownership evidenced by shares of stock. (p. 6)

Cost of goods available for sale Beginning inventory plus cost of goods purchased. (p. 208)

Cost of goods sold Cost of goods available for sale minus ending inventory. (p. 209)

Cost principle Assets are recorded at the cost to acquire them; also called *original cost* or *historical cost*. (p. 26)

Credit An entry on the right side of an account. (p. 117)

Credit card draft A multiple-copy document used by a company that accepts a credit card for a sale; also called an *invoice*. (p. 320)

Credit memoranda Additions on a bank statement for such items as interest paid on the account and notes collected by the bank for the customer. (p. 276)

Creditor Someone to whom a company or person has a debt; also called a *lender*. (p. 8)

Cumulative effect of a change in accounting principle A line item on the income statement to reflect the effect on prior years' income from a change in accounting principle. (p. 638)

Cumulative feature The right to dividends in arrears before the current-year dividend is distributed. (p. 505)

Current asset An asset that is expected to be realized in cash or sold or consumed during the operating cycle or within one year if the cycle is shorter than one year. (p. 67)

Current liability An obligation that will be satisfied within the next operating cycle or within one year if the cycle is shorter than one year; also called *short-term liability*. (pp. 69, 395)

Current maturities of long-term debt The portion of a long-term liability that will be paid within one year; also called *long-term debt, current portion*. (p. 398)

Current ratio Current assets divided by current liabilities. (pp. 72, 624)

Current value The amount of cash, or its equivalent, that could be received by selling an asset currently. (p. 156)

Debenture bonds Bonds that are not backed by specific collateral. (p. 458)

Debit An entry on the left side of an account. (p. 117)

Debit memoranda Deductions on a bank statement for such items as NSF checks and various service charges. (p. 276)

Debt securities Securities issued by corporations and governmental bodies as a form of borrowing; also called *bonds*. (p. 307)

Debt service coverage ratio A statement of cash flows measure of the ability of a company to meet its interest and principal payments. (p. 629)

Debt-to-equity ratio The ratio of total liabilities to total stockholders' equity. (p. 628)

Deferral Cash has either been paid or received, but expense or revenue has not yet been recognized. (p. 168)

Deferred expense An asset resulting from the payment of cash before the incurrence of expense. (p. 169)

Deferred revenue A liability resulting from the receipt of cash before the recognition of revenue. (p. 169)

Deferred tax The account used to reconcile the difference between the amount recorded as income tax expense and the amount that is payable as income tax. (p. 477)

Deposit in transit A deposit recorded on the books but not yet reflected on the bank statement. (p. 275)

Depreciation The process of allocating the cost of a long-term tangible asset over its useful life. (pp. 64, 353)

Direct method For preparing the Operating Activities section of the statement of cash flows, the approach in which cash receipts and cash payments are reported. (p. 560)

Direct write-off method The recognition of bad debts expense at the point an account is written off as uncollectible. (p. 312)

Discontinued operations A line item on the income statement to reflect any gains or losses from the disposal of a segment of the business as well as any net income or loss from operating that segment. (p. 638)

Discount The excess of the face value of bonds over the issue price. (p. 462)

Discount on notes payable A contra liability that represents interest deducted from a loan in advance. (p. 397)

Discounting The process of selling a promissory note. (p. 321)

Dividend payout ratio The annual dividend amount divided by the annual net income; the percentage of earnings paid out as dividends. (pp. 509, 636)

Dividend yield ratio The relationship between dividends and the market price of a company's stock. (p. 636)

Dividends A distribution of the net income of a business to its owners. (p. 20)

Double-declining-balance method Depreciation is recorded at twice the straight-line rate, but the balance is reduced each period. (p. 355)

Double-entry system A system of accounting in which every transaction is recorded with equal debits and credits and the accounting equation is kept in balance. (p. 119)

Earnings per share A company's bottom line stated on a per-share basis. (p. 658)

Economic entity concept The assumption that a single, identifiable unit must be accounted for in all situations. (p. 6)

Effective interest method of amortization The process of transferring

a portion of the premium or discount to interest expense; this method results in a constant effective interest rate. (p. 464)

Equity securities Securities issued by corporations as a form of ownership in the business; also called *stocks*. (p. 307)

Estimated liability A contingent liability that is accrued and reflected on the balance sheet. (p. 401)

Event A happening of consequence to an entity. (p. 106)

Expenses An outflows of assets or incurrences of liabilities resulting from the sale of goods, rendering services, or carrying out other activities. (pp. 9, 161)

External event An event involving interaction between an entity and its environment. (p. 106)

Extraordinary item A line item on the income statement to reflect any gains or losses that arise from an event that is both unusual in nature and infrequent in occurrence. (p. 638)

Face rate of interest The rate of interest on the bond certificate; also called *stated rate, normal rate, coupon rate*. (p. 460)

Face value The principal amount of the bond as stated on the bond certificate; also known as *par value*. (p. 458)

FIFO method An inventory costing method that assigns the most recent costs to ending inventory. (p. 220)

Financial accounting The branch of accounting concerned with the preparation of financial statements for outsider use. (p. 15)

Financial Accounting Standards Board (FASB) The group in the private sector with authority to set accounting standards. (p. 28)

Financing activities Activities concerned with the raising and repayment of funds in the form of debt and equity. (p. 559)

Finished goods A manufacturer's inventory that is complete and ready for sale. (p. 205)

FOB destination point Terms that require the seller to pay for the cost of shipping the merchandise to the buyer. (p. 213)

FOB shipping point Terms that require the buyer to pay for the shipping costs. (p. 213)

Future value of a single amount Amount accumulated at a future time from a single payment or investment. (p. 407)

Future value of an annuity Amount accumulated in the future when a series of payments is invested

and accrues interest; also known as *amount of an annuity*. (p. 411)

Gain on Sale of Asset The excess of the selling price over the asset's book value. (p. 360)

Gain or loss on redemption The difference between the carrying value and the redemption price at the time bonds are redeemed. (p. 468)

General journal The journal used in place of a specialized journal. (p. 123)

General ledger A book, file, hard drive, or other device containing all the accounts; also called *a set of accounts*. (p. 113)

Generally accepted accounting principles (GAAP) The various methods, rules, practices, and other procedures that have evolved over time in response to the need to regulate the preparation of financial statements. (p. 26)

Going concern The assumption that an entity is not in the process of liquidation and that it will continue indefinitely. (p. 26)

Goodwill The excess of the purchase price to acquire a business over the value of the individual net assets acquired; also called *the purchase price in excess of the market value of the assets*. (p. 363)

Gross profit Net sales less cost of goods sold; also called *gross margin*. (pp. 74, 207)

Gross profit method A technique used to establish an estimate of the cost of inventory stolen, destroyed, or otherwise damaged or of the amount of inventory on hand at an interim date. (p. 231)

Gross profit ratio Gross profit divided by net sales. (pp. 215, 622)

Gross wages The amount of wages before deductions; also known as *gross pay*. (p. 419)

Held-to-maturity securities Investments in bonds of other companies in which the investor has the positive intent and the ability to hold the securities to maturity. (p. 323)

Historical cost The amount paid for an asset and used as a basis for recognizing it on the balance sheet and carrying it on later balance sheets. (p. 155)

Horizontal analysis A comparison of financial statement items over a period of time. (p. 616)

Income statement A statement that summarizes revenues and expenses; also called *the statement of income*. (p. 19)

Indirect method For preparing the Operating Activities section of the statement of cash flows, the approach in which net income is reconciled to net cash flow from operations. (p. 560)

Intangible assets Assets with no physical properties. (p. 362)

Interest The difference between the principal amount of the note and its maturity value. (p. 318)

Interim statements Financial statements prepared monthly, quarterly, or at other intervals less than a year in duration. (p. 175)

Internal audit staff Department responsible for monitoring and evaluating the internal control system. (p. 284)

Internal auditing The department responsible in a company for the review and appraisal of its accounting and administrative controls. (p. 33)

Internal control report A report, required by Section 404 of the Sarbanes-Oxley Act, to be included in a company's annual report, in which management assesses the effectiveness of the internal control structure. (p. 280)

Internal control system Policies and procedures necessary to ensure the safeguarding of an entity's assets, the reliability of its accounting records, and the accomplishment of overall company objectives. (p. 279)

Internal event An event occurring entirely within an entity. (p. 106)

International Accounting Standards Board (IASB) The organization formed to develop worldwide accounting standards. (p. 28)

Inventory profit The portion of the gross profit that results from holding inventory during a period of rising prices. (p. 225)

Inventory turnover ratio A measure of the number of times inventory is sold during a period. (pp. 233, 627)

Investing activities Activities concerned with the acquisition and disposal of long-term assets. (p. 558)

Invoice Form sent by the seller to the buyer as evidence of a sale. (p. 290)

Invoice approval form Form the accounting department uses before making payment to document the accuracy of all the information about a purchase; also called a *voucher*. (p. 291)

Issued shares The number of shares sold or distributed to stockholders. (p. 503)

Journal A chronological record of transactions; also known as the *book of original entry*. (p. 123)

Journalizing The act of recording journal entries. (p. 123)

Land improvements Costs that are related to land but that have a limited life. (p. 353)

Leverage The use of borrowed funds and amounts contributed by preferred stockholders to earn an overall return higher than the cost of these funds. (p. 634)

Liability An obligation of a business. (p. 7)

LIFO conformity rule The IRS requirement that if LIFO is used on the tax return, it must also be used in reporting income to stockholders. (p. 223)

LIFO liquidation The result of selling more units than are purchased during the period, which can have negative tax consequences if a company is using LIFO. (p. 223)

LIFO method An inventory method that assigns the most recent costs to cost of goods sold. (p. 221)

LIFO reserve The excess of the value of a company's inventory stated at FIFO over the value stated at LIFO. (p. 224)

Liquidity The ability of a company to pay its debts as they come due; the nearness to cash of the assets and liabilities. (pp. 71, 623)

Long-term liability An obligation that will be settled within one year or the current operating cycle. (p. 457)

Loss on Sale of Asset The amount by which selling price is less than book value. (p. 361)

Lower-of-cost-or-market (LCM) rule A conservative inventory valuation approach that is an attempt to anticipate declines in the value of inventory before its actual sale. (p. 229)

Maker The party that agrees to repay the money for a promissory note at some future date. (p. 318)

Management accounting The branch of accounting concerned with providing management with information to facilitate planning and control. (p. 15)

Market rate of interest The rate that investors could obtain by investing in other bonds that are similar to the issuing firm's bonds; also called *yield, effective rate.* (p. 460)

Market value per share The selling price of the stock as indicated by the most recent transactions. (p. 519)

Matching principle The association of revenue of a period with all of the costs necessary to generate that revenue. (p. 161)

Materiality The magnitude of an accounting information omission or misstatement that will affect the judgment of someone relying on the information. (p. 64)

Maturity date The date that the promissory note is due. (p. 318)

Maturity value The amount of cash the maker is to pay the payee on the maturity date of the note. (p. 318)

Merchandise inventory The account wholesalers and retailers use to report inventory held for resale. (p. 205)

Monetary unit The yardstick used to measure amounts in financial statements; the dollar in the United States. (p. 26)

Moving average The name given to an average cost method when it is used with a perpetual inventory system. (p. 239)

Multiple-step income statement An income statement that shows classifications of revenues and expenses as well as important subtotals. (p. 74)

Natural resources Assets that are consumed during their use. (p. 361)

Net income The excess of revenues over expenses; also called *profits* or *earnings.* (p. 20)

Net pay The amount of wages after deductions. (p. 420)

Net sales Sales revenue less sales returns and allowances and sales discounts. (p. 207)

Nominal accounts The name given to revenue, expense, and dividend accounts because they are temporary and are closed at the end of the period. (p. 175)

Nonbusiness entity Organization operated for some purpose other than to earn a profit. (p. 7)

Note receivable An asset resulting from the acceptance of a promissory note from another company. (p. 318)

Note payable A liability resulting from the signing of a promissory note. (pp. 318, 396)

Number of days' sales in inventory A measure of how long it takes to sell inventory. (pp. 235, 627)

Number of days' sales in receivables A measure of the average age of accounts receivable. (p. 627)

Operating activities Activities concerned with the acquisition and sale of products and services. (p. 557)

Operating cycle The period of time between the purchase of inventory and the collection of any receivable from the sale of the inventory. (p. 66)

Operating lease A lease that does not meet any of the four criteria and is not recorded as an asset by the lessee. (p. 469)

Outstanding check A check written by a company but not yet presented to the bank for payment. (p. 275)

Outstanding shares The number of shares issued less the number of shares held as treasury stock. (p. 503)

Owners' equity The owners' claim on the assets of an entity. (p. 18)

Par value An arbitrary amount that represents the legal capital of the firm. (p. 503)

Participating feature Allows preferred stockholders to share on a percentage basis in the distribution of an abnormally large dividend. (p. 505)

Partnership A business owned by two or more individuals and with the characteristic of unlimited liability; organization form often used by accounting firms and law firms. (pp. 6, 522)

Partnership agreement Specifies how much the owners will invest, their salaries, and how profits will be shared. (p. 523)

Payee The party that will receive the money from a promissory note at some future date. (p. 318)

Periodic system System in which the Inventory account is updated only at the end of the period. (p. 210)

Permanent difference A difference that affects the tax records but not the accounting records, or vice versa. (p. 478)

Perpetual system System in which the Inventory account is increased at the time of each purchase and decreased at the time of each sale. (p. 210)

Petty cash fund Money kept on hand for making minor disbursements in coin and currency rather than by writing checks. (p. 278)

Posting The process of transferring amounts from a journal to the ledger accounts. (p. 123)

Premium The excess of the issue price over the face value of the bonds. (p. 462)

Present value of a single amount Amount at a present time that is equivalent to a payment or investment at a future time. (p. 409)

Present value of an annuity The amount at a present time that is equivalent to a series of payments and interest in the future. (p. 412)

Price/earnings (P/E) ratio The relationship between a company's performance according to the income statement and its performance in the stock market. (p. 635)

Principal The amount of cash received, or the fair value of the products or services received, by the maker when a promissory note is issued. (p. 318)

Profit margin Net income divided by sales; also called *return on sales.* (p. 76)

Profit margin ratio Net income to net sales. (p. 622)

Profitability How well management is using company resources to earn a return on the funds invested by various groups. (p. 631)

Promissory note A written promise to repay a definite sum of money on demand or at a fixed or determinable date in the future. (p. 318)

Public Company Accounting Oversight Board (PCAOB) The five-member body created by an act of Congress in 2002 that was given the authority to set auditing standards in the United States. (pp. 28, 280)

Purchase Discounts Contra-purchases account used to record reductions in purchase price for early payment to a supplier. (p. 213)

Purchase order Form sent by the purchasing department to the supplier. (p. 287)

Purchase requisition form Form a department uses to initiate a request to order merchandise. (p. 287)

Purchase Returns and Allowances Contra-purchases account used in a periodic inventory system when a refund is received from a supplier or a reduction given in the balance owed to a supplier. (p. 212)

Purchases Account used in a periodic inventory system to record acquisitions of merchandise. (p. 212)

Raw materials The inventory of a manufacturer before the addition of any direct labor or manufacturing overhead. (p. 205)

Real accounts The name given to balance sheet accounts because they are permanent and are not closed at the end of the period. (p. 175)

Recognition The process of recording an item in the financial statements as an asset, liability, revenue, expense, or the like. (p. 155)

Relevance The capacity of information to make a difference in a decision. (p. 63)

Reliability The quality that makes accounting information dependable in representing the events that it purports to represent. (p. 63)

Replacement cost The current cost of a unit of inventory. (p. 224)

Research and development costs Costs incurred in the discovery of new knowledge. (p. 364)

Retail inventory method A technique used by retailers to convert the retail value of inventory to a cost basis. (p. 233)

Retained earnings The part of owners' equity that represents the income earned less dividends paid over the life of an entity; also called *retained income.* (pp. 18, 504)

Retirement of stock When the stock is repurchased with no intention to reissue at a later date. (p. 508)

Return on assets ratio A measure of a company's success in earning a return for all providers of capital. (p. 631)

Return on common stockholders' equity ratio A measure of a company's success in earning a return for the common stockholders. (p. 633)

Return on sales ratio A variation of the profit margin ratio; measures earnings before payments to creditors. (p. 632)

Revenue An inflow of assets or settlement of liabilities from delivering or producing goods, rendering services, or conducting other activities. (pp. 8, 160)

Revenue expenditure A cost that keeps an asset in its normal operating condition and is treated as an expense; also called *item treated as an expense of the period.* (p. 359)

Revenue recognition principle Revenues are recognized in the income statement when they are realized, or realizable, and earned. (p. 160)

Revenues Inflows of assets or settlements of liabilities from delivering or producing goods, rendering services, or conducting other activities. (pp. 8, 160)

Sales Discounts Contra-revenue account used to record discounts given customers for early payment of their accounts. (p. 208)

Sales Returns and Allowances Contra-revenue account used to record both refunds to customers and reductions of their accounts. (p. 208)

Sales revenue A representation of the inflow of assets. (p. 207)

Sarbanes-Oxley Act An act of Congress in 2002 intended to bring reform to corporate accountability and stewardship in the wake of a number of major corporate scandals. (pp. 31, 279)

Securities and Exchange Commission (SEC) The federal agency with ultimate authority to determine the rules in preparing statements for companies whose stock is sold to the public. (p. 28)

Serial bonds Bonds that do not all have the same due date; a portion of the bonds comes due each time period. (p. 458)

Share of stock A certificate that acts as evidence of ownership in a corporation. (p. 6)

Simple interest Interest is calculated on the principal amount only. (p. 406)

Single-step income statement An income statement in which all expenses are added together and subtracted from all revenues. (p. 74)

Sole proprietorship Form of organization with a single owner. (pp. 5, 521)

Solvency The ability of a company to remain in business over the long term. (p. 628)

Source document A piece of paper that is used as evidence to record a transaction. (p. 107)

Specific identification method An inventory costing method that relies on matching unit costs with the actual units sold. (p. 219)

Statement of cash flows The financial statement that summarizes a company's cash receipts and cash payments during the period from operating, investing, and financing activities. (pp. 21, 554)

Statement of retained earnings The statement that summarizes the income earned and dividends paid over the life of a business. (p. 20)

Statement of stockholders' equity Reflects the differences between beginning and ending balances for all accounts in the Stockholders' Equity category of the balance sheet. (p. 513)

Stock dividend The issuance of additional shares of stock to existing stockholders. (p. 510)

Stock split The creation of additional shares of stock with a reduction of the par value of the stock. (p. 512)

Stockholder One of the owners of a corporation; also called a *shareholder*. (p. 8)

Stockholders' equity The owners' equity in a corporation; also called *shareholders' equity*. (p. 18)

Straight-line method A method by which the same dollar amount of depreciation is recorded in each year of asset use. (pp. 164, 353)

Subsidiary ledger The detail for a number of individual items that collectively make up a single general ledger account. (p. 310)

Temporary difference A difference that affects both book and tax records but not in the same time period; also known as *timing difference*. (p. 478)

Term The length of time a note is outstanding; that is, the period of time between the date it is issued and the date it matures. (p. 318)

Time period Artificial segment on the calendar, used as the basis for preparing financial statements. (p. 27)

Time value of money An immediate amount should be preferred over an amount in the future. (p. 405)

Times interest earned ratio An income statement measure of the ability of a company to meet its interest payments. (p. 629)

Trading securities Stock and bonds of other companies bought and held for the purpose of selling them in the near term to generate profits on appreciation in their price. (p. 323)

Transaction Any event that is recognized in a set of financial statements. (p. 106)

Transportation-in Adjunct account used to record freight costs paid by the buyer; also called *freight-in*. (p. 212)

Treasurer The officer responsible in an organization for the safeguarding and efficient use of a company's liquid assets. (p. 33)

Treasury stock Stock issued by the firm and then repurchased but not retired. (p. 507)

Trial balance A list of each account and its balance; used to prove equality of debits and credits. (p. 125)

Understandability The quality of accounting information that makes it comprehensible to those willing to spend the necessary time. (p. 63)

Units-of-production method Depreciation is determined as a function of the number of units the asset produces. (p. 354)

Vertical analysis A comparison of various financial statement items within a single period with the use of common-size statements. (p. 616)

Weighted average cost method An inventory costing method that assigns the same unit cost to all units available for sale during the period. (p. 220)

Work in process The cost of unfinished products in a manufacturing company; also called *work in progress*. (p. 205)

Work sheet A device used at the end of the period to gather the information needed to prepare financial statements without actually recording and posting adjustments. (p. 175)

Working capital Current assets minus current liabilities. (pp. 72, 623)

I N D E X

Absences, compensated, 422
ABC Transport, 4
Accelerated depreciation, 354–355
Account balances, normal, 118–119
Account receivable, 310
Accountants, report of
    independent, 83
Accounting, 14
    accrual, 159–160, 163–173,
        553–554
    as communication, 12–36
    as social science, 27
    career, 35–36
    cash and accrual bases compared,
        157–158
    conceptual framework, 26–28
    fair value, 328–329
    financial, 15
    for bad debts, allowance method,
        313–315
    management, 15
    payroll, 419–422
Accounting controls, 283
Accounting cycle, 174–175
    steps in, 174
Accounting ethics, 28–32
Accounting equation, 18
    and statement of cash flows,
        564–565
    effects of transactions, 107–110
    relationship with balance sheet, 19
Accounting for
    bad debts, allowance method,
        313–315
    investment in CD, 307
    investments, 306–307, 328
    in stocks and bonds, 323–329
Accounting information
    processing, 104–125
    qualitative characteristics, 62–65
    usefulness of, 62–65
    users of, 15–17
Accounting principles,
    alternative, 614
    cumulative effect of a change
        in, 638
    generally accepted, 27
Accounting profession, 31–36
Accounting requirements,
    summary, 328
Accounting system, 282–283
Account(s), 113
    allowance for doubtful, 312
    chart of, 113, 114
    control, 310
    nominal, 175
    normal balances, 118–119
    real, 175
    rules for increasing and
        decreasing, 118
    T, 116–117

Accounts payable, 396
Accounts receivable, 310–316
    aging of, 314–315
    analysis of, 626–627
    percentage of, 313–314
    turnover ratio, 316–317
    valuation of, 311
Accounts receivable turnover
    ratio, 626
Accrual, 169
Accrual accounting,
    and adjustments, 163–173
    and time periods, 159–160
    cash flows and, 553–554
Accrual basis, 158
    comparing, with cash basis,
        157–158
    ethical considerations, 173
    of accounting, 157–162
Accruals and deferrals, 168–169
Accrued asset, 168, 169
Accrued liability, 166, 169, 399
    other, 398–399
Accumulated benefit obligation
    (ABO), 482
Acid-test or quick ratio, 624
Acquisition cost, 351
    of intangible assets, 364–365
Additional paid-in capital, 504
Adjusting entries, 163
Adjustments
    and accrual accounting, 163–173
    example of, 170
    summary of, 169
    types of, 163–168
Administrative controls, 283
Aging of accounts receivable,
    314–315
Aging schedule, 314, 315
AICPA, 28
Albertsons', 4
Allowance
    for doubtful accounts, 312
    method, 312–315
Allowances and returns
    sales, 207
    purchase, 212
American Accounting Association, 35
American Express, 320, 336
American Institute of Certified
    Public Accountants (AICPA), 28
Amortization,
    bond, 464–467
    effective interest method of,
        464–467
    of lease, 471
    purpose of, 464
Amortization of intangibles, 365–366
Analyzing debt to assess a firm's ability
    to pay its liabilities, 473–474
Annual report, elements of, 82–85

Annuity, 410
    future value of an, 410–412
    future value of $1, 417
    present value of an, 412–413
    present value of $1, 418
Apple Computer Company, 305–306,
    309, 310, 311, 320, 322,
    343–344, 621
    consolidated balance sheet,
        306, 317
    consolidated statements of
        operations (partial), 317
    excerpt from statement of cash
        flows, 322, 344
    excerpt from notes to
        statements, 343
Arthur Andersen, 515
Asset(s), 8
    accrued, 168
    and records, safeguarding, 284
    contingent, 404
    contingent vs. contingent
        liabilities, 404
    current, 67–68
    gain on sale of, 360
    intangible, 362
    long-term, 367–368
    loss on sale of, 361
    noncurrent, 68–69
    rate of return on, 631–632
    return on, 633–634
Asset turnover, analyzing long-term
    assets for, 368–370
Asset turnover ratio, 632
Audit committee, 282
Audit staff, internal, 284
Auditing, 33
Auditors' report, 33, 281
Authorizations, proper, 283
Authorized shares, 502
Available-for-sale securities, 323
    investment in, 326–328
Average life, analyzing long-term
    assets for, 368–370

Bad debts,
    allowance method of accounting
        for, 313–315
    methods to account for, 311–312
Balance, trial, 124–125
Balance sheet, 18, 18–19
    and income statement, 111–113
    classified, 67–73
    effects of inventory error, 227
    relationship with accounting
        equation, 19
    retained earnings and, 503
    stockholders' equity on,
        501–502
Bank reconciliation, 276, 276–278
    adjustments to records, 278

Bank statement, **273,** 275
  reading a, 273–276
Bankers, 16
Beginning inventory, periodic
  system, 211
Best Buy, Inc., 165, 251, 260, 341,
  551–552, 553, 554, 578
  cash flow adequacy, 578
  consolidated statements of cash
    flow, 552, 559, 579
  notes to consolidated financial
    statements, 579
Blind receiving report, 290
Board of directors, 282
Boeing Company, 396, 494
Bond, 6
  callable, 459
  certificate, 459
  collateral, 458
  debenture, 458
  due date, 458
  other features, 459
  serial, 458
Bond amortization, 464–467
Bond issue price, 460
Bond price, factors affecting,
  460–462
Bondholder, 16
Bonds,
  accounting for investment in,
    308–309, 323–329
  characteristics of, 458–460
  discount on, 462–464
  investment in, 308–309
  issuance of, 460
  premium on, 462–464
  redemption of, 467–469
Bonds payable, 458–469
Book value, 354
  calculating with preferred stock,
    518
Book value per share, 516
Boston Chicken, 515
Boulder Company,
  balance sheet, 561
  income statement, 560
  statement of cash flows,
    560–562
Bristol–Myers Squibb, 160
Broadwing, Inc., 459
Business, 4
  types of, 5
Business activity
  model, 9
  nature of, 7–9
Business documents,
  computerized, 285–293
  design and use, 284
Business entity, 5, 5–6

Callable bonds, 459
Callable feature, 505
Campbell's, 211
Capital,
  additional paid-in, 504
  working, 71, 623–624
Capital expenditure, 359
Capital lease, 470
Capital stock, 7
Capital vs. revenue expenditures,
  358–360

Capitalization of interest, 352
Carrying value, 464
Carte Blanche, 320
Cash,
  control over, 273–279
  defined, 272–273, 556–557
  investing idle, 307
  operating cycle, 628
  received over the counter, 286
  received in the mail, 286
  stock issued for, 506
Cash basis, 158
  comparing, with accrual basis,
    157–158
  conversion of income statement
    items, 571
Cash disbursements, controlling,
  287–293
Cash discrepancies, 287
Cash dividends, 509
  for preferred and common stock,
    509
Cash equivalent(s), 272, 556
  and statement of cash flows,
    272–273
  defined, 556–557
Cash flow
  adequacy, creditors and, 577–578
  costing methods and, 222–223
  from financing activities,
    573–574
  from investing activities, 571–573
  from operating activities,
    566–570
  reporting, 560–562
  information, use of, 577–580
  per share, stockholders and, 580
**Cash flow from operations to capital
  expenditures ratio, 630**
**Cash flow from operations to current
  liabilities ratio, 625**
Cash flows,
  and accrual accounting, 553–554
  classification of, 557–560
  statement of, 21, 77–78
Cash flows statement, inventories
  and, 235–236
Cash from sales, accelerating the
  inflow of, 320–321
Cash management, 273
Cash operating cycle, 66, 628
Cash receipts, control over,
  286–287
Cash to cash operating cycle, 628
Certificate of deposit (CD), account-
  ing for investment in, 307
**Certified Public Accountant
  (CPA), 28**
Change in estimate, 357
Characteristics of bonds, 458–460
Chart of accounts, 113, 114
Check
  outstanding, 275
  with remittance advice, 291–293
Chicago Cubs, 3
Cincinnati Bell, Inc., 459
Circuit City, 260, 341
Citicorp, 4
Classified balance sheet, 67–73
Closing entries, 175
Closing process, 175

Coca-Cola Company, 366, 455–456,
  475–476, 647, 648
  annual report, 456
  consolidated statement of cash
    flows, 477
Collateral, 458
Common stock, cash dividends
  for, 509
Common stockholders' equity, return
  on, 633
Common-size and comparative
  statements, analysis of, 616–623
Communication, accounting as,
  12–36
Comparability, 64
Comparative and common-size
  statements, analysis of, 616–623
Compensated absences, 422
Compound interest, 406
Comprehensive income, 515
  defined, 514–516
Computerized business documents,
  and cash disbursements, 287–293
  and internal control, 285–293
Conservatism, 65
  and lower-of-cost-or-market rule,
    230–231
Consistency, 64
Consolidated financial statements,
  notes to, 84
Contingencies, note disclosure, 403
Contingent asset, 404
  note disclosure, 404
Contingent liabilities, 401–404
  disclosed, 402–404
  note disclosure, 403
  recorded, 401–402
  vs. contingent assets, 404
Contingent liability, 401
Contra account, 158
Control account, 310
Control environment, 282
Control over cash receipts, 286–287
Control over cash, 273–279
Control system, internal, 279
Controller, 33
Converse Inc., 349
Convertible feature, 505
Corporation, 6
Cost(s)
  acquisition, 351
  historical, 155
  inventory, 217
  replacement, 224, 229–230
  research and development, 364
  transportation, 213–214
Cost of goods available for sale, 208
Cost of goods purchased, 211–215
Cost of goods sold, 209, 208–216
  model, 208–210
  section of the income
    statement, 209
Cost principle, 26, 110
Costco Wholesale Corporation,
  consolidated statements of stock-
    holders' equity and comprehensive
    income, 542
Costing methods
  and cash flow, 222–223
  and inventory profits, 224–225
Coupons, 402

CPA, 28
Cramden Creamery, 4
Credit, 117
Credit card draft, 320
Credit card sales, 320–321
Credit memoranda, 276
Credit terms, 208
Creditor, 8
Creditors, other, 16
Creditors and cash flow adequacy,
    577–578
Credits and debits,
    and transactions, 119
    compared, 114
    for revenues, expenses, dividends,
    117–118
Cumulative effect of a change in
    accounting principle, 638
Cumulative feature, 505
Cumulative preferred stock, 510
Current asset, 67, 67–68
Current liabilities, 395–400
    cash flow from operations to, 625
    on statement of cash flows, 400
Current liability, 69, 395
Current maturities of long-term
    debt, 398
Current ratio, 72, 624
Current value, 156

Debenture bonds, 458
Debit, 117
Debit memoranda, 276
Debits and credits,
    and transactions, 119
    for revenues, expenses, dividends,
    117–118
Debt financing, stock vs., 501
Debt securities, 307
Debt service coverage, 629–630
    ratio, 629
Debt-to-equity ratio, 628–629
Deductions, voluntary, 420
Deferral, 168
Deferrals and accruals, 168–169
Deferred expense, 163–164,
    168–169
Deferred revenue, 148, 164–166, 169
Deferred tax, 477, 476–479
Dell Computer, 256
Delta Air Lines, 504
Deposit in transit, 275
Depreciation, 64, 353
    accelerated, 354–355
    and income taxes, 356
    estimate, change in, 357–358
    method,
        choice of, 356–357
        comparison of, 355–356
Difference,
    permanent, 478
    temporary, 478
Diners Club, 320
Direct method, 560, 561
    comparison with indirect method,
        576–577
    preparing statement of cash flows,
        565–574
Direct write-off method, 312
Discontinued operations, 638

Discount, 462
    amortization, 465
    purchase, 212–213
    on bonds, 462–464
    on notes payable, 397
    sales, 208
Discounting, 321
    notes receivable, 321
Discover Card, 320
Dixon Sporting Goods, 66
    classified balance sheet, 67–71
    current ratio, 72–73
    income statement, 74–75
    statement of cash flows, 77–78
    statement of retained earnings, 77
    working capital ratio, 71–72
Dividend payout ratio, 509, 636
Dividend yield ratio, 636
Dividends, 20, 509–513
    cash, 509–510
    debits and credits for, 117–118
    effect on retained earnings, 502
    stock, 510
Document,
    design and use of business, 284
    source, 107
Double–declining balance
    method, 355
Double-entry system, 115, 116–125
Doubtful accounts, allowance
    for, 312
Duties, segregation of, 283

Earnings, 20
    retained, 504
Earnings per share, 634
Economic entity concept, 6, 26
Economic events, 106–113
Effective interest method of
    amortization, 464–467, 471
Employer payroll taxes, 420–421
Ending inventory, periodic system, 211
Enron, 31, 279, 458
Environmental aspects of operating
    assets, 360
Equity,
    as source of financing, 500–504
    return on, 633–634
Equity securities, 307
Equivalent, cash, 556
Ernst & Young LLP, 34, 280, 281
Estimate, change in, 357
Estimated liability, 401
Ethics, 160, 395, 458, 515
    in accounting, 28–32
Event, 106
    external, 106
    internal, 106
Excel, using for interest calculations,
    423–428
Expenditures, capital vs. revenue,
    358–360
Expense(s), 9
    deferred, 163–164, 168-169
    debits and credits for, 117–118
Expense recognition and matching
    principle, 161–162
External event, 106
External users, 15–16
Extraordinary item, 638

Face rate of interest, 460
Face value, 458
Fair value accounting, controversy
    over, 328–329
FASB, 28
FICA,
    employees' share, 420
    employers' share, 421–422
FIFO costing with perpetual system,
    237–238
FIFO method, 220
Financial accounting, 15
Financial Accounting Standards
    Board (FASB), 28
Financial decision framework, 17
Financial position, statement of, 18
Financial ratios, summary of,
    636–637
Financial reporting,
    international perspective, 65
    objectives of, 61–62
Financial statement analysis,
    comparisons, 614–615
    effects of inflation, 615
    precautions in, 614–615
Financial statements, 18–23, 66–67
    conceptual framework, 26–28
    interim, 175
    notes to consolidated, 84
    recognition and measurement in,
        155–157
    relationships, 22
Financing, equity as source of,
    500–504
Financing activities, 7, 559
    cash flows from, 573–574
    noncash, 552–553
Finish Line (The), 3–4, 13–14, 59–61,
    105–106, 203–204, 207, 229, 231,
    234, 271–272, 273, 276, 279, 282,
    285, 302
    auditor's report, 34
    auditor's report on internal
        control, 281
    balance sheet, 23–24, 79–80,
        204, 234
    financial statements, 23
    income statement, 23, 25, 81
    management report on internal
        control, 280
    ratio decision model, 234–235
    statement of cash flows,
        236, 274
    statement of income, 204,
        216, 234
Finished goods, 205
Firm's ability to pay its liabilities,
    assessing, 473–474
First-in, first-out method (FIFO),
    220–221
Fitch Investors Service Inc., 577
FOB destination point, 213
FOB shipping point, 213
Foot Locker, 61, 153–154, 163–166,
    216, 265, 302
Future value of
    $1, 415
    a single amount, 407–409
    an annuity, 411, 410–412
    annuity of $1, 417

GAAP, 27
Gain on sale of asset, 360
Gain or loss on redemption, 467–469, 468
Gap Inc., 3, 19, 72
Gateway, 553, 554
General journal, 123
General ledger, 113
General Mills, 335
General Motors, 519
Generally accepted accounting principles, 27
Going concern, 26
Goodwill, 363
Government agencies, 16
Gross margin, 207
Gross profit, 74, 207
    method, 231, 231–233
    ratio, 215–216, 622
Gross profit percentage before and after price change, 230
Gross wages, 419
    calculation of, 419
Group purchase, 351
Guarantees, product, 401

Hang-Up Shoppes, Inc., 271
Held-to-maturity securities, 323
    investment in, 323–324
Hilton Hotels, 100
Historical cost, 26, 155
Horizontal analysis, 616–620

IASB, 28
IBM, 205, 343, 461, 621, 649
Idle cash, investing, 307
Improvements, land, 353
Income,
    comprehensive, 514–516
        effect on retained earnings, 502
    measurement of, 217
    net, 20
Income statement, 19, 19–20, 73–76, 158–159
    balance sheet and, 111–113
    comparing, with statement of cash flows, 159
    cost of goods sold section, 209
    discontinued operations, 638
    effects of inventory error, 226
    extraordinary items, 638
    for inventory costing methods, 222
    for merchandiser, 206–207
    format of, 73–75
    multiple-step, 74–75
    net sales section, 207
    relationship to statement of comprehensive income, 515
    retained earnings and, 503
    single-step, 74
    use of, 76
Income statement items,
    conversion to cash basis, 571
    reporting and analyzing, 638
Income tax, 420
Independent
    review and appraisal, 284
    verification, 284

Indirect method, 560, 562
    comparison with direct method, 576–577
    preparing statement of cash flows, 575–576
    summary of adjustments to net income, 576
Inflation, possible effects of, 615
Inflow of cash from sales, accelerating, 320–321
Intangible assets, 362
    acquisition cost of, 364–365
    balance sheet presentation, 363–364
    most common, 363
    operating assets, 362–366
Intangibles, 69
    amortization of, 365–366
Interest, 318
    capitalization of, 352–353
    compound, 406
    face rate of, 460
    market rate of, 460
    simple, 406
Interest calculation(s), 308
    using Excel, 423–428
Interim statements, 175
Internal auditing, 33
Internal audit staff, 284
Internal control,
    auditor's report, 281
    and computerized business documents, 285–293
    introduction to, 279–285
    limitations on, 284–285
    management report on, 280
    procedures, 283–284
Internal control report, 280
Internal control system, 279
Internal event, 106
Internal Revenue Service (IRS), 15, 16, 477, 479
Internal users, 15
International Accounting Standards Board (IASB), 28
Inventories,
    and the cash flows statement, 235–236
    periodic system, 211
Inventory,
    forms of, 205–206
    management of, 233–235
    merchandise, 205
    nature of, 204–206
    number of days' sales in, 627
    transfer of title, 214–215
    valuing at lower of cost or market, 229–231
Inventory analysis, 627–628
Inventory costs, 217
    relationship between business types and, 206
    types of, 205–206
Inventory costing methods
    income statements for, 222
    periodic system, 218–221
    perpetual inventory system, 236–239
    selecting, 221–229
Inventory errors, 226–228

    effects on balance sheet, 227
    effects on income statement, 226
    summary of effects, 228
Inventory method(s),
    retail, 233
    changing, 225
Inventory profit, 225
    costing methods and, 224–225
Inventory systems, 210–211
Inventory turnover ratio, 233, 627
Inventory valuation, 217
    in other countries, 226
Inventory value, methods for estimating, 231–233
Investing activities, 8, 558
    cash flows from, 571–573
    noncash, 552–553
Investing idle cash, 307
Investment, summary of accounting and reporting requirements, 328
Investment(s) in
    available-for-sale securities, 326–328
    CD, accounting for, 307
    held-to-maturity securities, 323–324
    highly liquid financial instruments, 307–308
    stocks and bonds, 308–309
    accounting for, 323–329
    trading securities, 324–326
Investments, 68
    accounting for, 306–307
    and receivables, 304–322
Invoice, 290
Invoice approval form, 291, 292
Issuance of bonds, 460
Issuance of stock, 506–507
Issued shares, 503

Jacuzzi Brands, Inc., 206, 393–394, 395, 396, 399, 402, 403, 499–500, 502, 503, 504, 507, 516
    consolidated balance sheet, 394, 500, 517
    consolidated statement of cash flows, 400
    note disclosure for contingencies, 403
    note disclosure for contingent asset, 404
    note disclosure for contingent liability, 403
Journal, 123
    general, 123
    posting from, 124
    record of transactions, 122–124
Journalizing, 123

Key Inc., 385
K-Mart, 197, 621
Kraft Foods, 613

Land improvements, 353
Last-in, first-out method (LIFO), 221
Lawsuits, 402
LCM rule, 229
    application of, 231
Lease(s), 469–473
    capital, 470
    operating, 469–470
    liability for, 469–473

Lease amortization, 472
Lease criteria, 469–470
Ledger
    general, 113
    posting to, 124
    subsidiary, 310
Legal claims, 402
Leverage, 634, 633–634
Liabilities,
    assessing a firm's ability to pay its,
        473–474
    contingent vs. contingent
        assets, 404
    current, 395–400
    long–term and the statement of
        cash flows, 474–476
    other, 476–479
Liability, 7
    accrued, 166–168, 169, 399
    contingent, **401**–404
    current, 69, 395
    estimated, 401
    for leases, 469–473
    long-term, 70, 457
    other accrued, 398–399
LIFO conformity rule, 223
LIFO costing with perpetual system,
    238–239
LIFO liquidation, 223
LIFO method, 221
    effect on income and taxes paid, 224
LIFO reserve, 224
Liquid assets, effect on statement of
    cash flows, 321–322
Liquidation, LIFO, 223
Liquidity, 71, 623
Liquidity analysis, management of
    working capital, 623–628
Long-term assets
    analyzing for average life and
        asset turnover, 368–370
    and the statement of cash flows,
        367–368
Long-term debt, current maturities
    of, 398
Long-term liability, 70, 457
    and the statement of cash flows,
        474–476
    balance sheet presentation,
        457–458
Loss on sale of asset, 361
Loss or gain on redemption, 467–469
Lower of cost or market, valuing in-
    ventory at, 229–231
**Lower-of-cost-or-market (LCM)
    rule, 229**
    application of, 231
    conservatism and, 230–231

Maker, 318
Man Alive, 59
Management accounting, 15
Management
    discussion and analysis, 84
    of cash, 273
    of inventory, analyzing, 233–235
Margin, gross, 207
Margin, profit, 76
Market, replacement cost as
    a measure of, 229–230

Market rate of interest, 460
Market value per share, 519
MasterCard, 320
Matching principle, 161
    expense recognition and, 161–162
Materiality, 64
Maturities of long-term debt,
    current, 398
Maturity, redemption at, 467
Maturity date, 318
Maturity value, 318
Maytag Corporation, 339
McDonald's Corporation, 648
Measure, unit of, 156
Measurement, 155–157
    in financial statements, 155–157
    of income, 217
Merchandise inventory, 205
Merchandise, net sales of, 207–208
Meredith Corporation, 165
Microsoft Corporation, 450
Monetary unit, 26
Money, time value of, 405
Money concepts, time value of,
    405–418
Moving average, 239
    with perpetual system, 239
**Multiple-step income statement,
    74**, 75

NASCAR, 455
Natural resources, 361
    balance sheet presentation, 361
    depletion of, 361–362
    operating assets, 361–362
NBA, 455
Net credit sales, percentage of, 313
Net income, 20
Net pay, 420
    calculation of, 419–420
Net sales, 207
    of merchandise, 207–208
New Balance, 204
New York Times Company, 265
Nike, Inc., 8, 204, 205, 206, 349–350,
    351, 366, 396
    consolidated assets section and in-
        tangibles note, 364
    consolidated balance sheet, 350
    consolidated partial statement of
        cash flows, 368
Nominal accounts, 175
Nonbusiness entity, 7
    employment by, 33
Noncash
    consideration, stock issued for,
        506–507
    investing and financing activities,
        552–553
Noncumulative preferred stock, 510
Noncurrent assets, 68–69
Nordstrom, Inc., 207, 513
    partial stockholder's equity section,
        513
Normal account balances, 118–119
Northwest Airlines, 553, 554
Note disclosure,
    for contingencies, 403
    for contingent asset, 404
    for contingent liability, 403

Note, promissory, 318
Note(s) payable, 318, 396–398
    discount on, 397
Note(s) receivable, 318, 318–319
    discounting, 321
Notes to consolidated financial
    statements, 84
**Number of days' sales in inventory,
    235, 627**
**Number of days' sales in
    receivables, 627**

Operating activities, 8–9, **557**
    determining cash flows from,
        566–570
    reporting cash flow from,
        560–562
Operating asset(s),
    environmental aspects of, 360
    intangible assets, 362–366
    natural resources, 361–362
    property, plant and equipment,
        350–361
Operating cycle, 66–67
    cash, 628
Operating lease, 469
Organization, forms of, 5–7
Organizations and social
    responsibility, 7
Outstanding check, 275
Outstanding shares, 503
Owners' equity, 18

Paiva, 59
Par value, 503
Participating feature, 505
Partnership, 6, 522, 522–524
Partnership agreement, 523
Pay, net, 419–420
Payee, 318
Payroll accounting, 419–422
Payroll taxes, employer, 420–421
PCAOB, 28, 280, 281
PepsiCo., Inc., 457, 474–475, 476,
    495, 520, 647, 648
    consolidated partial balance
        sheet, 457
    partial statement of cash
        flows, 520
Percentage of accounts receivable
    approach, 313–314
Percentage of net credit sales
    approach, 313
Periodic system, 210
    beginning and ending inventories,
        211
    inventory costing methods,
        218–221
Permanent difference, 478
Perpetual inventory system,
    236–239
Perpetual system, 210
    FIFO costing with, 237–238
    LIFO costing with, 238–239
    moving average with, 239
Petty cash fund, 278
    establishing, 278
Porsche, 28
Posting, 123, 124
Potential stockholders, 15

Preferred stock, 505–506
  cash dividends for, 509
  cumulative, 510
  noncumulative, 510
Premium(s), 402, **462**
  amortization, 466
  on bonds, 462–464
Prepaid expenses, 147
Present value of
  $1, 416
  a single amount, 409–410
  an annuity, 412–413
  annuity of $1, 418
Price,
  bond, 460–462
  bond issue, 460
Price change, gross profit percentage
  before and after, 230
Price/earnings (P/E) ratio, 635
Principal, 318
Principle
  cost, 26
  matching, 161
  revenue recognition, 160–161
Product warranties and
  guarantees, 401
Profit(s), 20
  gross, 74, 207
inventory, 225
Profit margin, 76
Profit margin ratio, 622
Profitability, 631
  analysis, 631–637
Promissory note, 318
  key terms, 318
Proper authorizations, 283
Property, plant, and equipment, 68,
  350–361
  acquisition of, 351–353
  balance sheet presentation,
    350–351
  disposal of, 360–361
  group purchase, 351–352
  use and depreciation of,
    353–358
Proprietorships, sole, 5, 521–522
Public accounting, employment in,
  33–35
**Public Company Accounting Over-
  sight Board (PCAOB)**, 28,
  280, 281
Purchase
  discounts, 212–213
  order, 287, 289
  **price in excess of the market
    value of the assets, 363**
  requisition form, 287, 289
  returns and allowances, 212
Purchasing function document
  flow, 288
Purchases, 212

Quick ratio, 624

Radio Shack, 553, 554
Rate of interest,
  face, 460
  market, 460
Rate of return on assets, 631

Ratio,
  accounts receivable turnover,
    316–317, 626
  acid-test, 624–625
  asset turnover, 632
  cash flow from operations to
    capital expenditures, 630
  cash flow from operations to
    current liabilities, 625
  current, 72, 396, 624
  debt service coverage, 629
  debt-to-equity, 628–629
  dividend payout, 509, 636
  dividend yield, 636
  gross profit, 215–216, 622
  introduction to, 71–73
  inventory turnover, 233, 627
  price/earnings (P/E), 635
  profit margin, 622
  quick, 396, 624–625
  summary of selected, 636–637
  return on assets, 631
  return on common stockholders'
    equity, 633
  return on sales, 632
  times interest earned, 629
Ratio decision model,
  accounts receivable, 316–317
  average life and asset turnover,
    369–370
  book value per share, 516–517
  cash flow adequacy, 578–579
  current ratio, 80–81
  debt–to–equity, 474
  debt service coverage, 474
  gross profit, 216
  inventory management, 234–235
  profit margin, 82
  times interest earned, 475
Raw materials, 205
Real accounts, 175
Receivables and investments, 304–322
Receiving report, 290–291
  blind, **290**
Recognition, 155
  and measurement in financial
    statements, 155–157
Reconciliation, bank, 276–278
Recording transactions, 106–113
  and source documents, 107
Records and assets, safeguarding, 284
Redemption
  at maturity, 467
  gain or loss on, 467–469
  of bonds, 467–469
Relevance, 63
Reliability, 63
Rent-Way, 395
Replacement cost, 224
  as a measure of market,
    229–230
Report of independent
  accountants, 83
Reporting requirements,
  summary, 328
**Research and development
  costs, 364**
Reserve, LIFO, 224
Retail inventory method, 233

Retained earnings, 18, 503, **504**
  effect of income and
    dividends, 502
  statement of, 20, 76–77
Retirement of stock, 509
Return on assets,
  components of, 632
  return on equity, and leverage,
    633–634
Return on assets ratio, 631
Return on common stockholders'
  equity, 633
**Return on common stockholders'
  equity ratio, 633**
Return on equity,
  return on assets, and leverage,
    633–634
Return on sales, 76
Return on sales ratio, 632
Returns and allowances,
  purchase, 212
  sales, 207
Revenue(s), 8, 160
  deferred, 148, 164–166, 169
  debits and credits for,
    117–118
Revenue expenditure, 359
**Revenue recognition principle,
  160**–161
Revenue vs. capital expenditures,
  358–359
Review and appraisal,
  independent, 284

Safeguarding assets and
  records, 284
Safeway, 4
Sale of asset,
  gain on, 360
  loss on, 361
Sales, 207
  accelerating the inflow of cash
    from, 320–321
  credit card, 320–321
  net, 207
  return on, 76
Sales discounts, 208
Sales returns and allowances, 207
Sales revenue, 207
Sara Lee Corporation, 396
Sarbanes-Oxley Act, 31, 279
Sears, Roebuck and Co.,
  197, 260
SEC, 28
Securities,
  available-for-sale, 323
  debt, 307
  equity, 307
  held-to-maturity, 323
  investment in
    available-for-sale, 326–328
  held-to-maturity, 323–324
  trading, 323, 324–326
**Securities and Exchange Commission
  (SEC)**, 16, 28, 233
Segregation of duties, 283
Serial bonds, 458
Share of stock, 6
Shareholder, 7

Shares,
    authorized, 502
    issued, 503
    outstanding, 503
Shipping terms, 213–216
Simple interest, 406
Single amount,
    future value of, 407–409
    present value of, 409–410
Single-step income statement, 74
Social responsibility, organizations
    and, 7
Sole proprietorship, 5, 521–522
Solvency, 628
    analysis, 628–631
Southwest Airlines, 73, 147
Source document, 107
    and recording transactions, 107
Specific identification method, 219
Starwood Hotels & Resorts, 100
Statement,
    bank, 273, 275
    income, 19
Statement analysis, precautions,
    614–615
Statement of cash flows, 21, 77–78,
    158–159, 274, **554**
    accounting equation and, 564–565
    and changes in current liabilities,
        400–401
    and changes in stockholders'
        equity, 519–520
    cash equivalents and, 272–273
    classification of items, 559
    comparing, with income
        statement, 159
    direct method, 561, 565–574
    effect of liquid assets on, 321–322
    format, 558
    indirect method, 562, 575–576
    long–term assets and, 367–368
    long–term liabilities and, 474–476
    purpose of, 554–555
    reporting requirements, 555–563
    structure of, 564–577
    work-sheet approach, 580–582
**Statement of comprehensive income,
    and income statement, 515**
Statement of financial position, 18
Statement of retained earnings, 20,
    20–21, 76–77
**Statement of stockholders' equity,
    513–514**
Stock,
    accounting for investment in,
        308–309, 323–329
    cash dividends for, 509–510
    investment in, 308–309
    issuance of, 505–506
    preferred, 505–506
    retirement of, 508
    share of, 6
    treasury, 507–508
    vs. debt financing, 501
Stock dividend, 510–512

Stock issued for
    cash, 506
    noncash consideration, 506–507
Stock split, 512–513
Stockholder, 8
Stockholders, 15
    and cash flow per share, 580
Stockholders' equity, 18, 70
    and firm's value, 516
    and the statement of cash flows,
        519–520
    number of shares, 502
    overview, 500–504
    relation to firm's value, 516–519
    return on common, 633
    statement of, 513–514
    on the balance sheet, 501–502
    identifying components, 502–504
Straight–line method, 158, 353–354
Subsidiary ledger, 310
    use of, 310–311

T account, 116–117
Target Corporation, 245, 262
Tax,
    deferred, 476–479
    income, 420
    unemployment, 421
Tax shield, 356
Taxes payable, 398
Temporary difference, 478
Term, 318
Texas Instruments, 408, 414
Time period, 27
Time periods, accrual accounting
    and, 159–160
Time value of money, 405
    concepts, 405–417
Time Warner, 4
Times interest earned, 629
    ratio, 629
Tommy Hilfiger Corporation, 396, 470
    note disclosure of leases, 471
Top of the World, 18
    balance sheet, 19
    income statement, 20
    statement of cash flows, 21
    statement of retained earnings, 21
Trading securities, 323
    investment in, 324–326
Transaction(s), 106
    and the accounting equation,
        107–110
    debits and credits applied
        to, 119
    for Glengarry Health Club,
        119–121
    record of (journal), 122–124
    recording, 106–113
Transaction effects equation, 115
Transportation costs, 213–214
Transportation–in, 212
Treasurer, 33
Treasury stock, 507–508
Trial balance, 124–125

Tribune Company and Subsidiaries,
    3, 259
Turnover ratio, accounts receivable,
    316–317

Uncollectible accounts, write-offs of,
    312–313
Understandability, 63
Unemployment tax, 421
Unincorporated businesses, 521–524
Unit of measure, 156
United Airlines, 4
Units-of-production method, 354
Unknowns, solving for, 413–414

Value,
    carrying, 464
    current, 156
    face, 458
    market, per share, 519
    maturity, 318
    par, 503
Valuing inventory at lower of cost or
    market, 229–231
Verification, independent, 284
Verizon, 72
Vertical analysis, 616, 621–622
VISA, 320
Voluntary deductions, 420

Walgreen Co. and Subsidiaries,
    263, 492
Wal–Mart Stores Inc., 76, 245, 262,
    538, 621
    consolidated statement of
        shareholders' equity, 538
Walt Disney, 4
Wages, gross, 419
Warranties, product, 401
Weighted average cost method, 220
Wendy's International Inc., 648
Weyerhauser, 362
    natural resources note, 362
Whirlpool Corporation, 338
Winnebago Industries, 224
    annual report excerpt, 224
Wm. Wrigley Jr. Company, 559,
    613–614, 617, 638, 642
    comparative financial statements,
        642–644
    financial highlights, 614
    financial summary, 618–619
WorldCom, 31
Work in process, 205
Work sheet, 175
Working capital, 71–72, 623–624
    management of, 623–628
WorldCom, 279
Write-offs of uncollectible accounts,
    allowance method, 312–313

Xcel Energy, 69